ENCYCLOPEDIA

OF

AMERICAN

HISTORY

CONSULTANT EDITORS

ENCYCLOPEDIA

☆ ——————— OF ——————— ☆

AMERICAN
HISTORY

Revised and Enlarged Edition

Edited by

RICHARD B. MORRIS

Gouverneur Morris Professor of History,
COLUMBIA UNIVERSITY

HARPER & BROTHERS · PUBLISHERS · NEW YORK

Library of Congress catalog card number: 61–10213

CONTENTS

I. *Basic Chronology*

II. *Topical Chronology*

III. *Four Hundred Notable Americans*

MAPS AND CHARTS

HOW TO USE THIS BOOK

Foreword to the Revised Edition

THE AIM of this *Encyclopedia* is to provide in a single handy volume the essential historical facts about American life and institutions. The organization is both chronological and topical. *Dates, events, achievements, and persons* stand out, but the text is designed to be read as a narrative.

The *Encyclopedia* is comprehensive in its coverage. There are three main divisions. Part I (Basic Chronology) presents the major political and military events in the history of the United States, introduced by an account of explorations, settlement, and colonial and Revolutionary problems. After reviewing the main political and constitutional developments in the original Thirteen Colonies, the focus is widened to encompass imperial and intercolonial issues. Thereafter the emphasis is upon national, Federal, or major sectional problems rather than on localized and isolated occurrences—on the President, Congress, the Supreme Court, and the issues of war and peace.

Events are arranged in time sequence, with annual coverage beginning with the year 1763. For purpose of clarity, however, as well as compression, many subjects are arbitrarily treated under the year in which they came to national attention; but, where feasible, the entire story is told only once even though it may be necessary to spread the net over more than one year. For instance, the removal of the Federal government's deposits from the 2nd Bank of the U.S. is treated under the year 1833 when it took place, but the censuring resolution of 1834 is thereunder included as well as the final expunging of that resolution in 1837. If, then, you do not find the entry under the year in which the event occurred, consult the Index.

The nonpolitical aspects of American life are examined in Part II (Topical Chronology), which organizes the facts about constitutional developments, American expansion, and demographic, economic, scientific, and cultural trends. Much of this information has never been presented before in a general chronological framework. Needless to say, social and cultural events and contributions often do not lend themselves to close dating.

A special feature of the *Encyclopedia* is Part III (Biographical Section), which furnishes data on 400 notable Americans chosen for their outstanding achievements in major fields of activity. Elsewhere, the names of significant persons not included in this section are followed (the first time cited) by the dates of birth and death and in many cases by brief biographical information.

Events Before 1752. The old Julian Calendar, in force in Great Britain and her colonies until 1752, overestimated the solar year by 11 minutes 14 seconds a year. Under that calendar the year technically began on 25 Mar. The New Style Calendar, which went into effect in 1752 (based upon the calendar ordained by Pope Gregory XIII in 1582), adjusted the errors in the old chronology by adding 10 days down through the year 1699 and 11 days beginning with 1700, and leaving 11 days out of the calendar in 1752 (3 Sept. became 14 Sept.). In addition, the new year once more began on 1 Jan. This chronology follows New Style usage for all dates prior to 1752. Thus, the Mayflower Compact, bearing the date of 11 Nov. 1620, was actually signed on 21 Nov. Under the Julian Calendar (Old Style), George Washington was born 11 Feb. 1731/2, but this book lists it as 22 Feb. 1732 (New Style).

Presidential Elections. Presidential and Congressional elections were originally held on varying days. For convenience the day when the electors cast their ballots has been designated election day (the 1st Wed. in Dec. under the Act of 1 Mar. 1792; the Tues. following the 1st Mon. in Nov. under the Act of 23 Jan. 1845).

Acts of Congress bear the date when they were signed by the President, although the dates of actual passage are indicated when deemed significant, as well as the division of the votes in Senate and House.

Revised Edition. This new and enlarged edition covers American historical events from the era of discovery and exploration to the inauguration of President John F. Kennedy (20 Jan. 1961). Complex, insistent, and worldwide issues dictated a new organization and synthesis of the period since the close of World War II, as well as numerous other changes and revisions throughout the *Encyclopedia*. New tables, charts, and maps have been added, the Biographical Section enlarged from 300 to 400 Notable Americans, and the Index considerably expanded.

A concluding word about historical facts. The *Encyclopedia* endeavors to incorporate the results of the latest research. This involves revisions of previously accepted historical data. For example, the "atomic time clock" and recent discoveries tend to support a much earlier date for the crossing of Bering Strait and the southward penetration into the Americas than had been accepted a decade ago. The extensive current publication programs of the writings of American statesmen are providing massive documentation of the authorship and dates of state papers, in some cases correcting previous information. Traditionally, John Dickinson has been accorded the lion's share of, if not complete, authorship of the "Declaration of the Causes and Necessities of Taking Up Arms," but Dr. Julian P. Boyd has conclusively demonstrated that Jefferson's contributions to the final draft were very substantial. The recent discovery of an affidavit in the Amsterdam archives indicates that Peter Stuyvesant was born around 1610 rather than in 1592, the generally accepted date. The court records of Saint Croix indicate that Alexander Hamilton was born in 1755 instead of 2 years later as commonly believed. The statistical data in this revised edition incorporate the latest findings of *Historical Statistics of the United States: Colonial Times to 1957* (1960).

For historians there is no quicksand more treacherous than a "first." In most cases "firsts" might more cautiously be phrased as "earliest known." Particularly in the field of science and technology must the researcher seeking to establish priority of discovery and invention be on guard against pitfalls. Priority is often a matter of definition. Whether one accepts 1636 or 1786 as the year of the earliest known strike depends on what kind of work stoppage constitutes a "strike." With this problem in mind the *Encyclopedia* attempts to define terms with some degree of precision. Thus, Royall Tyler's *The Contrast* was the 1st *American comedy* to be produced by a *professional company,* but it was not the 1st native play. That distinction must be awarded to Thomas Godfrey's tragedy, *The Prince of Parthia.* However, amateur performances of English plays had been given in the colonies as far back as 1665, more than 100 years earlier. Lastly, where the facts remain in the realm of conjecture (as in the Viking explorations and Polynesian contacts with South America), the *Encyclopedia* indicates how scholars still differ in interpreting the available evidence.

This enterprise has incurred numerous debts to scholars and librarians, above all to Cass Canfield, who conceived the project. The editor has constantly enlisted his sagacious judgment and been sustained by his unfailing encouragement. Many others in Harper & Brothers have cooperated in the preparation of both editions beyond the call of duty, among them Daniel F. Bradley and Beulah W. Hagen. The list of the editor's obligations in the preparation of the revised edition is extensive, starting with Henry Steele Commager and the other consultant editors. In the revisions of the opening section, "Original Peopling of the Americas," the editor enlisted the scholarship of Professor Helmut de Terra of Columbia University. The compilation of the 400 subjects of biographical treatment was based on an extensive poll among historians and specialists in a variety of fields. In making the selections in the categories of science, invention, and technology the editor leaned heavily upon the sagacious counsel of Professor I. I. Rabi of Columbia University and the Consultant Editor on Science and Invention, Mr. William L. Laurence, *The New*

York Times. Mr. Arthur Dreifuss of Hollywood, Calif., was indispensable in revising and updating the sections on the theater, motion pictures, and television. The editor's wife, Berenice Robinson Morris, has once more been recruited to bring the music section up to date, and his son, Jeffrey B. Morris of Princeton University, gave the entire book the benefit of a close and critical reading. Miss Harriet Schorr of Columbia University has been indefatigable as a research assistant on the revisions, and once again the text has benefited at many points by the expert copyediting of Mr. James Fergus McRee.

I
Basic Chronology

PHYSIOGRAPHIC MAP
OF THE
UNITED STATES

ORIGINAL PEOPLING OF
THE AMERICAS

c. 50,000–8,000 B.C. ASIATIC ORIGINS. The first human explorers entered this unpopulated region from northern Asia. Despite differences among scholars over the exact date, it now appears that the bulk of the early migration occurred during the last stages of the **Pleistocene glaciation** (the **last Ice Age**). Physical tests based on the half cycle of Carbon 14, which is present in all organic matter and disappears at a known rate, indicate that the centers of population around the edges of the Arctic Ocean, then a warm, open sea, began shifting south in relatively heavy waves, when **c.11,000 yrs.** ago the Arctic froze over, the Atlantic warmed, and the Ice Age ended (Ewing and Donn, 1956). The crossing of Bering Strait and the southward penetration of the Western Hemisphere introduced a somewhat mixed group from northern Asia into this region, but the predominating strain was **Mongoloid.** By 1492 this variable but basically Asiatic stock was dominant from Cape Horn to Point Barrow. The very early human remains found in archaeological deposits in the New World all belong to the modern human variety, **Homo Sapiens,** although physical anthropologists disagree on nomenclature. No Neanderthal, or other pre-Homo Sapiens, remains have yet been found in the Western Hemisphere. Since none of the tailless apes or anthropoid apes occur here either, it is generally believed that man evolved in the Old World and entered the New World fully developed physically, and in a **Late** or **Epi-Paleolithic** stage of culture.

LINGUISTIC STOCKS OF AMERICAN INDIAN are highly varied. The number of dialects, languages, and stocks increased greatly owing to the isolation or wanderings of these early hunters and gatherers. By a conservative estimate some 55 distinct linguistic stocks have been listed north of the Rio Grande. A few links have been postulated between Eskimo and Chukchee, and the Atha-baskan and Sino-Tibetan, but in general few linkages between Old and New World linguistic stocks have so far been fully demonstrated, indicating a considerable period of isolation.

c.50,000–8,000 B.C. EARLIEST SETTLEMENT. Carbon 14 tests indicate early-man sites in the Americas even prior to the ending of the **Ice Age,** and range in date from 35,000 to 8,000 B.C. The Folsom culture of the Lindenmeier site in Colorado flourished **c.8820 B.C.** (Haynes and Agogino, 1960) and a similar age is suggested for **Tepexpan Man** from the Valley of Mexico (de Terra, 1958). Those supporting the hypothesis of a considerably earlier date for man's migration to the Americas point to radiocarbon dates obtained for a Clovis-type fluted projectile point near Dallas, Tex., of **35,000 B.C.** (Humble Oil Co., 1956); the basin-shaped hearths on Santa Rosa Island off the southern Calif. coast, with a radiocarbon date of *c.*30,000 yrs.; and the occurrence near Puebla, Mex., of fossil bone fragments bearing engravings of animals which may possibly be of similar antiquity. Acceptance of these earlier datings would imply a very much greater age for man's migration to the Americas than previously supposed, possibly as early as 50,000 yrs. ago at the beginning of the last (Wisconsin) glaciation or even before. Despite current scientific controversy over such early datings, no doubt exists concerning the widespread dispersal of early man in both Americas 10,000 yrs. ago, as suggested by radiocarbon dates obtained from sites in Chile and southern Argentina. Tools fashioned either of stone or bone and classified according to types were found in direct association with extinct animals such as the mammoth, ground sloth, camel, and other forms which have long since disappeared.

HUMAN REMAINS OF EARLY MIGRATION. Great faunal interchanges took place between northern Asia and

North America in the closing stage of the Pleistocene glaciation. Man was only one of the many animals which moved either west into Asia or east into North America during such periods. Accurately recorded ancient skeletal remains of these early migrants are scarce and disputed. The fossil-man discoveries include the bones of the **Minnesota Woman** from the dried-up bed of glacial Lake Agassiz; the **Punin Calvarium** from fossil deposits near Quito, Ecuador; the **Lagoa Santo** skulls from coastal Brazil; the **Vero** and **Melbourne** finds in Florida; the **Midland Man** (Midland, Tex., *c.*12,000–20,000 yrs. old); and the **Tepexpan Man** from the Valley of Mexico. Racial admixture is indicated by the variety of the skulls.

c.9000–1500 B.C. EARLY KNOWN HUNTING AND GATHERING CULTURES. Archeological research has demonstrated that these early human immigrants were in a simple hunting, fishing, and gathering stage of culture. Their formidable prowess as hunters is indicated by the fact that they killed great animals like the mammoth, mastodon, and large extinct species of bison. Cultural remains in the form of camps, hearths, stone and bone tools, and slain-animal remains indicate that they had no knowledge of horticulture. Their weapons and tools were primarily chipped and, occasionally, ground stone and bone. Flint tools of a unique type were found underlying those of the Folsom culture (Sandia Cave, New Mexico). The people of the Folsom culture were hunters who used grooved, chipped darts with which they killed mammoth and bison. Remains of this culture have been found from Alaska south beyond the Great Plains. To the south, in Arizona and New Mexico, there were equally ancient peoples of the Cochise culture who used grinding stones and apparently were chiefly plant gatherers rather than hunters. Traces of early hunters and gatherers have been found in Texas, the deserts of California, in Mexico, Peru, Chile, and Argentina. This prehorticultural period persisted through many millennia. In marginal or other regions unfavorable to farming, it survived up to and beyond the time of the European invasion. However, in the Nuclear or heart regions of native American culture, primarily from Mexico south to Peru, it was gradually superseded by another mode of life.

c.3000 B.C. EARLIEST AMERICAN FARMERS. The earliest evidences of extensive New World horticulture are based on recent discoveries. The **Huaca Prieta horizon**, 1946, revealed people who lived on seafood, simple farming, and gathering. They grew and twined or wove cotton and bast; cultivated beans and gourds, but did not grow maize (Indian corn) nor manufacture pottery. Their stone industry was rudimentary. Further north in **Chiapas** (S.E. Mexico), **Honduras**, and **Tamaulipas** (N.E. Mexico) evidences suggesting preceramic cultivators have since come to light. At Chiapas maize was grown even in this early period. Still further north, at **Bat Cave**, in central New Mexico, very primitive types of pod corn have been found in association with chipped stone tools, both below and intermixed with the remains of pottery. Carbon 14 tests at Huaca Prieta give estimates of dates back to **2307 B.C.**, at Bat Cave perhaps back to about **1500 B.C.**; but such Carbon 14 datings may still require more adequate materials and further checking.

c.1000 B.C. FORMATIVE EPOCH. Based on this incipient farm pattern there developed in the Andean and Meso-American regions a series of Formative cultures sharing in common the **expansion of horticulture** (including cultivation of maize, squash, beans, and many other plants), and in the later stages of this Epoch developing **large settlements, irrigating systems,** and, in the Andean region, **metallurgy** based on gold, copper, and other minerals (save iron, which was never smelted in the aboriginal New World). Unlike the Old World, domesticated animals were few (mainly llama varieties in the Andes) and neither utilitarian wheel traction nor the potter's wheel was known in these or later native American cultures. Many of these long-flourishing Formative cultures have now been identified in Peru, Honduras, and Mexico.

c.1 A.D.–900 A.D. FLORESCENT, OR

CLASSIC, EPOCH IN MEXICO AND PERU. In Meso-America and Peru this culture dates around 1 A.D.; in the Maya region of the Petén and Yucatán, stone stelae carved with the glyphs of an accurate calendrical system date the most elaborate of the Maya temples, sculptures, and art forms from c.300–900 A.D. Teotihuacán, near Mexico City, the dead religious center with its huge pyramids and impressive mural paintings, belongs to this epoch as does the finest period Monte Albán III, in the vast ceremonial ruin in Oaxaca. Marked by great population, tremendous construction, and wide trade, this epoch constitutes the apogee of native American cultural progress and is comparable to that of the Bronze Age in the Old World which had flourished more than 3,000 years earlier in the Near East. On the northern coast of Peru the people of the Mochica kingdom built vast adobe-brick structures, made unsurpassed pictorial or modeled pottery, and practiced metallurgy; but unlike Teotihuacán, the Peruvian art forms depict an absorption in warlike activity and indicate the establishment of rigid priestly and other class distinctions. Classical remains from Mexico and Guatemala also provide evidence of a dominant priesthood. Later, throughout Nuclear America, a warrior class appears.

c.1300 A.D. EPOCH OF NATIVE EMPIRES. In this period Meso-America and the central Andean region remained the major centers of cultural progress and military and political activity.

Known as the Militaristic or Epoch of Fusion, this period in Mexico was marked by the Toltec rule at Tula (12th–13th centuries) and the Mexicanization of the Maya regions of Yucatán beg. 1204. Following came the little-understood barbarian Chichimec invasion from the north, and then the rise of the short-lived but barbarically picturesque Aztec Empire (c.1325–1521). Similar conflict to the south wiped out the Florescent Mochica, Nazca, and kindred cultures to be replaced by the so-called Tiahuanaco and related military conquerors. Finally, there emerged the far-flung Inca Empire, one of the most closely integrated totalitarian regimes of the pre-Columbian world. Zenith of Inca power: 11th to 15th centuries. After 1492 Spain pitted the small but desperately effective armies of Cortés and Pizarro against the more or less well organized native empires of the Aztecs (1518–21) and the Incas (1531–35), respectively, the latter then in the throes of bitter civil war.

c.1492. CULTURES AND POPULATIONS OF NATIVE AMERICA NORTH OF MEXICO. The regions north of the Rio Grande were occupied by largely unregimented native peoples, with strongly individualistic, if less complex, cultural patterns than the natives of the southern empires. On the basis of environmental and cultural similarities, the area now included within the United States and Canada can, in late pre-Columbian times, be broken up into five major cultural and ecological . areas (Kroeber, 1939, 1948).

TABLE I.   Major culture areas north of Mexico and estimated population in late pre-Columbian period (condensed from Kroeber, 1939, Table 9, p. 143).

Major Culture Areas	Estimated Population	Areas in 100 Kms.*	Density in 100 Kms.
1. Southwest (in U.S.)	103,000	9,671	10.71
2. Intermediate	158,350	19,411	8.10
3. Northwest Coast	129,200	4,560	28.30
4. Arctic Coast	89,700	22,288	4.02
5. a. Eastern	426,400	61,328	6.95
b. Northern	94,230	69,809	1.35
Total north of Mexico	1,000,880	187,067	5.35

* 100 sq. km. = 38.51 sq. mi., or 7% more than a U.S. township of 6 by 6 miles.

LINGUISTIC FAMILIES
OF
NORTH AMERICA

1. SOUTHWESTERN CULTURE AREA is an arid and elevated region where farming tribes lived in close juxtaposition to hunters (a northern advance of Mexicanlike cultures) and gatherers (a southward extension of simpler hunting and gathering patterns to the north). In the northeastern plateau, a region of summer rains, farming is possible in selected areas, as the long archaeological record of the Anasazi or **Basket Maker-Pueblo** sequence clearly indicates. In the southwestern desert lowland farming was only possible in the flood plains of a few rivers or where irrigation was practiced. This region was the center of another ancient subcultural province known, archaeologically, as the **Hohokam**. Between these farming peoples were a considerable number of other

AREAS OF
NATIVE CULTURE
IN
NORTH AMERICA

These two maps are adapted from A. L. Kroeber, *Anthropology*,
rev. ed., 1948, Harcourt, Brace and Co., Inc.

scattered tribes which eked out a living
through gathering and hunting, much
like the Intermediate area below.

First to attract the notice of the Spanish explorers when they pushed north
from Mexico were the **Pueblo,** or town-
dwelling and farming peoples of the
Anasazi province. In 1540 the Pueblos
occupied some 70 towns scattered in the
region of the present states of Arizona

and New Mexico. Various linguistic
stocks occupied this area, but, among
the Pueblos, the Shoshonean-speaking
Hopi to the north, the central **Zuni**
(probably Shoshonean), and the **Kere-
san**-speaking and other Pueblos of the
Rio Grande valley were outstanding.
The mythical riches of the Zuñi towns,
under the name of the **"Seven Cities of
Cibola,"** lured Coronado.

Pueblo Culture Pattern. The "Three Sisters," corn, beans, and squash, were the basic commodities of these skilled farmers, whose life was oriented around cultivating. Elaborate rituals were employed to bring the summer rains. Differing locally, Pueblo settlement patterns ranged from the contiguous stone masonry house of the Hopi, perched on top of high mesas, to the scattered adobe houses of the Rio Grande Pueblos. All were essentially town-minded, built no temples, but had underground **Kivas** or ceremonial rooms for their various clans and societies. The contiguous and sometimes several-storied buildings with roof entrances formed fortifications, further protected by their positions on high mesas or cliffs. Within the pueblos rule was **theocratic;** no classes other than the **priesthood.** Each Pueblo group was a rule unto itself; no large tribal groups or confederacies existed. In the west the social unit was the **maternal clan;** in the Rio Grande region a **dual organization** was dominant. **Religious rites** included rain-making rites in both east and west, curing ceremonies in the east, and throughout the region procreative rites. Although unwarlike, the Pueblos through their town organization and fortifications strove to hold off the nomadic tribes, such as the **Apache,** which surrounded them. Archaeology indicates that their territory had been drastically cut down long before the arrival of the white man. Intensely conservative, the twenty-odd surviving pueblos today constitute the most viable and truly native culture pattern to be observed in the territory of the U.S. Their neighbors, the Athabaskan-speaking **Navaho,** originally scattered nomads, far surpass all present North American tribes in numbers, but the basic Navaho economic patterns, farming and sheepherding, represent their respective debts, first to their Pueblo neighbor, and then to the white man.

2. INTERMEDIATE CULTURE AREA. North of the Southwestern area extends the arid intermontane Great Basin, and, to the north, the rugged Columbia and Fraser Plateau. These two regions, with that of central California across the Sierra Nevada range, represent a varied topographic but an essentially similar pre-Columbian culture pattern (Kroeber). (1) The **isolated Great Basin** proved one of the most unfavorable regions in North America for native culture; life based on intensive gathering of weed seeds, piñon nuts, insects, and small game; little leisure for broad cultural activities. (2) The **northern Plateau region** provided salmon runs that came up the great rivers which drained it, game, and access to the buffalo herds of the Great Plains after the white man brought the horse. (3) **Central California** abounded in a variety of oaks bearing acorns. The native, a balanophagist (acorn eater), supplemented his basic diet with deer and other game and locally abundant seafood. Aside from sporadic attempts to increase seed production, there was little plant cultivation in these three subareas.

Many **linguistic stocks** were represented in this region: Great Basin predominantly Shoshonean; Plateau largely Salish; Central California, a vast number of isolated languages and stocks. **Settlements** were small and scattered, brush shelters in the south, shelters and pit houses in the north. **Political organization** was based on small bands of bilateral family units, which, on the borders of the Great Basin and in the plateau, acquired some tribal polity when the horse was introduced. **Religion** was simple, primarily shamanistic, with some more elaborate cults among the central Californians, and certain Great Plains ceremonies adopted by the Plateau peoples after the introduction of the horse. **Warfare,** unimportant under native conditions, increased in the early 19th century with the advent of the horse. This area was among the last to feel the direct impact of U.S. expansion, but by the mid-19th century its effects were drastic. Tribal life has disappeared.

3. NORTHWEST CULTURE AREA (western British Columbia and Alaska), one of the most unique in the world, constituted a group of complex, competitive societies sustained without agriculture, dependent entirely on fishing (tremendous runs of salmon provided a food surplus), hunting, and gathering (abundant berries). The tribes of the Northwest Coast occupied a tortuous coast backed by the steep coast range located in a coniferous forest saturated but warmed by the Japanese Current. Facing the sea, all life focused on the beach. ("When the tide is out the table is set," Nootka expression.) **Northern regions** (despite lack of plant domestication) were the most complex culturally just prior to the white invasion, with the greatest population density in native North America (see Table I). At least 3 **major linguistic stocks**—(1) most northerly: **Tlingit** and **Haida** of Athabaskan stock; (2) central region: **Tsimshian** of Penutian stock and **Bella Coola** of Salish stock; (3) south: **Kwakiutl, Nootka** (Algonkian-Wakashan stock), and numerous other tribes in Puget Sound, western Oregon, and northern California.

Basic economy, salmon fisheries; secondary, whaling, sea fishing, berry gathering, and hunting. **Winter villages,** consisting of great plankhouses facing the beach, split from cedar and fir with fire, stone tools, and antler wedges, were often fortified or placed on protected points because of raiding parties. **Fishing stations** and **summer camps** located up the rivers were owned by individual families from time immemorial. Travel was by sea or along the fjords and rivers in great or small dugout canoes. **Northwest Coast art style,** highly symbolic: wood implements, particularly of cedar, characterized by a striking style of carved, painted, and shell-inlaid ornamentation, carried over into house facings, entrances, and especially the famous **totem poles,** or family crests, which marked the villages.

Organization was by independent villages, made up of graded groups of kinfolk and slaves, not tribally. North: local groupings crosscut by matrilineal clans and dual divisions, or moieties; Central region: both matrilineal and patrilineal groupings; South: patrilineal groupings predominant. **Class distinctions** emphasized: chiefs and nobles at the top; then commoners; lastly, slaves who were war captives or debtors. All rank rested on wealth, with an endless variation and shifting of grades. A comprehensive system of **private ownership** (embracing land, fishing stations, houses, masks, crests, names, etc.) carried prestige, and

was acquired by inheritance, purchase, and sometimes warfare. At **potlatches** (ceremonies or feasts) rival chiefs, supported by their respective kinsmen and slaves of all degrees, competed in ostentatious display of wealth and property exchanges. "Gifts" between rival chiefs had to be returned with compound interest, default leading to social degradation. In the later periods the white fur trade made this society even more highly competitive by producing greater surpluses of exchangeable goods and food. With its class stratification resting upon validated wealth and ostentatious exchange and destruction of property, the Northwest Coast economy was **capitalist** in form, with a trading acumen which matched the Yankees who in the late 18th century traded along its coast for sea-otter fur.

Religion ranged from the belief in a supreme deity to pure shamanism; rich in display, complex in masks and other equipment, and orgiastic in character. The winter season was taken up with elaborate ceremonies held by the graded societies, of which the **hamatsa,** or cannibal society, and the animal societies were the most numerous. Like the potlatch, these society affairs were competitive, each trying to outdo the other in richness of costume and ferocity of act and aspect. **Warfare,** sporadic, chiefly for purposes of revenge, to secure slaves, and, occasionally, crests or property. As a result of the impact upon this culture of the Russians coming from the north (after 1741), the Spanish from the south (1774), and the Anglo-Americans from the east (1786), tribal life is largely shattered, although a decimated population still occupies moldering villages.

4. ARCTIC COAST CULTURE AREA: THE ESKIMO.

A relatively small group, the Eskimo-Aleut, occupied the long northern coast from the Aleutians all the way east to Greenland and southern Labrador. Present archaeological evidence indicates that the early Eskimoan groups entered western Alaska shortly before 1 A.D., with the last eastward migration reaching Greenland about the same time as the Norsemen arrived from the east (*c.*1,000 A.D.). In **physical type** the Eskimo share most basic Mongoloid characteristics with the main Indian population, with certain minor, but distinctive, features. The Eskimoan **language** falls into three closely related divisions: Aleut, Western, and Eastern, the first being the most distinctive. **Occupations:** Primarily hunters and fishermen, with numerous variations based on differences in water, temperature, and ice conditions along their extended coastal terrain. **Open, western Pacific:** Eskimo hunted large sea mammals in skin-covered **kayaks** and open boats, seasonally going inland after the caribou, but also eating fish, birds, foxes, and polar bear. Similar open-water conditions prevailed in Greenland and Labrador. **Central region** (where the sea freezes all winter, typically Eskimoan): Eskimo are ice hunters, living in block-built snow **igloos**, traveling by dog sledge, and securing the seal through the ice and the walrus along the floe edges; in summer moving to caribou-skin tents and hunting caribou and fishing salmon in the interior. **Settlement pattern:** villages attaining considerable size in western Alaska and southern Greenland, but composed of small, shifting family groups in the north-central regions. Tailored fur and leather clothing, elaborate hunting gear including toggle harpoons, floats, sleds, and dog traction in winter and **kayaks** in summer, all speak of long and skillful adaptation to Arctic conditions. Hence, the most successful Arctic explorers like Peary not only were accompanied by Eskimo but employed clothing, food, equipment, and methods of transportation of Eskimo origin. **Political organization:** loose; shifting family groupings dominant. **Religion:** based in large part on fear of a hostile universe wherein many spirits dwell who must be propitiated. Contact with the supernatural is often attained through the **shaman**, who knows the speech of animals, and sends his soul away to treat with the recalcitrant spirits. The more elaborate ceremonies in western Alaska involve the use of masks, carvings, and equipment reminiscent of Northwest Coast culture. **Organized warfare:** rare or absent, although Indian-Eskimo conflicts were noted (by Samuel Hearne, 1771). Early European explorers, like

Frobisher (1576–78) and John Davis (1585), were attacked by the Eskimo of Baffin Land. Today, a somewhat mixed Eskimo population of less than half the numbers estimated for the first contact period (Table I) still survives in all but the southern limits of their former range. In the central Arctic, the old basic hunting pattern of life still continues in a few isolated places, but in general the Greenland, Canadian, and Alaskan Eskimo have today come under the influence of Euro-American culture although much of the native language, economy, and culture still persist.

5. EASTERN-NORTHERN CULTURE AREA comprises a great terrain which slopes east from the Rocky Mountains to the Atlantic Ocean. Variant but without drastic environmental or abrupt cultural breaks, this ecological area falls into 3 major subdivisions: (1) **Southeast**, (2) **Great Plains**, and (3) **Northeastern-Great Lakes** cultural provinces. From the palms of southern Florida to the dwarf-willow scrub of northern Labrador there is a gradual transition from tropical to subarctic conditions. Similarly, on the cultural plane, there is a gradual gradient from the elaborately class-structured society of the **Natchez** (Mississippi) to the wandering, classless **Naskapi** hunters (northern Labrador). The Great Plains to the west, due to the introduction of the horse and firearms in post-Columbian times (c.1540–1880), became for a time somewhat unique, but the original cultural pattern of the same fabric. **Ecologically**, the entire area is mainly woodland, deciduous trees predominating, with the addition of pine and spruce. Dominating the main regions were the hardwoods, thinning out into river-valley cover in the **tall-grass-prairie** regions from Illinois west, and, eventually, disappearing in the **short-grass** region of the **High Plains west of the 100th Meridian** (westward from the 20-in.-rainfall line to the Rockies, an area of scanty rainfall which later offered greater inducements to cattlemen than to farmers). In the central regions the bison was important for food; to the north, deer, moose, and caribou. Native means of navigation over the great rivers and lake systems served as a means of intercommunication: the birchbark canoe, best developed in the Great Lakes region, like the dugout canoes and rafts on the lower rivers, and the "bullboats" of the Missouri, reminiscent of but not historically related to the Welsh coracle. Owing to the preoccupation with war, the natives failed to exploit the rich agricultural potential of this region.

Linguistically, the northeastern and Great Lake regions were dominated by **Algonkian-**speaking tribes extending north to Labrador and as far south as the Carolinas. Splitting this distribution, from the Cherokee of Georgia north along the Great Lakes to the St. Lawrence, were a number of **Iroquoian-**speaking groups, most famous being the powerful **League of the Iroquois (Mohawk, Onondaga, Oneida, Cayuga, Seneca,** and, later, **Tuscarora**) in upper New York State. The southeastern subarea was dominated by **Muskogean-**speaking peoples, including the **Cherokee, Choctaw, Chickasaw, Creek,** and **Seminole** (later known as the "**Five Civilized Nations**"), and many others. Interspersed were peoples of **Siouan** and a considerable variety of other smaller linguistic stocks. On the Great Plains to the west, tribes of the **Caddoan** linguistic stock stretched from Arkansas to the Dakotas, with many Siouan tribes along the west bank of the Mississippi and on both sides of the Missouri River in both the tallgrass prairie and short-grass plains. Algonkian-speaking and other tribes were also interspersed throughout the Great Plains area. Most of these seem to have been latecomers, mainly after the advent of the horse, but some, like the **Blackfoot** (Algonkian), **Mandan** (Siouan), and **Pawnee** (Caddoan), appear to have been old residents. **Timetable of European exploration and settlement:** Southeast, by the French and Spaniards, beginning **1562;** the Northeastern Great Lakes and eastern Great Plains, by the French, beginning **1634** (Nicolet); the eastern maritime regions by the English, principally beginning **1607.** As in Meso-America, the Spanish encountered the most culturally advanced tribes.

Basic Economy. The aboriginal Southeast depended on the cultivation of **corn, beans,** and **squash,** supplemented by gathering, hunting, and fishing. Native farming by slash and burn methods soon exhausted the deciduous forest soil, causing villages to move frequently. Maize cultivation extended with lessening productivity north as far as the St. Lawrence River, and west along the river valleys of the Prairie-Plains. North and west of this area early frosts and drought prevented native farming. The extreme northern regions were dependent mainly on hunting the moose and caribou or fishing; the short-grass plains, primarily on the bison herds. The Great Lakes region had both farming and hunting, supplemented (in Wisconsin and Minnesota) by gathering "wild rice," which grows abundantly in shallow lakes. Because of farming, the southeastern subregion supported the larger population, while the forest and tundra of the northern subarea had the lowest population density in aboriginal North America (Table I). Considering its long occupation and rich agricultural food potential, even the eastern subarea seems amazingly underpopulated. Crude methods of cultivation and endless warfare combined to limit population.

The **settlement pattern** in the Southeast, and north to the St. Lawrence river, at the time of first European penetration seems mainly to have been one of **villages** (generally larger in the south) often surrounded with **stockades. Architecture:** In the southeast, round, semi-subterranean "**hothouses**" for winter; loosely constructed, rectangular bark or "**shake**" **houses** for summer were the rule. These family units were arranged in a square ground pattern with an open plaza in the center often surrounded by artificial mounds of earth within which the ceremonial "Chunkey" game was played. To the north, the Iroquois and many of their Algonkian neighbors made "**longhouses**" out of bark and poles to house many families. To the west, arbor-like houses of bark, matting, and poles were used. On the Great Plains even the earth lodge and the graceful skin **tipi** were employed. North of the St. Lawrence the conical **wigwam** covered with birchbark or caribou hide was most common. In the Southeast, the eastern prairies, and again north to the St. Lawrence, stockades with moats, bastions, and firing platforms protected the villages. In the south-central area quite elaborate temple mound structures were in use, often located on top of large artificial earth mounds with ramps leading up to them. The so-called ancient Indian "Mound builders" of the Ohio region left remains of just such mound structures as De Soto, Bartram, and other white explorers found actually in use in what is now the southeastern U.S.

Political Organization: Confederacy. Beginning with the **matrilineal** system, family, or clan, political organization passed on to the **moiety** or dual division, then to the **tribal** group, and, finally, to the **Confederacy**, or loose grouping of tribes, embodying certain concepts of the "state." In the South between **1836–40**, the **Creek Confederacy** included numerous tribes speaking 6 distinctive languages in some 50 towns. Others, like the **Powhatan Confederacy** (c.1607) in Virginia, were smaller. One of the most famous was the **League of the Iroquois** (beg. c.1559–70) in New York. Like the moiety divisions of White (Peace) and Red (War) towns among the Creeks, the Iroquois Confederacy, founded for peace, became a deadly instrument for war in the northeast. The unusual power exercised by the women in the latter tribes actually made or broke **sachems,** or chiefs. The northern peoples had a less complex political and social organization. Beyond the St. Lawrence it was based upon shifting family bands. To the west confederacies existed among the Caddoan peoples, matrilineal clans among certain Siouan peoples, and patrilineal and bilateral organizations among the bordering Plains tribes. Among some tribes on the lower Mississippi a true class system evolved; most celebrated was that of the **Natchez,** where by an imperative class-intermarriage system lineages passed from the top role of relatives of the sun to the lowest class of "Stinkards" within four generations.

Introduction of Horse. Archaeological research clearly indicates that the basic patterns of the eastern, or tallgrass-prairie, plains were horticultural and of a Southeastern semisedentary type (pre-1540). With the advent of the European horse (post-1540), the pattern

changed to equestrian, bison hunting. Many border tribes then first entered the plains from north, east, and west, to overrun the older, more settled Caddoan and Siouan peoples such as the Arikara, Pawnee, and the Mandan respectively. The early Spanish pioneers from the south encountered the semisedentary native peoples; the later modern American westward migration met the equestrian bison hunters in their militaristic prime.

Religious and Ceremonial Activities were varied and complex (see J. R. Swanton, *Indians of the Southeastern U.S.,* Bur. Amer. Ethnology, *Bull. 137,* 1946). **Southeast:** Temples and idols widely distributed, with a definite priesthood. Cultural climax attained by the **Natchez,** with their deified ruler representing the sun, living in a temple with sacred fetishes on top of a mound complex. Alongside supreme deities, a vast number of other deities, spirits, and sacred places were worshiped among the various tribes. Notable ceremonies: the "busk" or green-corn dance; and the "new fire" ceremony with its aim of "life renewal" and accompanying drinking of the "black drink," an emetic which led to purification. Ceremonies for both war and peace existed side by side. **West:** Basic in the religion of the Caddoan tribes were sacred bundles dedicated to agricultural pursuits. **North:** religion simpler and more shamanistic; great importance given to dreams in guiding all activity; the individual soul was identified with the breath. Among the most northeasterly Algonkians, the **Naskapi** combined an animalistic mythology, a shamanistic belief, with a native concept of a supreme deity associated with the caribou, the most important food animal.

WARFARE: SUBJUGATION OF TRIBES IN U.S. Warfare played a destructive role in the aboriginal Southeast, in the later phases of native life in the Iroquois region, and in the Great Plains, but to a much lesser extent in the northern areas. The fact that the eastern Indians cultivated less than 1% of the arable land available and achieved a population density of only 9 Indians per township in a region which today supports 400 persons per township is attributed by Kroeber to the "insane, attritional type of war" waged throughout the area, carried on incessantly by individuals for revenge, by small parties, towns, tribes, and confederacies. Warfare was highly ceremonialized, accompanied by elaborate torture rites (reaching a peak among the Iroquois), with war honors essential to almost every youth and the warpath the primary road to fame and honor. Aggressive behavior was somewhat canalized off in such ceremonial games as **lacrosse**. In addition, peace towns, moieties, and leagues were organized to maintain peace, but the eastern war pattern persisted to the end, latterly becoming blended with European war practices and weapons brought in by the new invaders. As a result of military defeat and white penetration native life as such has ended in most of the Eastern-Northern cultural provinces. The "Five Civilized Nations" were by 1838 moved over the "Trail of Tears" to the Indian Territory (Oklahoma), although the Seminoles, after prolonged warfare with the U.S., were all but exterminated by 1842. Other eastern groups, like the Iroquois, were confined to reservations or else have blended with the modern white and Negro populations of the area. Only in the far north do the old hunting and fishing patterns still persist, along with fur trapping, which is post-Caucasian, but even these faint marginal manifestations decrease from year to year. In addition to the Oklahoma Reservation for the Five Civilized Tribes, various reservations in the Dakotas and elsewhere were assigned to the Sioux and other tribes. Resisting the advancing mining frontier and the Federal government's reservation policy, the Indians of the West were finally overwhelmed by superior numbers and technology in a series of wars, 1861–68, 1875–90 (**Cheyenne-Arapaho War, 1861–64; Red River War, 1874; Sioux Wars, 1862–67 and 1875–76; Nez Percé War, 1877; Apache War, 1871–87; Ghost Dance Uprising, 1890,** also p. 458).

PRE-COLUMBIAN EXPLORATION

800–986. VIKING SETTLEMENT AND EXPLORATION. After occupying the Shetlands, the Faroes, and the Orkneys (by 800), the Vikings settled Iceland (874). **Eric the Red,** in exile from Iceland, after three years spent exploring the coasts of Greenland (982–85), led a group of settlers to the southwestern coast of that island, where the first Norse colony was planted (986). That same year **Bjarni Herjulfson** is credited with sighting the mainland of North America when blown off his course while seeking the new colony.

c.1000. LEIF ERICSON, the son of Eric the Red, either by accident (in 1000, according to the **Karlsevni Saga**) or with forethought (in 1002, according to the **Greenland Saga**), explored the North American coast, naming the regions, as he voyaged southward, **Helluland** (land of flat rocks), **Markland** (forest land), and **Vinland** (wineland). Experts differ as to the identity of Vinland: Newfoundland (Hovgaard), mouth of the St. Lawrence (Steensby), Nova Scotia (Storm), northern New England (Thorvarson), Cape Cod (F. J. Pohl), Rhode Island (Rafn), New York (Gathorne-Hardy), middle Atlantic coast (Haugen), Virginia (Mjeldi). **Thorvald Ericson,** Leif's brother, explored the coast of the continent (1004–07), using Leif's headquarters in Vinland. A second brother, **Thorstein,** tried unsuccessfully to find Vinland (1008).

1010–13. Thorfinn Karlsevni, a trader from Iceland, with 3 ships and 160 men, mostly Greenlanders, sailed on an exploratory trip to the North American mainland. Despite similarity between the names used to designate the regions Karlsevni visited and those explored by the sons of Eric, enough differences exist in their geographical descriptions to raise some doubt that they were in the same area. The operations of the Eric-sons, according to the prevailing view, were confined to the east coast of North America; but the possibility exists that Karlsevni, instead of coasting along Labrador or Newfoundland, sailed into Hudson's Bay. **Freydis,** Eric's daughter, believed to be a member of Karlsevni's group, is credited with making the last trip to the mainland described in the Sagas (1014–15).

1014–1415. DURATION OF NORSE SETTLEMENT. The Greenland Colony continued at least until the second decade of the 15th century, although its connection with Europe weakened during the 14th century. Its active role as a colony ceased with the sailing of the last royal ship to that island (1367). A party of Icelanders visited the colony, 1408, and a churchman appears to have sailed there in the second decade of the 15th century, but no further contacts are known. The North American mainland has yielded scores of Norse relics, most of which were either so patently spurious or found under such unverifiable circumstances that they have been dismissed by the majority of scholars. Nevertheless, the **Newport Tower** (a round stone structure in Rhode Island) has recently had its case revived and the **Kensington Stone,** a slab with Runic inscriptions dated 1362 (found in Minnesota, 1898), was originally pronounced a forgery but its case has also been revived, by H. R. Holand. A recent discovery at Copenhagen of a royal order indicates that a Norse searching party was sent in 1354 to find survivors of a colony on the west coast of Greenland. Any connection between the royal order and the Kensington Stone would involve accepting a route of the searching party from Hudson's Bay up the Nelson River to its source at Lake Winnipeg and crossing by a series of lakes and portages to central Minnesota. Recent discoveries at Beard-

14

more, in western Ontario, of a sword, ax-head, and shield grip (c.1000) are considered authentic. Their location is on an old route from James Bay to Lake Nipigon.

1447–98. PORTUGUESE EXPLORATION. Under the impetus of **Prince Henry the Navigator** (1394–1460), third son of John I, expeditions were sent down the west African coast, and the Azores, the Canaries, and Madeira were occupied. **Bartolomeu Dias** reached the Cape of Good Hope, 1488, and **Vasco da Gama** completed a voyage around Africa to India and return, 1498. Portuguese claims to the discovery of the New World are based on a number of westward explorations. On the basis of a map of the Venetian, Andrea Biancho (1448), in which a large island, **Ixola Otinticha** (authentic island), is shown lying a good distance southwest of Cape Verde, it has been suggested that the Portuguese already knew of the existence of South America. In 1452 Diogo de Teive and Pedro Vasquez sailed to the Azores, where they discovered two additional islands of that group (Corvo and Flores). After these discoveries they were blown northward, and Portuguese scholars (particularly Cortesão) believe that they reached the Grand Bank of Newfoundland before returning to Portugal. Sometime before 1460 a Portuguese ship is said to have reached Antillia, identified by the Portuguese with the legendary **Ilha das Sete Cidades** (Island of the Seven Cities). A Portuguese document credits João Vaz Corte-Real and Álvaro Martins Homem with the discovery of **Tiera de los Bacalfaos** (1472), a name applied to Newfoundland shortly after the voyages of Columbus. Lack of supporting data compels one scholar (Jansen) to place these explorers on a known Danish expedition as observers for the Portuguese Crown. In 1476 Fernão Teles sailed west in search of Antillia. Fernão Dulmo received a patent from the King (3 Mar. 1486) to explore islands or the mainland of Ilha das Sete Cidades. After entering into partnership with João Alfonso de Estreito, he had his plans approved by the King (24 July and 4 Aug. 1486), but there is no mention of this expedition. Admitting the possibility that Portugal may have wished to keep her territorial discoveries secret, scholars are hesitant about accepting claims to New World exploration put forth in behalf of the explorers of that nation.

1473–81. DANISH AND ENGLISH ACTIVITIES. Diderik Pining and Hans Pothorst, German mariners, sailed on an exploratory trip to Greenland for King Christian of Denmark, 1472. Cartographical sources indicating that Scolvus, possibly a Pole, sailed to the northwest at this time point to the probability that he went on this Danish voyage as a pilot. Possibly Corte-Real and Homem were also in the party. In 1480 Thomas Lloyd of Bristol, England, sailed in search of the island Antillia. Further exploratory trips were made annually in Bristol ships both to this island and to Brasil, another small island shown on contemporary maps (1491–98).

OTHER POSSIBLE PRE-COLUMBIAN CONTACTS. African contacts with the New World, based on the alleged presence of Negroes in pre-Columbian America, have been postulated by Leo Wiener. Claims have also been advanced that fishermen from the west coast of France sailed to the fishing waters off Newfoundland prior to 1492. Even had such trips been made, they failed to contribute to making Europeans aware of the existence of the New World. In fact, after the translation of Ptolemy's *Geography* (1410), and perhaps even before that date, such a possibility was suggested by available scientific knowledge. A connection between Inca and South Seas cultures has been argued by Thor Heyerdahl, who in 1947 sailed in an Inca-style raft in 101 days from the Peruvian port of Callao to one of the Tuamotu islands. Heyerdahl's thesis of a South American origin for Polynesian culture is disputed by Alfred Métraux (1957) and by Thomas S. Barthel's decipherment of the writing on the Easter Island statues, revealing that the people who made the mysterious statues spoke a Polynesian language. Hence, the evidence would point to a South Pacific westward cultural migration, with the likelihood that contacts came after the development of formative cultures on both sides of the Pacific.

COLUMBUS AND SUBSEQUENT EXPLORATION

Improvements in navigation which gave impulse to exploration included (1) the **magnetic compass;** (2) the **astrolabe,** a device for determining latitude; (3) the use of **portolani,** the first practical hydrographic charts; and (4) the construction of the fast Portuguese **caravel,** a small vessel with broad bows, high narrow poop, and usually triangular lateen sails, which could sail against the wind more efficiently than earlier ships. The early explorations to the New World were largely shaped by geographical factors—winds and ocean currents determined the landfalls and guided the interior exploration. Since chronometers and watches were not in common use, it was difficult to determine longitude at sea. Mariners would first strike the desired latitude and continue on the course until their goal was reached. Thus, Columbus, sailing for the latitude of Japan and then heading west, was helped along by the **northeast trade winds** and by ocean currents. On his return trip he was aided by the **westerly winds.** Once North America was reached, penetration and occupation were determined by opportunities for profitable exploitation and by natural advantages for travel. Thus, the accumulated wealth of Mexico and Central America repaid costly and laborious inroads and settlement, whereas similar expeditions from Florida and Mexico which ranged the lower half of the Mississippi Valley yielded nothing. The other two natural entries to the interior, the St. Lawrence-Great Lakes (with a branch by way of the Hudson River) and Hudson Bay, were first explored in vain as routes to Asia or to rich kingdoms, but remained unused until the North Atlantic fisheries stimulated a fur trade whose rapid drain of the supply drew traders along the waterways into the continent.

1451, c.25 Aug.–31 Oct. CHRISTO-PHER COLUMBUS (It., **Cristoforo Colombo;** Span., **Cristóbal Colón**) was born in or near Genoa of a family of wool weavers. The fact that he could write only one modern language, Spanish, even before he went to Spain, combined with vagueness and inconsistencies in his earliest biographies (his 2d son Fernando's *Historie* and Bartolomé de Las Casas' *Historia de las Indias*), have cast some doubt on his Genoese birth. On the other hand, the records of that city present a wealth of substantiating evidence which no other location can offer, including references to his family as well as several to Columbus himself in various notarial papers (31 Oct. 1470; 20, 26 Mar. 1472; 7 Aug. 1473). Fernando's assertion that his father attended the University of Pavia is not borne out by that institution's records. Columbus may have gone to sea in the service of René d'Anjou (1470–73), and made one or more trips to the island of Chios for the Centurione interests (1474–75).

1476–80. Following a naval battle off Cape St. Vincent between a Genoese fleet on which he was shipping and a Franco-Portuguese flotilla, Columbus arrived in Portugal (1476). Shortly thereafter (Feb. 1477) he made a trip to northern waters (possibly Iceland, but more likely England). Returning to Lisbon, he sailed (1478) once more for the Centurione, this time to Madeira. He married (1479 or 1480) Doña Felipa de Perestrello é Moñiz, daughter of the Captain of Porto Santo, to which he moved (1480), the year in which his son Diego was born. Probably (1481–82) he made a trip to the Guinea Coast.

1484. Columbus asked King João II of Portugal to sponsor a western voyage to the island of Cipangu (Marco Polo's Japan). The plan was rejected (1485) either because of lack of confidence in Columbus's geographical knowledge or because the crown was licensing self-financed voyages with similar objectives (Fernão Dulmo, 1486–87). Columbus' stay at Lisbon is believed to have furnished him with opportunities for acquiring knowledge of geography and navigation. Portugal was the home of the most advanced geographers, including José Vizinho and Diogo Ortiz de Vilhegas; was visited by the great Nuremberg cosmographer, Martin Behaim. The court corresponded with the Italian geographer, Toscanelli (1474), as did Columbus (c.1481).

1485–86. Columbus left Lisbon with his son Diego (his wife had already died) and landed at Palos, Spain, where he was befriended by a Franciscan friar, Antonio de Marchena. After unsuccessful negotiations with Don Enrique de Guzmán, Duke of Medina Sidonia, Columbus turned to Don Luis de la Cerda, Count of Medina Celi, who arranged a meeting between Columbus and Queen Isabella (c.1 May 1486). The result was inconclusive. For the next two years Columbus received a small yearly stipend from the Crown.

1488. Columbus attempted to re-open negotiations with King João II, and was in Lisbon to witness the triumphant return of Bartolomeu Dias. With India apparently within its grasp, Portugal was disinclined to back Columbus, who returned to Spain.

1490–92. Columbus' plan was twice rejected by the Castilian commission, but at the insistence of **Luis de Santangel,** Marrano treasurer of Aragon, the court, following the fall of Granada (2 Jan. 1492), marking the end of the reconquest of Spain from the Moors, agreed to sponsor his expedition. His voyage was financed by both the royal treasury and private sources. By the Capitulations of 17 Apr. and the Title of 30 Apr. 1492 Columbus was appointed Admiral of the Ocean Sea, Viceroy, and governor of whatever territory he might discover.

1492, 3 Aug.–1493, 15 Mar. 1ST VOYAGE. The 3 ships of Columbus' fleet (the *Niña,* commanded by Vincente Yáñez Pinzón; the *Pinta* by Martín Alonso Pinzón; and the *Santa Maria,* by Columbus), with a crew of 90, sailed from Palos. They arrived at the Canaries (12

Reconstruction of alleged Toscanelli map (1474?)
reputedly used by Columbus on his first voyage

Aug.), sailed west (6 Sept.), and during the first stage of the ocean crossing (9–19 Sept.) enjoyed favorable winds. With the next stage (20–30 Sept.) marked by unfavorable winds and calms morale dropped, with the crews at the point of mutiny 2 days before land was actually sighted. Columbus first sighted (12 Oct.) **Guanahani** (probably **Watlings Island**) in the Bahamas, which he named San Salvador. He explored the Bahamas (14–26 Oct.), discovered and explored the northeastern coast of **Cuba** (27 Oct.–5 Dec.), then (6 Dec. 1492–15 Jan. 1493) the northern coast of **Hispaniola** (Santo Domingo), where the *Santa Maria* was wrecked (25 Dec.) and a post established (**La Navidad**). On the homeward journey (16 Jan.–15 Mar.) stops were made at the Azores (18–24 Feb.) and Lisbon (4–13 Mar.). News of the voyage had already reached the court in a letter written by Columbus off the Canaries (15 Feb.), addressed to Luis de Santangel, a substantial backer of the expedition. This was printed at Barcelona in the original Spanish shortly after its receipt; reprinted, Valladolid, with slight corrections.

1493–94. DIPLOMATIC CONSEQUENCES OF THE DISCOVERY. At the urging of the Spanish rulers Pope Alexander VI (Rodrigo Borgia) issued (3–4 May) two bulls, **Inter Caetera** (granting Spain all lands not under Christian rule) and **Inter Caetera II** (setting a demarcation line at 100 leagues west of the Azores and Cape Verde Islands, beyond which all future discoveries not held by a Christian prince on 25 Dec. 1492 would belong to Spain). By the **Treaty of Tordesillas** (7 June 1494) between Portugal and Spain the line of demarcation was moved to 370 leagues west of the Cape Verde Islands, Portugal to have exclusive rights to all land east of the line.

1493, 25 Sept.–1496, 11 June. 2ND VOYAGE. Columbus sailed from Cadiz with 17 ships and some 1,200 men (including his brother Diego). The fleet stopped at the Canaries (2–7 or 10 Oct.) and reached the **Leeward Islands** (4 Nov.). After exploring the Leewards and **Puerto Rico**, Columbus anchored off La

Navidad (28 Nov.), where he found his post destroyed. Columbus planted (2 Jan. 1494) **Isabela**, a second colony on Santo Domingo, which served as a base for inland exploration, and explored the southern coast of Cuba, the coasts of Jamaica, and the remaining coastline of Hispaniola (29 Apr.–29 Sept.). The Isabela settlement faced serious difficulties from the start owing to its unsuitable location, sparse gold resources, and the resentment of the natives to enslavement by the conquerors. It was abandoned, and the city of **Santo Domingo** founded 1496. Leaving in command of the island his brother, Bartholomew, who had joined him in 1494, Columbus sailed for Spain (10 Mar. 1496) and reached Cadiz (11 June).

1498, 30 May–1500, 25 Nov. 3RD VOYAGE. Columbus, with a fleet of 7 ships, left the mouth of the Guadalquivir, touched at Madeira (7 June) and the Canaries (19 June), whence 3 ships proceeded directly to Santo Domingo and the remainder, with Columbus, took a more southerly route, touching the Cape Verde Islands (27 June–4 July) and reaching **Trinidad** (31 July). Columbus sighted South America (1 Aug.) at **Punta Bombeador**, explored the **Gulf of Paria** (1–13 Aug.), and sailed for **Santo Domingo**, where he arrived (31 Aug.) to find the colony in a state of rebellion. Some improvement in administration followed the granting of immunity to the rebel leaders (Sept. 1499), but news of unrest convinced the court of the need for a change in administration. The new governor, Francisco de Bobadilla, arrived 23 Aug. 1500, and the three brothers Columbus were sent home in chains (Oct.). They were ultimately restored to their honors but never to their old authority in the Indies, which the crown henceforth retained.

1502, 11 May–1504, 7 Nov. 4TH AND LAST VOYAGE. Columbus with a fleet of 4 ships sailed from Cadiz, stopped at the Canaries (20–25 May), and hit land at **Martinique** (15 June). After stopping at Hispaniola Columbus sailed past Cuba to the mainland of Central America on the **Honduran coast** (31 July) and explored southward as far as **central Panama** (31 July 1502–15 Apr.

1503). En route to Hispaniola he was shipwrecked and marooned in Jamaica (25 June 1503–29 June 1504), and returned to Spain 7 Nov. 1504.

1506, 20 May. DEATH AND BURIAL PLACE. Columbus died in Valladolid after spending his final days trying to regain his old privileges. Until his death he insisted that he had skirted the shores of Asia. However, recognition that the territory he had charted was in fact a New World was already gaining ground. His remains were sent to Santo Domingo some time after 5 Nov. 1540 along with those of his son, Diego (d.1526), and placed in the Cathedral. As a result of the Treaty of Basle (22 July 1795), under which the Spanish part of Santo Domingo was ceded to France, the Spanish authorities removed certain remains from the Cathedral in an unmarked lead casket and installed them in the Cathedral at Havana. Bones were later removed to Seville and deposited at the Cathedral in that city (1898). Meantime (10 Sept. 1877), a cask discovered on the Gospel side of the sanctuary of the Santo Domingo Cathedral bore markings indicating that it held the Discoverer's remains. Authorities are divided on the authenticity of the find. Hence, two Columbus shrines at the present day —one at Seville, the other at Ciudad Trujillo.

1497, 2 May–6 Aug. 1ST CABOT VOYAGE. John Cabot (b.c.1455, probably in Genoa), a resident (1461) and citizen (1472) of Venice, migrated to England (c.1484–90), where he lived chiefly in Bristol as a merchant or mariner. Henry VII issued (5 Mar. 1497) to the Cabots (John and his 3 sons, Lewis, Sebastian, and Sancio) a patent to discover for England regions to the east, west, and north (avoiding Portuguese claims). In return for a trade monopoly and customs exemptions the Cabots were to turn over to the crown 20% of all trading profits. John Cabot sailed from Bristol (2 May 1497) with a crew of 18, including some prominent Bristol merchants and possibly his son, **Sebastian,** on a voyage of general reconnaissance. He sighted land (24 June) probably in the vicinity of **Cape Breton** or **Newfoundland,** took possession of the

area for Henry VII, and then sailed southwest far enough to ascertain the direction of the coast, possibly reaching Maine before sailing for England (c.15 July), arriving at Bristol 6 Aug.

1498, early May. 2ND CABOT VOYAGE. Under new letters patent (3 Feb. 1498) Cabot left Bristol for Cipangu (Japan) and the Spice Islands via Newfoundland. From available evidence (La Cosa map, 1500, and the Hajeda patent, 8 June 1501), it appears that Cabot's company explored the coast of North America **as far south as the Delaware or Chesapeake Bay.**

1499–1501. SPANISH EXPLORATION AFTER COLUMBUS. Amerigo Vespucci (b.Mar. 1454 in Florence and employed by the Pier Francesco branch of the Medici, first in Italy, 1484–92, and then in Spain, 1492–99), sailed on an expedition commanded by **Alonso de Hajeda** (Ojeda), on which Juan de la Cosa, a member of Columbus' first and second expeditions, also participated. Before sighting land the party separated. Vespucci's company probably sighted land south of **Cape Cassipore** (c.27 June), journeyed down the South American coast, possibly exploring the mouth of the Amazon and the Pará, thence southeastward, passing the "Cape de la Vela" (19 Sept., possibly near Camocim, Brazil). Meantime, the Hajeda-La Cosa group had already arrived at Hispaniola (5 Sept.). Vespucci returned (end of Nov.), and, after sailing around the Bahamas and visiting the Azores, he reached Spain (mid-June 1500) several months after Hajeda and La Cosa. Two other expeditions sailing under the Spanish flag left in 1499 for the New World: (1) Peralonso Niño (former pilot of the *Santa Maria* and *Niña*) and Cristóbal Guerra went on an expedition to the Pearl Coast (Venezuela) in June and returned to Spain (Apr. 1500) laden with pearls. Vincente Yáñez Pinzón (captain of the *Niña* on Columbus' first voyage) sailed in Nov. or Dec. and reached the coast of Brazil (20 Jan. 1500) at ab. 8°S. and explored either the Amazon or the Marañón before returning to Spain (30 Sept. 1500). In 1500–01 Rodrigo de Bastidas explored the northern coast of South America from Maracaibo to the Gulf of Darien, and, possibly, Juan de la Cosa made another trip in 1501 (perhaps with Vespucci), in which he explored the Gulf of Darien and the Atrato River where he found traces of gold.

1499–1501. PORTUGUESE VOYAGES TO NEW WORLD. João Fernandes, a small landowner of the rank of **Llavrador,** i.e., peasant, and a seaman of the Azores, under a patent from King Manoel of Portugal (28 Oct. 1499) reached Greenland, initially called by his rank (Labrador). Under a patent from King Manoel (12 May 1500), **Gaspar Corte-Real** sailed (June 1500) to the east coast of Greenland, down and around its southern tip, and up the west coast until he encountered icebergs. On a second trip (15 May 1501) to Greenland he crossed Davis Strait to present Labrador, coasted south to Newfoundland, dispatched two boats home, continued southward in a third, and was never heard from again. His brother, **Miguel,** sailed (10 May 1502) to Newfoundland, but was also lost. A Portuguese expedition to locate the missing brothers (1503) presumably visited Newfoundland. In addition to their activity in northern waters, the Portuguese made voyages to South America. Pedro Alvarez Cabral reached the coast of Brazil (1500). **Amerigo Vespucci,** having switched flags, sailed west for the Portuguese (13 May 1501). He made his landfall a short distance south of **Cape São Roque** (16 Aug.) and, after sailing to the cape, he coasted southward as far as **Porto di San Giulian** (Puerto San Julián, Feb. 1502) in **Argentina.** Upon his return to Lisbon he wrote a letter (1502) to **Lorenzo di Pier Francesco de' Medici,** his former employer and patron, setting forth his conviction that what he had seen was a new land and a continent. This letter, along with two others to the same addressee, are generally accepted as authentic. Two others, the first called **Mundus Novus** (Aug. 1504) and addressed to de' Medici, and the second, called the **Four Voyages** (Sept. 1504) and addressed to Piero Soderini, are held to be forgeries, spiced-up versions of authentic letters, but not without evidential value. On the basis of these dubious letters four voyages are ascribed to Vespucci. On the

first (1497) he purportedly explored the Gulf of Mexico and voyaged north and eastward from Campeche, even reaching the Atlantic coast of the present U.S. The fourth voyage (1503) supposedly ended near Baía, Brazil. In 1507 Martin Waldseemüller, the geographer, proposed that the newly discovered world should be called "America, because Americus discovered it."

1501–04. ANGLO-PORTUGUESE VOYAGES FROM BRISTOL. Under letters patent of Henry VII (19 Mar. 1501) a mixed group of 3 merchants from Bristol and 3 men from the Azores, including João Fernandes, are presumed to have made 2 transatlantic voyages. Under a patent (9 Dec. 1502) to an Anglo-Portuguese group known as the "Company of Adventurers to the New Found Lands," trips were made annually to the New World (1502–05), possibly as far south as the Middle Atlantic states.

1503–04. Binot Paulmier de Gonneville, a merchant of Normandy, left Honfleur (June 1503) for a voyage around Africa to the Indies, was blown off his course, and arrived off the coast of Brazil, where he stayed for six months before sailing (3 July 1504) for home.

1509. SEBASTIAN CABOT (b.Venice, c.1483) sailed north and west from England (c.1509), and then southwest, returning to England (after 21 Apr. 1509). In later years he claimed to have reached Hudson Bay.

1508–13. SPANISH EXPLORATION FROM CARIBBEAN. Hispaniola was the center from which the Spaniards directed their explorations. By 1512 that colony was sending annually to Spain almost $1 million in gold and was raising sugar cane (introduced by the Spaniards from the Canaries), cotton, and cattle. In 1508 Sebastián de Ocampo circumnavigated Cuba, proving that it was not part of the mainland. Vincente Yáñez Pinzón and Juan Díaz de Solís explored the coasts of Honduras and Yucatan (1508–09). The conquest of the Caribbean Islands was the first military problem. Puerto Rico (1508–09), Jamaica (1510), and then Cuba (1511) were subjugated. **Juan Ponce de León,**

conqueror of Puerto Rico, sailed (3 Mar. 1513) to explore lands north of Cuba. Passing the Bahamas, he sighted **Florida** somewhere between St. Augustine and the St. Johns River, remaining a short time (2–8 Apr.). Thence he sailed north and, reversing his course, explored the entire eastern coast of Florida as well as the western shore as far north as Charlotte Harbor (23 May). In addition, he visited the Florida Keys and the Bahamas, and returned to Puerto Rico (21 Sept.) The Spanish set up temporary trading posts in present Venezuela and Colombia (at Santa Marta and Cartagena). From a third post, Santa Maria de la Antigua on the Gulf of Darien, **Vasco Nuñez de Balboa** pushed across the **Isthmus of Panama** to discover the **Pacific Ocean** (25 Sept. 1513). This discovery stimulated efforts to get around or through America.

1515–19. FURTHER SPANISH EFFORTS. Juan Díaz de Solís sailed from Spain (1515) and reached South America near present Rio de Janeiro, then sailed south to the mouth of the Rio de la Plata (Jan. 1516). Francisco Hernández Cordoba and Antón de Alaminos explored Yucatan (Sept. 1517), while Juan de Grijalva explored the Mexican coast from Yucatan to the Panuco River (Tampico, 1518). Alvárez Pineda explored the Gulf of Mexico from Florida to Vera Cruz (1519).

1519–22. MAGELLAN'S CIRCUMNAVIGATION. Fernando Magellan (Port. Fernão Magalhães), a Portuguese, sailed under the Spanish flag from St. Lucar (20 Sept. 1519), skirted the coast of South America (29 Nov. 1519–end of Mar. 1520), and wintered at Puerto San Julián (Apr.–Aug. 1520). Sailing through the strait that now bears his name and thence north and westward, he reached the Ladrones (Marianas) and **Philippines**, where he was killed (27 Apr. 1521). After many vicissitudes the remnants of his expedition returned to Spain (6 Sept. 1522). Permanent Spanish occupation of the Philippine Islands began with the expedition of Miguel López de Legaspi (1564).

1519–21. CONQUEST OF MEXICO. Hernando Cortés headed an expedition into the province of Tabasco, Mexico (Mar. 1519), defeated the Tabascan (25 Mar.) and Tlascala Indians (5 Sept.), but was amicably received by **Montezuma** (Moctezuma) in the Aztec capital of Tenochtitlán (Mexico City, 8 Nov.). After the death of Montezuma (30 June 1520) whom Cortés had imprisoned, the latter crushed an Aztec revolt at Otumba (7 July) and ended resistance by 13 Aug. 1521. This conquest opened to Spain the treasures of Mexico.

1521–30. SPANISH VOYAGES in these years include explorations of Francisco de Gordillo, along the Atlantic coast from Florida to South Carolina (1521); of Esteban Gómez, a Portuguese in Spanish service, from Nova Scotia to Florida (1524); of Pedro de Quexos as far north as 40°N. (1524–25); and of Sebastian Cabot, sailing under the Spanish flag, to the Río de la Plata, exploring the Paraná and Paraguay Rivers (1526–30).

1521–74. COLONIZING EFFORTS IN FLORIDA (see pp. 49–51).

1523, Dec.–1524, July. FRENCH EXPLORATION. French fishing vessels proceeded as far as Newfoundland (1504, p. 59). Efforts to find a route to the Indies through North America persisted. **GIOVANNI DE VERRAZANO** (Fr. Jehan de Varrasanne), b. near Florence, was dispatched by Francis I of France as pilot on a ship commanded by Antoine de Conflans to find such a route. After leaving Dieppe (Dec. 1523) he sailed west from Madeira (17 Jan. 1524) and reached North America, probably the Carolina coast (*c.*19 Mar.), thence proceeding southward "fifty leagues" before reversing his course and coasting north, reaching **New York Harbor** (*c.*17 Apr.) and **Narragansett Bay** (*c.*21 Apr.– 6 May), and continuing northward as far as **Nova Scotia** before returning to Dieppe. Copies of Verrazano's report to Francis I (8 July 1524) constitute the chief source of information about this voyage.

1527, 10 June. The English crown dispatched two ships from Plymouth, the *Samson* and the *Mary Guildford*. The former probably foundered, but the latter explored the North Atlantic coast from

Labrador south and arrived in the West Indies (19–26 Nov.).

1528–36. NARVÁEZ EXPEDITION. Pánfilo de Narváez sailed from Spain (1527) and landed near Tampa Bay, Florida (14 Apr. 1528) with a group of 400 colonists. They marched north and reached the village of Apalachee (25 June) near present Tallahassee. Unsuccessful in their quest for gold, they embarked, probably at Apalachee Bay, and sailed for Mexico (22 Sept.). As a result of shipwreck only 2 survived to reach Mexico City Apr. 1536, one of whom was **Cabeza de Vaca,** whose account of the expedition popularized the notion that New Mexico, specifically, the Seven Cities of Cibolá, were fabulously rich.

1534–43. INTERIOR EXPLORATION OF NORTH AMERICA: FRENCH. Jacques Cartier (b. St. Malo, Normandy, 1491), believed to have been on the Verrazzano expedition, was granted (Mar. 1534) 6,000 livres by Francis I to proceed to Newfoundland in search of islands and countries where it was hoped to find gold and "other riches." After sailing from St. Malo to the **Strait of Belle Isle** (20 Apr.–10 June 1534), he continued down the west coast of Newfoundland and passed Prince Edward Island, Chaleur Bay, and Gaspé Bay, and returned to St. Malo (5 Sept.). On his second voyage he sailed to Pillage Bay in the estuary of the St. Lawrence (19 May–9 Aug. 1535) and then proceeded up the river to **Quebec** (7 Sept.), where he left his ships and some men and proceeded in small boats as far as **Montreal.** After wintering in Quebec, he returned home (6 May–16 July 1536). His last trip was organized for the conquest of the kingdom of Saguenay, which Indians had led him to believe possessed great treasure. He left St. Malo (23 May 1541), reached Quebec (end of Aug.), set up a post at nearby Cap Rouge. En route home he stopped off at St. Johns, Newfoundland, where a few days before (8 June 1542) **Jean François de la Rocque, Sieur de Roberval,** commissioned (15 Jan. 1541) by Francis I to direct the conquest of Saguenay, had already arrived. Cartier brought back to France a shipload of iron pyrites (fool's gold) and some quartz crystals he believed to be diamonds. Roberval led one, apparently fruitless, expedition up the St. Lawrence (6 June 1543) toward the kingdom of Saguenay, but he was back in France in the fall of that year.

1539, May 28–1543, 10 Sept. INTERIOR EXPLORATION: SPANISH. **Hernando de Soto,** newly appointed governor of Cuba, landed with 600 soldiers on the Florida coast, either at Tampa Bay or Charlotte Harbor (28 May 1539), and, after exploring the western part of the peninsula, he wintered in Apalachee. The following spring he marched north to the vicinity of the Savannah River, thence west to the Blue Ridge Mountains, and southwest almost to the Gulf of Mexico near Mobile (17 Nov.), wintered (1540–41) probably in the Yazoo Delta country, and, proceeding north in the spring, crossed the **Mississippi** (May 1541) south of Memphis. He continued west through the Ozarks, wintered near the junction of the Arkansas and Canadian Rivers in eastern Oklahoma, and returned to the Mississippi where he died of fever (1542). With Luís Moscoso de Alvarado as their leader, the survivors journeyed west to the upper reaches of the Brazos River, but returned to spend a last winter (1542–43) at the mouth of the Arkansas. They sailed down the Mississippi (July 1543) and reached Panuco (10 Sept.).

1539–42. NEW MEXICO. The Franciscan, **Fray Marcos de Niza,** headed an expedition from Mexico into the Zuñi country, accompanied by Esteban, a Moorish or Negro companion of Cabeza de Vaca. Their discovery of a Zuñi pueblo at Hawikuh in western New Mexico was magnified in Mexico. **Francisco Vásquez de Coronado** led a force into New Mexico to conquer the Seven Cities of Cibola. He left Compostela (23 Feb. 1540) and captured the first city (Hawikuh, named Granada-Cibola, 7 July), which served as a base for further expeditions. Don García López de Cárdenas, proceeded westward and discovered the Grand Canyon; Hernando de Alvarado, going east, reached the Rio Grande around Albuquerque (region called Tiguex) and, continuing past the upper reaches of the Pecos, pushed into the Texas Panhandle in search of Quivera, a mythical kingdom of gold. After wintering at Tiguex, Coronado marched to the upper Brazos River (26 May 1541) where, separating from his main force, he moved north and northwest across the Arkansas River near Ford, Kan. (29 June), into the district of the Wichita Indians, returning to Tiguex (20 Oct.), which he finally abandoned (Apr. 1542), and returned to Mexico City (before 13 Oct.).

1539–43. SPANISH WEST COAST EXPLORATION. Francisco de Ulloa sailed from Acapulco (8 July) into the Gulf of California, circled the southern tip of Lower California, and sailed up its western shore possibly as far north as 30°N., thereby establishing its peninsularity. Hernando de Alarcón, heading an expedition from Acapulco to support Coronado, sailed up the Gulf of California and into the Colorado River (*c.*25 Aug. 1540), proceeding to some point between the junctions of the Gila and Williams with the Colorado, but left shortly before a Coronado searching party, headed by Melchior Díaz, reached the same area. In an exploration of the west coast **Juan Rodriguez Cabrillo** sailed (27 June 1542) up the California coast to Drake's Bay and took possession of the country for Spain. He died on San Miguel Island (3 Jan. 1543), and his successor in command, **Bartolomé Ferrelo**, sailed north, possibly to the California-Oregon border (1 Mar. 1543). Permanent Spanish settlement of the California coast did not start until a system of presidios and missions (Franciscan) was established at San Diego (1769), Monterey (1770), and San Francisco (1776).

1577, 13 Dec.–1580, 26 Sept. DRAKE'S CIRCUMNAVIGATION. Ostensibly on a voyage to Alexandria, Egypt, but actually to prey upon Spanish shipping in the Pacific (considerable following the conquest of Peru, 1530–32, by **Francisco Pizarro**), **Francis Drake** sailed through the Strait of Magellan and reached the Pacific (6 Sept. 1578). Raiding the west coast of South America—Valparaiso (5 Dec.), Tarapacá and Arica (4 and 5 Feb. 1579)—and capturing a rich treasure ship between Callao and Panama (1 Mar.), he continued north possibly to 40°N., then reversed his course, anchoring probably at **San Francisco Bay** (17 June). Upon taking possession of this territory in behalf of Queen Elizabeth he had a plaque struck off commemorating the event. (A brass plate answering its description was uncovered [1936] in the San Francisco Bay district, but its authenticity is not definitely established.) On leaving California (July 1579), Drake sailed north apparently to 48°N. in search of the western end of the Northwest Passage; then, heading eastward, he completed his circumnavigation (26 Sept. 1580).

1576–1606. ENGLISH SEARCH FOR NORTHWEST PASSAGE. (1) **Martin Frobisher** sailed from England (June 1576) and pressed northwest after sighting Greenland until, at 62°N., he reached **Baffin Land** and entered **Frobisher Bay**, believing it to be a strait between America and Asia. To exploit his discovery (including some ore brought back to England) the Company of Cathay was organized and Frobisher sailed under its auspices (May, 1577) both for further exploration and for mining operations, which he conducted in Baffin Land. He returned to Bristol (15 Oct.) with 200 tons of ore. On his 3rd voyage (1578) for the purpose of shipping ore Frobisher reached **Hudson Strait**, which he now considered a more likely passage to Asia. His ore proved worthless. (2) **John Davis** made 3 trips in search of the Northwest Passage (1585–87). The first led him to Baffin Land via the west coast of Greenland and the strait now bearing his name; on the second he followed the north coast of Labrador but missed Hudson Strait, and on the third he reached 73° in Baffin Bay. (3) **George Weymouth**, backed by the East India Co., sailed from Radcliffe, England (2 May 1602), reached Baffin Land, sailed south past Frobisher Bay and into Hudson Strait, where the mutiny of his crew forced him to return to England (autumn). (4) **John Knight**, sponsored by both the East India and Muscovy Cos., explored the shores of Newfoundland and Labrador.

1598–1610. SPANISH SETTLEMENT OF SOUTHWEST was begun in New Mexico by **Juan de Oñate** (1598), who dispatched an expedition which explored from Kansas to the Gulf of California. **Sante Fe** was founded (1609–10).

1608–11. VOYAGES OF HUDSON. In 1608 **Henry Hudson** made a voyage for the Muscovy Co. in search of the Northwest Passage, reaching the Kara Sea. With the same goal in view he sailed from Amsterdam for the Dutch East India Co. (25 Mar. 1609), reached Nova Zembla (Novaya Zemlya), where he was forced back by calms and mutiny. Sailing westward, he passed Newfoundland (3 July), continued south to the Carolina coast, reversed his course, entered **Delaware Bay** (28 Aug.), and the **Hudson River** (13 Sept.), up which he sailed as far as **Albany** (19 Sept.). Hudson's last voyage (begun 27 Apr. 1610) was under private English auspices and to locate the Northwest Passage. He reached Resolution Island (end of June), but was forced south by ice. Proceeding through Hudson Strait, he entered **Hudson Bay** (3 Aug.) and coasted along its eastern shore to **James Bay**, where he wintered. On the homeward journey he was set adrift by his own men (23 June 1611).

1603–35. CHAMPLAIN'S VOYAGES. After having sailed with a Spanish convoy to the West Indies (3 Feb. 1599–2 July 1601), **Samuel De Champlain** (b.*c.*1567) made 11 trips to eastern Canada. On the 1st, sailing from Honfleur (15 Mar. 1603) as a geographer on an expedition sponsored by Aymar de Chastes, he reached **Tadoussac** on the St. Lawrence, already a trading station for furs and fish. He then explored the St. Lawrence as far as **Lachine Rapids.** On his return to France (20 Sept.), he wrote his first book, *Des Sauvages,* re-

porting his voyage. On his 2nd trip (early June 1604–06) he sailed in the same capacity in an expedition to set up a fur-trading post for Pierre du Guast, sieur de Monts, who had received the trading patent previously held by Aymar de Chastes. Unsuccessful attempts were made to establish a post at New Brunswick and Annapolis Basin in Nova Scotia, but Champlain made 2 trips as far south as Nauset Harbor on Cape Cod (20 July 1605) and Vineyard Sound (20 Oct. 1606). On his 3rd voyage (13 Apr. 1608–15 Oct. 1609) he sailed in the service of De Monts, holder of a new monopoly. After erecting a fort at Quebec (8 July) and cementing friendly relations with the Indians (Algonquins of the lower St. Lawrence and Hurons and Algonquins of the Ottawa River), he voyaged up the Richelieu River into **Lake Champlain** (30 July 1609). On his 4th and 5th voyages (7 Mar.–27 Sept. 1610 and 1 Mar.–26 Sept. 1611) he devoted himself to the fur trade and Indian relations. On his 6th trip (6 Mar.–26 Sept. 1613) he pushed up the Ottawa River in quest of Hudson Bay (Northern Sea) above Waltham (7 June). On his 7th trip (24 Apr. 1615–3 Aug. 1616) he reached Georgian Bay via the Ottawa and Mattawa Rivers and Lake Nipissing. **Étienne Brûle,** who had accompanied Champlain on the 1608–09 trip and had traveled in the Huron region, and **Le Caron,** a Recollect (Franciscan) missionary, preceded Champlain by a week. Champlain joined the Hurons in raiding the Iroquois and, crossing Lake Ontario, penetrated south to Lake Oneida. After unsuccessfully besieging an Iroquois stronghold (probably on Lake Onondaga), 10–16 Oct. 1615, he wintered with the Hurons. In a trip growing out of this campaign, Brûle traveled (Sept.–Oct. 1615) down the Susquehanna as far as Chesapeake Bay.

THE FOUNDING
OF THE ENGLISH COLONIES
1578-1732

SETTLEMENT OF THE TOBACCO PROVINCES

VIRGINIA

1578–83. SIR HUMPHREY GILBERT obtained a patent (11 June) from Queen Elizabeth for discovery and colonization in northwest America. He made a voyage to the New World (1578–79), but his plan to establish a colony as a base against Spain had to await financial support. With meager funds raised in Bristol and Southampton, he sailed (June 1583) with 5 ships and 260 men, reached Newfoundland, and made exploratory trips, but his vessel was lost (Sept.) on the homeward journey.

1584–1602. RALEIGH'S COLONY. Sir Walter Raleigh, a half brother of Gilbert and a member of his last expedition, was granted a virtual renewal of the Gilbert patent (25 Mar.). With the aid of Walsingham, Drake, Sidney, and the elder and younger Richard Hakluyt, he equipped an expedition which sailed (27 Apr. 1584) under the command of **Sir Richard Grenville** and **Ralph Lane,** both to explore the North American mainland and reconnoiter Spanish Caribbean defenses. After accomplishing the latter mission, the expedition entered Albemarle Sound on the North Carolina coast, landed on Roanoke Island (July), and returned to England (mid-Sept.). Raleigh named his discovery **Virginia** and dispatched a colonizing expedition (9 Apr. 1585) under the same commanders, which landed at Roanoke Island (27 July). Grenville left Lane in charge of settlement. As a result of Indian troubles

and Spanish tension the colony was abandoned (June 1586) when Drake, stopping by after a raid on the Spanish West Indies, offered the settlers passage home. Returning with supplies a few weeks later, Grenville left 15 men at the deserted colony. A 4th expedition under **John White** (possibly the painter whose water colors of Indian life served as the conventional representation of the aborigines) sailed (8 May 1587), arrived at Roanoke Island (22 July), found no survivors of the previous Grenville expedition, but left a group of colonists. White sailed home to obtain supplies (25 Aug.) only a week after the birth of his grandchild, **Virginia Dare** (18 Aug.), the first English child born in the present U.S. His return to the colony was delayed by the threat and then the actuality of the Spanish Armada until 17 Aug. 1590, when he found no trace of the colonists, but noted the cryptic letters, CRO, cut in a tree and the word CROATOAN carved on a doorpost—apparently references to an island off the coast held by friendly Indians. Coincidental with the 350th anniversary of the colony's founding, a quartz stone was discovered in Chowan Co., N.C. (Sept., 1937), carved with what purported to be a message from Eleanore White Dare, Virginia's mother, describing the slaughter of the entire colony save 7, presumably saved by friendly natives. This "find" was followed by 48 others, all seeming to corroborate the first (1937–39), but they were exposed as forgeries (by Boyden

Sparkes, 1941). Raleigh dispatched a final expedition (Mar. 1602) in a futile search for survivors.

1605, 5 Mar.–1606, 18 July. GEORGE WEYMOUTH sailed under the auspices of the Earl of Southampton and the latter's Roman Catholic son-in-law, Sir Thomas Arundel, ostensibly to establish a colony for Catholics who found their position in England insecure (Catholic priests banished, 1604; Guy Fawkes' arrest, 4 Nov. 1605). The account of his voyage to Nantucket and the Maine coast, as narrated in James Rosier's *Relation,* prompted two interrelated groups of merchants, from London and Plymouth, to petition the crown (*c.*Sept. 1605) for a patent, which was conferred (20 Apr. 1606). Under its terms two **Virginia Companies**—the **London** (or South Virginia) **Company** and the **Plymouth** (or North Virginia) **Company** were established. The former was authorized to settle in a region between 34°N. and 41°N. (present New York City); the latter between 45°N. and 38°N. (present Washington, D.C.), but neither was to settle within 100 miles of the other, in effect creating a neutral zone between the two colonies. Each was to receive all lands 50 miles north and south of the first settlement and 100 miles into the interior.

1606, 20 Dec.–1609, 23 May. SETTLEMENT OF JAMESTOWN. The London Co. dispatched 3 vessels, which reached Virginia (26 Apr. 1607), entered Chesapeake Bay, and disembarked at **Jamestown** (24 May). During the first seven months famine and disease cut the number of settlers from the original 105 to 32 as the councilors chosen before sailing proved unable to cope with the situation. The arrival of two supply ships (Jan. and Apr., 1608), the compulsory work program instituted by Capt. **John Smith** (p. 780) upon his election as President of the Council (Sept.), and the emphasis upon self-sustaining agriculture, notably maize (1609), marked a turning point. Smith's capture by Powhatan, giving rise to the legend of Pocohontas' intercession, occurred when he left Jamestown (10 Dec. 1607) and ascended the Chickahominy to obtain

provisions. He explored Chesapeake Bay (24 July–7 Sept. 1608). A new charter granted to Virginia (2 June 1609) vested control in a council to be selected by the company and extended the colony's boundaries north and south from Old Point Comfort 200 miles in each direction and from "sea to sea."

1609–19. Dissension marked the period preceding the delayed arrival of **Thomas Lord De La Warr** (16 June 1610). Smith refused to yield authority, but left the colony (5 Oct. 1609). The "starving time" ran through the winter of 1609–10. **Sir Thomas Dale** assumed control (23 May 1611) as deputy for De La Warr, whom sickness had forced from Virginia. The "Dale Code" (**Laws Divine, Morall, and Martiall,** London, 1612) imposed severe penalties to check internal disorder. Dale began construction of a fort at Henrico, 50 miles up the James, and a system of stockades. Both projects were completed under **Sir Thomas Gates** (Governor from Aug. 1611 to early 1614). A third charter to the Virginia Company (22 Mar. 1612) placed Bermuda under its authority. During the administrations of Gates, Dale (early 1614–Apr. 1616), and **George Yeardley** (acting Governor, 1616–17), except for the misrule of **Sir Samuel Argall** (deputy Governor, 1617–Nov. 1618), such constructive developments occurred as the introduction of tobacco cultivation (credited to John Rolfe, 1612; first shipment to England, Mar. 1614; married Pocahontas, 14 Apr. 1614), individual allotments to tenant farmers (1613–14) supplementing the prevailing system of community labor, and fee simple grants (beg. *c.*1617).

1619–24. FINAL PERIOD OF COMPANY CONTROL. When, in 1618, **Sir Edwin Sandys** and the Earl of Southampton gained control of the Company, reforms were introduced through **George Yeardley,** newly appointed Governor (arrived Virginia 29 Apr. 1619). The harsh legal code was repealed. A **General Assembly,** comprising 22 burgesses (2 chosen by the planters from each town, hundred, or plantation) and the Governor and Council, met in Jamestown (9–14 Aug. 1619), constituting the first colonial legislature in the New

World, although it also served in a judicial capacity. In this period a previously inaugurated system of granting land to subordinate corporations (Society of Smith's Hundred, 1617; Martin's Brandon, 1617; Martin's Hundred, 1618) was extended, with 44 patents issued between 1619 and 1623. Heavy mortality from disease continued. An Indian massacre (22 Mar. 1622) provoked a series of retaliatory raids. A break in 1619 between the Sandys-Southampton group and that of Sir Thomas Smith, previous treasurer, was followed by several years of unprofitable operations, to which the suspension (8 Mar. 1622) by the Privy Council of the lottery, authorized in the charter of 1612 as a fundraising device, contributed. The Company went into receivership and was placed under the management of the Privy Council (July 1623). The charter was revoked 24 May 1624, and Virginia became a **Royal Colony.**

1624–42. SIR FRANCIS WYATT, who had been Company Governor, 1621–24, was appointed governor by James I (24 Aug. 1624). He in turn was superseded by **George Yeardley** (14 Mar. 1626). His successor, **Francis West** (Nov. 1627– 5 Mar. 1629) was instructed to call a General Assembly, which convened at the end of March, 1628. Pending the arrival of his successor, **John Harvey,** Dr. **John Pott** controlled affairs down to the spring of 1630, acting thereafter as opposition leader. Harvey was finally replaced (Jan. 1639) by **Sir Francis Wyatt** (1639–41), who was instructed to convene the burgesses "once a year or oftener."

1642–52. BERKELEY'S FIRST ADMINISTRATION. Wyatt's successor, **Sir William Berkeley** (1606–77), introduced a number of reforms, including the abolition of the poll tax. An Indian uprising (18 Mar. 1644) by Opechancanough was suppressed. The Indians ceded all lands between the York and the James from the falls to Kecoughton, but retained territory north of the York. Peace lasted until 1675. On 30 Jan. 1649 Virginia announced its allegiance to the Stuart house after the execution of Charles I and gave refuge to prominent Cavaliers. In retaliation, Parliament passed an act (Oct. 1650) imposing a blockade on Virginia and subsequently dispatched two armed vessels with commissioners who received the submission of Berkeley and the Council (12 Mar. 1652) upon liberal terms. Following a new election, the burgesses chose as Governor **Richard Bennett,** one of the Parliamentary commissioners. When the succeeding governor, **Samuel Matthews,** threatened to dissolve the burgesses (1658), he was temporarily removed as an object lesson, then reelected. With the collapse of the Protectorate and the death of Matthews (close of 1659) the burgesses asserted "supreme power" until lawful authority might be forthcoming from England, and elected the royalist, **Berkeley,** Governor (23 Mar. 1660). Upon the Restoration in England (29 May), Berkeley was commissioned by Charles II (31 July).

1660–75. DETERIORATING CONDITIONS. As a result of the Navigation Acts (p. 510) tobacco prices declined from 3d. per lb. previously paid by the Dutch to ½d. (1667). To meet the crisis attempts were made to limit tobacco acreage and establish cloth works in each county. The Dutch Wars (1664 and 1672) caused severe losses to the tobacco fleet. The crisis was further deepened by a cattle epidemic (1672–73), the reintroduction of the poll tax, and a number of servant uprisings (p. 546). Additional unrest was provoked by implementing the grant made by Charles II (1649) to Lord Hopton of a tract of more than 5 million acres between the Rappahannock and Potomac Rivers (assigned to Lord Culpeper, 1689, on whose death proprietary rights descended to his grandson, **Thomas Fairfax,** 1693–1781, 6th Baron Fairfax of Cameron, who settled in Virginia, 1747), and by a grant of all Virginia (25 Feb. 1673) to Lords Arlington and Culpeper for 31 years. This claim was reduced to quitrents and escheats and ultimately assigned to the king in payment to Culpeper of £600 for 20 years (1684). Despite growing discontent, Berkeley had stubbornly refused to call another election since the last one (1662).

1675-76. BACON'S REBELLION: PRELIMINARIES. Bands of Susquehannock Indians fleeing more powerful tribes to the north crossed the Potomac and committed atrocities. A joint force of Marylanders (under Thomas Trueman) and Virginians (under John Washington) failed at Piscatawy Creek (27 Sept.) to destroy the Indians, who now stepped up their attacks, killing in one January (1676) raid 36 Virginians on a single day. Frontier settlers deserted their homes, but Berkeley, who was accused of protecting the fur trade in which he was personally involved, refused to allow a force under Sir Henry Chicherley to march against the Indians.

1676, 10 May–18 Oct. BACON'S REBELLION. Nathaniel Bacon (1647–76), a recent settler in Henrico County and a member of the Council, marched without commission at the head of a force of frontiersmen to the Roanoke River, where he destroyed a body of Susquehannocks. Declared a traitor (26 May), he was arrested when he tried to take his seat in the burgesses, to which he had been elected, but was freed (5 June) on acknowledging his offense and pardoned by Berkeley. Returning to Henrico, he raised a force of 500 which he led unopposed into Jamestown (23 June), forcing Berkeley to sign his commission. The Assembly now enacted a number of democratic reforms. Again Berkeley proclaimed Bacon a rebel (29 July), but, failing to raise a force against him, fled to the Eastern Shore. Meeting at the Middle Plantation (3 Aug.), the large planters took oath to support Bacon. Returning (13 Sept.) from an expedition against the Indians on the upper reaches of the Potomac and Rappahannock, Bacon drove Berkeley's force out of Jamestown (18 Sept.), which he burned the next day. He died suddenly (18 Oct.)

1676, Oct.–1677, May. RESTORATION OF ORDER. The loss of its commander reduced the rebel army to a series of bands which were captured by treachery or surrendered piecemeal to Berkeley (Nov.–Dec.) under promise of amnesty. Commissioners John Berry and Francis Moryson arrived 29 Jan. 1677 to investigate the uprising, preceding by

a few days Col. **Herbert Jeffreys,** sent to restore order. Jeffreys brought with him royal pardons for the rebels which Berkeley (10 Feb.) nullified. Executions totaling 23 continued until Jeffreys formally took over the government (27 Apr.) just prior to Berkeley's departure (5 May).

1677–89. REVOLUTION OF 1689 IN VIRGINIA. Jeffreys and his successors, Sir **Henry Chicherley** (9 Nov. 1678–May, 1680) and **Lord Culpeper** (10 May 1680–28 Sept. 1683), enjoyed comparatively peaceful administrations, but that of **Lord Howard of Effingham** (1683–89) was marked by a struggle between the Governor and the legislature. A list of popular grievances was presented to James II (Sept. 1688), but before it could be acted upon William and Mary had landed in England. Their accession (13 Feb. 1689) and Howard's subsequent removal were hailed in Virginia.

MARYLAND

1620–32. PRELIMINARIES OF SETTLEMENT. George Calvert (c.1580–1632) became principal Secretary of State (1619), which office he resigned upon entering the Roman Catholic church (1625). By this act he did not lose favor with James I, who created him 1st **Lord Baltimore.** A member of the Virginia Co. (1609–20) and of the Council for New England (1622), Calvert bought from Sir William Vaughan (1620) the southeastern peninsula of Newfoundland, which he named Avalon. Because of the severity of the climate this colony did not prosper. After visiting Virginia (1628), Baltimore induced Charles I to grant him (1632) territory north of the Potomac River. The Maryland charter was granted (30 June) after his death. His son, Cecilius Calvert, 2nd **Lord Baltimore** (c.1605–75), became its first proprietor. The charter recognized Calvert as **proprietor;** conferred upon him the authority of the county Palatine of Durham, subject to the limitations that laws be made with the consent of the freemen and agreeable to the laws of England. The charter did not forbid the establishment of churches other than Protestant, and Baltimore took advantage of this to settle his coreligionists. The northern boundary was finally settled at 40°N., the southern at the Potomac River (conflicting with Virginia's claims), with a line drawn east of the mouth of the Potomac constituting the southern boundary on the Eastern Shore.

1634–40. EARLY PROBLEMS. The first group of some 200 colonists, including 2 Jesuits and many other Catholics, sailed from Portsmouth (22 Nov. 1633), arrived in Virginia (27 Feb. 1634), and went up Chesapeake Bay to Blakiston's Island, erecting a cross and celebrating mass (25 Mar.) before finally settling at St. Mary's (Yoacomaco). The 2nd Lord Baltimore never visited the colony himself, but governed by deputy. His brother, the first governor, **Leonard Calvert,** established the manorial government authorized by the charter, maintained friendly relations with the Indians, but came into conflict with Virginia. **William Claiborne** (c.1587–c.1677), a member of the Virginia Council, had established a trading post on Kent Island under royal license soon after the return of the 1st Lord Baltimore to England. Although this territory lay within Baltimore's patent, Claiborne refused to recognize his overlordship. His community sent representatives to the Virginia Assembly, which supported his claim. The controversy culminated in sea fights between Claiborne's and Baltimore's vessels (23 Apr. and 10 May 1635). Claiborne visited England (1637) in a vain attempt to substantiate his claims, was attainted by the Maryland Assembly (3 Apr. 1638), and the crown finally ruled against him (4 Apr.)

1640–60. UNDER LONG PARLIAMENT AND COMMONWEALTH. Baltimore's position in England grew increasingly insecure as Maryland suffered troubled times (1644–46). Claiborne proceeded to retake Kent Island and Capt. **Richard Ingle** (1609–c.1653), a Protestant tobacco trader, captured St. Mary's and plundered the colony, forcing Calvert to flee to Virginia. With the aid of Berkeley he recaptured the province, but Ingle, on return to England, almost succeeded (1647) in having the

charter revoked. During the administration of **William Stone,** a Protestant, as deputy governor (1648–52) a **Toleration Act** was passed (21 Apr. 1649), granting religious freedom to all Trinitarians. When Stone left the colony (Nov. 1651) he designated **Thomas Greene,** a Roman Catholic royalist, as his deputy. The latter, by recognizing Charles II as lawful heir to the throne (15 Nov.), precipitated an investigation in England and the dispatch to the province of Parliamentary commissioners, among whom was Claiborne. The commissioners ousted Stone (29 Mar. 1652), who still asserted his authority. William Fuller, designated Governor by the commissioners, called an Assembly (30 Oct. 1654), which repudiated the proprietor's authority, repealed the Toleration Act, and denied Catholics the protection of law. In the ensuing brief **Civil War** the Puritans were victors (25 Mar. 1655), Stone was wounded and imprisoned, and 4 of his supporters executed. Baltimore persuaded the Committee of Trade to restore his privileges (Jan. 1656) subject to the condition that **Josias Fendall** (who was actually chosen, 10 July) be governor in Stone's place. The new Assembly (10 Mar. 1660) declared itself free of proprietary control. On accepting his commission from that body, Fendall was promptly ousted and **Philip Calvert** appointed in his place (Nov.). In turn, he was succeeded by **Charles Calvert** (1637–1715), who, upon his father's death (1675), became proprietor and 3d **Lord Baltimore.**

1661–81. INCREASING TENSION. The proprietary regime became increasingly unpopular as a result of the decline in tobacco prices, the restriction of the suffrage to freeholders (18 Dec. 1670), Indian raids, absentee proprietorship and official nepotism, and continued anti-Catholic sentiment. A short-lived uprising under William Davyes and John Pate (Sept. 1676) was crushed and the two leaders hanged, but in Apr. 1681, Fendall, enemy of the proprietary party, staged an unsuccessful "rebellion" and was fined and banished.

1684–95. REVOLUTION OF 1689 IN MARYLAND. Baltimore returned to

England (May 1684) to settle boundary disputes with William Penn and the colony of Virginia and to answer charges of favoring Roman Catholics and interfering with the royal customs collectors. He was also called to account for the murder of Christopher Rousby (31 Oct. 1684), a collector, by the proprietor's nephew, **George Talbot**, acting Governor in his absence. The charges of pro-Catholicism were dropped, Baltimore was fined £2,500 for obstructing the customs, and Talbot was taken to Virginia and sentenced to death (24 Apr. 1686), only to have this sentence commuted by the king to five years' banishment (9 Sept.). While the Maryland-Virginia Eastern Shore boundary had been settled (1668, 1671), Baltimore's claim to the entire Potomac was not settled for 200 years (1878), and the complicated border dispute with Penn also remained unsettled. During the absence of Baltimore (1684–89) and the disgrace of his lieutenant, Talbot, antiproprietary sentiment mounted. When Baltimore finally dispatched (1688) **William Joseph,** an advocate of divine right, to act as his deputy, the Assembly (24 Nov.) voiced its disapproval, but took the oath (27 Nov.). Joseph then prorogued that body to meet in Apr. 1689, and again prorogued it until Oct. During the feverish period preceding the Glorious Revolution rumors were spread that the colony was to be turned over to the Roman Catholics. After the accession of William and Mary and the declaration of war with France (May 1689), an uprising led by **John Coode** (d.1709), with 250 recruits chiefly from Charles Co., marched on St. Mary's, where a surrender was signed by Joseph and 4 of his lieutenants (1 Aug.). The insurgent leaders (**Protestant Association**) called the Assembly into session (22 Aug.). That body petitioned the crown to take over the province, and proceeded to elect **Nehemiah Blakiston** its president. The Lords of Trade made Maryland a **Royal Province** (27 June 1691), with Sir **Lionel Copley** as first royal Governor, although Baltimore retained his property rights. In 1692 the Church of England was established, and in 1695 the capital moved from Catholic St. Mary's to Protestant Annapolis. With the death of Benedict Leonard Calvert (who had become a convert to the Church of England, 1713, and reared his children in his new faith) in 1715, leaving Charles, 4th Lord Baltimore (1699–1751), as his heir, the government was restored to the proprietor (May 1715) and the charter of 1632 again put into force.

SETTLEMENT OF NEW ENGLAND

PLYMOUTH

1606–20.   EARLY ACTIVITIES OF PLYMOUTH COMPANY. The first expedition of the Plymouth Co. (dispatched Aug. 1606) was captured by the Spaniards in the West Indies. A second (Oct.) sponsored by **Sir John Popham** explored the coast from Maine southward and returned with extensive data on the coastal areas. Sir **Ferdinando Gorges** fitted out the *Gift of God* (under George Popham) and the *Mary and John* (under Raleigh Gilbert), which sailed separately (1 May and 1 June 1607) and dropped anchor on the Maine coast north of Monhegan (7 Aug.), then sailed to Popham Beach (14 Aug.) on the Sagadahoc River (lower Kennebec). There a fort was erected, within which were constructed other buildings. The colony failed owing to idleness and factionalism. After George Popham's death (5 Feb. 1608), the venture was abandoned (Sept.). Sir Francis Popham, son of Sir John, sent trading and fishing expeditions to the mainland and islands off Maine (1608–14) as did Dutch, French, and Spanish traders and fishermen, with fairly permanent posts established on the islands of Damariscove and Monhegan, and at Pemaquid Point. Capt. **John Smith** sailed for the New England coast (3 Mar. 1614). On his return (*c.*Sept. 1614) he pointed out to Gorges settlement possibilities of the area. Richard Vines, a former Gorges' agent, spent a winter at the mouth of the Saco (1616–17). The richness of the cod fishery in these waters revived the interest of the Plymouth Co. Through Gorges the Company petitioned James I (3 Mar. 1620) for a charter according it privileges already granted the Virginia Co. A new charter, granted 13 Nov. to a **Council for New England** all land lying between 40°N. and 48°N. and from sea to sea.

1606–20. PILGRIM PRELIMINARIES. A group of separatists from the Church of England who had established a congregation at Scrooby, Nottinghamshire, emigrated to Amsterdam (Aug. 1608) and then removed to Leyden (1 May 1609). Although they enjoyed religious freedom in Holland, they found their children losing contact with English culture, were excluded from the local guilds, and feared the expiration of the 12 years' truce between Spain and the Netherlands (1609–21) would imperil their position and subject them to the rigors of the Inquisition. Leaders of the Leyden group—their pastor, John Robinson, and **William Brewster** (1567–1644) — sent agents to England (1616–19) to negotiate with the Virginia Co. for the right to plant a colony within its borders. Through the intervention of Sir Edwin Sandys they received a patent (19 June 1619) in the name of **John Wyncop**, an English clergyman. Pending royal approval, the Leyden group rejected an offer by the Dutch to settle under the States General (Feb. 1620). Meantime, **Thomas Weston**, a London ironmonger, in association with **John Peirce**, a London clothmaker, had received a patent from the Virginia Co. (20 Feb. 1620) and persuaded the Leyden group to join with them (July). Three groups were set up: (1) adventurers in England (70 in all) at £10 per share; (2) adventurer-planters, given 2 shares for each £10 in consideration of their settling; (3) planters, given 1 share each for their labor. Both capital and profits were to belong to the joint-stock for 7 years, at the end of which period they were to be divided proportionately.

1620, 22 July–9 Nov. VOYAGE OF THE PILGRIMS. Thirty members of the Leyden group (known henceforth as the **Pilgrims**), under the leadership of Brewster, left the Netherlands on the *Speedwell* (22 July) for England. When that ship proved unseaworthy, it was abandoned at Plymouth and the entire company crowded aboard the *Mayflower,* 180 tons burden, a ship provided by the adventurers. Sailing (16 Sept.), she carried, besides officers and crew, 101 persons (a majority non-Pilgrims, including Capt. **Miles Standish** [*c.*1584–1656], hired as their military leader), with 14 indentured servants and hired artisans. There were 35 from Leyden, 66 from Southampton and London. After Cape Cod was sighted (9 Nov.), decision was reached to land nearby despite the fact that this was outside the territory of the Virginia Co. This decision may have been inspired by a suggestion of Weston, who had reason to doubt the legality of their patent.

1620, 21 Nov. THE MAYFLOWER COMPACT. Fearing that the rebellious members of their company might prove even more untractable ashore, the Pilgrim leaders ("Saints") drafted an agreement which was signed in the cabin of the *Mayflower* by 41 adults. This preliminary plan of government, based on the social compact idea found in separatist church covenants, set up "a civil body politic" to frame "just and equal laws."

1620–24. PLYMOUTH, first sighted 11 Dec., was chosen as the site for the new settlement 25 Dec. The first winter (1620–21) was mild, but disease carried off half the settlers the first year. The Indians, decimated by a plague (1617–19), proved peaceful. Deacon **John Carver** (*c.*1576–1621), the first governor, was succeeded on his death (Apr. 1621) by **William Bradford** (p. 679), who held that office, with the exception of five years, down to 1656. A 2nd **Peirce Patent**, obtained (1 June) from the newly organized Council for New England, vested title to land jointly in the adventurers and planters (100 acres for each person transported and 1,500 for public use) at a yearly quitrent of 2s. per 100 acres, but the colony's boundaries remained undefined. A party of some 50 men under **Andrew Weston** landed at Plymouth in June, moved to Wessagusset to establish a fishing and trading post, but failed because of Indian troubles and poor management (1623). Another colony was established (1623) by Captain Wollaston at Passonagessit (Quincy). On Wollaston's departure within the year **Thomas Morton** assumed control at Mount Wollaston (Merrymount). The Pilgrims, outraged equally by his uninhibited life and his success at Indian trading, dispatched Miles Standish (June, 1628) to destroy the settlement and sent Morton back to England. **Robert Gorges**, son of Sir Ferdinando, sent out an expedition which moved into Weston's abandoned settlement at Wessagusset (end of Sept. 1623). Gorges abandoned the project (1624), but some settlers remained. In 1624 communal planting was modified and individual garden plots assigned. Meadow and pasture allotments were made (1632).

1626, 15 Nov. LIQUIDATION OF LONDON ADVENTURERS. Strengthened by a steady influx of settlers (since Aug. 1623), the Pilgrims were encouraged to make an agreement to buy out the London investors for £1,800 and assume the Company's debt of £600. Eight colonists underwrote the agreement in return for a monopoly of trade and a tax of 3 bu. of corn or 6 lbs. of tobacco per shareholder until the debt was paid (July 1627). This group established a trading post on the Kennebec (1628) and another on the Penobscot (c.1631).

1630, 23 Jan. NEW PLYMOUTH PATENT ("OLD CHARTER") granted by the Council for New England defined the colony's boundaries and confirmed title to land on the Kennebec.

1636. Adoption of a code, "Great Fundamentals," drawn up for the government of the colony established a General Court, comprising two deputies from each town chosen by the freemen together with the Governor and assistants sitting as a single house.

MAINE AND NEW HAMPSHIRE

1622–31. On 10 Aug. 1622 the Council for New England granted **John Mason** and **Sir Ferdinando Gorges** all land lying between the Merrimack and Kennebec Rivers. Special grants of 6,000 acres apiece were made to David Thomson (1622), who founded a plantation at the mouth of Piscataqua (Rye, 1623), and Christopher Levett (1623), who settled probably on an island at the mouth of Casco River (end of 1623). John Oldham and Richard Vines settled on the south side of the Saco (present Biddeford, 1623–24). In 1629 Mason and Gorges divided their northern holdings. Gorges received all land north of the Piscataqua; Mason all land to its south. A trading grant was conferred on Mason and Gorges (17 Nov.) of an indefinite area extending to Lake Champlain and the St. Lawrence. Under Walter Neale, settlements were made at present Portsmouth, c.1631, and present South Berwick, c.1632. After receiving a grant (2 Dec. 1631) of 24,000 acres on the Agamenticus (York) River, Gorges focused his colonizing activity in this area.

MASSACHUSETTS BAY

1624–26. DORCHESTER COMPANY planted a colony of Dorsetshire men on Cape Ann (present Gloucester). Proving ill-suited to both fishing and agriculture, most of the settlers returned to England, but the remainder (30–40) under Roger Conant removed to Naumkeag (Salem, 1626), where they set up a trading post.

1628, 19 Mar. THE NEW ENGLAND COMPANY. The Rev. **John White**, a Dorsetshire nonconformist who had been active in the first Dorchester Co., formed a new association, the New England Co., which received a patent to land extending from three miles north of the Merrimack River to three miles south of the Charles River. The company's ninety members (largely but not entirely Puritan) included 6 from the old Dorchester group.

1628, 20 June. JOHN ENDECOTT (c.1589–1665) sailed with a small group of colonists to Naumkeag (Salem). On arrival (6 Sept.) he served as Governor (1628-30), handing over the administration to John Winthrop.

1629, 14 Mar. MASSACHUSETTS BAY COMPANY, successor to the New England Co., received a royal charter which specified no location for its annual meeting. This oversight made it possible to transfer the government to New England and transform the company into a self-governing commonwealth. The Company dispatched its first fleet (Apr.), followed by two other ships (25 Apr. and middle May). The Salem church was organized along separatist lines, and two freemen were sent home (Aug.) when they insisted on conforming to the Anglican ritual.

1629, 26 Aug. THE CAMBRIDGE AGREEMENT. The position of the Puritans was becoming increasingly insecure after the dissolution of Parliament (10 Mar. 1629) and the growing influence of **William Laud** (Bishop of London, 1628), a zealous defender of conformity. In addition, the Thirty Years' War disrupted trade with the Continent and depressed the cloth industry. Twelve Puritan members of the Massachusetts Bay Co. signed the Cambridge Agreement, whereby they undertook to emigrate to America provided the charter and government were transferred thither. The Company ratified the agreement (29 Aug.).

1630-40. EARLY COLONIZATION. The first four of eleven ships outfitted at Southampton sailed (29 Mar. 1630) with **John Winthrop** (p. 803), the newly elected Governor. The remaining seven sailed a month later; other emigrants embarked at Bristol and Plymouth (Feb. and Mar. 1630). The *Arbella,* first of the Southampton ships, entered Salem Harbor (12 June). The population settled along the Massachusetts coast north of Plymouth. Endecott moved to Mishawum (Charlestown); others went to Shawmut (Boston), Mystic (Medford), Watertown, Roxbury, and Dorchester. The elevation of Laud to the primacy in England, combined with increasing economic difficulties, led to an influx of new settlers, beginning 1633, including such notable clergymen as

John Cotton (p. 691) from St. Botolph's Church, Boston in Lincolnshire (4 Sept.), and **Thomas Hooker** (1586-1647). In the first decade some 20,000 settlers emigrated to New England.

1630-34. CIVIL GOVERNMENT was rapidly established. The first meeting of the Governor and Assistants was held 2 Sept. 1630; the first General Court, 29 Oct. In addition to the twelve original freemen-settlers, 118 others were admitted to the freemanship (28 May 1631), but the freemanship was restricted to church members (in force until 1664), in violation of the charter. On 13 Feb. 1632 Watertown protested a tax levied by the Court of Assistants, and on 19 May the General Court regained the right of electing the Governor and deputy Governor. The freemen of each town were authorized to send deputies to the General Court (1644). Deputies and assistants (the latter elected by the freemen in a court of election) sat in one house until 1644, when, as a result of the "Sow Case" (*Shearman* v. *Keayne,* 1642-43), the legislature became bicameral.

1635. BANISHMENT OF ROGER WILLIAMS. Williams (p. 801) arrived in New England (5 Feb. 1631), served in the Salem and Plymouth churches, and became pastor of the former (early 1635). He attacked the validity of the charter, questioned the right of the civil authorities to legislate in matters of conscience, and urged the Salem church to separate from the rest. The General Court (12 Sept. 1635) expelled the Salem deputies, only seating them when they had repudiated Williams. The Court banished him (13 Sept.), but permitted him to remain over the winter. Fearing seizure and deportation to England, he fled from Salem (Jan. 1636) and wintered among the Indians. Joined by others in the spring, he first sought to settle at Plymouth, was warned off, and purchased land from the Indians at the site of the present Providence, which he founded (June 1636).

1635, May-1638, Apr. ATTEMPTS TO REVOKE CHARTER. Thomas Morton, who went back to New England (1629), was arrested by Endecott, had his house burned down, and was then deported, allied himself with Sir Ferdinando Gorges to secure revocation of the Massachusetts charter. On Gorges' complaint, the case came before the Privy Council (19 Jan. 1633). A Privy Council committee ("Lords Commissioners for the Plantations in General," known as "Laud Commission") ordered the recall of the charter on the ground that it had been surreptitiously obtained and unwarrantably overstepped (May 1635). Gorges was ordered to serve a writ of quo warranto on the Massachusetts officials, and the King's Bench ordered the charter canceled (3 May 1637). Meantime, Gorges' ship had broken in the launching, and he failed to secure the charter. Winthrop ignored a Privy Council order (4 Apr. 1638), but the outbreak of revolt in Scotland (signing of the Solemn League and Covenant, 28 Feb.) prevented the crown from taking further action.

1636–38. ANNE HUTCHINSON SEDITION TRIAL. Young Sir Henry Vane (1613–62), an aristocratic Puritan, elected Governor (25 May 1636), the year after his arrival, came under the influence of **Anne Hutchinson** (p. 731), along with most members of the Boston church including John Cotton. Her views, loosely called **"Antinomianism,"** stressed "grace" rather than "works," and her emphasis on personal revelation minimized the role of the orthodox clergy. When the Rev. **John Wheelwright** (*c.*1592–1679), her brother-in-law, in a sermon in Boston (20 Jan. 1637) denounced the doctrine of works, he was tried for sedition and contempt, convicted, but his sentencing was postponed. On election day (27 May 1637) Winthrop's faction had the voting transferred from pro-Hutchinson Boston to Newtown (Cambridge). Winthrop defeated Vane, who returned to England (3 Aug.). A synod of 25 ministers convened at Newtown (30 Aug.) defined orthodox Puritan doctrine. On 12 Nov. the General Court banished Wheelwright and ordered Anne Hutchinson to stand trial for sedition and contempt. She was sentenced to be banished (17 Nov.). After an ecclesiastical trial (Mar. 1638), in which she was excommunicated, the

sentence was put into effect. With her husband and children she journeyed to Roger Williams' new settlement on Narragansett Bay. In cooperation with another Boston exile, William Coddington, she founded the town of Pocasset (Portsmouth, 7 Mar.). Upon her husband's death she removed to Long Island (1642) and later to the vicinity of Eastchester, where she and her entire household (except one daughter ransomed by the Dutch, 1651) were murdered by the Indians (Aug. or Sept. 1643).

EXPANSION OF NEW ENGLAND, 1631–60

1631–60. FOUNDING OF CONNECTICUT. In the fall of 1632 Edward Winslow of Plymouth explored the Connecticut Valley probably as far north as Windsor. In support of their claim to the region the Dutch at New Amsterdam sent a ship up the Connecticut River (June 1633) and erected a small fort and trading post (Fort Good Hope, later Hartford). Although Winslow and Bradford sought unsuccessfully to organize a joint Plymouth-Massachussetts expedition to the Connecticut River (July), John Oldham of the Bay Colony took a small party overland (Sept.) and spent the winter (1634–35) at Pyquag (Wethersfield). Also in Sept. Lt. William Holmes, commissioned by Winslow, set up a trading post at Windsor above Hartford. Restlessness in Massachusetts seacoast towns where pasture lands were already proving inadequate caused a group from Dorchester (with perhaps a few from Newtown and Watertown) to settle in Windsor in defiance of Plymouth's claims (spring 1635) and a group from Newtown (Oct.) to settle around Hartford. Meantime, on 7 July a group headed by Lord Saye and Sele, who claimed rights to settle the region on the basis of a patent from the Council for New England assigned by the Earl of Warwick (1631), authorized **John Winthrop the Younger** (1606–76), son of the Bay Colony's Governor, to take control at the mouth of the Connecticut River. The settlers accepted Winthrop as Governor (before Mar. 1636) and the Massachusetts General Court laid down a plan of government (13 Mar.) and placed final authority in the hands of the "inhabitants." After the arrival (Oct. 1635) of Rev. Thomas Shepard, who settled his followers at Newtown, **Rev. Thomas Hooker** departed with the remainder of his Newtown followers, and reached Hartford (31 May 1636). Hooker's democratic views were reflected in a sermon (31 May 1638), in which he declared that authority should rest upon the free consent of the "people." His views, as well as those of his associates, **John Haynes** and **Roger Ludlow** (founded Fairfield and Stratford, 1638), were reflected in the **Fundamental Orders** (24 Jan. 1639), a frame of government adopted by Hartford, Windsor, and Wethersfield. (Springfield under **William Pynchon** refused to join, and by 1649 deputies from that town sat regularly in the Massachusetts General Court.) The Governor, who was to be of an approved congregation, and the magistrates were to be elected "by the vote of the country"; by this was meant the freemen, who were "admitted inhabitants" who had been selected for freemanship either by the General Court or by one or more of the magistrates. Voting in town affairs was open to "admitted inhabitants," i.e., Trinitarian male householders (after 1657 possessor of a £30 estate). In operation the franchise was as restricted as that of the Bay Colony. By 1662 (before the absorption of New Haven) 15 towns had been settled.

1636–56. RHODE ISLAND SETTLE-MENTS. Roger Williams established his colony at Seekonk (**Providence**) on Narragansett Bay (June 1636) solely on the basis of an Indian deed. He was joined (Apr. 1638) by a band of Boston exiles under William Coddington, who bought the island of Aquidneck (**Rhode Island**) from the Indians, and, in collaboration with Anne Hutchinson, founded Pocasset (**Portsmouth**). Splitting with Mrs. Hutchinson, Coddington founded **Newport** (8 May 1639). These two Rhode Island colonies were joined (12 Mar. 1640). A fourth town, **Warwick,** was founded by Samuel Gorton (1643). Imperiled by the hostile New England Confederacy, Roger Williams

left for England via New Amsterdam (Mar. 1643) to obtain a charter, which was granted him (24 Mar. 1644). Under its authority a general assembly composed of freemen from the four towns (Providence, Portsmouth, Newport, and Warwick (convened at Portsmouth (29–31 May 1647) and drafted a constitutional structure establishing freedom of conscience, separating church and state, providing for town referenda on laws passed by the assembly, and giving to towns as well as the assembly the right to initiate laws. William Coddington opposed the union, went to England (Oct. 1649), and obtained a separate charter for the island of Aquidneck (Mar. 1651), which Williams was able to have the Council of State revoke (Oct. 1652). Coddington finally accepted the authority of Providence Plantations (Mar. 1656).

1637–43. FOUNDING OF NEW HAVEN. Rev. **John Davenport** (1597–1670), a friend of John Cotton, sailed from England (Apr. 1636) with a group of followers, notably **Theophilus Eaton** (*c.*1590–1658), a London merchant, and, after stopping at Boston (26 June), established Quinnipiac (**New Haven**) as a colony and trading post. Land was purchased from the Indians, a town laid out in a modified grid pattern, and a government established which restricted the franchise to church members. In 1641 **Stamford** was founded and in 1643 the independent settlements of **Guilford** (6 July) and **Milford** (23 Oct.) joined New Haven colony. A General Court, comprising two deputies from each of the four towns, adopted (6 Nov.) a Frame of Government, established the Mosaic law as the basis of its legal system, and made no provision for trial by jury.

1636–37. PEQUOT WAR. A punitive expedition (24 Aug., led by John Endecott of Mass.) against the Pequots (who dominated the area between the Pequot [Thames] River and the present western boundary of Rhode Island, as well as eastern Long Island and Long Island Sound) in reprisal for the murder of a New England trader, John Oldham (20 July 1636), led to reprisals the following spring. A Connecticut force under Capt.

John Mason destroyed the main Pequot stronghold near the present village of Stonington (26 May). The fleeing remnants were slaughtered near New Haven (28 July) by a combined force from Plymouth, Massachusetts, and Connecticut.

1638–43. NEW HAMPSHIRE. After John Mason's death (Dec. 1635) his lands and buildings were appropriated by his colonists. In Apr. 1638 **John Wheelwright**, banished from Massachusetts Bay, established the town of **Exeter**. His settlers signed (14 July 1639) the **Exeter Compact** (based on the Mayflower Compact). Portsmouth and Dover conceded the authority of Massachusetts (1641), and Hampton (1642) and Exeter (1643) followed, causing Wheelwright to withdraw to Maine rather than submit. Merrimack, Salisbury, and Haverhill were then united with the Piscataqua settlements.

1640–51. MAINE. Despite the attempt of Gorges to govern Maine through his cousin, Thomas Gorges, and the establishment of a provincial court at York (25 June 1640), Massachusetts persisted in its expansionist aims. Despite an appeal by the Maine government to Parliament (5 Dec. 1651), the Massachusetts General Court held that Maine was legally included within the boundaries of the Bay Colony (31 May 1652). Ligonia was annexed (4 July); Kittery (20 Nov.) and York (22 Nov.) capitulated.

1641–60. MASSACHUSETTS AS AN INDEPENDENT COMMONWEALTH. In response to criticism that too much discretionary authority was lodged in the magistrates, the General Court adopted (Dec. 1641) the **Body of Liberties,** a code drawn up by **Nathaniel Ward**, in preference to an earlier proposed draft by John Cotton, "Moses his Judicialls" (1636), which was published in England inaccurately as *An Abstract of the Lawes of New England* (1641). While less wholly drawn upon Mosaic law, the Body of Liberties based its criminal code on the Pentateuch. On 14 Nov. 1646 **Robert Child** and other remonstrants attacked the Bay Colony for its civil and religious discrimination against non-Puritans and for not observing the laws of England. Winthrop and other magistrates framed a reply, and the General Court declared: "Our allegiance binds us not to the laws of England any longer than while we live in England." A more extensive code was adopted in 1648, which was influential throughout the Northern colonies with the exception of Rhode Island, whose code of 1647 adhered to the English common law. On 7 June 1652 the General Court set up a mint, and the "pine-tree shilling" was minted (down to 1684). On 29 Oct. Massachusetts, in defiance of Parliament, declared herself an independent commonwealth.

1643, 19 May. NEW ENGLAND CONFEDERATION. As a result of experience in the Pequot War, in which military action was not well coordinated, and the threat of Dutch expansion, representatives from Massachusetts, Plymouth, Connecticut, and New Haven, meeting at Boston, drew up 12 articles of confederation, which were ratified by the four colonies. The **United Colonies of New England** represented a union of the four colonies, each of whose territorial integrity was guaranteed. The government was a board of eight commissioners, two from each colony, chosen annually by their respective general courts. The commissioners were empowered to declare both offensive and defensive war, the expenses for which were to be borne by the colonies in proportion to the number of their male inhabitants between 16 and 60. In addition, the commissioners were given jurisdiction over interstate quarrels, fugitive servants, fugitives from justice, and Indian affairs. Six votes were required for a decision. Annual sessions were held until 1664, occasional meetings prior to King Philip's War, which served as a basis for renewed activity. Thereafter activity virtually ceased, and the union was terminated in 1684.

1644–52. CONVERSION OF INDIANS. As a result of orders of the Massachusetts General Court (29 Nov. 1644 and 14 Nov. 1646), the Rev. **John Eliot** (1604–90), pastor at Roxbury, who learned the Indian dialects and began to preach to the Indians at Nonantum

(Newton), settled a group of converts at Natick (1651), followed by 13 other colonies of "Praying Indians," comprising more than 1,000 in numbers. His efforts resulted in the founding in London (19 July 1649) of the Society for Propagating the Gospel in New England. His work was largely destroyed by King Philip's War (1675).

1649-60. TREATMENT OF RELIGIOUS MINORITIES. The independent government of Maine, organized after the death of Sir Ferdinando Gorges (July 1649), passed an act (16 Oct.) granting all Christians the right to form churches provided "they be orthodox in judgment and not scandalous in life." On 18 July 1651 the Massachusetts authorities heavily fined and banished three Baptists. The first Quakers to arrive in Boston (July–Aug. 1656) were imprisoned, brutally treated, and expelled, a step which was ratified by the Federal Commissioners (17 Sept.). The Massachusetts General Court imposed penalties on Quakers entering the colony (24 Oct.), forbade Quaker meetings (29 May 1658), and imposed the death penalty for Quakers who returned in defiance of expulsion (Oct. 1658). Two returning Quakers (William Robinson and Marmaduke Stevenson) were hanged (27 Oct. 1659), and thereafter Mary Dyer, onetime follower of Anne Hutchinson (1 June 1660), and William Leddra (24 Mar. 1661) suffered the same penalty. Similar laws in Plymouth (1657–58) and New Haven (1658) were not as ruthlessly enforced.

NEW ENGLAND UNDER THE RESTORATION, 1660–75

1660–61. CHARLES II PROCLAIMED. The Restoration imperiled the position of the New England colonies. The Puritans were sympathetic with the cause of the Commonwealth, and New Haven harbored the regicide judges, Whalley and Goffe (1661). First to proclaim Charles II was Rhode Island (18 Oct. 1660), followed by Connecticut (14 Mar. 1661), New Haven (5 June), and Massachusetts (7 Aug.).

1661, Sept.–1662, 18 Oct. SUSPENSION OF QUAKER PERSECUTION. A royal order which reached Boston 9 Sept. 1661 commanded that all Quakers under sentence of death or corporal punishment be remanded to England for trial. Massachusetts released all imprisoned Quakers, permitting them to leave the colony rather than sending them to England for trial, and suspended 7 Dec. the corporal punishment act of 1 June; but within a year (18 Oct. 1662) that penalty was revived.

1661–63. CONNECTICUT AND RHODE ISLAND CHARTERS. The Restoration threatened the independent existence of Connecticut (which had no charter) and Rhode Island (whose charter, 1644, now had no legality. Through the influence of Lord Saye and Sele, **John Winthrop, Jr.** (Governor since 1657), obtained a royal charter for Connecticut (3 May 1662), whose boundaries were defined as Massachusetts on the north, Long Island Sound on the south, Narragansett Bay on the east, and the South Sea on the west. Since this grant included Providence, an agreement was entered into between Winthrop and John Clark, Rhode Island agent, to limit Connecticut's eastern limits to the Pawcatuck. The charter granted Rhode Island (18 July 1663) guaranteed religious freedom regardless of "differences in opinion in matters of religion." In implementing the charter provisions, the General Assembly (Mar. 1664) repealed the law requiring approval by the towns of laws of the General Court.

1662, Oct.–1665, 5 Jan. CONNECTICUT ANNEXES NEW HAVEN. Connecticut demanded that New Haven be incorporated within her territory in accordance with the Charter of 1662. Despite a vote of the freemen to maintain independence (4 Nov.), Southold voted to join Connecticut. Rather than come under the jurisdiction of the Duke of York, whose grant (12 Mar. 1664) included all land lying between the Connecticut and Delaware Rivers, Stamford, Guilford, and part of Milford joined Connecticut (14 Dec.). New Haven formally submitted (5 Jan. 1665). Rather than yield, a group in Branford left for Newark in East Jersey.

1664–66. KING'S COMMISSIONERS.

The crown dispatched four commissioners to New England to secure aid in the war against the Dutch, investigate the governments of the colonies, settle boundary disputes, and see that the Navigation Acts were enforced. They laid down four conditions of compliance: (1) that all householders take an oath of allegiance to the crown, (2) that all men of competent estates be freemen, (3) that all of orthodox belief be admitted to existing churches or churches of their own choosing, and (4) that all laws derogatory to the crown be expunged. Plymouth (17 Feb. 1665), Connecticut (20 Apr.), and Rhode Island (3 May) agreed to comply, but Massachusetts, which had made a pretense of admitting nonchurch members to the franchise by qualifying all ratable at 10s. (23 July 1664), refused further compliance (19–24 May 1665). Three out of the four commissioners recommended the cancellation of the Massachusetts charter. When, in 1666, the king commanded the Bay Colony to send representatives to England to answer charges, the General Court refused to comply.

1665–69. MASSACHUSETTS ANNEXES MAINE.

The king's commissioners (following a regime set up, 1661, by commissioners of the Gorges' heirs) established a government in Maine which lasted from Oct. 1665 to May 1668. At a special convention at York the authority of Massachusetts was recognized (6 July 1668), and in May 1669 three Maine deputies were seated in the Massachusetts General Court.

1674, 29 June.

A patent was issued to the Duke of York confirming his title to all lands between the Connecticut and Delaware Rivers and (in Maine) between the St. Croix and the Kennebec. He proceeded to designate Sir Edmund Andros (1637–1714) his Governor General.

KING PHILIP'S WAR, 1675–76

1671, 10 Apr.–1675, 14 June. PRELIMINARIES.

Five tribes which increasingly felt the pressure of the New England settlers' expansionist activities were (1) the **Wampanoags**, who had been pushed from the east coast to the eastern shores of Narragansett Bay; (2) the **Narragansetts**, whose lands between the Thames River and Narragansett Bay were threatened by a large land company, the Atherton Co. (organized 1659), which was attempting to foreclose a mortgage on most of this area (1662–76); (3) the **Mohegans**, occupying the hill country between the Connecticut and Thames Rivers; (4) the **Podunks** to their north; and (5) the **Nipmucks**, who hunted in the country along the northern watersheds of the Thames and Pawtucket Rivers. **Philip**, son of the friendly sachem, Massasoit, became chief of the Wampanoags on his brother Alexander's death (1662). At the request of the Plymouth authorities that he yield his arms, he made a token delivery (10 Apr. 1671). Accusations of conspiracy against the colonists brought against Philip resulted in the murder of the accuser and, in turn, the trial and execution of 3 Indians (8 June 1675).

1675, 20 June–6 Sept. START OF HOSTILITIES.

When Philip attacked Swansea (20–25 June) a combined force of Plymouth and Boston troops attacked Mt. Hope, the Wampanoag stronghold on the Taunton River (28 June), but failed to destroy Indian forces. Philip now attacked the entire southern frontier, joined by the Nipmucks, who attacked Mendon (14 July) and Brookfield (2–4 Aug.). In turn, Lancaster (19 Aug.), Deerfield and Hadley (1 Sept.), and Northfield (2 Sept.) were attacked. The last was abandoned (6 Sept.).

1675, 9 Sept. NEW ENGLAND CONFEDERATION DECLARES WAR.

Massachusetts was assigned a quota of 527 men; Connecticut, 315; Plymouth, 158. Indian victories at **Bloody Brook** near Hadley (18 Sept.) and attacks on Springfield (5 Oct.), Hatfield (16 Oct.), and other settlements followed.

1675, 2 Nov.–1676, Jan. NARRAGANSETT CAMPAIGN.

A combined force under **Josiah Winslow** of Plymouth stormed the principal fort of the Narragansetts (present South Kingston, R.I.) on 19 Nov. Some 300 women and children were killed, but most of the warriors escaped. By the end of Jan. 1677 most of the tribe's women, children, and old men had been killed, while the warriors fled to the Nipmucks.

1676, 10 Feb.–30 Mar. THE INDIANS COUNTERATTACK. Driven by hunger the Indians attacked Lancaster (10 Feb. 1676), sacked the town, and took many captives, including Mrs. **Mary Rowlandson,** whose *True History* describing her captivity (ransomed, 2 May 1676) reveals the extent of Indian starvation. Attacks on Sudbury, Chelmsford, Medford, and Weymouth followed. Even Plymouth (12 Mar.) and Providence (29–30 Mar.) were attacked, as were Groton, Warwick, Marlboro, Sudbury, Rehoboth (the same month), and Wrentham, Seekonk, Andover, Chelmsford, Scituate, and Bridgewater (Apr. and May).

1676, 18 May–28 Aug. COLLAPSE OF INDIAN RESISTANCE. A force of 180 under Capt. Turner attacked a large body of Indians in the Connecticut Valley, near Deerfield, and destroyed many men and supplies, but subsequently were ambushed and annihilated. But the war of attrition stripped the Indians of their offensive power. After Major Talcot, with 250 men from the Connecticut Valley and 200 Mohegans, defeated the Indians at Hadley (12 June), chased the Valley tribes into the New Hampshire hills, and then, turning eastward, destroyed 250 Indians near Marlboro, Indians started surrendering in large numbers (410 from 16 June to 6 July). Philip, betrayed, was run down in the Assowamset Swamp and shot (12 Aug.), his wife and 9-year-old were sold into West Indian captivity, and the last sizable surrender took place 28 Aug.

1675, 5 Sept.–1678, 12 Aug. WAR IN THE NORTH. Following a raid on Falmouth (12 Sept.), 80 Maine settlers were killed by 10 Dec. The resumption of warfare (11 Aug. 1676) caused the abandonment of the region between Casco Bay and the Penobscot. Indian raids were renewed in the spring of 1677. Sir Edmund Andros constructed a fort at Pemaquid (Aug. 1677), negotiated for a release of prisoners, and concluded peace with the Indians (12 Apr. 1678),

by which they were to receive one peck of corn yearly for each family settled in Maine.

COST OF WAR. One out of every 16 men of military age was killed, over £90,000 were expended in prosecuting the war, 12 towns were completely destroyed, with half of the towns in New England suffering damage.

NEW ENGLAND TO THE GLORIOUS REVOLUTION, 1676–89

1676, June. EDWARD RANDOLPH (*c.*1632–1703) arrived in Boston as special agent of the Crown to convey royal instructions and check on the enforcement of the Navigation Acts. On return to England he submitted two reports (20 Sept. and 12 Oct.) charging Massachusetts with failing to enforce the Navigation Acts, putting English citizens to death for their religious views, denying the right of appeal to the Privy Council, and refusing the oath of allegiance.

1677. MASSACHUSETTS BUYS OUT GORGES HEIRS. The Lords of Trade upheld the title to Maine of the heirs of Sir Ferdinando Gorges. Through its agent, John Usher, Massachusetts proceeded to buy out the heirs for £1,250 (13 Mar.). Maine remained incorporated in Massachusetts until 1820 (pp. 159, 160).

1680, 4 Feb.–1686. ROYAL GOVERNMENT IN NEW HAMPSHIRE. By royal commission (Sept. 1680) New Hampshire was separated from Massachusetts. The administration of Governor John Cutt (1680–82) was comparatively peaceful except for the attempt of Robert Mason, John Mason's heir, to collect quitrents. Cutt's successor, Edward Cranfield (1682–85), ruled without an assembly when that body refused to pass his revenue bills (1683). Walter Barefoote, his deputy Governor, succeeded him, pending arrival of the Dudley Commission. New Hampshire was part of the Dominion of New England (1686–89); its royal authority was reestablished (1692), after which date it had no connection with Massachusetts except that from 1698–1741 both provinces had the same governor.

1684, 21 June. ABROGATION OF MASSACHUSETTS CHARTER. Edward Randolph, appointed collector and surveyor of customs (1678), wrote a series of hostile reports to the home authorities (11 Apr., 7 Aug. 1682) and returned to England to aid in the prosecution against the Bay Colony (13 June 1683). The Court of Chancery annulled the charter (21 June 1684; final decree, 18 Oct.).

1685-88. DOMINION OF NEW ENGLAND AND ANDROS REGIME. Joseph Dudley (1647-1720), who had been sent to England to protest the threatened loss of the charter (1682), was appointed by James II (Sept. 1685) Governor of Massachusetts, Maine, and New Hampshire. He was succeeded by **Sir Edmund Andros**, who arrived in Boston, 20 Dec. 1686, to assume the government of all the New England colonies (save Connecticut and Rhode Island) and to organize a Dominion of New England, to include New York, New Jersey, and Pennsylvania, for more effective military operations in the event of war with France and better enforcement of the Navigation Acts. Rhode Island was incorporated on 30 Dec., and Connecticut's government taken over (1 Nov. 1687), although the charter was successfully concealed in the **Charter Oak.** Other actions increasing his unpopularity were (1) his demand that Anglicans be permitted to share the Old South Meeting House (21 Dec. 1686), which he converted into an Anglican church (25 Mar. 1687); (2) his insistence that all land titles be reexamined and that the payment of a quitrent be a condition of regrants; (3) his imposition of assessments, which were resisted by an Ipswich town meeting (23 Aug. 1687), under the leadership of Rev. **John Wise**, 1652-1725 (arrested, tried, and fined £10 and costs; 4 others fined and disqualified from holding office); (4) an order limiting town meetings to one annually (17

Mar. 1688); (5) the placing of the militia under the direct control of the Governor (24 Mar.). Rev. **Increase Mather** (1639-1723), President of Harvard, eluding detection, sailed for England to place the grievances of New Englanders before the Lords of Trade (10 Aug.).

1689, 10 Jan.-25 July. GLORIOUS REVOLUTION IN NEW ENGLAND. Andros received news of the impending landing of William of Orange while he was at Pemaquid, Me. (10 Jan. 1689), and returned to Boston in the middle of March. On 18 Apr. an armed uprising in Boston forced Andros to take refuge in the fort. A manifesto (largely the work of **Cotton Mather** [1663-1728]), excoriating the Andros regime and justifying the uprising on the grounds of fear of a French alliance and a Popish plot, was read to the populace. At the end of the day Andros surrendered and was lodged in jail. Also jailed were Randolph and Dudley. A "Council for the Safety and the Conservation of the Peace" was set up (20 Apr.). Deputies to a General Court were elected (6 June) before receipt of an Order in Council (25 July) for the return of Andros and his councilors to stand trial.

1691, 17 Oct. ROYAL CHARTER. Efforts to have the old charter restored proved unavailing; a royal charter was issued which formally incorporated Maine and Plymouth within Massachusetts' boundaries, provided for a Governor to be appointed by the crown, a Council elected by the General Court subject to the Governor's veto, the substitution of a property for the religious qualification for voting, royal review of legislation, and appeals to the King in Council. As a result of opinions of the Attorney General (for Connecticut, 2 Aug. 1690; for Rhode Island, 7 Dec. 1693) that neither colony had been legally deprived of its charter, both colonies operated under their old charters until 1818 and 1842 respectively.

SETTLEMENT OF THE MIDDLE COLONIES

NEW NETHERLAND

1610–18. INDEPENDENT VOYAGES. Following the voyage of Henry Hudson for the Dutch East India Co. (25 Mar.–4 Nov. 1609), several exploring and trading voyages under Dutch auspices were made to the area (1610, 1611, 1613–14). **Adriaen Block** (d.1624) sailed to Manhattan (1613), braving the perilous passage named by him "Hellegat" (Hell Gate), discovered the Housatonic and Connecticut Rivers, Rhode Island, and Block Island (named for him). His map was the 1st to show Manhattan and Long Island as separate islands. A fort (Fort Nassau, later Orange) erected up the Hudson around this time (at Castle Island) was transferred (1617) to the west side of the river (present Albany). The 13 shipowners engaged in trade with the New World organized the New Netherland Co. (1614), with a 3-yr. trading monopoly between 40° and 45°N. At expiration date the charter was not renewed.

1621, 3 June. FOUNDING OF DUTCH WEST INDIA CO. Under the leadership of William Usselinx, a prominent merchant, the Dutch West India Co. was chartered by the States General, which participated in its financing. The charter conferred a trading monopoly and the right to colonize in the New World and along the west coast of Africa below the Tropic of Cancer. The Company was organized into 5 chambers. The most important, that of Amsterdam, had immediate control of New Netherland (which province played a minor role in the vast trading activities of the Company). The director-general of the colony, while chosen by the Company, had to be confirmed by the States General. The Council of Nineteen (the Company's executive body) adopted a resolution (3 Nov. 1623) authorizing the Amsterdam Chamber to dispatch 5 or 6 families to start a settlement and approved a **Provisional Order** (28 Mar. 1624), the first plan of government of the colony, based in large measure on the *Artikelbrief,* rules governing life aboard ship. Colonists were divided into 2 classes: (1) free colonists who received transportation, seeds, cattle, and necessities of life for the first two years and could own their own homesteads; (2) *bouwlieden* (indentured husbandmen) who were required to work for a stipulated term on the Company's own farms (*bouweries*) or on those of Company officials. Trading with outsiders was prohibited, and the export trade confined to the Company.

1624. FIRST PERMANENT SETTLEMENT. Some 30 families, mostly Walloons, sailed from Amsterdam (after 30 Mar. 1624) under the leadership of **Cornelis Jacobsen May,** a sea captain, named first director of the colony. On arrival in New York Bay, a small group was left at a fort on Nut (Governor's) Island, several families sent to the Delaware where they established Ft. Nassau (now Gloucester, N.J.), and 18 families proceeded up the Hudson to the older Fort Nassau. It is conjectured, but not established, that some members of this third group settled on Manhattan Island and that other Walloons (at this time or somewhat later) crossed the East River to Long Island, settling at Wallabout (Walloon's Cove).

1625, Jan.–1626, Sept. EARLY GOVERNMENT. Willem Verhulst, sent out as supercargo, became second director, with a council made up of available Dutch sea captains, a vice-director, and a vice-commissioner. As a result of his mismanagement the council ousted him (*c.*Sept. 1626), appointing in his place **Peter Minuit** (Pierre Minuyt, *c.*1580–1638), born Wesel on the Rhine of Dutch or Walloon ancestry. Minuit had arrived, 4 May 1626, on the *Sea-mew,* with a new group of emigrants who proceeded that summer to erect on Manhattan Island 30 houses. The same year he purchased Manhattan from native Indian chiefs for 60 guilders (*c.*$24) paid in trading goods, and changed its name to **New Amsterdam.** Settlement was reinforced by withdrawing settlers from Ft. Orange (leaving 16 men) and from the Delaware (completely abandoned by 14 June 1627).

1629, 7 June. ESTABLISHMENT OF PATROONSHIPS. To promote farm settlement with a view to making the colony self-sufficient as well as a supply base for the expanding merchant marine of the Company both in Brazil and the West Indies, the States General confirmed the **Charter of Freedoms and Exemptions,** under which the Company was empowered to grant to those transporting 50 settlers estates fronting 16 miles along navigable rivers, and extending inland as far as settlement would permit. The grantees (*patroons*) were given feudal rights, including the right to hold courts as well as exemption from taxation for 8 yrs. By the end of Jan. 1630 5 patroonships had been granted along the Hudson, Connecticut, and Delaware Rivers to directors of the Company. Three were settled (**Pavonia,** across the North River from Manhattan, incl. Staten Island; **Swaanendael,** on the west side of Delaware Bay; and **Rensselaerswyck,** near Ft. Orange, the patroonship of **Kiliaen Van Rensselaer** (1595–1644), Amsterdam diamond and gold merchant, who ruled as an absentee proprietor. Rensselaerswyck was the only patroonship that succeeded. Its tenants held perpetual leaseholds.

1629–37. UNDER MINUIT AND VAN TWILLER. Despite a generally constructive administration, Minuit was recalled by the Company (1631) for being too liberal in granting trading privileges to the patroons. He was succeeded, temporarily, by Bastiaen Janseen Krol (Mar. 1632–Apr. 1633), who, in turn, was followed by **Wouter Van Twiller** (1633–38), nephew of Van Rensselaer, who was elevated from a clerkship in Amsterdam. Trade expansion was promoted by the construction of Ft. Good Hope (present Hartford), 8 June 1633, and by the ouster of a party of Virginians who had occupied the abandoned Ft. Nassau (Aug. 1635). A garrison was placed on the Delaware and the settlement of Long Island begun by grants of patents (1636)

to Jacobus Van Curler and Wolfert Gerritsen in Flatlands and vicinity. Although exports increased during his regime (45,-000 guilders, 1626; 91,375 gldrs., 1634; 134,925 gldrs., 1635), Van Twiller was charged with illegal trading, incompetence, and hostility toward the Dutch Reformed Church, and was replaced (2 Sept. 1637) by **Willem Kiefft** (1597–1647), an Amsterdam merchant.

NEW NETHERLAND AND HER NEIGHBORS, 1638–64

1638–40. FOUNDING OF NEW SWEDEN. The New Sweden or New South Co. was organized (1633) as successor to a series of trading companies of which Willem Usselinx was the guiding spirit. The capital for the company was supplied by Dutch and Swedish investors in equal parts. Through the influence of Samuel Blommaert, who had a substantial interest in the patroonship of Swaanendael (destroyed by the Indians before 6 Dec. 1632), and Peter Minuit, who had now entered the Swedish service, the company was granted a charter for settlement on the Delaware (*c.*1637). Its first expedition sailed (31 Dec. 1637) under Minuit, arrived at the Delaware (mid-Mar. 1638), and, despite Dutch protests, built Ft. Christina (present Wilmington). Minuit was lost at sea on a return trip to Sweden (June), but the leaderless colony managed to survive until the arrival of a new expedition (spring 1640), bringing Peter Hollender Ridder, as Governor; Rev. Reorus Torkillus, a Lutheran minister; and much-needed livestock. A group of Dutch settlers from Utrecht were planted 20 miles north of Ft. Christina (Nov. 1640).

1640, 19 July. NEW CHARTER OF FREEDOMS AND EXEMPTIONS, granted to promote peopling of New Netherland, reduced the size of patroonships, provided grants of 200 acres to those transporting 5 persons, and liberalized commercial privileges.

1640–45. DUTCH EXPANSION. New settlements were established at Vriesendael on Tappan Zee, Hackensack, and at Staten Island (1641). The movement of English colonists into Westchester (the

Hutchinson, Throgmorton, and Cornell plantations) and on Long Island (Maspeth and Lady Moody's settlement at Gravesend) impelled Kiefft to appoint a special English secretary (11 Dec. 1642). Confronted with expanding European settlements in the southern part of the province and Iroquois ascendancy in the north, the Indians of the lower Hudson Valley raided Staten Island and Manhattan (summer 1641). Kiefft, who had levied tribute from the tribes, was accused by the settlers of provoking war. Twelve representatives of heads of families (**The Twelve**), called together by Kiefft (21 Jan. 1642), agreed to a campaign against the Indians, which proved ineffectual (Mar.). A year's truce was arranged by Jonas Bronck, a settler on the Bronx River. The Twelve were dismissed (18 Feb.) when they requested representation on the council and courts to prevent taxes being levied without their consent. In Feb. 1643 the Mohawks, armed by traders at Rensselaerswyck and Ft. Orange, attacked the Indians of the lower Hudson, forcing them to seek refuge among the Dutch at Pavonia (New Jersey) and Manhattan. They were slaughtered by Kiefft's men (25–26 Feb.), with resultant Indian reprisals throughout the area (Sept.). Kiefft was now forced to seek counsel from 8 men (**The Eight**). Despite reinforcements by a small English force under John Underhill of Connecticut (29 Sept.), the Dutch failed to prevent English plantations in Westchester (the Hutchinson, Throgmorton, and Cornell settlements) and Long Island from being destroyed (Lady Moody's at Gravesend was spared) as well as settlements on the west bank of the Hudson (17 Sept.–1 Oct.). Kiefft's disastrous policy brought him into conflict with The Eight, who refused approval of excises (18 June 1644) and appealed to the Amsterdam Chamber for relief (Oct.). Peace with the Indians was finally established (9 Aug. 1645) through the intervention of the Mohawks, but only after most settlers south of Ft. Orange and Rensselaerswyck had retired behind a wall built across Manhattan Island (1644).

1644, 16 Nov.–1646. RESETTLEMENT OF LONG ISLAND. After Kiefft purchased the western portion of Long Island (Coney Island to Gowanus), settlements were begun (Breukelen [northwest Brooklyn], 1646; Lady Moody's at Gravesend, chartered, 19 Dec. 1646), as well as English settlements at Heemstede (Hempstead, 16 Nov. 1644, and Flushing, 19 Oct. 1645). Meantime, the Dutch position on the Connecticut deteriorated with the expansion of English settlement in that area.

1646, 28 July–1664, 19 Mar. STUYVESANT'S REGIME. Kiefft was succeeded by **Peter Stuyvesant** (*c.*1610–72), Commissioner in Brazil (1635) and Governor of Curaçao (1643–44). On arrival at New Amsterdam (11 May 1647) he consented to an election (25 Sept.) by the Dutch householders of Manhattan, Breukelen, and Amersfort (Flatlands) of 18 men, who in turn chose 9 (**The Nine**) to advise the Governor and council and serve in a judicial capacity. The Nine soon complained to the States General (13 Oct. 1649), charging neglect by the Company, and proposed reforms, including the establishment of local self-government. Stuyvesant was ordered by the Amsterdam Chamber to grant New Amsterdam a city government (Apr. 1652). The director-general proclaimed New Amsterdam a municipality, appointed the municipal officials, and retained the right to enact ordinances (2 Feb. 1653). By Dec. 1661 5 Dutch and 6 English villages were incorporated on western Long Island, as were the villages of Bergen and Esopus. In addition to the sessions of The Nine, Stuyvesant called 3 assemblies of delegates from towns adjacent to New Amsterdam, the 1st (10 Dec. 1653), during the Anglo-Dutch War; the other 2 while the colony was in its last crisis (3 Nov. 1663, 19 Mar. 1664).

1647–63. END OF SWEDISH RULE ON THE DELAWARE. The Dutch members of the New Sweden Co. were bought out (1641) and the company reorganized (1642), with an increase of capital and an extension of control by the Swedish crown. **Johan Björnsson Printz** (1592–1663), a Swedish soldier of fortune, served as Governor of New Sweden (1643–53). He erected a series of blockhouses at Varkens Kill (Salem Creek), Upland, New Gothenburg on Tinicum

Island, 1643, and Ft. New Krisholm near the mouth of the Schuylkill (1647). Stuyvesant countered by building Ft. Beversrede across the river (at present Philadelphia, 27 Apr. 1648). Although the Swedes twice burned the post (May, Nov. 1648), the Dutch held the site until the establishment of Ft. Casimir (Newcastle, 5 Nov. 1651), controlling the approaches to New Sweden. This fort was captured by **Johan Classon Rising**, the newly appointed Governor of New Sweden (1654), but Stuyvesant proceeded to retake the fort (26 Sept. 1655), thereby ending Swedish rule in North America. In payment of debts incurred as a result of this campaign, the Dutch West India Co. transferred to the city of Amsterdam all lands west of the Delaware from Cristina Kill to Boomtje's (Bombay) Hook. The city sent out 167 settlers, who, on arrival at Ft. Casimir (21 Apr. 1657), reorganized the settlement as **New Amstel**, under Jacob Alrichs as vice-director (succeeded, 1659, by Alexander d'Hinoyossa). As a result of the transfer to the city of Amsterdam by the Company of all remaining lands on the west bank of the Delaware, as well as a tract 3 miles broad along the east bank (8 Feb. 1663), all authority in the area passed into the hands of d'Hinoyossa.

1650–64. ANGLO-DUTCH RELA-TIONS. Fearful of the encroachments of New Haven upon Westchester, Connecticut on Ft. Good Hope, and both colonies on Long Island, Stuyvesant at Hartford negotiated a boundary settlement (23–29 Sept. 1650) with the commissioners of the New England Confederacy whereby Long Island was divided by a line running north and south through Oyster Bay, and the mainland by a line 10 miles east of the Hudson (Ft. Good Hope to remain in Dutch hands). Although the English government never recognized this treaty, the boundaries were respected until shortly before the fall of New Netherland. During the **Anglo-Dutch War** (July 1652–Apr. 1654) the Confederacy refrained from declaring war on New Netherland, although Ft. Good Hope was seized (5 July 1653) by Connecticut and formally sequestered (Apr. 1654). In the spring of 1663 Connecticut dispatched Capt. John

Talcott into Westchester and James Christie into Long Island. The former dismissed the magistrates and took an oath of allegiance from the settlers; the latter forced Stuyvesant to recognize English suzerainty over the English towns on Long Island (3 Mar. 1664) pending negotiations between England and the Netherlands.

1658, 31 May–1664, 16 May. INDIAN RELATIONS. Increasing hostility of the Hudson Valley Indians (beg.1657) culminated in an attack on Wiltwyck, the village on the Esopus (7 June 1663). In 3 Dutch retaliatory expeditions (July, Sept., Oct.) 2 Indian forts were destroyed as well as most of their standing corn. On 16 May 1664 the Indians surrendered the whole of the Esopus Valley. Generally amicable relations with the Five Nations of the Iroquois, upon whom the Dutch were chiefly dependent for their furs, were marred by the activities of the *bosch loopers,* runners who intercepted Indians going to Ft. Orange to trade. Ordinances and prosecutions (June 1660) were instituted to end such illegal activities.

ESTABLISHMENT OF ENGLISH RULE

1661–64. CONQUEST OF NEW NETHERLAND. The English regarded the Dutch settlement as blocking westward expansion and interfering with the enforcement of the Navigation Acts through clandestine trade in tobacco. An open clash of national trading interests resulted from the chartering (1660) of "The Company of Royal Adventurers to Africa," with a monopoly of the African slave trade (reincorporated as the **Royal African Co.,** 1663; lost its monopoly, 1698). On 22 Mar. 1664 Charles II granted his brother, James, Duke of York, all of Maine between the Ste. Croix and Kennebec Rivers and from the coast to the St. Lawrence, all islands between Cape Cod and the Narrows, and all land from the western boundary of Connecticut (Connecticut's claims west of the Connecticut River were recognized, 30 Nov. 1667) to the eastern shore of Delaware Bay, with power to govern, subject to the reservation that judicial appeals might be taken to the crown. On 2 Apr. the Duke appointed Col. **Richard Nicolls** (1624–72) as chief of a commission to capture New Netherland and settle disputes in the New England colonies. A task force of 4 frigates reached New York Harbor (29 Aug.), and on 7 Sept. Stuyvesant, lacking support from the inhabitants, capitulated to Nicolls. Under the liberal surrender terms the Dutch were granted liberty of conscience, property and inheritance rights, and direct trade with Holland for 6 months (extended briefly, 1667; but canceled, 1668). Col. George Cartwright, another commissioner, took the surrender of Ft. Orange without incident (20 Sept.) and the British assumed the place of the Dutch as allies of the Five Nations of the Iroquois (24 Sept.). But Delaware did not yield until Sir Robert Carr had stormed Ft. Casimir (10 Oct.).

1664, 4 Oct.–1668, 21 Apr. ESTABLISHMENT OF ENGLISH RULE. Nicolls renamed New Amsterdam New York in honor of the Duke of York, but permitted the Dutch municipal officers to continue to function and even to name their own successors (2 Feb. 1665). Long Island, Staten Island, and Westchester, were constituted as "Yorkshire," with three ridings (East, Suffolk Co.; West, Staten Island, Brooklyn, and northwest Queens; and North, Westchester and central Long Island). A meeting at Hempstead (11 Mar. 1665) of 34 deputies from 17 towns from Westchester and Long Island (13 English and 4 Dutch) approved the **Duke's Laws** (a compilation by **Matthias Nicolls**), which contained a civil and criminal code, based in part on New England codes, provided for the election of overseers and a constable in each town, set up a general provincial organization of the courts and the militia, and assured freedom of conscience. Initially, the code applied only to "Yorkshire," but it was later extended to the Delaware (21 Apr. 1668). In June, 1665, the offices of mayor, alderman, and sheriff in New York City, all appointed for 1 year by the governor, replaced the schout, burgomasters, and schepens. As a result of the **Second Anglo-Dutch War** (Dec. 1664–July 1667) Nicolls confiscated all property of the Dutch West India Co.

(23 Feb. 1665) as well as the property of Dutch owners who had not taken the oath of allegiance to the British crown (10 Oct.). The **Peace of Breda** (21 July 1667) ending the war confirmed the English possession of New Netherland. Pursuing the same general policy of conciliation, Nicolls' successor, Col. **Francis Lovelace** (1668–73) refrained from extending the Duke's Laws to the predominantly Dutch areas of Kingston (Esopus, Wiltwyck), Albany, and Schenectady (settled 1661).

1673, 30 July–1674, 31 Oct. DUTCH REOCCUPATION OF NEW YORK. Following the outbreak of the **Third Anglo-Dutch War** (Mar. 1672), a Dutch fleet arrived at New York Harbor (7 Aug.), and after a brief exchange of fire (8 Aug.) the fort surrendered to the Dutch land force under Capt. **Anthony Colve**, designated Governor General (12 Aug.). Esopus and Albany were speedily occupied (15 Aug.) and Dutch officials appointed for both the province and city of **New Orange** (New York, 17 Aug.). Western Long Island and settlements in New Jersey submitted, but the 5 towns of the East Riding (Suffolk) resisted. The province was restored to England by the **Treaty of Westminster** (19 Feb. 1674) and formally surrendered (10 Nov.) to **Sir Edmund Andros**, the deputy of the Duke of York, to whom the province had been regranted by the king (9 July).

1674–87. STRUGGLE FOR REPRESENTATIVE GOVERNMENT. Andros confirmed the Duke's Laws, reappointed the previously ousted English officials, confirmed previous land grants, and secured the submission of towns on eastern Long Island which had claimed to be under Connecticut's jurisdiction. Despite popular demands for an assembly (as early as 1670), the Duke (Jan. 1676) indicated his opposition on the ground that such a body would "prove destructive . . . to the peace of the government." By the "Bolting Act" (1678) New York City was given a monopoly on flour milling for export and its position was reaffirmed by Andros as the sole port of entry. Although exonerated of charges of illegal trading with the Dutch and corruption in office, Andros was supplanted by Col. **Thomas Dongan** (1634–1715), an Irish Catholic, who arrived in New York, 28 Aug. 1683. Pursuant to instructions from the Duke he called a general assembly of delegates from each of the three ridings of Yorkshire and from New York and Harlem, Albany, Schenectady, Esopus, Martha's Vineyard, Nantucket, and Pemaquid (eastern Maine), which proceeded to enact the **Charter of Liberties** (30 Oct. 1683), largely the work of the speaker, **Matthias Nicolls.** The Charter, providing for a meeting at least once in 3 years of an assembly whose consent was necessary for the imposition of taxes, was approved by the Duke, but after his accession as James II (6 Feb. 1685) he disallowed the legislation of the assembly (29 May 1686) and expressly empowered the Royal Governor to exercise full legislative as well as executive power in conjunction with the council. The assembly was dissolved (Jan. 1687), never to meet again. Dongan granted municipal charters to New York City and Albany (1683), taking the latter out of the hands of the patroon.

1688, 11 Aug.–1691, 20 May. LEISLER'S REBELLION. Andros' commission as Governor of the Dominion of New England included New York (7 Apr. 1687). His 42-man council appointed by the king included 8 New Yorkers (16 Apr.). Andros went to Boston (1 Oct.), leaving his Lieutenant Governor, Capt. **Francis Nicholson,** in charge of affairs. When news of the Boston rising and the outbreak of war between England and France reached New York (26–27 Apr. 1689), Suffolk, Queens, and Westchester ousted their officials and elected others in their place. Dongan, retired to Hempstead, was rumored to be the center of a Catholic plot, which included Nicholson as well. **Jacob Leisler** (1649–91), a trader who had come from Germany, 1660, in the employ of the Dutch West India Co., seized Ft. James (31 May 1689), and was left in control of the city when Nicholson fled (11 June). Leisler called upon representatives from counties and towns to join the government in New York (12 June), proclaimed William

and Mary (22 June), and formed a Committee of Public Safety (26 June). Suffolk, Ulster, and Albany Counties and a few isolated towns refused to participate in Leisler's first assembly (27 July–15 Aug.), and Albany elected its own officials (14 Oct.). A letter from William III's secretary of state addressed to Nicholson (20 July 1689), or "in his absence to such as for the time being take care for preserving the peace and administering the laws," was intercepted by Leisler and interpreted as applying to himself. The burning of Schenectady by a mixed force of French and Indians (9 Feb. 1690) impelled Albany to accept Leisler. Representatives from Massachusetts, Plymouth, Connecticut, and New York convened at Albany (1 May); voted to prosecute an invasion of Canada by 2 land forces (from New York and New England), and to dispatch a naval force up the St. Lawrence. The expedition proved a fiasco (summer 1690). Meantime, the Lords of Trade had recommended sending a new Governor (31 Aug. 1689). Col. **Henry Sloughter** was commissioned (24 Nov.), but admiralty red tape and shipwreck delayed his arrival in the colony until 29 Mar. 1691. He was preceded by Maj. **Robert Ingoldesby,** who reached New York City with an English regiment (8 Feb.). Leisler refused Ingoldesby's request for the surrender of the fort on the ground that he lacked a royal commission as commander in chief or instructions from Sloughter to act as his deputy. Ingoldesby seized the City Hall, and hostilities broke out (27 Mar.) just two days before the arrival of Sloughter. Leisler surrendered to Sloughter (30 Mar.). He was tried, along with 9 of his supporters (10–27 Apr. 1691), and with 7 others sentenced to death. Leisler and Jacob Milborne, his lieutenant, were hanged (26 May), while the 6 others were reprieved and eventually pardoned by the crown (15 Mar. 1694). Sloughter's commission had empowered him to call an assembly. Such a call was issued, 30 Mar. 1691, a date which marked the beginning of representative government in New York.

NEW JERSEY

1664, 4 July–1665, 20 Feb. PROPRIETARY GRANT. The Duke of York granted to **John Lord Berkeley** and **Sir George Carteret** the region between the Hudson and Delaware Rivers, bounded on the north by a line running from 41°N. on the Hudson to the northernmost point of the Delaware. Technically, no governmental rights were conveyed, but the proprietors proceeded to issue their **Concessions and Agreements** (20 Feb. 1665), modeled on the Carolina Concessions, granting freedom of conscience, land on generous terms subject to quitrents, and the right of the freeholders to send deputies to a general assembly (first session 4 June 1668; last legal assembly until 1675 was held Nov. 1671). **Philip Carteret,** a distant relative of the proprietor (appointed Governor 10 Feb. 1665), was accepted by the Dutch in the northern section (around present Bergen), but his authority was contested by English settlers under grants from Governor Nicolls of New York.

1674–87. DEVOLUTION OF PROPRIETARY RIGHTS. Lord Berkeley sold his proprietary rights for £1,000 to **John Fenwick** (1618–83) and **Edward Byllinge,** fellow Quakers. On 8 Aug. 1674 the Duke of York then granted Sir George Carteret that part of New Jersey lying north of a line running from Barnegat Creek on the Atlantic to the mouth of Rankokus Kill on the Delaware. The province was divided (11 July 1676) between **East** and **West Jersey** by the **Quintipartite Deed** (between Carteret on one hand and Byllinge, William Penn, and two other Quakers on the other). The Duke recognized the new proprietors of West Jersey, but substituted as a boundary between the two sections a line running from Little Egg Harbor (in the Barnegat region) to the northernmost branch of the Delaware (16 Aug. 1680). After Byllinge's death (1685) his heirs sold his share to Dr. **Daniel Coxe** of London. On the death of Sir George Carteret (1680), the trustees for his heir sold his rights in East Jersey (1 Feb. 1681) to William Penn and 11 associates, for the most part highly connected Quakers (who enlarged their numbers, 1682, to

24 (confirmed by the Duke, 14 Mar. 1683).

1674–88 GOVERNMENT OF EAST JERSEY. Philip Carteret, recommissioned Governor (13 June 1674), resumed his post in the colony, but his authority was challenged by Gov. Andros of New York, who insisted on collecting duties on goods entering Jersey ports (5 Apr. 1679). Carteret was seized (30 Apr. 1680), tried in New York for illegally exercising governmental powers, but acquitted by a jury (May). Undeterred, Andros attended a session of the East Jersey assembly (2 June), which he dissolved when it refused to do his bidding, and continued in the exercise of executive powers (July–Aug.). Although Dongan's commission did not give him jurisdiction over East Jersey, he banned Jersey vessels from the Hudson (Aug. 1686) and proposed to the home authorities that the province be annexed to New York (19 Feb. 1688). James II had writs of quo warranto issued against the Jersey proprietors and secured the surrender of both Jersey charters (Mar. 1688), incorporating the area in the Dominion of New England. In the fall of 1692 the proprietors resumed control. **Andrew Hamilton,** a Scot, served as Governor until his death (Apr. 1703), save for a period in 1698 when Jeremiah Basse, one of the proprietors, acted in that capacity.

1675–1701. GOVERNMENT OF WEST JERSEY. The first English settlement in the western portion of the province was established by Fenwick at Salem (1675). On charges of illegally assuming governmental functions Fenwick was arrested (8 Nov. 1676), brought to New York (Jan. 1677), fined £40, and released on parole. Despite warnings to desist (3 June 1678) he attempted to function as Governor until Andros appointed his own officials (26 Oct.). Fenwick continued to make land grants until he had deeded most of his holdings to William Penn (1 Mar. 1682). On 13 Mar. 1677 the 4 proprietors of West Jersey issued the **Laws, Concessions, and Agreements,** largely the work of William Penn, providing for liberty of conscience, civil rights including trial by jury, and no taxation save with the consent of the representatives of the voters (proprietors, freeholders, and inhabitants). Byllinge, designated Governor (1680), dispatched Samuel Jennings to serve as his deputy. The assembly, with its first session, 1681, continued to meet at **Burlington** until 1701. In 1683 that body challenged the proprietors' right to govern and chose Jennings as Governor and its own councilors. On Byllinge's death Daniel Coxe, who had purchased his rights, including the title of hereditary Governor, proceeded to function through deputies. Coxe sold his interest (1692) to a group of 48 (West Jersey Society, largely Anglicans).

1701–38. NEW JERSEY AS ROYAL PROVINCE. In 1701 the Board of Trade recommended that the crown resume control of private colonies. On 26 Apr. 1702 the proprietors of both Jerseys surrendered governmental authority to the crown. Until 1738 the Governor of New York was also Governor of New Jersey, but under a separate commission. Thereafter, beginning with **Lewis Morris** (1671–1746), New Jersey had its own Royal Governor. Despite the loss of governmental rights the proprietors retained their property interest. A Board of Proprietors of East Jersey (est. 1684, headquarters Perth Amboy) and a similar organization for West Jersey (est. 1688, headquarters Burlington) have continued in existence to the present day.

PENNSYLVANIA

1680, 1 June–1682, 24 Aug. GRANTS TO PENN. William Penn (1644–1718), son of Admiral Sir William Penn, who had joined the Society of Friends, studied in France, then at Lincoln's Inn, received a charter from Charles II on 14 Mar. 1681, possibly in lieu of his father's claim against the exchequer for £16,000. Under its terms he was made absolute proprietor of an area between 43°N. and 40°N., running west from the Delaware through five degrees in longitude. The ambiguity of the description left the lower Delaware undecided. The charter included specific limitations on his governmental powers: (1) laws had to receive the approval of an assembly;

(2) the Navigation Acts were to be obeyed; (3) the Privy Council had the right to disallow all legislation within five years after passage; (4) the crown reserved the right to hear appeals from the courts of the province; (5) an ambiguous clause recognized the right of the king to impose taxes "by act of Parliament," an issue which remained academic until 1765.

1682–1704. PENN TAKES OVER DELAWARE. On 24 Aug. 1682 a grant to Penn of the region on the western shore of Delaware Bay, from New Castle to Cape Henlopen, was made by the Duke of York, who in fact lacked legal title to the area. These grants contained no rights of government. Hence, Penn's control over Delaware was of dubious legality. By the Charter of 1701 Delaware was empowered to have a government separate from Pennsylvania. On 22 Nov. 1704 the first independent assembly met at New Castle. Down to the Revolution both provinces were under the same Governor, save that the king had to approve for Delaware.

1682–88. EARLY CONSTITUTIONAL DEVELOPMENTS IN PENNSYLVANIA. Penn's **Frame of Government** (5 May, 1682) provided for a Governor (proprietor or his deputy), council (in which proprietor had a treble vote; 72 members, later reduced to 18; one third elected each year), and assembly (200–500 members; reduced in 1683 to 32), elected by the freeholders. The council was to initiate laws, act in an administrative and judicial capacity, and try officials impeached by the assembly, which could merely ratify or reject legislation. The assembly's right to initiate legislation was recognized in 1696. The right to amend and alter (exercised by 1688) was the subject of controversy for many years. William Markham, dispatched (10 Apr. 1681) to inform the inhabitants (c.500 Dutch and Swedes) of the Penn proprietorship, was succeeded by four commissioners (Sept. 1681), and, in turn, by Thomas Holme, who (early 1682) laid out the site for Philadelphia. Penn arrived on the Delaware (27 Oct. 1682), received the territory from the Duke of York's agent (28 Oct.), and proclaimed in assembly (2 Nov.) that the Duke's Laws were to be in force until the people decided otherwise. At Upland Penn called a general court (8 Nov.) to consist of representatives from six counties (3 from present Pennsylvania; 3 from present Delaware). The assembly (17 Dec. 1682) passed a declaration of liberty of conscience and placed the three lower counties under one administration. A new **Frame of Government**, reducing the size of council and assembly, was approved by a second assembly (12 Apr. 1683). Penn returned to England (16 Aug. 1684) to defend his southern boundary against Lord Baltimore, governing by deputy in his absence.

1682–83. EARLY SETTLEMENT. As the result of extensively publicizing his colonial venture in the British Isles, Holland, and Germany, immigration was sizable from the start. The first large contingent, Welshmen, arrived 13 Aug. 1682, settling on lands purchased from the Indians north and west of Philadelphia. Quakers from the Rhineland and lower Palatinate settled Germantown (fall, 1683) and groups of Irish and English Quakers established scattered settlements. Land grants were carelessly made; title quarrels were common. It remained for Penn's second son, **Thomas**

(1702–75), on his arrival in the province, 1732, to organize the land system and straighten out the claims.

1688–94. GLORIOUS REVOLUTION IN PENNSYLVANIA. Because of the friendship between Penn and James II and the passive stand of the Pennsylvania Quakers toward participating in the war against France, the crown appointed Gov. Benjamin Fletcher of New York as Governor of Pennsylvania (18 Mar. 1692). **Royal Rule** lasted until 20 Aug. 1694, when the proprietary government was restored. Penn returned to the colony as a resident Governor (1699).

1701, 8 Nov. CHARTER OF LIBERTIES, granted by Penn, remained the constitution of Pennsylvania down to the Revolution. Under its terms the legislature became **unicameral**, laws being passed by the Governor with the consent of the assembly alone. Except in the appointment of a Governor, proprietary rule, from a political point of view, virtually ceased. Penn returned to England (1701), leaving **James Logan** (1674–1751) as his agent. All but ruined by the chicanery of Philip Ford, a steward, Penn landed in the Fleet for debt, and had to mortgage the province to trustees (1708).

SETTLEMENT OF FLORIDA, THE CAROLINAS, AND GEORGIA

EARLY SPANISH COLONIZING EFFORTS

1521. PONCE DE LEÓN'S ATTEMPT. After a previous exploration of the Florida coast (1513, pp. 20, 21), Ponce de León received a patent from the crown of Spain (27 Sept. 1514) to settle the "islands of Bimini and Florida." Sailing from Puerto Rico (20 Feb.) with 200 men, he landed, probably at Charlotte Bay, where he was attacked by the natives, wounded, and forced to withdraw to Cuba, dying in May or June.

1526–27. DE AYLLÓN'S ATTEMPT. Lucas Vásquez de Ayllón received a

patent similar to de León's (12 June 1523), sailed from Hispaniola (July 1526) with some 500 settlers for the Cape Fear region, whence he coasted south probably to the Pedee River to establish a settlement. He died shortly thereafter (18 Oct.) and the remnant of 150 who survived a difficult winter (1526–27) abandoned the site and returned to Hispaniola.

1528. NARVÁEZ EXPEDITION (p. 22).

1539. DE SOTO IN FLORIDA. Under a grant to settle the entire region north of the Gulf of Mexico, Hernando de Soto landed at Tampa Bay (May), and headed north (1 Aug.) for his long march into the interior (p. 22).

1549. PIONEER MISSIONARY EFFORT. Fray Luis Cancer de Babastro, a Dominican, who had seen service in Guatemala (1535–38, 1542–46), sailed from Vera Cruz (spring) to convert the Florida Indians, coasted northward from Tampa Bay, then returned to that region where he was killed by the natives (26 June).

1558–61. SETTLEMENT FAILURES. In quest of Spanish treasure in the holds of ships wrecked along the Florida coast as well as for the conversion of the natives, **Don Tristán de Luna y Arellano** sailed from Vera Cruz (11 June 1559) with a party of 1,500 colonists with the immediate objectives of settling at Santa Elena and on the Gulf. Entering Pensacola Bay (14 Aug.), they failed to establish a permanent foothold, but explored the interior (northwest Alabama). Command passed to **Ángel de Villafañe**, who made an unsuccessful voyage, possibly as far north as Cape Hatteras (27 May–9 July 1561) to establish a settlement. The entire project was abandoned that year. On 23 Sept. Philip II issued a cedula barring further colonizing efforts in Florida.

STRUGGLE BETWEEN FRANCE AND SPAIN FOR CONTROL

1562–65. EARLY FRENCH ATTEMPTS AT SETTLEMENT. Gaspard de Coligny, Admiral of France, who had previously sent an unsuccessful expedition to Brazil (1555), dispatched five ships (16 Feb. 1562) under **Jean Ribaut** of Dieppe to establish a Huguenot colony. Landing on the north Florida coast (30 Apr.), they settled in S.C. at Santa Elena, whose name they changed to **Port Royal.** Failing to receive supplies, the colonists abandoned settlement early in 1564. A second expedition of Huguenots under **René de Laudonnière** was established at Ft. Caroline (1564) near the mouth of the St. Johns River (commanding the homeward route of the Spanish treasure ships) and was reinforced by supplies and settlers brought by Ribaut (spring 1565).

1565–67. FOUNDING OF ST. AUGUSTINE AND OUSTING OF THE FRENCH. The new French threat impelled Spain to reverse its policy toward Florida and to dispatch **Pedro Menéndez de Avilés** (20 Mar. 1565) both to settle Florida and to expel the French. Sailing from Cadiz (28 July 1565) with a party of 1,500, he arrived at St. Augustine Harbor (28 Aug.), which he named, inspected the approaches to the St. Johns River (4 Sept.), returned to St. Augustine, where he disembarked the colonists (7–8 Sept.). To destroy the Spanish colony Ribaut left 240 men at Ft. Caroline and sailed (10 Sept.) with the major part of his force for St. Augustine, but a storm (13 Sept.) wrecked his fleet. Menéndez countered with a march to Ft. Caroline (17–19 Sept.), which he captured (20 Sept.), killing 132 French defenders in the first hour of the attack and massacring those taken prisoner save for a few who managed to escape to some French vessels anchored in the river. Renaming the fort San Mateo, Menéndez established a garrison, hunted down French survivors of the Ribaut expedition, set up forts on the Indian River (Nov., removed to Santa Lucia, Feb. or early Mar. 1566) and at Santa Elena (San Felipe, Apr. 1566) and blockhouses at San Pedro and at the headwaters of the Broad River, as well as posts on the west coast at San Antonio (Charlotte Bay, 1566) and Tocobago (Tampa Bay, 1567) and to the south at Tegesta near Miami (early 1567).

1567, 22 Aug.–1568, 2 June. FRENCH RETALIATION. Dominique de Gourgues sailed to the West Indies from France with three vessels (crew of 80 and 100 arquebusiers), finally landed on an island near San Mateo (c.Apr. 1568), enlisted Indian aid, marched on two blockhouses at the mouth of the St. Johns, which he captured (12 Apr.), then advanced upon San Mateo, which fell to him (16 Apr.), and massacred his prisoners, taking similar revenge on crews from captured Spanish vessels (6 June).

1566–72. JESUIT ACTIVITIES. Efforts of the Jesuits at converting the Florida Indians were launched (1566–

68). Under **Fray Batista Segura** another group of Jesuits sailed from Santa Elena (5 Aug. 1570) to Axacan (Chesapeake Bay region), where all were murdered (in present Virginia, 14–18 Feb. 1571). As a result, all Jesuits were removed from Florida by the summer of 1572.

1576–81. FURTHER INDIAN AND FRENCH CONFLICTS. Indian unrest following the death of Avilés (1574) forced abandonment of the garrisons on the west coast of Florida, including San Felipe. **Pedro Menéndez Marqués**, acting Governor, rebuilt the fort at Santa Elena (July 1577), burned a large Indian village (Cocopay, *c.*Apr. 1578), taking many captives whom he traded for 12 Frenchmen previously captured by the Indians. In addition, French corsairs, including Nicolas Estrozi, were captured and killed (by early 1580). In a naval battle with a French force under **Gilberto Gil** at San Mateo (17 July), Marqués was the victor and Gil was killed. Another Indian uprising (4 Oct.) was quelled (by Jan. 1581).

1586, June–July. SIR FRANCIS DRAKE attacked and destroyed the fort and other buildings at Saint Augustine and looted the settlement at Santa Elena.

DEVELOPMENT OF SPANISH FLORIDA

1577–1655. SPANISH MISSIONARY EFFORTS. Franciscan missionary activity under **Fray Alonso de Reynoso**, with the support of the crown, was attempted (1577–92) without conspicuous success. A more intensive effort was begun under **Fray Juan de Silva** (23 Sept. 1595) with the establishment of mission provinces: Timucua (north-central Florida), Apalache (northwest Florida), Gualé (Georgia coast), Orista (South Carolina coast), and Tama (interior Georgia). Despite Indian hostility in the Gualé district 1,500 natives were converted (1595–96) and chapels were erected at San Pedro (Cumberland Island), Santiago de Ocone (Jekyll Island), Asao (St. Simon's Island), Tolomato (on the mainland above the mouth of the Altamaha River), and Tupique (north of Tolomato). As a re-

sult of attacks by the Gualé Indians (1597–1600), all missions north of Saint Augustine were abandoned except Santa Elena. A punitive expedition out of Saint Augustine (10 Oct.) destroyed Indian villages and supplies and forced the Indians to sue for peace (spring 1600). Thereafter (1603–06) Franciscan missions were established at San Juan and Santa Maria (below the St. Marys River), at San Pedro, Macoma, Talaxe (south bank of the Altamaha), and at Santa Catalina de Gualé (on St. Catherine Island). In the period, 1606–80, a chain of missions were pushed northward along the coast to Chatuache (Satuache, between the Combahee and Edisto Rivers, by 1650), with subsequent activity among the Tamali (in the area between the junction of the Ocmulgee and Oconee Rivers and the Gualé, 1680). A second line of advance went west from Saint Augustine across the northern neck of the Florida peninsula. Itinerant missionaries were active in Potano (1606–07), east of the Ocilla River, and at Apalachee (Oct. 1633), where (by 1655) 9 missions were established. Activity spread westward to the Chatot country around the Apalachicola River, where two missions (San Carlos de los Chacatos and San Nicolas de Tolentino) were established by 1674. Despite an Indian uprising (1647) 38 missions were established and some 26,000 Indians at least partly converted by 1655.

ENGLISH IN THE CAROLINAS

1629–39. EARLY PATENTS. In 1629 **Sir Robert Heath** was granted a patent to settle the area between 31° and 36°N. ("New Carolana"). On the basis of a conveyance from Heath (1630), **Samuel Vassal** and others made ineffectual efforts to explore and settle the area. In 1632 **Henry Lord Maltravers** is reputed to have been granted the "province of Carolana" by Heath, and by the Harvey Patent (1638), issued by Governor Sir John Harvey of Virginia, laid claim to land south of the James River to be called Norfolk County. But in neither area did he effect a settlement.

1653–54. ALBEMARLE COLONY. Settlers from Virginia began to move across the Nansemond Valley and the Dismal Swamp into present North Carolina, settling (by 1653) north of Albemarle Sound between the Chowan River and the sea. This movement was encouraged by the Virginia assembly for the protection of its southern frontier with offers of land grants to the first settlers between the Chowan and Roanoke Rivers (July) and by the expenditures of two Virginians, Francis and Argall Yeardley.

1655. FALL OF JAMAICA to England encouraged the belief that the Spaniards could be ousted from North America and promoted English expansion along the Southern frontier.

c.1660–63. CAPE FEAR COLONY. A group of New Englanders in association with London merchants organized the Cape Fear Co. and sent settlers from New England to the region around the Cape Fear River (*c.*1662), but the settlement was abandoned before the fall of 1663.

1663, 3 Apr.–1665, 10 July. CHARTERS OF THE CAROLINAS. As a result of a project formulated by Sir John Colleton, a Barbadian planter, Sir William Berkeley, former governor of Virginia, and **Sir Anthony Ashley Cooper** (later, 1672, **Earl of Shaftesbury**), an outstanding colonial promoter, Charles II granted to 8 proprietors—the 3 aforementioned prime movers as well as such high-ranking personages as the **Earl of Clarendon** (the King's chief minister), the **Duke of Albemarle** (General Monck), **John Lord Berkeley** (brother of Sir William and a high-ranking naval officer), the **Earl of Craven**, and **Sir George Carteret**—the area lying between 31° and 36°N. and extending westward to the "south seas." Maltravers' heir, the Duke of Norfolk, and Samuel Vassal both countered by filing claims to this territory (10 June) and the Cape Fear Co. likewise challenged the validity of the charter (6 Aug.). However, the Privy Council declared all previous patents void (22 Aug. 1665), but claims continued to be urged until 1768, when the descendants of Daniel Coxe of New Jersey, to whom the Heath patent had been transferred in 1696, received from the crown a grant of 100,000 acres in New York in satisfaction of their claim. By a 2nd charter (10 July 1665) the bounds were extended to include the northern end of Currituck Inlet (31°30′N.) and pushed south to 29° N. to include the entire settled part of Florida.

1663, 23 May–1665. PRELUDE TO SETTLEMENT. From their first meeting the proprietors sought to promote settlement from New England and Barbados (considered overpopulated) and were encouraged by the favorable report (6 Feb. 1664) from Capt. William Hilton, who had recently explored the area. Sir William Berkeley, authorized to name a Governor for the Chowan River settlement, designated (Oct. 1664) William Drummond as Governor of the province of **Albemarle** (later **North Carolina**). For the government of the entire chartered area the proprietors drew up the **Concessions and Agreements** (1665)—the same as those adopted by Berkeley and Carteret for New Jersey 6 weeks later— granting freedom of conscience, generous terms of land distribution subject to a quitrent (½d. per acre), and an assembly of freeholders' representatives.

1669–70. FUNDAMENTAL CONSTITUTIONS. To supplant the inadequate Concessions and Agreements the proprietors issued (11 Mar. 1669) the Fundamental Constitutions, generally attributed to **John Locke** in collaboration with Sir Anthony Ashley Cooper. This elaborate scheme of government blended advanced concepts with an artifically contrived aristocratic society. Religious freedom was guaranteed, but, under the revision of 1 Mar. 1670, the Church of England was established. A popular, as opposed to a standing, army was authorized. At the apex of Carolina society was a hereditary nobility: the **proprietors** (each with a seignory of 12,000 acres in each county); next came the **landgraves** (with 4 baronies apiece, 48,000 acres in all), followed by the **caciques** (Spanish for Indian chief, 2 baronies, 24,000 acres). Below them stood **lords of manors** (3,000 to 12,000 acres) and **freeholders** (with 50-acre minimum requirement for voting). Land and rank were synonymous; the loss of one meant the loss of the other. The 8 proprietors in England constituted a **Palatine Court** which appointed the Governor, disallowed laws, and heard appeals from the colony. The provincial assembly was to comprise the Governor, hereditary nobility, and the deputies (holders of 500-acre freeholds), but ultimately that body became bicameral (by 1693). The Governor's council came to be called the Grand Council. In all, 26 landgraves and 13 caciques were created. In a few cases the title descended to the 2nd and 3rd generations; in most they expired with the original holder. In fact, no seignory or barony above 12,000 acres was ever set up and no manors erected. The proprietors revised the Fundamental Constitutions (12 Jan. 1682); declared inoperative (1693); again revised in abridged form (1698); but they were never accepted by the assembly.

1669–80. FOUNDING OF CHARLESTON. A party of settlers under Joseph West left England (Aug. 1669), and finally settled at Port Royal Sound (by the end of Mar. 1670). Fear of the Spaniards caused them to move north to the Ashley, where at Albemarle Point their first settlement (Charles Town) was established (Apr. 1670, later called Old Charles Town). Subsequently (1680) this settlement was relocated at the junction of the Ashley and Cooper Rivers, present site of Charleston.

1670, 18 July. TREATY OF MADRID between England and Spain, temporarily recognizing the principle of effective occupation in the New World, served as a basis for future boundary discussions involving the Carolina-Florida border area.

1671–74. EARLY GROWTH AND FACTIONALISM. As a result of arrivals from Barbados (including Sir John Yeamans), England, and New York the population of Charles Town colony was close to 400 (by 1672). The first Governor, William Sayle, was succeeded on his death (4 Mar. 1671) by Joseph West, who summoned the 1st assembly (25 Aug.). On 14 Dec. Sir John Yeamans claimed the right as sole landgrave resident in the province to be Governor in place of West, a cacique whom he outranked. Yeamans, commissioned, reached the province Apr. 1672. He was supplanted by West (1674).

1671–83. INDIAN TRADE AND CONFLICT. A war against the **Kussos**, a tribe in the vicinity of Charles Town, who were believed to be conspiring with the Spaniards, resulted in their complete defeat (1671). Numerous captives were enslaved, marking the beginning of the experiment with Indian slavery. In May 1674 Dr. Henry Woodward was commissioned Indian agent to open trade with the Westos east of the lower Savannah in furs, deer hides, and slaves. Trade was also opened with the Kiowa to the north. A **Westo** uprising (Apr. 1680) was smashed by the end of that year and the natives along the Savannah persuaded to cooperate in trade with the western tribes.

1677–80. CULPEPER'S REBELLION. In protest against the arbitrary acts of Governor John Jenkins at Albemarle, Thomas Miller, a leader of the "proprietary faction," undertook to combine the functions of Governor and customs collector. The antiproprietary party set up a revolutionary government (3 Dec. 1677), and imprisoned Miller, who escaped to England and laid his case before the Privy Council. The rebels were defended before the proprietors by one of their leaders, **John Culpeper.** Through the conciliatory influence of Shaftesbury the proprietors decided that Miller had exceeded his authority and Culpeper, who was tried for treason before the king's bench, was acquitted.

1679, 10 Oct. An act passed in Virginia prohibiting the importation of Carolina tobacco made Carolinians increasingly dependent upon Massachusetts and Rhode Island sea captains and traders who carried their tobacco to New England and reshipped it to Europe in evasion of the Navigation Acts.

1682–86. PORT ROYAL COLONY. Under a patent from the Carolina proprietors (1682) a settlement of Scotsmen under Henry Erskine, Lord Cardross, was established (fall of 1684) at Port Royal on a site named Stuart's Town, despite the hostility of the Spaniards, who viewed this incursion as violating the Treaty of Madrid, and the antagonism of Charleston settlers, unwilling to divide their lucrative Indian trade with the Scotch Covenanters. As a result of the Westo War (1680) the Spanish authorities withdrew from their most northerly missions and sought to pull back their Indian allies. Rather than move south the Yamassees sought refuge among the English and Scots (the first Yamassee refugees arrived at Stuart's Town, Feb. 1685) and settled on former Westo lands. The Charleston authorities, who had ordered the arrest of Lord Cardross (5 May 1685) because of his refusal to submit to their control, now failed to heed appeals from Stuart's Town for aid against impending Spanish attack. The Spaniards, threatened in Gualé, which they finally abandoned (1684-85), and outflanked by Carolina traders (who had reached the Lower Creeks on the middle Chatahoochee River by 1685), had previously erected a new mission at the junction of the Flint and Chatahoochee (1681) and engaged in raiding coastal settlements in southern Carolina. Stuart's Town was completely destroyed (Sept. 1686). Only a storm saved Charleston.

1683-96. POLITICAL UNREST IN THE CAROLINAS. The colonists of Berkeley County (Charleston area) rejected the revised Fundamental Constitutions of 1682. On orders from the proprietors Gov. Joseph Morton dissolved the assembly (20 Sept. 1685) and Governor James Colleton (arrived Feb. 1687) refused to call an assembly (on orders, 1689). Under constant threat of Spanish invasion the colonists in this area made common cause with the corsairs who preyed on Spanish shipping, and juries acquitted those charged with violating the Navigation Acts. In the north Albemarle ousted (1689) its Governor, Seth Southel (arrived c.1683), who went to Charleston and proceeded

to oust Colleton, take over the government (Oct. 1690), and call an assembly. In Nov. 1691 he was suspended by the Palatine Court and charged with high treason. His death (1694) ended the controversy. The next three Governors (Philip Ludwell, 1691-93; Thomas Smith, 1693-94; and John Archdale, 1694-96) attempted to restore harmony.

1706-29. SOUTH CAROLINA AS A ROYAL COLONY. After 1706 proprietary control steadily weakened, accentuated by the crises of the French and Spanish attack (1706) and the Yamassee War (p. 63). In Nov. 1719 the colonists set up a revolutionary government, ousted the last proprietary Governor, Robert Johnson, and replaced him with James Moore as temporary Governor. The crown then appointed **Francis Nicholson** (1655-1728), who had been Governor or deputy Governor of 3 other colonies (proclaimed 29 May 1721), thus formally incorporating South Carolina as a **Royal Colony.** The proprietary charter was surrendered (1729), and 7 out of the 8 proprietors sold their claims for £2,500 apiece. The eighth, Lord Carteret, exchanged his portion (1743) for a tract south of Virginia's southern boundary, which he retained until the Revolution.

1691-1729. NORTH CAROLINA AS A ROYAL COLONY. Albemarle, known after 1691 as North Carolina and governed by a deputy, was torn by sectionalism and unrest. The passage of the Vestry Act (1701), making the Church of England the established church, aroused intense opposition on the part of the Quakers and other dissenters. Though disallowed, a second Vestry Act (1704) was passed. In attempting to enforce the act, **Thomas Cary,** deputy Governor, aroused the antagonism of the Quakers (now barred from office by a related act imposing an oath), who obtained from the proprietors an order for his removal. Cary refused to be supplanted by William Glover, chosen acting Governor, rebelled, and was convicted of high crimes and misdemeanors. Escaping to Virginia, Cary was seized, dispatched to England, but allowed to return home. The crisis in the northern colony was further intensified by the **Tuscarora War** (1711–12), in which, after the massacre of 200 settlers, the Indians were defeated with the aid of Virginia and South Carolina. Remnants of the Tuscaroras removed to New York and joined the Iroquois as a sixth nation. In 1712 a separate Governor was set up for North Carolina, with **Edward Hyde**

Lake Huron

Lake Ontario

Lake Erie

Fort Western (Augusta)

Falmouth (Portland)

Fort Stanwix

Rumford (Concord)

Portsmouth

Fort Oswego

Albany

Boston

Plymouth

Kingston

New York

Fort Bedford (Raystown)

Harris Ferry (Harrisburg)

Philadelphia

Fort Cumberland

Baltimore

A T L A N T I C

Charlottesville

Richmond

Colonies in 1660

Colonies, 1660 – 1700

Colonies, 1700 – 1760

Wachovia (Salem)

O C E A N

Wilmington

Fort Augusta

Charleston

Savannah

St Augustine

ENGLISH COLONIES

the first incumbent. North Carolina became a **Royal Colony**, 25 July 1729, with the formal surrender of the charter.

SETTLEMENT OF GEORGIA

20 June 1732. ROYAL CHARTER granted to trustees for 21 yrs. territory south of the Savannah River originally part of South Carolina, but retained by the crown when the Carolinas were surrendered by the proprietors in 1729, plus a one-eighth interest retained by Carteret at time of surrender, which he conveyed to the trustees. The charter was surrendered in 1752, when Georgia became a royal province. (See also p. 64.)

THE COLONIES

AND THE EMPIRE, 1624-1775

CENTRALIZED ADMINISTRATION

1624, 24 MAY. REVOCATION OF VIRGINIA CO. CHARTER, making Virginia a royal colony (p. 27).

1634, 28 Apr.–1641, Aug. LAUD COMMISSION. Under James I the Privy Council rather than Parliament had exercised control over trade and colonies. A Commission of Trade set up by Charles I (1625), subordinate to the Privy Council, considered the Gorges patent, and a special committee on New England Plantations (1632) served temporarily. On 28 Apr. 1634 there was set up as a subdivision of the Privy Council the **Commission for Foreign Plantations** ("Laud Commission" after its chairman, the primate, William Laud). Despite its broad powers, its 7 years of activity were marked by few achievements. Most supervisory activities were carried on by special Privy Council committees or occasional outside groups.

1643–59. PARLIAMENTARY COMMISSION FOR PLANTATIONS, comprising 18 members, assumed the functions of the Privy Council in colonial affairs. Save for the appointment of one Governor, Sir Thomas Warner, for the Caribbean islands (1643) and the granting of the charter of Providence Plantations (1644), it was virtually inactive, and its functions assumed by the **Council of State** (14 Feb. 1649), which set up a standing committee to handle trade (17 Dec. 1651) and plantations (4 May 1652). The **Protector's Council** (16 Dec. 1653) directed plantation affairs, assisted by the Committee for Foreign Plantations (10 May 1655) and the Committee for America (15 July 1656). It was replaced by the **Council of State** (May 1659).

1660, 4 July–1695, 15 May. THE LORDS OF TRADE. The king in council appointed a Committee for Trade and Plantations of the Privy Council (Lords of Trade) to report to the Council as a whole. A Council of Trade (7 Nov.) and a Council for Foreign Plantations (1 Dec.) were also subordinate to the Privy Council. When they ceased to function (1665), the Privy Council reappointed its own plantation committee (7 Dec. 1666), and on 31 Jan. 1668 a new standing committee was created similar to the Lords of Trade of 1660. It was assisted (1668) by a special Council of Trade and Plantations combining the functions of the two councils of 1660. These functions were again separated upon the revival (20 July 1670) of the **Council for Foreign Plantations,** but after considerable activity its commission was withdrawn (1674) and its functions assigned to the Lords of Trade (1675).

1696–1782. THE BOARD OF TRADE, commissioned by William III, comprised 15 members (7 high officials including Privy Councilors, 8 paid members, including a first Lord of Trade, president of the Board), was empowered to supervise (1) trade and the fisheries, (2) care of the poor, (3) plantation affairs, (4) recommend appointments of colonial officials, and (5) review colonial legislation and report to the Privy Council. Its first 20 years were marked by exceptional activity, although its powers were curbed as early as 1704 when the Secretary of State for the Southern Dept. assumed the right to appoint Governors (1704). With the accession of George I and the ascendancy of Newcastle the Board declined, reaching its nadir during the presidency of Baron Monson (1737–48). It was revived under **George Mon-**

57

tagu Dunk, Earl of Halifax (11 Nov. 1748). Under an order in council (11 Mar. 1752) nominations to colonial offices were to be made by the Board and transmitted (in the case of high officials) to the Privy Council or (in the case of lesser ones) to the Secretary of State. Nevertheless, the Seven Years' War marked a renewed decline of the Board's activity. With Halifax's resignation (Mar. 1761) the Board soon lost its right of nomination (22 May). The Board's powers were subsequently curtailed by an order in council (8 Aug. 1766), and correspondence was henceforth channeled through the Secretary of State. With the appointment of Hillsborough as both Secretary of State and president of the Board of Trade (20 Jan. 1768), both offices were held by the same person until 1782.

1673–76. THE TREASURY BOARD'S colonial functions were greatly expanded as a result of the Navigation Laws (particularly the Act of 1673). Immediately subordinate to that body were the **commissioners of customs** with jurisdiction over the collectors, searchers, and surveyors of customs in the colonies. Naval officers to enter and clear vessels were appointed (as early as 1676 for Jamaica) to enforce the Acts of Trade, eventually 6 for each colony.

1697. ESTABLISHMENT OF VICE-ADMIRALTY COURTS. Under the Navigation Act of 1696 the Privy Council directed the Board of Trade to establish vice-admiralty courts in the colonies. Acting under commission the Governors of New York, Massachusetts, Maryland, Pennsylvania, and Virginia designated judges and other officers of such courts. The vice-admiralty courts had jurisdiction over the Acts of Trade and ordinary maritime cases as well as prize (by act of 1708). In addition, the act of 1722 conferred jurisdiction over infringements on conserving timber—"broad-arrow policy" (p. 512). At first appeals lay to the High Court of Admiralty; after 1748 it shared appellate jurisdiction with the Privy Council, which assumed sole appellate jurisdiction (11 July 1766). But the new admiralty courts set up under the Townshend Acts (1767, p. 76) centered final control in America.

ROYAL DISALLOWANCE. The Board of Trade reviewed colonial legislation and made recommendations for disallowance where laws conflicted with imperial policy, were prejudicial to trade, or were in conflict with the law of England. Out of 8,563 acts submitted by the continental colonies (not including Pennsylvania prior to 1700 nor Maryland, 1691–1715), 469 were disallowed, with the highest percentage from Pennsylvania, 15.5 (E. B. Russell). Its application was more general in the first two decades (beg.1691) than at any later time. The existence of such machinery of review undoubtedly affected the course of later legislation and prompted colonial evasion by passage of temporary acts.

1696–1783. JUDICIAL APPEALS TO THE PRIVY COUNCIL were taken from all the colonies in some 1,500 cases. Civil cases were chiefly taken from Rhode Island, Virginia, and Massachusetts (among the continental colonies); criminal appeals were largely restricted to the early years (chiefly from Barbados); and Chancery appeals to the British West Indies.

THE ROYAL GOVERNOR, chief representative of the crown in the royal colonies and executive head of the provincial government, was guided by **instructions** generally formulated by the Board of Trade and transmitted by the Secretary of State for the Southern Dept. His authority came in the course of time to be undermined both by the home government and by the colonial assemblies. By the middle of the 18th century the Secretary of State came to appoint an increasing number of provincial officials, including the naval officer responsible for enforcement of the Navigation Acts. In the conflict with the assemblies the Governors gradually lost control over expenditures. The New York assembly forced the Governor, Lord Cornbury (1701–08), to accept its own treasurer (1706). Under George Clarke, acting Governor (1736–43), the assembly, by securing the right to pay salaries by name and amount, gained increasing control over all appointments. Both Governors Jonathan Belcher of Massachusetts (1730–41) and Lewis Morris of New Jersey (1738–46) failed to secure from the legislature other than temporary appropriations. In 1752 the Board of Trade instructed the governors to demand a fixed civil list (obtained nowhere except Jamaica) and in 1761 to appoint judges **during the pleasure of the crown** (a policy which aroused colonial antagonism reflected in the Declaration of Independence).

ANGLO-FRENCH COLONIAL RIVALRY TO 1763

1497–1604. RIVALRY OVER FISHERIES. John Cabot (p. 19) and his English crew, first Europeans definitely known to have visited the Newfoundland coast, reported its waters as "swarming with fish." The French, who fished these waters as early as 1504, were in a dominant position by 1540, although after 1560 Portuguese and Spanish fishermen entered the area. Until 1578 England was dependent upon the Iceland fisheries. To free themselves of dependence on France and Portugal for their solar salt used in "green fishing" (i.e., salting fish aboard ship without drying), English fishermen introduced "dry fishing" (i.e., drying fish on land with a minimum amount of salt) in the Newfoundland area. Such fish found a ready market in Mediterranean ports (c.1580–1604). To compete, the French now sought land bases on which to dry their catch. Since the English had already preempted some of the best bases in Newfoundland, they chose Cape Breton and the Gaspé Peninsula.

1534–99. START OF FUR TRADE. Trade in furs developed virtually with the first contacts between the French and the Indians (as far back as Cartier's voyage of discovery, 1534). As the French fishermen increased their land bases, the fur trade was expanded, notably at Tadoussac on the St. Lawrence (by the 1580s). European weapons hastened the extinction of the beaver, in immense demand for hatmaking, and drew the fur trade into the interior.

1598–1613. BACKGROUND OF FRENCH SETTLEMENT. Despite two unsuccessful attempts at settlement (under Baron de Léry, 1518, and Roberval, 1542–43, p. 22), the French crown granted (12 Jan. 1598) Troïlus du Mesgouez, Marquis de la Roche, a monopoly of the fur trade and settlement rights in Canada, Newfoundland, and adjacent lands. La Roche transported two shiploads of jailbirds (mostly beggars and vagabonds) to **Sable Island** off the coast of Nova Scotia and dominating Newfoundland, Acadia, and the Gulf of St. Lawrence, but, after an uprising, the settlement was abandoned. Another monopoly finally was assigned (1603) to **Pierre du Guast, Sieur de Monts,** who established a settlement at the mouth of the St. Croix River (June, 1604). This colony was moved across the Bay of Fundy to **Port Royal** (Annapolis Royal, Nova Scotia, Aug. 1607), but was abandoned when Monts' patent was canceled (1607), then reestablished (1610) with two subsequent stations set up on the west bank of the Bay of Fundy (by 1613).

1608–27. SETTLEMENT OF ST. LAWRENCE VALLEY. His monopoly restored for 1 year (7 Jan. 1608), Monts dispatched **François du Pontgravé** (5 Apr.) and **Samuel de Champlain** (c.1567–1635) (13 Apr.) to Canada. Champlain founded **Quebec** (3 July) and remained in charge of the new colony as lieutenant for a chain of successors of Monts as viceroys. However, stress on the fur trade discouraged permanent settlement and left the colony vulnerable to attack. With the outbreak of war between England and France (Mar. 1627), control was vested (25 Apr.) in **The Company of New France (The Hundred Associates),** a joint-stock company, which, in return for undertaking settlement, was given the fur monopoly.

1609–27. FRENCH-INDIAN RELATIONS. The entry of the French into the St. Lawrence challenged control of the area by the Five Nations of the **Iroquois.** The Montaignais (Saguenay Valley), the Algonquins of the Ottawa, and the Hurons (between the Ottawa and Georgia Bay) assured the French a steady flow of furs from the interior and sought to oust the Iroquois from the area. Before Champlain's arrival the Iroquois had been ousted from the St. Lawrence Valley, and Champlain undertook two expeditions (1609, with the Algonquins to Lake Champlain; 1615, with the Hurons into the Onondaga country), designed to push the Five Nations southward and protect the link with the friendly Indians. The arrivals of the Recollect friars (1615) and the Jesuits (1625) served as another link between France and her Indian allies. Missions were established as far west as Georgian Bay (by 1616), while further campaigns against the Five Nations (1618, 1627) guarded the trade route from the west (Georgian Bay–Lake Nipissing–Ottawa River–St. Lawrence–Quebec).

1613–29. EARLY ENGLISH ATTACKS. After the French settlements on either side of the Bay of Fundy had been totally destroyed in a raid conducted by Capt. Samuel Argall (1613), the English crown granted the region (1621) to **Sir William Alexander**, who, in the course of the war between France and England (1627–29), was given a monopoly of the St. Lawrence fur trade. On 20 July 1629 Sir David Kirke, who had joined forces with Alexander, captured Quebec, unaware that peace had already been established (24 Apr.) by the Treaty of Susa. By the Treaty of St. Germain-en-Laye (29 Mar. 1632) England restored Acadia and the St. Lawrence to France.

NEW FRANCE
TO KING WILLIAM'S WAR

1632–70. ACADIAN DEVELOPMENTS. Settlement of Acadia by the French began in earnest after the appointment of Isaac de Razilly as Governor (10 May 1632), but was halted by factionalism and civil war. A small force collected in Boston under Major Robert Sedgwick, originally intended to attack New Netherland but diverted to Acadia to eliminate French competition with New England in fish and furs, easily re-

duced the area (*c.*1 July 1654). The English held the province for 16 years until its return to France (1670) under provisions of the Treaty of Breda (July 1667).

1632–35. NEW FRANCE UNDER CHAMPLAIN. Champlain's return to Canada (22 May 1633), this time both as royal Governor and company Governor, inaugurated a period of expansion, with settlements founded at Beauport (near Quebec, 1634), Three Rivers (1634), and **Montreal** (14 Oct. 1641). Recollect and Jesuit missions were reestablished among the Hurons (1634) and as far west as the Algonquin tribes at Sault Ste. Marie (by 1641). Exploration of the interior was pressed, notably by **Jean Nicolet**, who journeyed as far west as Green Bay and the Fox River Valley, possibly even reaching the Mississippi (1634–35).

1642–53. IROQUOIS WAR. The Five Nations, armed by the Dutch, who sought to divert the northern and interior fur trade of the Huron and Algonquin to their own posts, with the Iroquois as intermediaries, attacked the Hurons on the Richelieu (3 Aug. 1642) and even raided Montreal (30 Mar. 1644). A short truce (14 July 1645–18 Oct. 1646) was broken by the Iroquois, Ft. Richelieu (erected by the French at the mouth of the Richelieu River, 1642) was burned (1647), with raids deep into the Huron country which forced the Jesuits to abandon their last Huron mission (1650) and the Hurons to retreat as far west as Wisconsin, where they were joined by other fugitive tribes from the Ottawa Valley, the Ohio, and southern Michigan. Raids along the St. Lawrence penetrated to the Saguenay-Rupert River country (1652). Victorious, though dangerously overextended, the Iroquois signed a peace with the French (5 Nov. 1653).

1654–72. RENEWED FRENCH EXPANSION. Revival of the fur trade by the Algonquins began in 1654. **Médard Chouart, Sieur des Grosseilliers,** and his brother-in-law, **Pierre-Esprit Radisson** set forth (Aug. 1659) for a journey into the interior to the western and southern shores of Lake Superior and into northwestern Wisc. On Mazarin's death (1661) Louis XIV assumed personal rule. His finance minister **Colbert** pressed French colonization. A base and settlement were established at Placentia, Newfoundland (1662–63), and a resident Governor appointed (1668). The government of Canada was placed under a Governor, appointed council, and an intendant (the king's personal representative). During his terms in office (1663–68, 1670–72) **Jean Baptiste Talon** (1625–91), the "great intendant," dominated the government of New France. To guard the old Iroquois route to the St. Lawrence, forts were erected on the Richelieu River and at the head of Lake Champlain (1665–66). Renewed war against the Five Nations, now in alliance with England, was prosecuted, and the tribes were forced to sue for peace (1666). Despite the gradual return to their original homes of tribes dispossessed by the Five Nations, the French now continued direct trade with the Indians of Lake Superior and Michigan. To establish more permanent relations with the interior tribes, Talon sent Nicolas Perrot to the Wisconsin region (1668–69) and François Daumont, Sieur de St. Lusson, to Sault Ste. Marie. Missions were founded on the upper Michigan peninsula (*c.*1668) and on Green Bay and the Fox River (1670–72). **René Robert Cavelier, Sieur de la Salle** (1643–87), temporarily established amicable relations with the Iroquois and penetrated south of Lake Erie to present Ohio (1669–70).

1673–83. EXPANSION IN THE MISSISSIPPI VALLEY. When the English established trading posts on Hudson Bay (1670–83), tapping the continent's richest fur area, the French accepted the challenge, notably during the governorships of **Louis de Buade, Comte de Frontenac** (1620–98, gov. 1672–82) and Jacques René de Brisay, Marquis de Denonville (gov. 1682–88). Frontenac favored the Recollects (allied in France with the King in the struggle for temporal power) to check the Jesuits, supported by the Papacy. In the beaver trade and the founding of missions the former outdistanced the latter in this period. **Père Jacques Marquette** (1637–75), a Jesuit missionary, and **Louis Joliet**

(1648–1700), trader and explorer, set out from Mackinac Straits (17 May 1673), voyaged down Lake Michigan through Green Bay, up the Fox River, and, after a long portage, down the Wisconsin to the Mississippi (17 June), which river they paddled down as far as the Arkansas (17 July). Convinced that the Mississippi flowed into the Gulf of Mexico rather than the Pacific, they returned to Mackinac Straits by way of the Illinois River and Lake Michigan. La Salle, who wished to erect a government in the Mississippi Valley free of Jesuit control, sailed across the Great Lakes with **Father Louis Hennepin** (1640–1701?), who was the first to describe Niagara Falls, which they passed (Dec. 1678), for Green Bay, Wis., continuing by way of Mackinaw to the Illinois River, where he built Ft. Crèvecoeur (15 Jan. 1680). Hennepin, detached to accompany an expedition to explore the upper Mississippi, discovered St. Anthony's Falls (present Minneapolis, 1680). On a later expedition La Salle descended the Illinois to its mouth, embarked upon the Mississippi, paddling to its mouth (9 Apr. 1682), and took possession of the entire region, which he named **Louisiana.**

1668–88. EARLY STRUGGLE FOR HUDSON BAY. Radisson and Grosseilliers secured the backing of an English syndicate headed by **Prince Rupert,** cousin of the king, for a voyage to Hudson Bay (June 1668–Oct. 1669). The syndicate, now enlarged, was chartered by the crown (2 May 1670) as the **Governor and Company of Adventurers of England into Hudson's Bay.** To divert the fur trade from the St. Lawrence posts were erected at the mouths of the Rupert, Moose, and Albany Rivers on James Bay and at the mouth of the Hayes River on the west side of Hudson Bay. After returning to French allegiance and capturing the Governor of the Hudson's Bay Co. (1682), Radisson switched back to the Company (1684). A French force under **Pierre le Moyne, Sieur d'Iberville** (1661–1706), captured the three James Bay posts (1686), leaving the English with lone posts at the mouth of the Hayes and the Severn. The French followed up their success with the setting up of two posts to the north, on Lake Abitibi (1686) and Lake Nipigon (1684).

1684–87. LA SALLE'S ATTEMPT TO SETTLE ON THE GULF. With a view to reaching the Spanish mines and establishing a base of operations against the Spaniards on the Gulf of Mexico (Spain and France were at war, Oct. 1683–Aug. 1684), La Salle sailed from France (July 1684) with a small fleet to the Gulf, failed to find the mouth of the Mississippi, landed at Matagorda Bay, Texas (Jan. 1685), continued on foot in an attempt to reach Canada, and

was murdered by his rebellious men on the banks of the Brazos (1687).

1684–89. RENEWED IROQUOIS HOSTILITIES. Encouraged by Gov. Thomas Dongan of New York, the Iroquois raided as far west as the Mississippi and across Lakes Erie and Ontario into the Huron country (1684), breaking the chain of trade that stretched along the lakes (by 1686). Nicolas Perrot conducted an ineffectual campaign against them (1687). In retaliation the Iroquois raided the St. Lawrence Valley (1688–89), slaughtering 200 at Lachine (Aug. 1689) and taking 90 prisoners.

THE FIRST TWO INTERCOLONIAL WARS

FRENCH ADVANTAGES. (1) Centralized control, contrasted with colonial decentralization and lack of unity; (2) strategically placed forts; (3) an army considered the most formidable on the European continent; (4) Indian alliances, extending from the Abenakis in Maine to the Algonquin in Wisconsin and north toward Hudson Bay; (5) *coureurs du bois* familiar with forests and trails in the area of conflict.

ENGLISH ADVANTAGES. (1) Overwhelming numerical superiority (over 100,000 in New England alone contrasted with 12,000 in New France, 1688); (2) the Iroquois alliance; (3) marked naval superiority in combination with the Dutch; (4) trading and financial superiority.

1689, 12 May–1697, 20 Sept. KING WILLIAM'S WAR (WAR OF THE LEAGUE OF AUGSBURG). The European phase of the war broke out first when William III joined the League of Augsburg and the Netherlands (Grand Alliance, 12 May 1689) to resist Louis XIV's invasion of the Rhenish Palatinate (25 Sept. 1688). In America hostilities broke out between the English and French on Hudson Bay and between the Iroquois and the French in the area from the Mohawk to the St. Lawrence. The French under Frontenac (returned as governor, Oct. 1689) struck with their

Indian allies along the northern frontier, with raids on Schenectady (9 Feb. 1690), Salmon Falls, N.H. (27 Mar.), and Falmouth (Portland, Me., 31 July), followed by Abenaki raids on Wells, Me. (21 June 1692), Durham, N.Y. (23 June 1694), and Haverhill, Mass. (15 Mar. 1697). On the western frontier Frontenac attacked the Iroquois (1693–96). On the part of the English the only successful colonial operation was the seizure of **Port Royal** (11 May 1690) by an expedition of Massachusetts troops under **Sir William Phips** (1651–95), recaptured a year later by the French. The three-pronged attack on the St. Lawrence projected at the Albany Conference (p. 46) failed (3 Aug.–23 Oct. 1690). Iberville ousted the English from their Hudson Bay posts at the mouths of the Severn (1690) and the Hayes (1694), but the English recaptured the James Bay area (1693). The inconclusive **Treaty of Ryswick** (30 Sept. 1697) restored the *status quo ante* in the colonies and turned the Hudson Bay dispute over to commissioners, who reached no agreement (1699).

1698–1702. FRENCH SETTLEMENT OF LOUISIANA. Fearing an influx of English traders into the West following a French order (1696) closing the western posts (owing to a glutted fur market; rescinded, 1699), the French were determined to secure the Mississippi Valley. A Sulpician mission was established at Cahokia (near present East St. Louis, 1699) and a Jesuit post at the mouth of the junction of the Kaskaskia and the Mississippi (1703). To protect the route to this region forts were built at Mackinac (1700) and Detroit (1701). Iberville established Ft. Maurepas on Biloxi Bay (1699), but the colony was moved (1702) to Ft. Louis on the Mobile River.

1702, 4 May–1713, 11 Apr. QUEEN ANNE'S WAR (WAR OF THE SPANISH SUCCESSION). To prevent the close cooperation, if not the amalgamation, of France and Spain on the death of Charles II of Spain (1 Nov. 1700), the Grand Alliance (7 Sept. 1701) declared war on France (4 May 1702). In New England the war followed the pattern of the previous conflict. The Abenakis raided Maine settlements (10 Aug. 1703), destroyed Deerfield, Mass. (28–29 Feb. 1704), and attacked Winter Harbor, Me. (21 Sept. 1707). To eliminate the source of Abenaki supplies and seize control of the Acadian fisheries, a force of 500 New Englanders under Col. Benjamin Church destroyed the French villages of Minas and Beaubassin (1, 28 July 1704). After two unsuccessful sieges of Port Royal (1704, 1707), a third expedition under Col. **Francis Nicholson** and **Sir Charles Hobby** reduced that stronghold (16 Oct. 1710). In **Newfoundland,** a mixed force of French and Indians operating out of Placentia destroyed an English settlement at Bonavista (18–29 Aug. 1704), and as a result of the capture of St. Johns (21 Dec. 1708) brought the eastern shore under French control. In the **South** the Carolina assembly authorized (10 Sept. 1702) an expedition to seize St. Augustine before it could be reinforced by the French. A mixed force of 500 colonists and Indians seized, burned, and pillaged the town (Dec.) after failing to capture the fort. Another mixed force under former Governor James Moore destroyed all but one of the 14 missions in the Apalache country (1704), opening the road to Louisiana. But the Carolinians were unable to penetrate the Choctaw screen protecting French Gulf settlements. By the **Treaty of Utrecht** (11 Apr. 1713) Newfoundland, Acadia, and Hudson Bay were ceded to Great Britain, but France retained Cape Breton Island and the islands of the St. Lawrence. The failure to define the boundaries of Acadia, Hudson Bay, and the interior of the continent left the door open to later conflict. Great Britain was also accorded (26 Mar.) the **Assiento,** a contract allowing the South Sea Co. (formed 1711) to import into the Spanish colonies 4,800 Negroes a year for 30 yrs. and to send 1 trading ship a year to the Spanish colonies.

INTERLUDE BETWEEN WARS (1713–39)

1718–29. FRENCH EXPANSION ON MISSISSIPPI. Prosperity in Louisiana was supported by the profits of John Law's Company of the Indies given royal permission to develop the Mississippi Valley. The founding of **New Orleans** (Nov. 1718) by **Jean Baptiste le Moyne, Sieur de Bienville,** brother of Iberville, marked intensive French expansion. Forts were erected at the mouths of the Kaskaskia and the Illinois (1720, 1726) and on the north bank of the Missouri (1723), and settlers from Canada relocated in the Illinois country (*c.*1735).

Following initial success with the Indians in the South (Ft. Toulouse erected among 'the Creeks on the Alabama River), the French were on the defensive as the result of being outbid by Carolina traders. The Yazoo and Natchez joined the Chickasaws in attacking French settlements (1729), ultimately confining the French to the Louisiana Valley area.

1715–28. THE CAROLINA FRONTIER: THE YAMASSEE WAR. Pressed by South Carolina settlers given large coastal grants for cattle ranches, the Yamassees joined the Lower Creeks, resentful of Carolinian trading practices, and raided the area northwest of Port Royal, ultimately ousting the Carolina traders from the entire area west of the Savannah. With the aid of the Cherokee located at the headwaters of the Savannah, the Carolinians defeated the Yamassees (Jan. 1716) and by spring had almost eliminated the Creeks from their frontier. Forts were built at present Columbia and Port Royal (1718) and, as a defense against the French and Spaniards, on the Altamaha, the Savannah, and the Santee (1716–21) despite Spanish protests. A brief **Anglo-Spanish War** (Feb. 1727–Mar. 1728) served as a pretext for the Carolinians to stage a deep march into Florida to destroy a Yamassee village near St. Augustine (9 Mar. 1728).

1732–52. FOUNDING OF GEORGIA. James Edward Oglethorpe (1696–1785), a Tory member of Parliament (since 1722), concerned with the problems of pauperism, relief for imprisoned debtors, imperial trade, and naval supremacy, received, along with 19 associates, including John, Viscount Perceval (first Earl of Egmont), a charter (20 June 1732), conferring upon them as **Trustees** for 21 years the right to settle the area between the Savannah and Altamaha Rivers, originally part of South Carolina, but retained by the crown when the Carolinas were surrendered by the proprietors (1729). The charter granted liberty of conscience to all except Catholics and limited individual grants to 500-acres. Sailing with the first group of settlers, Oglethorpe founded **Savannah** (12 Feb. 1733). During the first year the trustees prohibited the importation or use of rum or brandy as well as slaves. Gradually the landholding restrictions were relaxed. Seven-year tenancies were permitted on new land, size of holdings increased from 500 to 2,000 acres (1740), original grants in tail male (inalienable and restricted to male heirs) to serve as military fiefs were enlarged to fee simple (1750), rum importation permitted (1742), and, as a result of pressure from Carolinians settling in the province, the prohibition on slavery was repealed (1749). With the last meeting of the trustees (4 July 1752) control of the colony passed to the crown. In support of the project, which combined humanitarian and imperialist features, Parliament had by 1752 appropriated £136,608.

1733–39. MILITARY PREPARATIONS IN GEORGIA. Oglethorpe set about fortifying the southern frontier, erecting forts on St. Simon's, St. Andrew's, Cumberland, and Amelia Islands (by 1739), and founding Augusta on the Savannah and Ft. Okfuskee on the Talapoosa (present Alabama, 1735). A notable achievement was his establishment of peace with the interior tribes, particularly the Creeks (1739).

1719–41. RIVAL PREPARATIONS IN THE NORTH. The powerful fortress of Louisbourg on Cape Breton Island (constructed 1720) secured the St. Lawrence approaches, guarded from the south by a new fort at Crown Point on Lake Champlain (1731). To protect the route to the Mississippi (Lake Erie-Maumee-Wabash) the French built Ft. Miami (1704) at the portage, Ft. Ouiataon on the Wabash (*c.* 1719), and Ft. Vincennes (*c.*1724) on the lower Wabash. Ft. Niagara was built (1720) to secure the lower Great Lakes and serve as a base of operations against the Iroquois. The British countered by establishing Ft. Oswego on Lake Ontario (1725), and New Englanders built forts on the northern frontier against the Abenakis, who, as a result of Jesuit activities, remained loyal to France. In the West, **Pierre Gaultier de Varennes, Sieur de la Vérendrye,** French commander at Lake Nipigon, together with his three sons, readied both the Saskatchewan (1734) and the Missouri Valleys (1738) for defense.

WAR OF JENKINS' EAR AND KING GEORGE'S WAR

1739–42. WAR OF JENKINS' EAR. Great Britain, aroused by tales of mistreatment of her merchant seamen (notably Robert Jenkins) and other hostile acts, provoked by British abuses of the Assiento and activities of her logwooders on the Honduran coast as well as by the unsettled Florida border, declared war on Spain (19 Oct. 1739). His western flank protected by the friendly Creeks, Cherokee, and Chickasaw, Oglethorpe invaded Florida, captured Forts San Francisco de Pupo and Picolata on the San Juan River (Jan. 1740), and besieged Saint Augustine (May-July), breaking off when his rear was threatened. A Spanish counterattack was crushed at the **Battle of Bloody Swamp** on St. Simon's Island (1742).

1740–48. KING GEORGE'S WAR (WAR OF THE AUSTRIAN SUCCESSION). The invasion of Silesia by Frederick II of Prussia (16 Dec. 1740) following the death of Emperor Charles VI (20 Oct.) touched off a series of continental wars, with France, now allied with Prussia (5 June 1641), invading southern Germany. With the signing of the **Second Family Compact** (25 Oct. 1743) between France and Spain, France joined the war against England (15 Mar. 1744). Neither side prosecuted the war in America vigorously. The French made an unsuccessful assault on Annapolis Royal (Port Royal, Nova Scotia, 1744), and an expedition of New Englanders under **William Pepperrell** (1696–1759, baronet, 1746) in cooperation with a fleet under Sir Peter Warren captured Fort Louisbourg (16 June 1745). The Maine towns were raided by the French and Indians (from Aug. 1745). In New York **William Johnson** (1715–74), Mohawk Valley Indian trader and commissary of New York for Indian Affairs (1746), succeeded in getting the Iroquois on the warpath, with resultant French retaliatory raids on Saratoga (burned, 28–29 Nov. 1745) and Albany. The inconclusive **Treaty of Aix-la-Chapelle** (18 Oct. 1748) restored the *status quo ante* in the colonies and returned Louisbourg to France.

PRELUDE TO THE LAST WAR

1748–50. Although their area of effective control was confined to Nova Scotia the British claimed that Acadia included, in addition, present New Brunswick and the Gaspé Peninsula. To strengthen their hold on Nova Scotia Lord Halifax sent out 2,500 settlers (1749) to found the town of **Halifax.**

1744–54. WESTWARD MOVEMENT OF PENNSYLVANIANS AND VIRGINIANS. Ohio Valley traders from Pennsylvania, led by **George Croghan** (*c.*1718–82) and **Conrad Weiser** (1696–1760), rapidly expanded their posts in the Ohio area and as agents for the Pennsylvania legislature secured the allegiance of the Indians of the area (Aug. 1748). Virginians were equally interested in the area. The Ohio Co. (p. 435) obtained a huge grant on the upper Ohio and sent out **Christopher Gist** (1750) to explore the region. Erection of a trading house at present Cumberland, Md., and trail-blazing activities aroused the French to fortify present Toronto (1749), to divert trade from Oswego, to locate a post at Niagara portage, strengthen Detroit, and dispatch **Céloron de Bienville** to seize the Ohio Valley (1749). In the summer of 1752 the French attacked the trading post of Pickawillany and killed its defenders, and

North America
East of the Mississippi
in 1763

erected Ft. Presque Isle (Erie, Pa.) and Ft. Le Boeuf at the portage to French Creek (spring 1753), and Ft. Venango at the junction of French Creek and the Allegheny. Lt. Gov. **Robert Dinwiddie** (?1693–1770) of Virginia dispatched 21-year-old **George Washington** to protest these moves and to ascertain French intentions. He visited Ft. Venango and Ft. Le Boeuf (1753), reporting on his return (Jan. 1754) that the French pianned to occupy the entire Ohio and could not be removed except by force.

THE FRENCH AND INDIAN WAR (SEVEN YEARS' WAR)

1754, 17 Apr.–3 July. HOSTILITIES BEGIN. To forestall the French, Dinwiddie ordered construction of a fort at the Forks of the Ohio (junction of Allegheny and Monongahela, Feb. 1754), but the French seized the site and erected Ft. Duquesne. Dispatched with an advance party of 150 to occupy that post, Washington, following a successful skirmish with a French reconnaissance party (28 May), constructed Ft. Necessity at Great Meadows. Reinforced, he resisted a larger French force under Coulon de Villiers, but finally capitulated.

1754, 19 June–10 July. ALBANY CONGRESS. Advised by the British authorities to make a treaty with the wavering Iroquois, delegates from New England, New York, Pennsylvania, and Maryland met at Albany. **Benjamin Franklin** (p. 709), a Pennsylvania delegate, who had drawn up a plan of union (Mar. 1751), proposed (24 June) that the subject be considered. The "Plan of Union" finally approved (10 July) was based on Franklin's plan, with additions probably proposed by **Thomas Hutchinson** (1711–80), a Massachusetts delegate. The plan called for a union of all the colonies (except Georgia and Nova Scotia) under a president general appointed and paid by the crown. A grand council elected by the colonial assemblies (each colony to have from 2 to 7 delegates, depending on its contribution to the general treasury) was to have legislative power subject to approval by the president general and the crown. President general and grand council were to have jurisdiction over Indian affairs, including new land purchases "not now within the bounds of particular colonies." The plan was rejected both by the colonies and the home government. The Board of Trade countered with a proposal (9 Aug.) for a single commander in chief and a commissary of Indian affairs.

1755, 14 Apr.–9 Nov. CAMPAIGNS OF BRADDOCK AND SHIRLEY. Gen. **Edward Braddock** (?1695–1755) arrived in Virginia (14 Apr. 1755) as commander in chief of the British forces in America. At the head of 1,400 British regulars and 450 colonials under Lt. Col. Washington, he headed for Ft. Duquesne. On the Monongahela, about 8 miles below the fort, he was met by a mixed force of 900 French and Indians, surrounded, and defeated at the **Battle of the Wilderness** (9 July). With Braddock mortally wounded, Washington led the remnant back to Ft. Cumberland. Gov. **William Shirley** (1694–1771) of Massachusetts, replacing Braddock in command, was forced to postpone his campaign against Ft. Niagara owing to reinforcements which reached the French when their fleet slipped through a blockade established by Admiral Edward Boscawen (6–13 June). On 19 June Ft. Beauséjour was captured by a force of 2,000 New Englanders and a few British regulars under Colonels Robert Monckton (1726–62) and John Winslow (1703–74). By 30 June the Bay of Fundy area was completely in British hands. William Johnson, commanding a mixed force of 3,500 colonials, chiefly New Englanders, and 400 Indians, began constructing Ft. William Henry on Lake George in anticipation of a French attack. At the **Battle of Lake George (8**

Sept.) he defeated Baron Dieskau's mixed force of 1,400 French and Indian troops. But bad morale among the New England troops prevented Johnson from moving on Crown Point.

1755, July–8 Oct. EXPULSION OF THE ACADIANS. Fearing that a French attack would be supported by the Acadians acting as a fifth column, Col. Charles Lawrence, Governor of Nova Scotia, announced that all who refused to take the oath of loyalty to the British crown would be expelled (5 Sept.). Embarkation began (8 Oct.). In all some 6,000 Acadians were exiled and distributed among the Thirteen Colonies. Villages at the head of the Bay of Fundy were burned to the ground, but many of the inhabitants escaped to the woods. A sizable number eventually returned to Nova Scotia.

1756, 16 Jan.–29 Aug. WAR SPREADS TO EUROPE. The European phase of the war began following a new alliance between Britain and Prussia, on the one hand (16 Jan. 1756), and France and Austria, on the other (1 May), with a declaration of war by Great Britain on France (15 May). A British setback at Minorca, which fell 28 June, was matched by continued reversals in America.

1757–58. FURTHER BRITISH SET-BACKS IN AMERICA. To command French forces in America **Louis Joseph, Marquis de Montcalm** (1712–59), arrived in Canada with reinforcements (11 May 1756). He was opposed by **John Campbell, Earl of Loudoun,** who arrived in America on 23 July. Montcalm took and destroyed Forts Oswego and George (Aug.) and on 9 Aug. 1757 took and demolished Fort William Henry, whose outnumbered defender, Col. Monro, surrendered only to have his force treacherously set upon by the Indians. With 1,400 survivors he reached Ft. Edward. Under orders from Pitt to attack Louisbourg rather than Quebec, Loudoun assembled a large force at Halifax (30 June), but abandoned the attack on learning that the French navy had reached Louisbourg. Rear Adm. Francis Holborne proceeded to bottle up the French in Louisbourg Harbor, but a hurricane smashed

the British fleet (24 Sept.). Loudoun's preparations had been hampered by failure to receive wholehearted cooperation from colonial assemblies.

1757. PITT'S WAR LEADERSHIP. French success in Europe continued, with Hanover overrun and three armies converging on Frederick II. With his advent to power in the **Pitt-Newcastle Ministry** (29 June) **William Pitt** (1708–78, Earl of Chatham in 1766) committed the government to unlimited warfare, reinforcements in America, and subsidies to the continental allies, necessitating higher taxes and war loans.

1757, 30 Dec.–1758, 18 Sept. ABER-CROMBY IN COMMAND. James **Abercromby** (1706–81) supplanted Loudoun in command, and assembled about 12,000 troops at Lake George (1 July 1758) for a march on **Ticonderoga.** Electing to defend a low ridge outside the fort, Montcalm, with a greatly outnumbered force of 3,000, threw up breastworks. Abercromby's frontal attack (8 July) was routed by withering fire. The British withdrew with great casualties (464 killed, 29 missing, 1,117 wounded). This disaster was counterbalanced by Maj. Gen. **Jeffrey Amherst** (1717–97), who, with Brig. Gen. **James Wolfe** (1727–59), a fleet of 40 ships, and a force of 9,000 British regulars and 500 colonials, took **Louisbourg** (26 July). Col. **John Bradstreet** (1711–74) took Ft. Frontenac (27 Aug.), and Brig. Gen. **John Forbes** (1710–59), marching along a new road he constructed southwest from Raystown, forced the French to blow up Ft. Duquesne (25 Nov.). With the turn of the tide, Abercromby was relieved of his command (18 Sept.) and Amherst named his successor.

1759. YEAR OF FRENCH DISASTER. Pitt outlined a three-pronged campaign: (1) to capture Ft. Niagara and reinforce Oswego in order to sever the West from the St. Lawrence; (2) to strike through the Lake Champlain waterway to the St. Lawrence Valley; (3) to launch an amphibious attack against Quebec. **Ft. Niagara** fell (25 July) to a force of 2,000 regulars under Brig. Gen. John Prideaux (killed prior to the capitulation) and 100 Iroquois under Sir William Johnson.

BOUNDARIES PROPOSED IN THE PEACE NEGOTIATIONS OF 1872,
BETWEEN THE UNITED STATES AND ENGLAND

Meantime, Col. Frederick Haldimand had reinforced Oswego. Outnumbered by British attackers under Amherst the French blew up Ft. Carillon (**Ticonderoga**, 26 July) and Ft. St. Frederic (**Crown Point**, 31 July)—both refortified by Amherst—and retreated down the Richelieu. A combined force of 9,000 troops under Wolfe and a fleet under Rear Adm. Charles Saunders sailed up the St. Lawrence (16 June), anchoring off Bic and St. Barnabé, where Rear Adm. Durell landed a detachment of troops on the Île-aux-Coudres (28 May) and advanced to the Île d'Orléans to await the main force (25 June). Wolfe landed troops on Île d'Orléans (27 June); sent Monckton to occupy Pointe Lévis opposite Quebec, and Brig. Gen. George Townshend (1724–1807) to the north shore (9 July). After the failure of attempts by Montcalm to burn the British fleet (27 July) and by the British to storm the enemy position (31 July), Wolfe dispatched a force under Brig. Gen. James Murray (1719–94) to engage troops above Quebec. On their return (25 Aug.) he decided to attack. While the French were led to expect a major attack from the St. Lawrence, Wolfe moved his troops on the night of 12–13 Sept. downstream in small boats, landing before dawn on the north shore, and made a surprise ascent of the **Plains of Abraham**, a plateau about the city. Unwilling to await reinforcements by a force of 3,000 in the Cap Rouge area, Montcalm engaged the British with 4,500 troops. Superior discipline and arms won the day for the British, who lost only 60 killed and 600 wounded as against 200 killed and 1,200 wounded for the French. But these fatalities included both Wolfe and Montcalm. **Quebec** soon capitulated (18 Sept.).

1760. SURRENDER OF CANADA. Converging on Montreal, Amherst, striking from Lake Ontario, landed at Lachine (6 Sept.); William Haviland, marching north from Crown Point, captured Chambly (1 Sept.); and Governor Murray, pressing down from Quebec, made a junction with the others massed before Montreal, forcing Pierre François de Rigaud, Marquis de Vaudreuil, Governor of Canada, to surrender the entire province (8 Sept.). Maj. **Robert Rogers** (1731–95) took possession of Detroit and other Great Lakes posts (1760–61).

1761–62. INVOLVEMENT OF SPAIN. Apprehensive that a British victory would upset the balance of colonial power, Spain prepared to throw her weight on the side of France and Austria. Anticipating attack, Great Britain declared war (2 Jan. 1762). Martinique, principal French base in the lesser Antilles, fell to the British (15 Feb. 1762), followed by St. Lucia and Grenada, and, after a two-month siege, Havana capitulated (12 Aug.). Manila fell (5 Oct.) to a second fleet operating in the Far East. To compensate Spain for her loss France, anxious to end the war, ceded to her ally, by the secret **Treaty of Fontainebleau** (3 Nov. 1762), all her territory west of the Mississippi as well as the Isle of Orleans (ratified 13 Nov. 1762).

1763, 10 Feb. TREATY OF PARIS ended the west European and colonial phases of the Seven Years' War and the Treaty of Hubertusberg (15 Feb.) concluded its German phase. France ceded to Great Britain all claim to Acadia, Cape Breton, Canada, and the islands of the St. Lawrence, but retained fishing rights on Newfoundland's banks and was given the islands of St. Pierre and Miquelon. France further yielded all territory east of the Mississippi (including the port of Mobile) except the city of New Orleans. Pitt, preferring Canada to the French West Indies for reasons of military security as well as trade, returned to France Martinique and Guadeloupe. St. Vincent, Dominica, and Tobago were restored to Great Britain. France agreed to evacuate her positions in Hanover, restore Minorca to the British, and to the *status quo ante* in India. Cuba was restored to Spain in exchange for East and West Florida, and the British agreed to demolish fortifications on the Honduran coast, but the rights of her logwooders to operate in that area were specifically recognized by Spain.

THE ERA OF
THE AMERICAN REVOLUTION, 1763-89

1763

7 Oct. PROCLAMATION OF 1763.
The French and Indian War had revealed the insecurity of the frontiers against Indian raids. The first step in placating the Indians was the appointment by Gen. Braddock of **Sir William Johnson** as Indian Commissioner (Apr. 1755) and his reappointment as Commissioner for the North (spring 1756). Since land frauds were believed to lie at the root of Indian unrest Johnson's secretary, Peter Wraxall, urged (9 Jan. 1756) that henceforth land cessions require the approval of the Indian commissioners. By the **Treaty of Easton** (Oct. 1758) with its western Indians Pennsylvania agreed to make no settlements west of the Alleghenies. However, the abandonment of Ft. Duquesne (24 Nov.) and its occupation by the British resulted in an influx of settlers, compelling Col. **Henry Bouquet** (1719–65) to forbid settlement west of the mountains (13 Oct. 1761). The Earl of Egremont as Secretary of State for the Southern Dept. required royal approval for land grants in or adjacent to Indian territory (2 Dec.). To **William Petty, Lord Shelburne,** head of the Board of Trade in the Halifax-Grenville-Egremont ministry, was assigned the formulation of a policy for the newly acquired territory in North America resulting from the Treaty of Paris. Shelburne recommended (8 June 1763) that the Appalachians constitute the dividing line between the settlers and an Indian reservation save for a projected colonial settlement in the upper Ohio and some provision for Indian settlement east of that line. Out of the newly acquired territory three new prov-

inces were to be created: (1) Quebec; (2) East Florida; (3) West Florida, with boundaries confined within modest limits in no way encroaching upon the Thirteen Colonies. News of an Indian crisis reached the British ministry in August. Before the plan was put into effect Shelburne was replaced (2 Sept.) by the less-experienced **Earl of Hillsborough,** a close associate of Halifax, who prepared a proclamation which modified Shelburne's proposal by omitting provision for upper Ohio settlement and ordering colonists already settled in that area "forthwith to remove themselves." Purchases of land from the Indians east of the line were forbidden. Indian territory west of the line was placed under the control of the military commander in chief in America. English law was established in Quebec, a provision deemed unfair and anti-Catholic by French settlers. The proclamation was rushed through the cabinet and Privy Council and signed by the king (7 Oct.).

7 May–28 Nov. PONTIAC'S REBELLION. Following the surrender of Detroit to the English under Major Robert Rogers (29 Nov. 1760), the Indians demanded that the British authorities lower prices on trade goods and furnish them with ammunition. When these demands were not met at a conference at Detroit (9 Sept. 1761) the Indians grew increasingly restive, stirred up by the Delaware Prophet, a visionary living in the upper Ohio, and by his disciple, **Pontiac** (*c.*1720–69), chief of the Ottawa. After his plan to take Detroit by a surprise attack was betrayed (May), Pontiac took to open warfare. Within a few weeks every British post west of Niagara was destroyed (Sandusky, 16 May; Ft. St.

71

Joseph, 25 May; Ft. Miami, 27 May; Ft. Ouiatenon, 1 June; Ft. Venango, c.16 June; Ft. Le Boeuf, 18 June; Ft. Presque Isle, 20 June), save for Detroit, which, under Maj. Henry Gladwin, resisted a five months' siege, and Ft. Pitt, under Capt. Simeon Ecuyer. In retaliation Amherst proposed to Bouquet that "Small pox" be sent among the disaffected tribes, and the latter replied that he would try to distribute germ-laden blankets among them, but, because of the danger of exposure to British troops, preferred hunting the Indians "with English dogs" (13 July). As a result of reinforcements which reached Detroit (29 July), Gladwin made a sortie against Pontiac and was repulsed at **Bloody Ridge** (31 July). Marching to the relief of Ft. Pitt, Bouquet defeated (with heavy British losses) and routed the Indians at **Bushy Run**, east of present Pittsburgh (2–6 Aug.), and relieved the fort (10 Aug.). In Nov. Pontiac raised his siege of Detroit. A number of tribes had already signed treaties with Col. John Bradstreet at Presque Isle (12 Aug.). Pontiac finally submitted, concluding a peace treaty with Sir William Johnson at Oswego (24 July 1766). Subsequently he remained loyal to the British, but was murdered (1769) in Cahokia (Illinois), according to Parkman's version, by a Kaskaskia Indian bribed by an English trader.

5 Nov.–1 Dec. PARSON'S CAUSE. This case was the result of legislation in Virginia regulating salaries of Anglican ministers, which, from 1662, had by law been paid in tobacco, varying with the market value of that commodity. Owing to failure of the tobacco crop as a result of drought, the legislature (Oct. 1755) commuted such pay into currency at the rate of 2d. per lb.; reenacted, 1758. Acting on memorials from the Virginia clergy the Privy Council disallowed the act (10 Aug. 1759). As a result the clergy proceeded to sue for back salary even though the act had not been declared null and void *ab initio*. Most publicized was the case brought by Rev. **James Maury** in Hanover Co. Court. The bench held that the 1758 act was "no law," but a jury (swayed by the rhetoric of young **Patrick Henry** [1736–

99], who declared that by disallowing the act the king had broken the compact between the governed and the ruler, thereby forfeiting "all rights to his subjects' obedience") returned a verdict of 1d. for plaintiff. The action of the General Court (10 Apr. 1764) in giving judgment against the clergy was affirmed by the Privy Council (3 Dec. 1766).

13–27 Dec. FRONTIER DISORDER IN PENNSYLVANIA: THE PAXTON BOYS. As a result of the insecurity of the frontier against Indian attacks (1754–63), a mob from Paxton and Donegal attacked the Conestoga Indians in Lancaster Co. The assembly, which had failed to respond to the demand of frontiersmen for protection, ordered that the "Paxton Boys" be arrested and brought to Philadelphia for trial. Instead, the frontiersmen marched east, but were persuaded by Franklin to forego battle, and issued a formal protest by which they obtained greater representation in the legislature.

1764

5 Apr. REVENUE FROM AMERICA. Faced by a large postwar debt, heavy taxes at home, and the necessity of supporting an army in America, the Bute ministry sought revenue from the colonies. When the debate on the 1764 budget opened in the House of Commons (9 Mar.), the Chancellor of the Exchequer, George Grenville, presented an American Revenue Act (generally known as the **Sugar Act**) to become the 1st law ever passed by Parliament for the specific purpose of raising moneys in the colonies for the crown. The act (1) extended the Molasses Act of 1733 but reduced the 6d.-per-gallon duty upon foreign molasses to 3d., the old rate on raw sugar was continued, and an increased duty levied on foreign refined sugar; (2) placed new or higher import duties on non-British textiles, coffee, and indigo, and on Madeira and Canary wines imported directly; (3) doubled the duties on foreign goods reshipped in England to the colonies; (4) added iron, hides, whale fins, raw silk, potash, and pearl ash to the enumerated list;

(5) banned the import into the colonies of foreign rum and French wines. Grenville estimated that the act, if efficiently administered, would return *c.*£45,000 annually.

ENDING SALUTARY NEGLECT. More significant was Grenville's determination to enforce the trade laws by revitalizing the customs service (at that time the American customs returned little more than one fourth [£2,000] the cost of collecting them). A companion measure provided for tighter enforcement by (1) establishing a vice-admiralty court at Halifax with jurisdiction over all the American colonies and enabling prosecutors and informers to bring suit there at their option rather than in local colonial courts; (2) annulling the right of an accused to sue for illegal seizure; (3) placing the burden of proof upon the accused and obliging him to post bond for the cost of the trial; and (4) establishing stricter registration and bonding procedures for ships carrying nonenumerated as well as enumerated cargoes. Grenville ended the practice under which American customs officials were permitted to live in England and entrust their duties to a deputy in the colonies.

CURRENCY ACT widened the scope of colonial opposition as it affected the plantation as well as the commercial provinces. Aimed principally at Virginia, which had issued £250,000 of legal-tender paper money during the war, the act prohibited after 1 Sept. issues of legal-tender currency in all the American colonies (thereby extending the ban already operative in New England since 1751), as well as any extension of the recall date for outstanding issues. To guard against evasion, the act nullified all acts of colonial assemblies contrary to its terms and provided for a fine of £1,000 and dismissal from office (with ineligibility for any government position in the future) of any colonial Governor who assented to legislative acts in defiance of the law.

COLONIAL OPPOSITION. To Americans already distressed by a marked postwar business decline, the Grenville program, by combining higher imposts

and strict enforcement with the severe deflationary shock of the Currency Act, seemed calculated to ruin the colonial economy. Massachusetts led the way in protest. A Boston town meeting (24 May) denounced taxation without representation and proposed united action by the colonies in protest. The House of Representatives authorized a committee of correspondence (13 June) to contact the other provinces. In Aug. Boston merchants agreed to do without English lace and ruffles, an example which the town's mechanics followed (Sept.) in pledging to wear no leather work clothes not of Massachusetts make. By the end of the year **nonimportation** had spread to other colonies, notably New York.

1765

QUARTERING ACT. Requested by Gen. Thomas Gage, commander of the British forces in America, and not an integral part of the Grenville program, the Quartering Act added fuel to the rising fire of American resentment. Effective 24 Mar. for a 2-yr. term, the act required the civil authorities in the colonies to supply barracks and supplies for the British troops. A 2d act (1766) provided for quartering and billeting in inns, alehouses, and unoccupied dwellings.

22 Mar. STAMP ACT, the first direct tax ever levied by Parliament upon America, was designed to raise £60,000 annually, which, together with the return from the 1764 imposts, would produce an American return equal to about one third the £300,000 upkeep of the colonial military establishment. The act (passed the Commons, 27 Feb., the Lords, 8 Mar., to become effective 1 Nov.) placed a tax upon newspapers, almanacs, pamphlets and broadsides, legal documents of all types, insurance policies, ship's papers, licenses, and even dice and playing cards. The receipts were to be paid into the royal exchequer for the defense of the colonies. With the sensibilities of the colonists in mind Grenville appointed Americans to be the stamp agents. Penalties for infringements could be imposed by courts of vice-admiralty (which had no jury) as well as by colonial common-law courts.

STAMP ACT CRISIS. Factors underlying the virtually unanimous opposition to the act were (1) the novelty of direct taxation by Parliament and the fear that this tax was to be but the first of many; (2) its all-inclusive character transcended sectionalism; (3) by affecting groups which carried great weight throughout the colonies (lawyers, printers, tavern owners, and land speculators as well as merchants and shipowners) the act broadened the base of the opposition; (4) the grant of jurisdiction to vice-admiralty courts raised fears of an assault upon the right to trial by jury; and (5) the imposition of the tax at a time of economic stagnation and currency stringency convinced many that Britain was deliberately aiming to weaken the colonies.

NEW POLITICAL THEORIES. In 1764 Otis had raised the issue of no taxation without representation. But the Stamp Act impelled other American writers to draw distinctions aimed at establishing the measure's illegality. Widely read and quoted was the argument advanced (*Considerations*) by Daniel Dulany, a Maryland attorney, conceding the right of Parliament to regulate trade, even when such acts produced a revenue, but denying its authority to impose internal taxes for revenue upon the colonists inasmuch as the Americans were not and by their situation could not be represented in Parliament. The same distinction was expressed more militantly in the Virginia Resolutions (29 May) introduced before the House of Burgesses by **Patrick Henry** (p. 726) with the "Treason" speech in which he warned George III to note the fate of Cæsar and Charles I. Asserting that the right of Virginia to govern its internal affairs had always been recognized by the Crown, the Resolutions claimed for the province's General Assembly the sole power to tax Virginians. Upon further deliberation (30–31 May) the House rejected the more radical of these claims, contenting itself with stating that Virginians in the past had legislated respecting their own internal polity and approving the principle of no taxation without representa-

tion. Henry's complete set of resolutions were, however, published in the colonial newspapers.

SONS OF LIBERTY. During the summer of 1765 secret organizations known as the Sons of Liberty (the term had been used by Colonel Barré in a speech against the Stamp Act in the House of Commons) were formed in the provincial towns to organize the opposition to the Stamp Act. Often organized, sometimes personally led (as in New York City) by men of wealth and high position, these groups did not hesitate to resort to violence to force stamp agents to resign their posts and merchants to cancel orders for British goods. A notorious instance occurred in Boston on 26 Aug., when the records of the vice-admiralty court were burned, the home of the comptroller of the currency ransacked, and the elegant home and library of Chief Justice Thomas Hutchinson looted. The Boston stamp agent, Andrew Oliver (Hutchinson's brother-in-law) had been forced by mob violence to resign 15 Aug. Before the effective date of the Stamp Act (1 Nov.) all the stamp agents in the colonies had resigned.

7–25 Oct. STAMP ACT CONGRESS. Upon the motion of James Otis, the Massachusetts Assembly resolved (6 June) to propose an intercolonial meeting to seek relief from the Stamp Act. A circular letter was dispatched to each colonial assembly (8 June) suggesting that a congress meet at New York City in Oct. South Carolina endorsed the proposal promptly (2 Aug.), followed by Rhode Island, Connecticut, Pennsylvania, and Maryland. The assemblies of New Jersey, Delaware, and New York failed to take formal action, but were represented by delegates chosen informally. The other 4 provinces failed to act, and were not represented when the Congress opened.

The moderate character of the Stamp Act Congress was clearly reflected in the "Declaration of Rights and Grievances" (19 Oct.), chiefly the work of **John Dickinson** (Pa.). In 14 resolutions the delegates claimed all the rights and liberties of the king's subjects in Great Britain, stated that taxation without consent expressed personally or through representatives was a violation of these rights, pointed out that the colonists were not and could not be represented in the House of Commons, and concluded that no taxes could be constitutionally imposed on them but by their own legislatures. Specifically condemned was the provision in the Stamp Act giving jurisdiction to admiralty courts. Separate petitions embracing these resolutions and demanding repeal of the Stamp Act and the measures of 1764 were prepared for submission to the king, the House of Commons, and the House of Lords before the 27 delegates disbanded. On 11 Feb. 1766 the Northampton, Va., County Court declared the Stamp Act unconstitutional.

ECONOMIC SANCTIONS. The passage of the Stamp Act gave a new impetus to **nonimportation.** In New York City leading citizens signed an agreement (28 Oct.) banning the purchase of European goods until the Stamp Act was repealed and the trade regulations of 1764 modified. Following suit were 200 merchants (31 Oct.), some 400 Philadelphia merchants (Nov.), and 250 Boston merchants (9 Dec.). Business throughout the colonies was generally suspended when the Stamp Act went into effect (1 Nov.), owing to the practically universal refusal to use the stamps. Except in Rhode Island, where Gov. Hopkins refused to execute the act, the courts also closed rather than use the stamps as the law required. Before the end of the year, however, business was renewed without the stamps in open violation of the act.

BRITISH DEMANDS FOR REPEAL. When the Stamp Act became operative a movement in Britain for its repeal was already well along. Grenville's ministry, which had fallen from power in a crisis over a regency bill (10 July), was succeeded by a government under the Marquis of Rockingham. The decline in British exports to America (from £2,-249,710 in 1764 to £1,944,108 in 1765) spoke more eloquently than colonial resolutions. A committee of merchants, organized to work for the Stamp Act's repeal, called upon some 30 towns in Britain to petition Parliament for repeal. The petition of the London merchants (17 Jan. 1766) cited several bankruptcies resulting from shrunken American markets.

1766

18 Mar. REPEAL OF THE STAMP ACT. Parliament met on 14 Jan. and immediately debated the Stamp Act. Grenville demanded that the army be used to enforce it, while William Pitt, calling for repeal, commended the Americans for disobeying a tax framed by a body in which they were not represented. The colonial agents were called before the Commons sitting as a committee of the whole (beginning 3 Feb.) to give their views. The most telling testimony was given (13 Feb.) by **Benjamin Franklin** (p. 709), agent for Pennsylvania. Franklin stressed the heavy expenditures voted by the colonial assemblies during the French and Indian War (Pennsylvania spent £500,000, with a rebate of only £60,000 from the crown), pointed to the continuing expenses borne for prosecution of Indian wars, and declared that the Thirteen Colonies lacked sufficient specie to pay the stamp taxes for a single year. He warned that an attempt to carry out the Stamp Act by the use of troops might bring on rebellion, endorsed Dulany's distinction between internal and external taxes, and called for outright repeal.

A bill for full repeal was brought before the Commons by a vote of 275–167 (22 Feb.), passed the House (4 Mar.), and, as a result of pressure from the king, passed the Lords (17 Mar.). The repeal bill, effective 1 May, received the royal assent 18 Mar. America received the news (word reached New York 26 Apr.) with rejoicing. Nonimportation was immediately abandoned; the New York Assembly voted statues to honor the king and Pitt (30 June).

18 Mar. DECLARATORY ACT. Generally overlooked in the rejoicing over the Stamp Act's repeal was a statement of Parliament's authority over America enacted into law on the same day as the repeal measure (couched in the same terms as the Irish Declaratory Act of 1719), and asserting that Parliament had full authority to make laws binding the American colonists **"in all cases whatsoever."**

1 Nov. TRADE LAWS MODIFIED. The repeal of the Stamp Act was followed by another retreat on the government's part. The 3d. duty on foreign molasses imported by the colonists was now withdrawn (effective 1 Nov.) in favor of a uniform 1d.-per-gallon duty on all molasses, British as well as foreign, coming into the continental colonies. Export duties on British West Indian sugar were removed, thereby reducing its price on the American mainland. The act contained one notably unfavorable provision: all colonial products shipped to northern Europe henceforth had to clear through ports in Great Britain en route.

NEW YORK AND THE QUARTERING ACT CRISIS. Through Gov. Sir Henry Moore (1713–69) General Gage requested (13 Dec. 1765) that the N.Y. Assembly make provision for quartering and supplying his troops in accord with the Quartering Act. The Assembly, contending that this act weighed heaviest upon their province (New York was Gage's headquarters), refused full compliance (Jan. 1766). Tension mounted through the spring and summer. The destruction of a liberty pole by British soldiers (10 Aug.) led to a clash on the following day between citizens and bayonet-wielding redcoats in which Isaac Sears (c.1730–86), a leader of the Sons of Liberty, was wounded. On 15 Dec. the Assembly refused any appropriations for Gage's forces and was prorogued (19 Dec.). Not until 6 June 1767 did the Assembly vote £3,000. Ignorant of this step, Parliament suspended the Assembly's legislative powers (effective 1 Oct. 1767), but due to the grant of 6 June the suspension was not carried out by the Governor. On 7 May 1768 the Board of Trade sustained his decision by declaring invalid acts of the Assembly after 1 Oct. 1767.

1767

29 June. TOWNSHEND ACTS. When the Chatham ministry came into office (Aug. 1766) Charles Townshend became Chancellor of the Exchequer. By the beginning of 1767, due to Lord Chatham's illness, Townshend was the actual leader

of the government. In Jan., he attacked the distinction Americans (and Chatham himself, then William Pitt) had made between external and internal taxation and revealed that he was preparing a new revenue measure for America. A reduction in the British land tax, carried in defiance of the ministry (27 Feb.), made it imperative to carry out this pledge, for that revision involved a cut of £500,000 in home revenue.

The Townshend Acts conformed to the American position of 1765–66: the taxes were all **external**: import duties on glass, lead, paints, paper, and tea. The estimated annual return of £40,000 could be used (according to the bill's preamble) not only for the defense of the colonies but also for "defraying the charge of the administration of justice, and the support of civil government" in America. To provide for efficient collection of the new duties this bill and a companion measure (1) clearly affirmed the power of superior or supreme court justices to issue writs of assistance; (2) established new vice-admiralty courts; and (3) an American Board of Commissioners of the Customs at Boston, directly responsible to the British Treasury Board. The acts received the royal assent on 29 June and became effective 20 Nov.

28 Oct. REVIVAL OF NONIMPORTATION. Once more the colonists turned to nonimportation to force Parliament to retreat again. A Boston town meeting (28 Oct.) drew up a list of British products, chiefly luxury goods, which were not to be purchased after 31 Dec. In Providence a stringent nonimportation agreement was signed (2 Dec.) to become effective 1 Jan. 1768; Newport followed suit (4 Dec.); and a mass meeting in New York City (29 Dec.) appointed a committee to draw up a plan to promote domestic industry and employment.

5 Nov. FARMER'S LETTERS. The most significant statement of the constitutional basis for the opposition to the Townshend Acts was written by John Dickinson. First appearing in the *Pennsylvania Chronicle* (5 Nov. 1767–Jan. 1768), his 14 essays, entitled "Letters From a Farmer in Pennsylvania to the Inhabitants of the British Colonies," were widely reprinted in pamphlet form both in Britain and America during 1768. Dickinson conceded Parliament's authority to regulate trade, even if revenue was incidentally produced, but denied its right to tax in order to raise a revenue in America, declared the Townshend duties unconstitutional, and assailed the suspension of the New York Assembly as a blow to the liberties of all the colonies.

1768

11 Feb. MASSACHUSETTS CIRCULAR LETTER, drawn up by **Samuel Adams** (p. 667) and approved by the Mass. House of Representatives, informed the assemblies of the other 12 colonies of the steps taken by the Mass. General Court, denounced the Acts as violating the principle of no taxation without representation, reasserted the impossibility of representing America adequately in the British Parliament, attacked any move by the crown to make colonial governors and judges independent of the people, and concluded by soliciting proposals for united action. Gov. Francis Bernard (1712–79) condemned the Circular Letter as seditious and on 4 Mar. dissolved the General Court. This view was shared by the Secretary of State for the Colonies, Lord Hillsborough, who, in a dispatch to the colonial governors (21 Apr.), denounced the letter and ordered that their respective assemblies be prevented, by dissolution if necessary, from endorsing it. This order came too late. By May the assemblies of New Hampshire, New Jersey, and Connecticut had commended the stand of Massachusetts, and Virginia had drafted its own Circular Letter advising support of Massachusetts. On 22 Apr. Hillsborough ordered Gov. Bernard to dissolve the new General Court should the House of Representatives refused to rescind the Circular Letter. Bernard ordered the House to expunge the resolution embodying the letter from its journal (21 June), but after a protracted debate the Representatives voted 92–17 (30 June) to defy this command. The Court was then dissolved (1 July). The 17 "Rescinders"

came under heavy attack by the Sons of Liberty; 7 lost their seats in the election of May 1769.

10 June. SEIZURE OF THE "LIBERTY." Meanwhile, the obstructionist tactics of the people of Boston had led the Customs Commissioners there to request an armed force to protect them in carrying out their duties (Feb.); repeated in a memorial to the ministry 28 Mar. From Halifax the frigate *Romney*, 50 guns, was dispatched to Boston. Its arrival (17 May) made the customs officials overconfident. When they were informed (9 June) that a wharf official had been locked in a cabin of John Hancock's sloop *Liberty* while Madeira wine was landed without payment of duty, they ordered the seizure of Hancock's vessel (10 June). The *Liberty* was towed from her wharf and anchored close to the *Romney*. A crowd assaulted the customs officials on the dock and demonstrated before their homes. The next day (11 June) the customs officials fled to Castle William on an island in the harbor and again (15 June) appealed for troops.

1 Oct. BRITISH TROOPS IN BOSTON. On 12 Sept. the Boston town meeting, on the alleged ground of an imminent war with France, called upon the people to arm and requested the Governor to call the General Court into session. When he refused, 96 Massachusetts towns sent delegates to an informal Provincial Convention (23–28 Sept.), which broke up the very day British troopships arrived in the harbor. Despite threats of armed resistance made by the Sons of Liberty, 2 regiments of infantry with artillery landed without opposition (1 Oct.) and stationed in the town.

PROGRESS OF NONIMPORTATION. Boston merchants adopted (Mar.) a more stringent nonimportation agreement contingent upon similar action by New York and Philadelphia. In New York such an agreement was signed in Apr. (effective 1 Oct.), but meetings in Philadelphia (Mar.-June) failed to yield a similar compact. Thereupon the Boston merchants drew up their own plan (1 Aug.) barring the importation of the items bearing the Townshend duties from 1 Jan. 1769 until the duties were repealed, and of all but a brief list of British goods (mostly supplies for the fisheries) from 1 Jan. 1769 to 1 Jan. 1770. The merchants of New York countermanded all orders sent to Britain after 15 Aug. and agreed (28 Aug.) to import no British goods from 1 Nov. until the Townshend Acts were repealed. N.Y. tradesmen pledged not to deal with any merchant who refused to join in this accord (5 Sept.)

1769

COURSE OF NONIMPORTATION. By the end of 1769 New Hampshire alone remained aloof from nonimportation. The Philadelphia merchants finally took concrete action (6 Feb.) and on 10 Mar. banned most British goods from 1 Apr.; Baltimore merchants followed suit 30 Mar.

16–18 May. VIRGINIA RESOLVES AND ASSOCIATION. On 16 May George Washington introduced in the Virginia House of Burgesses a set of resolutions framed by **George Mason** (1725–92). Adopted unanimously, they asserted that the sole right of taxing Virginians lay with the Governor and provincial legislature; censured by inference the British ministry for its denunciation of the Massachusetts and Virginia Circular Letters; condemned the Parliamentary proposal that American malcontents be brought to England for trial under an act of Henry VIII. An address to the King was drawn up by **Patrick Henry** and **Richard Henry Lee** (1732–94) just before Gov. Botetourt (1718–70) dissolved the Assembly (17 May). The Burgesses met informally the next day in Williamsburg's Raleigh Tavern and adopted the Virginia Association, a nonimportation agreement banning the importation of British goods (except paper) upon which a duty was charged, of slaves (after 1 Nov.), and of a long list of European luxury goods.

June–Nov. THE SPREAD OF THE ASSOCIATION. A Maryland provincial convention meeting at Annapolis (22 June) drew up an association based on the Virginia model, augmented by a provision for boycotting those refusing to sign or keep the compact. South Carolina took similar action (22 July) and its agreement was copied by the citizens of Savannah, Georgia (19 Sept.). An informal meeting of the North Carolina Assembly endorsed the Virginia Association (7 Nov.). In Delaware and Connecticut nonimportation pledges were drawn up in the port towns (June–Aug.). Providence merchants acted 24 Oct. In Newport a very weak agreement was signed (30 Oct.). Threats of boycott by New York and Philadelphia merchants forced a tightening of its terms later in the year. The N.J. Assembly endorsed (18 Oct.) the sanctions against British imports entered into by the merchants of N.J., Pa., and N.Y.

EFFECTS OF NONIMPORTATION. Colonial imports from Britain fell from £2,157,218 in 1768 to £1,336,122 in 1769; in New York and Philadelphia from £490,673 to £75,930 and from £441,829 to £204,978, respectively. Though these American trade losses were largely offset by a rising market in Europe for British goods, the ministry, now led by the Duke of Grafton, was disturbed. As early as 13 May the Board of Trade informed the governors that modifications of the Townshend duties were under consideration.

1770

12 Apr. TOWNSHEND DUTIES LIMITED TO TEA ALONE. The movement for repeal of the Townshend measures gained new impetus when **Lord Frederick North** became head of the government (31 Jan.). North believed that complete repeal might be interpreted as a sign of weakness; his stand for partial repeal was sustained in the Cabinet by a 5–4 vote. In Commons (5 Mar.) he proposed a bill for the withdrawal of all the Townshend duties except that on tea and pledged that his ministry would lay no new taxes upon the colonists. The alteration in the Townshend duties received .the King's consent 12 Apr. At the same time the Quartering Act was allowed to expire without renewal.

COLLAPSE OF NONIMPORTATION.

Although most of the colonial nonimportation agreements had made repeal of all the Townshend duties a condition for dropping their sanctions against British goods, the withdrawal of all but the **tea tax** led to the abandonment of the program, despite Boston's attempt to hold the line (25 Apr.). Merchants in Albany, Providence, and Newport moved to abandon nonimportation (May); a house-to-house poll in New York City (7–9 July), which revealed that its inhabitants favored resuming imports of all but tea and other articles actually bearing a duty, led to an abandonment of the various associations, to which Philadelphia (12 Sept.), Boston (12 Oct.), South Carolina (13 Dec.), and finally Virginia (July 1771) bowed.

19 Jan. BATTLE OF GOLDEN HILL.

The contest in New York over the Quartering Act had been renewed late in 1768 when the Assembly once again refused to vote supplies (31 Dec.). This position was maintained by a new Assembly (elected Jan. 1769) until 15 Dec. 1769, when an appropriation of £2,000 was voted. **Alexander McDougall** (1732–86), a leader of the Sons of Liberty in New York, issued a broadside criticizing the Assembly, entitled "To the Betrayed Inhabitants of the City and Colony of New York" (16 Dec.). Clashes between citizens and soldiers broke out early in 1770. After one ineffectual attempt (13 Jan.) British soldiers succeeded in cutting down the town's liberty pole (17 January). A countermove by Sons of Liberty to prevent the posting of broadsides by soldiers (19 Jan.) led to a riot on Golden Hill in which some 30 or 40 soldiers used bayonets against citizens armed with cutlasses and clubs. Several on both sides were wounded seriously, but there were no fatalities. McDougall was arrested (8 Feb.) and charged with authorship of the broadside. He refused to post bond and remained in prison until 29 Apr., when he entered a plea of not guilty and was released on bail. The case never came to trial owing to the death of the state's witness. However, McDougall was called before the Assembly (13 Dec.) and imprisoned for contempt until 27 Apr. 1771.

5 Mar. BOSTON MASSACRE.

Minor clashes between citizens and soldiers were common occurrences in Boston following the arrival of the troops (1 Oct. 1768). In Oct. 1769 a serious encounter was only ended when the troops fired a volley into the air. Early in 1770 collisions between town laborers and soldiers seeking employment in off-duty hours became frequent. A fist fight between a worker and soldier at Grey's ropewalk on the afternoon of 5 Mar. quickly became a small riot. That evening belligerent bands of both civilians and soldiers roamed the streets of Boston. The pent-up tension exploded about 9 P.M. when a beleaguered sentry in King St. near the State House called the main guard, led by Captain Preston, to his aid. When the swelling crowd pressed upon this detachment, the soldiers, upon the command of a person never identified, fired into the mob, killing 3 outright and wounding 2 mortally. A general uprising was averted only when Lt. Governor Hutchinson bowed to a demand by Sam Adams and withdrew the troops from the town to islands in the harbor. Preston and 6 of his men were arrested for murder by the civil authorities (6 Mar.). Two outstanding patriot lawyers, **John Adams** (p. 666) and **Josia Quincy** (1744–75), agreed to undertake the defense. At the trial (24–30 Oct.) Preston and 4 soldiers were acquitted, while 2 of the guard, found guilty of manslaughter, pleaded their clergy (were branded on the hand) and were released.

1771

LULL IN AGITATION.

Despite exploitation of the "Boston Massacre" by Sam Adams as well as Paul Revere's engraving of the incident, tension relaxed between colonies and mother country. Compacts against the importation and use of dutied tea remained the sole significant vestiges of conflict.

16 May. BATTLE OF ALAMANCE.

In interior North Carolina a group known as the **Regulators**, active as an organized body since 1768 (under the leadership of **Herman Husbands** [1724–95]), had taken the law into their own hands, protesting lack of representation for the Piedmont areas in the Assembly and charging extortion and oppression by the eastern part of the province. Increasing disorders led to the passage of the Johnston Bill (the "Bloody Act"), which made rioters guilty of treason (15 Jan. 1771). Early in May Gov. **William Tryon** (1729–88) led a force of 1,200 militiamen into the heart of the Regulator country. On 16 May he met and crushed some 2,000 Regulators (many of whom had no firearms) at Alamance Creek near Hillsboro. One insurgent leader, James Few, was executed on the battlefield (17 May); 12 others were found guilty of treason (17 June) and 6 executed. The other 6 as well as some 6,500 Piedmont settlers were obliged to take an oath of allegiance to the government. The incident revealed deep-seated sectional differences.

1772

9 June. BURNING OF THE "GAS-PEE." On the afternoon of 9 June the customs schooner *Gaspee* ran aground on Namquit Point, 7 mi. below Providence, while pursuing another vessel. After nightfall 8 boatloads of men from Providence led by merchant **John Brown** (1736–1803) attacked the schooner. Lt. Dudingston, in command, was wounded. After the officer and crew were set ashore, the attackers set the *Gaspee* afire. A royal proclamation (26 Aug.) offered a £500 reward for the discovery of the culprits. On 2 Sept. Gov. Wanton (R.I.), the vice-admiralty judge at Boston, and the chief justices of Mass., N.Y., and N.J. were named as Commissioners of Inquiry. Those identified by the Commissioners were to be sent to England for trial. Two sessions were held at Newport (Jan. and May 1773) but, in the face of open hostility by Rhode Islanders, neither turned up any tangible evidence. The Commission finally adjourned June 1773.

13 June. CRIPPLING THE POWER OF THE PURSE. The proposal to try the case of the *Gaspee* in England alarmed even the moderates. More threatening to local self-rule was the announcement by Gov. Hutchinson of Mass. (13 June) that henceforth he would receive his salary from the crown, followed in September by a similar announcement relative to the Mass. judges. Thus executive and judiciary were at a stroke rendered practically independent of the General Court's power of the purse.

2 Nov. NEW COMMITTEES OF COR-RESPONDENCE. Sam Adams issued a call (5 Oct.) to the towns to form associations to discuss this new threat. Over considerable opposition (led by John Hancock) within the patriot circle, he succeeded (28 Oct.) in having a call issued for a Boston town meeting, at which (2 Nov.) he secured the appointment of a 21-man standing committee of correspondence to communicate Boston's position to the other towns in the province and "to the World" with the request that the other towns reciprocate. James Otis was made chairman of the Boston committee. On 20 Nov. three radical statements were reported from the committee to the town meeting, endorsed, and sent on to the other towns: Sam Adams' "State of the Rights of the Colonists," a "List of Infringements and Violations of those Rights" by **Joseph Warren** (1741–75), and a "Letter of Correspondence" by Dr. **Benjamin Church** (1734–76), later proved to be a British informer. The appointment of town committees of correspondence continued into 1773.

1773

EXPANSION OF COMMITTEES OF CORRESPONDENCE. Radicals elsewhere hastened to adopt the Massachusetts system. The Virginia House of Burgesses (12 Mar.) appointed an 11-man standing committee for intercolonial correspondence, including Patrick Henry, Thomas Jefferson, and Richard Henry Lee. By 8 July R.I., Conn., N.H., and S.C., in addition, had formed provincial committees, and by Feb. 1774 all but N.C. and Pa. had taken action.

10 May. TEA ACT. By early 1773 the East India Co. was on the verge of bankruptcy, its stock down from 280 to 160 on the London exchange. With a vast surplus of 17 million lbs. of tea on hand in England, the company sought relief from a government predisposed to save it because of its valuable hold on India. A bill passed by the Commons (27 Apr.) provided for full remission (after 10 May) of all British duties on teas exported to the American colonies. The import tax of 3d. per lb. in America was retained, however. More important was the provision giving the Company (obliged up to this time to sell its tea at public auction in England) the right to sell tea directly to agents or consignees in the colonies. With the drawbacks on the British duties enabling it to cut the price of its tea the Company was now in a position, even with the handicap of the 3d. duty in America, to undersell there both the law-abiding colonial merchant who had bought tea through middlemen at higher prices and the colonial smuggler who bought his tea in Holland. The Company, authorized (Sept.) to send half a million lbs. of tea to Boston, New York, Philadelphia, and Charleston, consigned the tea to a picked group of merchants.

TERRORIZING THE TEA CONSIGNEES. The American opposition to the Tea Act centered not upon the duty (now 6 yrs. old) but upon the threat of monopoly. A mass meeting in Philadelphia (16 Oct.) condemned the Act and appointed a committee to demand resignation of the Philadelphia consignees. The latter bowed to this demand. A Boston town meeting (5–6 Nov.) endorsed the Philadelphia resolves but was unable to secure the resignation of the Boston consignees, among whom were 2 sons and a nephew of Gov. Hutchinson. In New York City, a broadside (10 Nov.) warned harbor pilots against guiding any tea ship up the harbor. A meeting of the Sons of Liberty (29 Nov.) branded tea importers enemies of America and pledged a boycott. The New York consignees resigned their commissions (1 Dec.).

16 Dec. BOSTON TEA PARTY. The *Dartmouth*, 1st of 3 tea ships, arrived in Boston harbor 27 Nov. Two great mass meetings (29–30 Nov.) resolved that the tea must be sent back to England without payment of any duty. This Hutchinson refused to permit. He gave orders to the harbor authorities to allow the tea ships to pass outward only upon presentation of a permit certifying that the tea duties had been paid, a position he reiterated on 16 Dec. On the next day, in keeping with a 20-day waiting period under customs regulations, the tea aboard the *Dartmouth* became liable to seizure for nonpayment of customs duties. On the evening of the 16th some 8,000 people assembled in and near Boston's Old South Church heard Capt. Rotch of the *Dartmouth* inform Sam Adams, chairman of the meeting, of the Governor's final refusal. Thereupon, at a signal from Adams, a disciplined group of men disguised as Mohawk Indians rushed to Griffin's Wharf, boarded the tea ships, and, working through the night, dumped all the tea (342 chests) into the harbor. No other property aboard was damaged.

22 Dec. TEA LANDED AT CHARLESTON. Charleston's tea ship, the *London,* arrived 2 Dec. A mass meeting held the next day demanded and secured the resignations of the tea consignees. After the lapse of the 20-day period the customs officials, without opposition, landed the tea for nonpayment of the duties upon it. The tea was stored in government warehouses and remained there until the revolutionary government auctioned it off to raise funds (July 1776).

Dec. HUTCHINSON LETTERS SCANDAL. Late in 1772 Benjamin Franklin, as London agent for the Massachusetts House of Representatives, sent Speaker Thomas Cushing the originals of 6 letters written (1767–69) by Thomas Hutchinson (then Chief Justice) and 4 by Andrew Oliver (province secretary) to Thomas Whately, a member of the Grenville and North ministries. The letters were given to Franklin to show him that false advice from America went far toward explaining the obnoxious acts of the British government. Franklin sent the letters to Cushing, warning him that they were not to be copied or published but merely shown in the original to individuals in the province. But in June 1773 Samuel Adams read the letters before a secret session of the House of Representatives and later had the letters copied and printed. The House petitioned the king for the removal of Hutchinson and Oliver from office. When this petition reached London the affair of the letters became a scandal. Whately was now dead, but his brother William accused a John Temple of having stolen and released the letters. The pair fought a duel (11 Dec.), and when that was inconclusive plans were made for a 2nd encounter. Learning of this, Franklin announced (25 Dec.) that he alone was responsible for sending the letters to Boston.

1774

30 Jan. FRANKLIN DISCIPLINED. On 11 Jan. a committee of the Privy Council began hearings on the Massachusetts petition. Franklin was granted a postponement. The questioning was resumed on 29 Jan., by which date the news of the Boston Tea Party had reached London. Franklin disdained replying to a virulent attack by Solicitor General Alexander Wedderburn, who denounced Franklin as a man without honor and a thief. The committee's report to the Privy Council that the petition was based on false charges was approved (7 Feb.). On 30 January, Franklin was informed that he had been dismissed from his office of Deputy Postmaster General for America. In Massachusetts the House voted in Feb., 92-8, to impeach Oliver for accepting a salary from the crown, but before the case was tried Hutchinson prorogued (30 Mar.), and then dissolved the General Court.

Mar.–Dec. FURTHER TEA DISORDERS. March saw further Boston disorders. When a reckless private consignee elected to land a cargo of tea secretly in New York, Sons of Liberty disguised themselves as Indians and dumped the tea into the harbor (22 Apr.) A tea cargo brought into Annapolis aboard the *Peggy Stewart* (14 Oct.) was destroyed by fire along with the ship (19 Oct.). Flames consumed a shipment of tea (22 Dec.) temporarily stored at Greenwich, N. J.

31 Mar., 20 May. COERCIVE ACTS. Parliament met (7 Mar.) in an angry

mood. Chatham and Edmund Burke failed to dissuade it from endorsing the king's personal wish that Massachusetts be punished for the Tea Party in particular and for her long intransigence in general. The 1st of the "Coercive" measures, the **Boston Port Bill**, passed the Commons 25 Mar. and received the royal assent 31 Mar. Effective 1 June, this act prohibited the loading or unloading of ships in any part of Boston Harbor. Exceptions were made for military stores and for shipments of food and fuel which obtained clearance from the customs officials henceforth to sit at Salem rather than Boston. The king was authorized to reopen the port to trade when the East India Co. and the customs had been compensated for the losses incurred by the Tea Party.

Two months later more comprehensive measures were enacted. The **Administration of Justice Act** (20 May) was designed to encourage crown officials in Massachusetts by protecting them from major suits before hostile provincial courts. Upon the sworn statement of the Governor that the act upon which an indictment for a capital offense was based had been committed in putting down a riot or in collecting revenue, and that a fair trial could not be obtained in Massachusetts, the trial could be transferred to Britain (the Provincial Council's assent to the move was stipulated).

Massachusetts Government Act (20 May) worked even more drastic changes, virtually annulling the Massachusetts charter. Effective 1 Aug., members of the Council, heretofore elected by the House of Representatives, were to be appointed by the king and hold office at royal pleasure. Effective 1 July, the attorney general, inferior judges, sheriffs, and justices of the peace became appointable and removable by the Governor. The Governor was also empowered to nominate the Chief Justice and superior judges for appointment by the king. Juries were to be summoned by the sheriff rather than elected by the people of the towns. Finally, in a move designed to deprive the radicals of their most effective medium, the town meeting, the act provided that meetings in addition to the annual election session could not be held without the prior written consent of the Governor and, if approved, must be confined to the agenda which he approved.

20 May. QUEBEC ACT, though not a part of the coercive program, was regarded by the colonists as one of the "Intolerable" measures. The act provided a permanent civil government for Canada, ruled since 1763 by makeshift means. In keeping with the French tradition of the inhabitants the administration was made highly centralized. Legislative authority was vested in a council appointed by the crown. Its acts were subject to the royal veto and all but purely local taxation was specifically reserved to the British Parliament. Civil cases were to be tried without benefit of a jury. Catholics were granted religious toleration and civil rights; their church's privileges confirmed. American colonists looked askance at all these features so opposed to their own traditions. But perhaps the most objectionable feature of the Quebec Act in their eyes was the extension of Canada's boundaries to the Ohio River, an area in which Virginia, Connecticut, and Massachusetts had claims.

2 June. QUARTERING ACT applied to *all* the colonies. It legalized the quartering of troops not only in taverns and deserted buildings (as had the 1765–6 acts) but also in **occupied dwellings.**

COLONIAL PROTEST. On 13 May Gen. Thomas Gage arrived in Boston to supplant Hutchinson as Governor. On the same day a Boston town meeting called for new economic sanctions against Britain to force repeal of the Coercive Acts. The 1st of many public calls for an intercolonial congress came from Providence (17 May). Philadelphia (21 May) and New York City (23 May) sidestepped Boston's appeal for immediate nonimportation in favor of a congress at which common measures binding all the colonies might be framed. Massachusetts yielded. On 17 June the House of Representatives suggested that a congress be held in Sept. at Philadelphia. Boston's Committee of Correspondence, nevertheless, drew up a Solemn League and Covenant (5 June) which bound its subscribers to end all business dealings with Britain and stop consumption of

British imports after 1 Oct. In the other colonies provincial congresses or county conventions proceeded to name delegates to Congress (15 June–25 Aug.). Only in Georgia was the attempt (10 Aug.) to name delegates defeated.

5 Sept.–26 Oct. 1ST CONTINENTAL CONGRESS. Twelve colonies sent 56 delegates to the Congress, which opened in Carpenters Hall. Among them were conservatives, such as **Joseph Galloway** (Pa., *c.*1731–1803), **James Duane** (N.Y., 1733–97), and **George Read** (Del., 1733–98) and radicals like the two Adamses (Mass.), **Christopher Gadsden** (S.C., 1724–1805) and **Patrick Henry** and **Richard Henry Lee** (Va.). **Peyton Randolph** (Va., *c.*1721–1775) was elected president, and a nondelegate, **Charles Thomson** (Pa., 1729–1824), named secretary. The delegates decided to vote by provincial units, each having one vote, and pledged themselves to secrecy. On 17 Sept. the radical delegates succeeded in having the **Suffolk Resolves** endorsed by the Congress. These resolutions, the work of Joseph Warren, had been adopted by a convention in Suffolk County, Mass. (9 Sept.), and carried posthaste to Philadelphia by Paul Revere. The resolutions (1) declared the Coercive Acts unconstitutional and hence not to be obeyed; (2) urged the people of Massachusetts to form a government to collect taxes and withhold them from the royal government until the repeal of the Coercive Acts; (3) advised the people to arm and form their own militia; and (4) recommended stringent economic sanctions against Britain.

28 Sept. GALLOWAY'S PLAN OF UNION. The conservatives attempted to offset the endorsement of the Suffolk Resolves by uniting behind Joseph Galloway's "Plan of a Proposed Union between Great Britain and the Colonies" to regulate the "general affairs of America," each colony continuing to govern its internal affairs. The central administration would consist of (1) a president-general appointed by the king and holding office at the king's pleasure with a veto over the acts of (2) a grand council, whose members were to be chosen for 3-yr. terms by the assemblies of each province. The president and council would constitute an "inferior and distinct branch of the British legislature." Measures dealing with America might originate either with this body or the British Parliament, the consent of the other being required for a measure to become law. By a vote of 6–5 this plan was defeated, and subsequently (22 Oct.) expunged from the minutes of Congress.

14 Oct. DECLARATION AND RESOLVES adopted by the Congress denounced the Coercive Acts and the Quebec Act as unjust, cruel, and unconstitutional, and criticized the revenue measures imposed since 1763, the extension of vice-admiralty jurisdiction, the dissolution of colonial assemblies, and the keeping of a standing army in the colonial towns in peacetime. Ten resolutions set forth the rights of the colonists, among them to "life, liberty and property," and, of the provincial legislatures, to the exclusive power of lawmaking "in all cases of taxation and internal polity," subject only to the royal veto. Thirteen Parliamentary acts since 1763 were declared to violate American rights and economic sanctions pledged until they were repealed.

18 Oct. CONTINENTAL ASSOCIATION, closely modeled upon a Virginia Association framed 1–6 Aug., constituted a pledge by the delegates that their provinces would (1) cease all importation from Britain effective 1 Dec.; (2) totally discontinue the slave trade 1 Dec.; (3) institute nonconsumption of British products and various foreign luxury products (1 Mar. 1775); (4) embargo all exports to Britain, Ireland, and the West Indies effective 1 Sept. 1775. Notable were those clauses establishing extralegal machinery for enforcement. A committee was to be elected in each county, town, and city to execute the Association. Violators were to be punished by publicity and boycott. On the higher level, any province which failed to keep the Association was to be boycotted. By Apr. 1775 the Association was in operation in 12 colonies; even Georgia adopted a modified version (23 Jan. 1775).

26 Oct. ADJOURNMENT OF CON- GRESS. After preparing an address to the king and to the British and American peoples, Congress adjourned, but (22 Oct.) resolved to meet again 10 May 1775 if by that date American grievances had not been redressed.

DOMINION THEORY. The delegates at Philadelphia had been influenced by the constitutional viewpoints of **James Wilson** (Pa., 1742–98) and young **Thomas Jefferson.** Wilson's *Considerations on the Nature and Extent of the Legislative Authority of the British Parliament* (17 Aug.) rejected Parliament's authority over the colonies in favor of allegiance to the king alone. Jefferson expressed a similar view in his *Summary View of the Rights of British America* (July), an appeal to George III to heed "liberal and expanded thought." After Congress adjourned John Adams expressed the "dominion theory" in his **Novanglus** letters (Dec. 1774–Apr. 1775) written to answer the Tory viewpoint of "Massachusettensis" (Daniel Leonard, p. 563). The colonies, Adams contended, were not part of the British realm and hence not subject to Parliament, for "Massachusetts is a realm, New York is a realm . . ." over which the king is sovereign.

WAR PREPARATIONS IN NEW ENGLAND. On 1 Sept. British troops from Boston marched out to Charlestown and Cambridge and seized cannon and powder belonging to the province. Thousands of militiamen flocked to Cambridge but hostilities did not break out. Gen. Gage set about fortifying Boston Neck (Sept.). On 7 Oct. the Massachusetts House, meeting in Salem in defiance of Gage, constituted itself a Provincial Congress, and named John Hancock to head a Committee of Safety empowered to call out the militia. Special groups within the militia (Minute Men) were to be ready for instant call. On 14 Dec., warned on the 13th by Paul Revere of a plan to garrison British troops at Portsmouth, N.H., a band led by **John Sullivan** (1740–95) broke into Ft. William and Mary in Portsmouth, overpowered the small garrison without inflicting or suffering casualties, and carried away arms and gunpowder.

1775

27 Feb. LORD NORTH'S CONCILIA-TION PLAN. The petitions and Declaration of Congress were laid before Parliament on 19 Jan. The next day Chatham moved an address from the Lords to the king requesting immediate removal of the troops in Boston but was defeated by a 3–1 margin. Later (1 Feb.) he introduced a plan of reconciliation which embraced (1) a recognition of the Continental Congress, (2) a pledge by Parliament that no revenue measures would be levied upon America without the consent of the provincial assemblies, (3) American recognition of the "supreme legislative authority and superintending power" of Parliament, and (4) a plan by which the Continental Congress would vote a revenue for the crown. This measure was also rejected by the Lords. A declaration by both Houses (9 Feb.) termed Massachusetts to be in rebellion. On 20 Feb. Lord North presented the ministerial plan for reconciliation which had George III's grudging consent. By its terms Parliament, with royal approval, would "forbear" to lay any but regulatory taxes upon any American colony which, through its own assembly, taxed itself to provide for the common defense and for the support of the civil government and judiciary within its own province. The Commons endorsed the plan 27 Feb.

30 Mar. NEW ENGLAND RESTRAINING ACT. On the same day (27 Feb.) a bill was introduced forbidding the New England colonies to trade with any nation but Britain and the British West Indies after 1 July and barring New Englanders from the North Atlantic fisheries after 20 July. Despite a brilliant speech by Burke (22 Mar.) the bill was passed and received the royal assent (30 Mar.). Soon afterward (13 Apr.) the provisions of the act were made to apply to N.J., Pa., Md., Va., and S.C., news of their ratification of the Continental Association having reached London.

CRISIS IN NEW ENGLAND. A 2nd Mass. Provincial Congress met at Cambridge (1 Feb.), and under the leadership of Hancock and Warren framed measures to prepare the colony for war.

On 26 Feb. British troops landed at Salem to seize military supplies, but were turned back without violence. On 23 Mar. Patrick Henry predicted in his famous "Liberty or Death" speech before the Va. House of Burgesses that news of the outbreak of hostilities in New England could be expected momentarily. He proved to be a good prophet. On 14 Apr. General Gage received a letter of 27 Jan. from Lord Dartmouth, Secretary of State for the Colonies, ordering him to use force if necessary to execute the Coercive and other acts, to strike at once, even if that meant bringing on hostilities, rather than permit the rebellious faction time to perfect their organization.

19 Apr. LEXINGTON AND CONCORD. Aware that Concord (21 mi. from Boston by road) was a major supply depot for the militia organized by the Provincial Congress, Gage decided to strike quickly. On 14 Apr. he relieved the Light Infantry and Grenadiers from guard duty and had boats brought ashore from the transports (15 Apr.). On 18 Apr. Lt. Col. Francis Smith received secret orders to lead a force of some 700 men to Concord and destroy the supplies there the next morning. About 10 P.M. the troops marched to the edge of the Common and began embarking in boats for the short row across the Charles River to Cambridge. The Boston Committee of Safety, learning of their destination, sent **Paul Revere** and **William Dawes** (1745–99) to alert the countryside. Revere reached Lexington (5 mi. from Concord) at midnight and warned Sam Adams and John Hancock, who were staying there. About 1 A.M. (19 Apr.) Revere, joined by Dawes and Dr. Samuel Prescott, left Lexington for Concord. On the way a British mounted patrol surprised them. Prescott escaped and got through to Concord; Dawes eluded the British but had to turn back; Revere was captured and brought back to Lexington before being released.

Smith's forces reached Lexington at dawn and found 70 armed Minute Men under Capt. **John Parker** (1729–75) drawn up on the Common. Upon the repeated commands of Major John Pitcairn, commanding the British advance units, the Americans had begun to file off (though without dropping their weapons as ordered) when a report from an unidentified firearm brought, without a command by Pitcairn, a series of volleys from the British platoons. Only a few shots were returned from the American ranks where 8 lay dead and 10 were wounded. Only one British soldier was wounded. Smith reformed his men and marched on to Concord, where he destroyed some gun carriages, entrenching tools, flour, and a liberty pole. Late in the morning the steadily swelling American forces attacked a British platoon at Concord's North Bridge, inflicting 14 casualties. Smith left Concord for the return march to Boston shortly after noon and soon found the countryside swarming with militiamen who assailed his column from all sides. Only the arrival of reinforcements when he reached Lexington saved him from complete disaster. The relentless attacks continued until the expeditionary force reached Charlestown and the protection of the guns of the men-of-war in the harbor. Total British casualties for the day: 73 killed, 174 wounded, 26 missing. Almost 4,000 American militia saw action during the day; of these 93 were dead, wounded, or missing. The provincial forces closed in on Boston and began a siege which was to last until Mar. 1776. On 23 Apr. the Provincial Congress authorized the raising of 13,600 men, made **Artemas Ward** (1727–1800) commander in chief, and appealed to the other colonies for aid. By 20 May R.I., Conn., and N.H. had voted to send 9,500 men to Cambridge, Ward's headquarters.

10 May. CAPTURE OF FORT TICONDEROGA. Late in April the Massachusetts Committee of Safety authorized **Benedict Arnold** (1741–1801) to raise 400 men in western Massachusetts and attack Fort Ticonderoga on Lake Champlain, a strategic post rich in artillery and other military supplies. On 6 May Arnold learned that **Ethan Allen** (1738–89) was raising a force at Castleton, Vt., for an attack on Ticonderoga. Arnold hurried to Castleton and claimed command but without success. Nevertheless he accompanied Allen and was

with the force of 83 men with which the latter crossed the lake (9 May). Early on the 10th the Americans surprised the British garrison of 42 men, which yielded, according to Allen, upon his demand "in the name of the great Jehovah and the Continental Congress." One wounded British soldier was the only casualty. On 12 May Crown Point north of Ticonderoga was also seized and St. John's, across the Canadian border, was occupied by Arnold on 16 May.

10 May. 2ND CONTINENTAL CONGRESS. New figures at the 2nd Continental Congress, convened in the State House (Independence Hall), Philadelphia, included Benjamin Franklin, John Hancock, James Wilson, and, later in the session, Thomas Jefferson. Missing were conservatives like Galloway (Pa.) and Isaac Low (N.Y.). **Peyton Randolph** and **Charles Thomson** were again chosen president and secretary, but on 24 May Randolph withdrew from the Congress and **John Hancock** was elected to succeed him. On 15 May Congress resolved to put the colonies in a state of defense and on 29 May adopted an address to the people of Canada asking them as "fellow-sufferers" to join with rather than against the 12 colonies (Georgia was not yet represented at the Congress officially).

31 May. MECKLENBURG COUNTY RESOLUTIONS, Adopted by a convention in Mecklenburg County, N.C., and sent to the North Carolina delegation at Philadelphia (but never presented to Congress), declared all laws and commissions deriving their authority from the king or Parliament to be annulled and the royal government of the provinces "wholly suspended" for the present. Henceforth all legislative and executive power within each colony would devolve upon the Provincial Congress. Within Mecklenburg County anyone accepting a royal commission was branded an enemy and ordered to be apprehended.

15 June. WASHINGTON NAMED CHIEF OF THE CONTINENTAL FORCES. On 10 June John Adams proposed that the Congress accept the forces besieging Boston as a Continental

Army and appoint a general, hinting strongly that this appointment should go to **George Washington.** On 14 June Congress resolved to raise 6 companies of riflemen in Pa., Md., and Va. to march to New England and named a 5-man committee to draft rules for the administration of the Continental Army. On 15 June Thomas Johnson (Md.) nominated Washington to be commander in chief; seconded by John Adams and carried by a unanimous vote. The next day Washington formally accepted the command and offered to serve without a salary. The general organizational plan for the army was adopted; **Artemas Ward, Charles Lee** (1731–82), **Philip Schuyler** (1733–1804), and **Israel Put-**

nam (1718–90) were appointed major generals (17 June). To support the army Congress voted (22 June) to issue $2 million in bills of credit with the "12 Confederated Colonies" pledged to share the burden of redemption in proportion to population.

17 June. BATTLE OF BUNKER HILL. During May both the British in Boston and the American forces surrounding the city built up their strength. Three major generals (**Sir William Howe, Sir Henry Clinton,** and **John Burgoyne**) arrived 25 May to assist Gage. By the middle of June the American strength was about 10,000 men. On 12 June Gage issued a proclamation which (1) imposed martial law; (2) declared the

Americans in arms and those aiding them to be rebels and traitors; and (3) offered pardon to all those who returned to their allegiance with two exceptions: Sam Adams and John Hancock.

On 15 June the Committee of Safety learned that Gage intended to occupy Dorchester Heights on 18 June. The Council of War decided upon an immediate countermove against the high ground on Charlestown peninsula overlooking Boston. After dark on 16 June 1,200 men moved onto the peninsula and began to construct a redoubt on **Breed's Hill**, nearer Boston than Bunker Hill, the site originally chosen for this fortification. The work party was discovered at dawn on the 17th and the American position was at once brought under fire from the British ships in the harbor. Gage decided on a frontal assault to dislodge the Americans, but had to await a favorable tide after noon for landing his troops on the peninsula. The immediate command of the assault force, 2,400 in number, was given to Gen. Howe. The main American position, the redoubt, was garrisoned by 1,600 men with 6 cannon, under the command of Col. **William Prescott** (1726–95). Twice Howe's troops, burdened by heavy packs and advancing in tight formation, moved up the hill only to be turned back by a murderous fire. Reinforced by Clinton for a 3rd assault, Howe had his men drop their packs and ordered a bayonet charge. This time the fire from the redoubt slackened as the supply of powder gave out and the British seized the hill. Bunker Hill was then rapidly assaulted and won as the American retreat became a near rout. Howe decided against pressing on toward Cambridge and stopped the pursuit at the base of the peninsula. The British had won the field but at a cost of 1,054 casualties, a high proportion of them officers. The American losses, almost all of which were suffered after the fall of the redoubt, numbered 100 dead (including Joseph Warren), 267 wounded, 30 taken prisoner. Two weeks after the battle Washington reached Cambridge and took formal command of an army of 14,500 on 3 July.

5 July. OLIVE BRANCH PETITION, adopted by Congress and written by **John Dickinson,** professed the attachment of the American people to George III, expressed their hope for the restoration of harmony, and begged the king to prevent further hostile actions against the colonies until a reconciliation was worked out. On 6 July Congress adopted another important resolution, written jointly by Jefferson and Dickinson, a "Declaration of the Causes and Necessities of Taking Up Arms," which rejected independence but asserted that Americans were ready to die rather than be enslaved. A significant phrase touched upon the possibility of receiving foreign aid against Britain. On 15 July Congress voted to waive the provisions of the Continental Association where war supplies were concerned and on 31 July rejected Lord North's plan for reconciliation. Before adjourning (2 Aug.) Congress assumed 2 additional functions of an independent government: the appointment of commissioners to negotiate treaties of peace with the Indian tribes (19 July), and the establishment of a Post Office Department with Benjamin Franklin as Post Master General (26 July).

28 Aug.–31 Dec. MONTGOMERY'S EXPEDITION AGAINST QUEBEC. On 27 June, having received word that Sir Guy Carleton, British commander in Canada, was recruiting a Canadian force for an invasion of New York, Congress authorized Gen. Philip Schuyler to seize any points in Canada vital to the security of the colonies. Schuyler assembled an expeditionary force at Ticonderoga and began his advance from there (28 Aug.) with about 1,000 men. Crossing into Canada, he laid siege to St. John's (6 Sept.), garrisoned by about 600 British and Canadian troops. Ill health forced Schuyler to leave the army (13 Sept.) in the command of Brig. Gen. **Richard Montgomery** (1738–75), to whom the garrison of St. John's capitulated (2 Nov.). Carleton withdrew the remnants of his small force toward Quebec, thereby uncovering Montreal, which the Americans occupied 13 Nov. Carleton was almost captured when his flotilla of 11 small ships surrendered (19 Nov.), but managed to escape to Quebec.

12 Sept.–31 Dec. ARNOLD'S EXPEDITION AGAINST QUEBEC. Benedict Arnold recruited a force of about 1,100 volunteers at Cambridge with Washington's permission and set out for Maine (12 Sept.). From Gardiner he moved inland to Fort Western (Augusta), from which base the main trek began (24 Sept.) through country few white men had seen. The difficult terrain and shortness of provisions led one of the expedition's 4 divisions to turn back (25 Oct.). With 650 men Arnold reached the St. Lawrence opposite Quebec (8 Nov.) and crossed the river on the 13th. On 3 Dec. he was joined by Montgomery with 300 men from Montreal. At 5 A.M., 31 Dec., a combined assault was launched against Quebec but ended in disaster. Montgomery was killed, Arnold wounded, almost 100 men killed or wounded, over 300 taken prisoner. With the remnants of his force Arnold maintained a weak cordon around the city throughout the winter.

12 Sept. CONGRESS RECONVENES. The presence of a delegation from Georgia made Congress for the 1st time representative of all 13 colonies. On 9 Nov. news arrived that George III had refused to receive the Olive Branch Petition and had (23 Aug.) proclaimed the American colonies to be in open rebellion. (On 7 Nov. the House of Commons received the Petition but a motion that it constitute a basis for reconciliation was defeated 83–33.) Congress answered the royal proclamation on 6 Dec., disclaiming any intention to deny the sovereignty of the king, but disavowing allegiance to Parliament. The breach was further widened on 23 Dec. when a royal proclamation was issued closing the colonies to all commerce effective 1 Mar. 1776.

13 Oct. CONGRESS AUTHORIZES A NAVY. On 2 Sept. Washington authorized Col. **John Glover** (Mass., 1732–97) to convert fishing vessels into armed ships. In Congress a committee was appointed (5 Oct.) to prepare a plan for intercepting 2 British ships known to have military stores aboard, and another (13 Oct.) authorized to fit out 2 ships of 10 guns each, an authorization increased to 4

ships (30 Oct.). Congress resolved to raise 2 battalions of marines (10 Nov.) and on 25 Nov. formally declared British vessels open to capture in retaliation for British raids on American coastal towns. "Rules for the Regulation of the Navy of the United Colonies" were adopted 28 Nov. and a Marine Committee appointed (14 Dec.) to carry them out. On 22 Dec. Congress commissioned officers for the 4 Continental ships, naming **Esek Hopkins** (R.I., 1718–1802) commodore. Congress authorized privateering (19 Mar. 1776) and issued letters of marque and reprisal (23 Mar.).

29 Nov. CONGRESS LOOKS ABROAD. Congress appointed a 5-man Committee of Correspondence with wide discretionary powers to get in contact with "our friends" abroad. An appropriation of $3,000 for the use of agents was voted 11 Dec. On the 12th the Committee wrote to **Arthur Lee** (1740–92), agent for Massachusetts in London, requesting him to ascertain the attitude of the European powers toward America. Later that month a French agent, Archard de Bonvouloir, appeared before Congress and gave informal assurances that France would welcome American ships and might offer material aid to the colonies.

11 Dec. HOSTILITIES IN THE SOUTH. On 7 Nov. Gov. Dunmore (Va.) placed his colony under martial law, established a base at Norfolk, and began recruiting a Loyalist army. By a promise of freedom to those slaves who deserted their masters (17 Nov.) he raised a Negro regiment, but forfeited the support of almost the entire planter class. On 11 Dec. Dunmore was decisively defeated by a mixed force of 900 Virginians and North Carolinians at Great Bridge. He evacuated Norfolk, but on 1 Jan. 1776 landed there again and destroyed much of the town by fire. In Feb. the Americans reoccupied and completed the destruction of the town, rendering it practically useless as a base of operations.

1776

MILITARY BALANCE SHEET. The Patriots were favored by (1) campaigning on their own ground, (2) widespread acquaintance with firearms, (3) a great leader in George Washington, (4) the superiority (in both range and accuracy) of the American rifle over the British smoothbore musket, and (5) a significant number of officers and men with military experience gained against the French or Indians. Grave disadvantages: (1) lack of training and discipline; (2) short-term enlistments; (3) shortage of ammunition, food, clothing, and medical supplies; (4) the hostility or active opposition of perhaps one third of the colonial populace; and (5) the lack of an efficient naval arm.

British commanders in America possessed the advantages of (1) a well-equipped, trained, and disciplined force; (2) support of the British navy in landing and transporting troops and guarding communication and supply lines at sea; (3) a rich war chest which permitted the hiring of foreign troops to supplement their own forces; and (4) the cooperation of American Loyalists. Weighing against these advantages were (1) the distance of the theater of war from Britain; (2) its vast extent and varied nature; (3) a reluctance to adapt tactics to American conditions; (4) a disinclination to mobilize the Loyalists as an effective force; and (5) a tendency on the part of military and political leaders to underestimate the opponent.

15 Jan. "COMMON SENSE." The first clarion call for independence was voiced by **Thomas Paine** (p. 761) in *Common Sense*, a pamphlet which appeared in Philadelphia. Paine attacked George III (the "Royal Brute") as chiefly responsible for the obnoxious measures against the colonies and flayed the monarchical form of government. His simple yet electric presentation converted thousands to the cause of independence.

Feb.–June. HOSTILITIES IN THE SOUTH. Gen. **Henry Clinton** arrived off Cape Fear, N.C. (Mar.), with a British expeditionary force. Clinton had originally planned to land in North Carolina and join forces with a Loyalist army, but scrapped these plans when he learned that the Loyalists had been crushed at the Battle of Moore's Creek Bridge near

Wilmington (27 Feb.). After being joined by troops from Britain under Gen. **Cornwallis** (3 May) Clinton decided to attack Charleston, S.C., where defense preparations were well under way when the British appeared on 1 June. On 4 June Gen. **Charles Lee** arrived from New York to take command of the defense. On 28 June, the wind finally being favorable, the British warships under Sir Peter Parker moved against the main point of the American defenses, a palmetto log fort (later named **Ft. Moultrie** for its defender) on Sullivan's Island. Parker's fire was returned by the defenders with great effect, forcing him to abandon the attack at nightfall, with all his ships damaged and over 200 casualties. In the fort 10 were dead, 21 wounded. Clinton's troops likewise failed to achieve their objectives on the 28th and had to be withdrawn. The British failure at Charleston ended active operations by them in that theater for over 2 years.

17 Mar. BRITISH EVACUATE BOSTON. On 24 Jan. Gen. **Henry Knox** (1750–1806) reached Cambridge with 43 cannon and 16 mortars hauled laboriously overland from Fort Ticonderoga. On 16 Feb. a Council of War drew up plans for the seizure of Dorchester Heights, from which point Boston and most of its harbor would be within range of Knox's artillery. Under cover of a heavy cannonade the occupation was carried out by 2,000 men under Gen. **John Thomas** (1724–76) during the night of 4–5 Mar. Gen. Howe, who had succeeded Gage as British commander (10 Oct. 1775), gathered 2,400 men for an assault on the unfinished works on the 5th but heavy rains that day and the next forestalled the attack. On 7 Mar. Howe decided to evacuate Boston. By the 17th all his troops, plus some 1,000 Loyalists, were embarked on the troopships in the harbor. On 26 Mar. the fleet left for Halifax.

Mar.–May. FRANCE DECIDES TO AID AMERICA. On 1 Mar. the French Foreign Minister, Count Vergennes, wrote to the Foreign Minister of Spain, Grimaldi, asking his reaction to joint secret measures to provide help for Britain's rebellious colonists. Spain showed herself receptive. Thereupon Louis XVI ordered

(2 May) that 1 million livres' worth of munitions be supplied the Americans through a fictitious company, Roderigue Hortalez et Cie., actually administered by secret agent **Pierre de Beaumarchais.** Charles III of Spain made a similar arrangement shortly afterward. From these sources the American armies were to receive over 80% of their gunpowder, to mention but one type of military supplies, throughout 1776–77. Meanwhile Congress, ignorant of these developments, voted (3 Mar.) to send **Silas Deane** (1737–89) to Europe to purchase war matériel. This action made inevitable the resolution of 6 Apr., an important forerunner of the Declaration of Independence, opening the ports of the colonies to the trade of all nations but Britain. Deane arrived in Paris 7 July.

Apr.–July. RETREAT FROM CANADA. On 1 Apr. Gen. **David Wooster** (1711–77) arrived at Quebec with reinforcements for the Northern Army and to take over command from Arnold, but gave way to General John Thomas on 1 May. Thomas had already decided to abandon the siege of Quebec when British reinforcements reached Carleton (6 May) and enabled the latter to turn an orderly American retreat into a rout. Thomas retreated to Chambly and died there of smallpox (2 June). Gen. Sullivan, who succeeded him, attempted a counterattack against **Three Rivers** (7 June) but was defeated. He then retreated to St. John's, was joined there by Arnold and the Montreal garrison, and continued his retreat to Ticonderoga early in July. With command of Lake Champlain the key to all strategy, both Arnold and Carleton set to work to collect and build ships for a fleet.

Apr.–July. MOVEMENT TOWARD INDEPENDENCE. By the spring of 1776 sentiment for a break with Britain was clearly in the ascendant. On 12 Apr. the North Carolina Convention empowered its delegates in Congress to vote for a declaration of independence. Virginia followed suit (15 May). With this authorization Richard Henry Lee offered a resolution (7 June) that the United Colonies "are, and of right ought to be, free and independent States." While,

after some debate (7–10 June) it was decided to postpone a decision on the resolution until 1 July, a committee consisting of **Jefferson, Franklin, John Adams, Robert Livingston,** and **Roger Sherman** was appointed (11 June) to prepare a Declaration of Independence. Within the committee it was decided that Jefferson should write the draft of the Declaration. With a few changes by Adams and Franklin it was this draft which was presented to Congress on 28 June. Jefferson said he "turned to neither book nor pamphlet" in preparing the paper. He drew upon the prevalent "natural rights" political philosophy and compiled a long list of despotic "abuses and usurpations" by George III (Parliament received no direct mention) in asserting the right and the duty of the American people to dissolve their tie to Britain and declare the United Colonies free and independent States.

2 July. CONGRESS VOTES INDEPENDENCE. On 1 July Congress sat as a committee to debate the Lee resolution. When brought to a vote in committee the motion was carried, though Pennsylvania and South Carolina were in the negative and Delaware's vote was divided. On 2 July Congress, now sitting in formal session rather than as a committee, took the final vote for independence (12 for, none against). South Carolina shifted her vote, the arrival of a third delegate from Delaware (Caesar Rodney) threw the vote of that colony for independence, and Pennsylvania swung to the affirmative when John Dickinson and Robert Morris purposely absented themselves on the 2nd. The New York delegation, advised (11 June) by the N.Y. Provincial Congress to take no action for or against independence, abstained from voting.

Congress next debated the form and content of the Declaration prepared by Jefferson (2–3 July), making several changes. On 4 July the amended Declaration of Independence was approved without dissent (New York again abstained) and signed by Hancock (president) and Thomson (secretary). Copies were prepared (5–6 July) to be dispatched to all the states. The Declaration was first publicly proclaimed in

Philadelphia (8 July) and was read before Washington and his troops in New
York City the next day. On 9 July also
the Provincial Congress of New York
voted to endorse the Declaration, a decision of which Congress was informed
15 July. Congress then resolved (19
July) to have the "Unanimous Declaration" engrossed on parchment for the
signature of the delegates. On 2 Aug.
most of the 55 signatures were affixed.
One "Signer," Matthew Thornton of
N.H. (not a member of Congress when
the Declaration was adopted), added his
name as late as Nov.

27 Aug. BATTLE OF LONG ISLAND.
After evacuating Boston, Howe planned
to use strategic New York City as his
base of operations. Anticipating Howe's
movement, Washington shifted his army
from Boston (21 Mar.–13 Apr.). On 2
July Howe landed unopposed on Staten
Island with about 10,000 men. His
brother, Admiral **Lord Richard Howe,**
arrived with a strong fleet and 150 transports 12 July. Other reinforcements
reached Staten Island throughout July
and early August until Gen. Howe had
a command of 32,000 men, about 9,000
of whom were German mercenaries. Be-

BATTLE OF LONG ISLAND

→ British main advance
--→ British minor advance
····→ Hessian advance
⇒ American retreat

▪ British
▨ Hessians
▯ Americans

Scale of Miles
0   1   2   3   4

tween 22–25 Aug. he landed about 20,000 troops on Long Island. On the evening of the 26th he led a wide flanking movement around the left of the forces under Gen. Putnam before Brooklyn. On the morning of the 27th Howe fell upon the rear of Sullivan's position, routed his forces and took the general prisoner. Gen. **William Alexander** (1726–83, who claimed the title "Lord Stirling") fought a gallant delaying action to protect the escape route of the American forces, but finally surrendered to the Hessian general, De Hesiter. Howe cautiously halted the pursuit at the breastworks on Brooklyn Heights after inflicting 1,500 casualties upon an American force of about 5,000 at a cost of less than 400 of his own men. On the 28th Howe began constructing siegeworks. Having decided against making a stand in Brooklyn, Washington during the night of 29–30 Aug. skillfully withdrew Putnam's entire force to Manhattan Island unknown to the British.

11 Sept. STATEN ISLAND PEACE CONFERENCE. On 3 May Gen. and Adm. Howe had been appointed Peace Commissioners by the King with powers to pardon and protect those Americans who returned to their true allegiance, but without authority to negotiate with any colony until all extralegal congresses and conventions had been dissolved. After the Battle of Long Island the Howes sent their prisoner, Gen. Sullivan, to Congress with a proposal that an informal peace conference be held. On 6 Sept. Congress appointed Franklin, John Adams, and Edmund Rutledge to confer with Lord Howe. The meeting took place on Staten Island and, although cordial, was fruitless. Howe's demand for a revocation of the Declaration of Independence as a necessary preliminary to negotiations for peace left no ground for further conversations.

15 Sept. BRITISH OCCUPY NEW YORK CITY. On 12 Sept. Washington decided to evacuate New York City rather than risk being trapped on lower Manhattan Island. The movement of his troops to hilly northern Manhattan was still under way when the British landed at Kips' Bay on the eastern side of the

island (15 Sept.) and almost cut off a large section of the American army. Washington retreated to Harlem Heights, repulsed the British there (16 Sept.), and prepared new fortifications. Howe decided against an assault upon the American works and the next 3 weeks saw a lull in activity, marred by the great fire which destroyed almost 300 buildings in New York City (21 Sept.) and by the execution of **Nathan Hale** (1755–76) as an American spy (22 Sept.).

26 Sept. CONGRESS APPOINTS A DIPLOMATIC COMMISSION. On 12 June Congress appointed a committee to prepare plans for treaties of commerce and amity with foreign nations. The report of this committee (17 Sept.) was, after some alteration, adopted. On 26 Sept. 3 commissioners were appointed to negotiate treaties with European nations: **Silas Deane** (already in Europe), **Franklin**, and **Jefferson**. Jefferson declined the appointment and **Arthur Lee** (also in Europe) was named in his place. Franklin joined Deane and Lee in Paris on 21 Dec. Two days later Congress authorized the commission to borrow up to £2 million.

11 Oct. BATTLE OF VALCOUR BAY. The fleets which Arnold and Carleton had been gathering on Lake Champlain finally came to grips on 11 Oct. Arnold had placed his 83-gun fleet in the channel between Valcour Island and the western shore of Lake Champlain. Carleton's 87-gun fleet, manned by experienced sailors in contrast to Arnold's motley crews, attacked, and in a 7-hr. battle crippled most of the American flotilla. That night Arnold's remaining ships slipped by the British. Another engagement at **Split Rock** (13 Oct.) resulted in the complete destruction of the American flotilla as a fighting force. Carleton occupied Crown Point but then decided winter was too near at hand for a siege of Ticonderoga. He abandoned Crown Point (3 Nov.) and drew his forces back into Canada.

28 Oct. BATTLE OF WHITE PLAINS. In an effort to outflank Washington's strong position in northern Manhattan, Howe embarked the bulk of his army

(12 Oct.), sailed up the East River and Long Island Sound, and landed on the mainland (13 Oct.) at Pell's Point. To meet this threat to his rear Washington evacuated his main force from Manhattan (23 Oct.) and moved northward to White Plains, leaving a strong garrison at Ft. Washington on the island. Howe moved against Washington (28 Oct.) and, in a sharp battle in which he suffered over 300 casualties and inflicted about 200, captured a key hill position. While Howe awaited reinforcements, Washington again slipped away (1 Nov.) to a new line 5 mi. north at North Castle. On 16 Nov. Howe sent 13,000 troops against Ft. Washington, which capitulated. The British lost 458 in killed or wounded but took 2,818 prisoners. On 18 Nov. Howe sent Cornwallis across the Hudson with 4,500 men for an assault upon Ft. Lee. Gen. Greene evacuated the fort but was forced to abandon badly needed military supplies.

18 Nov.–20 Dec. RETREAT ACROSS NEW JERSEY. Greene and Washington joined forces at Hackensack and, with Cornwallis at their heels, retreated toward the Delaware River. After repeated commands from Washington, Gen. Charles Lee led the troops at North Castle across the Hudson (2 Dec.) and into Jersey. Washington crossed the Delaware into Pennsylvania 11 Dec. and 2 days later Lee was captured at Basking Ridge, N.J. by a British patrol. Sullivan took command of his troops on 20 Dec. joined Washington in Pennsylvania. Congress, fearing a British attack on Philadelphia, fled from that city to Baltimore (12 Dec.) after vesting Washington with virtually dictatorial powers.

26 Dec. COUP AT TRENTON. Howe sent the bulk of his army back to winter quarters in New York (13 Dec.) but left garrisons at Trenton, Princeton, Bordentown, Perth Amboy, and New Brunswick. Informed that the Hessian garrison (c.1,400) at Trenton under Col. Johann Rall was ill-prepared to meet attack, Washington decided on an assault by 3 forces, only one of which—the main body of 2,400 under Washington himself—succeeded in crossing the ice-choked Delaware. Washington crossed 9 mi. north of the town, split his force into

two divisions, and at 8 A.M. drove into Trenton from the north and northeast. The surprise was complete. After an hour of confused street fighting in which Rall was mortally wounded, the garrison surrendered. 918 of the Hessians were captured, 30 killed; while Washington suffered only 5 casualties. Washington recrossed into Pennsylvania with his prisoners and then once again crossed to the Jersey side and reoccupied Trenton (30–31 Dec.).

1777

3 Jan. COUP AT PRINCETON. Howe reacted to the news of the Trenton disaster with unusual celerity. On 1 Jan. he sent Gen. James Grant from New Brunswick toward Trenton and from New York dispatched a large force under Cornwallis to join Grant at Princeton. On 2 Jan. the British made contact with Washington's army of 5,200 men east of Trenton, but Cornwallis elected to wait until the next day for the attack which would "bag the fox." Leaving behind only enough men to give the illusion of an occupied camp, Washington stole around Cornwallis' flank that night and by dawn (3 Jan.) was close to Princeton. Near the town Patriot units under Gen. **Hugh Mercer** (c.1725–77) clashed with a British column under Col. Mawhood marching to join Cornwallis. Mercer was killed and the American vanguard routed. Then Washington appeared with the main body and drove the British back with heavy losses toward New Brunswick. Cornwallis, hearing the sounds of battle to his rear, also fell back to protect the supply depot there. Washington drew his tired troops off to the northeast and soon established winter quarters in the hills around Morristown (6 Jan.). His victories had cleared all but easternmost New Jersey of the enemy and had an incalculable effect in restoring the shattered-Patriot morale.

12 Mar. CONGRESS RECONVENES IN PHILADELPHIA. Congress returned to Philadelphia (4 Mar.), where it considered measures to obtain foreign aid. While at Baltimore Congress had resolved (30 Dec. 1776) to send commissioners to Austria, Prussia, Spain, and Tuscany. The commissioner to Spain was to be authorized to offer British-held Pensacola in Florida in return for a declaration of war by Spain against Britain. Similarly, the commissioners already in France were authorized to offer access to the Newfoundland fishing grounds and territorial gains as well if France would enter the war. On 1 Jan. Franklin was appointed to the Spanish in addition to the French mission, but on 1 May **Arthur Lee** was named to represent the U.S. at the Spanish court in his place. On 7 May **Ralph Izard** (1742–1804) was appointed commissioner to the Grand Duke of Tuscany, and on 9 May the Vienna and Berlin posts were assigned to **William Lee** (1739–95). Meanwhile, the Committee of Secret Correspondence had been reconstituted by Congress as the Committee for Foreign Affairs (17 Apr.).

14 June. STARS AND STRIPES. Congress resolved that the flag of the U.S. be "thirteen stripes alternate red and white, that the Union be thirteen stars white in a blue field. . . ."

RECRUITING FOREIGN OFFICERS. Congress had authorized Silas Deane to secure several European military experts for service in America, and by Mar. was swamped by applicants appearing in Philadelphia to claim commissions. On 13 Mar. Congress ordered that its agents send in the future only persons with the highest qualifications, including a knowledge of English. On 27 July two of the most famous foreign officers of the Revolution reached Philadelphia, the 20-yr.-old **Marquis de Lafayette** (1757–1834) and the veteran "Baron" **Johann de Kalb** (1721–80). Lafayette, who volunteered to serve without pay, was commissioned a maj. gen. (31 July), as was De Kalb (15 Sept.). Foremost among the other foreign officers were **Thaddeus Kosciusko** (1746–1817), commissioned col. of engineers (18 Oct. 1776), and **Baron Friedrich Wilhelm von Steuben** (1730–94), appointed inspector general 5 May 1778.

BRITISH PLAN KNOCKOUT BLOW. On 28 Feb. Gen. John Burgoyne, back in England, submitted to Lord George Germain, Secretary of State for the Colonies, his plan for a 3-pronged attack to isolate New England: (1) a main army of not less than 8,000 regulars to push southward down Lake Champlain and the upper Hudson; (2) an auxiliary force to operate from Oswego through the Mohawk Valley; (3) a strong force under Howe to move up the Hudson. Germain approved the plan; Burgoyne was given command of the main army to move from Canada; but Germain also approved (3 Mar.) Howe's plan for an attack on Philadelphia (by sea according to Howe's plan of 2 Apr.), hoping Howe could be finished in time to help Burgoyne.

23 July–26 Sept. HOWE'S CAMPAIGN AGAINST PHILADELPHIA. On 23 July Howe embarked from New York with 15,000 troops, sailed up Chesapeake Bay, and landed at Head of Elk on 25 Aug. Washington, with about 10,500 men, took up a defensive position barring the way to Philadelphia on the eastern side of **Brandywine Creek.** Howe attacked on 11 Sept., using a carefully planned flanking movement. The Germans under Gen. William von Knyphausen attacked the American center at Chad's Ford; Cornwallis routed Sullivan on the American right. Greene managed to turn the flight into an orderly if hard-pressed retreat, but the whole American army was forced back toward Philadelphia. Casualties: American, *c.*1,000; British, 576. The British scored again (21 Sept.), when a bayonet attack in the early hours of the morning routed a force under Gen. **Anthony Wayne** (1745–96) at Paoli. On 26 Sept. Howe occupied Philadelphia. Congress fled (19 Sept.) to Lancaster and then to York (30 Sept.).

4 Oct. BATTLE OF GERMANTOWN. On the night of 3 Oct. Washington began an intricate movement toward Howe's main encampment at Germantown. The battle began before dawn on the 4th with the Americans winning important initial successes. But the coordinated attack which Washington had planned did not materialize. Detachments became lost in a heavy fog and at one point American troops fired on each other. A retreat by several brigades forced the American detachments which had penetrated into the streets of Germantown to fall back. Again Greene distinguished himself in directing a stubborn retreat. Washington suffered almost 700 casualties and had 400 of his men taken prisoner against British losses of 534. The 400-man garrison of Ft. Mercer (on the Delaware below Philadelphia) repelled an attack by 1,600 Hessians (22 Oct.), but was forced to evacuate (20 Nov.) in the face of an assault by 5,000 men under Cornwallis. By 23 Nov. the Delaware as far north as Philadelphia was clear for British vessels. Washington meanwhile had withdrawn northwestward from Germantown and took up winter quarters at **Valley Forge** (mid-Dec.).

17 June–17 Oct. NORTHERN CAMPAIGN: BURGOYNE AND ST. LEGER. On 17 June, with a force of about 7,700 British and German troops, Canadians and Indians, Burgoyne left St. John's with a huge baggage train and 138 pieces of artillery. By 30 June his army had reached Ft. Ticonderoga commanded by Gen. **Arthur St. Clair** (1736–1818). On 2 July the British seized Mount Defiance, a strategic height south of the fort which the Americans had carelessly left unfortified and by 5 July had hauled cannon to the top, rendering the fort untenable. That night St. Clair evacuated, abandoning substantial supplies. Burgoyne, in pursuit, took Skenesborough and Ft. Anne 6–7 July. Thereafter, his advance was slowed by the forested terrain and trees felled by Schuyler's forces. On 4 Aug. Schuyler was replaced in command by **Horatio Gates** (1727–1805).

Meanwhile a British force of 1,800, mostly Loyalists and Indians, advanced eastward from Oswego on Lake Ontario under the command of Col. **Barry St. Leger.** On 3 Aug. St. Leger reached and besieged Ft. Stanwix on the Mohawk River, garrisoned by 750 men under Col. **Peter Gansevoort** (1749–1812). On 6 August 800 militiamen marching to the fort's relief under Gen. **Nicholas Herkimer** (1728–77) were caught in ambush at **Oriskany** by a force of Indians and Loyalists led by the Mohawk chief **Joseph Brant** (1742–1807). Herkimer, badly wounded at the outset of the battle, drew his men together on high ground and fought back fiercely. The Indians,

alarmed by firing from Stanwix, where the garrison made a sortie against the British camp, broke off the engagement. Herkimer retreated eastward with less than half his original strength. Schuyler now sent Arnold with a force of 1,000 volunteers to Gansevoort's aid. By a ruse the Indians were frightened off, and St. Leger abandoned the siege of Stanwix and retreated to Oswego (22 Aug.).

By early Aug. Burgoyne's supply problem became alarming. Learning that the Americans had quantities of military stores at Bennington, he detached some 700 men under the command of Lt. Col. Baum to capture them (11 Aug.). At **Bennington** were some 2,600 American troops under Gen. **John Stark** (1728–1822), most of them raw militiamen now taking up arms in increasing numbers as news of atrocities by Burgoyne's Indians (particularly the murder of Jane McCrea on 27 July) spread through New England. Stark launched an attack on Baum on 16 Aug. Baum was mortally wounded and, except for the Indians (most of whom fled), almost his entire force killed or taken prisoner. The reinforcements for Baum under Col. Breymann arrived too late and were in turn attacked by Stark, now reinforced by Seth Warner (1743–84) leading 400 veteran Massachusetts troops. Breymann, with the loss of a third of his 650 men, was forced to fall back on Burgoyne.

Burgoyne resolved to press on to Albany, crossed to the west side of the Hudson (13 Sept.), and moved against the entrenched position Gates had prepared on Bemis Heights. Gates, reinforced, now had over 6,000 men, with militiamen arriving daily. On 19 Sept. Burgoyne attempted to gain high ground on the American left but was checked short of his goal at **Freeman's Farm** by Gen. **Daniel Morgan** (1736–1802) and Col. **Henry Dearborn.** British casualties, c.600; American, 300. On 3 Oct. Gen. Clinton, commanding British troops in New York City, moved up the Hudson, taking Fts. Clinton and Montgomery on the 6th. Receiving an urgent appeal for help from Burgoyne on the 9th, he sent the fleet further up the Hudson to Esopus (Kingston), which the British burned (16 Oct.), but felt too insecure to push

CAMPAIGNS IN
NEW YORK STATE

Scale of Miles
0   10   20   30   40   50

on to Albany, and returned to New York for reinforcements.

Meanwhile Burgoyne had become desperate. On 7 Oct. he ventured out of his lines toward the American left again with 1,650 troops. A countermove by Gates, led by Morgan and Gen. Ebenezer Learned, repulsed the British. Then Benedict Arnold, though without a command that day, led a fierce assault which threw Burgoyne back upon **Bemis Heights.** The Americans continued to press on and carried the Breymann redoubt. That night, weakened by the day's toll of close to 600 (American casualties, *c.*150), Burgoyne withdrew northeastward about 1 mi. and on 8 Oct. retreated to Saratoga. On 13 Oct., surrounded by a force now 3 times his own, he asked for a cessation of hostilities. On 17 Oct., by the terms of the **"Convention of Saratoga,"** the 5,700 men constituting the remnants of Burgoyne's army laid down their arms. They were to be marched to Boston, shipped back to England, and pledged not to serve again in the war against America.

25 Sept.–23 Dec. "CONWAY CABAL." As a result of Congressional antagonism to the military direction of the war **Gates** was named (27 Nov.) president of the Board of War and **Thomas Conway,** previously an Irish colonel in the French army, inspector general (14 Dec.). Earlier Conway had written Congress (25 Sept.) disparaging his own commanding officer, Lord Stirling, and on 11 Oct. had sent Gates a letter attacking Washington. The rebuke by Washington (9 Nov.) forced Gates to disavow any connection with the affair. Doubt exists whether there was in fact any organized plot to supplant Washington. Conway, who resigned from the army, was wounded in the summer of 1778 in a duel with Gen. John Cadwalader, and later apologized to Washington.

15 Nov. ARTICLES OF CONFEDERATION. When Richard Henry Lee offered his resolution for independence (7 June 1776), he also proposed that "a plan of confederation be prepared and transmitted to the respective colonies for their consideration and approbation." Congress appointed a committee headed by John Dickinson (12 June). On 12 July 1776 the committee's report, "Articles of Confederation and Perpetual Union," was presented to Congress. For over a year the articles were debated intermittently. On 7 Oct. 1777 a vote was finally taken on the question of voting in the Congress under the Articles, 1 vote for each state winning acceptance. On 14 Oct. the apportionment of the expenses of the central government was settled on a basis of surveyed land in each state. Finally, on 15 Nov., the 13 articles were formally adopted and on 17 Nov. sent to each state for prompt ratification. Complete ratification did not occur until 1 Mar. 1781.

17 Dec. FRANCE AND U.S. INDEPENDENCE. When Lord North heard the news of Burgoyne's surrender (early Dec.) he began preparing a new offer of reconciliation. A British agent, Paul Wentworth, was sent to Paris to confer with Deane and Franklin, but found they stood squarely for full independence (15 Dec.–6 Jan. 1778). Fearful that the Americans might come to terms with the British, the French informed the American envoys (17 Dec.) that the king's council had decided to recognize the independence of the U.S.

1778

6 Feb. FRANCO-AMERICAN ALLIANCE. After an unsuccessful attempt by the French to induce Spain to join in a tripartite pact against Britain, Count Vergennes informed the American commissioners (8 Jan.) that France was prepared to enter into an alliance with the U.S. Two treaties resulted from the negotiations of the next 4 weeks: (1) a treaty of amity and commerce, under which each nation was granted most-favored-nation status by the other; and (2) a treaty of alliance to become effective if and when war broke out between France and Britain. Art. II of the latter declared its aim was to "maintain effectually the liberty, Sovereignty, and independence" of the U.S. The U.S. was given a free hand to conquer Canada and Bermuda; France, to seize the British West Indies, with mutual territorial guarantees and an agreement that neither would conclude a truce or peace with Britain without the other's consent. On 20 Mar. Franklin, Deane, and Lee were officially received by Louis XVI and within the week Conrad Gérard was named minister to the U.S. Congress received the news on 2 May, ratified the treaties unanimously on the 4th, voted (11 Sept.) to replace the commission in France by a minister, and elected (14 Sept.) Franklin to that post. Meanwhile, on 17 June a clash between French and British naval forces occurred; the two nations were at war.

12 Apr. CARLISLE PEACE COMMISSION. To forestall U.S. ratification of the French alliance, Lord North introduced (17 Feb.) in Commons a series of bills for effecting reconciliation with America, proposing (1) repeal of the Tea and Coercive Acts; (2) a pledge that Parliament would impose no revenue taxes upon the American colonies; (3) appointment of a peace commission with powers to negotiate with Congress, and, if necessary, to agree to suspension of all acts passed since 1763. The bills passed the Commons 16 Mar. The Earl of Carlisle was appointed to head the Commissioners (22 Feb.). William Eden, a member of the Board of Trade; George Johnstone, former Governor of West Florida; and the Howe brothers, already in America, were the other members of the group (commissioned 12 Apr.). When Carlisle, Eden, and Johnstone reached Philadelphia (6 June), they learned Congress was cold to conciliation and had resolved (22 Apr.) that any man or group who came to terms with the commission was to be branded an enemy of the U.S. To a request (9 June) for a conference, Congress replied (17 June) that the only negotiations it would undertake would be for the withdrawal of British forces and the recognition of U.S. independence. The British evacuation of Philadelphia by Clinton (who succeeded Howe 8 May) forced the commissioners to move to New York. Before leaving Philadelphia, however, George Johnstone tried to bribe Congressmen **Joseph Reed** (1741–85), **Robert Morris** (p. 756), and **Francis Dana** (1743–1811). His attempt failed and its revelation led him to resign from the commission (26 Aug.). On 3 Oct. Carlisle and Eden appealed to the people over the head of Congress in a Manifesto and Proclamation which threatened a war of great destructiveness if the Americans did not abandon their French allies and make peace with Britain. On 27 Nov. the commissioners left New York for England, their mission a complete failure.

23 Apr. JOHN PAUL JONES' RAIDS. The little squadron which Congress had put under Esek Hopkins' command late in 1775 was too weak to operate as a fleet. A successful raid was carried out by Hopkins on Nassau (Mar. 1776), but thereafter the U.S. navy generally operated in single units whenever a captain could slip out to sea through the British cordon off the American coast. American privateers proved much more vexing to the British. The House of Commons was informed (Feb. 1778) that they had taken 733 prizes, but even their numbers declined from 143 in 1775 to a low of 73 in 1777. The revival of American naval operations in 1778 (115 privateers were in action in that year) was highlighted by the exploits of Capt. **John Paul Jones** (p. 736) aboard the *Ranger*. Jones left Portsmouth, N.H., 2 Nov. 1777 and, after refitting at Nantes and Brest, sailed into the Irish Sea in Apr. He took two prizes (14–17 Apr.) and then on 23 Apr. landed at Whitehaven, England, spiked the guns of the fort, and set fire to a ship at anchor. That same evening he sailed to St. Mary's Island in Solway Firth, landing with the intention of kidnaping the Earl of Selkirk, who, in fact, was not on the island. Jones then crossed to the coast of northern Ireland, where, at Carrickfergus, he forced the British sloop *Drake* to strike after an hour's battle (24 Apr.) and took it to Brest (8 May).

28 June. BATTLE OF MONMOUTH. The agony at Valley Forge ended for Washington on 19 June. Though the shrinking American army, desperately short of food, clothing, and military supplies, was but 20 mi. from Philadelphia, Howe made no effort to disperse it during the winter. He was relieved by Clinton (8 May), who, concerned over reports of a French fleet heading for America, evacuated Philadelphia (18

June) and set out across New Jersey toward New York City. Washington broke camp at Valley Forge on 19 June and started in pursuit. Gen. Charles Lee (who had been exchanged and had returned to the army 20 May) was given command of a strong advance corps (26 June) with orders to press home at the first opportunity an attack on Clinton's extended column. On the 28th Lee attacked near Monmouth Court House. His orders to Lafayette and Wayne were vague and contradictory and early advantages were not followed up. As British reinforcements arrived, Lee suddenly ordered a retreat, a move which encouraged Clinton to engage his main army. Washington's arrival checked the flight of Lee's command and the discipline which Von Steuben had instilled at Valley Forge showed its worth when the Americans beat back Clinton's repeated attacks. The British, who stole away during the night, marched to Sandy Hook and boarded transports which took them to New York. Both sides had suffered about 350 casualties at Monmouth. After a court-martial suspended Lee from the service for disobedience and misbehavior (4 July), Washington led his army northward, crossed the Hudson, and on 30 July took up a position at White Plains above New York City.

3 July and 11 Nov. WYOMING AND CHERRY VALLEY MASSACRES. On 3 July Sir John Butler led Loyalists and Indians in a sweep through Pennsylvania's Wyoming Valley. In New York a series of raids planned by Sir John Johnson and Guy Johnson and executed by Butler's Rangers and Brant's Indians terrorized the outlying settlements from May through the culminating attack on Cherry Valley (11 Nov.) in which some 40 survivors were massacred after they had surrendered.

4 July. CLARK'S CAPTURE OF KASKASKIA. In the fall of 1777 **George Rogers Clark** (1752–1818), a militia leader at Harrodsburg, Ky., proposed to the Virginia authorities an expedition against the British, Indians, and Loyalists who, under the command of Col. Henry Hamilton (the "Hair Buyer"), Lt. Governor at Detroit, were raiding

western settlements. Commissioned lt. col. by Gov. Patrick Henry, Clark with 175 men moved (May) to the Ohio River, sailed down it almost to the Mississippi, and then struck northwestward. On 4 July he occupied Kaskaskia and, with the support of the French inhabitants, the other posts in the area within the next 6 weeks, organizing the territory as part of Virginia. On 17 Dec. Hamilton recaptured Vincennes with a force, more than half of which were Indians, numbering over 500. Clark gathered about 150 men at Kaskaskia, set out (6 Feb. 1779) across inundated plains for Vincennes, reached there 23 Feb., and by various ruses caused Hamilton's Indians to desert and Hamilton himself to surrender (25 Feb.).

29 July–29 Aug. FRANCO-AMERICAN ATTACK ON NEWPORT. On 11 July a French fleet of 17 ships under the Comte d'Estaing arrived off New York harbor, but the size of his ships made a crossing of the bar so hazardous that the plan of a sea-land assault on New York was abandoned (22 July) in favor of a joint operation against a British garrison of 3,000 men at Newport, R.I. D'Estaing arrived off that town on 29 July but it was 8 Aug. before the American land forces under Gen. Sullivan were grouped before Newport in sufficient numbers to begin the operation, by which date Howe's reinforced fleet was on its way to aid the garrison. D'Estaing moved out to meet Howe on the 10th and a decisive battle loomed when a fierce storm (11 Aug.) scattered both fleets. Without naval support Sullivan had to withdraw from Newport after an attack on the garrison (29 Aug.) in which each side suffered about 250 casualties. D'Estaing left Boston (where he had gone for repairs) for the West Indies (4 Nov.).

29 Dec. FALL OF SAVANNAH. Clinton now shifted British operations to the South, anticipating aid from large numbers of Loyalists. On 25 Nov. a detachment of 3,500 men embarked for Georgia under the command of Lt. Col. Campbell, landed near Savannah (29 Dec.), crushed 1,000 militia under Gen. **Robert Howe** (1732–86), and occupied the town.

1779

6 Jan.–19 June. BRITISH PROG-RESS IN THE SOUTH. On 6 Jan. Ft. Sunbury fell to a force under Gen. Augustine Prevost which pushed north-ward from Florida; Augusta was seized by Campbell 29 Jan. The Americans were heartened by Moultrie's successful defense of **Port Royal** (3 Feb.) and by Col. **Andrew Pickens'** victory over a Loyalist brigade at **Kettle Creek** (14 Feb.), both in South Carolina. However, an attempt to recapture Augusta from the British failed when Gen. **John Ashe** (*c.*1720–81) lost over 350 men and in-flicted less than 20 casualties at **Briar Creek** (3 Mar.). When Gen. **Benjamin Lincoln** (1733–1810) with a corps of Continental troops detached by Wash-ington moved inland for another attempt against Augusta (23 Apr.), Prevost struck northward along the coast and reached Charleston (12 May), but pulled back. Lincoln attacked the Brit-ish rear at **Stono Ferry** (19 June), but lost 300 men to 130 enemy casualties and failed to prevent Prevost from re-gaining Savannah. In isolated actions in the South during the spring a force of North Carolina and Virginia troops led by Col. **Evan Shelby** (1719–94) struck successfully at Chickamauga Indian vil-lages in Tennessee (Apr.), while the British captured and set fire to Ports-mouth and Norfolk, Va. (10 May).

31 May–15 Sept. WAR IN THE NORTH. On 31 May Clinton led 6,000 men up the Hudson and seized (1 June) 2 uncompleted American forts at Stony Point and Verplanck's Point. An-other force under William Tryon, Royal Governor of New York, was sent to rav-age (5–11 July) the Connecticut shore of Long Island Sound. On 15 July Gen. **Anthony Wayne** led 1,200 men in a night bayonet attack on **Stony Point** which bagged all but 1 man of the garrison of almost 700 at a cost of 15 killed, 83 wounded. Wayne dismantled the fort and evacuated it 18 July. While Clin-ton's attention was thus turned north-ward, Maj. **Harry Lee** (1756–1818) drove the British from their last major outpost in New Jersey, **Paulus Hook**, and took over 150 prisoners (19 Aug.).

More significant was the expedition led by Gens. **John Sullivan** and **James Clinton** (1736–1812) against the Loyal-ists and Indians who were ravaging the frontier settlements of Pennsylvania and New York. At Newtown (Elmira) a force of 1,500 Loyalists and Indians led by Sir **John Johnson** and **Joseph Brant** were defeated (29 Aug.). From Newtown, Sullivan moved northwestward meeting but scattered resistance. He destroyed 40 Seneca and Cayuga villages with their orchards and food plots and some 160,-000 bushels of beans and maize. Sullivan turned back (15 Sept.) after penetrating as far as Geneseo (without pressing on to Ft. Niagara). His expedition had ma-terially reduced the offensive threat from the Iroquois.

21 June. SPAIN ENTERS THE WAR. Fearful for her American possessions, Spain opposed American independence. When Britain refused to cede Gibraltar to her as the price of her neutrality or mediation, Spain delivered an ultimatum (3 Apr. 1779), which, if accepted, would have sacrificed U.S. interests. On 12 April the secret Convention of Aran-juez between France and Spain pro-vided for the entrance of the latter into the war if the ultimatum was rejected. When the British turned it down, Span-ish and French fleets began joint opera-tions in May. On 21 June Spain formally declared war on Great Britain, but re-fused to recognize U.S. independence or to pledge herself to fight on, as the French had, until that independence was secured. On 27 Sept. Congress appointed its president, **John Jay** (p. 734), as agent to Spain, but he was singularly unsuc-cessful in obtaining recognition, an alli-ance, or a substantial loan (he was able to borrow only $174,011) during his stay at Madrid (Jan. 1780–May 1782).

14 Aug. CONGRESSIONAL PEACE TERMS. On 15 Feb. a report of a committee of Congress to propose peace terms (presented 23 Feb.) set forth as minimum demands: independence, cer-tain minimum boundaries, complete Brit-ish evacuation of U.S. territory, rights to the fisheries, and free navigation of the Mississippi. Most of these terms were quickly approved by Congress, but those relating to the fisheries and the Mississippi occasioned long debate along sectional lines. Finally, on 14 Aug., Congress agreed on the instructions which were to guide the U.S. peace negotiator (still to be appointed). In these instructions the fisheries claim was removed from the minimum list, but that concerning the navigation of the Mississippi retained. On 27 Sept., **John Adams**, who had replaced Silas Deane as one of the commissioners in Paris (8 Apr. 1778), was named to negotiate the peace treaty with Britain.

23 Sept. "BONHOMME RICHARD" AND "SERAPIS." In Jan. Jones (in France) was given command of a decrepit French ship, the *Duc de Duras.* He refitted it, crowded 42 guns aboard, and renamed it the *Bonhomme Richard* in Franklin's honor. On 14 Aug. he sailed from L'Orient with 1 other American ship and 4 French ships. Two of the French ships soon turned back. On 23 Sept. Jones sighted a fleet of 39 merchant ships convoyed by the *Serapis* (44 guns) and the *Countess of Scarborough* (22 guns) off the east coast of England. Jones bore down on the *Serapis* and began action at close range. The early exchanges went heavily in favor of the *Serapis,* but a query as to surrender brought "I have not yet begun to fight" as Jones' reply. American marksmen in the rigging took a heavy toll on the enemy's deck, an American grenade touched off a powder explosion on the gun deck of the *Serapis,* and when its mainmast fell Capt. Pearson struck his flag. With the *Richard* in flames (it sank on the 24th) Jones transferred his 237-man crew, half of them casualties, to the *Serapis* and brought it to port 6 Oct. One of the French ships in Jones' squadron, the *Pallas,* took the *Countess of Scarborough* during the *Richard-Serapis* engagement.

3 Sept.–28 Oct. FAILURE AT SAVANNAH. On 3 Sept., off Savannah, Admiral d'Estaing returned to the American coast with a French fleet of 35 ships and 4,000 troops. He captured 2 British frigates and 2 supply ships and then moved against Prevost's 3,000-man garrison in Savannah (15 Sept.). On the 23rd 1,400 American troops under General Lincoln joined the French in be-

sieging the city. The siege proceeded too slowly for D'Estaing's timetable; assault was pressed on 9 Oct. D'Estaing was wounded, Count **Casimir Pulaski** (1749–79) killed, and the Allies suffered over 800 casualties to 155 of Prevost's. With the withdrawal of D'Estaing's fleet (28 Oct.) the initiative again passed to the British. Clinton evacuated Rhode Island (11 Oct.) to permit an increased effort in the South and on 26 Dec. left New York with nearly 8,000 troops with Charleston as his target.

1780

11 Feb.–12 May. FALL OF CHARLESTON. Clinton arrived off the Carolina coast on 1 Feb. By 11 Apr. he had completed the investment of the city with 14,000 attackers. On 6 May Ft. Moultrie fell; Lincoln capitulated on the 12th. At a cost of only 255 casualties Clinton captured the 5,400-man garrison and 4 American ships, making this the heaviest American defeat of the war. On 29 May a force of cavalry under Col. **Banastre Tarleton** destroyed a Virginian regiment at **Waxhaw Creek.** On 5 June Clinton left for New York, satisfied that South Carolina was rewon for the crown, leaving Cornwallis with about 8,000 men to maintain, and if possible extend, control.

28 Feb. RUSSIA'S ARMED NEUTRALITY. The declaration of Catherine II that the Russian navy would be used against all belligerents to protect neutral Russian trade was a blow to British blockade efforts against France and Spain, for Russia refused to recognize naval stores (required by the Allies) as contraband. More significant was Catherine's invitation to other European neutrals to join in a **League of Armed Neutrality.** Denmark (9 July) and Sweden (1 Aug.) promptly accepted; the Netherlands, Prussia, Portugal, Austria, and the Kingdom of the Two Sicilies joined in the next 2 yrs. Britain went to war with the Netherlands (20 Dec.) and was able to shut off the clandestine trade between the U.S. and the Dutch island of St. Eustatius in the West Indies, center of contraband trade with the U.S.

Although the League failed to aid the Dutch, its existence hampered British naval measures against the Allies. On 19 Dec. Congress appointed Francis Dana as minister to Russia, but he was ignored at St. Petersburg.

25 May. MUTINY AT WASHINGTON'S CAMP. The condition of Washington's army during the winter of 1779–80 at Morristown, N.J., was even more critical than at Valley Forge, as supplies failed to arrive (Mar.), owing to the drop in value of Continental currency (40 [Continental] to 1 [Specie]). Rations were cut to one eighth of normal quantity during the next 6 weeks. On 25 May 2 Connecticut regiments paraded under arms to demand a full ration and immediate payment of their salaries, then 5 mos. in arrears at the time, but were curbed by Pennsylvania troops.

11 July. FRENCH ARMY AT NEWPORT. Under the Comte de Rochambeau (1725–1807) 5,000 troops with a strong naval escort sailed from France on 2 May and arrived at Newport, R.I., 11 July. Washington planned to combine this army with his own for an attack on New York, but lacked adequate naval support. A British fleet under Adms. Arbuthnot and Rodney blockaded Newport within a few weeks of Rochambeau's arrival.

16 Aug. BATTLE OF CAMDEN. The British hold on Georgia and South Carolina was not seriously challenged (guerrilla bands led by **Andrew Pickens** [1739–1817], **Francis Marion** [p. 749], and **Thomas Sumter** [1734–1832] prevented consolidating British strength until Gates was commissioned by Congress [13 June] to lead a Southern Army with a core of Continental troops detached by Washington). Gates took over his command at Coxe's Mill, N.C. (25 July), and began a slow march against the British post and supply base at Camden, S.C. Cornwallis, with about 2,400 men, made contact with the Americans early on 16 Aug. north of that town. American troops broke when Tarleton's dragoons came crashing down upon their rear. Estimated U.S. losses: c.800–900 killed (including Kalb) and 1,000 captured. Gates fell back to Hillsboro, N.C., 160 miles from Camden.

Defeat by Tarleton of an American force under Sumter at Fishing Creek, S.C. (18 Aug.), opened the way for a British invasion of North Carolina, begun by Cornwallis 8 Sept. On 7 Oct. a Loyalist force of about 1,100 led by Major Patrick Ferguson, screening Cornwallis' left flank, was caught atop **King's Mountain** on the border between the Carolinas by a 900-man force of American frontiersmen under Col. **Isaac Shelby** (1750–1826) and Col. **William Campbell** (1745–81). The marksmanship of the backwoodsmen prevailed over Ferguson's bayonet charges. The Americans lost 28 killed, 62 wounded in killing or capturing the entire enemy force. Cornwallis retreated back into South Carolina and established winter quarters at Winnsborough (14 Oct.). On the same day capable **Nathanael Greene** was named to succeed Gates in the southern command.

21 Sept. TREASON OF ARNOLD. As early as May 1779 Benedict Arnold, then under fire for his administration as military commander of Philadelphia, opened negotiations with Gen. Clinton in New York and by 23 May was sending him information on Washington's movements. Relations were broken off for a time when Clinton refused (late July) to pay £10,000 to Arnold for his services and indemnify him as well for any losses he might suffer if detected. But after a court-martial found Arnold guilty on two charges of misusing his powers at Philadelphia (26 Jan. 1780) and after Washington, in keeping with the decision of the court, reprimanded Arnold officially (6 Apr.), Arnold reopened negotiations with the British in May. On 15 June he informed them that he expected to be put in command of West Point and on 12 July wrote Major John André, Clinton's adjutant, that he desired a conference with a British officer to plan the "disposal" of that key fortress. Arnold took up command at West Point 5 Aug. and on 21 Sept. met André on the west bank of the Hudson near Haverstraw to deliver plans of the fort and inform the British of its weak points. On his way back to the British lines André doffed his uniform in favor of civilian clothes against Clinton's specific orders. On 23 Sept. he was captured by 3 New York militiamen near Tarrytown and the incriminating papers discovered. His captors, not suspecting Arnold's part in the affair, sent word of André's apprehension to him at West Point. When Arnold received this information (25 Sept.) he fled to the *Vulture,* a British warship in the Hudson. On 29 Sept. André was convicted as a spy, and executed on the 30th. For his treachery Arnold was commissioned a brig. gen. in the British army and received £6,315 in cash, an annual pension of £500 for his wife Peggy (Shippen), army commissions for 3 sons by a previous marriage, and, beginning in 1783, pensions of £100 a year each for Peggy's 5 young children. Arnold led British raids against Virginia (Dec. 1780–Apr. 1781) and New London, Conn. (6 Sept. 1781).

1781

1 Jan. MUTINY OF THE PENNSYLVANIA LINE. The appearance of recruiting agents who paid $25 in coin to new enlistees provoked 2,400 veterans of the Pennsylvania division to quit their quarters, seize arms and artillery, wound several officers who tried to stop them, and march off under their sergeants toward Philadelphia. On 3 Jan. they made camp at Princeton and elected negotiators to treat with the officials of their state. Joseph Reed, president of Pennsylvania's Executive Council, who opened negotiations (7 Jan.) made concessions which ended the mutiny, though over half the Line left the service. When, on 20 Jan., troops of the New Jersey Line mutinied at Pompton, Washington dispatched Gen. Robert Howe with 600 men from West Point to put down the mutiny. Howe surprised the mutineers' camp (27 Jan.), forced them to parade unarmed, restored the officers to their commands, and had 2 men executed. Another outbreak among the Pennsylvania troops in May was similarly nipped by several executions.

20 Feb. ROBERT MORRIS MADE SUPERINTENDENT OF FINANCE. On 6 Feb. Congress resolved to establish a department of finance under a super-

intendent responsible to Congress. On 20 Feb. **Robert Morris** (p. 756) was named. He took office on 14 May at a critical time. Despite subsidies and loans from France and Spain (totaling for the entire period of the war almost $9 million), American finances were close to collapse after 1779. By the beginning of 1780 Congress had issued $191,500,000 in paper money ("Continentals"). Additional millions were outstanding in Quartermaster Certificates (receipts given in payment by the army for supplies it requisitioned), close to $50 million in loan-office certificates, most paying 6% interest, and more debits in the form of certificates given soldiers for their back pay. An attempt had been made (Jan. 1779) to retire some of the paper money, but when the failure of the states to provide for the current expenses of the war resulted in new issues exceeding the amount retired by over $35 million Continental currency dropped precipitately. On 14 Jan. 1779 it stood at 8–1 with specie but by the end of the year was down to 40–1. On 18 Mar. 1780 Congress resolved to retire the bills in circulation by accepting them in payments due it from the states at one fortieth their face value. About $120 million in Continental bills was thus retired while the remaining $71 million was worthless by the end of 1780. When Morris took office his first proposal (21 May) was for a national bank, which Congress approved (26 May), but did not actually charter the Bank of North America until 31 Dec. In June Morris received authorization to supply the army by contract rather than by the inefficient and expensive system of requisition from the states. A timely subsidy from France (May) and French backing for a large loan from the Netherlands (5 Nov.) enabled Morris to make some progress toward returning the country to a specie basis by the end of the year.

1 Mar. RATIFICATION OF THE ARTICLES OF CONFEDERATION, before the states ever since November 1777, was delayed by Maryland's refusal to ratify until the states claiming western lands ceded them to the U.S. With the cession by Virginia (2 Jan. 1781, and p. 440), Maryland signed the Articles 27

Feb. Congress then set 1 Mar. for final ratification and on 2 Mar. assumed a new title, "The United States in Congress Assembled." The president of the old Congress, **Samuel Huntington** (Conn., 1731–96) continued in office.

WAR IN THE CAROLINAS. After assuming command of the army in the south in Dec. 1780, Gen. Greene moved from North Carolina to Cheraw, S.C. Too weak to attack Cornwallis' main camp at Winnsborough, he detached Gen. **Daniel Morgan** with about 800 men for a sweep to the west and **Henry Lee** for guerrilla activity between Cornwallis and Charleston. Cornwallis ordered Tarleton to drive Morgan back against the main British force. But Morgan selected a position near **Cowpens**, disposed his force (now grown to 1,000) with great care, and met Tarleton's assault there on 17 Jan. By skillful handling of his militia and assisted by cavalry under Col. **William Washington** (1752–1810), Morgan won a smashing victory over the 1,100-man enemy force, suffering less than 75 casualties to Tarleton's 329, and capturing 600. Cornwallis now pursued Morgan into North Carolina. At Guilford Courthouse Greene and Morgan joined forces (9 Feb.) and retreated across the Dan River into Virginia. Lacking boats and supplies, Cornwallis was forced to discontinue the pursuit and withdrew into North Carolina. When reinforcements brought Greene's command up to 4,400 men he followed the British and offered battle at **Guilford Courthouse** (15 Mar.), where Cornwallis won the field but at a cost of almost 100 killed and over 400 wounded. Too weakened by these losses to continue the campaign, he retreated (18 Mar.) to Wilmington to receive reinforcements by sea.

Greene now marched into South Carolina, and though defeated at **Hobkirk's Hill** (19 Apr.), failed in his siege of the British post at **Ninety Six** (22 May–19 June), and lost again at **Eutaw Springs** (8 Sept.), he managed (aided by successes scored by Marion, Lee, and Sumter in capturing the smaller British posts in the state) by the fall to narrow British control in South Carolina to Charleston and its immediate vicinity.

2 Apr. "MARS" AND "MINERVA." In Apr. Capt. **John Barry** (1745–1803), returning from France on the *Alliance,* was attacked by 2 British privateers, the *Mars* and the *Minerva,* but soon had forced both to surrender (2 Apr.). On 29 May, while becalmed, two British men-of-war, the *Atalanta* and the *Trepassy,* attacked. Barry was badly wounded but held his rebellious crew to their guns until a breeze enabled him to drive between his attackers and force each to surrender. 1781 also saw a new high in the number of American privateers in action: 449. By the end of the war American privateers had accounted for about 600 British ships, worth, with their cargoes, over $18 million. The U.S. Navy captured or destroyed 196 enemy ships during the war.

14 June. U.S. PEACE COMMISSION. On 11 June Congress decided to entrust the peace negotiations to a commission rather than to John Adams alone. **John Jay** (13 June), **Benjamin Franklin, Henry Laurens** (1724–92), and **Thomas Jefferson** (14 June) were named in addition to **Adams.** On 15 June Congress modified the 1779 peace instructions. Only U.S. independence and sovereignty were deemed essential. Other matters were to be handled by the commissioners at their discretion without definite binding instructions. This change was made largely on the advice of the Chevalier Luzurne, French Minister to the U.S., who was also responsible for that section of the instructions which directed the commission to take no action without the "knowledge and concurrence" of the French ministry and which bound them to "ultimately govern yourselves by their advice and opinion."

10 May–1 Aug. CORNWALLIS' CAMPAIGN IN VIRGINIA. Convinced that British control could not be restored in the Carolinas while Virginia remained as a supply and training base for the Americans, Cornwallis left Wilmington 25 Apr. with 1,500 men and marched northward into Virginia. At Petersburg (20 May) he joined his small force to a body of over 4,000 British troops which had followed up Arnold's expedition. Further reinforcements brought his strength to about 7,500, much superior

to the small American forces under Lafayette and Von Steuben. He raided
deep into Virginia (Tarleton almost
captured Gov. Jefferson and the members of the legislature at Charlottesville,
4 June). But as Lafayette was reinforced by Anthony Wayne (10 June)
and then joined by Von Steuben (19
June), Cornwallis turned back to the
coast to establish a base from which he
could maintain communication by sea
with Clinton's force in New York. He
picked Yorktown, where he arrived 1
Aug.

**21 May. MEETING OF WASHING-
TON AND ROCHAMBEAU.** At a
conference at Wethersfield, Conn., Wash-
ington secured Rochambeau's reluctant
consent for a joint attack against New
York supported by the French West
Indian fleet under De Grasse. Rocham-
beau left De Grasse free either to sail to
New York or to operate against the
British in Virginia. Meanwhile the
French army moved from Rhode Island
and joined Washington's above New
York (5 July). Before a large-scale at-
tack could be mounted, a letter from De

THE SIEGE OF YORKTOWN

🛶 American Troops	🏰 French Troops	▬ British Troops
〰 Trenches	〰 Trenches	⚓ Defense works
△ Officers' H.Q.	△ Officers' H.Q.	◼ Redoubts
ılıılıᴾ Artillery	ılıılıᴾ Artillery	▲ Fusiliers
⊡ Technicians	◠ Ships	● Ships

Grasse reached Washington (14 Aug.) with news that he would leave the West Indies for Chesapeake Bay on 13 Aug. with 3,000 French troops and his entire fleet and would be available for operations in that area until mid-Oct. Washington immediately prepared to march both his and Rochambeau's troops to Virginia. Preserving the appearance of a movement against New York, the two armies crossed the Hudson (20–26 Aug.), feinted toward Staten Island, and then struck out southward across New Jersey.

30 Aug.–19 Oct. YORKTOWN CAMPAIGN. On 30 Aug. De Grasse arrived off Yorktown, set up a naval blockade of the garrison with his fleet, and landed (31 Aug.) his troops to join Lafayette's forces hemming in Cornwallis by land. On 5 Sept. the British fleet under Adm. Thomas Graves appeared and De Grasse sailed out to give battle. A sharp action that day was followed by 3 days of maneuvering. On 9 Sept. the French were strengthened by the arrival of Count Barras with the French squadron from Newport and on 10 Sept. Graves drew off toward New York for repairs, leaving the French in command of the sea off Yorktown. Cornwallis' fate was now quickly sealed. DeGrasse sent ships up Chesapeake Bay to bring the bulk of the forces under Washington and Rochambeau to Williamsburg (14–24 Sept.). From there the Allied army (about 9,000 American and 7,800 French troops) moved forward (28 Sept.) and began the siege of Yorktown. On 30 Sept. Cornwallis abandoned his outer line of fortifications, thereby permitting the Allies to bring up siege guns capable of hammering all parts of his inner line. These guns went into operation on 9 Oct. On 14 Oct. 2 redoubts on the left of the British line were taken in an assault in which Col. **Alexander Hamilton** (p. 719) distinguished himself. A British counterattack on the 16th failed to regain possession of these key points. Cornwallis now regarded his position as hopeless and when a storm later that day forced him to abandon a desperate plan for escaping across the York River, he opened negotiations (17 Oct.) for the surrender of his army. The capitulation was signed on the 18th and on the 19th the British force of almost 8,000 men laid down their arms. Total allied casualties were 262, against 552 British casualties (excluding prisoners). On 24 Oct. Clinton arrived off Chesapeake Bay with 7,000 reinforcements for Cornwallis, but put back to New York when he learned of the latter's surrender. Washington now urged an attack on New York, but De Grasse, now overdue in the West Indies, refused to participate. Washington marched his army northward to resume the envelopment of New York while Rochambeau's troops passed the winter in Virginia, returned to Rhode Island in the fall of 1782, and sailed from Boston for France 24 Dec.

1782

20 Mar. FALL OF LORD NORTH'S MINISTRY. With the capture of Cornwallis' entire army British hopes for victory in America collapsed. Defeats suffered at the hands of the French in the West Indies in 1781 and early 1782 further quickened Britain's desire for peace. The coercive policy of the North ministry was repudiated on 27 Feb. when the House of Commons voted against further prosecuting the war in America and passed a bill (5 Mar.) authorizing the crown to make peace with the former colonies. On 20 Mar. Lord North resigned. He was succeeded (22 Mar.) by Lord Rockingham, the minister who had secured the Stamp Act's repeal in 1766. The new ministry immediately decided to open direct negotiations with the American peace commissioners.

4 Apr. SIR GUY CARLETON SUCCEEDS CLINTON. Carleton arrived in New York (9 May) to assume his new commission (4 Apr.) as British commander in chief. With plans for continuing the war abandoned, he set about concentrating all British forces on the seaboard at New York. Wilmington, N.C., had been evacuated (Jan.), Savannah (11 July), and finally Charleston (14 Dec.). A skirmish at Combahee River, S.C. (27 Aug.), was the last land action of the war on the seaboard.

12 Apr. PEACE TALKS BEGIN IN PARIS. Richard Oswald, named by the Rockingham ministry to open peace negotiations with the American commissioners, began talks with Franklin (12 Apr.), at that time the only commissioner present in Paris. The British released Commissioner Henry Laurens, whom they had captured (3 Sept. 1780) and imprisoned in England, and sent him to The Hague to sound out John Adams. Laurens arrived in time to congratulate the latter on obtaining recognition by the Netherlands of U.S. independence (19 Apr.). Before leaving for Paris, Adams followed up this success by obtaining a loan of about $2 million from Dutch bankers (11 June) and a treaty of commerce and friendship with the Netherlands (8 Oct.).

27 Sept. START OF FORMAL NEGOTIATIONS. On 23 June, John Jay arrived from Madrid to join Franklin in Paris. Adams arrived on 26 Oct. (Laurens took no part in the Paris discussions until the preliminary peace treaty was virtually completed in Nov., and Jefferson, the 5th commissioner named by Congress, did not serve.) Meanwhile, Rockingham had died and was succeeded by the **Earl of Shelburne** as head of the British ministry (1 July). On 19 Sept. Oswald was authorized to treat with the commission of the "13 U.S." (tantamount to recognition of American

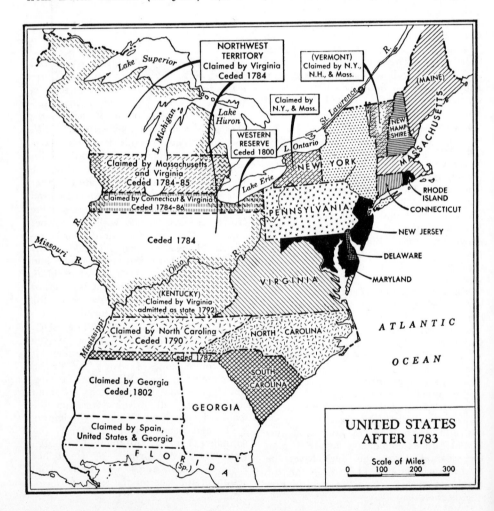

UNITED STATES AFTER 1783

independence) and opened formal negotiations with Franklin and Jay.

30 Nov. SIGNING OF THE PRELIMINARY ARTICLES OF PEACE. On 5 Oct. Jay presented Oswald with the draft of a preliminary treaty, to become effective when a similar treaty was signed by Britain and France. Upon the basis of these preliminary articles (which did not include an earlier demand by Franklin that Canada be ceded to the U.S.) negotiations continued. Oswald was joined by Henry Strachey (28 Oct.). About 1 Nov. the 3 U.S. commissioners (Adams was now on the scene) decided to disobey Congress's instructions concerning full consultation with the French and to proceed on their own initiative. A new set of articles was agreed to on 5 Nov. With a few last-minute changes these constituted the preliminary treaty of peace signed by Oswald for the British and by Adams, Franklin, Jay, and Laurens for the U.S. Without a single change these articles became the definitive peace treaty signed 3 Sept. 1783. Its most important provisions: (1) Britain recognized U.S. independence; (2) boundaries: the St. Croix River dividing Maine and Nova Scotia; the St. Lawrence-Atlantic watershed divide, the 45th parallel, a line through the Great Lakes and their connecting waterways, and a line from Lake Superior to the Mississippi dividing Canada and the U.S.; a line through the middle of the Mississippi River south to the 31st parallel to be the boundary with Spanish Louisiana; and the 31st parallel and the Apalachicola and St. Mary's Rivers as the boundary with Spanish Florida (Spain obtained Florida from Britain in the final peace treaty); (3) U.S. given the "right" to fish in their accustomed grounds off Newfoundland and Nova Scotia, and the "liberty" to dry and cure fish on any unsettled shore in Labrador, the Magdalen Islands, and Nova Scotia; (4) all debts due creditors of either country by citizens of the other were validated; (5) Congress was pledged to "earnestly recommend" to the legislatures of the states a full restoration of the rights and property of the Loyalists; and (6) hostilities were to cease and all British land and sea forces evacuated "with all convenient speed."

Vergennes, taken aback by the extremely favorable terms obtained for the U.S., criticized the commissioners (15 Dec.) for signing without consulting him. However, his own desire for a speedy settlement of the war and a tactful reply by Franklin (17 Dec.) prevented serious discord.

1783

20 Jan. EFFECTIVE DATE OF ARTICLES OF PEACE. The Anglo-American preliminary treaty was not to go into effect until Britain reached a settlement with France. On 20 Jan. preliminary articles of peace were signed between Britain and France and by Britain and Spain. Provisions were then made for a general armistice and on 4 Feb. Britain proclaimed a cessation of hostilities.

10, 12 Mar. NEWBURGH ADDRESSES. Early in Jan. a delegation of army officers memorialized Congress regarding grounds of their discontent: arrears in pay, unsettled food and clothing accounts, and Congress' failure to make provision for the life pension of half pay from the time of their discharge promised them 21 Oct. 1780. Their failure to obtain assurances of payment of sums owed officers and to secure a commutation of the pension for 6 yrs.' full pay (rejected 25 Jan. by Congress) led to the first anonymous address to the officers of the army circulated at Washington's main camp near Newburgh. Written by Maj. **John Armstrong** (1758–1843), the address attacked the "coldness and severity" shown by Congress, advised the officers to assume a bold tone and "suspect the man who would advise to more moderation and longer forbearance," and called upon them to meet the next day (11 Mar.) and draw up a "last remonstrance" which, if not well received by Congress, would justify the army in defying that body. Armstrong's call for pressure on Congress had the backing of Gen. Gates, Gouverneur Morris (1752–1816), and other civilian leaders who hoped to coerce the states into yielding more power to Congress. The address was well received by many of the officers, but Washington, with skill and tact, soon blunted the movement's force. On 11 Mar. he issued an order forbidding the unauthorized meeting called for by the anonymous address on that day, but went on to propose a regular meeting of the officers for the discussion of grievances on 15 Mar. A 2d anonymous address (also written by Armstrong) was issued on 12 Mar., expressing the opinion that Washington's action in calling for a meeting proved that he "sanctified" the claims of the officers. But when Washington unexpectedly addressed the meeting on the 15th in person, he soon made known his condemnation of the defiant tone of the Newburgh Addresses, expressed his confidence that Congress would treat the officers justly, called for patience, and counseled the officers to take no action which would sully the glory they had won. After Washington withdrew, the officers adopted resolutions, without dissent, affirming their patriotism, their confidence in Congress, and their disdain of the "infamous propositions . . . in a late anonymous address."

15 Apr. ARTICLES OF PEACE RATIFIED. On 13 Mar. Congress received the text of the provisional treaty from Paris. On 11 Apr. it issued a similar proclamation of the cessation of the war and on 15 Apr. ratified the provisional treaty after a debate in which the action of the commissioners in proceeding without consulting the French came in for considerable criticism. The treaty was signed at Paris 3 Sept., ratified by Congress 14 Jan. 1784, ratifications exchanged 12 May 1784.

26 Apr. 7,000 LOYALISTS SAIL FROM NEW YORK. Their departure was made necessary by the impending embarkation of the British army. This group was among the last of the total of almost 100,000 Loyalists who left the U.S. for Europe or Canada. The early "test acts" passed by the revolutionary state governments in 1776–77 requiring a repudiation of loyalty to George III had been followed by more severe repressive measures. Nine states had passed acts exiling prominent Tories, 5 had disfranchised all Loyalists, and in most of the states Loyalists were expelled from all offices, barred from the professions,

and forced to pay double or treble taxes. On 27 Nov. 1777 Congress recommended to the states that they appropriate the property of residents who had forfeited "the right to protection." By 1782 all the states had passed confiscation acts, some, in fact, antedating Congress' recommendation. New York obtained over $3,600,000 and Maryland over $2 million from the sale of Loyalist property. The British government established a commission (July) to which the Loyalists might present claims to cover their damages. The commission functioned until 1790, examined 4,118 claims, and authorized payment of a generous total of £3,292,452 in compensation.

13 June. ARMY DISBANDS. Congress voted (26 May) to give furloughs to soldiers who had enlisted for the duration until the signing of the peace treaty should permit their full discharge. Certificates for 3 mos.' pay were authorized for those furloughed. On 13 June, without waiting for these certificates to reach camp, most of Washington's army departed for their homes from the camps in the Hudson Highlands. On 18 Oct. Congress discharged all previously furloughed and on 3 Nov. discharged all other troops enlisted for the duration of the war. Only a small force of men serving time enlistments remained with Washington to await the evacuation of New York City by the British.

24 June. CONGRESS FLEES PHILADELPHIA. On 17 June about 80 soldiers began a march from Lancaster to Philadelphia to obtain justice from the state government and from Congress; they were joined (21 June) by an additional 200 from regiments in Philadelphia, and demonstrated before Independence Hall, where both the Executive Council of Pennsylvania and Congress were meeting. When the state authorities proved unwilling or unable to deal with the mutineers, President Elias **Boudinot** (1740–1821) changed the meeting place of Congress from Philadelphia to Princeton (24 June). Congress met there until 3 Nov., when it adjourned to meet 26 Nov. at Annapolis, Md., under a plan (adopted 21 Oct.) calling for alternate sessions there and at Trenton until dual permanent seats for the government (authorized 7 and 17 Oct.) were established on the Delaware and Potomac Rivers.

25 Nov. BRITISH EVACUATE NEW YORK CITY. On 21 Nov. the British drew back from northern Manhattan Island and from eastern Long Island into New York City and Brooklyn. Washington moved to Manhattan, taking up a position at Harlem Heights. Early in the afternoon of the 25th the last British troops left the docks of New York and Washington, accompanied by Gov. **George Clinton** (1739–1812), entered the city. By 4 Dec. the British had completed the evacuation of Staten Island and Long Island and were putting out to sea in their transports. On that same day Washington took leave of his officers at Fraunces' Tavern. After a triumphal tour to Annapolis where the Congress was in session, he appeared before that body (23 Dec.) to resign his commission as commander in chief and "take . . . leave of all the employments of public life."

SIGNIFICANT RESULTS OF THE REVOLUTION: (1) The 13 colonies became independent states and united under the Confederation of the U.S.; (2) the U.S. obtained title to a vast empire from the seaboard settlements to the Mississippi; (3) royal and proprietary colonial governments were replaced by republican state governments; (4) the overthrow of the royal and proprietary ruling class and the participation of men of all social levels in the Revolution brought a broader popular base to political life; (5) the confiscation of royal lands, proprietary estates, and Loyalist property, though chiefly designed as revenue-raising measures, brought, ultimately, a somewhat more democratic redistribution of property; (6) quitrents formerly collected by the crown and by colonial proprietors were abolished by the states; (7) entail and primogeniture, twin pillars of aristocratic land holding, were virtually abolished by state legislation, 1776–91; (8) the Anglican Church was disestablished in all colonies in which it had been tax-supported, 1776–86; (9) the slave trade was prohibited or heavily taxed in 11 states (1776–86), slavery abolished in Mass.

(1780), in N.H. (1784), and gradual emancipation adopted by Pa. (1780), Conn. (1784), and R.I. (1784); (10) the reform of penal codes and prisons was advanced as well as the secularization and democratization of education.

1784

STATE CONSTITUTIONS. During the Revolution 11 of the 13 states drew up new constitutions. (R.I. and Conn. continued to use the colonial charters of 1662 and 1663, merely deleting all references to the British Crown.) Except in the case of Mass., where a constitutional convention was called (1779) and its handiwork submitted to the people for ratification (1780), these new constitutions were the work of revolutionary congresses or conventions. Constitutions were adopted by N.H., N.J., Pa., Del., Md., Va., N.C., and S.C. in 1776; by N.Y. and Ga. in 1777.

Main features: (1) **Bicameral legislature** (exceptions: Pa., with a unicameral legislature and plural executive—executive council of 13; and N.H., with an executive council under 1776 Constitution). (2) **Weak chief executive:** in 9 of the 13 states his term was for 1 yr.; in 7 his reeligibility was variously limited; in 9 a veto power denied him. In 9 out of 11 the executive shared appointing power with the legislature; governors with greatest power were found in Mass. and N.Y., elected by the people rather than by the legislature. (3) **Strong legislature:** elected executive in 8 states; shared appointing power in 6; lower house originated all money bills in 9. (4) **Frequent elections:** in every state except S.C. (where both houses had 2-yr. terms) the lower house was elected annually, or semiannually (R.I. and Conn.); upper house elected annually in 8 states for terms of 2 yrs. (S.C.), 3 yrs. (Del.), and 4 yrs. (N.Y. and Va.). (5) **Property qualifications for officeholding** ranged as high as £10,000 for governor (S.C.), £2,000 (S.C.); £1,000 (N.J. and Md.) for the upper house; £500 (N.J. and Md.) for the lower. (6) **Property qualifications for voting** ranged from payment of a low poll tax (N.H.

and Pa., where sons of freeholders were eligible to vote without payment of taxes) to Va. requirement of 25 acres of settled or 500 acres of unsettled land. (7) an **appointive judiciary with tenure for good behavior** (8 states; annual appointment, Conn. and R.I.; for 5 yrs., N.H.; for 7 yrs., N.J. and Pa.).

Innovations: (1) **Bills of Rights** (beginning with Virginia, 12 June 1776, drafted by **George Mason,** 1725–92) included in many constitutions; (2) **Council of Appointment** in N.Y., chosen annually from Senate and Assembly, exercised (with the governor, who had but one vote) appointive power; (3) **Council of Censors** in Pa., elected by the people every 7th yr. and empowered to investigate actions of the Assembly and Executive Council and summon a convention to consider constitutional amendments.

23 Apr. JEFFERSON'S 1ST TERRITORIAL ORDINANCE. On 1 Mar., the day Congress accepted a revised version of Virginia's cession of her western lands, a committee headed by Jefferson proposed a plan for a temporary government in the West, the division of the domain into states to enter the Confederacy on equality with the original members. After amendments, the report was adopted 23 Apr. and, though never put into effect, served as the basis for the Northwest Ordinance (1787).

7 May. SECRETARY OF FOREIGN AFFAIRS. In Dec. 1783 **Robert Livingston** (N.Y., 1746–1813) resigned as first Secretary of Foreign Affairs (named 10 Aug. 1781). After long delay **John Jay,** then about to return to America from Europe, was named to succeed him.

May–July. WYOMING VALLEY VIOLENCE. On 30 Dec. 1782 a 5-man court appointed by Congress (Aug.) held unanimously that the disputed title to the Wyoming Valley claimed by both Pa. and Conn. should be awarded the former, whose territory was contiguous. Without awaiting settlement of individual claims, the Pa. Assembly approved a plan to oust the Connecticut settlers (1783). Militia actions against settlers were denounced by the Pa. Council of Censors, which forced the Assembly to enact measures (15 Sept.) restoring settlers to their lands under protection of a new commission (9 Sept.). After further violence in 1787, a Pa. act of that year brought an equitable and conclusive settlement.

28 May. TREASURY BOARD. At his own request Robert Morris was replaced as Superintendent of Finance by a board of 3 commissioners—**Samuel Osgood** (1748–1813), **Walter Livingston** (1740–97), named 25 Jan., and **Arthur Lee** (27 July). The central government was still dependent upon requisitions on the states. Of an $8 million requisition (Oct. 1781) only $1,486,512 had been paid by 1 Jan. 1784. Late in 1783 Morris had been forced to overdraw his account in Europe to provide for the army's demobilization pay. Negotiation of loans by John Adams in Holland (1784) enabled Morris to pay off $230,000 in notes (outstanding 1 Jan.) and leave office (1 Nov.) with a surplus of $21,000.

30 Aug. OPENING OF CHINA TRADE. Independence brought freedom from the British Navigation Acts but also the closing to the U.S. of the British West Indies. A British Order in Council (2 July 1783) banned importation of meats, fish, and dairy products from the U.S. into the West Indies and closed the trade in all other products to all but British ships. As a result, American businessmen looked to new markets, notably to the Orient. On 22 Feb. the *Empress of China,* Capt. John Greene, sailed from New York by way of Cape Horn and reached Canton 30 Aug. The profit from the cargo of tea and silks which it brought back (May 1785) prompted merchants of Philadelphia, Boston, and Providence to fit out ships for China. Despite gains in trade with France and Holland, Britain was still the best customer of the U.S., in part the result of an Order in Council (26 Dec. 1783) permitting the importation of American manufactured goods (with a few exceptions) into Britain on the same favorable terms as in colonial days. British exports to the U.S. amounted (1784) to £3,679,467 as against imports from the U.S. of only £749,345. The unbalance increased specie scarcity in the U.S. and led to overextension of inventories and credit.

23 Dec. NEW YORK TEMPORARY CAPITAL. Congress met in Trenton (1 Nov.) and voted (10 Dec.) to move from Trenton; on the 23rd it appointed commissioners to lay out a federal district on the banks of the Delaware and to move to New York until the federal city was ready.

1785

16 Feb. CONGRESS AND THE COMMERCE POWER. The weakness of the central government under the Articles of Confederation made it difficult to obtain commercial concessions from foreign nations. The British Ambassador in Paris told Franklin, Adams, and Jefferson (26 Mar.) that Britain could hardly enter into a treaty with Congress when one state could render "totally fruitless and ineffectual" any such agreement, and proposed that they obtain authorizations from the individual states as well. Congress unsuccessfully appealed in 1784 for a 15-yr. grant of power to regulate foreign commerce. On 24 Jan. a committee headed by **James Monroe** was appointed to consider a new appeal to the states. Its report called for an amendment to the 9th Article, which forbade Congress to enter into any treaty of commerce that deprived any state of its individual right to impose duties. No action was taken.

24 Feb., 10 Mar. MINISTERS TO BRITAIN AND FRANCE. On 31 July 1784, Jefferson reached Paris to serve with Franklin and Adams as commissioners to negotiate commercial treaties. On 24 Feb. Congress appointed John Adams Minister to the Court of St. James and granted Franklin's request to be replaced as Minister to France, appointing (10 Mar.) Jefferson to succeed him. Jefferson was received by Louis XVI on 17 May and Adams by George III on 1 June.

8 Mar. HENRY KNOX SECRETARY OF WAR. In 1781 Congress replaced the cumbersome Board of War by a Secretary heading a War Department. Gen. Lincoln held that office until 1783.

After a 2-yr. vacancy Knox was chosen to succeed him.

28 Mar. MT. VERNON CONFERENCE. Late in March 4 commissioners from Virginia, including Madison and Mason, met at Alexandria with 4 Maryland commissioners, including Samuel Chase (1741–1811), to consider problems relating to the navigation of Chesapeake Bay and Potomac River. On 28 Mar. the negotiators adjourned to **Mount Vernon,** where Washington acted as their host but apparently took no direct part in the discussions. Swift agreement was reached concerning the jurisdiction of the Potomac and the apportionment of expenses for marking the channel through Chesapeake Bay. The commissioners then drafted an agreement recommending to their respective legislatures uniform commercial regulations and imposts, a uniform currency, and annual conferences on common commercial problems. A request was also drawn up that Pennsylvania be invited to join Virginia and Maryland in a pact to establish water communication between the Chesapeake and the Ohio River. The Maryland legislature not only endorsed this plan (5 Dec.) but proposed the addition of Delaware. At Madison's behest, the Virginia legislature invited (21 Jan. 1786) all the states to discuss commercial problems at a convention to be held at Annapolis (Sept.).

20 May. BASIC LAND ORDINANCE provided for rectangular surveys dividing the land into townships of 6 mi. sq. Townships were to be divided into 36 lots of 640 acres each (1 lot set aside for maintaining public schools; but an attempt to include another lot for the support of the religion of the majority of resident adult males narrowly missed passage) and sale of minimum lots (640 acres) authorized at $1 an acre.

23 June–11 July. MASSACHUSETTS AND FOREIGN COMMERCE. As early as 1783 Md. laid discriminatory rates and port fees on British shipping and S.C. imposed a general duty of 2½% on foreign goods, with higher rates on specified articles. Pa., N.Y., and N.C. acted in 1784. On 23 June Mass. banned the export of U.S. products in British ships and doubled the tonnage duty on all goods imported in other than American ships. N.H. took similar steps the same day. Earlier in June R.I. passed a high protective tariff to encourage domestic industry. On 11 July the Mass. legislature passed a resolution favoring a convention to revise the Articles of Confederation, but her delegates at New York failed to offer this resolution. Pa. (20 Sept.) placed a discriminatory tonnage duty on ships of foreign nations which had no treaties with the U.S. U.S. imports from Britain totaled £2,308,023, a drop of £1,371,444 from the abnormally high figure of 1784, but exports to Britain rose from £749,345 (1784) to £893,594.

20 July. JAY-GARDOQUI NEGOTIATIONS. Spain refused to be bound by that part of the Anglo-American treaty which set the 31st parallel as the boundary between Spanish Florida and the U.S., claiming the territory 100 miles northward as far as the junction of the Yazoo River with the Mississippi (at 32°22'), and in 1784 refused to permit American shipping to pass freely through the lower Mississippi. On 15 May 1785 Don Diego de Gardoqui arrived as Spanish Minister to the U.S. with specific instructions to make no concession on the navigation of the Mississippi. Congress authorized John Jay to negotiate with Gardoqui (20 July) and instructed him (24 Aug.) "particularly to stipulate the right of the United States to . . . the free navigation of the Mississippi. . . ." A year of fruitless negotiation followed. Finally, on 29 Aug. 1786, Congress authorized Jay to "forbear" American navigation rights in return for a favorable commercial treaty with Spain. But the bitter debate on this authorization and the close vote (7–5) indicated the unlikelihood that 9 states (required by the Articles) would ratify the treaty. Hence, negotiations broke down, and the issues remained unsettled until the Pinckney Treaty of 1795.

10 Sept. TREATY WITH PRUSSIA. John Adams negotiated (1784) with Baron Thulemeier, Prussian Minister at The Hague, but was called to his English post before completing the treaty. Jefferson then sent his secretary William Short to complete negotiations. The treaty outlawed privateering and endorsed the principle of free ships-free goods.

30 Nov. NEGOTIATIONS WITH BRITAIN. In Britain Adams found that the inability of the U.S. to force the states to abide by those terms of the Treaty of Paris concerning the treatment of Loyalists and the removal of impediments to collection of debts to English creditors made it virtually impossible for him to obtain commercial concessions or British compliance with the treaty terms requiring them to evacuate Oswego, Niagara, Detroit, Michilimackinac, and other garrisons on U.S. soil. Adams' formal demand (30 Nov.) for the evacuation of the western posts brought the blunt reply (28 Feb. 1786) that the posts would be held until British creditors obtained payment from America. After 3 yrs., during which he pressed U.S. claims tenaciously but without success, Adams resigned and left for the U.S. (Apr. 1788).

1786

16 Jan. ADOPTION OF THE VIRGINIA STATUTE FOR RELIGIOUS FREEDOM. In 1779 an Ordinance of Religious Freedom written by Jefferson was proposed in the Virginia legislature and failed of adoption, but in Dec. 1785, virtually the same measure passed the House of Burgesses. Model for the 1st Amendment of the U.S. Constitution, the Statute declared that no man could be compelled to attend or support any church nor suffer any discrimination because of his religious beliefs. Jefferson ranked his authorship of this act with the drafting of the Declaration of Independence and the founding of the University of Virginia as his most significant accomplishments.

28 June. TREATY WITH MOROCCO. With the removal of the protection of the British fleet, American commerce in the Mediterranean and off the coasts of Spain and Portugal suffered substantial losses from pirates from Algiers, Tripoli, Tunis, and Morocco. On 22 Feb. John Adams had an interview in London with the Tripolitine Ambassador, Abdrahaman, who demanded £200,000 for the protection of U.S. commerce. Negotiations broke down. Jefferson proposed a plan for an international expedition against the Barbary states, but Congress balked at contributing a frigate. On 28 June, Thomas Barclay, in direct negotiations with the Emperor of Morocco, obtained a treaty in exchange for gifts worth about $10,000. With Algiers, Tripoli, and Tunis, however, the U.S. was unable to reach agreements until 1795, 1796, and 1797 respectively.

June–Sept. LOW POINT OF DEPRESSION (p. 536). Imports from and exports to Great Britain dropped to £1,-603,465 and £843,119 respectively compared to £2,308,023 and £893,594 (1785). Farm wages showed a decline of as much as 20% from the 1780 level. The combination of a money shortage, high taxes, and insistent creditors brought demands for relief through stay laws and paper money. The paper-money advocates succeeded in obtaining issues totaling £800,000 in Pa. (Mar. 1785), S.C. (Oct. 1785), N.C. (Nov. 1785), N.Y. (Apr.), R.I. (May), N.J. (May), and Ga. (Aug.). In the remaining 6 states the pressure for similar action was greatest in Mass. In R.I. the paper-money issue provided the background for the case of *Trevett* v. *Weeden,* in which the state's Supreme Court upheld the doctrine of judicial review propounded by counsel James Varnum in ruling (25 Sept.) that an act forcing a creditor to accept the paper money was unconstitutional.

7 Aug. PROPOSALS TO REVISE THE ARTICLES. On 26 June Congress debated a motion (3 May) by **Charles Pinckney** (S.C., 1746–1825) for a reorganization of the government. The debates and the proposed amendments submitted 7 Aug. by a special committee reveal the delegates' awareness of the weaknesses of the Articles of Confederation. One proposal would have set up a Federal court of 7 judges with appeal jurisdiction from the state courts in cases involving foreign nations and Federal matters; another would have given Congress power over foreign and domestic commerce; 2 others attempted to strengthen the requisition system to en-

sure payment of the state quotas. (The need for such measures had been highlighted when N.J. flatly refused, 20 Feb., to pay the requisition voted by Congress in September 1785. Congress, apparently despairing of winning that unanimous approval necessary under the Articles for adoption of an amendment, never submitted these proposals to the states.

11–14 SEPT. ANNAPOLIS CONVENTION. Virginia's invitation to an interstate commercial convention at Annapolis (issued on 21 Jan.) was accepted by 9 states. Ga., S.C., Conn., and, oddly enough, Md. took no action. The delegates named by N.H., Mass., R.I., and N.C. failed to reach Annapolis in time to participate. Hence, only N.Y., N.J., Del., Pa., and Va. were represented. When the convention opened on the 11th John Dickinson, now a resident of Delaware, was elected chairman. The slim attendance convinced the 12 delegates that it would be useless to proceed to a study of interstate commercial problems. A committee was appointed, however, on 13 Sept. to prepare an address to the states, which the Convention adopted 14 Sept. Drafted by **Alexander Hamilton,** a leading force at the meeting, the report called upon the states to send commissioners to a new convention at Philadelphia on the 2nd Monday in May, 1787, to discuss not only commercial problems but *all* matters necessary "to render the constitution of the Federal Government adequate to the exigencies of the Union." Congress referred this invitation to committee 11 Oct. Not until 21 Feb. 1787 was a cautious endorsement of the plan adopted. On that day Congress described as "expedient" a convention "for the sole and express purpose of revising the Articles of Confederation and reporting to Congress and the several legislatures such alterations and provisions therein." Five states (Va., N.J., Pa., Del., and N.C.) had already named delegates to the Philadelphia convention.

Aug.–Dec. SHAYS' REBELLION. When the Massachusetts legislature adjourned on 8 July without heeding the petitions of the debt-ridden farmers for a paper-money issue or laws to stay the mounting number of farm and home foreclosures, discontent mounted. A town meeting of protest at Worcester (15 Aug.) was followed by a Hampshire County convention of some 50 towns at Hatfield (22–25 Aug.). The delegates condemned the Massachusetts Senate, lawyers, the high costs of justice, and the tax system, and called for an issue of paper money. They also advised against violence, but mob action followed. On 31 Aug. armed men prevented the sitting of the court at Northampton and on 5 Sept. the court at Worcester was broken up. When similar mob actions occurred at Concord and Great Barrington, Gov. **James Bowdoin** (1726–90) sent 600 militiamen under Gen. **William Shepherd** (1737–1817) to protect the Supreme Court sitting at Springfield. About 500 insurgents gathered there under the leadership of **Daniel Shays** (1747–1825), a destitute farmer who had risen to the rank of captain during the Revolution, confronted the militia (26 Sept.), and obliged the court to adjourn. Shays' presence in Springfield, site of a Federal arsenal, prompted Congress to authorize Gen. Knox to raise 1,340 men, mostly in Mass. and Conn., ostensibly for service against the Indians (20 Oct.). Actually, the Federal forces never had to be used. The insurrection in eastern Massachusetts collapsed with the capture of Job Shattuck on 30 Nov. A greater threat to public order was posed in the western part of the state. At Worcester Shays gathered a force of about 1,200 men during Nov. and early Dec. On 26 Dec. he marched to Springfield to join forces with other insurgents led by Luke Day and threaten Shepherd's smaller force guarding the arsenal. The governor called for 4,400 men, enlisted for one month, to assemble at Boston and Springfield on 18–19 Jan. Command was given to Gen. **Benjamin Lincoln.**

1787

4 Feb. SHAYSITES ROUTED AT PETERSHAM. Shays and Day, their forces separated by the Connecticut River, planned to scatter Shepherd's force and seize the arsenal before Lincoln reached Springfield. On 24 Jan. Shays proposed a combined assault the next day. Day's reply that he could not attack until the 26th was intercepted, with the result that Shays went ahead confident of Day's cooperation. About 4 P.M. he led some 1,200 men toward the arsenal. When the insurgents approached to within 100 yards of the building (despite warnings), Shepherd opened fire with artillery. The Shaysites quickly broke and fled, leaving 4 dead. On 27 Jan. Lincoln arrived at Springfield and on the 28th moved on to Amherst, pushing Shays before him to Pelham and isolating Day, who fled to New Hampshire. On 3 Feb., in the midst of negotiations, Shays marched eastward to Petersham. Lincoln followed in a punishing night march and early on 4 Feb. surprised the insurgents, captured 150, scattered the rest, and sent Shays fleeing to Vermont. The uprising was completely crushed by the end of Feb. In Mar. the legislature offered a pardon to all Shaysites except Shays, Day, and 2 other leaders. Shays was finally pardoned 13 June 1788. The uprising had the effect of inducing the legislature not to impose a direct tax in 1787 and to enact laws lowering court fees and exempting clothing, household goods, and tools of one's trade from debt process.

Feb.–May. DELEGATES NAMED TO PHILADELPHIA CONVENTION. In addition to the 5 states that had already acted, 6 others (Mass., N.Y., Ga., S.C., Md., and Conn.) named delegates. N.H. and R.I. were the only states that failed to act by the date set (14 May) for the opening of the convention. N.H. finally fell into line in June (its delegates reached Philadelphia 23 July) but R.I. ignored the convention.

25 May. OPENING OF CONSTITUTIONAL CONVENTION. On 14 May only the delegates from Va. and Pa. were on hand at Philadelphia's State House (Independence Hall). Not until 25 May was a quorum of 7 states obtained. From 81-yr.-old Franklin to 26-yr.-old Jonathan Dayton (N.J., 1760–1824) the delegates included outstanding public figures. Most respected and influential men were Washington and Franklin, while the actual leaders in the floor debates proved to be **Madison** and **George Mason** (Va.),

Gouverneur Morris and James Wilson (Pa.), Roger Sherman (Conn., 1721–93), and Elbridge Gerry (Mass., 1744–1814). Of the 55 delegates 29 were college trained, over half were lawyers, while planters and merchants together with a few physicians and college professors made up the rest. When the convention opened Robert Morris nominated **Washington** as president; this won unanimous approval. **William Jackson** (1759–1828) was elected secretary. (The Journal kept by Jackson was meager; knowledge of the debates is derived very largely from notes taken each day by Madison. In keeping with the pledge of secrecy [29 May] these were not published until 1840, 4 years after his death).

29 May. VIRGINIA PLAN. Edmund Randolph (Va., 1753–1813) proposed 15 resolutions comprising the "Virginia Plan" of Union, which went beyond revision of the Articles and favored a new national government. Outstanding features: (1) a bicameral national legislature, representing the states proportionally, with the lower house elected by the people, and the upper house by the lower house from nominees proposed by the state legislatures; (2) an executive chosen by the legislature; (3) a judiciary including a supreme court and inferior courts; (4) a council of revision consisting of the executive and several members of the judiciary, with a veto over the legislature's acts. On 30 May the Convention resolved itself into a committee of the whole and debated the Virginia Plan until 13 June. On that date 19 resolutions based on Randolph's proposals were reported to the Convention.

15 June. NEW JERSEY PLAN. Opposition to the Virginia Plan came chiefly from the small states and centered upon the provision for proportional rather than equal representation of the states in both houses of the proposed legislature. On 15 June **William Paterson** (N.J., 1745–1806) introduced 9 resolutions which stressed retention of the Confederation but conferred upon Congress the powers to tax and regulate foreign and interstate commerce and to name a plural executive (without a veto) and a supreme court. U.S. treaties and acts of Congress were to be the supreme law in the states.

The issue before the Convention: whether to content themselves with amendments to the Articles or to draw up the framework of a new national government. After 3 days of debate (16–19 June) the Convention voted 7–3 to work toward a national government as visualized in the Virginia Plan. The committee of the whole now debated the issue of equal versus proportional representation in the legislature.

13 July. NORTHWEST ORDINANCE. While the Convention was debating a plan to supplant the Articles, the Congress of the Confederation registered its greatest achievement, the ordinance for the government of the territory north of the Ohio River. Based in part upon Jefferson's plan of 1784 and in part upon a committee report of 19 Sept. 1786, the Northwest Ordinance provided: (1) the territory to be governed initially by a governor, a secretary, and 3 judges appointed by Congress; (2) when there were 5,000 free adult males in the territory a bicameral legislature to be established; (3) ultimately, from 3 to 5 states to be created (a population of 60,000 free inhabitants was requisite for admission to the Union); (4) the new states to be "on an equal footing with the original states in all respects whatsoever"; (5) freedom of worship, right of trial by jury, and public support of education provided; and (6) involuntary servitude, save in punishment for crime, prohibited. On 5 Oct. **Arthur St. Clair** was elected 1st governor of the territory and **Winthrop Sargent** (1753–1820) named secretary.

16 July. CONNECTICUT COMPROMISE. A committee (appointed 2 July) reconsidered and rejected a proposal made on 11 June by Roger Sherman (Conn.): representation to be proportional to population in the lower house and one vote for each state in the Senate. On 5 July the committee reported in favor of this plan. On 12 July the Convention agreed that each state's representation in the lower house should be based on the total of its white population and three fifths of its Negro population. On 16 July it accepted as well the principle that in the Senate each state should have an equal vote. With this obstacle removed, the Convention pro-

RATIFYING THE
FEDERAL CONSTITUTION

- ■ Federal majority
- ▒ Anti-federal majority
- ▨ Evenly divided

NEW HAMPSHIRE
21 June, 1788

N E W   Y O R K
26 July, 1788

MASSACHUSETTS
6 Feb., 1788

PENNSYLVANIA
12 Dec., 1787

RHODE
ISLAND
29 May, 1790

CONNECTICUT
9 Jan., 1788

NEW JERSEY
18 Dec., 1787

DELAWARE
7 Dec., 1787

MARYLAND
28 Apr., 1788

VIRGINIA
25 June, 1788

KENTUCKY
DISTRICT

TENNESSEE
DISTRICT

NORTH CAROLINA
21 Nov., 1789

SOUTH CAROLINA
23 May, 1788

GEORGIA
2 Jan., 1788

ceeded (19–26 July) to draw up 23 "fundamental resolutions" forming a rough draft of a constitution. On 26 July these were submitted to a 5-man Committee of Detail which drafted a constitution of 23 articles and submitted it to the Convention 6 Aug.

6 Aug.–10 Sept. GREAT DEBATE. During the debates on the draft constitution, the specific provisions of the final constitution were hammered out: the 2-yr. term for representatives (8 Aug.); the 6-yr. term for senators (9 Aug.); the 4-yr. term for the President (6 Sept.); the power of Congress to regulate foreign and interstate commerce (16 Aug.); the prohibition of bills of attainder and ex post facto laws (22 Aug.).

17 Sept. FINAL APPROVAL. By 8 Sept. final agreement neared. A 5-man Committee on Style and Arrangement was appointed with **William Johnson** (1727–1819) as chairman, and **Hamilton, Madison, Rufus King** (1744–1814), and **Gouverneur Morris** as members. The Convention held its last day of debate on details 10 Sept. Johnson then assigned Morris to prepare the final draft. Working with great speed, Morris had the constitution before Congress on 12 Sept. It was examined clause by clause and a few changes made (13–15 Sept.). Finally, on 17 Sept., each of the 12 state delegations voted approval. Three of the 42 delegates present refused to sign the engrossed copy: Gerry (Mass.) and Randolph and Mason (Va.). When the 39 delegates had signed and a letter of transmittal to Congress had been prepared, the Convention formally adjourned. By the terms of Article VII the Constitution was to become operative when ratified by 9 states.

28 Sept. CALL FOR STATE RATIFYING CONVENTIONS. On 20 September Congress received the proposed Constitution. Attempts were made (26–27 Sept.) to have Congress censure the Convention for exceeding its authority, but on 28 Sept. Congress resolved to transmit the Constitution to the legislature of each state for submission to special ratifying conventions.

27 Oct. 1ST "FEDERALIST" PAPER.

Advocates (Federalists) and opponents (Antifederalists) of the Constitution quickly unleashed a flood of propaganda pro and con. Outstanding were the 77 masterly essays signed by "Publius" which appeared in New York newspapers (27 Oct.–2 Apr. 1788). With 8 additional essays these appeared in 2 vols., entitled *The Federalist* (Mar.–May 1788). The work of Hamilton (who wrote *c*.51), Madison (28), and John Jay (5), the essays stressed the inadequacy of the Confederation, the need for a strong government, and the conformity of the Constitution with the best principles of republican government.

7–18 Dec. EARLY RATIFICATION. To Del. went the honor of being first to ratify the Constitution. That action was taken by unanimous vote 7 Dec. Pa. was next to approve but opposition was considerable. In the convention, which met 21 Nov., the Federalist representatives from Philadelphia and the commercial towns defeated the Antifederalist moves for amendments and delays, and finally won on 12 Dec. by 46–23. In N.J., where Antifederalism was weak, the state convention required only a week's time to vote unanimously for ratification (18 Dec.).

1788

2 Jan.–6 Feb. FURTHER RATIFICATIONS. On 2 Jan., Ga. became the 4th state to ratify the Constitution and the 3rd to do so unanimously. Conn. was next to act favorably. Its convention met 4 Jan. and voted (9 Jan.) 128–40 for ratification. On that same day the Massachusetts convention met. Early estimates of Antifederalist strength gave opponents 192 votes against 144 for the Federalists, who reduced this opposition 30 Jan. by proposing that amendments to the Constitution be recommended along with ratification, a move which won over Sam Adams, and swung the convention for ratification. The Constitution was approved unconditionally (187–168) on 7 Feb. along with 9 recommended amendments, most significant, the reservation to the states of all powers not "expressly delegated" by the Constitution to the central government.

24 Mar. REJECTION BY RHODE ISLAND. Despite the failure of Rhode Island to send a delegation to the Philadelphia Convention, the commercial and professional groups of the state made a determined effort to have the legislature call a state convention, but the rural legislators rejected a convention and proposed instead (Feb.) a popular referendum (held 24 Mar.), in which the Federalists refused to participate. Out of 2,945 of the more than 6,000 eligible to vote, only 237 voted in favor of the Constitution. Not until Jan. 1790 was a state convention called. On 29 May 1790 Rhode Island finally ratified (34–32).

21 June. NINTH STATE RATIFIES. On 28 Apr. the Maryland convention ratified (63–11); South Carolina was next to act. Though the resolution for a convention passed by only one vote in the legislature (12 May), in the convention Antifederalist sentiment was much weaker, and ratification passed (23 May) by a large majority (149–73). With 8 states having ratified, one more was necessary for adoption of the Constitution. A New Hampshire convention, meeting 13 Feb., adjourned after a week until 18 June. The Federalists overcame an early majority against them and won by 57–47 on 21 June. Twelve amendments were proposed.

25 June, 26 July. RATIFICATION IN VIRGINIA AND NEW YORK. Virginia's convention met on 2 June with Patrick Henry leading the foes of the Constitution and Madison in the vanguard of its supporters. The latter's logical arguments counteracted Henry's eloquence; the vote on 25 June showed 89 for, 79 against. Virginia attached to ratification proposals for a bill of rights of 20 articles as well as 20 other changes. In New York the convention met at Poughkeepsie on 17 June with Governor George Clinton's Antifederalists holding a clear majority. Hamilton worked for delay, counting on the effect of news of affirmative action by N.H. and Va. His strategy turned the tide. A plan for conditional ratification was rejected (25 July) and on 26 July ratification was carried, 30–27.

2 Aug. RATIFICATION IN NORTH CAROLINA. In the N.C. convention, which met on 21 July, despite strong Federalist sentiment, the view prevailed that ratification should be withheld until the incorporation of certain amendments, particularly a bill of rights. The submission of 12 proposed amendments to the states by the new Congress on 25 Sept. 1789 led to a second convention (16–23 Nov. 1789) at which ratification was carried (194–77) 21 Nov.

13 Sept. CONGRESS PREPARES FOR THE NEW GOVERNMENT. On 2 July the President of Congress, Cyrus Griffin (Va., 1748–1810), announced that the Constitution had been ratified by the requisite 9 states. A committee, appointed to prepare the details for the change in government, reported (8 July), but not until 13 Sept. did Congress adopt an ordinance which set the site of the new government as New York and fixed the dates in 1789 for the appointment of Presidential electors (7 Jan.), for the balloting by the electors (4 Feb.), and for the meeting of the first Congress under the Constitution (4 Mar.). On 2 Oct. the last Congress under the Articles was unceremoniously moved from its rooms in New York's City Hall in order that the edifice might be renovated as the capitol for the incoming government. On 10 Oct. Congress transacted its last official business. The only significant political·action thereafter was the cession by Maryland (23 Dec.) of 10 sq. mi. to Congress for a Federal town, future site of the District of Columbia.

THE EARLY NATIONAL AND
ANTE-BELLUM PERIODS, 1789-1860

1789

7 Jan. FIRST PRESIDENTIAL ELEC-TION. Presidential electors, chosen in all of the ratifying states with the exception of New York, were named either by the state legislatures or directly by the people. On 4 Feb., as elections of senators and representatives progressed in the various states, the Presidential electors cast their ballots.

4 Mar. FIRST CONGRESS under the Constitution met in New York without a quorum (8 Senators and 13 Representatives present, the remainder still en route); 54 of the members of the 1st Congress had been members of the Federal Convention or state ratifying conventions; all but 7 had advocated ratification.

1 Apr. HOUSE OF REPRESENTA-TIVES organized, with 30 of its 59 members present. Frederick A. Muhlenburg (Pa.) was elected Speaker, and on 8 Apr. the House began its deliberations.

6 Apr. THE SENATE, with 9 of its 22 members present, elected as temporary presiding officer John Langdon (N.H.), who counted the ballots cast by the Presidential electors. **George Washington,** with 69 votes, was unanimously elected President; **John Adams,** receiving 34 votes, was chosen as Vice-President.

30 Apr. 1ST INAUGURAL. On 16 Apr. Washington set out from Mount Vernon for New York City, arriving there on 23 Apr. Adams, meanwhile, had taken his seat as Vice-President on 21 Apr. In a ceremony held on the balcony of Federal Hall, at the corner of Wall and Broad Streets, Washington was inaugurated as the 1st President of the U.S. The oath

of office was administered by Robert R. Livingston, chancellor of the State of New York. The first inaugural address was delivered in the Senate chamber housed in Federal Hall.

9 Sept.–22 Dec. BILL OF RIGHTS. The Constitution, already ratified by 11 states, was ratified by North Carolina (21 Nov.) and Rhode Island (29 May 1790), whose delay pointed to the active strength of the Antifederalists. Five state ratifying conventions had stressed the need for immediate amendments to the Constitution; Federalist leaders had pledged themselves to changes in the Constitution; and in his inaugural address Washington had alluded to such alteration. Moreover, the Federalists wanted to forestall action on demands for a second constitutional convention.

Chiefly at the instigation of James Madison, the House of Representatives decided (9 Sept.) to recommend for adoption by the various states 12 amendments originally suggested by the state ratifying conventions (submitted to states 25 Sept.). Of these amendments, ten were ratified by the states, and comprised a specific Bill of Rights. New Jersey was the first state to ratify these amendments (20 Nov.); Maryland followed on 19 Dec. and North Carolina on 22 Dec. On 15 Dec. 1791 the Bill of Rights became part of the Constitution.

EXECUTIVE DEPARTMENTS. The first executive department created under the new government was that of Foreign Affairs. Established on 27 July, it was officially redesignated (15 Sept.) as the Department of State. **Thomas Jefferson** was appointed (26 Sept.) to head the department, but did not take office until

22 March 1790. During the interim, John Jay handled the affairs of the State Department.

The War Department was set up on 7 Aug.; **Henry Knox** was named Secretary of War (12 Sept.). The Treasury Department was established on 2 Sept.; **Alexander Hamilton** was appointed Secretary of the Treasury (11 Sept.). The office of Postmaster General was created by Congress (22 Sept.); **Samuel Osgood** appointed to that office 26 Sept. The Post Office Dept. was permanently organized by Congress 8 May 1795.

24 Sept. FEDERAL JUDICIARY ACT made provision for the organization of the Supreme Court to consist of a Chief Justice and 5 associates, as well as 13 district and 3 circuit courts; and established the office of Attorney General. On 26 Sept. **John Jay** became Chief Justice of the U.S. and Edmund Randolph became Attorney General.

1790

HAMILTON'S FISCAL PROGRAM. The chief issue of Washington's first term was the fiscal program devised by Alexander Hamilton and submitted to the House of Representatives in a series of reports on the national and state debt, an excise tax, and a national bank. Controversy over these proposals ultimately led to the party cleavage between Federalists and Republicans.

14 Jan. 1ST REPORT ON THE PUBLIC CREDIT (14 Jan.) dealt with the debt inherited from the Confederation. The foreign debt, held chiefly by the French and Dutch, was set at $11,710,-378; the domestic debt, including arrears of interest and unliquidated claims and currency, was fixed at $44,414,085; state debts were estimated at $25 million. Hamilton recommended (1) funding of the foreign and domestic debt at par, enabling creditors to exchange depreciated securities for new interest-bearing bonds at face value; and (2) assumption by the Federal government, to the extent of $21,500,000, of debts incurred by the states during the Revolution.

These measures had a double purpose:

(1) to establish and maintain the public credit and thereby revive confidence in the government at home and abroad; (2) to strengthen and stabilize the central government by fostering a consciousness of national solidarity of interest among those business and commercial groups holding the greater part of the domestic debt.

While the proposal concerning the foreign debt was virtually unopposed, the plan to fund the domestic debt was bitterly attacked by debtor and agrarian groups compelled by necessity to sell their securities at a steep discount. James Madison's proposal to discriminate between original holders and subsequent purchasers was rejected (22 Feb.) by the House by almost 3 to 1.

Arousing even heavier opposition was the assumption scheme, which resulted in an approximately sectional alignment. The New England states, with the largest unpaid debts, generally favored assumption. But the Southern states, most of whom had made arrangements for discharging their indebtedness, were hostile to an immense increase in the national debt for which their inhabitants would be taxed. In addition, they feared that assumption would tend to aggrandize Federal power at the expense of the states.

Virginia led the opposition to the plan, and her leading Congressional spokesman, Madison, broke with the administration on this score. The assumption proposal was defeated in the House (12 Apr.) by a vote of 31 to 29.

SECTIONAL COMPROMISE. Hamilton's resourceful negotiations kept the assumption measure alive, and differences were finally settled by a compromise on the location of the permanent seat of the national government. Hamilton, consulting with Madison at a dinner party (c.20 June) arranged by Jefferson, agreed to exert his influence to secure enough Northern votes to assure location of the National Capital along the Potomac (instead of Philadelphia) in return for Madison's pledge to obtain a sufficient number of Southern votes to effect passage of assumption.

The House, 32–29 (10 July), fixed the site of the projected national capital in a district 10 mi. sq. along the Potomac, the precise area to be selected by the President. Philadelphia, where Congress assembled on 6 Dec., was named temporary capital until 1800. By 34–28 (26 July) the House adopted the assumption plan, and the funding provision for the debt became law on 4 Aug.

SOUTHERN FEARS. Despite the compromise, Southern apprehensions still remained, and found their voice in the Virginia resolutions (16 Dec.) framed by Patrick Henry. The Virginians protested that the assumption scheme established and perpetuated a moneyed interest, subordinated agricultural to commercial interests, and was inimical to republican institutions and the federal form of government, and that they could "find no clause in the constitution authorizing Congress to assume the debts of states!" Wrote Hamilton, privately: "This is the first symptom of a spirit which must either be killed, or will kill the Constitution."

1791

25 Feb. BANK OF THE U.S. On 13 Dec. 1790 Hamilton submitted to the House his report on a national bank. Before signing (25 Feb.) the bill chartering the Bank of the U.S., President Washington requested members of his Cabinet to submit written opinions on the constitutionality of the measure.

Jefferson's opinion (15 Feb.) maintaining that the bill was unconstitutional advanced the doctrine commonly known as "strict constructionist." Jefferson took as his main ground the 10th Amendment (not yet adopted). The incorporation of a bank, he argued, was not among the powers specifically delegated to Congress.

Hamilton's opinion (23 Feb.) elaborated the doctrine of "implied powers" (the so-called "loose constructionist" view of the Constitution). He contended that the proposed bank was related to Congressional power to collect taxes and regulate trade: a delegated power implied the employment of such means as were proper for its execution. He declared: "If the *end* be clearly comprehended within any of the specified

powers, and if the measure have an obvious relation to that *end,* and is not forbidden by any particular provision of the Constitution, it may safely be deemed to come within the compass of the national authority."

Although Washington was not fully convinced of the weight of argument on either side, he favored Hamilton's view on the ground that in such instances Presidential support should go to the Cabinet officer whose department was immediately and directly involved.

3 Mar. WHISKY TAX. Hamilton's 2d report on the public credit (13 Dec. 1790) recommended an excise tax on the manufacture of distilled liquors as a means of supplementing revenue yielded by the tariff. This levy, imposing a heavy burden on backwoods farmers for whom distilling was the chief mode of disposing of surplus grain (owing to poor roads and high shipment costs), stirred keen discontent among those affected by it.

EMERGING POLITICAL ALIGNMENTS. Dissatisfied with the administration's fiscal policies, Jefferson and Madison made a tour (May-June) of New York State, with excursions into New England, where they appear to have sounded out Antifederalist sentiment (particularly among the Clinton-Livingston-Burr faction in New York) for the purpose of forming a coalition on national lines. The political breach was widened with the establishment (31 Oct.) of the *National Gazette,* an antiadministration organ under the editorship of Philip Freneau, which soon crossed swords with the Federalist *Gazette of the United States* edited by John Fenno (begun 15 Apr. 1789).

The emerging **Jefferson-Hamilton feud** later became a personal quarrel, but its essential significance lay in its origin: a conflict of principle over the nature and ends of society and government. Jeffersonian principles embraced (1) a democratic agrarian order based on the individual freeholder; (2) a broad diffusion of wealth; (3) relative freedom from industrialism, urbanism, and organized finance; (4) sympathy for debtor interests; (5) distrust of centralized government; (6) belief in the perfectibility of man; and (7) confidence in the view that the people, acting through representative institutions, could be left to govern themselves. Hamiltonian principles included (1) a balanced and diversified economic order; (2) active governmental encouragement of finance, industry, commerce, and shipping; (3) sympathy for creditor interests; (4) advocacy of a strong national government under executive leadership; (5) distrust of the people's capacity to govern; and (6) a belief that the best government was that of an elite.

These views generally reflected the doctrines associated with the two national parties (in each case a larger grouping of local coalitions) formed during this period: the Republicans, also known as the Democratic-Republicans, under the leadership of Jefferson; and the Federalists, under the leadership of Hamilton. Competent latter-day authorities differ over the approximate date of origin of these parties. Among the dates indicated for their definite emergence are 1787–88 (C. A. Beard), 1791–92 (J. S. Bassett; D. Malone), and 1798 (O. G. Libby).

26 Nov. ORIGINS OF THE CABINET. As early as Oct. 1789 Washington consulted heads of depts. on the advisability of his making a tour of the U.S. He continued to consult them individually on matters of policy. On 26 Nov. and 28 Dec. 1791 he met with the dept. heads to consider foreign and military matters. At least 3 such meetings occurred in 1792. By the time Adams became President the practice of Cabinet meetings was well established.

5 Dec. REPORT ON MANUFACTURES submitted by Hamilton proposed a system of tariffs for industry, bounties for agriculture, and a network of internal improvements under Federal sponsorship. Hamilton's argument for encouraging manufactures made no marked impression at this time.

1792

21 Feb. PRESIDENTIAL SUCCESSION ACT (passed the House after previously passing the Senate 27–24) provided that in case of the removal, death, resignation, or disability of both President and Vice-President, the president pro tempore of the Senate would succeed; if there was no Senate president, then the speaker of the House. The Federalists defeated Jefferson's effort to have the Secy. of State made next in line of succession, a proposal finally put into effect by the Act of 1886.

8 May. MILITIA ACT. To cope with the growing Indian menace in the Northwest Territory (Gen. Arthur St. Clair had been defeated by Ohio Indians 4 Nov. 1791; Gen. Anthony Wayne was commissioned Apr. commander in chief of army to act against Ohio Indians), the Militia Act authorized state enrollment and organization of all able-bodied free white citizens between the ages of 18 and 45.

21 Aug.–15 Sept. RESISTANCE TO THE EXCISE TAX was manifested in the South (especially in the central counties of North Carolina) and in the 4 Pennsylvania counties west of the Alleghenies. At a Pittsburgh convention (21 Aug.) a series of resolutions drawn up by a committee of which **Albert Gallatin** (p. 712) was a member denounced the excise tax and declared that legal measures would be used to obstruct collections of the tax. Washington issued a proclamation (29 Sept.) warning against unlawful combinations and stating that the excise provision would be enforced.

JEFFERSON-HAMILTON FEUD. Violent attacks upon Hamilton's fiscal policies appearing in the *National Gazette* provoked Hamilton to rejoinder with a series of anonymous articles (July–Dec.) in the *Gazette of the United States*. Hamilton asserted that Jefferson had been opposed to the Constitution and its adoption, that he did not support the program of the administration, and was responsible for political intrigue disparaging the government.

Letters written by Jefferson (13 May) and Hamilton (30 July) to Washington, prevailing upon him to serve as President for a 2nd term, revealed the mutual animosity and distrust of the 2 Cabinet officers. Washington intervened, and in letters to Jefferson (23 Aug.) and Hamilton (26 Aug.) sought to heal their differences. Their replies (9 Sept.) indicated that the quarrel was still in progress.

Jefferson intimated his intention to retire after the close of Washington's first term. During a meeting with Jefferson at Mount Vernon (2 Oct.), Washington's attempt to mediate failed again.

5 Dec. PRESIDENTIAL ELECTION. Presidential electors cast their ballots. **Washington,** receiving 132 votes (with 3 abstentions), was reelected President; **John Adams,** with 77 votes, reelected Vice-President. The Antifederalist opposition gave 50 votes to George Clinton (N.Y.) for Vice-President.

1793

ATTACK ON HAMILTON. Rep. William Branch Giles (Va.) proposed a series of resolutions (23 Jan.) inquiring into the condition of the Treasury. The move climaxed the loose charges of corruption and mismanagement that had been made against Hamilton. In reports to the House (4, 13 Feb.) Hamilton made a detailed and factual defense of his official conduct. Giles and others submitted 9 resolutions (28 Feb.) censuring Hamilton's course, but none passed the House.

John Taylor of Caroline (Va., 1753–1824) published *An Examination of the Late Proceedings in Congress Respecting the Official Conduct of the Secretary of the Treasury.* An attack on the administration's fiscal measures, this pamphlet claimed that moneyed interests dominated Congress, and asked for a return to "genuine republicanism." Taylor wrote another pamphlet in a similar vein, *An Enquiry into the Principles and Tendency of Certain Public Measures* (1794).

IMPACT OF THE FRENCH REVOLUTION widened the cleavage between the Federalists and their antagonists, making party lines more definite. At its outset, the French Revolution had enlisted the sympathy of most Americans; but with the proclamation of the French Republic (21 Sept. 1792) and the execution of Louis XVI (21 Jan.), American opinion began to divide sharply. The French issue was injected into domestic affairs after France declared war (1 Feb.) on Great Britain, Spain, and Holland.

22 Apr. WASHINGTON'S NEUTRALITY PROCLAMATION. While both Hamilton and Jefferson desired to keep America neutral, Hamilton, unlike Jefferson, thought the occasion a good opportunity to repeal the treaties concluded with France in 1778. Hamilton's sympathies lay with Great Britain, those of Jefferson with France. Washington, however, steered an independent course. On 22 April he issued the Neutrality Proclamation (in which the word "neutrality" was not used) declaring that the U.S. was at peace with Great Britain and France and warning citizens to abstain from acts of hostility against any of the belligerent powers.

CITIZEN GENÊT AFFAIR. On 8 April Citizen Genêt (Edmond Charles Genêt), Minister of the French Republic to the U.S., landed at Charleston, S.C., under instructions from the Girondist regime to win U.S. amity and negotiate a new treaty of commerce. Even before presenting his credentials, he commissioned 4 privateers and dispatched them to prey upon British vessels along the U.S. coast. He also took steps to organize on American soil expeditions against Spanish and British territories.

En route (18 Apr.–16 May) from Charleston to Philadelphia, Genêt received a warm ovation. President Washington, however, received him (18 May) with cool formality; and on 5 June Jefferson presented Genêt with a communication from the President stating that Genêt's grants of military commissions on American soil constituted an infringement of U.S. national sovereignty. Genêt was also notified that the privateers commissioned by him would have to leave American waters and could not send their prizes to U.S. ports.

Genêt promised to comply but soon afterward authorized the arming of *The Little Sarah,* a prize that had been brought in by a French vessel and was being refitted as *La Petite Démocrate.* When Genêt was warned against dispatching the vessel, he threatened to appeal over the President to the people. In violation of a promise made to Jefferson, Genêt ordered the French privateer out to sea.

The newly established Democratic societies (from which the Democratic-Republican party later took its name) and Antifederalist newspapers attacked Washington's neutrality policy. Hamilton, writing a series of articles under the pseudonym "Pacificus," defended the Neutrality Proclamation and the President's right to decide the matter. He was answered by Madison, who wrote under the signature of "Helvidius." But both Jefferson and Madison agreed that Genêt's conduct and poor judgment had harmed the Antifederalist cause.

The Cabinet decided (2 Aug.) to demand Genêt's recall. Washington sent to Congress his full correspondence with the French minister, pointing out that Genêt's conduct had tended to involve the U.S. "in war abroad, and discord and anarchy at home." By this time the Jacobins had come to power in France. Genêt's successor, Joseph Fauchet, who arrived in 1794, carried orders for Genêt's arrest. Washington refused to extradite Genêt, who became an American citizen and married a daughter of Gov. George Clinton (N.Y.).

31 Dec. JEFFERSON'S RESIGNATION. President Washington, who had originally favored maintaining friendship with France, now veered toward the Federalists and henceforth tended to lean more heavily upon Hamilton for advice on foreign affairs. Jefferson submitted his resignation (31 July) as Secretary of State, but his withdrawal did not become effective until 31 Dec. He was succeeded (2 Jan. 1794) by Edmund Randolph.

POLITICAL OPINION split on the French issue. Most Federalists supported the British cause, regarding it as a bulwark against French anarchy and atheism. Most Republicans were in sympathy with the French, not so much from principle as from long-standing antagonism to the British.

1794

5 Mar. 11TH AMENDMENT, proposed by Congress to the states following protests from the legislatures of Georgia and other states against the Supreme Court decision in *Chisholm* v. *Georgia* (1793,

p. 487), provided in effect that a state was not suable by a citizen of another state. It was declared ratified on 8 Jan. 1798.

5 June. NEUTRALITY ACT forbade U.S. citizens to enlist in the service of a foreign power and prohibited the fitting out of foreign armed vessels in U.S. ports. This reinforcement of the Neutrality Proclamation, however, did not entirely ease tension between the U.S. and Great Britain.

July–Nov. WHISKY INSURRECTION, the result of discontent over enforcement of the excise tax, broke out among the backwoods farmers of the Monongahela Valley in western Pennsylvania. President Washington issued a proclamation (7 Aug.) ordering the insurgents to return to their homes, and called for 15,000 militia from Virginia, Maryland, New Jersey, and Pennsylvania. Negotiations with the leaders of the insurrection proving fruitless, Washington issued a second proclamation (24 Sept.) ordering the suppression of the rebellion. Government forces under the command of Henry Lee, who was accompanied by Hamilton, quelled the disorders. Of the insurgents tried for treason (May 1795), 2 were convicted, and were pardoned by Washington.

19 Nov. JAY'S TREATY. An old source of American grievance against England was the British refusal, despite the provisions of the peace treaty of 1783, to evacuate the Northwest military posts. The British justified their maintenance of garrisons on the ground that legal obstacles had been raised against the recovery of pre-Revolutionary debts owed to British merchants and Loyalist property confiscated by the states. Retention of the posts retarded Western settlement and kept the lucrative fur trade in the hands of the British. To assure their control of the posts and the fur trade, the British had encouraged the establishment of an Indian barrier state. American settlers in the Ohio country believed that Indian massacres of pioneers were instigated by the British.

Anglo-U. S. friction was intensified when the British issued Orders in Council (8 June, 6 Nov., 1793) interfering with neutral shipping. The enforcement of these orders resulted in the seizure of American vessels and the impressment and imprisonment of American crews. The two nations verged on war.

One of the leading motives behind the U.S. desire for a settlement was the maintenance of the fiscal structure. British exports to the U.S. were the chief source of tariff revenue, the main prop of Hamilton's fiscal system. For the negotiation of outstanding differences, President Washington named **John Jay**, Chief Justice of the U.S., as special envoy to Great Britain. Jay, whose nomination was confirmed in the Senate on 19 Apr., arrived in England in June. He was under instructions to make no commitment in violation of the treaties with France.

Jay's Treaty was signed on 19 Nov. The outstanding concession gained by the U.S. was the British withdrawal from the Northwest posts on or before 1 June 1796. The treaty also provided for (1) admission of U.S. vessels to British East Indian ports on a nondiscriminatory basis; (2) opening of the West Indian trade to U.S. vessels not exceeding 70 tons burden, on condition that Americans renounce their carrying trade in such staples as cotton, sugar, and molasses; (3) referral to joint commissions of the payment of the pre-Revolutionary debts (British claims settled at $2,664,000, 8 Jan. 1802), the northeast boundary question, and compensation for illegal maritime seizures; and (4) placing of British trade with the U.S. on a most-favored-nation basis. No provisions were made for impressment, the Indian question, the slaves removed by the British, or Loyalist claims.

When the terms of the treaty were made known (March 1795), the Republicans took the lead in whipping up popular opposition. Southern planters were chagrined by the treaty's provision for settlement of the debt (much of which was owed by Virginia) and its silence concerning the stolen slaves. Northern shipping and commercial interests as well as Southern Federalists attacked the treaty; even Washington and some Federalist legislators thought

the treaty unsatisfactory. Hamilton entered the controversy with the publication (22 July 1795 *et seq.*) of his "Camillus" papers in support of the treaty.

The Senate ratified the treaty (24 June 1795) only after long debate and after suspension of Article XII pertaining to the West Indian trade. The Republicans in the House attempted to block the treaty by denying the appropriation for enforcing its provisions. The House request (24 Mar. 1796) for papers relating to Jay's Treaty was refused by Washington; by asserting his executive prerogative, Washington thereby set an important precedent. The appropriation was approved on 30 Apr. 1796, following a supporting speech (28 Apr.) by Fisher Ames (1758–1808).

1795

CABINET REORGANIZATION. Timothy Pickering (Mass.) was named (2 Jan.) Secretary of War. Hamilton resigned (31 Jan.) as Secretary of the Treasury and was succeeded by Oliver Wolcott, Jr., but continued as unofficial adviser on major policy decisions. Secretary of State Edmund Randolph resigned (19 Aug.) on suspicion of corruption, a charge for which he was never tried. Washington believed that Randolph had intrigued with the French Minister, Joseph Fauchet, to block the ratification of Jay's Treaty. Some held that Randolph had been in the pay of the French (vindication of Randolph's conduct in Irving Brant's *Madison*, v. 3, 1950). Randolph was succeeded by Pickering, and James McHenry became (27 Jan. 1796) Secretary of War. The Cabinet as reorganized by Washington included only Federalists. After Adams took office as President, Pickering, McHenry, and Wolcott continued to be influenced by Hamilton.

29 Jan. NATURALIZATION ACT required 5 yrs.' residence.

27 Oct. TREATY OF SAN LORENZO (PINCKNEY'S TREATY), signed at Madrid, 27 Oct. The failure of the Jay-Gardoqui negotiations (1785–86) to adjust differences between the

U.S. and Spain left open the questions of the southern and western boundaries of the U.S. and the free navigation by Americans of the Mississippi from its source to its mouth. Negotiations for the U.S. were undertaken by **Thomas Pinckney** (1750–1828), U.S. Minister to Great Britain. Spain recognized the boundary claims of the U.S. under the Treaty of 1783 (the Mississippi at the west, the 31st parallel at the south) and gave to Americans free navigation of the Mississippi and the right of deposit for their goods at New Orleans for 3 yrs. and thereafter, if need be, at another point to be designated.

1796

8 Mar. *Hylton* v. *U.S.* (3 Dallas 171), a case involving the carriage tax imposed in 1794, in which the Supreme Court for the first time upheld the constitutionality of a Congressional act.

17 Sept. WASHINGTON'S FARE-WELL ADDRESS. Dated 17 Sept., it was first published (19 Sept.) in the Philadelphia *Daily American Advertiser*. Written with the aid of Madison (1792) and Hamilton (1796), it was never orally delivered before the public. The address (1) presented Washington's reasons for declining to stand for a 3rd term; (2) deplored the dangers of a party system, particularly a division along geographical lines; (3) counseled that the public credit be cherished; (4) advised the nation to steer clear of *permanent* alliances with foreign nations and trust to "temporary alliances for extraordinary emergencies." Nowhere did it contain the phrase "entangling alliances" (used by Jefferson in his 1st inaugural).

7 Dec. PRESIDENTIAL ELECTION indicated the rising strength of the Democratic-Republican party, much of it due to dissatisfaction with Jay's Treaty. **John Adams,** Federalist candidate, received 71 votes and was elected President; **Thomas Jefferson,** Democratic-Republican, with 68 votes, Vice-President. Among the other candidates were Thomas Pinckney (Federalist, 59 votes) and Aaron Burr (Democratic-Republican, 30 votes).

1797–1800

31 May. RELATIONS WITH FRANCE. The French Directory, angered by Jay's Treaty, interfered with American shipping and refused to receive **Charles Cotesworth Pinckney** (1746–1825) as U.S. minister to France when he arrived in Dec. 1796. President Adams appointed (31 May) a commission to France consisting of Pinckney and **John Marshall** (both Federalists) and **Elbridge Gerry** (Republican, 1744–1814), who were instructed to secure a treaty of commerce and amity with France.

18 Oct. XYZ AFFAIR. The commissioners arrived at Paris (4 Oct.) and were unofficially received (8 Oct.) by the French foreign minister, Talleyrand, who found a pretext for delaying the opening of official discussions. The commissioners were visited (18 Oct.) by three agents of Talleyrand (Hottinguer, Hauteval, and Bellamy; later designated in the mission's dispatches as X, Y, and Z) who suggested a U.S. loan to France and a bribe of $240,000. The Americans refused to make concessions; Marshall replied firmly (17 Jan. 1798); and on 19 Mar. President Adams reported to Congress the failure of negotiations. Only Gerry remained at Paris, Talleyrand having intimated that if he departed, a French declaration of war against the U.S. would ensue. On 3 Apr. 1798 Adams submitted to Congress the XYZ correspondence, which aroused American public opinion regardless of party.

UNDECLARED NAVAL WAR WITH FRANCE, 1798–1800. The prowar faction of the Federalists, headed in the Cabinet by Pickering, wanted an immediate declaration of war against France. Adams, however, favored a peaceful course while strengthening national defenses: if war were to come, France would have to take the initiative. **Defense measures:** 20 acts of Congress (passed 27 Mar.–16 July 1798) provided for consolidating the national defense. Washington was named (2 July 1798) commanding general; Hamilton, 2nd in command, inspector general. On 3 May the Navy Dept. was established, and on 21 May Benjamin Stoddert named Secretary of the Navy. Congress repealed (7 July 1798) the treaties with France, and thus terminated the alliance. An undeclared naval war began with the capture of the schooner *Retaliation* by the French off Guadeloupe (20 Nov. 1798) and the engagement (9 Feb. 1799) between the *Constellation* (Capt. Thomas Truxtun, commander) and *L'Insurgente*, in which the latter was captured. On 1 Feb. 1800 the *Constellation* fought a drawn battle with *La Vengeance,* and on 12 Oct. Capt. Little in the *Boston* captured the French ship *Le Berceau.*

CONVENTION OF 1800. A complete surprise to Hamilton's prowar faction was Adams' nomination (18 Feb. 1799) of **William Vans Murray** as minister to France, followed by publication of Talleyrand's assurance that a U.S. minister would be received with respect. Federalist pressure upon Adams to change his course failed, and the President appointed a commission to France consisting of Vans Murray, Chief Justice Oliver Ellsworth, and William R. Davie, governor of North Carolina (replacing Patrick Henry, who declined because of age). The negotiations bore fruit in the **Treaty of Morfontaine** (30 Sept. 1800, commonly known as the **Convention of 1800**), which superseded the treaties of 1778 and thus formally released the U.S. from its defensive alliance with France. The Senate ratified the convention on condition that the treaties of 1778 be not merely suspended but abrogated. The convention became effective on 21 Dec. 1801.

Adams' handling of the French crisis created a schism in the Federalist party. Adams finally concluded that he was the victim of a Cabinet conspiracy, and that Pickering and McHenry, in conjunction with Hamilton, were working for his defeat in the Presidential election of 1800. On 6 May 1800 he requested the resignation of McHenry (effective 31 May); on 10 May he asked for the resignation of Pickering (dismissed from office, 12 May). Pickering was succeeded in the State Dept. by John Marshall of Virginia (13 May).

1798

ALIEN AND SEDITION ACTS. Several of the leading Republican publicists were European refugees. The threat of war with France sharpened hostility to aliens and gave the Federalists an opportunity to impose severe restrictions:

18 June. Naturalization Act changed from 5 to 14 years the period of residence required for admission to full citizenship. It was repealed in 1802, when the naturalization law of 1795 was reenacted.

25 June. Alien Act authorized the President to order out of the U.S. all aliens regarded as dangerous to the public peace and safety, or suspected of "treasonable or secret" inclinations. It expired in 1802.

6 July. Alien Enemies Act authorized the President, in time of declared war, to arrest, imprison, or banish aliens subject to an enemy power.

14 July. Sedition Act made it a high misdemeanor, punishable by fine and imprisonment, for citizens or aliens to enter into unlawful combinations opposing execution of the national laws; to prevent a federal officer from performing his duties; and to aid or attempt "any insurrection, riot, unlawful assembly, or combination." A fine of not more than $2,000 and imprisonment not exceeding 2 yrs. were provided for persons convicted of publishing "any false, scandalous and malicious writing" bringing into disrepute the U.S. government, Congress, or the President; in force until 3 March 1801.

The Sedition Act was aimed at repressing political opposition, and its enforcement, carried out in a partisan manner, resulted in the prosecution of 25 persons and the conviction of 10, all of them Republican editors and printers. (Most notable: **James Thomas Callender,** tried before Judge Samuel Chase; fined $200 and sentenced to 9 mos. imprisonment; **Matthew Lyon,** imprisoned and fined $1,000; and Dr. **Thomas Cooper,** imprisoned for 6 mos. When Jefferson became President he pardoned all those convicted under the Act. Congress restored the fines with interest.) The Republicans attacked the Alien and

Sedition Acts as unnecessary, despotic, and unconstitutional. Their opposition was climaxed by the

KENTUCKY AND VIRGINIA RESOLUTIONS. The Kentucky resolutions (in 2 sets, passed by the state legislature on 16 Nov. 1798 and 22 Nov. 1799) were drafted by Jefferson. The Virginia resolutions (passed by the state legislature 24 Dec. 1798) were framed by Madison. Both invoked the compact theory of the Constitution and maintained that the Alien and Sedition Acts were unconstitutional. The Kentucky resolutions, the more forthright of the two, held that where the national government exercised powers not specifically delegated to it, each state "has an equal right to judge for itself, as well of infractions as of the mode and measure of redress." The Virginia resolutions pointed out that in such cases the states "have the right and are in duty bound to interpose for arresting the progress of the evil." The 2nd set of Kentucky resolutions was enacted after several Northern states repudiated the doctrines set forth by Kentucky and Virginia and indicated that the Federal judiciary was the exclusive arbiter of constitutionality. It was on this occasion that the Kentucky legislature added, as it restated the view that the states had the right to judge infractions of the Constitution: "That a nullification of those sovereignties, of all unauthorized acts done under color of that instrument, is the rightful remedy." Both states, however, declared their firm attachment to the Union and took no steps to nullify or obstruct the Alien and Sedition Acts.

14 Dec. 1799. DEATH OF WASHINGTON at Mt. Vernon; eulogized in Congress (26 Dec.) by Henry Lee as "first in war, first in peace, first in the hearts of his countrymen."

1799

Feb. FRIES UPRISING. John Fries (*c*.1750–1818) raised several hundred men in Northampton, Bucks, and Montgomery Counties, Pa., in opposition to the direct federal property tax established by acts of 9 and 14 July 1798 in anticipation of war with France. At Bethlehem he resisted the U.S. marshal. Convicted of treason, he was retried before Justice Samuel Chase, again convicted and sentenced to death, but pardoned by President Adams.

1800

4 Apr. 1ST FEDERAL BANKRUPTCY LAW enacted, extended only to merchants and traders; made possible the release of Robert Morris from prison; repealed 19 Dec. 1803.

17 Nov. Congress convened in Washington for 1st time.

3 Dec. PRESIDENTIAL ELECTION. Major campaign issues: (1) Alien and Sedition Acts, (2) increase by the Federalists of direct taxes occasioned by heavy defense expenditures, (3) reduction of trade with France, and (4) growth of anti-British sentiment over the impressment of American seamen. Federalist candidates: **John Adams** (Mass.) and **Charles Cotesworth Pinckney** (S.C.). Democratic-Republican: **Thomas Jefferson** (Va.) and **Aaron Burr** (N.Y.).

1801

20 Jan. One of Adams' last official acts was his appointment of **John Marshall** as Chief Justice of the Supreme Court.

11–17 Feb. ELECTORAL TIE. When the ballot count (11 Feb.) in the Electoral College resulted in a Jefferson-Burr tie (73 votes each; 65 for Adams, 64 for Pinckney, 1 for John Jay), the election was thrown into the Federalist-dominated House of Representatives. A deadlock followed; the Federalist caucus decided to back Burr; Hamilton, however, regarded Jefferson as the lesser evil, and used his influence to break the deadlock. It has been supposed that Jefferson made certain commitments to the Federalists, but there is no reliable evidence supporting this view. On the 36th ballot (17 Feb.) **Jefferson** was chosen President by ten states (each state having one vote). **Burr** was elected Vice-President.

The election demonstrated the inadequacy of the machinery provided by the Constitution for selecting the President. To prevent a similar situation in the Electoral College, the **12th Amendment** was proposed by Congress (9 Dec. 1803) and was declared ratified on 25 Sept. 1804. It provided for separate balloting for President and Vice-President.

27 Feb. JUDICIARY ACT reduced to 5 the number of Supreme Court justices, created 16 circuit courts (establishing a judgeship for each), and added to the number of marshals, attorneys, and clerks. In principle, the measure was justified, but it was exploited by Adams for political purposes, making under this law the so-called "midnight appointments" (3 Mar. until 9 P.M.) of Federalist judges and court officials.

4 Mar. Jefferson's inaugural was the 1st held at Washington, where the permanent capital had been officially established in the summer of 1800 (Congress assumed jurisdiction over District of Columbia 27 Feb. 1801; incorporation as a city 3 May 1802, its mayor to be appointed by the President). In his conciliatory inaugural address Jefferson stressed the need for a government of limited powers, economy in the national administration, support of state governments in all their rights, acquiescence in majority decisions, the preservation of civil liberties, and "peace, commerce, and honest friendship with all nations, entangling alliances with none."

8 Dec. Jefferson's 1st annual message to Congress broke the precedent, established by Washington and continued by Adams, of addressing Congress in person. Jefferson forwarded a written version to each House. This remained the custom until Woodrow Wilson reverted (1913) to the original practice.

TRIPOLITAN WAR, 1801-05. In order to buy immunity from interference with American commerce along the North African coast, Washington and Adams continued the custom, established by the British, of paying tribute to the pirates of the Barbary States (Algiers, Morocco, Tripoli, and Tunis). When the Pasha of Tripoli increased his demands for tribute and declared war (14 May 1801) against the U.S., Jefferson, although favoring economy and peace and opposed to a navy, decided to resist

and dispatched warcraft to Mediterranean waters. In 1803 Commodore Edward Preble was named commander of the Mediterranean squadron, and on his orders Lieutenant **Stephen Decatur** performed the most notable exploit of the war: the destruction (16 Feb. 1804) of the frigate *Philadelphia,* which had been captured and converted by the Tripolitans. A vigorous blockade brought the war to an end. A treaty of peace favorable to the U.S. was signed on 4 June 1805 (but the payment of tribute to other Barbary States continued until 1816).

1802

8 Jan.–29 Apr. REPEAL OF THE JUDICIARY ACT OF 1801 was moved (8 Jan.) in the Senate at Jefferson's insistence; upon a deadlock, an adverse vote by Burr blocked the measure temporarily; but it was repealed 8 Mar. A new Judiciary Act, passed 29 April, restored to 6 the number of Supreme Court justices, fixed 1 term annually for the high court, and set up 6 circuit courts, each headed by a Supreme Court justice.

NEW FINANCIAL POLICY framed by Gallatin carried out Jefferson's pledge of retrenchment. It called for reduction of the national debt, repeal of all internal taxes (with a corollary cut in expenditures by the War and Navy Departments), and a Congressional system of appropriations for specific purposes. Between 1801–09 the national debt was reduced from $83 million to $57 million, notwithstanding the acquisition of Louisiana and the Tripolitan War.

16 Mar. U.S. Military Academy established by act of Congress. On 4 July the Academy was formally opened at West Point, N.Y.

1803

24 Feb. MARBURY v. MADISON (1 Cranch 137). The conflict between President and judiciary was brought to a head after Jefferson ordered Secretary of State Madison to withhold from William Marbury the signed and sealed commission of his appointment (2 Mar. 1801) by President Adams under the Judiciary Act of 1801 as justice of the peace of the District of Columbia. Marbury sued for a writ of mandamus compelling delivery of his commission. In dismissing Marbury's suit on the ground that the court lacked jurisdiction, Chief Justice Marshall employed a strategy calculated to avoid an open struggle with the executive branch responsible for enforcement of the writ. The case is remembered, however, as the first occasion on which the high court held an act of Congress unconstitutional: Marshall declared that Section 13 of the Judiciary Act of 1789, empowering the court to issue such a writ, was contrary to the Constitution and therefore invalid. This is the 1st case in which the Supreme Court held a law of Congress void; it did not do so again until the Dred Scott decision (p. 221).

LOUISIANA PURCHASE. By the Treaty of Fontainebleau (1762) France ceded Louisiana to Spain, but by the secret Treaty of San Ildefonso (1 Oct. 1800) the province was returned to France. The transfer was made at the behest of Napoleon, who projected the revival of a French colonial empire in North America. The retrocession was confirmed (21 Mar. 1801) by the Treaty of Madrid; shortly afterward, Jefferson learned of the secret arrangement.

Jefferson was profoundly concerned over (1) the threat posed to American security by a neighboring imperial and aggressive power; (2) the possibility that the French possession of New Orleans would close the Mississippi to Western commerce. On 16 Oct. 1802, the Spanish intendant at New Orleans interdicted the right of deposit (restored 19 Apr. 1803). This action caused consternation in the West. In a letter to Robert R. Livingston (18 Apr. 1802) Jefferson declared: "The day that France takes New Orleans . . . we must marry ourselves to the British fleet and nation."

The President instructed Robert R. Livingston, American Minister at Paris, to negotiate for a tract of land on the lower Mississippi for use as a port or, failing this, to obtain an irrevocable guarantee of free navigation and the right of deposit. On 12 Jan. 1803 James Monroe was named Minister Plenipotentiary to France for the purpose of participating in the negotiations. He was instructed to purchase New Orleans and West Florida with the $2 million provided by a Congressional appropriation; if need be, he was to offer as much as $10 million. Even before Monroe arrived at Paris (12 April), Napoleon abandoned his scheme for a colonial empire. His decision to sell Louisiana and confine his sphere to the Old World was influenced by the costly French failure to suppress the slave revolt in Haiti (1794–1804), and by the impending resumption of hostilities with Great Britain. On 11 Apr. Talleyrand asked Livingston how much the U.S. was prepared to pay for the whole of Louisiana. With Barbé-Marbois, Napoleon's finance minister, acting for the French, Livingston and Monroe closed the negotiations. In sealing the bargain, the American envoys exceeded their instructions.

By the treaty of cession (signed 2 May, but antedated 30 Apr.), Louisiana was purchased by the U.S. for 60 million francs (approximately $15 million). The price for the territory itself was $11,250,-000; the remainder covered the debts, owed by France to U.S. citizens, which the U.S. government assumed.

The purchase of Louisiana doubled the area of the U.S. by the acquisition of a tract of some 828,000 square miles lying between the Mississippi and the Rocky Mountains. The treaty, however, did not define exact boundaries. While the Gulf of Mexico was fixed as the line to the south and the Mississippi as that to the east, there was no clear understanding as to whether the cession included West Florida and Texas.

The Constitution made no provision for the purchase and assimilation of foreign territory, and the constitutional aspect of the purchase perplexed Jefferson, who, although in principle committed to strict construction, took a broad constructionist view on this issue, while the Federalists took an equally inconsistent strict constructionist stand. The substance of the Republican position—that the power to govern territory flows from the right to acquire it—was upheld (1828) by Chief Justice Marshall in *American Insurance Co.* v. *Canter* (1 Peters 511).

The Senate approved the treaty (20 Oct.) 24–7. On 20 Dec. the U.S. took formal possession of Louisiana. William C. C. Claiborne was formally installed (1 Oct. 1804) as territorial governor. In 1812 the state of Louisiana became the 1st to be admitted from the territory.

NORTHERN CONFEDERACY SCHEME, 1803–04. Behind the constitutional controversy over Louisiana lay Federalist fears that the states carved out of the Western territories would inevitably change the political balance of power in Congress, with the agrarian and frontier interests of the South and West gaining ascendancy over the commercial and industrial interests of the Northeast.

ESSEX JUNTO, a name first applied by John Hancock in 1781 to a group in Essex County, Mass. (later anti-French Federalist extremists), under the leadership of Senator **Timothy Pickering** (Mass.), considered establishment of a Northern Confederacy including the 5 New England states, New York, and New Jersey, but such extremists as George Cabot and Theophilus Parsons refused to associate themselves with the plan. Hamilton's opposition to Pickering's scheme increased when it became apparent that the disunionists were counting on Burr's election as governor of New York, a state held essential to the formation of the confederacy.

11 July 1804. BURR-HAMILTON DUEL. Hamilton, who played a decisive role in securing Burr's defeat in the New York election (25 Apr. 1804), was reported to have said (16 Feb. 1804) that Burr was "a dangerous man, and one who ought not to be trusted with the reins of government." Burr's demand for an explanation led to the Burr-Hamilton duel (Weehawken, N.J., 11 July 1804), in which Hamilton was fatally wounded. With Hamilton's death (12 July), the Burr-Pickering coalition disintegrated completely.

LEWIS AND CLARK EXPEDITION, 1803–06. In his message to Congress (Jan.), Jefferson asked for an appropriation for an expedition for the purpose of cultivating friendly relations with the Indians and extending the internal commerce of the U.S. Congress lent its approval. Meriwether Lewis and William Clark (p. 741) were chosen to lead the expedition. On 31 Aug. the party began its descent of the Ohio and on 14 May 1804 began their ascent of the Missouri. They spent the following winter in the region of the Mandan Indians, near present-day Bismarck, N.D. On 7 Apr. 1805, they began their ascent of a Missouri River fork which they named the Jefferson (others named Madison and Gallatin), crossed the Rockies, and came within sight of the Pacific Ocean on 7 Nov. 1805. The expedition, which returned to St. Louis on 23 Sept. 1806, proved the feasibility of an overland route to the Far West, added to scientific knowledge, and ultimately stimulated Western settlement and commerce.

1804

12 Mar. IMPEACHMENT OF PICKERING AND CHASE. Jefferson's conflict with the Federalist judiciary was carried forward by the impeachment as unfit of Judge John Pickering, Federal district judge in New Hampshire, who was adjudged guilty by the Senate and removed from his post (12 Mar.). Also impeached was Judge Samuel Chase (Md.), Associate Justice of the U.S. Supreme Court, for his bias in the trials of Fries and Callender; his acquittal brought to a close the Republican campaign against the Federalist judges.

5 Dec. PRESIDENTIAL ELECTION. The 1st regular caucus of members of Congress for the nomination of Presidential candidates had (25 Feb.) unanimously nominated **Jefferson** for reelection and **George Clinton** as his running mate. **Thomas Jefferson,** opposed by the Federalist candidate **Charles Cotesworth Pinckney,** was reelected President, with 162 out of 176 electoral votes. Jefferson carried all the New England states except Connecticut. In the 1st election with separate ballots for President and Vice-

President, **George Clinton** was elected Vice-President, 162 to 14 for Rufus King. The Republican party won undisputed control of Congress.

1805

9 Aug. PIKE'S EXPEDITIONS. Lieut. Zebulon M. Pike (p. 766) was dispatched by Gen. James Wilkinson to explore (1805–06) the sources of the Mississippi. In a 2nd expedition (1806–07) he explored Colorado and New Mexico. Named after him was Pikes Peak, Colo., which he sighted 15 Nov. 1807.

1806

25 Jan.–21 Nov. COMMERCE AND NEUTRAL RIGHTS. With the resumption (1803) of the Napoleonic Wars, American neutrality faced new tests. Great Britain and France clamped further restrictions on the neutral carrying trade in order to deprive each other of the means of war. The overwhelming superiority of British over French naval power made its interference with American commerce the more serious invasion of neutral rights. There followed a renewal of the controversies with England over neutral trade, impressment, and blockade.

In a series of acts and orders (1804–05) the British evolved a West Indian trade policy calculated to destroy neutral commerce with French and Spanish colonies in America that furnished staples to Napoleon's armies. The "Rule of 1756," laid down by British courts during the Seven Years' War, to the effect that where a European nation has forbidden trade with its colonies in time of peace it shall not open it to neutrals in time of war, was enforced against U.S. neutral carriers (1793) after the outbreak of war between England and France. The latter had evaded this restriction by landing cargo at a U.S. port, passing it through the customs, and securing fresh clearance for a belligerent port. This principle of the "broken voyage" was upheld in British admiralty decisions in the cases of the *Immanuel* (1799) and the *Polly* (1800). There-

after the large number of American vessels plying between the French West Indies and France enjoyed relative freedom. British policy was abruptly reversed by the decision (23 July 1805) in the *Essex* case, when the British judge, Sir William Scott, declared that American cargo was subject to seizure and condemnation unless the shipper could prove that he had originally intended to terminate the voyage in an American port. Failing that, the voyage could be regarded as a **continuous** one between enemy ports. As a result of this decision, the seizures of American vessels increased sharply.

Madison's report (25 Jan.) on the British infringement of the rights of neutral commerce and the impressment of American seamen was followed (12 Feb.) by a Senate resolution attacking British seizures as "an unprovoked aggression" and a "violation of neutral rights." Great Britain took no heed. In retaliation, Congress passed the **Nicholson** (or 1st) **Non-Importation Act** (18 Apr.) prohibiting the importation from England of a long list of articles (including hemp, flax, tin, brass, and some classes of woolens) which could be produced in the U.S. or imported from other countries. It was to become effective 15 Nov.; upon the advice of Jefferson, it was suspended (19 Dec.) and was not again operative until 22 Dec. 1808. On 16 May British Foreign Minister Charles James Fox declared a blockade of the European coast from Brest to the river Elbe. Napoleon answered with the **Berlin Decree** (21 Nov.) declaring the British Isles in a state of blockade, forbidding all commerce and communication with them, and authorizing the seizure and confiscation of vessels and cargo.

31 Dec. M O N R O E - P I N K N E Y TREATY. At the instigation of Congress, Jefferson dispatched (May) William Pinkney (Md.) as special envoy to London to join James Monroe in negotiating a treaty with Great Britain. His instructions called for (1) British abandonment of the impressment of American seamen, (2) restoration of the West Indian trade on the basis of the "broken voyage," (3) indemnity payments **for**

seizures made after the *Essex* decision. Prolonged discussions with Lord Holland began 27 Aug.; as a bargaining point, the U.S. envoys used the threat of enforcing the Non-Importation Act. British refusal to make concessions finally moved Monroe and Pinkney to violate their instructions. The treaty was a defeat for U.S. diplomacy. It made no reference to impressment or indemnities and constituted a slight compromise on the West Indian trade. Jefferson received the treaty in March, 1807. Deeply embarrassed over its terms, he never submitted it to the Senate, but instructed the U.S. envoys (20 May 1807) that the treaty serve as a basis for reopening discussions.

1807-09

7 Jan.–17 Dec. BRITISH AND FRENCH COUNTERMEASURES. The British retaliated against the Berlin Decree with an Order in Council (7 Jan.) barring all shipping from the coastal trade of France and her allies. The enforcement of Napoleon's Continental system nevertheless became more effective after his Tilsit agreement (25 June) with Czar Alexander of Russia. The British struck back with new Orders in Council (11 Nov.) prohibiting commerce with Continental ports from which the British flag was excluded; only vessels which had first passed through a British port, and there paid customs duties and secured new clearances, were permitted to call at open ports on the Continent. Napoleon's **Milan Decree** (17 Dec.) declared that all vessels searched by the British or obeying the Orders in Council would be regarded as "denationalized" and subject to seizure and confiscation as British property.

19 Feb.–1 Sept. AARON BURR "CONSPIRACY" AND TRIAL, 1804–07. Shortly after slaying Hamilton, Burr, his political career now at an end, asked money of Anthony Merry, British Minister to the U.S., supposedly for the purpose of organizing a movement for separating the Western states from the U.S. The British never gave him funds; from the Spanish Minister, whom he subsequently approached, Burr received a

small sum. Whether Burr's aim was treasonable, or whether he was planning to lead a filibustering expedition against the Spanish dominions, is still a matter of dispute (Henry Adams, 1890, held that Burr plotted disunion; W. F. McCaleb, 1903, maintained that Burr, far from conspiring to commit treason, sought to build a Western empire through annexation of Spanish territories in the Southwest and Mexico). Burr is known to have conferred with General James Wilkinson, commander of U.S. forces in the Mississippi Valley, during a tour (May–Sept. 1805) of that region. At the end of Aug. 1806, Burr went to Blennerhasset's Island, in the Ohio River, the home of Harman Blennerhasset, one of his chief associates. Here he made preparations for a military expedition, his force consisting of some 60 to 80 men and about 10 boats, and then left for Tennessee. Wilkinson and others warned President Jefferson, who issued a proclamation (27 Nov. 1806) warning citizens against participating in an illegal expedition against Spanish territory. Burr was apparently unaware of the proclamation by the time he rejoined his followers for the journey down the Mississippi. The expedition passed several American forts without interference; when the party reached a point some 30 miles above Natchez, Burr learned that Wilkinson, at New Orleans, had betrayed him. Burr fled toward Spanish Florida, but was arrested in Alabama (19 Feb.) and taken to Richmond, Va., where he was brought (30 Mar. 1807) before Chief Justice. Marshall, presiding over the U.S. Circuit Court. Originally held for a misdemeanor in forming an expedition against Spanish territory, Burr was indicted (24 June) for treason. The trial (3 Aug.–1 Sept.), which ended in the acquittal of Burr and his associates, settled the U.S. law of treason, which Marshall strictly construed. Burr then went into European exile to escape further prosecutions (for murder of Hamilton in N.Y. and N.J., and for treason in Ohio, Ky., Miss., and La.).

22 June. CHESAPEAKE-LEOPARD AFFAIR. The U.S. frigate *Chesapeake*, commanded by Commodore James Barron, was hailed by the British frigate

Leopard outside the 3-mi. limit off Norfolk Roads. The British commander claimed that 4 men aboard the *Chesapeake* were British deserters, and demanded their surrender. When Commodore Barron refused to permit search of his vessel, the *Leopard* opened fire, killing 3 and wounding 18, and removed the 4 alleged deserters. The crippled *Chesapeake* returned to Norfolk. News of the incident aroused anti-British feeling. Jefferson issued (2 July) a proclamation ordering British warships to leave U.S. territorial waters. A British proclamation (17 Oct.) ordered a more vigorous prosecution of impressment of British subjects from neutral vessels. Discussions concerning reparations for the attack on the *Chesapeake* lasted until 1808, but satisfaction was blocked by the British demanding as a condition the withdrawal of Jefferson's proclamation. Not until 1 Nov. 1811 did the British present an offer of settlement which Secretary Monroe accepted (12 Nov.).

1807–09, EMBARGO. Jefferson decided to rely upon economic pressure to bring the belligerent powers to terms. While the Non-Importation Act had again become effective (14 Dec. 1807), its threatened use had already failed to move the British. Jefferson sent (18 Dec.) a message to Congress recommending an embargo. Federalist opposition failed to block speedy action on the measure. The bill was passed in the Senate (18 Dec.), 22–6; passage in the House (21 Dec.), 82–44, was supported chiefly by the South and West. The embargo became law on 22 Dec.

The Embargo Act interdicted virtually all land and seaborne commerce with foreign nations. It forbade all U.S. vessels to leave for foreign ports. U.S. ships in the coastwise trade were required to post bond double the value of craft and cargo as a guarantee that the goods would be relanded at a U.S. port. While importation in foreign bottoms was not prohibited, it was almost outlawed by the provision that foreign vessels could not carry goods out of an American port. The law was supplemented by the Embargo Acts of 9 Jan. and 12 Mar. 1808. Means were soon found for evading its provisions. A brisk smuggling trade was carried out by land and water, particularly across the Canadian border. U.S. ships which had been at sea when the act went into operation remained in foreign waters and continued their trade with the warring nations. The British government cooperated with merchants who violated the law. The effect upon the British economy was minor, as British shippers gained by the wholesale removal of U.S. competition, while their government was able to draw upon South America as a fresh source of supply. The French used the Embargo to their own advantage. Under the pretext of aiding the U.S. to enforce the law, Napoleon issued the **Bayonne Decree** (17 Apr. 1808) ordering the seizure of all U.S. vessels entering the ports of France, Italy, and the Hanseatic towns. Napoleon justified this move by accepting the Embargo as effective and declaring that any U.S. shipping in those ports must obviously be British vessels furnished with false papers. The strict enforcement of the Bayonne Decree resulted in French confiscation (1808–09) of some $10 million worth of U.S. goods and shipping.

Domestic opposition to the Embargo was strongest in the mercantile areas of New England and New York, where Eastern Republicans made common cause with Federalists on this issue. Although the Embargo stimulated New England industry, the benefits were outweighed by the heavy losses sustained by the carrying trade. Widespread economic distress brought the Federalists into power in the New England state governments after the elections of 1808. Popular hostility to the Embargo was increased by the **Enforcement Act** (9 Jan. 1809), which provided for strict enforcement and authorized severe penalties for evasions of the act. Numerous town meetings attacked the Embargo as a pro-French, anti-British measure, and state legislatures challenged its constitutionality. Resolutions drawn up by the Massachusetts legislature (Jan., Feb., 1809) characterized it as unjust and arbitrary. In his address to the Connecticut legislature (23 Feb. 1809) Gov. Jonathan Trumbull asserted that whenever Congress exceeded its constitutional powers, the state legislatures were in duty bound "to interpose their protecting shield between the rights and liberties of the people and the assumed power of the general government." Governors refused to furnish militia officers requested by collectors for enforcing the Embargo. Timothy Pickering proposed a New England convention for nullifying the Embargo.

Amid this flurry of states'-rights views, Chief Justice Marshall handed down his opinion (20 Feb. 1809) in *U.S.* v. *Peters* (5 Cranch 115). Although the case was not related to the Embargo (it involved the annulment of a Federal court order by the state of Pennsylvania), it was memorable for Marshall's pronouncement sustaining the power of the national over state authority. The Embargo itself was upheld (1808) by a Federalist Judge Davis in U.S. district court in Massachusetts, but appeal on the decision was never taken to the Supreme Court.

In Congress opposition came from (1) the Federalists, (2) the dissident "Quids," a faction led by **John Randolph** of Roanoke (1773–1833). Jefferson signed the **Non-Intercourse Act** (1 Mar. 1809) repealing the Embargo effective 15 Mar. 1809, reopening trade with all nations except France and Great Britain, and authorizing the President to proclaim resumption of trade with France or Great Britain in the event either power should cease violating neutral rights. The British Minister to the U.S., David M. Erskine, gave assurances to Secretary of State Robert Smith that the Orders in Council of 1807, as applicable to the U.S., would be revoked 10 June 1809. Unaware that Erskine had not been authorized to speak for his government, President Madison issued a proclamation (19 Apr. 1809) legalizing trade with Great Britain. British Foreign Secretary George Canning disavowed (30 May 1809) Erskine's arrangement and ordered him back to England. President Madison in turn issued a proclamation (9 Aug. 1809) reviving the Non-Intercourse Act against Great Britain.

1808

1 Jan. AFRICAN SLAVE TRADE. Congressional interference with the foreign slave trade before 1808 was forbidden under Art. I, Sect. 9 of the Constitution. In keeping with Jefferson's recommendation (2 Dec. 1806), Congress forbade (2 Mar. 1807) slave importations into U.S. on and after 1 Jan. 1808. The law provided a penalty of forfeiture of vessel and cargo, with disposal of the seized slaves to be left to the state in which the ship was condemned.

7 Dec. PRESIDENTIAL ELECTION. Confirming the precedent established by Washington, Jefferson refused to stand for a 3rd term. As his successor in the "Virginia dynasty" he supported **James Madison,** who was nominated by a Congressional caucus. Madison's nomination was opposed by 2 insurgent wings of the Republican party. The Southern "Old Republicans" (John Randolph-John Taylor of Caroline group) chose **James Monroe** (Va., who withdrew from the contest). The Eastern Republicans, smarting under the Embargo, nominated Vice-President **George Clinton** (N.Y.). The Federalist candidates were **Charles Cotesworth Pinckney** (S.C.) and **Rufus King** (N.Y.). Madison received 122 electoral votes to 47 for Pinckney and 6 for George Clinton. **Clinton** received 113 for Vice-President to 47 for Rufus King. The Federalists gained in the House, but did not secure a majority.

1810

1 May. MACON'S BILL NO. 2. Congress took its own course after the collapse of the Erskine agreement. Since the Non-Intercourse Act was due to expire at the close of the 2nd session of the 11th Congress in 1810, a substitute measure introduced by Nathaniel Macon (N.C.), chairman of the Foreign Affairs Committee, authorized the President to reopen commerce with Great Britain and France, adding that in the event either nation should before 3 Mar. 1811 modify or revoke its edicts so as to cease violations of American shipping, the President could prohibit trade with the other. If at the end of 3 mos. the other power failed to withdraw its edicts, the President was empowered to revive non-intercourse against it. The bill, which also excluded British and French naval craft from American territorial waters, passed the House 64–27, the Federalists voting solidly against it. The French regarded the act as discrimination in favor of Great Britain, whose naval power closed the sea routes to French shipping.

5 Aug.–2 Nov. NAPOLEON'S DECEPTION. Acting on the pretense of making reprisals against the Non-Intercourse Act, Napoleon issued (23 Mar.) the **Rambouillet Decree** ordering seizure and confiscation of all U.S. vessels entering any French port. The decree, published 14 May, was made retroactive to 20 May 1809. When Napoleon learned of Macon's Bill No. 2, he instructed (5 Aug.) his Foreign Minister, the Duc de Cadore, to notify John Armstrong, U.S. Minister at Paris, that the Berlin and Milan decrees would be revoked after 1 Nov. on condition that the U.S. declare non-intercourse against the British unless the Orders in Council were withdrawn. Yet on the same day Napoleon signed the **Decree of Trianon** ordering sequestration of U.S. vessels that had called at French ports between 20 May 1809 and 1 May 1810.

In communicating Napoleon's order to Armstrong, the Duc de Cadore took liberty with his phrasing and declared that the Berlin and Milan Decrees had been actually canceled. President Madison unsuspectingly accepted the French communication at face value and issued (2 Nov.) a proclamation reopening trade with France and declaring that commerce with Great Britain would come to a halt on 2 Feb. 1811. Non-intercourse against the British was sanctioned (2 Mar. 1811) by Congress. More than a year elapsed before the British revoked the Orders in Council. The delay proved costly. The immediate British response to the move was a renewal of the blockade of New York and a more vigorous impressment of American seamen.

Napoleon's duplicity was revealed after Joel Barlow, whom Madison had named minister to France, arrived at Paris (19 Sept. 1811) in order to seek clarification of the Berlin and Milan Decrees. The Duc de Bassano, Napoleon's Foreign Minister, showed Barlow the Decree of St. Cloud, supposedly signed by Napoleon 28 Apr. 1811. It stated that his earlier decrees had been declared nonexistent in regard to U.S. vessels since 1 Nov. 1810. The decree had never been published and, despite French assurances, had never been communicated to the U.S. government. Barlow's death (24 Dec. 1812) in Poland, where he had gone to confer with Napoleon, brought his mission to an end. By this time, however, Napoleon's involvement in the Russian campaign had terminated his influence in American affairs, and the U.S. was at war with Great Britain.

27 Oct. ANNEXATION OF WEST FLORIDA. The Louisiana treaty of 1803 made no reference to the status of Spanish-ruled East and West Florida. Jefferson supported the view that Louisiana included that portion of Florida between the Mississippi River to the west and the Perdido River to the east. In 1810 Southern expansionists led a revolt in the Spanish dominion, captured the fort at Baton Rouge, and proclaimed (26 Sept.) the independent state of the Republic of West Florida. Madison issued a proclamation (27 Oct.) announcing U.S. possession of West Florida from the Mississippi to the Perdido and authorizing its military occupation as part of the Orleans Territory. Congress assembled in secret session and adopted a resolution (15 Jan. 1811) authorizing extension of U.S. rule over East Florida as well in the event local authority consented or a foreign power took steps to occupy it. On 14 May 1812 West Florida was incorporated by Congress into the Mississippi Territory. After the outbreak of the War of 1812, Gen. James Wilkinson took the Spanish fort at Mobile (15 Apr. 1813) and occupied the Mobile district of West Florida to the Perdido River. This was the sole territorial conquest retained by the U.S. after the War of 1812.

YAZOO LAND FRAUD. The Georgia legislature (7 Jan. 1795) sold to 4 land companies (whose shareholders were discovered to include Georgia legislators) 35 million acres in the Yazoo River country (Mississippi and Alabama) for

$500,000. A new legislature rescinded (1796) this sale. When Georgia ceded (1802) to the U.S. her Western claims, the national government sought a final settlement by awarding 5 million acres to holders of Yazoo land warrants. With the support of other "Quids" John Randolph, who had already split with the administration over Louisiana, succeeded in blocking the bill (1804–05), which was not passed until 1814, when the claimants were awarded $48 million. Randolph's opposition precipitated a party schism and led to his removal as leader of the majority. The Yazoo affair was the subject of Chief Justice Marshall's opinion (1810) in *Fletcher* v. *Peck* (6 Cranch 87), in which he maintained that the judiciary could not inquire into the motives of legislators who made the original grant and construed the grant as a contract within the meaning of the Constitution and the rescinding law as impairing the obligation of the contract; hence void.

1811

24 Jan.–20 Feb. BANK DEBATE. The charter of the 1st U.S. Bank was due to expire 4 Mar. Petitions for extension of the charter had been made in 1808 and 1810, but Congressional consideration was postponed because of the pressure of foreign affairs. Secretary of the Treasury Gallatin, lauding the management of the Bank, endorsed renewal of the charter. Opposed to renewal were (1) "Old Republicans" who viewed the Bank as the last survival of Federalist power, denounced it on constitutional grounds, and desired to drive Gallatin from office on the issue; (2) Anglophobes who pointed to the fact that two thirds of the Bank stock was held by Britons and insisted that the measure would aid a potential enemy; (3) interests favoring the growth of state-chartered banks, which had increased rapidly, expanded their note issues, and were eager to share the profits of the Bank. The recharter bill died in the House (24 Jan.). In the Senate, where William Henry Crawford (Ga.) led the fight for the administration bill and William Branch Giles (Va.) opposed it, the tie (17 to 17) was broken by Vice-President Clinton, who voted (20 Feb.) against renewal. The Bank wound up its business and expired. Failure to recharter the Bank deprived the government of urgently needed financial resources during the War of 1812.

16 May. LITTLE BELT AFFAIR. In May, British cruisers off New York Harbor resumed more freely their impressment of American seamen. The British 38-gun frigate *Guerrière* overhauled (1 May) off Sandy Hook the American brig *Spitfire* and impressed a native-born American. Captain John Rodgers, commanding the U.S. 44-gun frigate *President,* was ordered (6 May) to cruise off Sandy Hook to give protection to American vessels. En route Rodgers sighted a ship he mistook for the *Guerrière* (actually the craft was the British 20-gun corvette *Little Belt*). Rodgers gave chase; the *Little Belt* refused to identify herself; and the pursuit ended in an evening engagement (16 May) off Cape Charles. The broadsides of the *President* disabled the *Little Belt,* killing 9 and wounding 23 of her crew. On 1 Nov. the U.S. government informed the British minister, Augustus John Foster, that it was willing to settle the matter amicably, provided the Orders in Council were revoked.

31 July–8 Nov. TECUMSEH AND THE NORTHWEST. Along the frontiers of the Old Northwest the Shawnee chief **Tecumseh** (?1768–1813) undertook the organization of a defensive tribal confederacy to resist the westward sweep of white settlement. The British governor in Canada, as well as the fur traders, were reputedly backing Tecumseh and his brother, the Prophet. When extensive Indian activity during the summer of 1811 created fear among frontier settlers, the people of Vincennes adopted resolutions (31 July) calling for the destruction of the Indian capital on Tippecanoe Creek. The settlers finally induced Gen. **William Henry Harrison,** governor of the Indiana Territory, to take the initiative against Tecumseh (who meanwhile had gone to the Southwest to seek support for his plan). Leading a force of some

1,000 men, Harrison set out (26 Sept.) from Vincennes for the Indian capital 150 mi. to the north, near the confluence of the Tippecanoe and the Wabash. Ft. Harrison, about 65 mi. above Vincennes, was established; on 28 Oct. the force resumed its march and encamped (6 Nov.) about a mile from the Indian village. In a surprise dawn attack (7 Nov.) the Indians descended upon the Americans. After a day-long battle, Harrison's men, despite heavy losses, beat back the Indians and razed the village (8 Nov.). The Americans then withdrew to Ft. Harrison. Westerners acclaimed the **Battle of Tippecanoe** as a great victory. Although the British authorities in Canada subsequently took steps to cut off aid to the Indians, the event increased anti-British sentiment along the frontier and resulted in louder demands for expelling the British from Canada. Indian raids broke out again (Apr. 1812) along the frontier, but Tecumseh chose to remain on the defensive. It was generally recognized that open war with the Indians would necessarily be part of a declared war against the British.

4 Nov. "WAR HAWKS." The prowar feeling that swept the country in 1810–11 left its mark on the Congressional elections. The 12th Congress numbered even fewer Federalists and, in place of many of the cautious legislators who had enacted Macon's Bill No. 2, brought to the fore a new type of Republican who espoused nationalism and expansionism. Upon these war Republicans John Randolph bestowed the epithet: "war hawks." Among them were **Henry Clay** (p. 686), **Richard M. Johnson** (Ky., 1780–1850), **John C. Calhoun** (p. 683), **William Lowndes** (S.C., 1782–1822), **Langdon Cheves** (S.C., 1776–1857), **Felix Grundy** (Tenn., 1777–1840), **Peter B. Porter** (1773–1844) from western New York. Notwithstanding their numerical minority the "war hawks" achieved a commanding position in the House. Clay was elected Speaker; the Foreign Relations Committee came under the control of Calhoun, Grundy, and Porter; Cheves was named chairman of the Naval Committee.

Most of the "war hawks" came from the agrarian areas of the South and West

whose people were hardly affected by maritime issues (although some Westerners claimed that the Orders in Council had crippled their markets for agricultural produce); yet they chose to view maritime seizure and impressment as outrages upon national rights and honor. Northern and Southern "war hawks" found common ground in expansionism (J. W. Pratt, 1925). Those from the Northwest, eager to destroy the frontier Indian menace they attributed to British intrigue and incitement, equated security with land hunger and demanded the conquest of Canada. The Southerners wanted to wrest Florida from Spain, Britain's ally.

5 Nov. Despite expansionist pressures, the U.S. would not have been involved in war had it not been for maritime and commercial issues. Madison was no tool of the war party (see Theodore Clarke Smith, 1931), although he ultimately supported its program. The President's message to Congress attacked Great Britain, had no friendly words for France, but made no express reference to impressment. The President requested preparations for the national defense, pointing to the "evidence of hostile inflexibility in trampling on rights which no independent nation can relinquish."

1812

1–10 Apr. WAR PREPARATIONS. Madison's message to Congress (1 Apr.) recommending an immediate and general embargo for 60 days was regarded by the "war hawks" as a prelude to armed conflict. The bill passed in the House (70–41). In the Senate, where the vote was 20–13, moderate Republicans, anxious to prolong negotiations with Great Britain, amended the bill to extend the embargo to 90 days. The embargo became law on 4 Apr. On 10 Apr. the President was empowered to call up for 6 mos.' service 100,000 militia from the states and territories.

10 Apr.–16 June. FAILURE OF DIPLOMACY. Madison's persistence in maintaining that the Berlin and Milan Decrees were not in force against the U.S. was countered by British denial that

Napoleon had unconditionally revoked them. Refusing to annul the Orders in Council, the British affirmed their view in a note (10 April) sent by Foreign Secretary Lord Castlereagh. Madison interpreted it as final notice of Britain's unyielding position, and toward the close of May drafted a message calling for an immediate declaration of war.

Under the impact of economic distress at home, the British government had begun to give way gradually, if reluctantly. The revival of non-intercourse, combined with the increased effectiveness of the Continental system, created severe hardships for English commercial and industrial interests. In 1810–11 factories and mills shut down; unemployment rose; the price of foodstuffs soared; and in one year alone (1811) British exports fell off by a third. Employers and workers joined in petitioning Parliament to consider repeal of the Orders. Prime Minister Spencer Perceval stood in danger of losing his office on the issue when he was assassinated (11 May) by a deranged malcontent. The consequent delay in taking up the question was crucial. Lord Castlereagh announced (16 June) suspension of the Orders in Council (formally suspended 23 June). Across the Atlantic the U.S. Congress, unaware of the British concession, had already moved for war.

18 June. DECLARATION OF WAR ON GREAT BRITAIN. Madison's message to Congress (1 June) listed 4 major grounds for war: (1) impressment of American seamen, (2) violation of U.S. neutral rights and territorial waters, (3) the blockade of U.S. ports, and (4) refusal to revoke the Orders in Council. The House (4 June) supported the declaration of war 79–49. In the Senate, where action was delayed by Federalist and "Old Republican" opposition, the vote (18 June) in favor of war was 19–13. The New England states (with the exception of inland Vermont) and other maritime and commercial states, such as New York, New Jersey, and Delaware, voted for peace. The vote of the Southern and Western states assured a declaration of war. On 19 June Madison proclaimed a state of war with Great Britain.

WAR OF 1812 (1812–14)

THE BALANCE SHEET. U.S. Advantages: (1) Great Britain's involvement in the Napoleonic wars prevented her from devoting her main resources to the war against the U.S.; (2) the U.S. had an initial advantage of proximity to the theater of war; (3) the U.S. population was overwhelmingly superior in numbers to that of Canada, the chief target of U.S. land operations; (4) the U.S. navy, although numerically inferior to the British (it had but 16 seagoing craft), was manned by efficient and well-trained officers and crews. **U.S. Disadvantages:** (1) a small and badly administered regular army composed of volunteers and raw militia with few experienced and capable commanders, and poorly equipped and supplied; (2) lack of united popular support, particularly in New England and New York, where the people spoke of "Mr. Madison's war" and accused the President of being a tool of the French; (3) lack of a national bank, which deprived the government of centralized financial machinery and compelled dependence upon borrowing by public subscription (a move that evoked a feeble response in the financial centers of the disaffected Northeast).

MILITARY SETBACKS. The improvised U.S. plan of operations called for a 3-pronged drive into Canada. In the east, a force under Gen. **Henry Dearborn** (1751–1829) was to use the Lake Champlain route for an assault on Montreal. In the center, troops under Gen. **Stephen Van Rensselaer** (1764–1839) were to attack the Canadians along the Niagara River frontier. In the west, an expedition under Gen. **William Hull** (1753–1825) was to launch from Detroit an attack against Upper Canada. The U.S. forces were composed mainly of ill-trained militia.

16 Aug. Hull's Surrender. The Canadian campaign began with a series of disasters. The surrender (17 July) of the U.S. post on Michilimackinac Island, in the Strait of Mackinaw joining Lakes Huron and Michigan, led the Northwest Indians under Tecumseh to align themselves definitely with the British. The British gained valuable intelligence when Hull's personal baggage (containing official papers and plans) was seized (1 July) as it was being conveyed to Detroit. With a force of 2,200 men, Hull crossed the Detroit River into Canada (12 July) and occupied Sandwich, but withdrew to Detroit (8 Aug.), apprehensive that the Indians would cut his line of communication with Ohio and of the Canadian force of some 2,000 under Gen. Isaac Brock. Fearing an Indian massacre of women and children, Hull surrendered Detroit (16 Aug.) to Brock without firing a shot. The garrison of Fort Dearborn (at the site of Chicago) was massacred (15 Aug.) as it evacuated the post, which was burned the next day. Hull's surrender left the British in control of Lake Erie and the Michigan country. A court-martial sentenced Hull to death for cowardice and neglect of duty (26 March 1814). The penalty was remitted because of Hull's Revolutionary War record but his name was dropped from the army roll.

13 Oct.–28 Nov. Niagara Campaign. Brock reached Ft. George on the Niagara River (23 Aug.), where, facing the U.S. line under Van Rensselaer in New York State, he established a strong defense. Van Rensselaer took the offensive (13 Oct.) with the occupation of Queenston Heights (Gen. Brock was killed in the engagement). Opposed by a British force of 1,000, the 600 Americans on the heights were crushed when New York State militia failed to reinforce them on the ground that their military service did not require them to leave the state. Van Rensselaer retired from his command and was succeeded by Gen. Alexander Smyth, an indecisive regular army officer who made a feeble attempt (28 Nov.) to cross the Niagara River. As a result of his failure, Smyth was relieved of his command and his name dropped from the army roll.

19 Nov. Montreal Fiasco. Stationed at Plattsburg, under the command of Gen. Dearborn, was the largest force of Americans under arms. Projecting a synchronized movement with Smyth's operation at Niagara, Dearborn led his army (19 Nov.) to the Canadian frontier, at which point the militia refused to proceed further. On 23 Nov. Dearborn returned his army to Plattsburg.

The military disasters of 1812 revealed the need for well-trained regular troops and an overhauling of the army command. Madison's dissatisfaction with the War Department led to the replacement (13 Jan. 1813) of Secretary Eustis by John Armstrong (N.Y.). Although he succeeded in invigorating the army command, Armstrong was tactless; upon his retirement in 1814, Monroe took charge of the War Department, remaining in that post until the appointment of William Henry Crawford (Ga.) in 1815.

NAVAL SUCCESSES. The skill and valor of U.S. seamanship were demonstrated in the engagement (19 Aug.) off Nova Scotia between the U.S. 44-gun frigate *Constitution,* Capt. **Isaac Hull** (1773–1843) commanding, and the British 38-gun frigate *Guerrière.* After a duel lasting about a half-hour, the *Guerrière* was so badly riddled and disabled that Hull had to abandon taking her as a prize and instead blew her up. The U.S. casualties numbered 14; the British, 79. News of the victory, coming hard upon reports of the fall of Detroit, helped to bolster sagging morale. The 18-gun sloop-of-war *Wasp,* Capt. Jacob Jones commanding, bested the British 18-gun brig *Frolic* in an encounter (17 Oct.) 600 mi. off the Virginia coast. The U.S. losses, 10 killed or wounded; British, *c.*90. The 44-gun frigate *United States,* Capt. **Stephen Decatur** (p. 694) commanding, subdued (25 Oct.) the British 38-gun frigate *Macedonian* off the Madeira Islands and brought her into New London as a prize. The *Constitution,* under her new commander Capt. **William Bainbridge** (1774–1833), destroyed (29 Dec.) the British 38-gun frigate *Java* in a duel off the coast of Brazil (American loss, 12 killed, 22 wounded; British loss, 48 dead, 102

THE WAR OF 1812

→ American routes   ⇨ British routes
—·— Hull's route, 1812   ······· Dearborn's route, 1812–13
▼▼▼ Harrison's route, 1813   ━I━ Wilkinson's route, 1813
——— British advance against Washington, 1814

wounded). Her performance on this occasion earned for the *Constitution* the sobriquet "Old Ironsides."

PEACE FEELERS. At the instruction of Secretary of State Monroe, the U.S. chargé at London, Jonathan Russell, informed Lord Castlereagh (24 Aug.) that the U.S. was willing to negotiate an armistice provided the British would abandon impressment and paper blockades and agree to indemnities for maritime spoliations. On his own initiative, Russell added informally that the U.S. would renounce the practice of naturalizing British seamen. Castlereagh rejected (29 Aug.) both proposals. From Halifax, Admiral Sir John Borlase Warren sent to Washington an offer of armistice and negotiation (30 Sept.). Monroe replied (27 Oct.) that the U.S. would accept only on condition that the British sus-

pend impressment. This peace overture also bore no result.

NEW ENGLAND DISAFFECTION. The declaration of war provoked sharp remonstrances in the Federalist stronghold. Gov. Strong (Mass.) issued a proclamation (26 June) declaring a public fast in view of the war "against the nation from which we are descended." The Mass. House of Representatives issued an "Address to the People" (26 June) terming the war as one against the public interest and asserting that "there be no volunteers except for defensive war." The General Assembly of Conn. condemned the war (25 Aug.). The governors of Conn. (2 July) and Mass. (5 Aug.) refused to furnish militia to the Federal government. In N.H. the Rockingham memorial (5 Aug.) protested against "hasty, rash, and ruinous measures" and made veiled hints of disunion.

2 Dec. PRESIDENTIAL ELECTION. At a Congressional caucus (18 May) where Southern Republican insurgents put aside their differences, **Madison** was renominated by unanimous vote. Vice-President **Clinton** having died in office (20 Apr.), **Elbridge Gerry** (Mass.) was chosen as Vice-Presidential candidate. The Federalist charge that Madison won renomination by truckling to Henry Clay and the war Republicans appears to be without foundation. In New York state the antiwar Republicans nominated (29 May) **De Witt Clinton** for the Presidency. At a secret meeting (Sept.) in New York, the Federalists threw their support to Clinton, and both groups endorsed Clinton's running mate, **Charles Jared Ingersoll** (Pa.), a moderate Federalist. The electoral vote: for President —Madison, 128; Clinton, 89. For Vice-President—Gerry, 131; Ingersoll, 86. Madison carried the Southern and Western states. Clinton carried all of New England and the Middle States to the Potomac, with the exception of Vermont and Pennsylvania. The sweeping Federalist victory in the Northeast doubled the party's strength in the new Congress.

1813

BRITISH BLOCKADE. The blockade of Chesapeake and Delaware bays (announced 26 Dec. 1812) shut off commerce from those waters and was marked by British raids along the shores of the upper Chesapeake by a naval force under Rear Adm. Sir George Cockburn. The blockade was extended (26 May) to the mouth of the Mississippi and to the ports and harbors of New York, Charleston, Port Royal, and Savannah. Chesapeake Bay was used as a British naval station, and from the early months of 1813 until the end of the war the Southern coast down to Georgia was kept in a constant state of panic. After the announcement (16 Nov.) of the blockade of Long Island Sound, only the ports along the New England coast north of New London remained open to neutral trade. The British hoped to exploit New England disaffection. When the Northeast failed to fulfill expectations of disunion, and when the British decided to use a complete blockade as a support for general offensive operations in 1814, the blockade was extended to New England (25 Apr. 1814).

Despite many individual exploits by U.S. naval vessels, the blockade was highly effective. It created a scarcity of goods that stimulated domestic manufactures and led to widespread speculation and price inflation, with consequent hardships on farmers. The sharp reduction in customs receipts weakened the Treasury, helping to bring the government to near bankruptcy in 1814.

The Americans retaliated by dispatching cruisers to prey on merchant convoys. Until its capture (28 Mar. 1814) off Valparaiso, the 32-gun frigate *Essex,* Capt. David Porter (1780–1843) commanding, captured or destroyed more than twoscore merchant ships or whalers in the Atlantic and South Pacific. But such individual ship actions did little to lessen British naval superiority. The Americans also resorted to privateering. Ineffective in 1813, privateering did not become a powerful weapon until 1814, when the U.S. blockade of British coasts made it unsafe for enemy shipping to sail without convoy from the English to the Irish Channel. By the summer of 1814 Lloyd's listed 825 vessels as captured by Americans. But even these inroads did not affect the tight British blockade of the U.S. coast.

HARRISON IN THE WEST. The fall of Detroit and Ft. Dearborn (Aug. 1812) compelled the Americans to fall back to the Wabash-Maumee line. Westerners took alarm. Shortly after learning of Hull's defeat, a group of Kentucky officials and citizens (including Henry Clay) commissioned William Henry Harrison a maj. gen. of militia and appointed him to head an expedition to Detroit. The move revived confidence along the frontier. When Madison and Secretary of War Eustis learned of Kentucky's action, they commissioned Harrison a brig. gen. (17 Sept. 1812) and gave him command of the northwestern army (Harrison was nominated a maj. gen. on 27 Feb.). Harrison's orders were simply to retake Detroit. At his disposal he had 10,000 men. The 1st battle, at **Frenchtown** on the Raisin River, at the western end of Lake Erie, resulted in defeat (22 Jan.) for the Kentucky force led by Gen. James Winchester. Some 500 Americans were taken prisoner; another 400 were killed in action or massacred by the Indians. The British and Tecumseh failed in their siege (1–9 May) of **Ft. Meigs,** at the mouth of the Maumee, where Harrison commanded the defense. The British assault (2 Aug.) on **Ft. Stephenson,** on the Sandusky River, was repulsed by a stout defense led by Maj. George Croghan. Harrison could not move on Detroit as long as the British remained in control of Lake Erie.

1 June. DESTRUCTION OF THE "CHESAPEAKE." The gloom that hung over the American cause in 1813 was darkened by news of the encounter between the U.S. 38-gun frigate *Chesapeake* and the British 38-gun frigate *Shannon,* 30 miles off Boston harbor. Acting against his better judgment, the commander of the *Chesapeake,* **James Lawrence** (1781–1813), accepted a challenge from Captain P. B. V. Broke of the *Shannon.* Lawrence's sole advantage lay in the number of his crew (379) as against that of the *Shannon* (330), but the recently acquired American crew was ill-trained and poorly disciplined. Powerful broadsides raked the *Chesapeake* from stem to stern with unerring effect. A British boarding party of 50 men captured the disabled *Chesapeake* and brought her into Halifax as prize. The British suffered 83 casualties; the Americans, 146. It is said that the last order of the dying Captain Lawrence was, "Don't give up the ship!" His words became the rallying cry of the U.S. navy.

10 Sept. BATTLE OF LAKE ERIE. Lawrence's last order was inscribed on the battleflag of the *Lawrence,* flagship of the 28-year-old Capt. **Oliver Hazard Perry** (p. 764) in the Battle of Lake Erie, the most important naval engagement on the Great Lakes during the war. Ordered from Newport (17 Feb.) to the Great Lakes, Perry reached Presque Isle (27 Mar.), where a flotilla of 2 brigs, a schooner, and 3 gunboats was under construction from materials (with the exception of timber) transported over land and water from Philadelphia by way of Pittsburgh. With the British evacuation of Ft. Niagara and Ft. Erie (27 May), Perry was able to remove 5 vessels from the navy yard at Black Rock (near Buffalo) and bring them to Presque Isle (5 June). During the temporary absence of the British blockading squadron (4 Aug.), Perry floated his heavier vessels over the harbor bar and brought them into deep water. He anchored off the island of Put in Bay, north of the mouth of the Sandusky River. The British squadron under Capt. Robert H. Barclay, consisting of 6 vessels (mounting a total of 65 guns), sailed for Perry's force (9 Sept.). Perry had at his disposal 10 vessels (mounting a total of 55 guns), improvised over the winter of 1812–13, but superior in tonnage and heavy armament. The engagement (10 Sept.), lasting more than 3 hrs., was one of the bloodiest naval actions of the war, and resulted in a decisive defeat for the British. Perry's flagship was riddled to pieces, and 80% of her crew were casualties. British casualties: 41 killed, 94 wounded. Perry sent to Gen. Harrison, at Seneca on the Sandusky River, the message (dispatched 10 Sept., received 12 Sept.) containing the words: "We have met the enemy and they are ours." Perry's victory placed Lake Erie under U.S. control and renewed the threat to Canada. It forced the British to evacuate Malden and Detroit and to fall back to a defensive line along the Niagara frontier.

5 Oct. BATTLE OF THE THAMES. Perry's triumph enabled Harrison to move his main force of about 4,500 infantry across Lake Erie to Middle Sister Island (20 Sept.) and to disembark them (27 Sept.) near Malden in Upper Canada. Meanwhile, against the protests of Tecumseh, Proctor had evacuated Detroit (18 Sept.). The British, with Harrison in pursuit, withdrew from Malden (24 Sept.) and retreated northward by way of Sandwich. Harrison overtook the British and Indians at Moravian Town on the north bank of the Thames River, defeating them in a battle marked by the prowess of a Kentucky mounted regiment under Col. **Richard Mentor Johnson** (1780–1850). U.S.

losses: 15 killed, 30 wounded; British: 12 killed, 36 wounded, 477 taken prisoner. The results of the battle were far-reaching. Tecumseh's death in this encounter brought about the collapse of the Indian confederacy and led the Indians to desert the British cause. The U.S. military frontier in the Northwest was made secure, and British power swept from that region (except at Ft. Michilimackinac, which the British occupied until the end of the war).

DRIVE ON UPPER CANADA. Despite their loss of Lake Erie, the British still maintained control of Lake Ontario. Their position was challenged by a combined military and naval action under Gen. **Henry Dearborn** and Capt. Isaac Chauncey, naval commander on Lake Ontario. Their plan was to gain U.S. control by seizing British naval craft at York (Toronto), capital of Upper Canada. About 1,600 troops embarked (22 Apr.) from Sackett's Harbor and raided York (27 Apr.), garrisoned by about 600 British troops. The U.S. descent upon York resulted in its surrender and the destruction of 1 ship and capture of another. But 320 Americans (including Gen. Zebulon M. Pike) were killed or wounded by the explosion of a powder magazine; the by-passing of Kingston wrecked the plan to gain control of the lake; and the burning of the public buildings at York (including the Assembly houses and the residence of the governor), put to the torch against Dearborn's orders, later gave the British their pretext for burning Washington in 1814. The raiding force returned to Niagara (8 May), where, during Dearborn's illness, the troops came under the immediate command of Col. **Winfield Scott** (p. 776), the general's chief of staff. Employing Chauncey's fleet, Scott moved a force of 4,000 men and attacked from the rear (27 May) the British force of 1,600 men stationed at Ft. George under command of Gen. John Vincent. Although the Americans failed to destroy the enemy body, the evacuation of Ft. George compelled the simultaneous withdrawal of the British from Ft. Erie to the south (opposite Buffalo), thus enabling Perry to liberate the vessels at the Black Rock navy yard.

A force of 2,000 Americans pursued Vincent. With only 700 men, Vincent attacked (6 June) at **Stony Creek**, 10 mi. from Hamilton, compelling the Americans to fall back on Ft. George. Two American generals, William H. Winder and John Chandler, were captured by the British. The U.S. force at Ft. Erie withdrew (9 June), and that post was occupied by the British over the following winter.

The outstanding action in this sector was the **Battle of Sackett's Harbor** (28–29 May), in which Gen. **Jacob J. Brown** (1775–1828) repulsed a British landing force commanded by Sir George Prevost, governor general of Canada.

2ND ATTEMPT TO TAKE MONTREAL. Dearborn was removed from his command (6 July) and replaced by Gen. **James Wilkinson.** The reorganization of the U.S. command also placed (3 July) Gen. **Wade Hampton** at the head of the force on Lake Champlain. Secretary of War John Armstrong, who arrived (5 Sept.) at Sackett's Harbor and established headquarters in the field, projected a combined attack on Montreal by Wilkinson and Hampton by way of the St. Lawrence. The strong Montreal position was supported by some 15,000 British troops in and around the city. Wilkinson's troops were to start from Sackett's Harbor and make the descent of the St. Lawrence; Hampton's force was to march northward from Plattsburg and effect a junction with them. The mutual dislike existing between the two generals made cooperation difficult.

Wilkinson left Sackett's Harbor (17 Oct.) at the head of 8,000 men and began (5 Nov.) the descent of the St. Lawrence. The flotilla stopped (10 Nov.) at Chrysler's Farm on the north bank of the river, about 90 mi. from Montreal. Learning of an enemy force advancing from the rear, Wilkinson ordered Gen. John Parke Boyd to take the offensive. Boyd's 3 brigades of regulars (about 2,000 men) were virtually routed (11 Nov.) by a British force of 800 led by Col. J. W. Morrison. U.S. casualties: 102 killed, 237 wounded, more than 100 taken prisoner; British: 22 killed, 48 wounded, 12 missing. Informed (12

Nov.) that Hampton had abandoned the attack on Montreal, Wilkinson went into winter quarters (13 Nov.) at French Mills, along the Salmon River.

Hampton had marched his force of about 4,000 men to the Canadian line (19 Sept.) and, instead of proceeding north, had moved west (26 Sept.) to the Chateaugay River, where he awaited news of Wilkinson's progress. Ordered by Armstrong (16 Oct.) to move down the Chateaugay, Hampton established his force about 15 mi. from the mouth of the river (22 Oct.). Although he theoretically menaced Montreal and British communications with Upper Canada, Hampton had a numerically inferior force and lacked water transportation. His position was untenable. After attacking a smaller British force (**Battle of the Chateaugay,** 25 Oct.), Hampton, without consulting Wilkinson, abandoned the drive on Montreal and fell back on Plattsburg. His decision may have been influenced by his receipt (25 Oct.) of Armstrong's order indicating that the army was going into winter quarters on the American side. Before resigning from the army (Mar. 1814), Hampton presided over the court-martial of Gen. Hull.

29–30 Dec. BURNING OF BUFFALO. When Gen. Vincent dispatched a British force to retake Ft. George, that post was evacuated (10 Dec.) by George McClure, a brig. gen. of N.Y. militia. Before withdrawing, McClure burned the village of Newark and part of Queenston. In retaliation, a British force under Colonel Murray captured Ft. Niagara (18 Dec.), killing 67, wounding 11, and taking 350 prisoners. Then the British set loose the Indians, who ravaged Lewiston and the surrounding countryside. Leading a British force of 1,500 men, Gen. Gordon Drummond burned Buffalo and Black Rock (29–30 Dec.), destroying ships and supplies. Ft. Niagara remained in British hands until the end of the war.

RUSSIAN MEDIATION. The diplomatic mission of John Quincy Adams, named minister to Russia (27 June 1809), benefited from the widening gulf between Napoleon and Czar Alexander I. The Czar courted French hostility by interfering on behalf of U.S. commerce in Denmark, giving orders to release U.S.

ships at Archangel, and issuing an imperial ukase (19 Dec. 1811) admitting U.S. goods to Russian ports. Following Napoleon's declaration of war on Russia (22 June 1812) the Czar learned (6 Aug. 1812) of the U.S. declaration of war on Great Britain, now Russia's ally, and took steps to end Anglo-U.S. differences in order to strengthen the Allied effort against Napoleon. Adams was notified (21 Sept. 1812) of the Czar's offer to mediate between the U.S. and Great Britain. Receiving Adams' communication (8 Mar.), Madison dispatched as peace commissioners James A. Bayard (Del.), a Federalist, and Secretary of the Treasury Gallatin. Bayard and Gallatin reached St. Petersburg on 21 July. In the meantime, however, Lord Castlereagh had declined mediation (5 July).

CASTLEREAGH'S PROPOSAL. Despite his resentment of the Czar's personal interference, Lord Castlereagh was becoming increasingly lukewarm toward the war with the U.S. British victories at Vittoria (21 June) and Leipzig (18–19 Oct.) were counterbalanced by reports of British defeats in the Lake Erie region. He sent (4 Nov.) an official letter to Monroe offering direct negotiation. The proposal was immediately accepted by Madison, who acted upon news of British victories on the Continent and the deteriorating U.S. military situation along the Niagara frontier and in the Lake Champlain region. The Senate confirmed (18 Jan. 1814) Madison's nomination of **J. Q. Adams, J. A. Bayard, Henry Clay,** and **Jonathan Russell** as peace commissioners. The addition of **Gallatin** to the commission was confirmed on 8 Feb. 1814 (Gallatin being replaced as Secretary of the Treasury by George W. Campbell, Tenn., 9 Feb. 1814). The Flemish town of Ghent was designated as the meeting place, and discussions began 8 Aug. 1814. The British were represented by Lord Gambier, Henry Goulburn, and William Adams.

1814

WAR EMBARGO. New England and New York contractors supplied beef, flour, and other provisions to the British armies in Canada and to enemy vessels off the East Coast. In a special message to Congress (9 Dec. 1813), President Madison recommended an embargo to interdict trade with the enemy. The measure passed in the House 85–57; in the Senate, 20–14; and became law on 17 Dec. 1813. It was modified (25 Jan.) when its strict enforcement along the coast resulted in the near starvation of the people of Nantucket. But the border trade with Canada persisted. Madison gradually recognized that his entire system of commercial restriction had failed in its aim both at home and abroad. His message to Congress (31 Mar.) recommended repeal of the Embargo and Non-Importation Acts. The only significant protest against repeal came from Representative Elisha Potter (R.I.), who spoke for newly developed manufacturing interests thriving under the exclusion of imports and for commercial interests profiting from the high prices created by scarcity. New England as a whole, however, supported repeal. As a protective measure for U.S. manufactures, the repeal bill guaranteed war duties for 2 yrs. after peace. The bill passed in the House (7 Apr.) 115–37; the Senate (12 Apr.), 26–4; and with Madison's approval (14 Apr.) commercial restriction came to an end. On 1 Sept. the British landed at the mouth of the Castine River in Maine, captured Castine, and advanced to Bangor. To the end of the war U.S. ships trading with the British paid out £13,000 in duties to the royal customs officials at Castine.

CREEK WAR. In 1811 Tecumseh had visited the Creek Indians in the Alabama country, apparently attempting to enlist Creek support for his confederacy. A year after the outbreak of the War of 1812, a war faction of the Creeks known as the "Red Sticks," numbering some 2,000 warriors from the Upper Creek country, took part in a general uprising along the frontier. A party of U.S. settlers clashed (27 July 1813) with some Indians at Burnt Corn, about 80 mi. north of Pensacola. This led directly to the Creek War, which was opened by the Creek attack (30 Aug. 1813) on Fort Mims, on the east bank of the Alabama River about 35 mi. above Mobile.

Of the 550 persons in the fort, 250 were massacred and many others burned to death. News of the affair reached **Andrew Jackson** at Nashville. As maj. gen. of Tennessee militia, he called out 2,000 volunteers. Frontier armies were organized also in Georgia and in what later became the state of Mississippi, but the major engagements against the Creeks were fought by the Tennesseans under Jackson.

Tennessee militia under Gen. John Coffee, Jackson's chief subordinate, destroyed the Indian village of **Talishatchee** (3 Nov. 1813). Jackson surrounded and destroyed (9 Nov. 1813) **Talladega**, killing more than 500 Indian warriors. The Tennesseans were repulsed at **Emuckfaw** (22 Jan.) and **Enotachopco Creek** (24 Jan.), and suffered heavy casualties at **Calibee Creek** (27 Jan.). Jackson's major effort came in the early spring of 1814, when he penetrated to the heart of the Upper Creek country. At the head of 3,000 men, Jackson and Coffee attacked (27 Mar.) the fortified position built by the Creeks and their Cherokee allies at the **Horseshoe Bend** of the Tallapoosa River. An estimated 850 to 900 warriors were killed, some 500 squaws and children were taken prisoner; U.S. casualties: 51 killed, 148 wounded. The campaign was brought to a close by the capitulation of the Creeks. Under the **Treaty of Ft. Jackson** (9 Aug.), signed by only part of the Creeks, two thirds of the Creek lands were ceded to the U.S. and the Indians agreed to withdraw from the southern and western part of Alabama. At almost the same time the Northwest Indians signed the **Treaty of Greenville** (22 July) restoring peace with the U.S. and requiring the Delaware, Miami, Seneca, Shawnee, and Wyandot Indians to declare war on the British. The treaty was signed for the U.S. by William Henry Harrison and Lewis Cass. Harrison had already resigned his army commission (11 May) and Jackson had been promoted to maj. gen. of the regular army (22 May).

BRITISH TAKE THE OFFENSIVE. The overthrow of Napoleon (6 Apr.) enabled the British to concentrate their resources on the war in North America. During the summer of 1814 some 14,000

British troops, veterans of the Duke of Wellington's Peninsular campaign, were sent across the Atlantic. The British planned concerted land and naval operations based on a triple thrust against Lake Champlain, Chesapeake Bay, and New Orleans. To support the general offensive, the blockade along the U.S. coast was enforced more rigorously.

U.S. MILITARY RESOURCES. While the U.S. military establishment was authorized at 58,254, the effective strength of the regular army (Jan.) stood at about 11,000. Under the law of 27 Jan., the army strength was authorized at 62,773; yet by 1 Oct. the regular army had only 34,000 men. The administration's proposal to raise 100,000 men by conscription was never accepted by Congress. Whenever possible, the government used the militia only as a last resort. In other respects, the military establishment had been improved. Secretary of War Armstrong divided the country into 9 military districts and revamped (Jan.–Feb.) the army command. Incompetent generals were removed from active sectors. Wilkinson, who was relieved from his command (24 March) and acquitted by a court of inquiry, was replaced by Maj.-Gen. **Jacob Brown,** who, with the newly promoted Brig.-Gen. **Winfield Scott,** was responsible for operations in the Niagara sector. Also promoted to maj.-gen. was George Izard of S.C., who replaced Hampton at Plattsburg (1 May).

NORTHERN CAMPAIGN: Niagara. Between Long Point on Lake Erie and York on Lake Ontario the British Gen. Gordon Drummond had under him in the spring of 1814 less than 4,000 troops. The first considerable body of British reinforcements did not begin to arrive in that sector until late in July. In the meantime, Brown and Scott took the offensive and invaded Canada.

5 July. Battle of Chippewa. The U.S. army under Brown, consisting of about 3,500 effectives, crossed the Niagara River and seized Ft. Erie (3 July). Gen. Riall established a British force along a defensive line on the north bank of the Chippewa River, 16 mi. north of Ft. Erie, then, after routing the brigade

under Gen. Peter B. Porter, he drew up his main force of 1,500 men on the Chippewa Plain about a mile from the river. He was engaged by Gen. Winfield Scott's brigade, called into action by General Brown as its 1,300 men were belatedly celebrating the 4th of July with a dinner and parade. The outnumbered Americans inflicted a severe defeat upon the British, whose lines crumbled after an action lasting a half hour. Scott's brigade lost 48 killed and 227 wounded; Riall's force lost 137 killed and 375 wounded. The Battle of Chippewa was the only one of the war in which approximately equal numbers of regular troops, neither enjoying the advantage of position, engaged in close combat in extended order. After Chippewa, no force of U.S. regulars was defeated by its British counterpart.

25 July. Battle of Lundy's Lane. In pursuit of Riall, Brown went as far north as Queenston (10 July). He requested (13 July) Commodore Isaac Chauncey, naval commander on Lake Ontario, to leave Sackett's Harbor and join his fleet with the army on the lake shore west of Ft. George, in order to work out a plan of operations for the conquest of Upper Canada. Chauncey's failure to cooperate was a decisive factor in the subsequent U.S. retreat from the Canadian side of the Niagara frontier.

With 2,600 effectives at his disposal, Brown moved on the village of **Lundy's Lane,** near Niagara Falls. In the most sharply contested land action of the war, he engaged 3,000 British troops under Riall and Drummond in a 5-hr. battle ending in a draw (although the Americans retired, leaving the British in possession of the field). U.S. losses: 171 killed, 572 wounded, 110 missing; British: 84 killed, 559 wounded, 193 missing, 42 taken prisoner.

2 Aug.–1 Sept. Siege of Fort Erie. The U.S. army fell back on Ft. Erie. A British force of 3,500 under Drummond entrenched before Ft. Erie (2 Aug.) and brought up 6 siege guns from which they laid down a heavy fire (13 Aug.) before assaulting the fort. The attack was repulsed (15 Aug.) by Gen. Edmund Pendleton Gaines, causing heavy losses to the enemy. The British continued their bombardment of the fort, which held about 2,000 Americans. Gen. Peter B. Porter led 1,600 men in a sortie (17 Sept.) that destroyed the enemy batteries and compelled Drummond to withdraw (21 Sept.). British losses: 609 killed, wounded, and missing; U.S.: 511 killed, wounded, and missing. Later in the year Ft. Erie was evacuated and destroyed by the Americans (5 Nov.) in final abandonment of the drive on Canada.

11 Sept. Lake Champlain and Plattsburg. The British offensive from Canada was planned as a joint land and water operation along the Lake Champlain route. The campaign was committed to Gen. Sir George Prevost, who had under him an army of 11,000 British veterans supported by a fleet of 4 ships and 12 gunboats (mounting a total of 90 guns and carrying about 800 men) commanded by Capt. George Downie. The Americans had at Plattsburg a mixed force of only 3,300 regulars and militia under Gen. Alexander Macomb, who took immediate command after Gen. Izard, with 4,000 troops, marched off for Buffalo (29 Aug.).

In order to meet the British attack, the U.S. required control of Lake Champlain. The naval commander on the lake was the 30-year-old Capt. **Thomas Macdonough** (1783–1825), who had taken his post on 12 Sept. 1812, and by the spring of 1814 had at his command a flotilla of 4 ships and 10 gunboats (mounting a total of 86 guns and carrying about 850 men). Macdonough sought to use to full advantage his powerful short-range guns against the long-range pieces of the British. Choosing his position carefully, he anchored his fleet in the narrow channel between Crab Island and Cumberland Head, across the bay from Plattsburg. His vessels were so deployed that the enemy fleet would be obliged to enter a narrow stretch of water under a raking fire and meet him at close range.

Meanwhile, Sir George Prevost, leaving the St. Lawrence frontier (31 Aug.), marched along the western edge of Lake Champlain, driving Macomb's army to a heavily defended position south of the Saranac River, just below Plattsburg. Prevost halted his army (6 Sept.) and waited for his naval support to appear. Downie's fleet rounded Cumberland Head (11 Sept.) and deployed his vessels within 300 yds. of Macdonough's fleet. The **Battle of Lake Champlain** lasted 2 hrs., 20 mins. For 2 hrs. the battle favored the British, but Macdonough won the victory by hauling about his flagship, the *Saratoga,* and bearing down with broadsides on the enemy flagship, the *Confiance,* which struck her flag. The British fleet received no support from Prevost's shore batteries at Plattsburg, at Macdonough's rear. The encounter resulted in the seizure or destruction of all of the British vessels except the gunboats. U.S. losses: 52 killed, 58 wounded; British: 57 killed, 72 wounded. The victory gave the U.S. undisputed control of Lake Champlain and compelled Prevost's army to retreat to Canada. Prevost left behind great quantities of supplies; many of his troops deserted. He was recalled to Canada and was replaced by Sir George Murray.

19–22 Aug. MARCH ON WASHINGTON AND BALTIMORE. A British force of 4,000 veterans commanded by Gen. Robert Ross left France (27 June) under instructions "to effect a diversion" on the U.S. coasts in support of the army in Canada. The instructions authorized quick descents upon selected points for the purpose of destroying naval and military property. The operation, as finally planned by Sir Alexander Cochrane, was in retaliation for York and for the unauthorized U.S. raid on Long Point on Lake Erie (15 May). Cochrane issued orders (18 July) directing his blockading squadron in Southern waters "to destroy and lay waste such towns and districts upon the coast as you may find assailable." This order was still in effect when Cochrane's squadron and the transports bearing Ross' troops moved up Chesapeake Bay to the mouth of the Patuxent River (Md.) and were landed at Benedict (19 Aug.). The British expedition had 3 aims: to seize or destroy the flotilla of gunboats under Commodore Joshua Barney that had taken shelter in the Patuxent, to descend on Baltimore, and to raid Washington and Alexandria. At the approach of Rear Adm. Sir George Cockburn's fleet, Barney blew up his gunboats (22 Aug.) in order to prevent their seizure by the British.

24 Aug. Battle of Bladensburg. Without encountering resistance, Ross marched to Marlboro (22 Aug.). Meanwhile, hasty preparations were being made at the poorly defended capital, where the incompetent Gen. **William H. Winder** held the command of the Potomac District. From nearby states Winder received militia reinforcements and Commodore Barney brought his 400 sailors to Washington. At the head of a mixed force of about 7,000 men, of whom only several hundred were regulars, Winder took up his position at Old Fields, about 8 mi. from Bladensburg, through which the British would inevitably pass. Learning that the British were advancing on Bladensburg (24 Aug.), Winder hastened there, followed by President Madison and most of the Cabinet. The Americans, despite the advantage of position, were routed by 3,000 of the enemy and withdrew to Georgetown. Barney, with his 400 sailors and 5 24-pound guns, was left to cover the road about a mile from the village, on the District of Columbia line. The sailors offered stout opposition, holding their ground for a half hour against 4,000 invaders. U.S. losses: 26 killed, 51 wounded; British: 64 killed, 185 wounded.

24–25 Aug. Capture and Burning of Washington. The British marched unopposed to Washington (the panic-stricken U.S. army, together with government officers, had fled to Virginia) and encamped a quarter of a mile from the national capital. Detachments under Ross and Cockburn entered the town and set fire to the Capitol, the White House, all of the department buildings (with the exception of the Patent Office), several private homes, and the office of the *National Intelligencer*. The navy yard was destroyed by Americans at the order of Secretary of the Navy Jones. The destruction (later estimated at more than $1,500,000) was completed on the morning of 25 Aug. A storm compelled the enemy to retire from the town. The British broke up their camp on the night of 25 Aug. and boarded their transports on the Patuxent. President

Madison and some of his Cabinet officers returned to Washington on 27 Aug. Denounced by an irate citizenry and militia, Secretary of War Armstrong announced (3 Sept.) his resignation. He had already been replaced by Monroe, who was named (27 Aug.) ad interim Secretary of War.

12–14 Sept. Attack on Baltimore. The British fleet under Cochrane sailed from the Potomac (6 Sept.) and reached the mouth of the Patapsco River, about 16 mi. from Baltimore. During the British march on Washington, Baltimore had prepared a formidable system of defense works. Gen. Samuel Smith had under him about 13,000 regulars and militia. A mixed force of about 1,000 men held Ft. McHenry, where a line of sunken hulks barred enemy vessels from the harbor. Ross's army disembarked (12 Sept.) at North Point, about 14 mi. from Baltimore, while the fleet moved up the river toward Ft. McHenry. The enemy land advance was opposed by 3,200 militia under Gen. John Stricker. The Americans fell back, but not before inflicting severe casualties on the British (Gen. Ross being mortally wounded), who were delayed until 13 Sept. When the enemy drew up within sight of the heavily defended heights, they halted. The British fleet's bombardment (13–14 Sept.) of Ft. McHenry was unsuccessful (inspiring a witness, Francis Scott Key, to write the verses of "The Star Spangled Banner"). The invaders abandoned their attempt to capture the town and its shipping and made a rapid withdrawal to their transports. On 14 Oct. the British army left Chesapeake Bay and sailed for Jamaica.

8 Jan. 1815. BATTLE OF NEW ORLEANS. In May, Gen. **Andrew Jackson** was named commander of Military District No. 7, embracing the Mobile-New Orleans area and the U.S. army in the southwest. He prepared an invasion of Spanish Florida and, disobeying Monroe's orders, seized Pensacola (7 Nov.). He then left Mobile (22 Nov.) for New Orleans, arriving there on 1 Dec. Jackson was unaware that a large British fleet carrying 7,500 veterans under Sir Edward Pakenham had sailed from Jamaica (26 Nov.) and was moving through the Gulf of Mexico for an assault on New Orleans. The British aim was to secure control of the Mississippi and its strategic river valley.

When he learned of the British move, Jackson established his main defense at Baton Rouge, 120 mi. away, with a view to opposing an enemy attack by way of the Mississippi. But instead the British fleet of more than 50 craft entered Lake Borgne (13 Dec.), about 40 mi. east of New Orleans. Jackson ordered (15 Dec.) his forces at Baton Rouge to speed to New Orleans, and proclaimed martial law in the city. Pakenham spent an entire week disembarking his troops. Without being detected, a British advance guard marched to 7 mi. below New Orleans, where the U.S. had no troops or defense works.

Acting swiftly, Jackson led 5,000 troops, supported by the 14-gun war schooner *Carolina,* in a night attack upon the enemy force (23–24 Dec.), checking the British advance. During the delay in enemy operations, Jackson withdrew to a point 5 mi. from New Orleans, where he utilized a dry, shallow canal to construct a line of breastworks between a cypress swamp and the east bank of the Mississippi. A furious artillery battle occurred on 1 Jan. 1815, in which the Americans outgunned the enemy. Pakenham waited for reinforcements and, on the morning of 8 Jan. 1815, attacked with his main force of 5,300 men. Behind Jackson's entrenchments were about 4,500 troops, many of them expert Tennessee and Kentucky marksmen armed with long rifles. The British regulars, in close ranks, made 2 direct assaults in the face of a withering rifle and artillery fire. The British were cut down and driven back. The battle lasted about a half hour. Gen. Pakenham and two other British generals were killed. In this action, and in a tributary engagement on the west bank of the river, British losses: 2,036 men killed and wounded; U.S.: 8 killed, 13 wounded. The surviving British senior officer, Gen. John Lambert, withdrew his troops and reembarked them on 27 Jan.

The Battle of New Orleans, the last major engagement of the war, was fought 2 weeks after the signing of the

peace at Ghent (24 Dec.). The greatest American land victory of the war, it had no effect upon its outcome, but acted as a powerful restorative to national pride and in Andrew Jackson created a military hero.

MILITARY LOSSES. U.S.: 1,877 killed in action, 4,000 wounded. The total number of enlistments was 531,622 (a misleading figure, for numerous militiamen served or reenlisted as many as 10 times).

24 Dec. PEACE OF GHENT. The peace negotiations opened with the envoys of both nations firmly insisting on leading demands. The U.S. commissioners were under instructions to obtain satisfaction on impressment, blockades, and other maritime grievances (although Monroe's instructions of 27 July sanctioned the withdrawal of the impressment issue if such a concession became necessary). The British demanded the establishment of a neutral Indian buffer state in the Northwest and territorial cessions along the line from Maine to west of Lake Superior (amounting to about one third of the territory held by the U.S.). Neither nation pressed for the other to carry out disarmament on the Great Lakes.

The attitude of the British was governed by reports of the prevailing military situation. When the British learned (27 Sept.) of the burning of Washington, they affirmed the principle of *uti possidetis* (retention of territories held in actual possession). The U.S. supported the principle of *status quo ante bellum* (restoration of prewar territorial conditions). The U.S. commissioners rejected the British terms after receiving news (21 Oct.) of Macdonough's victory on Lake Champlain. The Duke of Wellington, proffered the Canadian command, replied to his government that their waning military fortunes on the Great Lakes did not entitle the British to demand a cession of territory. This consideration, combined with the depletion of the British treasury and Castlereagh's diplomatic embarrassments at the Congress of Vienna, led the British envoys to concede (26 Nov.) to the U.S. view. Economic pressure on the U.S. commissioners by the British banker, Alexander

Baring, forced them to abandon U.S. rights to the fisheries.

The treaty restored the peace, but was silent on the issues over which Great Britain and the U.S. had clashed. No reference was made to impressment, blockades, indemnities, the right of search and visit, and other maritime differences. Nor did its clauses advert to military control of the Great Lakes or a neutral Indian barrier state. The treaty provided for the release of prisoners, a restoration of all conquered territory (although West Florida, taken from the Spanish, remained in U.S. hands), and for the appointment of an arbitral commission to settle the disputed northeastern boundary between the U.S. and Canada. By mutual understanding, the questions of the Great Lakes and the fisheries were left open for future negotiation.

News of the signing reached New York on 11 Feb. 1815. The treaty was unanimously ratified by the Senate (15 Feb. 1815) and was proclaimed by President Madison on 17 Feb. 1815.

15 Dec.–5 Jan. 1815. HARTFORD CONVENTION. Early in 1814 numerous Massachusetts towns sent memorials to the state legislature calling for a convention of the states to revise the Constitution. The convention, called by invitation of the Massachusetts legislature (17 Oct.), assembled in secret session at Hartford, Conn., and was attended by Federalist delegates from Conn., R.I., Mass., N.H., and Vt. Except for delegates from the last 2 states, chosen by local conventions, all were elected by their respective state legislatures.

The convention's proceedings and measures did not reflect the views of the extremist wing of the Federalist party. The Massachusetts delegation was headed by **George Cabot** (1752–1823), leader of the moderate element among the Federalists in the state. Cabot presided over the convention, and an influential role was played by his fellow delegate, **Harrison Gray Otis** (1765–1848). The report issued by the convention included a statement (echoing the states'-rights doctrine of the Kentucky and Virginia resolutions) that "in cases of deliberate, dangerous and palpable infractions of the Constitution, affecting the sovereignty of a State and liberties of the people; it is not only the right but the duty of such a State to interpose its authority for their protection, in the manner best calculated to secure that end."

The convention adopted a set of resolutions calling for (1) protection of the citizens of their states against military conscription unauthorized by the Constitution; (2) use of Federal revenue collected within these states to provide for the defense of their territory; (3) an interstate defense machinery, independent of Federal provisions, for repelling enemy invasion; (4) a series of amendments to the Constitution, including apportionment of direct taxes and representation among the states according to the number of free persons in each; (5) prohition of all embargoes lasting more than 60 days; requirement of a two-thirds vote of both Houses for declarations of war, restrictions on foreign commerce, and admissions of new states; (6) prohibition of the holding by naturalized citizens of civil office under Federal authority; and (7) limitation of Presidential tenure to one term. A committee of 3, headed by Otis, was appointed by the Massachusetts legislature to negotiate with the national government. News of Jackson's victory at New Orleans and the signing of the Treaty of Ghent brought an abrupt end to the work of the committee and made the Hartford Convention the butt of popular ridicule. That the convention had been conducted in secrecy gave its opponents a handle which they used for accusing the Hartford gathering of conspiracy, sedition, and treason (although there is no evidence supporting the charge).

1815

PEACETIME MILITARY ESTABLISHMENT. President Madison recommended a standing army of 20,000 men, but the House, by a vote of 70 to 38 (3 March), fixed the army strength at 10,000. Congress ordered (27 Feb.) the navy's gunboat flotilla to be put up for sale, and the armed vessels on the lakes were stripped of their equipment and laid up. No further reduction was made in the naval establishment; henceforth most of its vessels consisted of cruisers. A 3-man Board of Navy Commissioners was authorized (7 Feb.) to carry out, under the Secretary of the Navy, general supervision of the department.

3 Mar.–30 June. DECATUR'S ALGERINE EXPEDITION. During the War of 1812 the Dey of Algiers renewed his plunder of American Mediterranean commerce. He dismissed the U.S. consul, declared war, seized American vessels, and enslaved U.S. nationals on the pretext that he was not receiving sufficient tribute. An act of Congress (approved 3 Mar.) authorized hostilities against the Dey. Capt. Stephen Decatur sailed from New York (10 May) with 10 vessels, seized the Algerine 44-gun frigate *Mashouda* (17 June), captured the 22-gun brig *Estido* (19 June), and sailed into the harbor of Algiers. He exacted a treaty (30 June) whereby the Dey renounced molestation of U.S. commerce and tribute, and agreed to release all U.S. prisoners without ransom. Decatur received similar guarantees from Tunis (26 July) and Tripoli (5 Aug.), both states making compensation for U.S. vessels which they had permitted Great Britain to seize as prizes. Decatur's action brought to a close the troubles with the Barbary States.

3 July. COMMERCIAL CONVENTION WITH BRITAIN ended discriminatory duties and admitted U.S. commerce to the East Indies without making specific concessions regarding the West Indies.

1816

10 Apr. 2ND U.S. BANK. The wartime disorganization of the currency, bringing in its train a general suspension of specie payments, emphasized anew the need for a national bank. Secretary of the Treasury Dallas recommended (17 Oct. 1814) the creation of a bank capitalized at $50 million, under which the President would be empowered to suspend specie payments. His scheme was approved in principle by the House (24 Oct. 1814) by a vote of 66 to 40, but an emasculated compromise measure provided for a capitalization of $30 million and did not

grant the bank authority to suspend specie payments and to lend up to 60% of its capital to the government. The bill passed in the House (7 Jan. 1815), 120–38; and the Senate (20 Jan. 1815), 20–14. Madison vetoed the bill (20 Jan.), basing his objection on practical considerations, but conceding the constitutional authority of Congress to enact such legislation.

Madison's annual message (5 Dec. 1815) noted that if state banks could not restore a uniform national currency, "the probable operation of a national bank will merit consideration." Congressional debate witnessed a Republican reversal of objections to the measure on constitutional grounds. The debate was also noteworthy for the leading role played by the triumvirate of **John C. Calhoun** (p. 683), **Henry Clay** (p. 686) and **Daniel Webster** (p. 796), to dominate House and Senate proceedings until the decade before the Civil War.

The bill introduced by Calhoun (8 Jan.) followed in substance the recommendations of Dallas, and was supported by Clay, who in 1811 had maintained that the measure was unconstitutional. Calhoun backed the bill on the ground that it was necessary for the restoration of a sound and uniform circulating medium; for its constitutional sanction, he pointed to the power of Congress to regulate the currency. Clay, explaining his reversal, left the Speaker's chair to assert that a change in circumstances made the bank an indispensable necessity, and that Congress had the "constructive power" to authorize the bank. Webster opposed the bill, arguing that no currency reform was required in view of the constitutional and statutory provisions for gold and silver currency. He maintained that the currency problem could be solved by Congressional action against the note issues of suspended banks.

The bill, which passed in the House (14 Mar.) 80–71 (with 33 Republicans and 38 Federalists voting against it), and the Senate 22–12, created the 2nd Bank of the U.S. with an authorized capitalization of $35 million, of which the government was to subscribe one fifth. In return for its charter privileges, the Bank was to pay the government a bonus of $1,500,-000. The President was empowered to name 5 of its 25 directors. The Bank was authorized to act as a depository for government funds without paying interest for their use. In most other respects, the provisions followed the 1st Bank charter (1791). The central office remained at Philadelphia, and in time had 25 branches throughout the country. The bank began its operations on 1 Jan. 1817. Its first president was William Jones, whose inept management brought a Congressional threat to repeal the charter (Jan. 1819). The bank management was reorganized and performed capably under Langdon Cheves, who was named president in 1819. Cheves was succeeded (1823) by **Nicholas Biddle** (p. 676), who served until the expiration of the charter in 1836.

A bill introduced by Webster and adopted by Congress stipulated that after 20 Feb. 1817 the payment of public dues would be collected in either legal currency or in bank notes redeemable in specie. This measure virtually compelled the resumption of specie payments by state banks and resulted in a contracted note issue.

4 Dec. PRESIDENTIAL ELECTION. At the Republican Congressional caucus (16 Mar.) the younger element in the party supported William H. Crawford against **James Monroe.** Monroe won by a of vote 65 to 54, thus assuring the continuation of the "Virginia dynasty." **Daniel D. Tompkins** (N.Y.) was nominated for the Vice-Presidency. In the national elections, Monroe was opposed by the Federalist candidate, **Rufus King** (N.Y.). The waning strength of the Federalists, coupled with their popular discredit during the war years, gave **Monroe** an overwhelming victory. With 4 abstentions in the Electoral College, he received 183 electoral votes, King 34. Monroe carried all of the states except Mass., Conn., and Del. **Daniel D. Tompkins** (N.Y.) was elected Vice-President.

1817

3 Mar. BONUS BILL VETO. The rapid development of the West and the South created a need for adequate transportation facilities to link the outlying agricultural regions with the markets of the eastern seaboard, a need underscored by the military operations of the War of 1812. In his last annual message (3 Dec. 1816) President Madison recommended a Federally subsidized network of roads and canals, but his misgivings about its constitutionality led him to indicate the necessity for a constitutional amendment.

Calhoun reported a bill (23 Dec. 1816) to create a permanent fund for internal improvements by setting aside the $1,500,000 bonus paid by the Bank of the U.S. and all future dividends from Bank stock held by the government. Introducing the measure on 4 Feb., he declared that while the Constitution did not specifically authorize internal improvements, sanction could be drawn from the "general welfare" clause and from the power to establish post roads. Although Calhoun regarded the constitutional question as subsidiary to the value of internal improvements as a military necessity and a cement of national union, his argument showed the extent to which the Republican party had accepted the Hamiltonian doctrine of implied powers.

The bill passed in the House (8 Feb.), 86–84, and in the Senate, 20–15. Opposition to the bill was based on sectional rather than constitutional grounds. In the House, 34 opposing votes came from New England Federalists fearful of Western expansion; the South divided, 23 for, 25 against; the Middle States, 42 for, 6 against.

Performing his last act of office, President Madison vetoed the bill on constitutional grounds, stating that to draw authority from the "general welfare" clause for such a purpose "would be contrary to the established and consistent rules of interpretation, as rendering the special and careful enumeration of powers which follow the clause nugatory and improper."

4 Mar. Monroe's inaugural address revealed the Republican party's adoption of Federalist nationalist principles, including support of a standing army and an adequate naval establishment, and "the systematic and fostering care of the government for our manufactures."

ERA OF GOOD FEELINGS. During May-Sept. President Monroe toured the eastern seaboard north of Baltimore and visited the West as far as Detroit. The journey, undertaken ostensibly as an official tour of duty, soon became a popular symbol of the triumph of national feeling over party animosity. Enthusiasm, particularly marked in New England, where Federalists extended a warm welcome to the President, moved the Boston *Columbian Centinel* (12 July) to bestow upon the times the epithet "era of good feelings," a phrase commonly used to describe the state of the nation during Monroe's 2 terms in office (1817–25). The description is superficial and misleading. Although no formal political opposition existed during this period, new political factions and contenders were rising, as indicated by intra-Cabinet controversies and by the circumstances attending the Presidential election of 1824. During the same era, underlying sectional and economic issues were working basic transformations in the national life.

28–29 Apr. RUSH-BAGOT AGREEMENT. Among the sequels to the Treaty of Ghent was the arrangement for mutual disarmament on the Great Lakes effected by an exchange of notes between the British Minister to the U.S., Charles Bagot, and Acting Secretary of State Richard Rush, although the agreement was almost wholly the work of Monroe and Castlereagh, and was the direct outcome of a threatened naval armaments race on the Great Lakes. The British and U.S. agreed to limit their naval forces on inland waters to 1 vessel each on Lake Champlain and Lake Ontario and 2 vessels each on the Upper Lakes, none to exceed 100 tons or to have more than 1 18-pound gun. To allay British suspicion that succeeding U.S. administrations might not consider the arrangement binding, the Rush-Bagot agreement was submitted to the Senate, which gave it unanimous approval (16 Apr. 1818). The demilitarization of the Great Lakes, and the supposed extension of the principle to the land frontier, was thereafter regarded as an outstanding example of mutual disarmament. In reality, demilitarization of border fortifications and the equally important seaboard naval defenses was a lengthy and gradual process that did not produce genuine mutual disarmament until after the Treaty of Washington (1871).

1818

JACKSON AND THE FIRST SEMINOLE WAR. Ft. Apalachicola, on the river of that name in Spanish-held East Florida, had been built by the British during the War of 1812. After the war, the fort and the surrounding countryside occupied by Seminole Indians became a refuge for runaway slaves and hostile Indians. The threat to the Georgia border caused the U.S. government to dispatch an expedition which destroyed the fort (27 July 1816) and touched off armed conflict with the Negroes and Indians. A force led by Gen. Edmund P. Gaines was instructed to pursue hostile elements across the Florida boundary to the limits of the Spanish posts. On 26 Dec. 1817 command was transferred to Gen. Andrew Jackson, given similar orders. Upon receiving his instructions, Jackson wrote (6 Jan.) his **"Rhea letter"** to President Monroe, stating: "Let it be signified to me through any channel (say Mr. [Congressman] J. Rhea) that the possession of the Floridas would be desirable to the United States and in sixty days it will be accomplished." No immediate action on the letter was taken at Washington by President Monroe and Secretary of War Calhoun. Jackson chose to regard their official silence as tantamount to approval of his subsequent course in Florida. The letter was revived during the political controversies of 1831 when Calhoun, during his break with Jackson, published the Seminole correspondence.

Jackson marched into Florida and seized St. Marks (7 Apr.) and Pensacola (24 May), even as Secretary of State Adams was conducting discussions with the Spanish minister, Luis de Onís, concerning a settlement of the Florida question. During the campaign Jackson captured and court-martialed two British traders, **Alexander Arbuthnot** and **Robert Ambrister**, both of whom were accused of aiding the enemy. Arbuthnot was hanged and Ambrister was shot.

British public opinion was incensed, but Great Britain took no action. Jackson's raid also had domestic repercussions. His course met the disapproval of all Cabinet members except Adams. Two of its members, Calhoun and Crawford, believed Jackson merited stern disciplinary action. A House report (12 Jan. 1819) condemned Jackson's conduct. Anti-Jackson forces in the House, with Henry Clay at their head, proposed a resolution of censure during a debate (18 Jan.–8 Feb. 1819) on the question, and a Senate committee submitted a report (24 Feb. 1819) unfavorable to Jackson. No proceedings were taken against him.

Popular approval of Jackson's Seminole campaign, which brought all of East Florida under U.S. military control, influenced Monroe's decision not to punish Jackson. Actually, Jackson's raid strengthened the administration's hand in foreign affairs. Adams' firm instructions (28 Nov.) to the U.S. Minister at Madrid was virtually an ultimatum to the Spanish government. Accusing Spain of aiding and abetting hostilities against the U.S., Adams declared that the U.S. government had acted in self-defense. He defended Jackson's conduct and informed the Spanish government that it faced the alternatives of protecting and controlling Florida or ceding it to the U.S.

20 Oct. CONVENTION OF 1818. Another sequel to the Treaty of Ghent was the Convention of 1818, signed at London by Richard Rush, Minister to Great Britain, and Albert Gallatin, Minister to France. Under its terms, the northwest boundary between the U.S. and British North America was fixed along the 49th parallel from the Lake of the Woods to the crest of the Rocky Mountains (thus recognizing the northern line of the Louisiana Purchase). No boundary was established for the region west of the mountains, but the 2 powers agreed that the Oregon country was to be open to their subjects for 10 yrs., stipulating that such joint occupation would not be considered prejudicial to the territorial claims of either power in the Pacific Northwest. The convention gave U.S. nationals fishing privileges off sections of the coasts of Labrador and Newfoundland, and renewed the commercial treaty of 1815.

1819

PANIC OF 1819 was caused by commodity inflation, wild speculation in Western lands, overextended investments in manufacturing, mismanagement of the 2nd Bank of the U.S., collapse of foreign markets, and contraction of credit. The last factor was a result of the Congressional order (1817) for the resumption of specie payments, a move that strained the resources of state banks, caused many failures, and created hardships for debtors. The most severe effects of the panic were felt in the Southern and Western states. Many of the Western states, among them Missouri and Illinois, enacted legislation for the relief of debtors; in Kentucky such legislation led to the "relief war" (1823–26), a contest between the state legislature and judiciary over the constitutionality of replevin and stay laws. A more general result of the panic was widespread resentment against the National Bank in rural areas, where it became known as "The Monster," an epithet originated by **Thomas Hart Benton** (Mo., 1782–1858).

CESSION OF EAST FLORIDA. The Spanish posts seized by Andrew Jackson in East Florida were returned to Spain, but Adams' vigorous instructions, coupled with Spanish colonial difficulties in South America, led the Madrid government to accede to the U.S. demands. The extended negotiations which Adams had conducted with the Spanish minister resulted in the **Adams-Onís Treaty** (signed at Washington, 22 Feb.) whereby Spain renounced all claims to West Florida and ceded East Florida to the U.S. The U.S. renounced its claims to Texas and assumed the claims of its own citizens against Spain to the maximum amount of $5 million. The treaty also defined the western limits of the Louisiana Purchase. The boundary was established from the mouth of the Sabine River on the Gulf of Mexico, proceeding in a broken northwesterly line along the Red and Arkansas Rivers and the 42nd parallel, from which it was drawn due west to the Pacific Ocean. In effect, the Spanish claims to the Pacific Northwest were surrendered to the U.S. It was stipulated that the Treaty of San Lorenzo (1795) was to remain in force, except as altered by the Adams-Onís Treaty. The Senate ratified the treaty (24 Feb.); because of delays created by the Spanish government, the Senate again ratified on 19 Feb. 1821. The exchange of ratifications became final on 22 Feb. 1821.

2 Feb. THE DARTMOUTH COLLEGE CASE. In 1816 the Republican-dominated New Hampshire legislature altered the royal charter (1769) of Dartmouth College under which the college had been established, and vested the administration of the institution in a board of trustees appointed by the state. The old board of trustees, asserting that the legislative act was unconstitutional because it impaired the obligation of contracts, sued William H. Woodward, secretary of the university, for recovery of the seal, the charter, and other documents. The state court upheld the action of the legislature, declaring that the body established under the Dartmouth charter of 1769 was a public, not a private, corporation; and that as such its charter was not a contract within the meaning of the Constitution.

The case was appealed to the Supreme Court (*Trustees of Dartmouth College* v. *Woodward,* 4 Wheaton 518), with Daniel Webster as counsel for the college. Chief Justice Marshall, for the court, held that a charter to a private corporation constituted a contract and was therefore protected under the contract clause of the Constitution against impairment by state legislatures and declared the New Hampshire law invalid.

The decision appeared to place charters of existing private corporations outside the scope of control by the states that had chartered them. While it encouraged business growth, it also led to abuses of corporate privileges. Important modifications of Marshall's opinion in this case were made in *Charles River Bridge* v. *Warren Bridge* (p. 490) in 1837, and in *Munn* v. *Illinois* (p. 493) in 1877.

6 Mar. M'CULLOCH V. MARYLAND. During the postwar period of financial disorganization, state banks took advantage of popular feeling against the 2nd Bank of the U.S. to encourage legislation restricting its operations. A Maryland law provided that all banks not created by authority of the state were required to comply with restrictions concerning note issues or, in lieu of that, to pay an annual tax of $15,000. When the Baltimore branch of the National Bank ignored these provisions on the ground that the act was unconstitutional, the cashier of the branch, James W. M'Culloch, was sued by the state.

The case was appealed to the Supreme Court (*M'Culloch* v. *Maryland,* 4 Wheaton 316). The 2 leading points immediately at issue were the constitutionality of the act of Congress establishing the Bank, and the constitutionality of the tax imposed by the state legislature. Daniel Webster was among counsel representing the Bank, and the proceedings before the court included a notable 3-day argument by William Pinkney, senior counsel for the Bank.

The opinion, delivered by Chief Justice Marshall for a unanimous court, ranks among Marshall's most important pronouncements, and is commonly regarded as his most vigorous and detailed exposition of the Constitution. Drawing liberally upon the Hamiltonian doctrine of implied powers, Marshall expounded the origin and nature of the Federal union. The powers of the national government are derived from the people and are exercised directly on them, said Marshall; although the national government is limited in its powers, it is supreme within its sphere of action; and a government must be equipped with suitable and effective means to execute the powers conferred on it. He then proceeded to state the doctrine of "loose construction" based on Hamilton's opinion (1791) on the constitutionality of the 1st Bank of the U.S. "Let the end be legitimate," declared Marshall, "let it be within the scope of the constitution, and all means which are appropriate, which are plainly adapted to that end, which are not prohibited, but consist with the letter and spirit of the constitution, are constitutional." The act incorporating the Bank was therefore constitutional. As for the power of the Maryland legislature to tax the branch bank, Marshall declared that no state possessed that right, denying it on the ground that "the power to tax involves the power to destroy." Accordingly, he held the act of the Maryland legislature unconstitutional and void.

Of all his other opinions, only that pronounced (1821) in *Cohens* v. *Virginia* (p. 488) compares with this forthright assertion of nationalist doctrine. *M'Culloch* v. *Maryland* set off a nationwide controversy, with declarations by several states against inroads on state power. Marshall himself entered the argument with a series of anonymously published articles answering the criticisms of Judge Spencer Roane of Virginia.

1820

3 Mar. MISSOURI COMPROMISE. At the close of 1819, when the applications of Missouri and Maine for admission to statehood were before Congress, there were 22 states in the Union, 11 slave and 11 free. The slave states: Va., Md., Del., Ky., Tenn., N.C., S.C., Ga., Ala., Miss., and La. The free states: Mass., Conn., R.I., Vt., N.H., N.Y., N.J., Pa., Ohio, Ind., and Ill. The political balance between North and South had been maintained by admitting alternately (1802–19) slave and free states. But even with the three-fifths ratio operating in their favor, the slave states had only 81 votes in the House of Representatives as against 105 votes held by the free states. In addition, the population of the North was growing at a more rapid pace (free states: 5,152,000; slave states: 4,485,000). To preserve the sectional balance, the South looked to its equal vote in the Senate.

Late in 1819, the Missouri Territory embraced all of the Louisiana Purchase with the exception of the segments organized as the State of Louisiana (1812) and the Arkansas Territory (1819). The application of the Missouri Territorial Assembly (which had originally petitioned for statehood in 1817) raised the question of the legal status of slavery in Missouri and in the rest of the territory west of the Mississippi. In 1818 there were an estimated 2,000–3,000 slaves in

the upper Louisiana country (where slavery went back to Spanish and French rule).

13 Feb. 1819. Tallmadge Amendment. When the enabling legislation for Missouri came before Congress at the outset of 1819, Representative James Tallmadge (N.Y.) introduced an amendment (13 Feb. 1819) prohibiting the further introduction of slaves into Missouri and providing that all children born of slaves in Missouri after its admission should become free at the age of 25. The amendment set off a fierce debate. In the House, the 1st clause of the amendment was carried by 87–76 (16 Feb.) and the 2d clause 82–78 (17 Feb.); but the amendment was lost in the Senate (27 Feb.), 22–16 (1st cl.), 31–7 (2nd cl.).

26 Jan. 1819. Taylor Amendment. When the organization of Arkansas Territory came before Congress, Representative John W. Taylor (N.Y.) moved a proviso forbidding the further introduction of slavery. It was defeated (18 Feb. 1819), and Congress organized Arkansas as a territory (2 Mar. 1819) with its northern boundary at 36°30′ and with no restriction on slavery.

8 Dec. 1819–20 Mar. 1820. Missouri Debate. Senator Rufus King (N.Y.) maintained that Congress was empowered to forbid slavery in Missouri and to make the prohibition of slavery a prerequisite for admission. Senator William Pinkney (Md.) in reply asserted that the Union was composed of equal states and that Congress could not restrict Missouri's freedom of action.

17 Feb. 1820. Thomas Amendment. The 16th Congress, convened 6 Dec. 1819, faced the sectional issue with the presentation to Congress (8 Dec. 1819) of a memorial from the people of Maine petitioning for admission to statehood and the adoption (14 Dec. 1819) of a joint Congressional resolution admitting Alabama as the 22nd state. A proposition to combine the bill for the admission of Maine with that of Missouri (without restriction on slavery) was passed in the Senate, 23–21 (16 Feb.). Senator Jesse B. Thomas (Ill.) introduced a compromise amendment providing for the admission of Missouri as a slave state and for the prohibition of slavery in the Louisiana Purchase north of the line 36°30′.

The Thomas amendment passed in the Senate (17 Feb.) 34–10. On 18 Feb. the Senate agreed to admit Maine to statehood on condition that Missouri enter as a slave state.

The Senate bill was rejected by the House (28 Feb.). By 91–82, the House passed its own bill prohibiting slavery (1 Mar.), a measure incorporating the restrictive amendment proposed (26 Jan.) by Representative Taylor (N.Y.). Compromise elements arranged a conference and broke the deadlock. As a result, the Senate received the House bill, eliminated the Taylor amendment, and inserted the Thomas amendment. The Missouri bill was returned to the House, which passed the compromise measure, 90–87 (2 Mar.). The compromise became final 3 Mar., when by a House vote, 134–42, Maine was admitted as a free state, Missouri as a slave state, and slavery excluded from the line 36°30′. The decisive vote was made possible only by the defection of Northern representatives (whom John Randolph described as "doughfaces"). The admission of Maine as the 23rd state became effective 15 Mar.

19 July. Missouri Constitution. On 6 Mar. Congress authorized the people of Missouri to adopt a constitution. The Missouri convention at St. Louis (12 June) incorporated in the constitution (19 July) a provision excluding free Negroes and mulattoes from the state. This clause provoked antislavery sentiment in Congress when the Missouri constitution was presented to the Senate (14 Nov.) and the House (16 Nov.). A compromise formulated by Henry Clay resulted in the so-called "2nd Missouri Compromise" (2 Mar. 1821) providing that the state of Missouri should not gain admission to the Union until the legislature gave assurance that the offending clause would never be construed as sanctioning the passage of any law abridging the privileges and immunities of U.S. citizens. This condition was accepted by the Missouri legislature (26 June 1821), which qualified its pledge by insisting that it had no power to bind the people of the state. On 10 Aug. 1821 President Monroe proclaimed the admission of Missouri as the 24th state.

15 May. AFRICAN SLAVE TRADE. Under the act of 3 Mar. 1819, a $50 bounty was granted to informers for every illegally imported Negro slave seized in the U.S. or at sea, and the President empowered to return to Africa slaves captured under such circumstances. Under the 1820 act the foreign slave trade was declared piracy. In addition to the forfeiture of vessels authorized by the act of 1807, the death penalty was provided for all U.S. citizens engaging in the importation of slaves.

6 Dec. PRESIDENTIAL ELECTION. Because of the poor attendance at the Republican Congressional caucus called at Washington in Apr., no formal nominations were made. In the absence of old party distinctions, Monroe's candidacy for a 2nd term went unopposed. Out of 235 electoral votes (with 3 abstentions), Monroe received 231. One dissenting vote by a New Hampshire elector went to John Quincy Adams. Daniel D. Tompkins was reelected Vice-President, with 218 votes.

1821

5 Mar. The 4th of Mar. falling on a Sunday, Monroe postponed the inaugural exercises until the 5th, thereby setting a precedent.

28 Aug.–10 Nov. EXTENSION OF THE SUFFRAGE. The proposal to abolish the property qualification for voting in New York State, strenuously resisted at the New York Constitutional Convention by such conservatives as Chancellor James Kent (p. 737) and Chief Justice Ambrose Spencer, carried the day. For extension elsewhere, see p. 548.

1822

4 May. CUMBERLAND ROAD BILL VETO. Construction of the Cumberland Road, more commonly known as the National Road or Turnpike, came to a halt with the panic of 1819. The road extended from Cumberland, Md., to Wheeling, on the Ohio River. A bill for the repair of the road, authorizing establishment of toll gates and collection of tolls, passed in the House (29 Apr.), 87–68, and the Senate, 29–7. In his veto of the bill Monroe held that Congress did not have the right of jurisdiction and construction, but recommended a national system of internal improvements sanctioned by an appropriate constitutional amendment.

LATIN-AMERICAN REPUBLICS.

The success of the independence movements in Spanish America after 1817 led Henry Clay to advocate (1818) recognition of the revolutionary governments. In 1821, at Clay's instigation, the House of Representatives adopted a resolution expressing sympathy with the Latin-American republics and indicating the willingness of the House to support the President whenever he should decide to recognize the republics. It was clear that such a move would antagonize the Spanish government, but this consideration became a minor one after the final exchange of ratifications (1821) of the Florida treaty. President Monroe sent to Congress (8 Mar.) a special message proposing recognition of the Latin-American republics. A House resolution (28 Mar.) called for recognition, and the act of 4 May provided for establishment of diplomatic intercourse with those nations. The Republic of Colombia was formally recognized on 19 June and Mexico on 12 Dec. Chile and Argentina were recognized on 27 Jan. 1823, Brazil on 26 May 1824, the Federation of Central American States on 4 Aug. 1824, and Peru on 2 May 1826.

1823

RUSSIAN CLAIMS. The Czar issued an imperial ukase (4 Sept. 1821) extending Russian claims along the Pacific coast to north of the 51st parallel (which lay within the Oregon country) and closing the surrounding waters (of which the most important was Bering Strait) to the commercial shipping of other powers. The Russian claim was challenged by Secretary of State Adams, who informed the Russian minister to the U.S. (17 July) "that we should contest the right of Russia to **any** territorial establishment on this continent, and that

we should assume distinctly the principle that the American continents are no longer subjects for **any** new European colonial establishments." This principle regarding future European colonization in the New World was to become more familiar after its incorporation in the Monroe Doctrine. Under the treaty signed on 17 Apr. 1824, Russia agreed to a 54°40′ line and withdrew the maritime restriction. The U.S. renounced all claims to territory north of that line.

2 Dec. MONROE DOCTRINE. Great Britain was not sympathetic to the revolutionary governments in the former Spanish provinces; yet she was anxious to prevent the revival or extension of Spanish and French power in the New World, primarily in order to keep open to British commerce the rich markets of Latin America. This policy assumed a definite shape after George Canning became British Foreign Secretary (Sept. 1822).

At the Congress of Verona (Nov. 1822) the Quadruple Alliance (France, Austria, Russia, and Prussia) agreed to act to restore the authority of King Ferdinand VII of Spain, who in 1820 had been forced to accept a constitutional monarchy. The French were authorized to invade Spain, but no action was taken on the French request to intervene in South America. Canning protested against the Holy Alliance program of intervention and broke with the concert of European powers. Early in 1823, Canning attempted to obtain from France a promise barring the acquisition, either by cession or conquest, of any territory in Spanish America. France refused to make the pledge. (Authorities differ over the nature of the French threat to the Spanish colonies: H. W. V. Temperley, 1925, holds it serious; Dexter Perkins, 1927, no genuine peril; C. K. Webster, 1938, holds that the French failed to formulate specific plans.)

Canning's break with the Holy Alliance was followed by a move to come to an understanding with the U.S., with whom Great Britain had experienced difficulties (1822–23) concerning Cuba. Canning followed up an informal proposal (16 Aug.) to Richard Rush, U.S. Minister at London, with a note (20 Aug.) regarding the possibility of joint Anglo-U.S.

action against intervention of the Holy Alliance in the New World. Rush was not authorized to commit the U.S., but he indicated (23, 26 Aug.) that this proposition might meet with the favor of his government if the British recognized the Latin-American republics. Rush referred the matter to Monroe, who turned to his unofficial advisers, Jefferson and Madison. Both voiced support of close cooperation with the British.

Secretary of State Adams took a different view. Adams believed that the U.S. should assert its strength and independence by acting alone, in order to create an American system in the Western hemisphere, because (1) he was skeptical of Canning's apparently disinterested motives; (2) viewed the British proposal as a preliminary to exacting from the U.S. a pledge renouncing American designs on Cuba; and (3) felt that so long as the British maintained naval supremacy in the Atlantic, Russia's claims in the Pacific Northwest constituted a greater danger than possible French intervention in South America. Adams stated his position (7 Nov.): "It would be more candid, as well as more dignified, to avow our principles explicitly to Russia and France, than to come in as a cock-boat in the wake of the British man-of-war."

The U.S. government took no action on Canning's proposal. In the meantime, Canning secured his object in the **Polignac Agreement** (9 Oct.), whereby France renounced all intentions to conquer or annex the Spanish-American colonies. He did not resume his efforts to obtain a joint Anglo-American declaration.

The substance of Adams' views was adopted by Monroe and the Cabinet. In preparing an announcement of U.S. policy, Monroe acceded to Adams' suggestion that the formulation of views concerning European affairs (such as Greek independence) should be toned down. Adams held that the declaration of policy would be stronger were it based on wholly American interest. However, Monroe rejected Adams' recommendation that the declaration should be embodied in diplomatic communications to the various governments. With the support of Calhoun, Monroe decided to make the announcement in his annual message to Congress (2 Dec.). That portion of the message relating to foreign affairs was largely the work of John Quincy Adams (on the question of substantive authorship, see W. C. Ford, 1902, and S. F. Bemis, 1949, both of whom attribute it to Adams; W. A. MacCorkle, 1923, Dexter Perkins, 1927, and A. P. Whitaker, 1941, ascribe it to Monroe).

The Monroe Doctrine contained 4 major points: (1) the American continents were no longer to be considered as subjects for future colonization by European powers; (2) there existed in the Americas a political system essentially different and separate from that of Europe; (3) the U.S. would consider dangerous to its peace and safety any attempt on the part of European powers to extend their system to any point in the Western Hemisphere; (4) the U.S. would not interfere with existing colonies or dependencies of European powers in the New World; she would not interfere in the internal affairs of European nations; nor would she take part in European wars of solely foreign interest.

At the time of its announcement the Monroe Doctrine drew scant attention from the great powers. In Commons Canning, defending his Latin-American policy, declared (12 Dec. 1826): "I called the New World into existence to redress the balance of the Old." Although the Monroe Doctrine had no standing in international law until the Senate ratified the Act of Havana in 1940, that pronouncement served as the classic definition of the U.S. role in international affairs. But its major significance emerged only after the middle of the 19th century. Over the course of the years, it was modified and extended to meet changing circumstances.

1824

30–31 Mar. "AMERICAN SYSTEM." In a speech defending the protective features of the Tariff of 1824, Henry Clay applied the phrase "American system" to a combination of the protective tariff and a national system of internal improvements as a means of expanding the domestic market and lessening U.S. dependence upon overseas sources.

30 Apr. INTERNAL IMPROVE-MENTS. In 1818, William Lowndes (S.C.) submitted to the House 4 resolutions on internal improvements. The House (89–75) declared that Congress had authority to appropriate money for building military roads and other land routes, canals, and improved natural waterways. But following a debate on the constitutionality of these propositions, the House rejected all of them. Monroe's veto (1822) of the Cumberland Road Bill was sustained by both houses. The widespread demand, particularly from the West, for more and improved internal routes resulted in the introduction of the General Survey Bill empowering the President to initiate surveys and estimates of roads and canals required for national military, commercial, or postal purposes. By 115–86 (10 Feb.) the House passed the bill. The vote by sections: New England, 12 for, 26 against; the West, 43 for, none against; the South, 23 for, 34 against; the Middle States, 37 for, 26 against. The Senate passed the bill 24–18.

CABINET INTRIGUES. Between 1820 and 1822 political factionalism linked to Presidential ambitions caused dissension within the Cabinet. When the supporters of Secretary of War John C. Calhoun obtained his permission (28 Dec. 1821) to announce his Presidential candidacy, Calhoun was attacked by the adherents of Secretary of the Treasury William H. Crawford. The political rivalry between Calhoun and Crawford extended even to the administration of government business. The Senate, dominated by Crawford's followers, called for retrenchment in Calhoun's War Department expenditures and refused to approve nominations of military officers made by President Monroe at the recommendation of Calhoun.

Suspecting that Crawford was intriguing against the administration and was also attempting to establish a new political party, Monroe asked Crawford for an explanation. Crawford denied that he opposed the administration program, and assured the President of his loyalty. Monroe sought to remain neutral during the contest for power within the Cabinet, but the realization that he would soon be leaving office reduced his influence.

A direct outcome of factionalism at high levels was the "A.B." plot. Under the signature "A.B.," Senator Ninian Edwards (Ill.) published a series of articles (1823) in the Washington *Republican,* the organ of the Calhoun forces. The articles attacked Crawford for malfeasance in office. It was widely believed that Edwards' object in accusing Crawford was to injure the latter's standing as a Presidential candidate. Edwards, who was appointed Minister to Mexico 4 Mar., was recalled to Washington to testify before a House investigating committee. On 19 Apr. Edwards preferred charges against Crawford, but the Secretary of the Treasury was exonerated (25 May) by the House committee.

PRESIDENTIAL CAMPAIGN. The dissolution of the old party distinctions, and a rising opposition to the Congressional caucus as a means of choosing the Presidential candidate, left most of the nominations to the state legislatures. **John C. Calhoun** announced his candidacy in 1821. The Tennessee legislature nominated **Andrew Jackson** (20 July 1822), who was also chosen (4 Mar.) by a state nominating convention at Harrisburg, Pa. The action of the Tennessee legislature, which followed its move by a formal protest against the caucus procedure (1823), was the signal for other state and local resolves. The Kentucky legislature nominated **Henry Clay** (18 Nov. 1822); **John Quincy Adams** was nominated by a meeting (15 Feb.) at Boston. The rump Congressional caucus (attended by only 66 out of the 216 Republican representatives) that nominated **William H. Crawford** (14 Feb.) was the last one to nominate a Presidential candidate.

A paralytic stroke virtually eliminated Crawford (Sept. 1823). Calhoun withdrew and became Vice-Presidential candidate on the Jackson and Adams tickets. Adams held the strongest position; although he did not take part in trading for votes, he was to profit by the dissensions among the candidates from the South and West. In addition, his support of the "American system" brought him close to Clay, who had strong differences with Jackson. Most of the candidates supported a protective tariff and internal improvements. To these issues, Jackson added his attacks upon "King Caucus," and supported the right of the people to choose their own President.

1 Dec. PRESIDENTIAL ELECTION. Jackson received 99 electoral votes; Adams, 84; Crawford, 41; and Clay, 37. **Calhoun,** receiving 182 electoral votes, was chosen Vice-President. As no candidate had a majority the choice of the President was submitted to the House, which considered only the 3 leading candidates. Clay, eliminated, advised his friends (8 Jan. 1825) to vote for Adams; and the Kentucky representatives, acting under Clay's influence, disobeyed the instructions of their state legislature to vote for Jackson and instead cast their ballots for Adams. In the House vote (9 Feb. 1825), **Adams** received the votes of 13 states to 7 for Jackson and 4 for Crawford.

The charge that Clay had made a "corrupt bargain" by supporting Adams in return for the promise of the Secretaryship of State was made (Jan. 1825) by Representative George Kremer (Pa.) in an unsigned letter to a newspaper. Clay demanded a Congressional inquiry, but his accuser declined to appear. The charge received popular credence after Clay was appointed Secretary of State in the Adams Cabinet, and was repeated by Jackson in 1827. Although no persuasive evidence exists in support of the charge, the accusation clung to Clay's name until the end of his career.

The election of Adams ended the succession of the "Virginia dynasty." Over the winter of 1824–25, the Republican party divided into two groups. The Adams-Clay wing became known as the **National Republicans,** while the "Jackson men" emerged as the **Democratic Republicans.**

1825

CIVIL SERVICE POLICY. In keeping with his declared aim to lend a non-

political character to his administration, Adams refused to employ against his opponents the principle of political rotation in Federal appointive offices. He asserted that he would renominate any office-holder who did not warrant removal for official misconduct or incompetence (only 12 removals were made during his single term in office). Many of the incumbents were appointees of Crawford or McLean (a Jackson-Calhoun supporter) and used their influence against the President. Adams' deliberate refusal to have any connection with patronage cost him an essential means of building a political party.

AN OPPOSITION EMERGES. When the 19th Congress convened (5 Dec.) it soon became apparent that the forces opposed to Adams were beginning to coalesce. Adams' 1st annual message to Congress (6 Dec.) crystallized the opposition. Taking a broad nationalist view of Constitutional powers, Adams recommended construction of roads and canals, a national university, an astronomical observatory, standardization of weights and measures, the exploration of the U.S. interior and the Pacific Northwest coast, and the passage of laws for the promotion of agriculture, commerce, and manufacturing and the encouragement of the arts, sciences, and literature. These proposals antagonized Southern adherents of states' rights.

There were other signs of opposition to the President. Calhoun, using the recently granted powers of the Vice-President to appoint Senate committees, filled half of the important posts with senators who did not support the administration program. Adams, however, could count on the alliance of New England and the West based on common loyalty to the "American system"; so long as factionalism was rife in Southern politics, Adams still held the initiative.

1826

6 Jan. The 1st number of the *United States Telegraph* appeared at Washington, edited by Duff Green, a close friend of Calhoun and supported by senators and representatives opposed to the Adams administration.

PANAMA DEBATE. The 1st organized test of the Adams administration arose over the question of the mission to the Panama Congress. That assembly had been called for 1826 by Simon Bolívar, whose original invitation to the Latin-American republics (1824) had been extended by Colombia and Mexico to include the U.S. (1825). While not fully aware of the aims of the Congress, President Adams, with the support of Secretary of State Clay, believed that the dominant position of the U.S. in the Western Hemisphere demanded representation at the Congress. It was later revealed that the program of the Congress looked to a union of the Latin-American republics against Spain or other unfriendly nations and the establishment of a general assembly equipped with full war powers binding upon the member countries, neither of which were actually provided. Following his reference to the Congress in his annual message (6 Dec. 1825), Adams sent a special message to the Senate (26 Dec. 1825). He nominated 2 delegates to the Panama Congress and stressed the limited and consultative nature of U.S. participation.

The opposing coalition in the Senate, brought together on this issue by Calhoun and Senator Martin Van Buren (N.Y.), attacked the message on the ground (1) that since the Panama Congress would have the status of a government, U.S. participation would sharply diverge from traditional concepts of national independence and neutrality; (2) that Adams had accepted the invitation without consulting the Senate. On this score, Senator John Branch (N.C.) submitted a resolution affirming the authority of the Senate to pass upon appointments of ambassadors or other public ministers. Southern animosity was aroused on the slavery question. Adams' message had made no reference to slavery, but it was commonly known that the subject would enter into the proceedings at the Panama Congress, where some republics under the control of Negroes would be represented.

The Senate Committee on Foreign Relations reported unfavorably (11 Jan.) on the proposal, but the Senate approved the mission, 24–19 (14 Mar.), and the House approved the appropriation for it, 134–60 (25 Mar.). The U.S. was never represented at the Congress. Of the 2 delegates, Richard C. Anderson died enroute (24 July) and John Sergeant had not gone farther than Mexico City when the Congress adjourned.

During the Panama debate John Randolph made his famous charge against the Adams-Clay "corrupt bargain." Randolph declared from the Senate floor (30 Mar.) that the administration was "the coalition of Blifil and Black George," the combination "of the puritan with the black-leg." Randolph's accusation was followed by a challenge from Clay. The duel, fought on the Virginia bank of the Potomac (8 Apr.), left both contenders unharmed.

4 July. Death of Thomas Jefferson at Monticello and of John Adams at Quincy, Mass. Jefferson's death occurred a few hours before that of Adams. Shortly before he died, Adams is reported to have exclaimed: "Thomas Jefferson still survives."

1827

BROADENING OF DEMOCRACY. The movement against property-holding and taxpaying qualifications for voting was initiated before the War of 1812, with the abolition of those requirements in N.J. (1807) and Md. (1810), but even greater progress was made after 1815, with the admission of new Western states. The constitutions of Ind. (1816), Ill. (1818), and Ala. (1819) provided for white manhood suffrage; Me., in 1820, made the same provision. The era of state constitutional revision between 1816 and 1830 saw a liberalizing of the constitutions of Conn. (1818), Mass. (by amendments, 1821), and N.Y. (1821), all of which abolished property qualifications. Religious qualifications for voting and officeholding were removed, as in Md. (by constitutional amendment, 1826). There was also a trend toward apportionment on the basis of population rather than taxpayers, and an increase in popular elective offices. The selection of Presidential electors was gradually transferred from the state legislatures to the people. By 1828 only 2 of the 24 states in the Union (S.C. and Del.) still chose electors through their legislatures.

REVIVAL OF THE TARIFF QUESTION. Dissatisfied with the Tariff of 1824 because it failed to eliminate British competition, the wool-growing and woolen textile interests of the Northeast attempted to obtain higher duties. A bill introduced 10 Jan. incorporated 3 minimum valuations for woolen goods and made the importation of those articles virtually prohibitive. The bill was passed in the House (10 Feb.), but was lost in the Senate when Vice-President Calhoun, aligning himself with the antitariff forces, cast the decisive vote.

The rejection of this bill touched off a move for higher duties generally. At the call of the advocates of protection, a convention, dominated by the woolen interests, met at Harrisburg, Pa. (30 July–3 Aug.), with 100 delegates from 13 states in attendance. It called for the establishment of the minimum-valuation principle on textiles and proposed additional duties on hemp, flax, hammered bar iron and steel, and other goods. The memorial of the Harrisburg Convention was presented to Congress (24 Dec.). Dependent upon a world market for the disposal of its agricultural commodities, the South opposed a protective tariff which meant higher prices for manufactured goods.

South Carolina, whose economy had suffered gravely under the exhaustion of cotton lands (in general the effects of the Panic of 1819 lingered in the South longer than the North), took the lead against protectionism. In a speech made at Columbia, S.C. (2 July), **Thomas Cooper** (1759–1839), speaking for a small minority, condemned the economic ambitions of the North as a menace to Southern equality within the Union, and declared that the South would have to calculate the value of the Federal Union, for the "question is fast approaching the alternative of submission or separation."

1828

19 May. TARIFF OF ABOMINATIONS. The 20th Congress that convened on 3 Dec. 1827 witnessed the transfer of leadership from the administration forces to the "Jackson men." The protectionist scheme of the Harrisburg Convention having been rejected, the Jacksonians decided to exploit the tariff issue to discredit Adams. Crucial in the impending national elections were the Middle States. Jackson supporters reasoned that in any case the vote of New England would go to Adams and the vote of the South to Jackson. The Jacksonians who dominated the House Committee on Manufactures planned their tactics accordingly. They would report a bill with such excessively high duties (particularly at the cost of New England interests) that no section would vote for it; the responsibility for the defeat would be attributed to Adams; and the protectionist interests of the Middle States would be alienated from Adams. The Jacksonians, without offending Southern free-trade adherents, would then assure the Pennsylvanians that they favored protection of their iron interests.

The House committee framed a bill imposing very high duties on raw materials, iron, hemp, and flax, and eliminated some of the protective features pertaining to woolen goods. The bill was introduced in the House on 31 Jan., and discussion began on 4 Mar. The alliance of the Middle States and the South engineered by Martin Van Buren and Calhoun voted down every attempt by the New Englanders to amend the bill, and confidently awaited its defeat. To the surprise of the Jacksonians, New England voted for the bill despite its deficiencies, supporting it on the ground that it embodied the protective principle. The bill passed in the House, 105–94 (23 Apr.); the Senate, 26–21 (13 May). The Jacksonians of the West and the Middle States voted for the tariff, thereby depriving the Adams-Clay forces of a campaign issue. John Randolph asserted that "the bill referred to manufactures of no sort or kind, but the manufacture of a President of the United States."

19 Dec. Resolves of South Carolina Legislature. The South Carolina legislature promptly adopted a set of 8 resolutions (19 Dec.) terming the tariff unconstitutional, oppressive, and unjust. The Georgia legislature also protested (30 Dec.), as did Mississippi (5 Feb. 1829) and Virginia (4 Feb.). The Carolina resolutions were accompanied by the *South Carolina Exposition and Protest,* written (but not signed) by Calhoun. A lengthy essay on the theory of state sovereignty and minority rights, the *Exposition* expounded the doctrine of nullification by a single state. With it, Calhoun formally abandoned nationalism and identified himself with the particularist views of his state and section.

PRESIDENTIAL CAMPAIGN. Nominated for the Presidency by the Tennessee legislature (Oct. 1825), **Jackson** resigned from the U.S. Senate and began to build his political following for the election of 1828. His campaign was managed by a group of able editors and politicians including Amos Kendall, William B. Lewis, Duff Green, James Buchanan, and John H. Eaton. Jackson could count on the Southern vote, while in much of the West "Old Hickory" was acclaimed as a frontier military hero, a symbol of the common man, and a supporter of the "American system." **John C. Calhoun** was Vice-Presidential candidate on the Jackson ticket.

The National Republican Convention at Harrisburg, Pa., nominated **Adams** for a 2nd term with **Richard Rush** (Pa.) as his running mate. The Jacksonians, now called Democrats, based their campaign on personal grounds, and their opponents retaliated in kind. The "corrupt bargain" charge was used against Adams and Clay with telling effect.

3 Dec. PRESIDENTIAL ELECTION. **Jackson** received 647,231 popular votes and 178 electoral votes; Adams 509,097 popular votes, 83 electoral votes. **Calhoun**, with 171 electoral votes, was reelected Vice-President. The crucial states of Pennsylvania and New York went for Jackson. The vote in New York was close: 140,763 votes (20 electoral) for Jackson; 135,413 votes (16 electoral) for Adams. New York had been swung into the Jackson ranks by Martin Van Buren and William L. Marcy, leaders of the powerful "Albany Regency" that had succeeded the old Republican machine in the state and maintained its power by exercising the "spoils system."

1829

4 Mar. In his inaugural address, Jackson pledged himself to economy in government, a proper regard for states' rights, a "just and liberal policy" toward the Indians, and a revamping of the Federal civil service. The address contained no clear statement of policy on the tariff, internal improvements, the currency, or the Bank of the U.S. The boisterous reception at the White House, where Western frontiersmen mingled with Washington society, became a symbol of the common people's arrival at political power.

"KITCHEN CABINET." Shortly after taking office, Jackson suspended the practice of holding Cabinet meetings. For advice on policy he drew upon a small group of unofficial political confidants whom his opponents called the "Kitchen Cabinet" (also known as the "Lower Cabinet"). Among them were **Amos Kendall, Isaac Hill, William B. Lewis, Andrew J. Donelson,** and **Duff Green.** Some of them held minor government posts: Kendall was 4th auditor of the Treasury, while Lewis served as 2nd auditor. The "Kitchen Cabinet" was at the height of its influence between 1829 and 1831. With the reorganization of the Cabinet (1831), Jackson relied upon the members of that body for counsel.

THE "SPOILS SYSTEM." The phrase, "to the victor belongs the spoils," was used (1831) by Senator William Learned Marcy (N.Y.) during the course of a Congressional debate. The "spoils system" refers to the use of patronage for party purposes. First President to use the system was Jefferson, who employed it with restraint. By 1829, it was entrenched in the political machines of several states, including New York and Pennsylvania. Although Jackson introduced the system into national politics on a scale hitherto unmatched, he did not make wholesale political removals. The peak of Jackson's so-called "clean sweep" was reached during his 1st year in office, when only about 9% of the office holders were replaced. During Jackson's 2 terms (1829–37) not more than 20% of the office holders were removed on political grounds.

WORKINGMEN'S PARTY (also p. 519) was organized in Philadelphia (1828). Its candidates were defeated, but the party continued to agitate for free public education and for the protection of mechanics against competition from prison contract labor. In New York the Workingmen's party was formed in 1829, under the leadership of Robert Dale Owen, Thomas Skidmore, Fanny Wright, and George H. Evans. The Jacksonians attempted to exploit the party for their own ends. Erastus Root, speaker of the assembly and an adherent of Van Buren, sought to win the Workingmen's nomination (16 Apr. 1830) for governor. In turn, Fanny Wright and Robert Dale Owen split the party and nominated (14 Sept. 1830) Ezekiel Williams for governor.

1830

19–27 Jan. WEBSTER-HAYNE DEBATE had its inception when Senator **Samuel A. Foot** (Conn.) proposed a resolution (29 Dec. 1829) inquiring into the expediency of temporarily restricting the sale of public lands. The resolution, taken up on 13 Jan., came at a time when Jackson had not yet made any public announcement on the nullification stand taken by South Carolina. **Thomas Hart Benton** (Mo.) charged (18 Jan.) that Northeastern interests were attempting to check the settlement and prosperity of the West and was supported in this by **Robert Y. Hayne** (S.C.). In a speech (19 Jan.) invoking strict constructionist and states' rights views against Federal interference, Hayne asserted that "the very life of our system is the independence of the States, and that there is no evil more to be deprecated than the consolidation of this government." Hayne was answered (20 Jan.) by Daniel Webster (Mass.), who deplored the tendency of some

Southerners to "habitually speak of the Union in terms of indifference, or even of disparagement."

From this point onward the debate became a contest between Webster and Hayne, and was eventually confined to the origin and nature of the Constitution and the Union. Hayne's first reply (21, 25 Jan.) advanced the doctrine of state sovereignty and nullification. Webster's reply to Hayne (26, 27 Jan.) was one of the most eloquent orations ever delivered in the Senate. Passing over the Southerner's expression of economic grievances, Webster denied the validity of the constitutional doctrines advanced by Hayne, and expounded the nature of the Union. The states are sovereign only so far as their power is not qualified by the Constitution, said Webster, but only the Constitution and the national government are sovereign over the people. In the event of disagreement between the states and the national government, the settlement of the dispute rested with the agencies provided for that purpose in the Constitution: the Federal courts, the amending power, and regular elections. Attacking disunionist tendencies, Webster closed his oration with an eloquent peroration celebrating "Liberty *and* Union, now and forever, one and inseparable!"

Hayne's 2nd reply to Webster (27 Jan.) included the statement that the Federal government resulted from the compact between the states, and that each party to the compact was the rightful judge of infringements upon its rights. Questions of sovereignty, said Hayne, are not subject to judicial consideration; therefore the right of state interposition is "as full and complete as it was before the Constitution was formed." In his rebuttal (27 Jan.) Webster opposed Hayne's historical theory of the Constitution by attempting to show that the Constitution was not the result of a compact, but was established as a popular government with a distribution of powers binding upon the national government and the states.

13 Apr. "OUR UNION—" The Jefferson Day Dinner, held at Brown's Indian Queen Hotel in Washington, was arranged by Senators Benton and Hayne, ostensibly to align the Democratic party with Jeffersonian principles and to signify the alliance between the West and the South. Jackson gave much thought to the phrasing of his volunteer toast, given after he had heard 24 prepared toasts, many of them alluding to the propriety of state sovereignty and nullification. Jackson offered his toast: "Our Union: It must be preserved." Calhoun responded: "The Union, next to our liberty, most dear. May we always remember that it can only be preserved by distributing equally the benefits and burdens of the Union." At the request of Hayne, Jackson agreed to amend his toast for publication, to read: "Our Federal Union—." But the nullifiers could find only small comfort in this concession.

27 May. MAYSVILLE ROAD VETO. In his 1st annual message to Congress (8 Dec. 1829) Jackson referred to the constitutional objections that had been raised against internal improvements. He recommended the distribution of the surplus revenue among the states according to their Congressional apportionment, the states to use the funds at their own discretion. Meanwhile, he had been heeding Van Buren's advice to put an end to Congressional logrolling that resulted in the construction of internal improvements at Federal expense. Van Buren had a political object: to strike at the Clay party.

The opportunity arose when Congress passed a bill authorizing a government subscription of stock to the amount of $150,000 in the Maysville, Washington, Paris, and Lexington Turnpike Road Company, for the construction of a 60-mi. road in Kentucky. In his 1st veto, on expediency and strict constructionist grounds, Jackson declared that as the road lay within the limits of a single state and had no connection with any established system of improvements, it was not embraced by national jurisdiction. If Federally subsidized roads and canals were thought desirable, said Jackson, they should be sanctioned by a constitutional amendment.

Jackson's concession to Southern states' rights was made without withdrawing his general support of internal improvements. Thus Jackson kept his Southern political support and did not antagonize the North and the West. His subsequent policy on

internal improvements terminated sizable Federal expenditures on roads and canals, although it did not materially affect the improvement of harbors and rivers. The only large land-route project he approved was the Cumberland Road Bill (31 May).

7 Dec. Publication of the first number of the *Washington Globe*. The growing gulf between Jackson and Calhoun led the President and the "Kitchen Cabinet" to arrange for the establishment of an administration newspaper. Francis P. Blair, Sr., of Kentucky, was chosen to edit the *Globe*. After the formal break between Jackson and Calhoun, Duff Green's *United States Telegraph* (with the aid of a loan from the Bank of the U.S.) became an antiadministration organ.

1831

JACKSON'S BREAK WITH CALHOUN. In the spring of 1830 Jackson learned that in 1818 Calhoun, as Secretary of War, had favored punishing Jackson for his conduct in the Seminole War. The letter containing this charge was written by William H. Crawford and was made known by William B. Lewis and others for the purpose of discrediting Calhoun. Jackson, who hitherto believed that Calhoun had supported him in 1818, requested an explanation. Calhoun's defense of his position did not satisfy the President. "Understanding you now," wrote Jackson, "no further communication with you on this subject is necessary" (30 May 1830). At Calhoun's direction, a pamphlet containing the correspondence on the Seminole affair was published (15 Feb.). It angered Jackson, completed the breach between him and Calhoun, and helped to confirm Jackson in his choice of Van Buren as Presidential successor.

EATON AFFAIR. The split in Jackson's Cabinet between the supporters of Calhoun and those of Van Buren as heir apparent to the Presidency impinged upon a Washington social feud waged against Peggy O'Neale, a barmaid who had become (1829) the 2nd wife of Secretary of War John H. Eaton. Jackson supported Mrs. Eaton, whose status in society soon became a political issue. Mrs.

Calhoun and the wives of other members of the Cabinet refused to receive Mrs. Eaton. Jackson's stubborn efforts to compel recognition met with little success; he encountered resistance even in the White House, where Mrs. Andrew J. Donelson withdrew as hostess rather than call on Mrs. Eaton. When he raised the issue at a Cabinet meeting, the only Cabinet member to support Mrs. Eaton was the widower Martin Van Buren, who thereby increased Jackson's favor for him.

Van Buren, who saw the Eaton affair as a liability to the administration, submitted his resignation, aware that this would precipitate a reorganization of the Cabinet. When Eaton learned that Van Buren's resignation was impending, he offered his own.

CABINET REORGANIZATION. The resignations of Eaton (7 Apr.) and Van Buren (11 Apr.) were accepted by Jackson, who then requested and received those of Secretary of the Treasury Ingham (19 Apr.), Secretary of the Navy Branch (19 Apr.), and Attorney General Berrien (15 June). Van Buren was named Minister to England, and Jackson ended the Washington social war by appointing Eaton governor of Florida. A reorganized Cabinet was formed with an eye to harmony: Levi Woodbury of New Hampshire, Secretary of the Navy (23 May); Edward Livingston of Louisiana, Secretary of State (24 May); Roger B. Taney of Maryland, Attorney General (20 July); Lewis Cass of Ohio, Secretary of War (1 Aug.); and Louis McLane of Delaware, Secretary of the Treasury (8 Aug.). The only Cabinet member retained was Postmaster General William T. Barry.

JACKSONIAN DIPLOMACY. West Indian Trade. U.S. shipping interests suffered under the severe British restrictions on direct trade with the West Indies. The unsatisfactory results of the halfway measures adopted (1822–25) by the U.S. and Great Britain led both governments to make provisions (1826–27) for closing West Indian ports to direct trade. After taking office, Jackson adopted a moderate approach on the issue, basing his application for a reopening of trade on the grounds of a new administration, a change in public opinion, and the restoration of privileges rather than rights. Congress authorized Jackson (29 May 1830) to take reciprocal action in the event British colonial ports were reopened. After some months of negotiation Jackson announced by proclamation (5 Oct.) that trade was reopened with the West Indian ports on the basis of reciprocal privileges.

French Spoliation Claims. Claims against the French for depredations on U.S. commerce during the Napoleonic Wars had been pending since 1815. The negotiations lagged because of French counterclaims based on alleged U.S. violations of a commercial clause in the Louisiana Treaty. Jackson instructed William C. Rives, Minister to France, to secure a satisfactory adjustment. A treaty was concluded (4 July) whereby France agreed to pay 25 million francs and the U.S. 1,500,000 francs for spoliations committed against the subjects of either nation in 6 annual installments. Delay in the French payment of the 1st installment caused Jackson to recommend (annual message, 2 Dec. 1834) reprisals on French property in the event no provision was made for payment. The French voted an appropriation (25 Apr. 1835) on condition that Jackson apologize for certain expressions in his message. Jackson replied in his annual message (7 Dec. 1835): "The honor of my country shall never be stained by an apology from me for the statement of truth and the performance of duty." In a special message to Congress (15 Jan. 1836) Jackson again recommended reprisals and an expansion of naval and coastal defenses, but at the same time made an adroitly phrased offer of conciliation. Great Britain's offer of mediation (27 Jan. 1836) was accepted, and on 10 May 1836 Jackson announced that the French had paid four installments. Other spoliation claims to the amount of $5 million based on depredations committed before 1800 were incorporated in a bill that passed the Senate (28 Jan. 1835), but did not receive House action.

ANTI-MASONIC PARTY. The mysterious disappearance in western New York of **William Morgan** (Sept. 1826), who had prepared an exposé of Freemasonry, led to a series of official inquiries and court trials (1827–31) that threw no light on the fate of Morgan but revealed that virtually all of the officeholders in New York State were members of the order. During the subsequent popular reaction against Freemasonry opponents of Jackson (who was a Mason) exploited the issue. In mid-1830 the Anti-Masons appeared in New York State as a political party opposed to Jackson. Anti-Masonry and antipathy to all kinds of secret societies spread to other states, and a national convention of Anti-Masons assembled at Baltimore (26 Sept.), nominating **William Wirt** (Md., 1772–1834) for President and Amos Ellmaker (Pa.) for Vice-President. The Anti-Masonic party was the first 3d party in the U.S., the 1st to hold a national nominating convention, and the 1st to announce a platform. The party declined after the election of 1836 and was eventually absorbed by the Whigs.

ABOLITION MOVEMENT (p. 544).

13–23 Aug. NAT TURNER INSURRECTION (p. 544).

1832

INDIAN POLICY. Jackson's Indian policy was based mainly on the prospect of voluntary emigration to tracts west of the Mississippi set aside for permanent occupancy. Under the act of 28 May 1830 Congress made provision for removal; the act of 30 June 1834 established a special Indian territory in the Arkansas country.

Under a series of treaties (1791 *et seq.*) concluded with the U.S., the Cherokee inhabiting the state of Georgia were recognized as a nation with their own laws and customs. However, Georgia settlers encroached upon the Cherokee as well as the neighboring Creek Indians. Alabama and Mississippi likewise violated Federal treaties in annexing the lands of the Choctaw and the Chickasaw. Under a state law of 20 Dec. 1828, Georgia pronounced the laws of the Cherokee Nation null and void after 1 June 1830. After gold was discovered on the Cherokee lands (July 1829), the Cherokee sought relief in the Supreme Court. In an opinion delivered by Chief Justice Marshall (1831), an injunction against Georgia was denied on the ground that the court lacked jurisdiction because the Cherokee comprised a "domestic dependent" nation rather than a foreign state within the meaning of the Constitution (*Cherokee Nation* v. *Georgia,* 5 Peters 1).

A Georgia law (1830) ordered white residents in the Cherokee country to secure a license from the governor and to take an oath of allegiance to the state. Samuel A. Worcester and Elizur Butler, both New England missionaries, refused to obey the law and were convicted and sentenced to 4 years at hard labor. On appeal to the Supreme Court Chief Justice Marshall (3 Mar.) held that the national government had exclusive jurisdiction in the territory of the Cherokee Nation (*Worcester* v. *Georgia,* 6 Peters 515) and that the Georgia law was therefore unconstitutional. Georgia defied the court and was supported by Jackson, who is reported to have said: "John Marshall has made his decision, now let him enforce it!"

Jackson pursued a broad policy of extinguishing Indian land titles in states and in removing the Indian population. During his 2 terms 94 Indian treaties were concluded. In the Old Southwest, the Creeks, Choctaw, and Chickasaw signed treaties of evacuation. By the end of 1833 only the Cherokee insisted on retaining their lands. Finally, under the treaty of 29 Dec. 1835 the Cherokee surrendered to the U.S. all their lands east of the Mississippi in return for $5 million, transportation costs, and land in Indian territory. A **Bureau of Indian Affairs** was established in 1836. Some Indians resorted to armed resistance. Seeking to reoccupy their ceded lands in Wisconsin Territory and Illinois, the Sac and Fox Indians fought the **Black Hawk War** (6 Apr.–2 Aug. 1832) along the Upper Mississippi. They were beaten back. In Florida, the **Second Seminole War** broke out in Nov. 1835 and lasted until 14 Aug. 1843.

NULLIFICATION CONTROVERSY. In his annual message of 1830 Jackson affirmed the constitutionality of the Tariff of 1828 and protectionism. But to conciliate the South, he recommended tariff revision in his subsequent message.

During 1830–31, the nullification forces in South Carolina enlarged their following; but Union sentiment in the state was strong enough to prevent the calling of a convention. The Tariff of 1832, while somewhat milder than that of 1828, retained the protective principle. Its passage (14 July) encouraged the South Carolina nullifiers, who, under the leadership of Gov. James Hamilton, Jr., and Robert Barnwell Rhett, took a belligerent stand. The state elections (Oct.) resulted in a decisive victory for the nullification party.

Ordinance of Nullification. Meanwhile, Calhoun had reaffirmed and elaborated the doctrine of nullification in 2 important papers: the **Fort Hill Address** (26 July 1831), which contained the principle of the concurrent majority, and in a letter to Gov. Hamilton (28 Aug.) which defended nullification as a constitutional, conservative, and legitimate means of redress for acts deemed injurious to the state.

Gov. Hamilton called an extraordinary session of the legislature (22 Oct.), which promptly called for a state convention. The convention which assembled at Columbia (19 Nov.), attended by only a handful of Unionists, adopted (136–26) an ordinance nullifying the tariff acts of 1828 and 1832 (24 Nov.). The ordinance prohibited the collection of duties within the state, beginning 1 Feb. 1833; required a test oath for all state office holders except members of the legislature; forbade appeal to the U.S. Supreme Court of any case in law or equity arising under the ordinance; and asserted that the use of force by the Federal government would be cause for secession. The legislature (27 Nov.) passed laws for the enforcement of the ordinance. Among them were provisions authorizing the raising of a military force and appropriations for arms.

Jackson ordered the Secretary of War (29 Oct.) to alert the forts in Charleston Harbor. Maj. Gen. Winfield Scott was given the command of the army forces in South Carolina. Jackson's message to Congress (4 Dec.) again recommended downward revision of the tariff.

On 10 Dec. he issued his **Proclamation to the People of South Carolina**, which was drafted by Edward Livingston and ranks as Jackson's most important state paper. The proclamation characterized nullification as an "impractical absurdity" and asserted the supremacy of a sovereign and indivisible Federal government. No state, said Jackson, could refuse to obey the laws of the land, and no state could leave the Union. "Disunion by armed force is **treason,**" Jackson concluded.

The South Carolina legislature adopted a series of resolutions (17 Dec.) replying to the Nullification Proclamation, and the newly installed governor, Robert Y. Hayne, issued a counterproclamation (20 Dec.). Calhoun resigned the Vice-Presidency (28 Dec.), having been elected (12 Dec.) U.S. Sen. in place of Hayne (121–28). A call by South Carolina for a general convention of the states to consider relations between the Federal and state governments elicited a series of replies by various state legislatures unequivocally condemning nullification and secession.

Force Bill. Jackson asked Congress (16 Jan. 1833) for authority to enforce the revenue laws by the use of the military if necessary. The Congressional battle against the so-called Force Bill was led by Calhoun, who was engaged by Webster in a notable debate on nationalism and states' rights. Meanwhile, Henry Clay had formulated a compromise tariff. Introduced on 12 Feb. 1833, it passed the House, 119–85 (26 Feb. 1833), and the Senate, 29–16 (1 Mar.). The Force Bill was passed in the Senate, 32–1 (20 Feb. 1833; Calhoun, Clay, and others abstained from voting), and passed the House, 149–47 (1 Mar.). The compromise tariff of 1833 and the Force Bill were approved by Jackson on 2 Mar.

Upon learning that a compromise tariff was in the making, South Carolina suspended the ordinance of nullification (21 Jan. 1833). Calhoun supported the compromise, although he did not participate in the proceedings of the state convention which met on 11 Mar. and adopted (153–4) a rescinding ordinance (15 Mar.). As a face-saving gesture the convention (132–19) adopted (18 Mar.) an ordinance declaring the Force Bill null and void, and adjourned on the same day. The nullification episode was closed, with both sides claiming victory.

10 July. BANK VETO. The charter of the 2nd Bank of the U.S. was due to expire in 1836. Under the conservative management (1823 *et seq.*) of **Nicholas Biddle** (p. 676), the Bank had prospered and expanded. It aided business operations and reduced the threat of inflation posed by a disorganized currency. But there was a many-sided opposition to the Bank. Biddle's policy of branch drafts, which compelled state and local banks to contract their note issues, made the Bank unpopular among debtor groups, particularly in the South and West. Southern states' rights groups questioned its constitutionality. State banks sought government deposits. Van Buren and his New York supporters disputed Philadelphia's financial leadership. Biddle's personal domination of the Bank's policies, and his identification with conservative interests, ultimately made him a target for popular resentment against monopolies, corporations, and a moneyed aristocracy.

Jackson's 1st annual message (1829) questioned the Bank's constitutionality and expediency, and asserted that the Bank had failed to establish a sound and uniform currency. Jackson favored a government-owned institution with severely limited operations confined chiefly to deposit. When it became clear that Jackson was intent upon eliminating the Bank, Biddle embarked upon a policy of opposition. Until early in 1832, however, he planned to defer his application for renewal of the Bank charter until after the Presidential elections.

Senator Thomas Hart Benton launched an attack upon the Bank in a speech (Feb. 1831). Biddle, alarmed, and at Clay's advice, decided to make immediate application for renewal of the charter, thereby forcing the Bank issue upon Jackson.

A bill for recharter of the Bank was reported in the House (10 Feb.) and in the Senate (13 Mar.). The measure passed the Senate, 28–20 (11 June), and the House, 107–86 (3 July). Jackson ve-

toed the bill (10 July). Although his message showed no firm grasp of banking and finance, it was an indictment of monopoly and special privilege, and accepted the challenge of the opposition to make the Bank the major issue of the campaign of 1832. In referring to the Supreme Court's views on the constitutionality of the Bank, Jackson made a notable definition of the character of the Presidential office: "The Congress, the Executive, and the Court must each for itself be guided by its own opinion of the Constitution. Each public officer who takes an oath to support the Constitution swears that he will support it as he understands it, and not as it is understood by others. . . . The opinion of the judges has no more authority over Congress than the opinion of Congress has over the judges, and on that point the President is independent of both." The Senate vote of 22–19 (13 July) failed to override the veto.

PRESIDENTIAL CAMPAIGN. A National Republican Convention assembled at Baltimore (12 Dec. 1831), where its delegates nominated **Henry Clay** for President and **John Sergeant** (Pa.) for Vice-President. The Anti-Masonic party had already nominated (26 Sept. 1831) **William Wirt** (Md.) for President and **Amos Ellmaker** (Pa.) for Vice-President. The campaign of 1832 witnessed the adoption of the **national nominating convention** by the 3 parties in the field. The 1st platforms ever adopted by national conventions were by the Anti-Masons (Sept. 1831) and by a group of young National Republicans convened at Washington in May.

The 1st national nominating convention of the Democratic party (as it was now formally called) was held at Baltimore (21–22 May). It unanimously endorsed **Jackson** for a 2nd term and named **Martin Van Buren** for the Vice-Presidency. Van Buren's nomination as Minister to England had been rejected in the Senate 24–23 (25 Jan.). Calhoun, who had cast the deciding vote, thought the rejection would end Van Buren's political career; the move had an opposite effect. The convention adopted the **"two-thirds rule"** (which remained in force until 1936) requiring that "two-thirds of the whole number of votes in the convention shall be necessary to constitute a choice." No platform was adopted. The principal campaign issue was the Bank question, which struck a wide response from agrarian and frontier prejudice against the Bank and from Eastern feeling against privileged corporations. The National Republicans were identified with the conservative interests. Biddle printed and circulated campaign literature supporting Clay.

5 Dec. PRESIDENTIAL ELECTION was an overwhelming Democratic victory. Jackson won the electoral votes of 16 of the 24 states with 219 electoral votes (687,502 popular votes); Clay received 49 electoral votes (530,189 popular votes). William Wirt carried only Vermont (7 electoral votes). The South Carolina legislature cast 11 votes for John Floyd (Va.) and Henry Lee (Mass.). **Van Buren**, with 189 electoral votes, was elected Vice-President (Pennsylvania having thrown its 30 electoral votes to Senator William Wilkins, a native son).

1833

REMOVAL OF THE DEPOSITS. The Calhoun and Clay forces in the House united in adopting a resolution (2 Mar.) stating that government deposits might be safely continued in the Bank of the U.S. Jackson, however, interpreted his reelection as a popular mandate to proceed against the Bank. Biddle had already embarked upon a policy of tightening credit to bring the administration to terms.

Jackson asked (19 Mar.) the opinion of the Cabinet on the regulation of deposits and the establishment of a new bank. **Attorney General Taney** (3 Apr.) supported removal of the deposits and their distribution among selected state banks (a policy which Amos Kendall and Francis P. Blair, Sr., had already recommended). Secretary of the Treasury McLane (20 May) opposed removal and supported the formation of a new bank. Jackson then reorganized the Cabinet, appointing McLane as Secretary of State (1 June) and William J. Duane of Pa. Secretary of the Treasury. Upon receiving Jackson's instructions for removing the deposits, Duane replied with a letter (10 July) opposing the step.

On 10 Sept. Jackson submitted to the Cabinet a report by Kendall indicating the availability of state banks, and announced that on 1 Oct. the government would discontinue the Bank of the U.S. as a depository. Taney and Woodbury supported Jackson; McLane, Cass, and Duane were opposed. Jackson read to the Cabinet (18 Sept.) a paper drafted by Taney listing the reasons for removal. The document illuminated Jackson's concept of the role of the Cabinet: namely, that it was the personal organ of the President.

When Duane persisted in his refusal to carry out the removal, he was replaced (23 Sept.) by Taney as Secretary of the Treasury. Taney announced (26 Sept.) that the public funds would no longer be deposited in the Bank of the U.S., and issued the first order for removal (effected by transferring the funds). The Girard Bank of Philadelphia was the 1st state bank designated as a place of deposit. By the end of 1833, 23 state banks (popularly known as "pet banks") had been selected as depositories. By that time, too, Biddle's restrictions on credit had induced financial distress.

In his annual message (3 Dec.) Jackson assumed complete responsibility for removing the deposits, defending his action with the argument that the Bank was attempting to influence elections. The Senate issued a call (11 Dec.) for a copy of the paper which Jackson had read to the Cabinet. Jackson refused the request, declaring that "the executive is a co-ordinate and independent branch of the Government equally with the Senate, and I have yet to learn under what constitutional authority that branch of the Legislature has a right to require of me an account of any communication, either verbally or in writing, made to the heads of Departments acting as a Cabinet council."

Henry Clay introduced 2 **censuring resolutions** in the Senate (26 Dec.): The 1st, criticizing the action of the Treasury, was adopted 28 Mar. 1834,

28–18; the second, stating that "the President, in the late Executive proceedings in relation to the public revenue, has assumed upon himself authority and power not conferred by the constitution and laws, but in derogation of both," was adopted the same day, 26–20.

The Jackson supporters in the House pushed through 4 resolutions sustaining the administration's Bank Policy (4 Apr. 1834). Jackson made a formal protest (15 Apr. 1834), asserting that he had been charged with an impeachable offense but had been denied an opportunity to defend himself. On 21 Apr. 1834 he forwarded a supplementary message aimed at conciliating the Senate. By 27–16 (7 May 1834) the Senate rejected Jackson's power to question its authority and declined to enter the President's protest and message in the official record of its proceedings. In another move against Jackson, the Senate (24 June 1834) refused to approve Taney's nomination as Secretary of the Treasury. Through the repeated efforts of Senator Benton, the resolution of censure was finally expunged from the Senate journal (16 Jan. 1837).

The Bank of the U.S., having failed to secure a new charter, obtained a state charter (Feb. 1836) and, upon the expiration of its national charter (1 Mar. 1836), became the Bank of the U.S. of Pennsylvania. Under the **Deposit Act** (23 June 1836) the Secretary of the Treasury was required to designate at least one bank in each state and territory as a place of public deposit, and the banks were assigned the general services previously rendered to the national government by the Bank of the U.S. The act also provided for the distribution of the surplus revenue in excess of $5 million among the states, as a loan subject to recall by the Secretary of the Treasury. It was never recalled.

1834

RISE OF THE WHIG PARTY. The union of the National Republican and Calhoun forces which secured the passage of the Senate censuring resolutions was the genesis of the Whig coalition on a national scale. The name "Whig" was formally adopted in 1834, after Clay mentioned it approvingly in a Senate speech (14 Apr.), but it had been in use for at least 2 yrs. before that time. Gatherings of Northern and Southern opponents of the Jackson administration were held in the spring of 1834, apparently for the purpose of merging forces. By mid-1834 the Whig label was generally understood to refer to the coalition of the political groups led by Clay, Webster, and Calhoun, even though Calhoun preferred an independent course and acted with the Whigs when expedient. Included in this loose coalition: (1) National Republican supporters of Clay, Adams, and the "American system"; (2) states' rights groups opposed to Jackson's stand on nullification; (3) former administration supporters alienated by Jackson's Bank policy; (4) Southern planters and Northern industrialists; and, after 1836, (5) the remnants of the Anti-Masonic party.

1835

30 Jan. Attempted assassination of President Jackson. The assailant, Richard Lawrence, fired 2 pistols (both of which misfired) at the President as he was leaving the House chamber. Jackson was unharmed. Lawrence was adjudged insane and committed to a lunatic asylum.

ABOLITIONIST PROPAGANDA. The Southern states met abolitionist propaganda with regulatory or prohibitory laws. A Georgia code (1835) provided the death penalty for the publication of material tending to incite slave insurrections. Northern abolitionist editors and agents were expelled from the South. To the South Carolina legislature (1835) Governor McDuffie declared that "the laws of every community should punish this species of interference by death without benefit of clergy." At Charleston (29 July), a boatload of abolitionist tracts from New York impounded by the postmaster was seized by a mob and publicly burned. The Charleston postmaster, Alfred Huger, requested antislavery societies to discontinue their use of the mails; his appeal was rejected.

When Huger's report reached Postmaster General Kendall, the latter replied that he had no official authority to bar abolitionist propaganda from the mails; unofficially he advised Southern postmasters to intercept such material, having already declared, "We owe an obligation to the laws, but a higher one to the communities in which we live."

In his annual message (2 Dec.) Jackson recommended a law to prohibit the circulation of antislavery publications through the mails. A Senate committee headed by Calhoun presented (4 Feb. 1836) a minority report on abolitionist publications, which supported Jackson's opposition to the dissemination of antislavery literature but took objection on states' rights grounds to the recommended Federal law barring circulation through the mails and offered a bill for the interception by postmasters of any publication prohibited by the laws of a particular state. The bill was defeated in the Senate, 25–19 (8 June 1836).

29 Oct. LOCO-FOCOS. The radical wing of Jacksonian Democracy, an urban faction that inherited the mantle of the Workingmen's party in New York, emerged (1834–35) as the Equal Rights party. Its followers, dividing with the Democratic regulars chiefly over banking and currency questions, regarded Jackson's banking policy as inflationary. Called the "Loco-Focos," this faction fought those financial interests which, with the aid of the regular Democratic party in the state, applied for bank and corporation charters from the legislature, and advocated abolition of monopolies and special privileges, hard money, elections by direct popular vote, direct taxes, free trade, and Jeffersonian strict construction. The radical wing found a voice in the New York *Evening Post*. The origin of the name "Loco-Focos" dates from a primary meeting (29 Oct.) at Tammany Hall when the regulars, over the protests of the Equal Rights men, declared the ticket carried and the meeting adjourned. The dissidents remained in the hall. To oust them, the Tammany stalwarts turned out the gas lights, whereupon the Equal Rights men furnished candles which they lit with the new self-igniting friction matches

known as loco-focos, and proceeded to formulate their platform and nominate their own ticket.

1836

REPUBLIC OF TEXAS. The American settlement of Texas began when **Moses Austin** secured a charter (17 Jan. 1821) granting lands for colonization by 200 American families. The charter was obtained from the moribund government of New Spain, which soon became the independent state of Mexico. Upon Austin's death in Missouri (10 June 1821), his settlement scheme was carried forward by his son, **Stephen F. Austin** (p. 671), who arrived at Bexar, Texas (12 Aug. 1821), to take possession of the land grants. In 1822–23 Austin visited Mexico, where by a decree of the Emperor Iturbide he secured confirmation of his concession. Renewal was made during the subsequent revolutions in Mexico and the establishment of a federal republic under the constitution of 1824. A law (7 May 1824) made Texas part of a state in the Mexican republic, and a colonization law (24 Mar. 1825) threw Texas open to colonization. The success of Austin's venture attracted other *empresarios* who obtained charters or grants and brought in settlers to develop the rich lands. Both J. Q. Adams and Jackson negotiated unsuccessfully for the purchase of Texas.

A procession of revolutionary governments in Mexico finally resulted in restrictions on Texan colonization and a violation of what the settlers held to be their local rights. The Mexican Congress (8 Apr. 1830) enacted a law prohibiting slavery and the further settlement of Texas by U.S. citizens. The Texans remonstrated in petitions and memorials adopted (1 Oct. 1832) by a convention held at San Felipe; another convention held there (1–13 Apr. 1833) resolved to separate from Mexico. When Austin visited Mexico City to present the resolves to the new Mexican government under the Centralist party headed by **Santa Anna**, he was arrested (3 Jan. 1834) and imprisoned for 8 mos. The Centralist government took steps to maintain its authority in Texas, and relations worsened between the settlers and the Mexicans.

A group of Texan colonists led by William B. Travis seized the Mexican garrison at Anahuac (30 June 1835), and in the fall of that year other armed clashes occurred. At conventions (Oct.–Nov. 1835) Texans denied Mexican authority, supported local self-government, and asserted that Texas had the right to secede.

23 Feb.–6 Mar. The Alamo. Santa Anna replied by establishing a unitary state (15 Dec. 1835) which abolished all local rights. Then raising an army of about 6,000 men he marched against the Texans. A convention assembled at Washington, Texas (1 Mar.), adopted (2 Mar.) a declaration of independence and drew up a constitution based upon that of the U.S. A provisional government was established, and **Sam Houston** (p. 729) was named commander of the army (4 Mar.). Santa Anna began (23 Feb.) his **Siege of the Alamo** at San Antonio. The assaulting force of 3,000 Mexicans was held off by 187 Texans until 6 Mar., when the garrison commanded by William B. Travis (and including Davy Crockett) was massacred. Santa Anna also massacred (27 Mar.) more than 300 of the defenders of Goliad led by Captain James Fannin. By mid-April the Mexicans had swept through many of the American settlements and reached Galveston Bay.

21 Apr. Battle of San Jacinto, fought on the western bank of the San Jacinto River at its junction with Buffalo Bayou, near Galveston Bay. The Texans under Sam Houston went into battle with the cry, "Remember the Alamo!" defeated about 1,200 Mexicans, and captured Santa Anna. A treaty (14 May) pledging Santa Anna to secure the recognition of Texas, was repudiated by the Mexican Congress. Sam Houston was installed (22 Oct.) as president of the independent republic of Texas.

Resolutions calling for the U.S. recognition of Texas were adopted by the Senate (1 July) and the House (4 July). While Jackson was sympathetic to the Texans, he believed that the U.S. must honor its obligations to Mexico and maintain a strict neutrality. He feared that recognition might disrupt the Democratic party and involve the U.S. in a war with Mexico. He finally yielded, however, by nominating (3 Mar. 1837) Alcée La Branche (La.) as chargé d'affaires to the Texas republic. Texas petitioned for annexation to the U.S. (4 Aug. 1837), but her formal offer was refused (25 Aug. 1837).

28 June. Death of James Madison at Montpelier, his Virginia estate.

11 July. SPECIE CIRCULAR. Inflation and land speculation were fed by the expanded issue of paper money accepted as legal tender (also p. 533). The use of "land-office money" (currency based on speculators' notes) pyramided land sales from $2,623,000 in 1832 to $24,877,000 in 1836. The financial disorder was abetted by the employment of Federal deposits by the "pet" banks.

President Jackson ordered Secretary of the Treasury Levi Woodbury to issue the Specie Circular (11 July, after Congress adjourned) that had been drafted by Senator Thomas Hart Benton (whose resolution embodying the basic purpose of the circular had been rejected in the Senate on 22 Apr.). It provided that after 15 Aug. only gold, silver, and, in some cases, Virginia land scrip would be accepted by the government in payment for public lands, but permitted the receipt of paper money until 15 Dec. for parcels of land up to 320 acres purchased by actual settlers or bona fide residents of the state in which the sale was made. The circular declared that it was aimed at repressing "alleged frauds," withholding government approval or support "from the monopoly of the public lands in the hands of speculators and capitalists," and discouraging the "ruinous extension" of bank notes and credit.

The circular succeeded in reducing public-land sales in the West but taxed the inadequate resources of the "pet" banks, drained specie from the East, led to hoarding, and weakened public confidence in the state banks. The pressure on the deposit banks was increased by the scheduled payment (1 Jan. 1837) to the states of the 1st installment of the surplus revenue under the distribution provisions of the Deposit Act.

Jackson defended the circular in his annual message (5 Dec.), maintaining that it had "produced many salutary consequences" and strengthened the Western banks against the rising financial distress. He recommended that public land sales should be limited in quantity and confined to actual settlers. A Whig resolution for repeal of the circular was introduced in the Senate (12 Dec.). A House bill (reported 18 Jan. 1837) provided for government acceptance of the notes of specie-paying banks discontinuing note issues of less than $10 denominations. The bill was amended by Senator William C. Rives (Va.) to provide for rescinding of the Specie Circular. The measure passed the Senate, 41–5 (10 Feb. 1837), and the House (1 Mar. 1837), but was pocket-vetoed by Jackson. The Specie Circular was finally repealed by a joint resolution (21 May 1838).

PRESIDENTIAL CAMPAIGN. The Democratic Nominating Convention met at Baltimore (20 May 1835) and unanimously chose **Martin Van Buren** as Presidential candidate and **Richard M. Johnson** (Ky.) as the Vice-Presidential. No formal platform was adopted, but an address formulated by a committee and published in the Washington *Globe* (26 Aug. 1835) was the equivalent of the party's first platform. In his letter of acceptance Van Buren pledged himself to "tread generally in the footsteps of President Jackson."

The Whig coalition, unable to agree upon a single candidate, adopted the strategy of nominating candidates with strong local followings in the hope of throwing the election into the House. In Jan. 1835, **Daniel Webster** was nominated by a Massachusetts legislative caucus. In the same month **Hugh L. White** was chosen by anti-Jacksonian Democrats in the Tennessee legislature; the nomination was supported by Illinois and Alabama. Supreme Court Justice John McLean was nominated by an Ohio legislative caucus, but withdrew in Aug. 1836. The Anti-Masonic party met at Harrisburg, Pa. (16 Dec. 1835), and nominated **William Henry Harrison** (Ohio) for President and Francis Granger (N.Y.) for Vice-President.

7 Dec. PRESIDENTIAL ELECTION. Van Buren received 761,549 votes. The Whig candidates received 736,250 votes (Harrison, 549,567; White, 145,396; Webster, 41,287). **Van Buren** carried 15 of the 26 states, receiving 170 electoral votes, including 3 disputed Michigan votes; Harrison, 73; White, 26; Webster, 14; and South Carolina gave her 11 electoral votes to Willie P. Mangum (N.C.). Van Buren retired as Vice-President (28 Jan. 1837) and Senator William R. King of Alabama was chosen president *pro tempore* of the Senate. None of the 4 Vice-Presidential candidates received a majority of the electoral votes. The election, for the 1st and only time, was thrown into the Senate, which chose **Richard M. Johnson** by a vote of 33 to 16 (8 Feb. 1837).

1837

4 Mar. Jackson published his *Farewell Address* (drafted by Taney), a review of his 2 terms, which appealed for loyalty to the Union, condemned sectionalism, monopolies, paper currency, and speculation.

PANIC OF 1837 (also p. 537) resulted from reckless speculation. In the South the price of cotton fell by almost one half on the New Orleans market (Mar.). In New York there were demonstrations (Feb.–Mar.) by the unemployed. Protesting against high rents and the inflated prices of foodstuffs and fuel, a mob broke into the city's flour warehouses and sacked the supplies (12 Feb.). The New York banks suspended specie payments (10 May), and were followed by banks at Baltimore, Philadelphia, and Boston. The sale of public lands fell from 20 million acres (1836) to 3,500,000 (1838). The effects of the panic persisted until 1842–43, particularly in the Southern and Western states.

In a message to a special session of Congress (5 Sept.) Van Buren advocated a specie currency, criticized state-chartered banks, and alluded to a scheme to establish Treasury depositories independent of state banks. In every year between 1837 and 1841 (with the exception of 1839), the government had a deficit.

Numerous bank failures aroused dissatisfaction with the use of state banks as depositories for public funds and helped to develop sentiment for the Independent Treasury (1840). In 1841 Congress authorized the establishment of a bonded debt.

ABOLITIONIST CONTROVERSY IN CONGRESS. The steady flow of petitions to Congress requesting the abolition of slavery and the slave trade in the District of Columbia reached a crest in 1836. Up to that time such petitions were customarily referred to the standing Committee on the District of Columbia, and did not create serious dissension in either house of Congress. By 1836 the mounting apprehensions of the slave states had hardened the conviction of many Southerners that Congressional discussion of slavery was inimical both to the slave system and to the comity of the Union.

The Gag Rule. The Senate adopted a relatively satisfactory formula for disposing of the petitions. When Thomas Morris of Ohio (7 Jan. 1836) and James Buchanan (Pa.) presented (11 Jan. 1836) abolitionist petitions, Calhoun made a bitter attack upon the abolitionists and recommended the barring of future petitions. Calhoun's motion was defeated, 36–10 (9 Mar. 1836); but on the motion of Buchanan, the Senate, 34–6 (11 Mar. 1836), rejected the prayer of the petitioners. Thereafter the Senate adopted this as a regular practice. It enabled the abolitionists to exercise their constitutional right of petition, and at the same time gave the foes of the antislavery agitators an opportunity to register their firm disapproval.

The issue was more complicated in the House, where former President **John Quincy Adams** ardently defended the right of petition from the very outset of his 8 successive terms (1831–48) as representative from the Plymouth District, Mass. Adams held antislavery opinions, but was not sympathetic to the abolitionist cause. His view was that Congress had no authority to interfere with the institution in the slave-holding states, although he declared in a House speech (25 May 1836) that in the event those states ever became a theater of war, "the war powers of Congress [would] extend to interference with the institution of slavery in every way." His persistence in supporting the right of petition earned for him the sobriquet "Old Man Eloquent."

Adams' stubborn intention was one of the factors that led the House to establish (8 Feb. 1836) a special committee under Chairman Henry L. Pinckney (S.C.) to consider the question. Pinckney recommended the so-called "gag resolution" (18 May 1836), providing that "all petitions, memorials, resolutions, propositions or papers relating in any way or to any extent whatever to the subject of slavery or the abolition of slavery shall, without being printed or referred, be laid upon the table and that no further action whatever shall be had thereon."

The resolution was 1 of 3. The "gag resolution" itself was adopted (26 May 1836), 117–68. The resolution stating that Congress had no power over slavery in the states was adopted, 182–9; the one holding that interference with slavery in the District of Columbia was inexpedient was adopted, 132–45. When Adams' name was called on the roll, he withheld his vote with the response: "I hold the resolution to be a direct violation of the Constitution of the United States, of the rules of this House, and of the rights of my constituents."

When the 2nd session of the 25th Congress convened (4 Dec.), the "gag rule" was not immediately renewed (House rules required its renewal at each session). At this time Northern abolitionist feeling was inflamed by the murder (7 Nov.) of the abolitionist editor **Elijah P. Lovejoy** at Alton, Ill. Representative William Slade (Vt.) took advantage of the temporary lull in the "gag rule" and presented abolitionist petitions. The move culminated in an angry debate and led Southern representatives to consider an amendment for protecting the institution of slavery or, failing to gain that, to declare the expediency of dissolving the Union. Nothing came of this gesture. In reply to the abolitionists, a combination of Southern and Northern Democrats adopted a stricter "gag resolution," 122–74 (19 Dec.).

In the Senate, Benjamin Swift (Vt.) presented (19 Dec.) the resolutions of his state legislature opposing the annexation of Texas or the admission of any new slave state to the Union, upholding the constitutional authority of Congress to abolish slavery in the District of Columbia and to prohibit the interstate slave trade, and requesting Vermont representatives and senators to use their influence to promote these ends.

Calhoun responded by introducing into the Senate a set of 6 resolutions (27 Dec.). They reaffirmed the compact theory of the Union, the reserved-powers doctrine as it pertained to Southern action against abolitionist propaganda, and the theory that the Federal government, as the agent of the states, was bound "to resist all attempts by one portion of the Union to use it as an instrument to attack the domestic institutions of another"; declared that the institution of slavery was not to be attacked or interfered with; that the efforts to abolish slavery in the District of Columbia or the territories was a "direct and dangerous attack on the institutions of all the slave-holding States"; and denounced as detrimental to the Union interference with annexation which might expand slave territory. During the course of the discussion in the Senate (3–12 Jan. 1838) the first 3 of Calhoun's resolutions were adopted; the 4th and 5th were altered and adopted; the 6th tabled.

The House "gag rule" was renewed at each session of Congress between 1836 and 1844 over the opposition of Adams, Joshua Giddings (Ohio), and a small group of other Northern legislators. The "gag rule," by depriving the abolitionists of one of their civil rights, enabled the antislavery agitators to add this charge to their arsenal of indictments against the South. Finally, when Northern Democratic support was lessened, the "gag resolution" was rescinded (3 Dec. 1844) on the motion of Adams.

During the course of Senate debates on the slavery question, Henry Clay, with an eye to the Presidential nomination in 1840, attempted to placate Northern and Southern conservatives who tended to identify the Whig party with abolitionism. In a speech delivered on 7 Feb. 1839 he condemned the abolitionist agitators, accused them of being ready to risk a civil war, and denied Congressional authority to interfere with the institution of slavery where it was already established. It was in reference to this speech that Clay remarked to Senator William C. Preston (S.C.), when the latter suggested that the speech might injure Clay's following among Northern Whigs: "I trust the sentiments and opinions are correct; I had rather be right than be President."

1838

ANGLO-U.S. TENSIONS. In the wake of the panic of 1837, the default of American state governments and corporations on debts owed to British creditors revived Anglo-American differences, aggravated by numerous British travel accounts presenting the U.S. as a nation of boors and blusterers. A powerful voice was added by many of the 56 British authors whose memorial (1 Feb. 1836) asking for copyright protection in the U.S. had been ignored by Congress, and the literary war found the Americans replying in kind. The controversy was heightened by the addition of incidents involving disputed boundary claims and violations of neutrality.

Caroline Affair. With the failure of the insurrection led by William Lyon Mackenzie in Upper Canada in the autumn of 1837, the rebel leader and some of his followers, aided by American sympathizers, took refuge on Navy Island on the Canadian side of the Niagara River. Furnished with recruits, provisions and arms by their Anglophobe U.S. supporters, the insurrectionists proclaimed a provisional government and launched attacks against the Canadian frontier. A small American steamboat, the *Caroline,* was employed to transport supplies from the U.S. side to Navy Island. On the night of 29 Dec. 1837 a party of Canadian militia crossed the river to the American side, boarded the *Caroline,* set it afire, and then turned the vessel adrift.

In the course of overpowering the crew, the Canadians killed Amos Durfee, a U.S. citizen.

The *Caroline* affair touched off patriotic indignation and violent Anglophobe sentiment in the U.S. President Van Buren issued a neutrality proclamation (5 Jan.) warning Americans to desist from hostile acts against Great Britain. Militia called out by the President were posted along the Canadian frontier, where General Winfield Scott took immediate command of the U.S. forces. The Canadian rebels abandoned Navy Island (13 Jan.) and surrendered their arms to U.S. militia.

The British Foreign Office ignored the protests made by the State Department concerning the violation of U.S. neutrality. A number of incidents during the course of 1838 kept anti-British feeling at a high pitch. A group of Americans boarded and burned the Canadian steamer *Sir Robert Peel* on the American side of the St. Lawrence (29 May). Along the frontier Americans organized secret Hunters' Lodges for the purpose of overthrowing the British regime in Canada. The U.S. government adopted measures to prevent violation of the frontier. A few parties dispatched by the Lodges penetrated Canada (Nov.–Dec.), but were quickly repulsed or captured. President Van Buren issued a 2nd neutrality proclamation (21 Nov.) and ordered swift action against Americans violating the neutrality laws.

Anglo-U.S. tension lessened during 1839–40, but was renewed by the **McLeod case.** In Nov. 1840, Alexander McLeod, a Canadian deputy sheriff, was arrested in New York State on the charge of having murdered Amos Durfee and participated in the burning of the *Caroline.* He was jailed at Lockport, N.Y., to await trial. The British Minister to the U.S. asked (13 Dec. 1840) for McLeod's immediate release. Secretary of State John Forsyth replied (26 Dec. 1840) that the New York courts had exclusive jurisdiction over McLeod. Brought to trial at Utica, N.Y., McLeod was acquitted (12 Oct. 1841). Had he been found guilty, Gov. **William H.**

Seward (p. 777) was prepared to pardon him in order to forestall international complications.

Aroostook "War." The disputed northeastern boundary (between New Brunswick and Maine) had loomed as an Anglo-American issue since 1783, when the peace treaty incorporated a complicated and unsatisfactory provision. The Peace of Ghent did not touch on the question. Shortly after Maine became a state (1820), its legislature, together with that of Massachusetts, disregarded British claims in making land grants to settlers along the Aroostook River. The U.S. and Great Britain submitted the boundary differences to arbitration by the King of the Netherlands (29 Sept. 1827). His compromise award (10 Jan. 1831) was accepted by Great Britain, but was rejected by the Senate, 21–20 (23 June 1832).

During the winter of 1838–39 Canadian lumberjacks entered the disputed Aroostook region and began lumbering operations. Gov. Fairfield of Maine requested the legislature (Jan. 1839) to name a land agent and to provide a force for breaking up the Canadian camps. Rufus McIntire, who was appointed land agent with authority to expel the lumberjacks, was seized by the Canadians (12 Feb. 1839). His arrest, and the refusal of the Canadians to leave, marked the beginning of the so-called Aroostook war, an undeclared conflict without bloodshed. Maine and New Brunswick called out their militia. The Nova Scotia legislature made war appropriations. Congress authorized a force of 50,000 men and voted $10 million for a possible emergency.

President Van Buren dispatched Gen. Winfield Scott to the trouble zone. War might have broken out had it not been for the truce (Mar. 1839) Scott arranged between the governor of Maine and the lieutenant governor of New Brunswick. The British agreed to refer the dispute to a boundary commission, and the question was settled by the Webster-Ashburton Treaty (1842).

18 Aug. WILKES EXPEDITION (p. 800).

1839

13 Nov. LIBERTY PARTY. The entry of the antislavery forces into politics was signalized by the establishment of the Liberty party, which held its founding convention at Warsaw, N.Y., and nominated **James G. Birney,** a native of Kentucky and a former slaveholder, for President, and Thomas Earle (Pa.) for Vice-President. These nominations were confirmed at the party's 1st national convention at Albany (1 Apr. 1840). Liberty party conventions were subsequently held in Ohio and other states in the Northwest. The party was composed of moderate abolitionists who did not share Garrison's opposition to political action. Unlike Garrison, they professed loyalty to the Constitution and did not advocate secession or dissolution of the Union. By virtue of holding the balance of power, the party played an important part in the Presidential election of 1844, when it was responsible for the defeat of Clay. In 1848 it combined with the Free-Soil party and helped to defeat the Democratic candidate, Lewis Cass. The party's chief political issue was its stand against the annexation of Texas. Among its leaders were Gerrit Smith (N.Y.) and Salmon P. Chase (Ohio).

1840

4 July. INDEPENDENT TREASURY ACT. Van Buren's scheme to establish Federal depositories independent of state banks and private business, set forth in his message (5 Sept. 1837) to a special session of Congress, had the support of the Cabinet and of his Congressional managers, Sen. Silas Wright and Rep. Churchill C. Cambreleng, both of N.Y. The plan aroused the bitter opposition of the Whigs under the Congressional leadership of Henry Clay and Daniel Webster. While Calhoun and his followers still remained aloof from the Democratic party, they were in agreement with the administration on the Treasury issue, out of fear of the nationalist tendencies of the Whigs.

The independent treasury bill (also known as the subtreasury or divorce bill) was introduced in the Senate, where it passed, 26–20 (4 Oct. 1837), with incorporation of Calhoun's legal-tender amendment. This proviso called for a gradual reduction in the acceptance of notes of specie-paying banks in payment of government dues until 1841, when all payments should be made in legal tender. The amendment was later dropped, and the Senate (with Calhoun voting against the measure) passed the bill, 27–25. The bill was tabled in the House, 120–107 (14 Oct. 1837), and was rejected by that chamber, 125–11 (25 June 1838). Its defeat was caused largely by the split in the Democratic ranks: the conservative Democrats united with the Whig opposition, while the Loco-Focos supported the Van Buren plan.

A technicality that enabled the Democrats to organize the 26th Congress virtually assured its passage. Its enactment witnessed the reunion of the Calhoun wing with the Democratic party. The bill passed the Senate, 24–18 (23 Jan.), and the House, 124–107 (30 June), with Southern states' rights men joining Northern hard money Democrats to effect its passage.

The Independent Treasury Act entrusted the government with the exclusive care of its own funds and required the progressive enforcement of the legal-tender clause until all government payments and disbursements should be made in hard money after 30 June 1843. Subtreasuries were established at New York, Boston, Philadelphia, St. Louis, New Orleans, Washington, and Charleston. The act was repealed in 1841.

PRESIDENTIAL CAMPAIGN. When the Whig National Nominating Convention met at Harrisburg, Pa. (4 Dec. 1839), the Whig leaders, under the guidance of Thurlow Weed of New York, were determined to unite on a single candidate. Henry Clay was the leading contender, but his position on some issues, notably the protective tariff, impaired his availability. **William Henry Harrison** of Ohio had no substantial qualifications as a public servant, but he had no important political enemies, enjoyed a reputation as a military hero, and had received an encouraging vote in 1836. Clay had already indicated that in the interest of "union and harmony" he would if necessary defer to another candidate, and it was as the "union and harmony" convention that the Whig gathering went down in history. The convention adopted a rough equivalent of the "unit rule" by which the vote of the majority of each delegation was reported as the state's vote. Although Clay led on the 1st ballot, the convention finally nominated Harrison for President and **John Tyler** (Va.) for Vice-President. Tyler was a states' rights adherent who had turned against Jackson during the nullification episode. No platform was adopted. The Whigs, still a coalition rather than an organized political party, counted upon common opposition to the Democrats for their basic appeal.

The Democratic Convention at Baltimore (5 May) agreed on **Van Buren's** renomination, but failed to unite on a candidate for the Vice-Presidency. Because of strong opposition to the incumbent, Richard M. Johnson, the choice of a Vice-Presidential candidate was left to the state electors. The Democratic platform declared adherence to strict constructionist doctrine, opposed Congressional interference with slavery (thus formally introducing the slavery question into the platform of a major political party), opposed a national bank and internal improvements at Federal expense, and affirmed the principles of the Declaration of Independence (as no succeeding Democratic national convention during the pre-Civil War era would do).

Eschewing clear declarations on all leading issues, the Whigs waged their campaign on the basis of personalities. Ammunition for the Whig camp was unwittingly provided by a Democratic newspaper, the Baltimore *Republican,* which derisively remarked (23 Mar.) "that upon condition of his receiving a pension of $2,000 and a barrel of cider, General Harrison would no doubt consent to withdraw his pretensions, and spend his days in a log cabin on the banks of the Ohio." The Whigs turned this remark against their opponents, using the cider and log cabin symbols to present the hero of Tippecanoe as a sturdy son of the frontier and a simple man of the people.

In the rollicking **"Log Cabin and Hard Cider"** campaign that followed, the Whigs cleverly utilized many of the devices that later election contests featured as familiar means of stimulating popular enthusiasm: placards, emblems, campaign hats, effigies, floats, huge rallies, and transportable log cabins with the latchstring hanging out and furnished with coonskins and barrels of cider. The campaign slogan came into use ("Matty's policy, 50 cts. a day and soup; our policy, $2 a day and roast beef"), as well as newspaper advertisements with a political slant. ("The subscriber will pay $5 a hundred for pork if Harrison is elected, and $2.50 if Van Buren is.") The Whigs sang their way through the campaign to the words of "Tippecanoe and Tyler too," with its refrain of "Van, Van is a used up man."

In contrast to the studied simplicity of Harrison, the Whigs pictured Van Buren as an aristocrat of extravagant taste living amid the luxury of "the Palace" (as the Whigs called the White House) and supping with gold spoons. The campaign quickly degenerated into an exhibition of abuse, evasion, misrepresentation, and irrelevancies on a scale unparalleled in U.S. history up to that time.

2 Dec. PRESIDENTIAL ELECTION. Van Buren received 1,128,702 popular votes; **Harrison,** 1,275,017; and the 7,059 votes received by the Liberty party candidate, James G. Birney, were drawn from all of the free states except Indiana. Carrying 19 of the 26 states, **Harrison** won 234 electoral votes, as did **Tyler,** Van Buren, 60. The elections gave the Whigs a Congressional majority. The Whig victory was the 1st time since 1800 that a diffuse coalition defeated an organized political party holding power.

1841

4 Mar. Inauguration of William Henry Harrison, 9th President; John Tyler, Vice-President. Harrison's platitudinous inaugural address made it clear that the Executive would defer to Congressional leadership.

CABINET APPOINTMENTS. Named to office 5 Mar. were Daniel Webster, Secretary of State (a post that had been refused by Henry Clay); Thomas Ewing (Ohio), Secretary of the Treasury; John Bell (Tenn.), Secretary of War; George E. Badger (N.C.), Secretary of the Navy; and John J. Crittenden (Ky.), Attorney General. Francis Granger (N.Y.) was appointed Postmaster General (6 Mar.). All of the Cabinet members except Webster and Granger were supporters of Clay.

4 Apr. Death of President Harrison, caused by pneumonia. John Tyler became the 10th President, the 1st Vice-President to succeed to that office. A Virginia Democrat of the "old Republican" school, Tyler differed with the Whigs on constitutional principles and practical measures. In the quarrel between President and Congress that ensued, the minority of Whigs that supported Tyler was contemptuously termed "the Corporal's Guard." Tyler issued (9 Apr.) an address to the people indicating his intention of securing changes in the government fiscal structure compatible with the principles of "the fathers of the great republican school."

7 June. Clay introduced a set of resolutions embodying the essentials of Whig policy. He called for repeal of the Independent Treasury Act, the incorporation of a bank, customs duties designed to provide adequate revenue, and the distribution of the proceeds from the sale of public lands.

9 Mar. AMISTAD CASE. The Supreme Court sustained the lower courts and freed Negroes who in the course of being transported as slaves in Spanish ships mutinied and were captured by a U.S. warship (1839) off Long Island and carried to New London.

13 Aug. REPEAL OF THE INDEPENDENT TREASURY ACT. In order to clear the way for the incorporation of a national bank, the Whigs repealed the Independent Treasury Act. For 5 yrs. thereafter a Whig majority in Congress defeated efforts of Democrats to reestablish the subtreasury system. During this period the management of the public funds was left to the discre-

tion of the Secretary of the Treasury, who used the state banks as depositories. Until 1846 the deposit system of the government was not regulated by law.

16 Aug., 9 Sept. FISCAL BANK VETOES. The Whig program was launched with a bill for incorporating a fiscal agency in the District of Columbia under the name of the Fiscal Bank of the U.S. The projected institution was tantamount to a revival of the 2nd Bank of the U.S. Introduced in the Senate (12 June), the bill called for a bank capitalized at $30 million and authorized to set up state branches with deposit and discount functions, but only after obtaining the consent of the individual states in which branches were established (to satisfy Tyler's strict constructionist views). But this provision was eliminated, and a substitute measure stipulated that the consent of any state would be assumed unless its legislature registered explicit disapproval. The bill passed the Senate, 26–23 (28 July), and the House, 128–97 (6 Aug.). Tyler vetoed the bill on the grounds of constitutionality and expediency. The Senate (19 Aug.) failed to override the veto.

A 2nd bank bill was formulated to which Tyler, in an interview with Representative A. H. H. Stuart, a Virginian Whig, lent his apparent approval on condition of certain changes. The bill which was introduced provided for a fiscal corporation capitalized at $21 million. The provision for the establishment of offices only with state consent (one of the conditions Tyler had supposedly indicated as essential) was not included in the bill that passed the House, 125–94 (23 Aug.) and the Senate 27–22 (3 Sept.). The measure was vetoed by Tyler on substantially the same grounds as his veto of the 1st bill. The Senate (10 Sept.) failed to override his veto.

19 Aug. 2ND FEDERAL BANKRUPTCY LAW permitted, with few exceptions, any person to become a voluntary bankrupt, but allowed creditors to proceed against traders; repealed 1846.

11 Sept. CABINET RESIGNATIONS. Angry over what they regarded as a betrayal of faith, all the members of the Cabinet except Webster resigned (11

Sept.). All of the departing members (with the exception of Granger) made public statements charging that Tyler had committed himself to support the bank bill. The evidence on the circumstances attending Tyler's 2nd veto is conflicting, but it tends to clear Tyler of charges of duplicity.

Named to the Cabinet on 13 Sept. were Walter Forward (Pa.), Secretary of the Treasury; Abel P. Upshur (Va.), Secretary of the Navy; Hugh Swinton Legaré (S.C.), Attorney General; and Charles A. Wickliffe (Ky.), Postmaster General. Upon the death of Legaré (20 June 1843), John Nelson (Md.) was named Attorney General (1 July 1843). On 12 Oct. John C. Spencer (N.Y.) was appointed Secretary of War.

Tyler's administration witnessed frequent Cabinet shifts. Spencer was replaced in the War Department by James M. Porter (Pa., 8 Mar. 1843), who in turn was replaced (15 Feb. 1844) by William Wilkins (Pa.). Webster retired as Secretary of State (8 May 1843) and was replaced (24 July 1843) by Abel P. Upshur (Va.), who was succeeded as Secretary of the Navy by David Henshaw (Mass., 24 July 1843). Henshaw was replaced by Thomas W. Gilmer (Va., 15 Feb. 1844). Upshur and Gilmer were killed (28 Feb. 1844) by the explosion of a gun on the warship *Princeton.* John C. Calhoun was appointed Secretary of State (6 Mar. 1844) and John Y. Mason (Va.) was named Secretary of the Navy (14 Mar. 1844). Calhoun's entry into the Cabinet marked his final *rapprochement* with the Democratic party, and the rise of Southern influence in shaping Democratic policy.

1842

21–23 Mar. CREOLE CASE AND GIDDINGS RESOLUTIONS. The *Creole,* an American brig carrying a cargo of slaves, sailed from Hampton Roads, Va. (27 Oct. 1841), for New Orleans. During the voyage the slaves mutinied, killed a white crew member in taking possession of the ship, and forced the mate to proceed to Nassau in the Bahama Islands. The British authorities at Nassau freed all slaves except actual participants in the revolt, who were held on criminal charges. Secretary of State Webster protested and demanded the return of the slaves as "mutineers and murderers and the recognized property" of U.S. citizens. The British took no immediate steps to satisfy the demand, and the matter was not adjusted until 1855, with an award of $110,330 to the U.S.

Representative Joshua R. Giddings, a Whig from the Western Reserve district of Ohio, offered a series of resolutions (21–22 Mar.) based on the *Creole* case and directed against slavery and the coastal trade in slaves. The resolutions angered Southern representatives. When a censuring resolution against Giddings was adopted by a substantial House majority (23 Mar.), he resigned from Congress. A majority of more than 3,000 voters returned him to his seat in a special election (Apr.).

9 Aug. WEBSTER-ASHBURTON TREATY. Soon after taking office as Secretary of State, Webster initiated resumption of negotiations with Great Britain for settlement of the northeastern boundary question. A conciliatory atmosphere was created by the replacement (Sept. 1841) of the British government under Lord Melbourne by that headed by Sir Robert Peel. As special Minister, Alexander Baring, 1st Lord Ashburton, arrived at Washington in the spring of 1842 and began his informal discussions with Webster on 13 June. Commissioners from the states of Maine and Massachusetts, and, at one critical point, President Tyler, took part in negotiations eventuating in the Webster-Ashburton Treaty.

Under its terms, the controversial northeastern boundary provisions of the Treaty of 1783 were scrapped and the Maine-New Brunswick boundary was fixed along its present line. The U.S. received about 7,000 of the 12,000 sq. mi. of disputed territory, somewhat less than the award made by the King of the Netherlands in 1831. The compromise enabled the British to retain their military route between New Brunswick and Quebec. The claims of Maine and Massachusetts were satisfied in part by a U.S. payment of $150,000 to each state. The boundary line along the northern frontiers of Vermont and New York and thence westward to the Lake of the Woods was based on pre-1774 surveys and adjusted about a half mile north of the 45th parallel, thus leaving the U.S. in possession of its military works under construction at the northern head of Lake Champlain. Provision was made for a boundary commission to survey and mark the line.

Other articles gave the U.S. navigation rights on the St. John River (important for Maine's economy); provided for mutual extradition in cases involving 7 specified nonpolitical crimes; for a cruising convention authorizing the maintenance of joint squadrons for suppressing the slave trade along the African coast. The British without any reciprocal concession agreed to a line between Lake Superior and the Lake of the Woods (which gave the U.S. the Mesabi iron deposits). Through an exchange of notes, Lord Ashburton made an unofficial and carefully guarded apology that disposed of the *Caroline* affair and the McLeod case.

The treaty was approved by the Senate, 39–9 (20 Aug.), and promulgated in Nov. The acceptance of the treaty was accompanied in both the U.S. and Great Britain by the so-called "battle of the maps," in which each government answered domestic opposition by pointing to separate and conflicting maps indicating that the concessions were more than fair.

THE DORR REBELLION. The popular movement within the states to abolish limitations upon the suffrage resulted in serious disturbances in Rhode Island, where the charter granted (1663) by King Charles II that served as the state constitution restricted suffrage to freeholders and their eldest sons. This provision deprived more than half of the adult males of voting privileges. When petitions proved ineffective, a committee of the disfranchised called a convention at Providence (Oct. 1841) that framed the "People's Constitution" providing for white manhood suffrage. The instrument was ratified by a majority of the adult male citizens who voted on it (Dec. 1841). In a countermove, the state legislature called a convention at Newport for revising the constitution (Nov. 1841),

but the convention's decision to extend the franchise was defeated when the "Landholders' Constitution" was submitted to the vote of the freeholders (Mar.).

Both factions conducted separate elections for the legislature and state officers in the spring of 1842. The opponents of the old constitution chose **Thomas W. Dorr** as governor (18 Apr.). Dorr and his supporters, who controlled northwestern Rhode Island, established a state government basing its authority on the power residing in the people. Dorr was inaugurated at Providence. The old charter party reelected Gov. **Samuel W. King**, inaugurated at Newport. The conservative legislature of the King regime declared the Dorr party in a state of insurrection, imposed martial law, and called out the state militia to sustain its authority.

With Rhode Island under a dual government, both Dorr and King called upon President Tyler for help. Tyler replied in a letter to King which, despite its conciliatory tenor, made it clear that the national government would intervene if necessary on behalf of the old charter government to enforce Art. IV, Sect. 4 of the Federal Constitution.

When the Dorr party undertook military preparations, President Tyler issued instructions for the employment of Federal troops in support of state militia if circumstances required such action. The rebellion crumbled after the Dorrites made an unsuccessful attempt (18 May) to seize the Rhode Island state arsenal. After fleeing the state, Dorr returned and gave himself up to the authorities. He was tried and sentenced (25 June 1844) to life imprisonment, but amnestied and released in 1845. Meanwhile, a new constitution incorporating liberalized suffrage provisions was adopted (Apr. 1843). The suit arising from the contest of the two governments within the state led to the Supreme Court opinion (1848) in *Luther* v. *Borden* (7 Howard 1).

31 Mar. CLAY'S RESIGNATION. The defeat of the Whigs in the midterm Congressional elections enabled the Democrats to take control of the House. With the failure of the Whig program in Congress, Henry Clay, the chief proponent of party policy, resigned from the Senate to devote himself to consolidating the Whig party in preparation for the campaign of 1844. Clay took leave of the Senate in a speech that ranks among his most memorable. He was succeeded by John J. Crittenden.

1843

BEGINNINGS OF POLITICAL NATIVISM (also p. 584).

The **Native American Association** was formed at Washington in 1837. In the 1840's a variety of causes, including intensified anti-Catholic feeling and the influx of Irish immigrants, led to the establishment (June) of the **American Republican** party at New York. Its platform stressed opposition to voting and office-holding privileges for Catholics and foreigners. Nativist elements in New York and elsewhere frequently combined with the Whigs against the Democrats. The controversy was heightened by the public-school issue in New York state, where the Catholic demand for public funds to aid their parochial schools resulted in a movement to restrict voting privileges. Protestant resentment was also stirred by Catholic opposition to the reading of the King James version of the Bible in the public schools. In the local elections in New York City (1844), the American Republican party formed a coalition with the Whigs and succeeded in electing a nativist mayor.

The culmination of nativist agitation during the 1840's came at Philadelphia, where an American Republican Association was formed in Apr. 1844. A series of violent armed clashes between Protestants and Catholics (6–8 May, 5–8 July 1844) resulted in the death of about 20 persons and the injury of about 100. State militia were called out to suppress the disorders. The nativists called their 1st national convention at Philadelphia (5–7 July 1845) and adopted the name **Native American** party. Its platform called for changes in the naturalization laws. Nativist agitation was revived in the 1850's, which saw the rise of the **Know-Nothing (American)** party.

1844

OREGON DISPUTE.

The Anglo-American Convention of 1818, which established a 10-yr. joint occupation of the disputed Oregon country, was renewed (6 Aug. 1827) for an indefinite term with the stipulation that on a year's notice the occupation agreement might be unilaterally terminated. The Oregon country lay between the Rocky Mountains and the Pacific Ocean, and between the 42nd parallel and 54°40'. The treaties which the U.S. concluded with Spain (1819) and Russia (1824) narrowed the Oregon controversy to 2 parties: the U.S. and Great Britain. The disputed area was the region north of the Columbia River and south of the 49th parallel.

U.S. Claims were based on (1) explorations of Capt. Robert Gray, who in 1792 discovered and entered the mouth of the Columbia River, which was named for his vessel; (2) Lewis and Clark expedition (1804–06); (3) rights to the Pacific coast north of the 42nd parallel, under the treaty with Spain, and to the coast south of 54°40', under the treaty with Russia; (4) the fur-trading post of Astoria, established (1811) at the mouth of the Columbia by John Jacob Astor, head of the Pacific Fur Co., as the first permanent settlement along the lower Columbia; and (5) actual occupation by American settlers (including Methodist and Presbyterian missionaries), who after 1841 came to Oregon in growing numbers, establishing settlements in the Willamette Valley south of the Columbia River. By 1845 5,000 Americans were in the region below the Columbia River.

British Claims were based on (1) Nootka Sound Treaty (1790), under which Spain relinquished some of her claims; (2) voyage of Capt. Cook (1778); (3) explorations of Capt. George Vancouver (1792), who ascended part of the Columbia River shortly after its discovery by Gray, and of Sir Alexander Mackenzie (1793), who ascended part of the Fraser River; (4) fur-trading activities of the Hudson's Bay Co., which consolidated its power by absorbing (1821) the North West Co., an organization that earlier had amalgamated all

British and Canadian fur-trading operations; and (5) establishment (1805) by the North West Co. of Fort McLeod, the first settlement in the Oregon interior.

Beginning with the administration of John Quincy Adams, the U.S. government made repeated offers to fix the Oregon boundary along the 49th parallel. British refusal stemmed from unwillingness to sacrifice the trade of the Columbia River basin, access to a port on the Strait of Juan de Fuca, and the navigation of Puget Sound. The question did not cause serious controversy until the American population in Oregon began to increase rapidly.

A Senate bill introduced (16 Dec. 1841) by Lewis F. Linn (Mo.) provided for the militarization of the overland route from Missouri to Oregon and for land grants to male immigrants over 18 yrs. of age. The measure, which was before Congress, 1841–43, never became law, but encouraged immigration to Oregon and increased British apprehensions. Petitions for the establishment of a territorial government were submitted to Congress by the people of Oregon and by state legislatures. A meeting of Oregon settlers at Champoeg (5 July 1843) adopted a constitution for a **provisional government** to serve until the U.S. extended its jurisdiction over Oregon. In the same month a Cincinnati convention held on the Oregon issue adopted a resolution calling for 54°40′ as the American line.

Great Britain responded to U.S. offers by indicating her readiness to make a boundary adjustment along the Columbia River line. By the close of 1844 the development of serious Anglo-U.S. friction was intensified by the injection of the Oregon question into the Presidential campaign. Great Britain, rebuffed by the U.S. on an offer to reopen negotiations, took a more determined stand.

TEXAS QUESTION. Largely because of the opposition of the antislavery forces, the ambition of the Texas Republic under President Sam Houston for immediate annexation to the U.S. was not fulfilled. The abolitionists viewed the Texas settlements and revolution as a conspiracy of slaveholders. Northern Whigs opposed annexation from fear that several slave states would be carved from Texas territory. Resolutions calling for annexation adopted by Southern state legislatures were answered by opposing resolutions from Northern legislatures.

Rebuffed by the U.S., Texas formally withdrew its offer of annexation (12 Oct. 1838) and under **Mirabeau B. Lamar,** who succeeded Houston as president (Dec. 1838), proceeded to shape a foreign policy designed to assure its complete and permanent independence. Texas dispatched diplomatic agents to Europe, concluded treaties with France (1839), Holland and Belgium (1840), and Great Britain (1840), and secured loans for a program of commercial development. The British favored an independent Texas as a balance of power in North America, a buffer state against U.S. expansion, a valuable source of cotton production, and a duty-free market for British manufactured goods. In the lead of British public opinion supporting Texan independence were the abolitionists, who believed that Texas might accede to the abolition of slavery in return for a sizable loan and thus become a base of operations against the institution of slavery in the U.S. South.

Texas, however, never abandoned its willingness to become a part of the U.S. Its ends were furthered by British moves and American alarm after Houston returned to power (Dec. 1841). The Mexicans invaded Texas in 1842. In mid-1843 the British and French Ministers to Mexico arranged a truce between that country and Texas. Shortly afterward, Isaac Van Zandt, Texan Minister at Washington, was instructed to inform the U.S. authorities that the Texans were no longer interested in discussing annexation. The prospect of a close understanding between Texas and the 2 European powers caused anxiety at Washington and stirred fresh interest in annexation. Southern misgivings were increased by the circulation of reports that the British intended to use their influence to abolish slavery in Texas.

On 23 Aug. 1843, President Santa Anna notified the U.S. that the Mexican government would "consider equivalent to a declaration of war against the Mexican Republic the passage of an act of the incorporation of Texas in the territory of the United States; the certainty of the fact being sufficient for the immediate proclamation of war. . . ." On 16 Oct. 1843 Secretary of State Upshur informed Van Zandt that the U.S. was prepared to reopen negotiations for the annexation of Texas. Houston proceeded with caution, aware that if the treaty met rejection by the U.S. Senate, Texas would risk losing the support of Great Britain. He accordingly declined Upshur's proposal, thereby spurring the Secretary of State to make further efforts. On 16 Jan. Upshur informed William S. Murphy, the U.S. chargé in Texas, that "a clear constitutional majority of two-thirds" of the Senate favored the measure, and instructed Murphy to convey this information to Houston.

ANNEXATION OF TEXAS. On the basis of such assurance, Houston decided to accept the U.S. offer on condition that after the signing of the treaty but before its ratification the U.S. would take steps to furnish military and naval protection along the Gulf of Mexico and the southwestern border as a safeguard against a Mexican attack. With the death of Secretary Upshur, his successor, John C. Calhoun, successfully completed the negotiations. The treaty, signed 12 Apr., provided for the annexation of Texas "subject to the same constitutional provision" as other U.S. territories, the surrender by Texas of its public lands to the U.S., and the assumption by the U.S. of the Texan debt to a maximum of $10 million.

The treaty was submitted to the Senate (22 Apr.), accompanied by a message from President Tyler urging annexation on the ground of broad national interest. Tyler made brief reference to the security of the Southern states and to the abolitionist danger posed by British interference in Texas. These remarks, coupled with Calhoun's note (18 Apr.) to the British Minister vigorously defending the institution of slavery, strengthened the forces opposed to annexation. The abolitionists pointed to Calhoun's letter as proof of a slaveholders' conspiracy and succeeded in arousing Northerners who had been in-

different to annexation. The Senate rejected the treaty, 35–16 (8 June). Tyler then made a move to incorporate Texas in the Union by a joint resolution of both houses of Congress, but the measure failed to come to a vote by the time Congress adjourned (17 June). Meanwhile, Tyler carried out his pledge to send naval vessels to the Gulf of Mexico and troops to the Texas border. On 12 Dec. **Anson Jones** succeeded Houston as president of Texas.

Texas annexation, together with the Oregon dispute, became the leading issue in the Presidential campaign. The British continued to use their diplomatic resources to keep Texas out of the Union. But British success (May 1845) in winning Mexican recognition of Texan independence came too late, for by then the U.S. Congress had acted and the Texans had decided to enter the Union.

27 Apr. CLAY–VAN BUREN LETTERS. Tyler's alienation of the Democratic party and his firm opposition to the Whig program made him a President without a party, leaving him without vital political support for renomination. Van Buren, still the political heir of Jackson, loomed as almost certain choice for the Democratic nomination in 1844. In May 1842, Van Buren visited Clay at Ashland, Ky. It was generally surmised that the two rivals reached an agreement to bar the Texas annexation issue from the next Presidential campaign.

Van Buren's Southern opponents, aware of his hostility to annexation, obtained a letter from Jackson (12 Feb. 1843) favoring the acquisition of Texas. The letter, published in the Richmond *Enquirer* (22 Mar.), posed an immediate and crucial test for Van Buren on the eve of the Democratic National Convention. Approval of annexation would cost him his Democratic following in the key state of New York, where a party schism had begun to develop over the slavery question; rejection of the policy would lose him the Southern vote.

On 27 Apr. Van Buren and Clay published separate letters opposing the immediate annexation of Texas. Van Buren's letter (dated 20 Apr.), which appeared in the Washington *Globe,* maintained that annexation would probably involve the U.S. in an unjustifiable war with Mexico. His declaration, which incensed Southerners and alienated Jackson, was instrumental in depriving Van Buren of the Democratic nomination. When Jackson learned of the letter, he indicated that the candidate "should be an annexation man" and should be "from the Southwest," and finally threw his support to James K. Polk.

Clay's "Raleigh letter" (dated 17 April) was published in the *National Intelligencer*. It declared that the annexation of Texas without the consent of Mexico would lead to war with that nation, and was "dangerous to the integrity of the Union . . . and not called for by any general expression of public opinion." After winning the Whig nomination for the Presidency, Clay publicly qualified his position in the "Alabama letters" addressed to Stephen F. Miller of Tuscaloosa, Ala. In the 1st letter (1 July), Clay stated that while he was not opposed to annexation, he believed that the unyielding attitude of the abolitionists made the integrity of the Union the paramount consideration. His 2nd letter (27 July) asserted that "far from having any personal objection to the annexation of Texas, I should be glad to see it, without dishonor, without war, with the common consent of the Union, and upon just and fair terms. I do not think that the subject of slavery ought to affect the question, one way or the other." His explanation further embittered Northern antislavery sentiment and, derisively quoted out of context, was used by the Democrats to picture Clay as an opportunist.

PRESIDENTIAL CAMPAIGN. The national convention of the Liberty party met at Buffalo, N.Y. (30 Aug. 1843), and unanimously nominated **James G. Birney** for President and **Thomas Morris** (Ohio) for Vice-President. Its platform, consisting of 21 planks based almost entirely on the slavery question, made no direct reference to the annexation of Texas, but denounced the extension of slave territory.

The Whig National Convention met at Baltimore (1 May) and unanimously nominated **Henry Clay** for President; **Theodore Frelinghuysen** (N.J.) was chosen for Vice-President. The Whig platform, a general statement of party principles, advocated a single term for the Presidency, made no reference to the Texas issue, and was silent on the question of a national bank.

The Democratic National Convention, which assembled at Baltimore (27 May), was the 1st convention whose proceedings were reported by telegraph (over a line connecting Baltimore and Washington). Van Buren led on the first ballot, but Southern insistence on the application of the "two-thirds rule" disposed of his bid. On the 9th ballot (29 May), and on the 2nd ballot after his name had been placed before the convention, **James K. Polk** (Tenn.) was unanimously chosen as the Presidential candidate. Silas Wright (N.Y.), a Van Burenite and antislavery man, was chosen for Vice-President. He declined the nomination, and the convention chose instead **George M. Dallas** (Pa.). Polk, 1st "dark horse" nominee in the history of the Presidency, had the support of Andrew Jackson. The suggestion for his nomination came from the historian George Bancroft, a member of the Massachusetts delegation, in consultation with Gideon J. Pillow (Tenn.).

Robert J. Walker (Miss.), chairman of the executive committee of the Democratic party, formulated an expansionist platform designed to appeal to Northerners and Southerners alike. Its main plank declared that "our title to the whole of the Territory of Oregon is clear and unquestionable; that no portion of the same ought to be ceded to England or any other power; and that the reoccupation of Oregon and the reannexation of Texas at the earliest practicable period are great American measures, which this Convention recommends to the cordial support of the Democracy of the Union." The Democratic slogan of "54° 40' or Fight" (variously attributed to Senator William Allen [Ohio] and Samuel Medary, editor of the *Ohio Statesman*) was used to court Northern voters on the Oregon issue and to offset the Whigs' scornful query, "Who is James K. Polk?"

The Tyler Democrats also assembled at Baltimore on 27 May, to the rallying cry of "Tyler and Texas." Although the delegates represented every state in the Union, they had an estimated total following of only 150,000. **Tyler,** who had unsuccessfully attempted to establish a 3rd party by the use of patronage, accepted (30 May) the nomination. When it became clear that he could not hope to win over the annexationist element, he withdrew (20 Aug.) after reaching an understanding with Robert J. Walker, and brought his supporters into the Democratic fold. Tyler thus became the 1st President who failed to stand for a 2nd term.

4 Dec. PRESIDENTIAL ELECTION resulted in a close popular vote: **Polk,** 1,337,243; Clay, 1,299,068; Birney, 62,300. Polk's victory hinged upon the electoral vote (36) of New York, which Clay lost by 5,080 votes, and where Birney, by an accession of antislavery Whig strength in the western counties, received 15,812 votes. **Polk** received 170 electoral votes, carrying 15 of the 26 states; Clay 105 votes. Had Clay carried New York, he would have been elected President by 7 electoral votes.

1845

23 Jan. By act of Congress, the Tuesday following the 1st Monday in Nov. was designated the uniform election day for future Presidential elections.

1 Mar. ANNEXATION OF TEXAS. When the 2nd session of the 28th Congress convened (2 Dec. 1844), Tyler recommended that the Texas treaty be accepted by **joint resolution** of Congress. He made his plea on the grounds that (1) the Presidential election had demonstrated that "a controlling majority of the States have declared in favor of immediate annexation," and (2) that strained relations between Texas and Mexico weakened both powers, to the advantage of interested foreign nations (i.e., Great Britain).

A joint resolution (demanding a simple majority in both houses and the signature of the President) obviated the necessity of the two-thirds Senate vote required for ratification. The annexation resolution was passed by the House (25 Jan.), 120–98 (112 Democrats and 8

Southern Whigs in favor, 70 Whigs and 28 Northern Democrats opposed). In the Senate, Thomas Hart Benton posed the constitutional objection that Congress was not authorized to admit a state carved from foreign territory. An amendment offered by Robert J. Walker (Miss.) empowered the President to negotiate a new treaty which might either be ratified by the Senate or adopted by a joint resolution. In this form the measure, which made no reference to securing the consent of Mexico, was passed by the Senate by 27–25 (27 Feb.) and the House (28 Feb.), 132–76, indicating a restoration of party lines. It was the 1st time that a joint resolution had been employed to approve a treaty or to acquire territory. The resolution provided that Texas was to be admitted to statehood without a preliminary period of territorial status; that, with the consent of Texas, not more than 4 additional states might be formed from its territory; that Texas was to retain her public lands, but pay her own debt; and that the Missouri Compromise line of 36°30′ was to be extended to Texas territory.

Great Britain and France succeeded (Mar.–May) in inducing Texas and Mexico to sign the preliminaries of a treaty whereby Mexico would recognize the independence of Texas if the latter should promise to relinquish annexation. These negotiations were quickly abandoned by Texas after the Lone Star Republic received news of the Congressional action. A special session of the Texan Congress voted for annexation (23 June); a convention (4 July) called by President Jones accepted the terms; and the act of the convention was ratified by the people of Texas (13 Oct.). Texas was admitted to the Union (29 Dec.). A state government was formally installed at Austin on 19 Feb. 1846.

3 Mar. President Tyler vetoed (20 Feb.) a bill that prohibited payment for some naval craft that he had ordered built. The Senate and the House passed the measure over his veto on the last day of his administration, the 1st time a Presidential veto was overridden.

4 Mar. In his inaugural address, Polk reaffirmed the Democratic platform's declaration that the U.S. title to Oregon was "clear and unquestionable" and asserted that the question of Texas annexation belonged "exclusively to the United States and Texas" as the prerogative of two independent powers.

10 Oct. Formal opening of the "Naval School" at Ft. Severn, Annapolis, Md. Founded by Secretary of the Navy Bancroft, it became known (1850) as the U.S. Naval Academy.

"BARNBURNERS" AND "HUNKERS" were 2 factions (*c.*1843 *et seq.*) in the Democratic party in New York State whose electoral vote played a pivotal role in the Presidential election of 1844. In alliance with the Loco-Focos of the cities, the "Barnburners" were the radical and reform wing of the party. Leaders: Martin Van Buren and his son, John; Silas Wright; Benjamin F. Butler; and Azariah C. Flagg. Because of their uncompromising determination, the "Barnburners" were thus characterized by their opponents after the Dutch farmer who burned his barn in order to destroy the rats. The conservative "Hunkers" were so called by their antagonists after a corruption of the Dutch word *hunkerer*, meaning a self-seeking person, with particular application to politicians who "hunkered," i.e., "hungered" or "hankered" after office. Leaders: William L. Marcy and Daniel S. Dickinson.

Their initial differences stemmed from local issues, such as internal improvements and the chartering of state banks (both favored by the Hunkers) and the distribution of patronage. After the election of Polk, these disagreements were colored by national issues. The Barnburners opposed the annexation of Texas and the extension of slavery into the territories.

An open political contest between the 2 wings occurred in 1845, when they ran separate candidates for the state legislature in many districts. In Sept. 1847, the Barnburners withdrew from the Democratic state convention at Syracuse after the Hunkers defeated their resolution declaring "uncompromising hostility to the extension of slavery into territory now free." In 1848 the Barnburners seceded from the Democratic national convention and joined the Free-Soilers, whose vote held the balance of power in the Presidential election of 1848. The Barnburners later rejoined the Democratic fold, but their antislavery views led them into the Republican party in the mid-1850's.

ANTIRENT WAR, 1839–46, a culmination of agrarian unrest in upstate New York against the perpetual leases dating from the period of Dutch and English rule. The earliest serious disturbances connected with the Antirent War broke out (1839–40) in the manor of Rensselaerswyck in the Albany region when the heirs of Stephen Van Rensselaer precipitated tenant resistance by attempting to collect $400,000 in back rents. The ensuing "**Helderberg War,**" directed against the system of patroonships, was suppressed by militia called out by Gov. William H. Seward. Other revolts occurred in the area south of Albany, where farmers organized secret societies and, disguised as Indians, interfered with or attacked law-enforcement officers (a situation portrayed by James Fenimore Cooper in his novels *Satanstoe* [1845], *The Chainbearer* [1846], and *The Redskins* [1846]). The murder of a deputy sheriff (Aug.) caused Delaware County to be placed under martial law. Impact on state politics: Gov. Silas Wright called for legislation (1846) restricting the duration of farm leases and abolishing distress for rent in all new leases. The disturbances led to the adoption of the more liberal constitution of 1846. Perpetual leases were gradually replaced by fee-simple tenure.

2 Dec. "**POLK DOCTRINE.**" In his 1st annual message to Congress, Polk recommended tariff revision, the restoration of the Independent Treasury, urged Congress to take measures to protect the U.S. claim to the whole of the Oregon country, and proposed abrogation of the convention for joint occupation. Especially significant was his elaboration of the Monroe Doctrine: (1) "The people of *this continent* alone have the right to decide their own destiny." (2) "We can never consent that European powers shall interfere to prevent such a union [of an independent state with the U.S.] because it might disturb the 'balance of power' which they may desire to maintain upon this continent." (3) "No future European colony or dominion shall with our consent be planted or established on any part of the North American continent."

"MANIFEST DESTINY." The earliest known appearance of the phrase occurred in an unsigned editorial article published in the expansionist organ, *The United States Magazine and Democratic Review* (July–Aug.). The article, subsequently attributed to the magazine's founder and editor, **John L. O'Sullivan,** declared that foreign governments were attempting to obstruct the annexation of Texas in order to check "the fulfilment of our manifest destiny to overspread the continent allotted by Providence for the free development of our yearly multiplying millions." The phrase came into vogue after use in an editorial in the N.Y. *Morning News* (27 Dec.) on the Oregon dispute. Its 1st use in Congress supposedly dates from the speech (3 Jan. 1846) made by Representative Robert C. Winthrop (Mass.). During the debate on the resolution for terminating the joint occupation of Oregon, Winthrop referred to "the right of our manifest destiny to spread over this whole continent."

BREAK WITH MEXICO. On 28 Mar., soon after the passage of the joint resolution for the annexation of Texas, Mexico broke off diplomatic relations with the U.S. and took steps (June) to increase its armed forces in order to resist annexation. Major grievances: (1) **Boundary disagreements** stemmed from Mexican insistence on the Nueces River as the southwestern line of Texas. Under the treaty of 12 May 1836, which had been rejected by the Mexican government, the Texans laid claim to the Rio Grande as their lower frontier. The view of the U.S. government, as shaped by Secretary of State Buchanan, was that the annexation of Texas had revived legitimate territorial claims west of the Sabine River held by the U.S. before the signing of the Adams-Onís Treaty (1819). (2) **Halting by Mexico of payments** (1843) of more than $2 million in **adjusted damages to U.S. nationals** authorized by the claims conventions of 1839 and 1843 and the commission award of 1840. (3) **Status of California,** where the Mexican government had is-

sued orders for expulsion of U.S. settlers and exclusion of further immigrants. The U.S. government believed that the British were actively engaged in intrigues to take California.

Gen. **Zachary Taylor,** in command of the U.S. forces in the southwest, with headquarters at Fort Jesup, La., was ordered (28 May) to maintain his troops (known as the "Army of Observation") in a state of readiness for an advance into Texas to be made upon his receipt of official information that it had been invaded after consenting to annexation. On 15 June he was ordered to occupy a point "on or near the Rio Grande" for the defense of the territory of Texas. Taylor advanced into Texas (26 July); established his base (31 July) on the south bank of the Nueces, near Corpus Christi, about 150 mi. from the Rio Grande; and suggested (4 Oct.) that if the U.S. contemplated fixing the boundary line along the Rio Grande, an advantage would be secured by advancing to Point Isabel, on the Gulf of Mexico near the mouth of the Rio Grande. By mid-Oct. Taylor had under his command about 3,500 troops, approximately one half the U.S. Army.

Taylor was ordered (13 Jan. 1846) to advance from the Nueces to "positions on or near the left bank" of the Rio Grande, but did not receive his instructions until 3 Feb. and did not begin his advance until 8 Mar. Point Isabel was burned by the Mexicans before Taylor arrived there (24 Mar.). His 2nd in command, Gen. William J. Worth, proceeded to the left (or north) bank of the Rio Grande, opposite Matamoros, where the Mexicans had about 5,700 men. Both sides spent the following month building fortifications. On 12 Apr. 1846, Gen. Pedro de Ampudia, in command of the forces at Matamoros, warned Taylor to retire beyond the Nueces; otherwise, "arms and arms alone must decide the question." Taylor refused to comply, and requested U.S. naval forces to blockade the mouth of the Rio Grande.

SLIDELL MISSION. In Aug. the U.S. received confidential information that the Mexican government was apparently willing to resume diplomatic relations.

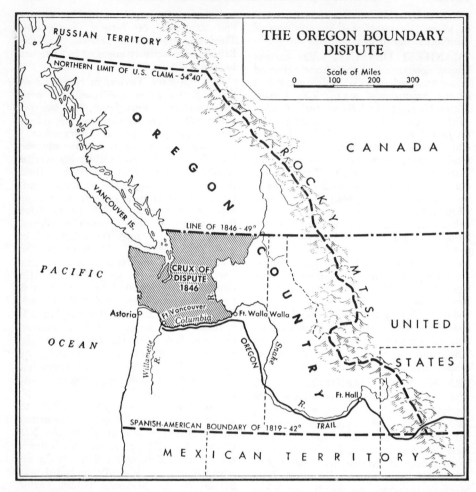

At the recommendation of Secretary of State Buchanan, President Polk appointed **John Slidell** (La., 1793–1871) to undertake a secret mission to Mexico for the purpose of purchasing Upper California and New Mexico, and adjusting the boundary line to run along the Rio Grande from its mouth to the 32nd parallel and thence westward to the Pacific. Polk, with the unanimous support of his Cabinet, was prepared to pay from $15 to 40 million.

John Black, U.S. consul at the City of Mexico, reported (17 Oct.) that Manuel de Peña y Peña, foreign minister of the Mexican government under President José J. Herrera, had agreed (15 Oct.) to receive a "commissioner" authorized to discuss the Texas boundary issue, on condition that the U.S. squadron off Vera Cruz should be removed. The recall of the naval force was ordered by Commodore David Conner immediately after he learned that the Mexicans had consented to negotiation.

President Polk and Secretary Buchanan agreed (7 Nov.) to dispatch Slidell at once. Despite the Mexican government's insistence on confining the discussions to the disputed Texas boundary, Slidell received amended instructions (10 Nov.) authorizing the purchase of New Mexico for $5 million and of California for $25 million, in return for Mexican approval of the Rio Grande as the Texas boundary. In addition, the U.S. would assume the claims of its nationals against Mexico. Slidell was accredited as envoy extraordinary and minister plenipotentiary. Meanwhile, Thomas O. Larkin, U.S. consul at Monterey, Calif., was appointed confidential agent (17 Oct.) with instructions to block the attempt by any foreign power to secure California. He was also informed that the U.S. policy envisaged the peaceful acquisition of California with the active support of the settlers, but in a manner that would not give the Mexicans cause for grievance.

When Slidell reached Mexico City (6 Dec.), the nature of his mission had already become known. After some delay caused by Herrera and his Cabinet, who refused to accept responsibility in the face of a hostile public opinion, Slidell was informed (16 Dec.) that the Mexican government could not receive him for the following reasons: his mission apparently lacked the consent of Congress; his appointment had not been confirmed by the Senate; and the Mexicans had agreed to receive a commissioner authorized to negotiate the Texas question rather than a minister plenipotentiary empowered to discuss extraneous issues. When Slidell's report reached Washington (12 Jan. 1846), Gen. Taylor was ordered (13 Jan. 1846) to proceed to the Rio Grande.

Slidell's appointment was confirmed by the Senate (20 Jan. 1846). The Mexican government, however, persisted in its refusal to discuss any question other than the Texas boundary. Meanwhile, the Herrera government was overthrown (31 Dec.) by Gen. Mariano Paredes, who assumed the Presidency (4 Jan. 1846) with a reaffirmation of Mexico's claim to Texas up to the Sabine River and a declaration of his purpose to defend all territory regarded by him as Mexican. Slidell informed Washington (6 Feb. 1846) that the inflexible attitude of the Mexicans was reinforced by their belief that the U.S. would become involved in war with Great Britain over the Oregon dispute. Upon Slidell's final inquiry (1 Mar. 1846), the Paredes government refused to receive him (12 Mar.), and late in Mar. he requested his passports and left Mexico.

1846

15 June. OREGON SETTLEMENT. In his 1st annual message to Congress (2 Dec. 1845) Polk claimed the whole of Oregon; recommended ending the Anglo-U.S. convention for joint occupation; called for extension of U.S. jurisdiction over the Oregon settlers, military protection of the Oregon Trail, and the establishment of an Indian agency beyond the Rocky Mountains. His unyielding attitude toward Great Britain was greeted by expansionist cries of "54°40' or fight!" Strong support of his position came from the states of the Old Northwest, whose prominent Democratic voices in Congress included Sen. **Lewis Cass** (Mich., 1782–1866) and Rep. **Stephen A. Douglas** (Ill., p. 696).

The resolution for terminating joint occupation was introduced in the House (5 Jan.) and, after lengthy debate (including a Senate filibuster), was passed (23 Apr.) in the Senate, 42–10, and in the House, 142–46. The resolution, signed by Polk on 27 Apr., authorized the President to give the required year's notice at his discretion. Polk served notice on 21 May.

Meanwhile, Richard Pakenham, British Minister to the U.S., requested (27 Dec. 1845) renewal of the U.S. offer of the 49th parallel as the boundary of Oregon and asked that the question be submitted to arbitration. Polk refused to renew the proposal. Secretary Buchanan (26 Feb.) then informed Louis McLane, U.S. Minister at London, that discussions would be reopened if the British took the initiative. There was strong resistance in Great Britain to concession on this score, but a truce in British party politics enabled the new Ministry under Lord Russell to adopt a conciliatory approach toward the U.S. Not less important in influencing the British attitude toward the U.S. was consideration of the economic ties between the two nations (British Corn Laws repealed 26 June). Lord Aberdeen, British Foreign Secretary, submitted his proposal in the form of a draft treaty that reached Washington 6 June. Almost at the same time, Aberdeen informed the British Minister to Mexico that Great Britain was unwilling to interfere between the U.S. and Mexico.

Because of the uncompromising stand he had taken on the Oregon question, Polk deemed it proper (at the suggestion of the Cabinet) to take the unprecedented course of laying the British proposal before the Senate (10 June) for its advice on the matter. The Senate, 37–12 (12 June), advised its acceptance, and ratified it, 41–14 (15 June). Opposition came from expansionist elements in the Old Northwest, who accused Polk of deception and betrayal.

The treaty provided (1) that the boundary between U.S. and British territory in Oregon should be an extension of the existing continental line along the 49th parallel to the middle of the channel between Vancouver Island and the mainland, and thence along a line running southward through Juan de Fuca Strait to the Pacific; (2) for free navigation of the channel and strait by both parties; and (3) by the British of the Columbia River below the 49th parallel. The water boundary, however, was not finally defined until the arbitration award of 1873.

6 Aug. INDEPENDENT TREASURY ACT. With the defeat of the Whigs in the election of 1844, the Congress organized by the Democrats proceeded to revive the Independent Treasury Act that had been repealed by the Whigs in 1841. The bill was in substance the act of 4 July 1840. Except for changes in the banking structure made during the Civil War, the act served without important change as the basis of the U.S. fiscal system until passage of the Federal Reserve Act (1913). The subtreasuries were not abolished until after the act of 1920.

24 Apr.–3 May. OPENING SKIRMISH. Gen. Mariano Arista succeeded Ampudia (24 Apr.) as commander of the Mexican forces at Matamoros, where the Mexicans had established Ft. Paredes. On the opposite bank of the river, Taylor's troops had erected Ft. Texas. Arista had orders (4 Apr.) from the Mexican minister of war authorizing him to attack. Arista notified Taylor (24 Apr.) that he considered hostilities as already begun. Pointing out that he had not committed any actions that could be construed as hostile, Taylor replied that "the responsibility must rest with them who actually commence them."

Arista dispatched a force of 1,600 cavalry under Gen. Torrejon to cross the Rio Grande above Matamoros (24 Apr.). A reconnoitering party of 63 dragoons under Captain Seth Thornton sent out by Taylor on the evening of the same day was surrounded and attacked (25 Apr.). Eleven Americans were killed, 5 wounded, the remainder captured. Upon receiving news of the Mexican attack, Taylor reported to Washington (26 Apr.) that "hostilities may now be considered as commenced." He immediately called upon the governors of Texas and Louisiana for a total of 5,000 volunteers. Taylor marched (1 May) to the relief of his supply base at Point Isabel. The Mexicans crossed the Rio Grande in force (30 Apr.–1 May) and on 3 May laid Ft. Texas (Maj. Jacob Brown commander) under siege.

THE WAR WITH MEXICO, 1846–48

11 May. POLK'S WAR MESSAGE. Slidell, reporting to Polk, 8 May, urged prompt action by the U.S. Taylor's report of the skirmish near Matamoros reached Washington Saturday, 9 May. The Cabinet, in an evening session, unanimously supported the adoption of war measures. President Polk prepared his war message on Sunday and delivered it at noon on Monday, 11 May. Asserting that the U.S. held legitimate title to the disputed territory beyond the Nueces, Polk declared: "Mexico has . . . shed American blood upon the American soil."

13 May. DECLARATION OF WAR ON MEXICO. By 174–14 (11 May) the House of Representatives (29th Congress, 1st sess.) declared that "by the act of the Republic of Mexico, a state of war exists between that government and the United States." All of the opposing votes were cast by Northern representatives. An amendment stating that nothing in the measure should be construed as approval of Polk's course in ordering the military occupation of the disputed territory between the Nueces and the Rio Grande was defeated, 97–27. The House authorized a call for accepting 50,000 volunteers and voted a $10 million appropriation. Voting against this measure were 67 Whigs, foreshadowing the opposition to the administration that would increase as the war progressed. During the discussion of the war measures, an outspoken Whig, Garrett Davis (Ky.), asserted: "It is our own President who began this war."

In the Senate, Calhoun took exception to the preamble of the war declaration. He maintained that while armed clashes had occurred, Congress had not yet recognized a state of war, and so war did not exist "according to the sense of our Constitution." The war declaration, including the preamble, passed the Senate (12 May), 40–2 (both Whigs), with 3 abstentions, including Calhoun.

8–9 May. 1ST BATTLES. Battle of Palo Alto. After hastening construction of the defense works at Point Isabel, Taylor, at the head of about 2,300 troops and 200 supply wagons, began (7 May) his return march to Ft. Texas to relieve the besieged force. Midway on the road to Matamoros, near the water hole of Palo Alto, he encountered (8 May) an enemy force of 6,000 placed across the route of march. The engagement began at 2 P.M. and lasted about 5 hrs. U.S. infantry broke up a Mexican cavalry attack across the prairie, and the Mexicans were finally repulsed by the superior fire of the U.S. guns, which easily won an artillery duel against the antiquated Mexican pieces. The U.S. losses: 9 killed, 45 wounded; Mexican: estimated c.300–400. The Mexicans retreated southward, to a natural strong point above Matamoros, in a sunken river bed or ravine called the Resaca de Guerrero, where a dense growth of chap-

arral afforded an excellent defensive position.

Battle of Resaca de la Palma. Instead of waiting for reinforcements, Taylor decided to pursue Arista's numerically superior force. At about 2 P.M. on 9 May, U.S. troops advanced to the edge of the Mexican position and occupied a ravine called the Resaca de la Palma.

About 1,700 Americans faced some 5,700 Mexicans in this engagement. Late in the afternoon, the Mexican army collapsed, fleeing across the Rio Grande with the Americans in close pursuit. U.S. losses: 39 killed, 83 wounded; estimated Mexican: 262 killed, 355 wounded, and c.150 captured or missing (in addition to many others lost by drowning during the crossing of the river). News of the battle made "Old Rough and Ready" Taylor a popular hero.

On the evening of 9 May, the siege of Ft. Texas was raised. The position was renamed Ft. Brown in honor of the officer who had commanded its defense. The Mexicans under Arista evacuated Matamoros (17–18 May), Taylor crossed the Rio Grande (18 May) and occupied the town.

MILITARY BALANCE SHEET. Mexican. At the outset of the war, the Mexican army had an initial numerical superiority. Its forces consisted of about 32,000 men, but the troops were defective in training, discipline, and equipment (most of its artillery pieces were obsolete and unreliable). It is estimated that during the war the peak strength of the Mexican army never exceeded 36,000 men. The officers were of a generally low quality (except for the engineers, who showed great skill in building entrenchments and fortifications), with a superabundance of high-ranking officers. The Mexicans had the advantage of fighting on familiar ground where the great distances involved afforded them a high degree of mobility.

U.S. At the outset of the war, the authorized U.S. regular army strength was 8,613, but the actual strength was 7,365 (8 regiments of infantry, 4 of artillery, 2 of dragoons). To fill the ranks, the government relied chiefly on short-term enlistments by volunteers (highly undependable). Six- and 12-mos.

volunteers were the rule, and not until 12 Jan. 1847 did Congress enact legislation authorizing 5-yr. enlistments. Total U.S. force employed during the war, including about 31,000 regulars and marines: *c.*104,000. Chief U.S. disadvantages: (1) inadequate transportation and communication (telegraph not yet applied to military purposes); (2) poor provisions for health and sanitation (percentage of deaths caused by disease was more than 10% of total enrollment); (3) friction among the generals, and between them and the administration. Both Taylor and Gen. Winfield Scott were Whigs, and did not have the full confidence of a Democratic President and his Cabinet. Scott was commanding general of the army, but because of strained relations with Polk and Marcy, was not permitted to depart for Mexico until late in 1846.

The Mexican campaigns gave U.S. officers who had never handled units larger than companies or battalions an opportunity to work with regiments and brigades. The war was valuable for its schooling of junior officers who later saw service as army or corps commanders with either side during the Civil War. Among those who later held commands in the Union armies were Lt. Ulysses S. Grant, Lt. William T. Sherman, Lt. George G. Meade, Lt. Joseph Hooker, Lt. George B. McClellan, Lt. John Pope, Lt. George H. Thomas, Lt. William B. Franklin, and Capt. Samuel P. Heintzelman. Those who afterward served with the Confederate forces included Capt. Robert E. Lee, Lt. Thomas Jonathan Jackson, Lt. Pierre G. Beauregard, Col. Albert Sidney Johnston, Lt. Col. Joseph E. Johnston, Lt. James Longstreet, Lt. Braxton Bragg, Lt. Richard S. Ewell, Lt. Daniel H. Hill, and Captain William J. Hardee.

CAMPAIGN PLANS. Despite months of tension preceding the outbreak of hostilities, no military plans had been drawn up by the War Department. Within 2 days after declaration of war, Col. (later Gen.) **Stephen Watts Kearny** (1794–1848), commanding a cavalry regiment at Ft. Leavenworth, was ordered to lead the "Army of the West" (consisting of his regular force and a body of Mis-

souri volunteers) on an expedition to New Mexico and to occupy its capital, Santa Fe. Commodore **David Conner** was ordered to blockade the enemy ports on the Gulf of Mexico, while Commodore **John D. Sloat** was ordered to blockade the Mexican ports on the Pacific and to seize and hold San Francisco Bay. Additional instructions (3 June) authorized Kearny to take possession of California in conjunction with anticipated naval support from Sloat.

President Polk, in conference (14 May) with Secretary of War Marcy and General Scott, formulated a plan of campaign, with the 1st major blow to be struck against the sparsely populated northern provinces of Mexico. At the urging of Scott, and after delays caused by friction between him and the administration, agreement was reached (20 Oct.–18 Nov.) on a joint army-navy expedition against Vera Cruz as the chief military objective. General Scott was placed in command of the operation, which called for a landing at Vera Cruz, a march through the Mexican interior, and the seizure of the City of Mexico.

7 July–6 Dec. MISSION TO SANTA ANNA. Col. A. J. Atocha, a U.S. citizen of Spanish birth and a friend of Santa Anna (in exile in Cuba) advised Polk (Feb.) that in return for $30 million Santa Anna would arrange that the U.S. would get the Rio Grande as the southwestern boundary of Texas and that the boundary line of California would run through San Francisco Bay. Santa Anna advised Commander Alexander Slidell Mackenzie (7 July) that he would cooperate with the U.S., even give military advice. Accordingly, he was permitted to pass through the blockade, arrived at Vera Cruz (16 Aug.), and then proceeded to denounce the treachery of former President Herrera in attempting to negotiate with the U.S. He replied (19 Sept.) unsatisfactorily to Secretary Buchanan's peace feeler (19 Sept.). On 6 Aug. Paredes was deposed, Gen. Mariano Salas became acting President, and Santa Anna led (28 Sept.) an expeditionary force northward from Mexico City to oppose Taylor. His election as President by the Mexican Congress (6 Dec.) ended hopes of early peace.

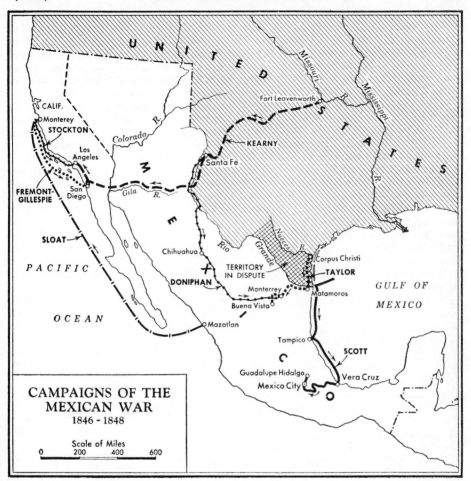

CAMPAIGNS OF THE
MEXICAN WAR
1846 - 1848

Scale of Miles
0   200   400   600

CONQUEST OF CALIFORNIA. Earlier History. Not until after 1840 did the American settlement of the Mexican province of California become numerically significant. The first important increase came with the colonization (1843) of the San Joaquin Valley. By the outset of 1846 there were approximately 500 American traders and settlers along the 500 miles of coast from Sonoma to San Diego, c.8,000–12,000 Mexicans of Spanish descent, and c.24,000 Indians. The weak government of the province was made even more vulnerable by the conflict of authority between Pío Pico, provincial governor at Los Angeles, and Gen. José Castro, military commandant at Monterey. Acting on the mistaken belief

that the U.S. and Mexico were at war, and that a British fleet was threatening to take possession of California, Commodore **Thomas ap Catesby Jones** proceeded from the Peruvian coast and landed a U.S. naval force at Monterey, where he seized the public buildings and raised the U.S. flag (20 Oct. 1842). Informed by Thomas O. Larkin, U.S. consul at Monterey, that relations between Mexico and the U.S. were still normal, Jones hauled down the flag (21 Oct. 1842). His act was disavowed by President Tyler, and reparation and apologies were made to the Mexican government. On 17 Oct. 1845 Polk appointed Larkin confidential agent to induce the California settlers to enter the Union or establish an independent state under U.S. protection. He learned of the appointment 17 Apr. 1846.

10 June–5 July. Bear Flag Revolt. Leading his 3rd surveying expedition to the West (May 1845 *et seq.*), Capt. **John Charles Frémont** (p. 710) reached Monterey (27 Jan.). With the apparent permission of Castro, he established his camp in the Salinas Valley. When Castro warned him (3 Mar.) to quit the area, his expedition erected breastworks atop Gavilan Mountain and hoisted the U.S. flag. In the face of a superior force, Frémont decided to withdraw (9 Mar.) and marched to the north. He had reached the edge of Klamath Lake, on the Oregon frontier, when he was overtaken (9 May) by Marine Lt. Archibald H. Gillespie, who conveyed to him dispatches and correspondence. Whether Frémont received from Gillespie secret verbal instructions to precipitate a revolt of the American settlers against Mexican authority has not been established, but he returned south and helped provoke resistance, at a time when the Pico-Castro feud was brought to a head by news of the revolution in Mexico (Dec. 1845) that deposed Herrera and installed Paredes as head of the government. Castro announced (April) his support of Paredes; Pico called a general convention (scheduled for 15 June at Santa Barbara) to establish California as an independent state under the protection of a foreign nation. Castro retaliated by dispatching an armed expedition to Los Angeles, seat of the Pico regime.

A party of U.S. settlers in the Sacramento Valley attacked a section of Castro's expedition (10 June). Another group, led by William B. Ide, seized Sonoma (14 June) and issued a proclamation declaring the independence of the American settlements. This so-called "Bear Flag Revolt" takes its name from the standard of the "Republic of California" raised at Sonoma. Designed by William Todd, this flag bore the name of the republic, a grizzly bear, and a star, on a field of white cloth. On 25 June, Frémont arrived at Sonoma, where he identified himself with the insurrection. A meeting of the settlers (5 July) chose

him to direct the affairs of the "Republic of California."

7 July–17 Aug. Naval Expedition to California. The commander of the U.S. naval force along the Pacific Coast, Commodore **John D. Sloat** (1781–1867), learned (17 May) of the opening skirmish of the war along the Rio Grande, but took no action because of his written instructions (24 June 1845) to avoid aggressive action and the lack of official confirmation. When informed (7 June) that Commodore Conner had blockaded Vera Cruz, Sloat sailed for California from the Mexican port of Mazatlán (8 June). He reached Monterey (2 July), sent a force ashore (7 July), raised the U.S. flag, and proclaimed California to be a part of the U.S. On 9 July, under Sloat's orders, Commander John B. Montgomery seized San Francisco and Lt. James W. Revere occupied Sonoma. The Stars and Stripes replaced the Bear Flag. Shortly afterward, a U.S. naval party took possession of Sutter's Fort on the Sacramento River.

In face of the common enemy, Castro and Pico submerged their differences and prepared their combined forces for a stand at Los Angeles. Sloat, who was in ill health, was replaced (23 July) by Commodore **Robert F. Stockton** (1795–1866), who issued a proclamation condemning Mexican resistance. The California Battalion was organized (24 July) under Frémont, given the rank of maj. Stockton's naval and military force occupied Santa Barbara and took Los Angeles (13 Aug.). Stockton issued a proclamation (17 Aug.) declaring the annexation of California by the U.S. and establishing a new regime with himself as governor. Frémont was named military commandant in the north and Gillespie in the south.

22–30 Sept. Mexican Revolt. Immediately after Stockton reported to the Navy Department (22 Aug.) that "peace and harmony" had been restored in California, a Mexican revolt against the U.S. authorities broke out (22–30 Sept.), and the insurgents, under the leadership of Capt. José Maria Flores, drove the Americans from Los Angeles, Santa Barbara, San Diego, and other points. By 29 Oct., when Flores was installed as governor and military commandant, all of California south of San Luis Obispo was in the hands of the Mexicans. Meanwhile, the expeditionary force under Kearny, which had been reduced in the belief that the conquest of California had been consolidated, was headed toward San Diego.

2 Aug.–13 Jan. 1847. Kearny's Expedition. After a month's march from Fort Leavenworth, the "Army of the West" under Kearny with a force of 1,700 reached Bent's Ft. (22–25 July) at the junction of the Arkansas River and the Santa Fe Trail, and he issued a proclamation (31 July) to the people of New Mexico declaring that he was entering the province "for the purpose of seeking union with and ameliorating the conditions of its inhabitants," and on 1 Aug. dispatched a letter to Gov. Manuel Armijo warning against resistance and pledging protection to those who cooperated.

Kearny's force began (2 Aug.) its march through the desert country, proceeding along the Arkansas to the mouth of the Timpas and thence southwest to the mountains, where the troops negotiated the Raton Pass (elevation, 8,560 ft.). Kearny reached Las Vegas (15 Aug.) and proclaimed New Mexico to be part of the U.S. The estimated 4,000 Mexican troops assembled at the Apache Canyon dispersed without offering battle, thus terminating all enemy resistance in the province (an uprising by the Mexicans during the winter of 1846–47 was suppressed by troops commanded by Col. Sterling Price, who ended all organized resistance by investing Taos, 4 Feb. 1847). On 18 Aug., after marching 29 mi. in less than a day, Kearny's troops occupied Santa Fe. Kearny issued a proclamation absolving the inhabitants of their allegiance to Mexico. After establishing a temporary territorial government under Gov. Charles Bent, Kearny left for California (25 Sept.) with 300 dragoons.

En route he encountered (6 Oct.) Kit Carson, bound for Washington with a dispatch from Frémont announcing the occupation of California. Kearny sent back 200 of his men. With the remaining 100 he crossed the Colorado (25 Nov.); entered Southern California, where the

Flores insurrection against the U.S. occupation was in progress; and defeated (6 Dec.) a Mexican force at the village of San Pascual. U.S. losses: 18 dead, 13 wounded. Kearny reached San Diego 12 Dec. His subsequent operations under the command of Stockton secured the reconquest of California. Stockton and Kearny left San Diego (29 Dec.) with a mixed force of 559 dragoons, sailors, marines, and volunteers, and advanced northward across the plain to Los Angeles, which was taken (10 Jan. 1847) after 2 brief clashes with the enemy along and above the San Gabriel River (8, 9 Jan. 1847). These were the concluding hostilities of the war in California. The remnants of the Mexican forces, under Andres Pico in the San Fernando Valley, capitulated to Frémont and signed (13 Jan. 1847) the **Treaty of Cahuenga,** which gave them generous terms.

KEARNY-STOCKTON AFFAIR grew out of a conflict of instructions concerning the establishment of a civil government in California. Stockton, following to the letter the Navy Department orders to Sloat, contested Kearny's right to organize a new territorial government, suspended Kearny from all command other than that over his small force of dragoons, and appointed Frémont governor (16 Jan. 1847). Kearny, after warning Frémont that he was guilty of disobedience to his superior officer, returned to San Diego. The arrival of fresh instructions (13 Feb. 1847) gave Kearny the duty of establishing a new government. He issued a proclamation setting up a provisional government with its capital at Monterey. At Los Angeles, however, Frémont persisted in executing his authority as governor and refused to carry out orders from Gen. Kearny. The controversy was prolonged until Kearny named Col. Richard B. Mason governor of California and, together with Stockton and Frémont, started out (31 May 1847) for Washington.

Frémont was tried by a court-martial (Nov. 1847–Jan. 1848) on charges of mutiny, disobedience, and prejudicial conduct; found guilty on all counts; and sentenced to dismissal from the service. President Polk approved the sentence (except for the charge of mutiny) and remitted the penalty with instructions to restore Frémont to duty. Frémont, however, resigned from the army. The affair precipitated open opposition between the Polk administration and Frémont's father-in-law, Senator Thomas Hart Benton.

8 Aug. WILMOT PROVISO. The prospect of acquiring additional territory as a result of the Mexican War precipitated a far-reaching Congressional debate occasioned by the Wilmot Proviso, introduced in the House as an amendment to the administration bill for a $2 million appropriation to facilitate negotiations with Mexico for territorial adjustments. Polk's request (known as the "Two Million Bill") was encouraged by the discussions with Santa Anna, which at that time seemingly augured a speedy peace settlement.

The Wilmot Proviso stated that "as an express and fundamental condition" to the acquisition of any territory from Mexico by the U.S. "by virtue of any treaty which may be negotiated between them, and to the use by the Executive of the moneys herein appropriated, neither slavery nor involuntary servitude shall ever exist in any part of said territory, except for crime, whereof the party shall first be duly convicted."

The proviso was drafted and introduced by **David Wilmot** (1814–68), a Democrat from northeastern Pennsylvania, previously a Polk supporter (some authorities credit the original proposal to Jacob Brinkerhoff [Ohio], a Van Buren Democrat).

Administration forces tried to amend the Wilmot Proviso by limiting its operation to territory north of the Missouri Compromise line. This attempt was defeated by a House vote, 89–54, and the proviso was adopted (8 Aug.), 87–64. The bill was lost in the Senate (10 Aug.) when discussion was terminated by the adjournment of the 1st sess. of the 29th Congress.

Polk's supporters in the House introduced a similar appropriation measure (8 Feb. 1847) raising the sum to $3 million. The more pronounced slavery-exclusion clause of a previous bill moved (3 Jan. 1847) by Preston King, a New York Democrat, was adopted and introduced by Wilmot in place of his original proposal. In this form, the Wilmot Proviso was passed as an amendment to the "Three Million Bill," 115–106, and the amended bill passed, 115–105 (15 Feb. 1847). In the Senate, which drew up its own bill, an attempt to add the Wilmot Proviso was defeated, 31–21, and the measure passed, 29–24 (1 Mar. 1847). The Senate bill was taken up in the House in committee of the whole, and was passed, 115–81 (3 Mar.).

In the heated debate in both houses Democrats defended the war as a just one; Whigs attacked it as an expansionist drive for territorial spoils, and accused the President of having initiated the war in violation of the Constitution.

19 Feb. 1847. Calhoun Resolutions. Southern Democrats and their Northern allies united in opposing the proviso as an unnecessary agitation of the slavery question and a threat to Southern rights. The defense of the Southern position was set forth by Calhoun in 4 resolutions on the slavery question (19 Feb. 1847). He asserted that the territories of the U.S. were the joint and common property of the states; that Congress, as the agent of the states, had no right to make any law discriminating between the states of the Union and depriving any of them of its full and equal right in any territory acquired or to be acquired by the U.S.; that the enactment of any law interfering with slavery would be a violation of the Constitution and states' rights, and inimical to the equality of the states within the Union; and that the people had an unconditional right to form and adopt their state governments as they chose, no condition being imposed by the Constitution for the admission of a state except that its government should be republican. Calhoun's remarks (19–20 Feb. 1847) forecast the position of the South: insistence on a positive protection of slavery; appeal to states' rights and constitutional-compact theory; the view of the section as the bulwark of conservatism within the Union; attack upon the "aggressive measures" of the nonslaveholding states. Pointing out that the South was already becoming a political minority in the national councils, Calhoun warned that were the balance between North and South destroyed, it would herald the approach of "political revolution, anarchy, civil war, and widespread disaster." The South, he said, was acting defensively and restricting itself to "repelling attacks . . . all we ask is to be let alone; but if trampled upon, it will be idle to expect that we will not resist it."

The fundamental principle of the Wilmot Proviso reappeared in later Congressional debates, and became a vital plank in the platforms of the Free-Soil and Republican parties.

25 Sept. CAPTURE OF MONTEREY. Taylor's army, increased (May–June) from 5,000 to 14,500 men, many being 3- and 6-mos. volunteers, and handicapped by lack of supplies and faulty transportation, began (6 July) its ascent of the Rio Grande from the advance base of Reynosa to Camargo, using a small fleet of river steamboats. Camargo, which the 1st troops reached 14 July, lay on the San Juan River, a branch of the Rio Grande, c.1,000 mi. north of Mexico City. It became Taylor's base for his march on Monterey. With a force of 3,080 regulars and 3,150 volunteers, Taylor began (19 Aug.) his advance on Monterey, reaching its outskirts on 19 Sept. The major fortification in the city was the Citadel (or Black Ft.). To the west of Monterey, the Mexicans had well-fortified defenses on Independence Hill and Federation Hill. Taylor took immediate command of the troops attacking from the east, and dispatched a force under Gen. William J. Worth to make the assault from the west. The attack on Monterey began 20 Sept.

Worth advanced along the Monterey-Saltillo road, took the redoubt on Federation Hill (21 Sept.), and seized Independence Hill (22 Sept.), thus securing control of the western approaches. In the east, the U.S. troops penetrated the town (21 Sept.), meeting heavy resistance in the fortified streets and houses. After a 4-day siege, during which the enemy fell back on the Citadel, the Mexicans capitulated (24 Sept.), the surrender being carried out 25 Sept. Estimated losses: U.S., 120 killed, 368 wounded; Mexican, 367 killed and wounded.

Taylor consented to an 8-wks. armistice, pledging that the U.S. forces would not penetrate southward beyond the mountains unless the armistice was disclaimed by either government. The armistice brought the disapproval of Polk, eager to press the war in order to exert pressure on the Mexican Congress. The War Department's notification (13 Oct.) did not reach Taylor until 2 Nov. The disapproval of the armistice increased Taylor's suspicion that the administration was engaged in intrigues against him because he had been mentioned in June by the Whig leader, Thurlow Weed, as that party's Presidential possibility.

Taylor informed Santa Anna (5 Nov.), who had reached San Luis Potosí (8 Oct.), that the armistice would be terminated effective 13 Nov. Taylor occupied Saltillo, capital of Coahuila (16 Nov.). Meanwhile, a force of about 3,000 troops under Gen. John E. Wool left San Antonio (23–28 Sept.) on an expedition against Chihuahua. Wool occupied Monclova (29 Oct.), but abandoned his march on Chihuahua under orders from the War Dept. approved by Taylor. Wool took Parras (5 Dec.), to the west of Monterey, and reinforced Taylor at Saltillo (21 Dec.).

12 Dec. TREATY OF NEW GRANADA. U.S. concern about Central America was revived by a growing interest in an isthmian transit route between the Atlantic and the Pacific, and by suspicion of British designs on the Caribbean area. The Republic of New Granada (Colombia) feared that Great Britain or some other foreign nation might take possession of the Isthmus of Panama. At the initiative of the New Granada government, Benjamin A. Bidlack, the U.S. Minister, signed (12 Dec.) a commercial treaty which conveyed to the U.S. the right of way across the isthmus. In return, the U.S. guaranteed the neutrality of the isthmus and the sovereignty of New Granada. The Senate approved the treaty (3 June 1848); ratifications exchanged 12 July 1848.

WHIG GAINS. State and Congressional elections indicated loss of support for Polk. In the state contests (Oct.–Nov.) the Whigs carried N.Y., N.J., Ohio, Md., Ga., and Fla., with strong gains in Pa. In the Congressional elections (Nov.) the Whigs made capital of the war (although

Polk's opposition to internal improvements and a high protective tariff were also under fire). The new House had a slim Whig majority.

7 Dec. NEW SESSION. The attack on Polk was resumed, with Whigs, notably Senators Robert Toombs (Ga., 8 Jan. 1847) and Thomas Corwin (Ohio, 11 Feb.), and antislavery Democrats joining forces. Nevertheless $5 million in war appropriations were voted (15 Feb., 3 Mar.) and Treasury notes to $23 million authorized (28 Jan.).

1847

Oct. 1846–1 Mar. 1847. DONIPHAN'S EXPEDITION. Before leaving New Mexico, Kearny ordered (23 Sept. 1846) Col. **Alexander W. Doniphan** (1808–87), commander of the 1st Regiment of Missouri Mounted Volunteers, to lead an expedition to the province of Chihuahua in support of Gen. Wool. Late in Oct. 1846, Doniphan's troops departed from Santa Fe on a march that was to take them through 3,000 miles of mountain and desert country. After signing (22 Nov. 1846) a treaty of peace with the Navajo chiefs assembled at Bear Springs, he left Valverde (14 Dec.) for El Paso, 90 mi. to the south, marched through virtually waterless country, and defeated the enemy in the **Battle of El Brazito** (25 Dec. 1846). U.S. loss: 7 wounded; Mexican, 43 killed. Occupying El Paso (27 Dec. 1846), Doniphan left the town (8 Feb.) on a march across desert wastes toward the provincial capital of Chihuahua. After defeating a defending Mexican force in the **Battle of the Sacramento** (28 Feb.)—U.S. loss: 1 killed, and 11 wounded; estimated Mexican: 300 killed, 300 wounded—he entered Chihuahua (1 Mar.).

22–23 Feb. BATTLE OF BUENA VISTA. In the late fall of 1846 Polk, convinced that Taylor could not bring the war to a successful conclusion, agreed to Gen. Winfield Scott's plan for an expedition to Vera Cruz. When Taylor learned (14 Jan.) that Scott had ordered (3 Jan.) the transfer of 9,000 of Taylor's troops to the Vera Cruz expedition and instructed him to remain on a "strict

defensive" on the line of Monterey, Taylor's suspicions of political and military intrigue against him were again aroused. Most of Taylor's troops joined the expeditionary force at Tampico after Taylor withdrew from Victoria (12 Jan.), the capital of Tamaulipas, which had been occupied on 29 Dec. 1846. The friction between Taylor and the administration was intensified with the publication (22 Jan.) in the N.Y. *Morning Express* of Taylor's letter to Gen. Edmund P. Gaines, in which he defended his agreement to the 8-wks. armistice, criticized the administration, and discussed military matters.

Taylor disobeyed orders (dated 20 Dec.) to communicate with Scott, and took the offensive, advancing (5–14 Feb.) to Agua Nueva, 18 mi. west of Saltillo. Meanwhile, Santa Anna massed about 20,000 troops at San Luis Potosí, with the aim of striking a decisive blow at Taylor's army. On 20 Feb., Santa Anna reached La Encarnación, 35 mi. from Taylor's encampment. Because of his poor defensive position at Agua Nueva, Taylor withdrew (21 Feb.) to La Angostura, a mountain defile along the Saltillo–San Luis Potosí road, in a valley 6,000 ft. above sea level. Here, 3 mi. north of the hacienda of Buena Vista, the U.S. forces (*c.*4,800 men, mostly untried volunteer infantry) entrenched along deep gullies and ravines.

Santa Anna, after leading more than 15,000 ill-trained men on an exhausting march, sent Taylor a demand for unconditional surrender. Taylor refused, and the ensuing battle ended in a hard-won U.S. victory, the retirement of Santa Anna's forces (23–24 Feb.), and termination of the war in northern Mexico. U.S. loss: 267 killed, 456 wounded, 23 missing; Mexican: estimated at 1,500, of whom at least 500 killed. Santa Anna returned to Mexico City, where he took the oath of office as President (21 Mar.).

Shortly after the battle, Taylor received from Secretary Marcy a reprimand (dated 27 Jan.) for the Gaines letter. For the next 9 mos. Taylor remained in command of the U.S. forces in northern Mexico. Relieved at his own request, he left for the U.S. on 26 Nov. and received a hero's welcome.

21 Feb.–29 Mar. SCOTT'S VERA CRUZ EXPEDITION. Influenced by the favorable progress of events in California, and finally yielding to repeated proposals made by Scott, Polk placed Scott at the head of an expedition to take Vera Cruz, at that time the most powerful fortress in the Western Hemisphere. From this point on the east coast of Mexico, Scott was to proceed along a direct but mountainous inland route to Mexico City. After a reconciliation with Polk (19 Nov. 1846), Scott was ordered (23 Nov. 1846) to take command of a force whose projected strength of 20,000 actually never exceeded 10,000. Scott left Washington (24 Nov. 1846) and reached Camargo (3 Jan.), where his progress was hindered by bad weather and inadequate water transportation.

Scott established headquarters at Tampico (18 Feb.) and, without express approval of the administration, issued **General Order No. 20** (19 Feb.). The order, which set up a system for dealing with crimes not defined in the Articles of War, was aimed at preventing the atrocities committed by some of Taylor's volunteer troops and at securing the cooperation of the native population along Scott's lines of communication. To an extent compatible with military necessity, local government was left to Mexican officials acting under army supervision. The order and the machinery for its execution constituted the **1st civil affairs administration** of enemy territory occupied by U.S. military forces.

Scott massed an invasion armada and 10,000 troops at the Lobos Islands, where he arrived 21 Feb. From this point, 50 mi. below Tampico, the fleet under Commodore Conner sailed (2–5 Mar.) to the final rendezvous at Antón Lizardo, 12 mi. south of Vera Cruz. Here Scott's operation was delayed by a serious outbreak of smallpox among the troops. At the advice of naval officers, Scott decided to abandon his plan to take the fortress city by direct assault from the sea. The Mexicans had 5,000 soldiers in the city.

The landings (9 Mar.), made on the beaches south of Vera Cruz, were virtually unopposed. The first large-scale amphibious operation in U.S. military history was carried out with special landing craft assembled at Sacrificios Island. Two wks. were spent in securing and building up the position on the beach. The Mexicans rejected a demand for surrender (22 Mar.). After a siege from U.S. land and naval batteries that began 22 Mar., Vera Cruz, with its strongly fortified seaward castle of San Juan de Ulúa, surrendered to Scott (27 Mar.) and was formally occupied (29 Mar.). U.S. losses: 82, of whom 19 were killed; Mexican: *c.*80 soldiers, 100 civilians.

18 Apr.–20 Aug. CERRO GORDO TO CHURUBUSCO. The route of Scott's march through the interior lay across an initial 55 mi. of lowland, which at the mountain pass of Cerro Gordo rises precipitously to slopes ultimately reaching a height of *c.*8,000 ft., and then across a heavily populated plateau between Perote and Mexico City. Scott's immediate objective was Jalapa, 75 mi. northwest of Vera Cruz and 4,250 feet above sea level.

Battle of Cerro Gordo. Leaving Vera Cruz 8 Apr., Scott's force of about 9,000 men marched along the National Road. On 13 Apr. they encountered the outlying enemy defenses at Plan del Rio, just below Cerro Gordo. Santa Anna, leaving the Mexican capital (2 Apr.), had reached Cerro Gordo (9 Apr.) and designated it as the point for containing the U.S. advance. The Mexican force numbered about 13,000 men. A skillful reconnaissance of enemy positions along the canyon near Cerro Gordo was made by U.S. engineer officers (including Capts. **Robert E. Lee** and **George B. McClellan**), but its value was partly vitiated by a premature action (17 Apr.). In an enveloping operation that witnessed much hand-to-hand combat, the U.S. forces carried Cerro Gordo by assault (18 Apr.), routing Santa Anna and his staff officers, capturing 204 enemy officers and 2,837 men, and seizing 43 artillery pieces and 4,000 small arms. U.S. losses: 63 killed, 337 wounded.

Scott's troops occupied Jalapa (19 Apr.), Perote (22 Apr.), and reached Puebla (15 May), 80 mi. from Mexico City. During this period Scott lost about one third of his effectives whose short-term enlistments had expired (7 regiments and 2 companies of volunteers). He was left with about 7,000 men, of whom some 1,000 were stricken with disease. Scott lacked money, supplies, and transportation; reinforcements from New Orleans were slow in arriving. Yet during a 3-mos. pause at Puebla, while the navy carried out operations along the southeastern coast of Mexico, Scott built up his force to 10,783 effectives. On 6 Aug. Gen. Franklin Pierce arrived at Puebla with 3,000 reinforcements.

Battles of Contreras and Churubusco. Scott began (7 Aug.) his advance from Puebla, cutting through the mountains and entering the Valley of Mexico at Ayotla, where he established his headquarters (11 Aug.). Santa Anna, who had again taken office as President (22 May) after some changes in the Mexican government, had about 20,000 men in the valley, concentrated in the vicinity of Contreras and Churubusco, along the roads leading to Mexico City. An American force of about 3,300 men stormed the Contreras position (19–20 Aug.) and routed the enemy, killing 700 and capturing 800 at a cost of 60 U.S. killed and wounded. The fighting at Churubusco (20 Aug.), where the enemy had converted a church and a convent into powerful defensive positions, also resulted in a U.S. victory, but at a heavy price. U.S. losses in both battles: 133 killed, 865 wounded, 40 missing (about one seventh of force engaged). Santa Anna lost more than 7,000 killed, wounded, or captured (about one third of his army). Santa Anna withdrew to Mexico City, now within 5 mi. of U.S. lines, and requested an armistice. Negotiations were conducted (22–23 Aug.), and the armistice of Tacubaya went into effect (24 Aug.) to enable the Mexican government to consider the peace proposals that had been entrusted to **Nicholas P. Trist** (1800–74), confidential commissioner accompanying Scott's army.

26 Aug.–6 Sept. TRIST MISSION. With the fall of Vera Cruz, Polk renewed his efforts for a peace settlement. He decided, with the agreement of his Cabinet, to dispatch a peace commissioner to Mexico. Chosen for the secret mission was Nicholas P. Trist, chief clerk of the State Department, who received his instructions from Polk and Buchanan (15 Apr.). The terms of the offer were essentially those that Mackenzie had made to Santa Anna, except that Trist was also authorized to negotiate for Lower California and the right of transit across the Isthmus of Tehuantepec. Trist's "confidential" mission became publicly known 4 days after he left Washington (16 Apr.).

Traveling under an assumed name, Trist reached Vera Cruz on 6 May. He was authorized, with certain reservations, "to enter into arrangements with the government of Mexico for the suspension of hostilities." There immediately ensued a controversy over Trist's authority, Scott regarding it as an invasion of his own and holding that an armistice was exclusively a military question. Relations between Trist and Scott were aggravated by an exchange of hostile correspondence. With the aid of the British legation in Mexico, a reconciliation was effected (25 June), and the armistice of Tacubaya was arranged by Scott. The negotiations (27 Aug.–6 Sept.) between Trist and the Mexican commission headed by former President Herrera ended with a Mexican rejection of the peace offer. The armistice was terminated 7 Sept.

8–14 Sept. MARCH ON THE MEXICAN CAPITAL. Battle of Molino del Rey. Scott resumed his march at once. A force of 3,447 men under Gen. William J. Worth was ordered to carry out a diversionary raid on the gun foundry of Molino del Rey, just outside the gates of the city, where the enemy was supposedly casting church bells into cannon. Here, and at the adjoining Casa Mata and the walled park of Chapultepec, an estimated 12,000 Mexicans were entrenched behind massive fortifications. The U.S. attack opened 8 Sept., and what had been conceived as a minor raid developed into a serious day-long battle. Although the Americans took the position, they withdrew to Tacubaya at the day's end. U.S. losses: 117 killed, 653 wounded, 18 missing; Mexican: c.2,000 men killed and wounded, c.700 captured.

Battle of Chapultepec. For the final assault on the capital, Scott had 7,180 men as against an estimated 15,000 enemy troops in the city. Scott decided to storm the fortified hill of Chapultepec (c.200 ft. high) commanding the causeways leading to the San Cosmé and Belén gates at the western outskirts of the capital. On Chapultepec there were some 1,000 troops, supported by 4,000 in the immediate area. Following an artillery bombardment (12 Sept.), the divisions commanded by Generals John A. Quitman and Gideon J. Pillow began their assault at 8:00 A.M. on the morning of 13 Sept. The storming parties scaled the rocky slopes with ladders and pickaxes. The summit was taken at 9:30 A.M. Gallant resistance was offered by "Los Ninos," about 100 boy cadets who defended the Mexican Military College on the crest of the hill. The Belén gate was taken at 1:30 P.M., and the San Cosmé gate by 6 P.M. U.S. losses: 130 killed, 703 wounded, 29 missing.

Capture of Mexico City. Scott immediately pressed on the capital (pop.: 200,000) with less than 6,000 effectives. Using picks and crowbars, the U.S. infantry hacked through the city walls and entered the capital during the night and early morning (13–14 Sept.). The U.S. flag was raised above the National Palace, where a battalion of U.S. Marines took guard over the "halls of Montezuma." After several days of disorder, the hostile population was brought under control. Gen. Scott reissued (16 Sept.) General Order No. 20; henceforth, military government became the chief function of his army. Scott remained in command until 18 Feb. 1848.

Even before the Americans occupied the capital, Santa Anna fled to the suburb of Guadalupe Hidalgo, where he renounced the Presidency (16 Sept.). At the head of about 8,000 men, he marched to Puebla, where the Mexicans under Gen. Joaquin Rea had begun a siege (14 Sept.) of the U.S. garrison (about 2,300 troops, mostly wounded and convalescent) under Col. Thomas Childs, who rejected a demand for surrender. Santa Anna left Puebla (1 Oct.) and the siege was raised (12 Oct.) by a relief expedition under Gen. Joseph Lane from Vera Cruz. Deposed as head of the army (7 Oct.), Santa Anna fled the country.

Pedro María Anaya was elected (11 Nov.) *ad interim* President of Mexico. The Anaya government informed Trist (22 Nov.) that it had named commissioners to negotiate peace on the basis of the original terms. Trist had received (16 Nov.) an order for his recall, but when the Mexicans pointed out that they had not received official notification of the withdrawal of his authority, Trist decided (4 Dec.) to remain in Mexico and negotiate a treaty.

1848

24 Jan. DISCOVERY OF GOLD in California by James W. Marshall, a New Jersey mechanic who was erecting a sawmill for **Johann Augustus Sutter** (1803–80) on a branch of the American River in Eldorado County, in the lower Sacramento Valley, about 40 mi. from present-day Sacramento. The news, announced by Marshall to Sutter (28 Jan.), soon spread and stimulated the great California gold rush. Impetus was lent by Polk's confirmation of the discovery in his annual message to Congress (5 Dec.). Adventurers came from all parts of the U.S. and from overseas places as distant as China and Australia. By the end of 1849, it is estimated, the California population had been swelled by 100,000. The influx of the "Forty-niners" continued for the next 2 yrs. In 1851 the annual output of gold rose to $55 million.

2 Feb. TREATY OF GUADALUPE HIDALGO resulted from the unauthorized negotiations between Trist and the Mexican commissioners begun formally 2 Jan., and the treaty was signed at the village just outside Mexico City. By that time, Peña y Peña had become (8 Jan.) acting President of Mexico. **Terms:** Mexico relinquished all claims to Texas above the Rio Grande and ceded New Mexico and California to the U.S. The territory (including the present states of Ariz., Nev., Calif., and Utah, and parts of N.M., Col., and Wyo.) added with Tex. 1,193,061 square miles to the national domain. In return for the territory, the U.S. agreed to pay $15 million and assume the adjusted claims of its citizens ($3,250,000) against the Mexican government. The U.S.-Mexican boundary was fixed along the Rio Grande to the southern line of N.M., thence westward and northward along the Gila and Colorado Rivers, and thence along the line between Upper and Lower California to the Pacific.

The treaty arrived at Washington on 19 Feb. Polk, doubtful and hesitant because the treaty was unauthorized, submitted it to the Senate (23 Feb.), which ratified the treaty, 38–14 (10 Mar.). For: 26 Democrats, 12 Whigs; against: 7 Democrats, 7 Whigs. A motion to add the Wilmot Proviso was defeated, 38–15. The opposition to the treaty stemmed from Secretary Buchanan and those senators who, supported by a growing expansionist demand, wanted to annex all of Mexico. The Mexican Congress ratified the treaty (25 May), ratifications were formally exchanged (30 May), and Polk proclaimed the treaty in effect (4 July). The final territorial adjustment under the treaty was made with the **Gadsden Purchase** (1853).

A military armistice suspending hostilities had been declared on 29 Feb., and the last action of the war was fought at Todos Santos in Lower California (30 Mar.). The U.S. forces evacuated Mexico City (12 June) and the last U.S. troops left Vera Cruz 2 Aug.

WAR COST. U.S. casualties: 1,721 killed or died of wounds; 11,155 died of disease; 4,102 wounded. Military and naval expenditures amounted to more than $97,500,000.

19 July. SENECA FALLS CONVENTION, held at the Wesleyan Chapel, Seneca Falls, N.Y., under the leadership of **Lucretia Mott** (1793–1880) and **Elizabeth Cady Stanton** (p. 782), adopted a group of women's rights resolutions.

14 Aug. THE OREGON BILL. In his annual messages (1846–48) Polk urged the establishment of a territorial government for Oregon, whose provisional laws excluded slavery. The ensuing debates raised the issue of the constitutional power of Congress to prohibit slavery in the territories. The Senate tabled a bill passed by the House (16 Jan. 1847) applying the restrictions of the Northwest Ordinance. Senator Stephen A. Douglas (Ill.) offered a bill (10 Jan.) providing that the Oregon laws should remain valid until the territorial legislature should change them.

The House (9 Feb.) reintroduced its Oregon bill. Senator Jesse D. Bright (Ind.), acting chairman of the committee on territories, introduced an amendment (27 June) extending the Missouri Compromise line through all newly acquired territory to the Pacific. Thus the Oregon bill raised anew the problem of the status of slavery in California and New Mexico. Under the Mexican laws of 1829 and 1837 slavery had been forbidden in those areas. Calhoun opposed Bright's amendment, denied (27 June) both the validity of Mexican laws in the conquered territories and Congressional authority over slavery in the territories, and insisted that slavery was not subject to Congressional or local action.

The Senate (12 July) referred the question of slavery extension to a committee headed by John M. Clayton (Del.). The "Clayton Compromise," adopted by the Senate, 33–22 (27 July), validated the provisional laws of Oregon insofar as they were compatible with the Constitution, but forbade the territorial legislatures of New Mexico and California to pass laws on slavery. The question of the status of slavery in those territories was referred to appeals from the territorial courts to the Supreme Court.

The Senate bill was tabled by the House (28 July), which by 129–71 passed its own bill (2 Aug.) for organizing Oregon with restrictions on slavery. The Senate amendment to the bill extended the Missouri Compromise line to the Pacific. The House refused to concur, and its bill incorporating the prohibition of slavery in Oregon was adopted by the Senate (13 Aug.). Despite Calhoun's view that the measure merited a veto on constitutional grounds, Polk signed the bill (14 Aug.) on the ground that it did not conflict with the Missouri Compromise because the territory in question lay north of 36° 30′.

PRESIDENTIAL CAMPAIGN. The slavery issue was injected into the Democratic National Convention at Baltimore (22 May) when the two factions of Barnburners (also known as the "Softs") and Hunkers (also known as the "Hards") from the key state of New York sent separate delegations. The antiadministration Barnburners were firm supporters of the Wilmot Proviso. When a compromise on seating the delegations failed, neither one took part in the convention; but the Hunkers, unlike their opponents, pledged their support to the nominees.

Polk, who in accepting the nomination in 1844 had pledged himself to a single term, declined to run for office. Gen. Lewis Cass (Mich.) was nominated for President and Gen. **William O. Butler** (Ky.) for Vice-President. Cass, a conservative and an expansionist, had approved the doctrine of "squatter sovereignty" (local determination of the status of slavery) in a letter (29 Dec. 1847) to A. O. P. Nicholson of Nashville. While his selection indicated the Democratic party's desire to win the Western vote and promote sectional harmony, the principle of "squatter sovereignty" was not incorporated in the Democratic platform. The platform, in substance that of 1844, denied the power of Congress to interfere with slavery in the states and criticized all efforts to bring the slavery question before Congress. In a move to quell the agitation of the slavery issue, the convention voted down a minority resolution of the Southern delegates favoring noninterference with slavery in the territories.

When the Whig National Convention met at Philadelphia (7 June), the 3 contenders for the nomination were Henry Clay, Gen. Zachary Taylor, and Gen. Winfield Scott. **Taylor,** whose political following grew rapidly after the battle of Buena Vista, was chosen as Presidential candidate; **Millard Fillmore** (N.Y.), as the Vice-Presidential nominee. A resolution affirming the power of Congress to control slavery in the territories was proposed by the antislavery Ohio delegation and voted down. Taylor's nomination was opposed by the antislavery delegations from New England and Ohio. The Whig platform was a recital of Taylor's military character and reputation.

The Barnburners, seceding from the Democratic convention, held their own convention at Utica, N.Y. (22 June), nominating **Martin Van Buren** for President and **Henry Dodge** (Wisc.) for Vice-President. Soon afterward the antislavery Democrats and Liberty party supporters joined with dissident New England Whigs (known as "Conscience Whigs" because of their opposition to slavery) in holding

a national convention of the **Free-Soil party** at Buffalo (9 Aug.). It was attended by 465 delegates from 18 states (including the 3 slave states of Virginia, Maryland, and Delaware). The Free-Soil opposition to Cass and Taylor united on the common basis of the Wilmot Proviso. John P. Hale (N.H.), who had been nominated for President by the Liberty party convention at New York City (Nov. 1847), withdrew in favor of **Van Buren,** who was nominated for President. **Charles Francis Adams** (Mass.) was nominated for Vice-President. Among the prominent members of the party were **Charles Sumner** (Mass.) and **Salmon P. Chase** (O.). The Free-Soil party was pledged to a "national platform of freedom in opposition to the sectional platform of slavery." It attacked the "aggressions of the slave power," upheld the substance of the Wilmot Proviso, and favored river and harbor improvements and free homesteads to actual settlers. For its slogan the party adopted "Free soil, free speech, free labor, and free men."

7 Nov. PRESIDENTIAL ELECTION (the 1st conducted on a uniform election day, in accord with the Congressional act of 1845). Popular vote: **Taylor,** 1,360,-101; Cass, 1,220,544; Van Buren, 291,-263. Electoral vote: Taylor, 163 (carrying 8 slave and 7 free states); Cass, 127 (carrying 8 free and 7 slave states). While Van Buren failed to carry a single state, the Free-Soil party was instrumental in winning the election for Taylor by depriving Cass of New York's 36 electoral votes. In that state, Van Buren received 120,510 votes to 114,318 for Cass, thus splitting the Democratic ranks.

1849

22 Jan. "ADDRESS OF THE SOUTHERN DELEGATES." A caucus (22 Dec. 1848) of 69 Southerners in Congress considered steps to oppose legislation prohibiting the slave trade in the District of Columbia. Spokesman for the caucus was Calhoun, whose "Address" listed the "acts of aggression" committed by the North against Southern rights—including (1) exclusion of slaves from the territories, (2) impediments to the return of fugitive slaves—and reaffirmed the right of slaveholders to take their property into the territories. Two additional meetings of the caucus (15, 22 Jan.) were attended by about 80 members, but owing to Whig opposition only 48 signed the "Address" (2 of them Whigs).

3 Mar. DEPT. OF THE INTERIOR created as the 6th with Cabinet status. Established at the recommendation of Secretary of the Treasury Robert J. Walker, it was originally called the Home Department, and brought under a single head diverse government bureaus, including the Office of the Census, the Office of Indian Affairs, and the General Land Office.

NEW CONGRESS. In the House of Representatives (31st Cong., 1st sess.) that convened on 3 Dec., there were 112 Democrats, 109 Whigs, and 13 Free-Soilers. The last group held the balance of power. The Democrats had a Senate majority of 10. The organization of the House revealed the bitter factionalism produced by sectional controversy. Southern Whigs under the leadership of Alexander Stephens and Robert Toombs opposed the Whig candidate for Speaker, Robert C. Winthrop (Mass.), because the Whig caucus had refused to pledge opposition to the Wilmot Proviso. The Free-Soilers refused to support Winthrop on the ground that he had not given adequate recognition to antislavery spokesmen during his previous service as Speaker. It took 3 weeks and 63 ballots before Howell Cobb (Ga.) was elected Speaker (22 Dec.). The debates, marked by threats of disunion, widened the breach between the Northern and Southern wings of the Whig party.

CALIFORNIA AND NEW MEXICO. Polk's efforts to secure territorial organization for California and New Mexico failed. The stumbling block was the status of slavery in the newly acquired regions. With the influx of settlers into California after the discovery of gold, territorial organization became a pressing need.

It was Taylor's view that Congress ought not to pass on the question of slavery in California and New Mexico. The people of these territories, he held, had the right to adopt their own constitution and form of government without Congressional authorization before ap-

plying for admission to the Union. The final decision would rest with Congress. Accordingly, he dispatched special messengers to California and New Mexico to inform the people that it was not necessary to await Congressional action before establishing a government.

The Californians took steps even before Taylor's special agent arrived. A convention met at Monterey (1 Sept.–13 Oct.) and adopted a constitution prohibiting slavery. The constitution was ratified by the people (13 Nov.) and a state government went into operation on 20 Dec. Taylor recommended in his annual message (4 Dec.) the immediate admission of California, and urged that Congress "should abstain from the introduction of those exciting topics of sectional character which have hitherto produced painful apprehensions in the public mind." Referring to threats of dissolution that had been freely made during the year, Taylor asserted that whatever dangers menaced the Union, "I shall stand by it and maintain it in its integrity to the full extent of the obligations imposed and the powers conferred upon me by the Constitution." Southerners at once attacked Taylor's proposal. (In the Union at this time there were 15 free and 15 slave states, and the admission of California would upset the balance.) On 12 Mar. 1850 California applied to Congress for statehood.

1850

29 Jan.–20 Sept. COMPROMISE OF 1850. Clay's Resolutions. Mounting sectional antagonism over territorial accessions alarmed moderates and conservatives. Returning to the U.S. Senate after a long absence, Henry Clay introduced (29 Jan.) a series of resolutions designed as a general formula for settling differences between North and South. These resolutions provided for (1) admission of California as a free state; (2) organization, without restriction on slavery, of the balance of the territory acquired from Mexico; (3) adjustment of the Texas-New Mexico boundary; (4) assumption by the U.S. of the Texas debt contracted before annexation, provided that Texas

SLAVERY
IN THE UNITED STATES, 1821
(AFTER THE MISSOURI COMPROMISE)

Dates indicate when freedom was granted,
or when gradual abolition began

States entirely
Free

States undergoing
Gradual Emancipation

Area Free by
Ordinance of 1787

Slave holding
Area

Occupied jointly
with Great Britain
1818–1846

relinquished her claim to any part of Mexico; (5) noninterference with slavery in the District of Columbia; (6) prohibition of the slave trade in the District of Columbia; (7) more effective provision for the return of fugitive slaves; and (8) declared that Congress had no authority to interfere with the interstate slave trade.

The Great Debate. The Senate debate on the resolution, the greatest in Congressional history, marked the last meeting of the Senatorial triumvirate of Calhoun, Clay, and Webster. Clay's speech (5–6 Feb.) made an appeal for mutual concessions and warned that secession was not a rightful remedy for Southern grievances. Calhoun, enfeebled by his final illness (he died 31 Mar.), sat in silence as his speech (4 Mar.) opposing the compromise was read by Senator James M. Mason (Va.). Calhoun maintained that the Union could be saved only by giving the South equal rights in the acquired territory, by halting the agitation of the slavery question, and by a constitutional amendment restoring "to the South, in substance, the power she possessed of protecting herself before the equilibrium between the sections was destroyed by the action of this government" (Calhoun did not elaborate on this last proposal; it was based on his doctrine of the "concurrent majority" expounded in his posthumous *Disquisition on Government*).

Webster's speech (7 Mar.) in support of the resolutions began: "I wish to speak today, not as a Massachusetts man, nor as a Northern man, but as an American. . . . I speak today for the preservation of the Union. 'Hear me for my cause.' " Contending that there was no necessity for Congressional action on slavery in the acquired territory, Webster held that slavery had been excluded by virtue of soil and climate.

William H. Seward (N.Y.) opposed the compromise in a speech (11 Mar.) which held "all legislative compromises radically wrong and essentially vicious." He supported the Wilmot Proviso and appealed to "a higher law" justifying refusal of constitutional protection to slavery. Also opposing the resolutions were Jefferson Davis (Miss.), whose speech (13–14 Mar.) advocated Congressional noninterference with slavery

and upheld equal rights for the South; and Salmon P. Chase (Ohio), who asserted (26–27 Mar.) that it was the duty of Congress to prohibit slavery in the territories. Other opponents of Clay's proposals included Thomas Hart Benton (Mo.), John Davis (Mass.), and John P. Hale (N.H.). Prominent among Clay's supporters were Lewis Cass (Mich.), Stephen A. Douglas (Ill.), and Henry S. Foote (Miss.).

The resolutions were referred (18 Apr.) to a Senate select committee of 13 (of which Clay was chairman) consisting of 7 Whigs and 6 Democrats representing 7 slave and 6 free states. The committee reported 2 bills (8 May): (1) the "Omnibus Bill," covering the organization of the territories; and (2) a bill to prohibit the slave trade in the District of Columbia.

Compromise Measures. President Taylor was opposed to the immediate territorial organization of New Mexico and Utah. His death (9 July) brought to the Presidency Millard Fillmore, who favored Clay's compromise. The "Compromise of 1850" is a collective term of later origin applied to the 5 laws enacted (9–20 Sept.) after Clay and Douglas succeeded in coalescing Union sentiment in Congress. With the exception of California, the territory won from Mexico was divided at the 37th parallel into a northern half (Utah) and a southern half (New Mexico). The compromise included the following measures:

9 Sept. (1) **Admission of California as a Free State.** The bill passed the Senate, 34–18 (13 Aug.); the House, 150–56 (7 Sept.).

9 Sept. (2) **Texas and New Mexico Act,** which organized New Mexico as a territory without restriction on slavery, adjusted the Texas-New Mexico boundary, and provided for the payment by the U.S. to Texas of $10 million in return for the abandonment by Texas of all claims to New Mexico territory. It included the "popular sovereignty" provision that was the substance of the compromise: "That, when admitted as a State, the said territory, or any portion of the same, shall be received into the Union, with or without slavery, as their constitution may prescribe at the time of their admission." The bill passed the Senate, 27–10 (15 Aug.); the House, 108–97 (6 Sept.).

9 Sept. (3) Utah Act, which established a territorial government with identical provisions.

18 Sept. (4) Fugitive Slave Act amended the original law of 1793; placed fugitive slave cases under exclusive Federal jurisdiction; provided for special U.S. commissioners who were authorized, following a summary hearing, to issue warrants for the arrest of fugitives and certificates for returning them to their masters. An affidavit by the claimant was accepted as sufficient proof of ownership. A feature of the law that abolitionists regarded as especially prejudicial was the authorization of a $10 fee for commissioners when such a certificate was granted, and of only $5 when it was refused. The commissioners were authorized to call to their aid bystanders, or to summon a *posse comitatus,* when deemed necessary for enforcing the law. Fugitives claiming to be freemen were denied the right of trial by jury, and their testimony was not to be admitted as evidence at any of the proceedings under the law. Heavy penalties were provided for evasion or obstruction. Marshals and deputies refusing to execute warrants were liable to a $1,000 fine; and in cases where the fugitives escaped through official negligence, the marshal might be sued for the value of the slave. Citizens preventing the arrest of a fugitive, or aiding in his concealment or rescue, were subject to a fine of $1,000, imprisonment up to six months, and civil damages of $1,000 for each fugitive so lost. The bill passed the Senate, 27–12 (23 Aug.); the House, 109–76 (12 Sept.).

20 Sept. (5) An Act Abolishing the Slave Trade in the District of Columbia after 1 Jan. 1851, passed the Senate, 33–19 (16 Sept.); the House, 124–47 (17 Sept.).

Both North and South hailed the "finality" of the measures, although acceptance was in reality conditional. Most Northern Whigs and Democrats viewed it as a permanent settlement of the slavery question. Northern radicals, however, condemned the Fugitive Slave Act and hinted at their intention to obstruct its enforcement. That a majority of Southern voters regarded the compromise as a welcome alternative to disunion was indicated by the defeat of the secessionists in the Southern state elections of 1851, when the Unionists won by narrow margins over the Quitman-Davis faction (Miss.), the Rhett wing (S.C.), and the Yancey radicals (Ala.). Northern radicals, however, gained a signal triumph with the election (1851) of Charles Sumner (Mass.) to the U.S. Senate. The chief political effect of the compromise was its hastening of the breakup of the Whig party.

19 Apr. CLAYTON-BULWER TREATY. U.S. interest in an interoceanic canal across the isthmian routes in Central America influenced Polk's foreign policy. Polk sent a special envoy, Elijah Hise, to Nicaragua to investigate British encroachments. The British, acting on the petition (1835) of the settlers of Belize (British Honduras), established a protectorate over the Mosquito Coast territory claimed by Nicaragua, drove the Nicaraguans from Mosquitia, and forced them (Jan. 1848) to renounce the area in the vicinity of the San Juan River, at the eastern terminus of the canal projected by the U.S.

Hise concluded with the Nicaraguans an unauthorized treaty granting the U.S. the exclusive right of way across the isthmus and the right to fortify the route, in return for the U.S. guarantee of the neutrality of the isthmus and the protection of Nicaraguan sovereignty. Polk never submitted the treaty to the Senate. A similar treaty was negotiated (1849) by E. G. Squier, an envoy sent by Taylor. Squier also obtained Tigre Island in the Gulf of Fonseca, at the western terminus of the projected canal. The island was seized (Oct., 1849) by British forces, who refused to leave despite Squier's contention that it belonged to the U.S.

Although the Taylor administration was anxious to reach an understanding with Great Britain, Secretary of State Clayton informed the British Foreign Secretary, Lord Palmerston, that the U.S. would not recognize the British protectorate over Mosquitia or its hold on the San Juan River. Clayton initiated discussions with the British Minister to the U.S., Sir

Henry Lytton Bulwer. The treaty was ratified by the Senate, 42–10, and ratifications were exchanged on 5 July. Terms: both nations (1) agreed never to obtain or exercise exclusive control over an isthmian ship canal, or to fortify it; (2) guaranteed the neutrality and security of the canal; (3) agreed to keep any future canal open to their nationals on terms of equality; and (4) pledged not to colonize, occupy, or exercise dominion over any part of Central America.

The British made the major concessions, but the treaty, unpopular in the U.S. with Anglophobes and expansionists, remained in effect until abrogated by the Hay-Pauncefote Treaty (1901). Anglo-U.S. friction was further allayed by cession (22 Nov. 1859) by Britain of the Bay Islands to Honduras.

10 June. NASHVILLE CONVENTION. Early in 1850 Southern advocates of a separatist program took steps to consider their position on Clay's compromise and the larger question of Southern rights. At the instigation of Calhoun, a Mississippi convention (1 Oct. 1849) and the state legislature (6 Mar.) adopted resolutions calling a convention of the slave states, to meet at Nashville, Tenn., 3 June. The extremists, led by **Robert Barnwell Rhett** (S.C.), saw an opportunity to broaden their support for secession. Nine slave states were represented, but the moderates were in control. The convention adopted (10 June) a resolution calling for the extension of the Missouri Compromise line westward to the Pacific. A 2nd convention, attended by a handful of delegates (11–18 Nov.), denounced the Compromise and asserted the right of secession.

9 July. Death of President Taylor at Washington, D.C., of cholera morbus. **Millard Fillmore** became the 13th President, taking the oath of office on 10 July.

13–14 Dec. GEORGIA PLATFORM. Indicative of Unionist sentiment among conservative Southerners was the Georgia Platform drawn up by Charles J. Jenkins and adopted by a state convention (10 Dec.) at Milledgeville. The resolutions stated that while Georgia did not wholly approve of the Compromise of 1850, she would "abide by it as a permanent adjustment of this sectional controversy";

however, they warned that Georgia "will and ought to resist, even (as a last resort) to a disruption of every tie which binds her to the Union," any future act of Congress that would repeal or substantially modify the fugitive slave laws, the suppression of the interstate slave trade, and the abolition of slavery in the District of Columbia. The Georgia Platform constituted the basis on which **Robert A. Toombs** (1810–85) and his colleagues, including the conservative Democrat, **Howell Cobb** (1815–68) formally established the Union Rights party.

"SILVER GRAY" WHIGS. The impact of the Compromise of 1850 upon the Whig party in the North was immediately reflected in the New York State Whig convention that met at Syracuse (Sept.). When the convention adopted resolutions approving Senator Seward's radical position, 40 conservative delegates of the Fillmore wing left the hall. They were led by Francis Granger, whose gray hair lent the name "Silver Gray" to the faction. The seceders held their own convention at Utica (Oct.), condemned Seward's policies and supported those of Fillmore, and shortly after backed a fusion ticket that included Horatio Seymour, the Democratic candidate for governor. The "Silver Grays" lost their influence in the state Whig party and later seized control of the American (Know-Nothing) organization in New York.

FUGITIVE SLAVE RESCUES. Most controversial aspect of the Compromise of 1850 was the adoption and subsequent enforcement of the Fugitive Slave Law. Although the number of runaway slaves was small (estimated, 1850, by the census of 1860 as only 1,000 out of c.3 million slaves, most of whom were ultimately returned to their masters), the South regarded Northern interference with the rendition of fugitive slaves as a violation of a constitutional guarantee. Sectional strife was increased by the further enactment of more stringent "personal liberty" laws in Vermont (1850) and other free states during the decade. Southern slaveholders who entered free states to seize runaway slaves risked being mobbed, sued for false imprisonment, or prosecuted for kidnaping. Outstanding rescues or attempted rescues of fugitive slaves (some leading to riots and loss of life): **James Hamlet** at New York City (1850), **Rachel Parker** at Baltimore, **Shadrach** and **Thomas Sims** at Boston (1851), **"Jerry"** at Syracuse (1851), the **Christiana** (Pa.) **affair** (1851), **Anthony Burns** at Boston (1854), and the **Oberlin** rescue (1858).

21 Dec. THE HÜLSEMANN LETTER. While the Hungarian revolution of 1848 was still in progress, the Taylor administration instructed (1849) its special agent, A. Dudley Mann, to give the revolutionary regime discretionary assurance of U.S. recognition. Mann never entered Hungary, but the offended Austrian government instructed Chevalier Hülsemann, its chargé d'affaires in the U.S., to register a firm protest against interference in its affairs. Secretary Webster's reply to Hülsemann's letter defended the U.S. right to take an interest in the European revolutions and asserted that these "events appeared to have their origin in those great ideas of responsible and popular governments on which the American constitutions themselves are founded. . . . The power of this republic, at the present moment, is spread over a region, one of the richest and most fertile on the globe, and of an extent in comparison with which the possessions of the House of Hapsburg are but as a patch on the earth's surface." Webster's letter received support in the U.S. Senate and was endorsed by both parties. U.S. sympathy with the revolutions of 1848 reached its height with the public reception (5 Dec. 1851) accorded **Louis Kossuth,** the Hungarian patriot.

1851

LOPEZ FILIBUSTERING EXPEDITIONS. Southern annexationists were involved in the armed expeditions undertaken against Cuba by the adventurer Gen. Narciso Lopez, a leader of Spanish refugees in the U.S. who claimed that Cuba was ripe for revolt against Spanish oppression. His 1st filibustering venture collapsed after President Taylor issued a proclamation (11 Aug. 1849) and Federal authorities intervened. His 2nd,

manned by many Southern volunteers, failed after a landing was made at Cardenas, Cuba (19 May 1850). A proclamation by President Fillmore (25 Apr.) notwithstanding, Lopez sailed from New Orleans (3 Aug.) and landed (11–12 Aug.) about 60 mi. from Havana. A Cuban uprising failed to materialize. Col. William L. Crittenden (Ky.) and 50 other Southern volunteers were captured (13 Aug.), tried and sentenced by a military court, and executed at Havana (16 Aug.). The news of the executions caused anti-Spanish riots at New Orleans (21 Aug.) and the wrecking of the Spanish consulate there. Lopez was captured (28 Aug.) and publicly garroted at Havana (1 Sept.). Nearly half his 162 supporters sent to Spain as prisoners were Americans. Their release was secured only after Congress voted a $25,000 indemnity for the damage at New Orleans.

1852

20 Mar. Publication in book form of *Uncle Tom's Cabin,* by **Harriet Beecher Stowe** (p. 785), a work originally serialized in the antislavery newspaper, the *National Era* (Washington, D.C.). A sentimental novel directed against the brutality and injustice of slavery, it was inspired by the Fugitive Slave Act of 1850. By mid-1853 some 1,200,000 copies of the work had been published. As a stage play it was first presented 24 Aug. Mrs. Stowe wrote *Key to Uncle Tom's Cabin* (1853) in an attempt to show that she had relied on factual evidence.

"YOUNG AMERICA" was the name given to an amorphous movement that began in the mid-1840's identified with aggressive nationalism, manifest destiny, and sympathy with the European revolutions of 1848. The term is thought to have originated in an address (1845) made by Edwin de Leon. Most of its adherents were Democrats; most prominent, Stephen A. Douglas. Its chief spokesman was George N. Sanders (Ky.); its organ the *Democratic Review*. In 1852 the movement reached its high point when Sanders formulated a program of southward expansion, aid to republican elements in foreign countries, and free trade.

PRESIDENTIAL CAMPAIGN. The Democratic National Convention assembled at Baltimore (1 June) and nominated **Franklin Pierce** (N.H.) for President (49th ballot) and **William R. King** (Ala.) for Vice-President on a platform accepting the finality of the Compromise of 1850, affirming opposition to attempts to renew Congressional agitation of the slavery question, and endorsing the Kentucky and Virginia resolutions. The Whig national convention met at Baltimore (16 June) and nominated Gen. **Winfield Scott** for President (53rd ballot) and **William A. Graham** (N.C.) for Vice-President on a platform accepting the Compromise of 1850, condemning further agitation of the slavery question, affirming states' rights, and supporting river and harbor improvements. The Free-Soil convention met at Pittsburgh (11 Aug.) and nominated **John P. Hale** (N.H.) for President and **George W. Julian** (Ind.) for Vice-President on a platform condemning slavery and the Compromise of 1850, and supporting free homesteads for "landless settlers" and unimpeded entry for immigrants.

2 Nov. PRESIDENTIAL ELECTION. Popular vote: Pierce, 1,601,474; Scott, 1,386,578; Hale, 156,149. Electoral vote: **Pierce,** 254 (27 states); Scott, 42 (4 states). The results indicated the further disintegration of the Whig party (the Unionists of the South having merged with the Democrats) and the decline of the Free-Soilers.

1853

4 Mar. Pierce's inaugural address (the 1st delivered by a President from memory) pledged full support to the Compromise of 1850 and favored new territorial acquisitions by peaceful means.

30 Dec. GADSDEN PURCHASE. James Gadsden (S.C., 1788–1858), named (19 May) to negotiate with Mexico a settlement of a boundary question arising from the Treaty of Guadalupe Hidalgo, signed a treaty whereby Mexico, for a payment of $15 million (later reduced to $10 million), ceded to the U.S. a rectangular strip of territory (area: about 29,640 sq. mi.) in the Mesilla Valley, south of the Gila River. The line established marks the existing boundary with Mexico. The region, which includes the southern part of present-day Arizona and New Mexico, was regarded as a desirable route for a southern railroad to the Pacific. The treaty was ratified on 29 June 1854.

1854

31 Mar. PERRY'S REOPENING OF JAPAN. Since the early 17th century Japan had been virtually isolated from the Western world. U.S. concern about its shipwrecked nationals, and interest in the commercial potentialities of Japan, led the Fillmore administration to authorize (Jan. 1852) a special expedition commanded by Commodore **Matthew C. Perry** (p. 764). He sailed from Norfolk (24 Nov. 1852) and reached Yedo Bay (later Tokyo Bay) on 8 July 1853. In the face of considerable distrust he presented (14 July 1853) Fillmore's letter to representatives of the Japanese emperor and then withdrew to give the government time to reach a decision. To forestall Russian maneuvers he returned to Japan (Feb.) with a fleet of 7 ships, and at a conference near present-day Yokohama (8 Mar.) he gave the authorities American presents (including a miniature telegraph and railroad) which the Japanese accepted as impressive evidence of the civilized arts of the Western world. Perry signed a treaty of peace, friendship, and commerce (**Treaty of Kanagawa,** 31 Mar.) that opened the ports of Shimoda and Hakodate to U.S. trade and made provision for shipwrecked U.S. seamen. Officially promulgated 22 June 1855, the treaty laid the foundation for future U.S. demands, pressed shortly thereafter by **Townsend Harris** (1804–78), appointed (4 Aug. 1855) consul general to Japan, and resulting in agreements signed 18 June 1857 and 29 July 1858. The 1st opened Nagasaki to U.S. commerce; the 2nd opened additional ports, granted Americans residence rights, and established diplomatic representatives at the respective capitals.

30 May. KANSAS-NEBRASKA ACT.
The slavery extension issue was reopened
with the introduction (23 Jan.) by Senator **Stephen A. Douglas** (p. 696) of a
bill for organizing the territories of Kansas and Nebraska. (His 1st bill, introduced 4 Jan., provided for organizing
the single territory of Nebraska; the 2nd
authorized its division at the 40th parallel.) The measure incorporated the
"squatter" or "popular sovereignty"
principle originated by Lewis Cass and
permitted the admission of the territories
with or without slavery. By implication,
the bill repealed the Missouri Compromise (which was expressly repealed in
the bill's final version) and thus formally
established the doctrine of Congressional
nonintervention in the territories. Passed
after 3 mos. of bitter debate, the bill also
provided that in all cases involving slavery, there might be appeal to the territorial courts and the Supreme Court.

The "Appeal of the Independent Democrats," published 24 Jan., condemned
the measure as a "gross violation of a
sacred pledge" and the work of a slaveholders' "plot," and maintained that the
Compromise of 1850 had specifically affirmed the Missouri Compromise. Signers
included Sens. Charles Sumner and Salmon P. Chase. Widely reprinted, the Appeal was partly responsible for the organization of the Republican party.

Among the motives attributed to Douglas for sponsorship of the bill are (1)
his belief in the principle of self-government; (2) his courting of Southern support for Presidential ambitions; (3) his
conviction that by force of geography
and nature, the territories would remain
free soil; (4) his interest in the building
of a transcontinental railroad along a
central route (as opposed to a southern
one advocated by Pierce and Jefferson
Davis) with Chicago as its eastern terminus, impelling him to take steps to
open to settlement the region west of
Iowa.

The Kansas-Nebraska bill passed the
Senate, 37–14 (3 Mar.), and the House,
113–100 (22 May). The Senate (25
May) approved the Clayton amendment
denying voting and office-holding privileges to aliens.

**26 Apr. MASSACHUSETTS EMI-
GRANT AID SOCIETY** organized by
Eli Thayer (1819–99) of Worcester,
Mass., an adherent of "popular sovereignty." Reincorporated (21 Feb. 1855)
as the **New England Emigrant Aid Co.,**
it promoted the settlement of antislavery
groups in Kansas with the ultimate object of making it a free state. It founded
Lawrence and other Free State communities and was active in Kansas until 1857,
bringing some 2,000 settlers there. The
activities of the company led in turn to
the organization of secret societies in
Missouri for the purpose of establishing
slavery in Kansas.

**5 June. CANADIAN RECIPROCITY
TREATY.** The prolonged Anglo-U.S.
dispute over fishing privileges granted by
the Convention of 1818 was settled by
the Reciprocity Treaty of 1854 signed
at Washington. The negotiations were
handled by Secretary Marcy and a special British delegation headed by Lord
Elgin, governor general of Canada. The
agreement gave the U.S. offshore sea-
fishing privileges along the inlets of
Canada, New Brunswick, Nova Scotia,
Prince Edward Island, and several adjacent small islands. The British were
granted fishing privileges along U.S.
shores to the 36th parallel. The reciprocity arrangement provided for the duty-
free entry of many articles, chiefly agricultural commodities. The treaty was to
remain in force for 10 yrs., and thereafter until terminated by either country.
It was abrogated by the U.S. on 17
Mar. 1866:

6–13 July. REPUBLICAN PARTY.
Popular dissatisfaction with the Kansas-
Nebraska Act caused realignment of political forces in the North and West. The
immediate impact was felt in the Northwest, where "anti-Nebraska" men of all
parties united on the common platform
of opposing the extension of slavery into
the territories. A coalition meeting of
Whigs, Free-Soilers, and antislavery
Democrats held at Ripon, Wis. (28
Feb.); recommended the organization of
a new party on this single principle and
suggested the name "Republican." A state
meeting of Michigan citizens held at Jackson (6 July) officially adopted the name.
The Jackson platform called for the re-

peal of the Kansas-Nebraska Act and the Fugitive Slave Law and demanded the abolition of slavery in the District of Columbia. Similar meetings were held (13 July) in Ohio, Wis., Ind., and Vt. By the end of the year the organization had begun to spread throughout the North. Among its leaders were radical antislavery men such as **Charles Sumner** and **George Julian;** Free-Soilers such as **Salmon P. Chase** and **Lyman Trumbull;** and conservative Whigs such as **Edward Bates** and **Orville H. Browning.**

KNOW-NOTHING PARTY. The anti-Catholic and anti-immigrant movement of the 1840's was revived on a national scale after the election of 1852, and by 1854 had emerged as an important political force. Officially called the American party, it was popularly known as the Know-Nothing party because of the password "I don't know" used by members of secret lodges that were active in nearly every state. These bodies stemmed from a clandestine organization, the Order of the Star Spangled Banner, established at New York in 1849. Its rise was symptomatic of the breakup of the 2 major parties over the slavery issue. The party program called for the exclusion of Catholics and foreigners from public office and for a 21-yr. residence for immigrants as qualification for citizenship. Internal divisions over the slavery issue ultimately weakened the party, which reached its zenith in 1854–55. Its disruption came after the election of 1856. The Republicans drew accessions of strength from its ranks.

18 Oct. OSTEND MANIFESTO. When the U.S. merchant vessel *Black Warrior* was seized and condemned by authorities at Havana (28 Feb.) for an error in her manifest, a clamor for war with Spain broke out among expansionists in Congress. **Pierre Soulé** (1802–70), U.S. Minister to Spain, presented a claim for damages (8 Apr.) followed by an ultimatum demanding immediate satisfaction. Secretary Marcy checked Soulé, and in 1855 the U.S. accepted a Spanish apology and reparation.

Soulé was instructed by Marcy (16 Aug.) to meet at Ostend, Belgium, with **John Y. Mason** (1799–1859) and **James Buchanan,** U.S. Minister to France and Great Britain, respectively, for the purpose of shaping a policy on the acquisition of Cuba. The meeting (9 Oct.), with the approval of President Pierce, resulted in the Ostend Manifesto, sent as a confidential diplomatic dispatch from Aix-la-Chapelle (its common designation was of later origin). Declaring Cuba indispensable for the security of slavery, the Ministers recommended that the U.S. should make every effort to buy Cuba; should Spain refuse, "then by every law human and divine, we shall be justified in wresting it from Spain, if we possess the power." The aggressive pronouncement of the document was the work of Soulé. The document brought Marcy's disavowal, and Soulé resigned (17 Dec.). Publication (3 Mar. 1855) of the manifesto aroused Northern feeling and intensified Spanish resentment of the administration's annexationist policy. The newly born Republican party pointed to the manifesto as proof that a Southern-dominated administration had surrendered to pressure for more slave territory; Buchanan's participation recommended him to Southern Democrats.

16 Oct. LINCOLN'S "PEORIA SPEECH." Speaking at Springfield, Ill. (4 Oct.), **Abraham Lincoln,** whose reputation as a politician and lawyer was still confined largely to Illinois, condemned the Kansas-Nebraska Act. The speech, delivered again at Peoria (16 Oct.), was Lincoln's 1st public denunciation of slavery. He denied that the Kansas-Nebraska Act was the result of a slaveholders' conspiracy. "I have no prejudice against the Southern people. . . . I surely will not blame them for not doing what I should not know how to do myself." He acknowledged the constitutional rights of the Southerners; with careful qualification favored gradual emancipation; and supported a fair and practical Fugitive Slave Law, but opposed slavery in free territory.

1855

"KANSAS QUESTION." The opening of Kansas to settlement under the "popular sovereignty" formula put that principle to a severe test. With Congressional nonintervention a declared policy, control of the territorial government became a vital necessity. Armed contests between proslavery and antislavery settlers converted Kansas into a cockpit of civil war.

Proslavery Legislature. Andrew H. Reeder (Pa.), 1st territorial governor of Kansas, was appointed in June 1854. The election of **John W. Whitfield**, the proslavery candidate, as territorial delegate (29 Nov. 1854) was accompanied by fraud and violence, most of it the work of about 1,700 armed men from western Missouri. Like methods were used by some 5,000 Missouri "Border Ruffians" in the election (30 Mar.) of a territorial legislature. Under armed intimidation, Reeder refused to declare the election fraudulent, and Kansas was organized with a proslavery legislature, which disregarded his conciliatory plea when it convened (2 July) at Pawnee and later (16 July) at Shawnee Mission, and enacted proslavery statutes providing severe penalties for antislavery agitation and authorizing a test oath for office holders.

In convention at Big Springs (5 Sept.) the antislavery colonists repudiated the territorial legislature as illegal and asked admission to the Union under a free state constitution. Mass conventions (Sept.–Oct.) organized a Free State party. Arms poured in from the North. **James H. Lane** (Ind.) was appointed military commander of the Free State forces.

Antislavery Legislature. The **Topeka Constitution,** drawn up by a Free State convention (23 Oct.–2 Nov.), prohibited slavery. That the Free State colonists were not abolitionists was indicated by the ordinance prohibiting entry of Negroes which was submitted to popular vote together with the constitution. Both were adopted (15 Dec.) and a Free State governor and legislature were elected (15 Jan. 1856). Kansas now had dual government.

Meanwhile Reeder had been removed from office (31 July), ostensibly because of his implication in land speculation but actually because of his opposition to the proslavery legislature. He was succeeded by **Wilson Shannon** (Ohio), a proslavery man (arrived in Kansas 3 Sept.). On 9 Oct. Reeder was elected Congressional delegate from Kansas Territory by the Free State men, while on 1 Oct. Whitfield had been reelected by proslavery men.

The so-called **"Wakarusa War"** (26 Nov.–7 Dec.), limited to a few shootings and brawls along the Wakarusa River near Lawrence, brought about 1,500 "Border Ruffians" into Kansas, who refrained from attacking Lawrence when they found that the town was heavily defended by Free State settlers. The "war" was terminated by the intervention of Gov. Shannon.

WALKER'S FILIBUSTERING EXPEDITIONS. American filibustering in the Caribbean region was climaxed by the expeditions against Nicaragua (1855–57) led by the military adventurer **William Walker** (1824–60). Although his incursions received some support in the South, they were widely misinterpreted in the North as part of a slaveholders' "plot" to extend slavery southward. Actually, Walker was backed by U.S. isthmian-transit interests (the Accessory Transit Co.).

Walker, who had led an unsuccessful filibustering expedition against Lower California (1853), exploited a Civil War in Nicaragua to his own end, subjugated the divided country (June–Oct. 1855), and set himself up as dictator. Though President Pierce issued a proclamation (8 Dec.) against the invasion of Nicaragua, his reception of Walker's emissary (14 May 1856) amounted to virtual recognition. Walker became President (July 1856) and issued a decree opening Nicaragua to slavery. His downfall was brought about by **Cornelius Vanderbilt** (now in control of Accessory Transit Co.), who promoted the formation of a coalition of neighboring republics that ousted Walker, who surrendered 1 May 1857 to the U.S. naval commander.

Acclaimed in the South as a hero, Walker raised a new expedition and landed (25 Nov. 1857) at Greytown, at the mouth of the San Juan River. By this time Walker had seriously embarrassed U.S. isthmian policy. His expedition was broken up by the U.S. Navy. Again, in Aug. 1860, he landed at Honduras at the head of a filibustering expedition, was captured, courtmartialed, and executed (12 Sept.).

1856

"BLEEDING KANSAS." In a special message to Congress (24 Jan.) Pierce condemned the Topeka government as an act of rebellion and in effect recognized the proslavery legislature. Although he issued (11 Feb.) a proclamation warning both Free State men and "Border Ruffians" to disperse, it was now clear that Pierce was committed to support of the proslavery element in Kansas.

21 May–15 Sept. Civil War. Actual civil war broke out in Kansas in the late spring of 1856, by which time the Free State party had received from the East fresh shipments of arms (the Sharps rifles popularly known as "Beecher's Bibles"). On 21 May, Lawrence was taken and sacked, as "Border Ruffians" joined Kansas proslavery men (including Col. Jefferson Buford's company and the Kickapoo Rangers) in burning down the Free State Hotel, pillaging many homes, and destroying the offices and presses of *The Herald of Freedom* and *The Kansas Free State*. One man was killed. Exaggerated accounts of the Lawrence affair inflamed Northern antislavery sentiment.

In retaliation for proslavery depredations, the fanatical **John Brown** (1800–59), with 6 companions (4 of them his sons), carried out the Pottawatomie massacre on the night of 24–25 May with midnight executions of 5 proslavery colonists who lived near Dutch Henry's Crossing at Pottawatomie Creek. Free State men disavowed this act of terrorism, but the incident raised feeling to a pitch and caused both parties to alert their military forces.

Governor Shannon issued a proclamation (4 June) warning all irregular armed bodies to disperse. The Free State party seized Franklin (13 Aug.), a proslavery stronghold. About 300 proslavery men attacked the town of Osawatomie (30 Aug.), which was defended by John Brown and about 40 other Free State men, drove off their opponents, and pillaged the settlement. Guerrilla warfare was now raging throughout the territory. The total loss (Nov. 1855–Dec. 1856) was estimated at 200 killed and $2 million in property destroyed.

Shannon resigned as governor (18 Aug.) and was replaced by Daniel Woodson, a proslavery man who became acting governor. Woodson issued a proclamation (25 Aug.) declaring Kansas in a state of open insurrection and called out the proslavery militia. **John W. Geary** (Pa.), appointed territorial governor by Pierce, assumed his official duties on 11 Sept. With the aid of Federal troops, Geary intercepted (15 Sept.) an army of 2,500 "Border Ruffians" who were marching on Lawrence and persuaded them to return to their homes. By his intervention, Geary brought temporary peace to Kansas.

Congressional Reaction. The Topeka Legislature adopted (4 Mar.) a memorial requesting statehood and elected Lane and Reeder U.S. senators. Douglas introduced (17 Mar.) an enabling act for Kansas, providing for the election of a constitutional convention and the formation of a state government. He denounced the Topeka government and the New England Emigrant Aid Co. as lawless bodies.

The Congressional opposition to Pierce and Douglas supported the admission of Kansas under the Topeka constitution. An amendment to the Douglas bill was formulated by Robert Toombs (Ga.). Its substance provided for a free and open election for a constitutional convention. Introduced on 30 June, the Toombs amendment was approved in the Senate, 33–12 (2 July), but never considered in the House.

The House (19 Mar.) appointed a special 3-man committee to investigate the conduct of the Kansas elections. Its report, confirming the charges of fraud and violence, provided material for Republican electioneering. The House passed a bill (3 July) to admit Kansas under the Topeka constitution, but the measure was quashed in the Senate. The House (1 Aug.) refused to seat either the proslavery or Free State territorial delegate.

The Republicans held up an army appropriation bill (18 Aug.) by attaching a rider forbidding the use of the army in aid of the proslavery Kansas legislature. The bill was finally passed (30 Aug.) without the Kansas rider only after an extra session of Congress had been called.

When Congress adjourned (30 Aug.), Kansas still had no settled government. The Democrats charged that the Republicans had deliberately left "Bleeding Kansas" to anarchy in order that they might exploit a catch phrase in the approaching elections.

19–20 May. "The Crime Against Kansas." During the Congressional debates on Kansas, Sen. Charles Sumner delivered a speech that later became known by the title, "The Crime Against Kansas." It was a bitter denunciation of the "Slave Oligarchy" and its "rape" of Kansas. Sumner's tirade included coarse and insulting aspersions upon the character of several senators, particularly the absent Andrew P. Butler (S.C.). In retaliation, Representative Preston S. Brooks (S.C.), Butler's nephew, assaulted Sumner as the latter sat at his desk in the Senate chamber (22 May). Sumner collapsed under the heavy blows of a cane. House attempts to expel or censure Brooks failed. His act brought general approval throughout the South. Brooks resigned his seat (14 July) and was unanimously reelected by his district. In the North, news of the assault created widespread indignation that became even more inflamed when it was reported that Lawrence had been pillaged. The Brooks-Sumner affair was condemned as a gross violation of liberty of speech. Except for a single day in Feb. 1857, Sumner did not again attend Congressional sessions until Dec. 1859. During that time his empty chair in the Senate remained a symbol of Northern opinion of the attack upon him.

PRESIDENTIAL CAMPAIGN. The National Convention of the American (Know-Nothing) party met at Philadelphia (22 Feb.) and nominated **Millard Fillmore** (N.Y.) for President and **Andrew J. Donelson** (Tenn.) for Vice-President on a nativist platform. These candidates were also nominated by the Whig National Convention that met at Baltimore (17 Sept.) and adopted a platform eschewing specific planks and warning against the sectionalization of parties.

The Democratic National Convention at Cincinnati (2 June) nominated **James Buchanan** (Pa.) for President on the 17th ballot (Pierce and Douglas being rejected because of their close association with the Kansas issue) and **John C. Breckinridge** (Ky.) for Vice-President. The Democratic platform affirmed the Compromise of 1850 and supported the Kansas-Nebraska Act as "the only sound and safe solution of the slavery question."

The Republican National Convention met at Philadelphia (17 June) and unanimously nominated Col. **John C. Frémont** (Calif.) for President and **William L. Dayton** (N.J.) for Vice-President on a platform upholding Congressional authority to control slavery in the territories. Other planks condemned the Ostend Manifesto and favored a railroad to the Pacific and the admission of Kansas as a free state.

The chief campaign issue was "Bleeding Kansas," as Republican electioneers called it. The American party split on the slavery issue and in the Northeast supported the Republicans. The Democrats and Fillmore supporters attacked the "Black Republicans" as a sectional threat to the Union.

4 Nov. PRESIDENTIAL ELECTION. Popular vote: Buchanan, 1,838,169; Frémont, 1,335,264; Fillmore, 874,534. Electoral vote (counted 11 Feb. 1857): Buchanan, 174 (14 slave and 5 free states); Frémont, 114 (11 free states); Fillmore, 8 (1 slave state, Md.). The election results forecast the speedy demise of the Whig organization and the hardening of sectional lines.

1857

4 Mar. Buchanan's inaugural address condemned the slavery agitation and supported the policy of noninterference with slavery in the states and "popular sovereignty" in the territories.

6 Mar. DRED SCOTT DECISION. Dred Scott, a Negro slave and the household servant of Dr. John Emerson, an army surgeon, was taken (1834) by his master from St. Louis, Mo., to Rock Island, Ill. (where slavery had been forbidden by the Ordinance of 1787), and later to Fort Snelling, in Wisconsin Territory (where slavery was prohibited by the Missouri Compromise). Scott remained on free soil during most of the period 1834–38.

In 1846 Scott sued for his liberty in the Missouri courts, holding that he had become free because of his stay in a free state and free territory. A lower court's judgment in favor of Scott was overruled (1852) by the state supreme court, which had previously ruled that under such circumstances a slave became free upon his return to Missouri. The case was appealed to the Federal district court and finally to the Supreme Court of the U.S. (*Dred Scott* v. *Sandford*, 19 Howard 393). Scott's nominal owner at this time was John F. A. Sanford of New York (whose name is misspelled in the official reports).

The case involved three leading issues: (1) whether Scott was a citizen of the state of Missouri and thus entitled to sue in the Federal courts; (2) whether his temporary stay on free soil had given him a title to freedom that was still valid upon his return to the slave state of Missouri; and (3) the constitutionality of the Missouri Compromise, whose prohibition of slavery applied to Wisconsin Territory.

Each of the justices handed down a separate opinion (that of Chief Justice Roger B. Taney is customarily cited for the majority). The majority held that Scott (and hence all Negro slaves or their descendants) was not a citizen of the U.S. or the state of Missouri, and thus was not entitled to sue in the Federal courts (on this point, only 3 justices explicitly denied such citizenship, while only 2 affirmed it). Having refused jurisdiction, the majority passed on other issues: (1) Scott's temporary residence in free territory had not made him free upon his return to Missouri, since his status was determined by the laws of the state in which he resided when the question of his freedom was raised (on this point, the decision was 6 to 3); and (2) the Missouri Compromise was unconstitutional on the ground that under the 5th Amendment Congress was prohibited from depriving persons of their property without due process of law (on this point, the decision was 6 to 3), a principle first enunciated as regards a state

law in *Wynehamer* v. *The People*, 13 N.Y. 378 (1856).

The dissenting opinions of Justices John McLean and Benjamin R. Curtis, both of whom are generally held responsible for introducing the thorny issue of the Missouri Compromise, maintained that free Negroes were citizens of the U.S. and that Congress was constitutionally empowered (Art. IV, Sect. 3) to regulate slavery in the territories. Curtis' opinion was subsequently used by Republican and abolitionist elements as one of their chief grounds for attacking the Court decision.

Northern denunciation of the decision included charges of "conspiracy." Opponents pointed to the fact that Buchanan's inaugural had predicted that the slavery controversy would be "speedily and finally settled" by the Court. It has been established that Justices Robert C. Grier and John Catron violated judicial ethics in confidentially advising the President as to the intention of the Court; there is no substance to the charge of collusion. The decision, 1st since *Marbury* v. *Madison* (1803) in which the Court declared an act of Congress unconstitutional, lowered the Court's prestige among Northerners and widened the sectional cleavage.

19 Oct.–21 Dec. LECOMPTON CONSTITUTION. In Kansas, Gov. Geary's recommendations for a thorough revamping of the laws to assure free elections and genuine self-government were ignored by the proslavery legislature. Meeting at Lecompton (12 Jan.–14 Feb.), the legislature called for a census enumeration (Mar.) and an election (15 June) for delegates to a constitutional convention. No provision was made for submitting the constitution to a popular vote. Geary, whose sympathy with the proslavery party had been replaced by a desire for impartial justice, vetoed the bill, which was promptly passed over his objection. Geary's efforts to follow a nonpartisan course in Kansas failed to secure the support of the Pierce administration. He resigned (4 Mar.) and was succeeded (26 Mar.) by a Buchanan appointee, Robert J. Walker (Miss.).

Walker's inaugural address (26 May) made a plea for cooperation and pledged that any constitution adopted would be submitted to a fair vote. A Free State convention met at Topeka (15 July), but Walker finally persuaded its leaders to abandon their refusal to participate in the election of a new legislature. Walker's policy brought from the South demands that any constitution drawn up by the proslavery convention should go into force without being submitted to the people.

The territorial elections were held (5 Oct.) under fairly strict supervision. Walker and the territorial secretary, Frederick P. Stanton (Tenn.), threw out thousands of fraudulent votes cast by the proslavery party. The final results gave the Free State party a decisive majority in both houses of the legislature.

The Lecompton convention (19 Oct.– 8 Nov.) recognized that a proslavery constitution would be rejected if submitted to a fair vote. Instead of arranging to place the constitution as a whole before the people, the convention drafted a special article on slavery which alone was to be submitted to a popular vote. The article guaranteed the right of property in slaves. Should it be rejected (the "constitution without slavery"), slavery would exist "no longer," but the right of property in slaves already in the territory would not be abolished. This arrangement gave the proslavery party an obvious advantage; in addition, the elections were to be conducted by officials named by the convention.

The Lecompton convention was denounced throughout the North. Walker, opposed to the Lecompton proposal, went to Washington to place the question before the President. Buchanan was anxious to preserve party unity and harmony; moreover, he was under the influence of his pro-Southern Cabinet. He decided to reverse his earlier pledge to Walker, and upheld the Lecompton convention. Walker resigned (17 Dec.). Buchanan's fateful step precipitated a party crisis by placing Douglas (who had come out against the Lecompton constitution, 9 Dec.) in open opposition, and helped to bring on the disruption of the Democratic party.

The vote on the Lecompton constitution was held on 21 Dec. Free State men and others among its opponents refused to participate. Results: for the constitution with slavery, 6,226 (of these, 2,720 were later shown to be fraudulent); for the constitution without slavery, 569.

Rejection. The Free State party induced Stanton, now acting governor, to convene the territorial legislature on 7 Dec., in advance of its scheduled date. The legislature called another election, permitting unequivocal voting for or against the Lecompton constitution. The administration punished Stanton by removing him from office. The Kansas election was held on 4 Jan. 1858. Results: for the constitution with slavery, 138; for the constitution without slavery, 24; against the constitution, 10,226.

24 Aug. PANIC OF 1857 (also pp. 537, 550). The failure of the New York City branch of the Ohio Life Insurance and Trust Company precipitated a commercial and financial panic.

"THE IMPENDING CRISIS." *The Impending Crisis of the South: How to Meet It,* by Hinton Rowan Helper (a native of N.C.), published at New York in mid-1857, sought to prove by statistics (drawn largely from the Census of 1850) that slavery had degraded and impoverished broad sections of Southern whites. A compressed version of the book (the *Compendium*) was endorsed by 68 House Republicans (1859) and 100,000 copies distributed as electioneering material. The South banned the book on the ground that it was insurrectionary. In Dec. 1859, John Sherman (Ohio) was denied the House Speakership because of his endorsement of the work. The Southern outcry against "Helperism" brought the publication of several rejoinders, among them *Helper's Impending Crisis Dissected,* by Samuel M. Wolfe.

1858

DOUGLAS AND LECOMPTON. In support of the Southern extremist position, President Buchanan submitted the Lecompton constitution to Congress (2 Feb.), recommending the admission of Kansas as a slave state. His policy stirred Douglas to open revolt. Taking his stand on principle, Douglas condemned the Lecompton constitution (3 Feb.) as a violation of "popular sovereignty" and a mockery of justice. The executive patronage was brought to bear against Douglas and his supporters. The Senate, 33–25 (23 Mar.), voted to admit Kansas under the Lecompton constitution.

1 Apr. Crittenden-Montgomery Amendment, providing for resubmission of the constitution to popular vote, passed the House, 120–112.

4 May. English Bill, an administration compromise measure, sponsored by William H. English (Ind.), a moderate Democrat, was reported to both houses on 23 Apr. Designed to quell party upheaval, the English bill provided for a popular vote on the Lecompton constitution as a whole. In the event of ratification Kansas was assured of *c.*4 million acres of public land grants (Lecomptonites had requested 23½ million acres) and 5 per cent of the net proceeds from about 2 million acres to be sold by the government in July. Rejection would delay admission to the Union until a census indicated that Kansas had a population (about 90,000) required for a Congressional representative. By winning the votes of 9 anti-Lecompton Democrats, the compromise broke the House deadlock. In the Senate, Douglas wavered, but finally opposed the measure. On 30 Apr. the English bill passed the House, 112–103, and the Senate, 31–22.

16 June. "A HOUSE DIVIDED." Abraham Lincoln (p. 741), whose political reputation was still confined largely to the Northwest, in a speech before the Republican state convention at Springfield that nominated him for U.S. senator, took a radical stand on the institution of slavery, but scrupulously refrained from criticizing slaveholders. Lincoln asserted that under the Kansas-Nebraska Act the slavery agitation "has not only not ceased, but has constantly augmented. In my opinion, it will not cease until a crisis shall have been reached and passed. 'A house divided against itself cannot stand.' I believe this government cannot endure permanently half slave and half free. I do not expect the Union to be dissolved; I do not expect the house to fall; but I do expect it will cease to be

divided. It will become all one thing, or all the other." Both as phrase and concept, the Biblical "house divided" passage was not new in the slavery controversy. It had been used, e.g., by Edmund Quincy, Theodore Parker, and the New York *Tribune.*

2 Aug. Lecompton Constitution rejected by Kansas voters (in favor, 1,926; against, 11,812). The decision to remain in territorial status brought the disturbances virtually to an end. Under the Dred Scott decision slavery was legal in Kansas; practically, it was excluded because of free soil domination. Kansas did not enter the union until 29 Jan. 1861, when it was admitted under the free state **Wyandotte Constitution** (ratified 4 Oct. 1859). Political results of the Kansas controversy (1) gave the Republicans a powerful campaign issue; (2) encouraged Southern extremists; (3) lost Buchanan the support of Northern Democrats; and, by way of the Douglas-Buchanan feud, (4) disrupted the Democratic party.

21 Aug.–15 Oct. LINCOLN-DOUGLAS DEBATES. On 24 July Lincoln challenged Douglas, his opponent in the Illinois senatorial race, to a series of joint debates. Douglas accepted. Seven debates were held during the course of a statewide campaign: Ottawa (21 Aug.), Freeport (27 Aug.), Jonesboro (15 Sept.), Charleston (18 Sept.), Galesburg (7 Oct.), Quincy (13 Oct.), and Alton (15 Oct.). The debates covered the ground of the slavery controversy and its impact on politics, law, and government. From them dates Lincoln's emergence as a national figure.

The most memorable debate was held at Freeport, where Lincoln asked Douglas how he could reconcile the doctrine of "popular sovereignty" with the Dred Scott decision. The question evoked from Douglas his formulation of what became known as the "**Freeport doctrine**": the people of a territory could, by lawful means, exclude slavery prior to the formation of a state constitution. The right to admit or bar slavery existed despite the Dred Scott decision, "for the reason that slavery cannot exist a day or an hour anywhere, unless it is supported by local police regulations," which could only be established by the local legislature. The "Freeport doctrine" provoked a storm of Southern criticism, and was instrumental in depriving Douglas of Southern backing for the Presidential nomination in 1860.

The debates as a whole illuminated the sharp difference between Lincoln and Douglas: where Lincoln regarded slavery as "a moral, a social, and a political wrong" (Quincy, 13 Oct., although he avoided a radical position, and at Charleston rejected Negro equality), Douglas evaded the moral issue. Lincoln lost the election by a narrow margin, winning the larger popular vote but failing to carry the legislature, where the vote was 54–41.

It was during this campaign, between the 2nd and 3rd debates, that Lincoln is supposed to have said at Clinton (2 Sept.): "You can fool all of the people some of the time, and some of the people all of the time, but you cannot fool all of the people all the time."

25 Oct. "IRREPRESSIBLE CONFLICT." Speaking at Rochester, N.Y., Sen. William H. Seward, at that time the leading contender for the Republican Presidential nomination, delivered a radical pronouncement on the sectional controversy: "It is an irrepressible conflict between opposing and enduring forces, and it means that the United States must and will, sooner or later, become either entirely a slaveholding nation or entirely a free-labor nation."

REPUBLICAN SUCCESS. The results of the autumn elections indicated the rapidly growing strength of the Republican party. The chief campaign issue was the Lecompton constitution. In some areas the Republicans also stressed the protective tariff (Pa., N.J., and New England) and the homestead policy (Western states). Except for Illinois (where the prestige of Douglas was an important factor) and Indiana, every Northern state election was carried by the Republicans, even Buchanan's own state, Pa. In New York, the Republicans and antiadministration Democrats won 29 of the 33 Congressional seats. In all, the Republicans gained 18 seats in the Congressional elections. With a dozen anti-Lecompton Democrats in the House, the administration lost control of that body.

1859

16–18 Oct. JOHN BROWN'S RAID. Obtaining money from a number of New England and N.Y. abolitionists (including Theodore Parker, Thomas W. Higginson, Samuel G. Howe, and Gerrit Smith), John Brown formulated a plan for instigating a slave insurrection in Va., establishing a free state in the southern Appalachians, and spreading a servile rebellion southward. Collecting arms and equipment at the Kennedy farm in Md., across the Potomac from Harper's Ferry, Va., he led 18 of the 21 men in his band (including 5 Negroes) in an attack on Harper's Ferry. They seized the Federal arsenal and armory and held some of the local citizenry as hostages. No slaves came to the aid of the attackers. After 2 days of battle, Brown and his surviving followers were taken prisoner by a force of U.S. marines commanded by Col. Robert E. Lee.

25 Oct.–2 Dec. Treason Trial. Brown was indicted for treason against the state of Va. and criminal conspiracy to incite a slave insurrection. He was tried (25–31 Oct.) at Charles Town, Va., convicted, and hanged (2 Dec.). Four of his band were hanged on 16 Dec.; 2 others on 16 Mar. 1860. Brown's raid spread alarm throughout the South, which fixed responsibility not only on the abolitionists but also on the "Black Republicans." Conservative Northerners deplored the raid, but antislavery groups mourned Brown as a hero and a martyr.

AFRICAN SLAVE TRADE. The **Southern Commercial Convention** at Vicksburg, Miss. (9–19 May), urged the repeal of all laws prohibiting the foreign slave trade. This move was in accord with the growing Southern view that the Federal government's sole relation to slavery should be that of positive protection (on this score, Southern extremists were also demanding a Federal slave code for the territories). Some Southerners, notably Jefferson Davis and William L. Yancey, condemned the slave importation act of 1820 as unconstitutional and called for its repeal.

The Buchanan administration was on the whole firmly opposed to the foreign slave trade. It increased the naval patrols off the African coast. In his message to Congress (19 Dec.), Buchanan declared that all lawful means would be employed to suppress the illicit traffic. But the administration also ordered that U.S. merchant ships were to be protected against detention or search, thus giving them immunity to the more effective British patrols. Under such circumstances, there was little recourse against non-American vessels which used the U.S. flag fraudulently.

1860

2 Feb. DAVIS RESOLUTIONS. The program of the Southern extremists was embodied in the set of resolutions introduced in the Senate by **Jefferson Davis** (p. 693), asserting that (1) no state had a right to interfere with the domestic institutions of other states; (2) any attack on slavery within the slave states was a violation of the Constitution; (3) it was the duty of the Senate to oppose all discriminatory measures against persons or property in the territories; (4) neither Congress nor a territorial legislature was in any way empowered to impair the right to hold slaves in the territories, and the Federal government should extend all needful protection (i.e., a slave code) to slavery in the territories; (5) the territories might not decide on the question of slavery until admission to the Union; and (6) all state legislation interfering with the recovery of fugitive slaves was inimical to the constitutional compact. The resolutions, adopted 24 May, touched off an extensive Senate debate on the constitutional and political aspects of the slavery controversy, and widened the breach between the Northern and Southern wings of the Democratic party.

SECESSION THREATS. In the winter and spring of 1860 political leaders and state legislatures in the Lower South openly avowed the right of secession and the idea of Southern solidarity.

The more radical resolutions were adopted in S.C. and Miss.; in these states and a few others, the legislatures passed appropriations for raising military forces. Many of the states (e.g., Ala. and Fla.) asserted that the election of a "Black Republican" President would be considered just cause for dissolving the Union.

Prominent among the leaders who began an exchange of opinion on a course of future action was Gov. **William H. Gist** (S.C., 1807–74). However, the states of the Upper South (notably Virginia) did not support Gist's project for a convention on Southern rights. At this time the overwhelming mass of opinion in the Upper South believed that Southern grievances could be remedied within the Union. Even in the Lower South (particularly Ga.) sentiment was divided.

27 Feb. LINCOLN'S COOPER UNION SPEECH. Appearing before a distinguished audience at Cooper Union in New York City, Abraham Lincoln, still a virtual stranger to Eastern audiences, delivered a carefully weighed speech refuting Douglas' "popular sovereignty" doctrine and examining Southern attitudes toward the North and the Republican party. Lincoln condemned Northern extremism and made an appeal for sectional understanding, but did not minimize the gravity of Southern disunionist threats and indicated that no compromise with principle on the slavery extension issue was possible.

PRESIDENTIAL CAMPAIGN. The disruption of the Democratic party was formalized at the national nominating convention at Charleston, S.C. (23 Apr.). The Southern Democrats, now under the dominant influence of the radicals, insisted on a platform supporting positive protection to slavery in the territories. The Douglas Democrats reaffirmed the party platform of 1856 approving Congressional nonintervention, abiding by Supreme Court decisions, and acquiring Cuba. When the Douglas forces carried the convention, the delegations of 8 Southern states withdrew to meet in a separate convention. The Charleston convention adjourned (3 May), having failed to agree on a nominee after 57 ballots. The Democrats reassembled at Baltimore (18 June) and, following another secession of Southern delegates, nominated **Stephen A. Douglas** (Ill.) for President (2nd ballot) and **Herschel V. Johnson** (Ga.) for Vice-President.

The Charleston seceders, after meeting at Richmond (11 June), convened at Baltimore (28 June) and nominated **John C. Breckinridge** (Ky.) for President and **Joseph Lane** (Ore.) for Vice-President on a platform supporting slavery in the territories, the admission of states into the Union on an equal footing with the rest, and the acquisition of Cuba.

The remnants of the Whig and American parties convened at Baltimore (9 May) and established the Constitutional Union party, nominating **John Bell** (Tenn.) for President and **Edward Everett** (Mass.) for Vice-President on a platform condemning sectional parties and upholding "the Constitution of the country, the Union of the States and the enforcement of the laws."

The Republican National Convention met at Chicago (16 May) and nominated **Abraham Lincoln** (Ill.) for President (3rd ballot) after William H. Seward (N.Y.) had led on the first two ballots. Lincoln's "availability," as opposed to Seward's long political career and his identification with antislavery radicalism, was a prime factor in winning the nomination. **Hannibal Hamlin** (Me.) was chosen for Vice-President.

The skillfully drawn Republican platform was calculated to win support in the East as well as the West, from conservatives as well as radicals. It reaffirmed the principles of the Declaration of Independence, the Wilmot Proviso, and the right of each state to control its domestic institutions. It supported internal improvements, a railroad to the Pacific, a homestead law, and a liberal immigration policy. Its reference to a tariff adjustment which would "encourage the development of the industrial interests of the whole country" was interpreted as support of a protective tariff (a leading issue in the doubtful states of Pa. and N.J.). The platform condemned attempts to reopen the African slave trade and denied the authority of Congress or a territorial legislature to give legal status to slavery in the territories.

6 Nov. PRESIDENTIAL ELECTION. The division among his opponents made Lincoln's election almost certain. The state elections (Sept.–Oct.), bringing Republican victories in Me., Vt., Ind., and Pa., indicated the impending result. Popular vote: **Lincoln**, 1,866,352; **Douglas**, 1,375,157; **Breckinridge**, 847,953; **Bell**, 589,581. The electoral vote (Lincoln failing to secure a single Southern vote) demonstrated the sectional character of the contest: **Lincoln**, 180 (carrying 18 free states); **Breckinridge**, 72 (carrying 11 slave states); **Bell**, 39 (carrying 3 border slave states); **Douglas**, 12 (carrying Mo., and 3 N.J. votes). Had the Lincoln opposition combined on a fusion ticket (attempted unsuccessfully in several states), it would have changed the result only in N.J., Calif., and Ore. for a total of 11 electoral votes. Lincoln would still have had 169, a clear majority.

THE CIVIL
WAR AND RECONSTRUCTION, 1861–77

1860, 13 Nov.–24 Dec. SOUTH CARO-LINA SECESSION CRISIS. On news of Lincoln's election the South Carolina legislature by unanimous vote called for a state convention, which met at Columbia and passed (20 Dec.) without a dissenting vote an ordinance declaring that "the union now subsisting between South Carolina and the other States, under the name of the 'United States of America,' is hereby dissolved." The convention then issued (24 Dec.) a "Declaration of Immediate Causes" reiterating the arguments for state sovereignty and justifying secession on grounds of the North's long attack on slavery, the accession to power of a sectional party, and the election of a President "whose opinions and purposes are hostile to slavery."

1861

9 Jan.–1 Feb. EXTENSION OF SE-CESSION. South Carolina was followed by the other 10 states which ultimately formed the Confederate States of America. The 7 states of the Lower South (S.C., 20 Dec.; Miss., 9 Jan.; Fla., 10 Jan.; Ala., 11 Jan.; Ga., 19 Jan.; La., 26 Jan.; and Tex., 1 Feb.) grounded secession on Northern aggression against their "domestic institutions." The 4 states of the Upper South (Va., Ark., Tenn., and N.C.), though not seceding at this time, warned they would oppose any attempt of the Federal government to coerce a state. In only 3 states (Tex., Va., and Tenn.) were the ordinances of secession submitted to the voters for ratification; elsewhere public opinion was registered through the election of delegates to state conventions. The votes in these 3 states: Tex. (23 Feb.), 34,794

for, 11,255 against; Va. (23 May), 96,750 for, 32,134 against; Tenn. (8 June) 104,913 for, 47,238 against (on 9 Feb. a call to consider secession was rejected, 68,282 to 59,449), but in every case the referenda were held after the state governments had already committed themselves to the Confederacy. Sizable Unionist minorities existed in some areas (notably N.C., Va., and Tenn.), and some outstanding Southern leaders opposed secession, including **Alexander H. Stephens** (p. 782, in a speech as late as 14 Nov. 1860), **Benjamin H. Hill** (1823–82), and **Herschel V. Johnson** (1812–80) of Ga.; **Benjamin F. Perry** of S.C.; and Gov. **Sam Houston** of Tex.

BUCHANAN'S LAST DAYS. President Buchanan in his message to Congress (3 Dec. 1860) recognized the grievances of the slave states, deprecated the disruption of the Union, but announced the impotence of the Federal government to prevent secession by force (relying upon an opinion of Attorney General Jeremiah S. Black). On 18 Dec. Senator **John J. Crittenden** (Ky., 1787–1863) introduced a peace resolution which would have recognized slavery in territories south of 36°30'. This was unacceptable to Lincoln, who, through Thurlow Weed, advised its rejection. A Senate committee of 13 (appointed 20 Dec. 1860 to consider the Crittenden proposal) disagreed 31 Dec.

4 Feb. MONTGOMERY CONVENTION AND CONFEDERATE CONSTITUTION. Motivated by Southern nationalism and the need for united action, the seceding states called a convention which met at Montgomery, Ala., framed a constitution, and set up a provisional government (8 Feb.). The Confederate Constitution resembled the U.S. Constitution, with significant differences. It stressed "the sovereign and independent character" of each state while establishing a federal government and obliging state officers to swear to support the new constitution, which, together with the laws and treaties, was declared "the supreme law of the land." No specific provision was included for state secession, but that right was implied. Several clauses recognized and protected slavery, but Art. 1, cl. 1, sect. 9 prohibited "the importation of negroes of the African race from any foreign country." This clause was inserted to conciliate British and French opinion. The President was empowered to disapprove of specific appropriations in a bill which he signed.

4 Feb. PEACE CONVENTION, called at the urging of the Va. Assembly, met in Washington behind closed doors, with ex-President John Tyler as its chairman. Border and Northern states were represented as well as the South. On 23 Feb. the delegates called on President-elect Lincoln for a frank exchange of views. The convention failed to agree upon an acceptable compromise to save the Union.

9 Feb. JEFFERSON DAVIS (p. 693) elected provisional President of the Confederacy; **Alexander H. Stephens** provisional Vice-President; inaugurated 18 Feb. Until regular elections were held (6 Nov. 1861) the Montgomery convention acted as a provisional Congress.

SEIZURE OF FEDERAL FORTS AND ARSENALS. On 28 Dec. South Carolina commissioners presented demands on President Buchanan for removal of U.S. troops from Charleston Harbor and delivery of forts within the state. Buchanan refused (31 Dec.), but on 30 Dec. South Carolina troops seized the U.S. arsenal at Charleston. Other seizures: 3 Jan., Ft. Pulaski by Georgia state troops; 4 Jan., Mt. Vernon arsenal and 5 Jan., Ft. Morgan and Ft. Gaines by Alabama troops; 6 Jan., Apalachicola arsenal by Florida troops; 10 Jan., Baton Rouge arsenal and barracks by Louisiana troops; 24 Jan., Augusta arsenal by Georgia troops; 8 Feb., Little Rock ar-

senal by Arkansas troops; 16 Feb., San Antonio arsenal by Texas troops. On 18 Feb. Gen. David E. Twiggs surrendered to Texas U.S. military posts in that state.

Fort Sumter. On 26 Dec. Maj. **Robert Anderson** (1805–71), commander of U.S. troops in Charleston Harbor, withdrew his garrison from Ft. Moultrie to the more formidable Ft. Sumter. On 5 Jan. President Buchanan ordered the dispatch to Sumter of the *Star of the West,* an unarmed ship with reinforcements and provisions. But on 9 Jan. the ship was repulsed with fire from South Carolina shore batteries and returned to New York. Buchanan's policy was to collect public revenues and protect public property "so far as . . . practicable under existing laws."

11–23 Feb. LINCOLN'S JOURNEY TO WASHINGTON. President-elect Lincoln took leave (11 Feb.) from his neighbors in Springfield, "not knowing when or whether I ever may return, with a task before me greater than that which rested upon Washington," and began his journey to the Capital. In brief speeches en route (Indianapolis, Cincinnati, Columbus, Cleveland, Pittsburgh, Buffalo, Rochester, Syracuse, Albany, Troy, New York, Trenton, Philadelphia, Harrisburg) he avoided disclosure of plans and policies. Warned (22 Feb.) of an assassination plot in Baltimore, he was secretly put aboard a special train at night, arriving at Washington at 6 A.M., 23 Feb.

4 Mar. LINCOLN'S 1ST INAUGURAL was firm but conciliatory toward the South. He assured the South that the rights of that section would be protected and declared: "I have no purpose directly or indirectly to interfere with the institution of slavery in the States where it exists." On the other hand, secession would not be countenanced. "Physically speaking," he insisted, "we cannot separate. . . . No State, upon its own mere action, can lawfully get out of the Union." But there need be no violence "unless it be forced upon the national authority."

THE CIVIL WAR, 1861–65

1–15 Apr. FORT SUMTER AND THE CALL TO ARMS. Desirous of avoiding an overt act, Lincoln delayed a decision on Ft. Sumter. On 1 Apr. Secretary of State Seward proposed that Sumter be evacuated, but that the Gulf ports be reinforced and a strong stand adopted toward foreign nations in the interest of national unity. Lincoln, in reply, made clear that he intended to run his own administration. The President considered (4 Apr.) a proposal that Sumter be yielded in exchange for a loyalty pledge from Virginia, but rejected it as indicative of fatal weakness. When he decided to provision the fort he notified South Carolina (6 Apr.) that an expedition was on the way solely to provision the Sumter garrison. Fearing a ruse or prolonged Federal occupation, South Carolina (11 Apr.) requested Major Anderson to surrender at once. Anderson's offer to surrender upon exhaustion of his supplies (a matter of a few days) was rejected by the state authorities, aware that provisions were on the way. At 4.30 A.M. 12 Apr. the shore batteries under command of Gen. **Pierre G. T. Beauregard** (1818–93) opened fire. The Civil War began. Anderson was forced to surrender at 2.30 P.M. 13 Apr., after 34 hrs. of intense but bloodless bombardment. **Lincoln's role:** Some historians (Masters, 1931; Ramsdell, 1937) charge that Lincoln deliberately maneuvered the South into the role of aggressor; others (Potter, 1942; Randall, 1945; Stampp, 1951) dispute the charge. The attack on Sumter galvanized the North to spring to defense of the Union. On 15 Apr. Lincoln declared that "insurrection" existed, and called for 75,000 3-month volunteers.

17 Apr.–21 May. BORDER STATES. The outbreak of hostilities drove Va. (17 Apr.), Ark. (6 May), Tenn. (7 May), and N.C. (20 May) over to the side of the Confederacy despite Unionist sentiment which had prevailed prior to the attempted reinforcement of Ft. Sumter.

The declaration of Va.'s convention (17 Apr.) that the President's call for volunteers constituted a signal for the invasion of the South and its vote to secede (103–46) led to the resignation of some of the ablest officers in the U.S. Army, including **Robert E. Lee** (p. 740), who had been offered command of the Federal forces, and **Joseph E. Johnston** (p. 735). **Richmond** was chosen (21 May) as the new capital of the Confederacy; the government moved from Montgomery in early June.

West Virginia. The mountainous western section of Va., tied economically to the Ohio Valley and traditionally opposed to Tidewater and Piedmont, refused to recognize secession. A convention called at Wheeling (11 June) organized a Union government and elected Francis H. Pierpont governor (19 June). Ultimately the 50 western counties of Va. were admitted into the Union as the state of West Virginia (20 June 1863), with a constitution providing for gradual emancipation of slaves.

3 June–11 Sept. Loyal Slave States. 4 slave states (Del., Md., Ky., and Mo.) remained loyal to the Union, but not without prolonged contests in the last 3. Delaware's legislature unanimously rejected secession (3 Jan.) and in Apr. raised troops to defend the Union.

Maryland, in a strategic position to cut the National Capital off from the North, was divided. A majority opposed secession, but pro-Confederates were prominent, particularly in Baltimore where a mob attacked the 6th Mass. Reg. 19 Apr. as it passed through the city en route to Washington (militia casualties: 4 killed, 36 wounded). To avoid repetition of the riot the Maryland authorities burned down the railroad bridges connecting Baltimore with Philadelphia and Harrisburg. Gov. Thomas Hicks, a Unionist, was opposed by a legislature ready to accept Southern independence or to remain "neutral" in the conflict (10 May). The Federal government felt obliged to suspend habeas corpus in that state, followed, in the summer and fall of 1861, with arrest and imprisonment of numerous state and local officials. By the end of 1861 the state's position in the Union was assured. Maryland contributed 46,000 men to the Union army.

Kentucky, native state of both Lincoln and Jefferson Davis, was economically oriented to the South but strongly nationalistic. The legislature resolved (20 May) to be neutral. Lincoln gave assurances that no troops would be sent into Kentucky provided it remained peaceful, and pointed out that the war was fought to preserve the Union, not to free the slaves. When on 3 Sept. Confederate forces crossed from Tennessee into Kentucky and occupied Hickman and Columbus, Gen. **Ulysses S. Grant** (p. 716) countered by occupying Paducah (6 Sept.). The legislature demanded (11 Sept.) the ouster of the Confederates, and on 18 Sept. took steps to expel them. Ultimately 75,000 Kentuckians served with the Union forces. In a convention held at Russellville (18 Nov.) the Kentucky soldiers in the Confederate army adopted an ordinance of secession.

Missouri became a theater of civil war. Attempts of Gov. Claiborne F. Jackson to lead the state out of the Union failed (22 Mar.). The state soon divided into opposed armed groups headed by Gen. Nathaniel Lyon, a Unionist, and Gov. Jackson, respectively. Two major battles were fought at **Wilson's Creek,** where Lyon was killed (10 Aug.), and at **Pea Ridge, Ark.** (6–8 Mar. 1862), a Union victory leading to Union control of the state. Guerrilla warfare thereafter necessitated the establishment of martial law. 109,000 Missourians joined the Union army; 30,000 fought for the Confederacy.

OPPOSING FORCES. The North was predominant in numbers and economic power. Population of 23 Northern and border states, 22 million, augmented by heavy foreign immigration during the war years (400,000 foreign-born served in the Union army). The North had the advantage of a **balanced economy** (advanced industrial development, prosperous agriculture, strong banking institu-

tions), a **railroad grid** (an immense logistical advantage, with the Northeast closely bound to the Mississippi and Ohio Valleys), a **merchant marine,** and **naval supremacy** which handicapped the South from the start of the war.

The South. The 11 seceded states numbered 9 million (with few immigrants), of whom 3,500,000 were Negro slaves. An **agricultural economy** (based on the staples: cotton, tobacco, rice, sugar cane, and naval stores), its industrial resources were stunted, in part due to lack of banking capital (one third that of the North) and in part to lack of technological skills and equipment (despite abundant resources in iron, coal, and timber). An **inadequate railroad system,** despite expansion in the 50's, progressively deteriorated during the war. In addition, the Mississippi and Tennessee Rivers and the Great Valley of Virginia offered invasion routes by the Union armies. Its few good harbors could be easily blockaded.

Calculated Risk. Despite preponderant Northern strength the South risked war as a result of underrating the North and overestimating its own strength. Secessionists were convinced (1) that the North would not fight to maintain the Union; (2) if it did, Great Britain and France, dependent on Southern staples, would recognize Confederate independence and give material aid; (3) that the South's control of the mouth of the Mississippi would swing the Great Valley to the Confederacy (overlooking the new East-West orientation resultant upon the railroad building of the 50's). Confederate optimism rested on (1) the fact that it stood on the defensive; (2) it could afford to lose battles and campaigns if only it could wear down the Union in the process; (3) its men were trained in arms and outdoor living and predisposed toward military careers (182 general Confederate officers had begun their careers in the U.S. Army).

ENLISTMENTS (reduced to 3-yrs. service equivalent and taking into account desertions—Livermore): **Union,** 1,556,-678; **Confederate,** 1,082,119, distributed as follows:

		Union	Confederate
July	1861	186,751	112,040
Jan.	1862	575,917	351,418
Mar.	1862	637,126	401,395
Jan.	1863	918,121	446,622
Jan.	1864	860,737	481,180
Jan.	1865	959,460	445,203

A relatively higher proportion of Southern than Northern men served in the army. Considering the requirements of offensive warfare, invasion, and maintaining long lines of communication, the North had far less effective numerical superiority than the figures would suggest.

WAR AIMS. The North: Originally, the restoration of the Union; after 1862 freeing of the slaves became a secondary objective. President Lincoln insisted that only *individuals* not *governments* had taken up arms in rebellion and that the Union army was in effect an enlarged sheriff's posse. Yet in proclaiming a **blockade** of the South (19, 27 Apr.) and forbidding trade with the seceded states (16 Aug.), Lincoln in fact recognized the existence of a state of war. The conflict was conducted in accord with the rules of war—captured Confederate soldiers and privateersmen were treated as prisoners of war; prisoners were exchanged. The South: Recognition by the North of the independence and sovereignty of the Confederacy.

STRATEGY. The **major military operations** took place in 2 theaters: (1) east of the Appalachians, particularly in the vicinity of the rival capitals of Washington and Richmond; (2) between the western slope of the Appalachians and the Mississippi. **Lesser operations:** (1) isolated trans-Mississippi region; (2) amphibious operations along the coasts and inland waters; (3) war on the high seas waged by cruisers, privateers, and blockade runners. **Northern military strategy** aimed at (1) starving the South by blockading her coastline; (2) dispatching an army to seize Richmond in the East; and (3) another force in the West, aided by gunboats, to capture the Mississippi and Tennessee Rivers and divide and subdivide the Confederacy. Then the 2 armies would join and crush the South. **Confederate strategy** proposed

to seize Washington and move northward into Maryland and central Pennsylvania, thus cutting the Northeast off from the Northwest and forcing the Federal government to sue for peace. A large part of the Confederate forces were to be employed for defense only.

15 Apr.–20 July. EARLY SKIRMISHING. Minor actions were fought in western Virginia, where 20,000 troops led by Maj. Gen. **George B. McClellan** (1826–85), a West Pointer who had retired to railroad management in the 50's but was recalled to service at the start of the war as commander of the Department of the Ohio, cleared the enemy from the Valley of the Kanawha, with a victory at Philippi (3 June).

21 July. 1ST BATTLE OF BULL RUN. Demand of press and politicians for a march on Richmond overruled the caution of General-in-Chief **Winfield Scott,** who wanted more time to train the green Union troops. Gen. **Irvin McDowell** (1818–85), in command of a force of 30,000, was ordered to advance from his position southwest of Washington against a Confederate force under Beauregard stationed at Manassas Junction, Va. Another Federal force under Gen. Patterson was ordered to prevent Confederate general **Joseph E. Johnston** from bringing a force of 9,000 from the Shenandoah Valley. Patterson permitted Johnston to evade him and join Beauregard (20 July). Before dawn (21 July) McDowell attacked and by 3 P.M. seemed to have carried the day. Then the arrival of Confederate reinforcements and Gen. **Thomas J. Jackson's** (p. 733) magnificent stand, which earned him the sobriquet of "Stonewall," turned an apparent Southern rout into victory. McDowell's men began an orderly retreat, which quickly became a confused, panicky stampede toward Washington.

24 July. McCLELLAN IN COMMAND. First Bull Run aroused the North to the peril to the Capital and to the seriousness of the war and convinced Lincoln of the need for more thorough training for the army. McDowell was replaced by McClellan, who, upon retirement of Gen. Scott, became general-in-chief (1 Nov.).

NAVAL BLOCKADE. To enforce the blockade of the Confederate coast (proclaimed by Lincoln 19 Apr.) the Navy Dept. had to convert a small, and, for the main, obsolete, collection of ships into an effective force. Loss to the Virginia authorities of the Norfolk navy yard with its vast stores and the hull of the frigate *Merrimac* was a severe setback. A large naval construction program was launched (on 7 Aug. building of 7 ironclad gunboats by the engineer **James Buchanan Eads** [1820–87] was authorized), but for immediate use ships of all types were purchased and assigned to blockade duty. By July the blockade of the 3,550 mi. of Confederate coastline was well under way. The Confederates built numerous speedy ships to run the Federal gauntlet, with Nassau in the Bahamas becoming a major supply port. About 800 vessels managed to evade the blockade in its 1st yr. of operation; by comparison, in 1860, last year of peace, 6,000 ships entered and cleared Southern ports. By Nov. 1861 the Union navy had set up bases on the Southern coast after the capture of Forts Clark and Hatteras, N.C. (28–29 Aug.), Ship Island on the Gulf (17 Sept.), and Port Royal, S.C. (7 Nov.). The Union gained control of Albemarle and Pamlico Sounds when Gen. Burnside's naval and military expedition (Feb.–Mar. 1862) captured Roanoke Island (8 Feb.) and New Bern, N.C. (14 Mar.). With the fall of Fort Pulaski (11 Apr.) commanding approaches to Savannah, Fort Macon, N.C. (26 Apr.), and New Orleans (29 Apr.), the effectiveness of the blockade increased. Chances of capture were estimated as 1 in 10 (1861), later 1 in 3 (1864).

EUROPE AND THE CIVIL WAR. The war divided British opinion. The upper class favored the Confederacy; the commercial interests, irked at the new high tariffs imposed by the Union, looked to the opening of a vast free-trade market in the Confederacy; British manufacturers and shippers expected to benefit from the defeat of their Northern competitors. The working class, however, and a large proportion of the middle class, favored the Union. A British declaration of neutrality (13 May) aroused the North by its mention of the belligerent status of the Confederacy. On 21 May Secretary Seward instructed U.S. minister **Charles Francis Adams** (p. 665), who arrived at Liverpool 12 May, that he should "desist from all intercourse whatever, unofficial as well as official, with the British Government, so long as it shall continue intercourse of either kind with the domestic enemies of this country." On representations to Lord John Russell, the latter replied that the British government had no intention of seeing the Confederate agents again (on 3 and 9 May Russell had received William L. Yancey and Pierre A. Rost, Confederate commissioners to Great Britain). On 1 June Great Britain forbade the armed ships of either side to bring their prizes to British ports, a heavy blow to Confederate privateering.

8 Nov.–25 Dec. "Trent" Affair. A 2nd crisis with Britain arose when the U.S.S. *San Jacinto*, commanded by Capt. **Charles Wilkes** (p. 800), stopped the British steamer *Trent* and removed James M. Mason and John Slidell, Confederate commissioners en route to England. News of the seizure provoked war fever in England, but war was abated when Secretary Seward ordered (26 Dec.) the release of Mason and Slidell on the ground that the two commissioners were "personal contraband" and, therefore, Wilkes had erred in not bringing the ship as well as the passengers to port for adjudication.

20 Dec. JOINT COMMITTEE ON CONDUCT OF THE WAR. As a result of growing dissatisfaction at the inactivity of the Union armies and a defeat at **Ball's Bluff** just above Washington (21 Oct.), a group of radical Republicans led by Sens. **Benjamin F. Wade** (Ohio, 1800–78) and **Zachariah Chandler** (Mich., 1813–79) and Rep. **Thaddeus Stevens** (Pa., p. 783) pressed the administration for military action and emancipation of the slaves. Resentment at Lincoln's assumption of vast powers led Congress to set up the Joint Committee on the Conduct of the War, dominated by radical Republicans.

CIVIL WAR
1861-1862

Scale of Miles
0   50   100   150   200

All dates 1862 except where noted

CIVIL WAR
1863

Scale of Miles
0   50   100   150   200

KEY TO ALL MAPS
SYMBOLS INDICATE VICTOR

Federal		Confederate		Federal		Confederate
——•——	Major Advance	——•——•		O	Point taken by force	☐
————	Minor Advance	——·——·		⌣	Unsuccessful siege	·.·
■—■—■—■	Major Retirement	••••••••		◌	Successful siege	:.:
——————	Minor Retirement	•••••••••••		F.S.	Surrender	C.S.
✗	Battle	☒		F.E.	Evacuation	C.E.
■	Point Occupied	☐		◄—■	Continuation of troop movement	☐—►
▲	Point occupied, later yielded	△			Confederate names and dates in italics	

1862

15 Jan. STANTON AS WAR SECRETARY. The inefficiency and corruption of the War Dept. under Simon Cameron was ended when **Edwin M. Stanton** (1814–69) replaced him.

27 Jan. LINCOLN'S WAR ORDER NO. 1 set 22 Feb. for the launching of a general Union offensive. McClellan ignored this as well as subsequent orders.

WAR IN THE WEST. On 19–20 Jan. Union troops under Gen. **George H. Thomas** (p. 790) decisively defeated the Confederates at the **Battle of Mill Springs,** Ky. A flanking movement by Union forces began in Feb. when Gen. **Ulysses S. Grant,** in conjunction with a gunboat flotilla under Commodore A. H. Foote, moved against Confederate positions on the Mississippi, Tennessee, and Cumberland. A joint attack captured **Ft.**

Henry on the Tennessee (6 Feb.), but most of its garrison retreated to **Ft. Donelson** on the Cumberland, regarded by Confederate Gen. **Albert S. Johnston** (1803–62) as the major defense of Nashville. Another large Confederate force at Bowling Green, Ky., menaced by Gen. Don Carlos Buell from the north and by Grant from the south, retreated toward Tennessee to join the defense of Nashville and Ft. Donelson. After 4 days of siege Ft. Donelson surrendered to Grant (16 Feb.) with some 14,000 men. Johnston was forced to retreat from Kentucky and to evacuate Nashville, which fell 25 Feb.

6–7 Apr. SHILOH. Grant was prevented from striking a decisive blow against the main Confederate army of the East when his superior, Gen. Henry W. Halleck, given command of the armies in the West (11 Mar.), diverted part of the Union army under Pope to the task of expelling the enemy from the upper Mississippi. Pope, supported by Foote's fleet, besieged **Island No. 10** in the Mississippi (16 Mar.–7 Apr.). The Confederates surrendered, giving Johnston time to draw up his forces at Corinth, Miss., together with Beauregard's and Polk's. Grant marched to Pittsburg Landing just over the Tennessee border from Corinth, where he planned his attack without preparing suitable defenses. The Confederates struck (6 Apr.), and after a day of confused fighting in which Gen. A. S. Johnston was killed, the Union forces were close to defeat. During the night of 6–7 Apr. reinforcements from Gen. Buell's Army of the Ohio as well as Gen. Lew Wallace's division arrived. With the resumption of battle at dawn the tide turned. By evening the Confederates withdrew to Corinth, with the Union army too exhausted for pursuit. Heavy losses sustained on both sides: 13,000 out of 63,000 Union troops engaged; 11,000 out of 40,000 Confederates.

26 Apr. OCCUPATION OF NEW ORLEANS. Flag Officer (later Adm.) Farragut (p. 704) ran the forts below New Orleans; bombarded the city (24–25 Apr.), which was occupied by Gen. **Benjamin F. Butler** (1818–93).

WAR IN THE EAST. Peninsula Campaign. Impatient with McClellan for his continued inactivity, Lincoln on 8 Mar. issued an order reorganizing the Army of Virginia into 4 corps. On 11 Mar. McClellan was relieved of supreme command except for the Army of the Potomac, and ordered to begin immediate operations against Richmond. McClellan preferred an advance by way of the peninsula between the James and York Rivers instead of a frontal assault from Washington (Lincoln's preference). His opponents persuaded the President to withhold McDowell's corps in order to protect Washington.

9 Mar. "MONITOR" AND "MERRIMAC." The water route to Richmond up the James was guarded by the Confederate ironclad *Virginia* (formerly U.S.S. *Merrimac*), which on 8 Mar. had sunk the Federal ship *Cumberland* and burned the *Congress* off Hampton Roads. The

next day, when the *Virginia* sailed out to complete the destruction of the Union flagship *Minnesota,* which had run aground, she was met by the U.S.S. *Monitor,* another armored, raftlike craft with a revolving turret amidships. The ensuing 5-hr. battle, the 1st naval engagement between ironclads, resulted in a draw, although the *Virginia* was driven back to Norfolk for repairs. The latter still closed the James and kept the Federal fleet in Hampton Roads until burned by the Confederates to keep her from falling into Union hands when Norfolk fell 10 May.

17 Mar.–31 May. McCLELLAN'S ADVANCE. Embarkation of McClellan's army began from Alexandria, Va. On 5 Apr. McClellan began the siege of **Yorktown**, which he occupied 4 May. At a stubborn rear-guard action at **Williamsburg** (5 May) the Confederates frustrated McClellan's plans to come in contact with the main part of Johnston's army. By 14 May the Army of the Potomac had reached its advance base at White House on the Pamunkey River (20 mi. from Richmond), where, despite overwhelming strength, McClellan awaited reinforcement by McDowell's corps.

23 Mar.–9 June. JACKSON'S VALLEY CAMPAIGN. "Stonewall" Jackson, in command in the Shenandoah Valley with some 18,000 men, kept 2½ times that many Union troops engaged and pinned down the forces of Generals Banks and Frémont. In late Mar. his cavalry attacked at Winchester; his main force hit Banks at Kernstown, forcing the Union general to bring his full forces back into the Valley. On 23 May he struck Banks at **Front Royal**, forcing him to retreat to **Winchester**, where Jackson again struck (25 May), routing the Union forces, who were forced to retreat across the Potomac. Stanton that same day telegraphed Northern governors to send militia to defend the Capital. From McDowell's command 20,000 men were detached and rushed to the Valley.

31 May–1 June. BATTLE OF SEVEN PINES (FAIR OAKS). McClellan's lines were extended along both sides of the Chickahominy River in a great V, the upper arm stretching out along the north bank to meet McDowell, the lower reaching out to within 5 mi. of Richmond, just beyond Fair Oaks Station. On 31 May Johnston attacked the 2 Union corps on the south bank isolated by the flooded river from the main part of McClellan's army. Only the fortuitous arrival of another corps which managed to cross the river prevented a disastrous Union defeat. Heavy losses were sustained on both sides: Union, under 6,000; Confederate almost 8,000, including Johnston, who was severely wounded. **Robert E. Lee** was given command of the Army of Northern Virginia (1 June).

26 June–2 July. 7 DAYS' BATTLES. In an offensive move to drive McClellan off the Peninsula, Lee sent Jackson to attack the Union right flank while he himself struck at McClellan's center. The Union army was alerted by a cavalry raid by **James E. B. ("Jeb") Stuart** (1833–64) which misfired. McClellan withdrew to protection of Union gunboats on the James River. On 26 June Lee struck at the Union's extreme right at **Mechanicsville** and for 6 days attacked the smaller Union forces. At Mechanicsville (26–27 June), Gaines' Mill (27 June), Savage's Station (29 June), and Frayser's Farm (30 June) McClellan inflicted heavy losses on the Confederates while withdrawing across the Chickahominy to a new base at Harrison's Landing on the James. At Malvern Hill (1 July), supported by Union gunboats on the James, he withstood Lee's last desperate attacks. The next day the Confederates withdrew toward Richmond, marking the end of the Peninsula Campaign. Casualties of 7 Days' Battles: Union, killed 1,734; wounded 8,062; missing 6,053. Confederate, killed 3,478; wounded 16,261; missing 875.

11 July. Maj.-Gen. Halleck was named general-in-chief of the U.S. Army.

29–30 Aug. 2nd BULL RUN. Halleck consolidated the Armies of Virginia under Gen. **John Pope** (1822–92), ordered Burnside north from Fortress Monroe to Falmouth, and directed McClellan to bring his army to Alexandria and join Pope for an overland march on Richmond. Determined to strike quickly, Lee moved his army toward the Valley. Jackson defeated Banks at **Cedar Mountain** (9 Aug.) and struck at Pope's rear (26 Aug.), destroying his headquarters and supply base at Manassas Junction. When Pope moved to attack Jackson in the belief that he was isolated from the main Confederate army, he was drawn into a trap. Maj.-Gen. **James Longstreet** (1821–1904) forced Thoroughfare Gap (left practically undefended by Pope), struck at Pope's flank, and sent the Union army reeling toward Bull Run. Gen. **Fitz-John Porter** (1822–1901), who failed to throw his corps into battle the 1st day was made the scapegoat of Pope's defeat (cashiered 21 Jan. 1863). McClellan also had failed to get substantial forces to Pope in time.

14–15 Sept. MARYLAND INVADED. Pope withdrew (3 Aug.) to the defenses of Washington, and was supplanted (5 Aug.) by McClellan as commander of the Army of the Potomac. The latter reorganized the army and moved to meet Lee, who had begun a general invasion in the hope of cutting railroad lines and isolating Washington, with Harrisburg as his probable ultimate objective. Overestimating Confederate strength, McClellan proceeded with his customary caution. Federal victories over Lee at **South Mountain** and **Crampton's Gap** (14 Sept.) did not come in time to save **Harper's Ferry**, which fell to Jackson (15 Sept.), with its 11,000-man garrison and immense body of equipment.

17 Sept. ANTIETAM. The Confederates (40,000) were caught by McClellan (70,000) near **Sharpsburg, Md.**, the bloodiest day of the war. Union casualties, 2,108 killed, 9,549 wounded; Confederate, 2,700 killed, 9,029 wounded. McClellan failed to use his reserves, Lee held his lines, and the battle was a draw. But Lee pulled back to Virginia (18 Sept.), giving McClellan a technical victory. Although inconclusive from a military standpoint, Antietam had repercussions both at home and abroad. The British and French governments, on the verge of recognizing the Confederacy and intervening to force mediation (early Sept.), now held back. The Union victory also enabled Lincoln to issue (22 Sept.) his **Preliminary Emancipation Proclamation**, freeing as of

1 Jan. 1863 all slaves in areas still in rebellion against the U.S. Lincoln had submitted the 1st draft of the proclamation to his Cabinet on 22 July, but was persuaded to withhold it because of military reverses. On 1 Dec. the President appealed to Congress for passage of a constitutional amendment providing for **compensated emancipation**, but the border states opposed the plan.

8 Dec.–3 Jan. 1863. OPERATIONS IN THE WEST. Tied to Richmond by railroad, **Chattanooga** was the gateway to the nearer Southwest and a base to threaten Ohio and bar Union penetration of the lower South; while **Vicksburg** dominated the connections with the farther Southwest and Texas, important supply sources. On 11 July Grant had been promoted to command the Army of West Tennessee. Gen. Braxton Bragg (successor to Beauregard), in an advance on Louisville from Chattanooga, was stopped by Gen. Buell's Army of the Ohio at **Perryville** (8 Oct.), but Bragg continued to dominate central Tennessee until forced to withdraw after the costly engagement with Rosecrans at **Murfreesboro** (31 Dec.–3 Jan. 1863). Casualties, Union, 1,677 killed, 7,543 wounded; Confederate, 1,294 killed, 7,945 wounded.

13 Dec. FREDERICKSBURG. The North, dismayed at Lee's escape, was further shocked by McClellan's procrastination (Oct.), and by "Jeb" Stuart's daring cavalry raid around the Union army into Pennsylvania close to Gettysburg (10–12 Oct.). On 7 Nov. Lincoln replaced McClellan with Maj. Gen. **Ambrose E. Burnside** (1824–81). At Fredericksburg Burnside's overwhelming force (113,000 Union–75,000 Confederate) was shattered in a series of desperate attacks against the Confederate position, with losses of 1,284 killed, 9,600 wounded as against Confederate losses of 595 killed, 4,061 wounded. Burnside was replaced (25 Jan. 1863) by Gen. **Joseph Hooker** (1814–79).

17 Dec. CABINET CRISIS. A delegation of 7 radical Republican senators demanded that Lincoln reorganize the Cabinet, replace Seward by Chase, and fill the other Cabinet posts with radicals. Lincoln confronted the committee with his whole Cabinet (save Seward), who assured them that complete harmony existed. With the President declining the proffered resignations of Seward and Chase, the crisis was weathered.

1863

1 Jan. EMANCIPATION PROCLAMATION. To retain the loyalty of the border states Lincoln had resisted demands of the radical Republicans for abolition. **Military Action.** On 25 May 1861 Gen. B. F. Butler, in command of Fortress Monroe, Va., ruled that slaves escaping to his lines were "contraband of war" which he would not return to their masters. On 30 Aug. 1861 Gen. John C. Frémont issued a proclamation declaring that slaves of Missourians taking up arms against the U.S. were free. Lincoln modified this order (2 Sept.) to conform to existing law. On 9 May 1862 Gen. David Hunter proclaimed the emancipation of slaves in his Department (including Ga., Fla., and S.C.), but Lincoln disavowed this action 19 May. **Congressional Action.** The confiscation act of 6 Aug. 1861 provided for the emancipation of slaves employed in arms or labor against the U.S. A 2nd confiscation act of 17 July 1862 liberated slaves of all persons who committed treason or supported the rebellion. Lincoln's plan of compensated emancipation was embraced by the act of 16 Apr. 1862 abolishing slavery in the District of Columbia, but no such compensation was provided in the act of 19 June 1862 abolishing slavery in the territories of the U.S. In vain Lincoln appealed to the loyal states to enact gradual and compensated emancipation. Aware of the public shift toward the radical position on slavery and of the need to influence European opinion, Lincoln followed his Preliminary Emancipation Proclamation (22 Sept. 1862) with his Proclamation (1 Jan. 1863) declaring that all slaves in areas still in rebellion were "then, thenceforward, and forever free." The Proclamation actually freed no slaves; in fact, it went no further than Congress had already gone in legislation on the subject, for it applied *only* to areas over which the Federal government exercised no control, specifically exempting all regions under Federal military occupation.

RAISING THE ARMIES. Recruiting systems proved inefficient and inequitable. The state militia provided the bulk of the troops at the outbreak of war on a 3-mos.' to 9-mos.' basis. Ill-trained and often poorly led by officers who were political appointees or elected by the men they commanded, the militia marched home when their terms expired, sometimes on the eve of important battles.

3 Mar. 1st Conscription Act made all men, 20–45, liable to military service, but service could be avoided by payment of $300 or procuring a substitute to enlist for 3 yrs. State quotas were fixed (proportionate to total population) and states given credit for previous enlistments. The draft was regarded as inequitable to the poor. The 1st drawings provoked serious riots in working-class quarters in New York City, culminating (13–16 July) in the **New York City Draft Riots,** 4 days of pillaging and Negro lynching, chiefly participated in by Irish-Americans, requiring the dispatch to New York of regiments detached from Meade's army sorely needed to pursue Lee after Gettysburg. Although there were 4 drafts in all, a very small proportion of the Union Army was furnished through that means, although many "volunteered" under pressure (including **"bounty-jumpers"** who enlisted and deserted again and again).

Confederate Manpower Problems. The Confederacy first relied on enlistments; then, on 16 Apr. 1862, drafted into military service every white man (18–35) for 3 yrs. This 1st Confederate Conscription Act placed requisitions on the states but was administered and enforced by national authority. The lower classes denounced the long list of exempted occupations as well as the privilege of sending substitutes; many Southern leaders questioned the constitutionality of conscription; widespread fraud and evasion marked its administration. **Desertions** ran to about 10% in both Confederate and Union armies.

FINANCING THE WAR (also p. 530). An act of Congress (25 Feb.; amended 3 June 1864) established a **National Banking System,** requiring national banks to have one third of their capital invested in U.S. securities and authorizing them to issue notes up to 90% of such U.S. bond holdings. The imposition of a 10% tax (3 Mar. 1865) on state bank notes drove them out of circulation. Handicapped by inability to raise substantial loans abroad, by inadequate banking facilities, and opposition to taxation, the Confederate government resorted to **inflation.** Loans provided about $100 million (19 Aug. 1861) and an additional $15 million from abroad (authorized 29 Jan. 1863); taxation a similar sum, including the 10% tax "in kind" on the produce of land (24 Apr. 1863 and 17 Feb. 1864). On the other

UNION CONSCRIPTION AND ENLISTMENTS

	Draft of	1863 July	1864 14 Mar.	1864 18 July	1864 19 Dec.
Number called for		700,000		500,000	300,000
Reduced by credits to		407,092		234,327	300,000
Names drawn		292,441	113,446	231,918	139,024
Failed to report		39,415	27,193	66,159	28,477
Examined		252,566	84,957	138,536	46,128
Exempted for physical disability, etc.		164,855	39,952	82,531	28,631
Exempted by paying commutation		52,288	32,678	1,298	460
Substitutes furnished by registered men			84,733	29,584	12,997
Substitutes furnished by draftees		26,002	8,911	28,502	10,192
Draftees held to personal service		9,881	3,416	26,205	6,845
Voluntary enlistments			489,462	188,172	157,058
Total number obtained			537,672 *	272,463	187,092

* The excess, 130,579, credited to call of 18 July 1864.

hand, over $1 billion in paper was issued by the Confederacy, beginning 9 Mar. 1861 with an authorization of $1 million in treasury notes. These notes, which were not legal tender, depreciated to 33 cts. in gold by 1863 and to 1.6 cts. by Appomattox. U.S. "greenbacks" (p. 530) dropped to a low of 39 cts. 11 July 1864.

HOME FRONT. The North enjoyed a war boom, as production, prices, and profits soared; only wages lagged. Between 1860 and 1865 prices rose 117%; wages 43%. A continuous flow of immigrants (almost 800,000 during the war) and the adoption of labor-saving devices by industry and agriculture compensated for the manpower drain by the armed forces. Passage of the **Homestead Act** (20 May 1862, p. 463) promoted westward agricultural expansion. Bumper crops met not only the increased home demand but also that from abroad occasioned by poor European harvests. Great Britain's dependence on **Northern wheat** counterbalanced her need for **Southern cotton.**

The South, by diversifying her agriculture, raised sufficient food. Her supply of white manpower was depleted by the war, but women supervised farming and most slaves remained loyal and productive. But by 1863 the breakdown of the railroad system brought hardship and near starvation to some cities.

FOREIGN AFFAIRS. On 3 Feb. 1863 Napoleon III, through the French Minister at Washington, proposed mediation of the conflict, but was rebuffed by Seward (6 Feb.) and by a concurrent resolution of Congress (3 Mar.) which branded as "foreign intervention" offers of mediation. The French Emperor permitted French shipyards to build ships for the Confederates and forcibly intervened in Mexican affairs, occupying Mexico City with a French army (7 June) and placing Archduke Maximilian of Austria on the throne as Emperor of Mexico (10 Apr. 1864). U.S. protests went unheeded until after the war (see p. 280).

4 Apr. BRITAIN AND CONFEDERATE COMMERCE RAIDERS. In July 1862 the new raider, *Alabama,* had been permitted to slip out of Liverpool to join her sister ship, *Florida,* which had left England (Mar.), on a career of destruction of Union shipping. These and several other raiders destroyed 257 ships and impelled Union shipowners to transfer over 700 American vessels to foreign registries. The U.S. merchant marine did not recover from this blow for over half a century. Despite pro-Northern sentiment in Britain following the Emancipation Proclamation, the construction of Confederate naval vessels in British shipyards continued. When (Apr. 1863) it appeared that the *Alexandra,* another raider, would put to sea, the protest of U.S. Minister Adams resulted in the seizure (5 Apr.) of the ship by the British government. But the courts freed her and she put to sea.

2–4 May. CHANCELLORSVILLE. Following his victory at Fredericksburg, Lee clung to strong positions below the Rappahannock. Gen. Hooker crossed the river to attack (27 Apr.) with 130,000 men as against Lee's less than 60,000. Lee split his forces, sending Jackson through the Wilderness to hit the Union right, while he rolled up the Union center and left. Jackson struck on 2 May, completely surprising the Union troops under Howard and Sickles, who were sent reeling back in confusion. Gen. Pleasanton's stand prevented a Union catastrophe. On 5 May Hooker pulled his battered army back across the Rappahannock. Chancellorsville was the South's costliest victory: Confederate casualties, 1,665 killed (including Jackson, mortally wounded by his own men on 2 May), 9,081 wounded; Union, 1,575 killed, 9,594 wounded.

VICKSBURG CAMPAIGN. Failure had marked attempts to take Vicksburg by naval assault (May–June 1862) and by land (Dec.–early 1863). The river city, held by Gen. **John C. Pemberton,** was strongly fortified and protected by natural defenses. Most vulnerable were the approaches from south and east, remote from Grant's supply base at Memphis. Grant cut loose from his base (29 Mar.), crossed the Mississippi above Vicksburg, and marched down along the Louisiana shore of the river to a point south of the city where the fleet, which ran the Vicksburg batteries on the night of 16–17 Apr., ferried him across the river (30 Apr.). With 20,000 men he advanced northeastward on the rear of Vicksburg, living off the country. His 5 victories inside 3 weeks (**Port Gibson**, 1 May; Raymond; Jackson; **Champion's Hill**, 16 May; and **Big Black River**, 17 May) separated the armies of Johnston and Pemberton, driving the latter back into the Vicksburg perimeter.

22 May–4 July. Siege of Vicksburg. After 2 futile assaults (19, 22 May) Grant settled down to a siege. After a 6-wks.' bombardment Gen. Pemberton surrendered the city and over 30,000 troops (4 July). Union casualties of the Vicksburg campaign (Oct.–July), *c.*9,000; Confederate, 10,000, not counting prisoners. On 9 July Gen. Banks, after a siege begun in mid-May, captured **Port Hudson**, La. The entire Mississippi was now under Union control and the Confederacy split.

27 June–4 July. GETTYSBURG CAMPAIGN. Partly in the hope of winning foreign recognition, partly to encourage dissension and appeasement in the North, Lee decided to carry the war to the enemy. Early in June the Army of Northern Virginia began a move up the Shenandoah Valley. Confederate Gen. Richard S. Ewell crushed the Union garrison at **Winchester** (13–15 June), crossed the Potomac (17 June), and by 23 June neared Chambersburg, Pa. Hooker, preferring to stage a counterblow against Richmond, was ordered instead to follow on Lee's flank. On 25 June he crossed the Potomac, coming between Lee and his cavalry chief, "Jeb" Stuart, who was off on one of his audacious but costly forays, as a result of which Lee was deprived for 3 days of information about enemy movements. Hooker established headquarters at Frederick (27 June) before Lee (at Chambersburg) learned his whereabouts. The next day Hooker, at odds with Halleck, resigned the command, and Lincoln appointed Maj. Gen. **George G. Meade** (1815–72) to command the Army of the Potomac. An aroused North responded promptly to Lincoln's call (15 June) for 100,000 volunteers for 6 mos.' service. Carlisle and York fell 27–28 June, and the next day Ewell's cavalry came within 10 mi. of Harrisburg.

1–3 July. Gettysburg. Lee took up a strong defensive position along the east-

ern slope of South Mt., near Cashtown. Meade planned to take a defensive position behind Pipe Creek. On 30 June a chance contact at Gettysburg of a part of Confederate Gen. Ambrose P. Hill's force in search of boots and saddles with John Buford's cavalry division drew both into that town, where the battle began. On the **1st day** (1 July), the Confederates drove the Union forces back through Gettysburg to strong defensive positions on Cemetery Hill and Culp's Hill. The Confederates occupied Seminary Ridge, a long, partially wooded rise running north and south parallel to the Union position. In the crucial battle that followed Meade enjoyed the advantage of a numerical superiority of 15,000, greater fire power, and a strong defensive position, with Cemetery Ridge and Culp's Hill heavily reinforced. Gettysburg was won and lost the **2nd day** (2 July). Lee attacked. Early was finally driven off Cemetery Ridge. Longstreet drove back Sickles' corps, but failed to take Little Round Top, which would have enabled him to enfilade the entire Union position. Ewell attacked Culp's Hill on the Union right; again on the **3rd day** (3 July), being repulsed. At Lee's insistence Longstreet reluctantly ordered a direct attack on the strongest part of the Union center, with Pickett's, Pettigrew's, and Trimble's divisions (15,000 strong). At 1 P.M. the Confederates opened up with an unprecedentedly heavy artillery barrage. As 3 gray lines of Confederate infantrymen approached Cemetery Ridge, they were mowed down by artillery fire and volleys of musketry. Less than a half company managed to reach the crest of Cemetery Ridge, only to be killed or captured. On 4 July Lee remained in position, but that afternoon retired to a position west of Sharpsburg. There the flooded Potomac blocked his retreat. Lincoln and Halleck ordered Meade to attack, but Meade procrastinated inexcusably, the river subsided, and Lee escaped into Virginia (13 July). Casualties: Union, 3,155 killed, *c.*20,000 wounded and missing; Confederate, 3,903 killed, *c.*24,000 wounded and missing. On 19 Nov. the cemetery at the Gettysburg battlefield was dedicated. The principal oration was delivered by Edward Everett, but Lincoln's brief remarks, in the course of which he referred to "a new birth of freedom," constituted the most memorable of all American addresses.

5 Sept. Diplomatic Fruits of Gettysburg. The Union victories at Vicksburg and Gettysburg decisively tipped the diplomatic balance in favor of the North. On 5 Sept. U.S. Minister Adams warned Russell that the ironclads under construction in England for the Confederacy (the "Laird rams") meant "war." Russell ordered that the rams be not permitted to leave Liverpool, and in Oct. the British government took over the ships. Similarly, Napoleon III ordered 6 naval vessels under construction for the Confederacy to be sold to European governments. The close of 1863 saw Confederate hopes for foreign recognition and aid irretrievably shattered.

19–20 Sept. CHICKAMAUGA. Gen. William S. Rosecrans' Army of the Cumberland moved east from Murfreesboro at the end of June and maneuvered the unresourceful Braxton Bragg out of Chattanooga (9 Sept.), gateway to the East, without a battle. Alarmed at the loss of this key point, Davis rushed Longstreet and 11,000 troops from the East to reinforce Bragg. The armies clashed on the field of Chickamauga, northeast of Chattanooga, where the Union line cracked and broke, but Gen. **George H. Thomas**, who earned for himself the sobriquet "Rock of Chickamauga," used the bayonet to hurl back the Confederate attack until reserves saved the day. The Union forces retired into Chattanooga, and Bragg invested the city. Casualties: Union, 1,657 killed, almost 15,000 wounded and missing; Confederate, 2,312 killed, c.16,000 wounded and missing.

23–25 Nov. BATTLE OF CHATTANOOGA (LOOKOUT MOUNTAIN-MISSIONARY RIDGE). Grant, given command of the western armies (16 Oct.), replaced Rosecrans with Thomas; forced open communications with Chattanooga; and, reinforced by 2 corps under Hooker, prepared for the offensive. On 23 Nov. the armies came to grips. Hooker, Sherman, and Thomas drove Bragg off **Lookout Mountain** and the knolls south of Chattanooga, but Bragg

concentrated his forces on **Missionary Ridge.** On 25 Nov. Thomas started a limited attack to clear the Confederates from the foot of the ridge, but continued to the crest, putting Bragg to rout. Casualties: Union, 753 killed, c.5,000 wounded and missing; Confederate, 361 killed, c.6,000 wounded and missing. The Union conquest of the Mississippi had split the Confederacy vertically. After Chattanooga, the Union armies of the West were poised to bisect the upper and lower South by marching across Georgia to the sea. On 3 Dec. Longstreet abandoned his siege of Knoxville, Tenn., and began a retreat.

1864

5–6 May. BATTLE OF THE WILDERNESS. Operations on the Virginia front bore little resemblance to the rapid movements of Sherman and Thomas. By comparison Grant's campaign before Richmond was slow and costly. Promoted (9 Mar.) to the newly revived rank of lieutenant general and given supreme command of the Union armies, Grant proposed to hammer away at Lee's army until it was decimated. The Army of the Potomac, over 100,000 strong, was assembled at Culpeper for its advance southward. Gen. Butler's Army of the James with some 36,000 men was to march up the south bank of the James and cut Lee off from the Lower South. Maj. Gen. **Franz Sigel** (1824–1902) was to move up the Shenandoah Valley and seize Lynchburg. To meet Grant, Lee had a force of 60,000, and was supported by Beauregard with 30,000 troops in the Richmond-Petersburg area. Grant and Meade crossed the Rapidan (4 May) and entered the Wilderness. Lee attacked Grant's right flank. In the ensuing indecisive 3-day battle Lee outmaneuvered his opponents, inflicting c.18,000 Union casualties (over 2,000 killed) to some 10,000 of his own men.

8–12 May. SPOTSYLVANIA. Disregarding losses, Grant futilely attempted to flank Lee at Spotsylvania Court House. Five bloody days of trench warfare followed. On 11 May Grant sent word to Halleck: "I propose to fight it out along this line if it takes all summer." Union losses, *c*.12,000, as Lee parried the Union blows.

1–3 June. COLD HARBOR. At the Chickahominy, Grant again assaulted a well-entrenched foe, losing on 3 June alone 12,000 men. In one month ending 12 June Grant's losses amounted to nearly 60,000 (equal to Lee's total strength) as against Confederate casualties of *c*.25,000–30,000, but Lee's Army of Northern Virginia never really recovered from the heavy punishment.

15–18 June. PETERSBURG. Grant decided to move his army south of the James to Petersburg, 20 mi. below Richmond, approach the Confederate capital from the rear, and cut transportation connections with the South. Faulty generalship by Butler in his advance up the James prevented Grant from taking Petersburg, which withstood 4 days of battering and cost Grant 8,000 more men. Grant now dug in for a 9-mos.' siege, longest of the war. On 30 July a huge mine was exploded in a costly but futile Union attempt to take the city.

2–13 July. EARLY'S RAIDS. Confederate Gen. **Jubal A. Early** (1816–94) who had defeated Sigel in the Shenandoah Valley (15 May) and driven Hunter, Sigel's successor, into West Virginia (16–18 June), suddenly struck north into Maryland. Moving from Winchester (2 July), he crossed the Potomac, exacted tribute from Hagerstown and Frederick; then swung southeast and reached the District of Columbia, within 5 mi. of Washington on 11 July. A thrust by Lew Wallace at Monocacy, Md., 9 July, slowed up Early and gave Grant time to assemble troops to defend the Capital. Two divisions hastily returned from the Petersburg front helped drive Early back to Virginia on 13 July. Given command of the Army of the Shenandoah (Aug.), Gen. **Philip H. Sheridan** (1831–88) defeated Early at **Winchester** (19 Sept.) and **Fisher's Hill** (22 Sept.), and rallied his men at **Cedar Creek** (19 Oct.), turning defeat into victory. Sheridan then proceeded to scorch the Valley as thoroughly as Sherman laid waste Georgia.

7 May–2 Sept. SHERMAN'S MARCH THROUGH GEORGIA. With 100,000 men Gen. **William T. Sherman** (p. 778) set out from Chattanooga (May 1864) and began his invasion of Georgia. Joseph E. Johnston, who had replaced Bragg after Chattanooga, faced Sherman with some 60,000 men, but fought a skillful series of defensive actions at **Resaca** (13–16 May), **New Hope Church** (25–28 May), and **Kenesaw Mountain** (27 June), where, momentarily forsaking his flanking movements designed to cut the enemy's communications, Sherman assaulted Johnston and was repulsed with 2,000 killed and wounded, compared with 270 Confederate casualties. On 17 July the Union army crossed the Chattahoochee River, only 8 mi. from Atlanta. Davis, impatient at Johnston's masterfully executed Fabian tactics, replaced him with **John Bell Hood** (1831–79), who attacked Sherman in 2 pitched battles (20, 22 July), but, after suffering heavy losses, pulled back into Atlanta's entrenchments. On 1 Sept. he was forced to evacuate Atlanta; the next day Sherman occupied the city. The fall of Atlanta lifted Northern morale, staggered by Grant's losses before Richmond, and contributed to the Republican success in the Presidential campaign.

14 Nov.–22 Dec. MARCH TO THE SEA. Changing his strategy, Hood decided to strike at Sherman's long lines of communication stretching back to Tennessee. Dispatching Thomas to hold Hood and protect Tennessee, Sherman set out (14 Nov.) with 60,000 men in his march to the sea. Before leaving Atlanta he destroyed or confiscated all supplies useful to the enemy. On his march across Georgia his army cut a swath to the sea, 300 mi. in length, 60 mi. in width. Factories, cotton gins, warehouses, bridges, railroads, and some public buildings were systematically destroyed. His soldiers were ordered to "forage liberally on the country," and wild looting resulted. Sherman's advance was virtually unopposed. On 10 Dec. he reached Savannah, which fell (22 Dec.).

15–16 Dec. BATTLE OF NASHVILLE. In pursuit of Thomas, Hood made contact with part of the Union forces under Gen. John M. Schofield at Franklin,

Tenn. (30 Nov.), and was repulsed with heavy Confederate losses (*c*.5,500 killed and wounded, as against *c*.1,200 Union killed and wounded). Schofield then joined Thomas at Nashville, where in a 2-day battle he all but destroyed Hood's army. Mopping up operations against Confederate forces in Tennessee were accomplished by Gen. James H. Wilson's cavalry.

PRESIDENTIAL CAMPAIGN. On 7 June the Republican or National Union Convention at Baltimore nominated **Lincoln**, with **Andrew Johnson** (Tenn.), a War Democrat, as his running mate. The Democratic National Convention at Chicago, nominated (29 Aug.) Gen. **McClellan** for President and **George H. Pendleton** (Ohio) for Vice-President. Under Copperhead influence the Democrats adopted a platform calling for immediate cessation of hostilities and the restoration of peace "on the basis of the Federal Union of the States." McClellan repudiated the peace plank but sought to capitalize on Northern defeatism. Pacifism and defeatism in midsummer made the outlook for Lincoln's reelection seem dark. On 4 July the President pocketvetoed the **Wade-Davis Bill**, a measure for the Radical reconstruction of the South. A manifesto by the bill's authors denouncing him was published by **Horace Greeley** (p. 717) in the N.Y. *Tribune* (5 Aug.). The Radicals covertly circulated a call for a new convention to replace Lincoln with another nominee. However, Sherman's success in Georgia in Sept. changed the election outlook and induced the Radicals to unite behind Lincoln.

8 Nov. PRESIDENTIAL ELECTION. Lincoln was reelected by 212–21 electoral votes, but with a popular majority of but 400,000 out of 4 million votes.

1865

LAST DAYS OF THE CONFEDERACY. The breakdown of transportation, the blockade (tightened by the capture of **Ft. Fisher**, N.C., 15 Jan., and the closing of the port of Wilmington, captured 22 Feb.), and Federal occupation of important producing areas and devas-

tation of others spread hunger throughout large sections of the South. Riots and demonstrations against the Confederate government or the food speculators broke out in Southern cities. Army morale was shattered by food and clothing shortages. Increasing desertions had forced Davis to admit (Sept. 1864) that "two-thirds of our men are absent . . . most of them absent without leave." In desperation he approved the **arming of the slaves** (7 Nov. 1864), but the Confederate Congress failed to authorize such action until 20 Mar. 1865, too late to take effect before the close of the war. The Richmond government tightened its laws against conspiracy and suspended habeas corpus with increasing frequency. Disunion tendencies appeared. South Carolina virtually nullified (23 Dec. 1864) an act of the Confederate Congress which had authorized the central government to impress goods and services.

16 Jan.–21 Mar. SHERMAN'S DRIVE THROUGH THE CAROLINAS. Sherman's corps fanned northward through South Carolina, wreaking even greater destruction than in Georgia. More than a dozen towns were burned in whole or part, including (17 Feb.) a large part of **Columbia**, the state capital. Whether Union soldiers (with or without orders) set the blaze or, as Sherman later claimed, retreating Confederates were responsible, has never been definitely established. The fall of Columbia led to the evacuation of Charleston, which fell to the Union (18 Feb.). Sherman advanced into North Carolina, his progress somewhat slowed by Johnston, whom Lee, now commander in chief of all Confederate forces, had restored to command. At **Bentonville** (19–20 Mar.) Sherman and Johnston met in their last battle. The smaller Confederate force was pushed back, but not crushed. Sherman entered Goldsboro (21 Mar.), where he joined Gen. Schofield.

3 Feb. HAMPTON ROADS CONFERENCE. Jefferson Davis, while agreeing to send Vice-President Stephens, R. M. T. Hunter, and J. A. Campbell to confer with Lincoln and Seward aboard the Union transport *River Queen*, stubbornly insisted on recognition of Southern independence. This was, of course, unacceptable to Lincoln, and the conference broke up.

4 Mar. LINCOLN'S 2ND INAUGURAL. The President appealed to the nation to forget vengeance. "With malice toward none; with charity for all . . . let us strive on to finish the work we are in; to bind up the nation's wounds . . . to do all which may achieve and cherish a just and lasting peace."

2 Apr. PETERSBURG AND RICHMOND ABANDONED. On 25 Mar. Lee tried to break through Grant's besieging army by an attack on Ft. Steadman, east of Petersburg, but was badly beaten. Holding an advantage of 115,000 men to Lee's 54,000, Grant systematically battered the Confederate lines. On 1 Apr. Lee made his last assault of the war, hitting Grant's left flank at **Five Forks** near Petersburg, but was repelled by Sheridan, who arrived from the Valley. On 2 Apr. Lee evacuated Petersburg and Richmond and headed toward Lynchburg, whence he hoped to move by rail to North Carolina and join forces with Johnston.

9 Apr. SURRENDER AT APPOMATTOX COURTHOUSE. With Grant in pursuit of Lee, Sheridan's force took Burkesville, a railway junction, preventing Lee from moving south toward Danville. He then blocked Lee's path westward, and the Confederates were virtually surrounded. Lee's forces had now shrunk to less than 30,000, with few rations remaining. On 7 Apr. Grant requested Lee to surrender. Lee asked for terms. On 9 Apr. he met Grant at Appomattox Courthouse and quickly came to terms, by which Lee's soldiers were paroled to return home, officers were permitted to retain side arms, and all soldiers allowed to retain private horses and mules. All equipment was to be surrendered. 25,000 rations were issued by the Union army to the Confederates.

14 Apr. ASSASSINATION OF LINCOLN. The President visited Richmond on 5 Apr., then returned to Washington (where news of Appomattox arrived by noon 9 Apr.) and worked on plans for restoration of peace. In his last public address (11 Apr.) and at his final Cabinet meeting on the morning of 14 Apr. the President repeated his plea for conciliation. At 10.15 P.M. that evening, as he was sitting in his box at Ford's Theater in Washington, watching a performance of *Our American Cousin,* he was shot by **John Wilkes Booth** (1838–65), carried unconscious to a lodging-house across the street, and died there just before 7.30 A.M. 15 Apr. Vice-President Johnson took the oath of office as President 3 hrs. later. Simultaneously with the assassination of Lincoln, Secretary Seward was attacked and severely wounded at his home by Lewis Powell (alias Payne), a fellow conspirator of Booth. Booth escaped to Virginia, but was caught in a barn near Bowling Green. On his refusal to surrender, the barn was fired and (probably) he shot himself (26 Apr.). Of the 9 other persons implicated in the assassination 4 were hanged (7 July), 4 imprisoned, and a jury failed to convict the 9th suspect, John H. Surratt.

26 Apr.–26 May. FINAL CAPITULATION. Sherman drew closer to Johnston's army when he occupied Raleigh on 13 Apr. Despite Davis' plea for continued resistance, Johnston surrendered to Sherman (18 Apr.), with 37,000 men, and was granted liberal terms, including unauthorized political concessions disavowed by President Johnson. Final surrender terms along the lines of the Appomattox capitulation were agreed upon (26 Apr.) near Durham Station, N.C. Gen. Taylor surrendered the remaining Confederate forces east of the Mississippi to Gen. Canby at Citronelle, Ala., 4 May. Resistance ended (26 May) with the capitulation of Gen. Kirby Smith to Gen. Canby at New Orleans. Jefferson Davis was captured in Georgia on 10 May.

WAR LOSSES. In the proportion of casualties to participants the Civil War was the costliest U.S. war, with casualties totaling between 33% and 40% of the combined Union and Confederate forces. Union dead, 359,528 (including 110,070 killed in battle or died from wounds); wounded, 275,175. Confederate dead, 258,000 (94,000 in battle or from wounds); wounded, 100,000 minimum.

RECONSTRUCTION, 1865–77

1863, 8 Dec.–1865, 4 Dec. PRESIDENTIAL RECONSTRUCTION. Two constitutional issues were involved: (1) Were the rebellious states in the Union? (2) Was the President or Congress responsible for direction of Reconstruction (involving both the status of the freedmen and the restoration to the Union of the 11 Confederate states)? Lincoln consistently maintained that these states had never left the Union, but was little concerned with the "pernicious abstraction" of constitutional theory. In 1862 he appointed provisional military governors for La., N.C., and Tenn. On 8 Dec. 1863 he announced his plan of Reconstruction: (1) amnesty, with certain exceptions, to Southerners taking a prescribed loyalty oath; (2) executive recognition of state governments in cases where 10% of the 1860 electorate had taken the oath and where the state agreed to emancipation. These steps were taken by Ark. and La. in 1864, but Congress refused to seat their representatives.

WADE-DAVIS BILL (4 July 1864) represented the Congressional blueprint for reconstruction. It required a majority of the electorate in each Confederate state to take an oath of past as well as future loyalty as a condition precedent to restoration. Lincoln pocket-vetoed the bill, and was excoriated by Radical Republicans, who considered him too lenient. Republicans of all shades feared a revived Democratic party. In addition, many in Congress resented the wartime expansion of the executive power.

JOHNSON'S POLICIES. Andrew Johnson quickly disabused the Radicals of any idea that he favored their program. In fact, he adopted Lincoln's Reconstruction plan with minor changes. During the recess of Congress he recognized the loyal governments of Ark., La., Tenn., and Va. set up by Lincoln.

29 May–13 July. RECONSTRUCTION PROCLAMATION. Johnson granted amnesty to Confederates who took the oath of allegiance, with several excepted classes (among them holders of taxable property exceeding $20,000) who could petition him for special pardons. These he granted liberally. He proceeded to organize provisional governments for the 7 remaining states. Provisional governors were empowered to convene conventions composed of delegates elected by "loyal" citizens (including those pardoned by the President) to amend the state constitutions, abolish slavery, and repudiate the state war debt. By Dec., every Confederate state except Texas had fulfilled these requirements. Texas conformed 6 Apr. 1866. In his 1st annual message to Congress (6 Dec.) Johnson announced that the Union was restored; the delegates of the ex-Confederate states awaited admission to Congress.

4 Dec. JOINT COMMITTEE OF FIFTEEN. When the 39th Congress convened it refused to endorse Johnson's actions. Republicans secured the appointment of a joint committee of 6 senators and 9 representatives to examine the issues of suffrage and Southern representation in Congress. Controlled by the Radicals, this committee was dominated by **Thaddeus Stevens** (p. 783), who during this period came to exercise almost dictatorial powers both over the House and the Republican party.

RADICAL THEORIES OF RECONSTRUCTION. To Stevens the ex-Confederate states were "conquered provinces"; to Senator Charles Sumner (Mass.) the seceding states had committed "suicide." Either interpretation put the South under the control of Congress. The joint committee declared that the South had no state governments and that Congress alone could restore them and impose such conditions for readmission as it deemed necessary.

18 Dec. 13TH AMENDMENT, abolishing slavery, ratified by 27 states, was formally proclaimed in effect.

1866

19 Feb. NEW FREEDMEN'S BUREAU BILL. Beginning with Miss. (24 Nov. 1865), Southern state legislatures enacted "Black Codes," a body of vagrancy and apprenticeship laws which bound the freedmen to the land. These codes varied in harshness; were notably lenient in Ga., severe in La. and Miss. To protect the Negro, Congress sought to enlarge the scope of the **Freedmen's Bureau** (est. 3 Mar. 1865) as a temporary bureau to care for the freedmen and the abandoned lands of the South. Congress sought to empower the bureau to try by military commission persons accused of depriving freedmen of civil rights. Johnson vetoed the bill on the ground that Congress had no power to legislate with 11 states unrepresented, and that the provisions for military trials violated the 5th Amendment. On 16 July the bill was passed over his veto.

9 Apr. CIVIL RIGHTS ACT, bestowing citizenship upon the Negro (legislation necessitated by the Dred Scott decision) and granting the same civil rights to all persons born in the U.S. (except Indians) was passed by Congress over Johnson's veto, which had condemned the measure as an unwarranted invasion of states' rights. The Supreme Court held the act unconstitutional (**Civil Rights Cases,** 1883, p. 493).

16 June. 14TH AMENDMENT was formulated by the joint committee of 15 because of widespread doubt as to the constitutionality of the Civil Rights Act. It passed Congress 13 June and was submitted to the states for ratification (16 June). Rejected by most of the Southern states, its ratification was made a condition of restoration to the Union (ratification announced 28 July 1868). The amendment for the 1st time defined national citizenship (to include Negroes) and threw the protection of the Federal government around rights that might be invaded by the states. The charge has been made, with little support in fact, that the framers deliberately phrased the 1st section to protect property and the rights of corporations against state legislation. Subsequent judicial decisions did in fact so interpret the amendment. Sect. II abrogated the "three-fifths" clause, increasing Southern representation in the House by some 12 seats, but provided a proportionate reduction in representation when a state denied suffrage "except for participation in rebellion or other crime." This section has never been applied.

20 June. REPORT OF THE JOINT COMMITTEE OF 15 recommended that the Confederate states were not entitled to representation, and maintained the authority of Congress rather than the Executive over the process of Reconstruction. Tennessee, under Radical control, ratified the 14th Amendment (19 July) and was restored to the Union (24 July). The other Southern states rejected the amendment, counting upon the approaching Congressional election to repudiate the Radical program.

CONGRESSIONAL ELECTIONS. Johnson's abortive attempt to join all moderates in a new party at a National Union Convention meeting in Philadelphia (14 Aug.) convinced many Northerners that his supporters were primarily ex-rebels and Copperheads. Republicans also capitalized upon the President's maladroit speaking tour (28 Aug.–15 Sept.). In contrast, the Radicals' skillful campaign stressed the connection between the Republican party and the Union cause. Race riots in New Orleans (30 July) and Memphis supported the Radical contention that the South was unregenerate. While Johnson failed to capitalize on the discontent of Western farmers, the Republicans were more successful in persuading industrial interests that a Democratic victory would lead to a reversal of policies favoring business. In the fall elections the Republicans captured two thirds of each house, giving the Radicals effective control of Reconstruction.

1867–68

2 Mar. 1ST RECONSTRUCTION ACT, passed over Johnson's veto, divided the South into 5 military districts subject to martial law. To achieve restoration the Southern states were required to call new constitutional conventions, elected by universal manhood suffrage, which were to establish state governments guaranteeing Negro suffrage and ratifying the 14th

Amendment. Excluded from voting were ex-Confederates disqualified under the proposed 14th Amendment. Congress reserved to itself the power to review each case, end military rule, and seat representatives.

23 Mar., 19 July 1867; 11 Mar. 1868. SUPPLEMENTARY RECONSTRUCTION ACTS. On failure of the South to call such conventions, Congress passed the first supplemental act requiring the military commanders to initiate the enrollment of voters; then a second act giving the commanders broad powers to discriminate between voters and office holders; and lastly, a measure declaring that a majority of votes cast was sufficient to put a new state constitution into effect, regardless of the numbers participating.

MILITARY RECONSTRUCTION. Despite doubts as to their constitutionality, President Johnson conscientiously executed these laws. He appointed military commanders who led 20,000 troops (as well as Negro militia) into the South. The governments previously set up by Johnson were supplanted. A total of 703,000 Negroes and 627,000 whites were registered as voters. In 5 states (Ala., Fla., La., Miss., and S.C.) Negro voters were in the majority. In the other states a Negro-white coalition constituted Radical majorities. Southern whites allying with Radicals were called "scalawags"; Northerners who went South to participate in Reconstruction, "carpetbaggers."

1867, 4 Dec. GRANGER MOVEMENT. The Patrons of Husbandry, popularly called the Grangers, a secret association devoted to the promotion of agricultural interests, was organized in Washington, D.C. Typical of its objectives were the resolutions adopted at the Springfield, Ill., Farmers' Convention (2 Apr. 1873) attacking "all chartered monopolies," and urging laws "fixing reasonable maximum rates" for freight and passengers. The Declaration of Purpose of the National Grange (1874) stressed (1) cooperation, (2) reduction of the number of middlemen, (3) opposition to monopoly, (4) establishment of agricultural and technical colleges. Associated with this movement was the rise of independent farmers' parties, which, by 1874, had been organ-

ized in 9 prairie states and in Oregon and California under the leadership of **Ignatius Donnelly** (Minn., 1831–1901) and **Newton Booth** (Kan.). First Granger legislation was enacted in Illinois (7 Apr. 1871), setting up a railroad and warehouse commission to fix maximum rates. Intrastate railroad freight rates were regulated by law in Wisconsin (11 Mar. 1874) and Iowa (23 Mar. 1874). For the early validation of Granger laws by the courts, see p. 468.

NEW SOUTHERN STATE CONSTITUTIONS. In late 1867 the Southern states voted to call conventions, which met in 1868 and established new constitutions. These conventions were Radical-dominated. Negroes participated in every such convention and formed a majority in that of South Carolina. The new constitutions were similar to those in effect in the North except for guarantees of civil rights for Negroes, universal manhood suffrage, and the disqualification of ex-rebels.

1868, 22–25 June. OMNIBUS ACT. Seven states (Ark. [22 June] and Ala., Fla., Ga., La., N.C., and S.C. [25 June]) satisfied the requirements of the Reconstruction Acts and were readmitted by Congress. On 26 Feb. 1869 Congress proposed the **15th Amendment** forbidding any state from depriving a citizen of his vote because of race, color, or previous condition of servitude. By 1870 Miss., Tex., and Va., whose readmission had been held up by their refusal to approve the disfranchising clauses of the new constitutions, were restored to the Union following ratification of the 15th Amendment, proclaimed 30 Mar. 1870. Following her restoration in 1868, Ga. was once more returned by Congress to military rule when, after withdrawal of Federal military forces, Negroes were expelled (Sept.) from the state legislature. With the return of troops, both the Reconstruction Acts and the 14th Amendment were enforced and the state (by Act of Congress, 22 Dec. 1869) compelled to ratify the 15th Amendment and restore the expelled Negro members in order to gain readmission to the Union (15 July 1870).

1868

24 Feb.–16 May. IMPEACHMENT OF JOHNSON. The Radical sweep in the 1866 election resulted in their overriding Johnson's vetoes and enacting legislation curbing the power of the executive, who was prevented from appointing new Supreme Court justices (23 July 1866). Congress called itself into special session (22 Jan. 1867) and virtually deprived the President of command of the army (**Command of the Army Act,** 2 Mar. 1867) by requiring that he issue all military orders through the General of the Army (U. S. Grant). Furthermore, the President (by the **Tenure of Office Act,** 2 Mar. 1867) was prohibited from removing officials appointed by and with the advice of the Senate without Senatorial approval. Johnson decided to test the constitutionality of the latter measure and dismissed Secretary of War Stanton (21 Feb., previously suspended [12 Aug., 1867], appointed Gen. Grant to act *ad interim,* and then reinstated Stanton [13 Jan.]).

24 Feb. Covode Resolution, carried in the House, 126–47, impeached Johnson on 11 charges, including alleged violations of the Tenure of Office Act and Command of the Army Act and with attempting to bring disgrace and ridicule upon Congress.

30 Mar.–16 May. Impeachment. Chief Justice Chase presided over the Senate proceedings, and his insistence on the observance of legal procedure maintained some semblance of nonpartisanship. Johnson's counsel (Benjamin R. Curtis, William Maxwell Evarts (p. 704), W. S. Groesbeck, and Henry Stanbery) disputed the evidence offered by the House managers (J. A. Bingham, G. S. Boutwell, B. F. Butler, J. A. Logan, T. Stevens, T. Williams, and J. F. Wilson). Voting (16 May) on the 11th article of impeachment as to whether the President was guilty of high misdemeanor as charged, the Senate voted 35 for conviction, 19 (including 7 Republicans and 12 Democrats) for acquittal, short by one vote of the two thirds necessary.

CAMPAIGN OF 1868. The Republican National Convention at Chicago nominated Gen. **U. S. Grant** for the Presidency on the first ballot, with an Indiana Radical, **Schuyler Colfax** (1823–85) as his running mate (20–21 May). The platform endorsed Radical Reconstruction, condemned Johnson and the Democrats, advocated payment of the national debt in gold, and equivocated on the tariff and Negro suffrage. The Democratic Convention, meeting in New York City (4 July), adopted a platform attacking Radical Reconstruction and endorsing Congressman **George H. Pendleton's** (1825–89) **"Ohio Idea"** (payment of the national debt in greenbacks). Their nominee for President on the 22nd ballot (9 July) was **Horatio Seymour** (1810–86), former governor of New York and a hard-money man. **Francis P. Blair** (Mo., 1791–1876) won second place. The Republicans made "the bloody shirt of the rebellion" their main campaign issue.

3 Nov. PRESIDENTIAL ELECTION. Grant captured 26 out of 34 states, with an electoral vote of 214–80, but a popular majority of only 306,000 out of 5,715,000 votes. A Negro vote exceeding 500,000 decided the election, in which 3 Southern states did not participate and 6 others were under Radical domination.

SUPREME COURT AND RECONSTRUCTION. In *ex parte Milligan* (Dec. 1866, p. 492) the court declared unconstitutional the resort to martial law where the civil courts were in operation. Nevertheless, the defiant Radicals made military tribunals a prominent feature of Reconstruction legislation. The court denied jurisdiction (*Georgia* v. *Stanton, Mississippi* v. *Johnson*) when two Southern states sought to enjoin executive enforcement of the Reconstruction Acts (Apr., May 1867). In Feb. 1868 the court agreed to consider *ex parte McCardle.* Fearing that a review of this case might invalidate Reconstruction measures, Congress deprived the court of jurisdiction (27 Mar. 1868). In *Texas* v. *White* (1869) the court affirmed Lincoln's position that the Union was indissoluble, but at the same time upheld Congress' authority to reconstruct the states. In *ex parte Garland* and *Cummings* v. *Missouri* (1867) the court invalidated Federal and state loyalty oaths which effectively barred ex-Confederates from pursuing their vocations.

Harris (1883) the Supreme Court held part of the act of 1871 unconstitutional.

1869

18 Mar. CURRENCY ISSUE. The Grant regime supported "hard" money. Congress, by the Public Credit Act, provided for payment of government obligations in gold, thus repudiating the "Ohio Idea." Bitter debate ensued over the question of whether the remaining $356 million in "greenbacks" still in circulation should be redeemed.

24 Sept. "BLACK FRIDAY." In an attempt to corner gold **Jay Gould** (1836–92) and **James** ("Jubilee Jim") **Fisk** (1834–72), stock manipulators, induced Abel Rathbone Corbin, lobbyist brother-in-law of President Grant, to exert himself to prevent the government from selling gold. Despite Grant's refusal to agree, they spread the rumor that the President opposed such sales. With Grant's approval, Secretary of the Treasury **George S. Boutwell** (1818–1905) ordered the sale of $4 million in gold, and the gold price plunged from 162 to 135, with the ruin of many speculators.

1870–71

KU KLUX KLAN was founded at Pulaski, Tenn. (1866); constitution adopted May 1867. Ex-Confederate Gen. **Nathan Bedford Forrest** (1821–77) was the first Grand Wizard. Aimed to destroy Radical political power and establish white supremacy, the order was used as a cloak for lawlessness and violence and formally disbanded (1869), although its activities continued for some time after that date. Congress took cognizance of the order and similar secret societies, such as the Knights of the White Camelia, by passing the **Ku Klux Klan Acts** of 31 May 1870 and 20 Apr. 1871, to enforce the 15th and 14th Amendments, respectively. A Congressional committee sat during the summer of 1871 and took 13 vols. of testimony on conditions in the South. Certain sections of the act of 1870 were declared unconstitutional (*U.S.* v. *Reese; U.S.* v. *Cruikshank,* 1876). In *U.S.* v.

1871

3 Mar. CIVIL SERVICE REFORM. Spoils politics and corruption led to a demand for civil service reform voiced by such leaders as **E. L. Godkin** (p. 715) of the *Nation,* **Carl Schurz** (p. 776), Sumner, and Lyman Trumbull. Grant appointed (4 Mar.) **George William Curtis** (1824–92) to head the first Civil Service Commission, authorized by Act of Congress, which failed to make an appropriation, but he resigned (1875) when his recommendations were ignored, and the commission was discontinued.

8 July. TWEED RING. George Jones of *The New York Times* initiated his exposé of the regime of Tammany Boss **William Marcy Tweed** (1823–78) in New York City, where, through a new city charter creating a Board of Audit, he had seized control of the municipal treasury, which was systematically plundered to the extent of from $75 million to $200 million through faked leases, padded bills, false vouchers, unnecessary repairs, and kickbacks. Tweed was arrested 27 Oct., convicted (5 Nov. 1872), and died in jail. Others spent their plunder abroad.

1872

22 May. AMNESTY ACT removed disability from all but the most prominent (*c.*500) ex-Confederates.

LIBERAL REPUBLICAN MOVEMENT represented a reaction from the Radical Republican policy toward the South as well as from the corruption of the Grant administration. It had its genesis in Sumner's break with Grant over Santo Domingo (p. 281) and in party division in Missouri. Leaders included **Schurz, Gideon Welles** (1803–78), **Charles Francis Adams** (p. 665), **Godkin,** and **Horace Greeley.**

4 Sept. CRÉDIT MOBILIER. A New York *Sun* exposé charged Vice-President Colfax, Vice-Presidential nominee Wilson, Rep. James A. Garfield (Ohio), and other prominent politicians with accepting stock of the Crédit Mobilier (a construction company, organized 1864 by the promoters of the Union Pacific Railway to divert to themselves the profits from building that line) in return for political influence. An investigation which followed resulted in the censure (27 Feb. 1873) of Reps. **Oakes Ames** (Mass.) and **James Brooks** (N.Y.).

CAMPAIGN OF 1872. Convening at Cincinnati (1 May) the Liberal Republicans nominated **Horace Greeley**, protectionist and reformer, for President and **B. Gratz Brown** (Mo.), for Vice-President, and adopted a platform favoring civil service reform, return to specie payments, and reservation of the public domain for the actual settler. The Greeley-Brown slate was also picked by the Democratic National Convention at Baltimore (9 July) despite Greeley's tariff views and long association with the Republicans, and by the Liberal Colored Republicans at Louisville, Ky. (25 Sept.). A "Straight" Democratic National Convention, meeting at Louisville (3 Sept.), nominated **Charles O'Conor** (N.Y.) for President and **John Quincy Adams, II** (Mass.), for Vice-President. The Republicans at Philadelphia (5 June) renominated **Grant** on the 1st ballot and named **Henry Wilson** (Mass.) as his running mate. Natl. Labor Reform ticket, p. 550.

5 Nov. PRESIDENTIAL ELECTION. Grant was the victor, with 286 electoral votes to 66 for Greeley, and a popular majority of 763,000. As Greeley died 29 Nov. his electoral votes were cast as follows: Thomas A. Hendricks, 42; B. Gratz Brown, 18; Charles J. Jenkins, 2; David Davis, 1.

1873

12 Feb. "THE CRIME OF '73," the Coinage Act, demonetized silver (omitting the standard silver dollar from the coinage) and made gold the sole monetary standard, despite the increase in U.S. silver production resultant upon new discoveries in the West (p. 451). The charge that this act was part of a "gold conspiracy" was without foundation, but was an article of faith of many Americans for 20 years.

3 Mar. "SALARY GRAB" ACT doubled the President's salary to $50,000 a year and increased other government officials, including Congressmen (from $5,000 to $7,500). Public indignation forced Congress to repeal the law (20 Jan. 1874) except for the increases voted the President and Supreme Court justices.

18 Sept. PANIC OF 1873. Unbridled railroad speculation, notably in the field of construction, combined with overexpansion in industry, agriculture, and commerce weakened the U.S. financial structure, further shaken by the contraction of European demand for U.S. farm products after 1871. The failure (18 Sept.) of the powerful banking firm of **Jay Cooke** (p. 689) precipitated a fall in security prices, ultimately affecting national income and leading to substantial unemployment (p. 539). As a palliative the government released $26 million in greenbacks (20 Sept.–15 Jan. 1874).

1875

14 Jan. RESUMPTION OF SPECIE PAYMENTS was recommended by President Grant on 6 Dec. 1869 and 7 Dec. 1874. The financial stringency resulting from the Panic of 1873 led to passage of a bill (14 Apr. 1874) to increase the issuance of legal tender notes to $400 million, which Grant vetoed (22 Apr. 1874). Instead, Congress (20 June 1874) placed a ceiling of $382 million on greenbacks in circulation, and by the Specie Resumption Act provided for the resumption of specie payments (by 1 Jan. 1879) and the reduction of greenbacks in circulation to $300 million. (For the Legal Tender Cases, see p. 492.)

1 Mar. CIVIL RIGHTS ACT (Sumner's Bill) guaranteed equal rights in public places (inns, public conveyances, theaters, etc.) without distinction of color and forbade exclusion of Negroes from jury duty. (For the 5 cases involving the validity of the act, see p. 493.)

1 May. WHISKY RING. A conspiracy of revenue officials (chief among them John McDonald, a Grant appointee) and distillers, formed in St. Louis to defraud the government of the internal revenue tax, spread rapidly to other leading cities. As a result of an exposé by the *St. Louis Democrat,* Secretary of the Treasury **Benjamin H. Bristow** (1832–96) ordered an investigation, resulting in the indictment (10 May) of 238 persons, as well as Grant's private secretary, Gen. **O. E. Babcock** (indicted 9 Dec.), who was saved from conviction through the President's intervention.

1876

2 Mar. IMPEACHMENT OF BEL-KNAP. As a result of a House investigation disclosing that Secretary of War **William W. Belknap** (1829–90) had received bribes for the sale of trading posts in the Indian Territory, a resolution of impeachment passed the House. Belknap resigned the same day to avoid trial. Later (1 Aug.) he was acquitted by vote of the Senate, but 23 out of 25 senators who voted not guilty declared that they did so because they believed they had no jurisdiction over an official who had previously resigned.

PRESIDENTIAL CAMPAIGN. The Prohibition party meeting at Cleveland nominated Gen. Green Clay Smith (Ky.) for President and Gideon T. Stewart (Ohio) for Vice-President. The National Greenback Convention at Indianapolis (18 May) nominated Peter Cooper (N.Y., p. 690) for President and Samuel F. Carey (Ohio) for Vice-President. The Republican National Convention at Cincinnati nominated (16 June) **Rutherford B. Hayes** (Ohio) for President on the 7th ballot and **William A. Wheeler** (N.Y.) for Vice-President. Up to the final balloting the leading Presidential candidate had been James G. Blaine, who had been discredited by testimony (31 May) before a house committee by James Mulligan, a bookkeeper for Warren Fisher of Boston. Mulligan charged that Blaine had indirectly sold Little Rock and Fort Smith R.R. bonds to the Union Pacific and had borrowed from him and refused to return incriminating letters. On 5 June Blaine defended himself before the House, reading selected portions of the "Mulligan letters." The Democratic National Convention meeting at St. Louis (27–29 June) nominated **Samuel J. Tilden** (N.Y., 1814–86) for President and **Thomas A. Hendricks** (Ind.) for Vice-President.

7 Nov.–6 Dec. DISPUTED ELECTION OF 1876. The Presidential election gave Tilden a popular-vote margin of 250,000. More decisive, however, was the electoral vote. Tilden carried N.Y., N.J., Conn., Ind., and, apparently, the South; but Republican headquarters refused to concede his election on the ground that the returns were in dispute in Fla., La., S.C., and Ore. (without these electoral votes Tilden, with 184, would be 1 short of the necessary majority). On 6 Dec. 2 sets of electoral returns were reported from the 4 disputed states (in the 3 Southern states Republican election boards threw out sufficient Tilden votes on the ground of irregularities to certify Hayes; in Ore., which the Republicans had unquestionably carried, the Democratic governor, violating Oregon law, disqualified 1 Republican elector and certified a Democrat in his place).

1877

29 Jan. Electoral Commission. The Constitution offered no clear guide for the disputed election of 1876. It provided that "The President of the Senate shall, in the presence of the Senate and the House of Representatives, open all certificates and the votes shall then be counted." But counted by whom? If by the Senate (Republican), the Hayes electors would be sustained; if by the House (Democratic since 1875), the Tilden electors. To break an alarming deadlock Congress set up an **Electoral Commission** consisting of 5 members of the House, 5 of the Senate, and 5 justices of the Supreme Court. Four of the justices were designated in the bill: 2 Republicans, 2 Democrats. The House selected 3 Democrats and 2 Republicans; the Senate, 3 Republicans and 2 Democrats. The 15th member, the 5th justice, was to be selected by the other 4 justices, with the tacit understanding that Justice David Davis, an independent, would be chosen.

But owing to his election by the Illinois state legislature to the U.S. Senate, Davis was replaced by Justice Bradley, a Republican.

9–28 Feb. Commission Award. Under pressure from Republican politicians Bradley, who had first written an opinion favoring Tilden, switched to the Hayes' side. Deciding by a vote of 8–7 (along straight party lines) not to "go behind the returns" and investigate the count in each disputed state, the Commission (9 Feb.) awarded the vote in Florida to Hayes, and later (16, 23, 28 Feb.) gave similar decisions for the 3 remaining states.

2 Mar. HAYES DECLARED ELECTED (185–184). Support by Southern Democrats for the Electoral Commission's decision was the result of Republican promises (1) to withdraw Federal troops from the South, (2) appoint at least 1 Southerner to the Cabinet, and (3) make substantial appropriations for Southern internal improvements. A lobby headed by Thomas A. Scott, president of the Pennsylvania Railroad, and Grenville M. Dodge, chief engineer of the Union Pacific (1866–70), persuaded many Southern Congressmen that the construction of the proposed route of the Texas & Pacific R.R. (chartered 1871) from East Texas to the Pacific coast was dependent on Republican victory. Hayes was inaugurated 5 Mar., after having taken the oath privately on 3 Mar., since 4 Mar. was a Sunday. On 5 Mar. he appointed David M. Key (Tenn.) Postmaster General, and in Apr. withdrew the last Federal troops from the South.

10–24 Apr. END OF "BLACK RECONSTRUCTION." The period of Radical control of the ex-Confederate states had been under attack for corruption, incompetence, and extravagance. Corrupt financial practices were notorious in South Carolina, where the public debt rose from $7 million (1865) to $29 million (1873); but in other states extravagant governments had raised tax burdens and increased state debts (in Ark., from $3.5 million, 1868, to $15.7 million, 1875—$115 per voter; in La., from $11 million to $50 million, 1875, and the state tax rose almost 5-fold, treble the N.Y. real property tax in 1870), while property values declined sharply. But maladministration and corruption were not confined to the South in that period. On the credit side, it should be pointed out that large sums were needed for rebuilding devastated areas and for essential public services in many cases hitherto not adequately provided, such as public education, hospitals, and asylums. By 1876 the constitution in nearly every Southern state contained provisions making tax-supported free public schools for both whites and Negroes mandatory.

In reaction against Radical rule the conservatives won control in Ga., N.C., Tenn., and Va. (1869–71); and in Ala., Ark., Miss., and Tex. (1874–75). By the summer of 1876 only Fla., La., and S.C. remained in Radical hands. On 2 Jan. 1877 carpetbag rule ended in Fla. with the inauguration of George F. Drew, Democratic governor, and the radicals also lost control in the 2 remaining states of the South. Federal troops were withdrawn from S.C. (10 Apr.) and La. (24 Apr.).

DOMESTIC ISSUES FROM HAYES TO WILSON, 1878-1918

1878

28 Feb. BLAND-ALLISON ACT. The demonetization of silver excited little controversy when adopted, but within a few years was characterized as the "Crime of '73" by Western silver-mine operators. Chief factor in the agitation for resuming the unlimited coinage of silver was the discovery, during the middle 70's, of new deposits in Nev., Col., and Utah. The expansion of silver production coincided with a growing international trend toward adoption of the gold standard. Declining market prices for silver bullion led Western mining interests to call for a return to bimetallism. The silverites found natural allies in inflationist-minded agrarian and labor groups who viewed an increase in the volume of circulating money as the best means of raising farm prices and industrial wages. The House of Representatives, dominated by inflationist elements, passed a bill (13 Dec. 1876) sponsored by **Richard P. Bland** (Mo., 1835–99), providing for the free and unlimited coinage of silver at the ratio of 16 to 1. When the Senate took no action, the House again passed the bill (5 Nov. 1877). Weakened by a Senate amendment introduced by Senator **William B. Allison** (Iowa, 1829–1908), the bill was finally passed over President Hayes' veto.

The Bland-Allison Act required the Secretary of the Treasury to make monthly purchases of not less than $2 million and not more than $4 million worth of silver at the market price, such purchases to be converted into standard dollars. Thus, unlimited purchase and coinage, the original goal of the inflationists, was not attained. The act also provided for an international monetary conference (which met without achieving conclusive results).

The effect of the act was not inflationary because of the discretionary powers granted to the Secretary of the Treasury and his conservative use of them. Monthly purchases were made at the minimum amount authorized by law. A revival of prosperity beginning in 1879 staved off further agitation.

GREENBACK LABOR MOVEMENT. The labor unrest of 1877 helped to create labor support for the Greenback program. The Greenback Labor party, organized at the Toledo convention (22 Feb.) attended by some 800 delegates from 28 states, adopted a platform reflecting inflationist and labor viewpoints. The party denounced the resumption of specie payments, and called for the free coinage of silver on a parity with gold, the suppression of national bank notes, restrictions on the hours of industrial labor, and checks on Chinese immigration.

In the Congressional elections of 1878, the Greenback party reached peak strength, with a total of 1,060,000 votes. Fourteen candidates won seats in Congress, where **James B. Weaver** (Iowa, (1833–1912) became the standard bearer of the movement. In 1880 the party broadened its program by endorsing such issues as woman suffrage, Federal regulation of interstate commerce, and a graduated income tax, but after that year declined in strength. In 1884 the Greenback Labor party ran its last independent Presidential candidate, **Benjamin F. Butler** (Mass., 1818–93).

11 July. HAYES AND THE SPOILSMEN. By taking steps to separate the civil service from the domination of the

Radical Republican machine leaders, President Hayes widened his differences with the Senate oligarchy. One of the most flagrant examples of corrupt patronage was the New York custom house, where appointments were controlled by the state political machine under Senator **Roscoe Conkling** (1829–88). When Hayes asked for the resignations of **Chester A. Arthur** (p. 669), port collector of customs, and Alonzo B. Cornell (1832–1904), port naval officer, his request was ignored. The Tenure of Office Act prevented Hayes from removing them. Hayes' own nominations were blocked by the Senate Radicals (12 Dec. 1877), but soon after Congress adjourned in 1878, Hayes suspended Arthur and Cornell (11 July). Later, with Democratic support, Hayes secured confirmation of his appointments. This blow at the Conkling machine and the "Stalwart" faction within the Republican party weakened the Radical hold over the Senate and strengthened the Executive, but it left Hayes without the support of a united party.

1879

1 Jan. RESUMPTION OF SPECIE PAYMENTS began, as authorized by the act of 1875, with no wholesale attempt to reclaim greenbacks (now on a par with the national dollar). On 31 May 1878 Congress had enacted that the $346,681,000 outstanding in greenbacks should remain a permanent part of the currency. Because Secretary of the Treasury **John Sherman** (1823–1900) had accumulated a gold reserve of about $200 million, public confidence was restored in the government's ability to redeem the currency, reflected in the fact that on 17 Dec. 1878 greenbacks reached face value in gold, for the first time since 1862.

HAYES' "RIDER" VETOES. In 1879 the Democrats gained control of both Houses of Congress. They attached to the Army Appropriation Act for 1880 a "rider" which in effect nullified the Force Acts of 1865 and 1874 authorizing the President to use Federal troops in Congressional elections. Hayes' veto

(29 Apr.) invoked the constitutional principle of the equal independence of the various branches of the government. Hayes subsequently vetoed 4 other measures by which Congress attempted to repeal the Force Acts. In his avowal of the principle of military intervention in the South, Hayes drew the support of his party.

1880

PRESIDENTIAL CAMPAIGN. When the Republican National Convention met at Chicago (2 June), the field was open, for Hayes had earlier pledged not to run for a 2nd term. There were 2 rival factions in the party—one headed by the supporters of James G. Blaine; the other by the "Stalwart" leader, Roscoe Conkling, who nominated Ulysses S. Grant. The Grant supporters failed in their effort to secure the adoption of the unit rule. Grant led on the 1st ballot, but **James A. Garfield** of Ohio, a "dark horse," was drafted on the 36th ballot (8 June) after the Blaine and Sherman forces threw their support to him. The "Stalwart" faction was appeased with the nomination of **Chester A. Arthur** (N.Y.) for Vice-President. The Republican platform advocated civil service reform, a protective tariff, veterans' legislation, and the restriction of Chinese immigration.

The Greenback Labor party met at Chicago (9 June) and nominated James B. Weaver (Iowa) for President and B. J. Chambers (Tex.) for Vice-President. The Prohibition party met at Cleveland (17 June) and nominated Neal Dow (Me.) for President and A. M. Thompson (Ohio) for Vice-President.

The Democratic National Convention met at Cincinnati (22 June) and nominated **Winfield Scott Hancock** (Pa., 1824–86) for President and **William H. English** (Ind.) for Vice-President on a platform which, except for demanding a tariff for revenue purposes only, followed that of the Republican party.

The campaign indicated that the Republican tactic of "waving the bloody shirt" was losing its effectiveness, but the revival of prosperity favored the Republicans.

2 Nov. PRESIDENTIAL ELECTION. Popular vote: Garfield, 4,449,053; Hancock, 4,442,035; Weaver, 308,578; Dow, 10,305. Electoral vote: Garfield, 214; Hancock, 155. Victory in N.Y. and Ind. decided the extremely close election for Garfield, whose plurality was under 10,000 out of over 9 million votes. The Republicans regained control of the House for the 1st time since 1874.

1881

23 Mar.–16 May. "HALF-BREEDS" AND "STALWARTS." Blaine's appointment to the Cabinet as Secretary of State (5 Mar.) was regarded by the "Stalwarts" as a victory for the "Half-Breed" wing, and his prominent influence over the administration led to a reopening of political strife between the rival factions of the Republican party. The struggle, revolving about the spoils of office, came to a head when Garfield challenged Conkling's control of the New York patronage by naming (23 Mar.) a Conkling opponent, William H. Robertson, as collector of the port of New York over the protests of Conkling and Thomas Platt, junior senator from New York, who succeeded in blocking the appointment until May and then resigned (16 May) in protest. The New York legislature refused to reelect the pair. The result spelled Conkling's retirement from politics and the decline of the "Stalwart" faction. Garfield's determined stand was as much a victory for Presidential power as it was for the "Half-Breeds."

2 July. ASSASSINATION OF GARFIELD. President Garfield was shot at the Washington railroad station by **Charles J. Guiteau**, a mentally unstable and disappointed office seeker who boasted that he was a "Stalwart" and wanted Arthur for President. Garfield died (19 Sept.) at Elberon, N.J. His assassin was tried (14 Nov.), convicted, and executed 30 June 1882. The murder of Garfield resulted in a strong wave of public opinion against "Stalwartism."

20 Sept. Vice-President **Chester A. Arthur** took oath of office as President; 21st occupant of the office.

CABINET CHANGES. With Arthur's accession to the Presidency, the "Half-Breeds" and independents left the Cabinet. Arthur's choices, however, showed surprising caution and independence of the "Stalwarts."

1882

15 May–4 Dec. TARIFF COMMISSION. Congress authorized appointment by the President of a 9-man Tariff Commission, which on 4 Dec. recommended substantial tariff reductions. (For tariff of 1883, see p. 519.)

1883

16 Jan. PENDLETON ACT. Public reaction to Garfield's assassination, combined with Democratic victories in the fall elections of 1882, impelled the outgoing Republican Congress to adopt civil service reform legislation. The Pendleton Act, drafted by **Dorman B. Eaton** (1823–99), secretary of the Civil Service Reform Association, and sponsored by Senator **George H. Pendleton** (Ohio, 1825–89), provided for a bipartisan 3-man Civil Service Commission (of which Eaton was named head) for drawing up and administering competitive examinations to determine on a merit basis the fitness of appointees to Federal office. A limited classified civil service list was set up, which the President was empowered to extend at his discretion. The act forbade the levying of political campaign assessments on Federal office holders and protected the latter against ouster for failure to make such contributions. Appointments were to be made on the basis of an apportionment among the states according to population. The act immediately affected only larger units and about one tenth of the total number of Federal employees. In addition, it governed only future appointments. Despite its weaknesses, the Pendleton Act enabled the Chief Executive to broaden the merit system and provided the foundation for the Federal civil service in its present form.

1884

RESURGENCE OF AGRARIAN DIS-CONTENT. Five years of farm prosperity (1879–84) were followed by a decline in the prices of agricultural commodities that was to continue steadily until 1896, the result of overproduction and rising competition of foreign wheat-growing countries. The long drought (1887 *et seq.*) caused heavy damage and losses. (For other factors, see p. 508.) When attempts to revive the cooperatives of the Granger era failed to alleviate their plight, farmers banded together in state and regional organizations such as the **Agricultural Wheel,** the **Farmers' Union,** the **Texas State Alliance,** the **Farmers' Mutual Benefit Association,** and the **National Colored Farmers' Alliance.** There finally emerged two great regional bodies, the **Southern Alliance** and the **National Farmers' Alliance of the Northwest.** The farmers aimed their attacks against Eastern moneyed interests, the middlemen, the railroads, industrial monopolies, and advocates of the gold standard.

6 Oct. U.S. Naval War College established at Newport, R.I., with Commodore Stephen B. Luce (1827–1917) as first president. The first institution of its kind, it was founded to provide naval officers with postgraduate training in advanced naval science and warfare, international law, and history.

PRESIDENTIAL CAMPAIGN. The National Greenback Labor party met at Indianapolis (28 May) and nominated Benjamin F. Butler (Mass.) for President and A. M. West (Miss.) for Vice-President. The Republican National Convention met at Chicago (3 June) and on the 4th ballot (6 June) nominated **James G. Blaine** (Me.) for President. **John A. Logan** (Ill.) was nominated for Vice-President. The Republican choice alienated the Independent Republicans, a reform group that regarded Blaine as inimical to the cause of good govern-

ment. Among the Independents, who were shortly dubbed "Mugwumps," were George William Curtis, E. L. Godkin, Carl Schurz, and Charles F. Adams, Jr. Valuing civil service reform above party regularity, the Mugwumps backed the Democratic candidate. The Democratic National Convention, meeting at Chicago (8 July), nominated **Grover Cleveland,** governor of New York, on the 2nd ballot (11 July) and chose **Thomas A. Hendricks** (Ind.) for Vice-President. The Prohibition party national convention met at Pittsburgh (23 July) and nominated John P. St. John (Kan.) for President and William Daniel (Md.) for Vice-President.

The campaign promptly degenerated into one of the most scurrilous in American political history. The "Mulligan letters" (1876), illuminating Blaine's corrupt dealings during his service as Speaker of the House, were fully exploited by the Democrats. The Republicans in turn charged that Cleveland, as a young bachelor in Buffalo, had fathered an illegitimate child. With characteristic honesty, Cleveland acknowledged the truth of the accusation.

The key state in the election was New York, where the Tammany machine headed by John Kelly opposed Cleveland. Shortly before election day, Rev. **Samuel D. Burchard,** leader of a delegation of clergymen who called on Blaine at the Fifth Avenue Hotel in New York (29 Oct.), referred to the Democrats as the party of "Rum, Romanism, and Rebellion." Blaine's failure to disavow the remark or to rebuke Burchard cost him many votes in the Irish-American stronghold of New York. Blaine later said it cost him the election.

4 Nov. PRESIDENTIAL ELECTION. Popular vote: **Cleveland,** 4,911,017; Blaine, 4,848,334; Butler, 175,370; St. John, 150,369. Electoral vote: **Cleveland,** 219; Blaine, 182. The Democrats carried New York by 1,149 out of a total of 1,125,000 votes. Cleveland was the 1st Democratic candidate since Buchanan to win a Presidential election. The Republicans gained 18 seats in the House, but that body still remained under Democratic control (since 1882).

1885

25 Nov. Death of Vice-President Thomas A. Hendricks at Indianapolis, Ind.

1886

19 Jan. PRESIDENTIAL SUCCESSION ACT, which replaced the statute of 1792, provided that in the event of removal, death, resignation, or inability, both of the President and Vice-President, the heads of the executive departments, in order of the creation of their offices, should succeed to the duties of the office of the President. This law remained in effect until 1947.

TREASURY SURPLUS. The accumulation of a large Federal surplus, most of it the result of the continuance of internal revenue taxes levied to finance the Civil War, began to loom as a major political question. The revival of national prosperity in 1879 swelled the surplus (see p. 530), now attacked for withdrawing large sums from general circulation and promoting extravagant government spending. Cleveland referred to the problem in his annual message to Congress in 1886, and looked to a reduction of tariff duties as a means of dealing with it. The Republicans were unwilling to modify protectionism.

WHITNEY AND THE "STEEL NAVY." After the Civil War the U.S. Navy, consisting of obsolescent wooden ships, fell into disrepair. In 1880 the U.S. stood 12th among the world's naval powers. In 1881 a naval advisory board recommended the construction of steel cruisers. On 3 Mar. 1883 Congress, taking initial steps toward the creation of a modern navy, authorized the building of 3 steel cruisers; further shipbuilding authorized 3 Aug. 1886. Constructive reforms and advances awaited the reorganization of the Navy Department by Secretary **William C. Whitney** (1841–1904). He coordinated the bureaus, rid the fleet of antiquated vessels, and embarked on the rapid construction of modern steel ships incorporating advances in naval armament (22 such vessels had been built or authorized by the time Whitney left office, 1889). By insisting upon naval armor of American manufacture, Whitney encouraged the development of domestic steelworks capable of producing heavy ship plates and huge naval guns, thereby eliminating American dependence upon European steelmakers. Whitney's naval policy was continued by succeeding administrations. By 1900 the U.S. ranked 3rd among world naval powers.

1887

3 Feb. ELECTORAL COUNT ACT, designed to prevent a disputed national election (as in the instance of the Hayes-Tilden election of 1876), made each state the absolute judge over appointment or returns, specifying Congressional acceptance of electoral returns certified by a state in accordance with its own electoral law. Congress can intervene only if the state itself is unable to decide or has decided irregularly. In such cases, a concurrent vote of Congress is decisive, but should the 2 Houses disagree, the votes of those electors whose appointment is certified by the governor shall be counted.

4 Feb. INTERSTATE COMMERCE ACT. Public resentment of abuses in railway transportation led to numerous bills and resolutions being placed before Congress. In 1874 a special Senate Committee headed by **William Windom** (Minn., 1827–91) had advocated competitive routes to the seaboard, development of waterways, and establishment of a statistical bureau; but this report failed to satisfy the demand of agrarian groups for government regulation. The McCrary Bill, introduced in 1874, provided for the establishment of a Federal commission empowered to fix maximum rates, investigate complaints, and call witnesses. The measure passed the House by a narrow margin, but was never considered by the Senate. The Senate likewise failed to act on the Reagan Bill (1878), which called for the prohibition of railroad pools, rebates, drawbacks, and discriminatory rates.

In the absence of Federal legislation, the movement for railroad regulation within the states gained momentum during the 70's with the passage of the so-called **Granger laws**, which received judicial approval in the Supreme Court decision in **Munn v. Illinois** (1877, p. 493). However, the states were virtually stripped of their restraining power over the railroads by the Supreme Court decision in the **Wabash Case** (1886, p. 494). Continuing public dissatisfaction made itself felt through the Cullom Committee headed by Senator **Shelby M. Cullom** (Ill., 1829–1914), which in 1885 conducted hearings throughout the country and submitted a report recommending the Federal regulation of interstate commerce.

The result was the Interstate Commerce Act, which passed the House, 219–41, and the Senate, 43–15. Applying only to railroads passing through more than one state, the act provided that all charges made by railways must be reasonable and just (but did not authorize rate-fixing); prohibited pooling operations, discriminatory rates, drawbacks, and rebates; and made it illegal to charge more for a short haul than for a long haul over the same line. Railroads were required to post their rates, and could not change them until after a 10-day public notice. The act created the **Interstate Commerce Commission**, the first regulatory commission in U.S. history. The commission was authorized to investigate the management of railroads, summon witnesses, and compel the production of company books and papers, but its orders did not have the binding force of a court decree. However, it could invoke the aid of equity proceedings in the Federal courts. The commission was empowered to require railroads to file annual reports of operations and finances and to adopt a uniform system of accounting.

At the outset, the railroads conformed to the law, but after 1890 difficulties in interpretation and application made the practical results of the act feeble and disappointing. Railroad operators used a variety of devices for circumventing the provisions of the act. The decisions of the commission met serious reversals at the hands of the Supreme Court, as in the Maximum Freight Rate case (1897) and the Alabama Midlands case (1897). By 1898 the commission had been reduced to virtual impotence, and was active chiefly as a body for the collection and publication of statistics.

11 Feb. CLEVELAND'S PENSION VETOES. By the middle 80's Union veterans on the pension rolls constituted a heavy drain on the national Treasury. Veterans' appropriations increased markedly after the passage of the Arrears of Pension Act (1879), enacted under pressure from the Grand Army of the Republic. Cleveland, insofar as pressure of duties permitted, followed a policy of investigating individual claims and vetoing those which appeared to be fraudulent. While he approved more special pension bills than did any of his predecessors, he also vetoed more. In 1885, annual expenditures for pensions stood at $56 million; by 1888, they had increased to $80 million. Cleveland's vetoes earned him the bitter antagonism of the organized "old soldier" interests.

The climax came when Senator Henry W. Blair (N.H.) introduced the **Dependent Pension Bill**, passed by Congress in Jan. 1887. This measure provided a pension for all honorably discharged veterans with at least 90 days' service who were then unable to earn their support and depended on manual labor for a living. It established a precedent for pensioning without regard to service-connected disability. Cleveland vetoed the bill (11 Feb.), declaring it would make the pension list a refuge for frauds rather than a "roll of honor."

2 Mar. HATCH ACT for the promotion of agricultural science provided Federal subsidies for the creation of state agricultural experiment stations.

5 Mar. TENURE OF OFFICE ACT (1867), as amended in 1869, was repealed after Cleveland's contest with the Senate over appointments and removals from office. Cleveland's message to the Senate (1 Mar. 1886) had insisted that under the Constitution the President had the sole power of suspension or removal. By his action, Cleveland strengthened the independence of the Executive.

7–15 June. CONFEDERATE BATTLE FLAGS. Cleveland again incurred the enmity of the organized Union veterans' interests when he approved a War Department order (7 June) for the return of captured Confederate battle flags to the South. Even though the order was by way of executive routine, and had been initiated at the behest of Adj. Gen. Richard C. Drum, a Republican and a member of the G.A.R., it brought angry protests from Republican politicians and leaders of the G.A.R. Cleveland revoked the order (15 June). The flags were finally returned in 1905 during the administration of Theodore Roosevelt.

6 Dec. After long deliberation, and without consulting the leaders of his party, Cleveland devoted his entire annual message to a plea for a lowered protective tariff, pointing out that the existing rates had encouraged the creation of trusts and the maintenance of high prices. His advocacy of tariff reform alienated protectionist elements within the Democratic party.

1888

PRESIDENTIAL CAMPAIGN. The Union Labor party convention met at Cincinnati (15 May) and nominated Alson J. Streeter (Ill.) for President and C. E. Cunningham (Ark.) for Vice-President. The United Labor party, also meeting at Cincinnati (15 May), nominated Robert H. Cowdrey (Ill.) for President and W. H. T. Wakefield (Kan.) for Vice-President. The national convention of the Prohibition party met at Indianapolis (30 May) and nominated Clinton B. Fisk (N.J.) for President and John A. Brooks (Mo.) for Vice-President. The Democratic National Convention met at St. Louis (5 June) and nominated President **Grover Cleveland** for reelection and **Allen G. Thurman** (Ohio) for Vice-President. The Republican National Convention met at Chicago (19 June) and nominated **Benjamin Harrison** (Ind.) for President and **Levi P. Morton** (N.Y.) for Vice-President.

The Republicans made the high protective tariff the chief plank in their platform, and the campaign thus became the first in U.S. history waged on this issue. The Republicans also included a promise of generous pensions for Civil War veterans. A huge Republican campaign fund, which found ready contributors among the enemies of tariff reform, was employed to denounce Cleveland's stand on the tariff, his pension vetoes, and the Confederate battle flag order. On the eve of the election the Democratic cause was dealt a severe blow by the **"Murchison letter"** involving the British Minister to the U.S., Sackville-West. The letter was written ostensibly by "Charles F. Murchison," a naturalized Englishman (in reality George A. Osgoodby, a California Republican) seeking Sackville-West's counsel on how to vote in the approaching election. The British Minister's reply (13 Sept.) intimated that "Murchison" should vote for Cleveland. The correspondence was published (24 Oct.) by the Republicans and aroused public indignation against foreign interference in internal affairs. Sackville-West was handed his passports (24 Oct.), but the damaging political blunder cost the Democrats many Irish-American votes.

6 Nov. PRESIDENTIAL ELECTION. Popular vote: Cleveland, 5,540,050; **Harrison,** 5,444,337; Fisk, 250,125; Streeter, 146,897; Cowdrey, 2,808. Electoral vote: **Harrison,** 233; Cleveland, 168. Harrison carried the key states of New York and Indiana.

1889

11 Feb. Department of Agriculture raised to Cabinet status. Norman J. Coleman (Mo.) named first Secretary of Agriculture.

22 Feb. OMNIBUS BILL provided for the admission of North Dakota, South Dakota, Montana, and Washington.

1890

19 June. FORCE BILL, reported in the House, provided for supervision of Federal elections by the national government in order to protect Negro voters in the

South against state measures designed to deprive them of the vote. It passed the House (2 July), but failed of adoption by the Senate.

27 June. DEPENDENT PENSION ACT. Upon taking office, Harrison appointed as Commissioner of Pensions James "Corporal" Tanner, a past commander of the G.A.R., who declared, "God help the surplus!" During his 6 mos. in office, Tanner pursued a liberal private pension policy. The administration's debt to the "old soldier" vote was discharged with the passage of the Dependent Pension Act, which granted pensions to veterans of the Union forces with at least 90 days' service who were then or thereafter disabled because of physical or mental reasons (without regard to origin) and were unable to earn a livelihood by manual labor. The Act, which inaugurated the principle of the service pension, also provided that pensions of varying amounts were to be granted to minor children, dependent parents, and widows who had married veterans before the passage of the Act and had to work for a living. Between 1891 and 1895 the number of pensioners rose from 676,000 to 970,000. By the time Harrison left office, the annual appropriation for pensions had increased from $81 million to $135 million.

2 July. SHERMAN ANTITRUST ACT. With the establishment of the first industrial combination, the Standard Oil Trust (1879), there followed in rapid succession other large combinations controlling such commodities as whisky, sugar, lead, beef, and linseed oil. In protest many Western and Southern states enacted antitrust laws, the first in Kansas in 1889. By 1893 similar legislation had been enacted in 15 other states and territories. Since such state laws were powerless to deal with trusts and monopolies engaged in interstate commerce, the demand for governmental regulation of national scope became insistent.

The result was the first Federal measure that undertook to regulate trusts. Although the Sherman Antitrust Act was named for Sen. **John Sherman** (Ohio, 1823–1900), the bill was drafted by the Senate Judiciary Committee, the larger share of the work being credited to Sen. **George F. Hoar** (Mass., 1826–1904) and George F. Edmunds (Vt., 1828–1919). The Act, consisting of eight major provisions, declared: "Every contract, combination in the form of trust or otherwise, or conspiracy, in restraint of trade or commerce among the several states, or with foreign nations, is hereby declared to be illegal." The Act authorized the Federal government to proceed against a trust to obtain its dissolution, and invested Federal circuit courts with jurisdiction to prevent and restrain violations of the law.

The most critical weakness of the act was its obscure and ambiguous phrasing, its failure clearly to define words like "trust," "combination," and "restraint." It was not clear whether the act was intended to apply to labor combinations and railroads as well as to combinations of capital. That its provisions embraced labor unions and railroads, respectively, was the decision of the Federal courts in *U.S.* v. *Debs* (1894) and in the Trans-Missouri Freight Association case (1897). In the case of *U.S.* v. *E. C. Knight Company* (1895), among the first in which the Supreme Court interpreted and applied the act, the effectiveness of the law was seriously limited. Between 1890 and 1901, the act was not vigorously enforced. During that period only 18 suits were instituted, 4 against labor unions. The existence of the statute did not prevent the continued growth of combinations and monopolies under other names. (See also p. 524.)

14 July. SHERMAN SILVER PURCHASE ACT. The Bland-Allison Act satisfied neither silverites nor gold standard advocates. Meanwhile, the steady decline in the market price of silver bullion (by 1890 it stood to gold at a ratio of 20 to 1), combined with the deepening economic depression, helped to increase the political strength of the silver and inflationist forces (reinforced by senators from the recently admitted Omnibus states [1889]). In the House, which still remained under the control of gold standard men, the silverites gained new accessions from representatives voted into office by the Farmers' Alliances.

The prosilverite Senate passed a bill

(June) for the free and unlimited coinage of silver, but the House blocked its passage. By threatening to vote against the McKinley tariff bill, Western interests were able to wrest a concession from conservative Easterners, and a compromise was arranged to permit a more liberal purchase policy. The Sherman Silver Purchase Act, while it did not provide for free silver, required the Treasury to purchase 4,500,000 ounces of silver each month at the prevailing market price and to issue in payment legal tender Treasury notes redeemable in gold or silver at the option of the Treasury. The amount of bullion specified was the currently estimated total U.S. production of silver.

The act had the effect of increasing the circulation of redeemable paper currency and weakening the Federal gold reserve. Among Eastern business and financial groups it created a fear that the silver inflation might take the country off the gold standard. Nor did the act satisfy the demands of those who advocated free coinage and a bimetallic standard. Cleveland made his position clear. In a public letter (10 Feb. 1891) he attacked the "dangerous and reckless experiment of free, unlimited, and independent coinage."

4 Nov. Congressional elections in 39 states resulted in a Democratic landslide that cost the Republicans their control of the House. Public reaction against the McKinley Tariff of 1890 was blamed for the Republican defeat.

1892

PEOPLE'S (POPULIST) PARTY. The sectional struggle between debtor and creditor, intensified by the continuing agricultural depression, led the agrarian protest movement to take political action. Beginning in 1889–90, efforts were made to unite farmer and labor organizations on the basis of common objectives. The agrarian organizations of the West and South, together with labor, Granger, and Greenback representatives, held a meeting at St. Louis (Dec. 1889). In June 1890, the statewide People's party was formed in Kansas. In Dec.

1890, the Southern Alliance, the Farmers' Mutual Benefit Association, and the Colored Farmers' Alliance convened at Ocala, Fla., and drew up a list of grievances resembling the platform approved at St. Louis. These included cheap currency, the abolition of national banks, and the restriction of land ownership to American citizens. Labor men who attended the Ocala meeting called for the establishment of a 3rd party, but the Southern Alliance, fearing such a movement might bring the Negro into power, opposed independent action. The Alliance advised its members to support instead candidates of either major party who would pledge themselves to policies benefiting agriculture. In general, Southern agrarian leaders adopted the tactic of attempting to capture the Democratic machinery.

A national convention was held at Cincinnati (19 May 1891) to plan independent action. More than 1,400 delegates from 32 states adopted resolutions supporting a new party. The **People's Party of the U.S.A.** was formally organized at St. Louis (22 Feb.) and held its 1st national convention at Omaha (2 July). Present at Omaha were the outstanding leaders of the Populist movement, including **Ignatius Donnelly** (Minn.), **Thomas E. Watson** (Ga.), **"Sockless Jerry" Simpson** (Kan.), **Mary Ellen Lease** (Kan.), **William A. Peffer** (Kan.), and **James Kyle** (S.D.). Only a small minority of the Southern Alliance backed the third-party movement.

The Populist convention nominated **James B. Weaver** (Iowa) for President and **James G. Field** (Va.) for Vice-President. The Populist platform (4 July) demanded free and unlimited coinage of silver at 16 to 1, and an increase in the circulating medium of not less than $50 per capita; a national currency issued by the Federal government only and without the use of banking corporations; government ownership and operation of all transportation and communication lines; a graduated income tax; establishment of a postal savings system; direct election of U.S. senators; adoption of the secret ballot, the initiative, and referendum; prohibition of the alien ownership of land; a shorter working day for industrial labor; and restrictions on immigration.

PRESIDENTIAL CAMPAIGN. The Republican National Convention met at Minneapolis (7 June) and on 10 June nominated President **Benjamin Harrison** for reelection and **Whitelaw Reid** (N.Y.) for Vice-President. The party's chief plank was the high protective tariff. The Democratic National Convention met at Chicago (21 June) and nominated **Grover Cleveland** for President and **Adlai E. Stevenson** (Ill.) for Vice-President. The straddling plank on the tariff, opposed by the radical wing of the Democratic party, was dropped in favor of a stronger declaration "that the federal government has no constitutional power to impose and collect tariff duties, except for purposes of revenue only." During the campaign, however, Cleveland took a moderate stand on the tariff. The National Prohibition Convention met at Cincinnati (29 June) and nominated John Bidwell (Calif.) for President and James B. Cranfill (Tex.) for Vice-President. The Socialist Labor Convention met at New York and nominated Simon Wing (Mass.) for President and Charles H. Matchett (N.Y.) for Vice-President.

Cleveland's unswerving position on the gold standard won him the heavy support of conservative Eastern financial and business groups. The Democrats kept the silver issue in the background except in those states where the inflationist forces were strong. Factors which militated against Republican success included public reaction to the McKinley Tariff of 1890 and the labor disturbances of 1892.

8 Nov. PRESIDENTIAL ELECTION. Popular vote: **Cleveland**, 5,554,414; Harrison, 5,190,802; Weaver, 1,027,329; Bidwell, 271,058; Wing, 21,164. Electoral vote: **Cleveland**, 277; Harrison, 145; Weaver, 22. The Democrats secured control of both houses of Congress.

1893

PANIC OF 1893: U.S. GOLD RESERVE. U.S. fiscal conditions were adversely affected by (1) failure (Nov. 1890) of the British banking house of Baring Bros., causing British investors to unload American securities, with a resultant drain of gold from the U.S.; (2) a sharp decrease in U.S. revenues attributed to the McKinley Tariff Act; (3) depletion of government surplus by pension grants of the Harrison administration. The decline of the U.S. gold reserve below the $100 million mark (21 Apr.) helped precipitate the panic. On 5 May stocks on the New York Stock Exchange dropped suddenly, crashing 27 June (see also p. 538). By 30 Dec. the gold reserve fell to $80 million.

1 Nov. REPEAL OF SHERMAN SILVER PURCHASE ACT. To stem the drain on the gold reserve Cleveland summoned (30 June) an extra session of Congress to convene 7 Aug., requesting repeal of the Sherman Silver Purchase Act. The struggle over repeal, centered in the Senate, proved the grimmest of Cleveland's Presidential career. Repeal passed the House, 239–108 (28 Aug.), and the Senate, 48–37 (30 Oct.), but the administration's victory split the Democratic party.

1894

25 Mar.–1 May. "COXEY'S ARMY." Over the winter of 1893–94 growing economic distress and mass unemployment brought the formation of scattered groups of jobless men into "armies" whose leaders were known as "generals." Of these, the best known was "Coxey's Army," led by the Populist **Jacob S. Coxey** of Massillon, Ohio. Coxey called upon the unemployed to march upon Washington and deliver to Congress their demands for relief. Although many small detachments of the "army" started out from various points throughout the country, only 400 reached the national capital (30 Apr.). Coxey advocated a public works relief program of road construction and local improvements financed by a Federal issue of $500 million in legal tender notes. The program had a twofold purpose: to provide jobs and to increase the amount of money in circulation. "Coxey's Army" disbanded after its 3 leaders (Coxey, Carl Browne, and Christopher Columbus Jones) were arrested for trespassing on the Capitol grounds.

FREE-SILVER PROPAGANDA. *Coin's Financial School* (1894), by William H. Harvey of Chicago, which soon became the infallible guide of the bimetallists, was followed by similar tracts, including *The American People's Money* (1895), by Ignatius Donnelly. Among the magazines that served as a platform for the silverites were the *Arena* and the *National Bimetallist*.

BEGINNINGS OF CONSERVATION. Early conservation measures included the establishment of the **Division of Forestry** (1887) in the Department of Agriculture and, shortly afterward, the survey of irrigation sites by Maj. **John W. Powell** (p. 767) of the U.S. Geological Survey. The **Forest Reserve Act** (3 Mar. 1891) repealed the Timber Culture Act of 1878 and authorized the President to set apart forest reserve lands in any part of the public domain. The **Carey Act** (18 Aug.) authorized the President to grant to each public-land state a maximum of 1 million acres within its boundaries for irrigation, reclamation, settlement, and cultivation. The surplus funds accruing to each state from this program were to be used for reclaiming other lands in the state.

1895

5 Mar. APPEAL OF THE SILVER DEMOCRATS. The broadening cleavage in the Democratic party between the gold and silver factions was indicated by the "Appeal of the Silver Democrats" framed by **Richard P. Bland** (Mo.) and **William Jennings Bryan** (Neb., p. 680), leaders of the silver bloc in the House. The appeal, signed by a minority of House Democrats, called for the immediate restoration of the free and unlimited coinage of silver at the ratio of 16 to 1. During the year a number of free-silver conventions were held in the South and West.

GOLD RESERVE. Repeal of the Sherman Silver Act failed to halt depletion of the gold reserve. Confronted by declining government revenues, the Treasury was compelled to use the gold reserve not only for redemption but also for meeting operating expenses. After unsuccessfully attempting to win Congressional authority to sell bonds, Secretary of the Treasury Carlisle took steps to maintain a normal gold reserve. Invoking the unrepealed provisions of the Resumption Act of 1875 for borrowing gold, he invited bids for a bond issue of $50 million (Jan. 1894), and in Nov. 1894 asked for a similar loan; but owing to lack of public response to the offerings, had to place the loans with New York bankers. Successive withdrawals finally caused the gold reserve to fall to $41 million early in 1895. Cleveland moved to cope with the Treasury crisis by calling J. Pierpont Morgan, the New York banker, to a White House interview (7 Feb.). The result was a 3rd loan placed with a banking syndicate headed by Morgan and August Belmont. The arrangement called for the purchase of 3,500,000 ounces of gold, to be paid for in bonds. One half of the gold was to be purchased abroad. It is estimated that the bankers realized a profit of some $1.5 million on the $62 million loan. While the loan succeeded in relieving the Treasury emergency for a time, it was condemned by Populists and bimetallists. Upon the expiration of the Morgan-Belmont contract, the government was again compelled to resort to a loan when the reserve dipped to $79 million (Dec.), but this time the administration threw the $100 million loan open to the public (6 Jan. 1896). Its quick subscription indicated a restoration of public confidence. But the Treasury had to resume withdrawal of gold to pay for bonds; consequently, by July 1896, the reserve fell below the $90 million mark. The situation was not serious because of the revival of business activity, but gold hoarding did not cease until after the election of 1896, when the future of the gold standard was assured.

1896

PRESIDENTIAL CAMPAIGN. The Prohibition National Convention met at Pittsburgh (27 May) and nominated

Joshua Levering (Md.) for President and Hale Johnson (Ill.) for Vice-President. A free-silver minority, organized as the National party, nominated Charles E. Bentley (Neb.) for President and J. H. Southgate (N.C.) for Vice-President. The Republican National Convention met at St. Louis (16 June) and nominated **William McKinley** (Ohio) for President and **Garret A. Hobart** (N.J.) for Vice-President on a platform upholding the single gold standard (although the Republicans promised to promote the free-silver policy by international agreement), the high protective tariff, and a vigorous foreign policy (calling for U.S. control of the Hawaiian Islands). The way for McKinley's nomination had been prepared by the maneuvers of the Cleveland industrialist and financier, **Marcus A. Hanna** (p. 721), named Republican party campaign manager. Adoption of the gold plank caused Western silver Republicans under Sen. **Henry M. Teller** (Colo.) to bolt the party. Organized as the National Silver Republicans, they held a national convention at St. Louis (22 July) and endorsed the Democratic candidates. The Socialist Labor National Convention met at New York (4 July) and nominated **Charles H. Matchett** (N.Y.) for President and **Matthew Maguire** (N.J.) for Vice-President.

When the Democratic National Convention met at Chicago (7 July), it was clear that the free-silver faction was in control of the party organization. The Democratic platform called for the free and unlimited coinage of silver at the 16 to 1 ratio; condemned trusts, monopolies, and the high protective tariff, as well as the use of injunctions against labor; and attacked the Supreme Court ruling in the income tax case. The dominant issue was the money question. In support of the adoption of the free-silver plan, William Jennings Bryan (Neb.) delivered his eloquent **"Cross of Gold"** speech (8 July), closing with this challenge to the advocates of the gold standard: "You shall not press down upon the brow of labor this crown of thorns, you shall not crucify mankind upon a cross of gold." **Bryan** was nominated for President and **Arthur Sewall** (Me.) for

Vice-President. The gold Democrats withdrew from the convention, organized the National Democratic party, and in convention at Indianapolis (2 Sept.) nominated **John M. Palmer** (Ill.) for President and **Simon B. Buckner** (Ky.) for Vice-President on a platform supporting the gold standard. The People's (Populist) National Convention, meeting at St. Louis (22 July), endorsed Bryan's nomination and chose Thomas E. Watson (Ga.) for Vice-President.

Supported by 3 parties, Bryan, the "Boy Orator of the Platte," waged a vigorous and strenuous campaign, traveling 13,000 miles in 14 weeks, making 600 speeches in 29 states. Against Bryan the Republicans, under Hanna's political generalship, and with a much larger campaign fund, pictured Bryan as an "anarchist" and a "revolutionist." McKinley staged a front-porch campaign from his home in Canton, Ohio. The campaign arrayed creditor against debtor, the moneyed East against the agrarian West and South.

3 Nov. PRESIDENTIAL ELECTION. Popular vote: **McKinley,** 7,035,638; Bryan, 6,467,946; Levering, 141,676; Palmer, 131,529; Matchett, 36,454; Bentley, 13,969. Electoral vote: **McKinley,** 271; Bryan, 176. The Republicans retained control of both houses of Congress which they had previously won in 1894.

1898

12 May. Louisiana adopted constitution disfranchising Negroes under property and literacy tests and the "grandfather clause."

1 June. ERDMAN ACT (p. 553).

1 July. FEDERAL BANKRUPTCY ACT extended to traders and nontraders, allowed voluntary and involuntary bankruptcy, and provided for creditor participation and discharge of the debtor; amended by Act of 22 June 1938.

1900

14 Mar. CURRENCY ACT (GOLD STANDARD ACT) declared the gold dollar of 25.8 grains, nine tenths fine, the standard unit of value and placed all forms of money issued by the U.S. on a parity with gold. A gold reserve (fixed at $150 million and to be set apart from other funds), whose maintenance was authorized by the sale of bonds, was provided for the redemption of legal tender notes. Agrarian financial needs were partly satisfied by the authorization of national banks with a capital of not less than $25,000 in towns of under 3,000 population.

PRESIDENTIAL CAMPAIGN. The Social Democratic National Convention met at Indianapolis (9 Mar.) and nominated Eugene V. Debs (Ind., p. 693) for President and Job Harriman (Calif.) for Vice-President. The People's (Anti-Fusion) National Convention met at Cincinnati (9 May) and nominated Wharton Barker (Pa.) for President and Ignatius Donnelly (Minn.) for Vice-President. The Socialist Labor National Convention met at New York (2 June) and nominated Joseph P. Maloney (Mass.) for President and Valentine Remmel (Pa.) for Vice-President. The Republican National Convention met at Philadelphia (19 June) and nominated President **McKinley** for reelection and **Theodore Roosevelt** (N.Y.) for Vice-President on a platform upholding the gold standard, the administration's foreign policy, and a U.S.-built-and-controlled isthmian canal. The Prohibition National Convention met at Chicago (27 June) and nominated John G. Woolley (Ill.) for President and Henry B. Metcalf (R.I.) for Vice-President. The Democratic National Convention met at Kansas City, Mo. (4 July), and nominated **William Jennings Bryan** (Neb.) for President and Adlai E. Stevenson (Ill.) for Vice-President on a platform condemning imperialism and the Currency Act, and calling for the free coinage of silver. The Fusion Populists also endorsed Bryan. The Democrats made imperialism the "paramount issue"; the Republicans stressed the "Full Dinner Pail" as symbol of the administration's success.

6 Nov. PRESIDENTIAL ELECTION. Popular vote: **McKinley,** 7,219,530; Bryan, 6,358,071; Woolley, 209,166;

Debs, 94,768; Barker, 50,232. Electoral vote: **McKinley,** 292; Bryan, 155. The Republicans retained control of both houses of Congress.

1901

6 Sept. ASSASSINATION OF McKINLEY. President McKinley, while attending a reception at the Pan-American Exposition, Buffalo, N.Y., was shot by Leon Czolgosz, an anarchist. McKinley died 14 Sept.

14 Sept. Theodore Roosevelt took oath as 25th President.

27 Nov. ARMY WAR COLLEGE. The defects in the U.S. military structure, as revealed during the Spanish-American War, led Secretary of War **Elihu Root** (p. 773, succeeded 1 Aug. 1899 Russell A. Alger, who resigned 19 July 1899 under public criticism) to undertake reorganization of the army. An initial step was to open the Army War College (Tasker H. Bliss, president) to advance the higher instruction and training of officers under a unified system.

1902

ROOSEVELT'S TRUST POLICY. The trend toward industrial mergers and combines (p. 524), culminating (1901) in the formation of the U.S. Steel Corp., first billion-dollar company, and the Northern Securities Co., a railroad holding company, was considered by Roosevelt in his 1st annual message to Congress (3 Dec. 1901), in which he recommended legislation to abolish abuses without destroying combinations. Failing to get Congressional action, he directed Attorney General Knox to file suit (10 Mar.) for dissolution of the Northern Securities Co. On 19 Aug. Roosevelt left Washington on a tour of New England and the Middle West to bring the trust issue directly to the people. Demanding a "square deal" for all, he pledged strict enforcement of existing antitrust laws and called for stricter supervision and control of big business. "We do not wish to destroy corporations," he said, "but we do wish to make them subserve the public good." The adamant stand of the mine owners during the anthracite coal strike of 1902 (p. 553) created broad support for Roosevelt's program, which was strengthened by the Supreme Court decision in the government's favor in the Northern Securities case (1904, p. 495).

17 June. NEWLANDS ACT (p. 465). **REFORM MOVEMENT IN THE STATES** attacked the alliance between organized wealth and machine politics. An outstanding example was the "**Wisconsin Idea**," a term applied to the legislative and administrative advances (including an **income tax** and a **railroad commission**) adopted in Wisconsin during the governorship of **Robert M. La-Follette** (p. 701). In keeping with what became the Progressive ideal of returning government to the electorate, Wisconsin was the 1st state to adopt the **direct primary** (23 May 1903). Oregon was the first state to adopt the **initiative** and **referendum** on a general scale (2 June 1902), and in 1904 instituted the **preferential primary**. The movement against municipal boss rule also gained impetus during this period, as exemplified in the reforms initiated by Mayor **Samuel** ("**Golden Rule**") **Jones** (1846–1904) of Toledo, who was elected in 1897, and by Mayor **Tom L. Johnson** (1854–1911) of Cleveland, who took office in 1901.

1903

MUCKRAKERS, a group of writers who aroused public opinion with exposures of dishonesty, greed, and corruption in machine politics and business and also attacked social evils like slums, juvenile delinquency, and prostitution. Magazines of wide circulation (*Collier's, McClure's, Cosmopolitan,* the *American,* and *Everybody's*) threw their pages open to disclosures, in time weakened by appeals to the purely sensational. One of the pioneer muckrakers was Ida M. Tarbell, whose *History of the Standard Oil Company* began in McClure's in 1903. Other noted exposures were Lincoln Steffens' *The Shame of the Cities* (1904), David Graham Phillips's *The Treason of the Senate* (1906), Thomas W. Lawson's

Frenzied Finance (1902), Gustavus Myers' *History of the Great American Fortunes* (1910), Burton J. Hendrick's *Story of Life Insurance* (1907), Charles Edward Russell's *The Greatest Trust in the World* (1905; on the beef trust), and Ray Stannard Baker's "The Railroads on Trial" (*McClure's,* 1906). The muckraking impulse also appeared in fiction, most sensationally in Upton Sinclair's *The Jungle* (1906), exposing conditions in the Chicago stockyards and meat-packing plants. Muckraking literature reached its height between *c.*1904 and *c.*1910. Increasing stress on sensationalism led President Roosevelt (14 Apr. 1906) in a public address caustically to compare some of these writers to the man with the muckrake (in Bunyan's *Pilgrim's Progress*) who was so busy raking the filth off the floor that he could look no way but downward, and to suggest that constructive effort was more important than mere exposure.

11 Feb. EXPEDITION ACT, designed to expedite prosecution of Federal antitrust suits, gave such proceedings precedence (at the request of the Attorney General) on the dockets of the circuit courts.

14 Feb. DEPARTMENT OF COMMERCE AND LABOR established by act of Congress. It included a Bureau of Corporations empowered to investigate and report upon the operations of corporations (with the exception of common carriers) engaged in interstate commerce. The first Secretary of Commerce and Labor, George B. Cortelyou (N.Y.), was appointed 16 Feb.

14 Feb. Army General Staff Corps established by act of Congress at behest of Secretary of War Root. The move was part of the War Department reorganization based to some extent on Root's study of *The Military Policy of the United States,* by Emory Upton (1904). The act created a corps charged with the preparation and execution of military plans, and discarded the system of divided authority that had created conflict between the Secretary of War and the commanding general.

19 Feb. ELKINS ACT, aimed primarily at eliminating the rebate evil, reinforced the Interstate Commerce Act by defining unfair discrimination between shippers engaged in interstate commerce and by providing for the punishment of shippers and railway officials and agents, as well as railroad corporations, for the giving or receiving of rebates. The act made it a misdemeanor for railroads to deviate from published rates and invested the Federal courts with the power to issue injunctions against violators.

8 Nov. PRESIDENTIAL ELECTION. Popular vote: **Roosevelt**, 7,628,834; Parker, 5,084,401; Debs, 402,460; Swallow, 259,257; Watson, 114,753; Corregan, 33,724; Holcomb, 830. Electoral vote: **Roosevelt**, 336; Parker, 140. The Republicans retained control of both Houses of Congress. On the night of his election Roosevelt pledged that "under no circumstances will I be a candidate for or accept another nomination."

1904

PRESIDENTIAL CAMPAIGN. The Socialist National Convention met at Chicago (1 May) and nominated **Eugene V. Debs** (Ind.) for President and Benjamin Hanford (N.Y.) for Vice-President. The Republican National Convention met at Chicago (21 June) and by acclamation nominated President **Theodore Roosevelt** for re-election and **Charles W. Fairbanks** (Ind.) for Vice-President on a platform shaped by party conservatives. The Prohibition National Convention met at Indianapolis (29 June) and nominated Silas C. Swallow (Pa.) for President and George W. Carroll (Tex.) for Vice-President. The Socialist Labor National Convention met at New York (2 July) and nominated Charles H. Corregan (N.Y.) for President and William C. Cox (Ill.) for Vice-President. The People's (Populist) National Convention met at Springfield, Ill. (4 July), and nominated **Thomas E. Watson** (Ga., 1856–1922) for President and Thomas H. Tibbles (Neb.) for Vice-President. The Democratic National Convention met at St. Louis (6 July) and nominated Judge **Alton B. Parker** (N.Y., 1852–1926) for President and **Henry G. Davis** (W. Va.) for Vice-President on a platform which, at Parker's insistence, accepted the gold standard. The Democratic platform assailed the trusts and demanded supplementary powers for the Interstate Commerce Commission. The Continental Party National Convention met at Chicago (31 Aug.); its candidates were Austin Holcomb (Ga.) for President and A. King (Mo.) for Vice-President.

1906

29 June. HEPBURN ACT, a compromise measure adopted after Roosevelt's demand for stricter railroad regulation met the opposition of Congressional conservatives, reinforced the Interstate Commerce Act. The Act increased the membership of the Interstate Commerce Commission from 5 to 7 and vested in that body the authority to fix just and reasonable maximum railroad rates and to prescribe uniform methods of accounting. The Commission's jurisdiction was broadened to include express and sleeping-car companies, oil pipe lines, ferries, terminal facilities, and bridges. Its orders governing carriers were made binding pending a court decision, thereby placing the burden of proof upon the carrier. The act restricted sharply the granting of free passes, and prohibited railroad from carrying any commodities produced by themselves or by companies in which they held an interest, with the exception of timber and other products necessary for railway operation. A serious limitation was the failure of the Act to authorize the Commission to fix physical valuations of railroads.

30 June. PURE FOOD AND DRUG ACT forbade the manufacture, sale, or transportation of adulterated or fraudulently labeled foods and drugs sold in interstate commerce.

30 June. MEAT INSPECTION ACT aimed at discreditable and dangerous conditions in the meat-packing industry provided for the enforcement of sanitary regulations in packing establishments and Federal inspection of all companies selling meats in interstate commerce.

30 June. IMMUNITY OF WITNESSES ACT required corporation officers to testify to company operations and conduct without invoking plea of immunity.

1907

PANIC OF 1907. Stock market drop (beg. 13 Mar.) and business failures in mid-1907 were followed by the suspension (22 Oct.) of the Knickerbocker Trust Co. in New York. In order to avoid a more serious decline, Roosevelt permitted (4 Nov.) the U.S. Steel Corp. to acquire the Tennessee Coal and Iron Co., with the understanding that no antitrust action would be instituted. The panic revealed flaws in the currency and credit structure, and was directly responsible for the passage of the Aldrich-Vreeland Act.

1908

13 May. WHITE HOUSE CONSERVATION CONFERENCE. In 1901, at the outset of his administration, Roosevelt announced that the conservation of forest and water resources was a national problem of vital importance. The conservation program carried out under his leadership was instrumental in educating the country in the need for the planned protection and development of physical resources. During his incumbency more than 148 million acres were set aside as national forest lands and more than 80 million acres of mineral lands withdrawn from public sale. Also withdrawn were some 1,500,000 acres of water-power sites.

An important step in the conservation program was initiated with the appointment (14 Mar. 1907) of the **Inland Waterways Commission** for the study of such routes with a view to relieving transportation congestion. When the commission's 1st report indicated that water transportation was related to the general problem of natural resources, Roosevelt summoned the White House Conservation Conference (13 May). Among those in attendance were members of the Cabinet, the justices of the Supreme Court, Congressmen, and the governors of 34 states. The conference succeeded in bringing the problem to wide public attention.

A direct outgrowth of the conference was the **National Conservation Commission** (8 June), of which **Gifford Pinchot** (1865–1946) was named chairman. The commission's systematic study of mineral, water, forest, and soil resources was supplemented by the work of local conservation commissions in 41 states. The commission's 1st report, submitted to President Roosevelt on 11 Jan. 1909, was the 1st attempt to inventory U.S. natural resources. Organized later in 1909 was the National Conservation Association, a private body (Charles W. Eliot, president).

30 May. ALDRICH-VREELAND ACT, passed as an emergency currency measure, authorized national banks for a period of 6 yrs. to issue circulating notes based on commercial paper and state, county, and municipal bonds. In order to limit bank note emission based on securities other than Federal bonds, a graduated tax up to 10% was levied on such notes. While the Act introduced some elasticity into the national currency, it provided no safeguards for the credit supply. The most important provision was the establishment of a **National Monetary Commission** authorized to investigate and report upon the banking and currency systems of the U.S. and European countries. The commission, consisting of 9 sens. and 9 reps., was headed by Sen. **Nelson W. Aldrich** (R.I., 1841–1915). Its report, submitted to Congress on 8 Jan. 1912, contained legislative proposals (notably, a national reserve association with branches throughout the country) later incorporated in modified form in the Federal Reserve Act of 1913.

PRESIDENTIAL CAMPAIGN. The People's (Populist) National Convention met at St. Louis (2 April) and nominated **Thomas E. Watson** (Ga.) for President and Samuel W. Williams (Ind.) for Vice-President. The United Christian National Convention met at Rock Island, Ill. (1 May), and nominated Daniel B. Turney (Ill.) for President and L. S. Coffin (Iowa) for Vice-President. The Socialist National Convention met at Chicago (10 May) and nominated **Eugene V. Debs** (Ind.) for President and Benjamin Hanford (N.Y.) for Vice-President. The Republican National Convention met at Chicago (16 June) and nominated **William H. Taft** (Ohio) for President and **James S. Sherman** (N.Y.) for Vice-President. Taft was largely the personal choice of President Roosevelt, who had announced his intention not to serve for a second elective term. The Republican platform pledged tariff revision, stricter enforcement of antitrust legislation, and a furthering of Roosevelt's conservation program. The Democratic National Convention met at Denver (7 July) and nominated **William Jennings Bryan** (Neb.) for President and **John W. Kern** (Ind.) for Vice-President on a platform that condemned monopolies and unequivocally pledged a reduction in tariff rates. The Prohibition National Convention met at Columbus, Ohio (15 July), and nominated Eugene W. Chafin (Ill.) for President and Aaron S. Watkins (Ohio) for Vice-President. The Socialist Labor Convention met at New York (24 July) and nominated August Gillhaus (N.Y.) for President and Donald L. Munro (Va.) for Vice-President. The Independence Party Convention met at Chicago (27 July) and nominated Thomas L. Hisgen (Mass.) for President and John Temple Graves (Ga.) for Vice-President.

3 Nov. PRESIDENTIAL ELECTION. Popular vote: **Taft**, 7,679,006; Bryan, 6,409,106; Debs, 420,820; Chafin, 252,683; Hisgen, 83,562; Watson, 28,131; Gillhaus, 13,825; Turney, 461. Electoral vote: Taft, 321; Bryan, 162. The Republicans retained control of both Houses of Congress.

1910

TAFT'S TRUST POLICY. Under Roosevelt, 44 antitrust suits were started; under Taft, 90 proceedings were initiated against monopolies. The Taft program was carried out by Attorney General **George W. Wickersham** (1858–1936). Taft proposed requiring Federal incorporation of companies engaged in interstate commerce, and the establishment of a Federal Corporation Commission to supervise companies holding national charters, but Congress failed to act. The two major Supreme Court decisions of the Taft administration were the **Standard Oil Co.** case (1911, p. 496) and the **American Tobacco Co.** case (1911, p. 496). The suit for dissolution against the U.S. Steel Corp. (1911) had political overtones. The bill filed by the government charged that the Steel Trust had been strengthened by its absorption of the Tennessee Coal and Iron Co. during the panic of 1907, and alleged that the corporation had used misleading statements in order to secure Roosevelt's consent. The implication that Roosevelt had been hoodwinked served to widen the rift between Taft and Roosevelt after the latter's return from abroad in 1910.

COMMISSION ON EFFICIENCY AND ECONOMY. In his 1st annual message to Congress (1909), Taft stressed "economy in expenditures" and issued an executive order directing that all estimates must first be submitted to him. By this method the administration succeeded in saving more than $42 million during the fiscal year ending 30 June 1911 as compared to estimates for the preceding year. In June 1910, Taft secured a Congressional appropriation of $100,000 to investigate Federal spending, and appointed (Mar. 1911) a Commission on Efficiency and Economy to carry out a survey of administrative organization. Its members included Frederick A. Cleveland, William F. Willoughby, and Frank J. Goodnow. The reports of the Commission pointed to outmoded business methods employed in numerous departments and recommended the establishment of a national budget. Partly because of the Taft-Roosevelt schism, partly because of patronage interests, the Commission failed to secure Congressional support and was finally dissolved. The detailed budget that Taft transmitted to Congress during his last year in office was ignored. Although Taft's attempt to establish a national budgetary system failed, it encouraged similar fiscal innovations in state and local governments.

moreover, it paved the way for the Budget Act of 1921.

18 June. MANN-ELKINS ACT, recommended by Taft, placed telephone, telegraph, cable, and wireless companies under the jurisdiction of the Interstate Commerce Commission. It gave the Commission authority to suspend new rates pending a court decision and provided for effective enforcement of the long and short haul clause. The act created a Federal Court of Commerce to pass upon appeals arising from rate disputes; this tribunal, however, was abolished in 1912.

25 June. POSTAL SAVINGS bank system, recommended by Taft and established by act of Congress, authorized 2% interest on funds deposited at specified post offices.

25 June. PUBLICITY ACT, recommended by Taft, required filing of statements concerning election campaign contributions for Representatives. Previously state corrupt practices acts had been passed (beg. N.Y. 1890).

25 June. MANN ACT (WHITE SLAVE TRAFFIC ACT) prohibited interstate transportation of women for immoral purposes.

REPUBLICAN INSURGENCY. When Roosevelt left office, it was with the conviction that Taft, as his personally chosen successor, would carry forward the reform policies of the Roosevelt administration. Taft did not share Roosevelt's concept of the Presidency as a stewardship of the public welfare, and early in his administration became involved in a party split that weakened his prestige and contributed to his break with Roosevelt.

During the Senate hearings and debates on the Payne-Aldrich Tariff (1909), open dissension within the Republican ranks emerged under the leadership of Sen. Robert M. La Follette (Wis.). Insurgent hostility toward Taft was hardened when he signed the tariff bill and then, in a speech at Winona, Minn. (17 Sept. 1909), termed it "the best bill that the Republican party ever passed." The Insurgents, most of whom came from the Midwest, later combined with the Democrats (1911–13) in enacting tariff revision measures which Taft vetoed.

19 Mar. REVOLT AGAINST "CANNONISM" in the form of an amendment (19 Mar.) to the House rules, offered as a resolution (17 Mar.) by George W. Norris (Neb.), deprived Speaker **Joseph G. Cannon** (Ill., 1836–1926) of his dictatorial power to appoint the Committee on Rules. This committee was made elective by the House itself and the Speaker was barred from serving on it.

31 Aug. ROOSEVELT-TAFT SPLIT. In his "New Nationalism" speech at Osawatomie, Kan. (31 Aug.), Roosevelt, who had returned from Africa in June, attacked the Supreme Court's attitude toward social legislation and declared that the New Nationalism "maintains that every man holds his property subject to the general right of the community to regulate its use to whatever degree the public welfare may require it." The speech was interpreted as an assault upon the conservatism of the Taft administration.

BALLINGER-PINCHOT CONTROVERSY arose from charges made against the conservation policy pursued by Secretary of the Interior Richard A. Ballinger. Under the Roosevelt administration certain water-power sites in Wyoming and Montana had been withdrawn from sale by Secretary of the Interior James R. Garfield. Ballinger doubted the legality of the action and reopened the lands to public entry. Gifford Pinchot, chief of the U.S. Forest Service, publicly accused Ballinger of injuring the conservation program in order to aid corporation interests. Siding with Pinchot was **Louis R. Glavis**, a special agent of the Field Division of the Interior Department who, after being dismissed by order of Taft, charged in an article in *Collier's* (13 Nov. 1909) that Ballinger had favored the patenting of claims to Alaskan coal lands by interests alleged to include the Guggenheims. Taft upheld Ballinger. When a letter written by Pinchot in criticism of Ballinger's conduct was read to the Senate (6 Jan.) by Sen. Jonathan P. Dolliver (Iowa), an Insurgent Republican, Taft ordered Pinchot's removal from office (7 Jan.). A joint Congressional committee was established (26 Jan.) to inquire into the administration of the Interior Department. While a majority of the committee exonerated Ballinger, the controversy had already become a major political issue that widened the breach between Taft and the Insurgent Republicans and ultimately contributed to the break between Taft and Roosevelt. Public feeling toward Ballinger was so unfavorable that he resigned (6 Mar. 1911) to relieve the Taft administration of political embarrassment.

8 Nov. MID-TERM ELECTIONS. The Democrats gained control of the House; the Senate, while nominally Republican, was actually under the control of a Democratic-Insurgent Republican bloc. In the state elections of 1910, the Democrats elected 26 governors, including **Woodrow Wilson** (N.J.).

1911

21 Jan. National Progressive Republican League founded at Washington, D.C., by Insurgent Republicans under the leadership of Sen. Robert M. La Follette (Wis.). Sen. Jonathan Bourne (Ore.) was elected president of the organization, whose professed chief object was "the promotion of popular government and progressive legislation." Its platform: direct election of U.S. senators; direct primaries for the nomination of elective officers; direct election of delegates to national conventions; amendment of state constitutions to provide for the initiative, referendum, and recall; and a corrupt practices act. The Progressives sought to gain control of the Republican organization, block the nomination of Taft, and choose their own candidate, at this time, La Follette, whom they endorsed 16 Oct.

22 Aug. President Taft vetoed the joint resolution of Congress admitting Arizona to statehood, on the ground that the provision in its constitution authorizing the recall of judges was a blow at the independence of the judiciary. Arizona removed the offending clause and was ad-

mitted to statehood (14 Feb. 1912), but afterward restored the article.

1912

SOCIAL LEGISLATION IN THE STATES. By 1912, height of the Progressive movement, there had been enacted in the states a considerable body of social legislation relating to wages and hours, the employment of women and children, and safety and health conditions in factories. A few landmarks among state laws: the adoption by Maryland (1902) of the 1st state workmen's compensation law; the adoption by Oregon (1903) of a 10-hour law for women in industry (upheld by the Supreme Court in 1908, in *Muller* v. *Oregon*); the enactment by Illinois (1911) of the 1st state law providing public assistance to mothers with dependent children; the 1st minimum wage law in the U.S., adopted by Massachusetts (1912), which established a commission to fix wage rates for women and children (this and similar legislation in other states invalidated by the Supreme Court, 1923, in *Adkins* v. *Children's Hospital*).

ROOSEVELT ENTERS THE RACE. Early in 1912 the La Follette boom among the Progressives began to weaken. At the same time Roosevelt, whose alienation from Taft and the conservative Republican leadership had brought him close to the Progressive camp, decided (letter to William B. Howland, 23 Dec. 1911) to oppose Taft for the Republican Presidential nomination. A Chicago meeting (10 Feb.) of Republican leaders sent Roosevelt a letter (signed by 7 Republican governors) declaring "that a large majority of the Republican voters of the country favor your nomination, and a large majority of the people favor your election as the next President of the United States." In an address (21 Feb.) before the Ohio constitutional convention at Columbus, Roosevelt reaffirmed the principles of the New Nationalism and laid special emphasis on the recall of judicial decisions. The speech, which widened the gulf between Roosevelt and Republican conservatives, was followed by Roosevelt's reply (24 Feb.) to the Chicago letter: "I will accept the nomination for President if it is tendered to me, and I will adhere to this decision until the convention has expressed its preference." The Roosevelt boom gained pace during the preconvention campaign, with Roosevelt carrying 4 state conventions and the preferential primaries in 6 states.

PRESIDENTIAL CAMPAIGN. The Socialist Labor National Convention met at New York (7 Apr.) and nominated Arthur E. Reimer (Mass.) for President and August Gillhaus (N.Y.) for Vice-President. The Socialist National Convention met at Indianapolis (12 May) and nominated **Eugene V. Debs** (Ind.) for President and Emil Seidel (Wis.) for Vice-President. The Prohibition National Convention met at Atlantic City (10 July) and nominated Eugene W. Chafin (Ariz.) for President and Aaron S. Watkins (Ohio) for Vice-President.

When the Republican National Convention met at Chicago (18 June), the party's national committee, under conservative control, excluded most of the Roosevelt support represented by contested delegations. As a result, President **Taft** was renominated (22 June). Vice-President **James S. Sherman**, also renominated, died at Utica, N.Y., on 30 Oct. The Roosevelt following met on 22 June, condemned the nomination of Taft as having been gained by fraudulent means, and called upon Roosevelt to assume the leadership of a third party. On 5 Aug. the Progressive ("Bull Moose") party met in national convention at Chicago and nominated **Roosevelt** for President and **Hiram W. Johnson** (Calif., 1866–1945) for Vice-President. The Progressive platform, called "A Contract with the People," included demands for tariff revision; stricter regulation of industrial combinations; direct election of U.S. senators; nationwide preferential primaries for Presidential candidates; the initiative, referendum, and recall; woman suffrage; recall of judicial decisions; prohibition of child labor; and minimum wage standards for working women.

When the Democratic National Convention met at Baltimore (25 June), the 2 chief contenders were **Beauchamp ("Champ") Clark** (Mo., 1850–1921)

and **Woodrow Wilson** (N.J.). Clark held the initial lead, but partly because Bryan shifted his support, **Wilson** was nominated for President on the 46th ballot (2 July). **Thomas R. Marshall** (Ind.) was nominated for Vice-President. The two major party platforms were almost alike in their support of conservation measures, a corrupt practices act, and banking and currency reform; but where the Republicans called for a stricter regulation of trusts and for a milder protective tariff, the Democrats asked for a virtual abolition of monopolies and declared in favor of a tariff for revenue only (pledging "immediate downward revision"). During the campaign Wilson shaped the creed known as the "New Freedom." It differed from Roosevelt's "New Nationalism" chiefly on the issue of monopoly control. Roosevelt believed that trusts were not harmful as long as they were subject to Federal regulation; Wilson tended to view monopolies as positive evils inimical to the existence of free competition.

5 Nov. PRESIDENTAL ELECTION. Popular vote: **Wilson,** 6,286,214; Roosevelt, 4,126,020; Taft, 3,483,922; Debs, 897,011; Chafin, 206,275; Reimer, 29,-079. Electoral vote: **Wilson,** 435; Roosevelt, 88; Taft, 8. In point of the popular vote, Wilson was a minority President, but his electoral majority was the largest in U.S. Presidential history up to that time. The Democrats gained control of both Houses of Congress.

1913

25 Feb. 16TH AMENDMENT to the Constitution, proposed 12 July 1909, was declared adopted and in effect. This so-called **"income tax"** amendment authorized Congress to impose taxes on incomes, from whatever source derived, without apportionment among the states and without regard to any census or enumeration.

28 Feb. PUJO COMMITTEE REPORT. Charges of the existence of a "money trust" led the House (Feb. 1912) to authorize its Committee on Banking and Currency to inquire into the concentration of financial and banking resources. A subcommittee under Rep. Arsène Pujo

(La.) began its investigations on 27 Apr. 1912. In the course of the inquiry prominent financiers, including J. P. Morgan, testified at the hearings. The committee's report stated that the concentration of money and credit was increasing. Cited among the methods that had been used to establish concentration were the consolidation of banks and trust companies; the acquiring of control through purchase of stock in competitive units; interlocking directorates; extension of control into insurance companies, railroads, public utilities, and industrial corporations; and joint arrangements for purchasing security issues. The report lent added cogency to the incoming Wilson administration's program of currency and banking reform.

1 Mar. PHYSICAL VALUATION ACT empowered the Interstate Commerce Commission to make thorough investigations of property held or used by railroads under its jurisdiction with a view to establishing cost and physical valuation as a basis for rate making and the fixing of a reasonable profit.

1 Mar. WEBB-KENYON INTERSTATE LIQUOR ACT, passed over President Taft's veto, forbade interstate shipment of liquor into states where sale was illegal.

4 Mar. Department of Commerce and Labor divided by act of Congress into 2 departments, each with Cabinet status.

4 Mar. Wilson's inaugural address projected a broad program for the conservation of human and natural resources and the restoration of free competition.

8 Apr. Appearing in person before a special session of Congress to deliver his message on tariff revision, President Wilson broke the precedent set by President Thomas Jefferson in 1801. The last personal appearance of a President before the national legislature had been made by John Adams in 1800; since that time transmitted Presidential messages had been read by clerks.

31 May. 17TH AMENDMENT to the Constitution, proposed on 16 May 1912, was declared adopted and in effect. It provided for the **popular election of U.S. senators.**

23 Dec. FEDERAL RESERVE ACT. Wilson asked Congress (23 June) for a measure that would create a government-controlled, decentralized banking system capable of assuring an elastic currency. The Congressional debate lasted some 6 mos., during which time banking interests fought to defeat the measure.

The **Owen-Glass Act** establishing the Federal Reserve System was the first thorough reorganization of the national banking system since the Civil War. The act provided for the establishment of not less than 8 and not more than 12 districts or regions with a Federal reserve bank in each (12 centers were set up at Boston, New York, Philadelphia, Richmond, Atlanta, Dallas, Kansas City, St. Louis, Chicago, Cleveland, Minneapolis, and San Francisco). At the apex of the system was a Federal Reserve Board consisting of 7 members (subsequently increased to 8) including the Secretary of the Treasury and the Comptroller of the Currency. This central board was authorized to raise or lower the rediscount rate prevailing at the district reserve banks, thus giving it direct control over the credit supply.

The district banks were to serve as bankers' banks, i.e., as depositories for the cash reserves of the national banks (which were required to join the system) and of state banks (whose membership was optional). Each Federal reserve bank was to be governed by a board of 9 directors, 6 of them appointed by the Federal Reserve Board. A member bank was required to subscribe to the capital stock of its district Federal reserve bank in an amount equal to 6% of its own capital and surplus. The Federal reserve banks were empowered to rediscount the commercial and agricultural paper of member banks, and the system's currency was to be based upon approved rediscounted paper deposited by member banks. Against such paper the reserve banks could issue Federal Reserve notes (accepted as government obligations) as part of the circulating money supply. The amount could be expanded and contracted in keeping with the changing requirements of business activity. Each reserve bank was required to maintain a gold reserve of 40% against Federal

Reserve notes outstanding, although it was specified that this provision might be suspended in time of emergency.

1914

8 May. SMITH-LEVER ACT provided for a system of agricultural extension work based on cooperation between the Department of Agriculture and the land-grant colleges. Federal grants-in-aid were to be matched by state appropriations in carrying out the program.

26 Sept. FEDERAL TRADE COMMISSION ACT, passed at Wilson's recommendation as part of his trust regulation program, was designed to prevent unfair methods of competition in interstate commerce. The Bureau of Corporations was eliminated, and in its place was established the Federal Trade Commission, a bipartisan body consisting of 5 members, authorized to demand annual and special reports from corporations, investigate the activities of persons and corporations (except banks and common carriers), publish reports on its findings, and issue cease and desist orders (subject to judicial review in the Federal courts) to prevent unfair business practices. Among the practices which the commission subsequently singled out were trade boycotts, mislabeling and adulteration of commodities, combinations for maintaining resale prices, and false claims to patents.

15 Oct. CLAYTON ANTITRUST ACT, which supplemented and strengthened the Sherman Antitrust Act, was aimed at corporate methods hitherto not specified as illegal practices. It also contained provisions relating to labor and agricultural organizations. The act prohibited the following: price discriminations substantially tending to create a monopoly, tying contracts (i.e., contracts based on the condition that purchasers would not buy or handle the products of sellers' competitors), interlocking directorates in industrial aggregations capitalized at $1 million or more, and the acquisition of stockholdings tending to lessen competition. Officials of corporations violating antitrust statutes could be held individually responsible. The following remedies were provided whereby injured parties might secure relief: court injunctions, the issuance of cease and desist orders by the Federal Trade Commission, and civil suits for 3-fold damages in instances where the existence of price discrimination and tying contracts was established.

In regard to labor and agriculture, the act specified that "the labor of a human being is not a commodity or article of commerce; nothing contained in the antitrust laws shall be construed to forbid the existence and operation of labor, agricultural and horticultural organizations . . . nor shall such organizations or the members thereof be held or construed to be illegal combinations in restraint of trade under the antitrust laws." The act also forbade the use of the injunction in labor disputes unless the court decided that an injunction was necessary to prevent irreparable injury to property; made strikes, peaceful picketing, and boycotts legal under Federal jurisdiction; and provided for trial by jury in contempt cases, except in instances where contempt was committed in presence of the court. Hailed by organized labor as its "Magna Carta," the Act's labor provisions were substantially weakened by court interpretation.

1915

PREPAREDNESS MOVEMENT. Shortly after the beginning of World War I, the issue of military preparedness was introduced into public debate in the U.S. Private organizations and individuals pointed to occupied Belgium as an example of the fate in store for an unprepared nation, and undertook a campaign for strengthening the national defense. Among such organizations were the National Security League (est. Dec. 1914), the American Defense Society (est. Aug. 1915), the League to Enforce Peace (est. June 1915), and the American Rights Committee (est. Dec. 1915). Individuals prominent in the preparedness movement included **Theodore Roosevelt, Henry Cabot Lodge,** and **Henry L. Stimson.** The "**Plattsburg idea**" (military training camps for civilians) came into being at Plattsburg on 10 Aug. Preparedness was opposed by organized pacifist and antimilitarist groups who contended that the war did not involve vital U.S. interests. The most spectacular effort of the peace associations was Henry Ford's chartering of the "peace ship," *Oskar II,* which sailed for Europe (4 Dec.) in an ill-fated attempt to end the war by a negotiated peace. On 10 May Wilson in an address at Philadelphia declared: "There is such a thing as a man being too proud to fight. There is such a thing as a nation being so right that it does not need to convince others that it is right." But his opposition to a large standing army and advocacy of unarmed neutrality changed after the *Lusitania* incident (7 May, p. 303). On 7 Dec. he laid before Congress a comprehensive plan for national defense, and on 27 Jan. 1916 began a tour of the country to urge preparedness.

1916

10 Feb. Lindley M. Garrison resigned as Secretary of War. Garrison's advocacy of a volunteer force under direct national control, as opposed to the state-controlled National Guard units, was not accepted by Wilson, who feared loss of Congressional support on the issue.

7 March. Newton D. Baker (Ohio, 1871–1937) appointed Secretary of War.

3 June. NATIONAL DEFENSE ACT, first major result of the administration's preparedness program, provided for expansion of the regular army to 175,000 men, and its further enlargement to 223,000 over a five-year period. It also authorized a National Guard of 450,000 men; established an Officers Reserve Training Corps at universities, colleges, and military camps; and made provisions for industrial preparedness.

17 July. FEDERAL FARM LOAN ACT provided farmers with long-term credit facilities similar to those made available to industry and commerce by the Federal Reserve Act. The country was divided into 12 districts under the general administration of a Federal Farm Loan Board consisting of the Secretary of Treasury and 4 members. In each district there was established a Farm Loan Bank (capitalized at $750,000) in which cooperative farm loan associations held membership.

Farmers belonging to these associations could secure long-term loans (5–40 yrs.) on farm-mortgage security at interest rates (5%–6%) lower than those prevailing in commercial banks.

11 Aug. WAREHOUSE ACT authorized licensed and bonded warehouses to issue against specified agricultural commodities (including grain, cotton, tobacco, and wool) warehouse receipts negotiable as delivery orders or as collateral for loans. The measure assisted farmers in financing their crops.

29 Aug. COUNCIL OF NATIONAL DEFENSE established under the Army Appropriation Act. Organized (11 Oct.) under the chairmanship of Secretary of War Baker, this advisory body consisting of 6 Cabinet members was charged with coordinating industry and resources for the national security and welfare. Its Advisory Commission, consisting of 7 civilian experts headed by Daniel Willard, was responsible for mapping preparedness plans in fields including transportation, munitions and manufacturing, labor, raw materials, supplies, engineering and education, and medicine and surgery.

7 Sept. SHIPPING ACT authorized the creation of the U.S. Shipping Board, a 5-man body empowered to build, purchase, lease, or requisition vessels through the agency of the Emergency Fleet Corporation, capitalized at $50 million.

PRESIDENTIAL CAMPAIGN. The Socialist Labor National Convention met at New York (23 Apr.) and nominated Arthur E. Reimer (Mass.) for President and August Gillhaus (N.Y.) for Vice-President. The Socialist party held no convention; its candidates, nominated by a mail referendum, were Allen L. Benson (N.Y.) for President and George R. Kirkpatrick (N.J.) for Vice-President. The Republican National Convention met at Chicago (7 June) and nominated Supreme Court Justice **Charles E. Hughes** (N.Y.) for President and **Charles W. Fairbanks** (Ind.) for Vice-President. The Progressive National Convention, also meeting at Chicago (7 June), nominated Theodore Roosevelt for President and John M. Parker (La.) for Vice-President. Roosevelt, however, declined the nomination, and gave his support to Hughes.

Roosevelt's defection led to the rapid dis-integration of the Progressive party. The national committee of the Progressive party endorsed (26 June) Hughes' nomination, but an Indianapolis conference of the Progressive party (3 Aug.) repudiated this step. The Democratic National Convention met at St. Louis (14 June) and renominated President **Woodrow Wilson** and Vice-President **Thomas R. Marshall.** The Prohibition National Convention met at St. Paul (19 July) and nominated J. Frank Hanly (Ind.) for President and Ira D. Landrith (Tenn.) for Vice-President.

Wilson's supporters defended his record on neutrality and preparedness, waging the campaign with the slogan, "He kept us out of war." The slogan was highly effective in attracting the support of women's groups, particularly in those Western states where the vote had been conferred on women. Some of the strongest opposition to Wilson came from Irish-American and German-American elements critical of his foreign policy. The Democrats, however, turned against Hughes his failure to repudiate (until late in the campaign) the support of these so-called hyphenate groups.

7 Nov. PRESIDENTIAL ELECTION. Popular vote: Wilson, 9,129,606; Hughes, 8,538,221; Benson, 585,113; Hanly, 220,-506; Reimer, 13,403. Electoral vote: Wilson, 277; Hughes, 254. So close was the election that the final result was in doubt until it was definitely known that California had gone Democratic (by only 3,773 votes). The Democrats retained control of both Houses of Congress.

1917

23 Feb. SMITH-HUGHES ACT provided for Federal grants-in-aid, to be matched by the contributions of individual states, for promoting instruction in agriculture and the trades. It established a Federal Board for Vocational Education.

8 Mar. SENATE CLOTURE RULE, adopted by special session of Senate, permitted a majority to terminate debate.

31 Mar. General Munitions Board established by Council of National Defense.

Organized 9 Apr., it was responsible for coordinating the procurement of war materials for the War and Navy Departments and for assisting them to acquire raw materials and manufacturing plants. Its purpose, however, was weakened by conflicting authority and by the Board's lack of power to enforce its decisions.

14 Apr. COMMITTEE ON PUBLIC INFORMATION, established by executive order of the President, was headed by the journalist **George Creel** (1876–   ) and consisted of the Secretaries of State, War, and Navy. Responsible for uniting American public opinion behind the war effort, the committee employed an elaborate nationwide publicity apparatus based on pamphlets, news releases, posters, motion pictures, and volunteer speakers.

24 Apr. THE LIBERTY LOAN ACT, a war finance measure, authorized the issue of bonds to be sold by public subscription and provided for loans to the Allied powers to enable them to purchase food and war supplies. The Liberty Loan drives were as follows: 1st, June 1917 ($2 billion); 2nd, Nov. 1917 ($3.8 billion); 3rd, May 1918 ($4.2 billion); 4th, Oct. 1918 ($6 billion); Victory Loan, Apr. 1919 ($4.5 billion).

18 May. SELECTIVE SERVICE ACT provided for the registration and classification for military service of all men between the ages of 21 and 30, inclusive; as amended by the Man Power Act (31 Aug. 1918) it required the registration of all men between the ages of 18 and 45. The 1st registration (5 June) enrolled 9,586,508 men; the 2nd (5 June 1918) added well over a million who had come of age; and the 3rd (12 Sept. 1918) enrolled 13,228,762. Of the 24,234,021 registered during the war, 2,810,296 were called up for service in the army.

15 June. ESPIONAGE ACT, aimed at treasonable and disloyal activities, provided severe penalties (up to $10,000 fine and 20 yrs. imprisonment) for persons found guilty of aiding the enemy, obstructing recruiting, or causing insubordination, disloyalty, or refusal of duty in the armed services. The act empowered the Postmaster General to exclude from the mails newspapers, periodicals, and other material alleged to be treasonable or seditious. The constitutionality of the act was upheld in *Schenck* v. *U.S.* (1919).

28 July. WAR INDUSTRIES BOARD, established by the Council of National Defense as successor to the General Munitions Board, was directed to act as a clearing agency for the nation's war industries and to take steps to increase production and eliminate waste. A reorganization of the War Industries Board (4 Mar. 1918) placed at its head **Bernard M. Baruch** (1870–   ), who was given authority for all major controls. The board was endowed with wide powers over the determination of priorities, the conversion of existing facilities, the manufacture of war materials, price fixing, and the purchase of supplies for the U.S. and the Allies.

10 Aug. LEVER FOOD AND FUEL CONTROL ACT, effective for the duration of the war, empowered the President to make regulations and issue orders to stimulate and conserve the production, and control the distribution, of foods and fuels necessary to the war effort. The President was authorized to fix the price of wheat at not less than $2 a bushel (a provision effective until 1 May 1919; in practice, the guaranteed price was $2.20); to fix the price of coal, coke, and other commodities; to license producers and distributors; and to prohibit unfair trade practices. The Act forbade the use of foodstuffs in the manufacture of distilled liquors, whose importation was also forbidden. **Herbert Hoover** was appointed Food Administrator (10 Aug.) and Harry A. Garfield named Fuel Administrator (23 Aug.). Among the other agencies employed in administering the Act were the Grain Corporation (for the financing of wheat crops) and the Sugar Equalization Board (for stabilizing the price of sugar and regulating its distribution).

3 Oct. WAR REVENUE ACT, which made the income tax the chief source of revenue during the war, authorized a graduated income tax beginning at 4% on personal incomes of more than $1,000; raised the corporation tax to 6%; imposed a graduated excess profits tax of from 20% to 60% on corporations and persons; raised postal rates; and provided for sharp increases in excise taxes on luxuries, transportation, amusements, alcoholic beverages, and tobacco.

6 Oct. TRADING WITH THE ENEMY ACT forbade commerce with enemy nations or their associates and empowered the President to impose an embargo on imports and to establish censorship of material passing between the U.S. and any foreign nation. The War Trade Board assumed the task of licensing imports and halting commercial intercourse with the enemy. The Act also created the Office of Alien Property Custodian to take possession and dispose of the property held in the U.S. by persons residing in enemy countries. A. Mitchell Palmer was named (12 Oct.) to the post.

18 Dec. PROHIBITION AMENDMENT. The war against Germany created wider support for the prohibition movement, which by the outset of 1917 had succeeded in establishing prohibition in 19 states. The **Anti-Saloon League** (est. 1895) had long been agitating for a national prohibition amendment. With U.S. involvement in the war, there were added to the arguments of moral and social reformers the need for conserving food and the patriotic condemnation of individuals of German extraction prominent in the brewing and distilling industry. On 18 Dec. Congress adopted and submitted to the states an amendment to the Constitution prohibiting the manufacture, sale, or transportation of alcoholic liquors. This, the 18th Amendment, was declared ratified on 29 Jan. 1919 and went into operation on 16 Jan. 1920. It was repealed with the adoption of the 21st Amendment (1933).

26 Dec. U.S. RAILROAD ADMINISTRATION. An impending crisis in the national transportation system led President Wilson to place the railways under government operation. He named Secretary of the Treasury **William Gibbs McAdoo** (1863–1941) as director-general of the U.S. Railroad Administration, which controlled 397,014 miles of track operated by 2,905 companies. On 21 Mar. 1918 the **Railroad Control Act** provided for fixing compensation to the railroads during the period of government management (to end not later than 1 yr. and 9 mos. after ratification of a peace treaty), and established a regional system of administration. The U.S. Railroad Administration was subsequently authorized to control railway express companies and inland waterway systems.

1918

5 Apr. WAR FINANCE CORPORA-TION, created to finance war industries, was capitalized at $500 million and authorized to issue $3 billion in bonds and to make loans to financial institutions to cover commercial credits extended to war industries.

8 Apr. NATIONAL WAR LABOR BOARD appointed by President Wilson to act as court of last resort for labor disputes, Frank P. Walsh and ex-President Taft named cochairmen. On 8 June the **War Labor Policies Board** was constituted to standardize labor conditions, with Felix Frankfurter chairman.

10 Apr. WEBB-POMERENE ACT, authorized exporters to organize associations for export trade without becoming liable for violation of antitrust laws. Unfair methods of competition were prohibited.

16 May. SEDITION ACT, an amendment to the Espionage Act of 1917, provided severe penalties for persons found guilty of making or conveying false statements interfering with the prosecution of the war; willfully employing "disloyal, profane, scurrilous, or abusive language" about the American form of government, the Constitution, the flag, or the military and naval forces; urging the curtailed production of necessary war materials; or advocating, teaching, defending, or suggesting the doing of any such acts or things. The enforcement of the Act was aimed chiefly at Socialists and pacifists, and resulted in the trial and imprisonment of the Socialist leaders Eugene V. Debs and Victor L. Berger. The case of *Abrams* v. *U.S.* (1919, p. 497) involved application of the Sedition Act.

20 May. OVERMAN ACT authorized the President to coordinate or consolidate executive bureaus, agencies, and offices in the interest of economy and the more efficient concentration of governmental operations in matters relating to the conduct of the war.

5 Nov. CONGRESSIONAL ELECTIONS gave the Republicans control of both Houses of Congress. The result, coming after Wilson had appealed (25 Oct., p. 315) to the country to return a Democratic Congress, was interpreted as repudiation of the President.

THE UNITED STATES IN WORLD AFFAIRS, 1866-1918

1866

31 May. FENIAN UPRISING. The Fenians, a secret Irish brotherhood organized in the 50's to achieve independence for Ireland, crossed the Niagara River with an army of several hundred and fought an engagement with Canadian militamen ("Battle of Limestone Ridge") before fleeing back to New York. After the repulse of another Fenian attack (25 May 1870) under John O'Neill, the leaders were arrested by the U.S. Marshal for Vermont.

1866-67

NAPOLEON III AND MEXICO. On 12 Feb. 1866 Secretary Seward delivered an ultimatum demanding French withdrawal from Mexico following the dispatch to the Mexican border under Gen. Sheridan of 50,000 U.S. troops. Napoleon withdrew his forces in the spring of 1867. Maximilian, Austrian Archduke, established on the Mexican throne as a result of the occupation of Mexico City by French forces (7 June 1863), was executed by Mexican partisans under Benito Juárez (19 June).

1867

TERRITORIAL EXPANSION. Acquisition of Alaska. In Dec. 1866 Baron Edoard de Stoeckl, Russian Minister to the U.S., was instructed to negotiate with Secretary Seward, an ardent expansionist, for the sale of Alaska, regarded by Russia as an economic liability. A treaty for the purchase of Alaska for $7,200,000 was submitted to the Senate (30 Mar.). With the aid of Sumner and a propaganda campaign, the treaty was ratified (9 Apr.), and formal transfer of "Seward's Folly" accomplished (18 Oct.). A similar campaign, aided by Stoeckl's judicious use of funds to buy votes, resulted in the adoption by the House of the necessary appropriation bill (14 July 1868).

28 Aug. Midway. Midway Islands, 1,134 mi. west of Hawaii, were occupied in the name of the U.S. by Capt. William Reynolds of the U.S.S. *Lackawanna* after discovery by the U.S. 1859.

24 Oct. Danish West Indies. Seward negotiated a treaty with Denmark for the acquisition of the Danish West Indies (now the Virgin Islands) for $7,500,000, but it died in the Senate.

1869-72

"ALABAMA" CLAIMS. The U.S. pressed claims against Great Britain for damage (estimated at 100,000 tons with cargoes) done to the Northern merchant marine by British-built Confederate raiders, including the *Alabama*. Seward negotiated the **Johnson-Clarendon Convention** (14 Jan. 1869) providing for adjudication of the claims, which the Senate, led by Sumner, rejected (13 Apr.). In the Grant administration Secretary Fish reopened negotiations. The **Treaty of Washington** (8 May 1871), which represented a triumph for Fish over Sumner, provided for the submission of all outstanding differences between the U.S. and Great Britain to an international arbitral tribunal (representatives from Italy, Switzerland, Brazil, and the interested parties). That tribunal decided (25

Aug. 1872) that Great Britain failed to use "due diligence" to prevent the Confederate raiders from going to sea, and awarded the U.S. $15,500,000. This amount was far below Sumner's demands (which included **collateral damage**, estimated at $2,125 million), but the tribunal refused to pass upon indirect claims.

1870

SANTO DOMINGO AFFAIR. Desirous of annexing Santo Domingo, Grant dispatched his secretary, Babcock, to survey the situation. On Babcock's return from the island Grant submitted a treaty of annexation to his Cabinet, which was unanimously rejected. A more formal treaty was then drawn up and submitted to the Senate (10 Jan.). On 15 Mar. the Committee on Foreign Relations reported adversely on ratification and Sumner delivered his famous **"Naboth's Vineyard"** speech, which cost him the chairmanship of that committee (deposed 9 Mar. 1871). Another opponent of ratification, Attorney General E. R. Hoar, was forced to resign from the Cabinet. Despite Grant's insistence (31 May) that ratification would be "an adherence to the Monroe Doctrine," the treaty was defeated (30 June). On 14 July Secretary Fish submitted a memorandum upholding the no-transfer corollary (no territory shall be subject to transfer to a European power) as part of the Monroe Doctrine.

1873

CUBA AND THE "VIRGINIUS" IN-CIDENT. When revolt broke out in Cuba (1868) Fish persuaded Grant to abstain from recognition (1869). When Spanish authorities in Cuba captured (31 Oct. 1873) the arms-running ship *Virginius*, illegally flying the American flag, and summarily shot 53 of the crew (among them Americans) as pirates, Fish moderated U.S. demands and secured (29 Nov.) an indemnity of $80,000 for the families of the executed Americans.

1875

30 Jan. TREATY WITH HAWAII of commercial reciprocity signed, providing that no Hawaiian territory should be disposed to a 3rd power. Senate approval 18 Mar.

1878

17 Jan. SAMOAN TREATY. U.S. interest in the Samoan Islands began as early as 1838 and was renewed after the Civil War. A U.S. naval officer, Commander Richard W. Meade, negotiated a treaty (17 Feb. 1872) with the Samoan chieftains giving the U.S. exclusive rights to a naval station at the strategic harbor of Pago Pago on the island of Tutuila. The Senate failed to ratify the treaty. U.S. penetration was extended by Col. A. B. Steinberger, dispatched by President Grant as a special agent to the islands (1873). The U.S. and the native chieftains had a mutual interest in confining German influence in Samoa. Accordingly, a treaty of amity and commerce was signed (17 Jan.) and approved (30 Jan.) by which the U.S. was given nonexclusive rights to a naval station at Pago Pago.

1880

3 July. MADRID CONVENTION. U.S. joined European powers in restricting extraterritorial rights of Moroccans. Senate approval 5 May 1881.

17 Nov. CHINESE TREATY. Anti-Chinese agitation, chiefly on the Pacific Coast, led to pressure by Western interests on President Hayes for abrogation of the Burlingame Treaty (1868) giving the Chinese the right of unlimited immigration to the U.S. Hayes vetoed (1 Mar. 1879) a Congressional measure restricting the number of Chinese passengers aboard U.S.-bound ships on the ground that it was equivalent to exclusion and hence violative of the Burlingame Treaty. Hayes dispatched a mission to China to consider the revision of the treaty. The result was the Treaty of 1880, giving the U.S. the right to "regulate, limit or suspend" but not absolutely to prohibit entry of Chinese laborers. On 6 May 1882 the Exclusion Act restricted such immigration for a 10-yr. period.

1881

BLAINE'S FOREIGN POLICY. Secretary of State James G. Blaine, the most influential figure in the Garfield administration, advocated closer commercial and cultural ties with Latin-America. His program had a dual aim: to strengthen the competitive position of the U.S. export trade, and to increase U.S. prestige by attempting to arbitrate Latin-American disputes threatening war or European intervention. Blaine failed to settle the War of the Pacific (begun by Chile against Bolivia and Peru in 1879), and made a fruitless attempt to intercede in the Costa Rica-Colombia and Mexico-Guatemala disputes.

He invited (22 Nov.) the Latin-American nations to a peace conference at Washington scheduled for 22 Nov. 1882. Invitations had already been accepted by 9 countries by the time Blaine left office (12 Dec.), but his successor, Frederick T. Frelinghuysen, revoked the invitations.

Blaine endeavored to secure British consent to modification of the Clayton-Bulwer Treaty. Hayes had asserted in a message to Congress (8 Mar. 1880) that since an isthmian canal would be virtually part of the U.S. coastline, it must on that account be under U.S. control. In Apr. 1880, the House adopted a resolution authorizing the President to "take immediate steps for the formal and final abrogation" of the treaty. When Blaine learned of reports that Colombia was sounding out several European nations on assuming the guarantee of an isthmian canal, he invoked (24 June) the U.S. "paramount interest" interpretation of the Monroe Doctrine. The British Foreign Secretary, Earl Granville, dispatched a note (10 Nov.) insisting on the finality of the Clayton-Bulwer Treaty. The Frelinghuysen-Zavala Treaty (1884), signed with Nicaragua, violated the Clayton-Bulwer Treaty, but died in the Senate.

1882

22 May. KOREAN-U.S. TREATY of commerce and amity signed; recognized independence of Korea. Senate approval 13 Feb. 1883.

26 July. GENEVA CONVENTION OF 1862 for care of wounded proclaimed after Senate approval 16 Mar.

1884

1 Oct.–1 Nov. INTERNATIONAL PRIME MERIDIAN CONFERENCE, at Washington, recommended meridian of Greenwich as basis for counting longitude and mean time.

15 Nov.–26 Feb. 1885. CONGO CONFERENCE at Berlin, called by Germany to consider commerce and navigation in the Congo area and procedures for acquiring African territory, was participated in by the U.S., which had (22 Apr.) recognized the International Association of the Congo. The U.S. was instrumental in bringing conference agreement on freedom of trade and abolition of slave traffic in Central Africa, but declined to ratify the general act. On 2 July 1890 the U.S. signed an international agreement for suppression of the African slave trade; Senate approval 11 Jan. 1892.

1887

20 Jan. PEARL HARBOR. The Hawaiian Reciprocity Treaty of 1875, which had been renewed in 1884 but not approved by the Senate, was ratified when it was amended to give the U.S. the exclusive right to establish a fortified naval base at Pearl Harbor, near Honolulu.

RIVALRY IN SAMOA. Mutual suspicion and consular intrigues marked the activities of the U.S., Great Britain, and Germany in the Samoan Islands after 1879. A tripartite agreement reached in that year provided for a protectorate over the municipal government of Apia (an arrangement later extended to all of the islands), but it never received Senate approval. A German-instigated revolt brought the protest (19 June 1885) of Secretary of State Thomas F. Bayard, who proposed a 3-power meeting. Before discussions began at the Washington conference (25 June–26 July), the British and Germans came to an understanding whereby Britain supported Germany's ambition for a mandate over Samoa in return for German recognition of British interests in Africa and the Near East. The Washington conference terminated without reaching a decision. Germany then renewed her interference in Samoan affairs by deporting the resisting ruler and establishing a government under direct German influence. Tension rose after the new regime discriminated against U.S. and British commercial interests. By the close of 1888, warships of the 3 powers were stationed in Apia Harbor, and a conflict threatened.

1888

BAYARD-CHAMBERLAIN TREATY.
Difficulties with Great Britain over the Canadian fisheries question arose after the U.S. served notice that beginning 1 July 1885 it would terminate the fishing clauses of the Treaty of Washington (1871). The Canadians then fell back on a narrow interpretation of the Treaty of 1818 and began seizing U.S. fishing vessels for technical violations. American resentment, especially in maritime New England, was aroused. On 2 Mar. 1887 Congress authorized President Cleveland to take retaliatory steps against Canada (by excluding her vessels from U.S. waters and halting the importation of Canadian products). A joint Anglo-American commission met at Washington (22 Nov. 1887). On 15 Feb. the Bayard-Chamberlain Treaty and a *modus vivendi* were concluded with Great Britain. The treaty was rejected (21 Aug.) by the Republican majority in the Senate, partly because it provided for a reciprocal tariff, partly because of anti-British feeling. But the *modus vivendi*, giving the U.S. privileges in Canadian ports, remained the basis for use of the fisheries until abrogated by Canada (1923) in retaliation against the Fordney-McCumber Tariff.

For Hague Tribunal award (1910, p. 299).

1889

BERLIN CONFERENCE ON SAMOA.
Germany's policy of armed intervention in Samoa with the tacit approval of the British led President Cleveland to lay the question before Congress (15 Jan.). Terming the situation "delicate and critical," Cleveland asserted that the U.S. insisted upon the preservation of Samoan autonomy and independence. The threatened naval clash in Apia Harbor was averted by a hurricane (15–16 Mar.) that wrecked the U.S. warships *Trenton* and *Vandalia*, caused the *Nipsic* to be run ashore, and destroyed all of the German ships. Only the British *Calliope* escaped disaster. But even before the hurricane struck, President Harrison had already dispatched (14 Mar.) 3 American commissioners to the Berlin conference, which opened 29 Apr. The agreement, signed on 14 June, provided for the independence and autonomy of the Samoan Islands under a tripartite protectorate (the U.S., Great Britain, and Germany). The chief agents of the 3-power condominium were to be the chief justice and the president of the Apia municipal council. The agreement also provided for a foreign adviser to the Samoan king and a court for the settlement of land titles.

BLAINE'S LATIN-AMERICAN POLICY.
Blaine's plan to call a Latin-American conference, which had been scrapped by his successor in the Department of State, finally won the approval of Congress, which on 24 May 1888 authorized President Cleveland to summon a conference for discussing measures for the promotion of the common peace and prosperity. Secretary of State Bayard issued invitations (13 July 1888); by the time the 1st International American Conference met at Washington (2 Oct. 1889–19 Apr. 1890), Blaine was again Secretary of State. Seventeen Latin-American nations were represented, Santo Domingo being the sole absentee. The major U.S. goal, to establish a customs union, was defeated by the opposition of the other delegates. The conference likewise failed

to establish machinery for the arbitration of disputes, but set up the International Bureau of American Republics (later called the **Pan-American Union**), which served as a permanent agency for exchanging and disseminating information regarding each country; and paved the way for a U.S. policy of reciprocal tariff arrangements by executive agreement, as authorized by the McKinley Tariff Act of 1890.

1891

CONTROVERSIES WITH ITALY AND CHILE. Italy. The slaying (15 Oct. 1890) of the police chief at New Orleans, who had been investigating the activities of persons suspected of affiliation with the secret Mafia (Black Hand) Society, resulted in the trial and acquittal of the Italian suspects. A New Orleans mob broke into the jail (14 Mar.) and lynched 11 persons (3 of them Italian nationals). The Italian government demanded indemnity for the victims and punishment of the responsible parties. While Blaine deplored the action of the New Orleans mob, he refused to take action on the ground that the crime fell under state rather than Federal jurisdiction. The Italian government withdrew its Minister to the U.S. (31 Mar.), and the U.S. took similar action, but there was no formal diplomatic break. President Harrison's annual message (9 Dec.) condemned the New Orleans lynching and assured the Italian government of the good faith of the U.S. government. The incident was closed with the offer (12 Apr. 1892) of a $25,000 indemnity that was accepted by the Italian government.

Chile. Following the outbreak of civil war in Chile (1891), the rebel Congressionalist party sent a vessel, the *Itata,* to San Diego to take on a shipment of arms. The U.S.S. *Charleston* was ordered to pursue and seize the *Itata.* The rebel vessel was escorted back to San Diego but later released on the ground that there had been no violation of the neutrality laws. The incident gave the Congressionalists (who took over the Chilean government) reason for harboring resentment against the U.S. This hostility was brought to a head when a Valparaiso mob attacked (16 Oct.) sailors on shore leave from the U.S. cruiser *Baltimore,* killed 2, and injured 17. In his annual message to Congress (9 Dec.), President Harrison defended the conduct of the U.S. naval commanders. In reply, the Chilean Foreign Minister, M. A. Matte, sent a denunciatory telegram (11 Dec.), which aroused indignation in the U.S. Blaine's note to the Chilean government (21 Jan. 1892) stated that unless a retraction and apology were forthcoming, the U.S. would terminate diplomatic relations. In a special message to Congress (25 Jan. 1892) Harrison virtually asked for a declaration of war. The Chilean government submitted an official apology, and the incident was closed with the payment of an indemnity of $75,000.

1892

29 Feb. BERING SEA DISPUTE. The U.S. acquisition of the Pribilof Islands as a result of the Alaska purchase led to an Anglo-American controversy concerning jurisdiction over pelagic (i.e., ocean) sealing in the Bering Sea. The U.S., which exercised jurisdiction within the 3-mile limit, leased sealing rights to a private company. As the commercial value of sealskins rose, pelagic sealing vessels of other nations (principally Canada) began to operate in the waters beyond the 3-mile limit. The dispute was touched off when U.S. revenue cutters seized Canadian pelagic sealers in the Bering Sea (1886).

On 2 Mar. 1889 Congress empowered the President to take steps to protect U.S. rights and declared U.S. dominion over the waters of the Bering Sea. In a note to the British government (22 Jan. 1890), Secretary of State Blaine characterized its course as just short of piracy. In reply, British Foreign Secretary Lord Salisbury stated that Great Britain would hold the U.S. "responsible" for acts contrary to "established principles of international law." An Anglo-American arbitration treaty (29 Feb.) referred the question to a mixed international tribunal (French, Swedish, and Italian), whose decision (15 Aug. 1893) denied the U.S. claim to exclusive rights to a closed sea; provided for the assessment of damages against the U.S.; and prohibited pelagic sealing in a 60-mi. zone around the Pribilof Islands for a specified period during each year. This protective regulation remained in force until 1908. The controversy was terminated with the payment (16 June 1898) of $473,151 by the U.S. to Great Britain.

1893

30 Mar. Senate confirmation of the appointment of Thomas F. Bayard as U.S. Ambassador to Great Britain, first American to hold that rank.

HAWAIIAN QUESTION. The most vital link between the U.S. and Hawaii was the Hawaiian sugar planters, mostly Americans. The planters, ranged against native dynastic interests, brought off a revolution (1887) that succeeded in securing a liberal constitution and a government under their influence. However, they lost power in 1891. Meanwhile, the McKinley Tariff Act of 1890, which put imported sugar on the free list and authorized a bounty of 2 cts. a lb. for home-grown sugar cane, wiped out the reciprocity advantages hitherto enjoyed by Hawaiian sugar planters and broke sugar prices, with an estimated loss of $12 million.

Queen Liliuokalani, exponent of a firm pronative policy, came to the Hawaiian throne in 1891. She revoked the liberal constitution of 1887 and by royal edict (14 Jan.) promulgated a new constitution giving her autocratic powers. The Americans, under the leadership of **Sanford B. Dole** (1844–1926), had already established a revolutionary committee of safety to overthrow the native government, with the apparent support of the U.S. Minister to Hawaii, the proannexationist **John L. Stevens** (1820–95). He ordered U.S. marines to be landed from the cruiser *Boston* (16 Jan.), ostensibly to protect American life and property. Aided by the marines, the committee of safety occupied the government buildings; and Stevens, without permission from the State Department, recognized the revolutionary regime (17 Jan.). On 1 Feb. Stevens raised the U.S. flag over the government buildings and proclaimed Hawaii a U.S. protectorate. Dole became president of the new government.

On 15 Feb. a treaty of annexation (signed 14 Feb.) drawn up by diplomatic commissioners of the Hawaiian provisional government was submitted to the U.S. Senate. Chiefly because of Democratic opposition, the Senate failed to act on the treaty by the time Harrison left office. President Cleveland withdrew the treaty (9 Mar.) and appointed ex-Congressman James H. Blount (Ga.) as special commissioner to Hawaii to conduct a thorough investigation. Blount ordered the withdrawal of the marines and the lowering of the American flag. After an inquiry lasting 4 mos., he reported that Stevens's conduct had been improper; that the majority of Hawaiians were opposed to annexation; and that the Hawaiian sugar planters and their U.S. associates had been the chief force behind the revolution, hoping to secure the sugar bounty through annexation.

Independence of the provisional government was recognized when President Cleveland sent Albert S. Willis as the new Minister to Hawaii. Willis was instructed to take steps to restore Queen Liliuokalani to power, with the proviso that she assume the obligations of the provisional government, grant amnesty to its leaders, and sustain the constitution of 1887. In return, the provisional regime was to abdicate. Queen Liliuokalani acceded to Cleveland's request on 18 Dec. President Dole, however, refused to surrender power, pointing out that the provisional government had received U.S. recognition and that the U.S. had no right to interfere in the internal affairs of Hawaii. Cleveland was unwilling to employ force to carry through his policy. In a special message to Congress (18 Dec.), he condemned the means by which the provisional government had been brought into power and stated he would not again submit the annexation treaty to the Senate. On 4 July 1894 the Republic of Hawaii was proclaimed, and on 7 Aug. 1894 Cleveland formally recognized the new government.

1895

VENEZUELAN BOUNDARY DIS-
PUTE. The controversy between Venezuela and Great Britain over the boundary line of British Guiana went back to
1814 when the British took over that
possession from the Dutch. In 1840 a
survey made by Sir Robert Schomburgk, a
British engineer, was rejected by Venezuela, and the dispute remained unsettled. With the discovery of gold in the
contested region, Great Britain withdrew
its offer of the Schomburgk line and
claimed areas west of it. In 1887 Venezuela broke off diplomatic relations with
Great Britain and asked the U.S. to arbitrate, but the U.S. offer to use its good
offices was rejected by the British
(1887). In his annual message to Congress in 1894 Cleveland declared that he
would renew his attempt to bring about
arbitration. A joint Congressional resolution (20 Feb.) approved Cleveland's
recommendation. Again Great Britain
refused to arbitrate.

Largely under the influence of Secretary of State Richard Olney, Cleveland
based the U.S. position on a broad construction of the Monroe Doctrine. Olney
sent a note (20 July) to the British government stating that British pressure on
Venezuela would be regarded by the
U.S. as a violation of the Monroe Doctrine and that peaceful arbitration (with
U.S. intercession toward that end) was
the only way of settling the controversy.
The belligerent tenor of the dispatch
was evident in this: "Today the United
States is practically sovereign on this
continent, and its fiat is law upon the
subjects to which it confines its interposition. Why? . . . It is because, in
addition to all other grounds, its infinite
resources combined with its isolated position render it master of the situation and
practically invulnerable as against any or
all other powers."

The reply (26 Nov.) of Lord Salisbury, the British Prime Minister and
Foreign Secretary, asserted that the Monroe Doctrine was not applicable to the
boundary dispute and rejected the U.S.
offer of arbitration. The diplomatic correspondence was laid before Congress
(17 Dec.) by President Cleveland, who
affirmed the applicability of the Monroe
Doctrine and recommended the creation
of an independent commission to determine the boundary. "When such report
is made and accepted," said Cleveland,
"it will . . . be the duty of the United
States to resist by every means in its
power, as a wilful aggression upon its
rights and interests, the appropriation by
Great Britain of any lands or the exercise of governmental jurisdiction over
any territory which after investigation
we have determined of right belongs to
Venezuela."

The American outburst caught the
British off guard. In the eyes of Great
Britain, whose imperial preoccupations
lay elsewhere, the Venezuelan dispute
was a relatively minor matter. Furthermore, her rivalry with Germany and
other powers in Africa and the Near East
made American friendship desirable. This
became doubly clear when Kaiser Wilhelm II sent to President Kruger of the
Boer Republic an indiscreet congratula-
tory telegram (3 Jan. 1896) that offended
the British. On 25 Jan. the British Colonial Secretary, Joseph Chamberlain,
publicly asserted that war between the
U.S. and Great Britain "would be an absurdity as well as a crime. . . . The two
nations are allied and more closely allied
in sentiment and interest than any other
nations on the face of the earth."

The Venezuelan boundary commission
was appointed on 1 Jan. 1896 and held
its first meeting on 4 Jan. 1896. The
British aided the U.S. authorities by fur-
nishing data. A treaty signed by Great
Britain and Venezuela (2 Feb. 1897)
through the good offices of the U.S. provided for submitting the dispute to a
board of arbitration. The awards (3 Oct.
1899) were in substantial accord with
the original British claims and placed
the boundary roughly along the Schomburgk line (Venezuela, however, being
awarded the mouth of the Orinoco
River).

CUBAN QUESTION. American interest in Cuba declined after the U.S. attempt (1875–76) to terminate the Cuban
rebellion (1868–78), but was revived
following the outbreak (24 Feb.) of the
native insurrection against Spanish rule.
Added to Spanish oppression as a cause

of revolt was the severe impact upon the sugar economy of the panic of 1893 and the high protective Wilson-Gorman Tariff of 1894. American sympathy favored the rebels. Financial contributions from Americans aided Cuban *juntas* (committees of revolutionists) in organizing filibustering expeditions on American soil, but these ventures were blocked by the U.S. navy and revenue service.

The revolutionists followed a policy of widespread and thorough destruction of sugar plantations and mills (in which American interests had extensive holdings), hoping by this method to induce U.S. intervention and to break the will of the Spanish rulers. The task of suppressing the uprising was assigned to Gen. Valeriano ("Butcher") Weyler, who established (after 10 Feb. 1896) concentration camps where he indiscriminately confined revolutionists, sympathizers, and neutrals, including women and children, many of whom became victims of disease, semistarvation, and ruthless treatment. American sympathy for the rebels was fanned by the "yellow press" (William Randolph Hearst's New York *Journal* and Joseph Pulitzer's New York *World*).

By concurrent resolution, the Senate (28 Feb. 1896) and the House (6 Apr. 1896) called for the U.S. to accord belligerent rights to the Cuban revolutionists and offer its good offices to Spain for the recognition of an independent Cuba. Spain declined the U.S. offer (22 May 1896).

1898

RELATIONS WITH SPAIN. The liberal Sagasta ministry, which came into power at Madrid (Oct. 1897), made important concessions on Cuban policy (25 Nov. 1897), including the recall of Gen. Weyler, a measure of autonomy, release of imprisoned U.S. nationals, and reform of the concentration camp policy. These concessions satisfied neither the insurrectionists nor the loyalists in Cuba. Loyalists at Havana held a violent demonstration (12 Jan.) condemning Weyler's recall and the grant of autonomy. The yellow press in the U.S. renewed its attack on Spain. Within the Republican party a group of younger politicians (including Theodore Roosevelt and Henry Cabot Lodge), who regarded Cuba as the key to domination of the Caribbean and favored expansionism, called for a firm attitude.

9 Feb. DE LÔME LETTER, written by the Spanish Minister to the U.S., Dupuy de Lôme, was published (9 Feb.) in Hearst's N.Y. *Journal.* This was a private communication that had been stolen from the mails in Havana and released to the Hearst press by Cuban revolutionists in the U.S. Dupuy de Lôme called President McKinley "weak and a bidder for the admiration of the crowd, besides being a would-be politician who tries to leave a door open behind himself while keeping on good terms with the jingoes of his party." De Lôme immediately cabled his resignation to the Spanish government.

15 Feb. SINKING OF THE "MAINE." After the Havana riot of 12 Jan., the U.S. battleship *Maine* was ordered to Havana harbor, ostensibly to protect American life and property. On 15 Feb. at 9:40 P.M. the *Maine,* while at anchor in the harbor, was destroyed by an explosion which killed 260 officers and men. The Navy Department appointed a court of inquiry (17 Feb.). Although the government urged the public to reserve judgment, the yellow press attributed the disaster to enemy agents and demanded U.S. intervention in Cuba. "Remember the *Maine!*" became a popular slogan. Congress without dissent voted a $50 million defense appropriation (9 Mar.).

The naval court of inquiry reported (21 Mar.) that the *Maine* had been destroyed by the explosion of a submarine mine, but was "unable to obtain evidence fixing the responsibility . . . upon any person or persons." Despite strong pressure from the public, Congress, and a prowar group within the Republican party, the McKinley administration followed an antiwar policy. The U.S. Minister to Spain, Stewart L. Woodford, was instructed (27 Mar.) to notify the Madrid government that the U.S. had no territorial ambitions in Cuba and that it sought the following: a Cuban armistice until 1 Oct. and the revocation of the concentration camp policy. On the latter point, Spanish agreement came on 5 Apr., and on 9 Apr. the Spanish yielded to the U.S. demand for an armistice. This information was cabled to McKinley on 10 Apr.

11 Apr. McKINLEY'S WAR MESSAGE. Swayed by the powerful demand for war in and out of Congress, McKinley reversed his antiwar policy even before learning of the Spanish concessions. His message to Congress asked for the "forcible intervention" of the U.S. to establish peace in Cuba.

20 Apr. WAR RESOLUTION. Congress adopted a joint resolution that (1) recognized the independence of Cuba; (2) demanded the withdrawal of the Spanish armed forces; (3) empowered the President to use the army and navy to carry out these demands; and (4) disclaimed any intention on the part of the U.S. to exercise sovereignty or control over Cuba, asserting that the government and control of the island would be left to its people after peace had been restored. (This last clause was the **Teller Amendment.**) McKinley signed the war resolution on 20 Apr.; and on the same day a formal ultimatum was served on Spain to the effect that if she did not grant Cuban independence and quit the island, the U.S. would take the necessary steps to carry the joint resolution into effect. On 21 Apr. Spain broke diplomatic relations with the U.S.; 22 Apr. the U.S. inaugurated blockade of Cuban ports; 24 Apr. Spain declared war against the U.S.; 25 Apr. formal U.S. declaration of war against Spain, made retroactive to 21 Apr.

THE SPANISH-AMERICAN WAR, 1898

BALANCE SHEET. The opening of the war found the U.S. modern "steel navy" in an advanced state of readiness and efficiency. The navy consisted of about 2,000 officers and 24,000 men. The preparations of the Asiatic squadron, based at Hong Kong under the command of Commodore **George Dewey** (p. 695), were enhanced by a secret order (25 Feb.) sent by Assistant Secretary of the Navy **Theodore Roosevelt,** who instructed Dewey to keep his fleet intact and to engage the Spanish fleet in the Philippines should war break out. In contrast, the U.S. Army, consisting of about 2,100 officers and 28,000 men, was ill-prepared. Its high command, training, and equipment were inadequate, and it lacked proper supply and medical services for waging a tropical campaign. Congress authorized (22 Apr.) a volunteer force of 200,000 men, and approved (26 Apr.) an increase of the regular army to 60,000. The decisive battles of the war were naval engagements. On this score, the U.S. enjoyed the advantage, for the Spanish navy was outmoded in armament and had poorly trained crews.

1 May. BATTLE OF MANILA BAY. Dewey's Asiatic squadron at Hong Kong consisted of 4 cruisers (*Olympia, Boston, Baltimore,* and *Raleigh*) and 2 gunboats (*Petrel* and *Concord*). This force departed from Mirs Bay, China (27 Apr.), with orders to capture or destroy the Spanish squadron thought to be in Manila Bay under the command of Adm. Montojo. The U.S. squadron entered Manila Bay on the evening of 30 Apr. The Spanish fleet (consisting of 10 vessels, including cruisers and gunboats) lay off Cavite Point. Early on the morning of 1 May the U.S. fleet laid down a powerful broadside, methodically raking the Spanish line from end to end. The battle, beginning 5:40 A.M., was over in 7 hrs. The Spanish suffered 381 men killed; all of the Spanish craft were destroyed, silenced, or captured. None of the American ships was damaged; U.S. casualties: 8 wounded.

13 Aug. FALL OF MANILA. Lacking the necessary support for land operations,

Dewey imposed a blockade on Manila Bay. Gen. Wesley Merritt was ordered (11 May) to the Philippines to support Dewey and take Manila. Merritt arrived at Manila Bay (25 July) with the final American contingent, bringing the total U.S. military strength there to 10,700 men. Dewey and Merritt sent (9 Aug.) the Spanish commander at Manila a formal demand for surrender. U.S. troops, reinforced by Filipino guerrillas under Gen. Emilio Aguinaldo, assaulted and occupied Manila (13 Aug.). On 14 Aug. Gen. Merritt received the Spanish capitulation and proclaimed the military occupation of the Philippines.

SPANISH FLEET IN CUBA. The blockade of Cuba was assigned to Rear Adm. **William T. Sampson** (along the northern shores) and Commodore **Winfield S. Schley** (along the southern shores). Sampson moved at once to hunt out the Spanish fleet; it was known that the enemy ships would have to recoal at Cuba or Puerto Rico after making the transatlantic voyage. Schley did not leave Key West until 19 May and did not arrive off Santiago de Cuba until 28 May. His delay gave the Spanish fleet its opportunity.

Commanded by Adm. Cervera, the Spanish force departed from the Cape Verde Islands (29 Apr.) and entered the harbor of Santiago de Cuba (19 May), where it lay under the protection of land batteries. Cervera's fleet of 4 cruisers and 3 destroyers was bottled up by Schley's force (29 May). Adm. Sampson arrived at Santiago (1 June) and assumed command of the blockading squadron. The capture or destruction of the Spanish fleet was the main task confronting the U.S. Navy.

14 June. CUBAN EXPEDITION. A land force of 17,000 regulars and volunteers, including the "Rough Riders" (the 1st U.S. Volunteer Cavalry Regiment under Col. **Leonard Wood** and Lt. Col. **Theodore Roosevelt**), was marshaled. at Tampa, Fla., awaiting the end of the tropical rains before undertaking the invasion of Cuba. Commanded by Gen **William Shafter**, this force was improperly trained, organized and equipped. When the U.S. Navy blockaded the enemy fleet at Santiago, Shafter was ordered to reinforce Sampson and seize the port. The expeditionary force sailed from Tampa on 14 June.

1 July. BATTLES OF EL CANEY AND SAN JUAN HILL. Shafter's force arrived off Santiago oñ 20 June and two days later began disembarking at Daiquiri and Siboney Bay, to the east of their main objective. Unloading operations were completed on 26 June; on 30 June the force began its march on Santiago. In the day-long battle of El Caney (1 July) about 7,000 U.S. troops took a strongly fortified village garrisoned by about 600 of the enemy. In the battle of San Juan Hill (1 July), in which the dismounted Rough Riders under Col. Theodore Roosevelt took part, the Americans seized the position under heavy fire. At a total cost of 1,572 ċasualties, the U.S. succeeded in winning command of the heights to the east and north of Santiago and were now in position to place the city and the Spanish fleet under artillery bombardment.

3 July. DESTRUCTION OF THE SPANISH FLEET. Sampson's blockading force outside Santiago harbor consisted of the battleships *Indiana, Iowa, Massachusetts, Oregon,* and *Texas,* and the cruisers *New York* and *Brooklyn.* Adm. Cervera, who was under orders not to surrender, decided to make an attempt to escape to the open sea. On the morning of 3 July the Spanish fleet left the harbor and tried to run the U.S. blockade. In a battle along the coast that lasted about 4 hrs., the enemy fleet was destroyed by the superior fire of the American guns. The Spanish losses, 474 killed and wounded, 1,750 taken prisoner; the U.S. casualties, 1 killed, 1 wounded. The destruction of the Spanish fleet virtually terminated the war. Santiago and its garrison of 24,000 troops surrendered on 17 July.

4 July. WAKE ISLAND, 2,325 mi. west of Honolulu, was acquired by the 2d U.S. expedition to the Philippines and formally occupied in 1900.

7 July. ANNEXATION OF HAWAII. While Cleveland remained in the Presidency, he checked all attempts to annex Hawaii. His successor, McKinley, favorably disposed to annexation, negotiated

a new treaty of annexation (signed 16 June 1897), but Democratic and anti-imperialist Republican opposition in the Senate delayed its ratification. When the Japanese government protested against the treaty, McKinley pressed even harder for ratification. During the Spanish-American War Hawaii's use as a naval installation lent emphasis to its strategic value and brought increased demand for annexation. In order to preclude defeat under the rule requiring a two-thirds vote for ratification by the Senate, the treaty was adopted by a joint resolution of Congress, which required a simple majority vote. On 30 Apr. 1900 Congress granted territorial status to Hawaii, to take effect 14 June 1900.

25 July. A. U.S. force under Gen. Nelson A. Miles occupied Puerto Rico after encountering minor enemy opposition.

4 Aug. Disease and food poisoning took such a high toll of U.S. troops in Cuba that the War Department instructed the Cuban expeditionary force to embark for Montauk Point, L.I. Such conditions, both in Cuba and in army camps in the U.S., were among those investigated by a commission appointed (8 Sept.) to inquire into the conduct of the war.

10 Dec. TREATY OF PARIS. On 26 July the Spanish government, making its approach through Jules Cambon, French Ambassador at Washington, requested the U.S. to name peace terms. A protocol signed on 12 Aug. provided for a peace treaty to be concluded at Paris and terminated hostilities on the following terms: Spain was to relinquish Cuba, and cede Puerto Rico and one of the Ladrone Islands to the U.S.; and the U.S. was to hold and occupy Manila pending the conclusion of a peace treaty that would determine the disposition and control of the Philippines.

When the peace commission met at Paris (1 Oct.), U.S. policy on the Philippines was vague and divided. Guided by economic, strategic, and humanitarian considerations, McKinley decided to demand the cession of the Philippines. The demand, made by the U.S. commissioners on 1 Nov., encountered strong Spanish opposition; but with the conclusion of the treaty (10 Dec.), the Spanish agreed to cede the Philippines to the U.S. for a payment of $20 million. Spain surrendered all claim and title to Cuba and agreed to assume the liability for the Cuban debt amounting to about $400 million. As indemnity, Spain ceded Puerto Rico and Guam to the U.S.

WAR COST. Of the more than 274,000 officers and men who served in the army during the Spanish-American War and the period of demobilization, 5,462 died in the various theaters of operation and in camps in the U.S. Only 379 of the deaths were battle casualties, the remainder being attributed to disease and other causes. The total wounded was 1,604. The immediate cost of the war was about $250 million.

1899

TREATY FIGHT. The Senate debate over the Treaty of Paris revealed the sharp division between the imperialists and anti-imperialists. The former stressed national prestige, the civilizing mission of the U.S., economic and strategic advantages, and the contention that foreign powers active in the Far East would establish a foothold in the Philippines if the U.S. withdrew. The anti-imperialists maintained that the acquisition of non-contiguous areas peopled by alien stocks incapable of assimilation was contrary to the traditional U.S. isolationism, inimical to the Monroe Doctrine, and contrary to U.S. principles of self-government. Democrats and Populists were generally opposed to the treaty, and were joined by a minority group of New England Republicans. The leader of the Democratic party, William Jennings Bryan, succeeded in influencing a sufficient number of opponents of the treaty to vote for it on the ground that it would end the war. The question of the independence of the Philippines, Bryan pointed out, could be left to the national election of 1900. The treaty was ratified (6 Feb.) by the close vote of 57–27 (thus securing confirmation by a 2-vote margin).

PHILIPPINE QUESTION. At the outbreak of the Spanish-American War the U.S. returned the insurrectionist leader,

Emilio Aguinaldo, to the Philippines to direct the native uprising against the Spanish. Aguinaldo organized a Filipino army and on 12 June 1898 established a provisional government, proclaiming its independence of Spain. The Filipino rebels believed that the U.S. would grant freedom and independence to the islands. When Aguinaldo learned (4 Jan.) that the Treaty of Paris gave the U.S. control of the Philippines, he called upon the natives (5 Jan.) to declare their independence. President McKinley appointed (20 Jan.) a Philippine Commission headed by Jacob G. Schurman to study the situation in the islands and to submit a report to serve as a basis for setting up a civil government. On 4 Feb. the Filipinos broke out in armed revolt against U.S. rule.

To suppress the uprising the U.S. employed a force of 70,000 men against a Filipino army almost as large. Organized Filipino resistance came to an end by the close of 1899, but guerrilla warfare that led to ruthless measures on both sides continued until mid-1902, despite the earlier capture (23 Mar. 1901) of Aguinaldo. The administration's Philippine policy was condemned by the Anti-Imperialist League, an organization established on 17 Feb. that included many influential citizens among its members. The report of the Philippine Commission (June) recommended ultimate independence for the islands, but suggested the continuation of U.S. rule for an indefinite period until the Filipinos were ready for self-government.

20 Mar. OPEN DOOR POLICY. Growing political and military weakness of China revealed during and after the Sino-Japanese War (1894–95) left her powerless to resist the demands of foreign powers for political and economic concessions in the form of leaseholds and spheres of influence. In 1898 and 1899 the British made overtures to the U.S. with a view to securing Anglo-American guarantees of equal commercial opportunity in China, but these proposals were rejected as contrary to the established U.S. policy of noninvolvement. But the U.S., despite the fact that its trade with China was relatively small, was disturbed by the possibility that the foreign powers might establish discriminatory tariffs and other commercial barriers in the Chinese regions under their influence.

The Open Door policy of securing equal commercial opportunity was more English than American in its origin. It was chiefly the work of Alfred E. Hippisley, a British citizen who had served in the Chinese customs service; and its fundamental idea had already been publicized in *The Break-up of China,* an influential book by Lord Charles Beresford, who visited the U.S. in 1899. Hippisley's views reached the U.S. administration through the offices of W. W. Rockhill, private adviser to Secretary of State John Hay on Far Eastern affairs. Hippisley drafted a memorandum (17 Aug.) that was revised by Rockhill (28 Aug.) and accepted by Hay (5 Sept.). In his circular letter of 6 Sept., Hay instructed the U.S. embassies at Berlin, St. Petersburg, and London (and subsequently those at Paris, Rome, and Tokyo) to request formal assurances from each power as regards their respective spheres of influence in China: (1) that each power would in no way interfere with any treaty port or vested interests; (2) that the existing Chinese treaty tariff would apply to such spheres of interest, and the duties would be collected by the Chinese government; and (3) that no power would discriminate in favor of its own subjects regarding railroad charges and harbor dues. The various powers gave evasive and qualified replies, but Hay saw fit to construe their answers as approval of his proposals. He announced (20 Mar. 1900) that the acceptance of the Open Door policy was "final and definitive."

18 May–29 July. 1ST HAGUE CONFERENCE, called at the invitation of Czar Nicholas II of Russia (24 Aug. 1898) to consider disarmament, the limitation of methods of warfare, and the creation of machinery for the arbitration of international disputes, was participated in by 26 nations, including the U.S. The conference failed to enlist the support of most of the nations on the prohibition of certain instruments of war (e.g., poison gas and balloon-launched missiles) or disarmament, but established the **Permanent Court of International Arbitration** The U.S., which lent its weight to securing such a body, signed a convention (29 July) providing for the peaceful settlement of international disputes by the following means: mediation by a 3rd party, international commissions, and the international tribunal at The Hague. It was stipulated, however, that arbitration was not to be compulsory and was not to extend to any question involving national honor or integrity. In addition, the U.S. delegation insisted on a reservation concerning disputes involving application of the Monroe Doctrine.

2 Dec. PARTITION OF SAMOA. Continuing differences among the U.S., Germany, and Great Britain after 1899 created dissatisfaction with the tripartite protectorate over Samoa. In 1899 Germany proposed the partition of the islands. By the Anglo-German treaty of 14 Nov., the Samoan Islands were divided between the U.S. and Germany, with Britain surrendering her claims in return for (1) rights in West Africa and elsewhere in the Pacific, and (2) relinquishment by Germany of rights in certain areas of Samoa. Several islands, including Tutuila (with its harbor of Pago Pago), went to the U.S.; the islands of Upolu and Savaii went to Germany. This agreement was confirmed by a treaty signed (2 Dec.) by the U.S., Germany, and Great Britain, and ratified (16 Jan. 1900) by the Senate. American Samoa, placed under the control of a naval commandant, became a strategic U.S. naval base in the Pacific.

1900

COLONIAL PROBLEM. Imperialists contended that acquisition did not automatically incorporate the new possessions into the U.S. and endow them with the constitutional privileges of U.S. citizens. Anti-imperialists argued that the "Constitution followed the flag," i.e., that territorial acquisition made these dependencies an organic part of the U.S. and hence entitled to all constitutional guarantees. A halfway group held that only "fundamental" constitutional guarantees, as distinguished from "formal" privileges, were applicable to the insular possessions.

The constitutional status of the dependencies was settled by the Supreme Court in the so-called **Insular Cases** (1901 *et seq.*, p. 495).

12 Apr. FORAKER ACT provided for the establishment of civil government in Puerto Rico, to take effect on 1 May. The island was made an unorganized territory and its residents made citizens of Puerto Rico (U.S. citizenship was extended to them in 1917). The President was empowered to appoint a governor-general and a council. The council was to serve as the upper house of the legislature; the lower house was made popularly elective. Both the executive and the legislature were endowed with the veto power. The act extended the Dingley Tariff to Puerto Rico, providing for duties amounting to 15% of authorized levies.

TAFT COMMISSION. On 7 Apr. President McKinley appointed a Second Philippine Commission headed by Federal Circuit Judge William Howard Taft. The commission was directed to establish a civil government in the islands. Under the guidance of Secretary of War Root, the Commission organized municipal administrations, and by progressive stages created a government for the Philippines. Taft encouraged native participation; ultimately permitted Filipinos to take seats on the commission. On 21 June 1901 military government was terminated in the Philippines (except in those areas where rebellion was still in progress), to take effect 4 July 1901.

BOXER REVOLT. In the spring of 1900 an aggressively antiforeign group of Chinese revolutionists known as Boxers rose in revolt to expel the "foreign devils" from China. The Boxers occupied Peking and laid the foreign legations under siege. An international expedition that included U.S. troops relieved Peking (14 Aug.). Secretary of State Hay, fearing that the foreign powers would use the Boxer incident as a pretext to abandon the Open Door policy and carve up China, dispatched a circular letter (3 July) stating it to be the policy of the U.S. "to seek a solution which may bring about permanent safety and peace to China. preserve Chinese territorial and administrative entity [an elaboration of the Open Door], protect all rights guaranteed to friendly powers by treaty and international law, and safeguard for the world the principle of equal and impartial trade with all parts of the Chinese Empire."

The **Boxer Protocol** (7 Sept. 1901) provided a total indemnity of $333 million. The U.S. share was set at $24,500,-000, but the U.S. subsequently reduced this to $12 million and in 1924 remitted the unpaid balance. The Chinese government used about $18 million of the U.S. share to educate Chinese students at U.S. colleges and universities.

1901

2 Mar. PLATT AMENDMENT. At the end of the Spanish-American War Cuba remained under the control of a U.S. military administration headed by Gen. Leonard Wood. Cuban finances were reorganized and a public health and sanitation campaign (in which **Dr. Walter Reed** [p. 770] and Maj. **William C. Gorgas** [1854–1920] figured) succeeded in exterminating the yellow-fever menace. While the U.S., by the Teller Amendment (1898), had disclaimed all intention of exercising sovereignty over Cuba, it feared that rapid and complete withdrawal might jeopardize Cuban political stability and threaten American strategic and financial interests.

Gen. Wood was instructed to authorize the Cubans to call a constitutional convention. The convention met on 5 Nov. 1900 and ultimately adopted a constitution based upon that of the U.S., but made no provisions for continuing future relations with the U.S. At the behest of Secretary of War Root, Wood informed the convention that the withdrawal of American control was conditional upon the adoption of such provisions. These provisions, known as the Platt Amendment, were incorporated in the Army Appropriation Bill and sponsored by Senator Orville H. Platt (Conn.), though most of the clauses were drawn up by Secretary Root. Its

more important provisions: (1) Cuba would never enter into any treaty with any foreign power impairing Cuban independence; (2) the Cuban government would not contract any public debt in excess of the capacity of its ordinary revenues to discharge; (3) the U.S. was authorized to intervene to preserve Cuban independence and maintain law and order; and (4) Cuba agreed to sell or lease to the U.S. lands necessary for naval or coaling stations. In effect, the Amendment gave the U.S. a quasi-protectorate over Cuba.

The Cuban convention appended the amendment to the constitution (12 June); the U.S. withdrew from Cuba (20 May 1902); and, to preclude its elimination by the amending power, the Platt Amendment was incorporated into a treaty between the U.S. and Cuba (22 May 1903). The amendment was abrogated on 29 May 1934.

18 Nov. HAY-PAUNCEFOTE TREATY. U.S. pressure for the modification of the Clayton-Bulwer Treaty to secure exclusive control over an isthmian canal resulted in the signing (5 Feb. 1900) of the 1st Hay-Pauncefote Treaty. Great Britain agreed to renounce all joint rights to a canal which the U.S. was to construct, control, and maintain. The U.S. pledged to maintain the neutrality of the canal and was forbidden to fortify it. The treaty was ratified by the Senate (20 Dec. 1900); an amendment permitting U.S. fortification as well as other changes proved unacceptable to the British (Mar. 1901). Because of mounting difficulties with Germany and Russia, Great Britain was anxious to remain on friendly terms with the U.S. Following negotiations in Apr., the 2nd Hay-Pauncefote Treaty was concluded (18 Nov.) and ratified by the Senate (16 Dec.). It abrogated the Clayton-Bulwer Treaty; permitted the U.S. to construct and control the canal; stipulated that neutrality would be maintained under U.S. auspices; and provided that the canal was to be free and open to ships of all nations on equal terms. In a memorandum of 3 Aug. the British conceded the right to fortify the canal.

1902

1 July. PHILIPPINE GOVERNMENT ACT (also known as the Organic Act) passed by Congress constituted the Philippine Islands an unorganized territory and made its inhabitants citizens of the islands. It confirmed the President's appointment of the Taft Commission and provided for the retention of the commission as a governing body. When the first Philippine assembly met in 1907, the commission continued to serve as the upper house of the legislature.

1903

22 Jan. HAY-HERRAN CONVENTION. With the ratification of the Hay-Pauncefote Treaty, Congress had to choose between Panama (then a province of Colombia) and Nicaragua as the route for the isthmian canal. At first, on the recommendation of the Walker Commission (16 Nov. 1901) the Nicaraguan right of way was favored, chiefly because the New Panama Canal Co., successor to the bankrupt De Lesseps venture, asked the exorbitant price of more than $109 million for its holdings and franchises. But when the Panama Co. (4 Jan. 1902) lowered its price to $40 million, the Commission recommended (18 Jan. 1902) the Panama rather than the Nicaragua route. Congress passed the Spooner Act (28 June 1902), stipulating 2 conditions for the construction of a Panama Canal: (1) purchase of the property and rights of the New Panama Canal Co. (for which Congress made an appropriation of $40 million), and (2) a Colombian grant to the U.S. of perpetual control over the right of way. The Act, which also established the Isthmian Canal Commission, authorized the President, if negotiations for the Panama route failed, to purchase the Nicaraguan route.

It was now necessary to obtain an agreement whereby Colombia would relinquish sovereignty over the proposed Panama canal zone. The Hay-Herran Convention provided that in return for a payment of $10 million and an annual rental of $250,000 the U.S. would receive a 99-yr. lease (with option of renewal)

over a canal zone 6 mi. in width. Under this arrangement Colombia was not to receive any part of the money paid to the Panama Co. The convention was ratified by the U.S. Senate; after much delay, it was rejected by the Colombian Senate (12 Aug.). The Colombians, who wanted at least $25 million, believed that by deferring action until after Sept. 1904 (expiration date of the New Panama Canal Co.'s charter), they could then receive the full price offered by the U.S. The Colombian Senate adjourned (31 Oct.) without having taken further action.

PANAMA REVOLT. Colombia's effective rejection of the Hay-Herran Convention aroused the strong displeasure of President Roosevelt, who for a time contemplated recommending the forcible seizure of Panama. On 3 Nov. the province of Panama rose in revolt and declared itself independent of Colombia. The revolution was accomplished by native groups and foreign promoters linked to the Panama Co. who acted with the tacit approval of the Roosevelt administration. Even before the revolution broke out, Roosevelt ordered (2 Nov.) U.S. warships to Panama to maintain "free and uninterrupted transit" across the isthmus, guaranteed by the Treaty of New Granada (1846). On 6 Nov. the U.S. recognized the Republic of Panama and on 13 Nov. formally received Philippe Bunau-Varilla (a onetime associate of the New Panama Canal Co.) as Minister from Panama.

18 Nov. HAY–BUNAU-VARILLA TREATY granted to the U.S. in perpetuity the use and control of a canal zone 10 mi. wide across the Isthmus of Panama, giving it full sovereignty (including the right of fortification) over that zone as well as all rights to the holdings of the New Panama Canal Co. and the Panama R.R. Co. The neutrality of the zone was to be maintained in conformity with the Hay-Pauncefote Treaty. The U.S. guaranteed the independence of Panama and agreed to pay $10 million and an annual fee of $250,000 beginning 9 yrs. after the exchange of ratifications. The treaty was ratified by the Senate on 23 Feb. 1904.

ALASKAN BOUNDARY DISPUTE arose after the Klondike gold rush of 1896 showed that the Alaskan Panhandle (lying in U.S. territory) commanded the water routes to the goldfields. The Canadians invoked the Anglo-Russian Treaty of 1825 to support their contention that the shoreline ran in such a fashion as to give them practical control of the important harbors of the Alaskan Panhandle (the Canadians maintained that the boundary followed the outer edges of the promontories; the U.S. claimed it followed the heads of the bays and inlets).

The U.S. and Great Britain signed (24 Jan.) a convention providing for a joint commission of 3 Americans and 3 Britons to arbitrate the questions. When the commission met at London, its British representation consisted of 2 Canadians and Lord Alverstone, the Lord Chief Justice of England. During the commission's deliberations (3 Sept.–20 Oct.) President Roosevelt intimated that if the U.S. did not receive satisfaction, it would employ military force in the disputed area. This was among the first demonstrations of "big stick" diplomacy (a term derived from a statement made by Roosevelt in 1900: "I have always been fond of the West African proverb: 'Speak softly and carry a big stick, you will go far' ").

The U.S. claims were given a 4-2 majority when they were upheld by Lord Alverstone. The award ran a line excluding Canada from the ocean inlets of the Alaskan Panhandle.

1904

6 Dec. ROOSEVELT COROLLARY. During the rule of the dictator Cipriano Castro, Venezuela was plunged into heavy debt to European investors. Castro's unwillingness to meet these financial obligations led the European powers to consider taking forcible action, but they were mindful of the Monroe Doctrine, as indicated by the German memorandum to the State Department (Dec. 1901) disclaiming any intention of permanent occupation. At this time President Roosevelt did not regard such in-

tervention as a violation of the Monroe Doctrine, for in his 1st annual message (1901) he observed that the U.S. did "not guarantee any State against punishment if it misconducts itself, provided that punishment does not take the form of acquisition of territory by any non-American power."

When Castro refused to submit the claims of the foreign powers to arbitration by the Hague Tribunal, Great Britain and Germany imposed a blockade (Dec., 1902) subsequently joined by Italian warships. Following the bombardment of Venezuelan ports and the destruction of Venezuelan naval craft, Castro asked Roosevelt to propose arbitration by the U.S. Minister to Venezuela. This proposal was transmitted by Roosevelt (12 Dec. 1902) to Great Britain and Germany. Both powers accepted the principle of limited arbitration, and the matter was settled by the Hague Tribunal in 1904.

Similarly burdened by debts to European powers was the Dominican Republic, whose financial obligations were serviced chiefly by customhouse receipts pledged to various creditors (with the provision that default would permit the creditors to demand control of the customhouses). Political instability pointed to the likelihood of default by Santo Domingo. A proposal by Belgium (17 Oct. 1903) that the U.S. join in seizing all customhouses and provide for the governing of Santo Domingo by an international commission was refused by the U.S. A change in the Dominican regime brought into power a ruler (Gen. Morales) willing to accede to the U.S. administration of the customhouses.

The situation came to a head in 1904 when the debts payable to an American firm were given a preferred position over those owed to other creditors. The protests of European investors foreshadowed armed intervention, as in Venezuela. To forestall a threat to U.S. interest in the Caribbean, Roosevelt proclaimed in his annual message the dictum later known as the Roosevelt Corollary to the Monroe Doctrine (by which he transformed the Doctrine from one of nonintervention by European powers to one of intervention by the U.S.): "Chronic wrongdoing, or an impotence which results in a general loosening of the ties of civilized society, may in America, as elsewhere, ultimately require intervention by some civilized nation, and in the Western Hemisphere the adherence of the United States to the Monroe Doctrine may force the United States, however reluctantly, in flagrant cases of such wrongdoing or impotence, to the exercise of an international police power."

The Corollary was one of the outstanding examples of Roosevelt's "big stick" diplomacy. Santo Domingo signed an agreement with the U.S. (1905) providing for the U.S. administration of the customs and management of debt payments. Roosevelt carried out the protocol despite the fact that it was rejected by the Senate. A permanent treaty including the protocol in revised form was ratified (25 Feb. 1907) and on 31 July 1907 the U.S. withdrew from Santo Domingo.

1905

ROOSEVELT AND THE RUSSO-JAPANESE WAR.

The Russo-Japanese War (10 Feb. 1904) jeopardized the Open Door policy. Roosevelt was perturbed by complaints of American commercial interests that the Russian advance into Manchuria endangered the Open Door. In a circular note (20 Feb. 1904) the U.S. asked the belligerents to respect "the neutrality" and "administrative entity" of China. However, each made its acceptance conditional upon the other's, and Russia went so far as to reject the proposed neutralization of Manchuria.

In Roosevelt's view, the complete defeat of either Russia or Japan was not desirable, since it would upset the balance of power in the Far East and endanger U.S. interests. On 25 Apr. Japan informed the U.S. that it would maintain the Open Door in Manchuria and restore that province to China. After the Japanese victory over the Russian fleet at the Battle of Tsushima Strait (27–29 May), the Japanese government formally asked Roosevelt (31 May) to take the initiative in acting as mediator. Roosevelt's proposal was accepted by Russia

(6 June) and on 8 June he formally invited both powers to open joint negotiations.

In the interim, the secret Taft-Katsura Memorandum was concluded (29 July) by Secretary of War Taft, then on a mission to the Philippines, and the Japanese Foreign Minister. It stipulated that the U.S. would not interfere with Japanese ambitions in Korea in return for a Japanese promise to disclaim territorial conquest in the Philippines. This executive agreement was endorsed by Roosevelt (31 July) despite his earlier insistence on a Japanese pledge of support for the Open Door policy. The Japanese construed the Taft-Katsura Memorandum as U.S. approval of a Japanese protectorate over Korea (proclaimed 21 Dec.).

9 Aug. PORTSMOUTH PEACE CONFERENCE

(held at the navy yard at Portsmouth, N.H.) was concluded by a Russo-Japanese peace treaty signed 5 Sept. Japan secured recognition of her dominant rights in Korea and, through the acquisition of Russia's Liaotung leasehold and the South Manchurian Ry., consolidated her economic and territorial position in Manchuria. Partly because of Roosevelt's opposition, the Japanese failed to obtained an indemnity and all of the island of Sakhalin (only its southern half was ceded to Japan). For his work as mediator, Roosevelt was awarded (1906) the Nobel Peace Prize.

1906

16 Jan. ROOSEVELT AND THE ALGECIRAS CONFERENCE.

Since the turn of the century France had been engaged in securing agreements with Italy, Great Britain, and Spain looking toward the establishment of a French protectorate over Morocco, in return for recognizing the interests of these powers elsewhere in North Africa. German opposition to French ambitions and to the economic partition of North Africa grew stronger, particularly after the conclusion of the Anglo-French Entente (1904). Tension was heightened after Kaiser Wilhelm II made a speech at Tangier

(31 Mar. 1905) proclaiming support of Moroccan independence.

Germany demanded an international conference on Morocco and asked Roosevelt to secure French participation. Although reluctant to intervene, Roosevelt feared that a Moroccan crisis might touch off a general European war. Through Roosevelt's efforts, France and Great Britain agreed to attend a conference at Algeciras, Spain, with U.S. delegates in attendance. Roosevelt was instrumental in securing German acceptance of the settlement (Act of Algeciras, 7 Apr.) affirming the independence and territorial integrity of Morocco, guaranteeing equality of commercial opportunity, establishing an international bank for the stabilization of Moroccan finances, and providing for the training and control of the Moroccan police by France and Spain. The Algeciras convention was ratified by the U.S. Senate (Dec. 1906) with the proviso that such approval was not to be construed as departure from the traditional U.S. policy of noninvolvement in purely European affairs.

RELATIONS WITH JAPAN. By the treaty of 1894 citizens of the U.S. and Japan were permitted mutual free entry, although both governments were empowered to protect domestic interests by legislating against excessive immigration of laborers. Because of American protests, Japan inaugurated a policy of voluntary limitation of emigration (Aug. 1900), but this move failed to halt the flow of emigrant laborers to Hawaii, Canada, or Mexico, whence entry to the U.S. could not be effectively controlled. The growth of anti-Japanese antagonism led West Coast labor to organize a Japanese and Korean Exclusion League (1905). Similar pressures, coinciding with the increasing fear of Japan as a military power ("the Yellow Peril"), resulted in a movement for the statutory exclusion of Japanese.

11 Oct. SAN FRANCISCO SCHOOL SEGREGATION. The San Francisco schools, disrupted by the earthquake and fire (18–19 Apr.), were reopened in July. On 11 Oct. the school board ordered the segregation of all Japanese, Chinese, and Korean children in a separate Oriental school. The Japanese government (25 Oct.) charged that the board's action violated the treaty of 1894. Faced with an impending international crisis, Roosevelt invited the San Francisco School Board to Washington for a conference (Feb. 1907), and effected an arrangement whereby the segregation order would be rescinded locally but the Federal government take action on the immigration question. The result was an amendment to the Immigration Act of 1907 (20 Feb.) authorizing the President to exclude from the U.S. immigrants holding passports to any country other than the U.S., any insular possession of the U.S., or the Canal Zone, and attempting to use such passports to enter the U.S. to the detriment of internal "labor conditions." By executive order (14 Mar.) Roosevelt put this authorization into effect.

"GENTLEMEN'S AGREEMENT" was embodied in a Japanese note (24 Feb. 1907) whereby Japan promised to withhold passports from laborers intending to migrate to the U.S., and recognized the American right to refuse admission to Japanese immigrants using passports originally issued for travel to any country other than the U.S. The San Francisco School Board order was formally rescinded 13 Mar. 1907. However, it was not until 18 Feb. 1908 that a Japanese note provided the basis for the effective restriction of immigration. To offset any Japanese surmisals that the concessions extended by the U.S. in the Far East signified a fear of Japan, Roosevelt sent the bulk of the U.S. Navy on a world cruise (16 Dec. 1907–22 Feb. 1909) which demonstrated that the U.S. was now the 2nd naval power in the world (Japan ranked 5th).

1907

15 June–15 Oct. 2ND HAGUE PEACE CONFERENCE. Called by the Czar of Russia, this meeting, attended by 46 nations, was originally suggested by President Roosevelt in 1904 but had been postponed because of the Russo-Japanese War. The U.S. efforts for the establishment of a world court were unsuccessful. Of particular interest to the U.S. was the adoption by the conference of a revised version of the **Drago Doctrine** (reinforcing the Monroe Doctrine), which had been formulated (29 Dec. 1902) by Luis M. Drago, Foreign Minister of Argentina, during the dispute over the collection of the Venezuelan debts. The essence of the doctrine was that armed force must not be employed by a European power to collect national debts owed by American nations to foreign creditors.

PANAMA CANAL. Preliminary work on the Panama Canal was virtually halted in 1905 because of the heavy mortality rate caused by disease. In addition, opinion was divided over a sea-level canal as opposed to a lock canal. The sanitation program carried out under Col. **William C. Gorgas** of the U.S. Army Medical Department sharply reduced the deaths caused by malaria and yellow fever and enabled a long-term construction program under safe conditions. President Roosevelt signed a bill (29 June 1906) authorizing the construction of a lock canal. With the reorganization of the Canal Commission (1 Apr.), the entire project was placed under the direct authority of the Secretary of War. Appointed as chief engineer was Lt. Col. (later Col.) **George W. Goethals** (p. 715) of the U.S. Army Corps of Engineers, under whose immediate direction the canal was built. The Panama Canal, 40.3 mi. from shore to shore, links Cristobal, on the Caribbean, with Balboa, the Bay of Panama terminus. The total cost of original construction was more than $365 million. The canal was opened to traffic 15 Aug. 1914.

14 Nov.–20 Dec. CENTRAL AMERICAN PEACE CONFERENCE. The outbreak of war in Central America prompted Secretary of State Root to propose, in conjunction with Mexico, the meeting of a peace conference in Washington. The participating powers were Costa Rica, Guatemala, Honduras, Nicaragua, and Salvador. The U.S. was not a signatory party. The 8 conventions concluded by the conference included a general treaty of peace and amity and the establishment of a Central American Court of Justice.

1908

30 Nov. ROOT-TAKAHIRA AGREEMENT, was an executive agreement concluded by an exchange of notes (30 Nov.) between Secretary of State Root and Ambassador Takahira. Carrying a step further the concession granted by the Taft-Katsura Memorandum, it provided that Japan and the U.S. would (1) maintain the "existing *status quo*" in the Pacific, (2) respect the territorial possessions belonging to each other in the Pacific, (3) uphold the Open Door policy in China, and (4) support by peaceful means the independence and integrity of China. The phrase, "existing *status quo*," was interpreted by Japan as U.S. recognition of Japan's paramount imperialist influence in Korea and southern Manchuria.

1909

TAFT'S FAR EASTERN POLICY. President Taft and his Secretary of State, Philander C. Knox, reaffirmed the Open Door with a policy subsequently known as "**Dollar Diplomacy**"—increasing U.S. trade by supporting American enterprises abroad, and including Latin America as well as the Far East.

Shortly after Taft's inauguration an international consortium composed of French, British, and German bankers took steps to float a loan for building the Hukuang Railways in southern and central China. At the suggestion of the State Dept. an American banking group was organized to finance railroad concessions in China. The bankers' agent, Willard Straight, who played a dominant role in Far Eastern "Dollar Diplomacy," unsuccessfully asked the European interests for admission to the consortium. Only after Taft took the unprecedented step of making a personal appeal (15 July) to the Chinese regent, Prince Chun, was American participation permitted in a 4-power consortium agreement (signed on 20 May 1911). American bankers had already declined Straight's proposal (1909–10) to build a rail line in northern Manchuria. As a direct result of this attempted U.S. penetration of Manchuria, Russia and Japan concluded a treaty (4 July 1911) staking out spheres of influence in deliberate defiance of the Open Door. This treaty weakened U.S. prestige in the Far East. Japan's position in Manchuria was strengthened by the fact that France and Great Britain favored giving Japan a free hand there in order to safeguard their own spheres of influence elsewhere in the Far East.

Despite these setbacks, Secretary Knox encouraged the Chinese government to request (22 Sept. 1910) a large loan to underwrite currency reform in China and industrial development in Manchuria. Japan and Russia registered their opposition, and U.S. bankers announced that they would not be bound to participate in contracts objectionable to other powers. Although a 6-power consortium was established (20 June 1912), the final agreement was signed (26 Apr. 1913) without U.S. participation. Eager to avoid further commitments in China, American bankers informed President Wilson (5 Mar. 1913) that they would remain active there only under official pressure. Wilson withdrew U.S. support of the consortium (18 Mar. 1913) on the ground that its terms endangered China's "administrative independence." This step terminated the Taft-Knox policy in the Far East. The coming of World War I shifted U.S. interest to Europe and permitted Japan to expand at China's expense.

1910

7 Sept. NEWFOUNDLAND FISHERIES. The continuing controversy over the North Atlantic fisheries was finally resolved after the U.S. and Great Britain agreed (27 Jan. 1909) to submit the question to the Hague Tribunal. The decision was a compromise award upholding the Newfoundland claim to local regulation and authorizing the provisions of the rejected Bayard-Chamberlain Treaty (1888) pertaining to the definition of territorial bays. The award was confirmed by an Anglo-American convention (20 July 1912).

1911

U.S. INTERVENTION IN NICARAGUA. Nicaragua was the object of special U.S. interest because of the disturbing possibility that its canal route might fall under foreign control. In 1909 José S. Zelaya, an opponent of foreign penetration, was deposed as dictator of Nicaragua. The ensuing political turmoil brought to the Presidency (1911) Adolfo Díaz, whose friendly policy toward the U.S. matured in the **Knox-Castrillo Convention** (6 June). This agreement gave the U.S. the right of intervention and provided for refunding of the national debt, payment to be secured by a customs receivership under U.S. protection. On 1 July the Nicaraguan government defaulted on a loan made by a British syndicate. Without waiting for the Senate to act, Knox persuaded a group of New York bankers to implement the treaty's provisions before formal ratification. The Senate adjourned without taking any action. Desperate for financial aid, the Nicaraguan government secured a loan of $1,500,000; in return, the U.S. bankers received control of the National Bank of Nicaragua and the government-owned railway. Customs receipts were pledged in payment, collection to be carried out under American auspices. The Knox-Castrillo Convention was rejected by the Senate, as was a similar one made with Honduras.

When native dissatisfaction with the agreement touched off a Nicaraguan revolt, the U.S. intervened. A force of marines was landed (14 Aug. 1912) to protect American interests. Knox then attempted to negotiate a treaty granting the U.S., in return for a payment of $3 million, the exclusive right of way for an interoceanic canal, a 90-yr. lease of the Great Corn and Little Corn Islands in the Caribbean, and a naval base on the Gulf of Fonseca. The Senate failed to act on this agreement. To insure the regular operation of the financial arrangements, a small detachment of marines remained in

Nicaragua until 1925, and did not finally leave until 1933.

7 July. PELAGIC SEALING AGREEMENT. The controversy regarding pelagic sealing in the North Pacific persisted after Blaine's unsuccessful attempt to deal with it, and became acute as the steadily dwindling herds of seals were threatened with extinction. In 1911 a 4-power conference on the sealing industry was called at Washington and, participated in by the U.S., Great Britain, Russia, and Japan, agreed to a treaty, to continue in force subject to one year's notice, which outlawed for 15 years pelagic sealing north of the 30th parallel, established a U.S. monopoly of the catch, and authorized an allocation of profits to Great Britain and Japan in return for their withdrawal from pelagic sealing in the area. Japan abrogated the convention on 23 Oct. 1940.

CANADIAN RECIPROCITY. Anxious to forestall the breakup of trade with Canada, threatened in retaliation against the Payne-Aldrich Tariff of 1909, the Taft administration signed a reciprocity agreement (26 Jan.) providing for the reduction or elimination of duties on many Canadian items, chiefly agricultural commodities, and for reduced rates on U.S. manufactures. Because it involved fiscal matters, the agreement was subject to approval by both Houses of Congress. The House approved, as did the Senate (22 July), despite opposition from Midwestern agricultural interests; but when Taft and several Congressmen publicly referred to the reciprocity agreement as a prelude to the U.S. annexation of Canada, national feeling was aroused in Canada. In the elections of 1911 the Liberal party, in favor of the agreement, was defeated by the antireciprocity Conservatives (21 Sept.), ending for the time being Canadian-American reciprocity.

ARBITRATION TREATIES. The arbitration treaties which Secretary of State Root negotiated (1908–09) with 25 nations, providing for the referral of controversies to the Hague Tribunal, were weakened by reservations concerning disputes involving national interests, honor, and independence. When Taft became President, he made efforts to obtain arbitration agreements of a more general

character. The impetus was provided by the Anglo-Japanese Alliance, by which Great Britain was bound to aid Japan in the event of war. The U.S. was anxious to employ diplomatic means to restrain Japan. An opportunity arose with the renewal (13 July) of the Anglo-Japanese Alliance containing a proviso that neither nation would fight a 3rd power with whom a general arbitration treaty was in force. The U.S. signed such treaties (3 Aug.) with Great Britain and France, but these agreements were vitiated by amendment in the Senate (which ratified them on 7 Mar. 1912), where Senator Henry Cabot Lodge (Mass.) led the fight for reservations on matters involving Oriental exclusion and the Monroe Doctrine, and for determination by the Senate of the character of controversies before their submission to arbitration.

1912

2 Aug. LODGE COROLLARY. In 1911 it became known that a Japanese syndicate was conducting negotiations for the purchase of a large site near strategic Magdalena Bay, Lower California. The negotiations came to an end when the State Department registered its disapproval. A Senate resolution introduced by Senator Lodge declared the U.S. viewed with "grave concern" the possession of strategically important areas "by any corporation or association which has such a relation to another Government, not American, as to give that Government practical power of control for national purposes." The Lodge Corollary extended the Monroe Doctrine's scope to non-European powers and to foreign companies as well as foreign nations.

1913

24 Apr. BRYAN'S "COOLING OFF" TREATIES. As early as 1905 William Jennings Bryan recommended that the U.S. take the initiative in establishing a system of arbitration providing for the referral of all international differences to a permanent court of arbitration. Shortly after becoming Secretary of State, he negotiated with 30 nations separate treaties (differing in detail, but similar in their broad features) providing for the referral of all international disputes, without exception, to a permanent investigating commission. Resort to armed conflict was prohibited until the commission submitted its report within a year. Twenty-one ratifications were finally exchanged.

MEXICAN REVOLUTION. Since 1877 Mexico had been almost without interruption under a dictatorship headed by President Porfirio Díaz, who had granted foreign investors liberal concessions for the development of Mexican resources including oil, mines, land, and railways. By 1913 a total of some $2 billion (of which more than half came from the U.S.) had been invested by foreign interests. A revolution led by the democratic reformer, Francisco I. Madero, broke out Nov. 1910. Americans were compelled to abandon their holdings and flee the country; some lost their lives. The revolution culminated in Díaz' resignation (25 May 1911) and the establishment of a liberal government.

The Taft administration recognized the Madero regime and embargoed the shipment of munitions to Madero's opponents; for the rest, the U.S. adhered to a policy of nonintervention. Madero was assassinated (22 Feb.) by agents of the reactionary Gen. Victoriano Huerta, who seized power and held it amid revolutionary upheaval. European powers recognized Huerta, but President Taft refused recognition despite pressure by American business interests.

When Wilson became President, he decided to follow a policy of cooperating with only such governments as rested upon the undoubted consent of the governed. In a speech (11 Mar.) he tacitly disapproved of Huerta and indicated the termination of Dollar Diplomacy with the announcement that the U.S. would not lend support to special interests. After a revolution headed by Venustiano Carranza gathered force, Wilson proposed an immediate armistice, to be followed by a free election in which Huerta should not be a candidate. In return the U.S. would encourage American bankers to extend loans to the Mexican government.

Huerta's refusal (16 Aug.) evoked from Wilson a policy of "watchful waiting" and the application of a strict arms embargo. Huerta dissolved the Mexican Congress (10 Oct.) and was elected President (26 Oct.). American business interests renewed their demand for intervention, but Wilson, in a speech delivered at Mobile, Ala. (27 Oct.), asserted that the U.S. "will never again seek one additional foot of territory by conquest."

Wilson applied sharper pressure in a note (7 Nov.) requesting Huerta's retirement from power. The Mexican ruler was further notified (24 Nov.) that it was the policy of the U.S. to isolate him from material aid and foreign sympathy, and to force him out of office. Early in 1914 Wilson lifted the arms embargo to permit munitions to reach the opponents of Huerta and stationed U.S. naval units off Vera Cruz to block the entry of European shipments of war materials to the Huerta regime.

1914

9–21 Apr. TAMPICO AND VERA CRUZ INCIDENTS. An unarmed party from the U.S.S. *Dolphin,* one of the vessels stationed in Mexican waters, went ashore at Tampico (9 Apr.) to secure supplies, and by error entered a restricted area. Despite the cover of the U.S. flag, they were arrested by Huerta's troops on the charge of violating martial law. Although they were released promptly, with apologies from a superior officer, Adm. Henry T. Mayo peremptorily demanded that the port commander apologize formally, promise to punish the responsible officer, and hoist the American flag ashore, giving it a 21-gun salute. Mayo made these demands without consulting Washington, but the Wilson administration felt that he must be supported to preclude Huerta's exploitation of the incident. However, Huerta succeeded in evading the salute, despite a warning that a refusal would probably result in intervention.

Congress granted (22 Apr.) Wilson's request for permission to use force to uphold U.S. rights and secure redress of grievances. Meanwhile, U.S. forces had already landed on Mexican soil. Informed that a German ship was approaching with munitions, Bryan advised Wilson (21 Apr.) to use the navy to prevent delivery. On 21 Apr. the American forces bombarded Vera Cruz and occupied the city. Huerta promptly broke off diplomatic relations with the U.S. The incident united Mexican opinion behind Huerta and brought Mexico and the U.S. close to war.

20 May–30 June. ABC CONFERENCE. Wilson accepted the offer of the ABC Powers (Argentina, Brazil, and Chile) to mediate the dispute. At a meeting at Niagara Falls, Ontario, attended by representatives of the U.S., Mexico, and the ABC Powers, the mediators proposed the retirement of Huerta, establishment of a Mexican provisional government in favor of agrarian and political reforms, and no indemnity to the U.S. for occupation costs at Vera Cruz. This plan, agreed to 24 June, was rejected by Mexico, but its moral effect was instrumental in compelling Huerta to leave office (15 July). The U.S. occupation forces withdrew from Vera Cruz (23 Nov.) and on 19 Oct. 1915 the U.S. and several Latin-American nations recognized Carranza as *de facto* president.

15 June. PANAMA TOLLS ACT. On 24 Aug. 1912, Congress passed the Panama Canal Act, exempting U.S. coastwise shipping from payment of tolls, in apparent contravention of the Hay-Pauncefote Treaty provision that the canal should be free and open to the vessels of commerce and of war of "all nations" on terms of entire equality. The British protested on the ground that "all nations" should include, rather than exclude, the U.S. American supporters of the Act (which was approved by both major parties in the election of 1912) maintained that the equality provisions referred to uniformity of rates. Disturbed by the charges of bad faith brought against the U.S., Wilson recommended (5 Mar.) repeal of the tolls exemption. Repeal passed the Senate on 11 June. Settlement of the controversy helped win British backing for the U.S. course in Mexico. The Panama Canal was officially opened to traffic on 15 Aug.

4 Aug. U.S. NEUTRALITY. With the outbreak of World War I (Germany declared war on Russia 1 Aug., on France 3 Aug., and invaded Belgium 3 Aug.; Britain declared war against Germany 4 Aug.), President Wilson issued a proclamation of neutrality. On 19 Aug. he publicly appealed to Americans to be "impartial in thought as well as in action."

6 Aug. CONTROVERSY OVER NEUTRAL RIGHTS. Great Britain justified her blockade of Germany by the "unusual" conditions of warfare. Secretary Bryan asked the belligerents (6 Aug. 1914) to accept the Declaration of London (drafted in 1909 and signed by the leading powers but not ratified) as a code of naval warfare. Because its guarantees gave the Central Powers their only chance for large-scale trade with neutrals, they promptly accepted, conditional upon enemy agreement. France and Russia made acceptance conditional upon Great Britain, whose position was clarified by an Order in Council (20 Aug. 1914). The order, setting the pattern of British trade regulation for the duration of the war, accepted the Declaration but made exceptions to its contraband provisions, extending the list of conditional contraband beyond the categories specified in the Declaration.

A vigorous protest (26 Sept. 1914) by the State Department was withheld at the suggestion of Col. **Edward M. House** (1858–1938), private diplomatic adviser to President Wilson. The note sent instead (28 Sept. 1914) stressed the evil effects of British policy upon American public opinion rather than neutral rights. When the U.S. abandoned (22 Oct. 1914) its efforts to make the Declaration of London effective, the British, in successive Orders in Council (29 Oct., 23 Dec. 1914), further extended the contraband list and revived the **doctrine of the continuous voyage** by proceeding to intercept neutral ships going to Germany and to neighboring countries (Denmark, Holland, and the Scandinavian nations, which lay in the Baltic area under the control of the German navy). This enabled the British to seize many goods (especially foodstuffs) previously considered fair trade for neutrals. The British declared (3 Nov. 1914) the North Sea a military area and presently mined it and proclaimed (11 Mar.) a blockade of all German ports, with all merchant vessels bound for or coming from a German port liable to seizure and confiscation.

15 Aug. LOANS TO BELLIGERENTS. The U.S. government announced that "loans by American bankers to any foreign nation which is at war are inconsistent with the true spirit of neutrality." This policy was modified (Oct.) at the behest of Robert Lansing, then counselor for the State Dept. Advised that the U.S. would not object to short-term credits, the National City Bank (4 Nov.) advanced $10 million to the French government. In Sept. 1915 Wilson reluctantly agreed to the floating of general loans by the belligerents, and on 25 Sept. 1915 a group of American bankers completed negotiations for a loan of $500 million to France and Britain. By Apr. 1917 U.S. investors had purchased $2,300 million in bonds from the Allies in contrast with only about $20 million in German bonds. U.S. trade with the Allies rose from c.$800 million (1914) to c.$3 billion (1916), while direct exports to Germany and Austria-Hungary dropped from $169,289,775 to $1,159,653.

1915

10 Feb. "STRICT ACCOUNTABILITY." The German government proclaimed (4 Feb.) the waters around the British Isles a war zone and announced that beginning 18 Feb. enemy merchant ships would be destroyed on sight in the forbidden area without provision for the safety of passengers and crew. Warning of the dangers resulting from the misuse of neutral flags and from the accidents of warfare, the German government declared that neutral craft entering the war zone would do so at their own risk. In contrast with the temporizing position on British interference with American rights on the high seas, the U.S. government registered a sharp protest (10 Feb.). The note stated that in the event American vessels or the lives of American

citizens were destroyed by Germany on the high seas, the U.S. would view the act as "an indefensible violation of neutral rights" and hold Germany strictly answerable.

The German ambassador, Count von Bernstorff, promptly urged the State Dept. to warn Americans against travel on belligerent ships, but his advice was not heeded. On 28 Mar. an American citizen perished in the sinking of the British liner *Falaba* in the Irish Sea. On 1 May the American tanker *Gulflight* was struck by a torpedo launched in a fight between a submarine and a British naval patrol off the Scilly Isles, causing the death of two Americans.

7 May. SINKING OF THE "LUSITANIA." The German embassy at Washington issued a warning (1 May) that Americans entering the war zone around the British Isles would do so at their own risk. On 7 May the British transatlantic steamer *Lusitania* was sunk off the Irish coast without warning by a submarine, with the loss of 1,198 lives, including 128 Americans. The act precipitated a revulsion of public opinion against Germany.

13 May, 9 June, 21 July. "LUSITANIA" NOTES. The first *Lusitania* note (13 May) was drafted by Wilson and signed by Bryan against his own inclination. It demanded that Germany abandon unrestricted submarine warfare, disavow the sinking of the *Lusitania,* and make reparation for the loss of U.S. lives. The note insisted upon the right of Americans to sail on the high seas and reiterated the "strict accountability" position. The German reply (28 May) excused the torpedoing on the ground that the *Lusitania* was armed and carried contraband (the vessel, in fact, was unarmed, but carried a shipment of rifles and cartridges). Wilson regarded the reply as evasive and unsatisfactory. A 2nd note (also drafted by Wilson) took issue with the German contention that special circumstances imposed the necessity for unrestricted submarine warfare and demanded specific pledges. Bryan informed Wilson that he could not sign the note because he feared that it might involve the U.S. in war. His resignation, tendered on 7 June, was promptly accepted, and the 2nd *Lusi-*

tania note (9 June) was dispatched over the signature of Secretary Robert Lansing. The 3rd note (21 July), virtually an ultimatum, warned Germany that a repetition of such acts would be regarded as "deliberately unfriendly."

24 July–1 Dec. GERMAN ESPIONAGE AND SABOTAGE. The U.S. Secret Service obtained possession of documents signed by Ambassador Bernstorff and Capt. Franz von Papen, revealing German sabotage activity in the U.S. Publication (beg. 15 Aug. in N.Y. *World*) led to the recall of the Austro-Hungarian Ambassador, Dr. Constantin Dumba (8 Sept.), and of the German attachés, Capts. von Papen and Boy-Ed (1 Dec.). On 30 July 1916 a munitions explosion on **Black Tom** Island, N.J., attributed to German sabotage, resulted in property loss of $22 million. On 11 Jan. 1917 an explosion wrecked the Canadian Car & Foundry plant at Kingsland, N.J. A Mixed Claims Commission (15 June 1939) found Germany guilty of both explosions, but Germany never paid the $55 million damage award.

19 Aug.–5 Oct. "ARABIC" CRISIS. Anxious to avoid the consequences of similar incidents, the German government privately instructed its submarine commanders (6 June) not to sink liners, even those under the enemy flag, without warning. When 2 American lives were lost in the sinking of the British steamer *Arabic* (19 Aug.), German Ambassador von Bernstorff rendered the so-called *Arabic* pledge (1 Sept.) on his own authority: "Liners will not be sunk by our submarines without warning and without safety of the lives of non-combatants, provided that the liners do not try to escape or offer resistance." During the remainder of 1915 the German U-boats concentrated on freighters in the Atlantic. The German government (5 Oct.) offered apologies and indemnity for the loss of American lives in the *Arabic* disaster, and this outcome was regarded as a diplomatic victory for the U.S.

INTERVENTION IN HAITI. A Haitian revolution raised Vibrun Guillaume Sam to power as President (5 Mar.), by which time Haiti's foreign debt had risen to *c.*$24 million. American financial in-

terests held investments in the Haitian national bank and railroad, and the U.S., countering a Franco-German proposal (Mar. 1914) for joint customs, proposed a customs receivership. Following another revolution, resulting in the overthrow and assassination of President Sam (28 July), the U.S. marines, at Wilson's order, landed in Haiti (29 July) and imposed a military occupation. Sudre Dartiguenave, elected President (15 Aug.), signed a treaty (16 Sept.) by which Haiti became for all practical purposes a U.S. protectorate. The treaty, which went into effect for a 10-yr. period (with option of renewal) on 3 May 1916, stipulated that the Haitian public debt might not be increased, nor its tariff diminished, without U.S. consent.

1916

15 Mar. MEXICAN BORDER CAMPAIGN. Revolutionary opposition to Carranza was continued by a number of freebooting chieftains, particularly by **Pancho Villa** in northern Mexico. Villa was responsible for the deaths of Americans on both sides of the border. When 18 American engineers were invited by Carranza to return and operate the abandoned mines, Villa's band shot and killed them at Santa Ysabel (10 Jan.). Villa was also credited with repeated raids into Texas and New Mexico in the spring of 1916. A raid on Columbus, N.M. (9 Mar.), resulted in 17 deaths. Congressional pressure for intervention mounted, and Wilson was compelled to abandon his policy of "watchful waiting."

With Carranza's reluctant consent, Gen. John J. Pershing was ordered to head a punitive expedition of 15,000 men and pursue Villa into Mexico. Wilson called out 150,000 militia and stationed this force along the border. The pursuit of Villa (begun 15 Mar.) aroused the antagonism of Carranza and intensified anti-American feeling. Carranza refused to accept a proposal signed (24 Nov.) by joint commissioners of Mexico and the U.S. for withdrawal of U.S. troops and joint but independent guarding of the border. As war with Germany became imminent, Wilson finally withdrew the U.S. expeditionary force (Jan.–5 Feb. 1917). A new Mexican constitution was proclaimed (5 Feb. 1917), Carranza was elected President (11 Mar. 1917), and the U.S. extended *de jure* recognition to the new government.

LATIN-AMERICAN RELATIONS.
Nicaragua: Bryan-Chamorro Treaty (signed 5 Aug. 1914) perpetuated the Taft-Knox policy of Dollar Diplomacy. An unsuccessful attempt to insert Platt Amendment provisions delayed Senate ratification until 18 Feb. 1916. Nicaragua received $3 million in return for granting the U.S. exclusive rights to a canal route and a naval base. The U.S. secured a 99-yr. lease (with option of renewal) to the Great Corn and Little Corn Islands and to the Gulf of Fonseca. The treaty evoked the protests of Costa Rica and Salvador, both claiming that it infringed upon their territorial rights. An adverse decision of the Central American Court of Justice was disregarded by the U.S. and Nicaragua.

Intervention in Santo Domingo. The financial protectorate set up in Santo Domingo in 1907 temporarily relieved that country of political instability. But renewal of domestic disorders led to a further increase in the public debt. By Sept. 1912, revolutionary forces had seized 2 customhouses and laid two others under siege. The Dominican Republic accepted (June 1914) the temporary appointment of a new American official who exercised a check on expenditures; but when the U.S. Minister again demanded (Nov. 1915) the acceptance of a financial adviser, the Dominican President was reluctant to comply. Internal disorder forced his resignation (May); partial occupation of the country followed; and U.S. officials began collecting internal revenue, putting the financial advisership into practical operation. Secretary Lansing recommended (22 Nov.) full military occupation of Santo Domingo. The occupation was proclaimed on 29 Nov. and an internal administration was established under U.S. naval officers, who remained in charge until 1924 (p. 321).

22 Feb. HOUSE MISSION AND MEMORANDUM. President Wilson, anxious to avoid U.S. involvement in the European War and concerned with the necessity of a negotiated peace, dispatched (Dec. 1914) his private adviser and close friend, Col. Edward M. House, as an unofficial emissary on a secret mission to the foreign offices of the major belligerent powers. House arrived in London (6 Feb. 1915), where he conferred with the British Foreign Secretary, Sir Edward Grey. These discussions were inconclusive, as were those held (Mar.–Apr. 1915) at Paris and Berlin. House again went to Europe and conducted (Jan.–Feb.) another series of discussions with British, French, and German statesmen. House proposed an understanding by which Germany would be granted wider scope in colonial areas and overseas markets in return for a pledge to reduce her naval construction. While the scheme lacked precise formulation, it proposed the following peace terms: the restoration of Belgium and Serbia, the cession of Alsace-Lorraine to France, and of Constantinople to Russia. House's conversations at London resulted in the **House-Grey Memorandum** (22 Feb.), which promised on Wilson's behalf that, "on hearing from France and England that the moment was opportune," the President would summon a peace conference. Should Allied acceptance be followed by German refusal, the U.S. "would probably enter the war against Germany." Wilson's endorsement (6 Mar.) of the Memorandum was communicated to Grey 8 Mar. However, the Allies and the Central Powers still believed that they could break the military deadlock by force of arms; hence, the U.S. proposal for a negotiated peace fell on deaf ears.

3–7 Mar. GORE-McLEMORE RESOLUTIONS. A German declaration (8 Feb.) to the effect that all armed enemy merchant vessels would be sunk without warning after 1 Mar. raised fears in Congress that the further loss of American lives on the high seas would draw the U.S. into war and touched off a revolt within Democratic ranks.

Representative Jeff McLemore (Tex.) introduced a resolution (17 Feb.) requesting the President to warn Americans not to travel on armed vessels. At a stormy White House conference with party leaders (21 Feb.), Wilson made it clear that he was adamant in his interpretation of U.S. rights. Construing the McLemore resolution as a challenge to U.S. sovereignty and a test of his Presidential leadership, Wilson informed the Senate Committee on Foreign Relations (24 Feb.) that he could not "consent to any abridgement of the rights of American citizens in any respect. . . ."

Senator Thomas P. Gore (Okla.) introduced a resolution (25 Feb.) to deny passports to Americans seeking passage on armed belligerent vessels and demanded protection of American trade in noncontraband from the Allied restrictions. (In a direct challenge to the administration, this resolution was later modified to read that the loss of American life because of the sinking of an armed merchant vessel by Germany "would constitute a just and sufficient cause of war between the United States and the German Empire"; by such a positive declaration, the opponents of Wilson's position hoped to embarrass the administration.) Wilson decided (29 Feb.) to bring the fight over the resolutions to a head. Under pressure from the White House, the Gore resolution was tabled in the Senate (3 Mar.), 68–14, and the McLemore resolution tabled in the House (7 Mar.), 276–142.

24 Mar. "SUSSEX" AFFAIR. A secret German order (21 Nov. 1915) authorized submarine commanders to regard as troop transports that could be sunk without warning all ships plying the English Channel. A German submarine torpedoed (24 Mar.) the *Sussex,* an unarmed French cross-channel passenger ship, causing injury to several Americans. The U.S. regarded the attack as a violation of the *Arabic* pledge. Secretary Lansing called for drastic action, informing President Wilson (27 Mar.) that he favored an immediate severance of diplomatic relations with Germany. Wilson resisted the pressure for a break, and substituted an ultimatum (18 Apr.) that unless Germany immediately abandoned its present methods of submarine warfare, the U.S. would sever relations. Germany agreed (4 May) to the U.S. demands, but laid down the countercondition that the U.S. compel the Allies to respect the "rules of

international law." Wilson accepted the pledge, but refused (8 May) to accept the condition.

18 July. BRITISH BLACKLIST of 85 American individuals and firms (30 commercial firms) which because of suspected dealings with the Central Powers were to be denied the use of British banking, shipping, and cable facilities. Responding to U.S. public opinion, Wilson considered asking Congress to prohibit loans and cut exports to the Allies. Two retaliatory laws were passed. The **Shipping Board Act** (7 Sept.) empowered the President to deny clearance papers to any ship refusing to accept cargo from blacklisted firms. The **Revenue Act** (8 Sept.) authorized the President to withhold clearance or port facilities from any ship guilty of unfair discrimination against American commerce. However, these discretionary powers were never exercised, partly because the British government, under the pressure of this legislation, began to make concessions, and partly because Secretary of Commerce William C. Redfield reported (23 Oct.) that retaliation would invite counter-reprisals without guaranteeing the desired concessions. In addition, the naval appropriation of 1916, the largest in U.S. peacetime history to date, served as an implied warning to Great Britain.

29 Aug. JONES ACT (known as the Organic Act of the Philippine Islands) reaffirmed the U.S. intention to withdraw its sovereignty over the islands and to recognize their independence as soon as a stable government should be established. The act conferred Filipino citizenship upon all inhabitants who had been Spanish subjects on 11 Apr. 1899, provided for a bill of rights and male suffrage, established an elective senate in place of the Philippine Commission, and vested the supreme executive power in the governor-general of the Philippine Islands, who was to be appointed by the President of the U.S.

2 Sept.–12 Dec. GERMAN PEACE OVERTURES. At the behest (2 Sept.) of Chancellor Theobald von Bethmann-Hollweg, the German Ambassador to the U.S., Count Bernstorff, inquired whether the good offices of the U.S. would be offered if Germany guaranteed the restoration of Belgium. Bernstorff was informed that President Wilson would not take any steps toward mediation until after the fall elections. By 25 Nov. Wilson had completed the first draft of his proposal for mediation and a program for an equitable peace, but the Allies were uncompromisingly hostile toward peace overtures. The fall of the Asquith Cabinet in Great Britain (5 Dec.) and the accession of Lloyd George as Prime Minister brought no change in policy. Before Wilson could release his peace proposal, the German government published a statement (12 Dec.) directed to all neutral powers announcing the willingness of Germany and the other Central Powers to enter immediately upon peace negotiations. The Allies declined the proposal because of the German refusal to state her peace terms.

18 Dec. WILSON'S PEACE NOTE to the belligerent powers was neither a peace proposal nor a mediation offer. It abandoned his proposed call for a general conference and put forward a simple request to both parties to state their war aims. The move was futile. The Germans refused a statement. An Allied joint reply (30 Dec.) rejected the German note of 12 Dec. In a joint note (10 Jan. 1917) to the U.S., the Allies outlined peace terms clearly unfavorable to the Central Powers: (1) the restoration of Belgium, Serbia, and Montenegro with appropriate indemnities; (2) the evacuation of the invaded territories of France, Russia, and Rumania with just reparations; (3) the restitution of territories or provinces taken from the Allies by force; (4) the liberation of Italians, Slavs, Rumanians, and Czecho-Slavs from foreign domination; (5) the expulsion from Europe of the Ottoman Empire; and (6) the reorganization of Europe, guaranteed by a stable regime founded upon respect of nationalities and full security to all nations, great or small.

1917

17 Jan. PURCHASE OF THE VIRGIN ISLANDS. U.S. desire to annex the Danish possessions in the Caribbean was heightened by fears that Germany had a long-standing ambition to use them as a naval base. By a treaty signed on 4 Aug. 1916, Denmark agreed to cede the Virgin Islands to the U.S. in return for $25 million. The U.S. took official possession on 31 Mar. The administration was placed under a governor appointed directly by the President. The inhabitants, chiefly Negroes, were granted limited home rule on a local basis (in 1927 they were given U.S. citizenship).

22 Jan. "PEACE WITHOUT VICTORY." Shortly after receiving the Allied reply (10 Jan.) Wilson prepared his own program for a desirable peace settlement. In an address to the Senate (22 Jan.) he referred to the need for international organization as a guarantee of an enduring world peace and insisted upon "peace without victory."

1 Feb. RESUMPTION OF UNRESTRICTED SUBMARINE WARFARE. Early in 1917 the struggle between German civilian and military leaders over the unlimited use of the submarine came to a head. A conference at Pless (31 Aug. 1916) had agreed that the Supreme High Command of the German army should have the power to decide when the submarine campaign was to be opened. The leaders of the armed services agreed (Nov. 1916) that unless Germany's peace moves were successful, unrestricted U-boat warfare must be launched by the end of Jan. At a conference of political and military leaders, held (8–9 Jan.) at Pless, field headquarters of Gen. Paul von Hindenburg, Gen. Erich von Ludendorff supported the demand of the German admirals for resumption of unrestricted submarine warfare. Chancellor Bethmann-Hollweg, spokesman of the civilian opposition, agreed reluctantly when it became apparent that the advantages likely to accrue (chiefly the destruction of the British means and will to fight) outweighed the dangers of U.S. entry into the war. Accordingly, Ambassador Bernstorff notified (31 Jan.) Secretary Lansing that, effective 1 Feb., submarine assaults against all neutral and belligerent shipping would be renewed. The Germans specified that the U.S. would be permitted to send 1 ship to England each week, provided the vessel observed certain conditions set by the German government.

3 Feb. BREAK WITH GERMANY. The violation of the *Sussex* pledge made U.S. relations with Germany increasingly intolerable. On 3 Feb. U.S.S. *Housatonic* was sunk after warning. Wilson resisted (31 Jan.) Secretary Lansing's recommendation for a break, but soon made his own decision, and in an address to Congress (3 Feb.) announced the severance of diplomatic relations with Germany. He plainly implied that "actual overt acts" by the German government would bring positive steps by the U.S. A Senate resolution (7 Feb.) endorsed Wilson's action.

1 Mar. ZIMMERMANN NOTE was a code message (dated 19 Jan.) sent to von Eckhardt, German Minister in Mexico, by German Foreign Secretary Alfred Zimmermann. If war between Germany and the U.S. broke out, Eckhardt was to propose an alliance with Mexico on the following basis: "That we shall make war together and together make peace. We shall give generous financial support, and it is understood that Mexico is to reconquer the lost territory in New Mexico, Texas, and Arizona." Mexico was to urge Japan to switch to Germany's side. This message was intercepted and decoded by the British naval intelligence, and a copy given (24 Feb.) to **Walter Hines Page** (1855–1918), U.S. Ambassador to Great Britain, who immediately transmitted it to the State Department, which, in turn, released it to the press (1 Mar.).

26 Feb.–13 Mar. ARMING OF U.S. MERCHANTMEN. Moving to prevent an overt act which would precipitate war with Germany, Wilson asked Congress (26 Feb.) for authority to arm American merchantmen in the hope of deterring submarines from attack. Publication of the Zimmermann note lent added force to his request. The House acted promptly (1 Mar.), passing the **Armed Ship Bill** by a vote of 403 to 13. In the Senate, however, a "little group of willful men" (as Wilson characterized these 7 Republicans and 5 Democrats) led by Robert M. La Follette filibustered the bill from 28 Feb. until the end of the session (4

Mar.). Wilson was then advised by Secretary Lansing (6, 8 Mar.) that under statute law he could arm merchant ships without the specific approval of Congress. The State Department announced (12 Mar.) that all American merchant vessels sailing through war zones would be armed. The Navy Department issued instructions (13 Mar.) authorizing such vessels to take action against submarines.

SUBMARINE TOLL. On 25 Feb., S.S. *Laconia* (British), with 2 U.S. dead, announced 26 Feb., day of Wilson's message to Congress; 12 Mar., S.S. *Algonquin*, unarmed, with warning; 16 Mar., sinkings reported of *City of Memphis, Illinois,* and *Vigilancia;* 21 Mar., Standard Oil steamer, *Healdton,* in safety zone off Dutch coast.

2 Mar. JONES ACT (known as the Organic Act for Puerto Rico) made Puerto Rico a U.S. territory and conferred U.S. citizenship on its inhabitants. Male suffrage was instituted, and a bill of rights gave the Puerto Ricans virtually all of the civil rights prescribed by the U.S. Constitution, with the exception of the right to demand a trial by jury. The upper house of the legislature was made elective; legislative acts were made subject to Presidential veto. The governor and the supreme court were to be appointed by the President, who also had the power of appointment over four of the six executive departmental heads. The act provided for the payment into the local treasury of U.S. internal revenue collections.

2 Apr. WILSON'S WAR MESSAGE. Secretary Lansing favored war with Germany, maintaining that U.S. participation would encourage the democratic elements within Germany and lend support to the new democratic government in Russia, where the March Revolution brought a provisional regime into power on the 12th. Wilson delayed his commitment. The unanimous advice of his Cabinet (20 Mar.) for war was influential, and on 21 Mar. Wilson issued a call for a special session of Congress to convene on 2 Apr. In a message asking for a declaration of war Wilson condemned the German submarine policy as "warfare against mankind," stated that the U. S. was joining the fight for ultimate world peace, and declared: "The world must be made safe for democracy."

4–6 Apr. WAR RESOLUTION, which passed the Senate (4 Apr.), 82–6, was concurred in by the House (6 Apr.), 373–50.

THE UNITED STATES IN WORLD WAR I, 1917–18

6 Apr. U.S. DECLARATION OF WAR ON GERMANY. The joint Congressional resolution declaring a state of war was signed by President Wilson. War against Austria-Hungary was declared on 7 Dec. During World War I the U.S. was not formally a member nation of the Allies. To the end of that conflict she was known as an "Associated Power" in a group of "Allied and Associated Powers."

MILITARY SITUATION. The U.S. entry into the war came at a time when the prospects for an Allied victory took a decided turn for the worst. The peak of the German destruction of Allied shipping (chiefly British) was Apr., when 881,000 gross tons were lost. Although the monthly losses declined thereafter, averaging about 200,000 tons a month over the following year, they still exceeded the Allied capacity for replacement. French failure in the Aisne and Champagne offensives (Apr.) caused a sharp drop in morale and led to mutinies in the French army. The Flanders offensive (June–Nov.) by the British was indecisive, and won little ground at the cost of enormous casualties. Brusilov's offensive (July), launched by the Russians, was smashed by the Germans; the defeat contributed to an upsurge of peace sentiment in Russia. Following the November Revolution (6–7 Nov.), the Bolsheviks negotiated a separate peace (**Treaty of Brest-Litovsk,** 3 Mar. 1918). Not only was Russia lost as a military ally; her defection enabled the release of masses of German troops for use on the Western Front. At the close of the year (Oct.–Dec.) the Italians suffered a crushing disaster in the Caporetto campaign, which gave northeastern Italy above Venice to the enemy. The Allies were reduced to defensive tactics, and the winter of

1917–18 saw a lull in military operations on the Western Front. At the outset of 1918, the balance of strength on land appeared to lie with the Germans. U.S. participation gave the Allies fresh resources of man power, finances, raw materials, and munitions, and offset depressed morale.

U.S. MILITARY CONTRIBUTION. When war was declared, there were about 200,000 men in the army. During the war this number was expanded to 4 million. A total of 4,791,172 men served in the armed forces of the U.S. during World War I; of these, about 2,800,000 were inducted through Selective Service; 32 camps and cantonments, with facilities for 1,800,000 men, were built to carry out the training program. The number of American soldiers who went to France was 2,084,000. By May 1918, the U.S. had 500,000 men in France, and the peak of overseas movement was reached in July 1918, when 313,410 troops arrived in France. In all, 42 infantry divisions were sent to France (each division consisting of about 1,000 officers and 27,000 men). Of these, 29 took part in active combat (7 regular army, 11 national guard, and 11 national army), bringing to 1,390,000 the number of men who saw active combat service. The **AMERICAN EXPEDITIONARY FORCE (A.E.F.)** was commanded by Gen. **John J. Pershing** (p. 765). From June 1917 until 11 Nov. 1918, more than 4,400,000 tons of cargo were shipped directly to France for the A.E.F. Adm. **William S. Sims** (1858–1936) commanded the U.S. naval forces abroad. The navy, which had a wartime strength of about 500,000, convoyed troop transports, chased submarines, and aided the British fleet in keeping German craft out of the North Sea.

A.E.F. When General Pershing arrived at Paris (14 June) as commander of the U.S. overseas forces, his army was non-existent (the 1st U.S. troops, units of the 1st Div., did not arrive in France until 26 June). Pershing's orders for cooperation with the Allied forces in operations against the enemy specified that the U.S. forces "are a distinct and separate component of the combined forces, the identity of which must be preserved." Against Allied opposition, Pershing vigorously maintained his demand for an integral U.S. army and a U.S. sector on the Western Front. He received the full support of Wilson to use his forces according to his own judgment. In July Pershing won Allied consent for concentrating the U.S. forces in eastern France, in the area east of Verdun known as the Toul sector. General orders issued on 5 July created the general staff of the A.E.F. On 1 Sept. Pershing established his general headquarters at Chaumont.

The 1st U.S. troops to go to the front were units of the 1st Div. They moved (21 Oct.) into the Toul sector, relieving French units holding the line. Pershing did not participate in the conversations (Nov.) that resulted in the creation (27 Nov.) of the Supreme War Council, on which civilian and military leaders served. This group, an inadequate attempt to unify the Allied military command, left the conduct and control of each army to its respective government. The Supreme War Council decided that it would be inadvisable to undertake an offensive until a sufficient number of U.S. troops arrived in France.

2 Nov. LANSING-ISHII AGREEMENT. Japan joined (23 Aug. 1914) the Allies in the war against Germany and then attempted to expand her power in China and the North Pacific. Her policy of aggression was evident in the **21 Demands** on China (18 Jan. 1915). In revised form, these were embodied in a Sino-Japanese treaty (25 May 1915) by which Japan secured reluctant Chinese recognition of her position in South Manchuria and Shantung. This contributed to a renewal of U.S.-Japanese rivalry in the Far East and resulted in a U.S. note (11 May 1915) registering disapproval of the Japanese move and declaring that the U.S. would refuse to recognize any agreement impairing the political or territorial integrity of China, the Open Door policy, or the treaty rights of the U.S. in China.

The American position remained for some time the only foreign obstacle to Japan's realization of her objectives in China. To safeguard her territorial and economic ambitions, Japan took advantage of the submarine crisis and signed (1916–17) a number of secret treaties with the Allied powers designed to guarantee her succession to German rights in Shantung and the Northern Pacific islands. Her efforts to commit the U.S. to recognition of Japanese "paramount interests" in China resulted in the Lansing-Ishii Agreement.

Viscount Kikujiro Ishii was sent on a mission to Washington. Out of his discussions (6 Sept.–2 Nov.) with Secretary Lansing came an agreement by which the U.S. recognized that "territorial propinquity creates special relations between countries, and consequently, the Government of the United States recognizes that Japan has special interests in China, particularly in the part to which her possessions are contiguous." Japan affirmed respect for the Open Door policy and the independence and territorial integrity of China.

Lansing viewed the agreement as a stopgap measure designed to prevent full recognition of Japan's position in China. But the terms of the agreement were ambiguous. According to the U.S. interpretation, Japan was conceded only an economic hold on China. The Japanese, on the other hand, construed the agreement as a political concession. When translated into Chinese the word "special" appeared as "paramount." Yet the agreement left the U.S. at the end of World War I as the only important nation holding reservations of this kind.

1918

8 Jan. 14 POINTS. The year 1917 was marked in Europe by a growing demand for a statement of war aims and a negotiated peace. In May the Kerensky government took office in Russia with a pledge to promote a peace based on the self-determination of peoples and without annexation or indemnities. Pope Benedict XV circularized (1 Aug.) the leaders of the belligerent powers, suggesting the following as a basis for a just and durable peace: renunciation of indemnities; disarmament; the substitution of arbitration for war; the evacuation of Belgium, and a guarantee for its complete independence; the evacuation of occupied territories; freedom of the seas; and the examination of territorial claims in a "spirit of equity and justice." The U.S. reply (27 Aug.) expressed the desire for a just peace but asserted that the word of the German government could not be accepted as a guarantee.

When, following the November Revolution in Russia, the Bolsheviks published the secret treaties concluded by the Allies and condemned these arrangements as evidence of imperialist designs, the need for a statement of Allied war aims became exigent. When an Interallied Conference at Paris (29 Nov.–3 Dec. 1917) was unable to agree upon such a statement, Col. House urged Wilson to issue a formulation. Lloyd George, in a speech (5 Jan.) before British labor representatives, announced his nation's war aims.

Addressing Congress (8 Jan.), Wilson set forth 14 points "as the only possible program" for peace from the U.S. standpoint. The address was based upon consultations with Col. House and a report furnished by a group of academicians and publicists called The Inquiry. The 14 Points were as follows: (1) open covenants of peace openly arrived at; (2) absolute freedom of navigation of the seas alike in peace and war, except as the seas might be closed by international action for the enforcement of international covenants; (3) removal, so far as possible, of all economic barriers and the establishment of equality of trade; (4) adequate guarantees that national armaments would be reduced to the lowest point consistent with domestic safety; (5) an absolutely impartial adjustment of all colonial claims, based on the principle that the interests of the population must have equal weight with the equitable claims of the government; (6) evacuation of all Russian territory and the independ-

ent determination by Russia of her own political development and national policy; (7) evacuation and restoration of Belgium; (8) evacuation and restoration of all French territory and return to France of Alsace-Lorraine; (9) readjustment of the Italian frontiers along clearly recognizable lines of nationality; (10) opportunity of autonomous development for the peoples of Austria-Hungary; (11) evacuation of Rumania, Serbia, and Montenegro, restoration of occupied territories, and free access to the sea for Serbia; (12) the Turkish portions of the Ottoman Empire to be assured a secure sovereignty, but the other nationalities under Turkish rule to be given free opportunity of autonomous development, and the Dardanelles to be permanently opened as a free passage to the ships of all nations under international guarantees; (13) establishment of an independent Poland, to include territories having an indisputably Polish population, with free and secure access to the sea; and (14) a general association of nations to be formed under specific covenants for the purpose of affording mutual guarantees of political independence and territorial integrity to great and small states alike.

21 Mar. GERMAN SPRING OFFENSIVE. The growing effectiveness of the British blockade and the lessening force of the U-boat campaign led the German military leaders to undertake a series of great offensives on the Western Front in the hope of decisively crushing the Allies before U.S. troops could arrive in force. The Germans enjoyed superiority of numbers in the West. The German assault, under the command of General Ludendorff, was launched (21 Mar.) along a 50-mi. front on the Somme battlefield, with the immediate objective of splitting the French and British armies at their junction point and breaking through to the vital rail center of Amiens and, ultimately, to the Channel ports. By 6 Apr. the Germans had smashed the lines of the British 5th Army and had penetrated the Allied lines to a depth of about 35 mi., advancing beyond Noyon and Montdidier and coming within 12 mi. of Amiens with its vast stores of British supplies. In this action (also known as the Picardy offensive), approximately 2,200 U.S. troops served with the British and French.

The critical situation led the Allied statesmen and military leaders to confer (26 Mar.) at Doullens-en-Picardie, where Gen. **Ferdinand Foch** was assigned the task of coordinating the Allied armies on the Western Front. Wilson gave his approval (29 Mar.) to the Doullens agreement and on 14 Apr. Foch was formally appointed supreme commander for the Western Front. Although Gen. Pershing never yielded his intention of having a separate U.S. army with its own front, American units, at his decision (28 Mar.), were placed at the disposal of Foch and thrown into action wherever needed during the enemy spring offensive. However, the Beauvais agreement (3 Apr.) concluded by an Interallied Conference contained a reference to a separate U.S. army, which was endorsed at the conference (1 May) of the Supreme War Council at Abbeville.

9–29 Apr. The attack upon Amiens had been only partly checked when the Germans struck again to the north in the Armentières sector and advanced for 17 mi. up the Lys Valley; but the enemy was unable to exploit the wide gap in the British lines. About 500 Americans, serving with the British, participated in the Lys defensive.

27 May–5 June. The next German drive was directed against the French front along the Chemin des Dames north of the Aisne. In this, the 3rd battle of the Aisne, the line from Rheims to a little east of Noyon was forced back. Soissons fell (29 May), and the Germans reached the Marne (31 May) on a 40-mi. front about 50 mi. from Paris. At this critical moment the U.S. 2nd Div. and elements of the 3rd and 28th Divs. were thrown into the line. By blocking (3–4 June) the German advance at **Chateau-Thierry,** the Americans helped the French to stem the enemy drive.

6 June–1 July. BELLEAU WOOD. The 1st sizable U.S. action of the war was fought when the 2nd Div. recaptured **Vaux, Bouresches,** and **Belleau Wood,** with the 4th U.S. Marine Brigade attached to the 2nd Division playing a notable role. About 27,500 Americans were

engaged in the 3rd battle of the Aisne. **9–15 June.** The 3 enemy offensives established 2 salients threatening Paris, and the Germans now sought to convert them into one by a 4th massive blow delivered on a 27-mi. front between Montdidier and Noyon. Even before the drive began the U.S. 1st Div. demonstrated the fighting qualities of American troops by capturing (28 May) and holding the town of **Cantigny.** This 1st U.S. success reinforced the decision to permit Pershing to establish a separate army. In the Noyon-Montdidier offensive the French and Americans resisted firmly and the attack was halted after an initial German advance of about 6 mi. Throughout this operation the extreme left line of the salient was defended by the U.S. 1st Div. About 27,500 U.S. troops participated.

18 July–6 Aug. TURNING POINT: 2ND BATTLE OF THE MARNE. On 15 July the Germans attacked simultaneously on both sides of Rheims, the eastern point of the Aisne salient. To the east of Rheims the Germans made slight gains; to the west they crossed the Marne, but made little progress. Stabilization of the Marne salient brought to an end the great German offensive. In this action some 85,000 American troops were engaged.

18 July–6 Aug. AISNE-MARNE OFFENSIVE. During the months of May and June more than 500,000 men were embarked from the U.S. for France, and in July the millionth American soldier arrived in France. The initiative passed from Ludendorff to Foch, who on 18 July launched his 1st counteroffensive, choosing as his point of attack the west flank of the German pocket from the Aisne to the Marne. About 270,000 U.S. troops, together with selected. French units, were engaged in the Aisne-Marne offensive. When the operation was completed (6 Aug.), bringing to an end the 2nd Battle of the Marne, the salient had been eliminated and the Allied line ran from Soissons to Rheims along the Vesle.

8 Aug. SOMME OFFENSIVE. The British, under Gen. Haig, struck at the Somme salient, initiating an offensive which, with intermittent lulls, lasted un-

THE WESTERN FRONT IN 1918
WORLD WAR I
SHOWING ACTION BY
UNITED STATES TROOPS

Scale of Miles
0   25   50   75

til 11 Nov. About 54,000 U.S. troops participated.

10 Aug. 1ST U.S. ARMY was organized, with Foch's consent, under the command of Gen. Pershing, who remained commander of the A.E.F.

18 Aug. OISE-AISNE OFFENSIVE was begun under Gen. Mangin, at the head of the French 10th Army. Starting from the Soissons-Rheims line, the French advanced by successive stages to the Aisne, to Laon, and on 11 Nov. were approaching the Belgian frontier. About 85,000 U.S. troops participated in the first stages of this advance, but by 15 Sept. all of these were withdrawn for the impending U.S. Meuse-Argonne offensive.

19 Aug. YPRES-LYS OFFENSIVE, launched by the British, lasted until 11 Nov. About 108,000 U. S. troops participated.

24 Oct.–4 Nov. BATTLE OF VITTORIO-VENETO on the Italian front ended in the rout of the Austrian army. About 1,200 U.S. troops participated.

12–16 Sept. ST. MIHIEL SALIENT. The 1st distinctively U.S. offensive was the reduction of the St. Mihiel salient, carried through largely by U.S. troops and wholly under the command of Gen. Pershing. The Americans were aided by French colonial troops and by British and French air squadrons. St. Mihiel, on the right bank of the Meuse, was at the tip of a salient below Verdun (in French hands) to the northwest and Metz (in German hands) to the northeast. Within 24 hrs. after the offensive began, the salient had been cut off, and the completion of the operation removed a German threat of long standing. About 550,000 American troops were engaged at St. Mihiel; U.S. casualties: about 7,000. The Americans captured 16,000 prisoners and 443 guns. The operation demonstrated the ability of U.S. commanders and troops to plan and execute a major military undertaking.

26 Sept.–11 Nov. MEUSE-ARGONNE OFFENSIVE. After the St. Mihiel victory, U.S. troops were removed from the line and largely concentrated along a sector between the Meuse River and the Argonne Forest. Every available American division was employed. The goal of the American attack was the Sedan-Mézières railroad, main line of supply for the German forces on the major segment of the Western Front. Cutting this line would force a general retirement that would include German evacuation of the Briey and Longwy iron fields, which the enemy had been using to supplement its iron supply. The U.S. offensive, part of a larger advance planned by Foch to compel a general withdrawal by the Germans, involved 1,200,000 U.S. troops. Its 1st and middle stages comprised a battle of attrition. The final phase of the offensive began 1 Nov. Within a week, the Americans were in hot pursuit of the enemy east of the Meuse, while toward the north they reached the outskirts of Sedan and cut the Sedan-Mézières railroad, making the German line untenable. The armistice (11 Nov.) brought the offensive to a halt. The operation cost 120,000 U.S. casualties and resulted in the capture of 16,000 prisoners and 468 guns.

29 Sept.–8 Nov. GERMAN PEACE MOVE. The rapid deterioration of the military position of the Central Powers during the summer of 1918 impelled Gen. Ludendorff, who foresaw imminent collapse, to press his government (29 Sept.) for an armistice. The situation became more critical with the surrender (30 Sept.) of Bulgaria. A new German regime headed by Prince Max of Baden took office on 2 Oct. and through Swiss auspices requested Wilson (6 Oct.) for an armistice preliminary to a conference which would use the 14 Points as a basis of peace. Austria made a similar request 7 Oct. Wilson spent about a month in negotiations. **Reasons for delay:** (1) Reluctance of the Allies to accept Wilson's war aims. The British pointed out that approval of the proposed armistice carried tacit acceptance of the 14 Points, and both the British and the French denied they had ever been asked to accept the 14 Points. However, a threat that the U.S. would take separate action finally compelled the Allies to accept (5 Nov.) the 14 Points as a basis for an armistice, but with 2 vital reservations. The Allies insisted upon reserving to themselves the unqualified right to discuss freedom of the seas in the peace conference, and they demanded that German restoration of evacuated territory include reparation for war damages to the civilian population. Wilson accepted these conditions and transmitted them to the German government (5 Nov.) ; thereafter responsibility for the truce was left to Gen. Foch. (2) Wilson's refusal to deal with a German government unless he was satisfied that it represented the German people. Following a mutiny in the German fleet that began at Kiel (3 Nov.), a revolution broke out (7 Nov.) in Bavaria. Austria had already surrendered (4 Nov.). Kaiser Wilhelm II abdicated and fled from Germany (9 Nov.), and a German republic was proclaimed. Meanwhile, a German armistice commission met with General Foch in the Forest of Compiègne (8 Nov.).

11 Nov. ARMISTICE. Signing (5 A.M.) of the armistice brought the cessation of hostilities at 11 A.M.

The armistice terms were as follows: (1) German evacuation of occupied territory; (2) evacuation of the left bank of the Rhine and of the bridgeheads of Mainz, Cologne, and Coblenz; (3) reservation to the Allies and the U.S. of full right to make claim for damages; (4) surrender of submarines and internment of the German fleet; (5) abrogation of the treaties of Bucharest and Brest-Litovsk; (6) destruction of German aircraft, tanks, and heavy artillery; (7) maintenance of the Allied blockade until conclusion of the peace; (8) return of prisoners of war and deported civilians; and (9) 150,000 railway cars, 5,000 locomotives, and 5,000 trucks to be turned over to the Allies.

U.S. WAR COST. Total deaths for the U.S. armed forces (including army, navy, and marines) were 112,432—more than half caused by disease (chiefly the influenza-pneumonia pandemic that swept U.S. military camps). The battle casualties of the A.E.F. were 48,909 dead, 230,074 wounded. The total direct war expenditures (Apr. 1917–Apr. 1919), $21,850 million. (For loans to Allies, see pp. 319, 320.)

25 Oct. WILSON'S APPEAL TO THE ELECTORATE. Anxious that the position of the U.S. should not be weakened at the approaching peace conference, President Wilson decided to make the Congressional elections a test of confidence in his policies. He issued an appeal to the voters to return a Democratic majority to both Houses of Congress. The appeal evoked widespread disapproval, the Republicans condemning it as a violation of Wilson's declared wartime truce on politics. The election (5 Nov.) resulted in the Democratic loss of the House by 50 seats and of the Senate by 2 seats.

REPUBLICAN OPPOSITION. Wilson's announcement (18 Nov.) that he would attend the peace conference provoked a storm of Republican criticism, as did the announcement that in addition to Wilson the U.S. peace commission would consist of **Col. House, Secretary Lansing, Gen. Tasker Bliss,** and **Henry White.** No member of the Senate was included, and the only Republican member was White. Wilson sailed for Europe 4 Dec. on the *George Washington.*

AMERICA BETWEEN TWO WORLD WARS, 1919-1939

FOREIGN RELATIONS

1919

18 Jan. BEGINNING OF THE PEACE NEGOTIATIONS at Paris. All major decisions were made by the "Big Four," Wilson, Georges Clemenceau (for France), David Lloyd George (for Great Britain), and Vittorio Orlando (for Italy). Wilson's idealism was quickly challenged. France and Britain were determined to punish Germany. France wanted territorial concessions and reparations, as well as permanent military security against Germany. In addition, many of the provisions of the so-called "Secret Treaties" entered into by the Allies and known in broad outline to American leaders shortly after America's entry into the war ran counter to Wilsonian principles.

25 Jan.–14 Feb. DRAFT COVENANT OF THE LEAGUE OF NATIONS. Wilson insisted that the League must be central to the peace negotiations, a position which the other Allies accepted only after exacting serious concessions. On 25 Jan. the 2nd Plenary Session voted to include the League in the peace settlement. Beginning on 3 Feb., a commission, presided over by Wilson, worked out a draft covenant submitted to the Plenary Session on 14 Feb., based upon the work of **David Hunter Miller** and **Lord Robert Cecil.** Wilson then returned to the U.S. on the *George Washington,* arriving at Boston on 24 Feb. Opposition was already mounting in the U.S. At a dinner meeting between Wilson and members of the Senate and House committees on foreign relations (26 Feb.) the President was grilled by his Republican critics. On 2 March 37 Republican senators and 2 senators-elect signed a Senatorial **Round Robin,** proposed by **Henry Cabot Lodge** (Mass., 1850–1924) and **Frank B. Brandegee** (Conn.), and drafted by **Philander C. Knox,** which rejected the League in its existing form and opposed further consideration until after the final peace settlement; read in the Senate 2 days later. On 4 Mar. Wilson defiantly predicted in an address in New York that it would not be possible to "dissect the covenant from the treaty without destroying the whole vital structure."

Mar.–Apr. WILSON'S RETURN TO EUROPE. French Demands. The President arrived at Brest on 13 Mar. The next day he was presented in Paris with a bill of particulars by Marshal Foch including (1) heavy but undefined reparations for German destruction of French property; (2) either an Allied occupation of Germany to the Rhine or the creation of a Rhineland buffer state. A bitter battle followed, in the midst of which Wilson became ill (3 Apr.). On 7 Apr. the President was reported to have ordered the *George Washington* to Europe, presumably to take him home unless a compromise could be worked out. The French yielded to Wilson's threat and agreed to a series of compromises. In return for a terminable occupation of German territory Wilson agreed to a treaty binding Britain and the U.S. to defend France against a future unprovoked German attack. This treaty was pigeon-holed by the U.S. Senate.

Italian Demands. The Italians insisted on territorial commitments of the Treaty of London (26 Apr. 1915), by which Italy was promised a strategic boundary running to the Brenner Pass, including some 200,000 Germans, as well as territory on the head and eastern shore of the Adriatic. In addition, Italy now demanded the port of **Fiume.** Wilson agreed to the Brenner line before his own experts had clarified this violation of his own principle of self-determination, but on 19 Apr. he informed the American delegation that he would stand fast against Fiume. When Italy's peace delegates, **Vittorio Orlando** and **Sidney Sonnino,** continued to press their claims, Wilson appealed directly to the Italian people (23 Apr.) to desert their leaders in favor of a peace of justice. The Italians quit the conference at once, but returned on 6 May. They were unsuccessful in their demand for Fiume. That port did not pass under Italian control until 1924. Under the Italo-Jugoslav Treaty of Rapallo (1920) it had been nominally independent.

Japanese Demands. Japan insisted on recognition of her right to **Shantung,** which she had occupied during the war. Defeated, 11 Apr., in her effort to obtain the passage of a resolution on **race equality,** Japan on 15 Apr. refused to agree to have German rights in Shantung turned over to the Allied powers. She rested her claim on the Secret Treaties of 1917, on agreements with China of 25 May 1915 and 24 Sept. 1918, and on the **Lansing-Ishii** Agreement with the U.S. (see p. 310). On 28 Apr. Wilson surrendered to Japan, but exacted a promise that Shantung would be eventually returned to China, with Japan retaining only her economic concessions in the province.

Compromises on the League Covenant. In response to proposals of such pro-League Republicans as William Howard Taft and A. Lawrence Lowell, Wilson proposed amendments to the Covenant to overcome opposition in the Senate. These included: (1) permission of the U.S. to refrain fom participating in the mandate system established to administer the conquered colonies; (2) restraints upon League interference with such matters as tariffs and immigration; (3) granting permission to a state to withdraw from the League upon 2 yrs.' notice; (4) excepting "regional understandings like the Monroe Doctrine" from the League's jurisdiction.

7 May–28 June. TERMS OF THE VERSAILLES TREATY. The treaty was presented to the Germans on 7 May; they signed on 28 June. Wilson returned to the U.S. on 8 July, and presented the treaty to the Senate on 10 July. The final treaty (1) forced Germany to admit her **war guilt** (Art. 231); (2) stripped her of her **colonies, Alsace-Lorraine,** the **Saar Basin** (its final disposition to be determined by a plebiscite in 1935), **Posen,** and parts of **Schleswig** and **Silesia;** (3) exacted **reparations,** later fixed at $56 billion; (4) substantially **disarmed** her. Attached to the treaty was the **Covenant of the League of Nations,** which provided for: (1) an **Assembly** in which all member nations had an equal voice; (2) a **Council** made up of representatives from the U.S., Great Britain, France, Italy, Japan, and 4 other nations elected by the Assembly; (3) a **Secretariat,** permanently located at Geneva. Members pledged themselves to (1) respect and preserve against external aggression the territorial integrity and political independence of all member nations (**Art. X**); (2) submit to the League all disputes threatening war; (3) employ military and economic sanctions against nations resorting to war; (4) reduce armaments; and (5) cooperate in setting up a **Permanent Court of International Justice.**

10 July–19 Nov. SENATE OPPOSITION. The Senate divided on the League issue into 3 groups: (1) Democratic supporters of Wilson who favored immediate ratification, led by **Gilbert M. Hitchcock** (Neb., 1859–1934), who succeeded Thomas S. Martin as minority leader when the latter died during the course of the Senate debate on the issue; (2) moderates, headed by **Henry Cabot Lodge,** chairman of the Senate Committee on Foreign Relations, who favored participation in the League with reservations to protect American interests; and (3) "irreconcilables," including **Hiram**

W. Johnson (Calif., 1866–1945), William E. Borah (Ida., 1865–1940), and Robert La Follette (Wis.), who advocated complete rejection of the Covenant. On 19 Aug. Wilson at a luncheon conference with the Senate Committee agreed to accept interpretative reservations not requiring consent of the other parties to the treaty nor embodied in the resolution of ratification. This failed to satisfy the irreconcilables, who now launched a nationwide propaganda campaign against ratification, financed by Andrew Mellon and Henry C. Frick. Since 6 of the 10 members of the Senate Committee were irreconcilables, action was held up until 10 Sept., when the Committee proposed 45 amendments and 4 reservations to protect traditional American policies. Wilson took the case to the people in a 9,500-mile tour of the West, commencing 4 Sept., in the course of which he delivered 37 speeches in 29 cities. On 10 Sept. Sens. Johnson and Borah began a tour in opposition to the League and the treaty. On 25 Sept. Wilson broke down at Pueblo, Colo., and was rushed back to Washington, suffering a stroke on 2 Oct. which incapacitated him during this crucial period. A combination of Democrats and moderate Republicans voted down the reservations. On 6 Nov. Lodge reported a resolution of ratification accompanied by 14 reservations, which, while circumscribing somewhat American obligations under the Covenant, did not seriously impair the League. On 18 Nov. Wilson, in a letter to his supporters, expressed the view that the Lodge resolution "does not provide for ratification but, rather, for the nullification of the treaty," and urged its defeat. As a result, a combination of Wilson Democrats and irreconcilable Republicans defeated the resolution on 19 Nov. Had the Democrats voted for the Lodge resolution the League and the Treaty would have been carried, 81–13. Unconditional acceptance was defeated, by 38–53.

1920

Jan.–May. **SENATE AND THE TREATY.** A bipartisan approach to ratification was wrecked in January when Lodge yielded to threats by the irreconcilables and refused to modify his original reservations. On 9 Feb. the Senate voted to reconsider the treaty and referred it back to the Committee, which reported it the following day with the reservations intact. Wilson remained adamant. In a message to the Jackson Day Dinner (8 Jan.) he insisted that the treaty must not be rewritten by the Senate, and again on 8 March reiterated his opposition to the Lodge reservations. On 19 March 21 Democrats deserted Wilson to join the Republican reservationists in a vote on the Lodge resolution, which was again defeated, 49–35. When, on 20 May, Congress declared the war at an end by joint resolution, Wilson vetoed the action. Finally, on 2 July 1921, Congress, by a joint resolution, terminated war with Germany and Austria-Hungary, reserving for the U.S. any rights secured by the armistice, the Versailles Treaty, or as a result of the war. Separate treaties concluding peace with Germany, Austria, and Hungary were ratified 18 Oct.

June–Nov. **"SOLEMN REFERENDUM."** Wilson urged the Democratic Convention which met in San Francisco on 28 June to endorse his views on the League. The party platform pledged unequivocal ratification of the Treaty of Versailles with only such reservations as should be found necessary under the U.S. Constitution. The party nominee, **James M. Cox,** publicly promised that as soon as possible after 4 Mar. 1921 the U.S. would enter the League. The Republicans were divided on the issue, Root, Taft, and Hughes, on the one hand, supporting the League, the irreconcilables opposing it. Hence, the Republican platform straddled the issue. It criticized the Covenant, but favored the formation of "an international association" to prevent war. Its candidate, **Warren G. Harding,** had no deep convictions either way. But when once in office, he promptly abandoned any attempt to bring the U.S. into the League, and retreated into what Wilson stigmatized as "sullen and selfish isolation." In his inaugural address Harding declared: "We seek no part in directing the destinies of the world." Again, in a special message to Congress on 2 Feb. 1923, he stated that the League "is not for us. Nothing could be more decisively stamped with finality."

1921–22

12 Nov.–6 Feb. 1922. WASHINGTON ARMAMENT CONFERENCE. On 14 Dec. 1920 Sen. Borah introduced a resolution requesting the President to call an international conference for the reduction of naval armaments. The resolution was appended to the Naval Appropriations Bill for 1921. In accordance therewith President Harding (11 Aug.) invited the principal powers, except Russia, to a conference to consider not only naval disarmament, but questions concerning the Pacific and the Far East. The American delegation included Secretary of State **Charles Evans Hughes,** Elihu Root, Henry Cabot Lodge, and Oscar Underwood. Hughes, who was designated chairman of the conference, proposed at the first session (12 Nov.) not only a limitation upon future naval building but also a substantial scrapping of ships already built or in construction. The U.S. offered to scrap ships amounting to 845,000 tons; Great Britain was asked to scrap 583,000 tons; Japan, 480,000 tons. This program was immediately accepted in principle. It was further agreed to fix the tonnage of capital ships (over 10,000-tons displacement or having guns larger than 8-in. cal.) at a ratio of 5 (U.S.)— 5 (Britain)—3 (Japan)—1.67 (France) —1.67 (Italy). France agreed to her ratio under pressure, but would not permit any limitation on cruisers, destroyers, or submarines, nor have land armaments placed on the agenda. As a result of the conference **9 treaties** were drafted and signed: (1) a **naval armaments** treaty between the 5 powers (U.S., Great Britain, Japan, France, and Italy) providing for a 10-yr. naval holiday during which no new capital ships were to be built, and establishing a ratio of capital ships (6 Feb. 1922); (2) a 5-power treaty between the same nations restricting the use of submarines in war by the accepted rules of naval warfare and outlawing asphyxiating gases; (3) a 4-power treaty (13 Dec.) between the U.S., Britain, France, and Japan, by which the signa-

tories agreed to respect each other's rights over Pacific island possessions; (4) a 4-power treaty providing for consultation in the event of "aggressive action" in the Pacific (carrying with it the abrogation of the existing Anglo-Japanese alliance); (5) a 9-power treaty (6 Feb.) signed by all the states at the conference guaranteeing China's independence and territorial integrity, and reiterating the "Open Door" principle; (6) a similar treaty granting China greater control over her customs; (7) a treaty between Japan and China providing for the restoration of Kiachow and the Shantung peninsula to China (4 Feb.); (8) a treaty between Japan and the U.S. confirming American cable rights on the island of Yap; and (9) a 6-power treaty between the U.S., Britain, Japan, France, Italy, and China allocating the former German cable lines in the Pacific. The U.S. Senate ratified all the treaties, the 4-power treaty passing by the narrow margin of 4 votes, and with a reservation stating that "there is no commitment to armed force, no alliance, no obligation to join in any defense."

U.S. AND INTERALLIED WAR DEBTS. In addition to the war loans to the Allied governments, the U.S. also made loans after the Armistice for relief purposes or as advances for the payment of surplus American war materials left in Europe at the close of the war:

To Allies	Total Indebtedness
Great Britain	$4,277,000,000.00
France	3,404,818,945.01
Italy	1,648,034,050.90
Belgium	379,087,200.43
Russia	192,601,297.37
Rumania	37,911,153.92
Greece	27,167,000.00
Cuba	10,000,000.00
Nicaragua	431,849.14
Liberia	26,000.00

To Countries Formed out of Allied Territory	
Estonia	13,999,145.60
Finland	8,281,926.17
Latvia	5,132,287.14
Lithuania	4,981,628.03

To Countries or Areas Formed
Partially or Wholly Out of
Enemy Territory

Poland	159,666,972.39
Czechoslovakia	91,879,671.03
Yugoslavia	51,758,486.55
Austria	24,055,708.92
Armenia	11,959,917.49
Hungary	1,685,835.61

Total $10,350,479,074.70

As early as Dec. 1918 the British proposed to Wilson that they would agree to cancel debts due them from their Allies, virtually uncollectible claims approximating $10 billion, in return for the cancellation of British debts to the U.S. of about $4 billion. Wilson refused, insisting that the interallied debts were unrelated to German reparations. France also argued strongly for debt cancellation. To deal with this issue the World War Foreign Debt Commission, authorized by Act of Congress, 9 Feb. 1922, was set up to negotiate specific agreements. Based on their capacity to pay, the debtor nations accepted obligations of over $11.5 billion, payable over a 62-year period at an average interest rate of 2.135%. Under these agreements principal and interest totaled in excess of $22 billion. On 1 Aug. Great Britain (**Balfour Note**) agreed to remit, "as part of a satisfactory international settlement," both debts and reparations due herself, and in no case to ask more from her debtors than was necessary to pay her creditors. The U.S. remained adamant. President Coolidge continued the Harding policy. ("They hired the money, didn't they?") Finally, owing to the increasingly serious European financial situation, drastic reductions in principal were agreed to by the U.S. On 14 Nov. 1925 Italy's interest rate was reduced to .4% and 80.2% of the debt was canceled; in Apr. 1926, the French interest rate was reduced to 1.6%, and 60.3% of the debt was canceled. Despite these concessions, the insistence by the U.S. on partial debt payments promoted anti-U.S. feeling in Europe, isolationism in America.

1922–23

1922, 4 Dec.–7 Feb. 1923. SECOND CENTRAL AMERICAN CONFERENCE convened at Washington to settle issues between Nicaragua and Honduras. The U.S. and all Central American republics participated. The conference drew up a treaty of neutrality and provided for the establishment of a Central American court of justice and limitation of armaments.

1924

24 May. FOREIGN SERVICE ACT (Rogers Act) reorganized and consolidated the diplomatic and consular services and provided for initial appointment after examination, a period of probation, and promotion on merit.

15 Dec. 1923–9 Apr. 1924. GERMAN REPARATIONS: THE DAWES PLAN. On 27 Apr. 1921 the Allied Reparations Commission set up under the Treaty of Versailles submitted a report fixing Germany's obligations at **132,000,000,000 gold marks.** On 31 May 1922 the Commission, to check the further collapse of the mark, granted Germany a moratorium for the remainder of the year despite protests from France. On 26 Dec. and, again, on 9 Jan. 1923, Germany was declared in default. Two days later French and Belgian troops began the **occupation of the Ruhr.** By 26 Sept., as a result of Germany's passive resistance, the mark had become worthless; the franc had depreciated 25%. On 15 Dec. 1923 President Coolidge announced that **Charles G. Dawes** (1865–1951), Henry M. Robinson, and Owen D. Young would serve as experts on a commission to investigate German finances. The **Dawes Plan,** reported on 9 Apr. 1924, proposed (1) to stabilize German currency by reorganizing the Reichsbank under Allied supervision; (2) a schedule of payments for reparations, graduated from 1 billion gold marks in the 1st year (1924–25) to 2½ billion in the 5th year (1928–29). This plan was accepted by the Germans on 16 Apr. and adopted at a London conference (16 July–16 Aug.). Of a foreign loan totaling 800,000,000 gold marks to be advanced Germany under the Plan, $110,000,000 was taken up in the U.S. To carry out the plan the Allied powers selected an American, S. **Parker Gilbert** (1892–1938), as Agent General of Reparations. At an Interallied Financial Conference at Paris (7–14 Jan. 1925) it was agreed that the U.S. should receive 2¼% of the annual payments made by Germany under the plan to satisfy American claims—$255,000,000 for American Army of Occupation costs, $350,000,000 for war damages.

U.S. AND THE LEAGUE. Although both Presidents Coolidge and Harding had favored entry into the League in 1920, neither took active measures to ratify the Covenant. On 11 Nov. 1929 Hoover declared that "public opinion will suffice to check violence" (similarly, on 14 Apr. 1930). Nevertheless, this period was marked by increasing U.S. participation in League affairs. On 17 Nov. 1924 U.S. delegates were represented at the International Opium Conference of the League, withdrawing on 6 Feb. 1925 when the U.S. proposal was not accepted. The U.S. participated in conferences on communication and transit (1926), in 3 conferences on the abolition of import and export prohibitions (1927), and in a conference on double taxation and fiscal evasion (1928). By 1931 212 persons had been officially appointed to represent the U.S. in more than 40 League conferences (Ellery C. Stowell), and the U.S. government maintained 5 permanent officials stationed at Geneva to represent American interests at the League (D. F. Fleming).

END OF DOMINICAN OCCUPATION. President Wilson directed (Dec. 1920) that preparations be made for ending military government in the Dominican Republic. An agreement on evacuation procedure was worked out by the State Dept. with a group of Dominican political leaders (30 June 1922). The military government delegated to a provisional president sufficient authority to permit the holding of elections. In July 1924 Gen. Horacio Vásquez was inaugurated as constitutional president and the U.S. Marines withdrawn. A new treaty (27 Feb.) between the U.S. and the Dominican Republic superseded that of 1907.

1926

27 Jan.–Jan. 1935. U.S. AND THE WORLD COURT. The League Covenant provided for the establishment of a permanent Court of International Justice to consist of 15 members, to be elected by the Council and Assembly from a list of persons nominated by the Hague Court of Arbitration. The court was given jurisdiction over all international disputes submitted to it by states subscribing to the protocol, which was approved by the Council and Assembly in Dec. 1920. The U.S. had instructed its delegates to the 1st Hague Conference, 1899, and the 2nd, 1907, to set up a permanent court of arbitration. On 17 Feb. 1923 Secretary of State Hughes wrote Harding urging U.S. membership in the World Court with the distinct understanding that such action would not involve any legal relation to the League. President Coolidge in 3 successive annual messages favored Senate action. On 3 Mar. 1925 the House supported a resolution of adherence by a vote of 303–28. Finally, on 27 Jan. 1926, the Senate approved adherence by 76–17, but attached reservations to safeguard U.S. interests. All were acceptable to members of the World Court except a reservation relating to advisory opinions. Since no agreement could be reached on this point, the U.S. did not join. In 1928 Hughes was chosen by the Council and Assembly to fill the vacancy in the World Court caused by the resignation of another American, **John Bassett Moore** (1860–1947). In Feb. 1929 Elihu Root sailed for Europe to join a commission to revise the statute of the court. His formula provided that the Court shall not, without the consent of the U.S., render an advisory opinion touching any dispute to which the U.S. is a party, and reserved to the U.S. the right to withdraw from the Court protocol if the interested parties insisted on an advisory opinion in a matter in which the U.S. claimed an interest. On 4 Mar. 1929

Hoover urged Court membership in his inaugural address, and on 9 Dec. the U.S. charge d'affaires in Switzerland, upon authorization of the President, signed the protocol of adherence with revisions agreed to both by the U.S. and the Court members. Hoover submitted the protocol to the Senate on 10 Dec. 1930, but Sen. Borah blocked action. On 1 June the Senate Foreign Relations Committee finally came out for adherence. Involved in critical domestic affairs, President Roosevelt delayed risking debate on the issue until 16 Jan. 1935, when he urged ratification. Led by Huey P. Long (La.), the Senate rejected membership, 52–35. Although press opinion had favored the Court, 3–1, the Hearst newspapers and the radio activities of Father Charles E. Coughlin kept the "irreconcilables" in line.

1927

20 June–4 Aug. NAVAL DISARMAMENT: GENEVA CONFERENCE. On 10 Feb. President Coolidge called for a 5-power conference to be held at Geneva to consider limitations on the building of cruisers, destroyers, and submarines, not curbed at the Washington Conference. France and Italy refused to attend; Great Britain and the U.S. failed to agree on cruiser restrictions. The conference adjourned without accomplishment. In Feb. 1929 the U.S. authorized the construction of 15 cruisers of 10,000-ton displacement.

Mar.–27 Aug. 1928. OUTLAWRY OF WAR. As a result of conversations with Professor **James T. Shotwell** (1874–   ) of Columbia University in Mar., French Foreign Minister **Aristide Briand** released 6 Apr. a proposal for the "outlawry of war" (a phrase attributed to Salmon O. Levinson). On 25 Apr. President **Nicholas Murray Butler** (p. 682) of Columbia University revived the issue in a letter to *The New York Times*. On 11 June Secretary of State **Frank B. Kellogg** (1856–1937) made a formal acknowledgment. Briand submitted a draft treaty on 20 June. As a result of a conference with Senator Borah, Kellogg sub-

stituted a **multinational** for a bilateral agreement in a note of 28 Dec. On 11 Jan. 1928 he published a draft treaty, which was brought to the attention of other powers on 13 Apr. On 27 Aug., 14 nations signed; eventually 62 nations signed. The sanctions of the **Kellogg-Briand Pact** rested on the moral force of world opinion.

31 Jan. 1917–26 Dec. 1927. MEXICAN-U.S. RELATIONS. The new Mexican Constitution of 1917 not only provided for radical political and social reforms but curbed foreign ownership of lands, mines, and oil fields. By a decree, 19 Feb. 1918, oil was declared an inalienable national resource, and titles to oil lands were to be converted into concessions. British and American companies promptly protested. Following the death of Carranza (21 May 1920) **Alvaro Obregón** was elected President (5 Sept.). He was recognized by the U.S., 31 Aug. 1923, upon an executive agreement (**Bucareli Agreement**) to respect subsoil rights acquired before 1917 and confirmed by some "positive act." After the election of **Plutarco Calles** in 1924, Secretary Kellogg warned Mexico (12 June) that the U.S. would continue its support "only so long" as Mexico "protects American lives and American rights." In retaliation the Mexican Congress passed two laws, to become effective 1 Jan. 1927, to implement the 1917 Constitution: the Petroleum Law, by which permanent foreign concessions were limited to 50 years and alien corporations required to waive their right of appeal to the home government (**Calvo Clause**); the Land Law, designed to break up the huge estates, restricted alien land ownership. A U.S. Senate resolution (27 Jan. 1927) unanimously recommended arbitration of the dispute with Mexico. In Sept. President Coolidge appointed **Dwight W. Morrow** (1873–1931) of J. P. Morgan & Co. as Ambassador to Mexico. His conciliatory efforts quickly produced results. On 17 Nov. the Mexican Supreme Court declared the limitation on concessions under the Petroleum Law unconstitutional. On 25 Dec. the Mexican Congress granted unlimited confirmatory concessions to lands on which "positive" acts had been performed prior to 1 May 1917. Morrow's efforts to compose the differences between the Church and the Mexican government, growing out of the act of 11 Feb. 1926 nationalizing church property, were interrupted by the assassination of President-elect Obregón, 17 July 1928.

1927–28

NICARAGUAN RELATIONS. The U.S. refused to recognize the government of Emiliano Chamorro, which assumed power after a revolt on 25 Oct. 1925. After Chamorro became President (14 Jan. 1926), a Liberal insurrection was started by Gen. **Augustino Sandino.** The U.S. landed troops and supported **Adolfo Díaz,** Conservative, as President. On 4 May 1927 President Coolidge sent Henry L. Stimson to bring the two factions together. Under an agreement Díaz was to complete his term, the rebels were to disarm, and the U.S. was to supervise the next election. When, 4 Nov. 1928, José Moncada (Liberal) was elected President, Sandino left the country. Again, in 1931, he started a revolt, which was suppressed by 1933. Under President Hoover **U.S. troops were finally withdrawn from Nicaragua in 1933.** Meantime, the U.S. had been impliedly criticized at the **Havana Conference,** opened by President Coolidge, 16 Jan. 1928, in a proposed resolution declaring that "no state has the right to intervene in the internal affairs of another." Charles Evans Hughes, heading the U.S. delegation, managed to block its passage. Immediately after his election on 6 Nov. Herbert Hoover embarked on a good-will tour (19 Nov.–6 Jan. 1929) of 11 Latin-American countries, where he received a cordial welcome.

17 Dec. 1928. CLARK MEMORANDUM of the U.S. State Department, drafted by **J. Reuben Clark** (1871–   ), defined the Monroe Doctrine as stating "a case of the U.S. v. Europe, and not of the U.S. v. Latin America," in effect **repudiating the Roosevelt Corollary.**

1929

YOUNG PLAN. German dissatisfaction with the operation of the reparations program resulted in a new series of negotiations. On 19 Jan. **Owen D. Young** (1874–   ) and J. P. Morgan were named as American experts on a Committee on German Reparations, which met in Paris (11 Feb.) to revise the Dawes Plan, and designated Young as chairman. The report aimed at a final settlement of German reparations. It reduced the amount due from Germany to **$8,032,500,000,** payable over 58½ **years** at 5½% **interest;** set up a **Bank for International Settlements** from the profits of which Germany's payments during the final 22 years should be made; and provided for a further reduction should the U.S. consent to scaling down the inter-allied war debts. In ratifying the debt settlement agreement with the U.S. (21 July) the French Chamber of Deputies resolved that the amounts paid to the U.S. should be covered by German reparation payments. At the **Lausanne Conference** (16 June 1932) **over 90%** of the reparations required to be paid under the Young Plan were **canceled.**

1930

21 Jan.–22 Apr. LONDON NAVAL CONFERENCE. On a visit to the U.S. (4–6 Oct. 1929) Prime Minister Ramsay MacDonald of Great Britain discussed with President Hoover the issue of naval disarmament. On 7 Oct. 1929 Great Britain issued a formal invitation to the other 4 major naval powers. The U.S. delegation was headed by Secretary of State Stimson, and included Charles Francis Adams, Secretary of the Navy, Dwight W. Morrow, Hugh Gibson, and Sens. David A. Reed (Rep.) and Joseph T. Robinson (Dem.). France refused to accept Italy's demands for parity with any continental power, and neither nation signed the more important provisions of the treaty. The U.S., Great Britain, and Japan adopted a program of cruiser limitation; an "escalator" or escape clause permitted Britain to start construction should France or Italy threaten her traditional policy of a navy equal to both continental powers. In cruisers Japan was restricted to a 10–6 ratio, but in other auxiliaries except submarines received a 10–7 ratio. In submarines parity at an upper limit of 52,700 tons was adopted. The capital-ship ratio remained at 10–10–6, but no new ships were to be built until 1936 (except French and Italian battleships authorized at Washington but not yet begun). As a result, 5 British, 3 American, and 1 Japanese capital ship were scrapped. The treaty's expiration date was 31 Dec. 1936. President Hoover called a special session to secure favorable action by the Senate (21 July). **Further disarmament efforts** were continued by the League's Preparatory Commission on Disarmament. A general disarmament conference assembled at **Geneva**, 2 Feb. 1932, with U.S. participation. When the U.S. proposal for **abolition of all offensive armaments** failed of adoption, President Hoover countered with a proposal for a 30% over-all reduction. The conference adjourned in July, resumed negotiations in Feb. 1933, adjourned from June until Oct. (by which time Germany had announced her withdrawal from the League), and broke up without accomplishment in the spring of 1934.

1931

20 June. HOOVER DEBT MORATORIUM. The deepening worldwide economic crisis made the payment of either reparations or war debts an impossibility. The repercussions of the New York stock market crash of Oct. 1929 were soon felt abroad. On 11 May 1931 the Austrian Credit-Anstalt failed. Foreign funds were hastily withdrawn from Germany. On 16 June the Bank of England, to stem the financial panic, advanced 150,000,000 schillings to the Austrian National Bank. On 20 June President Hoover proposed a **1-yr. moratorium** on both interallied debts and reparations. French opposition, delaying acceptance until 6 July, contributed to the closing of all the German banks by mid-July. The crisis seriously affected Great Britain, forcing the Bank of England off the gold standard on 21

Sept. The French position was presented to the U.S. by Premier Pierre Laval, who had a conference at the White House with the President, 23–25 Oct. As a result a statement was issued that, when the moratorium ended, some agreement on the interallied debts "covering the period of business depression," not merely the moratorium year, might be necessary.

1931–32

18 Sept. JAPANESE AGGRESSION IN MANCHURIA. In violation of the Washington treaties, the Kellogg-Briand Pact, and the League Covenant Japanese army leaders occupied major Manchurian cities, in effect launching an unofficial war between Japan and China. Military control of South Manchuria was completed by 4 Jan. 1932. On 15 Sept. 1932 Japan formally recognized the new puppet state of **Manchukuo.**

7 Jan. 1932. STIMSON DOCTRINE. Secretary Stimson addressed an identical note to Japan and China declaring that the U.S. does not "intend to recognize any treaty or agreement . . . which may impair . . . the sovereignty, the independence, or the territorial and administrative integrity of the Republic of China . . . or the Open Door policy. . . ." Instead of supporting Stimson, the British Foreign Office on 11 Jan. professed its faith in Japan's assurances regarding the Open Door. On 29 Jan. naval and military intervention by the Japanese took place at Shanghai, where the Chinese forces were expelled, 3 Mar. Stimson proposed to **Sir John Simon,** British Foreign Secretary, that a joint protest be made on the basis of the 9-Power Treaty of 1922, but the British government, preferring to work within the League, was unresponsive. On 23 Feb. Stimson, in a letter to Senator Borah, chairman of the Senate Foreign Relations Committee, declared that the U.S. would stand by its treaty rights in the Far East, and urged other nations to follow the Stimson Doctrine of nonrecognition. On 11 Mar. the League of Nations Assembly unanimously adopted a resolution incorporating this doctrine.

On 31 May Japan, bowing to world opinion, withdrew from Shanghai.

10 Dec. 1931–27 Mar. 1933. LYTTON REPORT. The League attempted to end hostilities in the Far East, formally inviting the U.S. on 16 Oct. 1931 to appoint a representative to sit with the Council in considering the Manchurian crisis. The U.S. accepted. **Prentiss B. Gilbert**, consul at Geneva, was authorized to participate in such discussions as related to U.S. obligations under the Kellogg-Briand Pact; otherwise to act as an observer. Meantime, a ground swell was developing in the U.S. for an economic boycott of Japan, which President Hoover opposed. When it appeared that the League might impose sanctions, Stimson, on 19 Nov., told Charles G. Dawes, American Ambassador to Great Britain: "We do not intend to get into war with Japan." On 10 Dec. the League appointed the Lytton Commission, including Gen. **Frank Ross McCoy** (1874–1954), an American, to investigate the Manchurian crisis. The **Lytton Report**, 4 Oct. 1932, condemned Japan, but proposed a settlement recognizing Japan's special interest in Manchuria, which was to become an **autonomous** state under Chinese sovereignty but Japanese control. The report was adopted by the League on 24 Feb. 1933, and on 27 Mar. Japan gave notice of withdrawal from the League.

1933

4 Mar. GOOD NEIGHBOR POLICY. In his first inaugural Franklin D. Roosevelt declared: "In the field of world policy I would dedicate this nation to the policy of the good neighbor—the neighbor who resolutely respects himself and, because he does so, respects the rights of others." The implementation of this policy meant a further improvement in relations with Latin America. At the **Montevideo Conference** Secretary of State **Cordell Hull** (1871–1955) favored declaration: "No state has the right to intervene in the internal or external affairs of another." This pact was unanimously adopted, 26 Dec. "The definite policy of the U.S. from now on is one

opposed to armed intervention," declared F. D. R. on 28 Dec.

12 June–27 July. LONDON ECONOMIC CONFERENCE. President Hoover had pledged American participation in this conference called by the League at the request of the Lausanne Conference. Between 4 Mar. and 12 June the U.S. had abandoned the gold standard. Hence, Roosevelt was disinclined to support a currency stabilizing program supported by the gold-bloc nations (France, Belgium, the Netherlands, Italy, and Switzerland). Secretary Hull received instructions en route to the Conference to limit participation to negotiating bilateral tariff treaties. On 2 July President Roosevelt, in a radio message, rebuked the delegates for concentrating on currency stabilization. Since the other participating nations would not agree to consider tariff reductions until *after* currency stabilization, the Conference broke up without substantial accomplishment. Its failure marked a blow at international cooperation and signalized the American drift toward isolation.

16 Nov. RECOGNITION OF SOVIET RUSSIA. Following the overthrow of the Kerensky regime in 1917, U.S. administrations had refused to recognize the Soviet Union on various grounds, including Russia's refusal to assume the obligations incurred by former governments as well as her revolutionary program for the overthrow of capitalist nations. Roosevelt's communication of 16 May addressed to 54 heads of states, urging military and economic disarmament, was sent, among others, to **Mikhail Kalinin**, titular head of the Russian government. On 10 Oct. the President requested Kalinin to send an envoy to the U.S. **Maxim Litvinov**, Commissar for Foreign Affairs, arrived in Washington on 7 Nov. In a formal exchange of notes (16 Nov.) Russia promised (1) not to interfere with the domestic affairs of the U.S., including abstaining from propaganda; (2) to extend religious freedom to American citizens in the Soviet Union and to negotiate an agreement to guarantee a fair trial to Americans accused of crime in Russia; (3) to negotiate a settlement of mutual claims (no specific agreement on debts outstanding was ever made).

The expected increase in American foreign trade failed to materialize, and the Soviet Union violated her pledge on propaganda and interference in U.S. internal affairs.

1933-38

DECLINE OF DOLLAR DIPLO-MACY. Cuba. As a result of the collapse of sugar prices in the 1920's Cuban economic conditions deteriorated and were further damaged by the Hawley-Smoot Tariff (1930). In Aug. 1931 dictator **Gerardo Machado** suppressed a revolt against his regime. To stabilize Cuban internal conditions President Roosevelt sent **Sumner Welles** (1892–   ) as Ambassador to Cuba. Arriving in Havana on 1 June 1933, Welles served as mediator between the Cuban administration and various opposition groups. A general strike and an army revolt forced Machado out of office (12 Aug.). On 5 Sept. another army coup forced out his successor, Cárlos Manuel de Céspedes, and a practical dictatorship was established under **Fulgencio Batista**. The radical government of President **Grau San Martín** was not recognized by the U.S. On 20 Jan. 1934 this regime was overthrown by Carlos Mendieta, favored by the U.S., Batista, and Cuban conservatives, who successfully negotiated a treaty with the U.S. **abrogating the Platt Amendment** (29 May) and removing limitations previously imposed on Cuban sovereignty. Chief credit for these negotiations belongs to Sumner Welles. On 25 Aug. the U.S. and Cuba signed a reciprocal trade agreement by which duties on sugar were reduced from 2.5 cts. to .9 cts. per lb. Cuban sugar production was finally stabilized by the **Jones-Costigan Sugar Control Act** (in effect 8 June).

Haiti. As the result of the restoration of order and the stabilizing of finances with U.S. aid, U.S. troops were withdrawn on 6 Aug. 1934.

Panama. As a result of a conference in Washington between President **Harmodio Arías** and President Roosevelt, a declaration was issued (17 Oct. 1933) that Panama should be permitted the commercial rights of a sovereign state in the Canal Zone. Negotiations between the two nations were soon entered into to secure a modification of the Hay-Bunau-Varilla Treaty of 1903. In a new treaty signed 2 Mar. 1936 some of the inequities were eliminated, but this treaty was not ratified by the U.S. Senate until 25 July 1939, owing in part to opposition from U.S. military and naval authorities.

HEMISPHERE SOLIDARITY. Early Phases. The rise of fascist and totalitarian regimes in Europe underscored the need for unity among the nations of the Western Hemisphere. Three Pan-American conferences prior to the outbreak of World War II dealt with this new world peril: (1) The **Montevideo Conference,** which denied the right of any state to intervene in the "internal or external affairs of another" (26 Dec. 1933); (2) the **Buenos Aires Conference,** opened by President Roosevelt (1 Dec. 1936) in a speech in which he declared that non-American states seeking "to commit acts of aggression against us will find a Hemisphere wholly prepared to consult together for our mutual safety and our mutual good," and which adopted a pact pledging consultation whenever war threatened; (3) the **Lima Conference** (24 Dec. 1938), which adopted the **Declaration of Lima,** not only reaffirming the absolute sovereignty of the American states but expressing their determination to resist "all foreign intervention or activities that may threaten them." It provided for consultation where the "peace, security, or territorial integrity" of any state should be threatened. Actually, the Argentina delegation blocked an even stronger declaration desired by Secretary Hull, who headed the U.S. delegation.

Closer Ties with Brazil. As a result of radical unrest in Brazil, President **Getulio Vargas** was granted almost dictatorial powers, which were enlarged by a new constitution proclaimed 10 Nov. 1937. The U.S. refused to label Vargas' government as fascist, and moved quickly to supplant German influence in that strategic area. Largely as a result of the efforts of Sumner Welles, Brazil concluded a series of agreements with the U.S., 9

Mar. 1939, by which it obtained financial aid for economic development.

SETTLEMENT OF THE MEXICAN EXPROPRIATION CONTROVERSY.

Under a 6-Year Plan launched by President Lázaro Cárdenas (inaugurated 11 Nov. 1936) numerous social reforms were introduced. Acting under authority of a statute passed in 1936, Cárdenas nationalized most of the properties of British and U.S. oil companies, valued at $450 million (18 Mar. 1938). Secretary Hull admitted the right of expropriation, but insisted on fair compensation (30 Mar.). On 1 Apr. the U.S. discontinued purchasing Mexican silver at a price above the world level, an act which threatened Mexico's financial stability. Certain aspects of the controversy were settled by a joint commission, and payments by the Mexican government began in 1939; other aspects were settled by agreement between the U.S. and President Avila Camacho (19 Nov. 1941). Mexico agreed to pay $40 million in settlements of agrarian claims; the U.S. to establish a $40-million fund to support the peso, to resume purchase of Mexican silver at a price above the world market, and to issue through the Export-Import bank a $30-million credit for Mexican highway construction. Each party agreed to appoint an expert to arrive at an equitable valuation of the U.S.-owned oil properties. On 18 Apr. 1942 a figure of $23,995,991 for subsoil rights was announced, in addition to $9,600,000 paid by Mexico in individual settlements with 2 U.S. oil companies.

U.S. COLONIAL POLICY. Philippine Independence Movement.

Following the election of 1932 a movement gained ground to implement the promise of independence for the Philippines contained in the Jones Act, 1916 (see p. 306). Joining forces to promote independence were U.S. beet-sugar and dairy interests seeking to bar Philippine cane sugar and coconut oil, respectively; organized labor favoring immigration curbs; and anti-imperialists. The immediate result was the **Hawes-Cutting Act,** passed by a Democratic Congress over the President's veto in the closing days of the Hoover administration, 13 Jan. 1933. The Act provided for independence after 12 years, but reserved to the U.S. the right to military and naval bases, and to the U.S. Supreme Court the right to review the decisions of the Philippine courts. The Philippine legislature rejected the measure in Oct. on the ground that its real aim was to exclude Philippine products and labor from the U.S. To meet some of these criticisms, Congress (24 Mar. 1934) passed the **Tydings-McDuffie Act,** which substantially reenacted the Hawes-Cutting bill, but provided for the removal of U.S. military posts and the settlement by negotiation of the future status of U.S. naval bases. This Act was unanimously accepted by the Philippine legislature (1 May). Under its authority a convention met on 30 July to frame a constitution, which President Roosevelt approved on 8 Feb. 1935. The constitution was ratified, 14 May, and the first President, **Manuel Quezon,** elected on 17 Sept. On 14 Apr. 1937 President Roosevelt appointed the Joint Preparatory Commission on Philippine Affairs to recommend a program for economic adjustment. The Committee proposed that the 75% of preferences existing on 4 July 1946 (the date when Philippine independence was to go into effect) be gradually eliminated by 31 Dec. 1960.

Virgin Islands. U.S. prohibition seriously curtailed the demand for sugar products from these islands; the depression deepened economic deterioration. A civil government was established by the U.S. in Feb. 1931, with St. Thomas as the capital. By Mar. President Hoover referred to the island as "an effective poorhouse." New Deal relief measures, together with an expanded rum industry after 1933, brought substantial amelioration. On 22 June 1936 the **Organic Act** revised the political structure of the islands and set up a territorial legislature to act with the governor. On 1 June 1938 universal suffrage went into effect.

Puerto Rico. Suffering acutely from the depressed condition in the sugar industry, Puerto Rico was rent by nationalist propaganda. Riots and demonstrations occurred during 1936–37. Demands were made by a committee of the legislature on 4 June 1939 for statehood, and, in the interim, for an elective governor.

Hawaii. In 1937 a bill was introduced

to change the status of the islands from that of a territory to that of a state. A congressional committee reported adversely on the grounds of the mixed character of the population and the strategic position of the islands.

ISOLATION AND NEUTRALITY. As totalitarian regimes increasingly threatened the peace of Europe, the U.S. adopted a series of isolationist measures to avoid involvement in war. The **Johnson Debt Default Act** (13 Apr. 1934) prohibited loans to any foreign government in default to the U.S. Previously (June 1933) Britain, Czechoslovakia, Italy, Rumania, Latvia, and Lithuania had made token payments, their last on debts to the U.S. All formally defaulted on 15 June 1934. Only Finland continued to meet her payments in full. The new approach to neutrality, in part the result of the work of the **Nye Committee** (p. 348), sought to disentangle U.S. economic interests from foreign wars and constituted an abandonment of traditional concepts of neutral rights.

Neutrality Act of 1935. When Italy attacked Ethiopia (May 1935) the U.S. State Department drafted a bill which would have given the President power to embargo arms against one or all belligerents in future wars. Introduced in the House on 17 Aug., it was rejected by the Foreign Relations Committee, which substituted a resolution authorizing the President, after proclaiming the existence of a state of war, to prohibit all **arms** shipments and to forbid U.S. citizens from traveling on belligerent vessels except **at their own risk.** Yielding to the administration, Congress placed a 6-mos. limit on such embargo. Roosevelt signed the measure, 31 Aug., but characterized it as calculated to "drag us into war instead of keeping us out." The embargo did not include primary materials such as oil, steel, copper, easily converted to military use.

Neutrality Act of 1936. The Act of 1935 was extended on 29 Feb. 1936 to 1 May 1937, and forbade the extension of loans or credits to belligerents. On 14 Aug. 1936, in an address delivered at Chautauqua, N.Y., President Roosevelt pointed to the dangers of being drawn into war and declared: "I hate war."

Neutrality Acts of 1937. On 18 July 1936 the Spanish Civil War broke out, with a revolt of army chiefs in Spanish Morocco. Foreign powers soon intervened on both sides. Since the U.S. neutrality acts applied only to wars **between nations,** not to civil wars, new legislation was deemed necessary. On 6 Jan. 1937 Congress passed a joint resolution forbidding the export of munitions "for the use of either of the opposing forces in Spain." Under this Act Roosevelt embargoed shipments to both sides. The embargo worked to the particular disadvantage of the Loyalist government in Madrid, as the rebels secured supplies from Italy and Germany. The deficiencies of each of the neutrality acts called for a more realistic and flexible measure, which was adopted on 1 May 1937. This Act (1) authorized the President to list commodities **other than munitions** to be paid for on delivery (limited to 2 years); (2) made travel on belligerent vessels **unlawful.** Again, the ineffectiveness of the new act was demonstrated when, on 7 July 1937, fighting broke out between Japanese and Chinese troops near Peiping. The President declined to invoke the Neutrality Act of May 1937 on the ground that it would have worked to China's disadvantage. However, on 14 Sept. he forbade transport of munitions to China and Japan on U.S. government vessels, and notified private shippers that they acted at their own risk. Japan, with her large merchant marine, benefited by this ruling.

ROOSEVELT AND COLLECTIVE SECURITY: THE QUARANTINE SPEECH. In complete disagreement with the isolationist trend of the neutrality legislation, President Roosevelt, in a speech in Chicago, 5 Oct. 1937, urged an international quarantine of aggressors as the only means of preserving peace. Roosevelt soon recognized that he had moved ahead of public opinion, although his address undoubtedly encouraged a widespread U.S. boycott against Japanese goods.

NAVAL EXPANSION. Japan, on 29 Dec. 1934, denounced the Washington Naval Treaty of 1922. The U.S. refused to grant parity to Japan at the discussions preliminary to the 2nd London Naval Conference, from which Japan withdrew, 15 Jan. 1936. Great Britain, the U.S., and France signed (25 Mar.) a treaty providing for minor limitations, largely made ineffective by numerous "escape clauses." In 1938 Congress voted a billion-dollar naval-building program (see p. 359).

DETERIORATING JAPANESE RELATIONS. Panay Incident. On 12 Dec. 1937 Japanese planes bombed a U.S. river gunboat, the *Panay*. The vessel sank with a loss of 2 killed, 30 wounded. (For the **Ludlow Amendment** [14 Dec.], see p. 358.) On 14 Dec. the U.S. formally demanded apologies, reparations, and guarantees against further incidents. On the same day Japan formally apologized and gave the necessary assurances. On 25 Dec. Secretary Hull acknowledged the reply. On 6 Oct. 1938 U.S. Ambassador **Joseph Clark Grew** (1880–   ) protested against Japanese violations of the Open Door in China. The Japanese note of 18 Nov. declared that the Open Door was "inapplicable" to the conditions "of today and tomorrow." The State Department, in its reply of 31 Dec., refused to recognize the "new order."

1938–39

DETERIORATING EUROPEAN CONDITIONS. On 11 Jan. 1938 President Roosevelt proposed to the British government a program for a world conference to reduce armaments, promote economic security, and ameliorate the more inhumane aspects of any war that might break out. Prime Minister Chamberlain rejected this proposal. The **German war timetable:** 7 Mar. 1936, German reoccupation of the Rhineland; 17 Nov. 1936, Anti-Comintern Pact of Germany, Japan, and Italy against communism; Mar.

1938, annexation of Austria by Germany; Sept. 1938, the German-Czech crisis, which caused Chamberlain to intervene (at Berchtesgaden, 15 Sept.; at Godesberg, 22–23 Sept.). On 27 Sept. President Roosevelt appealed to Hitler and Mussolini for a peaceful solution of the issues. As a result of the **Munich Conference** and Agreement, 29 Sept., the Sudetenland and all vital Czech fortresses were yielded to Germany. Despite French and British guarantees of the new frontiers of Czechoslovakia, that nation came to an end in Mar. 1939, when Slovakia and Carpatho-Ukraine declared their independence, and Bohemia and Moravia became a German protectorate. On 23 Mar. Germany annexed Memel, and made stiff demands to Warsaw regarding Danzig and the Polish Corridor. On 31 Mar. Britain pledged Anglo-French aid to the Poles in case their independence was threatened, a pledge extended to Rumania and Greece on 13 Apr. Meantime, 7 Apr., Italy invaded Albania. On 15 Apr. President Roosevelt, in a letter to Hitler and Mussolini, asked assurances against attack on 31 nations of Europe and the Near East. Denying warlike intentions, Hitler, in reply, restated German grievances. On 22 May a military alliance was concluded between Germany and Italy. On 23 Aug. a **Russo-German** pact was signed at Moscow. This provided that (1) either party would abstain from attacking the other; (2) either party would remain neutral if the other were attacked by a third party. The next day President Roosevelt addressed an appeal to President Moscicki of Poland, to Hitler, and to King Victor Immanuel proposing direct negotiations between Germany and Poland, arbitration or conciliation. Poland accepted conciliation. On 31 Aug. the Poles decreed partial mobilization.

DOMESTIC ISSUES

1919

28 Oct. NATIONAL PROHIBITION ENFORCEMENT ACT (VOLSTEAD ACT) was passed over President Wilson's veto (27 Oct.). Designed to provide the enforcement apparatus for the 18th Amendment, the Act went into effect on 16 Jan. 1920. It defined as intoxicating liquor any beverage containing more than ½ of 1% of alcohol and placed the administration of the law under the Bureau of Internal Revenue, in which the post of commissioner of prohibition was created. A supplementary Act (23 Nov. 1921) limited the use of liquor by medical prescription and extended prohibition to the Hawaiian and Virgin Islands. The **Jones Act** (2 Mar. 1929) increased the penalties for violation. Widespread evasion of the Volstead Act was evidenced by the growth of bootlegging (i.e., the illicit liquor traffic) on a vast scale during the 1920's, when the organized distilling and distribution of liquor fell under the control of criminal elements.

24 Dec. President Wilson announced that on 1 Mar. 1920 the railroads and express companies would be returned to private operation.

1920

13 Feb. Robert Lansing resigned as Secretary of State, at Wilson's request, after the President had charged him with holding unauthorized meetings of the Cabinet following Wilson's physical collapse in 1919.

28 Feb. TRANSPORTATION ACT (ESCH-CUMMINS ACT) provided for the return of the railroads to private control on 1 Mar. and widened the powers of the Interstate Commerce Commission. The Commission was authorized to draw up plans for the consolidation of all railroads into about a score of competing groups exempt from antitrust legislation; was empowered to make evaluations of the aggregate value of railroad properties, to set minimum and maximum rates, and to establish a fair return to stockholders; and was given jurisdiction over pooling, regulation of service and traffic, and new issues of securities. A recapture clause required carriers to turn over to the Interstate Commerce Commission one half of all net earnings in excess of 6%, these to be set aside as a revolving fund for the benefit of railroads handicapped by low income. A **Railroad Labor Board** was created for the adjustment of wage disputes.

5 June. MERCHANT MARINE ACT (JONES ACT) repealed emergency war legislation relating to shipping, reorganized the U.S. Shipping Board and extended its life, and authorized the sale of government-built ships to private operators, the proceeds up to $25 million to be used for loans to private owners for the construction of new craft. The Shipping Board was empowered to propose the establishment of shipping routes for the purpose of promoting mail and trade service and to operate the shipping service until private interests took over. The Act provided that coastwise commerce was to be carried in U.S. vessels, as well as the mails where practicable.

10 June. WATER POWER ACT established a **Federal Power Commission** consisting of the Secretaries of War, Interior, and Agriculture, with an executive secretary directly responsible for its administration. The Act applied to water power reserves on public lands of the U.S. (except reservations) and to navigable streams, including falls, rapids, and shallows. The Commission was empowered to issue licenses, limited to 50 years, for the construction and operation of facilities (e.g., power houses, dams, reservoirs, and transmission lines) for improving navigation and developing and utilizing power. Upon expiration of the lease, the government reserved the right to take over and operate these facilities. The commission was authorized to regulate rates and security issues of licensees under its jurisdiction.

26 Aug. 19TH AMENDMENT to the Constitution, providing for woman suffrage, was declared ratified.

PALMER RAIDS. Following the Bolshevik Revolution in Russia, the Soviets carried out an intensive propaganda campaign against the Western nations. In 1919 the Workers' (later the Communist) party was established in the U.S. Beginning in the fall of 1919, the Department of Justice under A. Mitchell Palmer made countrywide mass arrests of political and labor agitators. In instances where arrested persons were aliens, they were deported; on 22 Dec. 1919 the U.S. transport *Buford,* with 249 deportees aboard, including the anarchists Emma Goldman and Alexander Berkman, sailed for Russia. One of the largest mass arrests came on 2 Jan., when government agents carried out raids in 33 cities and took 2,700 persons into custody. The raids were terminated in May. Within individual states, criminal syndicalist laws were invoked against radicals.

PRESIDENTIAL CAMPAIGN. The Socialist Labor Party Convention met at New York (5 May) and nominated W. W. Cox (Mo.) for President and August Gillhaus (N.Y.) for Vice-President. The Socialist Party Convention met at New York (8 May) and unanimously nominated Eugene V. Debs (Ind.) for President. Debs was then serving a 10-year sentence in Federal prison for having engaged in seditious activity in violation of the wartime Espionage Act. Seymour Stedman (Ohio) was chosen as the Socialist candidate for Vice-President.

The Republican Convention met at Chicago (8 June) and on the 10th ballot nominated Sen. **Warren G. Harding** (Ohio) for President. Gov. **Calvin Coolidge** (Mass.) was nominated for Vice-President on the 1st ballot. The Republican platform rejected the Covenant of the League of Nations and made a vague declaration favoring an "agreement among the nations to preserve the peace of the world." Harding waged a front-porch campaign; in a well-calculated appeal to the postwar temper, he called for a "return to normalcy."

The Democratic National Convention met at San Francisco (28 June) and on the 44th ballot nominated Governor **James M. Cox** (Ohio) for President. **Franklin D. Roosevelt** (N.Y.), assistant secretary of the navy, was nominated for Vice-President by acclamation. The Democratic platform unequivocally endorsed the Versailles Treaty and the League of Nations, but did not "oppose the acceptance of any reservations making clearer or more specific the obligations of the United States to the League associates."

The Farmer Labor Party Convention met at Chicago (11 July) and nominated P. P. Christensen (Utah) for President and Max S. Hayes (Ohio) for Vice-President. The Single Tax party convention met at Chicago (12 July) and nominated Robert C. Macauley (Pa.) for President and Richard Barnum (Ohio) for Vice-President. The Prohibition Party Convention met at Lincoln, Neb. (21 July), and nominated A. S. Watkins for President.

2 Nov. PRESIDENTIAL ELECTION. Popular vote: **Harding,** 16,152,200; Cox (D.), 9,147,353; Debs, 919,799; Watkins, 189,408; Cox (S.L.), 31,175; Christensen, 265,411; Macauley, 5837. Electoral vote: **Harding,** 404; Cox (D.), 127.

1921

BUSINESS RECESSION. The sharp deflation, 1920–21 (p. 539), was the result of stringent credit, a glutted domestic market and heavy inventories, and a sharp drop in the export trade. Wages dropped; about 20,000 business failures occurred in 1921; and some 4,750,000 persons were unemployed. The recession's impact upon agriculture was more lasting (p. 509).

10 June. BUDGET AND ACCOUNTING ACT, the first material step in the reform of the national budget, created a Budget Bureau in the Treasury Department, with a director appointed by the President. At each regular session of Congress the President was to submit to the legislators a budget including estimates of expenditures and receipts for the following year together with estimates for the current and last fiscal years. The President was also to present a complete statement of the government's financial condition and, when deemed advisable, recommendations for loans, tax revision, and other financial measures. Except on special request of either House of Congress, no financial recommendation or request for appropriations was to be made by any government officer except through the budget. The Act also created a General Accounting Office, under the Comptroller General of the U.S., for carrying out an independent audit of government accounts. **Charles G. Dawes** (1865–1951) was named (21 June) as 1st director of the Bureau of the Budget.

9 Aug. VETERANS BUREAU was established as an independent unit, directly responsible to the President, for assuming the administration of all forms of veterans' relief. Col. **Charles R. Forbes** was named as its head.

15 Aug. PACKERS AND STOCK-YARDS ACT related to livestock, livestock products, poultry, and dairy products. Its enforcement was vested in the Department of Agriculture. The Act forbade unfair and discriminatory practices, the manipulation and control of prices, and other devices creating a monopoly and acting in restraint of trade. Operators of stockyards and other marketing facilities were required to register with the Department of Agriculture and to file their schedule of charges.

24 Aug. GRAIN FUTURES TRADING ACT was designed to regulate all contract markets authorized to sell grain for future delivery, in order to prevent market manipulation and monopoly practices. It discouraged speculative transactions by levying a prohibitive tax on grain sold for future delivery except by owners or certain authorized contract markets. The Act was invalidated by the Supreme Court in 1922 and superseded by a 2nd Grain Futures Act (21 Sept. 1922) regulating trading under the interstate commerce power.

23 Nov. SHEPPARD-TOWNER ACT for the promotion of the welfare and health of maternity and infancy extended Federal aid to states. The Act authorized annual Federal appropriations of $1 million. The Act, which lapsed in 1929, was attacked as constituting Federal interference in state affairs.

1922

18 Feb. COOPERATIVE MARKETING ACT (CAPPER-VOLSTEAD ACT) exempted agricultural producers, cooperatives, or associations from the operations of antitrust laws and allowed cooperative buying and selling by farmers in interstate commerce. Administration of the act was vested in the Department of Agriculture.

22 Sept. CABLE ACT granted married women U.S. citizenship independent of their husbands' status.

1923

KU KLUX KLAN EXPOSÉS. The Ku Klux Klan, a secret nativist organization patterned upon the rituals of its post-Civil War predecessor, and active against minority groups (Negroes, Catholics, Jews, and immigrants) as well as against certain tendencies in modern thought (e.g., birth control, pacifism, internationalism, Darwinism, and the repeal of prohibition), was revived at a meeting on Stone Mountain, Ga., Nov. 1915. At peak strength in the 1920's it was reported to have had 5 million members in the North, South, and Midwest, with political power in several states (including Ind., Okla., and Tex.). Exposés of its activities appeared in 1923. The Baltimore *Sun* (7 Jan.) exposed the reign of terror in Morehouse Parish, La., where despite evidence of torture and murder of marked victims, a grand jury refused to indict. Concurrently the N. Y. *World* exposed Klan activities in the North. In Vincennes, Ind., Grand Dragon David C. Stephenson was convicted on a charge of murder in the 2nd degree (21 Nov. 1925). By 1926 Klan membership was on the decline. By 1930 it was estimated at only 9,000.

4 Mar. INTERMEDIATE CREDIT ACT was designed to facilitate loans for crop financing by means of an intermediate credit system that liberalized the use of short-term agricultural paper. It established 12 intermediate credit banks, 1 in each Federal reserve bank district, under the jurisdiction of the Federal Farm Loan Board. Each bank, with a capital of $5 million subscribed by the government, was authorized to make loans (ranging from 5 mos. to 3 yrs.) to cooperative producing and marketing associations. The act also authorized the creation of agricultural credit corporations by private interests.

2 Aug. DEATH OF PRESIDENT HARDING at San Francisco, while on a return trip from Alaska. Embolism was listed as the cause of death.

3 Aug. Vice-President **Calvin Coolidge** took the oath of office as President at Plymouth, Vt., becoming the 29th President of the U.S.

5 Dec. In his 1st annual message to Congress, President Coolidge voiced his support of U.S. adherence to a world court, the tax reduction plan of Secretary of the Treasury **Andrew W. Mellon** (1855–1937), and prohibition enforcement. He opposed the cancellation of Allied debts and the payment of a veterans' bonus. His program called for a scaling down of government expenditures, a minimum of government interference in business, and government aid to industry and commerce.

1924

HARDING ADMINISTRATION SCANDALS. Early in 1924 Congressional committees, acting upon persistent rumors of graft and corruption in the Harding administration, brought to light scandals in the departments of Justice, Navy, and the Interior, and in the Veterans Bureau and the Office of the Alien Property Custodian. Col. Charles R. Forbes, former chief of the Veterans Bureau, who had resigned in 1923, was indicted for fraud, conspiracy and bribery, and sentenced (4 Feb. 1925) to 2 yrs. in a Federal penitentiary and a fine of $10,000. Col. Thomas W. Miller, the

Alien Property Custodian, was also sent to prison (1927) on charges of conspiring to defraud the government.

The major scandals involved the lease of naval oil reserve lands by private interests and the influence over the Department of Justice wielded by the Ohio gang, a group of self-seeking politicians close to Harding. A Senate investigating committee disclosed that President Harding, acting with the approval of Secretary of the Navy Denby, had transferred (1921) to Secretary of the Interior **Albert B. Fall** (1861–1944) the administration of oil reserves at Teapot Dome, Wyo., and Elk Hills, Calif. During the Taft and Wilson administrations these reserves had been set aside for the use of the navy. The Teapot Dome reserve was secretly leased by Fall (7 Apr. 1922) to oil operator Harry F. Sinclair; the California fields were likewise leased (25 Apr., 11 Dec. 1922) to Edward L. Doheny.

The scandal came to light when a Senate committee headed by **Thomas J. Walsh** (Mont., 1859–1933) found that in 1921 Doheny had lent Fall $100,000 without interest or collateral, and that Fall, after retiring from the Cabinet in March, 1923, had received a "loan" of $25,000 from Sinclair. A joint Congressional resolution charged fraud and corruption. The government secured cancellation of the oil leases in 1927. Fall was indicted (30 June) for bribery and conspiracy, convicted of bribery, and sentenced to 1 yr. in prison and $100,000 fine. Sinclair and Doheny were acquitted of bribery; Sinclair sentenced to 9 mos. in prison and $1,000 fine for contempt of court.

An investigation revealed that Attorney General **Harry M. Daugherty** (1860–1941), acting in concert with members of the Ohio gang, had received payments from violators of the prohibition statutes. It was also disclosed that he had failed to prosecute for graft in the Veterans Bureau. Daugherty was tried for conspiracy, but acquitted (4 Mar. 1927). He resigned (Mar. 1924) at the request of President Coolidge.

The Supreme Court declared the Elk Hills lease invalid 28 Feb. 1927; the Teapot Dome lease, 10 Oct. 1927.

19 May. WORLD WAR ADJUSTED COMPENSATION ACT. (SOLDIERS BONUS ACT). Shortly after the close of World War I organized veterans' groups, including the American Legion and the Veterans of Foreign Wars, initiated a demand for an ex-servicemen's bonus. The move was made on the assumption that veterans ought to be compensated for the differential between their service pay and the wages received by war workers who had remained in civilian life.

On 19 Sept. 1922 President Harding vetoed a bonus bill. Veterans' groups continued to exert pressure on Congress. On 18 Mar. a bonus bill was passed by the House, and on 23 Apr. it was approved by the Senate. It was vetoed (15 May) by President Coolidge, but was passed over his veto by the House (17 May) and Senate (19 May).

The Act provided for the payment of adjusted compensation to all veterans (excluding officers above the rank of captain) on the basis of $1.25 a day for overseas service and $1 a day for service in the U.S. The bonus was made in the form of 20-year endowment policies on which ex-servicemen might borrow from the government up to about 25% of full value. Cash payment, which became a major issue in 1931–32, was finally authorized in 1936.

McNARY-HAUGEN BILL. The postwar depression in agriculture, deepened by a glutted market and a continuing slump in crop prices, and farm mortgages on expanded acreage, led spokesmen of farmer interests to consider basic legislation for coping with agricultural distress. The **Capper-Volstead Act** (1922) and the **Intermediate Credit Act** (1923) failed to satisfy agrarian discontent, mobilized by such organized groups as the American Farm Bureau Federation and the Farmers' National Council. A bipartisan agrarian bloc in Congress undertook to deal with the problem by 2 means: the control of the surplus and the stabilization of prices. The **McNary-Haugen Farm Relief Bill**, sponsored by Sen. **Charles L. McNary** (Ore., 1874–1944) and Rep. **Gilbert N. Haugen** (Iowa), was introduced in both Houses

of Congress (16 Jan.). The measure featured the equalization fee scheme, whereby a proposed Federal farm board would purchase the annual surplus of specified commodities during years of large output and either keep it off the market until prices rose or sell it abroad at the prevailing world price. The equalization fee (i.e., the difference between the fixed domestic price and the free international price) was to be paid by producers of individual commodities in the event that the government suffered losses in selling at lower world prices. The bill was defeated in the House (3 June) when Western farm interests failed to muster adequate support. It suffered successive defeats in the House (21 May 1926) and Senate (24 June 1926). Passed by the Senate (11 Feb. 1927) and the House (17 Feb. 1927), it was vetoed by President Coolidge (25 Feb. 1927) on the ground that it incorporated a price-fixing principle and benefited special groups.

PRESIDENTIAL CAMPAIGN. The Commonwealth Land party (formerly the Single Tax party) met in convention (8 Feb.) and nominated W. J. Wallace (N.J.) for President and J. C. Lincoln (Ohio) for Vice-President. The Socialist Labor Party Convention met at New York (11 May) and nominated Frank T. Johns (Ore.) for President and Verne L. Reynolds (Md.) for Vice-President. The American Party Convention met at Columbus, Ohio (3 June) and nominated Judge Gilbert O. Nations (Washington, D.C.) for President and Charles H. Randall (Calif.) for Vice-President. The Prohibition Party Convention met at Columbus, Ohio (5 June), and nominated Herman P. Faris (Mo.) for President and Miss Marie C. Brehm (Calif.) for Vice-President.

The Republican Party Convention met at Cleveland (10 June) and nominated President **Coolidge** for re-election and Gen. **Charles G. Dawes** (Ill.) for Vice-President. The Republican platform supported reduced taxes and retrenchment in government expenditures, the Fordney-McCumber tariff, the limitation of armaments, U.S. adherence to the World

Court, and international action for the prevention of war.

The Democratic Party Convention met at New York (24 June) and, after a prolonged contest between the partisans of William G. McAdoo (Tenn.) and Alfred E. Smith (N.Y., 1873–1944), nominated **John W. Davis** (W. Va., 1873–1955) for President on the 103rd ballot (9 July). Gov. **Charles W. Bryan** (Neb.) was nominated for Vice-President. The Democratic platform favored a competitive tariff and endorsed disarmament and the League of Nations. It denounced the Ku Klux Klan and condemned the corruption of the Harding administration.

The Conference for Progressive Political Action, representing dissident agrarian and labor elements, met at Cleveland (4 July) and launched a new Progressive party that was endorsed by the Farmer Labor party, the Socialist party, and the American Federation of Labor. The Progressives nominated Senator **Robert M. La Follette** (Wis.) for President and Senator **Burton K. Wheeler** (Mont.) for Vice-President. The Progressive platform called for government ownership of railroads and water power resources, the abolition of the use of the injunction in labor disputes, freedom for farmers and labor to organize and bargain collectively, ratification of the child labor amendment, limitation of judicial review, and tighter controls over futures trading in agricultural commodities. It denounced corruption in government, condemned the Mellon financial program, and attacked "the control of government and industry by private monopoly."

The Workers' (Communist) party met on 11 July and nominated William Z. Foster (Ill.) for President and Benjamin Gitlow (N.Y.) for Vice-President.

4 Nov. PRESIDENTIAL ELECTION. Popular vote: **Coolidge,** 15,725,016; Davis, 8,385,586; La Follette, 4,822,856; Faris, 57,551; Johns, 38,958; Foster, 33,361; Nations, 23,867; Wallace, 2,778. Electoral vote: **Coolidge,** 382; Davis, 136; La Follette, 13. Both houses of Congress remained under Republican control.

1925

10–21 July. SCOPES TRIAL (p. 586).

28 Oct.–17 Dec. "BILLY" MITCHELL TRIAL. Differences among military and naval authorities over the role of the airplane in warfare set the background for the court-martial of Col. William ("Billy") Mitchell of the Army Air Service. A forthright critic of U.S. aviation policy, Mitchell publicly contended (5 Sept.) that the military high command was incompetent, criminally negligent, and almost treasonable in its administration of the national defense. An exponent of air power, he insisted that capital ships were vulnerable to air attack. Summoned to Washington, D.C., by the National Air Board, Mitchell advocated (29 Sept.) an independent department for aviation and a unified command of the armed services. A court-martial found him guilty of conduct prejudicial to good order and military discipline. He was suspended from the service for 5 yrs. Mitchell resigned from the service (29 Jan. 1926). He died in 1936. In 1942 he was posthumously restored to the service with the rank of maj. gen.

1926

26 Feb. REVENUE ACT, in keeping with the Coolidge-Mellon fiscal program, reduced personal income and inheritance taxes and abolished a wide variety of excise imposts. It also repealed the publicity clause relating to income tax returns. Additional reductions were made in the Revenue Act of 29 May 1928.

2 Nov. CONGRESSIONAL ELECTIONS cut Republican majorities in both houses, with gains for Progressives.

1927

2 Aug. COOLIDGE'S WITHDRAWAL. It was generally assumed that Coolidge would seek the Presidential nomination in 1928. While on a vacation in the Black Hills of South Dakota, Coolidge issued the following statement to newspaper reporters at Rapid City, S.D.: "I do not choose to run for President in 1928."

SACCO-VANZETTI CASE. Nicola Sacco and Bartolomeo Vanzetti, 2 Italian anarchists, were arrested (5 May 1920) for having allegedly murdered (15 Apr.) a paymaster and guard at a shoe factory in South Braintree, Mass. They were convicted (14 July 1921) on what many regarded as insubstantial evidence. It was charged by liberals and radicals in the U.S. and abroad that Sacco and Vanzetti had been tried for their radical views rather than for any actual crime. During the 20's, when defense committees succeeded in securing a stay of the death sentence, the Sacco-Vanzetti case became a *cause célèbre*. Mass demonstrations for the convicted were held in the U.S., Latin America, and Europe. Under pressure of widespread protest that the convicted had not received a fair trial, Gov. Alvan T. Fuller (Mass.) appointed (1 July 1927) a commission (Pres. Abbott Lawrence Lowell of Harvard, chairman), which examined the evidence and conduct of the trial and sustained the verdict (27 July). Sacco and Vanzetti were put to death in the electric chair at the Charlestown State Prison (23 Aug.).

1928

FINAL DEFEAT OF THE McNARY-HAUGEN BILL. As the situation of the American farmer showed no sign of general improvement, agrarian spokesmen in Congress renewed efforts to enact the McNary-Haugen Farm Relief Bill. In a 5th attempt, the bill passed the Senate (12 Apr.), 53–23, and the House (3 May), 204–121, but was again vetoed by President Coolidge on the following grounds: that it sanctioned price fixing; was an improper delegation of the taxing power; would lead to overproduction and profiteering; and would antagonize overseas agricultural producers and thus invite retaliation. Coolidge's persistent opposition to this mode of farm relief was a leading issue in the Presidential election of 1928.

15 May. FLOOD CONTROL ACT appropriated $325 million for levee work in the Mississippi Valley over a 10-yr period.

22 May. MERCHANT MARINE ACT (JONES-WHITE ACT) was designed to encourage private shipping. It increased from $125 million to $250 million a ship construction loan fund from which private builders could borrow up to three quarters of the cost of constructing, reconditioning, or remodeling a vessel. It also permitted the sale of government owned craft at low prices and liberalized long-term mail-carrying contracts.

PRESIDENTIAL CAMPAIGN. The Socialist Party Convention met at New York (13 Apr.) and nominated Norman Thomas (N.Y.) for President and James H. Maurer (Pa.) for Vice-President. The Workers' (Communist) Party Convention met at New York (27 May) and nominated William Z. Foster (Ill.) for President and Benjamin Gitlow (N.Y.) for Vice-President.

The Republican Party National Convention met at Kansas City, Mo. (12 June), and nominated Secretary of Commerce Herbert C. Hoover (Calif.) for President on the 1st ballot (14 June). Sen. Charles Curtis (Kan., 1860–1936) was nominated for Vice-President. The Republican platform rejected the McNary-Haugen scheme for farm relief but supported the creation of a Federal farm board authorized to promote the establishment of a farm marketing system and of farmer owned and controlled stabilization corporations or associations to prevent and control surpluses through orderly distribution. The platform upheld prohibition, the protective tariff, and the Coolidge foreign policy. During the campaign Hoover made his "rugged individualism" speech at New York (22 Oct.) in which he condemned the Democratic platform as state socialism and upheld free competition and private initiative as the traditional American way.

The Democratic Party Convention met at Houston, Tex. (26 June), and nominated Gov. Alfred E. Smith (N.Y.) for President on the 1st ballot (28 June) and Sen. Joseph T. Robinson (Ark.) for Vice-President. The Democratic platform, although not committed to the McNary-Haugen plan, pledged that "farm relief must rest on the basis of an economic equality of agriculture with other industries," and advocated the creation of a Federal farm board with powers somewhat similar to those proposed in the McNary-Haugen Bill. The platform pledged enforcement of the prohibition laws; and while Smith supported this pledge, he called for repeal of the 18th Amendment. His position cost him the "dry" vote, particularly in the South. Also favored by the Democratic platform were collective bargaining for labor and the abolition of the use of the injunction in labor disputes, "except upon proof of threatened irreparable injury"; the stricter regulation of water power resources; and immediate independence for the Philippines. Republican foreign policy was condemned.

The Prohibition Party Convention met at Chicago (12 July) and nominated William F. Varney (N.Y.) for President and James A. Edgerton (Wash.) for Vice-President. The Farmer Labor candidate for President was Frank E. Webb. The Socialist Labor party nominated Verne L. Reynolds for President.

5 Nov. PRESIDENTIAL ELECTION. Popular vote: **Hoover, 21,392,190;** Smith, 15,016,443; Thomas, 267,420; Foster, 48,770; Reynolds, 21,603; Varney, 20,-106; Webb, 6,390. Electoral vote: **Hoover, 444;** Smith, 87. In part because of religious prejudice against Smith, a Roman Catholic, the electoral vote of 5 Southern states went to Hoover. The Republicans maintained control of both houses of Congress.

1929

15 Apr. Special session of the 71st Congress convened at call of President Hoover to deal with farm relief and limited revision of the tariff.

EXPORT DEBENTURE PLAN. The agrarian relief scheme favored by the Congressional farm bloc differed fundamentally from that advocated by President Hoover. Exponents of the subsidy principle, the farm bloc introduced in the Senate the export debenture plan initially advanced in 1926 and again in 1928. This scheme called for export bounties on specified commodities. Equal to one half of the tariff duties on such commodities, these bounties were to be added to the prevailing world price. Payment was to be made in the form of debentures receivable in payment of import duties. Thus the difference between the domestic and world price would be met by the government out of customs receipts. The proposal of this plan by the farm bloc touched off a heated contest between the Senate and House. The House 3 times (25 Apr., 17 May, 13 June) rejected the debenture plan passed by the Senate, and President Hoover made it clear that he would veto the measure. The Senate finally abandoned the scheme.

15 June. AGRICULTURAL MARKETING ACT was an administration measure which eliminated the subsidy and price-fixing principle of the McNary-Haugen and export debenture plans. The act established a **Federal Farm Board** (consisting of 8 members and the Secretary of Agriculture) for promoting the marketing of farm commodities through agricultural cooperatives and stabilization corporations. It authorized a revolving fund of $500 million for low-interest loans to such agencies in the interest of the orderly purchasing, handling, and selling of surpluses of cotton, grain, livestock, and other specified commodities. The Board was authorized to make agreements with cooperatives and stabilization corporations in order to prevent losses resulting from price fluctuations. As a means of maintaining an even level of staple prices, the Federal Farm Board created (1930) the **Cotton Stabilization Corp.,** the **Grain Stabilization Corp.,** the **Wool Marketing Corp.,** and similar bodies for the purpose of making purchases in the open market. However, the price support program did not succeed, partly because farmers were reluctant to reduce their acreage. In 1931 the Board terminated its purchasing program; in 1933, after spending more than $180 million, it went out of existence.

PANIC OF 1929. (For the boom, 1922–29, fed by unprecedented securities speculation, see p. 539.) The Wall Street stock market crash (Oct.–Nov.) was the overt inception of the worldwide Great

Depression. Severe breaks occurred on 24 Oct., when 13 million shares changed hands, and 29 Oct. (16 million shares traded). By 13 Nov. about $30 billion in the market value of listed stocks had been wiped out; by mid-1932 these losses had increased to *c.* $75 billion. (For the deepening depression, see p. 539.)

1930

3 July. VETERANS ADMINISTRA-TION ACT consolidated all Federal functions for ex-servicemen's relief in a single agency known as the Veterans Administration.

4 Nov. CONGRESSIONAL ELEC-TIONS. In their 1st setback since 1916, the Republicans lost eight seats in the Senate and their majority in the House. The vote on prohibition in states such as R.I., Ill., and Mass. pointed to lessening support for the 18th Amendment.

HOOVER RELIEF POLICY. Opposed to direct Federal relief for unemployed persons suffering from genuine distress, President Hoover advocated a policy of decentralized work relief. In Oct. he formulated a relief program that called for Federal leadership of a national voluntary effort by agencies operating on a self-help basis in state and local communities. His object was to "preserve the principles of individual and local responsibility." On 2 Dec. Hoover requested an appropriation of $100–$150 million for construction of public works. Hoover created national emergency relief organizations headed at various times by Walter S. Gifford, Newton D. Baker, and others. However, when early in 1932 unemployment rose to 10 million, Hoover approved the Relief and Construction Act (p. 339).

1931

19 Jan. WICKERSHAM REPORT. By 1929 it was clearly evident that the enforcement of the 18th Amendment had broken down, creating a set of serious social and political problems. In May 1929, President Hoover appointed a Law Observance and Enforcement Commission headed by former Attorney General George W. Wickersham (1858–1936) to conduct a survey to serve as the basis for formulating public policy on the 18th Amendment. In its report the Commission stated that effective enforcement was hindered by the lucrative returns of the illicit liquor traffic, by public antipathy or hostility, and by the belief that enforcement of the 18th Amendment ought to be the function of the Federal government alone rather than a joint Federal-state undertaking. The Commission opposed repeal of the Prohibition Amendment; a majority of the Commission, however, favored its revision. In submitting the report to Congress (20 Jan.), President Hoover stated that he did not favor repeal.

VETERANS' BONUS. As the depression deepened, veterans' groups demanded immediate enactment of a bill authorizing a loan of 50% on the adjusted compensation ("bonus") certificates provided for by the act of 1924. Congress passed such a bill but Hoover vetoed it (26 Feb.) on grounds that it would be a blow to government economy and benefit many veterans not actually in distress. Congress passed the bill (27 Feb.) over his veto. Later in the year Democratic Congressional leaders proposed that the entire bonus be paid in cash. The pressure for legislative approval resulted in the "Bonus March" on Washington in 1932.

1932

2 Feb. RECONSTRUCTION FINANCE CORPORATION. President Hoover advocated an economic recovery program based on the assumption that government loans to banks and railroads would check deflation in agriculture and industry and ultimately restore the levels of employment and purchasing power. He proposed to Congress (8 Dec. 1931) the creation of a government lending agency with authority to issue tax-exempt bonds and with wide powers to extend credit. The Senate (11 Jan.) and the House (15 Jan.) passed the measure establishing the Reconstruction Finance Corporation, capitalized at $500 million and authorized to borrow to the extent of $2 billion to provide emergency financing for banking institutions, life insurance companies, building and loan societies, railroads, and farm mortgage associations. It was also empowered to subscribe the capital for government-owned corporations. The measure was signed by President Hoover on 22 Jan. The RFC was established on 2 Feb. with **Charles G. Dawes** as its head. Within 6 months it had authorized a total of $1.2 billion in loans to about 5,000 life insurance companies, agricultural credit corporations, and other financial institutions.

27 Feb. GLASS-STEAGALL ACT, a credit expansion measure, broadened the acceptability of commercial paper for rediscount by the Federal Reserve System and made available for industrial and business needs about $750 million of the government gold supply hitherto used to support the currency. This act was designed to counteract the contraction of credit due to foreign withdrawals and the domestic hoarding of gold and currency.

7 July. The House, 202–157, passed the Wagner-Garner Bill to extend the work of Federal employment agencies to states which did not sponsor such units. The Senate passed it (9 July), 43–31. President Hoover vetoed the measure (11 July) on the ground that it would interfere with state control over unemployment problems.

21 July. RELIEF AND CONSTRUCTION ACT extended the scope and functions of the RFC and authorized it to incur a total indebtedness of $3 billion. The RFC was empowered to provide $1.5 billion in loans for the construction by state and local agencies of public works of a self-liquidating character, and to furnish $300 million in temporary loans to states unable to finance the relief of economic distress. The act also broadened the powers of the RFC to assist agriculture.

22 July. FEDERAL HOME LOAN BANK ACT, a measure recommended to Congress by President Hoover (8 Dec. 1931), established a 5-man Home Loan Bank Board and created a series of discount banks for home mortgages that pro-

vided for home owners a service similar to that performed for commercial interests by the Federal Reserve discount facilities. It authorized the establishment of 8 to 12 banks set up in different parts of the country with a total capital of $125 million. Eligible for membership in the system were building and loan associations, savings banks, and insurance companies. The measure was designed to reduce foreclosures, stimulate residential construction (and thus increase employment), and encourage home ownership by providing the facilities for long-term loans payable in installments.

28–29 July. "BONUS ARMY." The demand for the immediate cashing of adjusted compensation certificates in full provided the impetus behind the "Bonus March" on Washington, D.C. About 1,000 ex-servicemen descended on the national capital (29 May) with the avowed purpose of remaining there until Congress authorized the cash payment. Other groups of veterans who arrived in June from all parts of the country brought the total number in the "Bonus Expeditionary Force" to an estimated 17,000. Many camped on the Anacostia Flats, on the edge of the city, and others made their homes in shacks and unused government buildings near the Capitol.

The House (15 June) passed the **Patman Bonus Bill** providing for the issuance of $2.4 billion in fiat money to pay off the remainder of the soldiers' bonus certificates. The Senate (17 June) defeated the measure. The government then provided funds for returning the veterans to their homes. Most of the ex-servicemen departed, but about 2,000 refused to disband. An attempt by the Washington police to evict them forcibly resulted in the death of 2 veterans and 2 policemen. President Hoover called out Federal troops (28 July), who completed the removal of the veterans with the use of infantry, cavalry, and tanks.

PRESIDENTIAL CAMPAIGN. The Socialist Labor Party Convention met at New York (30 Apr.) and nominated Verne L. Reynolds (N.Y.) for President and J. W. Aiken (Mass.) for Vice-President. The Socialist Party Convention met at Milwaukee (21 May) and nominated

Norman Thomas (N.Y.) for President and James H. Maurer (Pa.) for Vice-President. The Communist Party Convention met at Chicago and nominated (28 May) William Z. Foster (N.Y.) for President and James W. Ford, a Negro and native of Ala., for Vice-President.

The Prohibition Party Convention met at Indianapolis (5 July) and nominated William D. Upshaw (Ga.) for President and Frank S. Regan (Ill.) for Vice-President. The Farmer-Labor Party National Committee met at Omaha (9 July) and nominated Jacob S. Coxey (Ohio) for President. The Liberty Party Convention met at St. Louis and nominated (17 Aug.) W. H. Harvey (Ark.) for President and Frank B. Hemenway (Wash.) for Vice-President.

The Republican Party Convention met at Chicago (14 June) and renominated President **Hoover** (on the 1st ballot) and Vice-President **Charles Curtis.** The Republican platform called for a sharp reduction in government expenditures, a balanced budget, the maintenance and extension of the protective tariff to stabilize the home market, U.S. participation in an international monetary conference, the gold standard, restriction of immigration, revision of the Prohibition Amendment, and veterans' pensions for service-connected disabilities.

The Democratic Party Convention met at Chicago (27 June) and nominated Gov. **Franklin Delano Roosevelt** (N.Y.) for President on the 4th ballot (30 June) and **John Nance Garner** (Tex., 1868–) for Vice-President. Breaking the tradition that a Presidential nominee must await formal notification of his selection, Roosevelt flew from Albany to Chicago (2 July) and delivered an acceptance speech stressing the need for the reconstruction of the nation's economy. "I pledge you, I pledge myself," he told the convention, "to a **new deal** for the American people."

The Democratic platform advocated a drastic cut in government spending, a balanced budget, a competitive tariff for revenue, unemployment and old-age insurance under state laws, a sound currency, U.S. participation in an international monetary conference, repeal of the Prohibition Amendment, and veterans' pensions for service-connected disabilities.

It called for the "enactment of every constitutional measure that will aid the farmer to receive for basic farm commodities prices in excess of the cost of production." The platform advocated banking and financial reforms including the Federal regulation of holding companies, of exchanges trading in securities and commodities, and of the rates of interstate utility companies. It supported protection of the investing public by requiring full publicity and filing with the government of all offerings of foreign and domestic stocks and bonds.

During the campaign Roosevelt delivered numerous speeches in which he set forth a program of economic nationalism and social reconstruction shaped by him with the aid of a group of assistants (including **Rexford G. Tugwell, Raymond Moley,** and **Adolf A. Berle, Jr.**) known as the **"Brains Trust."** Roosevelt's appeal was made to the "forgotten man at the bottom of the economic pyramid" (a phrase he first used on 7 Apr., before his nomination). In an address delivered (23 Sept.) at the Commonwealth Club of California, at San Francisco, he said that the function of government was to meet "the problem of underconsumption, of adjusting production to consumption, of distributing wealth and products more equitably, of adapting existing economic organizations to the service of the people. . . ." However, such economic regulation was to be assumed "only as a last resort."

Hoover condemned Roosevelt's philosophy of government as a "radical departure" from the American way of life and called for the decentralization of government to permit the free expansion of private enterprise. Should the New Deal come to power, Hoover warned (31 Oct.), "the grass will grow in streets of a hundred cities, a thousand towns; the weeds will overrun the fields of millions of farms. . . ."

8 Nov. PRESIDENTIAL ELECTION. Popular vote: **Roosevelt,** 22,809,638; Hoover, 15,758,901; Thomas, 881,951; Foster, 102,785; Upshaw, 81,869; Harvey, 53,425; Reynolds, 33,276; Coxey, 7,309. Electoral vote: **Roosevelt,** 472; Hoover, 59. Roosevelt carried 42 states; Hoover carried Me., Vt., N.H., Conn.,

Pa., and Del. The Democrats secured majority control of both branches of Congress. The composition of the 73rd Congress was as follows: in the Senate, 60 Democrats, 35 Republicans, and 1 Farmer-Laborite; in the House, 310 Democrats, 117 Republicans, and 5 Farmer-Laborites.

1933

6 Feb. 20TH AMENDMENT to the Constitution, sponsored by George W. Norris (Neb.) and proposed on 2 Mar. 1932, was declared ratified. This so-called **"Lame Duck" Amendment** provided that effective 15 Oct. 1933 Congress would convene each year on 3 Jan. and that the terms of the President and Vice-President would begin on 20 Jan. following the national elections.

15 Feb. At Miami, Fla., an assassin, Giuseppe Zangara, fired 6 shots at close range at President-elect Roosevelt and the party in the latter's open touring car. Roosevelt was uninjured, but several others were wounded, including Mayor **Anton Cermak** of Chicago, who died on 6 Mar. Zangara was put to death in the electric chair at Raiford, Fla. (20 Mar.).

ECONOMIC CRISIS. In the interim between the Presidential election and the inauguration of President Roosevelt economic conditions reached gravely critical proportions. From Dec. 1932 to Mar. 1933 the index of industrial production dropped from 64 to an all-time low of 56. The nation's banking system revealed signs of alarming weakness as runs on banks became increasingly frequent and the hoarding of currency set in on a large scale. From 1930 until the eve of Roosevelt's inauguration, a total of 5,504 banks shut down. These banks had total deposits of $3,432,000,000. On 4 Feb. Louisiana declared a 1-day bank holiday. In Michigan, Gov. W. A. Comstock issued a proclamation (14 Feb.) calling for an 8-day bank holiday. By 2 Mar. 21 other states had suspended or drastically restricted banking operations. In New York, Gov. Herbert H. Lehman proclaimed (4 Mar.) a 2-day bank holiday. By Inauguration Day virtually every bank in the Union had been closed or placed under restrictions by state proclamations.

4 Mar. In his inaugural address, Roosevelt affirmed that "the only thing we have to fear is fear itself," and called for vigorous national leadership.

5 Mar. President Roosevelt summoned the 73rd Congress to convene in special session on 9 Mar. Invoking powers granted by the Trading with the Enemy Act of 1917, Roosevelt prepared a proclamation, effective 6 Mar., declaring a 4-day national banking holiday suspending all transactions in the Federal Reserve and other banks, trust companies, credit unions, and building and loan associations. In order to permit the continuance of business operations, the use of scrip was allowed (e.g., clearing house certificates or other evidence of claims against the assets of banks). The proclamation also placed an embargo for a like period (6–9 Mar.) on the export of gold, silver, and currency, and ordered that gold and silver could be exported or withdrawn only on a license from the Treasury Department. During the 1st 3 days after the banking holiday, 4,507 national banks and 567 state member banks were opened (i.e., about 75% of all the member banks of the Federal Reserve System). Within 2 weeks stock prices rose 15%, with a return flow of hoarded currency and a rapid return of gold and gold certificates to the Treasury and the Reserve banks.

12 Mar. 1ST "FIRESIDE CHAT." Initiating a practice that became customary during his administration, President Roosevelt addressed the American people by nationwide radio broadcast. On this occasion he explained the steps he had taken to meet the financial emergency.

THE NEW DEAL

INAUGURATION OF THE NEW DEAL. The special session of the 73rd Congress that met on 9 Mar. was called by the President to deal with the banking crisis, but Roosevelt decided to hold Congress in session to deal with unemployment and farm relief. By the time this session (later known as the "Hundred Days") ended its deliberations (16

June), it had enacted a comprehensive body of legislation affecting banking, industry, agriculture, labor, and unemployment relief. This was the initial phase of "1st New Deal" (1933–35), aimed primarily at relief and recovery.

9 Mar.–16 June. "HUNDRED DAYS" produced the following body of legislation:

9 Mar. EMERGENCY BANKING RELIEF ACT, introduced, passed, and approved on the same day, confirmed all of the emergency steps taken by the President and the Secretary of the Treasury since 4 Mar. The Senate vote was 73–7; the House vote was unanimous. The Act, affecting all national banks and Federal Reserve Banks, gave the President broad discretionary powers over transactions in credit, currency, gold, and silver, including foreign exchange. Gold hoarding and export were forbidden. A maximum penalty of $10,000 fine and 10 years in prison was provided. The Act permitted sound banks in the Federal Reserve System to open only under licenses from the Treasury Department; gave the Comptroller of the Currency authority to appoint conservators to care for the assets of insolvent national banks; authorized the Secretary of the Treasury to call in all gold and gold certificates in the country; enlarged the open market operations of the Federal Reserve banks; and empowered the RFC to subscribe to the preferred stock of national banks and trust companies. This Act, combined with the proclamation of 6 Mar., succeeded in checking the money panic.

20 Mar. ECONOMY ACT, requested by President Roosevelt on 10 Mar., was passed by the House (11 Mar.), 266–138, and by the Senate (15 Mar.), 62–13. It was designed to balance the budget of normal expenditures through (1) reductions of up to 15% in the salaries of government employees; (2) cuts in veterans' pensions and other allowances, particularly pension payments based on nonservice-connected disabilities; and (3) the reorganization of government agencies with a view to economy. Roosevelt estimated that the savings effected under this Act would total $500 million. The amount actually saved was about $243 million.

22 Mar. BEER-WINE REVENUE ACT, aimed at securing additional revenue, amended the Volstead Act to legalize wine, beer, lager beer, ale, and porter of 3.2% maximum alcoholic content by weight, or 4% by volume, and levied a tax of $5 per barrel of 31 gallons. The Act left to the states all regulatory and control measures, especially those relating to sale and distribution, and incorporated safeguards for states whose prohibition laws stipulated a lesser alcoholic content. The measure took effect on 7 Apr.

31 Mar. CIVILIAN CONSERVATION CORPS REFORESTATION RELIEF ACT, passed as an unemployment relief measure, established the Civilian Conservation Corps (CCC), authorized to provide work for 250,000 jobless male citizens between the ages of 18 to 25 in reforestation, road construction, the prevention of soil erosion, and national park and flood control projects under the direction of army officers. Work camps were established for those enrolled in the CCC; the youths received $30 per month, part of which went to dependents. 4 govt. depts. (War, Interior, Agriculture, and Labor) cooperated in carrying out the program. CCC had as many as 500,000 on its rolls at one time; by end of 1941 had employed over 2 million youths.

Apr.–May. BLACK-CONNERY-PERKINS WAGES AND HOURS BILL was displaced on the legislative program by the NIRA.

19 Apr. The U.S. officially abandoned the gold standard, causing a decline in the exchange value of the dollar abroad and an increase in the prices of commodities, silver, and stocks on American exchanges.

12 May. FEDERAL EMERGENCY RELIEF ACT created the Federal Emergency Relief Administration (FERA) and authorized an appropriation of $500 million, allotting half this amount as direct relief to the states and the balance for distribution on the basis of $1 of Federal aid for every $3 of state and local funds spent for relief. The FERA was based on the system of outright grants to states and municipalities, as differentiated from the loan policy initiated under the Hoover administration. The Act left the establishment of work relief projects for employables to state and local bodies and authorized the RFC to supply the funds for distribution to the states through a relief administrator. **Harry L. Hopkins** (N.Y., 1890–1946) was appointed Federal Relief Administrator.

12 May. AGRICULTURAL ADJUSTMENT ACT was designed to restore the purchasing power of agricultural producers. Its chief objects were the elimination of surplus crops of basic commodities through curtailed production and the establishment of **parity prices** for enumerated basic commodities. Parity price was based on the purchasing power of the farmers' dollar at the level of 100 cts. during the base period of 1909–14 for corn, cotton, wheat, rice, hogs, and dairy products; and the base period of 1919–29 for tobacco. The Act incorporated the **subsidy principle**: in return for voluntarily reducing acreage or crops, farmers were to be granted direct benefit or rental payments. The funds for such payments were to be derived from levies on the processors of specified farm products. The Act established the Agricultural Adjustment Administration (AAA). In 1934 the list of enumerated commodities was extended by the Jones-Connally Farm Relief Act and the Jones-Costigan Sugar Act.

The Act relieved the credit situation by providing for the refinancing of farm mortgages through the agency of the Federal Land Banks. In addition, the Thomas Amendment to this Act permitted the President to inflate the currency by the following means: devaluation of the gold content of the dollar, free coinage of silver at a ratio to gold determined by the President, and the issuance of paper currency to the amount of $3 billion. This last provision was never implemented by Roosevelt. The devaluation provision, however, enabled the President to make attempts to raise prices through control of the so-called "commodity dollar."

The processing tax and production control features of the Agricultural Adjustment Act were declared unconstitutional by the Supreme Court in *U.S.* v. *Butler* (1936).

18 May. TENNESSEE VALLEY AUTHORITY. During World War I the national government, at a cost of $145 million, built a large hydroelectric power plant and two munitions plants at Muscle Shoals, on the Tennessee River in Alabama. During the 20's the government unsuccessfully attempted to dispose of the Muscle Shoals facilities to private interests. Senator **George W. Norris** (Neb., p. 759) conducted a campaign to place the power resources of the Tennessee River at the service of the watershed's inhabitants, and to devote the World War I plants to the manufacture of fertilizer. On 25 May 1928 and again on 3 Mar. 1931 a group of legislators headed by Norris secured the passage of bills providing for government operation of Muscle Shoals, but the measures were vetoed by Presidents Coolidge and Hoover, respectively, on the ground that government operation would constitute competition with private enterprise. As governor of New York, Roosevelt sponsored and executed a statewide planning movement and helped to establish a state power authority. In Jan. 1933, he visited Muscle Shoals with a group of officials and experts. Before his accession to the Presidency, Roosevelt envisioned for the Tennessee River drainage basin and adjoining territory a program embracing not merely power development but a plan of regional development based on the control and use of water resources. Aimed at furthering the general social and economic welfare of the region, the program contemplated flood control, land reclamation, the prevention of soil erosion, afforestation, the elimination of marginal lands from cultivation, and the distribution and diversification of industry.

The aims of Roosevelt and Norris were embodied in the act establishing the **Tennessee Valley Authority** (TVA), an independent public corporation with a board of three directors (the initial board consisted of Arthur E. Morgan, chairman; Harcourt Morgan, and David E. Lilienthal). The TVA was authorized to construct dams and power plants and to develop the economic and social well-being of the Tennessee Valley region (covering the states of Tenn., N.C., Ky., Va., Miss., Ga., and Ala.). It was authorized to produce, distribute, and sell electric power and nitrogen fertilizers to the industry and people of the region, and to sell explosives to the Federal government. A "yardstick" for public utilities was embodied in the provisions for the construction of transmission lines to farms and villages not supplied with electricity at rates that were reasonable and fair, and for the selling of power to municipalities and other public bodies.

Between 1933 and 1944 9 main-river dams and many subsidiary ones were built along the water system. During World War II, TVA supplied the power facilities for the manufacture of munitions and aluminum and for the atom bomb plant at Oak Ridge, Tenn.

27 May. FEDERAL SECURITIES ACT was designed to compel full disclosure to investors of information relating to new securities issues publicly offered or sold through the mails or in interstate commerce. It required that with certain exceptions (e.g., Federal, state, and municipal bonds; railroad securities; securities of religious, charitable, and educational bodies) all new issues were to be registered with the Federal Trade Commission by the filing of sworn statements placed on public file (in 1934 this function was transferred to the Securities and Exchange Commission).

5 June. GOLD REPEAL JOINT RESOLUTION, another move for making the abandonment of the gold standard effective, canceled the gold clause in all Federal and private obligations and made contracts and debts payable in legal tender.

6 June. NATIONAL EMPLOYMENT SYSTEM ACT authorized a national employment system, established as the U.S. Employment Service, based on cooperation with states maintaining such agencies. It required matching of state appropriations for employment services.

13 June. HOME OWNERS REFINANCING ACT created the Home Owners Loan Corporation (HOLC), with a capital stock of $200 million and an author-ized issue of $2 billion in bonds, to refinance home mortgage debts for nonfarm owners. Refinancing was accomplished by the exchange of HOLC bonds for mortgages and all other obligations (up to a total of $14,000), which were then converted into a single first mortgage. The HOLC was also empowered to furnish cash advances for taxes, repair, and maintenance up to 50% of appraised values on unencumbered properties. By the time the HOLC terminated its activities in June 1936, it had made loans covering 1 million mortgages.

16 June. BANKING ACT OF 1933 (GLASS-STEAGALL ACT) created the **Federal Bank Deposit Insurance Corporation** for guaranteeing individual bank deposits under $5,000. It also extended the open-market activities of the Federal Reserve Board to enable it to prevent excessive speculation on credit; permitted branch banking; divorced deposit from investment affiliates; and widened the membership of the Federal Reserve System to include savings and industrial banks.

16 June. FARM CREDIT ACT was designed to facilitate short-term and medium-term credits for agricultural production and marketing, thereby refinancing farm mortgages on long terms at low interest. On 27 Mar. President Roosevelt had by executive decree consolidated in a single agency, the Farm Credit Administration (FCA), the functions of all Federal units dealing with agricultural credit (e.g., the Federal Farm Board, the Federal Farm Loan Board).

16 June. EMERGENCY RAILROAD TRANSPORTATION ACT, applying to carriers and subsidiaries subject to the Interstate Commerce Act, was designed to avoid unnecessary duplication of services and facilities; to promote financial reorganization of the carriers; and to provide for the study of other means of improving conditions pertaining to rail transportation. The Act repealed the "recapture" clause of the Transportation Act of 1920, placed railroad holding companies under the supervision of the Interstate Commerce Commission, provided for a simpler rule of rate making, and created the office of Federal Co-

Tennessee Valley Authority (TVA)

ordinator of Transportation (a post to which **Joseph B. Eastman** was appointed).

16 June. NATIONAL INDUSTRIAL RECOVERY ACT (called the NIRA) was designed to revive industrial and business activity and to reduce unemployment. It was based on the principle of industrial self-regulation, operating under government supervision through a system of fair competition codes. The act created the National Recovery Administration (NRA) and formalized the fair trade codes that had been used by many industrial and trade associations in the period after World War I. Under the NIRA, fair competition codes drawn up by such associations and approved by the President were enforceable by law. The President was also empowered to prescribe codes for industries and to make agreements or approve voluntary agreements. Actions under codes and agreements were exempt from the operations of the antitrust laws. The courts could issue injunctions against violators. When business pressure compelled the administration to abandon the Black-Connery-Perkins Bill, provision for labor was made in Section 7a of the NIRA guaranteeing labor's right "to organize and bargain collectively through representatives of their own choosing." Gen. **Hugh S. Johnson** (1882–1942) was appointed (16 June) head of the NRA, an agency which ultimately affected about 500 fields and a total of 22 million employees. Sen. Robert F. Wagner (N.Y.) was appointed chairman of the **National Labor Board,** established (5 Aug.) by the President under NIRA to enforce the right of collective bargaining.

While the NRA was initially successful, code violations soon became increasingly frequent; complaints of cutthroat competition and unfair price fixing became numerous. The National Recovery Review Board, established on 19 Feb. 1934, reported (21 May 1934) that the NRA was encouraging monopoly and cartelization to the detriment of the small businessman. The Supreme Court held the NIRA unconstitutional in *Schechter Poultry Corp.* v. *U.S.* (1935).

Title II of the NIRA established the **Public Works Administration** (PWA) for the construction of roads, public buildings, and other projects, for which a fund of $3,300 million was authorized. Secretary of the Interior **Harold L. Ickes** (1874–1952) was named (16 June) to head the agency. The PWA was created for the purpose of increasing employment and business activity by means of "pump priming" (i.e., the raising of popular consuming power). During its recovery phase, the PWA spent a total of more than $4,250 million on some 34,000 public projects.

16 June. Special session of the 73rd Congress adjourned.

18 Oct. COMMODITY CREDIT CORPORATION, an agency organized under the AAA with a capitalization of $3 million (increased in 1936 to $100 million), was authorized to use RFC funds for extending loans to farmers on their crops. Its purpose was to support farm prices by enabling producers to retain commodities. At the outset, loans were extended chiefly to cotton farmers; as a result cotton prices were bolstered.

22 Oct. "COMMODITY DOLLAR." President Roosevelt announced that he had authorized the RFC to establish a government market for gold newly mined in the U.S. and to buy and sell gold on the world market if necessary in order to enable the government to take "in its own hands the control of the gold value of our dollar."

The new gold policy was put into effect on 25 Oct., when the government set the price at $31.36 an ounce (as compared with $29.01 an ounce on the world market on 21 Oct.). The price was subsequently increased until it reached $34.06 on 18 Dec. The gold value of the dollar was set at 66 cts. This forced devaluation of the dollar, however, did not accomplish its object of raising farm commodity prices above the world level. Moreover, the measure provoked complaints from foreign nations (which feared that cheaper American goods gave U.S. exporters an unfair advantage in world trade); brought "sound money" elements in the Democratic party into open conflict with the administration; and ultimately led inflationist groups to increase their pressure for silver legislation.

8 Nov. CIVIL WORKS ADMINISTRA-TION (CWA) was established as an emergency unemployment relief program for the purpose of putting 4 million jobless persons to work on Federal, state, and local make-work projects. **Harry L. Hopkins** was appointed (8 Nov.) as its administrator. Funds were allocated from FERA and PWA appropriations supplemented by local governments. The CWA was created to offset a drop in the business revival of mid-1933 and to cushion economic distress over the winter of 1933–34. The CWA was terminated in Mar. 1934, and transferred its functions to the FERA. Of the more than $933 million spent on 180,000 work projects, more than $740 million went directly into wages and salaries.

5 Dec. 21ST AMENDMENT to the Constitution, proposed on 20 Feb. 1933 and providing for the **repeal of the 18th (Prohibition) Amendment,** was declared ratified.

21 Dec. Acting under the Thomas Amendment to the Agricultural Adjustment Act, President Roosevelt ordered the Treasury to buy at 64½ cts. an ounce (21½ cts. above the prevailing market price) all the silver mined in the U.S. during the ensuing 4-yr. period.

1934

30 Jan. GOLD RESERVE ACT OF 1934 was designed to give the government full control over dollar devaluation and to increase commodity prices without relying on inflationary measures. The Act empowered the President to do the following: to set the limits for devaluation of the dollar at from 50 to 60 cts. in relation to its gold content; to change the value within these limits from time to time, as deemed necessary by him; to impound in the Treasury the gold stocks held by the Federal reserve banks; to assure to the government any profit that might accrue to the Treasury from an increase in the value of gold; and to use part of this profit to set up a fund (the Exchange Stabilization Fund) of $2 billion with which to stabilize the dollar. By proclamation (31 Jan.) Roosevelt fixed the value of the dollar at 59.06 cts.

31 Jan. FARM MORTGAGE REFINANCING ACT established the Federal Farm Mortgage Corporation (FFMC) under the Farm Credit Administration and authorized it to issue up to $2 billion in bonds guaranteed in principal and interest. The purpose of the FFMC was to further the refinancing of farm debts by exchanging its bonds for consolidated farm loan bonds and investing them directly in mortgage loans.

2 Feb. EXPORT-IMPORT BANK, established by President Roosevelt under powers granted to the RFC and NRA, was created to encourage the flow of overseas commerce by financing trade with foreign nations in the following ways: short-term credits in connection with the exportation of agricultural commodities, extension of longer-term credit to American firms desiring to export industrial manufactures, and loans to American exporters where foreign governments failed to provide their own nationals with sufficient exchange to permit them to meet dollar obligations. Two banks were set up, one to provide credits for trading with the Soviet Union, which had recently received formal diplomatic recognition by the U.S.; another (12 Mar.) to provide credit facilities for trading with Cuba and ultimately other foreign nations. Both banks were consolidated in a single bank in 1936.

15 Feb. CIVIL WORKS EMERGENCY RELIEF ACT authorized $950 million for use by the FERA until the end of the fiscal year 1935 for operating the program of civil works and direct relief. This program emerged (1935) as the Works Progress Administration (WPA). Under the Emergency Work Relief Program authorized by the Act of 15 Feb., a total of 2,500,000 unemployed were on the rolls by Jan. 1935, when direct relief was returned to state and local governments.

23 Feb. CROP LOAN ACT authorized the Farm Credit Administration to extend loans to agricultural producers in 1934 for crop production and harvesting. A fund of $40 million was set up for this purpose. Approximately $37,900,000 was loaned.

27 Mar. VINSON NAVAL PARITY ACT authorized the building of a full-treaty-strength navy within the limits set by the Washington Naval Limitation Treaty of 1922 and the London Naval Limitation Treaty of 1930. It provided for the construction of 100 warships and more than 1,000 airplanes over a 5-yr. period. Congress, however, did not appropriate sufficient funds, and until 1938 naval construction was carried out chiefly on a replacement basis.

28 Mar. INDEPENDENT OFFICES APPROPRIATIONS ACT represented the 1st defeat President Roosevelt sustained at the hands of Congress. The Senate and House passed (26 Mar.) the Independent Offices Bill restoring the cuts made under the Economy Act of 1933. It increased salaries of government employees by $125 million and the allowances of World War I veterans by $228 million. President Roosevelt vetoed the bill (27 Mar.) on the ground of economy. The House (310–72, 27 Mar.) and the Senate (63–27, 28 Mar.) overrode the veto.

7 Apr. JONES-CONNALLY FARM RELIEF ACT extended the list of enumerated basic agricultural commodities subject to the Agricultural Adjustment Act, adding barley, flax, peanuts, grain sorghums, rye, and beef and dairy cattle.

21 Apr. COTTON CONTROL ACT (BANKHEAD ACT) provided for the compulsory reduction of surplus cotton crops through the licensing of individual producers who in turn received benefit payments. The Act, a departure from the voluntary principle of the AAA, authorized the fixing of a national limitation on the cotton crop and provided for the allocation of crop and marketing quotas for cotton-growing states, counties, and farmers. A tax of not less than 5 cts. a pound was authorized for production in excess of stipulated quotas.

27 Apr. HOME OWNERS LOAN ACT guaranteed the principal and interest of the $2 billion in bonds authorized for the refinancing of home mortgages. From the funds made available as a result of the guarantee, the HOLC was enabled to extend further assistance for the repair and maintenance of homes and to pro-vide funds to savings and loans associations operating under Federal sponsorship.

9 May. JONES-COSTIGAN SUGAR ACT extended the list of enumerated basic crops subject to the Agricultural Adjustment Act to include sugar cane and sugar beets, and authorized benefit payments allocated from funds derived from a processing tax on sugar. It sought to stabilize the price of sugar by authorizing limitation on the national production of these sugar crops and empowered the Secretary of Agriculture to put all sugar imports on a quota basis. The decision of the Supreme Court in *U.S.* v. *Butler* (1936) invalidated the tax features of this act.

NYE MUNITIONS INVESTIGATION. The Senate voted (12 Apr.) an inquiry into the manufacture and traffic in arms in the U.S. Sen. **Gerald P. Nye** (N.D.) was appointed (23 Apr.) chairman of the Senate Munitions Investigating Committee, whose public hearings stressed the heavy profits made by American financiers and armament makers during World War I and sought to show, although without conclusive evidence, that the U.S. entry into World War I was due to the covert pressures they exerted. The activities of the Nye Committee, which continued until 1936, strengthened isolationist sentiment and set the domestic background for the neutrality legislation of 1935, 1936, and 1937 (see p. 328).

18 May. CRIME CONTROL ACTS. To counteract the widespread rise of racketeering, kidnaping, and other forms of crime, 6 new crime laws were enacted, among others empowering the Federal government to punish persons assaulting, resisting, killing, or interfering with Federal agents performing their law-enforcement duties and authorizing the death penalty for kidnapers taking their victims across state lines (the last as a result of the kidnaping and murder of the son of Charles A. and Anne Morrow Lindbergh (1 Mar. 1932). The Federal criminal code was further strengthened by the Crime Prevention Compact Act (16 June) which permitted the states to enter into compacts for the prevention of crime and the enforcement of criminal laws.

24 May. MUNICIPAL BANKRUPTCY ACT permitted cities and other local government units to petition the Federal courts for the ensuing 2 years to approve plans for readjusting their debt burden, providing that holders of 51% of outstanding obligations gave their consent.

6 June. SECURITIES EXCHANGE ACT provided for Federal regulation of the operations of exchanges dealing in securities and for the correction of unfair practices in the securities markets. It established the **Securities and Exchange Commission** (SEC) and authorized that unit to license stock exchanges. It made trading in securities subject to the regulations of the SEC and prohibited price manipulation. It empowered the Federal Reserve Board to regulate the use of credit in financing trading in securities by prescribing regulations governing margin requirements (a move designed to curb speculation).

7 June. CORPORATE BANKRUPTCY ACT permitted the reorganization of corporations, provided that at least two thirds of their creditors consented, and stipulated that a petition for reorganization might be filed in court by a creditor or stockholder if approved by at least one fourth of other stockholders (10% where the corporation was not insolvent but unable to meet maturing obligations).

12 June. FARM MORTGAGE FORECLOSURE ACT authorized the Land Bank Commissioner to extend loans to farmers to enable the recovery of farm properties owned by them prior to foreclosure.

15 June. NATIONAL GUARD ACT made that military organization a part of the Army of the U.S. in time of war or during a national emergency declared by Congress.

19 June. COMMUNICATIONS ACT abolished the Federal Radio Commission and established the **Federal Communications Commission** (FCC) for the regulation of interstate and foreign communications by telegraph, cable, and radio. The act transferred to the FCC the authority of the Interstate Commerce Commission for control of communications,

and imposed new regulations for the control of radio broadcasting.

19 June. SILVER PURCHASE ACT, a compromise measure passed to meet the demands for additional inflation voiced by farmer and silver interests in Congress, empowered the President to increase the monetary value of the Treasury's silver holdings until they should reach one third the value of its gold stocks; to nationalize silver stocks and purchases of domestic and foreign silver; and to impose a 50% profits tax on certain transfers of silver in order to preclude a windfall for silver speculators. By Presidential order (9 Aug.) the Treasury was directed to buy all silver in the U.S. at 50 cts. an ounce, all newly mined silver at 64.64 cts. an ounce, and to pay for it with silver certificates at the rate of $1.29 an ounce (thereby placing silver on a 27–1 ratio with gold). This move benefited U.S. silver producers.

19 June. LABOR DISPUTES JOINT RESOLUTION established the National Labor Relations Board, replacing the National Labor Board, 1933.

27 June. RAILROAD RETIREMENT ACT OF 1934 was declared unconstitutional in *Railroad Retirement Board* v. *Alton R.R. Co.* (1935).

27 June. CROSSER-DILL RAILWAY LABOR ACT (p. 553).

28 June. FEDERAL FARM BANKRUPTCY ACT (FRAZIER-LEMKE FARM BANKRUPTCY ACT), designed to prevent foreclosures, provided additional relief to farmers by enabling them to secure credit extensions. Provision was made whereby farmers could repurchase their properties at a newly appraised value with small annual payments, at an interest rate of 1%, distributed over a 6-yr. period. In the event creditors opposed such a settlement, farmers could retain possession on fair and reasonable terms for 5 yrs., during which time bankruptcy proceedings were suspended. This act was declared unconstitutional in the case of *Louisville Joint Stock Land Bank* v. *Radford* (1935).

28 June. NATIONAL HOUSING ACT was designed to stimulate residential construction, promote improvement in housing standards, and create a sound system of home financing. It established the Federal Housing Administration (FHA) for the purpose of insuring loans made by banks, trust companies, building and loan associations, and other private lending institutions for new construction, repairs, alterations, and improvements. The Act, which enabled the modernization of farm properties and of small business plants and equipment, increased the borrowing power of the HOLC to $3 billion.

28 June. TOBACCO CONTROL ACT (similar to the Cotton Control Act of 1934) authorized a compulsory production quota system for tobacco planters and subjected to an ad valorem tax producers who did not agree to crop reduction.

6 Nov. CONGRESSIONAL ELECTIONS gave the Democrats a gain of 9 seats in the Senate and 9 seats in the House. The 74th Congress was the 1st to convene (3 Jan. 1935) under the provisions of the 20th Amendment.

1935

4 Jan. 2ND NEW DEAL. In his annual message to Congress, President Roosevelt outlined a program of **social reform** that signalized the launching of the 2nd New Deal, designating 3 major goals: security of livelihood through the better use of national resources; security against unemployment, old age, illness, and dependency; and slum clearance and better housing. He also recommended a national works program for absorbing the needy unemployed. The chief beneficiaries of the 2nd New Deal were labor and the smaller farmers.

8 Apr. EMERGENCY RELIEF APPROPRIATION ACT signalized the withdrawal of the Federal government from the arena of direct relief, which was left to the states and local communities, and provided for the establishment of a large-scale national works program for jobless employables, who were required to meet a means test in order to qualify for work relief. Established as the major agency of the program was the **Works Progress Administration** (WPA), which beginning

in 1939 was called the **Works Projects Administration. Harry L. Hopkins** was appointed (6 May) administrator of the WPA. About 85% of the funds spent on WPA projects went directly into wages and salaries. Beginning in 1936 the "security wage" of WPA workers was based on the prevailing hourly rate, at reduced hours of work (the average monthly maximum schedule ranging between 120 and 140 hours). By Mar. 1936, the WPA rolls reached a total of more than 3,400,000 persons; after initial cuts in June 1939, it averaged 2,300,000 monthly; and by 30 June 1943, when it was officially terminated, the WPA had employed more than 8,500,000 different persons on 1,410,000 individual projects, and had spent about $11 billion. While most of the projects were geared to the employment of manual labor, provision was made by way of arts projects for writers, actors, artists, and musicians. In addition to the WPA, other participating agencies in the national works program included the Public Works Administration, the Civilian Conservation Corps, and the National Youth Administration. During its 8-yr. history, the WPA built 651,087 miles of highways, roads, and streets; and constructed, repaired, or improved 124,031 bridges, 125,110 public buildings, 8,192 parks, and 853 airport landing fields. It operated community recreation and educational centers and carried out numerous surveys of Federal, state, and local archives. The WPA was attacked on the grounds of inefficiency, extravagance, waste, and political corruption. Defenders pointed to its constructive achievements and to the rise in national purchasing power.

27 Apr. SOIL CONSERVATION ACT established the Soil Conservation Service as a permanent unit of the Department of Agriculture for the control and prevention of soil erosion.

1 May. RESETTLEMENT ADMINISTRATION (known as the RA) was established by executive order under powers granted by the Emergency Relief Appropriation Act of 1935. Undersecretary of Agriculture **Rexford G. Tugwell** was appointed administrator. The general objectives of the RA included the improvement of the conditions of impoverished farm families that had not been materially aided by the AAA, and the prevention of waste due to unprofitable farming operations and improper land use. The RA was authorized to administer projects involving resettlement of destitute or low-income families from rural and urban areas, or soil erosion, flood control, stream pollution, and reforestation; and to grant loans to enable the purchase of farm lands and equipment by smaller farmers, farm tenants, sharecroppers, or farm laborers. Among the activities of the RA were the establishment of subsistence homestead communities and the construction of suburban communities for low-income city workers—"Greenbelt towns," including Greenbelt (near Washington, D.C.), Greenhills (near Cincinnati), and Greendale (near Milwaukee). The functions of the RA were absorbed by the Farm Security Administration in 1937.

11 May. RURAL ELECTRIFICATION ADMINISTRATION (called the REA) was established by Executive order under powers granted by the Emergency Relief Appropriation Act of 1935. Its purpose was to formulate and administer a program of generating and distributing electricity in isolated rural areas which were not served by private utilities. The REA was authorized to lend the entire cost of constructing light and power lines in such areas, on liberal terms of 3% interest, with amortization extended over a 20-yr. period. Priority was given to publicly owned plants distributing electricity.

22 May. VETO OF THE PATMAN BONUS BILL. The Patman Bill provided for the full and immediate payment in cash by issuance of $2,200 million greenbacks of the adjusted compensation certificates held by World War I veterans, which, under the act of 1924, were not due to mature until 1945. President Roosevelt, establishing a precedent by appearing before a joint session of Congress to deliver a veto message in person, rejected the bill, chiefly on the grounds that enactment of the measure would spur inflation and increase the national deficit. The House (322–98, 22 May) overrode the veto, but the Senate (54–40, 23 May) sustained it.

27 May. The NIRA was invalidated by the Supreme Court decision in the case of *Schechter Poultry Corp.* v. *U.S.* (p. 498).

7 June. NATIONAL RESOURCES COMMITTEE was created by Executive order under powers granted by the Emergency Relief Appropriation Act of 1935 for the purpose of collecting and preparing plans, data, and information relating to the planned development and use of land, water, and other national resources. The successor to the National Resources Board set up on 30 June 1934, it later became known as the National Resources Planning Board and was entrusted with the preparation of long-range plans for the development of national resources and the stabilization of employment. It was terminated on 1 July 1943 upon failure of Congress to appropriate further funds.

26 June. NATIONAL YOUTH ADMINISTRATION (called the NYA) was established by Executive order under powers granted by the Emergency Relief Appropriation Act of 1935. It was created as a part of the WPA and was placed under the direction of **Aubrey Williams**. The purpose of the NYA was to administer a work-relief and employment program for persons between the ages of 16 and 25, chiefly from relief families and no longer in regular full-time attendance at school, and to provide part-time employment for needy school, college, and graduate students to help them continue their education. By 1936, some 600,000 persons were engaged in NYA activities, with a peak in 1939–40 when about 750,000 students in 1,700 colleges and universities and more than 28,000 secondary schools received NYA benefits. In 1939 the NYA was transferred to the Federal Security Agency, and in 1942 became part of the War Manpower Commission. During 1941–43 it trained workers for national defense activities at an average rate of 30,000 a month. The NYA was terminated Sept. 1943.

5 July. NATIONAL LABOR RELATIONS ACT (WAGNER-CONNERY

ACT) created a new National Labor Relations Board (NLRB) with power to determine appropriate collective bargaining units subject to elections it supervised at the request of the workers, to certify the duly chosen trade union, and to take testimony about unfair employer practices and issue cease and desist orders. Sec. 7 upheld the right of employees to join labor organizations and to bargain collectively through representatives of their own choosing. Sec. 8 defined unfair labor practices on the employers' part. The constitutionality of the act was upheld by the Supreme Court (Mar. 1937, p. 498). This legislation was soon complemented by state "Wagner Acts."

9 Aug. MOTOR CARRIER ACT placed buses and trucks engaged in interstate commerce under the authority of the Interstate Commerce Commission, which was empowered to regulate finances, labor, and minimum and maximum rates.

ANTI-NEW DEAL COALITION. Dissatisfaction with the social, fiscal, and other aspects of the New Deal led to the emergence of several organized antiadministration groups during 1934–35. The **Liberty League** (est. Aug. 1934), which drew its following from industrialists, financiers, corporation lawyers, conservative Democrats, and others, attacked the New Deal as a departure from the Constitution and actively opposed the passage of such measures as the Wagner-Connery Labor Relations Bill and the Wealth Tax Bill. The **Old Age Revolving Pension** scheme proposed by Dr. Francis E. **Townsend** of Long Beach, Calif., called for payments of $200 a month to persons 60 yrs. of age and over, the pensions to be drawn from a national 2% tax on commercial transactions. The **Share-Our-Wealth** movement inspired by Senator **Huey P. Long** (La., b.1893; assassinated at Baton Rouge, 8 Sept. 1935) demanded that the Federal government make "Every Man a King" by guaranteeing a minimum annual income of $5,000 to every family. Rev. **Gerald L. K. Smith** succeeded to Long's leadership of the Share-Our-Wealth clubs and formed an alliance with the Townsend movement, later to include Rev. **Charles E. Coughlin**, of Royal Oak, Mich., who in 1934

organized the **National Union for Social Justice.** Coughlin advocated a program of social reform that was specific in its support of silver inflation but vague on most other points. His radio speeches, directed against international bankers, Communists, labor unions, and the Roosevelt administration, attracted a national audience. The Smith-Townsend-Coughlin coalition gained in strength during 1935 and in 1936 emerged as a 3rd-party movement. However, it never succeeded in uniting under a single and continuous leadership.

14 Aug. SOCIAL SECURITY ACT (an administration measure motivated in part by an attempt to win over the Townsend-Long following) created the Social Security Board as a general administrative agency and provided for the following in relation to unemployment compensation, old-age security, and various social services: (1) Establishment of a cooperative Federal-State system of **unemployment compensation** designed to promote substantial uniformity of unemployment insurance plans among the various states and to invite the states to legislate in this field. The Act levied a Federal tax on total payrolls of employers of 8 or more workers (with certain exceptions, including agricultural laborers) equal to 1% in 1936, 2% in 1937, and 3% thereafter. Each state was to administer its own insurance system, and was to receive credit up to 90% of the Federal tax. The Act authorized grants to the states to enable them to meet administrative costs in providing unemployment insurance. (2) A tax for **old-age and survivors' insurance** to be levied in equal amounts upon all employers and employees (with specified exceptions) commencing at 1% in 1937 and gradually increasing to 3% in 1949. This part of the Act was exclusively Federal in scope and character. Out of the national fund created by these taxes the Federal government was to pay to retired individuals 65 yrs. of age and over a retirement pension (beg. 1 Jan. 1942) ranging from a minimum of $10 to a maximum of $85 per month, depending upon the number of working years during which the employee contributed. (3) Authorized money grants to states to help them meet the cost of **old-age pensions allowed under state laws** to aged persons in need of relief, the grants to match the amount contributed by the state, with a maximum Federal contribution of $15 per month for each individual plus a small amount for administrative purposes. (4) Authorized money grants to the states to assist them in relief of the destitute blind and of homeless, crippled, dependent, and delinquent children, and in services such as public health work, vocational rehabilitation, and maternity and infant care. The tax features of the Act were upheld by the Supreme Court in *Steward Machine Co.* v. *Davis* and *Helvering et al* v. *Davis* (1937).

23 Aug. BANKING ACT OF 1935 included the following provisions: (1) The title of the Federal Reserve Board changed to the Board of Governors of the Federal Reserve System, the board's ex-officio members were eliminated, and its membership increased from 6 to 7, with 1 member to serve as chairman for 4 yrs.; (2) control over the regulation of credit vested in an Open Market Committee consisting of the Board of Governors and 5 representatives of the Federal reserve banks; (3) purchase of government securities by the Federal reserve banks confined to open market operations; (4) Board of Governors empowered to increase the reserve requirements of member banks up to a limit of twice existing maximums; (5) Federal reserve banks permitted to lend to member banks on time or demand notes with maturities not exceeding 4 mos.; (6) national banks authorized to make real estate loans.

28 Aug. PUBLIC UTILITY HOLDING COMPANY ACT (WHEELER-RAYBURN ACT), designed to counteract the monopolistic public utility holding company device for controlling gas and electric operating companies, vested in the Federal Power Commission authority to regulate interstate transmission of electric power; in the Federal Trade Commission authority over gas; in the SEC authority over financial practices of such holding companies. The Act restricted electric and gas holding companies to operations as single and concentrated systems confined to a single area, and called for simplification of the corporate structure of utility holding companies in order to eliminate pyramiding. The **"death sentence"** clause set a term of 5 yrs., at the end of which any holding company which could not demonstrate its localized, useful, and efficient character would be dissolved. In compliance public utility holding companies had by 1952 divested 753 affiliates, with assets of $10.3 billion.

29 Aug. FARM MORTGAGE MORATORIUM ACT OF 1935 (FRAZIER-LEMKE ACT OF 1935) was passed following the Supreme Court decision invalidating the Federal Farm Bankruptcy Act of 1934. It provided for a 3-yr. moratorium against seizure for farmers who secured court permission, thus enabling debt-burdened farmers to keep possession of their properties by paying a fair and reasonable rental determined by the court.

29 Aug. WAGNER-CROSSER RAILROAD RETIREMENT ACT provided pensions for railroad employees after retirement and established a **Railroad Retirement Board** of 3 members appointed by the President to administer the law; amended and incorporated in the Railroad Retirement Act of 1937 (24 June).

30 Aug. GUFFEY-SNYDER BITUMINOUS COAL STABILIZATION (or CONSERVATION) ACT, popularly known as the "little NRA," created the **Bituminous Coal Labor Board** and the **National Bituminous Coal Commission** to administer production quota, price-fixing, and labor regulations based on the NRA soft coal code. The act sought to stabilize the bituminous coal-mining industry. A 15% tax based on the market value of coal was levied on producers, with 90% of the tax being remitted to producers complying with the code. The act was invalidated by the Supreme Court decision in the case of *Carter* v. *Carter Coal Co. et al.* (1936) and was succeeded by the Guffey-Vinson Act (1937).

30 Aug. REVENUE ACT OF 1935 (WEALTH TAX ACT). In his message to Congress on tax revision (19 June), President Roosevelt declared: "Our revenue laws have operated in many ways to the unfair advantage of the few, and they have done little to prevent an unjust concentration of wealth and economic power." His recommendations were embodied in the Revenue Act, which increased the surtax rate on individual incomes over $50,000 and affected individual estates of decedents over $40,000. Taxes on individual incomes above $1 million were graduated steeply to 75% on income in excess of $5 million. Although an inheritance tax feature proposed by the President was eliminated from the bill, estate and gift tax rates were increased. In place of the existing uniform tax of 13¾ %, income tax rates for small corporations were lowered to 12½%; rates on all corporation incomes above $50,000 raised to 15%; additional taxes of 6% were levied on profits in excess of 10%, graduated to 12% on profits in excess of 15%.

1936

6 Jan. The Agricultural Adjustment Act was invalidated by the Supreme Court in *U.S.* v. *Butler* (p. 498)

24 Jan. ADJUSTED COMPENSATION ACT. A bill calling for full and immediate cash payment of adjusted service (bonus) certificates held by World War I veterans demanding payment before the maturity date (1945) was passed by the Senate (20 Jan.) and the House (22 Jan.), but was vetoed by President Roosevelt (24 Jan.). Both branches of Congress immediately overrode his veto. The Act authorized the issuance of 9-yr. interest-bearing bonds convertible into cash at any time. On 15 June more than $1,500 million in bonus bonds were distributed to some 3 million World War I veterans.

29 Feb. SOIL CONSERVATION AND DOMESTIC ALLOTMENT ACT, designed to replace the invalidated AAA, enabled the continued restriction of agricultural output, not by contracts with farmers for the control of crop production, but by **benefit payments** to growers who practiced soil conservation in cooperation with the government program. Farmers participating in the program through their county agricultural associations leased to the government land

withdrawn from use for soil-depleting crops (such as corn, cotton, tobacco, wheat, and oats), and in return received compensation for their efforts to check wastage of fertility and erosion. Payments depended upon acreage withdrawn from soil-depleting crop production and turned over to soil-conserving crops. Provision was made whereby sharecroppers and tenants received part of the payments.

20 June. FEDERAL ANTI-PRICE DISCRIMINATION ACT (ROBINSON-PATMAN ACT), aimed primarily at chain stores engaged in interstate commerce, made illegal unreasonably low prices tending to destroy competition and empowered the Federal Trade Commission to abolish price discrimination tending to promote monopoly or reduce competition.

22 June. REVENUE ACT OF 1936 included among its provisions an undistributed profits tax on corporate income that added to the normal corporation income tax a scale of surtaxes ranging from 7% to 27%—attacked by business groups as penalizing the setting aside of corporate profits for expansion or as reserves for slack periods.

26 June. MERCHANT MARINE ACT OF 1936, substituted for the U.S. Shipping Board the **U.S. Maritime Commission,** an independent regulatory agency empowered to carry out a program to develop an American merchant marine through government aid. The Act eliminated subsidies in the form of ocean mail contracts and provided instead outright subsidies based on differentials between foreign and domestic operating and construction costs. Other provisions of the Act related to labor standards for seamen. As amended 23 June 1938 a **Maritime Labor Board** was established, primarily as a mediatory agency. In 1941 the Board was shorn of its mediatory functions.

30 June. WALSH-HEALY GOVERNMENT CONTRACTS ACT provided that all persons employed by a contractor dealing with the U.S. government shall be paid not less than the prevailing minimum wages as determined by the Secretary of Labor and shall not be permitted to work in excess of 8 hrs. a day or 40 hrs. a week; child labor (boys under 16, girls under 18) and convict labor barred in government contracts.

PRESIDENTIAL CAMPAIGN. The Socialist Labor Party Convention met at New York City (26 Apr.) and nominated John W. Aiken (Mass.) for President and Emil F. Teichert (N.Y.) for Vice-President. The Prohibition Party Convention met at Niagara Falls, N.Y. (5 May), and nominated Dr. D. Leigh Colvin (N.Y.) for President and Claude A. Watson (Calif.) for Vice-President. The Socialist Party National Convention met at Cleveland (23 May) and nominated Norman Thomas (N.Y.) for President and George Nelson (Wis.) for Vice-President.

The Republican National Convention met at Cleveland (9 June) and on 11 June nominated Gov. **Alfred M. Landon** (Kan., 1887–   ) for President; on 12 June Col. **Frank Knox** (Ill.) was chosen for Vice-President. The Republican platform condemned the New Deal, accused President Roosevelt of usurping the powers of Congress, and charged that regulated monopoly had displaced free enterprise and unconstitutional laws been passed. The platform called for return of responsibility for relief administration to nonpolitical local agencies, the protection of the rights of labor to organize and to bargain collectively, a balanced budget, farm subsidies, a revamped system of social security, opposed further devaluation of the dollar; but made no specific proposals for repealing New Deal legislation except for revising corporate and personal income taxation policies. During the campaign the Republicans were supported by conservative Democrats (including Alfred E. Smith, Bainbridge Colby, and John W. Davis) active in the Liberty League.

Representative **William Lemke** (N. D.), a Republican, announced (19 June) that he would be Presidential candidate on the Union party ticket and that the Vice-Presidential candidate would be Thomas C. O'Brien (Mass.). Lemke's candidacy was endorsed by Rev. Charles E. Coughlin, whose organization, the National Union for Social Justice, backed the endorsement at its first national convention, held at Cleveland (14 Aug.).

The Union party platform, which denounced the New Deal, was drawn up with an eye to attracting the supporters of Coughlin, Townsend, and Gerald L. K. Smith.

The Democratic National Convention met at Philadelphia (23 June) and renominated President **Roosevelt** on 26 June and Vice-President **John N. Garner** on 27 June. The convention abolished the two-thirds rule for choosing candidates, in force since 1832, and restored the simple majority rule. In his acceptance speech (27 June), President Roosevelt attacked "economic royalists" who, he claimed, had "created a new despotism and wrapped it in the robes of legal sanction." The Democratic platform took its stand on the administration's record. Labor's Nonpartisan League (which included the American Labor party in New York State) and the National Progressive Conference endorsed Roosevelt's candidacy.

The Communist Party National Convention met at New York City (24 June) and nominated Earl Browder (Kan.) for President and James W. Ford (N.Y.) for Vice-President.

The campaign ranked among the most bitterly waged in U.S. political history. The Republicans attacked the New Deal as a bureaucratic planned economy. About 80% of the press opposed Roosevelt. In defense, Roosevelt declared in his opening speech of the campaign (Syracuse, N.Y., 29 Sept.): "The true conservative seeks to protect the system of private property and free enterprise by correcting such injustices and inequalities as arise from it."

3 Nov. PRESIDENTIAL ELECTION. Popular vote: **Roosevelt,** 27,751,612; Landon, 16,681,913; Lemke, 891,858; Thomas, 187,342; Browder, 80,181; Colvin, 37,609; Aiken, 12,729. Electoral vote: **Roosevelt,** 523; Landon, 8. Roosevelt carried every state but Maine and Vermont, winning the most overwhelming electoral majority since Monroe's victory in 1820 and the greatest in any national contest in which there were 2 or more separate tickets. The election gave the Democrats majorities of 76–16 in the Senate and 331–89 in the House.

1937

20 Jan. Inauguration of President Franklin D. Roosevelt, serving his 2nd term; John N. Garner, Vice-President. Roosevelt was the 1st President inaugurated on this day, set by the 20th Amendment. In his inaugural address, Roosevelt reemphasized his objectives of social justice. The challenge to American democracy, he said, is the "tens of millions of its citizens . . . who at this very moment are denied the greater part of what the very lowest standards of today call the necessities of life. . . . I see one-third of a nation ill-housed, ill-clad, ill-nourished. . . ."

5 Feb.–22 July. SUPREME COURT FIGHT. The continued invalidation by the Supreme Court of major New Deal economic and social legislation led to the severest test of President Roosevelt's political leadership. On 5 Feb. Roosevelt submitted to Congress a plan for reorganizing the Federal judiciary. His proposal included the following: (1) an increase in the membership of the Supreme Court from 9 to a maximum of 15 if judges reaching the age of 70 declined to retire; (2) addition of a total of not more than 50 judges to all classes of the Federal courts; (3) sending of appeals from lower-court decisions on constitutional questions directly to the Supreme Court; (4) requiring that government attorneys be heard before any lower court issued an injunction against the enforcement of any act of Congress where the question of constitutionality was involved; and (5) assigning district judges to congested areas in order to expedite court business.

Announcement of the plan aroused widespread and bitter debate. The opposition concentrated on the proposal for increasing the Supreme Court membership. Roosevelt was accused of perverting the Constitution, and of attempting to "pack" the Supreme Court, to destroy judicial independence and integrity, and to aggrandize the power of the Executive. Even administration adherents in and out of Congress who believed that the court plan had its merits insisted that the proper mode of making the change lay in a constitutional amendment. By early

Mar. the bill had produced serious disunity in Democratic ranks in Congress. Sen. Burton K. Wheeler (Mon.), a New Dealer, took the lead in campaigning against the measure. At the hearings which the Senate Judiciary Committee conducted on the proposal the weight of recorded opinion was against the plan. The opposition took heart from a personal letter (21 Mar.) which Chief Justice Charles E. Hughes sent to Sen. Wheeler pointing out that the Supreme Court was fully abreast of its work and needed no new justices.

When it became clear that the drift of Congressional opinion was against the Judiciary Reorganization Bill, President Roosevelt took personal command of the campaign for the measure. In an address at the Democratic Victory Dinner held at Washington, D.C. (4 Mar.), he asserted that the "personal economic predilections" of the Court majority had rendered the national and state governments powerless to deal with pressing problems. In a fireside chat to the nation (9 Mar.), he declared that the courts had "cast doubts on the ability of the elected Congress to protect us against catastrophe by meeting squarely our modern social and economic conditions," and maintained that the purpose of the bill was to restore that balance of power among the 3 major branches of the Federal government intended by the framers of the Constitution.

A number of developments contributed to the weakening of the claims for the urgency of the bill. The Supreme Court Retirement Act (1 Mar.), approved by Roosevelt, permitted Supreme Court justices to retire at the age of 70. The impending retirement of Justice Willis Van Devanter, a foe of the New Deal, was announced on 18 May. The death (14 July) of Sen. Joseph T. Robinson (Ark.), majority leader of the Senate fight for the reorganization plan, weakened further the administration forces. But even more compelling, the Supreme Court in a number of leading decisions (29 Mar.–24 May) sustained important New Deal and State legislation, including the Washington State minimum-wage law for women, the Frazier-Lemke Farm Mortgage Moratorium Act of 1935, the Social

Security Act, and the Wagner Labor Relations Act. These decisions, tantamount to judicial approval of the 2nd New Deal, indicated that the Court personnel was responsive to the national temper, and induced the administration to compromise. On 22 July the Senate (70–20) recommitted the original reorganization bill to the Judiciary Committee, where it died. On 26 Aug. President Roosevelt signed the **Judicial Procedure Reform Act,** a modified measure that reformed the procedure of the lower courts but made no provision for the appointment of new justices and judges.

Political costs of the court battle: (1) brought into the open a break on domestic policy in the Democratic ranks that, except for the liberal wing of the party, was never fully repaired and became especially evident in the Congressional elections of 1938; (2) enabled Republicans and conservative Democrats to block other administration-sponsored legislation, such as the Executive Reorganization Bill (finally passed in 1939), whose merits were overlooked in the heat of feeling against the proposal for revamping the courts.

Although Roosevelt failed to secure provisions for adding new judges to the Supreme Court, he filled 7 vacancies on the Court within the following 4 years. Among the justices appointed by him were Hugo Black (Ala.) in 1937, Stanley Reed (Ky.) in 1938, Felix Frankfurter (Mass.) in 1939, William O. Douglas (Conn.) in 1939, Frank Murphy (Mich.) in 1940, Robert H. Jackson (N.Y.) in 1941, and James F. Byrnes (S.C.) in 1941.

26 Apr. GUFFEY-VINSON BITUMINOUS COAL ACT reenacted all of the chief provisions of the outlawed Guffey-Snyder Act of 1935 with the exception of the wages-and-hours clause. It authorized the promulgation of a new code of fair competition for the bituminous coal industry (promulgated on 21 June), placed the output of soft coal under Federal regulation, laid a revenue tax of 1 ct. a ton on soft coal, and imposed on noncode producers a penalty tax of 19½% of the sales price.

22 July. BANKHEAD-JONES FARM TENANT ACT, designed to cope with the steady decline in U.S. farm ownership and the rise of farm tenancy and sharecropping, established the **Farm Security Administration** (FSA), under which the Resettlement Administration was placed. The Act authorized low-interest loans repayable in small installments over a 40-yr. period to farm tenants, sharecroppers, and farm laborers whose applications for the purchase of farms were approved by committees of local farmers. The Act also authorized rehabilitation loans for operating expenses and educational assistance. The FSA, often against heavy opposition from Southern conservatives, developed a program of regulating the supply and wages and hours of migrant workers, of aid to migrants by way of sanitary camps and medical services, and of cooperative homestead communities.

18 Aug. MILLER-TYDINGS ENABLING ACT, reluctantly signed by President Roosevelt as a "rider" to an appropriations bill for the District of Columbia, amended the Federal antitrust laws so as to legalize contracts made by producers or distributors for the resale price maintenance of branded nationally advertised goods traded in interstate commerce in states where such contracts, authorized by state laws, were illegal under existing Federal statutes. The number of states immediately affected was 42. The Act was supported by influential trade associations on the ground it would end destructive competition brought on by price cutting.

26 Aug. REVENUE ACT OF 1937 was aimed at closing loopholes in the income-tax laws which permitted evasion of tax payments.

1 Sept. NATIONAL HOUSING ACT (commonly known as the WAGNER-STEAGALL ACT), designed to alleviate housing conditions in low-income groups, established the **U.S. Housing Authority** (USHA) under the Department of the Interior, authorized to extend low-interest 60-yr. loans to local public agencies meeting at least 10% of the cost of low-cost slum clearance and housing projects, and to grant subsidies for setting rents geared to low-income levels in areas where local agencies provided an amount equal to 25% of the Federal grant. By 1 Jan. 1941 the USHA had made loan contracts for 511 low-rent public housing projects containing a total of 161,162 dwelling units whose estimated development cost was $767,526,000. During World War II the USHA was active in planning, constructing, and operating defense housing facilities.

15 Nov.–21 Dec. SPECIAL SESSION OF CONGRESS. On 12 Oct. President Roosevelt issued a proclamation calling Congress to convene in extra session on 15 Nov. On that date he submitted a message recommending the passage of legislation including a new agricultural program, wages-and-hours standards, reorganization of the executive branch, and planning for the conservation and development of national resources. During the 5-week session, Congress failed to enact any of the recommended measures, largely owing to the defection of Southern Democratic conservatives who joined with Republicans in blocking the administration's program.

1938

3 Jan. Although his annual message to Congress was for the most part concerned with domestic issues, President Roosevelt opened it with a reference to unsettled world conditions, declaring: "We must keep ourselves adequately strong in self-defense." On 28 Jan. he submitted to Congress recommendations for increased expenditures for armaments, including $8,800,000 for antiaircraft matériel, $6,080,000 for defense industry tools, and a 220% increase in the authorized naval construction program.

10 Jan. LUDLOW RESOLUTION. Beginning in 1935, the Ludlow Resolution for a national referendum on a declaration of war, sponsored by Representative **Louis Ludlow** (Ind.), was introduced several times but failed of passage. The proposed resolution, in the form of a constitutional amendment, stated that except in the event of an invasion of the U.S. or its territorial possessions, the authority of Congress to declare war should not become effective until confirmed by a majority vote in a nationwide referendum. After the amendment was reintroduced in 1937, a national poll revealed that 73% of those polled favored a popular referendum of this type (however, the poll also showed that majority opinion favored a larger army and navy for defense). With the convening of the 2nd session of the 75th Congress passage seemed assured. President Roosevelt sent a letter (6 Jan.) to Speaker William B. Bankhead asserting: "Such an amendment to the Constitution as that proposed would cripple any President in his conduct of our foreign relations, and it would encourage other nations to believe that they could violate American rights with impunity." The House (209–188) returned the resolution to committee. The vote for consideration of the resolution came from most Republican members and from most Democratic members from Western areas; opposed were representatives from the South and Northeast.

16 Feb. AGRICULTURAL ADJUSTMENT ACT OF 1938. When it became apparent that the Soil Conservation and Domestic Allotment Act of 1936 had proved unable to curb farm surpluses and price declines during the recession of 1937–38, that Act was superseded by an administration-sponsored measure which revived the Agricultural Adjustment Act of 1933 in modified form. The processing taxes of the original AAA were eliminated, and financing provided out of the Federal Treasury. The Act (1) empowered the Secretary of Agriculture to fix a marketing quota whenever it was determined that a surplus of any export farm commodity (such as cotton, wheat, rice, tobacco, and corn) threatened the price level; (2) authorized acreage allotments to each grower after two thirds of the farmers had by referendum expressed their approval of the marketing quota; (3) incorporated the **"parity payment"** principle and established the **"ever-normal granary"** arrangement by the following means: the Commodity Credit Corporation was authorized to make loans to farmers on their surplus crops at a level slightly below "parity" (a price based on the Aug.

1909–July 1914 level of farm purchasing power). Such excess crops were to be stored under government auspices, and the farmer was to repay the loan and market the surplus during crop failure years when the price was at "parity" or above. Since such disposal of surpluses would prevent the market price from rising too high above "parity," this arrangement stabilized agricultural prices and stored surplus crops without loss to individual farmer income.

The Act also established the **Federal Crop Insurance Corporation** (FCIC) as an agency of the Department of Agriculture with a capitalization of $100 million, authorized to insure wheat crops only, beginning with the harvest of 1939, by accepting wheat in payment of premiums on insurance policies taken out against crop losses from unavoidable causes (such as drought, flood, hail, and plant diseases) ranging from 50% to 75% of the average yield.

14 Apr. ROOSEVELT AND BUSINESS RECESSION. To combat the business recession under way since Aug. 1937, President Roosevelt sent to Congress a series of recommendations, which he outlined to the nation in a fireside chat the same day. They involved a reversal of the administration's deflationary policy, the expansion of WPA rolls from 1,500,000 to 3 million, a $3-billion recovery and relief program, "desterilizing" more than $3 billion in idle gold in the Treasury, "pump-priming" through RFC loans, and a "loose money" policy authorized by the Board of Governors of the Federal Reserve System. On 21 June the Emergency Relief Appropriation Act became law.

17 May. NAVAL EXPANSION ACT OF 1938 (also known as the VINSON NAVAL ACT) authorized a $1,090,656,000 expansion of a "2-ocean" navy over the ensuing 10 yrs. and provided for a maximum increase of 135,000 tons in capital ships up to a tonnage of 660,000, a maximum increase of 68,754 tons in cruisers up to a tonnage of 412,500, and an increase of 40,000 tons in aircraft carriers up to a tonnage of 175,000.

26 May. HOUSE COMMITTEE TO INVESTIGATE UN-AMERICAN ACTIVITIES, popularly known as the Dies Committee after its chairman, **Martin Dies** (Tex.), was established for the purpose of conducting investigations into Nazi, Fascist, Communist and other organizations termed "un-American" in character.

27 May. REVENUE ACT OF 1938, supported by Democratic and Republican opponents of the New Deal on the ground that tax concessions to business were necessary for the stimulation of the national economy, was passed by Congress on 11 May and became law without the signature of President Roosevelt. It repealed the progressive normal tax and undistributed profits tax authorized in 1936 and substituted a tax of 19% on corporations whose income exceeded $25,000, with the tax being reduced by a flat 2½% of dividends paid out of income subject to the tax (in effect it reduced taxes on large corporations and increased them on smaller firms). The measure also drastically modified the progressive tax provisions applicable to capital gains and losses.

16 June. TEMPORARY NATIONAL ECONOMIC COMMITTEE (TNEC) was a joint legislative-executive body authorized by joint Congressional resolution and established under the chairmanship of Sen. **Joseph C. O'Mahoney** (Wyo.), with **Leon Henderson** serving as executive secretary. Earlier, 29 Apr., President Roosevelt had submitted to Congress recommendations for curbing monopolies and the growing concentration of economic power. The TNEC conducted public hearings (1 Dec. 1938–26 Apr. 1940) to determine the effects of monopoly on prices, wages, profits, consumption, investment, cartels, patents, and many other aspects of the national economy with a view to improving Federal antitrust policy and procedure. In its final report (31 Mar. 1941) the committee included the following among its recommendations: (1) amendment of the patent laws and revision of Patent Office procedure; (2) amendment of the Clayton Antitrust Act to lessen centralization of corporate resources; (3) prohibition of specified activities of trade associations tending to violate the antitrust laws; (4) legislation authorizing the Federal Trade Commission to forbid corporations from acquiring the assets of competing corporations over a certain size, unless it could be shown that such acquisition was in the public interest; (5) legislation to deal with the control exercised by foreign governments and their industry over American concerns through patent laws; (6) repeal of the Miller-Tydings Act of 1937; (7) allocation of defense funds in such a way as to eliminate monopoly control of basic products; (8) legislation prohibiting the use of "basing point" and other industrial pricing systems resulting in the elimination of competition; and (9) additional appropriations to strengthen the machinery for enforcing the antitrust laws by the Department of Justice and the Federal Trade Commission. Some antitrust suits initiated as a direct result of the TNEC's activities were suspended during World War II.

24 June. FOOD, DRUG, AND COSMETIC ACT (WHEELER-LEA ACT) superseded and widened the scope of the Pure Food Act of 1906. It prohibited misbranding of products; required manufacturers of foods, drugs, and cosmetics to list on their products' labels the ingredients used in processing; and forbade the use of false and misleading advertising claims disseminated in more than 1 state. Enforcement of provisions relating to misbranding was left to the Food and Drug Administration; those relating to advertising to the Federal Trade Commission, which was also given extended powers over unfair trade practices injuring competitors or consumers.

25 June. FAIR LABOR STANDARDS ACT (WAGES AND HOURS LAW), applied to enterprises which engaged in, or which affected, interstate commerce, with many occupations exempted (including farm laborers, domestic servants, and professional workers), established (1) a minimum wage of 40 cts. an hr. (amended to 75 cts. an hr., 1949; to $1, 1955) and (2) a maximum work week of 40 hrs., to be put into effect, for wages, within 8 yrs. beginning at 25 cts. an hr., and for hours, at 3 yrs. beginning at 44 hrs. per week, with time and a half

for overtime (750,000 workers received wage increases when the law went into effect in Aug.); (3) forbade labor by children under 16, and restricted to nonhazardous occupations those under 18. Constitutionality upheld by the Supreme Court in *U.S.* v. *Darby Lumber Co.* (1941, p. 499).

4 July. "THE NATION'S NO. 1 ECONOMIC PROBLEM." As a result of a request by President Roosevelt (22 June) to the National Emergency Council to prepare a report on the problems and needs of the South, the Conference on Economic Conditions in the South met at Washington. In a message (4 July) to the Conference, Roosevelt declared: "It is my conviction that the South presents right now the nation's No. 1 economic problem." The findings of the Conference, set forth in the comprehensive *Report on Economic Conditions of the South,* issued 12 Aug., pointed out that despite the South's good natural and human resources and potential untapped market, its people suffered from inadequate living standards.

8 Nov. CONGRESSIONAL ELECTIONS. To lessen the dependence of the New Deal domestic and foreign program on conservative Democrats (alienated from the administration over such issues as the Fair Labor Standards Act, the Anti-Lynching Bill [defeated by a Southern filibuster], and appropriations for the Farm Security Administration), President Roosevelt decided to participate actively in the Democratic primary campaign in order to effect the nomination of party liberals, with a fireside chat (24 June). The primary campaigns in selected districts in which Roosevelt made direct appeals included New York City, Georgia, Maryland, and Kentucky. Roosevelt's personal intervention fell far short of its intended goal. He failed to defeat Walter F. George (Ga.) and Millard F. Tydings (Md.), but scored a victory over Rep. John J. O'Connor of New York City. Although the Democrats retained control of both branches of Congress, the elections indicated the first Republican gains since 1928. The Democrats lost 7 seats in the Senate, 80 in the House. The composition of the 76th Congress was as follows: Senate, 69 Democrats, 23 Republicans, 2 Farmer-Laborites, 1 Progressive, 1 Independent; House, 261 Democrats, 164 Republicans, 4 others.

1939

4 Jan. In his annual message to Congress, President Roosevelt for the 1st time since taking office proposed no new domestic reforms, but stressed the dangers posed to democracy and international peace by the forces of aggression.

5 Jan. The $9-billion budget submitted to Congress by President Roosevelt for the fiscal year 1940 included $1,319,558,000 for national defense.

12 Jan. President Roosevelt urged Congress to pass additional appropriations, amounting to $525 million for an emergency program of national defense. He proposed that $300 million of this sum be used for military aviation to strengthen the air defenses of the continental U.S. and outlying possessions and territories, and suggested that the balance be devoted to the "2-ocean" navy, the training of civilian air pilots, the facilitating of matériel procurement, and the improvement and strengthening of the seacoast defenses of Panama, Hawaii, and the continental U.S. On 4 Mar. he requested further appropriations to increase the national defense, and on 26 Apr. signed an appropriations bill for $549 million. On 29 Apr. he submitted an additional request for defense appropriations.

3 Apr. ADMINISTRATIVE REORGANIZATION ACT OF 1939. On 12 Jan. 1937 the report of the President's Committee on Administrative Management was submitted to Congress with President Roosevelt's recommendation for the enactment of most of its proposals. The Executive Reorganization Bill aimed to increase government efficiency by regrouping and simplifying the many Federal agencies, boards, commissions, and other units that had come into existence since the turn of the century, and thereby reduce or eliminate overlapping and waste. In 1937, and again in 1938, the measure was not passed, largely owing to the fight over the reorganization of the judiciary and to opposition from conservative Democrats and Republicans, who charged that the bill would make Roosevelt a "dictator." Following the 1938 elections, there was little opposition to the measure, and the bill, in modified form, was approved.

Plans I and II for the regrouping of 50 government units were submitted to Congress by President Roosevelt on 25 Apr. and 9 May, respectively, and went into effect by Presidential order on 1 July failing the passage of concurrent resolutions nullifying these plans. Under Plans I and II the President set up a **Federal Security Agency**, a **Federal Works Agency**, and a **Federal Loan Agency**, under all of which a total of 24 units was placed; and by transfer, consolidation, or abolition distributed among these 3 new agencies and the Executive Department the major independent establishments of the government. The Bureau of the Budget was transferred to the Executive Office of the President from the Treasury Department. By Presidential order (8 Sept.) the reorganization of the Executive Office of the President established the following principal divisions: the White House Office, the Bureau of the Budget, the National Resources Planning Board, the Liaison Office for Personel Management, the Office of Government Reports, and an optional office for emergency management (established 25 May 1940 as the Office for Emergency Management). The President was provided with 6 administrative assistants. Three additional reorganization plans were submitted in 1940 and became effective that year.

16 May. FOOD STAMP PLAN, a New Deal scheme established for the purpose of disposing of surpluses of agricultural commodities to persons on relief, was inaugurated in Rochester, N.Y. Recipients of relief were permitted to buy each week between $1 and $1.50 worth of "orange stamps" for each member of the family unit. For each $1 worth of these stamps the purchaser received gratis 50 cts. worth of "blue stamps" redeemable for foods officially designated as surplus commodities. By the end of 1940 the plan had been adopted in more than 100 cities. World War II forced its discontinuance.

CUT IN RELIEF EXPENDITURES. Although employment began to increase in Sept. 1938, it failed to reach the level of Sept. 1937. President Roosevelt requested (5 Jan.) a deficiency appropriation of $875 million for the Works Progress Administration. Congress reduced this to $725 million. Further requests by President Roosevelt (7 Feb., 14 Mar.) for $150 million to avoid drastic reduction of WPA employment were scaled down by Congress (11 Apr.) to $100 million. The lack of sufficient funds necessitated a reduction of WPA rolls to 2,578,000 in June, 1939. On 27 Apr. Roosevelt recommended an appropriation of $1,477 million for the WPA for the fiscal year 1940. Although the Emergency Relief Appropriation Act of 1939 (30 June) allotted this sum, it abolished the Federal Theater Project, reduced the security wage, and set an 18-mo. limit for continuous WPA employment. (The Act also changed the name of the Works Progress Administration to the Works Projects Administration.) The measure brought a nationwide strike of WPA workers and resulted in the dismissal of many.

2 Aug. HATCH ACT was passed chiefly as a direct result of alleged political malpractices involving the votes of WPA workers in the border states of Ky., Tenn., and Md. during the elections of 1938. The Act prohibited Federal office holders below the policy-making echelon in the Executive branch of the government to participate actively in political campaigns, to solicit or accept contributions from work relief employees, and to make use of official authority or favors in order to interfere with or influence the outcome of Presidential or Congressional elections. On 19 July 1940 an amendment to the act extended its scope to state and local government workers whose salaries were drawn in whole or in part from Federal funds, and limited the annual expenditures of political parties to $3 million and individual campaign contributions to a maximum of $5,000.

10 Aug. SOCIAL SECURITY AMENDMENTS. Most of the improvements proposed by the Social Security Board in its report transmitted to Congress (16 Jan.) by President Roosevelt were embodied in amendments to the Social Security Act passed by the House (10 June) and the Senate (13 July). The amendments included the following provisions: (1) the date for starting monthly old-age benefit payments was advanced to 1 Jan. 1940; (2) supplementary old-age benefits provided for aged wives; (3) average wages replaced total wages as the basis for computing old-age benefits; (4) old-age insurance coverage extended to maritime workers, persons earning wages after they reached 65, and employees of Federal instrumentalities, e.g., member banks in the Federal Reserve System; (5) the increased taxes to be paid by employers and employees postponed until 1943; (6) the maximum Federal grant for each aged or blind person increased by $15 to $20 per month; and (7) the Federal contribution toward state aid to dependent children increased from one third to one half the amount granted each individual. The Social Security Act of 1950 raised employers' and employees' 1¼% payroll tax to 2% in 1954, 2½% in 1960, 3% in 1965, 3¼% in 1970, and extended coverage. By the Social Security Act of 1952 (signed by President Truman, effective 1 Sept.) old age and survivor insurance benefits were increased $5 per month or 12½% (whichever is greater), and beneficiaries permitted to earn $75 a month instead of $50. Liberalized and expanded by Act of 1954 (1 Sept.), extending benefits to 7 million additional workers, including farm workers and household domestics, permitting retired persons over 65 to receive benefits while earning up to $1,200 per yr.; and by Act of 1956 (1 Aug.), providing old-age and survivors' insurance benefits for totally and permanently disabled workers beginning at age 50 and reducing from 65 to 62 the age at which women are eligible for OASI benefits. Act of 1958 (29 Aug.) increased benefits c.7% and raised earnings from $4,200 to $4,800; further liberalizations provided under Act of 1960 (13 Sept.).

THE UNITED STATES IN WORLD WAR II

PRELUDE TO GLOBAL WAR, 1939–41

1939

1 Sept.–5 Oct. WAR BEGINS: POLAND CRUSHED. Germany invaded Poland (1 Sept.). Great Britain and France declared war on Germany; Belgium proclaimed its neutrality (3 Sept.). The Germans crossed the Vistula (11 Sept.), the San (16 Sept.), and demanded the surrender of Warsaw (17 Sept.). Soviet forces invaded Poland (17 Sept.). With the fall of Warsaw (27 Sept.) main organized resistance in Poland ended. Soviet-German partition of Poland (28 Sept.). Polish Government-in-Exile formed in Paris (30 Sept.). Last Polish forces east of the Vistula surrendered (5 Oct.).

3–21 Sept. U.S. POSITION. In a fireside chat (3 Sept.) President Roosevelt declared: "This nation will remain a neutral nation, but I cannot ask that every American remain neutral in thought as well." On 5 Sept. the U.S. proclaimed its neutrality. Under the Neutrality Act of 1937 President Roosevelt prohibited the export of arms and munitions to belligerent powers. On 8 Sept. he proclaimed a limited national emergency, and on 21 Sept. urged a special session of Congress to repeal the arms embargo.

3 Oct. DECLARATION OF PANAMA, issued by the Inter-American Conference, announced sea safety zones in the Western Hemisphere, south of Canada. Belligerent powers were warned to refrain from naval action within these zones.

11 Oct. President Roosevelt was informed by **Albert Einstein** and other scientists of the possibilities of developing an atomic bomb.

14 Oct.–12 Mar. 1940. RUSSO-FINNISH WAR. On 14 Oct. Russia presented Finland with demands for military and territorial concessions, and invaded Finland 30 Nov. The war terminated with the signing of a treaty at Moscow 12 Mar. 1940.

4 Nov. NEUTRALITY ACT OF 1939 repealed the arms embargo and authorized "cash and carry" exports of arms and munitions to belligerent powers. The bill passed the Senate, 63–30 (27 Oct.), and the House, 243–181 (2 Nov.).

1940

26 Jan. U.S.-Japanese commercial treaty of 1911 expired. Secretary Hull notified the Japanese government that trade between the two nations would rest on a day-to-day basis.

9 Feb. WELLES MISSION. President Roosevelt announced that Under Secretary of State Sumner Welles would leave for Europe to gather information concerning the war aims of the belligerent powers and the possibility of a just and lasting peace. He reported to Roosevelt 28 Mar.

30 Mar. A Japanese-dominated government in China was established at Nanking under Wang Ching-wei.

9 Apr.–11 June. INVASION OF NORWAY. German troops invaded Denmark and Norway by sea and air 9 Apr. An Anglo-French expeditionary force which came (18–20 Apr.) to the aid of the resisting Norwegian troops was evacuated on 2 May. On 9 May British troops occupied Iceland. On 29 May the British announced the capture of Narvik, but withdrew on 11 June. A puppet regime under Vidkun Quisling was established in Norway on 1 Feb. 1942.

17 Apr. Secretary Hull announced that any change in the *status quo* of the Netherlands East Indies would be prejudicial to the peace and security of the Pacific area.

10 May–4 June. FALL OF THE NETHERLANDS AND BELGIUM. Germany invaded Luxembourg, the Netherlands, and Belgium by land and air (10 May). British Prime Minister Neville Chamberlaign resigned, and was succeeded (11 May) by **Winston Churchill,** who headed a coalition government. The Netherlands government fled to Great Britain (14 May) and the army capitulated on the 15th. On 27–28 May King Leopold III ordered the Belgian army to capitulate, thus forcing the withdrawal of the Anglo-French expeditionary force from Belgium. The **Evacuation from Dunkirk** of 338,226 British and French troops (28 May–4 June) was completed with the use of 861 vessels of all types.

16 May–3 June. U.S. PREPAREDNESS AND AID TO BRITAIN. President Roosevelt, who in his annual budget message (3 Jan.) had requested $1,800 million for national defense, asked for new appropriations of $1,182 million and called for a production program of 50,000 planes a year. On 31 May he requested an additional $1,277,741,170 for the acceleration and development of military and naval requirements. In response to Prime Minister Churchill's appeal for military supplies, the War Department (3 June) released to Great Britain surplus or outdated stocks of arms, munitions, and aircraft. More than $43 million worth was sent in the month of June alone.

5 June–10 July. FALL OF FRANCE. Battle of France opened (5 June) with German crossings of the Somme and the Aisne-Oise canal. Italy declared war on France and Great Britain (10 June) and Italian forces penetrated southern France.

On 13 June Premier Paul Reynaud of France appealed to President Roosevelt for aid. Following a breakthrough at Sedan, German troops entered Paris (14 June), compelling transfer of the French government to Bordeaux. On 16 June France requested release from obligations under the Anglo-French agreement barring a separate peace, and Marshal Henri-Philippe Pétain succeeded Reynaud as head of the French government. On 17 June he asked for armistice terms. An armistice with Germany was signed at Compiègne (22 June); with Italy on 24 June. In London the French National Committee under Gen. Charles de Gaulle pledged (18 June) continued French resistance against Germany. On 2 July the Pétain government established its headquarters at Vichy; on 10 July Pétain was granted dictatorial powers.

15–22 June. U.S. DEFENSE MEASURES. On 15 June President Roosevelt established the **National Defense Research Committee,** with Dr. **Vannevar Bush** (1890–   ) as chairman. In May 1941 this body was supplanted by the Office of Scientific Research and Development. The **Pittman Resolution** (16 June), designed to strengthen the military defenses of the Latin-American republics, authorized the sale of munitions to the governments of the republics of the Western Hemisphere. The U.S. notified Germany and Italy that it would refuse to recognize transfer of title from one non-American power to another of any geographic region of the Western Hemisphere. On 20 June **Henry L. Stimson** (N.Y., 1867–1950) was named Secretary of War; **Frank Knox** (Ill., 1874–1944) Secretary of the Navy. On 22 June Congress adopted national defense tax measures designed to yield $994,300,000 a year. The national debt limit was raised from $45 billion to $49 billion.

17 June. Soviet forces completed the occupation of Lithuania, Latvia, and Estonia, which were incorporated into the Soviet Union 25 Aug.

28 June. ALIEN REGISTRATION ACT (commonly called the **SMITH ACT**) strengthened existing laws governing the admission and deportation of aliens and required the fingerprinting of all aliens in the U.S. The measure, however, was designed primarily to check subversive activities. The Act made it unlawful for any person to advocate or teach the overthrow or destruction of any government in the U.S. by force or violence, and to organize or become a member of any group dedicated to teaching such doctrine.

30 July. ACT OF HAVANA was unanimously approved by delegates of the 21 republics of the Pan-American Union gathered at an Inter-American Conference. It provided that the American republics, collectively or individually, might in the interest of the common defense take over and administer any European possession in the New World endangered by aggression. The measure was designed to prevent the transfer to Germany of European colonies in the Western Hemisphere.

4 Aug. Italian troops invaded British Somaliland and completed its occupation on 19 Aug.

8 Aug.–31 Oct. BATTLE OF BRITAIN. The Luftwaffe, with more than 2,600 operational fighters and bombers at its disposal, opened a vast air offensive against British shipping, RAF installations, factories, land transportation, and cities in the British Isles. The Nazi objective was to soften Great Britain in preparation for an invasion of England by sea and air. The Battle of Britain came to a climax on 15 Sept. when 56 German aircraft were destroyed (the original British claim was 185). Aircraft losses, 10 July–31 Oct. (Churchill):

British fighters lost by RAF 915
Enemy aircraft actually destroyed
 (according to German records) 1,733
Enemy aircraft claimed by British 2,698

Defeat in this crucial battle compelled the Germans to abandon plans for the invasion of the British Isles.

18 Aug.–29 Oct. U.S. DEFENSE MEASURES. Meeting at Ogdensburg, N.Y. (18 Aug.), to discuss defense problems common to Canada and the U.S., Prime Minister W. L. Mackenzie King and President Roosevelt agreed to establish a **Permanent Joint Board on Defense.** On 27 Aug. Congress authorized induction of the National Guard into Federal service. Initial units were called out 31 Aug. On 3 Sept. a defense agreement between the U.S. and Great Britain provided for the transfer of 50 U.S. overage destroyers to the British; in exchange, the U.S. acquired the right to take 99-year leases on naval and air bases in Newfoundland, Bermuda, the Bahamas, Jamaica, St. Lucia, Trinidad, Antigua, and British Guiana. On 16 Sept. the **Selective Training and Service Act** (the **Burke-Wadsworth Bill**) was approved. The first peacetime program of compulsory military service in the U.S., it provided for the registration of all men between 21 and 35, and for the training over a 1-yr. period of 1,200,000 troops and 800,000 reserves. The 1st registration (16 Oct.) resulted in a listing of 16,400,-000 men; the 1st draft numbers were selected on 29 Oct.

4–27 Sept. JAPANESE AGGRESSION. Secretary Hull advised the Japanese government (4 Sept.) that aggression against French Indo-China would bring adverse reaction in the U.S. On 12 Sept. Joseph C. Grew, U.S. Ambassador to Japan, warned Secretary Hull that Japan might interpret a drastic embargo on oil as sanctions and retaliate. On 22 Sept. Japan concluded with Vichy France an agreement giving the former air and troop maintenance bases in Indo-China. On 27 Sept. Japan signed at Berlin a 3-power pact with Germany and Italy providing for a 10-yr. military and economic alliance. By this pact, which made Japan a member of the Axis, each of the signatories pledged mutual assistance in the event of war with a nation not then a belligerent. The pact was subsequently signed by other nations, including Bulgaria, Rumania, Hungary, and Yugoslavia. On 26 Sept. President Roosevelt proclaimed an embargo, effective 16 Oct., on exports of scrap iron and steel to all countries outside the Western Hemisphere except Great Britain. The ban was aimed at Japan. Ambassador Horinouchi protested the move as an "unfriendly act" (8 Oct.).

8–28 Oct. AXIS MOVES IN THE BAL-KANS. On 8 Oct. German troops began occupation of Rumania. On 28 Oct. Italy invaded Greece from Albania. British forces were landed on Crete and other Greek islands. Fighting between Greeks and Italians continued through the winter and spring.

PRESIDENTIAL CAMPAIGN. The Republican National Convention met at Philadelphia (28 June) and nominated **Wendell L. Willkie** (N.Y., 1892–1944) for President and Sen. **Charles L. McNary** (Ore.) for Vice-President on a platform that attacked the New Deal administration but supported most of its major reforms. The Democratic National Convention met at Chicago (15 July) and received a message (16 July) from President Roosevelt stating that he had no desire to be a candidate for a 3rd term. On 18 July **Roosevelt** was nominated for a 3rd term; Secretary of Agriculture **Henry A. Wallace** (Iowa) was nominated for Vice-President. Both major parties supported the national defense program, aid to Britain, and hemispherical defense, but opposed participation in foreign wars. Other Presidential candidates: Norman Thomas (N.Y.), Socialist; Roger Babson (Mass.), Prohibition party; Earl Browder (N.Y.), Communist; and John W. Aiken, Socialist Labor.

5 Nov. PRESIDENTIAL ELECTION. Popular vote: **Roosevelt,** 27,244,160; Willkie, 22,305,198; Thomas, 100,264; Babson, 57,812; Browder, 48,579; Aiken, 14,861. Electoral vote: **Roosevelt,** 449 (38 states); Willkie, 82 (10 states).

20 July. President Roosevelt approved a bill authorizing a 2-ocean navy for the defense of the U.S. and the Western Hemisphere at a cost of $4 billion. The measure increased the authorized U.S. warship tonnage by 70% to a level of 3,500,000, and provided for the construction of about 200 warships, including 7 battleships of 55,000 tons each.

13 Nov.–8 Feb. 1941. BRITISH MEDITERRANEAN OFFENSIVE. British naval aircraft dealt a severe blow to the Italian fleet at Taranto (13 Nov.). Wavell's offensive began 9 Dec., with a surprise attack around the Italians' southern flank in North Africa. By 8 Feb. the British had occupied El Agheila, 500 miles from Matrûh, their starting point, and destroyed Graziani's army, capturing 133,000 prisoners.

20–29 Dec. U.S. DEFENSE PRODUCTION. The Office of Production Management, with **William S. Knudsen** (1879–1948) as director, was set up by President Roosevelt (20 Dec.) to coordinate defense production and speed all material aid "short of war" to Great Britain and other anti-Axis nations. On 21 Dec. Germany asserted U.S. aid to Great Britain was "moral aggression." In a fireside chat on national security (29 Dec.) President Roosevelt stressed the Axis threat to the U.S. and called for an immense production effort that would make the U.S. "the great arsenal of democracy."

1941

6 Jan. "FOUR FREEDOMS." In his annual message to Congress President Roosevelt recommended Lend-Lease for the Allies and enunciated the "Four-Freedoms": freedom of speech and expression, freedom of worship, freedom from want, and freedom from fear.

27 Jan.–29 Mar. SECRET U.S.-BRITISH STAFF TALKS, held in Washington, produced a plan known as ABC-1, suggesting the strategy for war. In the event of Anglo-U.S. involvements in war with both Germany and Japan the concentration of force should be on **Germany first.**

Feb.–27 May. BATTLE OF THE ATLANTIC. Although the battle had assumed grim proportions as early as Nov. 1940, when the pocket battleship *Scheer* attacked a convoy and sank the *Jervis Bay,* it was at a critical stage at the time of the secret U.S.-British staff talks. In Feb.-Mar. the *Scharnhorst* and *Gneisenau* sank or captured 22 ships (115,000 tons). U-boats, using "wolf-pack" tactics, reached great effectiveness. To 9 Apr. 1940 total Allied and neutral shipping losses had amounted to 688,000 gross tons. Between 10 Apr. 1940 and 17 Mar. 1941 losses amounted to 2,314,000 gross tons. On 11 Apr. Roosevelt informed Churchill that the U.S. would extend security zone and patrol areas to a line covering all North Atlantic waters west of about West Long. 26° (thereafter "the sea frontier of the U.S."). On 21 May the *Robin Moor,* an American merchant ship, was sunk by a German submarine in the South Atlantic, off the coast of Brazil. On 24 May the British warship *Hood* was sunk by the German battleship *Bismarck* in the North Atlantic. The *Bismarck* was sunk (27 May) while attempting to return to port.

5 Mar. The Republic of Panama agreed to permit the U.S. to extend air defenses beyond the limits of the Canal Zone. The agreement was limited to the duration of the war.

11 Mar. LEND-LEASE ACT approved by President Roosevelt. It was drawn up primarily to offset the exhaustion of British credits for the purchase of war supplies. The measure passed the Senate, 60–31 (8 Mar.), and the House, 317–71 (11 Mar.). Lend-Lease enabled any country whose defense the President deemed vital to that of the U.S. to receive arms and other equipment and supplies by sale, transfer, exchange, or lease. An initial appropriation of $7 billion was authorized. Total Lend-Lease aid during the course of the war amounted to $50,-226,845,387. On 15 Mar. President Roosevelt promised increasing aid to the Allies for a total victory.

24 Mar.–15 Apr. ROMMEL'S COUNTEROFFENSIVE. A North African offensive by German and Italian forces under Gen. Erwin Rommel compelled the British (whose strength was drained by the dispatch of 60,000 troops to help Greece resist the Germans) to evacuate Bengasi and to withdraw to Egypt by the end of May. British troops aided by the Royal Navy held out at Tobruk.

6 Apr.–1 June. Germany invaded Greece and Yugoslavia (6 Apr.). The Yugoslavian army surrendered on 17 Apr.; Greek resistance ended on 23 Apr. The British withdrew from the Greek mainland (29 Apr.). German airborne troops landed in Crete (20 May) and by 1 June had conquered the island.

9 Apr. GREENLAND. Signing of U.S.-Danish agreement pledging the U.S. to defend Greenland against invasion. In return, the U.S. was granted the right to construct, maintain, and operate in Greenland air, naval, radio, and other defense installations. President Roosevelt announced that the defense of Greenland was essential to the security of the Western Hemisphere.

13 Apr. Mutual nonaggression pact signed at Moscow by Japan and Russia.

21–27 Apr. U.S., Dutch, and British military planning officers met at Singapore and drew up a strategic plan for combined operations against Japan should the latter commit aggression against the U.S.

27 May–16 June. President Roosevelt proclaimed (27 May) an unlimited national emergency and ordered (16 June) the closing of German and Italian consulates in the U.S. by 10 July. In retaliation, the German and Italian governments ordered the closing of U.S. consulates in European areas under Axis control.

22 June. INVASION OF RUSSIA. Germany invaded the Soviet Union. Together with Finnish and Rumanian troops, the German forces penetrated Russia along a 2,000-mile front extending from the Arctic to the Ukraine. By mid-Aug. the Germans had overrun most of the Ukraine; by early Sept. they reached Leningrad; by mid-Nov. they had laid Sevastopol under siege and reached the outskirts of Moscow. Rostov fell on 22 Nov., but was retaken by the Russians on 29 Nov. In Dec. the Russians launched a counteroffensive.

24 June–6 Nov. AID TO RUSSIA. On 24 June President Roosevelt promised U.S. aid to the Soviet Union. On 12 July Great Britain and Russia signed a mutual assistance pact at Moscow barring a separate peace with Germany. British and Soviet forces occupied Iran (25–29 Aug.). U.S.-British missions conferred in Moscow (29 Sept.) to determine Russian defense needs, and on 1 Oct. decided to grant Russian requests for matériel. The U.S. granted Lend-

Lease credit of $1 billion to the Soviet Union (6 Nov.).

7 July. ICELAND. By agreement with the Icelandic government, the U.S. landed forces in Iceland to prevent its occupation by Germany for use as a naval or air base against the Western Hemisphere. The agreement stipulated that the U.S. would withdraw following the close of the European war.

24 July–24 Aug. U.S.-JAPANESE RELATIONS. Japan occupied French Indo-China (24 July). Two days later President Roosevelt froze all Japanese credits in the U.S., thus bringing Japanese-American trade to a virtual halt. Simultaneous action was taken by Great Britain. Japan ordered freezing of all U.S. and British funds. President Roosevelt nationalized (26 July) the armed forces of the Philippines for the duration of the emergency, placing them under the command of Gen. **Douglas MacArthur** (p. 745), who was named commander in chief of U.S. forces in the Far East. The Japanese ambassador to the U.S., Adm. Kichisaburo Nomura, was informed by President Roosevelt that additional attempts to extend Japanese military control in the Far East would compel the U.S. to take immediate steps to protect American rights and interests. On 24 Aug. Prime Minister Churchill promised that Great Britain would come to the aid of the U.S. should the negotiations with Japan break down.

14 Aug. ATLANTIC CHARTER, a joint statement of principles issued by President Roosevelt and Prime Minister Churchill, formulated the broad postwar aims of the U.S. and Great Britain. The Charter was not an alliance nor a binding legal commitment. It was drawn up at secret meetings (9–12 Aug.) that took place aboard the U.S. cruiser *Augusta* and the British battleship *Prince of Wales* at Argentia Bay off Newfoundland. Drafted by Roosevelt and Churchill with the aid of Sumner Welles and Sir Alexander Cadogan, the document included the following points: (1) renunciation of territorial or other aggrandizement; (2) opposition to territorial changes contrary to the wishes of the people immediately concerned; (3) sup-

port of the right of peoples to choose their own form of government; (4) support, with due respect for existing obligations, of the easing of restrictions on trade, and access to raw materials on equal terms; (5) support of cooperative efforts to improve the economic position and social security of the peoples of the world; (6) freedom from want and fear; (7) freedom of the seas; and (8) disarmament of aggressor nations pending the establishment of a permanent peace structure. On 24 Sept. it was announced that 15 anti-Axis nations, among them the Soviet Union, had endorsed the Atlantic Charter.

18 Aug. SELECTIVE SERVICE EXTENSION. President Roosevelt approved a bill extending for 18 months the army service of draftees. The House vote (12 Aug.) on the extension of Selective Service was 203–202.

4 Sept.–30 Oct. WARFARE IN THE ATLANTIC. A German submarine attacked the U.S.S. *Greer,* a destroyer on duty in waters off Iceland (4 Sept.). On 11 Sept. President Roosevelt announced a "shoot-on-sight" order to U.S. naval forces in U.S. defensive waters, stating that German and Italian vessels would enter these areas at their own risk. Five days later the U.S. Navy undertook merchant convoy duty as far as Iceland. On 9 Oct. President Roosevelt asked Congress to modify the Neutrality Act of 1939 to permit arming of U.S. merchantmen engaged in overseas commerce and their passage through combat zones. The U.S. destroyer *Kearny* was torpedoed and damaged by a German submarine in waters west of Iceland (17 Oct.), causing the loss of 11 American lives. On 30 Oct. the U.S. destroyer *Reuben James,* on convoy duty in waters off Iceland, was attacked and sunk by a German submarine, with about 100 American lives lost. The Senate, 50–37, approved repeal of restrictive sections in the 1939 Neutrality Act (7 Nov.), and the House followed (13 Nov.), 212–94. The measure, which became law on 17 Nov., authorized the arming of U.S. merchant vessels and permitted them to carry cargoes to belligerent ports.

11 Oct. President Roosevelt privately proposed that Great Britain and the U.S.

pool their resources and research facilities to develop the atomic bomb.

18 Oct.–6 Dec. JAPANESE ATTITUDE HARDENS. On 18 Oct. the Japanese Cabinet headed by Prince Fumimaro Konoye resigned. General Hideki Tojo became Prime Minister. U.S. Ambassador Grew warned Washington (17 Nov.) of the possibility of a sudden attack by the Japanese. On 20 Nov. discussions in Washington were opened between Secretary Hull and the two Japanese negotiators, Ambassador Nomura and a special envoy, Saburo Kurusu. Japan demanded that the U.S. abandon China; lift the orders freezing Japanese credits in the U.S.; resume full trade relations with Japan; exert pressure to aid Japan in securing supplies from the Netherlands East Indies; and bring a halt to U.S. naval expansion in the Western Pacific. On 26 Nov. Hull countered with a set of proposals that included the withdrawal of Japanese troops from China and Indo-China and the conclusion of a multilateral nonaggression pact. The U.S. proposals restated the following principles: respect for the territorial integrity and sovereignty of all nations; support of the principle of noninterference in the internal affairs of other countries; support of the principle of equality, including equality of commercial opportunity; nondisturbance of the *status quo* in the Pacific except by peaceful means. In return, Hull promised to free frozen Japanese assets and to resume treaty-based commercial relations. Asking for two weeks in which to study the proposals, Japan in the meantime went ahead with military and naval preparations in Asia and the Pacific. On 25 Nov. (Washington time) carrier force that attacked Pearl Harbor left Kurile Islands. The next day U.S. warned Great Britain of an impending Japanese attack. War and Navy Departments, believing it likely that the Japanese would strike in the Philippines or Southeast Asia, sent (27 Nov.) warnings of imminent war to commanders of U.S. forces in the Pacific. On 29 Nov. Premier Tojo publicly asserted that U.S. and British influence must be eliminated from Asia, and on 1 Dec. Japan publicly rejected the Hull proposals. The next day the U.S. requested an explanation by Japan for increasing its forces in Indo-China, and on 6 Dec. President Roosevelt made a direct appeal to Emperor Hirohito, asking him to use his influence to preserve the peace and to withdraw troops from French Indo-China.

7 Dec. ATTACK ON PEARL HARBOR. On the morning of Sunday, 7 Dec., Japanese naval and air forces made a sneak attack on the U.S. fleet at the Pearl Harbor naval base in Hawaii. On the same day (8 Dec., Far Eastern time) the Japanese launched assaults on the Philippines, Guam, and Midway Island, and on British forces at Hong Kong and in the Malay Peninsula. The air attack at Pearl Harbor began at 7:55 A.M. (local time; 1:20 P.M. Washington time) and continued until 9:45 A.M. Of the 8 battleships at Pearl Harbor, the *Arizona, California* and *West Virginia* were sunk; the *Nevada* was grounded; the *Oklahoma* capsized; others were damaged. Altogether 19 ships were sunk or disabled. 5 battleships were later raised; 4 restored to the fleet. About 150 U.S. planes were destroyed, 2,335 soldiers and sailors and 68 civilians were killed, and 1,178 were wounded. During the morning of 7 Dec., the official Japanese reply to the U.S. proposals of 26 Nov. arrived at Washington, with instructions to the Japanese envoys to present it to Secretary Hull at 1 P.M. (Washington time). Nomura and Kurusu, however, did not appear in Hull's office until 2:05 P.M., just as Hull received reports of the attack on Pearl Harbor. On 24 Jan. 1942 a Presidential commission headed by Supreme Court Justice Owen J. Roberts attributed the effectiveness of the Japanese attack to the failure of the naval and military commanders at Hawaii (Rear Adm. Husband Kimmel and Lt. Gen. Walter Short) to adopt adequate defense measures. Previously (17 Dec. 1941) **Chester W. Nimitz** (1885–   ) had succeeded Kimmel in command of the Pacific fleet.

8 Dec. With only 1 dissenting vote, the U.S. Congress declared war on Japan.

11 Dec. Germany and Italy declared war on the U.S., which then recognized a state of war with these nations.

19 Dec. Congress extended military conscription to men between the ages of 20 and 44.

THE WAR IN THE PACIFIC AND THE FAR EAST, 1941–45

1941

8–25 Dec. JAPANESE GAINS. Thailand and Malaya were invaded by the Japanese (8 Dec.). On 10 Dec. the British battleship *Prince of Wales* and the battle cruiser *Repulse* were sunk by Japanese torpedo planes in the South China Sea. This blow to Allied naval strength enabled the Japanese capture of Singapore and other enemy successes in Southeast Asia. The Japanese made landings on the Philippines (10–23 Dec.); took Guam (13 Dec.), Wake Island (22 Dec.), and Hong Kong (25 Dec.).

2 Jan. Supreme command for American, British, Dutch, and Australian forces in the Far East (ABDACOM), headed by Gen. Sir Archibald P. Wavell, with Maj. Gen. George P. Brett, deputy, was announced following a meeting at Washington.

1942

2 Jan.–6 May. BATAAN AND CORREGIDOR. Manila and Cavite fell to the Japanese (2 Jan.). Gen. MacArthur's forces retired to Bataan Peninsula, where MacArthur established headquarters at the fortress of Corregidor ("The Rock") in Manila Bay. On 17 Mar. MacArthur arrived in Australia after secretly leaving Bataan Peninsula, and took command of the Allied forces in the Southwest Pacific. After resisting a siege of more than three months, Bataan fell 9 Apr. American forces under Gen. Jonathan M. Wainwright withdrew to Corregidor Island in Manila Bay. On 6 May Wainwright surrendered Corregidor and its garrison of 11,500 to the Japanese.

11 Jan.–3 May. JAPAN'S ADVANCE. Japanese forces occupied the Netherlands East Indies (11–31 Jan.). In the 1st major sea battle between the Allies and Japan, the Battle of **Macassar Strait** (between Borneo and Celebes), Allied sea and air forces inflicted severe damage on a large Japanese invasion convoy (24–27 Jan.). On 31 Jan. British troops withdrew from Malaya to Singapore and on the same day Vice-Adm. **William F. Halsey, Jr.,** carried out a bombardment of the Marshall and Gilbert Islands. Singapore and its British garrison unconditionally surrendered (15 Feb.). A naval battle was fought in Badoeng Strait (19–20 Feb.). On 24 Feb. the British withdrew from Rangoon, in Burma. Its occupation by the Japanese (9 Mar.) cut off supplies from the Burma Road. Mandalay fell 3 May. The **Battle of the Java Sea** (27 Feb.–1 Mar.), fought as a delaying action by the U.S. fleet under Adm. **Thomas C. Hart,** resulted in the most severe U.S. naval losses since Pearl Harbor. On 6 Mar. Batavia, capital of the Netherlands East Indies, fell. By 9 Mar. the Japanese conquest of Java had been completed. On 8 Mar. Japanese troops landed at Lae and Salamaua in New Guinea. On 10 Mar. Lt. Gen. **Joseph W. Stilwell** ("Vinegar Joe") was made chief of staff of Allied armies in the Chinese theater of operations.

18 Apr.–6 June. STIFFENING ALLIED RESISTANCE. On 18 Apr. carrier-based U.S. army bombers (B-25's) led by Maj. Gen. **James H. Doolittle** raided Toyko. On 7–8 May was fought the **Battle of the Coral Sea,** the 1st naval engagement in history in which surface ships did not engage enemy ships (all fighting was done by carrier-based planes). One Japanese carrier was sunk, 2 damaged, as well as a number of other ships. The U.S. carrier *Lexington* was lost in this engagement, which halted the enemy advance upon Australia by frustrating the Japanese attempt to seize Port Moresby in southern New Guinea in order to cut the Australian supply line. The naval and air **Battle of Mid-**

way (3–6 June), in the Central Pacific, resulted in the 1st major defeat of Japanese naval forces. The attempted enemy seizure of Midway Island ended in failure, with the loss of 4 aircraft carriers and 275 planes. This action checked the Japanese advance across the Central Pacific, eliminated the threat to Hawaii, and restored the balance of naval power in the Pacific.

3–21 June. The Japanese bombed Dutch Harbor and Ft. Mears, Alaska (3–4 June), and occupied the islands of Attu and Kiska in the westernmost Aleutians (12–21 June). On 21 June the Oregon coast was shelled. Previously (23 Feb.) an oil refinery near Santa Barbara, Calif., had been shelled by a Japanese submarine.

22 July. Japanese forces in northern New Guinea began an overland push against Port Moresby on the southern coast. After crossing the Owen Stanley Mountains they were halted by Australian forces who counterattacked from Port Moresby (29 Sept.) and crossed the Owen Stanley Range (10 Oct.).

7 Aug.–9 Feb. 1943. GUADALCANAL, FIRST MAJOR OFFENSIVE. Countering Japanese advances in the Solomons, U.S. marines landed at Guadalcanal (7 Aug.) and seized the airport, renaming it Henderson Field. Marines also landed on Tulagi, Florida, and other nearby islands. Two days later occurred the naval **Battle of Savo Island**, north of Guadalcanal, resulting in the loss of 4 heavy cruisers (3 U.S., 1 Australian), a Japanese victory which temporarily deprived U.S. forces on Guadalcanal of air and naval support. A 6-mo. fight for the island followed. A naval battle of the Eastern Solomons (23–25 Aug.) resulted in damage to Japanese carriers and cruisers by aircraft from the U.S. carriers *Enterprise* and *Saratoga*. On 26 Aug. Japanese landed at Milne Bay in New Guinea, but were defeated after a 2-wk. battle. The naval **Battle of Cape Esperance** (11–12 Oct.), in the Solomons, resulted in a U.S. victory over the Japanese, who lost 1 carrier and 4 destroyers. Strong Japanese attacks (21–25 Oct.) failed to take Henderson Field. The naval **Battle of Santa Cruz** (26–27 Oct.), in

the Solomons, resulted in the sinking of 2 Japanese destroyers and damage to 8 other enemy warships. The naval **Battle of Guadalcanal** (12–15 Nov.), a decisive U.S. victory, prevented the Japanese from landing substantial reinforcements and made possible the conquest of Guadalcanal by U.S. troops. This action cost the U.S. 2 cruisers and 7 destroyers. The Japanese lost 2 battleships, 1 cruiser, 2 destroyers, and 10 transports. By 9 Feb. 1943 Japanese forces completed the abandonment of Guadalcanal.

1943

23 Jan.–16 Sept. GAINS IN NEW GUINEA. Ground fighting ended in Papua (23 Jan.), with the Japanese cleared out. The air **Battle of the Bismarck Sea** (2–3 Mar.), in the New Guinea area, resulted in the destruction of 12 Japanese troop convoys and 10 warships and the death of Adm. Yamamoto. On 16 Sept. U.S. forces under Gen. MacArthur took Lae in New Guinea, completing reconquest of Lae-Salamaua area.

24 Mar.–15 Aug. STRUGGLE FOR THE ALEUTIANS. Naval battle of the Komandorski Islands in the western Aleutians resulted in a U.S. victory. U.S. forces landed on Attu (11 May), in the western Aleutians. By 3 June all organized enemy resistance on Attu had ended. On 15 Aug. U.S. and Canadian troops reoccupied Kiska without resistance, the Japanese having already left the island.

30 June–26 Dec. U.S. SOUTH PACIFIC OFFENSIVE began 30 June with the landing of U.S. troops on Rendova Island, in New Georgia. The naval **Battle of Kula Gulf** (6 July) was followed by other U.S. naval victories (Aug.–Oct.) which gave the Allies control of the waters adjacent to the central Solomons. On 1 Nov. U.S. marines landed at Bougainville, in the northern Solomons, in a thrust toward the bastion of Rabaul. The Japanese struck back, but the naval **Battle of Empress Augusta Bay** (2 Nov.), off Bougainville, resulted in a decisive Japanese defeat and enabled the Allies to cut the supply lines to Rabaul, thus isolating

all enemy forces remaining in the Solomons and securing the U.S. flank for an advance toward the Philippines. The next steps were landings by U.S. forces at Arawe (15 Dec.) and Cape Gloucester (26 Dec.) in New Britain.

21 Nov. U.S. CENTRAL PACIFIC OFFENSIVE, under Admiral **Chester W. Nimitz,** commander in chief, Pacific fleet, aimed at capturing islands "up the ladder" of the Solomons, the Gilberts and Marshalls, the Marianas, and the Bonin Islands to within effective bombing distance of Japan, began with landings on **Tarawa** and **Makin** in the Gilbert Islands. At Tarawa, which was not secured until 24 Nov., the direct assault on heavily fortified positions cost the U.S. 2nd Marine Division 913 killed and missing, and 2,037 wounded.

25 Aug.–21 Dec. Lord Louis Mountbatten was appointed (25 Aug.) supreme Allied commander, Southeast Asia. On 21 Dec. Gen. Stilwell began his campaign in northern Burma.

1944

31 Jan.–25 Nov. CENTRAL PACIFIC ADVANCE. U.S. forces invaded (31 Jan.) the Marshall Islands, taking Roi and Namur (3 Feb.), Kwajalein (6 Feb.), and Eniwetok (17–22 Feb.); landed on the air and naval base of Saipan (15 June), in the Mariana Islands, completing its conquest 9 July, on Guam (21 July), completing its reoccupation 9 Aug. The invasion of the Palaus began with the landing of U.S. marines on Peleliu (15–17 Sept.), finally taken on 25 Nov.

1 Mar.–22 Apr. SOUTHWEST PACIFIC GAINS. U.S. troops invaded the Admiralty Islands (1 Mar.), completing their occupation on 25 Mar., and landed at Hollandia (22 Apr.), Dutch New Guinea, seizing enemy airfields.

17 May–3 Aug. BURMA CAMPAIGN. The capture (17 May) by Allied forces of Myitkyina airstrip in northern Burma gave them an air route to China. After severe fighting Myitkyina was retaken by Allied forces 3 Aug.

16 June. The U.S. air offensive against cities in the Japanese home islands was opened with an attack on Kyushu by U.S. Superfortresses (B-29's).

19 June–15 Dec. PHILIPPINES CAMPAIGN. Naval and air **Battle of the Philippine Sea** (19–20 June), fought entirely by carrier-based planes, cost the Japanese 3 carriers, 200 planes, and badly crippled its battleships and cruisers. On 18 July Premier Tojo resigned together with the entire Japanese Cabinet, and was relieved as chief of staff. Gen. Kuniaki Koiso became Premier. On 20 Oct. U.S. forces under Gen. MacArthur returned to the Philippines. Invading Leyte, in the central Philippines, they opened the drive for retaking the islands. The naval **Battle of Leyte Gulf** (23–25 Oct.), the last and greatest naval engagement of the war—in reality 3 separate engagements—resulted in decisive defeat for the Japanese. The battle caused the destruction of most of Japan's remaining sea power and gave the U.S. control of Philippine waters. After losing 2 battleships, 4 carriers, 9 cruisers, and 9 destroyers, the remnants of the Japanese fleet withdrew. On 15 Dec. U.S. forces landed on Mindoro Island in the Philippines.

28 Oct. Gen. Stilwell was recalled to Washington. Command of U.S. forces in China was assumed by Maj. Gen. **Albert C. Wedemeyer.**

24 Nov. Air offensive launched from Saipan in the Marianas began with Superfortress (B-29) attacks on Tokyo.

1945

9 Jan.–23 Feb. END OF PHILIPPINES CAMPAIGN. Landing at Lingayen Gulf (9 Jan.), U.S. forces invaded Luzon, main island of the Philippines, and took Manila (5–23 Feb.).

28 Jan. 1st convoy of trucks carrying war material over the Ledo (renamed Stilwell) Road across Burma from northeast India reached China.

10 Feb. Tokyo raided by 90 Superfortresses (B-29's).

19 Feb.–17 Mar. IWO JIMA. U.S. marines of the 4th and 5th Divisions landed on Iwo Jima, 750 miles from Tokyo. After bitter fighting, the U.S. forces took Mt. Suribachi (23 Feb.) and completed their conquest of the island on 17 Mar. Marine casualties: 4,189 killed, 15,308 wounded, 441 missing.

19 Mar.–21 June. BATTLE FOR THE RYUKYUS. U.S. carrier planes made extensive attacks on Japanese shipping and airfields in the Ryukyus (19–21 Mar.). On 1 Apr. the U.S. Tenth Army invaded **Okinawa,** main island of the Ryukyus, 360 miles southwest of Japan, completing their conquest on 21 June. Heavy air attacks by the Japanese, who used many suicide planes, made the campaign the costliest engagement of the war in point of losses in ships and sailors. The total U.S. casualties were 11,260 killed and 33,769 wounded.

5 Apr. Premier Koiso and the entire Japanese Cabinet resigned.

30 Apr. The Fourteenth British Imperial Army in Southeast Asia, aided by U.S. and Chinese forces, completed the expulsion of Japanese armies from that sector.

May–Aug. AIR OFFENSIVE AGAINST JAPAN, the greatest in the Pacific and Far East war, was launched against the Japanese home islands by the U.S. Twentieth Air Force, supported by British and U.S. naval units which carried out attacks along the Japanese coast. On 5 July Gen. **Carl Spaatz** was appointed commander of the Strategic Air Forces in the Pacific. In accordance with the terms of the Cairo Declaration, the U.S., Great Britain, and China demanded (26 July) that Japan surrender unconditionally. Japan formally rejected the Potsdam surrender ultimatum on 29 July. An **atomic bomb** with an explosive force of 20,000

tons of TNT was dropped (6 Aug.) on the Japanese city and military base of **Hiroshima,** the first time this weapon, until then held secret, was used for a military purpose. The bomb destroyed over 4 square miles of the city and brought death or injury to over 160,000 persons.

8 Aug. Russia declared war on Japan. Soviet armies invaded Manchuria.

9–15 Aug. An **atomic bomb** was dropped on the Japanese city and naval base of **Nagasaki.** On 10 Aug. the Japanese Cabinet under Premier Suzuki offered to surrender on condition that Emperor Hirohito keep his throne. The Japanese accepted the Allied terms on 14 Aug. **V-J Day** (15 Aug.).

15 Aug. U.S. CASUALTIES (in the Pacific theater: 41,322 dead out of total casualties 170,596); in all theaters by 15 Aug.: 321,999 dead; 800,000 wounded, captured, or missing; 111,426 of the 124,079 captured returned to U.S. control. The ratio of fatalities per 100 wounded in World War II was less than one half the ratio of World War I, owing, among other reasons, to **penicillin,** the **sulfa** drugs, early use of **blood plasma,** and an efficient system of evacuation (much of it by air). Total maximum **enrollment** in all U.S. forces was 12,466,000 (army, 8,300,000; navy, 3,500,000; marine corps, 486,000; coast guard, 180,000).

27 Aug.–9 Sept. U.S. forces began occupation of Japan (27 Aug.). The Japanese Premier and military leaders signed the formal surrender on board the U.S.S. *Missouri* in Tokyo Bay (2 Sept.). Surrender terms for Japanese forces in China were signed at Nanking (9 Sept.).

EUROPEAN AND MEDITERRANEAN THEATERS OF WAR, 1942–45

1942

7 Jan.–29 June. BRITISH VS. ROMMEL IN AFRICA. On 18 Nov. 1941 the British Eighth Army had opened its offensive in Libya, reached Agheila (7 Jan.), but held it for only two weeks. On

21 Jan. Rommel struck against the British and pressed them back in the neighborhood of Tobruk. A new offensive was launched in Libya by Rommel (26 May). Axis troops took Tobruk and Bardia (21 June), and Matrûh, in Egypt (29 June). The Axis advance was checked at El

Alamein (29 June), 70 miles west of Alexandria.

20 Jan.–12 May. RUSSIAN COUNTER-ATTACK. The Russians retook Mozhaisk (20 Jan.), claimed Dorogobuzh (23 Feb.), advanced near Kursk (29 Apr.), and attacked near Kharkov (12 May).

26 Jan. U.S. forces arrived in Northern Ireland.

27 Feb.–19 Aug. COMMANDO RAIDS. Allied paratroopers raided Bruneval, France (27 Feb.); British commandos raided St. Nazaire (28 Mar.); and on 19 Aug. Dieppe was raided by about 6,000 British and Canadian troops and a small force of U.S. Rangers. About 3,350 invaders were killed, wounded, or taken prisoner.

30 May–17 Aug. ALLIED AIR WAR. First 1,000-bomber raid carried out by the British on Cologne (30 May), followed the next day by a 1,000-bomber raid on Essen and the Ruhr, and a 1,000-plane raid on Bremen (25 June). The first independent U.S. bombing attack in Europe was carried out (17 Aug.) by Eighth Air Force Flying Fortresses (B-17's) in raid on railroad yards near Rouen.

10 June. LIDICE, town in Czechoslovakia, laid waste by the Germans in reprisal for the assassination (27 May) of Reinhard Heydrich, Gestapo official.

28 June–13 Sept. GERMAN SUMMER OFFENSIVE AGAINST RUSSIA started from Kirsh (28 June). Sevastopol fell to the Germans (1 July) after an 8-month siege. The Germans took Voronezh (7 July), Rostov (24 July), Markov (9 Aug.), crossed the Don River (20 Aug.), and opened the siege of Stalingrad (22 Aug.). On 1 Sept. they crossed the Kerch Straits from the Crimea and invaded the south Caucasus. They entered Stalingrad (13 Sept.).

23 Oct.–24 Dec. ALLIED CAMPAIGNS IN NORTH AFRICA. British Eighth Army under Gen. Bernard L. Montgomery launched (23 Oct.) 3rd Allied offensive in North Africa. British victory at El Alamein (4 Nov.) forced Rommel's forces to make a full retreat from Egypt by 12 Nov. The British took Bardia (12 Nov.), Tobruk (13 Nov.), Bengasi (20 Nov.).

8 Nov.–1 Dec. Operation TORCH. In the first major Allied amphibious operation in this theater, commanded by Gen. **Dwight D. Eisenhower,** with Admiral Sir Andrew Cunningham, naval commander, U.S. and British forces landed (8 Nov.) in North Africa. The main landings were made at Casablanca, Oran, and Algiers. On 10 Nov. fighting ceased at Oran. On 15 Nov. Allied troops advanced into Tunisia. Earlier, on 11 Nov., an armistice was arranged with Adm. Jean-François Darlan, Vichy representative in French North Africa, and the same day German forces entered Unoccupied France. Final agreement with Darlan was reached 13 Nov. On 27 Nov. the French fleet at Toulon was scuttled by its crews to prevent seizure of warships by Germans. With U.S. and British approval, Darlan became chief of state in French North Africa (1 Dec.), but he was assassinated in Algiers (24 Dec.), and Gen. Henri Giraud was appointed temporary administrator of North Africa.

19 Nov.–3 Mar. 1943. RUSSIAN COUNTEROFFENSIVE began on the Stalingrad front (19 Nov.), on Velikie Luki–Rzhev front (25 Nov.), and on Middle Don River (16 Dec.). On 18 Jan. 1943 the Russians raised the 17-month siege of Leningrad, the Germans at **Stalingrad** surrendered (2 Feb.), and the Russians retook Rostov (14 Feb.), Kharkov (16 Feb.), and Rzhev (9 Mar.).

1943

24 Jan.–13 May. END OF THE AFRICAN WAR. Tripoli fell to the British Eighth Army (24 Jan.). On 6 Feb. Gen. Eisenhower was appointed commander in chief of all Allied forces in North Africa. On 14 Feb. U.S. II corps, commanded by Maj. Gen. Lloyd R. Fredendall, was thrown back by Rommel's Afrika Korps at **Kasserine Pass.** The Americans retook the position on 19 Feb. and by 23 Feb. had checked Rommel's drive. In March Fredendall was replaced by Maj. Gen. **George S. Patton, Jr.** (1885–1945). On 19 Mar. U.S. forces took El Guettar in Tunisia. On 21 Mar., from the east, Gen.

RECONQUEST OF
THE AXIS
PRINCIPAL ALLIED THRUSTS

Scale of Miles
0   200   400

Montgomery launched an offensive against Axis forces on the Mareth Line in Tunisia. The British breakthrough took place on 29 Mar. On 7 Apr. U.S. First Army and British Eighth Army joined lines near Gafsa, thus encircling the Axis forces in Tunisia. Tunis fell to the British, and Bizerte to the Americans (7 May). The main Axis forces under Gen. Jurgen von Arnim (Rommel having fled) retreated into the Cape Bon peninsula. About 250,000 Axis troops surrendered. 13 May marked the formal end of the North African campaign. Total U.S. casualties: about 18,500.

5 July–29 Dec. TURN OF THE TIDE IN RUSSIA. The German summer offensive in Russia, launched 5 July, made little headway. The Russians smashed back, retook Orel and Belgorod (4 Aug.), Smolensk (25 Sept.), cleared the German forces from the east bank of the Dnieper (29 Sept.), recaptured Dnepropetrovsk (26 Oct.), Kiev (7 Nov.), and broke enemy lines west of Kiev (29 Dec.), entering Poland on 3 Jan. 1944.

10 July.–17 Aug. INVASION OF SICILY by air and sea was begun by Anglo-American forces (Operation HUSKY) on 10 July, under the immediate command of deputy commander Gen. Sir Harold R. L. G. Alexander, with British forces led by Montgomery and U.S. by Patton. Palermo fell to U.S. troops (24 July), Catania to British (5 Aug.). Fall of Messina to the U.S. (17 Aug.) completed the conquest of Sicily, assured greater safety to Allied shipping in the Mediterranean, and provided a springboard for attacks on Italy and Sardinia. U.S. casualties totaled about 7,400.

25–28 July. King Victor Emmanuel II announced (25 July) the resignation of Premier Mussolini and his Cabinet. Marshal Pietro Badoglio became head of the Italian government. On 28 July Badoglio ordered the dissolution of the Fascist party.

17 Aug.–15 Oct. U.S. Eighth Air Force raided ball-bearing works at Schweinfurt and Regensburg (17 Aug.). On 15 Oct. U.S. Flying Fortresses (B-17's) bombed Schweinfurt.

3 Sept.–2 Dec. ITALIAN CAMPAIGN. The British Eighth Army invaded Italy from Sicily across the Straits of Messina (3 Sept.)—Operation BAYTOWN. On 8 Sept. Italy accepted the Allied terms of unconditional surrender. Operation AVALANCHE was begun 9 Sept. when the U.S. Fifth Army under Gen. **Mark Clark** made amphibious landings at Salerno, about 30 miles below Naples. Strong German resistance at Salerno ended on 18 Sept. On 10 Sept. the Germans seized Rome. The bulk of the Italian fleet surrendered the next day. On 12 Sept. Mussolini, who had been placed under arrest by the Italian government, escaped with the aid of a raiding party of German paratroopers, and on 15 Sept. he proclaimed the establishment of a Fascist Republican regime in Italian areas under German domination. Allied crossings of the Volturno River (north of Naples) took place (12–14 Oct.) and by 25 Dec. an Allied front bisected Italy along the Garigliano and Sangro rivers. On 2 Dec. 1943 an air raid against Allied-held Bari resulted in the loss of 16 vessels. An Allied Control Commission for Italy was established 10 Nov.

9 Oct. Yugoslav partisans under Marshal Tito began assault against Axis forces near Trieste.

1944

11 Jan. ALLIED AIR OFFENSIVE. Strategic air offensive from the British Isles in preparation for Allied invasion of the Continent began 11 Jan., and reached its peak in Apr. and May. On 6 Mar. 800 U.S. planes bombed Berlin.

16 Jan. Gen. Eisenhower arrived in Britain to assume his duties as Supreme Commander, Allied Expeditionary Forces. He established SHAEF (Supreme Headquarters, Allied Expeditionary Forces).

22 Jan.–4 June. CAMPAIGN IN CENTRAL ITALY. On 22 Jan. Allied amphibious landings were made at Nettuno-Anzio beachhead 30 miles south of Rome. The successful Allied assault on Cassino, in central Italy, a key position in the German Gustav Line, begun 15 Mar., ended 18 May. On 4 June Rome was liberated by the U.S. Fifth Army.

29 Jan.–9 May. FURTHER SOVIET GAINS. On 29 Jan. the Russians announced the Moscow-Leningrad area had been cleared of German troops. The Russians recaptured Odessa (10 Apr.) and Sevastopol (9 May).

22 Mar. German forces occupied Hungary.

6 June. OPERATION OVERLORD. Allied forces concentrated in southern England invaded Europe on a 60-mi. line along the coast of Normandy, from the mouth of the river Orne to the beaches near Ste-Mère-Église on the Cotentin Peninsula. The spearhead assault by a force of 176,000 troops was made with 4,000 invasion craft supported by 600 warships and an air cover of 11,000 planes, and was preceded by the descent of U.S. and British parachute and glider troops. The entire action was under the unified command of Gen. Eisenhower and was the largest amphibious operation of the war and all history. The ground forces (21st Army Group) were under the command of Gen. Montgomery. The American land contingent (U.S. First Army) was commanded by Gen. **Omar N. Bradley** (1893–   ). The Germans countered (14 June) by initiating the bombing of southern England with jet-propelled pilotless aircraft (V-1's), launched across the Channel from special sites in France and Belgium, with London as chief target. The U.S. forces reached the west shore of the Cotentin Peninsula (18 June). On 27 June Cherbourg and its demolished harbor works were captured by U.S. forces. By 2 July the Allies had landed in Normandy about 1 million troops, 566,648 tons of supplies, and 171,532 vehicles. The British forces captured Caen (9 July); the U.S. forces took St. Lô (18 July), road center linking Normandy with Brittany. U.S. "breakout" from St. Lô (25 July) enabled powerful armored thrust toward Avranches and into Brittany, which by 10 Aug. had been overrun and cut off by the U.S. Third Army under Gen. Patton. The St. Lô action concluded the Allied offensive in Normandy and opened the **Battle of France.**

23 June. The Russians opened their summer offensive along an 800-mi. line south of Leningrad.

19 July. Leghorn taken by the U.S. Fifth Army.

20 July. Attempted assassination of Hitler and plot to overthrow the Nazi regime ended in failure.

2 Aug. Polish underground army in Warsaw area commanded by General Bor (Komorowski) opened fight against the Germans. The Polish forces surrendered on 2 Oct.

3–23 Aug. Allies closed the Falaise-Argentan pocket, causing heavy German losses.

12 Aug. Florence fell to British forces. German troops in Italy pulled back to the Gothic Line.

15 Aug. OPERATION DRAGOON. Allied forces, including the U.S. Seventh Army under Gen. **Alexander M. Patch,** landed in southern France, between Marseilles and Nice, and drove up the Rhône Valley.

25 Aug.–11 Sept. LIBERATION OF FRANCE, BELGIUM, AND LUXEMBOURG. On 25 Aug. Paris was liberated. On 28 Aug. the U.S. Third Army reached the Marne. Brussels and Antwerp were liberated by British and Canadian troops (4 Sept.). By 5 Sept. the Allies had landed 2,086,000 men and 3,466,000 tons of supplies in Western Europe. Luxembourg was liberated 11 Sept.

7 Sept. Germans fired first V-2 (p. 570) on London.

8 Sept. Bulgaria surrendered to the Allies.

12 Sept.–3 Dec. BATTLE FOR GERMANY. U.S. forces entered Germany near Eupen and Trier (12 Sept.). In an attempt to turn the flank of the Westwall and gain a bridgehead on the Rhine, the Allies landed 34,000 airborne troops in Holland (17–28 Sept.) The U.S. forces took Eindhoven and Nijmegen. The British were defeated at Arnhem. The Canadian First Army cleared the Scheldt Estuary (9 Oct.–9 Nov.), thus enabling the Allies to use the urgently needed port facilities of Antwerp. The U.S. First Army took Aachen (21 Oct.) after a battle that began on 2 Oct. and required penetration of the Siegfried Line. Aachen was the first large German city taken by the Allies. The U.S. Third Army entered Metz (22 Nov.) and Strasbourg (23 Nov.), and U.S. forces reached the Roer River (3 Dec.).

22 Sept.–29 Dec. SOVIET ADVANCES. Russians took Tallinn (22 Sept.) and entered East Prussia (20 Oct.). Russian and Yugoslav forces seized Belgrade (20 Oct.), and the Russians entered Budapest 29 Dec.

3 Dec. Civil war broke out in Greece and lasted until 12 Jan. 1945.

16–26 Dec. BATTLE OF THE BULGE. A German counteroffensive under the command of Gen. Karl von Rundstedt was launched in the Ardennes along an 80-mi. front held by an inadequate number of U.S. troops, many of whom lacked battle experience. By this surprise attack the Germans hoped to split the Allied armies and take Liége and Antwerp. After advancing 50 mi. to a point near Dinant, within 4 miles of the Meuse, the German drive was checked, largely owing to the defense of ringed Bastogne, which was relieved on 26 Dec. The original Allied line in the Ardennes was not restored until 21 Jan. 1945. The Battle of the Bulge resulted in about 77,000 U.S. casualties, including 8,000 killed, 48,000 wounded, and 21,000 captured or missing.

1945

12–23 Jan. Russians launched general offensive in Poland (12–15 Jan.), took Warsaw (17 Jan.), Lodz (19 Jan.), and reached the Oder River (23 Jan.).

8 Feb.–26 Apr. GERMANY CRUSHED. British offensive launched in Holland (8 Feb.); U.S. Third Army crossed the Saar River (22 Feb.). The Saar-Palatinate area was cleared of German troops by 25 Mar. U.S. forces penetrated the Ruhr Valley (23 Feb.) and reached the Rhine near Düsseldorf (2 Mar.). Cologne and Düsseldorf fell on 7 Mar.; on the same day U.S. forces captured the **Remagen Bridge** across the Rhine before the Germans could demolish it, and secured a bridgehead on the east bank. On 23 Mar. Allied forces crossed the Rhine between Rees and Wesel by water and air. The Ruhr was enveloped and reduced (24 Mar.–18 Apr.), with the surrender of 325,000 German troops. On 27 Mar. U.S. forces took Mannheim and Frankfurt am Main. The U.S. Ninth Army reached the Elbe (11 Apr.). The Russians launched (13 Apr.) a drive on Berlin, entering the city on 24 Apr. U.S. forces took Nuremburg (21 Apr.). U.S. and Russian troops met at Torgau, on the Elbe (25 Apr.). On 26 Apr. the British took Bremen.

3 Mar. Finland, which had quit the war against Russia 4 Sept. 1941, declared war against Germany.

28 Apr. Mussolini and his mistress, Clara Petacci, captured and killed by Italian partisans in the town of Dongo, on Lake Como, as he tried to flee to Switzerland. Allied forces invaded the Po Valley.

1 May–5 June. GERMAN CAPITULATION. On 1 May the provisional German government under Adm. Karl Doenitz announced Hitler's death. It was reported that he had committed suicide in Berlin. On 2 May Berlin fell and the German forces in Italy surrendered. The German forces in the Netherlands, Denmark, and northwest Germany surrendered 4 May. Field Marshal Jodl signed (7 May, 2:41 A.M. French time) the instrument of unconditional surrender of Germany in the Allied headquarters at Reims. 8 May, **V-E Day**—formal end of the war in Europe. The German surrender was formally ratified at Berlin (9 May). On 5 June Germany was placed under an Allied Control Council and divided into four occupation zones.

THE UNITED STATES AND THE WESTERN HEMISPHERE, 1942–45

HEMISPHERE SOLIDARITY. On 12 Jan. 1942 the U.S. and Mexico established a joint defense commission. At the **Rio de Janeiro Conference** (15–28 Jan.) of American foreign ministers, delegates of all 21 American republics, under the leadership of Sumner Welles and Oswaldo Aranha, chairman, voted to recommend to their respective governments a break in diplomatic relations with the Axis powers. All of the governments involved, with the exception of Chile and Argentina, severed relations. Chile broke off relations with the Axis (20 Jan. 1943); Argentina not until 26 Jan. 1944. The U.S. revealed (19 Mar. 1942) establishment of air bases in Guatemala to defend the Panama Canal Zone. On 30 Mar. the Inter-American Defense Board held its first session at Washington, D.C. President Roosevelt and President Getulio Vargas of Brazil, in conference aboard a U.S. destroyer off Natal, Brazil, announced (28 Jan.) agreement on common defense aims. The friendly relations between the U.S. and Mexico were stressed at a meeting (21 Apr.) of President Roosevelt and President Avila Camacho. On 16 Aug. 1944 the U.S. government froze Argentina's gold assets in the U.S. in retaliation against the Argentine government's refusal to cooperate fully against the Axis. On 29 Sept. President Roosevelt expressed concern over the continuing spread of Nazi and Fascist influence in Argentina and accused its government of having failed to fulfill its "solemn inter-American obligations." The Inter-American Conference on Problems of War and Peace met (21 Feb.–8 Mar. 1945) at Chapultepec Castle, Mexico City. All of the American republics except Argentina were represented. The conference adopted (3 Mar.) the **Act of Chapultepec,** a regional security agreement binding for the duration of the war. It provided that aggression upon one American state by another would be regarded as aggression against all and specified the "use of armed force to prevent or repel aggression." On 27 Mar. 1945 Argentina declared war on Germany and Japan, was admitted to the Pan-American Union (4 Apr.), and recognized (9 Apr.) by the U.S., other American republics, and Great Britain.

WAR MOBILIZATION. By Executive order the 9-man **War Manpower Commission** (WMC) was established (18 Apr. 1942) for the more effective utilization of manpower resources. Federal Security Administrator **Paul V. McNutt** was named chairman. Later that year its powers were extended to include jurisdiction over Selective Service, the U.S. Employment Service, and other war recruiting and training agencies. Voluntary male enlistments in the military services were ended. All males 18–38 became subject to selective service (draft age lowered to 18, 13 Nov. 1942), with deferments limited to war industries, agriculture, hardship cases, and the clergy. After a trial, drafting of 38–45 was ended, but all males between 45 and 64 were registered (25 Apr.). Women were enlisted for noncombat duties in the Women's Auxiliary Army Corps (WAACS, by act of 15 May 1942), Women Appointed for Voluntary Emergency Service (WAVES), Women's Auxiliary Ferrying Squadron (WAFS), *Semper Paratus* Always Ready Service (SPARS), and the Women's Reserve of the Marine Corps. To deal with the labor shortage, President Roosevelt decreed (9 Feb. 1943) for the duration of the war a minimum work week of 48 hours, applicable immediately in U.S. areas where labor shortages prevailed, but specified time-and-a-half for the extra 8 hours. Following Roosevelt's "hold-the-line" order (8 Apr. 1943), the WMC adopted regulations to "freeze" 27 million workers in war jobs.

WAR PRODUCTION. On 13 Jan. President Roosevelt appointed **Donald M. Nelson** chairman of the **War Pro-**

duction Board (WPB) with authority to mobilize the nation's resources for a total war effort. WPB was the principal agency in the field of production and supply. On 21 Jan. Nelson abolished the Office of Production Management, whose functions were absorbed by the WPB. On 8 Apr. the WPB halted nonessential residential and highway construction in a move to conserve materials for the war effort. On 14 Aug. 1944 Nelson issued orders permitting limited reconversion of industry from war to civilian output. Nelson resigned (30 Sept.) and was succeeded by Julius A. Krug. On 2 Nov. President Roosevelt appointed Nelson his "personal representative" and requested him to organize war production in China. The WPB was terminated 4 Oct. 1945, and its functions transferred to the Civilian Production Administration. On 3 Oct. 1944 James F. Byrnes was named head of the newly established Office of War Mobilization and Reconversion.

STRATEGIC AND CRITICAL WAR MATERIALS. In June 1942 the WPB substituted for general priorities a classified system of specific allocations of all strategic materials. The problem was also tackled by other officials and war agencies. On 7 Jan. 1942 Federal Loan Adminstrator Jesse H. Jones announced a $4-billion program for increasing production of synthetic rubber. On 14 Apr. control of the U.S. stockpile of critical and essential materials was transferred to the Board of Economic Warfare headed by Vice-President Henry A. Wallace. On 15 Sept. William M. Jeffers, president of the Union Pacific Railroad, was appointed Rubber Administrator with full authority over the entire U.S. rubber program. On 15 July 1943 President Roosevelt abolished the Board of Economic Warfare and created the Office of Economic Warfare (OEW), headed by Leo T. Crowley, which absorbed its predecessor's functions as well as the foreign subsidiaries of the RFC on 25 Oct. Other war agencies concerned with war materials included Petroleum Administrator for War (Exec. order, 2 Dec. 1942, preceded, 28 May 1941, by Office of Petroleum Coordinator for War, with the Secretary of the Interior as coordinator); Solid Fuels Administrator for War (es-

tablished in the Department of the Interior by Exec. order, 19 Apr. 1943, with power over coal and certain other solid fuels, including supervision of operations when mines were placed under government control). Financing for war industries was facilitated by the RFC and the Smaller War Plants Corp., established by Act of Congress, 11 June 1942 and terminated 27 Dec. 1945, when its functions were transferred to the RFC.

PRICE CONTROL AND RATIONING. The Emergency Price Control Act (30 Jan. 1942) established the Office of Price Administration (OPA) to fix price ceilings on all commodities (except farm products) and to control rents in defense areas. This Federal agency was originally created (11 Apr. 1941) as the Office of Price Administration and Civilian Supply, with Leon Henderson as first Federal Price Administrator; succeeded (Jan. 1943) by Prentiss M. Brown, in turn by Chester Bowles (Oct. 1943), and by Paul A. Porter (Feb. 1946). Rationing began 27 Dec. 1941, with auto tires. The first war ration book (1942) provided coupons for sugar, then coffee, with separate books for gasoline (1 Dec.), and coupon sheets for fuel oil. Point rationing was started early in 1943 with meat, fats and oils, butter, cheese, and processed foods. Shoes were later added. At its peak 13 rationing programs were administered. Before the close of Nov. 1945 all rationing programs were ended except for sugar and rubber tires. Tire rationing ended 31 Dec. 1945; sugar, 11 June 1947. As compared with World War I considerable price stabilization was obtained. By V-J Day consumer prices had risen 31% as against 62% by the Armistice of 1918. (See also p. 541.)

LABOR CONTROLS. In Mar. 1941 the National Defense Mediation Board, a tripartite body, with William H. Davis as chairman, was given investigatory and mediatory powers to deal with labor disputes in defense industries. In Nov. 1941 it rejected the United Mine Workers' demand for a union shop in the steel companies' "captive mines." C.I.O. members resigned and the Board's usefulness was destroyed. It was replaced (12 Jan. 1942) by a 12-man National War Labor

Board (NWLB), equally divided among public, employers, and labor representatives, with Davis as chairman (to 8 Mar. 1945), with authority to settle disputes by mediation and arbitration. In the **International Harvester Case** (15 Apr.) the Board granted the union **maintenance of membership** on condition that a majority of union employees, voting in a secret election, approved; modified in June to provide a 15-day period when employees could resign from union membership, after which maintenance of membership would go into effect. The Board tied wage increases to the rise in the cost of living since 1 Jan. 1941 (**"Little Steel" formula**, 16 July). On 8 Apr. 1943 President Roosevelt issued his "hold-the-line" order freezing prices, wages, and salaries; modified in effect (12 May). Because of a strike involving 450,000 soft-coal miners and 80,000 anthracite miners, President Roosevelt ordered (1 May) Secretary of the Interior Harold L. Ickes to take over all coal mines in the Eastern U.S. Roosevelt placed responsibility for the stoppage upon John L. Lewis, who called off the strike on 2 May. The **War Labor Disputes Act** (**Smith-Connally Anti-Strike Act**), passed over Roosevelt's veto (25 June), broadened Presidential power to seize plants where interference with war production was threatened by a labor disturbance; made illegal the instigation of strikes in plants seized by the government; and made unions liable for damage suits for failure to give 30 days' notice of intention to strike in war industries. By order of President Roosevelt (27 Dec.) the U.S. Army took temporary possession of all railroads in the U.S. in order to prevent a strike of railway workers. The railroads were returned to private management on 18 Jan. 1944. On 28 Dec. 1944 the U.S. Army took possession of Montgomery Ward establishments in Chicago and elsewhere following the firm's refusal to obey WLB directives.

FEPC. The migration of Negroes from rural sections to industrial areas led to a demand for ending racial discrimination in war industries and the armed services. The **Fair Employment Practice Committee**, originally established (25 June 1941) to curb discrimination in war production and government employment, was strengthened by an Executive order (27 May 1943) calling for the mandatory incorporation of nondiscrimination clauses in war contracts and subcontracts. Race riots broke out in Detroit (20–21 June). President Roosevelt ordered out Federal troops to quell the disturbance. A strike in the transportation field in protest against the upgrading of Negroes occurred in Philadelphia 1 Aug. 1944, and the U.S. Army quickly restored order and normal transportation facilities. In Feb. 1946 a bill for a permanent FEPC was killed in the Senate by a filibuster. Again in 1950 the Senate blocked passage, and a modified plan was blocked in 1952. By the end of 1946 5 states (N.Y., N.J., Mass., Conn., and Wash.) had enacted Fair Employment Practice acts.

OTHER WAR AGENCIES. Office of Civilian Defense (28 Jan. 1942), with Mayor **Fiorello H. La Guardia** (N.Y.) director; succeeded by James N. Landis. **Director of Economic Stabilization**, filled (4 Oct. 1942) by Supreme Court Justice **James F. Byrnes** (S.C.), who (28 May 1943) headed the **Office of War Mobilization** (OWM), established to unify the activities of Federal agencies engaged in the production or distribution of civilian supplies. **Office of Scientific Research and Development** (28 June 1941). **Office of Lend-Lease Administration** (Exec. order 8 Oct. 1941). **Office of Censorship** (Exec. order 19 Dec. 1941), with Byron Price director until Nov. 1945. **Office of Defense Transportation** (Exec. order 18 Dec. 1941). **War Shipping Administration** (Exec. order 7 Feb. 1942), with Rear Adm. **Emory S. Land** as administrator. **National Housing Agency** (Exec. order 24 Feb. 1942). **Office of Alien Property Custodian** (Exec. order 11 Mar. 1942). **Office of Foreign Relief and Rehabilitation** (by State Dept. order 4 Dec. 1942). **Office of Coordinator of Inter-American Affairs** (Exec. order 30 July 1941), **Nelson A. Rockefeller**, coordinator (1940–44). **Office of War Information** (OWI, Exec. order 13 June 1942), to consolidate in one agency the information activities, both foreign and domestic, of the government (Office of

Facts and Figures, Office of Government Reports, Division of Information of the Office of Emergency Management, and the Foreign Information Service), **Elmer Davis**, director. **Office of Strategic Services** (Exec. order 13 June 1942), placed under the jurisdiction of the Joint Chiefs of Staff, to engage in intelligence operations abroad and in the analysis of strategic information; **William J. Donovan**, director.

ATOMIC BOMB PROJECT. The Manhattan Engineer District for the development of the atomic bomb was placed under the command of Brig. Gen. Leslie R. Groves (13 Aug. 1942). Construction was begun (Sept.–Dec.) on the 3 chief installations of the Manhattan District: the U-235 separation plant (Oak Ridge, Tenn.), the bomb development laboratory (Los Alamos, N.M.), and the plutonium production works (Hanford, Wash.). Scientists working on the Argonne Project at the University of Chicago effected the first self-sustaining nuclear reaction (2 Dec.). The first atomic bomb was exploded (16 July 1945) in a test at Alamogordo, N.M.

G.I. LEGISLATION. The "state rights" soldier vote bill became law (31 Mar. 1944) without President Roosevelt's signature. Roosevelt approved (22 June) the "GI Bill of Rights" authorizing educational and other benefits for World War II veterans.

1942 ELECTION TREND. Congressional, state, and local elections (3 Nov.) indicated a swing toward the Republicans, who gained 46 seats in the House, 9 in the Senate. The Democrats, however, retained control of both houses.

RELOCATION AND ENEMY ALIENS. By order of President Roosevelt (19 Feb. 1942), the Secretary of War was authorized to prescribe restricted military areas from which persons might be excluded. About 110,000 Japanese-Americans living in Calif., Ore., Wash., and Ariz. were by 29 Mar. transferred to relocation camps in the U.S. interior. On 12 Oct. Attorney General Francis Biddle announced that, effective 19 Oct., 600,000 unnaturalized Italians in the U.S. would no longer be considered as enemy aliens. On 17 Dec. 1944 the U.S. Army an-

nounced the termination, effective 2 Jan. 1945, of the mass exclusion from the West Coast of persons of Japanese ancestry.

INTERNAL SECURITY MEASURES. On 27 June 1942 J. Edgar Hoover, director of the FBI, announced the arrest of 8 Nazi saboteurs who had been landed from submarines on the Long Island and Florida coasts. Convicted by a secret military tribunal appointed by the President, 6 were electrocuted and the other 2 given long prison terms. On 23 July, 28 persons, including George Sylvester Viereck, William Dudley Pelley, and Gerald Winrod, were indicted as seditionists. In the course of their trial in 1944 Judge Edward C. Eichers died, and the indictments were dismissed (1946) by Chief Justice B. L. Laws of the Circuit Court of Appeals, who rebuked the Department of Justice for "lack of diligence" in prosecution. On 15 May 1943 the 3rd International (Comintern) was dissolved in Moscow. On 20 May 1944 the Communist party of the U.S. dissolved as a political party but was reconstituted as a supposedly nonparty group under the name of the Communist Political Association, headed by Earl Browder. Congressman Martin Dies' **Committee on Un-American Activities** was given permanent status by a House vote, 207–186 (3 Jan. 1945). The Dies Committee recommended dismissal of some 3,800 government employees; but after a Department of Justice investigation, only 36 were found to warrant dismissal. On 27 July 1945 the Communist Political Association voted to disband and to reconstitute the Communist Party of the U.S. On 29 July William Z. Foster replaced Earl Browder as head of the Communist organization.

PLANNING FOR PEACE: CONNALLY-FULBRIGHT RESOLUTION. On 16 Mar. 1943 Sens. Joseph Ball (Rep., Minn.), Harold Burton (Rep., Ohio), Carl Hatch (Dem., N.M.), and Lister Hill (Dem., Ala.) began a bipartisan movement to commit the U.S. Senate to participation in an international organization. On 21 Sept. the House of Representatives adopted the Fulbright Resolution (introduced by J. W. Fulbright [Ark.]) favoring "the creation of appropriate international machinery with power adequate to establish and to maintain a just and lasting peace," and U.S. participation "through its constitutional process." A similar resolution (introduced by Tom Connally [Tex.]), was adopted in the Senate, 85–5 (5 Nov.), with the express stipulation that any treaty made to carry out its purpose would require a vote of two thirds of the Senate. On 21 July 1945 the Senate approved U.S. membership in the United Nations Food and Agriculture Organization. On 28 July the Senate ratified the United Nations Charter by a vote of 89 to 2. President Truman signed the Charter (8 Aug.)

PRESIDENTIAL CAMPAIGN OF 1944. The Republican National Convention met at Chicago (26 June) and nominated (27 June) Gov. **Thomas E. Dewey** (N.Y.) for President and Gov. **John W. Bricker** (Ohio) for Vice-President. The Democratic National Convention met at Chicago (19 July) and on 20 July renominated President **Roosevelt.** Sen. **Harry S. Truman** (Mo.) was chosen as Vice-Presidential candidate. Minor

party candidates: Norman Thomas (N.Y.), Socialist; Claude A. Watson (Calif.), National Prohibition; and Edward A. Teichert (Pa.), Socialist Labor. Both major parties backed U.S. participation in some form of postwar international organization to maintain world peace and security. Organized labor took part in the campaign through the agency of the C.I.O. Political Action Committee (PAC), which claimed that its support helped to elect 17 candidates for the Senate and 120 for the House.

7 Nov. PRESIDENTIAL ELECTION. Included in the national vote were 2,691,160 soldiers' ballots. Popular vote: **Roosevelt,** 25,602,505; Dewey, 22,006,-278; Thomas, 80,158; Watson, 74,758; and Teichert, 45,336. Electoral vote: **Roosevelt,** 432 (36 states); Dewey, 99 (12 states). The Democrats retained control of both Houses of Congress.

1945, 12 Apr. DEATH OF PRESIDENT ROOSEVELT. President Roosevelt died suddenly of a cerebral hemorrhage at Warm Springs, Ga. Vice-President **Harry S. Truman** took the oath of office as 32nd President of the U.S.

INTERNATIONAL CONFERENCES, DECLARATIONS, AND AGREEMENTS, 1941–45

1941

22 Dec. Prime Minister Winston Churchill arrived in Washington for a series of conferences with President Roosevelt. The fundamental basis of joint strategy was affirmed: to concentrate upon the defeat of the Axis in Europe (which was viewed as the decisive theater of war), and to follow a policy of containment in the Far East until military successes in Europe or mounting Allied resources permitted stronger blows against Japan. The last of this series of conferences was held on 14 Jan. 1942. The Declaration of the United Nations was drafted and the Combined Chiefs of Staff and the Munitions Assignment Board were set up.

1942

1 Jan. UNITED NATIONS DECLARATION was signed at Washington. Twenty-six nations, including the U.S., Great Britain, the Soviet Union, and China, affirmed the principles of the Atlantic Charter, pledged the employment of their full military and economic resources against the Axis, and promised not to make a separate armistice or peace with the common enemies.

27 Jan. Anglo-American Combined Raw Materials Board established at Washington.

6 Feb. Joint Anglo-American War Council established at Washington.

23 Feb. Master Mutual Lend-Lease

Agreement signed by the U.S. and Great Britain, Australia, and New Zealand.

29 Apr. Hitler and Mussolini conferred at Salzburg.

26 May. Great Britain and Russia signed a 20-year mutual aid pact.

29 May. The Soviet Foreign Minister, Vyacheslav M. Molotov, arrived in Washington for conferences with President Roosevelt and other high U.S. officials. Among the results of the meetings was a new Lend-Lease protocol with Russia. The agreement provided that materials or data received from the U.S. would not be transferred to other parties without U.S. consent and that materials still available at the end of the war would be returned to the U.S. The new agreement went into effect on 1 July.

9 June. U.S. and Great Britain established a Combined Production Resources Board and a Combined Food Board.

18–27 June. Anglo-American conference at Washington discussed strategy problems. Roosevelt and Churchill participated, as did Russian and Chinese representatives.

July. The Combined Chiefs of Staff, meeting in London, decided to invade North Africa and to postpone a 2nd front in Europe as well as the Pacific offensive.

12–15 Aug. 1ST MOSCOW CONFERENCE. Principal participants were Soviet Premier Joseph V. Stalin, Prime Minister Churchill, and W. Averell Harriman, who represented President Roosevelt. Churchill, with the support of Harriman, informed Stalin that it was not possible to open a 2nd front in Europe in 1942.

9 Oct. U.S. and Great Britain announced they would abandon extraterritorial rights in China. A treaty incorporating this provision was signed by the U.S. and China on 11 Jan. 1943.

1943

14–24 Jan. CASABLANCA CONFERENCE was held in French Morocco. President Roosevelt and Prime Minister Churchill declared that the war would be fought until the **"unconditional surrender"** of the enemy had been secured. Agreement in principle was reached on a second front, but not on its location. U.S. officials favored an invasion of the Continent through France. The British urged an assault on the "soft underbelly" of Europe (i.e., Italy and the Balkans). A compromise was reached on the invasion of Sicily and Italy without prejudice to the ultimate invasion of Europe from the west. No agreement was worked out on the conflicting claims for leadership of Gens. Charles de Gaulle and Henri Giraud, who also attended the conference. Gen. Dwight D. Eisenhower was placed in supreme command of the North African theater.

25 Apr. The Soviet Union broke off relations with the Polish government-in-exile.

12–25 May. ANGLO-AMERICAN CONFERENCE (TRIDENT) at Washington planned global strategy and the opening of a 2nd front in Europe. President Roosevelt, Prime Minister Churchill, the Combined Chiefs of Staff, and many U.S. and British officials took part. The date (1 May 1944) for the Normandy invasion was definitely set and the seizure of the Azores authorized unless Portugal could be persuaded by negotiation to grant the use of bases on the islands. The conference also agreed to step up the quantity of aviation gasoline being flown over "the hump" from India to China.

18 May–3 June. The United Nations Conference on Food and Agriculture met at Hot Springs, Va. It established the Food and Agriculture Organization (FAO) of the United Nations.

22 May. Moscow announced the dissolution 15 May of the 3rd International (Comintern).

31 May. In French Algiers, Gens. Charles de Gaulle and Henri Giraud announced their agreement on the formation of a French Committee of National Liberation, of which they were copresidents. The committee, which became (2 June 1944) the French Provisional Government-in-Exile, promised full support to the war against the Axis. On 23 Oct. 1944 the U.S., Great Britain, and Russia recognized the committee as the French provisional regime.

11–24 Aug. 1ST QUEBEC CONFER-ENCE (QUADRANT) attended by President Roosevelt, Prime Minister Churchill, and top-ranking advisers including the Combined Chiefs of Staff, reaffirmed 1 May 1944 as the target date for the Normandy invasion (OVERLORD), which was to be supplemented by landings in Southern France (ANVIL, later DRAGOON). Agreement was reached on stepping up military operations in the Far East, particularly in Burma, and a Southeast Asia Command was established, with Lord Louis Mountbatten as Supreme Allied Commander. The Chiefs of the Naval Staffs reported that the Battle of the Atlantic against the U-boat had turned in favor of the Allies.

19–30 Oct. MOSCOW CONFERENCE OF FOREIGN MINISTERS was the first Allied 3-power meeting of World War II. It was attended by Secretary of State Cordell Hull, Foreign Minister Anthony Eden, and Foreign Minister V. M. Molotov, together with U.S., British, and Soviet military officials. The most controversial point in the discussions involved the status of the Polish government-in-exile at London, which the Soviet Union refused to recognize. The U.S. and Great Britain assured the Russians that preparations for opening a 2nd front in Europe were under way. Stalin made an unconditional promise that after Germany's defeat Russia would enter the war against Japan. The conference established a European Advisory Commission for the purpose of formulating a postwar policy for Germany. The Moscow Declaration issued at the close of the conference recognized "the necessity of establishing at the earliest practicable date a general international organization, based on the principle of the sovereign equality of all peace-loving states, and open to membership by all such states, large and small, for the maintenance of international peace and security."

9 Nov. The United Nations Relief and Rehabilitation Administration (UNRRA) was established with the signing of an agreement at Washington by 44 nations. Its purpose was to aid liberated populations in war-devastated areas of Europe and the Far East. **Herbert H. Lehman** (1878–   ), former governor of New York, was named director general of UNRRA. By agreements of Mar. 1944 and Dec. 1945 the member countries contributed $4 billion. The U.S. paid 72% of UNRRA's operating expenses; 90% of all food and other supplies distributed were products of U.S. farms or factories.

22–26 Nov. 1ST CAIRO CONFER-ENCE. President Roosevelt and Prime Minister Churchill conferred with Generalissimo and Madame Chiang Kai-shek regarding the war in the Far East. The **Declaration of Cairo** (1 Dec.) affirmed that the 3 powers would prosecute the war against Japan until her unconditional surrender and that they had no desire for territorial expansion; that Japan should be deprived of all Pacific islands acquired since 1914, whether by capture or League of Nations mandate; that all territories which Japan had taken from the Chinese, such as Manchuria, Formosa, and the Pescadores, should be restored to China; and that the 3 powers were "determined that in due course Korea shall become free and independent."

At the **2nd Cairo Conference** (4-6 Dec.) Roosevelt and Churchill held discussions with the president of Turkey, Ismet Inönü. This conference affirmed the alliance between Great Britain and Turkey and noted "the firm friendship existing between the Turkish people," the U.S., and the Soviet Union. As a result of military decisions taken at the 2nd Cairo Conference, the command of the invasion of Western Europe was conferred on Gen. **Dwight D. Eisenhower.**

28 Nov.–1 Dec. TEHERAN CONFER-ENCE, held at the capital of Iran, was attended by President Roosevelt, Prime Minister Churchill, and Premier Stalin. It was the 1st 3-power war conference in which Stalin took a personal part. The chief subject of the meeting was the projected Anglo-American invasion of Western Europe, supported by a flanking invasion through Southern France, and the timing of this assault with the Soviet offensive against Germany. Stalin re-affirmed his promise to enter the war against Japan. The conference formulated a plan for an international organization to keep the peace.

1944

1–22 July. UNITED NATIONS MONETARY AND FINANCIAL CONFERENCE, (BRETTON WOODS CONFERENCE), held at Bretton Woods, N.H., was attended by representatives of 44 nations. The conference established an International Monetary Fund of $8.8 billion (of which about 25% was contributed by the U.S.) for the stabilization of national currencies (it effected a general evaluation of the currencies of Western Europe late in 1949) and the fostering of world trade. It also set up an International Bank for Reconstruction and Development with a capitalization of $9.1 billion (of which about 35% was supplied by the U.S.) for extending loans to nations requiring economic rehabilitation. By 1950 the Bank had made loans of only $700 million. Russia refused to participate in these financial arrangements.

27 July. The Polish Committee of National Liberation, organized at Moscow, was recognized by the Soviet government. The committee, which later transferred its headquarters to Lublin, was entrusted with administrative control of Polish areas taken by the Red Army.

21 Aug.–7 Oct. DUMBARTON OAKS CONFERENCE, held near Washington, D.C., was attended by representatives of the U.S., Great Britain, the Soviet Union, and China (with the last 2 meeting separately, since Russia was still at peace with Japan). The conference discussed the draft of a charter for a permanent postwar international organization for maintaining world peace and security. The tentative proposals (known as the Dumbarton Oaks Plan) served as the basis for the Charter of the United Nations. Agreement on the veto issue could not be reached, Russia refusing to agree to bar a member of the Security Council from voting on a question to which it was itself a party.

11–16 Sept. 2ND QUEBEC CONFERENCE, attended by President Roosevelt and Prime Minister Churchill, considered strategic plans for final victory over Germany and Japan. The chief subjects of the conference were the demarcation of the zones of occupation following the conquest of Germany and the policy governing the postwar treatment of that nation. The **Morgenthau plan** (sponsored by Secretary of the Treasury Henry Morgenthau, Jr.) for reducing Germany to an agrarian economy was tentatively approved at this conference, but was rejected by President Roosevelt a month later.

9–18 Oct. 2ND MOSCOW CONFERENCE, attended by Prime Minister Churchill and Premier Joseph Stalin, divided the Balkans into spheres, Russia to predominate in Rumania, Bulgaria, and Hungary, Great Britain in Greece, with Yugoslavia to be shared. It was generally agreed that the Curzon Line should bound Poland on the east and the Oder River on the west. Roosevelt, who was not a party to these arrangements, let it be known that he would not be bound by them.

1945

Jan. Malta Conference. Combined Chiefs of Staff planned final campaign against Hitler.

4–11 Feb. YALTA CONFERENCE, held in the Crimea, was attended by President Roosevelt, Prime Minister Churchill, and Premier Stalin, together with their top diplomatic and military advisers. Most of the important agreements remained secret until the postwar period. In exchange for her pledge to enter the war in the Far East, Russia was given the Kurile Islands, the southern half of Sakhalin, and an occupation zone in Korea, and was granted privileged rights in Manchuria and in the Chinese cities of Dairen and Port Arthur. In addition, the U.S. and Great Britain agreed to recognize the autonomy of Outer Mongolia, which had severed its connections with China and come under Soviet influence. The U.S. and Great Britain also agreed to award eastern Poland to the Soviet Union. Poland's eastern border was fixed on the Curzon Line; and that nation was to receive territorial compensation in the north and west at the expense of Germany. Agreement was reached for reorganizing the Polish (Lublin) government on a broader democratic basis. The Russian demand of $20 billion in reparation payments from Germany, to be taken out of current production, was referred to a reparations commission. The 3 powers reaffirmed the "unconditional surrender" formula and issued a Declaration of Liberated Europe pledging the Big Three to support postwar governments in the liberated states which would be representative of the popular will through free elections. The conferees announced they had worked out a formula for voting procedure in the Security Council and that a conference to elaborate the United Nations Charter would convene at San Francisco on 25 Apr. It was secretly agreed that the Ukraine and Byelo-Russia would be accorded full and equal membership in the United Nations organization on the footing of independent nations.

5 Apr. The Soviet Union denounced its 5-year nonaggression pact with Japan.

21 Apr. The Soviet Union concluded a 20-year mutual assistance pact with the Polish Provisional Government (the Lublin regime).

25 Apr.–26 June. UNITED NATIONS CONFERENCE ON INTERNATIONAL ORGANIZATION, attended by delegates of 50 nations, assembled at San Francisco to draft the Charter of the United Nations Organization (UNO). The Russians at San Francisco interpreted the Yalta voting formula to mean that a nation could use the veto to forbid the Security Council from even discussing questions which might require force in their settlement. Secretary of State Edward R. Stettinius, Jr., threatened that the U.S. would not participate in the organization unless the Russians yielded. The deadlock was broken when President Truman directed Harry L. Hopkins, then in Moscow, to take the issue to Stalin. The latter agreed that the veto should not be used to prevent discussion. Following the announcement

(7 June) of this compromise, a draft Charter was worked out. The Charter of the United Nations provided for six chief organs: (1) a **General Assembly** of all member nations as the policy-making body, each nation to have a single vote; (2) a **Security Council** of 11 members in continuous session for deciding diplomatic, political, or military disputes, the Big Five (the U.S., Great Britain, the Soviet Union, France, and China) to have permanent seats, the other 6 to be held for 2-yr. terms; (3) an **Economic and Social Council** of 18 members elected by the General Assembly for the purpose of dealing with human welfare and fundamental rights and freedoms; (4) an **International Court of Justice** (sitting at The Hague) for dealing with international legal disputes, its 15 judges to be elected by the General Assembly and the Security Council; (5) a **Trusteeship Council** made up of states administering trust territories, the permanent members of the Security Council, and members elected by the General Assembly for a 3-yr. term; and (6) a **Secretariat,** headed by the Secretary-General, for performing the routine administrative work of the UNO, the staff to be selected from nations holding membership in the UN. The Charter was unanimously approved on 25 June and signed on the following day.

5 June. EUROPEAN ADVISORY COMMISSION established German occupation zones, assigning eastern Germany to Russia, dividing the south between the U.S. and France, and placing Great Britain in charge of the west. Berlin was shared among the occupying powers and placed in the heart of the Soviet zone, leaving all ground approaches dominated by the Russians. The administration of Berlin was entrusted to a military Kommandatura.

17 July–2 Aug. POTSDAM CONFERENCE, held near Berlin, was attended by President Harry S. Truman, Prime Minister Churchill (who after 28 July was replaced by the newly chosen British Prime Minister, Clement R. Attlee, head of the Labour government), and Premier Stalin. Also present, in addition to other top-ranking officials, were Secretary of State James F. Byrnes, Foreign Secretary

Anthony Eden (who after 28 July was replaced by Ernest Bevin), and Foreign Secretary V. M. Molotov. The first declaration issued by the conference was the "unconditional surrender" ultimatum (26 July) presented to Japan. The chief questions before the conference were the plan for the occupation and control of Germany and the settlement of various European problems. A Council of Foreign Ministers, its members drawn from the Big Five, was established and entrusted with the preparation of draft treaties with Austria, Hungary, Bulgaria, Rumania, and Finland, and with the proposal of settlements of outstanding territorial questions. The Council was also authorized to negotiate an agreement with a central German government whenever the latter should come into being. The occupation authorities were to conduct programs designed to denazify, decentralize, disarm, and democratize Germany, which was to be treated during the occupation period as a single economic unit. Provision was made for the trial of war criminals (shortly after the conference an International Military Tribunal was set up). Final delimitation of

the Polish-German frontier was left to the peace treaty. The Soviet Union abandoned its $20-billion reparations demand in exchange for a reparations schedule based on a percentage of useful capital equipment in the Western zone and materials in the Eastern zone. The conference agreed that Germany should make good for losses suffered at its hands by the United Nations. Provision was made for the mandatory transfer of 6,500,000 Germans from Hungary, Czechoslovakia, and Poland to Germany. Economic agreements were reached concerning German industry, foreign trade, finance, communications, and transportation. At the earliest practicable date the German economy was to be decentralized for the purpose of eliminating excessive centralization of economic power as exemplified by cartels, syndicates, and trusts. Primary emphasis in the German economy was to be given to the development of agriculture and peaceful domestic industries.

14 Aug. The Sino-Soviet treaty signed at Moscow formalized China's consent to the concessions granted to the Soviet at the Yalta Conference.

FOUR-POWER OCCUPATION of GERMANY

THE UNITED STATES IN
THE NUCLEAR SPACE AGE

RELIEF AND RECONSTRUCTION

1945, 21 Aug. LEND-LEASE TERMINATED. Total Lend-Lease aid by U.S. (Mar. 1941–Sept. 1946) amounted to $50.6 billion; reverse Lend-Lease received by U.S., $7.8 billion. On 27 Dec. 1946 President Truman reported to Congress that settlements had been made with 7 nations (representing 70% of U.S. Lend-Lease aid) including Great Britain (27 Mar.), but as yet not with the Soviet Union (received $11.1 billion; supplied *c.*$2.2 million as reciprocal Lend-Lease). Coincident with settlement of the British agreement the U.S. granted Britain an additional loan of $3.7 billion payable at 2% in 50 annual installments beginning 31 Dec. 1951.

UNRRA. From V-E Day to the spring of 1947 the U.S. provided Europe with over $11 billion in the form of UNRRA aid, loans, etc. Opposition to UNRRA arose from the fact that the bulk of its relief supplies were distributed in Eastern Europe (ex-enemy countries were outside its functions; liberated countries in Western Europe had refused UNRRA assistance). On 12 Nov. 1946 Under Secretary of State Dean Acheson proposed further international relief action, advocating for the future bilateral arrangements, and on 8 May 1947 publicly advocated the essentials of the **European Recovery Program**. A post-UNRRA Relief Bill (31 May 1947) appropriated $350 million relief for Austria, Greece, Italy, Hungary, and Poland.

DISPLACED PERSONS (p. 475).

1947, 5 June. MARSHALL PLAN was launched by Secretary of State George C. Marshall in an address at Harvard University in which he declared that U.S. policy was directed "not against any country or doctrine but against hunger, poverty, desperation, and chaos. Its purpose should be the revival of a working economy in the world so as to permit the emergence of political and social conditions in which free institutions can exist."

27 June–2 July. The Foreign Ministers of Great Britain, France, and the Soviet Union met at Paris to consider Marshall's proposal of U.S. economic aid. Great Britain and France invited 22 nations to join a Committee for European Economic Cooperation to draft plans for reconstruction. On 3 July Soviet Foreign Minister Molotov walked out of the preliminary meeting, charging that the Marshall Plan was an "imperialist" plot for the enslavement of Europe. The Soviet satellites refused to participate.

12 July. Marshall Plan Conference, in which 16 nations participated, set up a Committee for European Economic Cooperation, which submitted (22 Sept.) a report on Europe's needs, with estimated dollar aid needed for the next 4 yrs. between $16.4 and $22.4 billion.

17 Dec. On basis of reports of the Krug Committee (9 Oct.), the House Select Committee on Foreign Aid (Herter Committee, 10 Oct.), the Nourse Committee (28 Oct.), and the Harriman Committee (7 Nov.), a special session of Congress convened to deal with aid to Europe as well as inflation, and enacted the Foreign Aid Act of 1947 providing interim relief for France, Italy, and Austria ($540 million), part to go to China. On 19 Dec. President Truman submitted to Congress a $17-billion European Recovery Program (ERP).

1948–60. FOREIGN AID PROGRAMS.
From the end of World War II through Dec. 1959, U.S. expended $72.5 billion in foreign aid.

1949, 20 Jan. President Truman in his inaugural address outlined the "Point Four" program for economic assistance to underdeveloped areas throughout the world.

25 Jan. Under Soviet influence the Council of Mutual Economic Assistance was set up as a counterweight to the Marshall Plan. The Council included the USSR, Poland, Czechoslovakia, Bulgaria, Hungary, and Rumania.

New Funds Available for Mutual Security, 1948–60
(in $ million; *Statistical Abstract, 1960*)

Year	Military	Non-military	Total
1948–49	—	6,461	6,461
1950	1,314	3,785	5,099
1951	5,223	2,136	7,359
1952	5,268	2,015	7,283
1953	4,098	1,914	6,012
1954	3,219	1,504	4,724
1955	950	1,855	2,805
1956	1,024	1,688	2,712
1957	2,022	1,750	3,772
1958	1,317	1,458	2,775
1959	1,558	1,922	3,480
1960	1,361	1,789	3,274

PEACE SETTLEMENTS

U.S. AND THE UN. The UN charter went into effect 24 Oct. 1945. The UN Educational and Cultural Conference met at London (1–16 Nov.) and adopted a constitution for UNESCO. The 1st meeting of the General Assembly was held in London 10 Jan. 1946. The Security Council convened the same month, and on 1 Feb. **Trygve H. Lie** of Norway was elected Secretary-General of the UN. The International Court of Justice met at the Hague (3 Apr.–6 May) to set up its organization and rules of procedure.

Control of Atomic Energy. On 24 Jan. 1946 the UN General Assembly created a commission to study the control of atomic energy. On 28 Feb. the State Dept. issued the Acheson-Lilienthal report on the international control of atomic energy. On 14 June **Bernard M. Baruch** (1870–   ), U.S. delegate to the UN Atomic Energy Commission, proposed an International Atomic Development Authority to which the U.S. would turn over its atomic bomb secrets provided there was international control and inspection not subject to the big-power veto, and that further manufacture of bombs should cease and existing bombs be destroyed. A Soviet counter-proposal for outlawry of atomic weapons made no provision for international control and inspection. On 1 Aug. President Truman approved the McMahon Act, sponsored by Senator **Brien McMahon** (Conn., 1903–52), setting up a 5-man Atomic Energy Commission. **David E.**

Lilienthal (1899–   ) was named (28 Oct.) head of the AEC. **Timetable of atomic explosions:** 4th U.S. atomic explosion in tests with warships at Bikini Atoll, 1 July 1946; 5th, 25 July. New and improved bomb exploded in 3 tests at Eniwetok, Apr.–May 1948. On 24 Sept. 1949 an atomic explosion in Russia was disclosed; a 2nd blast was revealed by the U.S. on 4 Oct. 1951. On 31 Jan. 1950 President Truman announced that the U.S. would undertake development of the **hydrogen bomb.** On 6 Apr. 1952 it was announced that the U.S. was manufacturing the H-bomb. On 3 Oct. Great Britain exploded its 1st atomic weapon in the Monte Bello Islands, off Australia. On 4 Nov. 1948 the UN General Assembly backed the U.S. plan for international control of atomic energy. On 12 Jan. 1952 Andrei Y. Vishinsky proposed to the UN a plan for international control and inspection to operate under the Security Council (with big-power veto); not acceptable to the U.S. On 1 Nov. U.S. exploded on Eniwetok its most advanced atomic bomb, incorporating **hydrogen** ingredients.

Iran. The Security Council considered a protest of Iran (19 Jan. 1946) charging that Soviet troops were kept in her territory after date agreed upon with Britain, U.S., and Iran for withdrawal. The complaint was considered despite Soviet abstention. On 3 Apr. Russia announced that its troops would be withdrawn from Iran on 6 May.

Greece. A UN investigating commission reported 25 June 1947 that Albania, Bulgaria, and Yugoslavia had supported guerrilla warfare in Greece. A resolution proposed by the U.S. (29 July) to accept the findings and implement the commission's recommendation failed in the Security Council (9 for, 2 against) but carried in the UN Assembly (21 Oct., 40–6).

Indonesia. A U.S. offer of mediation between the Republic of Indonesia and the Netherlands government was rejected by the former. On 1 Aug. 1947 the UN set up a Good Offices Commission of 3 members (from Belgium, Australia, and the U.S.) to mediate the dispute, as a result of which a truce agreement was signed aboard the U.S. transport *Renville* (17 Jan. 1948) recognizing the sovereignty of the Netherlands until the U.S. of Indonesia was organized. On 28 Jan. 1949 the UN Security Council condemned the military action taken by the Dutch government against republican areas of Sumatra and Java as a violation of the *Renville* truce. The Netherlands accepted a compromise proposal by the Council (23 Mar. 1949), evacuated Jogjakarta (24 June), and terminated hostilities in Java (10 Aug.) and Sumatra (14 Aug.). On 2 Nov. 1949 the Netherlands transferred sovereignty over the Netherlands East Indies (except Dutch New Guinea) to the Republic of the U.S. of Indonesia, which accepted a state of union with the Netherlands and was admitted to UN membership 25 Sept. 1950.

Israel was the subject of a special session of the UN Assembly beginning 28 Apr. 1947, which adopted (29 Nov.) a plan for the partition of Palestine into Jewish and Arab states, with Jerusalem internationalized. The new state of Israel, proclaimed upon termination of the British mandate (15 May 1948), was recognized that day by the U.S. After UN mediator Count Folke Bernadotte of Sweden was assassinated in Jerusalem (17 Sept.), **Ralph J. Bunche (1904–)** of the U.S. succeeded him as mediator and effected armistice agreements between Israel and her Arab neighbors. Israel was admitted to the UN 11 May 1949.

Kashmir. In Mar. 1949 Adm. Chester W. Nimitz was appointed UN administrator to conduct a plebiscite to determine the disposition of the border state of Kashmir claimed by both Pakistan and India. At the end of 1949 the UN commission reported that Indian and Pakistani troops prevented holding the plebiscite. On 18 Oct. 1951 UN mediator Frank P. Graham of the U.S. reported no progress but suggested that negotiations be continued.

North Korean Aggression, 25 June 1950 (p. 398). The absence of the Soviet representative permitted the Security Council to adopt the resolutions of 25 and 27 June and 7 July under which military action was taken. On 27 June President Truman announced: "I have ordered United States air and sea forces to give the Korean Government troops cover and support." As the return to the Council (1 Aug.) of Yakov A. Malik, Soviet representative, blocked further Council action, the General Assembly, by resolution 7 Oct., laid down the objectives of UN action in Korea, and, following Chinese intervention, a UN Council resolution (30 Nov.) calling for withdrawal of Chinese Communists from Korea and promising to safeguard Chinese border interests was vetoed by the Soviet delegate. On 3 Nov. the UN General Assembly adopted the "Uniting for Peace" Resolution, asserting the right to deal with any threat to the peace where failure of the permanent members of the Security Council to agree prevented the Council from functioning. A U.S. proposal for an arms embargo against Communist China (urged by resolutions of both houses of Congress, 15 May 1951) was adopted by the UN General Assembly 18 May.

China. On 20 May 1946 Gen. George C. Marshall, in China, accused both Nationalists and Communists of fomenting hate campaigns. On 24 June Mao Tsetung, Chinese Communist head, demanded that the U.S. halt military aid to Nationalist China and that all U.S. forces leave. On 29 Jan. 1947 the U.S. informed both sides that it was abandoning mediation efforts. Lt. Gen. Albert C. Wedemeyer, appointed 11 July to appraise the situation in China and Korea,

ondemned (24 Aug.) the use of force
y the Chinese Communists and stressed
he need for thoroughgoing political and
conomic reforms on the part of the Na-
onalists. The Chinese Communists chal-
enged (9 Nov. 1949) the right of the
Nationalists to represent China in the
UN, and on 18 Nov. demanded their
uster. The Nationalists fled the Chinese
mainland (8 Dec.) and moved their cap-
al to Formosa. On 13 Jan. 1950 Soviet
elegate Malik walked out of the Secur-
y Council, declaring that the Soviet
Union would not participate so long as
he Chinese delegates remained. He did
ot return until 1 Aug., when he as-
umed the presidency of the Council.

WAR CRIMES TRIALS. Nazis. Acting
under a charter adopted in London (Aug.
1945) to bring to trial the German and
Japanese war criminals for crimes against
1) peace, (2) humanity, and (3) the
ws of war, an International Military
Tribunal at Nuremburg, Germany, tried
principal Nazi offenders (20 Nov.
1945–1 Oct. 1946). U.S. prosecutor was
ssociate Justice **Robert H. Jackson**
1892–1954). 12 Nazis were sentenced
o be hanged: Reichsmarschall Hermann
Göring (committed suicide by poisoning
n the eve of his execution), Martin
Bormann, *in absentia,* and the 10 who
ere hanged 16 Oct. 1946: Joachim Rib-
entrop, Field Marshal Wilhelm Keitel,
ol. Gen. Alfred Jodl, Ernst Kalten-
runner, Alfred Rosenberg, Hans Frank,
Wilhelm Frick, Arthur Seyss-Inquart,
ulius Streicher, and Fritz Sauckel; 3
ere acquitted: Franz von Papen, Hjal-
mar Schacht, Hans Fritsche; 3 escaped

trial: Martin Bormann, whereabouts unknown, Gustav Krupp because of advanced age and ill health, and Robert
Ley, who committed suicide after indictment. In addition, the U.S. conducted
a series of 12 trials, each centered on an
occupation group. In all, 836,000 former
Nazis were tried in the U.S. zone, of
whom 503,360 were convicted, 430,890
fined less than 1,000 Rm., 27,413 sentenced to perform some community work,
7,768 given short terms in labor camps,
18,503 pronounced ineligible to hold office, and 20,865 suffered partial property
confiscation.

Japanese war leaders were tried by an
International Military Tribunal for the
Far East (est. 19 Jan. 1946). Trials (3
June 1946–12 Nov. 1948) resulted in
death sentences being meted out to former Premier Hideki Tojo and Gens.
Seishiro Itagaki, Kenji Doihara, Heitaro
Kimura, Iwane Matsui, and Akira Muto;
on appeal the U.S. Supreme Court denied
jurisdiction 20 Dec. 1948; the 7 were
hanged in Tokyo 23 Dec. Adm. Shigetaro
Shimada and Army Chief of Staff Yoshi-
jiro Umezu and 14 others were given life
sentences, former Foreign Minister Shi-
genoi Togo sentenced to 20 yrs., and
former Foreign Minister Mamoru Shige-
mitsu 7 yrs. (paroled Nov. 1950). In addition, a large number of high-ranking
Japanese army and navy officers were
tried before special tribunals in Japan
and throughout the areas of Japanese
military operations for offenses against
the laws of war. As of 19 Oct. 1949,
4,200 Japanese had been convicted, 720
executed.

NEGOTIATIONS, CONFERENCES, AND TREATIES
1945–52

1945, 11 Sept.–2 Oct. LONDON CON-
FERENCE. The 1st meeting of the
ouncil of Foreign Ministers failed to
ring agreement on treaties with Italy,
ulgaria, Hungary, and Rumania. The
onference broke up over the issue of
hinese and French participation and
evealed a cleavage between Russia and
he West.

16–26 Dec. MOSCOW CONFERENCE.
The 2nd meeting of the Council of Foreign Ministers considered international
control of atomic energy, a new 4-power
control commission for Japan, trusteeship
for Korea, and the drafting of European
peace treaties by a 5-power conference
for submission to a peace conference of
the 21 Allied nations.

1946, 25 Apr.–16 May, 15 June–12 July, 29 July–15 Oct. PARIS PEACE CONFERENCE, attended by Foreign Ministers of Great Britain, France, the Soviet Union, and the U.S., considered peace treaties for the Axis satellites, agreed (1 July) on terms of the treaties, and called a 21-nation conference to study the drafts. The 21-nation conference revealed increasing disagreement between Russia and the West, and the conference broke down when the Soviet Union objected to participation by the smaller powers.

4 Nov.–12 Dec. The Council of Foreign Ministers, at New York, completed peace treaties with minor Axis nations. Secretary Byrnes, supported in his firmer stand against the U.S.S.R. by President Truman's dismissal (20 Sept.) of Secretary of Commerce Wallace, who had opposed a "get tough with Russia" policy, succeeded in reaching agreement with Soviet Foreign Minister Molotov. The treaties were signed for the U.S. in Washington by Secretary Byrnes (20 Jan. 1947), for the other powers in Paris (10 Feb.), and were ratified by the U.S. Senate on 4 June. Italy. The Republic of Italy (formed 14 July 1946) agreed to make reparations in kind to Yugoslavia ($125 million), the U.S.S.R. ($100 million), Greece ($105 million), Ethiopia ($25 million), and Albania ($5 million); to restrict its armed forces; to cede the Dodecanese Islands to Greece; Fiume, the Istrian peninsula, and much of Venezia Giulia to Yugoslavia; and to set up Trieste provisionally as a free territory under UN guarantee. She renounced all claims to her former colonies. A UN Assembly resolution provided for a united and independent Libya (Cyrenaica, Tripolitania, and Fezzan), and Italian Somaliland was placed under Italian trusteeship for 10 yrs. Hungary agreed to pay reparations in kind to the Soviet Union of $200 million and $50 million each to Czechoslovakia and Yugoslavia. Northern Transylvania was returned to Rumania and the Carpatho-Ukraine became part of the Soviet Ukraine. Rumania agreed to make reparations to the U.S.S.R. ($300 million) and confirmed the cession of Bessarabia and northern Bucovina to the Soviet Ukraine and of southern Dobruja to Bul-

garia. Bulgaria was required to pay in reparations $25 million to Czechoslovakia and $45 million to Greece. Finland agreed to pay reparations to Russia of $300 million and to cede to the Soviet Union the Arctic port of Petsamo, her part of the Rybachi peninsula west of Murmansk, and the Karelian peninsula including the port of Viipuri. The U.S.S.R. gave up its lease on Hangö but took a 50-yr. lease on a naval base at Parkkala on the Gulf of Finland.

1947, 10 Mar.–24 Apr. MOSCOW CONFERENCE. Secretary Marshall and British Foreign Minister Bevin advocated a federal form of government for Germany, as opposed to Russia's demand for a centralized state, and rejected the Soviet claim for $10 billion reparations.

29 May. Secretary Marshall instructed Gen. Lucius D. Clay to strengthen the bizonal organization in Germany and expedite upward revision of the level of bizonal industry. A directive of the Joint Chiefs of Staff to Gen. Clay (11 July) urged him to work toward "an increasing standard of living in Germany" and "a self-sustaining German economy." Under orders of U.S. and British commanders (29 Aug.) the maximum production was fixed at the 1936 level of German industry, thus increasing Germany's potential by one third over the 4-power level of Mar. 1946. A new level was introduced by the Allied powers on 3 Apr. 1951, and restrictions further relaxed.

1947, 25 Nov.–Dec. LONDON CONFERENCE. The 5th session of the Council of Foreign Ministers was marked by Soviet charges that the Allies had violated the Potsdam Agreement. The meeting adjourned without fixing a time or place for another meeting.

1949, 8 Apr. By agreement of the Allied powers in Washington the dismantling process of German industry was scaled down and reparations payments reduced.

23 May–20 June. PARIS CONFERENCE. The 6th session of the Council of Foreign Ministers failed to reach agreement on the German question. Russian proposals for German unification and withdrawal of Allied troops were unacceptable to the West. In turn, Russia

ejected Western proposals for the extension of the Bonn Constitution to Eastern Germany.

950, 11–14 May. LONDON CONFERENCE of Foreign Ministers of Great Britain, France, and the U.S. considered mutual defense problems and declared that Germany should "reenter progressively the community of free peoples of Europe."

2 Sept. NEW YORK CONFERENCE of Foreign Ministers of Great Britain, France, and the U.S. considered Secretary Acheson's proposal of 10 German divisions for service in NATO. France objected. However, it was announced that any attack on West Germany or Berlin would be considered an attack on the Western Powers.

5–26 Sept. NORTH ATLANTIC COUNCIL, at New York, agreed on setting up an integrated European defense force under a supreme commander, with Germany contributing to the defense effort. On 6 Dec. France accepted a compromise plan for German rearmament.

8 Dec. BRUSSELS CONFERENCE of Foreign Ministers of North Atlantic Pact nations approved plan for arming Western Europe. On 19 Dec. the conference agreed on Gen. **Dwight D. Eisenhower** as supreme commander of the North Atlantic Pact forces. He took formal command of SHAPE (Supreme Headquarters, Allied Powers in Europe) at Paris on 2 Apr. 1951, but resigned in the spring of 1952 to campaign for the Republican nomination for the Presidency, and was replaced by Gen. **Matthew B. Ridgway** (1895–   ).

951, 8 Sept. JAPANESE PEACE TREATY, signed at San Francisco by 49 nations (not including the U.S.S.R.), provided for withdrawal of occupation forces not later than 90 days after a majority of the signatories ratified and recognized Japan's "full sovereignty." Japan in turn acknowledged the independence of Korea and renounced all claims to Formosa, the Pescadores, the Kuriles, Sakhalin, and the Pacific islands formerly under her mandate, and agreed to UN trusteeship over the Ryukyu and Bonin Islands. By the **U.S.-Japanese Treaty** signed the same day at San Francisco

Japan granted the U.S. the right to maintain armed forces in Japan. Previously, on 1 Sept., a **Tripartite Security Treaty** (U.S., Australia, and New Zealand) provided for mutual assistance. A similar pact was signed between the U.S. and the Philippines (30 Aug.), implementing the Philippines Trade Act (continuing free trade between the U.S. and the Philippines until 1954, with gradual imposition of tariff duties over a 20-yr. period thereafter), the Philippines Rehabilitation Act (both acts, 30 Apr. 1946), and the Philippines Military Assistance Act (26 June 1946).

1952, 5–8 Jan. President Truman and Prime Minister Churchill reviewed the world situation in a conference at Washington and reported (9 Jan.) an agreement by which U.S. air bases in Britain would not be used for atomic bombing of Communist Europe without British consent.

20 Feb. The NATO Council in Lisbon agreed upon West Germany's financial and military contribution to mutual defense and set up permanent council headquarters in Paris.

13 Mar. AUSTRIAN TREATY NEGOTIATIONS. Big Three Western powers proposed a short treaty draft to Moscow restoring Austrian independence. A peace commission had been set up in Vienna in May 1947.

27 May. U.S., Britain, West Germany, and 5 other West European states signed an agreement to create a European Defense Community with a joint army.

2 Aug. WEST GERMAN PEACE CONTRACT was signed by President Truman, along with a protocol to the North Atlantic Treaty extending its mutual defense guarantees to the European Defense Community. The pact gave West Germany virtual freedom, ended Allied occupation, reserved Allied military rights in that territory, and provided for West German contributions to the cost of Western defense. In a covering letter the Allied powers promised to protect West Berlin.

4 Aug. ANZUS (PACIFIC) COUNCIL, created by the mutual security pact between the U.S., Australia, and New Zealand, met at Honolulu and planned organization and functions.

COLD WAR: OPENING PHASE

1946, 28 Feb. Secretary Byrnes declared that the U.S. would not and could not "stand aloof if force or the threat of force is used contrary to the purposes and principles" of the UN Charter.

3 Nov. Soviet Foreign Minister V. M. Molotov, in an address to the UN Assembly, attacked U.S. foreign policy.

1947, 12 Mar. TRUMAN DOCTRINE, enunciated by President Truman, called for the containment of Soviet imperialist expansion and pledged the employment of U.S. economic and military resources to aid Greece and Turkey and resist aggression elsewhere in Europe, whether by overt attack or subversion. The Senate formally endorsed the Truman Doctrine, 67–23 (23 Apr.), in a vote on a bill to strengthen Greece and Turkey; the House followed, 287–107 (9 May). On 22 May President Truman approved an initial appropriation of $400 million for Greek-Turkish aid.

Soviet Reaction. On 18 Sept. Andrei Y. Vishinsky, Deputy Soviet Foreign Minister, attacked U.S. "warmongers" in the UN Assembly. On 5 Oct. Moscow announced formation of the Cominform successor to the Comintern dissolved in 1943, and proclaimed its determination to block the Marshall Plan. A *coup d'état* (25 Feb. 1948) gave the Communists control of the government of Czechoslovakia. The new regime was headed by Klement Gottwald. On 10 Mar. Czech Foreign Minister Jan Masaryk committed suicide in Prague.

Western Military Alliances. Franco-Belgian Treaty of Dunkirk, 4 Mar. 1947; Brussels Treaty joining France, Britain, Belgium, the Netherlands, and Luxembourg in a 50-yr. defense alliance, 7 Mar. 1948. On 11 June 1948 the Senate

NATO COUNTRIES

adopted (64–4) the **Vandenberg Resolution** (introduced by Sen. **Arthur H. Vandenberg** (Mich., 1884–1951) supporting the principle of U.S. association with certain types of regional collective security arrangements as stipulated under Art. 51 of the UN Charter.

4 Apr. 1949. NORTH ATLANTIC TREATY, signed in Washington by the Foreign Ministers of the U.S., Great Britain, Canada, France, Belgium, the Netherlands, Luxembourg, Italy, Denmark, Norway, Iceland, and Portugal, obligated the signatories to rearm. By Art. 5 the parties agreed that an attack upon any of them would be considered an attack upon all, to be followed by individual or collective resistance under Art. 51 of the UN charter. A North Atlantic Treaty Organization (NATO), headed by the Council of Ministers, was set up to integrate Atlantic nations' defenses. On 8 June the Senate Foreign Relations Committee unanimously recommended ratification. The Senate ratified (82–13) 21 July and the pact went into effect 24 Aug. Greece and Turkey joined NATO Feb. 1952.

GERMANY. The U.S. announced 27 May 1946 it would suspend dismantling in its German zone, thus ending this mode of reparations payment in its occupation area. On 2 Dec. the U.S. and Great Britain agreed to merge their occupation zones.

1948, 24 June–1949, 12 May. Berlin Blockade and Airlift. Upon Russia's refusal to consider a Western proposal for a 4-power agreement for Berlin and her insistence that Russian currency be used throughout the city, the U.S., Great Britain, and France inaugurated currency reform in West Berlin (23 June). On 24 June Russia clamped a total blockade on all land traffic between Berlin and West Germany (these land routes not having been guaranteed by the Potsdam Agreement or the Allied Control Council), charging that the Western Powers had violated the Potsdam Agreement. The Western Powers began the Berlin airlift (which lasted 321 days) to supply 2,100,-000 residents of the blockaded areas and instituted a counterblockade against the Russian zone. The Soviet government announced (1 July) that it would no longer participate in the meetings of the Berlin Kommandatura. When the Western Powers took the blockade issue to the UN Security Council (4 Oct.), Russia vetoed the compromise proposal (25 Oct.) and boycotted the discussions. Tension mounted steadily. On 5 May 1949, in a sudden reversal, the Russians announced they would reopen land communications on condition that the Council of Foreign Ministers renew discussion of Berlin as well as the entire German question and take up the Austrian peace treaty. On 8 May the Basic Law prescribing a federal system of government for Germany was adopted by the German Parliamentary Council at Bonn. On 7 Sept. the West German parliament convened. East Germany countered by proclaiming (7 Oct.) the "German Democratic Republic." On 21 Sept. U.S. military government in Germany was replaced by a High Commission (agreed upon in Washington 8 Apr.), with John J. McCloy as U.S. High Commissioner (named 18 May).

AGGRESSION IN KOREA

1946–49. CONDITIONS BEFORE AGGRESSION. On 1 Oct. 1946 Under secretary of State Acheson reasserted U.S. intention to stay in Korea until it was united and free. On 17 Sept. 1947 the U.S. informed the Soviet Union of its intention to refer the question of Korean independence to the UN. On 23 Jan. 1948 the Soviet government informed the UN that the UN Temporary Commission on Korea would not be permitted to visit North Korea. On 22 Mar. the U.S. military governor in Korea announced an extensive land-reform program. On 1 May the North Koreans announced adoption by a "North and South Korean Conference" at Pyongyang of a constitution for the "People's Democratic

Republic of Korea" with jurisdiction over all Korea. On 10 May elections held in U.S.-occupied South Korea under the observation of the UN Temporary Commission were boycotted in North Korea. On 15 Aug. the Republic of Korea was proclaimed at Seoul, South Korea, with **Syngman Rhee** as President. On 9 Sept. a "People's Republic" claiming authority over the entire country was set up in North Korea. On 10 Dec. the Rhee government signed an agreement with the U.S. providing for a program of economic assistance to be carried out by the ECA and the War Dept. In a speech on 12 Jan. 1949 Secretary Acheson declared that Korea would be expected to defend itself, backed by "the commitment of the entire civilized world" under the UN charter. A Soviet veto (19 Apr.) blocked admission of the Republic of Korea into the UN. The U.S. completed withdrawal of its forces from Korea 29 June, leaving only an American military advisory group. The UN Commission on Korea reported 2 Sept. failure to settle differences between the Korean Republic and the North Korean Communist regime and stressed the danger of civil war.

1950, 25 June. NORTH KOREAN AGGRESSION. North Korean Communist forces equipped with Soviet-made weapons invaded South Korea. The UN Security Council emergency session ordered an immediate cease-fire and the withdrawal of North Korean forces and called on UN members (27 June) to "furnish such assistance to the Republic of Korea as may be necessary to repel the armed attack and to restore international peace and security in the area." President Truman the same day ordered U.S. air and naval forces into Korea. Seoul fell to the North Koreans on 28 June. On 30 June U.S. ground forces were ordered into the fighting and authorized to conduct missions above the 38th parallel. On 7 July the U.S. government announced that the draft would be employed to enlarge the army. The UN voted for a unified UN command in Korea under a commander to be designated by the U.S. Gen. **Douglas MacArthur** (p. 745) was so designated 8 July. On 20 July President Truman proposed partial mobilization of

U.S. resources to meet the Korean crisis and urged Congress to enact a $10-billion rearmament program.

MILITARY OPERATIONS. Battle of **the Pusan Beachhead** (6 Aug.–15 Sept.) in Southern Korea. Red offensive, which captured Pohang 6 Sept., failed to drive UN forces off the peninsula. Launching a counteroffensive (15 Sept.), UN forces made an amphibious landing at **Inchon** and began an eastward sweep across the peninsula. The operation was timed with the breakout of UN forces from the beachhead in southeastern Korea. On 26 Sept. Gen. MacArthur announced the capture of Seoul.

Chinese Communist Intervention. On 30 Sept. Foreign Minister Chou En-lai of the Chinese Communist regime implied that Chinese Communists would intervene. On 11 Oct. Peiping denounced the crossing of the 38th parallel by UN forces and declared that China "cannot stand idly by." On 14 Oct. President Truman and Gen. McArthur held a meeting at Wake Island. On 20 Oct. UN troops captured Pyongyang, Communist capital in North Korea, and advanced toward the Manchurian border. On 26 Oct. Chinese Communist divisions intervened in Korea, crossing the Yalu River from Manchuria. On 24 Nov. Gen. MacArthur ordered an "end-the-war" offensive. On 26 Nov. Chinese Communist forces opened a massive counteroffensive against UN troops in the **Yalu Valley.** The operation ended in a general UN retreat toward the 38th parallel and the abandonment (5 Dec.) of Pyongyang. A UN Security Council resolution (30 Nov.) calling for withdrawal of Chinese Communists and promising to safeguard Chinese border interests was vetoed by the Soviet delegate. On 11 Apr. 1951, after he had threatened (25 Mar.) Communist China with naval and air attack, Gen. MacArthur was recalled and replaced by Gen. **Matthew B. Ridgway.**

Casualties. Total U.S., UN, and Republic of Korea military battle casualties to 21 Mar.: 417,356. North Korean and Chinese casualties (to 20 June): est. 1,659,837. Total U.S. casualties to 31 Mar. 1954: 33,237 dead, 103,376 wounded, 410 missing.

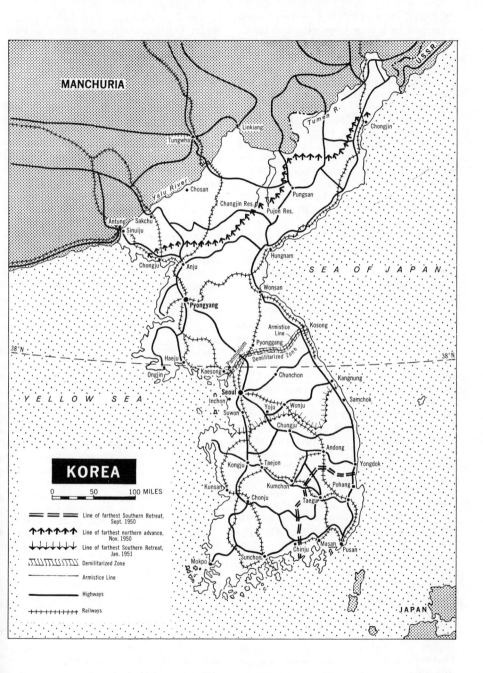

MANCHURIA

Linkiang

Tumen R.

Chongjin

Tungwha

Yalu River

Chosan

Pungsan

Changjin Res.

Pujon Res.

Antung

Sakchu

Sinuiju

Hungnam

Chongju

Anju

SEA OF JAPAN

Wonsan

Pyongyang

Armistice
Line

Kosong

Pyonggang

Haeju

Panmunjom

Demilitarized Zone

38°N

38°N

Ongjin

Kaesong

Chunchon

Kangnung

Seoul

YELLOW SEA

Inchon

Samchok

Suwon

Yoju

Wonju

Chungju

Andong

KOREA

0   50   100 MILES

Kongju

Taejon

Yongdok

Kunsan

Kumchon

Pohang

Chonju

Taegu

≡≡≡ Line of farthest Southern Retreat,
       Sept. 1950

↑↑↑↑↑ Line of farthest northern advance,
       Nov. 1950

↓↓↓↓↓ Line of farthest Southern Retreat,
       Jan. 1951

⊓⊔⊓⊔⊓ Demilitarized Zone

——— Armistice Line

——— Highways

+++++ Railways

Chinju

Masan

Pusan

Mokpo

Sunchon

JAPAN

"GREAT DEBATE." U.S. military commitments in Korea were attacked on 12 Dec. 1950 by Joseph P. Kennedy and on 20 Dec. by ex-President Hoover, who advocated reliance upon naval and air power for Western Hemisphere defense. Contrary views were expressed by Gov. Thomas E. Dewey on 14 Dec., by Secretary Acheson (22 Dec.), and by John Foster Dulles, adviser to the State Dept. (28 Dec.). The Congressional phase of the debate largely narrowed down to the specific issue of implementing NATO with U.S. troops. Senate Resolution 8, introduced 8 Jan. 1951 by Sen. Kenneth S. Wherry (Neb.), opposed assignment of U.S. ground forces to duty in Europe pending adoption of Congressional policy. Leading debate in favor of the resolution was Sen. Robert A. Taft (Ohio, 1889–1953). President Truman attacked the proposal in his State of the Union message (8 Jan.), as did Gen. Eisenhower at a joint meeting of both Houses of Congress (1 Feb.). A substitute resolution endorsing assignment of U.S. troops to NATO, but calling upon the President to consult with Congress and the military authorities, and amended to restrict U.S. ground troops to 4 divisions, was adopted 4 Apr. (69–21). The debate was revived when Gen. MacArthur, after being relieved of his command, addressed a joint session of Congress (19 Apr.) and advocated naval and air action against Communist China. On 27 June the Senate committee which conducted the inquiry into MacArthur's removal issued a unanimous statement assuring the world that U.S. objectives remained unchanged.

10 July 1951–26 July 1953. ARMISTICE NEGOTIATIONS. After UN forces (Apr.-May) hurled back 2 Red attacks, truce negotiations began at Kaesong, 10 July 1951, and were resumed at Panmunjon 25 Oct. Negotiations, with interruptions, continued in 1952. Negotiators were deadlocked over the issue of the forced repatriation of prisoners, which Communists demanded. On 8 June 1953, despite South Korean opposition, an agreement was reached on prisoners of war, under which those refusing to return to Red territory would be freed as civilians after 120 days if a major political conference failed to solve the problem. On 17–18 June, South Korean guards allowed 25,000 anti-Communist North Korean prisoners to escape. Finally, on 26 June 1953 an armistice was signed by the truce delegates in Panmunjon, and hostilities halted at 10 P.M. Under its terms a demilitarized zone of 4 km. separating the Communists from the Allies was set up; a neutral repatriation committee was to control the remaining prisoners, including those refusing repatriation, the strength of both sides was to be frozen, and the administration of the truce was to be entrusted to a military armistice commission consisting of 5 from each side. The armistice gave South Korea about 1,500 sq. mi. more territory than it had before the fighting began, when the 38th parallel was the dividing line.

1953–60. UNEASY TRUCE. Charges of inhumane practices were made by both sides. On 21 Feb. 1953, Chou En-lai accused the U.S. of having used germ warfare. This charge was explicitly denied by the U.S., which demanded a UN inquiry (27 Mar.). In turn the U.S. charged (30 Nov.) the Reds with the murder of over 35,000 Allied troops and Korean civilians, and its condemnatory resolution was adopted by the UN Assembly, 42–5 (3 Dec.). Acting on the recommendation of President Eisenhower Congress voted (3 Aug. 1953) $200 million for relief and rehabilitation for the Republic of Korea, and on 19 Jan. 1954 the Senate Foreign Relations Committee approved a U.S.-Korean mutual defense treaty, with the stipulation that armed aid should be provided only in case of "external armed attack" against the Republic of Korea. Ratifications were exchanged, 17 Nov., when the U.S. agreed to expand its military and economic aid to Korea in 1955. On 26 Oct. 1958, Red China announced the withdrawal of the "Chinese People's Volunteers" from North Korea, but as late as 19 Oct. 1959 the Military Armistice Commission accused the Communists of no fewer than 218 violations of the armistice between 17 Sept. 1958 and 29 Sept. 1959.

AMERICA IN A DIVIDED WORLD, 1953-60

NEW ERA IN MOSCOW. The death of Stalin (announced 5 Mar. 1953) resulted in a revamped Soviet government in the hands of a new 5-member Presidium of the Council of Ministers, headed by Georgi Maximilianovich Malenkov, and including Deputy Premiers Lavrenti P. Beria, Vyacheslav M. Molotov, Marshal Nikolai A. Bulganin, and Lazar M. Kaganovich. Beria was dismissed and arraigned on treason charges, 10 July. In an apparent reversal of the cold war policies of Stalin, the new government seemed more conciliatory. On 8 Aug. Malenkov declared that the U.S.S.R. stood for "a peaceful co-existence of two systems," but demanded acceptance of Red China as a Big Five Power and the banning of "atomic and other arms of mass destruction," positions the Soviet Union unswervingly held to through the decade of the '50's.

CAPTIVE PEOPLES" RESOLUTION. On 27 Jan. 1953, Secretary of State John Foster Dulles in a radio-TV talk held out to "captive" people behind the Iron Curtain a promise that "you can count on us." On behalf of the administration a resolution was introduced into both houses of Congress, 20 Feb., deploring "the forcible absorption of free peoples into an aggressive despotism" and denouncing Soviet interpretations of wartime agreements to "bring about the subjugation of free peoples." On 7 Mar., 2 days after news of Stalin's death, the resolution was shelved. However, on 16 Apr. President Eisenhower urged "full independence of the East European nations." When, 18–24 June, strikes, arson, and rioting broke out in numerous East German cities, including Berlin, and Russian and East German troops restored order only after shooting, Eisenhower told the press (1 July) that the U.S. planned no physical intervention in East Europe. Again on 30 Nov. Secretary Dulles declared the U.S. would not "confirm their captivity" by recognizing Russia's incorporation of Lithuania, Estonia, and Latvia.

FORMOSA (TAIWAN), QUEMOY, and MATSU. On 2 Feb. 1953, President Eisenhower announced his decision to lift the U.S. 7th Fleet's blockade of Taiwan, making possible Nationalist attacks against the Red Chinese mainland. On 11 Aug. 1954 Chou En-lai declared that Taiwan must be liquidated. President Eisenhower rejoined (17 Aug.) that "any invasion of Formosa would have to run over the 7th Fleet." Red China then turned attention to the Nationalist-held islands, launching, 3 Sept., a bombardment of Quemoy and Little Quemoy. The Nationalists retaliated 7 Sept. against Amoy. At a meeting of the National Security Council on 12 Sept. the President rejected proposals for military action against Communist China because of the dangers of atomic war. On 2 Dec. 1954 the U.S. and Nationalist China signed a mutual defense treaty pledging U.S. action if the Reds attacked Nationalist Chinese territory. The treaty did not apply to the islands along the Chinese mainland, from Quemoy northward to Shanghai, recently under attack. To clarify the U.S. position the President in a message to Congress, 24 Jan. 1955, asked Congress for authority to use armed force to "assure the security of Formosa and the Pescadores." The resolution passed both houses overwhelmingly and was signed by the President 29 Jan. On 3 Mar. Secretary Dulles announced in Taipei that the defense policy would not be "static" or confined to Taiwan itself. As a result the Communists chose not to risk a general war.

Following Soviet-Red Chinese discussions in Peiping 31 July-3 Aug. 1958, bombardment of Quemoy and Matsu was renewed 23 Aug. In Sept. the U.S. fleet

TAIWAN STRAIT

MILES

0   50   100   150

CHINA

EAST CHINA
SEA

TAIWAN STRAIT

TACHEN IS.

NANKI IS.

MATSU IS.

HAITAN IS.

Foochow

QUEMOY IS.

Amoy

Swatow

Hong Kong

PESCADORES IS.

Keelung

Taipei

TAIWAN

Tainan

began to furnish naval escort to Nationalist convoys to the beleaguered garrison
of Quemoy, but stopped 3 mi. short of
the objective to remain outside Chinese
territorial waters. A more cautious policy
on both sides soon became evident. After
Secretary Dulles criticized the concentration of large military forces on the offshore islands, President Eisenhower (1
Oct.) noted that a cease-fire would provide "an opportunity to negotiate in good
faith." A brief cease-fire was ordered by
the Red Chinese on 6 Oct., and on 25
Oct. Red China announced that it would
reserve the right to bombard the islands
on alternate days of the month. This signaled the end of the acute phase of the
Taiwan crisis, but the smoldering issue
flamed up again during the Presidential
campaign in the fall of 1960. Senator
John F. Kennedy in a TV debate (7
Oct.) maintained that the U.S. was not
obligated to defend Quemoy and Matsu
unless an attack upon them could be construed as an attack on Formosa and the
Pescadores. His opponent, Vice-President Richard M. Nixon, declared that
the U.S. should not abandon even one
"island of freedom."

NUCLEAR STALEMATE. The Soviet
government announced (20 Aug. 1953)
that it had tested an H-bomb "within the
last few days"; confirmed by the U.S.
Atomic Energy Commission. On 1 Mar.
1954 the U.S. set off its 2nd H-bomb
explosion at Bikini atoll, a blast in the
megaton range, which revealed considerable "fallout" peril. Widespread fallout
was reported from Soviet nuclear tests
beginning mid-Sept. Great Britain successfully tested an H-bomb on 15 May
1957; France an A-bomb on 11 Feb.
1960.

DISARMAMENT DEADLOCK. Development of nuclear weapons combined
with anti-inflationary considerations
prompted the "New Look" revealed in
President Eisenhower's budget message,
22 Jan. 1954, involving a reduction in
armed forces man power and greater
reliance on atomic weapons, while at the
same time encouraging the adaptation of
atomic energy to peacetime uses. To the
latter end the President had urged (8
Dec. 1953) that part of the nuclear
stockpiles be donated to an international
"bank of fissionable materials."

A 5-power subcommittee of the UN
Disarmament Commission held 19 secret
meetings in London, 13 May–22 June
1954. While favoring the banning of
atomic and nuclear weapons, it failed to
agree on the issue of inspection and a
one-third cut in conventional forces. Because of the failure to come to agreement
with the U.S.S.R. on the "atoms for
peace" program, the U.S. on 6 Sept.
1954 disclosed that an agreement had
been reached with Great Britain, France,
Canada, Australia, and South Africa to
set up an international agency to foster
the spread of atomic technology for
peaceful uses. Belgium and Portugal were
soon included in the discussions. The U.S.
now advanced a proposal for an International Atomic Energy Agency to encourage research and the exchange of
information, the donor states to earmark
fissionable materials for the agency's
operation and transfer them directly to
the project approved by the agency. This
was done to conform with the U.S.
Atomic Energy Act (30 Aug. 1954),
which imposed stringent restrictions on
the transfer of nuclear materials outside
the jurisdiction of the U.S. On 15 Nov.
1954 the U.S. announced that the
Atomic Energy Commission had allocated 110 kilograms of fissionable materials to serve as fuel in experimental
reactors to be installed abroad. Great
Britain, 16 Nov., pledged 20 kilograms.
The Geneva Conference on Peaceful
Uses of Atomic Energy, 8–20 Aug. 1955,
dramatized technological progress
achieved to date.

**18–23 July 1955. THE "SUMMIT"
AT GENEVA.** At a conference of the
heads of state Premier Bulganin proposed a definite prohibition on the manufacture and use of atomic weapons and
a limitation of 1,500,000 men each in the
armed forces of the U.S., the U.S.S.R.,
and Communist China, with 650,000
apiece permitted to the United Kingdom
and France and 150,000 to 200,000 each
for other states. President Eisenhower
then declared that "the United States
will never take part in an aggressive
war," which evoked Bulganin's reply:
"We believe the statement." President
Eisenhower proposed to the Soviet Union
that each nation give the other "a complete blueprint" of its military establish-

ments, and that each permit the other freedom of photographic reconnaissance over its national territory. These proposals, although rejected by Bulganin, 4 Aug., triggered a long series of disarmanent talks by the major powers. Broken off from time to time, but always resumed on some level, they suggested that the disarmament issues between East and West were narrowing, as evidenced by the earlier acceptance in principle (30 Sept. 1954) by Andrei Y. Vishinsky of an Anglo-French two-stage disarmament proposal. On 17 Nov. 1956 the U.S.S.R. announced its acceptance in a very limited way of the principle of mutual aerial inspection as a safeguard against massive surprise attack. However, after extended private conferences between Harold E. Stassen, head of the U.S. disarmament delegation, and Valerian A. Zorin of the Soviet delegation the proposal appears to have been discarded by the latter on 27 Aug. 1957.

Disengagement. On 14 Feb. 1958 Polish Foreign Minister Adam Rapacki in a formal note to the U.S. and other powers proposed a "denuclearized zone" in Central Europe, including E. and W. Germany, Poland, and Czechoslovakia. U.S. in reply (3 May) stressed "limited scope" of plan and its dependence on "the good intentions" of the Soviet Union. The Rapacki plan was incorporated in Soviet proposals (15 July) for an all-European treaty. Revival of disengagement proposals was spurred by plans to provide West Germany with nuclear arms. On 3 Mar. 1959 an Anglo-Soviet communiqué referred to possible arms limitations in an agreed area of Europe under appropriate inspection.

Suspension of Nuclear Testing. During the Presidential campaign of 1956 Adlai E. Stevenson, the Democratic nominee, proposed the suspension of nuclear tests. At the London Disarmament Conference the West (2 July 1957) proposed a 10-month suspension of nuclear testing. On 21 Aug. the White House proposed a 2-yr. suspension. Following the U.S.S.R. election (17 Mar. 1958) to the Supreme Soviet, Premier Bulganin resigned (27 Mar.) and **N. S. Khrushchev,** secretary of the Communist party, was elected to succeed him as premier. His first move in his anti-Western "peace" campaign was

to announce, 31 Mar., the unilateral suspension by the U.S.S.R. of nuclear tests. On 29 April the U.S. proposed at the UN Security Council the setting up of a northern (Arctic) inspection zone without waiting for agreement on other areas; vetoed by the Soviet Union (2 May). "Conference of Experts to Study the Possibility of Detecting Violations of a Possible Agreement on Suspension of Nuclear Tests" met at Geneva 1 July. The UN Scientific Committee on the Effects of Atomic Radiation reported 10 Aug. that "even the smallest amounts of radiation are liable to cause deleterious genetic, and perhaps also somatic, effects." A more conservative view was presented, 27 Mar. 1958, by Dr. Willard F. Libby of the U.S. Atomic Energy Commission, who reported that the total yearly dosage of nuclear test products to fresh human bone is at most 5% of the natural radiation dosage. These assertions were disputed by Dr. Linus Pauling, who warned that carbon-14 already released would cause 5 million genetically defective children in the next 300 generations. UN report of 10 Aug. pointed out that the relative danger of fallout varied from region to region, but that further studies were needed to determine the effect on man. The fear of the effect of H-bomb tests on pollution of the atmosphere led, 1957–58, to a quest in the U.S. for a "clean" H-bomb, a weapon in the megaton range giving rise to at most a small percentage of radioactivity. The feasibility of such a bomb was reported to President Eisenhower by his scientific advisers.

1960, 1–11 May. U-2 INCIDENT. Failure of the U.S.S.R. to accept the "open skies" proposal of 1955 led the U.S. to undertake photographic reconnaissance flights over the Soviet Union. The fact of these secret flights over a period of nearly 4 yrs. was revealed on the eve of the Summit Conference held in Paris in May, 1960. On 5 May the U.S.S.R. announced that an American U-2 (Lockheed high altitude) plane used for photographic reconnaissance had been brought down (1 May) 1,200 mi. inside the Soviet Union. Previously, on 3 May, the U.S. issued a cover story to the effect that a plane on a meteorological mission might have been forced down inside the

Soviet border owing to mechanical failure. On 7 May Premier Khrushchev announced that the pilot, Francis Gary Powers, was alive and had confessed. President Eisenhower (11 May) stated that he himself had authorized the U-2 flight, an unprecedented avowal of espionage activities by a head of state. In retaliation the U.S.S.R. canceled an invitation to Eisenhower to visit the Soviet Union. The incident provided Khrushchev with a pretext for denouncing the President and torpedoing the Summit Conference. Khrushchev who had previously visited the U.S. (Sept. 1959) and had held private talks with President Eisenhower at Camp David (25–27 Sept.), attended the UN sessions in New York Sept.-Oct. 1960. He again denounced the U-2 flights and expressed the hope that he could resume top-level negotiations with President Eisenhower's successor. With this prospect in mind he declared at a New Year's party in the Kremlin (1 Jan. 1961) that the U.S.S.R. was dropping the complaint against the U.S. over the U-2 incident.

Reflecting tension over the U-2 incident, the Ten-Nation Disarmament Conference (15 Mar.–27 June 1960) remained deadlocked over controls and compliance (U.S. proposing control organization within UN framework; U.S.S.R., controls to follow 1st-stage measures) and Soviet demand for elimination of foreign bases. No agreement was reached either on proposals for banning the orbiting of destructive weapons in outer space or on control of missile and delivery systems.

On 1 July the Russians shot down a U.S. RB47, a reconnaissance plane on a flight to the Barents Sea. Two surviving U.S. airmen were imprisoned, but released by the Soviet govt. 25 Jan. 1961.

AUSTRIAN PEACE TREATY. As a result of the firmness of the West in insisting on Big Four negotiations, with Austria sitting in, the U.S.S.R., after bilateral negotiations of its own, agreed on a treaty with Austria. President Eisenhower signed the U.S. instrument on 24 June 1955. Under the terms of the treaty Austria was re-established, with the 1 Jan. 1938 frontiers, and the 4 powers undertook to respect her independence and territorial integrity.

FOREIGN BASES. On 26 Sept. 1953 Spain authorized the U.S. to develop, maintain, and use military bases in that country in return for at least $226 million worth of economic and military aid. Executive agreements, effective upon signature, were to be in force for 10 yrs. and continue automatically for 2 successive 5-yr. periods unless terminated by either govt. On 9 Sept. 1954 Libya gave the U.S. long-term rights (until 1970) to the Wheelus Air Force base near Tripoli in exchange for annual economic aid. Following the independence of Morocco in 1956, negotiations were entered into between that nation and the U.S. for the eventual evacuation of the U.S. base. On 26 Mar. 1956 the Icelandic parliament approved a resolution demanding the withdrawal of all NATO (U.S.) forces from the country. This meant the abandonment of the U.S. air base of Keflavik, a key element in the U.S. global air network. Neutralist and leftist forces formed a coalition govt. 24 June pledged to work for the removal of U.S. forces. However, on 6 Dec. an agreement was reached with the U.S. on a new formula under which the U.S. forces would be able to operate the base on much the same terms as before. On 2 Apr. 1957 the U.S. renewed for a 5-yr. term its use of the air base at Dhahran in Saudi Arabia. On 9 Nov. 1960 the U.S. agreed to give up most of the bases in the British West Indies it had secured for 99 yrs. as part of the destroyers-for-bases deal of 1941. The U.S. planned to continue to use the Chaguaramas naval base on Trinidad, while quitting other bases on Antigua, Jamaica, Saint Lucia, and Trinidad.

HUNGARIAN REVOLT. Anti-govt. demonstrations in Budapest 23 Oct. 1956 forced a reshuffling of the govt. Revolutionaries demanded that the govt. denounce the Warsaw Pact as well as seek the complete liberation of the country from Soviet troops. On 30 Oct. Moscow promised major concessions. The next day President Eisenhower hailed these developments as "the dawning of a new day" in Eastern Europe, but earlier, on 21 Oct., in connection with Polish uprisings, Secretary Dulles had made it clear that the U.S. would not give military aid. On 4 Nov. Soviet troops and tanks opened a violent assault on Budapest, and a new all-Communist govt. was set up. The revolt was crushed. It was revealed on 16 June 1958 that ex-Premier Imre Nagy was executed following a secret trial.

BERLIN AND WEST GERMANY. Central to all disarmament talks conducted since World War II was the issue of Berlin and the unification of Germany. At the Berlin Conference of Foreign Ministers, 25 Jan.–18 Feb. 1954, agreement between East and West could not be reached on the reunification of Germany. The U.S.S.R. proposed a 50-yr. all-European security treaty, which would exclude the U.S. from the defense of Europe and make Red China and the U.S. equal "observers" of the pact's application. This proposal was rejected by Great Britain and France. At the London Conference of Foreign Ministers, 3 Oct., West Germany was admitted to NATO; formally on 6 May 1955. On 7 Apr. 1955 the U.S. Senate ratified the protocol formally ending the occupation of West Germany, with the occupation troops of the Western powers becoming "security forces," and sovereignty restored to West Germany.

At the "Summit" meeting at Geneva, 18–23 July 1955, attended by President Eisenhower, Prime Minister Eden, Premier Edgar Faure, and Premier Bulganin, the West proposed German unification with 3 safeguards: a 5-power mutual defense pact, an agreement as to the total forces and armaments permitted in Germany, and the setting up of a demilitarized zone between East and West. The U.S.S.R. again proposed an all-European treaty of mutual defense, excluding the U.S. except as an "observer." At the Paris meeting of foreign ministers in Oct. the West insisted that Germany be unified on the basis of free elections; that it keep the place in NATO that West Germany held. It proposed a 9-power treaty renouncing the use of force, and a demilitarized zone along the boundary between Germany on the West and Poland and Czechoslovakia on the East. On 10 Nov. 1958 Premier Khrushchev stated that the Soviet Union intended to hand over its powers in Berlin to the "sovereign German Democratic Republic." This warning carried an im-

plied threat that the East German govt. might impose a full-scale blockade of West Berlin by land, water, and air. On 21 Nov. the White House stated the intention of the West to "maintain the integrity" of West Berlin. On 27 Nov. the U.S.S.R. in a note to the U.S., Britain, and France granted a 6-mo. breathing spell. Germany was included in the series of atomic cooperation agreements which the U.S. made early in May with the Netherlands, Greece, Turkey, and Canada as a step toward the preparation of their forces to participate in nuclear warfare. On 12 Dec. 1960 the U.S. offered NATO allies nuclear submarines armed with Polaris missiles, and on 28 Dec. the U.S. signed an agreement with 4 of its NATO allies to produce fighter jets in Europe.

THE U.S. AND THE FAR EAST. Indo-China. President Eisenhower informed the Senate Foreign Relations Committee, 8 May, 1953, that he had given France a special aid grant of $60 million to support the Indo-Chinese campaign against the Vietminh rebels. Further disclosures of substantial military aid were made on 30 Sept. and 6 Feb. 1954, although on 10 Feb. the President stated that he was opposed to involving the U.S. in a "hot" war in Indo-China. According to a report of the French National Assembly, 16 Mar. 1954, the U.S. had paid to date 78% of the cost of the anti-Communist fighting in Indo-China. Although Secretary Dulles predicted (23 Mar.) that the French would win in Indo-China, their defenses collapsed and on 7 May the French Union fortress at Dienbienphu was captured by Vietminh rebels. At the Geneva Conference, 26 Apr.–21 July 1954, 19 nations were represented, including the U.S.S.R., Red China, North Korea, and the 16 Allies in the Korean War. Neither side was prepared to compromise on Indo-China, but direct truce talks were ordered 29 May. On 21 July armistice agreements halting the 7½-yr. war in Indo-China were signed dividing Vietnam, the northern part, including Hanoi and the delta area, going to the Vietminh rebels, the southern part to the French-backed govt. of Vietnam.

Laos. Following coup (9 Aug. 1960) in which the pro-Western govt. in Laos was overthrown, the neutralist govt. formed a coalition (18 Nov.) with Communist elements. The neutralist govt. accepted arms from the U.S.S.R., the 1st shipment arriving 4 Dec., and demanded (5 Dec.) that the U.S. halt shipment of arms to the right-wing rebel forces, while at the same time agreeing to a cease-fire. The U.S. announced (15 Dec.) full support for the pro-Western government of Premier Boum Oum which quickly gained control (16 Dec.) of Vientiane, the administrative capital. Following an appeal of the new government to the UN (30 Dec.) for support against reported troup movements from North Vietnam, the U.S. warned (31 Dec.) Red China and North Vietnam to keep their troops out of Laos, and called upon SEATO for further action.

SEATO Pact. A U.S.-sponsored Southeast Asian collective defense treaty was signed 8 Sept. 1954 in Manila by the delegates of 8 nations: Australia, Great Britain, France, New Zealand, Pakistan, Philippines, Thailand, and the U.S. The pact pledged joint action against aggression to any member nation, but promised "practical measures to insure conditions favorable" to self-determination by colonial peoples. Taiwan was excluded from the treaty region, defined as "the general area of Southeast Asia . . . and the Southwest Pacific not including the Pacific areas north" of 21° 31' N. lat.

U.S.-Japanese Relations. The U.S.-Japanese security treaty of 8 Sept. 1951 allowed the U.S. virtually a free hand in disposing of its armed forces in and about Japan. A Mutual Defense Assistance Agreement (8 Mar. 1954) provided for U.S. military aid in development of Japan's self-defense forces. Negotiations looking toward a revision of the 1951 treaty to give Japan a larger voice in military arrangements on its territory began in Tokyo in Oct. 1958 and continued through 1959, with Ambassador Douglas MacArthur II representing the U.S. Previously, as a result of an agreement with Japan, 21 June 1957, U.S. combat troops were withdrawn (1 Aug.). The U.S.S.R. had advised Japan to abrogate the 1951 treaty and adopt a neutral position. Opposition to the treaty was widespread among many elements in Japan who also opposed allowing the U.S. to equip Japanese forces with atomic weapons and demanded that the U.S. abandon

Okinawa and other Ryukyu and Bonin islands, which the U.S. had occupied since the war. Anti-U.S. riots broke out in Japan on 27 Nov. 1959. The new U.S.-Japanese pact included an undertaking to consult Japan about any major changes in the deployment or equipment of U.S. forces in that country, as well as any use of Japanese bases for combat operations. On the verge of ratification by both nations, new anti-American demonstrations occurred in Japan, forcing the Japanese govt. to withdraw (6 June 1960) the invitation it had extended to President Eisenhower to visit that nation. The President, who was in Manila preparatory to flying to Japan, returned to the U.S. 26 June. The Japanese govt. ratified (18 June) the treaty, but the U.S. position in Japan was considered to have been seriously weakened by the incident. However, on 14 Nov. a record turnout of voters in the U.S.-governed Ryukyu Islands returned to power by a big majority the most pro-American of the contending parties. The victorious party advocated reversion of the islands to Japan, but only after a step-by-step process extending over a period of yrs. Again, on 20 Nov., Premier Hayato Ikeda's pro-U.S. Liberal-Democratic party was continued in power in Japan, increasing its strength in the Diet from 283 to 296 seats.

Indonesia. Operations of the U.S.-owned oil companies in Sumatra were threatened as anti-Communist forces made headway (beg. 15 Feb. 1958) in their civil war with Moscow-oriented Premier Sukarno. On 26 Feb. Secretary Dulles expressed sympathy with the rebels, but the U.S. followed a hands-off policy in the civil war. By early May the back of the rebellion was broken. Abandoning its neutrality, the U.S. (13 Aug.) made an agreement with the Sukarno govt. for sale of U.S. military equipment to Indonesia for internal security and self-defense purposes.

THE U.S. AND THE MIDDLE EAST. Relations with Israel. On 20 Oct. 1953 Secretary Dulles disclosed that the U.S. had decided to withhold economic aid to Israel, variously estimated at $15–$50 million, because Israel had defied a UN order to halt a Jordan River hydroelectric project. When, on 28 Oct., Israel

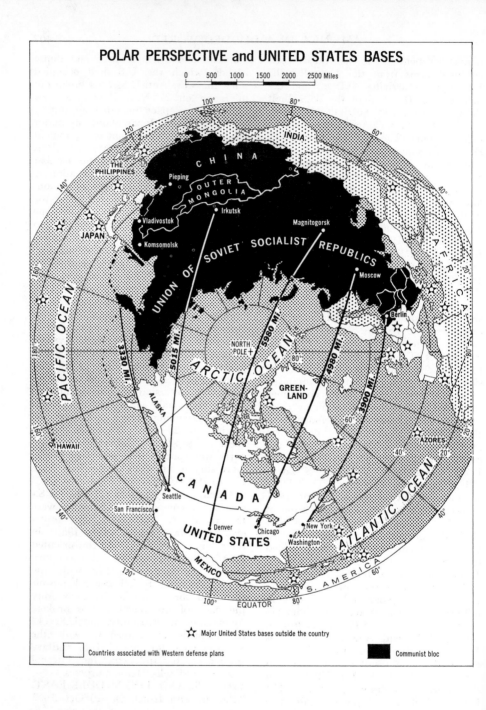

POLAR PERSPECTIVE and UNITED STATES BASES

0   500   1000   1500   2000   2500 Miles

☆ Major United States bases outside the country

☐ Countries associated with Western defense plans

■ Communist bloc

suspended work on the project, the U.S. resumed such aid. Again on 18 Nov. the U.S. joined Great Britain and France in proposing a resolution in the UN Security Council censuring Israel for a raid on the Jordan village of Kibya; adopted by the Council 24 Nov. When, on 28 Feb. 1955, fighting broke out between Israel and Egypt in the Gaza strip, the UN Security Council condemned Israel (29 Mar.). Following the cease-fire agreement, 4 Sept., the U.S., 7 Nov., agreed to sell arms to Israel.

Suez Crisis. On 17 Dec. 1955 the U.S. and Great Britain offered financial assistance to Egypt for constructing the Aswan Dam. On 17 July 1956 the Egyptian government accepted the offer, but Secretary Dulles, 19 July, announced the withdrawal of the offer, as did Great Britain and the International Bank. In retaliation President Gamal Abdel Nasser on 26 July announced that he was nationalizing the Suez Canal and would use the tolls to defray the expenses of constructing the dam. The issues over the Canal were not resolved at an international conference in London 16–23 Aug. On 29 Oct. an Israeli army invaded the Gaza strip and the Sinai Peninsula, hurling back the Egyptians to the Canal. This was followed, 31 Oct., by an Anglo-French attack on Egypt, the same day President Eisenhower declared himself opposed to the use of force as an instrument for settlement of international disputes. Yielding to American pressure and Russian threats of intervention (5 Nov.), Prime Minister Eden announced (6 Nov.) that a cease-fire would go into effect at midnight. On 10 Apr. 1957 the Suez Canal was again open, following clearance operations by a UN salvage team. The enhancement of Nasser's prestige as a result of the Suez fiasco was evidenced by the formation (22 Feb. 1958) of the United Arab Republic (Egypt and Syria), with Nasser as President. On 2 July 1959 the U.S. announced resumption of its technical cooperation program in the U.A.R., and on 22 Dec. the International Bank approved a loan of $56.5 million for improvement of the Suez Canal.

Iran. The U.S. mediated the British-Iranian oil dispute (5 Aug. 1954). A new agreement provided for oil production and marketing by an 8-firm consortium (including 5 American firms), with a 50–50 split of payments with Iran.

Baghdad Pact. Treaties of cooperation to protect the northern tier of the Middle Eastern states were signed between Turkey, Pakistan, Iraq, Iran, and the United Kingdom in 1954. The U.S. declined to join formally at that time. On 21–22 Nov. 1955 the Baghdad Pact Council held its first meeting in Baghdad, with U.S. observers present. On 29 Nov. 1956 the U.S. issued a declaration of support for the pact and for the independence and integrity of its members. At a meeting of the Council of Ministers in Karachi (3–6 June 1957) the U.S. formally joined the Military Committee. On 5 Mar. 1959 the U.S. signed bilateral cooperation agreements with Turkey, Iran, and Pakistan in Ankara. On 24 Mar. Iraq announced its withdrawal from the Baghdad Pact, and canceled its military and economic agreements with the U.S. (30 May). The Baghdad Pact was officially changed to **Central Treaty Organization** (CENTO), 18 Aug.

5 Jan. 1957. The Eisenhower Doctrine. President Eisenhower in an address to Congress warned the Communist powers that the U.S. would permit no further Communist conquests in the Middle East. A resolution was introduced by Rep. Thomas A. Gordon (Ill.) on the same day embodying the President's request for authority to undertake "programs of military assistance and cooperation with any nation or group of nations which desires such aid," including the employment of the armed forces of the U.S. to secure and protect the territorial integrity and political independence of such nations requesting such aid against overt armed aggression from any nation "controlled by international communism." After debate in the Senate a modified version of the resolution was adopted 7 Mar., authorizing the President to assist any nation or group of nations in the Middle East in developing economic or military power. $200 million was made available for this purpose.

The Eisenhower Doctrine was subjected to 2 tests in 1957. On 10 Apr. King Hussein of **Jordan** requested the resignation of Premier Salayman al-

Nabulsi. Rioting ensued. President Eisenhower sent the 6th Fleet to the eastern Mediterranean, although Hussein did not request aid. Order eventually was restored. In Aug. Communists took over key governmental positions in **Syria.** Both crises were internal and did not justify intervention under the Eisenhower Doctrine.

On 9 May 1958 armed rebellion broke out in **Lebanon.** Again the U.S. moved the 6th Fleet to the eastern Mediterranean, and on 15 July the U.S. marines landed in response to a request from President Camille Chamoun for assistance under the Eisenhower Doctrine. The landing of the marines touched off a pro-Nasser coup in Iraq on 14 July. King Feisal II and Crown Prince Abdul Illad were murdered. When a revolt against King Hussein threatened, the British rushed in troops. With the restoration of order in Lebanon and Jordan the U.S. and British troops were gradually withdrawn.

UPHEAVAL IN LATIN AMERICA.
British Guiana. 30 Apr. 1953. After elections under a new constitution gave the leftist People's Progressive party a clear majority, the British government sent troops and suspended the constitution to prevent a coup. The People's Progressive party again captured control of the legislative council, 12 Aug. 1957.

Guatemala. On 17 May 1954 the U.S. Department of State regarded as "a development of gravity" the arrival 15 May at Puerto Barrios of a vessel containing arms from a Soviet-controlled territory in Europe. On 18 June an insurgent force under Col. Carlos Castillo Armas invaded Guatemala from Honduras. On 26 June the U.S. and 9 other American governments requested a special meeting of the Council of the Organization of American States to consider the threat to peace and security created by the situation in Guatemala. On 29 June the pro-Communist government was overthrown, and on 1 Sept. Col. Castillo Armas became President, with the dissolution of the military junta. On 30 Oct. the U.S. promised Guatemala $6,425,000 in economic aid, and on 18 June 1955 the U.S. and Guatemala signed a military assistance pact. On 26 July 1957 President Armas was assassinated by

an alleged Communist, and a military junta temporarily took over.

Panama. On 25 Jan. 1955 the U.S. and Panama signed a treaty of cooperation concerning the Panama Canal. On 26 Apr. 1959 a small insurgent force from Cuba landed in Panama, but surrendered 1 May following intervention by an O.A.S. observation group. On 3 Nov. mobs attacked the U.S. embassy in Panama City and attempted to invade the Canal Zone. To allay Panamanian feeling President Eisenhower (7 Sept 1960) ordered that the Panamanian as well as the U.S. flag should henceforth be flown in the Canal Zone.

Nixon Visit. Vice-President Nixon made a good-will tour of 8 South American countries, 27 Apr.–15 May 1958, but encountered hostile demonstrations, particularly in Peru (7–8 May) and Venezuela (13 May). A precautionary movement of U.S. forces into Caribbean bases was ordered by President Eisenhower in view of the virulence of the demonstrations in Venezuela.

Venezuela. The dictatorial regime of President Marcos Pérez Jiménez was overthrown on 23 Jan. 1958. In Dec. the military-civilian junta promulgated new tax rules giving Venezuela 60% of the profits of foreign-owned oil companies instead of the 50% customary hitherto. Some temporary stability was provided by the election, 7 Dec., of Rómulo Betancourt of the Democratic Action party to the Presidency, and leftist demonstrations against the regime (Nov.-Dec. 1960) failed.

Cuban Crisis. On 2 Dec. 1956 a small revolutionary expedition headed by Fidel Castro landed in Oriente Province. By 24 Dec. 1958 military operations had reached a decisive stage, with insurgent attacks in Las Villas and Oriente provinces. On 1 Jan. 1959 President Fulgencio Batista (assumed office 10 Mar. 1952) resigned and fled the country. Executions of Batista supporters began. On 16 Feb. Fidel Castro became Premier. Executions continued. During months of Feb. and Mar. an agrarian reform program was enacted. Castro visited the U.S. (15–20 Apr.), but shortly after his return a serious deterioration of U.S.-Cuban relations set in, accompanied by the establishment of close economic and military ies between Cuba and the U.S.S.R. On 7 June the U.S. denounced Cuba before the O.A.S. as contributing to Caribbean tensions and for its policy of slander of the U.S. In retaliation for the confiscation of U.S.-owned oil refineries 29 June, followed by widespread seizure of most of the remaining American business firms, Congress voted 3 July to cut the quota of Cuban sugar to the U.S. This was cut by Presidential order (6 July) by 700,000 tons; subsequently, further purchases of Cuban sugar were suspended and an embargo placed (12 Oct.) on the export of all products except medical supplies and food to the island. Threats made by Castro and members of his govt. against the continued U.S. occupation of the naval base at Guantanamo, held under the U.S.-Cuban treaty of 1903, prompted White House announcement (26 Oct.) to the effect that it was "firm administration policy" to fight to defend the base. In a note 28 Oct. to the O.A.S. the U.S. charged that the Cuban govt. had created and armed a military force ten times the size of that of Batista, with a stepped-up delivery of arms since Aug. As a result of increased Caribbean tension President Eisenhower ordered (17 Nov.) U.S. naval units to patrol Central American waters and shoot if necessary to prevent any

Communist-led invasion of Guatemala or Nicaragua. On 2 Dec. President Eisenhower announced that he had authorized the use of $1 million for the relief and resettlement in the U.S. of refugees from the "Communist-controlled" regime of Fidel Castro. U.S. broke off diplomatic relations with Cuba 3 Jan. 1961, when Castro demanded a drastic cut in personnel of American embassy in Havana.

THE U.S. AND AFRICA. 13 new African nations were admitted to the UN at its fall session, 1960. The Republic of the Congo, which was precipitously granted its independence by Belgium in June, 1960, was soon torn by a secessionist move on the part of mineral-rich Katanga Province and by a civil war between the forces of President Joseph Kasavubu and Prime Minister Patrice Lumumba. With U.S. support the Kasavubu regime was seated at the UN (22 Nov.) by a vote of 53–24 (19 abstentions), the Soviet and neutralist block in opposition. In recognition of the importance of Africa to the U.S., President-elect Kennedy named (1 Dec.) Gov. G. Mennen Williams (Mich.) Asst. Secy. of African Affairs. On Dec. 14, UN Assembly voted, 89–0, to end colonialism, U.S. abstaining.

DOMESTIC ISSUES
AND NATIONAL POLITICS SINCE 1945

ANTI-INFLATION MEASURES. On 1 Dec. 1945 the National War Labor Board was abolished and replaced by the Wage Stabilization Board (WSB), which in turn was replaced (29 July 1952) by a new board with circumscribed powers. On 21 Feb. 1946 the Office of Economic Stabilization was established by executive order. **Chester Bowles** (1901–   ) was named director. Price control ended 30 June after President Truman vetoed a new measure, but was revived in modified form 25 July. On 15 Oct. meat price controls were ended and all other price and wage controls save on rents, sugar, and rice terminated 9 Nov. On 26 July 1948 President Truman urged a special session of Congress to enact an inflation-control program calling for revival of excess profit taxes, priorities, and ration-

ing. On 16 Aug. the **Anti-Inflation Act,** a compromise bill, became law; on 17 Aug. the Board of Governors of the Federal Reserve System ordered curbs on installment buying. The **Defense Production Act of 1950** (8 Sept.) gave the President broad economic powers, including authority to stabilize wages and prices. On 21 Dec. **Charles E. Wilson** (1886–   ) was named director of the newly established Office of Economic Stabilization (26 Jan. 1951). On 30 June 1952 a compromise 1-yr. extension of the Defense Production Act with economic controls weakened was signed by President Truman. Last price controls ended 17 Mar. 1953.

MOBILIZATION AND REARMAMENT. On 31 Mar. 1947 the Selective Service Act expired. The National Security Act (26 July) coordinated the army, navy, and air force into a single National Military Establishment under the **Secretary of Defense** with Cabinet status. A new Selective Service Act (24 June 1948) provided for registration of all men between 18 and 25, with induction restricted to those between 19 and 25, for 21 mos. service. By the National Security Act (10 Aug. 1949) the National Military Establishment was renamed the Dept. of Defense and reorganized. A nonvoting chairman of the Joint Chiefs of Staff was set up, to which post President Truman named Gen. **Omar N. Bradley** (1893–   ). On 30 June 1950 the draft was extended by law to 9 July 1951 and the President authorized to call out the National Guard and organized reserves for 21 mos. active service. The draft was further extended (19 June 1951) to 1 July 1955 and the draft age lowered to 18½, paving the way for possible institution of universal military training (UMT). Armed forces appropriations mounted following the Korean War (fiscal years in $billion): 1950, $14.8; 1951, $26.6; 1952, $56.9; 1953, $46.6, including a plan for a 143-wing air force by mid-1955.

INTERNAL SECURITY. The **Loyalty Order** for investigation of employees in the Executive branch of the Federal service was promulgated by President Truman 22 Mar. 1947 and the loyalty check to remove disloyal and subversive persons began on 22 Aug.

Hiss Case. On 3 Aug. 1948 Whittaker Chambers, admitted former Communist courier, named Alger Hiss as a member of a prewar Communist apparatus in Washington. A libel suit brought by Hiss against his accuser led to the production by Chambers of State Dept. classified documents or copies thereof allegedly turned over to him by Hiss. On 15 Dec. Hiss was indicted on 2 counts of perjury by a Federal grand jury in New York. His 1st trial ended 8 July 1949 in a hung jury; he was found guilty at his 2nd trial and sentenced (17 Nov.) to 5 yrs. in prison.

Communist trials. The trial of 11 top leaders of the U.S. Communist party on charges of violating the Smith Act of 1940 began 17 Jan. 1949. They were convicted 14 Oct. and sentenced 21 Oct. to prison terms.

Espionage Cases. On 7 Mar. 1950 Judith Coplon and Valentin Gubichev, the latter a Soviet consular official, were found guilty of conspiracy and attempted espionage against the U.S. Gubichev was expelled from the U.S.; Miss Coplon on 28 Jan. 1952 was granted a new trial. Klaus Fuchs, a German-born physicist, was sentenced 1 Mar. 1950 by a British court to a 14-yr. term in prison after being convicted of atomic espionage for the Soviet Union. His trial was followed by the arrest in the U.S. of his confederate Harry Gold, sentenced to 30 yrs. in prison (9 Dec. 1950), and by the trial and conviction (29 Mar. 1951) for atomic espionage of Julius Rosenberg and his wife Ethel, who were sentenced to death, and of Morton Sobell, to a 30-yr. term. The Rosenbergs were executed in Sing Sing Prison, 19 June 1953.

1950, 23 Sept. INTERNAL SECURITY ACT OF 1951 (McCARRAN ACT), passed over President Truman's veto, provided for registration of Communist and Communist-front organizations, and for the internment of Communists during national emergencies and prohibited employment of Communists in national defense work. The Act prohibited from entry into the U.S. anyone who had been a member of a totalitarian organization; but by amendment, 28 Mar. 1951, anyone who was under 16 when forced into such a group, or who joined to maintain his livelihood was not banned for that reason alone.

1950, 1 Nov. ASSASSINATION ATTEMPT. Two Puerto Rican Nationalists, Oscar Collazo and Griselio Torresola, attempted to assassinate President Truman at Blair House, Washington, D.C. Torresola was killed instantly; Collazo was tried and sentenced to death for the killing of a guard, but on 24 July 1952, the same day that President Truman signed an act enlarging the self-government of Puerto Rico, he commuted the sentence to life imprisonment.

GOVERNMENT REORGANIZATION. The Legislative Reorganization Act (2 Aug. 1946) modified Congressional procedure. The **Hoover Commission** on organization of the Executive branch of the government was provided for by act of Congress (7 July 1947). The President's salary was increased to $100,000 with a tax-free expense allowance of $50,000 by Act of 19 Jan. 1949, which also raised the salaries of the Vice-President and Speaker of the House to $30,000. The Reorganization Act of 20 June 1949 authorized the President to reorganize the Executive branch of the government subject to Congressional approval. Legislation enacted (1952) by the 82nd Congress included approval of a Presidential plan to reorganize the Bureau of Internal Revenue, with provision for selection of all officers of the agency, with the exception of the commissioner, from Civil Service.

1947, 18 July. PRESIDENTIAL SUCCESSION ACT revised the law of 1886 and made the Speaker of the House first and the president *pro tempore* of the Senate second in line of succession of President and Vice-President, followed by the Secretary of State and other Cabinet members according to rank.

1951, 26 Feb. 22ND AMENDMENT made 2 terms the maximum for the Presidency and barred election for more than 1 term of a person who held that office for more than 2 yrs. of a term to which some other person was elected. The amendment did not apply to President Truman.

CORRUPTION. The Senate Subcommittee to Investigate Interstate Crime, headed by Sen. **Estes Kefauver** (Tenn., 1903–   ) attracted nationwide attention (1950–51) when its hearings were televised. Evidence of corruption among Federal officials was highlighted by the demand (Aug. 1950) by Secretary of the Treasury Snyder for the resignation of James P. Finnegan, St. Louis collector of internal revenue. Finnegan finally resigned 24 Apr. 1951. On 31 July George J. Schoeneman, commissioner of internal revenue, resigned. In addition, collectors of internal revenue at Boston (27 June), San Francisco (28 Sept.), and Brooklyn (23 Oct.) were removed, along with 31 other Revenue Bureau officials (28 Nov.), as well as T. Lamar Caudle, Assistant Attorney General in charge of the Justice Dept.'s Tax Division, and Charles Oliphant (5 Dec.), chief counsel of the Revenue Bureau. On 1 Feb. 1952 President Truman appointed Newbold Morris

(N.Y.) to investigate corruption among Federal officials, but he himself was removed by Attorney General J. Howard McGrath (3 Apr.) and McGrath was replaced (4 Apr.) by James P. McGranery.

1946, 5 Nov. Victories in the national elections gave the Republicans control of both Houses for the 1st time in 14 yrs.

1948 PRESIDENTIAL CAMPAIGN. The Republican National Convention met at Philadelphia (21 June) and on 24 June nominated Gov. **Thomas E. Dewey** (N.Y.) for President and Gov. **Earl Warren** (Calif.) for Vice-President. The Democratic National Convention met at Philadelphia (12 July) and on 15 July renominated President **Harry S. Truman** and chose Sen. **Alben W. Barkley** (Ky.) for Vice-President. Several Southern delegations walked out of the convention in protest against the strong civil rights plank and nominated Gov. **J. Strom Thurmond** (S.C.) for President on a States' Rights ("Dixiecrat") ticket. Other minor party Presidential candidates: Henry A. Wallace (N.Y.), Progressive; Norman Thomas (N.Y.), Socialist; Claude A. Watson (Calif.), National Prohibition; Edward A. Teichert (Pa.), Socialist Labor.

2 Nov. PRESIDENTIAL ELECTION. Popular vote: **Truman,** 24,105,812; Dewey, 21,970,065; Thurmond, 1,169,063; Wallace, 1,157,172; Thomas, 139,414; Watson, 103,224; Teichert, 29,244; Dobbs, 13,613. Electoral vote: Truman 303; Dewey 189; Thurmond 39. The Democrats regained control of Congress, securing a majority of 12 in the Senate and 93 in the House.

1950, 7 Nov. The Republicans made wide gains in Congressional and state elections, increasing their representation by 5 seats in the Senate and 28 in the House, but the Democrats retained control of both Houses.

1952 PRESIDENTIAL CAMPAIGN. The Republican National Convention convened at Chicago (7–11 July). Preceding the convention the National Committee ruled on disputed credentials of delegates from the Southern states, awarding most of the delegates from the crucial states of Ga., La., Miss., and Tex. to Sen. **Robert A. Taft** despite the claims of Gen. **Dwight D. Eisenhower**, whose backers carried the fight to the floor of the convention. In an initial test of strength the Eisenhower forces (658–548) secured adoption of a rule barring disputed delegates from voting on contested seats until their own credentials had been decided. Thereafter the convention sustained Eisenhower delegates in Ga. and Tex., and the General was the victor over Taft on the 1st ballot as a result of a switch by Minnesota from Harold E. Stassen to Eisenhower. Vice-Presidential nominee was Sen. **Richard M. Nixon** (Calif.). The Republican platform attacked the stands of the Truman administration on China and Korea, advocated a balanced budget, reduced national debt, "progressive tax relief," retention of the Taft-Hartley Act, and Federal legislation in the matter of discriminatory employment practices while conceding the right of "each state to order and control its own domestic institutions."

On 30 Mar. President Truman announced: "I shall *not* be a candidate for reelection," leaving the race for a Democratic nominee wide open for the 1st time since 1932. At the Democratic National Convention at Chicago (21–26 July) Gov. **Adlai E. Stevenson** (Ill., 1900–   ), Truman's own choice, was nominated on the 3rd ballot after trailing Sen. Estes Kefauver on the first 2. Stevenson, who did not seek the nomination, was the 1st Presidential nominee to be drafted since Garfield (1880). A Southern bolt failed to develop after the convention permitted delegations from Va., S.C., and La. to vote despite their refusal to take an oath to support the party's candidates. Sen. **John J. Sparkman** (Ala.) was nominated for Vice-President. The platform endorsed the domestic and foreign policies of the New and Fair Deals; advocated repeal of the Taft-Hartley Act and Federal legislation to secure civil rights.

Minor party candidates: Progressive (and American Labor): Vincent W. Hallinan; Socialist Worker, Farrell Dobbs; Socialist, Darlington Hoopes; Christian Nationalist (in 5 states) and Constitution (2 states): Gen. Douglas MacArthur; Prohibition, Stuart Hamblen.

4 Nov. PRESIDENTIAL ELECTION. Gen. **Eisenhower** scored a sweeping personal victory, with 442 electoral votes to Stevenson's 89. The Republican candidate carried 4 Southern states: Tenn., Va., Fla., and Tex. Both candidates received the highest popular vote for a winner and loser respectively in U.S. history: Eisenhower, 33.9 million; Stevenson, 27.3 million; Hallinan, 140,123; Hoopes, 20,203; Dobbs, 10,312; Hamblen, 72,949; MacArthur, 17,205. The Republicans captured both Houses by a slim majority: Senate, 48 Rep., 47 Dem., 1 Ind. (Wayne L. Morse, Ore.).

2–5 Dec. President-elect Eisenhower visited Korea, carrying out a campaign pledge (24 Oct.).

1953, 7 Jan. BRICKER AMENDMENT. An amendment to the Constitution to limit the scope of international treaties to which the U.S. could be a party and to impose novel controls on the power of the President to negotiate treaties and executive agreements was proposed by Senator John W. Bricker (Ohio). The amendment was opposed on 6 Apr. by Secretary of State John Foster Dulles as "dangerous to our peace and security." After extended debate the Senate (26 Feb. 1954) rejected the amendment, 60–31, one vote short of the two-thirds majority required.

3 Mar. PUERTO RICO. President Truman signed a Congressional resolution approving the new constitution drafted by Puerto Rico and elevating the island to the status of a free commonwealth voluntarily associated with the U.S.; became effective 25 July 1953. **Luis Muñoz Marín** (1898–   ) was re-elected governor of the island in 1952, 1956, and 1960 (the last time despite the open opposition of the Catholic church in Puerto Rico). As a result of "Operation Bootstrap" (1947), granting income tax exemption for 10 yrs. on earnings from new plants and expansion of old ones, the island moved from a one-crop to a diversified economy, with 581 new factories established, 1947–Sept. 1959.

1 Apr. DEPT. OF HEALTH, EDUCATION, AND WELFARE created by joint Congressional action. Mrs. Oveta Culp Hobby sworn in, 11 Apr., as 1st secy.

1954, 11 Jan. REPUBLICAN FARM PROGRAM. President Eisenhower in a message to Congress proposed to replace rigid, mandatory farm price supports with flexible supports based on "modernized parity" instead of the "old" parity (the 1910–14 relationship between prices farmers received for their products and prices they paid for the articles they bought). The bill finally enacted by Congress substituted 82½–90% of parity for rigid 90% props for wheat, cotton, rice, and peanuts; 75–90% for dairy products instead of prevailing 75% level; and gave the Dept. of Agriculture authority to barter surplus crops to foreign nations for strategic goods. President Eisenhower signed the bill 28 Aug.

1 Mar. 5 Congressmen were shot on the floor of the House of Representatives by Puerto Rican nationalists; all recovered. **McCARTHY INVESTIGATION.** Senator **Joseph R. McCarthy** (Wis., 1908–57), chairman of the Senate Permanent Investigating Subcommittee, conducted during 1953–54 a long series of hearings, public and secret, on the role of Communism in government and in other areas of American life. During the same period the Senate Internal Security Subcommittee under Senator William F. Jenner (Ind.) investigated Communism in education, and the House Un-American Activities Committee, under the chairmanship of Rep. Harold R. Velde (Ill.) looked into Communist activities in the entertainment field. Because of its sensationalism the McCarthy committee stirred up exceptional controversy. On 25 Mar. 1953 McCarthy had publicly opposed the confirmation of Charles E. Bohlen as Ambassador to the U.S.S.R., alleging that his close association with the foreign policy of F.D.R. and Truman disqualified him, but Bohlen was confirmed (27 Mar. 1953) by the Senate, 74–13. Again, on 4 Feb. 1954, McCarthy set off on a Lincoln Week speechmaking tour, whose theme, he announced, was the Democratic party's "twenty years of treason." McCarthy's tactics were denounced by President Eisenhower, who on 14 June 1953 assailed "the book burners," on 23 Nov. asserted the right of everybody to meet his "accuser face to face," and on 31 May 1954 attacked "thought control."

Climax of the McCarthy hearings was the investigation (Dec. 1953–Jan. 1954) of alleged subversion in the Signal Corps Engineering Laboratories at Ft. Monmouth, N.J. Army Secretary Robert T. Stevens appeared before the McCarthy subcommittee 25 Feb. and again for 13 consecutive days beginning 22 Apr. Much of the hearings was devoted to airing charges that Stevens and his aides, including Brig. Gen. Ralph W. Zwicker, attempted to cover up evidence of espionage activities which McCarthy and his staff had allegedly uncovered at Ft. Monmouth and countercharges by the army that Roy M. Cohn, chief counsel to the subcommittee, had exerted improper pressure on the Army and the War Dept. Cohn resigned 20 July, but in Aug. McCarthy and his aides were cleared of the army's charges. However, on 27 Sept. a Senate committee headed by Senator Arthur V. Watkins (Utah) recommended unanimously that the Senate censure McCarthy for contempt of the Senate Privileges and Elections Subcommittee and for unwarranted abuse of Brig. Gen. Zwicker. On 2 Dec. the Senate "condemned" but did not "censure" McCarthy by a vote of 67–22; the Zwicker count was dropped.

1 Apr. AIR FORCE ACADEMY. President Eisenhower signed a bill authorizing the establishment of an Air Force Academy, similar to West Point and Annapolis; first class sworn in at Lowry Air Force Base, Denver, Colo., 11 July 1955, and Academy moved 1958 to permanent site near Colorado Springs.

12 Apr. OPPENHEIMER CASE. Dr. Robert J. Oppenheimer (1904–   ), wartime head of the Los Alamos atomic laboratory, was suspended in Dec. 1953 by the Atomic Energy Commission as an alleged security risk. He had served as chairman of the AEC's General Advisory Commission. The action was taken under the President's Executive Order of 27 Apr. 1953, which required a recheck of employees and consultants who had substantial derogatory information against them. Oppenheimer was informed by Rear Admiral **Lewis L. Strauss** (1896–   ), AEC chairman, that he could avoid facing charges if he resigned as a government consultant within 24 hrs. Oppenheimer declined. A special AEC panel headed by ex-Army Secretary Gordon Gray began secret hearings on 12 Apr. Oppenheimer was charged with being associated with Communists, with hiring Communists and ex-Communists, with aiding Communist causes, and with actively opposing the H-bomb project even after President Truman had ordered work started on it. While admitting association with Communists and aiding some Communist causes, Oppenheimer denied being a Communist party member or subscribing to Communist dogma, and declared he was completely disillusioned by the Communists. The Gray committee cleared Oppenheimer as "loyal," but decided, 2–1, against his reinstatement as an AEC consultant, it was disclosed 1 June. The testimony of **Edward Teller** (1908–   ), Hungarian-born nuclear physicist and key figure in the development of the H-bomb, weighed heavily in the committee's findings that Oppenheimer had shown insufficient "enthusiasm" for the H-bomb project. The AEC, by a 4–1 decision, upheld the findings of the special panel.

2 Aug. HOUSING LEGISLATION. The Housing Act of 1954 authorized the construction over a 1-yr. period of 35,000 houses to serve families displaced by programs of urban redevelopment, slum clearance, or urban renewal, increased the amount of the maximum mortgage on both sale and rental housing, lowered down payments, and lengthened amortization periods. Provisions were included to curb future abuses under FHA operations as a result of disclosures of irregularities in the administration of the FHA home-loan insurance program. An additional 45,000 public housing units for the next 2 yrs. were authorized by the Housing Act of 1955 (11 Aug.). The Housing Act of 1957 (12 July) raised maximum permissible mortgage amounts in a number of FHA programs and cut required cash payments. As a result of the increase under the act of existing $900-million capital-grant authorization for urban renewal by another $350 million, urban renewal programs were sharply stepped up. The Housing Act of 1958 (1 Apr.) further liberalized minimum down payments and increased the funds available for

home mortgages. Another housing bill providing $650 million for slum clearance and urban renewal was signed by President Eisenhower on 24 Sept. 1959 after his veto of two other bills had been sustained. A stopgap housing bill extending the FHA loan improvement program 1 yr. was signed 14 Sept. 1960.

24 Aug. COMMUNIST CONTROL ACT deprived the Communist party of rights, privileges, and immunities, subjected Communists to penalties under the Internal Security Act, and provided that Communist-infiltrated organizations lose their rights under the National Labor Relations Act. On 11 Oct. the Civil Service Commission reported that 2,611 security risks had been dismissed from Federal positions in the period 28 May 1953–30 June 1954, and 4,315 other civilian employees had resigned before determination was completed about "unfavorable" information in their files.

30 Aug. ATOMIC ENERGY ACT permitted private power companies to own reactors for production of electric power, to own nuclear materials, and to obtain patents on their own atomic inventions, which had to be shared with others for 5 yrs. In addition, the law authorized the release of certain information on atomic weapons to European allies and the sharing of information on the peaceful use of atomic energy with friendly nations.

2 Nov. DEMOCRATIC GAINS. In exceptionally close elections the Democrats narrowly regained control of Congress, with a 29-seat margin in the House and a 1-seat margin in the Senate. The Democrats won 19 gubernatorial contests, including the Maine election (13 Sept.), against 15 victories for the Republicans.

1955, 9 Apr. CIVIL DEFENSE CO-ORDINATING BOARD, to be headed by the Civil Defense Administrator, Val Peterson, was set up by Presidential order.

11 July. DIXON-YATES CONTRACT. On 5 Oct. 1954 the AEC approved a contract under which the Middle South Utilities, Inc., and the Southern Co. (Dixon-Yates group) were to build a generating plant at West Memphis to feed power into the TVA system to supply Memphis, Tenn. The contract was an issue during the Congressional elections of 1954, when the Democrats raised the cry of "Nixon, Dixon and Yates." In Feb. 1955 the Joint Congressional Atomic Energy Committee disclosed that Adolph H. Wenzell, Bureau of the Budget consultant, had participated in the Dixon-Yates negotiations, although he was also vice-president of the First Boston Corp., Dixon-Yates' financial agent. Following an announcement that the city of Memphis had voted to build its own steam-generating plant, the contract was canceled by President Eisenhower 11 July. Generating capacity of TVA system rose from 2.9 million kilowatts (1950) to 11.3 million kilowatts (1960). On 15 Nov. 1960, TVA sold publicly an initial issue of $50 million bonds to be secured by net power revenues. TVA's expansion brought steam-generating projects of great magnitude, accounting in 1960 for 10% of all power production by the nation's utility systems, and servicing an area of 80,000 sq. mi. in 7 states.

4 Aug. HELL'S CANYON. Proponents of public power were unable to secure passage in 1955 and 1957 of a bill providing for a single high Federal dam at Hell's Canyon in the Snake River, about 100 mi. below Weiser, Ida. The Federal Power Commission awarded, 4 Aug. 1955, a license to the Idaho Power Co. to build 3 small dams.

24 Sept. EISENHOWER'S ILLNESSES. President Eisenhower suffered a coronary thrombosis in the early hours of 24 Sept. on vacation in Colorado. He entered Fitzsimons Army Hospital near Denver, began to resume limited official activities 30 Sept., and returned East in Nov. On 10 June 1957 the President was seized by an attack of ileitis, was operated upon for removal of part of the intestinal tract, and entered a period of convalescence. In his 2nd term he suffered a slight stroke on 25 Nov. 1957.

1956, MONTGOMERY BUS BOYCOTT. A boycott by Negroes of buses in Montgomery, Ala., began 1 Dec. 1955, when a Negro woman refused to relinquish her seat to a white man. Under the leadership of **Rev. Dr. Martin Luther King** (1929–   ) the boycott resulted in the bus company's loss of 65% of its normal income. In response

to a Supreme Court decision of 13 Nov., unsegregated bus service was begun on 21 Dec. Spearheading the drive for desegregation was the Natl. Assn. for the Advancement of Colored People (NAACP) with a membership *c.* 310,000 in 1956. In response to desegregation decisions of the Supreme Court, White Citizens' Councils, originating in Miss., 1954, spread to much of the South. This prosegregationist movement used economic pressures against proponents of desegregation, including mortgage foreclosures, withdrawal of credit, job dismissals, and business boycotts.

17 Feb. NATURAL GAS BILL VETO. President Eisenhower vetoed bill to exempt independent producers of natural gas from federal utility rate control after Sen. Francis Case (S.D.) revealed he had been offered $2,500 campaign contribution by the oil interests.

11 Apr. UPPER COLORADO PROJECT. Congress appropriated $760 million for an Upper Colorado River irrigation and reclamation project, including dams, reservoirs, power plants, and transmission facilities.

28 May. SOIL-BANK BILL set up an acreage reserve or "soil bank" program to compensate producers for reducing their 1956–59 crops of basic commodities below their allotments or base acreage.

29 June. FEDERAL-AID HIGHWAY ACT provided $32.5 billion over the next 13 yrs. for construction of a 41,-000-mi. interstate system of highways and for completing construction of the Federal-aid system of highways, the government to contribute 90% of construction of the interstate system and 50% of the Federal-aid system. The act provided for new taxes on gasoline and other highway user items to yield an estimated $14.8 billion over a 16-yr. period. As of 1 Jan. 1960, 7,570 mi. of the interstate system were open to traffic, 4,770 mi. under construction, 18,-370 mi. in various stages of preliminary engineering and right-of-way acquisition.

1956 PRESIDENTIAL CAMPAIGN. The Democratic National Convention convened at Chicago (13–17 Aug.). **Adlai E. Stevenson** was nominated on the

1st ballot with 905½ votes to 200 for Gov. Averell E. Harriman of N.Y., supported by ex-President Truman. Prior to the balloting Senator Estes Kefauver (Tenn.) withdrew his name and asked his 200 delegates to support Stevenson. Senator Kefauver was named for 2nd place on the ticket, defeating Senator John F. Kennedy (Mass.) by a narrow margin. The Republican National Convention, opening in San Francisco on 20 Aug., renominated **Dwight D. Eisenhower** and **Richard M. Nixon.**

Platform differences were not sharp. The Democrats asserted the right of all citizens to "equal opportunities for education"; the Republicans declared their approval of the Supreme Court decision that segregation must be "progressively eliminated." The Democrats favored public as opposed to private development of water power; the Republicans advocated partnership among federal agencies, the states, and private enterprise. The Democrats supported 90–100% parity payments to farmers; the Republicans, the flexible parity payments.

In the ensuing campaign Stevenson proposed an international ban on the testing of H-bombs. Late in Oct. Marshal Bulganin impliedly endorsed Stevenson's position and was rebuked by Eisenhower. The election, coming at a time of international tension, with eruptions in Poland, Hungary, and the Middle East, was a personal victory for President Eisenhower but not for the Republican party. **Eisenhower** secured a landslide electoral vote of 457–74, and a popular vote of 35,590,472 to 26,022,752 for Stevenson. Minor party vote: Andrews, 107,929; Holtwick, 41,937; Haas, 44,300; Hoopes, 1,763. The Democrats carried both House and Senate, 232–199, 49–47, presaging 4 yrs. of divided rule in Washington.

1957, 18 June. Ratification by the Senate of the Intl. Atomic Energy Agency statute, signed by the U.S. and 79 other nations, authorized a director and bd. of governors to work toward harnessing the atom for peaceful purposes on a world-wide scale; members authorized to make fissionable material available at their discretion.

30 Aug. RESTRICTION ON USE OF

F.B.I. FILES. An amendment to the U.S. Code was enacted to clarify **Jencks v. U.S.** (353 U.S. 657), 1957, which gave defendant in a Federal trial the right to see all evidence in govt. files. The new section provided that only material in F.B.I. files relating to the subject of a witness's testimony at a trial might be produced in court after his direct examination.

1–12 Aug. NIAGARA POWER BILL authorized N.Y. State Power Authority to build a $532 million power project at Niagara Falls, N.Y.; formally opened 1961.

12 Aug. DEFENSE CUTBACKS. Defense Secy. Charles E. Wilson directed that total defense expenditures for the fiscal yr. 1958 be limited to $38 billion.

9 Sept. CIVIL RIGHTS ACT, the 1st since 1875, established a 6-man bipartisan Commission on Civil Rights with power of subpoena to investigate denial of voting rights and equal protection of the laws because of color, race, religion, or national origin; authorized injunctive proceedings in Federal district courts if the vote was interfered with, as well as civil contempt proceedings, without a jury, to secure compliance with its orders. In criminal contempt, trial might be with or without jury, except in case of a fine of more than $300 or jail term in excess of 45 days, when the defendant could demand jury trial. A Reconstruction statute of 1866, giving the President power to use troops to enforce civil rights laws, was repealed. Number of Southern Negroes who registered to vote rose from 595,000 (1947) to 1,200,000 (1956), or 25% of the c. 5 million Negroes reported by census of 1950 as of voting age.

24 Sept. LITTLE ROCK. Sporadic violence broke out in 1956 at such places as the Univ. of Ala., Mansfield, Tex., and Clinton, Tenn., when Negro students sought admission to all-white schools. In 1957, with the start of the fall term, the school integration issue erupted at Little Rock, Ark. A Federal district judge nullified a state court injunction forbidding the school board to start integration beginning with the upper grades of high school. Gov. Orval M. Faubus on the eve of the school opening called out the

National Guard to maintain order, although not a single case of interracial violence had been reported to the police. As a result the 9 Negro students were prevented from entering the high school. Despite a meeting of Gov. Faubus with President Eisenhower at Newport 14 Sept., the governor did not withdraw the troops until the Federal court issued an injunction barring him from obstructing the Negro students' entry. Rioting broke out on 23 Sept. after the National Guard was withdrawn. On 24 Sept. the President dispatched 1,000 U.S. paratroopers of the 101st Airborne Division to Little Rock and put the Ark. National Guard under Federal command. The Negroes entered the guarded school 25 Sept. Gradually the troops were reduced. Elsewhere in the South integration made slow progress. A start was made in Sept. in N.C. at Charlotte, Greensboro, and Winston-Salem, but in the lower South there was massive resistance. Of the border states, West Va., Md., Mo., and Okla. had made the most progress by the fall of 1957; Ky., Del., Ark., and Tenn. the least. Token integration, begun in New Orleans schools 14 Nov. 1960, sparked rioting and heavy absenteeism. On 1 Dec. the U.S. Circuit Court of Appeals declared unconstitutional a series of segregation laws and interposition resolutions adopted by the La. legislature.

1958, 5 Mar. President Eisenhower vetoed Congressional appropriation to make the U.S. the 1st nation to put a nuclear-powered airplane in the air.

6 Aug. DEFENSE REORGANIZATION ACT put into effect a plan to subordinate the uniformed services to a central civilian authority. Previously, 29 July, the National Aeronautics and Space Administration was established to develop research and technology, the Dept. of Defense to be responsible for military space activity.

25 Aug. A law granting pensions to ex-Presidents of the U.S. became effective, the first ever enacted to provide pensions for the former Chief Executives.

28 Aug. AGRICULTURE ACT modified price supports on basic crops for 1959 and 1960, giving farmers choice between modified price supports and increase of crop allotments. Supports on dairy prod-

ucts were raised 31 Aug. 1960.

28 Aug. LABOR PENSION REPORTING ACT required the reporting and disclosure of employee welfare and pension plans covering more than 25 employees, whether operated by unions, employers, or both in combination.

2 Sept. NATIONAL DEFENSE EDUCATION ACT provided $295-million loan fund to lend college students $1,000 at 3% interest over 10 yrs., with 50% reduction if the student later teaches in an elementary or secondary school for 5 yrs. after graduation. In addition, $280 million was voted for grants to state schools for facilities in sciences or modern foreign languages, with matching grants by states, 5,500 fellowships for graduate students planning to go into college or university teaching, *c.* $28 million for language study in higher institutions, and $18 million for utilization of TV, radio, motion pictures, and related media for educational purposes.

2 July. ATOMIC ENERGY COOPERATION. The exchange of atomic information and materials with military allies was authorized. The European Atomic Energy Community (Euratom) Act authorized $3 million for research, to be matched by a similar amount by the Euratom countries, and the sale or lease of 30,000 kilograms of U-235 and 1 kilogram of plutonium for fueling reactors. On 8 Nov. the U.S. signed an aid agreement.

4 Nov. CONGRESSIONAL ELECTIONS strengthened the Democratic party's control of Congress by 15 seats in the Senate and 48 in the House, with a net gain of 6 governorships (including Alaska). Accountable in part for Democratic victories were the 1958 recession, farm opposition to the administration policy of lowered price supports for farm products, labor opposition to state right-to-work laws prohibiting union membership as a condition of employment, and dissatisfaction with administration leadership in foreign affairs. Senator **John F. Kennedy** (Dem., Mass.) gained in political stature as a result of his re-election by a record margin of 860,000 votes. Reversing the national trend, **Nelson A. Rockefeller** (Rep., 1908–   ) was elected governor of N.Y., defeating incumbent Gov. W. Averell Harriman.

1959, 29 Aug. VETERANS PENSION ACT made major revisions in benefits of needy veterans for nonservice-connected disabilities, or of their widows and children.

14 Sept. LABOR MANAGEMENT REPORTING AND DISCLOSURE ACT, designed to suppress gangsterism, racketeering, and blackmail in labor organizations, enacted a cluster of proposals, including the anticorruption, fair election, and trusteeship guarantees proposed by Senator John F. Kennedy (Mass.), 15 Apr.; the "Bill of Rights" of Senator Thomas H. Kuchel (Calif.), 22 Apr., setting criminal penalties to protect union members against unfair actions by their unions; and the amendment of Senator John L. McClellan (Ark.), 24 Apr., revising the ban on secondary boycotts under the Taft-Hartley Act to prohibit unions from inducing or coercing an employer or employee to stop doing business with another firm or handling its goods, and to extend the secondary-boycott prohibitions to all unions.

1960, 13 Sept. MEDICAL CARE BILL established federal-state medical care program for the needy aged, with federal contributions granted to existing state medical-care programs for needy persons 65 and over, and federal grants authorized on matching basis to help states start new programs for "medically needy," payments to go to the health-care vendors, not to the beneficiaries.

1960 PRESIDENTIAL CAMPAIGN. The Democratic National Convention convened at Los Angeles (11 July). Sen. **John F. Kennedy** was nominated (13 July) on the 1st ballot, 806 to 409 votes for his nearest rival, Sen. **Lyndon B. Johnson** (Tex.), who won the nomination for Vice-President. Despite a strong civil rights plank, the Southern delegates failed to walk out. The platform favored placing medical care for the aged under Social Security and criticized the administration's tight-money policy. At the

Republican National Convention in Chicago **Richard M. Nixon** was nominated (27 July) on the 1st ballot, after Governor Nelson A. Rockefeller had eliminated himself from consideration on the ticket. **Henry Cabot Lodge** (Mass.) was nominated for Vice-President. Reaffirming the Eisenhower foreign policy, the platform pledged a health program "on a sound fiscal basis and through a contributory system," an expanded national defense program, and a strong civil rights bill, including enforcement of the right to vote and desegregation in the public schools.

8 Nov. PRESIDENTIAL ELECTION. In the closest Presidential election since 1884, **Kennedy** was elected, with a margin over Nixon of 112,881 votes out of a record 68.8 million votes cast. Minor party candidates: Eric Haas (Socialist Labor), 48,031; Farrell Dobbs (Socialist Workers), 39,692; Dr. Rutherford B. Decker (Prohibition), 46,197; Gov. Orvil Faubus (National States Rights), 227,-881. Because of demands for recount in some of the close states, such as Ill. and Tex., and the role of unpledged electors from Miss., the final issue was in some doubt until the Electoral College vote, 19 Dec., which gave Kennedy 300 (22 states); Nixon, 219 (26 states); Senator Harry F. Byrd, 15 (unpledged electors in Ala. and Miss. and 1 Nixon vote in Okla.). Hawaii's vote was withheld at that time as a recount was still in progress. Official count, 6 Jan. 1961, gave Kennedy 303 (including Hawaii), Nixon 219.

1961, 20 Jan. KENNEDY'S INAUGURAL ADDRESS called for "a grand and global alliance" to combat tyranny, poverty, disease, and war, served notice on the world that the U.S. was ready to "pay any price" to assure survival and "the success of liberty," but also to resume negotiations with the Soviet Union to ease world tensions. "Let us never negotiate out of fear. But let us never fear to negotiate," the President declared.

PRESIDENTS
AND THEIR CABINETS

PRESIDENT AND VICE-PRESIDENT	SECRETARY OF STATE	SECRETARY OF TREASURY	SECRETARY OF WAR
George Washington-John Adams ...1789	T. Jefferson ....1789 E. Randolph ....1794 T. Pickering 1795	Alex. Hamilton .1789 Oliver Wolcott ..1795	Henry Knox ....1789 T. Pickering ...1795 Jas. McHenry ..1796
John Adams-Thomas Jefferson 1797	T. Pickering ....1797 John Marshall ..1800	Oliver Wolcott ..1797 Samuel Dexter ..1801	Jas. McHenry ...1797 John Marshall ..1800 Sam'l Dexter ...1800 R. Griswold 1801
Thomas Jefferson-Aaron Burr ......1801 George Clinton 1805	James Madison ..1801	Samuel Dexter ..1801 Albert Gallatin .1801	H. Dearborn ...1801
James Madison-George Clinton .....1809 Elbridge Gerry 1813	Robert Smith ..1809 James Monroe ..1811	Albert Gallatin .1809 G. W. Campbell.1814 A. J. Dallas ...1814 W. H. Crawford .1816	Wm. Eustis ....1809 J. Armstrong ...1813 James Monroe ..1814 W. H. Crawford..1815
James Monroe-D. D. Tompkins 1817	J. Q. Adams ...1817	W. H. Crawford .1817	Isaac Shelby ...1817 Geo. Graham ...1817 J. C. Calhoun...1817
John Q. Adams-John C. Calhoun....1825	Henry Clay 1825	Richard Rush ..1825	Jas. Barbour ...1825 Peter B. Porter..1828
Andrew Jackson-John C. Calhoun...1829 Martin Van Buren 1833	M. Van Buren ..1829 E. Livingston ...1831 Louis McLane ..1833 John Forsyth ...1834	Sam. D. Ingham.1829 Louis McLane ..1831 W. J. Duane ...1833 Roger B. Taney..1833 Levi Woodbury ..1834	John H. Eaton ..1829 Lewis Cass .....1831 B. F. Butler ...1837
Martin Van Buren-R. M. Johnson..1837	John Forsyth ...1837	Levi Woodbury ..1837	Joel R. Poinsett.1837
Wm. H. Harrison-John Tyler 1841	Daniel Webster ..1841	Thos. Ewing 1841	John Bell 1841
John Tyler 1841	Daniel Webster ..1841 Hugh S. Legaré..1843 Abel P. Upshur..1843 John C. Calhoun.1844	Thos. Ewing ....1841 Walter Forward...1841 John C. Spencer.1843 Geo. M. Bibb ..1844	John Bell .....1841 John McLean ...1841 J. C. Spencer ..1841 Jas. M. Porter ..1843 Wm. Wilkins ...1844
James K. Polk-George M. Dallas...1845	James Buchanan .1845	Robt. J. Walker .1845	Wm. L. Marcy..1845
Zachary Taylor-Millard Fillmore ...1849	John M. Clayton.1849	Wm. M. Meredith.1849	G. W. Crawford..1849
Millard Fillmore 1850	Daniel Webster ..1850 Edward Everett ..1852	Thomas Corwin .1850	C. M. Conrad ..1850
Franklin Pierce-William R. King....1853	W. L. Marcy ...1853	James Guthrie ..1853	Jefferson Davis ..1853
James Buchanan-J. C. Breckinridge .1857	Lewis Cass .....1857 J. S. Black 1860	Howell Cobb ....1857 Philip F. Thomas.1860 John A. Dix ...1861	John B. Floyd ..1857 Joseph Holt 1861
Abraham Lincoln-Han'b'l Hamlin ...1861 Andrew Johnson 1865	W. H. Seward ..1861	Salmon P. Chase.1861 W. P. Fessenden.1864 Hugh McCulloch .1865	S. Cameron ....1861 E. M. Stanton ..1862
Andrew Johnson 1865	W. H. Seward ..1865	Hugh McCulloch .1865	E. M. Stanton ..1865 U. S. Grant ....1867 L. Thomas .....1868 J. M. Schofield..1868
Ulysses S. Grant-Schuyler Colfax...1869 Henry Wilson 1873	E. B. Washburne.1869 Hamilton Fish ..1869	Geo. S. Boutwell.1869 W. A. Richardson.1873 Benj. H. Bristow.1874 Lot M. Morrill..1876	J. A. Rawlins ..1869 W. T. Sherman..1869 W. W. Belknap..1869 Alphonso Taft ..1876 J. D. Cameron..1876

SECRETARY OF NAVY	SECRETARY OF INTERIOR	POSTMASTER GENERAL	ATTORNEY GENERAL	OTHER MEMBERS
	Established 3 Mar. 1849	Samuel Osgood ..1789 Tim. Pickering ..1791 Jos. Habersham .1795	E. Randolph ...1789 Wm. Bradford ..1794 Charles Lee 1795	SECRETARY OF AGRICULTURE
Benj. Stoddert ..1798		Jos. Habersham .1797	Charles Lee ....1797 Theo. Parsons ..1801	Established 11 Feb. 1889.
Benj. Stoddert ..1801 Robert Smith ...1801 J. Crowninshield..1805		Jos. Habersham .1801 Gideon Granger .1801	Levi Lincoln ...1801 Robt. Smith ...1805 J. Breckinridge .1805 C. A. Rodney ..1807	N. J. Colman...1889 J. M. Rusk ....1889 J. S. Morton ...1893 J. Wilson ......1897 J. Wilson 1901
Paul Hamilton ..1809 William Jones ..1813 B.W. Crowninshield '14		Gideon Granger .1809 R. J. Meigs, Jr..1814	C. A. Rodney ..1809 Wm. Pinckney ..1811 Richard Rush ..1814	J. Wilson .....1909 D. F. Houston ..1913 E. T. Meredith..1920 H. C. Wallace ..1921 H. M. Gore 1924
B.W. Crowninshield '17 Smith Thompson..1818 S. L. Southard ..1823		R. J. Meigs, Jr..1817 John McLean ...1823	Richard Rush ..1817 William Wirt ...1817	W. M. Jardine ..1925 A. M. Hyde ...1929 H. A. Wallace ..1933 Claude R. Wick--
S. L. Southard ..1825		John McLean ...1825	William Wirt ...1825	ard ....1940 Clinton P. Ander- son 1945
John Branch ...1829 Levi Woodbury ..1831 Mahlon Dickerson.1834		Wm. T. Barry ..1829 Amos Kendall ..1835	John M. Berrien .1829 Roger B. Taney..1831 B. F. Butler ...1833	Charles F. Bran- nan ....1948 Ezra T. Benson ..1953 Orville L. Free- man 1961
Mahlon Dickerson.1837 Jas. K. Paulding.1838		Amos Kendall ..1837 John M. Niles ..1840	B. F. Butler ...1837 Felix Grundy ...1838 H. D. Gilpin ...1840	SECRETARY OF COMMERCE AND LABOR
George E. Badger.1841		Francis Granger .1841	J. J. Crittenden .1841	
George E. Badger.1841 Abel P. Upshur..1841 David Henshaw ..1843 Thos. W. Gilmer.1844 John Y. Mason..1844		Francis Granger .1841 C. A. Wickliffe..1841	J. J. Crittenden .1841 Hugh S. Legaré..1841 John Nelson 1843	Established 14 Feb. 1903.
George Bancroft..1845 John Y. Mason ..1846		Cave Johnson ...1845	John Y. Mason ..1845 Nathan Clifford .1846 Isaac Toucey ...1848	George B. Cor- telyou ....1903 Victor H. Met- calf ....1904 O. S. Straus ....1906 Chas. Nagel 1909
Wm. B. Preston..1849	Thomas Ewing ..1849	Jacob Collamer .1849	Reverdy Johnson .1849	
Wm. A. Graham .1850 John P. Kennedy.1852	A. H. H. Stuart.1850	Nathan K. Hall..1850 Sam D. Hubbard.1852	J. J. Crittenden .1850	
James C. Dobbin.1853	R'bt. McClelland.1853	James Campbell .1853	Caleb Cushing ..1853	
Isaac Toucey ...1857	Jacob Thompson..1857	Aaron V. Brown .1857 Joseph Holt 1859	J. S. Black ....1857 Edw. M. Stanton.1860	
Gideon Welles ..1861	Caleb B. Smith..1861 John P. Usher ..1863	Horatio King ...1861 M'tgomery Blair .1861 Wm. Dennison ..1864	Edward Bates ...1861 Titian J. Coffey .1863 James Speed ...1864	(Department divided, 1913.)
Gideon Welles ..1865	John P. Usher ..1865 James Harlan ..1865 O. H. Browning .1866	Wm. Dennison ..1865 A. W. Randall ..1866	James Speed ...1865 Henry Stanbery .1866 Wm. M. Evarts..1868	
Adolph E. Borie..1869 Geo. M. Robeson.1869	Jacob D. Cox ...1869 C. Delano .....1870 Zach. Chandler ..1875	J. A. J. Creswell.1869 Jas. W. Marshall.1874 Marshall Jewell .1874 James N. Tyner..1876	E. R. Hoar ....1869 A. T. Ackerman .1870 Geo. H. Williams.1871 Edw. Pierrepont .1875 Alphonso Taft ..1876	

PRESIDENT AND VICE-PRESIDENT	SECRETARY OF STATE	SECRETARY OF TREASURY	SECRETARY OF WAR
Rutherf'd B. Hayes-Wm. A. Wheeler.1877	W. M. Evarts...1877	John Sherman ..1877	G. W. McCrary..1877 Alex. Ramsey ..1879
Jas. A. Garfield-Chester A. Arthur..1881	James G. Blaine.1881	Wm. Windom ...1881	R. T. Lincoln ..1881
Chester A. Arthur 1881	F. T. Frelinghuy- sen 1881	Chas. J. Folger..1881 W. Q. Gresham..1884 Hugh McCulloch .1884	R. T. Lincoln ..1881
Grover Cleveland-T. A. Hendricks...1885	Thos. F. Bayard.1885	Daniel Manning .1885 Chas. S. Fairchild 1887	W. C. Endicott..1885
Benjamin Harrison-Levi P. Morton..1889	James G. Blaine.1889 John W. Foster..1892	Wm. Windom ..1889 Charles Foster ..1891	R. Proctor .....1889 S. B. Elkins....1891
Grover Cleveland-Adlai E. Stevenson.1893	W. Q. Gresham..1893 Richard Olney ..1895	John G. Carlisle .1893	D. S. Lamont ..1893
Wm. McKinley-Garret A. Hobart ..1897 Theodore Roosevelt.1901	John Sherman ..1897 Wm. R. Day ...1897 John Hay 1898	Lyman J. Gage..1897	R. A. Alger ...1897 Elihu Root 1899
Theodore Roosevelt ....1901 Chas. W. Fairbanks.1905	John Hay .....1901 Elihu Root .....1905 Robert Bacon ...1909	Lyman J. Gage..1901 Leslie M. Shaw..1902 G. B. Cortelyou..1907	Elihu Root ....1901 Wm. H. Taft...1904 Luke E. Wright..1908
William H. Taft-James S. Sherman.1909	P. C. Knox 1909	F. MacVeagh ...1909	J. M. Dickinson..1909 H. L. Stimson ..1911
Woodrow Wilson-Thos. R. Marshall.1913	Wm. J. Bryan ..1913 Robert Lansing ..1915 Bainbridge Colby.1920	W. G. McAdoo ..1913 Carter Glass ..E1918 D. F. Houston ..1929	L. M. Garrison ..1913 N. D. Baker ...1916
Warren G. Harding-Calvin Coolidge.1921	Charles E. Hughes 1921	Andrew W. Mellon 1921	John W. Weeks..1921
Calvin Coolidge-Charles G. Dawes ..1923	Chas. E. Hughes 1923 Frank B. Kellogg.1925	Andrew W. Mellon 1923	John W. Weeks..1923 Dwight F. Davis.1925
Herbert C. Hoover-Charles Curtis...1929	Henry L. Stimson 1929	Andrew W. Mellon 1929 Ogden L. Mills..1932	James W. Good..1929 Pat. J. Hurley..1929
Franklin Delano Roosevelt- John Nance Garner ....1933 Henry A. Wallace....1941 Harry S. Truman....1945	Cordell Hull 1933	Wm. H. Woodin.1933 Henry Morgenthau, Jr. 1934	Geo. H. Dern...1933 Harry A. Wood- ring ....1936 Henry L. Stim- son 1940
Harry S. Truman ....1945 Alben W. Barkley....1949	James F. Byrnes.1945 Geo. C. Marshall.1947 Dean G. Acheson.1949	Fred M. Vinson..1945 John W. Snyder.1946	Robert P. Pat- terson ....1945 Kenneth C. Royall 1947*
Dwight D. Eisenhower- Richard M. Nixon 1953	John F. Dulles..1953 Christian A. Herter 1959	Geo. M. Hum- phrey ....1953 Robert B. Ander- son 1957	
John F. Kennedy-Lyndon Johnson ..1961	Dean Rusk 1961	Douglas Dillon ..1961	

* On 26 July 1947 the War and Navy Depts. were incorporated in the Dept. of Defense.

SECRETARY OF NAVY	SECRETARY OF INTERIOR	POSTMASTER GENERAL	ATTORNEY GENERAL	OTHER MEMBERS
W. Thompson.1877 than Goff, Jr...1881	Carl Schurz 1877	David M. Key...1877 Horace Maynard 1880	Chas. Devens ...1877	SECRETARY OF COMMERCE William C. Redfield 1913
, H. Hunt ...1881	S. J. Kirkwood..1881	T. L. James....1881	W. MacVeagh ...1881	Joshua W. Alexander 1919
, E. Chandler..1881	Henry M. Teller.1881	T. O. Howe.....1881 W. Q. Gresham..1883 Frank Hatton ...1884	B. H. Brewster..1881	H. C. Hoover ..1921 H. C. Hoover ..1925
, C. Whitney..1885	L. Q. C. Lamar..1885 Wm. F. Vilas...1888	Wm. F. Vilas...1885 D. M. Dickinson.1888	A. H. Garland..1885	W. F. Whiting..1928 R. P. Lamont ..1929 R. D. Chapin ..1932
nj. F. Tracy ..1889	John W. Noble..1889	J. Wanamaker ..1889	W. H. H. Miller.1889	D. C. Roper ...1933 Harry L. Hopkins 1939
lary A. Herbert.1893	Hoke Smith ....1893 D. R. Francis...1896	W. S. Bissell ..1893 W. L. Wilson ..1895	R. Olney.......1893 J. Harmon 1895	Jesse Jones ....1940 Henry A. Wallace.1945 W. A. Harriman.1946
hn D. Long...1897	C. N. Bliss.....1897 E. A. Hitchcock.1899	James A. Gary...1897 Chas. E. Smith..1898	J. McKenna ....1897 J. W. Griggs....1897 P. C. Knox 1901	Charles Sawyer...1948 Sinclair Weeks...1953 Luther Hodges...1961
hn D. Long...1901 m. H. Moody..1902 ul Morton....1904 J. Bonaparte.1905 ctor H. Metcalf.1907 H. Newberry..1908	E. A. Hitchcock.1901 J. R. Garfield...1907	Chas. E. Smith..1901 Henry C. Payne..1902 Robt. J. Wynne.1904 G. B. Cortelyou..1905 G. von L. Meyer.1907	P. C. Knox ....1901 W. H. Moody ..1904 C. J. Bonaparte..1907	SECRETARY OF LABOR Established 4 Mar. 1913. William B. Wilson 1913
von L. Meyer.1909	R. A. Ballinger..1909 W. L. Fisher ...1911	F. H. Hitchcock.1909	G. W. Wickersh'm.1909	J. J. Davis ....1921 J. J. Davis ....1923 J. J. Davis 1929
sephus Daniels.1913	F. K. Lane ....1913 J. B. Payne....1920	A. S. Burleson..1913	J. C. McReynolds.1913 Thos. W. Gregory.1914 A. M. Palmer...1919	Wm. N. Doak...1930 Frances Perkins..1933 Lewis B. Schwellenbach .1945
lwin Denby ...1921	Albert B. Fall..1921 Hubert Work 1923	Will H. Hays...1921 Hubert Work....1922 Harry S. New...1923	H. M. Daugherty.1921	Maurice J. Tobin.1948 Martin P. Durkin.1953 James P. Mitchell.1953 Arthur J. Goldberg 1961
lwin Denby ...1923 rtis D. Wilbur.1924	Hubert Work ...1923 Roy O. West ...1928	Harry S. New...1923	H. M. Daugherty.1923 Harlan F. Stone.1924 John G. Sargent..1925	SECRETARY OF DEFENSE Established 26 July 1947.
as. F. Adams.1929	Ray L. Wilbur..1929	Walter F. Brown.1929	Wm. D. Mitchell.1929	James V. Forrestal ....1947 Louis A. Johnson.1949 George C.
aude A. Swanson 1933 arles Edison ..1940 ank Knox 1940	Harold L. Ickes.1933	James A. Farley.1933 Frank C. Walker.1940	H. S. Cummings.1933 Frank Murphy...1939 Robert H. Jackson.'40 Francis Biddle ..1941	Marshall ....1950 Robert A. Lovett.1951 C. E. Wilson ...1953 Neil H. McElroy.1957
s. V. Forrestal ...1945*	Harold L. Ickes.1945 Julius C. Krug..1946 Oscar L. Chapman 1949	Frank C. Walker.1945 Robert E. Hannegan ....1945 Jesse M. Donaldson ...1947	Tom C. Clark ..1945 J. Howard McGrath ....1949 J. P. McGranery.1952	Thomas S. Gates, Jr. ....1959 Robert S. McNamara 1961
	Douglas McKay..1953 Fred A. Seaton.1956	A. E. Summerfield.1953	Herbert Brownell, Jr. ....1953 William P. Rogers.1957	SECRETARY OF HEALTH, EDUCATION, AND WELFARE Established 1 Apr. 1953 Oveta Culp Hobby.1953 Marion B. Folsom.1955 Arthur S. Flemming 1958
	Stewart L. Udall.1961	J. Edward Day..1961	Robert F. Kennedy 1961	Abraham A. Ribicoff 1961

[Ad-Administration; AM-Anti-Masonic; C-Coalition; D-Democratic; DR-Democratic-Republican; F-Federalist; J-Jacksonian; NR-National Republican; Op-Opposition; R-Republican; U-Unionist; W-Whig]

CONGRESS	YEAR	PRESIDENT	SENATE			HOUSE		
			Majority party	Principal Minority party	Others	Majority party	Principal Minority party	Others
1	1789–91	F (Washington)	Ad 17	Op 9	0	Ad 38	Op 26	0
2	1791–93	F (Washington)	F 16	DR 13	0	F 37	DR 33	0
3	1793–95	F (Washington)	F 17	DR 13	0	DR 57	F 48	0
4	1795–97	F (Washington)	F 19	DR 13	0	F 54	DR 52	0
5	1797–99	F (J. Adams)	F 20	DR 12	0	F 58	DR 48	0
6	1799–01	F (J. Adams)	F 19	DR 13	0	F 64	DR 42	0
7	1801–03	DR (Jefferson)	DR 18	F 14	0	DR 69	F 36	0
8	1803–05	DR (Jefferson)	DR 25	F 9	0	DR 102	F 39	0
9	1805–07	DR (Jefferson)	DR 27	F 7	0	DR 116	F 25	0
10	1807–09	DR (Jefferson)	DR 28	F 6	0	DR 118	F 24	0
11	1809–11	DR (Madison)	DR 28	F 6	0	DR 94	F 48	0
12	1811–13	DR (Madison)	DR 30	F 6	0	DR 108	F 36	0
13	1813–15	DR (Madison)	DR 27	F 9	0	DR 112	F 68	0
14	1815–17	DR (Madison)	DR 25	F 11	0	DR 117	F 65	0
15	1817–19	DR (Monroe)	DR 34	F 10	0	DR 141	F 42	0
16	1819–21	DR (Monroe)	DR 35	F 7	0	DR 156	F 27	0
17	1821–23	DR (Monroe)	DR 44	F 4	0	DR 158	F 25	0
18	1823–25	DR (Monroe)	DR 44	F 4	0	DR 187	F 26	0
19	1825–27	C (J. Q. Adams)	Ad 26	J 20	0	Ad 105	J 97	0
20	1827–29	C (J. Q. Adams)	J 28	Ad 20	0	J 119	Ad 94	0
21	1829–31	D (Jackson)	D 26	NR 22	0	D 139	NR 74	0
22	1831–33	D (Jackson)	D 25	NR 21	2	D 141	NR 58	14
23	1833–35	D (Jackson)	D 20	NR 20	8	D 147	AM 53	60
24	1835–37	D (Jackson)	D 27	W 25	0	D 145	W 98	0
25	1837–39	D (Van Buren)	D 30	W 18	4	D 108	W 107	24
26	1839–41	D (Van Buren)	D 28	W 22	0	D 124	W 118	0
27	1841–43	W (W. Harrison) W (Tyler)	W 28	D 22	2	W 133	D 102	6
28	1843–45	W (Tyler)	W 28	D 25	1	D 142	W 79	1
29	1845–47	D (Polk)	D 31	W 25	0	D 143	W 77	6
30	1847–49	D (Polk)	D 36	W 21	1	W 115	D 108	4
31	1849–51	W (Taylor) W (Fillmore)	D 35	W 25	2	D 112	W 109	9
32	1851–53	W (Fillmore)	D 35	W 24	3	D 140	W 88	5
33	1853–55	D (Pierce)	D 38	W 22	2	D 159	W 71	4
34	1855–57	D (Pierce)	D 40	R 15	5	R 108	D 83	43
35	1857–59	D (Buchanan)	D 36	R 20	8	D 118	R 92	26
36	1859–61	D (Buchanan)	D 36	R 26	4	R 114	D 92	31
37	1861–63	R (Lincoln)	R 31	D 10	8	R 105	D 43	30
38	1863–65	R (Lincoln)	R 36	D 9	5	R 102	D 75	9
39	1865–67	R (Lincoln) R (Johnson)	U 42	D 10	0	U 149	D 42	0
40	1867–69	R (Johnson)	R 42	D 11	0	R 143	D 49	0
41	1869–71	R (Grant)	R 56	D 11	0	R 149	D 63	0
42	1871–73	R (Grant)	R 52	D 17	5	R 134	D 104	5
43	1873–75	R (Grant)	R 49	D 19	5	R 194	D 92	14
44	1875–77	R (Grant)	R 45	D 29	2	D 169	R 109	14
45	1877–79	R (Hayes)	R 39	D 36	1	D 153	R 140	0
46	1879–81	R (Hayes)	D 42	R 33	1	D 149	R 130	14
47	1881–83	R (Garfield) R (Arthur)	R 37	D 37	1	R 147	D 135	11
48	1883–85	R (Arthur)	R 38	D 36	2	D 197	R 118	10
49	1885–87	D (Cleveland)	R 43	D 34	0	D 183	R 140	2
50	1887–89	D (Cleveland)	R 39	D 37	0	D 169	R 152	4
51	1889–91	R (B. Harrison)	R 39	D 37	0	R 166	D 159	0
52	1891–93	R (B. Harrison)	R 47	D 39	2	D 235	R 88	9
53	1893–95	D (Cleveland)	D 44	R 38	3	D 218	R 127	11
54	1895–97	D (Cleveland)	R 43	D 39	6	R 244	D 105	7
55	1897–99	R (McKinley)	R 47	D 34	7	R 204	D 113	40
56	1899–01	R (McKinley)	R 53	D 26	8	R 185	D 163	9
57	1901–03	R (McKinley) R (T. Roosevelt)	R 55	D 31	4	R 197	D 151	9
58	1903–05	R (T. Roosevelt)	R 57	D 33	0	R 208	D 178	0
59	1905–07	R (T. Roosevelt)	R 57	D 33	0	R 250	D 136	0
60	1907–09	R (T. Roosevelt)	R 61	D 31	0	R 222	D 164	0

[Ad-Administration; AM-Anti-Masonic; C-Coalition; D-Democratic; DR-Democratic-Republican; F-Federalist; J-Jacksonian; NR-National Republican; Op-Opposition; R-Republican; U-Unionist; W-Whig]

CONGRESS	YEAR	PRESIDENT	SENATE			HOUSE		
			Majority party	Principal Minority party	Others	Majority party	Principal Minority party	Others
61	1909–11	R (Taft)	R 61	D 32	0	R 219	D 172	0
62	1911–13	R (Taft)	R 51	D 41	0	D 228	R 161	1
63	1913–15	D (Wilson)	D 51	R 44	1	D 291	R 127	17
64	1915–17	D (Wilson)	D 56	R 40	0	D 230	R 196	9
65	1917–19	D (Wilson)	D 53	R 42	0	D 216	R 210	6
66	1919–21	D (Wilson)	R 49	D 47	0	R 240	D 190	3
67	1921–23	R (Harding)	R 59	D 37	0	R 303	D 131	1
68	1923–25	R (Coolidge)	R 51	D 43	2	R 225	D 205	5
69	1925–27	R (Coolidge)	R 56	D 39	1	R 247	D 183	4
70	1927–29	R (Coolidge)	R 49	D 46	1	R 237	D 195	3
71	1929–31	R (Hoover)	R 56	D 39	1	R 267	D 167	1
72	1931–33	R (Hoover)	R 48	D 47	1	D 220	R 214	1
73	1933–35	D (F. Roosevelt)	D 60	R 35	1	D 310	R 117	5
74	1935–37	D (F. Roosevelt)	D 69	R 25	2	D 319	R 103	10
75	1937–39	D (F. Roosevelt)	D 76	R 16	4	D 331	R 89	13
76	1939–41	D (F. Roosevelt)	D 69	R 23	4	D 261	R 164	4
77	1941–43	D (F. Roosevelt)	D 66	R 28	2	D 268	R 162	5
78	1943–45	D (F. Roosevelt)	D 58	R 37	1	D 218	R 208	4
79	1945–47	D (F. Roosevelt)						
		D (Truman)	D 56	R 38	1	D 242	R 190	2
80	1947–49	D (Truman)	D 45	R 51	0	D 188	R 246	1
81	1949–51	D (Truman)	D 54	R 42	0	D 263	R 171	1
82	1951–53	D (Truman)	D 49	R 47	0	D 235	R 199	1
83	1953–55	R (Eisenhower)	R 48	D 47	1	R 221	D 212	1
84	1955–57	R (Eisenhower)	D 48	R 47	1	D 232	R 203	0
85	1957–59	R (Eisenhower)	D 49	R 47	0	D 232	R 199	0
86	1959–61	R (Eisenhower)	D 62	R 34	0	D 280	R 152	0
87	1961–63	D (Kennedy)	D 65	R 35	0	D 261	R 176	0

II
Topical Chronology

THE EXPANSION
OF THE NATION

TERRITORIAL EXPANSION, TRANSPORTATION, AND COMMUNICATIONS

GEOGRAPHICAL FACTORS. English settlement was favored by a heavily forested coastal area abounding in good ports and river systems leading into the interior. For the first 150 years the English colonists were largely confined within a strip running from the Atlantic coast inland to the Appalachian Mountains. First to be settled was the southern Tidewater region and the northern coastal lowlands; second, the Piedmont area above the fall line, a rolling elevation extending to the mountain barrier. The French ascended the St. Lawrence and the Great Lakes, and by easy portages were able to settle the interior as far as the upper Mississippi long before the English. For the English colonists the chief natural passages across the mountain barrier were: **To Canada**—Hudson-Lake George-Lake Champlain-Richelieu River. **To the Ohio Valley**—(1) Mohawk-Lake Ontario; (2) Susquehanna-Monongahela; (3) Potomac-Monongahela; (4) Roanoke-Kanawha. **To the South**—Valley of Virginia-upper Tennessee-Cumberland.

STAGES OF FRONTIER EXPANSION. The **frontier** (usually defined as an area containing not less than 2 nor more than 6 inhabitants to the sq. mi., and actually a plurality of lines) was constantly pushing into the interior, and generally according to the following stages: (1) initial zone—hunters, trappers, fur traders; (2) cattlemen; (3) miners (less significant in the colonial period than later); (4) **farmers**; (5) town dwellers.

EARLY NORTHERN FRONTIER EXPANSION: 1630–77. Advancing New England settlements spread over the coastal lowlands and up river valleys, thus isolating Indian tribes that occupied the highlands of the interior. The natives struck back in two wars—the Pequot War (1637, pp. 35, 36) and King Philip's War (1675–77, pp. 38, 39). In the latter the Wampanoags (east of Narragansett Bay), Narragansetts, and Nipmucks (between coast and Conn. Valley) were virtually exterminated.

1677–1704. Indian defeat allowed peaceful expansion over the remaining river valleys and into the highlands of Mass. and Conn. When wars with French Canada (pp. 62, 63) brought new Indian attacks (1689–1713), Mass. and Conn. designated 19 towns as frontier forts, forming a fortified ring between York, Me., and Plainfield, Conn. Behind this the frontier advanced steadily.

1704–76. By 1750 the interior of Conn. and Mass. was so well settled that expansion turned northward, where between 1750 and 1776 74 new towns were established in Vt., 100 in N.H., and 94 in Me.

EARLY SOUTHERN FRONTIER EXPANSION SOUTHWARD: 1646–76. Settlement followed river valleys south and west. Indian attacks were prevented by granting 600-acre plots to adventurers who would establish **forts** on the western edge of the Tidewater.

431

TERRITORIAL GROWTH
OF THE UNITED STATES

1663–90. Establishment of the colony of Carolina, with centers of settlement at Albemarle Sound and Charleston (1670), pushed back the Spaniards who had been advancing northward from Florida.

1689–1713. Border warfare along the **Carolina frontier**, as part of the Intercolonial Wars (p. 63), resulted in the destruction of Spanish missions in northern Georgia and western Florida.

1713–32. Continued Indian warfare along the Spanish borderland, highlighted by the massacre of several hundred Carolinians by Yamassee Indians (1715), led to the founding of Georgia (p. 64) in 1732. This resulted in pushing the Spanish frontier back beyond the Altamaha River (1739–42).

EARLY SOUTHERN FRONTIER EXPANSION WESTWARD: 1650–76. Exploration of the Piedmont began in 1650 when Capt. Abraham Wood and Edward Bland explored to the forks of the Roanoke. A more important expedition under Thomas Batts and Robert Fallam (1671–73) followed the Staunton River through the Blue Ridge to emerge on the westerly-flowing New River. By 1673 the Yadkin River had been explored, and a pass opened through the Carolina Blue Ridge.

1676. BACON'S REBELLION (p. 28), caused in part by failure to maintain a peaceful frontier with the Indians. The defeated rebels fled westward, stimulating the frontier advance.

1716. Governor Alexander Spotswood (1676–1740) of Va. led an expedition up the James into the Shenandoah Valley, advertising the West.

1750. Engrossment of the Virginia and Carolina Piedmont by the mid-18th century, with 2 huge grants: (1) Lord Fairfax—"Northern Neck" of Virginia between the Rappahannock and Potomac Rivers; (2) Earl of Granville—most of northern N.C. Hence, exploration and settlement of the West deemed imperative. In N.Y. land system had discouraged settlement by small farmers in the western part of the colony. The settlement, Oct. 1710, of 3,000 Palatines near Livingston Manor, to produce naval stores, soon failed, some settlers moved into the Schoharie Valley, but could not get title. By 1750 all the river valleys and principal arable areas in New York had been engrossed by speculators and insiders, causing immigration to be deflected to Pa. But cheaper lands to the south drew immigrants (Germans and Scotch-Irish) into the Valley of Virginia (by 1727; Winchester settled 1731). In 1751 German Moravians purchased 100,000 acres near Yadkin River, N.C. Scotch-Irish settled the western fringes of the Appalachians and built outposts along the rivers of the upper Tennessee system.

EARLY INTERIOR TRANSPORTATION. River systems preferred to overland passage. Original roads were based on Indian trails. Intertown and intercolonial roads were developed in the 1st half of the 18th century.

1732. First stagecoach line for the conveyance of the public opened between Burlington and Amboy, N.J. Connections made by boat from Amboy to N.Y. and from Burlington to Philadelphia.

1756. Through stage, Philadelphia to New York, took 3 days (coach traveling 18 hours a day).

1760–76. Three roads to the West through western Pennsylvania had now been opened: **Forbes Road** (from Ft. Loudoun to Ft. Pitt), **Braddock's Road** (from Ft. Cumberland on the Potomac to Ft. Pitt), and **Gist's Road** (from Ft. Cumberland to the upper Monongahela).

c.1776. A continuous system of highways extended from Boston to Savannah, but no hard-surfaced turnpike existed, except for a hard-graveled road leading out from Portsmouth, Me. (*c.*1760).

1672–83. ORIGINS OF THE POSTAL SYSTEM. Temporary mail route opened between New York and Boston, 1672; discontinued upon recapture of New York by the Dutch, 1673. No organized postal system in early period. Mass. (1673) and Conn. (1674) provided for transmission of official documents by riders. Mass., by act of 1677, fixed a price for private letters and appointed a postmaster; similarly, Pa., 1683.

1691–1706. Colonial Postal System Under Proprietary Management. Thomas Neale granted a monopoly for 21 years; operation proved profitless, and Neale gave up patent before expiration date.

1707–75. Colonial Postal System Linked with Imperial System. By Act of Parliament, 1710, the postmaster gen-

ROUTES TO
THE WEST

eral of London was made postmaster general for the whole empire. Plan to extend postal system to Southern colonies blocked by Va. until 1732 when ex-Governor Spotswood became postmaster general. The appointment in 1753 of Benjamin Franklin and William Hunter as joint postmasters general resulted in improving efficiency and increasing revenues. By 1758 newspapers were admitted to the mails at fixed rates. Franklin was removed from office in 1774 as a result of his release of the Hutchinson letters (pp. 81, 82). In 1764 a 2nd postal district was set up south of Virginia, including the Floridas and Bahamas, with headquarters at Charleston. Regular monthly packets were running to both New York and Charleston (by 10 Jan. 1769), and Suffolk, Va., was established as the transfer point between the 2 districts.

1774–75. William Goddard, publisher of the *Maryland Journal,* proposed (2 June 1774) that a "Constitutional Post Office" be set up to replace the "uncon-stitutional" British system. By 18 May 1775 all colonies to the north of the Carolinas had established their own postal systems. On recommendation of a committee headed by Franklin the Continental Congress approved a plan (26 July) establishing a postal system for the United Colonies with Franklin as postmaster general. All inland service of the British system came to a halt (25 Dec.). Plagued by wartime inflation, postal rates by 1779 rose to 20 times the '75 level. Rates again revised (12 Dec. 1780, 24 Feb. 1781). System reorganized in 1782; franking privileges curtailed. Within a year the service was flourishing, although foreign mails continued to be carried by British and French packets.

1745–49. LAND COMPANY RIVALRY. To contest the claims of Lord Fairfax, Va. granted lands beyond the 1st ridge of mountains to such Tidewater families as the Carters, Beverleys, Pages, and Robinsons. By 1754 grants totaled 2.8 million acres. The latter phases of the Intercolonial Wars were marked by ambitious efforts of land speculators to exploit the trans-Appalachian area and by the formation of grandiose land companies. Early in 1747 the **Ohio Company** was organized by Thomas Lee. Its traders under Hugh Parker and Thomas Cresap (*c*.1702–90) reached the Ohio country (by 20 Oct. 1748). On 16 Mar. 1749 the Privy Council granted the Company 200,000 acres in the area bounded by the Ohio and Great Kanawha Rivers and the Allegheny Mts., on condition that they be settled and a fort built. Opposing crown grants of her territory Va. granted (12 July) 800,000 acres to run west from the Va.-N.C. border to the **Loyal Company**, formed by John Lewis (d. 1753) and Dr. Thomas Walker (1715–94), with the support of John Robinson (1704–66), president of Virginia Council, and son, John, speaker of the Burgesses. (See also p. 65.)

1750–53. Ohio Co. Developments. Christopher Gist (*c*.1706–59) explored the Ohio country as far west as Pickawillany for the Company (31 Oct. 1750–51). The **Treaty of Logstown** between Va. and the Iroquois and Delaware Indians (13 June 1752) ceded to Va. lands south of the Ohio and authorized the Ohio Co. to build a fort and settle that area. Cutting a road over an old Indian route from the mouth of Wills Creek to the mouth of Red Stone Creek on the Monongahela (1753), Gist persuaded 11 families to settle near him on Red Stone Creek.

1744–54. ADVANCE OF PENNSYLVANIA TRADERS. The French who occupied the Ohio Valley resented the Ohio Co. intrusion, but were more alarmed by an influx of Pennsylvania traders under George Croghan and others. To protect the interior from this invasion, they decided to throw a line of forts across the back country of Pa. Ft. Le Boeuf at the French Creek portage and Ft. Venango at the junction of that stream with the Allegheny were built in 1753. **George Washington** was sent by Lt. Gov. Dinwiddie of Va. (a member of the Ohio Co.) to warn away the French (p. 67). At the Winchester Conference (10 Sept.) the Indians abrogated the Treaty of Logstown and moved into the French camp.

1754–63. FRENCH AND INDIAN WAR (pp. 67–70) at its outset brought a cessation of land grants as well as settlement in the West. French seizure of the forks of the Ohio (17 Apr. 1754) and the defeat of Washington at Ft. Necessity (3 July) and of Braddock at Ft. Duquesne (9 July 1755) drove the earliest settlers on the Monongahela back to the Atlantic watershed. To the north, the fall of Oswego (14 Aug. 1756) and the abandonment of the Mohawk by Gen. Webb. (*c*.31 Aug.) forced the settlers to flee toward Schenectady and Albany. To the south, after suffering raids from Indians operating out of Ft. Duquesne (winter, spring 1755–56), the colonies, largely through the prodding of Washington, built a string of forts running from the mouth of Wills Creek on the Potomac (Ft. Cumberland) south along the south branch of the Potomac and the headwaters of the James and Roanoke Rivers to Ft. Prince George in S.C. Ft. Loudoun on the Little Tennessee (completed summer 1757) served as an advance base to secure friendship of the Cherokee and Creeks. Cherokee raids on the Virginia frontier (spring 1758–Sept. 1759) and the retaliations of the frontiersmen led Gov. Lyttleton of S.C. to make a treaty with the Cherokee (26 Dec. 1759) whereby the Indians agreed to surrender those guilty of disorders. Lyttleton held some of the negotiators hostage at Ft. Prince George. Cherokee attacked the fort (19 Jan. 1760) unsuccessfully and turned to the westernmost settlements for vengeance. The slaying of the hostages (16 Feb.) brought a full-scale attack on the western forts, and Ft. Loudoun, isolated and reduced to starvation, surrendered (7 Aug.); its garrison slaughtered en route to Ft. Prince George (10 Aug.). The relief sent by Amherst (1 Apr. 1760) was ineffective, and war continued until Col. Grant, after a series of destructive raids, forced all the tribes to sue for peace (1761). After the abandonment of Ft. Duquesne by the French (24 Nov. 1758), settlers poured into the Monongahela and Youghiogheny valleys over roads built by Braddock and Forbes (p. 68) in spite of the Treaty of Easton (1758) and Col. Bouquet's proclamation (1761) forbidding settlement. By 1763 over 200 houses had been erected around Ft. Pitt alone. The recapture of Oswego and the fall of Ft. Niagara (1759) had a similar effect on the Mohawk Valley.

1755–62. Other Land Projects. Samuel Hazard, Philadelphia merchant, and Lewis Evans (c.1700–56), surveyor and mapmaker, proposed a new trans-Appalachian colony to include the Ohio and part of the Mississippi valleys. Franklin requested the crown to create two new colonies, one along the Scioto, the other south of Lake Erie (1756).

1762. Route for a canal from the Susquehanna at Middletown to the Schuylkill at Reading surveyed by Pennsylvania to prevent diversion of Western trade to Baltimore (settled, 1730); project postponed until 1791.

SUSQUEHANNA CO., under a charter from Connecticut, began the settlement of the Wyoming Valley over the protests of Pennsylvania.

1763. MISSISSIPPI CO., headed by **George Washington,** which had purchased military-bounty grants to the Virginia militia for a fraction of their value, petitioned the crown (9 Sept.) for 2.5 million acres at the junction of the Ohio and Mississippi to satisfy their claims.

7 May. Beginning of **Pontiac's Rebellion** (pp. 71, 72).

7 Oct. ROYAL PROCLAMATION OF 1763 (p. 71).

Dec. "Suffering Traders," including **George Croghan** (c.1718–82), Sir William Johnson's deputy, and 2 Pennsylvania mercantile firms, Baynton, Wharton & Morgan and Simon, Trent, Levy & Franks, organized to seek compensation for losses suffered at the hands of the Indians. **Illinois Co.** (Mar. 1766) and **Indiana Co.** (1763–67) resulted from this group's activities.

1764, 10 July. Adoption by the Board of Trade of a plan by Croghan, Johnson, and Col. John Stewart (1718–98), Indian Commissioner for the southern district, for subdividing the northern and southern districts and placing trade under the supervision of the commissioners. The plan broke down in the South owing to the refusal of the Governors to curb

illicit trade; in the North as a result of Johnson's order that all Great Lakes' trade be transacted at Detroit and Mackinac. Result: New York and Montreal traders and Frenchmen operating from beyond the Mississippi captured the fur trade. Peltry exports declined from £28,067 (1764) to £18,923 (1768).

20 July. Order in Council placed region west of the Connecticut River and north of Mass. (Vt.) within boundaries of N.Y. Patents had been issued (since 1750) by Gov. **Benning Wentworth** (1696–1770) of N.H. for 119 townships, or about one half the region.

1765. By a preliminary agreement with the Choctaw and Chickasaw, Stuart secured acceptance of the high-tide line as the boundary of the Floridas.

1766, 17 Apr. Opinion of R. Cholmondely, Auditor General of North America, that the Proclamation of 1763 did not void prior land grants encouraged speculators to press their claims both in England and the colonies.

1767, 11 Sept. Lord Shelburne (Secretary of State for the Southern Department) proposed abolition of the Indian Department, withdrawal of most troops from Indian territory, and creation of 3 new colonies (Upper Ohio, Illinois country, Detroit district) to be open for settlement. No action taken.

Fall. All licensed traders permitted by Johnson to operate north of Lake Superior and the Ottawa River.

1767–68. EXPLORATION OF KENTUCKY. Daniel Boone (1734–1820), a frontiersman from the Upper Yadkin Valley, on his first trip into trans-Appalachian country (winter) proceeded along the present border of Kentucky and West Virginia without entering the bluegrass region. At least 4 parties of hunters had preceded him (1766), including **Benjamin Cutbird,** who had traveled along the Tenn.-Ky. border to the Mississippi, and thence south to New Orleans to market furs.

1768, Mar. Lord Hillsborough, first Secretary of State for the Colonies (since Jan.) secured Cabinet acceptance of a new plan for the West: (1) Indian superintendents restricted to imperial affairs; (2) fur trade reverted to the colonies; (3) Proclamation Line to be moved west by treaties with the Indians.

MODIFICATIONS OF THE PROCLAMATION LINE. By the **Treaty of Hard Labor** (14 Oct.) between Stuart and the Cherokee the Va. border was pushed west to a line running from Chiswell's mine to the mouth of the Big Kanawha on the Ohio. The Creeks agreed at Pensacola (Nov.) to have the S.C. border run from Ft. Tryon south to the Savannah; Ga.'s western border fixed at the Ogeechee River. By the **Treaty of Ft. Stanwix** (5 Nov.) between Johnson and the Iroquois the crown secured all land east of a line drawn near Ft. Stanwix, south to the Unadilla River, along that stream to the town of Unadilla, thence south to the Delaware near Hancock, N.Y., westward to Oswego, southwest to the west branch of the Susquehanna near Williamsport and along that river to its head, thence west to Kittanning on the Allegheny, and along that river and the Ohio west to the mouth of the Tennessee—including much of western New York, the region between the branches of the Susquehanna, and the area west of the Big Kanawha—beyond what the British Ministry had proposed. Meanwhile, on 3 Nov. the Indiana Co., with Johnson's aid, purchased from the Iroquois 1,800,000 acres southeast of the Ohio from an extension of the Mason-Dixon Line (southern boundary line of Pa.) to the Little Kanawha.

1769. VANDALIA. Samuel Wharton formed "Walpole group" (including Thomas Walpole, British banker; Lord Hertford, Lord Chancellor; and George Grenville), organized as **Grand Ohio Co.** (27 Dec.) to obtain a crown grant of 20 million acres under the Treaty of Ft. Stanwix. On 4 Jan. 1770 the Lords of the Treasury approved the grant, to be organized as the proprietary colony of **Vandalia.**

1769–73. SETTLEMENT AND SPECULATION. Pittsburgh land office stormed by purchasers (Apr. 1769). Population of western Pa., end of 1769, 5,000 families; 1771, 10,000 families. Other Western settlements: Lewisburg and Peterstown (W. Va.), 1769–70; along the Watauga (1768), Holston, and Noli-

chucky Rivers (1769). Judge **Richard Henderson** (N.C., 1735–85) sponsored a hunting expedition led by **Daniel Boone** (with John Stewart and John Finley) which used the Cumberland Gap and crossed the Licking, Kentucky, Green, and Cumberland river valleys before returning (spring 1771). In Aug. 1771 a proprietary force failed to oust the Conn. settlers from the Wyoming Valley, Pa.

PROCLAMATION LINE CHANGES. The **Treaty of Lochaber** between Stuart and the Cherokee (18 Oct. 1770) modified the line by pushing the border westward to a line running from a point near the forks of the Holston to the mouth of the Great Kanawha, adding 9,000 sq. mi. to Virginia, including most of the lands claimed by the Greenbrier and Loyal Cos. In surveying this line John Donelson tripled the acreage acquired under the treaty by running it along the Kentucky River to its mouth (with the connivance of Indian companions). In addition, the transmission to Croghan (9 Apr. 1772) of the **Camden-Yorke opinion** (1757, by the British Attorney General and Solicitor General), with the omission of the word "Grand Mogul," encouraged land companies to interpret crown authorization of the purchase of lands from Indian princes without crown patents (applicable originally to India) as being applicable to America. Pa. speculators immediately made capital of this interpretation: Wabash and Illinois land companies organized 1774, and the George Croghan-William Trent interests accumulated 6 million acres, chiefly in western Pa. **Watauga Association** was a squatters' agreement, 1772, to obtain from the Indians by lease a tract embracing the northeast corner of Tenn., south and east of the south fork of the Holston River, and a second tract including the headwaters of the Nolichucky River and Lick Creek. On 14 Aug. 1772 the crown approved the **Vandalia** grant in payment of £10,460 7s. 3d.; Board of Trade fixed boundaries and drafted charter (3 Apr. 1773), but actual title never conferred. The coming of the Revolution killed this project. By a treaty with the Creeks (1 June 1773) Ga.'s boundary was moved west from the Ogeechee to the Oconee River.

1774, Jan.–10 Oct. LORD DUN-MORE'S WAR. In an effort to control the northwest, Virginia's Royal Governor, **John Murray, Earl of Dunmore** (1732–1809), seized western Pa., appointing John Connolly Governor at Pittsburgh. This action, combined with the entry of colonial hunters into Ky., goaded the Shawnee and Ottawa into war (by 10 June). Neutralization of Cherokee in the south obtained by **James Robertson** (1742–1814), negotiator of Watauga lease; in the north by Johnson and Croghan. On 24 July Maj. Angus Mc-Donald marched into the Muskingum Valley. In a 2-pronged attack, Col. Andrew Lewis descended the Great Kanawha while Dunmore led a column down the Ohio. **Chief Cornstalk,** Shawnee leader, attacked Lewis at Pt. Pleasant (W. Va.) and was defeated (10 Oct.) at the **Battle of Point Pleasant.** By the **Treaty of Camp Charlotte** the Indians yielded hunting rights in Ky. and agreed to allow unmolested transportation on the Ohio.

20 May, Quebec Act (p. 83), which extended the boundaries of Quebec to the Ohio and Mississippi, antagonized colonies claiming Western lands under charters (notably Va.) as well as speculators who had made purchases under the Camden-Yorke opinion (e.g., Wabash-Illinois and Croghan-Trent interests).

16 June. Harrodsburg, Ky., founded by **James Harrod** (1742–93). Burned during Lord Dunmore's War, it was rebuilt the following year.

1775. Transylvania Co. under Judge Richard Henderson (Jan.) sent out **Daniel Boone** (10 Mar.) to blaze a trail through Cumberland Gap to the bluegrass country of Kentucky (**Wilderness Road**). By the **Treaty of Sycamore Shoals** (17 Mar.) the Cherokee for £10,000 conveyed an area between the Kentucky River and the southern border of the Cumberland Valley, as well as a strip through Cumberland Gap. At the same conference the Watauga settlers converted their lease into a purchase (19 Mar.). **Boonesborough** founded by Boone (6 Apr.), where he was joined by Henderson (20 Apr.) and the first settlers.

A 2nd group under **Benjamin Logan** (c.1743–1802) founded St. Asaph's Station (Apr.). An offshoot of Henderson's emigrants settled at Boiling Springs Station (Mercer Co., Ky.). Delegates from these new settlements met at Boonesborough (23 May) under Henderson and set up a proprietary government for **Transylvania.** Delegates to Continental Congress were rejected (25 Sept.). Population, back country, Md.-Ga., est. 250,-000.

1776–83. THE WEST IN THE AMERICAN REVOLUTION. In the early phases of the war British advantages in the West stemmed from (1) loyalty of the Indian Commissioners, Stuart and Guy Johnson (succeeded his uncle, Sir William, 1774) to the crown; (2) traditional animosity to frontiersmen; (3) superiority of British goods. American military achievements had sufficiently overcome these handicaps to permit (by 1779–80) a resumption of migration into Ky. and Tenn. over the Wilderness Road. Land companies continued their activities and the states engaged in a struggle for control of the West. **Frontier Military Incidents:** The Watauga settlements, forewarned by Stuart, withstood Cherokee attacks at Eaton's Station at the forks of the Holston (20 July **1776**) and at Ft. Watauga (21 July). N.C. troops retaliated by burning the Middle Cherokee towns and, acting with South Carolinians, attacked the Lower Cherokee (Sept.–Oct.). In Nov. the Watauga settlements were incorporated into N.C. Dissatisfied with Transylvania Co. domination, Ky. settlers at a conference (6 June) called by **George Rogers Clark** (1752–1818) petitioned Va. for annexation. The area was organized as a county (6 Dec.) and formally incorporated into Va. (early 1777). By the end of 1776 Ky. settlers, as a result of Shawnee and Delaware raids, were concentrated in three main centers—Harrodsburg, St. Asaph's, and Boonesborough. **George Rogers Clark,** appointed (2 Jan. 1778) by Gov. **Patrick Henry** of Va., surprised the British and captured their base at **Kaskaskia** (4 July) and **Vincennes** (20 July). By the middle of Aug. he was in control of the Illinois country; established as Illinois County by Va. (9 Dec.) Vincennes was retaken by the British

under Capt. Henry Hamilton (Dec.).
Boonesborough withstood a Shawnee
siege (7–16 Sept.) after being warned by
Boone, who escaped captivity (winter to
16 June). **Joseph Brant** (1742–1807), a
Mohawk chief, with 300 Iroquois, destroyed Cobleskill (30 May) and continued depredations down the Mohawk Valley. A second column under Col. **John
Butler** (1728–96), moving farther south,
slew 360 settlers in the **Wyoming Massacre** (3 June). Joining Brant, they
raided **Cherry Valley**, N.Y. (11 Nov.),
costing the defenders 30 killed, 71
wounded. On 29 Jan. **1779** George
Rogers Clark captured Hamilton's force
at Vincennes. The neutralization of the
southern Indians for the remainder of
the war resulted from a combined Va.-
N.C. attack under Col. Evan Shelby
which destroyed 11 Chickamauga villages
in the Tennessee Valley (Apr.) and the
destruction of 6 more villages by a S.C.
force in the fall. Settlers now moved into
the Tenn. and Ky. area over the Wilderness Road and down the Ohio. Nashville
founded by Judge Henderson and James
Robertson (1779–80); Louisville now
assumed an urban character. Population
of Kentucky, 1780: 20,000. **Further Frontier Raids:** British force attacked the Illinois country; repulsed at Cahokia and
St. Louis (May, **1780**). Marching over
the Maumee-Miami route, Henry Bird
captured the Ky. posts of Riddle's Station (20 June) and Martin's Station (27
June) along the Licking River. **Battle of
King's Mountain** (7 Oct., p. 103) ended
Loyalist raids in the Carolina back country. Retaliatory raids upon the Cherokee
conducted by the Watauga settlers under
Col. **John Sevier** (1745–1815) led to further land cessions by the second **Treaty
of Long Island** (26 July **1781**). The Mohawk Valley, virtually in British hands
as far east as Schenectady (as late as
Aug.) was cleared (Aug.–Oct.) by a
force under Col. **Marinus Willett** (1740–
1830). Open conflict between the Delaware Indians and frontiersmen broke out
in May **1782** as a result of the unprovoked slaughter of 96 Christian Delawares at Gnadenhutten (early spring).
Marching into the Ohio country to bolster the frontier, William Crawford was
defeated on the Upper Sandusky (4

June). During 1782 Brant's raiders penetrated Pa. as far east as Hannastown;
others, operating from Detroit, pushed
into Ky. as far south as Bryant's Station,
defeating a Ky. force at the **Battle of
Blue Licks** (19 Aug.). The situation was
critical when news of peace talks reached
the West (*c*.Nov.).

**1776–83. CONTROVERSY OVER
WESTERN LANDS.** John Dickinson's
draft of the Articles of Confederation (12
July 1776) proposed limiting the Western
boundaries of the states; rejected by committee. **Land Bounties:** Congress granted
land to British military deserters (12, 27
Aug.) and 100–500 acres, depending on
rank, to all soldiers up to the rank of
col. who would serve in the Continental
Army for the duration of the war or until
discharged (7, 18 Sept.). Land bounties
were granted gens. under the same conditions (12 Aug. 1780; 850–1,100 acres).
Larger grants were offered by the states
(N.Y., 600 acres; Pa., 200–2,000; Va.,
100–1,500; N.C., 640–12,000). Continental and state grants underscored the
need for political organization of the
West. In Aug. **1777** states whose charters
gave them no Western lands (Pa., N.J.,
Del., Md., N.H., R.I.) proposed that
Congress be empowered to limit the
Western boundaries of the states. The
motion failed, but over their protests, a
clause was added to the Articles of Confederation (27 Oct.) providing that no
state be deprived of Western lands for
the benefit of the U.S. By the **Treaty of
DeWitts Corner** (20 May) the Lower
Cherokee ceded their remaining land in
S.C., and by the **Treaty of Long Island**
(20 July) the Overhill Cherokee surrendered lands east of the Blue Ridge
and the Watauga-Nolichucky region. On
4 Nov. **1778** the Virginia Assembly
voided all Indian sales within her charter limits, in effect curbing land engrossment under the Camden-Yorke opinion.
On 15 Dec. Md. announced her refusal
to ratify the Articles of Confederation
until Western lands were ceded to Congress by the states. On 17 Dec. Va. offered to provide Western lands for soldiers
of the Revolution, but Md. remained
adamant (6 Jan. **1779**). As a result of
the activities of the Illinois and Wabash
Cos., the Virginia Assembly nullified all

Indian purchases in the Northwest (May, June). On 14 Sept. the Indiana and Vandalia Cos. petitioned Congress for a confirmation of land grants. In Nov. a committee of Congress recommended that Va. make no further grants until the end of the war. On 1 Feb. **1780** the N.Y. legislature ceded to the U.S. all claims to Western lands (based on her overlordship of the Iroquois). Conn. followed (10 Oct.), excepting a 3-million-acre tract in Ohio (the Western Reserve). On 2 Jan. **1781** Va. ceded her claims north of the Ohio River (p. 104). On 30 Dec. **1782** the commissioners appointed under the Articles of Confederation awarded to Pa. all lands claimed by Conn. within the charter limits of the former colony. The conditional offer of land cession by Va. was rejected by Congress (13 Sept. **1783**); a revised offer (20 Oct.) was accepted 1 Mar. **1784**, Congress agreeing to reserve as bounty land for Va. a tract between the Scioto and Little Miami, along with a small tract opposite Louisville. By the **Treaty of Augusta** with the Creeks (1 Nov.) Ga. extended her northern boundary west from the Tugaloo to the Oconee River. As a result of dissatisfaction with this treaty the Creeks raised to "kingship" **Alexander McGillivray** (c.1759–93), a half-breed and implacable foe of land cessions, who (June 1784) accepted a Spanish colonelcy.

1784–86. INLAND NAVIGATION. Potomac Co. (organized, 1784, with charters from both Md. and Va. and a grant of £6,666 by each state; **George Washington**, first president) publicly raised £40,300 to build a route from the headwaters of the Potomac to the Cheat or Monongahela Rivers (connecting the Potomac Valley with the West); constructed by 1808 canal along the Potomac with the first water locks in the U.S., but the project was not a paying one. (For steamboat franchise to John Fitch, 1786, see p. 565; for **Annapolis Convention,** 11–14 Sept. 1786, p. 115.)

1784–88. ORGANIZATION OF THE WEST. On 20 Feb. 1784 Ga. created Tennessee County to include the region of the big bend of the Tennessee, with authority to grant land entrusted to 3 commissioners associated with a land-engrossing project launched (1783) by **William Blount** (1749–1800) of N.C. On 2 June the N.C. legislature ceded its western lands (most of which had been disposed of to speculators, 1783–84), with the proviso that Congress accept within 12 mos. Under the leadership of **John Sevier** the trans-Allegheny settlers, in convention at Jonesboro (Tenn., 23 Aug.), set up the independent state of **Franklin** (including a southwest fringe of Va.) and continued down to 1787 to seek admission to the Union. On 20 Nov. N.C. repealed its cession law and attempted to re-establish control over Franklin. By the **2nd Treaty of Ft. Stanwix** (22 Oct.) the Six Nations of the Iroquois ceded to the U.S. all lands west of the Niagara River (rejected by the Ohio tribes). On 21 Jan. **1785** the Wyandot, Chippewa, Delawares, and Ottawa at Ft. McIntosh ceded to the U.S. all the present state of Ohio except for a strip south of Lake Erie between the Maumee River and a line drawn along the Cuyahoga and Tuscarawas Rivers. On 7 Feb. Ga. created the county of Bourbon on land ceded by the Indians between the 31st parallel and the Yazoo, but in control of Spain, which ordered the Georgia commissioners to leave (10 Oct.). In 1788 Ga. repealed the act. Led by Col. McGillivray, the Creeks were defeated in a short war with Ga. (May–Nov.) and signed the **Treaty of Galphinton** (12 Nov.), recognizing the cession of the Treaty of Augusta and yielding a strip on the coast from the Altamaha to the St. Mary's. **Mass.-N.Y. Controversy:** Mass. cession of Western lands completed (19 Apr.), excepting claims in N.Y. By agreement with N.Y. (1786) the western part of the state was divided by a line running north and south through Sodus Bay. N.Y. retained sovereignty over the whole region, but Mass. was awarded land west of the line.

Land Ordinance of 1785 (20 May, p. 113).

Treaty of Dumpling Creek (May 1785) between "State of Franklin" and the Cherokee extended the former's borders south and west along the Holston to the watershed of the Little River; disallowed by U.S. commissioners at the **Treaty of Hopewell** (28 Nov.), which confirmed Cherokee rights to most of the land held in 1777. Dissatisfied with the Treaties of Augusta and Galphinton, the Creeks resumed hostilities (summer

1786). On 28 Feb. the British government notified the U.S. that it would refuse to comply with the Treaty of Paris (Art. 7) and give up posts in the Great Lakes region which were centers of Indian unrest (notably in Ohio) until the U.S. honored British debts (Art. 4). On 8 Mar. 1787 S.C. ceded its narrow strip of Western claim to the U.S., leaving only N.C. and Ga. with western claims. On 15 July 1788 Congress rejected the Ga. cession of its Western lands (1 Feb.). Such cessions were not completed until the acceptance (2 Apr. 1790) of the 2nd N.C. act of cession (22 Dec. 1789) and the ratification by the Ga. legislature (16 June 1802) of the Articles of Agreement and Cession (24 Apr. 1802) between U.S. and Ga. On 20 June 1788 Congress granted 4,000 acres to each head of a family settling the Illinois country before 1783 (c.150 French families), a privilege extended to those at Vincennes and along the Wabash (1790), although, for the most part, the grants were not actually made. By making bounty warrants transferable (9 July), Congress eased operations for the big land companies.

1786–88. SETTLEMENTS IN OHIO.

Formation in Boston (1 Mar. 1786) of a new **Ohio Co.**, organized by Genls. **Benjamin Tupper** (1738–92) and **Rufus Putnam** (1738–1824), to dispose of $1 million worth of stock in exchange for Continental certificates redeemable at par in exchange for public lands. In behalf of the company Rev. **Manasseh Cutler** (1742–1823) petitioned Congress (5–14 July 1787) for 1½ million acres at $.66⅔ an acre. In a deal with Col. **William Duer** (1747–99), secretary of the Board of Treasury, the Ohio Co. was authorized to act for a group of insiders with whom Cutler organized the **Scioto Co.** Under authority of Congress (23 July) the Board sold (27 July) to Cutler 1,500,000 (actually 1,781,760) acres for $1 million with an option on another 5 million acres. The lands lay between the first 7 ranges of townships (already surveyed) and the Scioto River. By agreement the option was assigned to the Scioto Co. In Oct. **John Cleve Symmes** (1742–1814) of N.J. petitioned Congress for land on similar terms; granted (1788)

a 20-mile strip east of the Great Miami. The first auctions of land surveyed in Ohio (the 7 Ranges) brought in only $176,090 in inflated currency (Sept.–Oct.). To offset lawlessness and "facilitate the surveying and selling" of public lands Congress resolved (3 Oct.) to station troops on the frontier. On 7 Apr. 1788 **Marietta**, Ohio, was founded by settlers sent out by the Ohio Co.

1787, 13 July. NORTHWEST ORDINANCE (p. 117).

1789. First Yazoo land grant (25,400,-000 acres) to a group of speculating companies authorized by Ga. legislature; additional grant made in 1795; immediate settlement impeded by Indian wars and Spanish diplomatic intrigues.

1789–1829. EXTENSION OF POSTAL SERVICE. As late as 1792 Vt., Ky., Tenn., and the entire West had no post office, but the Federal government rapidly expanded the mail routes. The Act of 1794 established additional post roads and provided for stage transportation; the Act of 1814 provided that mail service be arranged from the nearest post office to the courthouse of any county in any state or territory. As a result, many new mail lines were extended to outlying regions. Miles of post roads in operation: 1790–94, 5,001; 1825–29, 104,521. Postal rates, 1825–38 (about half the rate prevailing in 1815): up to 30 mi., 6 cts.; 30–80 mi., 10 cts.; 80–150 mi., 12½ cts.; 150–400 mi., 18¾ cts.; over 400 mi., 25 cts.

ACQUISITION OF THE TERRITORY AND PUBLIC DOMAIN OF THE U.S.

Year and How Acquired	Total Area (Acres)
1781–1802 State cessions	236,825,600
1783 Treaty of Paris with Gt. Britain	541,364,480
1803 Louisiana Purchase 1	529,911,680
1803 Red River Basin 2	29,601,920
1819 Cession from Spain	46,144,640
1845 Annexation of Texas	249,066,240
1846 Oregon Compromise	183,386,240
1848 Mexican Cession	338,680,960
1850 Purchase from Texas	78,926,720
1853 Gadsden Purchase	18,988,800

1 Data exclude areas eliminated by the Treaty of 1819 with Spain. Such areas are included in figures for annexation of Texas and the Mexican Cession.

2 Drainage basin of the Red River of the North, south of the 49th parallel, sometimes considered part of the Louisiana Purchase.

1790. Southwest Territory organized.

Settlement of Gallipolis, in the Ohio country, by French immigrants on lands fraudulently claimed by Scioto Co. promoters; some eventually resettled on the "French Grant" authorized by Congress (1795).

1790–95. EARLY TURNPIKES. Opening of the **Philadelphia-Lancaster Turnpike** (1790), completed, 1794. Its financial success encouraged considerable building of toll roads, especially in New England and the Middle States. Construction of the **Knoxville Road** (1791–95), linking the Wilderness Road to the Cumberland settlements. **Wilderness Road** opened to wagon traffic (1795), facilitating settlement in the lower Ohio Valley. In the same year the **Old Walton Road** was opened, connecting Knoxville and Nashville, serving as route for settlers in the Tenn. interior.

1791, 4 Nov. A mixed force of regulars and militia led by Gen. **Arthur St. Clair** (1736–1818), governor of the Northwest Territory, was defeated by Indians of the Maumee and Wabash Rivers. St. Clair was replaced (5 Mar. 1792) by Gen. **Anthony Wayne** as commander of troops in the Ohio country.

Vermont admitted to the Union.

1792. Kentucky admitted to the Union.

Capt. **Robert Gray** (1755–1806), of the ship *Columbia* out of Boston, discovered and named the Columbia River.

1792–1800. EARLY CANALS. Western Inland Lock Navigation Co., chartered in New York, 1792, opened canal (1796) around the Little Falls in the Mohawk River. Santee Canal constructed (1792–1800), joining the Cooper and Santee Rivers in S.C. Middlesex Canal constructed (1793), linking Boston with the Merrimac River.

1794, 20 Aug. BATTLE OF FALLEN TIMBERS, won by Gen. Anthony Wayne at the rapids of the Maumee, in northwest Ohio, hastened to a close Indian resistance in the area, secured the Northwest frontier, and gave added proof of the national government's stability.

19 Nov. By Jay's Treaty (p. 126) the British agreed to evacuate the Northwest posts by 1 June 1796. The securing of the military frontier encouraged steady settlement of the upper Ohio Valley and freed the Old Northwest from diplomatic intrigues and Indian threats until shortly before the War of 1812.

1795, 3 Aug. TREATY OF GREENVILLE, signed by 12 Indian tribes, set up a definite boundary in the Northwest Territory between Indian lands and those available to U.S. settlers.

27 Oct. Treaty of San Lorenzo, also called **Pinckney's Treaty** (p. 127), signed with Spain; its favorable commercial and boundary provisions allayed Western discontent and separatist feeling.

Organization of the Connecticut Land Company, which purchased the **Western Reserve** in northeast Ohio. Its general agent was **Moses Cleaveland** (1754–1806), who laid out and named the city of Cleveland (1796).

1796. Tennessee admitted to the Union.

U.S. Military Reserve laid out in the Ohio country; set apart for land bounties to Revolutionary veterans.

Congress authorized construction of **Zane's Trace,** first road running through Ohio. Connecting Wheeling and Limestone (later Maysville), it was one of the main routes taken by emigrants.

1796–1803. Holland Land Company organized by Dutch bankers, to whom Robert Morris sold in 1792–93 the greater part of a tract west of the Genesee River, helped to advance the settlement of western New York and Pennsylvania.

1798. Establishment of the **Mississippi Territory** opened the Old Southwest to settlement, but large-scale colonization came only after the pacification of the Georgia Indians and the elimination of Spanish control of the West Florida ports.

1800. Liberal provisions of the Land Act of 1800 (p. 461) stimulated settlement of the Old Northwest.

Establishment of the Indiana Territory.

1803, 30 Apr. LOUISIANA PURCHASE secured the Mississippi Valley against foreign economic and diplomatic pressures, ushered in period of Western settlement temporarily halted by the War of 1812.

7 June. Treaty of Vincennes, signed by 9 Indian tribes of the Old Northwest, gave the U.S. title to disputed lands along the Wabash River, beyond the line established by the Treaty of Greenville. Ohio admitted to the Union.

1803–06. LEWIS AND CLARK overland expedition to the Far Northwest (p. 133).

1804–05. Lower Red River and Ouachita River explored by government scientific expedition under **William Dunbar** (1749–1810).

1805. Creation of the territories of Louisiana and Michigan.

1805–06. Government expedition to the upper Mississippi led by Lt. **Zebulon M. Pike** (p. 134), who also conducted an expedition to the Southwest (1806–07).

1806. Government expedition led by Thomas Freeman (?–d.1821) produced first accurate map of the lower Red River.

1807. John Colter (c.1775–1813), one of the pioneer fur traders in the Far West, traveled through the country south of the Yellowstone River, penetrating the valley of the Big Horn.

17–21 Aug. New York-to-Albany and return voyage of the *Clermont*, designed by **Robert Fulton** (p. 711); inaugurated era of successful steamboat navigation on a commercial basis.

1807–08. Encouraged by the achievements of the Lewis and Clark expedition, parties of trappers and traders penetrated the region of the Missouri and Yellowstone Rivers; led to the organization of the Rocky Mountain fur trade, active until c.1840.

1808. Incorporation of the **American Fur Co.**, organized by **John Jacob Astor** (p. 670).

1809. Establishment of Illinois Territory.

Treaty of Ft. Wayne, signed with Indians of the Old Northwest, gave the U.S. title to large tract in southern Indiana.

Formation of the Missouri Fur Company; declined after c.1812.

First successful sea voyage (New York to Philadelphia) by a steamboat made by the *Phoenix*, designed by **John Stevens** (1749–1838).

1809–11. Exploration of the Missouri River beyond the Mandan villages made by **Thomas Nuttall** (1786–1859), natural scientist, who later carried out explorations along the Arkansas and Red Rivers (1818–20).

1811. Fur trading post of **Astoria** established at the mouth of the Columbia River by Astor's Pacific Fur Co. (1810).

7 Nov. BATTLE OF TIPPECANOE (p. 140).

Construction at Pittsburgh of the sidewheeler *New Orleans*, the 1st steamboat used on Western waters; made voyage between Louisville and New Orleans. First voyage on the upper rivers made in 1815 by the *Enterprise*, from Brownsville on the Monongahela to New Orleans and return.

1811–18. TURNPIKES. Construction of the **Cumberland Road** (also called the **Old National Road**), a paved highway connecting Cumberland, Md., with Wheeling on the Ohio River. Subsequent extensions brought it to Columbus, Ohio, and to its final terminus at Vandalia, Ill. One of the chief arteries of Western colonization, it was later neglected, only to become a part of U.S. Highway No. 40 in the era of the motor car. By 1821, 600 miles of new turnpike construction had been authorized, 4,000 completed. Shortly thereafter the **turnpike boom** came to an end.

1812. Louisiana admitted to the Union. Creation of the Missouri Territory.

1812–13. Expedition under the fur trader **Robert Stuart** (1785–1848) made eastward journey from Astoria to St. Louis over route virtually unknown to white men; discovered **South Pass**, later used by Calif. and Ore. immigrants.

1812–14. War of 1812 (pp. 141–153) brought Western expansion to a temporary halt. The war was in part a result of frontier expansionist sentiment (Southern ambitions to secure East and West Florida; Western "land hunger" for Canadian territory) and of Western desire for security against Indian attacks.

1813. West Florida seized by the U.S. British and Indians defeated at **Battle of the Thames** (5 Oct.), breaking power of Indians of Northwest and opening region to settlement.

1814. Battle of Horseshoe Bend (27 Mar.) ended in defeat of Creek Indians by force under Andrew Jackson, and led to drafting of **Treaty of Ft. Jackson** (9 Aug.) in which Creeks ceded large tracts in Mississippi Territory. These events ended Indian resistance in Southwest and opened region to pioneers after War of 1812.

1815. Treaties of Portage des Sioux terminated virtually all Indian resistance in the Old Northwest; enabled rapid settlement of the westernmost part of the upper tier of trans-Appalachia.

c.1815–50. End of the War of 1812 brought resumption of westward expansion and large-scale settlement of the Lake Plains, the Mississippi Valley frontier, the Gulf Plains, and the Southwest. The northern areas were settled chiefly by emigrants from the Northeast (although many Southerners emigrated to the lower tiers of Ohio, Indiana, and Illinois) and, after 1848, by immigrants from Northern Europe. The Gulf Plains and Southwest were settled mostly by emigrants from the Southern seaboard and Piedmont. This period witnessed the rapid expansion of the "Cotton Kingdom" in the deep South.

1816. Indiana admitted to the Union.

1816–18. First Seminole War ended in defeat of Florida Indians by expedition under Gen. **Andrew Jackson** (p. 732).

1816–21. Series of treaties with Indians of the Southwest encouraged settlement in middle Ga. and in western Ala. and Tenn.

1817. Mississippi admitted to the Union.
Creation of Alabama Territory.

STEAMBOAT. The *Washington,* designed by Henry M. Shreve (1785–1851) and launched at Wheeling, made return voyage between Louisville and New Orleans, initiating successful commercial steam navigation on the Ohio-Mississippi route. Quickly following was the inauguration of steam navigation on Lakes Ontario and Erie. Technical developments, such as a more efficient high-pressure engine (by 1825), stimulated steamboat building and operation. **Rates of speed** of fastest steamboats: On Hudson, 30 miles an hour; on Mississippi, 25

miles downstream, 16 upstream. **Passenger fares** fell rapidly from high initial levels: New Orleans to Louisville before 1818, $100–$125; 1825, $50; 1830's, $25–$30. Pittsburgh to Cincinnati, 1825, $12; 1840's, $5. Middle Western cities served by the Mississippi steamboat system outdistanced others before 1850. **Population,** 1850: Cincinnati, 115,000; St. Louis, 78,000; Louisville, 43,000; New Orleans, 116,000. Great Lakes Ports: Chicago, 30,000; Buffalo, 42,000.

1817–18. Explorations of southern Mo. and Ark. by **Henry R. Schoolcraft** (1793–1864), geologist and ethnologist, who made pioneer studies of the North American Indians.

1817–25. Construction of the **Erie Canal,** extending from Albany to Buffalo and linking the Hudson River with Lake Erie; was authorized by an act of the N.Y. legislature of 1817, and vigorously pushed by **De Witt Clinton** (1769–1828). Formally opened in Oct. 1825, the canal made Buffalo and New York entrepôts of Western commerce, quickly became the chief route for emigrants from New England to the Great Lakes country, and was instrumental in creating an agricultural boom in the West. Its success set off a **canal-building boom.**

1818. Illinois admitted to the Union.

1819. ADAMS-ONÍS TREATY (p. 157) provided for cession of **East Florida** to the U.S. and defined western borders of Louisiana Purchase.

Alabama admitted to the Union.
Creation of Arkansas Territory.

24 May–20 June. The *Savannah,* 1st steamship to cross the Atlantic, made voyage from Savannah to Liverpool.

1820. Maine admitted to the Union.

Moses Austin (1761–1821) granted Spanish charter to settle 300 families in Texas; colonization scheme carried out by his son, **Stephen F. Austin** (p. 671).

Army expedition under Major Stephen H. Long (1784–1864) explored the region between the Missouri River and the Rocky Mountains. Its report originated the myth of the "Great American Desert," a misnomer for the Great Plains.

Completion of **Jackson's Military Road,** connecting Florence, Ala., and the Gulf region near New Orleans.

CANALS AND THE CUMBERLAND ROAD
1785–1850

CANALS
Completed
Uncompleted
Canalized rivers
CUMBERLAND ROAD
Macadamized
Not macadamized

Scale of Miles
0   50   100   150

1821. Missouri admitted to the Union.

1821–22. Opening of the **Santa Fe Trail** to the commerce of the Southwest. Although parts of the trail had been in use, it remained for **William Becknell** (c.1790–c.1832), a Missouri trader, to define the route that was soon plied by trade caravans.

1822. Organization of the trapping and trading business that later became known (1830) as the **Rocky Mountain Fur Co.**, which originated the rendezvous method (as distinguished from trading posts). It dominated the trade in the central portion of the Rockies, finally yielding (1834) to the superior resources of the American Fur Co.

1822–23. Expeditions up the Missouri River to the Yellowstone led by **William H. Ashley** (c.1778–1838), one of the founders of the Rocky Mountain Fur Co.

1824. **South Pass,** at the lower point of the Wind River range of the Rockies, rediscovered by Thomas Fitzpatrick (c.1799–1854) and Jedediah Smith (1798–1831), active in the Rocky Mountain fur trade. It was later used by emigrants taking the Oregon Trail.

James Bridger (1804–81), fur trader and guide, credited with discovery of the Great Salt Lake. Another fur trader, **Peter S. Ogden** (1794–1854), for whom Ogden, Utah, is named, credited with being one of the 1st white men to explore the region of the Great Salt Lake.

Gibbons v. Ogden (p. 489), by ending private monopolies in interstate shipping, contributed to the expansion of steam navigation on Eastern rivers, harbors, and bays.

1824–50. CANALS TO TIDEWATER. Construction of the **Morris Co. Canal** across N.J. (1824–32), connecting N.Y. Harbor with the mouth of the Lehigh River, served as important route for Lehigh coal. Other canals between up-country and tidewater included the **New Haven and Northampton** (1835, abandoned 1847); the **Delaware and Hudson,** connecting Honesdale, Pa., and Kingston, N.Y., and used chiefly for transportation of anthracite coal, reaching peak traffic, 1872; the **Lehigh** and the **Morris** in Pa. and N.J.; the **James River and Kanawha** from Richmond to Buchanan,

Va., 1832–51; the **Chesapeake and Ohio Canal** (1828–50), linking Georgetown with Cumberland, Md., based on a route begun earlier by the Potomac Co., suffered heavily from the competition of the B. & O. R.R., whose tracks paralleled its route; the **Pennsylvania Portage and Canal System** (Philadelphia to Pittsburgh, 1826–40), the eastern and western sections of which were joined by the **Allegheny Portage Railway** (1831–35), projected as a competitor of the Erie Canal in a bid for Western commerce, but burdened with high construction costs and strong railroad competition almost from the beginning.

1825. Definite adoption by U.S. government of **removal policy** providing for transfer of eastern Indians to trans-Mississippi regions in order to facilitate advance of white settlement and to fix a permanent Indian frontier beyond the 95th meridian. Originated by Secretary of War John C. Calhoun in 1823, the policy was announced by President Monroe (1825), and carried out on an extensive scale by President Jackson. Most of the Indians of the Old Northwest and Southwest were resettled in present-day Kan. and Okla.

Treaties of Prairie du Chien established boundaries of Indian lands in Old Northwest. This division of tribal lands enabled the U.S. government to make individual treaties for land cessions.

Establishment of Ft. Vancouver by Hudson's Bay Co. on Columbia River solidified British control of the Oregon country.

1826. Treaty of Washington, signed by the Creek Indians, whose removal from Georgia to beyond the Mississippi was accomplished during 1827–29.

1825–56. WESTERN CANALS, linking the Ohio and Mississippi with the Great Lakes. The original **Welland Canal** around Niagara Falls, connecting Lakes Erie and Ontario, was built by Canada, 1829–33. Other interior canals included the Ohio Canal, connecting Portsmouth and Cleveland, 1825–32; Miami Canal (Cincinnati and Toledo, 1825–45); Louisville and Portland Canal around the falls of the Ohio River, 1826–31; 'the **Wabash and Erie Canal,** linking To-

RAILROAD LINES IN
ACTUAL OPERATION
OCT. 1860

In operation, 1827–1850
Completed, 1850–1860

Scale of Miles
0 50 100 200 300

The gauge of all the principal Southern railroads was changed, June 1886, to 4 ft. 9 in. to conform to
Northern railroads; previously it was generally 5 ft.

ledo, Ohio, with Evansville, Ind. (452 miles), the longest canal in the U.S. (1832–56), helped open up northern Indiana, but a financial failure; the **Illinois and Michigan Canal**, linking Lake Michigan and the Illinois River (1836–48), contributed to the rapid growth of Chicago (still in active use).

1826–40. EARLY RAILROAD ERA. In 1825 the Stockton and Darlington R.R. began operations in England. U.S. railroad building quickly rivaled European construction. Early efforts included **Mohawk and Hudson R.R.**, chartered in N.Y. (1826), built in 1830; began operations (Albany to Schenectady) in 1831.

1827. Construction of short-line railway in Mass., from Quincy to the Neponset River, used for transporting granite; construction of the short-line Mauch Chunk R.R. in Pa., from Carbondale to the Lehigh River, used for transporting coal; incorporation of the **Baltimore and Ohio Railroad**, the first passenger railway in the U.S. Construction began on 4 July 1828, lagged after the panic of 1837, and was resumed in 1848. In 1853 the connection between Baltimore and Wheeling was completed. Chartering of the South Carolina Canal and R.R. Co., which by 1833 completed a rail link from Charleston to Hamburg, S.C.; later became the South Carolina R.R. Co.

1828. Philadelphia and Columbia R.R., chartered in N.J., opened 1834.

1829–57. Construction of the Memphis and Charleston R.R.

1830. Incorporation of the **Boston and Worcester R.R.**, opened in 1835.

1830–32. Construction of the Lexington and Ohio R.R.

1832–52. Construction of the **New York and Harlem R.R.**

1833. Organization of the **Western Railroad Corporation**, which built (1835–42) a connection between **Boston and Albany**; incorporation of the **Philadelphia and Reading R.R.**; formation of the **Central of Georgia R.R.**, which by 1843 linked Savannah and Macon.

1835–36. Chartering of the **Louisville, Cincinnati and Charleston R.R.**, projected by Southern interests to enable local centers to compete with Northern ports as entrepôts for the commerce of the Ohio and Mississippi Valleys. Although state particularism and financial obstacles brought the venture to an end in 1839, the separate state roads built by local interests served as the foundation for the Southern rail network built in the 2 decades before the Civil War.

1836. Erie and Kalamazoo R.R. connected Toledo, Ohio, with Adrian in Michigan Territory; Richmond and Petersburg R.R. chartered by the state of Virginia, later the **Atlantic Coast Line R.R.** (1900).

1836–51. Construction of the Western and Atlantic R.R., connecting Atlanta and Chattanooga.

1837. As part of a state internal improvements program, Michigan projected 3 railroads: the Michigan Northern (Port Huron-Grand Rapids), the **Michigan Central** (Detroit-St. Joseph), and the Michigan Southern (Monroe-New Buffalo). Under separate private ownership, the Michigan Central and the Michigan Southern were completed to Chicago in 1852. Chartering of the **New Orleans and Nashville R.R.**, aimed at tapping the trade of the Tennessee and Cumberland regions; failed after the panic of 1837.

1840. Completion of the **Vicksburg and Jackson R.R.**, traversing central Mississippi.

U.S. had 3,328 miles of railroad; all Europe only 1,818.

1826–30. Explorations of California and the Pacific Northwest by **Jedediah Smith** (1798–1831).

1827. American Fur Co. absorbed the Columbia Fur Co.; thereafter dominated the upper Missouri trade.

1830. Congressional enactment of the Removal Bill empowering the President to transfer any eastern Indian tribe to trans-Mississippi areas.

Maysville Road Bill vetoed by President Jackson (p. 169).

1831–32. Expedition to the upper Mississippi led by **Henry R. Schoolcraft**, who discovered the source of that river to be a lake, which he named Itasca.

1832. Black Hawk War in the upper Mississippi Valley. The defeat of the Sauk and Fox led by the chieftain Black Hawk ushered in an active period (1832–37) of Indian removal to trans-Mississippi areas. By 1846 Indian removal from the Old Northwest had been completed.

Completion of the **Chicago Road, a** military highway facilitating the settlement of southern Michigan and upper Indiana.

1832–33. Treaties of Payne's Landing and **Ft. Gibson,** authorizing removal of the Seminoles from Florida to beyond the Mississippi, led to resistance culminating in the **2nd Seminole War.**

1832–35. Rocky Mountain trapping and hunting expedition led by Captain **Benjamin L. E. Bonneville** (1796–1878), subject of Washington Irving's *The Adventures of Captain Bonneville* (1837).

1833. Opening of the Black Hawk Purchase on the west bank of the Mississippi inaugurated large-scale settlement of Iowa country.

Organization of the village of **Chicago;** incorporated as a city in 1837.

1833–34. Expedition under the Rocky Mountain fur trader **Joseph R. Walker** (1798–1876) climbed the Sierra Nevada (believed to be the 1st ascent from the east made by white men), penetrated the Yosemite Valley, and on the return journey crossed the Sierra through the gap later called Walker Pass.

1834. With others, Rev. **Jason Lee** (1803–45), a Methodist missionary, explored the Willamette Valley and established the 1st mission and the 1st American agricultural settlement (near present-day Salem, Ore.) in the Oregon country.

Overland expedition to Oregon led by **Nathaniel J. Wyeth** (1802–56) from Independence, Mo., to Fort Vancouver. A member of this expedition was the ornithologist John K. Townsend (1809–51), who wrote *Narrative of a Journey across the Rocky Mountains to the Columbia River* (1839). Wyeth attempted to establish in the Pacific Northwest a project for exploiting the natural resources of the Columbia River region. His venture, the Columbia River Fishing and Trading Co. (1834–37), was unsuccessful due to the opposition of the Hudson's Bay Co.

The **Territorial Road,** a land route facilitating settlement in southern Michigan, opened to traffic.

1835. Treaty of New Echota ceded to the U.S. all Cherokee lands and provided for the transportation of the Cherokee Indians to areas beyond the Mississippi; removal completed by 1838.

Completion of the removal of Alabama Creek Indians to beyond the Mississippi.

Overland journey from St. Louis to the Green River under the leadership of **Dr. Marcus Whitman** (1802–47) and Rev. Samuel Parker (1779–1866), sponsored by the American Board of Commissioners for Foreign Missions. Whitman's next expedition from St. Louis (1836), the 1st party with women to cross the Rockies, reached Oregon, where Whitman established the Walla Walla mission.

1835–40. Final period of the Rocky Mountain fur trade.

1835–42. Second Seminole War ended with removal of last resisting Seminole Indians from Florida to beyond the Mississippi.

c.1835–c.1841. State-assisted internal improvement programs in the states of the Old Northwest stimulated a **Transportation Boom,** particularly in Western canal building, resulting in heavy speculation in both lands and transportation facilities, many of the latter being built with funds from British investors. These elaborate programs collapsed after the **Panic of 1837,** burdening the states with heavy indebtedness. Between 1816 and 1840, about $125,000,000 was spent on canal projects alone. In the following decade some of the uncompleted projects were resumed by private interests, but railroad competition ultimately made canal operations unprofitable.

1836. Establishment of the independent **Republic of Texas** (pp. 176, 177); recognized by the U.S. in 1837.

Arkansas admitted to the Union.

Territories of Iowa and Wisconsin organized.

1837. Michigan admitted to the Union.

1837–40. Opening of the **Lumbering Frontier** in northern Wisconsin and Minnesota, which in turn attracted farmers by creating a demand for foodstuffs.

1840–46. Father Pierre-Jean De Smet (1801–73), Jesuit missionary, founded

Catholic missions in the Oregon country and the Great Plains.

1841, 4 Sept. Distribution-Preemption Act (p. 455).

Bidwell-Bartleson party inaugurated overland migration to California, opening California Trail through South Pass and across Humboldt region of Nevada; followed by numerous emigrants in next years.

1842. Exploring expedition to the Wind River range of the Rockies led by **John C. Frémont**. Second expedition (1843–44) took Frémont from the Missouri River to the Oregon country, thence to Pyramid Lake, into present-day Nevada, and across the Sierra into California. He returned to St. Louis by way of Nevada and Utah. The expeditions contributed valuable scientific observations and stimulated popular interest in the Far West, although Frémont saw no territory not previously explored by fur traders.

1842–43. Beginning of the "great migration" to the Oregon country as the "Oregon fever" spread throughout the Midwest, bringing settlers from Mo., Ohio, Ky., and other states. The **Oregon Trail**, parts of which had been used by fur traders and explorers, became the main route for emigrants. The trail extended from **Independence, Mo.**, to **Astoria**, at the mouth of the Columbia River.

1844. First successful transmission of message by telegraph (p. 566).

1845. ANNEXATION OF TEXAS (p. 191); admitted to the Union.

Florida admitted to the Union.

3 Mar. **Postal Act** reduced postage to 5 cts. a ½ oz. for 300 mi. and authorized mail subsidies for transatlantic steamers; discontinued in 1859.

1846. OREGON TREATY gave U.S. undisputed claim to Pacific Northwest south of 49th parallel (p. 195); stimulated migration to region.

Bear Flag Revolt in the Sacramento Valley; conquest of California by the Americans (p. 200).

Iowa admitted to the Union.

Pennsylvania R.R. chartered. Under the direction of **John Edgar Thomson** (1808–74) a link between Pittsburgh and Philadelphia was built; opened to passenger traffic, 18 July 1858, but the road's major expansion came after the Civil War.

1846–47. Donner party, a group of emigrants bound for Calif., suffered extreme hardships during winter at Truckee Lake.

1847. First Mormon settlers arrived in the Salt Lake Valley after overland trek from Kanesville (now Council Bluffs, Iowa). Under the leadership of **Brigham Young** (p. 805), Salt Lake City was founded (1847) and the State of Deseret established (1847) with Young as governor.

Collins Line opened transatlantic steamship service between New York and Liverpool. Ocean Steam Navigation Co. opened similar service between New York and Bremen. These routes were abandoned after the reduction of Federal mail subsidies in 1857–58.

Formation of the railway co. later known (1851) as the Chicago and Rock Island R.R., the 1st to reach the Mississippi River (1854), across which it constructed the 1st bridge (1856).

Mobile and Ohio R.R. chartered; projected by Southern interests, it later received land grant subsidies from Ala. and Miss.

Hannibal and St. Joseph R.R. (built 1851–59) incorporated in Mo.

1847–51. Construction of the Hudson River R.R., connecting New York and Albany.

1848, 24 Jan. DISCOVERY OF GOLD in California by James W. Marshall on property of **Johann Augustus Sutter** (1803–80); announced by President Polk in farewell message to Congress (Dec.), starting **gold rush** (1849).

2 Feb. TREATY OF GUADALUPE HIDALGO gave U. S. large domain in the Southwest (p. 207).

Wisconsin admitted to the Union.

Oregon Territory established.

1848–49. Frémont's expedition explored railroad route across the Rockies; followed by similar venture in 1853–54.

1848–56. As part of a state program of internal improvements, the North Carolina R.R. was built from Charlotte to Goldsboro.

1849. Minnesota Territory established.

Pacific R.R. Co. (later the **Missouri Pacific R.R.**) chartered in Missouri. Built during 1851–56, it eventually linked St. Louis with Kansas City, and was the first railroad west of the Mississippi River.

Incorporation in Pennsylvania of the railway later known (1853) as the Delaware, Lackawanna and Western R.R.

1849–55. Consolidation of 4 railways in Illinois resulted in creation (1855) of the **Chicago, Burlington and Quincy R.R.;** furnished the Midwest with important connections to Eastern markets.

1850. 9 Sept. California admitted to the Union.

TEXAS CESSION of all claims to New Mexico territory for $10 million (also p. 211).

Territories of Utah and New Mexico established.

20 Sept. Congressional Act authorized land grants to Ill., Miss., and Ala., for railroad construction between Chicago and Mobile; permitted state grants to railways of tracts in the public domain in alternate sections not exceeding 6 miles. Between 1850–57 some 21 million acres were granted to subsidize the construction of railroads in the Mississippi Valley.

Louisville and Nashville R.R. chartered; completed in 1859.

1851. Chartering of the **Illinois Central R.R.,** the 1st land-grant railway. Completed in 1856, it linked Chicago, Galena, and Cairo. It received more than 2.5 million acres and, in the course of selling these lands in order to provide for construction costs, carried out extensive colonization work.

1853. Washington Territory organized.

GADSDEN PURCHASE (p. 216).

Consolidation of 3 New York railways connecting New York with Buffalo brought creation of the **New York Central Co.,** which in 1867 came under the control of Commodore **Cornelius Vanderbilt** (1794–1877).

The Cleveland, Columbus and Cincinnati R.R. joined with the Pittsburgh, Ft. Wayne and Chicago R.R. at Crestline, Ohio, to form the 1st rail connection between Pittsburgh and Cincinnati.

Opening of the Cleveland and Erie R.R.

1854. Territories of Kansas and Nebraska organized; "popular sovereignty" principle inflamed issue of slavery in the territories (p. 217).

Assassination of James King, editor of *San Francisco Bulletin,* marked the apogee of desperado activity in California; led to setting up of **Vigilance Committee** utilizing quasi-legal process to restore order.

1854–57. War Dept. explorations for a railroad route to the Pacific constituted the Federal govt.'s 1st attempt at a comprehensive and systematic geographical examination of the West.

1855. Opening of the St. Marys Falls Ship Canal, linking Lake Huron with Lake Superior.

1857–58. Conflict of authority with the Federal government resulted in dispatch of U.S. troops to Utah Territory; virtually bloodless "Mormon War" ended in compromise.

1858. Minnesota admitted to the Union.

Inauguration of mail service to California by the **Butterfield Overland Mail,** until 1861 active between St. Louis-Memphis and the Pacific coast.

Opening of the **mining frontier** following the discovery of gold in **Colorado, Nevada,** and **British Columbia; Pikes Peak gold rush** (1858–59). **Comstock Lode** (Virginia City) yielded $300 million in gold and silver in 20 years; continuous and profitable mining made possible by **Sutro Tunnel** (1869–79), built by **Adolph Sutro** (1830–98). Leadville, Colo., silver production peak 1880–93.

1859. Oregon admitted to the Union.

Establishment of the Leavenworth and Pikes Peak Express, a stage-line company operating between Leavenworth and Denver.

1860. Establishment of the **Pony Express,** relay mail service between St. Joseph, Mo., and San Francisco; 1st run inaugurated on 8 Apr. 1860.

Kansas territorial legislature chartered the Central Overland, California and Pikes Peak Express, a consolidation of stage lines between St. Joseph and Salt Lake City.

RAIL TRANSPORTATION ON THE EVE OF THE CIVIL WAR. Between 1840–60 an additional 28,000 miles were added to the U.S. railroad system, representing capital expenditures of close to a billion dollars. Originally, most of the railroads were extensions of existing lines of water transportation, but by 1855 New York was joined by a continuous line of rails to Chicago. The rapid expansion of East-West rail connections outpaced direct rail connections between North and South. As yet no direct rail connection existed along the coast between Washington, Charleston, and Savannah. How-ever, the trunk lines from Chicago to New Orleans linked the South with the Middle West. The farthest Western extension of the railroads by 1860 was to St. Joseph on the Missouri, but on the Pacific coast a short road near Sacramento, Calif., had already been built, signalizing the beginning of West-East construction.

Rail vs. Water-Turnpike Transportation by 1860: Rates per ton-mile ranged from about 15 cts. for turnpikes, 2 cts. for railroads, and from ¼ ct. to 1 ct. for canals.

TIME REQUIRED FOR FREIGHT SHIPMENTS FROM CINCINNATI TO NEW YORK CITY, 1815–1860, BY VARIOUS ROUTES AND METHODS *

Date	Route	Average Time Elapsed
1817	Ohio River keelboat to Pittsburgh, wagon to Philadelphia, wagon or wagon and river to N.Y.	52 days
1843–51	Ohio River steamboat to Pittsburgh, canal to Philadelphia, railroad to N.Y.	18–20 days
1852	Canal across Ohio, Lake Erie, Erie Canal, and Hudson River	18 days
1850's	Steamboat to New Orleans and packet to N.Y.	28 days
1852	All rail via Erie R.R. and connecting lines	6–8 days

* By permission of George R. Taylor, *The Transportation Revolution* (N.Y., Rine-hart, 1951).

1860–64. MINING FRONTIER. Gold discovered (1860), in Humboldt and Esmeralda, Nev., intensified rush to mining areas. Government over these areas evolved through (1) mining camps; (2) vigilance committees providing a speedy trial for law-and-order offenders; (3) permanent government, territorial and state. In 1861–64 gold was discovered in Snake River Valley, **Idaho** (Clearwater and Salmon River gold fields; pop. Idaho City, 1863, 6,000). **Montana** gold rush (1863). Main camps: **Virginia City, Helena** (1864). Gang terrorism led by **Henry Plummer** put down by vigilantes, 1864.

1860–66. Pacific Telegraph Act, 16 June 1860, authorized the U.S. to construct a telegraph line from Missouri to San Francisco. The first telegraph message, San Francisco–Washington, D.C., was transmitted 24 Oct. 1861. The merger in 1866 of the **Western Union Telegraph Co.** (1856), controlling Western lines, with the American Telegraph Co. (1855) in control of the East, led to rapid expansion of telegraph service. **Postal Telegraph** organized, 1881.

1861. Kansas admitted to the Union. Colorado, Dakota, and Nevada organized as territories.

Merchandise admitted to the U.S. mails.

Beginning of the **Cheyenne-Arapaho War,** caused by the influx of miners into Col.; climax in 1864 when Denver was isolated. On 28 Nov. the **Chivington Massacre** of 450 Indians took place, when Col. militia under Col. J. M. Chivington attacked the main Indian encampment; submission of Indians by Oct., 1865.

1862–93. WESTERN RAILROAD BUILDING. (1) **Central Route:** Chicago to San Francisco via lowlands near South Pass. Pacific Railroad Act (1 July 1862) authorized the **Union Pacific R.R.** to build a line from Neb. to Utah, where it was to meet the **Central Pacific** (organized, 1861, and directed by **Collis P. Huntington** [1821–1900] and **Leland Stanford** [1824–93]) building east from Calif. Land grants of 10 alternate sections per mile on both sides of the entire distance were made (also p. 464). The route was completed, 10 May 1869, by a junction of the 2 lines at **Promontory**, Utah. Corrupt practices of **Crédit Mobilier**, Union Pacific's construction company, came into the open in Dec. 1867; scandal also attached to the operations of the **Crocker Corp.**, responsible for Central Pacific building. The latter used Chinese labor; the Union, Irish. In 1880 U.P. absorbed the Kansas Pacific and Denver Pacific, giving it access to Kansas City. By 1893 it had over 8,000 miles of track.

(2) **Northern Route: Northern Pacific R.R.** (chartered, 1864), to utilize route from Lake Superior to Portland, Ore., financed by **Jay Cooke** (1821–1905); reorganized, 1881, by **Henry Villard** (1835–1900); route completed, 1883. An additional northern route was started in 1878 by the St. Paul, Minneapolis, and Manitoba R.R. (reorganized, 1889 as **Great Northern R.R.**), as a result of the seizure of control of the bankrupt St. Paul and Pacific R.R. by **James J. Hill** (1838–1916). By 1893 the line reached the Pacific at Seattle, Wash. To compensate for the lack of a land grant Hill promoted farm settlement along the entire route to create traffic.

(3) **35th Parallel Route:** The **Atchison, Topeka and Sante Fe R.R.**, promoted by **Cyrus K. Holliday** (1826–1900), received a land grant from Congress in 1863 of 3 million acres in alternate sections in Kan. By 1872 the line reached Col. Over a combination of its own and leased tracks it ran to Los Angeles via Needles and Yuma by 1883, by which date the line had 7,100 miles of track, from Kansas City to the West Coast.

(4) **Southern Route** (32nd parallel) was granted the **Texas & Pacific R.R.** (organized, 1871), to build to Calif. and meet the tracks of the **Southern Pacific R.R.**, a line operated by the controllers of the Central Pacific. Acquired by Jay Gould, 1879, T. & P. later shared track privileges with S.P. east of El Paso, which the latter railroad had reached in 1881, joining Eastern lines in 1882 to complete a route to New Orleans.

1863. West Virginia admitted to the Union. Arizona and Idaho territories or-

ganized, the latter being separated from the Oregon Territory.

1863–73. Congress authorized, 1863, free-carrier mail service direct to addressee. By 1871, 51 cities had carrier service. In 1873 the **postal card** was introduced from Europe.

1864. Nevada admitted to the Union to ensure the ratification of the 13th Amendment.

Montana Territory organized.

Railway mail service, proposed by George B. Armstrong in 1862, inaugurated by Postmaster General Montgomery Blair (1813–83). **Money order** system went into operation 1864.

1865. Submission of the Indians marked the end of the **Apache** and **Navaho** wars and the establishment of reservations (1866–67). **First Sioux War**, caused in part by U.S. project to construct a road from Fort Laramie, Wyo., to Bozeman, Mont., ended on 29 April 1868, when Sioux agreed to accept permanent reservation in Dakota Territory.

CATTLE KINGDOM. Beginning of the "Long Drive" of cattle from Texas to railroads of Kan. and Neb. The transfer of cattle was caused by (1) a price decline in Texas, (2) scarcity and price rise in the Middle West, (3) the Civil War. Between 1865 and 1879, 4 million head of cattle were thus transported. A by-product of the Long Drive was the "cow towns"—Abilene (1867), Ellsworth, Newton (after 1872), and **Dodge City**, Kan. (after 1875). From these centers live cattle were shipped to slaughterhouses in Chicago. The **refrigerator car** (by 1875) delivered Western dressed beef to the East.

1867. Nebraska admitted to the Union.

30 Mar. ALASKA PURCHASE (p. 280).

Establishment by Congress of the **Oklahoma Reservation** for members of the Five Civilized Tribes (eventually settled by 75,000 Indians), of the Black Hills Reservation for the Sioux, and 5 smaller reservations.

Beginning of the extermination of the buffalo. Hides worth $1 to $3 per head. By 1883, about 13 million buffalo had been killed.

1867–69. FOUR GREAT WESTERN SURVEYS by the Federal govt.: (1) by **Clarence King** (1842–1901), of 40th Parallel (1867–78); (2) by **Dr. Ferdinand V. Hayden** (1829–87) of a geological survey of Neb. and Wyo. (1867–78); (3) by **Lt. George M. Wheeler**, of the 100th Meridian (1872–79); (4) by **Maj. John W. Powell** (p. 767) of Utah, Nev., and Ariz. (1869–78).

1867–1910. EASTERN RAILROAD CONSOLIDATION. Organization, 1867, of the **New York Central & Hudson River R.R.** by **Cornelius Vanderbilt** (1843–99), subsequently adding the N.Y., West Shore, and Buffalo R.R. By 1885 control over the Michigan Central and the "Big Four" system (connecting Cleveland, Cincinnati, Chicago, and St. Louis) had been obtained. In 1898 the Boston and Albany R.R. was leased. The **Pennsylvania Company**, a pioneer holding company (1870), was organized by the Pennsylvania R.R. for rail lines leased or controlled. Rapid expansion of lines to Pittsburgh, Cincinnati, Chicago, St. Louis, and to Baltimore and Washington followed. Having acquired terminal facilities on the west shore of the Hudson, it constructed a tunnel under the river and opened a terminal in New York City in 1910. By 1866 **Erie** was in control of stock manipulator **Daniel Drew** (1797–1879), who was associated with **Jay Gould** (1836–92) and **James Fisk** ("Jubilee Jim," 1834–72) in stock manipulations at the expense of Cornelius Vanderbilt, operations which threw the line into bankruptcy in 1875; reorganized by J. P. Morgan, 1894.

1868. Wyoming Territory organized.

Beginning of **1st Dakota Boom.** By 1873, population of the Dakotas rose to 20,000.

1870. Beginning of the **Texas boom.** During the next decade the number of Tex. farms increased from 61,125 to 174,184.

23 May. Start of the 1st transcontinental railroad trip from Boston to Oakland.

1871–86. Apache War in N.M. and Ariz. began 30 Apr. 1871 with the massacre of over 100 Apaches at Camp Grant, Ariz. The conflict ended with the capture of the Apache leader, **Geronimo,** in 1886, and the remnants of the tribe were assigned small reservations in the Southwest.

1873. Passage of the **Timber Culture Act,** 1887 (p. 464).

Panic of 1873 interrupted railroad construction. By that date the Rock Island R.R. extended to Council Bluffs (1869); the Chicago, Burlington & Quincy to south-central Neb.; the Illinois Central to Sioux City; the Chicago, Milwaukee & St. Paul into Iowa; the Chicago & Northwestern across Minnesota and into the Dakotas; the Northern Pacific had reached Bismarck, N.D.; the Lake Superior & Mississippi had extended to Duluth; and the Sante Fe had completed the trans-Kansas line.

1873–1907. SOUTHERN RAILROAD EXPANSION. The Baltimore & Ohio completed its line to Cincinnati (1873); later extended its lines north to Lake Erie and west to Chicago, Cincinnati, and St. Louis. Chesapeake and Ohio crossed the Appalachians, reaching Asheville, N.C., 1892; Norfolk and Western extended to the Ohio Valley, 1892. In 1900 the Clinchfield completed crossing from N.C. to Tenn.; in 1907 the Virginian completed the last Appalachian route. The main North-South route of the Southern Railway was completed to Atlanta, 1873; the Atlantic Coast Line consolidated more than 100 smaller lines, 1898–1900; Seaboard Airline, 1900. By the 1890's southern Fla. was reached by the Florida East Coast. Another line from Atlanta to Cincinnati had been completed in 1880.

1874. The worst grasshopper plague in U.S. history spread devastation among Great Plains farmers from the Dakotas to northern Tex.

Joseph F. Glidden (1813–1906) marketed his first **barbed wire** and solved the problem of fencing the cattle range. Ultimately the American Steel and Wire Co. (U.S. Steel subsidiary) established a virtual monopoly of barbed wire based on the Glidden patents.

1875. Opening of the **Black Hills** area in S.D. to gold seekers, after gold was reported (Aug.) by U.S. military expedition headed by **Gen. George A. Custer**

(1839–76). By fall over 15,000 prospectors entered the region. Main camps: **Custer City** and **Deadwood** (resort of desperadoes, one of whom killed **James Butler** ["Wild Bill"] **Hickok**, scout and U.S. marshal, in 1876; vigilantes restored order). Ultimately the **Homestead Mining Co.** assumed control of operations in this area.

1875–76. Second Sioux War caused by (1) the gold rush into the Black Hills reservation; (2) extension of the route of the Northern Pacific R.R.; (3) corruption in the Department of the Interior. U.S. troops finally defeated Chiefs **Sitting Bull** and **Crazy Horse** (31 Oct. 1876), but not before Custer and a contingent of 264 men were annihilated at the **Battle of the Little Big Horn** (26 June).

1876. Colorado admitted to the Union.

1877. Passage of the **Desert Land Act** Act (p. 464).

Nez Percé War, fought in the Pacific Northwest. Nez Percé Indians under **Chief Joseph** were defeated (Oct.) and assigned a reservation in Oklahoma.

1877–1915. EARLY TELEPHONE EXPANSION. Operation in 1877 of the 1st practical intercity telephone lines—Salem to Boston (Bell), Chicago to Milwaukee (Gray)—led to establishment by 1880 of 148 telephone companies operating 34,305 miles of wire. These systems were ultimately consolidated by the **American Telephone & Telegraph Co.** By 1895 long-distance telephone lines were in operation between New York and Chicago; connections extended to Denver, 1911; to San Francisco, 1915. Number of telephones in the U.S.: 1900, 1,355,900; 1932, 17,424,406; 1952, 43,003,800.

1878. Timber and Stone Act (p. 464).

1878–85. 2nd Dakota Boom, promoted by entry of Northern Pacific R.R. and Great Northern into territory by 1882, followed by other lines. Peak in homestead grants in the Dakotas was reached in 1884 when 11,083,000 acres were granted to settlers. Population, 1890, 539,583; Montana, 142,924.

1881–87. Publication of Helen Hunt Jackson's *A Century of Dishonor* (1881) aroused new concern over Indian problems. Agitation of the Indian Rights

Association, organized within a year, led to the enactment of the **Dawes Severalty Act,** 1887 (p. 464).

1883. Four standard time zones established, facilitating railroad operations.

1883–86. Coeur d'Alene gold rush to northern Ida. In 1885 the **Bunker Hill** and **Sullivan Mines** were discovered, eventually yielding $250 million in silver and lead.

1883–87. END OF THE CATTLE BOOM marked by big business control of ranching. In Wyo. 23 stock-raising corporations were organized with a total capital of $12 million. Overstocking the range was followed by serious drought, 1885–86, and a cold winter, 1886–87. Prices crashed in 1885. Result: the end of the open range and the introduction of fenced pastures, better cattle breeding, and the substitution of rail transportation for the Long Drive to market.

1884. RAILROAD LAND GRANTS. Estimate of all public lands granted to railroads: 155,504,994 acres (Donaldson), almost the area of Tex. (Union Pacific, 20 million; Sante Fe, 17 million; Central and Southern Pacific, 24 million; Northern Pacific, 44 million, sales of which by 1917 had brought the last-named railroad over $136 million). Western states also granted roads 49 million acres. Because of noncompletion of a number of projected roads, the final,Federal total: 131,350,534 acres (U.S. General Land Office, *Ann. Rep.,* 1943). In addition, loans totaling $64,623,512 were advanced to 6 companies to build the Pacific routes, which were repaid with interest by 1898–99. In return, the land-grant railroads agreed to transport U.S. property and troops "free," a clause which was adjusted to 50% of normal commercial rates. In 1940 Congress eliminated reductions on U.S. government's civilian passenger and freight traffic, but low rates continued during World War II for U.S. Army and Navy freight and personnel; discontinued 1 Oct. 1946.

17 May. Organic Act applied the laws of Oregon to Alaska after a period of government by the War Dept.

1887. Dawes Severalty Act (p. 464); **Interstate Commerce Act** (p. 258).

1889. North Dakota, South Dakota, Montana, and Washington admitted to

THE TERRITORIAL POSSESSIONS

THE UNITED STATES IN 1917

the Union (with Idaho and Wyoming admitted, 1890)—known as the **Omnibus States.**

22 Apr. In 1884 "Boomers" led by **David L. Payne** and W. L. Couch entered Oklahoma but were dispersed by Federal troops. Constant pressure led to the **opening of Oklahoma District** to homesteaders at noon. Within a few hours 1,920,000 acres were settled under bedlam conditions (Oklahoma city by nightfall—population, 10,000).

1890, 2 May. Oklahoma Territory organized.

U.S. Census Director, in his report, announced that "there can hardly be said to be a frontier line."

The **Ghost Dance War** on the Black Hills Reservation arose when U.S. Army authorities sought to curb religious rites of the Teton Sioux; came to an end with an Indian massacre at the **Battle of Wounded Knee** (29 Dec.).

1891, 22 Sept. Lands of the Sauk, Fox, and Pottawatomie in Oklahoma Territory (900,000 acres) opened to settlement.

1892. Opening of the Cheyenne-Arapaho Reservation of 3 million acres.

1893, 16 Sept. Second major "Boomer" invasion of Oklahoma on 6 million acres of the **Cherokee Outlet.**

1896. KLONDIKE GOLD RUSH. Gold discovered 16 Aug. 1896 on Bonanza Creek, near Dawson, Canada, 50 mi. east of Alaska border; followed by gold rush. Peak production, 1900, $22 million; total production, 1885–1929, exceeded $175 million.

Utah admitted to the Union.

Rural free delivery est.

1900. LAND SETTLEMENT. In the 30 years ending 1900, 430 million acres had been occupied; 225 million placed under cultivation. For the entire period, 1607–1870, 407 million acres occupied; 189 million improved.

1900–52. HIGHWAY CONSTRUCTION AND MOTOR TRANSPORTATION. Twentieth-century highway construction augmented the use of the automobile, the motor truck, and the bus as formidable competitors to railroad transportation. Asphalt roads had been introduced in New York City in the 1870's; Portland cement in the U.S. in 1894. Surface roads increased in mileage from

161,000 (1905) to 521,000 (1925), and 1,527,000 (1945). Most notable of numerous recent highway projects was the **Alaskan Highway (Alcan)**, work upon which was started on 12 Mar. 1942 and completed 1 Dec., 1,523 mi. from Dawson Creek, B.C., through Canada and the Yukon Territory to Fairbanks, Ala. Constructed as a military supply route during World War II at a cost of $138 million, it was opened to tourists, summer 1948. **Passenger car registrations:** 1900, 8,000; 1913, 1,258,062; 1930, 26,545,281; 1951, 42,700,000. **Motor truck registrations:** 1904, 700; 1913, 67,667; 1952, 9,116,000. Regular route intercity passengers carried by **intercity bus** averaged 425 million (1944–48).

1901–34. INDIAN REFORMS. Oct. 1901, admission of Five Civilized Tribes to U.S. citizenship. Mar. 1923, defeat, as a result of strong Indian protests, of the Fall Indian Omnibus Bill (Bursum Bill), which in effect would have transferred Pueblo titles to white settlers. Under Act of 1924 a Pueblo Land Board was set up to establish compensation for lands; such compensation was awarded in 1933. By Act of 2 June 1924 all Indians born in the U.S. were admitted to full U.S. citizenship. In 1926 the Indian Bureau inaugurated drive to curb Pueblo religious rites. Publication, 1928, of Brookings Institution report, *The Problem of Indian Administration,* revealed deficiencies in Federal administration of Indian lands. **Indian Reorganization (Wheeler-Howard) Act** (18 June 1934) ended land allotments in severalty and provided for revestment to tribal ownership of surplus lands hitherto open to sale.

1906. Alaska permitted to elect a delegate to Congress.

1907. Oklahoma and Indian Territory admitted to the Union as 1 state.

1911–52. AIRPLANE TRANSPORTATION, following the 1st successful airplane flight by the **Wright brothers**, 1903, at Kitty Hawk (p. 569), made rapid strides in the U.S. The 1st air-mail service, N.Y. to Washington, 1918; across the continent, 8 Sept. 1920. 15 Oct., 1st contracts for international air mail (Western Hemisphere) awarded to private operators. By the **Kelly Act** (1925) air-mail contracts were to be awarded on the basis of private bidding. Factors promoting air transport in this period include (1) inauguration of regular night flying (Chicago to Cheyenne), 1923; (2) installation of radio beacons for aerial navigation (Washington, D.C.), 1925; (3) passage of the **Air Commerce Act**, 1926, which inaugurated a government program of aid to civil air transport and navigation, including the establishment of airports. Rapid expansion followed.

1927, 21 May. First nonstop flight, New York to Paris, by **Charles A. Lindbergh, Jr.** (1902–   ).

1 Sept. Air express established by arrangement between American Railway Express Agency and airlines.

1934, 19 Feb. All domestic air-mail contracts canceled by Postmaster General **James A. Farley** (1888–   ) on the ground of collusion. U.S. Army Air Corps assumed operations pending new arrangements with private operators, who began to handle air mail by 8 May. The **Air Mail Act** of 12 June provided that the ICC was to determine "fair and reasonable" air-mail rates and to review them periodically, and reduced air-mail postage to 6 cts. an oz.

1935. Inauguration of transpacific air service (San Francisco to Manila) by Pan American Airways.

1938, 23 June. Civil Aeronautics Act created **Civil Aeronautics Authority (CAA)** empowered to regulate rates of air transport and foster stability in the field.

1939. Inauguration of transatlantic air service (New York-Southampton) by Pan American Airways and Imperial Airways.

1947. First fully automatic (without pilot control) transport flight (U.S. Army C-54), Newfoundland to England.

Airlines carried 12,890,208 **revenue passengers** that year as against 5,782 in 1926 and 1,365,706 in 1938.

1948–52. First U.S. jet-propelled commercial air transport—Consolidated Vultee Convair; 1st British DeHaviland Comet (1949); revised version ordered by several U.S. airlines (1952).

Domestic air routes in operation: 139,030 mi. (1948) as compared with

8,252 mi. in 1926 and 35,492 in 1938. **Domestic cargo,** exclusive of mail (estimated), 30,637,879 (ton-miles) for express, 69,023,000 for freight.

1912. New Mexico and Arizona admitted to the Union, completing the political organization of the West. Alaska given territorial status (population: 1920, 55,000, as against 30,000 in 1867).

1913. Establishment of **domestic parcel post** by Act of 24 Aug. 1912. Parcel post arrangements between the U.S. and the United Kingdom had been in existence since 1902.

1919–50. EXPANSION OF RADIO COMMUNICATION SYSTEMS. After initial broadcast by **Lee De Forest** on 5 Mar. 1907 (p. 656) the field of radio communication entered a period of consolidation. In 1919 the **Radio Corporation of America** was organized by Owen D. Young (1874–   ), with David Sarnoff (1891–   ) president, 1930; chmn. bd. since 1947. It in turn set up a subsidiary, the **National Broadcasting Co.** (NBC) in 1926, the 1st major radio network. In 1927 **Columbia Broadcasting System** (CBS) was organized with William S. Paley (1901–   ) president, 1928–46; chmn. bd. since 1946. As of 1 Aug. 1950 radio stations in the U.S. totaled: standard broadcast, 2,160; TV, 106; FM, 687. The first commercial station to begin regular broadcasting was WWJ in Detroit, 20 Aug. 1920. In Nov. Westinghouse sent out its first national broadcast by reporting the Presidential elections. In 1922 station WEAF put on the air the 1st known commercial program. Basic developments since 1940 include:

1940, 5 Jan. Introduction of "staticless" FM (frequency modulation) radio developed by **Edwin H. Armstrong** (1890–1954) successfully demonstrated by station WIXOJ near Worcester, Mass., linking with New York.

1951, 18 Aug. First call placed over the microwave radio relay system, consisting of 107 steel and concrete towers, 30 mi. apart, between New York and San Francisco, constructed at cost of $40 million.

1952. The FCC ended curb on the building of new TV stations put into effect in 1948 and permitted an increase in number of stations in the U.S. and territories from 108 to 2,051 by (1) making maximum use of VHF band frequencies; and (2) opening UHF band. Two types of licenses were to be issued: (1) for commercial stations (1,809); (2) for noncommercial stations (educational institutions and groups, 242). Eight million TV sets enabled an estimated 60 million persons to see and hear the political conventions and the Presidential Candidates. For development of TV, see p. 570.

1953. NEW INDIAN POLICY. A concurrent resolution of 1 Aug. declared it to be the "sense of Congress" that certain Indian groups should "at the earliest possible time" be freed from "all disabilities and limitations especially applicable to Indians." In compliance with this mandate the Bureau of Indian Affairs initiated consultations with tribal groups to shape legislation providing for the eventual dissolution of their special ties with the Federal government. The Bureau also stepped up the transfer of responsibility over the Indians to state or local agencies.

1954, 27 Sept. "DEW LINE." Supplementing the Pinetree Chain of radar stations extending across the continent north of the U.S.-Canadian border (work begun 1950) and the "Mid-Canada Line" 500 mi. farther north (1953), the U.S. and Canada agreed in principle on establishing a 3rd radar line, "Distant Early Warning" (DEW) Line, across Arctic Canada from Alaska to Greenland. DEW Line went into operation 1 July 1957.

1954, 13 May. ST. LAWRENCE SEAWAY. The Wiley-Dondero Act established the St. Lawrence Seaway Development Corp. to finance and construct navigational improvements along the St. Lawrence in U.S. territory. This action reflected growing dependence of Midwestern steel mills on iron ore of the Quebec-Labrador region. St. Lawrence Seaway and St. Lawrence power project formally opened 26–27 June 1959. Seaway made possible the navigation of ships of 27-ft. draft from Montreal to Lake Superior except in winter months.

1958, 3 May. ANTARCTICA. The U.S. proposed to the other 11 involved nations that a treaty be formulated to preserve the present legal status of the continent. Political claims would be frozen, and the continent would remain a scientific laboratory for an indefinite period. At a conference in Washington (15 Oct.–1 Dec. 1959) attended by 12 nations (7 of which had made territorial claims in Antarctica; the remainder had conducted scientific work there), a treaty was adopted and signed which reserved that continent exclusively for peaceful purposes and froze territorial claims for the duration of the treaty (34 yrs.).

1958, 13 Dec. OUTER SPACE. The U.S. regarded the Antarctica treaty as a precedent for cooperation in outer space. UN Committees on the Peaceful Uses of Outer Space were set up, 13 Dec. 1958, and again on 12 Dec. 1959 (the latter with a membership of 12 pro-Western, 7 Communist, and 5 neutral states) to avoid projecting national rivalries into this new field.

1959, 3 Jan. ALASKA admitted to the Union as the 49th state.

21 Aug. HAWAII admitted to the Union as the 50th state.

1940–57. HOMESTEAD ENTRIES, except on ceded Indian lands, totaled 1,898,000 acres.

1953, 16 Jan. TIDELANDS OIL. Before leaving office President Truman issued an executive order "setting aside the submerged lands of the Continental Shelf as a naval petroleum reserve." This policy was reversed with the advent of the Eisenhower administration. A bill to give the states title to submerged lands passed the House 1 Apr. and the Senate 5 May, after a 22-hr., 26-min. filibuster speech (24–25 Apr.) by Sen. Wayne Morse (Ore.), opponent of the bill. President Eisenhower signed the measure 22 May. The act asserted U.S. jurisdiction over the resources of the outer Continental Shelf.

FEDERAL LAND LEGISLATION AND POLICY
SINCE 1789

With the establishment of the national government, the disposal of the public domain was regulated under the Ordinance of 1785, which was accepted by the Federal Congress but not recognized as binding. In practice, this conservative and orderly land policy favored the speculator at the expense of the actual settler.

New land legislation became urgent to meet both Treasury needs and the prospect of large-scale Western settlement. Wayne's defeat of the Northwest Indians (1794) and the signing of the **Treaty of Greenville** (1795) gave the U.S. secure occupancy of the lands northwest of the Ohio River and encouraged Western pioneering.

Alexander Hamilton's "Report of a Uniform System for the Disposition of the Lands" (1790–91) had ignored the accurate and uniform survey procedure of the Ordinance of 1785 in favor of a modified system of indiscriminate location. His policy reflected the conservative views of Eastern business interests desiring a check on the agricultural class and the systematic regulation of the labor supply. Its complete adoption would have meant the priority of revenue from sales to large speculators over actual settlement by cultivators.

1796, 18 May. After a lengthy House debate on land policy, Congress passed the **Land Act of 1796.** It provided for rectangular survey and public auction sales, but raised the minimum price from $1 to **$2 an acre,** payable within a year. The lands were to be divided into township units 6 miles square, and half of these were to be divided into single sections of **640 acres.** Intervening townships were to be disposed of in single sections, alternate townships in units of 8 sections. Land offices were established at Cincinnati and Pittsburgh. The attempt of frontier interests to secure an amendment for the sale of half of the 640-acre tracts in quarter sections (160 acres) was defeated in the Senate. Because of poor administrative machinery and inadequate credit provisions, only 48,566 acres were sold by 1800.

1800, 10 May. The needs of Western interests led to the adoption of a more liberal policy under the **Land Act of 1800** (also known as the **Harrison Land Act**). It retained the minimum price of **$2 an acre,** but authorized minimum purchases of **320 acres, a 4-yr. credit,** and a discount of 8% for cash payment. A frontier demand for the incorporation of the preemption principle was defeated. Land offices were established at Cincinnati, Chillicothe, Marietta, and Steubenville. This Act served as the model for similar legislation until 1820. Sales under it began in Apr. 1800; by 1 Nov. 1801, 398,466 acres had been sold. Although its provisions were calculated to favor revenue rather than actual settlement, in practice the system encouraged the latter. The more important modifications of the Act were:

Ohio Enabling Act (30 Apr. 1802). With the admission of the 1st public land state, the Federal government adopted the policy of retaining title to all ungranted tracts within state boundaries, except 1 section in each township set aside for educational purposes.

Act of 3 Mar. 1803. Provided for the survey and sale of ungranted lands in the Mississippi Territory.

Public Land Survey System

Land Act of 1804 (26 Mar.). Reduced the minimum cash payment to **$1.64 per acre** and authorized minimum sales of **160 acres**.

Act of 2 Mar. 1805. Provided for the determination and confirmation of Spanish and French land grants in Louisiana, extended the U.S. land surveys over the Louisiana Purchase, and authorized penalties for squatters (illegal settlers).

Intrusion Act (3 May 1807). Authorized penalties for unregistered squatters; poorly enforced.

Act of 25 Apr. 1812. Established the General Land Office as a bureau of the Treasury Dept. The central executive and administrative duties pertaining to public lands were transferred from the Secretary of the Treasury to a commissioner. In 1849 the Land Office was transferred to the Department of the Interior.

The liberal credit provisions of the Act of 1800 stimulated **widespread speculation,** weakened the national land system, and contributed to the Panic of 1819. Secretary of the Treasury W. H. Crawford reported that since 1789 the government had disposed of $44 million worth of land, but up to 30 Sept. 1819 had been paid only half that amount. By 1820 Congress had passed 12 relief acts for land purchasers. The precarious financial condition of the government after the War of 1812 made reform imperative.

1820, 24 Apr. Under the **Land Act of 1820,** the **credit system was abolished,** but the minimum price was reduced to **$1.25 an acre** and minimum purchases were fixed at **80 acres.** In principle, this benefited the pioneer, but heavy and almost universal indebtedness made the full cash payment stipulation a hindrance to the actual settler and benefited the speculator.

1821–32. Eleven relief acts were passed by Congress to meet Western demands for (1) cheap land; (2) **preemption** (the legal confirmation of squatter claims on public lands as opposed to engrossment by nonresident purchasers). Except for some special instances, the national government had since its foundation opposed demands for granting preemption or donations to actual settlers.

After 1820 public land policy was linked to (1) the maneuvering of North and South for sectional balance, and (2) the rise of the West as a distinctive section, with its own special interests. Sen. **Thomas Hart Benton** (Mo., 1782–1858), champion of the West, introduced (1824) his first bill providing for grading the price of land, whereby public lands would be sold at less than $1.25 an acre or even given away, after such tracts had failed to draw purchasers at the legal minimum price.

Western demands were echoed in urban areas. The Jacksonian era witnessed the rise in Northeastern centers of workingmen's groups supporting the agrarian program for more land. In New York City, labor publicists such as **Thomas Skidmore** denounced land monopoly, while another, **George Henry Evans** (1805–56, later the leader of the Land Reform movement), advocated free homesteads for Eastern surplus labor.

1829, 29 Dec. The Eastern conservative viewpoint was reflected in the resolution introduced by Senator **Samuel A. Foot** (Conn., 1780–1846) proposing an inquiry into the advisability of temporarily restricting the sale of public lands (a proposal that touched off the Webster-Hayne debate, p. 168)—a resolution denounced by Western spokesmen.

1830. An alliance of South and West enabled the Senate to pass Benton's **Graduation Bill** (May), but the measure was tabled in the House. This sectional alliance, however, effected the passage of the **Pre-emption Act of 1830** (29 May), authorizing settlers who had cultivated land on the public domain in 1829 to enter as many as **160 acres** at the minimum price of **$1.25 an acre**. Although the Act was adopted as a temporary measure, its substance was renewed at regular intervals (1832–40), and it remained in force until 22 June 1842.

1836, 23 June. Henry Clay's **SURPLUS REVENUE ACT** provided for the distribution of the Treasury surplus in excess of $5 million as a **loan** to the states according to population. This was a modification of Clay's earlier proposals to distribute the proceeds of land sales to the states. However, the surplus disappeared in the Panic of 1837 and payments were discontinued. Western pressure caused the passage of further legislation combining the ideas of **Benton** (preemption) and **Clay** (distribution).

1841, 4 Sept. **DISTRIBUTION-PRE-EMPTION ACT** authorized settlers to stake claims on most surveyed lands and to purchase up to **160 acres** at the minimum price of **$1.25 an acre** (except for alternate sections of land grants to canals and railroads, which could be preempted at $2.50 an acre). The Act, constituting a signal victory for the West, recognized (1) settlement before purchase was not illegal (making **permanent** the preemption feature of the Act of 1830); (2) actual settlement was now given priority in official policy over revenue. The distribution provisions authorized the grant of 500,000 acres to each new state for the construction of internal improvements; 10% of the proceeds of land sales were apportioned to the states in which the lands were located, and the remainder, minus administrative costs, to be divided among the states according to their representation in Congress. At the behest of the South, a stipulation was included that such apportionment was to be repealed in the event that the tariff should exceed the 20% level. The distribution provisions were repealed in Aug. 1842.

1854, 3 Aug. **GRADUATION ACT** marked the emerging sectional alliance of the Northeast and the West (against Southern opposition). It provided that all unsold lands on the market for **10 years or more** were to be sold at **$1 an acre; 15** years or more, 75 cts. an acre; 20 years or more, 25 cts. an acre; **30 years or more, 12½ cts. an acre.** The provisions applied preemption to graduated lands but did not cover mineral lands and grants for internal improvements and railroads. As a result, 30 to 40 million acres were sold a year. Repealed, 2 June 1862.

1860. Land Reform movement (1840–60) gained ground with Eastern labor and by support from **Horace Greeley.** The program included free homesteads of 160 acres, homestead exemption from attachment for debts, and limitation on land grants to large interests. A Homestead Act that finally passed both Houses was vetoed (22 June 1860) by President Buchanan. The Republican platform of 1860 included a homestead plank.

1862, 20 May. **HOMESTEAD ACT** offered any citizen or intending citizen who was the head of a family and over 21 years of age **160 acres** of surveyed public domain **after 5 yrs.** of continuous residence and payment of registration fee ranging from $26–$34. As an alternative, land under the Act could be acquired **after 6 mos.** residence at **$1.25 an acre.** Such homesteads were to be exempt from attachment for debt.

2 July. MORRILL ACT granted to each loyal state 30,000 acres for each senator and representative then in Congress for the purpose of endowing at least 1 agricultural college. Under its provisions **69 land-grant colleges** have been established.

1862–64. PACIFIC RAILWAY ACTS. By Act of 1 July 1862 a central transcontinental railroad was authorized with rights of way and 10 alternate sections per mi. of public domain on both sides of the railway granted. A 2nd Act (2 July 1864) doubled the land grants and gave the government a 2nd instead of a 1st mortgage on railroad property. The Northern Pacific, chartered by Congress 1864, was granted 20 sections per mi. in the states, 40 sections per mi. in the territories.

1862–1904. DISTRIBUTION OF THE PUBLIC DOMAIN. During this period 610,763,183 acres were acquired **by purchase** as against only 147,351,370 acquired **free** (except for fees). More acreage was patented under the Homestead Act **after 1904** than before that date, although most of these newer lands were inferior.

1864, 21 Mar. A homestead bonus provided for soldiers with 2 yrs. service, subject to a yr.'s residence.

1866. Mining lands on public domain opened to occupation.

21 June. Congress extended the Homestead Act to public property in the Confederate States. The Act was repealed, 1872, after most of the lands had been distributed.

1870, 9 July. Congress authorized a survey of mineral lands to be sold at **$2.50 per acre.** Later amendment raised the price of land with lodes to $5 an acre, and reduced iron areas to the usual $1.25.

1871. Termination of land grants to railroads (also p. 455).

1872. Yellowstone National Park created.

1873, 3 Mar. TIMBER CULTURE ACT authorized any person who kept 40 acres of timber land in good condition to acquire title to 160 acres thereof. The minimum tree-growing requirement was reduced in 1878 to 10 acres.

Coal Lands Act provided for sale of coal lands belonging to the U.S. Individuals could acquire up to 160 acres, associations, 320 acres, at $10–$20 an acre, depending on the distance of the land from railroads.

1877, 3 Mar. DESERT LAND ACT authorized individuals to acquire 640 acres at 25 cts. an acre, provided the land was irrigated within 3 yrs.

1878, 3 June. TIMBER CUTTING ACT allowed bona fide settlers and miners to cut timber on the public domain, free of charge, for their own use. **TIMBER AND STONE ACT,** applicable to Calif., Ore., Nev., and Wash., provided for the sale of timber and stone lands unfit for cultivation at $2.50 an acre, with a limit of 160 acres.

1879, 3 Mar. Establishment of the U.S. Geological Survey, with **Clarence King** (1842–1901) as 1st director.

1885, 3 Apr. Suspension by **William Andrew Jackson Sparks,** Land Commissioner, of all entries of titles where fraud was suspected, by this action preserving 2,750,000 acres for bona fide settlers. Sparks was dismissed in Nov. 1887, and the reforms were revoked.

1887, 8 Feb. DAWES SEVERALTY ACT provided for the dissolution of the Indian tribes as legal entities and the division of the tribal lands among individual members—160 acres to each head of family and 80 acres to each adult single person. Right of disposal was withheld for 25 years, after which time the Indian was to become an unrestricted owner.

1891, 3 Mar. Repeal of the Pre-emption and Timber Culture Acts and reduction of the maximum entries under the Desert Land Act. Passage of the **Forest Reserve Act,** permitting the President to close timber areas to settlers and establish them as **national parks.** During Harrison's administration 13 million acres were set aside.

1894, 18 Aug. CAREY ACT (p. 264).

1897. Publication of Capt. Hiram Martin Chittenden's (1858–1917) report on irrigation (*Reservoirs in Arid Regions*) served as the basis of later legislation, particularly the National Reclamation Act (1902).

The Pettigrew Amendment, a rider on an appropriation bill, permitted the President to change or revoke land reservations and excluded agricultural and mineral lands from reservations. Passed by the Senate and defeated by the House, a compromise was finally reached. The delegation of power to the President was held unconstitutional in *U.S.* v. *Grimond,* 1911.

1901. THEODORE ROOSEVELT'S CONSERVATION POLICY (p. 269).

15 Feb. Congress passed an Act establishing a licensing system for the use of water power on public lands.

1902, 17 June. NATIONAL RECLAMATION ACT (NEWLANDS ACT) set aside almost the entire amount of proceeds of public land sales in 16 Western and Southwestern states to finance construction and maintenance of irrigation projects in arid states.

1904. KINKAID HOME ACT provided for grants of 640 acres of desert land in Neb. after 5 yrs. residence and improvements valued at $800; extended, 1909, to the rest of the public domain.

1906, 11 June. FOREST HOMESTEAD ACT provided for the opening, at the discretion of the Secretary of Interior, of forest lands of agricultural value under the provisions of the Homestead Acts.

29 June. By executive order all coal lands were withdrawn from entry to permit their appraisal; later opened to buyers at from $35–$100 an acre.

1907, 19 June. A protest meeting against the land reservation policy, led by Western grazing interests, convened in Denver. A rider on an appropriation bill repealed the Forest Reserve Act of 1891. Before signing the bill, President Roosevelt added 21 reserves.

1908, May. The White House Conference of Governors called for the creation of the National Conservation Commission. In its report (Dec.) the Commission urged the repeal of the Timber Culture Act of 1878, the valuation of land at title value instead of $1.25, and the repeal of the Desert Land Act.

1909, 19 Feb. ENLARGED HOMESTEAD ACT, to satisfy Western cattle interests, increased the maximum permissible homesteads to 320 acres in portions of Col., Mont., Nev., Ore., Utah, Wash., Wyo., and Ariz. Of these, 80 acres were to be cultivated. Timber and mineral lands were specifically excepted.

25 Aug. First National Conservation Congress convened in Seattle under the leadership of lumber interests.

1910, 25 June. An Act of Congress authorized the President to withdraw public lands subject to further legislation and prohibited the creation of further reserves in Ore., Wash., Idaho, Col., and Wyo.

1916, 29 Dec. STOCK-RAISING HOMESTEAD ACT enlarged the maximum permissible homestead to 640-acre tracts of grazing or forage land not suitable for irrigation, and reserved mines and coal deposits.

1933–36. NEW DEAL CONSERVATION PROGRAM. TVA, p. 343; Soil Conservation program of AAA, p. 354; Civilian Conservation Corps, p. 342; Conservation programs of FERA, CWA, PWA, pp. 342, 346, 347; Soil Conservation Service, p. 350; Resettlement Administration, p. 350. The **Taylor Grazing Act** (28 June 1934) provided for the segregation of up to 8 million acres (later raised to 142 million) for grazing purposes under the jurisdiction of the Interior Dept. Indian Reorganization Act, p. 458.

1935. President Roosevelt withdrew the remainder of the public domain for purposes of conservation. As of 1949, 455 million out of 1.9 billion acres were under Federal ownership or 23.89% of the total U.S. land area. By 1950 no less than 181.2 million acres were reserved in national forests. Mineral, water power, and oil reserves (mostly subsoil rights) affected another 47,948,454 acres; about 20 million acres under irrigation.

DISPOSITION OF THE PUBLIC LANDS OF THE U.S., 1940
(General Land Office, Department of the Interior)

	Acres
Title passed from the United States:	
Homesteads (approx.)	285,000,000
Cash sales and miscellaneous disposals (approx.)	419,117,998
State grants for educational or other purpose	181,975,263
Canal and river improvement grants to states	6,842,921
Wagon-road grants to states	3,359,188
Grants to states in aid of railroads	38,208,638
Railroad grants to corporations	94,239,448
Total area disposed of	1,028,743,456
Pending and unperfected entries	2,373,542
Title remaining in the United States:	
National forests, estimated net area of public lands	134,515,000
National Parks and Monuments	13,864,245
Indian reservations (estimated net)	55,192,183
Military, naval, miscellaneous reservations (approx.)	3,336,000
Unappropriated, but withdrawn (part estimated)	199,842,600
Miscellaneous disposals	4,333,294
Grand total (exact public land area)	1,442,200,320

POPULATION AND IMMIGRATION

Figures prior to the 1st Census, 1790, are computed on the basis of militia, polls, tax-ables, families, and houses (Greene and Harrington).

AREA OF THE 13 COLONIES

1625	1,980	(Va., 1,800; Plymouth, 180)	1754	1,485,634	
1641	50,000	(English settlers)	1774	2,600,000	(Bancroft; 3,016,678, informal Congress poll)
1688	200,000		1783	2,389,300	(Continental Congress)
1715	434,600		1790	3,929,625	

790. Regional Distribution of Population: New England, 25.7%; Middle states, 5.9%; Southern states, 48.5%.

ORIGINAL THIRTEEN STATES IN ORDER OF POPULATION

Va.	747,610	(inc. W. Va.)	Conn.	237,655	
Mass.	475,199	(inc. Maine)	N.J.	184,139	
Penn.	434,373		N.H.	141,885	
N.C.	393,751		Ga.	82,548	
N.Y.	340,120		R.I.	68,825	
Md.	319,728	(inc. Dist. of Columbia)	Del.	59,096	
S.C.	249,073				

URBAN POPULATION TRENDS TO 1790

	Phila. (1682)	N.Y. (1624)	Boston (1630)	Charleston (1680)	Baltimore (1730)
1730	8,500	8,500	13,000	c.4,000	
1750	13,400	13,300	15,731	8,000	c.100
1770	28,000	21,000	15,520	10,863	c.5,000
1790	42,444	33,131	18,038	16,359	13,503

URBAN POPULATION (8,000 INHABITANTS OR MORE) COMPARED WITH TOTAL POPULATION, 1710–1900 (*A Century of Population Growth*)

Year	% of Total	Year	% of Total
1710	2.5	1860	16.1
1740	4.3	1900	32.9
1790	3.3		

Using the more recent classification of the Census Bureau (Urban Population, 2,500 inhabitants or more), the urban percentage, 1790, was 5.4 as against 56%, 1940.

LEADING U.S. CITIES SINCE 1790

1820 (De Bow, Statistical View)		1860 (8th Census)	
New York	123,700	New York	1,080,330
Phila.	112,800	Phila.	565,529
Baltimore	62,700	Baltimore	212,418
Boston	43,300	Boston	177,840
New Orleans	27,200	New Orleans	168,675

LEADING U.S. CITIES SINCE 1790 (*Cont.*)

	1900			*1960*	
	New York	3,437,202		New York	7,781,984
	Chicago	1,698,575		Chicago	3,550,404
	Phila.	1,293,697		Los Angeles	2,479,015
	St. Louis	575,238		Phila.	2,002,512
	Boston	560,892		Detroit	1,670,144

POPULATION OF THE U.S. SINCE 1790

Year	Population (in thousands)	% Increase over Preceding Census	Year	Population (in thousands)	% Increase over Preceding Census
1790	3,929	....	1880	50,155	30.1
1800	5,308	35.1	1890	62,947	25.5
1810	7,239	36.4	1900	75,994	20.7
1820	9,638	33.1	1910	91,972	21.0
1830	12,866	33.5	1920	105,710	14.9
1840	17,069	32.7	1930	122,775	16.1
1850	23,191	35.9	1940	131,409	7.3
1860	31,443	35.6	1950	150,697	14.5
1870	38,558	22.6	1960 (1 Mar.)	179,647	19.6 (est.)

Decade, 1941–60, marked reversal of downward birth-rate trend (*Stat. Abstr. of the U.S., 1949, 1951, 1960*):

	Birth Rate (per 1,000 population)	Death Rate (per 1,000 population)		Birth Rate (per 1,000 population)	Death Rate (per 1,000 population)
1915	25.0	13.2	1947	25.8	10.1
1936	16.7	11.6	1959	24.1	9.4

Decade, 1951–60, kept pace with population growth of preceding decade, with an indicated yearly growth of 1.9% compared with 1.4%, 1941–50.

LIFE EXPECTANCY, 1789–1956
(*Historical Statistics of the U.S., to 1957*)

	At birth Male	Female	Age 20 Male	Female	Age 40 Male	Female	Age 60 Male	Female
1789 (Mass.)	34.5	36.5	34.2	34.3	25.2	26.9	14.8	16.1
1900–02	48.23	51.08	42.19	43.77	27.74	29.17	14.35	14.23
1945	64.4	69.5	48.6	52.9	30.6	34.4	15.4	17.8
1956	67.3	73.7	50.1	55.9	31.6	36.7	15.9	19.3

INTERNAL MIGRATION WITHIN THE U.S., 1870–1940

	East-West Movement (Net gain of states west of Mississippi River)[1]	North-South Movement (Net gain of the North)[2]		East-West Movement (Net gain of states west of Mississippi River)[1]	North-South Movement (Net gain of the North)[2]
1870	2,298,952	752,455	1910	4,592,106	77,878
1880	3,300,378	639,018	1920	4,188,945	430,200
1890	4,078,157	500,026	1930	3,497,090	1,419,137
1900	3,993,554	274,403	1940	2,731,002	1,381,500

[1] Excess of persons born east and living west of the Mississippi over persons born west and living east.
[2] Excess of persons born in the South and living in the North over persons born in the North and living in the South.

1941–60. NEGRO MIGRATION. 43 cities outside the South doubled their Negro population as against 2 in the South, 1941–50. Negro increase was greater in central part of cities, showing 48.3% increase, 1940–50, as against 10.1% for whites. Nonwhite population was 10% of central parts of cities (1940), 33⅓% (1950). In the period 1950–58, nonwhite population increased 21.9% in U.S. as against 14.2% for white, with greatest nonwhite percentage gains in Pacific (53.3), N.E. (49.7), East North Central (47.6), Middle At-

lantic (38.2), and the lowest in the East South Central (4.9). The South contained 6% less of the nation's nonwhite population in 1958 than in 1950.

1951–60. POPULATION SHIFTS. Final 1960 census returns brought the loss of 3 House of Representative seats for Pa.; 2 for N.Y., Mass., and Ark.; and 1 each for 12 other states. Chief gainers: Calif., 8; Fla., 4. Largest percentage population gains scored by Fla., 78.7; Nev., 78.2; Alaska, 75.8; Ariz., 73.7; Calif., 48.5; Del., 40.3. Losses: Ark., 6.5; W. Va., 7.2; D.C., 4.8.

IMMIGRATION OF NON-ENGLISH STOCK

1624. Walloon settlement of New Amsterdam (p. 41).

1624–64. Dutch settlement of New Netherland (pp. 41, 42); on the Delaware, 1657–64 (pp. 42, 43). Dutch cultural decline in N.Y.C. noted by 1763, when an invitation was extended to Rev. Archibald Laidlie, English-speaking Scottish minister, to preach in the Dutch Reformed Church. In Hudson and Hackensack valleys Dutch language persisted until 1835–41.

1637–55. Swedish settlement on the Delaware (p. 42).

1682. First Welsh settlement near Philadelphia.

1683–84. Settlement of **Germantown** (13 families from Crefeld, Germany) by Rhinelanders and Palatines under **Francis Daniel Pastorius** (1651–*c*.1720) and **Johann Kelpius** stamped Pennsylvania-Dutch settlement with cultural and linguistic persistence down to the 20th century.

1685. FRENCH HUGUENOT settlement following the revocation of the Edict of Nantes (18 Oct.), chiefly to New York (N.Y.C. and New Rochelle), Mass. (Boston, Salem, and Oxford), and S.C. (Charleston and along Santee River).

1689. Beginning of sizable emigration from Scotland of Covenanters (opposing Anglican Church rule) and Jacobites (supporters of Stuart cause), and from Northern Ireland (Ulster) of Scotch-

Irish Presbyterians (est., 1607–09); especially significant after Act of Parliament, 1704, barring Presbyterians from public office. English Navigation Acts caused economic deterioration in Ireland and the exaction of tithes for the support of the Church of England was resented.

1709. Passage of Parliamentary Act of 1709 (Whig) extended the privilege of natural-born subjects to strangers who took the oath of allegiance and partook of the Sacrament (naturalizing German Protestant refugees); repealed by Tories, 1711. More liberal naturalization laws had been passed in the colonies beginning with the 17th century.

1710. Over 3,000 **GERMAN PALATINES**, given temporary refuge in England (1709) from devastations of War of Spanish Succession and severe winter, 1708–09, were transported to N.Y. to produce naval stores in Hudson Valley. Unfavorable economic conditions caused their migration under **Conrad Weiser** (1696–1760) to Schoharie Valley (1713), then to the Mohawk Valley, and ultimately in some instances to Bucks (1723) and Berks Counties, Pa. (1728–29).

Settlement of 650 Palatines by **Baron de Graffenried** at New Bern, N.C.; attacked and nearly destroyed by Indians in Tuscarora War, 1712, and colonists scattered throughout southeastern N.C.

1714–20. Start of **MAIN EXODUS OF SCOTCH-IRISH** (including Jacobites after suppression of revolts of 1715 and 1745 on behalf of the 2 Stuart Pretenders), spurred by expiration, beg. 1717, of leases and increased rent demands by landlords in Ireland. A small portion went to New England but the bulk settled the counties of western Pa., between the Susquehanna and Alleghany Mts., moving down the Shenandoah Valley (1732) into Va., the Carolinas, and Ga. The famines, 1740–41, and the decline of the Irish linen industry, c.1771, assured the continuance of this emigration momentum.

1727–75. HEAVY GERMAN MIGRATION continued, including settlers from the German-Swiss cantons of Bern and Zurich, with substantial Pietist representation.

1735–53. MORAVIAN COLLECTIVIST EXPERIMENTS, under the leadership of **Augustus Gottlieb Spangenberg** (1704–92), at Savannah (1735), Bethlehem, Pa. (1744), and vicinity of Winston-Salem, N.C. (1753).

1740. Act of Parliament specifically provided for naturalization in the colonies, with 7-yr. residence provision, and the usual oaths not to be required of Jews or Quakers.

1768. 1,400 settlers from **Minorca, Leghorn,** and **Greece** established by Dr. **Andrew Turnbull** at New Smyrna, East Florida, the 2nd largest mass migration to the colonies. After an insurrection (p. 546), the colony was eventually abandoned (by 1777), and Turnbull lost his holdings.

NATIONAL OR LINGUISTIC STOCKS IN THE U.S., 1790
(Based upon nomenclature, Census of 1790, as computed in Amer. Hist. Assn., *Ann. Rep., 1931,* I). 1

State	English	Scotch	Irish Ulster	Irish Free State	German	Dutch	French	Swedish	Spanish	Unassigned	Total
Maine	60.0	4.5	8.0	3.7	1.3	0.1	1.3	....	....	21.1	100.0
New Hampshire	61.0	6.2	4.6	2.9	.4	.1	.7	....	....	24.1	100.0
Vermont	76.0	5.1	3.2	1.9	.2	.6	.4	....	....	12.6	100.0
Massachusetts	82.0	4.4	2.6	1.3	.3	.2	.8	....	....	8.4	100.0
Rhode Island	71.0	5.8	2.0	.8	.5	.4	.8	0.1	....	18.6	100.0
Connecticut	67.0	2.2	1.8	1.1	.3	.3	.9	....	....	26.4	100.0
New York	52.0	7.0	5.1	3.0	8.2	17.5	3.8	.5	....	2.9	100.0
New Jersey	47.0	7.7	6.3	3.2	9.2	16.6	2.4	3.9	....	3.7	100.0
Pennsylvania	35.3	8.6	11.0	3.5	33.3	1.8	1.8	.8	....	3.9	100.0
Delaware	60.0	8.0	6.3	5.4	1.1	4.3	1.6	8.9	....	4.1	100.0
Maryland and District of Columbia	64.5	7.6	5.8	6.5	11.7	.5	1.2	.5	....	1.7	100.0
Virginia and West Virginia	68.5	10.2	6.2	5.5	6.3	.3	1.5	.6	....	.9	100.0
North Carolina	66.0	14.8	5.7	5.4	4.7	.3	1.7	.2	....	1.2	100.0
South Carolina	60.2	15.1	9.4	4.4	5.0	.4	3.9	.2	....	1.4	100.0
Georgia	57.4	15.5	11.5	3.8	7.6	.2	2.3	.6	....	1.1	100.0
Kentucky and Tennessee	57.9	10.0	7.0	5.2	14.0	1.3	2.2	.5	....	1.9	100.0
Area enumerated	60.9	8.3	6.0	3.7	8.7	3.4	1.7	.7	....	6.6	100.0
Northwest Territory	29.8	4.1	2.9	1.8	4.3	....	57.1	....	....	....	100.0
Spanish, United States	2.5	.3	.2	.1	.4	....	....	....	96.5	....	100.0
French, United States	11.2	1.6	1.1	.7	8.7	....	64.2	....	12.5	....	100.0
Continental United States	60.1	8.1	5.9	3.6	8.6	3.1	2.3	0.7	0.8	6.8	100.0

1 W. S. Rossiter, *A Century of Population Growth* (1909), had previously estimated English and Welsh stock at 82.1% of total; Scotch and Irish, 8.9%, and the Germans, 5.6% (1790).

IMMIGRATION TO U.S., 1790–1820 (8th Census, 1860, Prelim. Report, based upon a "survey of the irregular data previous to 1819"—a deduction of 14.5% for transients should be made from the following approximations): 1790–1800, 50,000; 1800–10, 70,000; 1810–20, 114,000.

IMMIGRATION TO U.S., 1820–1959
(U.S. Bureau of the Census, *Hist. Statistics of the U.S., to 1957; Statistical Abstract, 1958–60.*)

Year	No. of persons 1	Year	No. of persons 1	Year	No. of persons 1
1820	8,385	1867	315,722	1914	1,218,480
1821	9,127	1868	138,840	1915	326,700
1822	6,911	1869	352,768	1916	298,826
1823	6,354	1870	387,203	1917	295,403
1824	7,912	1871	321,500	1918	110,618
1825	10,199	1872	404,806	1919	141,132
1826	10,837	1873	459,803	1920	430,001
1827	18,875	1874	313,339	1921	805,228
1828	27,332	1875	227,498	1922	309,556
1829	22,520	1876	169,986	1923	522,919
1830	23,322	1877	141,857	1924	706,896
1831	22,633	1878	138,469	1925	294,314
1832	60,482	1879	177,826	1926	304,488
1833	58,640	1880	457,257	1927	335,175
1834	65,365	1881	669,431	1928	307,255
1835	45,374	1882	788,992	1929	279,678
1836	76,242	1883	603,322	1930	241,700
1837	79,340	1884	518,592	1931	97,139
1838	38,914	1885	395,346	1932	35,576
1839	68,069	1886	334,203	1933	23,068
1840	84,066	1887	490,109	1934	29,470
1841	80,289	1888	546,889	1935	34,956
1842	104,565	1889	444,427	1936	36,329
1843	52,496	1890	455,302	1937	50,244
1844	78,615	1891	560,319	1938	67,895
1845	114,371	1892	579,663	1939	82,998
1846	154,416	1893	439,730	1940	70,756
1847	234,968	1894	285,631	1941	51,776
1848	226,527	1895	258,536	1942	28,781
1849	297,024	1896	343,267	1943	23,725
1850	369,980	1897	230,832	1944	28,551
1851	379,466	1898	229,299	1945	38,119
1852	371,603	1899	311,715	1946	108,721
1853	368,645	1900	448,572	1947	147,292
1854	427,833	1901	487,918	1948	170,570
1855	200,877	1902	648,743	1949	188,317
1856	200,436	1903	857,046	1950	249,187
1857	251,306	1904	812,870	1951	205,717
1858	123,126	1905	1,026,499	1952	265,520
1859	121,282	1906	1,100,735	1953	170,434
1860	153,640	1907	1,285,349	1954	208,177
1861	91,918	1908	782,870	1955	237,790
1862	91,985	1909	751,786	1956	321,625
1863	176,282	1910	1,041,570	1957	326,867
1864	193,418	1911	878,587	1958	253,265
1865	248,120	1912	838,172	1959	260,686
1866	318,568	1913	1,197,892		

1 From 1820–67, figures represent alien passengers arrived; 1868–91 and 1895–97, immigrant aliens arrived; 1892–94 and 1898 to present, immigrant aliens admitted.

IMMIGRATION BY COUNTRY OF ORIGIN, 1820–1950

(U.S. Bureau of the Census, *Hist. Stat. of the U.S., 1789–1945; Statistical Abstract*, 1946–50.)

(Figures are totals, not annual averages, and were tabulated as follows: 1820–67, alien passengers arrived; 1868–91 and 1895–97, immigrant aliens arrived; 1892–94 and 1898 to present, immigrant aliens admitted. Data below 1906 relate to country whence alien came; since 1906, to country of last permanent residence.)

Countries	1820–1900	1901–1910	1911–1920	1921–1930	1931–1940	1941–1950	1820–1950
Europe: Albania 1	....	....	....	1,663	2,040	85	3,788
Austria 2	1,027,195	2,145,266	453,649	32,868	3,563	24,860	4,172,104
Belgium	62,161	41,635	33,746	15,846	4,817	12,189	170,394
Bulgaria 3	160	39,280	22,533	2,945	938	375	66,231
Czechoslovakia 1	....	....	3,426	102,194	14,393	8,347	128,360
Denmark	192,768	65,285	41,983	32,430	2,559	5,393	340,418
Estonia 1	....	....	....	1,576	506	212	2,294
Finland 1	....	....	756	16,691	2,146	2,503	22,096
France	397,489	73,379	61,897	49,610	12,623	38,809	633,807
Germany 2	5,010,248	341,498	143,945	412,202	114,058	226,578	6,248,529
Great Britain: England	1,824,054	388,017	249,944	157,420	21,756	112,252	2,753,443
Scotland	368,280	120,469	78,357	159,781	6,887	16,131	749,905
Wales	42,076	17,464	13,107	13,012	735	3,209	89,603
Not specified 4	793,741	....	....	....	....	....	793,741
Greece	18,685	167,519	184,201	51,084	9,119	8,973	439,581
Hungary 2	....	....	442,693	30,680	7,861	3,469	4,172,104
Ireland	3,873,104	339,065	146,181	220,591	13,167	25,377	4,617,485
Italy	1,040,479	2,045,877	1,109,524	455,315	68,028	57,661	4,776,884
Latvia 1	....	....	....	3,999	1,192	361	4,952
Lithuania 1	....	....	....	6,015	2,201	683	8,899
Luxembourg 1	....	....	....	727	565	820	2,112
Netherlands	127,681	48,262	43,718	26,948	7,150	14,860	268,619
Norway 5	474,684	190,505	66,395	68,531	4,740	10,100	814,955
Poland 6	165,182	....	4,813	227,734	17,026	7,571	422,326
Portugal	63,840	69,149	89,732	29,994	3,329	7,423	263,467
Rumania 7	19,109	53,008	13,311	67,646	3,871	1,076	158,021
Spain	41,361	27,935	68,611	28,958	3,258	2,898	173,021
Sweden 5	771,631	249,534	95,074	97,249	3,960	10,665	1,228,113
Switzerland	202,479	34,922	23,091	29,676	5,512	10,547	306,227
Turkey in Europe	5,824	79,976	54,677	14,659	737	580	156,453
U.S.S.R. 8	761,742	1,597,306	921,201	61,742	1,356	548	3,343,895
Yugloslavia 3	....	....	1,888	49,064	5,835	1,576	58,363
Other Europe	1,940	665	8,111	9,603	2,361	5,573	28,253
Total Europe	17,285,913	8,136,016	4,376,564	2,477,853	348,289	621,704	33,246,339
Asia: China	305,455	20,605	21,278	29,907	4,928	16,709	398,882
India	696	4,713	2,082	1,886	496	1,761	11,634
Japan 9	28,547	129,797	83,837	33,462	1,948	1,555	279,146
Turkey in Asia 10	29,088	77,393	79,389	19,165	328	218	205,581
Other Asia	5,883	11,059	5,973	12,980	7,644	11,537	55,076
Total Asia	369,669	243,567	192,559	97,400	15,344	31,780	950,319
America: Canada & Newfoundland 11	1,051,275	179,226	742,185	924,515	108,527	171,718	3,177,446
Central America	2,173	8,192	17,159	15,769	5,861	21,665	70,819
Mexico 12	28,003	49,642	219,004	459,287	22,319	60,589	838,844
South America	12,105	17,280	41,899	42,215	7,803	21,831	143,133
West Indies	125,598	107,548	123,424	74,899	15,502	43,725	496,696
Other America 13	....	....	....	31	25	29,276	29,332
Total America	1,219,154	361,888	1,143,671	1,516,716	160,037	354,804	4,756,270
Africa	2,213	7,368	8,443	6,286	1,750	7,367	33,427
Australia & New Zealand	19,679	11,975	12,348	8,299	2,231	13,805	68,337
Pacific Islands	7,810	1,049	1,079	427	780	5,437	16,582
Countries not specified	219,168	33,523 14	1,147	228	....	142	254,208
Total all countries	19,123,606	8,795,386	5,735,811	4,107,209	528,431	1,035,039	39,325,482

1 Countries added to list since beginning of World War I are theretofore included with countries to which they belonged. 2 Data for Austria-Hungary not reported until 1861. Austria and Hungary recorded separately after 1905. Austria included with Germany 1938–45. 3 Bulgaria, Serbia, Montenegro first reported in 1899. Bulgaria reported separately since 1920. In 1920, separate enumeration for Kingdom of Serbs, Croats, Slovenes; since 1922, recorded as Yugoslavia. 4 For United Kingdom. 5 Norway included with Sweden 1820–68. 6 Included with Austria-Hungary, Germany, and Russia 1899–1919. 7 No record of immigration until 1880. 8 Since 1931, U.S.S.R. has been broken down into European Russia and Siberia (Asiatic Russia). 9 No record of immigration until 1861. 10 No record of immigration until 1869. 11 Includes all British North American possession 1820–98. 12 No record of immigration 1886–93. 13 Included with "Countries not specified" prior to 1925. 14 Includes 32,897 persons returning in 1906 to their homes in U.S.

IMMIGRATION TO U.S., 1790–1820
8th Census, 1860, Prelim. Report, based
upon a "survey of the irregular data
previous to 1819"—a deduction of
4.5% for transients should be made
from the following approximations):
790–1800, 50,000; 1800–10, 70,000;
810–20, 114,000.

798. Alien and Sedition Laws (p. 129)
providing for the deportation of subversive aliens.

819–60. IMMIGRATION LAWS.
State immigration laws, continuing colo-
ial practices (Pa., head tax, 1729), generally required a bond upon entry of passengers deemed likely to be a public
charge. Federal laws, 1819, 1847, 1848,
1855, were designed to protect immigrants from overcrowding and unsanitary
conditions of the Atlantic crossing which
had led to heavy mortality rate; largely
ineffective.

827–38. Beginning of **GREAT IRISH
AND GERMAN MIGRATION** to the
U.S. Causes included (1) cold winter,
1829–30; (2) restrictive legislation
against German Jews; (3) economic distress in Northern Ireland; (4) increasing
factionalism in Southern Ireland.

843–82. "OLD IMMIGRATION"—
Scandinavian, Irish, and **German.** (1)
Scandinavian: Although the settlement
of 53 Scandinavians in western N.Y.,
1825, marked the beginning of the inflow to the U.S., a more substantial
Swedish inflow began c.1841 with a settlement of a small group at Pine Lake,
Wis., and the main Scandinavian migration setting in, 1843, with a total of
1,777 in that yr. The number rose to
1,106, 1852, and then leveled off until
the post-Civil War period, with peak immigration, 1868–83 (1882, 105,326),
again leveling off to 29,391 by 1914.
Settlement primarily in Wisconsin and
Minnesota. (2) **Irish:** Although substantial Irish immigration began in 1809 and
was resumed at the close of the War of
1812, the main flow started in the 1820's,
representing 44% of the total immigration, 1830–40. Irish immigration (largely
Roman Catholic) reached its peak after
the great famine of 1846, constituting
49% of the total, 1841–50. Such emigration was in part assisted by British
and Irish authorities. The emigrants were

employed on canal and railroad construction projects. All-time peak year,
1851, 221,253. Highest post-Civil War
year, 1883, 81,486. (3) **German** emigration amounting to 30% of the total,
1830–40, was augmented by bad farm
conditions in the 40's and by political
refugees from the Revolution of 1848
(e.g., **Carl Schurz**), with German colonies formed in N.Y., Baltimore, Cincinnati, St. Louis, and a completely Ger-
manized Milwaukee (by 1850). Peak
German migration, 1853–54, 356,955 for
the two years, with revival beginning
1866, reaching 149,671 in 1873, and
setting a pre-World War I peak in 1882
of 250,630.

1854–68. Chinese immigrant labor
(largely employed on transcontinental
railroad projects, but in at least 1 case
in a New England textile mill) totaled
75,000 in this period.

1865–85. CONTRACT LABOR. Office
of Commissioner of Immigration established 4 July 1864; authorized to admit
contract laborers under agreements based
on a maximum of 12 mos. labor for the
immigrant's passage to the U.S.

1866. Most Southern states, notably
South Carolina, attempted to attract Eu-
ropean immigrants to take the place of
Negro workers, but without success.

1868–82. CHINESE EXCLUSION. The
Burlingame Treaty, 1868, gave Chinese
the right to immigrate to the U.S., but
anti-Chinese sentiment on the Pacific
coast ("Sandlot Riots," San Francisco,
July 1877) resulted in the enactment by
Congress, 1879, of a bill abrogating the
provision; vetoed by President Hayes,
who appointed a commission to negotiate
a new treaty. The result was the Treaty
of 17 Nov. 1880 permitting the U.S. to
"regulate, limit or suspend" but not to
prohibit the entry of Chinese laborers.
Chinese immigration in this period,
160,000, with 1882 the peak year, of
39,579. In 1882 a bill to prohibit the
immigration of Chinese laborers for a
period of 10 years received the signature
of President Arthur. New treaty, 1894,
recognized a 10-yr. exclusion period.
Upon China's termination of this agreement, 1904, an exclusion act of 1902
was reenacted without terminal date. By
Act of Congress, 17 Dec. 1943, Chinese

immigration was permitted within the strict limitations of the quota system, with an annual quota of 105.

1882, 18 Aug. Federal Act excluded criminals, paupers, the insane, and other undesirables, and imposed a head tax of 50 cts. upon those entering; subsequently raised to $2 (1903) and to $4 (1907).

1885–1914. "NEW IMMIGRATION" from Eastern and Southern Europe developed in the middle and late 80's as prosperity dried up the source of German immigration. Heavy inflow now developed from Russia, Russian Poland, Austria-Hungary, the Balkans, and Italy. The persecution of the Jews in Russia also contributed to large migrations. **1901–05:** from Italy, 959,763; Russia, 658,735; Austria-Hungary, 944,239; Germany, 176,995; Great Britain and Ireland, 385,469. Concentration of sizable foreign-born blocs appeared in the larger cities: Chicago (Poles, Bohemians, Hungarians), New York (Italians and Jews), Boston (Irish). **1905–14:** zenith of U.S. immigration, with the million mark exceeded in 6 separate years. In the peak year, 1914, 73.4% of the total immigrants came from Southern and Eastern Europe as against 13.4% from Northern and Western Europe.

1885, 26 Feb. CONTRACT LABOR ACT forbade the importation of contract laborers, but exempted professional, skilled, and domestic labor; modified, 1891, with respect to certain professional categories; again in 1907 and 1917.

1903, 3 Mar. Act providing for U.S. inspection of immigrants at European ports of departure, with the U.S. government given the right to deport any immigrant illegally entering. Anarchists and prostitutes added to the list of excluded persons.

1906. Establishment of the Bureau of Immigration to keep records and statistical data.

1906–24. JAPANESE EXCLUSION. No significant Japanese immigration appeared until the decade 1891–1900, during which period 25,942 Japanese entered the U.S., a total which rose to a peak of 129,797 in the following decade. By the 1st "Gentlemen's Agreement" (Aug. 1900) Japan agreed to inaugurate

a policy of voluntary limitation of emigration through refusal to issue passport to emigrant laborers. On 7 May 1905 the Japanese and Korean Exclusion League was organized on the West Coast. On 11 Oct. 1906 the San Francisco School Board ordered that Chinese, Japanese and Korean children attend a separate public school. As a result of a conference with President Theodore Roosevelt the Board rescinded this action (13 Mar. 1907), and in a series of notes, 1907-08 (the "Gentlemen's Agreement"), Japan affirmed her intention of stopping the emigration of laborers. This arrangement continued until superseded by the Immigration Act of 1924, excluding Japanese immigrants as "aliens ineligible to citizenship." Meantime, state laws, notably in California, had limited the right of the Japanese to own (1913) and then to lease (1920) farm lands; upheld by the Supreme Court, 1923. The result was "Humiliation Day" in Tokyo, 1 July 1924, marked by "Hate American" mass meetings.

1917–20. LITERACY TEST AND FURTHER BARS. Bills imposing a literacy test were vetoed by Cleveland (1896) and Taft (14 Feb. 1913). On 28 Jan. 1915 President Wilson vetoed such a bill on the ground that it constituted a fundamental reversal of historical policy without popular mandate. Again on 29 Jan. 1917, Wilson vetoed a similar measure on the ground that it was "not a test of character, of quality, or of personal fitness." The Act, passed over the President's veto, required aliens over 16 years of age to read "not less than 30 nor more than 80 words in ordinary use" in the English language or some other language or dialect. As a war measure an Act of 16 Oct. 1918 excluded alien anarchists and others advocating the overthrow of the government. An Act of 10 May 1920 provided for the deportation of alien enemies and anarchists.

1921, 19 May. 1ST "QUOTA LAW" limited immigration in any year to 3% of the number of each nationality according to the Census of 1910, with maximum quota of 357,000.

1924, 26 May. NEW QUOTA LAW halved 1921 quota (1923, 357,803; 1924–25, 164,447) and limited immigra ion in any year to 2% of the **Census of 1890** (in order to reduce quotas from Eastern and Southern Europe); to remain in force until 1927, when an apportionment on the basis of 1920 distribution of "national origins" would serve as the basis for a maximum quota of 150,000 per annum. Owing to opposition this law did not go into effect until 1 July 1929, since which date the annual quota of any nationality for each fiscal year has been a number which bears the same ratio to 150,000 as the number of inhabitants in 1920 having that origin bears to the total number of inhabitants in the U.S. in 1920. Under an Act of 1929 consuls were empowered to refuse visas to all applicants who may become "public charges." The quota laws did not apply to immigration from Canada or Latin America, and provided a few minor exceptions for ministers, professors, and bona fide college students.

1945–52. DISPLACED PERSONS. Under directive of President Truman, 22 Dec. 1945, measures were taken to facilitate the entrance under quota of displaced persons. Under the directive 42,000 persons were admitted to the country. By Act of 25 June 1948, visas were authorized for the admission of 205,000 European displaced persons, including 3,000 nonquota orphans; the number of visas authorized was increased by Act of 16 June 1950 to 341,000 to be issued by 30 June 1951. Certain discriminatory provisions were eliminated and new categories of expellees and war orphans added with total visas of 54,744

and 5,000 respectively to be issued by 30 June 1952. By Act of 28 June 1951, issuance of visas to displaced persons was extended to 31 Dec. 1951.

1952, 30 June. McCARRAN-WALTER ACT, passed over the veto of President Truman (House vote, 278–133; Senate, 57–26), codified U.S. immigration laws and generally retained the provisions of the 1924 Act on maximum immigration and the quota system, but removed the ban against immigration of Asian and Pacific peoples. Screening measures to keep out "subversives" and other undesirables were incorporated and the Attorney General empowered to deport immigrants for "Communist and Communist-front" affiliations even after they acquired U.S. citizenship.

1953, 7 Aug. REFUGEE RELIEF ACT provided for entry into the U.S., on an emergency basis outside regular immigration quota, of 186,000 escapees from Communist persecution, as well as selected persons in other groups up to a total of 214,000. Under accelerated procedure adopted late in 1956 to cope with a mass influx of refugees from Hungary into Austria, 21,500 Hungarian refugees were admitted into the U.S., with an emergency air- and sea-lift instituted by the Defense Dept. Total displaced persons admitted, 1948–55, 406,028; refugees, 1954–59, 234,145.

1950–59. Immigration to U.S. by countries of last permanent residence in order of rank: (1) Germany, 448,313; (2) Canada, 331,284; (3) Mexico, 267,103; (4) Italy, 172,122; (5) Great Britain, 144,631.

THE CONSTITUTION AND
THE SUPREME COURT

THE CONSTITUTION OF THE UNITED STATES

Preamble

We the People of the United States, in Order to form a more perfect Union, establish Justice, insure domestic Tranquility, provide for the common defence, promote the general Welfare, and secure the Blessings of Liberty to ourselves and our Posterity, do ordain and establish this Constitution for the United States of America.

Article I

Section 1. All legislative Powers herein granted shall be vested in a Congress of the United States, which shall consist of a Senate and House of Representatives.

Section 2. The House of Representatives shall be composed of Members chosen every second Year by the People of the several States, and the Electors in each State shall have the Qualifications requisite for Electors of the most numerous Branch of the State Legislature.

No Person shall be a Representative who shall not have attained to the Age of twenty five Years, and been seven Years a Citizen of the United States, and who shall not, when elected, be an inhabitant of that State in which he shall be chosen.

Representatives and direct Taxes shall be apportioned among the several States which may be included within this Union, according to their respective Numbers, [which shall be determined by adding to the whole Number of free Persons, including those bound to Service for a Term of Years, and excluding Indians not taxed, three fifths of all other Persons.] [1] The actual Enumeration shall be made within three Years after the first Meeting of the Congress of the United States, and within every subsequent Term of ten Years, in such Manner as they shall by law direct. The Number of Representatives shall not exceed one for every thirty Thousand, but each State shall have at Least one Representative; and until such enumeration shall be made, the State of New Hampshire shall be entitled to chuse three, Massachusetts eight, Rhode-Island and Providence Plantations one, Connecticut five New-York six, New Jersey four, Pennsylvania eight, Delaware one, Maryland six Virginia ten, North Carolina five, South Carolina five, and Georgia three.

When vacancies happen in the Representation from any State, the Executive Authority thereof shall issue Writs o Election to fill such Vacancies.

The House of Representatives shall chuse their Speaker and other Officers and shall have the sole Power of Impeachment.

Section 3. The Senate of the United States shall be composed of two Senator from each State, [chosen by the Legislature thereof,] [2] for six Years; and eacl Senator shall have one Vote.

Immediately after they shall be assembled in Consequence of the first Election they shall be divided as equally as ma be into three Classes. The Seats of th Senators of the first Class shall be vacated at the Expiration of the second Year, of the second Class at the Expira

1 Superseded by the Fourteenth Amendment.
2 Superseded by the Seventeenth Amendment

476

tion of the fourth Year, and of the third Class at the Expiration of the sixth Year, so that one third may be chosen every second Year; [and if Vacancies happen by Resignation, or otherwise, during the Recess of the Legislature of any State, the Executive thereof may make temporary Appointments until the next Meeting of the Legislature, which shall then fill such Vacancies.] [3]

No Person shall be a Senator who shall not have attained to the Age of thirty Years, and been nine Years a Citizen of the United States, and who shall not, when elected, be an Inhabitant of that State for which he shall be chosen.

The Vice President of the United States shall be President of the Senate, but shall have no Vote, unless they be equally divided.

The Senate shall chuse their other Officers, and also a President pro tempore, in the Absence of the Vice President, or when he shall exercise the Office of President of the United States.

The Senate shall have the sole Power to try all Impeachments. When sitting for that Purpose, they shall be on Oath or Affirmation. When the President of the United States is tried, the Chief Justice shall preside: and no Person shall be convicted without the Concurrence of two thirds of the Members present.

Judgment in Cases of Impeachment shall not extend further than to removal from Office, and disqualification to hold and enjoy any Office of honor, Trust or Profit under the United States: but the Party convicted shall nevertheless be liable and subject to Indictment, Trial, Judgment and Punishment, according to Law.

Section 4. The Times, Places and Manner of holding Elections for Senators and Representatives, shall be prescribed in each State by the Legislature thereof; but the Congress may at any time by Law make or alter such Regulations, except as to the Places of chusing Senators.

[The Congress shall assemble at least once in every Year, and such Meeting shall be on the first Monday in December, unless they shall by Law appoint a different Day.] [4]

Section 5. Each House shall be the Judge of the Elections, Returns and Qualifications of its own Members, and a Majority of each shall constitute a Quorum to do Business; but a smaller Number may adjourn from day to day, and may be authorized to compel the Attendance of absent Members, in such Manner, and under such Penalties as each House may provide.

Each House may determine the Rules of its Proceedings, punish its Members for disorderly Behaviour, and, with the Concurrence of two thirds, expel a Member.

Each House shall keep a Journal of its Proceedings, and from time to time publish the same, excepting such Parts as may in their Judgment require Secrecy; and the Yeas and Nays of the Members of either House on any question shall, at the Desire of one fifth of those Present, be entered on the Journal.

Neither House, during the Session of Congress, shall, without the Consent of the other, adjourn for more than three days, nor to any other Place than that in which the two Houses shall be sitting.

Section 6. The Senators and Representatives shall receive a Compensation for their Services, to be ascertained by Law, and paid out of the Treasury of the United States. They shall in all Cases, except Treason, Felony and Breach of the Peace, be privileged from Arrest during their Attendance at the Session of their respective Houses, and in going to and returning from the same; and for any Speech or Debate in either House, they shall not be questioned in any other Place.

No Senator or Representative shall, during the Time for which he was elected, be appointed to any civil Office under the Authority of the United States, which shall have been created, or the Emoluments whereof shall have been encreased during such time; and no Person holding any Office under the United States, shall be a Member of either House during his Continuance in Office.

Section 7. All bills for raising Revenue shall originate in the House of Rep-

[3] Modified by the Seventeenth Amendment.

[4] Superseded by the Twentieth Amendment.

resentatives; but the Senate may propose or concur with Amendments as on other Bills.

Every Bill which shall have passed the House of Representatives and the Senate, shall, before it become a Law, be presented to the President of the United States; If he approve he shall sign it, but if not he shall return it, with his Objections to that House in which it shall have originated, who shall enter the Objections at large on their Journal, and proceed to reconsider it. If after such Reconsideration two thirds of that House shall agree to pass the Bill, it shall be sent, together with the Objections, to the other House, by which it shall likewise be reconsidered, and if approved by two thirds of that House, it shall become a Law. But in all such Cases the Votes of both Houses shall be determined by yeas and Nays, and the Names of the Persons voting for and against the Bill shall be entered on the Journal of each House respectively. If any Bill shall not be returned by the President within ten Days (Sundays excepted) after it shall have been presented to him, the Same shall be a Law, in like Manner as if he had signed it, unless the Congress by their Adjournment prevent its Return, in which Case it shall not be a Law.

Every Order, Resolution, or Vote to which the Concurrence of the Senate and House of Representatives may be necessary (except on a question of Adjournment) shall be presented to the President of the United States; and before the Same shall take Effect, shall be approved by him, or being disapproved by him, shall be repassed by two thirds of the Senate and House of Representatives, according to the Rules and Limitations prescribed in the Case of a Bill.

Section 8. The Congress shall have Power To lay and collect Taxes, Duties, Imposts and Excises, to pay the Debts and provide for the common Defence and general Welfare of the United States; but all Duties, Imposts and Excises shall be uniform throughout the United States;

To borrow Money on the credit of the United States;

To regulate Commerce with foreign Nations, and among the several States, and with the Indian Tribes;

To establish a uniform Rule of Naturalization, and uniform Laws on the subject of Bankruptcies throughout the United States;

To coin Money, regulate the Value thereof, and of foreign Coin, and fix the Standard of Weights and Measures;

To provide for the Punishment of counterfeiting the Securities and current Coin of the United States;

To establish Post Offices and post Roads;

To promote the Progress of Science and useful Arts, by securing for limited Times to Authors and Inventors the exclusive Right to their respective Writings and Discoveries;

To constitute Tribunals inferior to the supreme Court;

To define and punish Piracies and Felonies committed on the high Seas, and Offences against the Law of Nations;

To declare War, grant Letters of Marque and Reprisal, and make Rules concerning Captures on Land and Water;

To raise and support Armies, but no Appropriation of Money to that Use shall be for a longer Term than two Years;

To provide and maintain a Navy;

To make Rules for the Government and Regulation of the land and naval Forces;

To provide for calling forth the Militia to execute the Laws of the Union, suppress Insurrections and repel Invasions;

To provide for organizing, arming, and disciplining, the Militia, and for governing such Part of them as may be employed in the Service of the United States, reserving to the States respectively, the Appointment of the Officers, and the Authority of training the Militia according to the discipline prescribed by Congress;

To exercise exclusive Legislation in all Cases whatsoever, over such District (not exceeding ten Miles square) as may, by Cession of particular States, and the Acceptance of Congress, become the Seat of the Government of the United States, and to exercise like Authority over all Places purchased by the Consent of the Legislature of the State in which the

Same shall be, for the Erection of Forts, Magazines, Arsenals, dock-Yards, and other needful Buildings;—And

To make all Laws which shall be necessary and proper for carrying into Execution the foregoing Powers, and all other Powers vested by this Constitution in the Government of the United States, or in any Department or Officer thereof.

Section 9. The Migration or Importation of such Persons as any of the States now existing shall think proper to admit, shall not be prohibited by the Congress prior to the Year one thousand eight hundred and eight, but a Tax or duty may be imposed on such Importation, not exceeding ten dollars for each Person.

The Privilege of the Writ of Habeas Corpus shall not be suspended, unless when in Cases of Rebellion or Invasion the public safety may require it.

No Bill of Attainder or ex post facto Law shall be passed.

No Capitation, or other direct, Tax shall be laid, unless in Proportion to the Census or Enumeration herein before directed to be taken.[5]

No Tax or Duty shall be laid on Articles exported from any State.

No Preference shall be given by any Regulation of Commerce or Revenue to the Ports of one State over those of another; nor shall Vessels bound to, or from, one State, be obliged to enter, clear, or pay Duties in another.

No money shall be drawn from the Treasury, but in Consequence of Appropriations made by Law; and a regular Statement and Account of the Receipts and Expenditures of all public Money shall be published from time to time.

No Title of Nobility shall be granted by the United States: And no Person holding any Office of Profit or Trust under them, shall, without the Consent of the Congress, accept any present, Emolument, Office, or Title, of any kind whatever, from any King, Prince, or foreign State.

Section 10. No State shall enter into any Treaty, Alliance, or Confederation; grant Letters of Marque and Reprisal; coin Money; emit Bills of Credit; make any Thing but gold and silver Coin a

[5] Modified by the Sixteenth Amendment.

Tender in Payment of Debts; pass any Bill of Attainder, ex post facto Law, or Law impairing the Obligation of Contracts, or grant any Title of Nobility.

No State shall, without the Consent of the Congress, lay any Imposts or Duties on Imports or Exports, except what may be absolutely necessary for executing it's inspection laws; and the net Produce of all Duties and Imposts, laid by any State on Imports or Exports, shall be for the Use of the Treasury of the United States; and all such Laws shall be subject to the Revision, and Control of the Congress.

No State shall, without the Consent of Congress, lay any Duty of Tonnage, keep Troops, or Ships of War in time of Peace, enter into any Agreement or Compact with another State, or with a foreign Power, or engage in War, unless actually invaded, or in such imminent Danger as will not admit of delay.

Article II

Section 1. The executive Power shall be vested in a President of the United States of America. He shall hold his Office during the Term of four Years, and, together with the Vice President, chosen for the same Term, be elected, as follows.

Each State shall appoint, in such Manner as the Legislature thereof may direct, a Number of Electors, equal to the whole Number of Senators and Representatives to which the State may be entitled in the Congress: but no Senator or Representative, or Person holding an Office of Trust or Profit under the United States, shall be appointed an Elector.

[The Electors shall meet in their respective States, and vote by Ballot for two Persons, of whom one at least shall not be an Inhabitant of the same State with themselves. And they shall make a List of all the Persons voted for, and the Number of Votes for each; which list they shall sign and certify, and transmit sealed to the Seat of the Government of the United States, directed to the President of the Senate. The President of the Senate shall, in the Presence of the Senate and House of Representatives, open all the Certificates, and the Votes shall then be counted. The person having the greatest Number of Votes shall be the President, if such Number be a Majority of the whole Number of Electors appointed; and if there be more than one who have such Majority, and have an equal Number of Votes, then the House of Representatives shall immediately chuse by Ballot one of them for President; and if no Person have a Majority, then from the five highest on the List the said House shall in like Manner chuse the President. But in chusing the President, the Votes shall be taken by States, the Representation from each State having one Vote; A quorum for this purpose shall consist of a Member or Members from two thirds of the States, and a Majority of all the States shall be necessary to a Choice. In every Case, after the Choice of the President, the Person having the greatest Number of Votes of the Electors shall be the Vice President. But if there should remain two or more who have equal Votes, the Senate chuse from them by Ballot the Vice President.] 6

The Congress may determine the Time of chusing the Electors, and the Day on which they shall give their Votes; which Day shall be the same throughout the United States.

No Person except a natural born Citizen, or a Citizen of the United States, at the time of the Adoption of this Constitution, shall be eligible to the Office of President; neither shall any Person be eligible to that Office who shall not have attained to the Age of thirty five Years, and been fourteen Years a Resident within the United States.

In Case of the Removal of the President from Office, or of his Death, Resignation, or Inability to discharge the Powers and Duties of the said Office, the Same shall devolve on the Vice President, and the Congress may by Law provide for the Case of Removal, Death, Resignation or Inability, both of the President and Vice President, declaring what Officer shall then act as President, and such Officer shall act accordingly, until the Disability be removed, or a President shall be elected.

The President shall, at stated Times receive for his Services, a Compensation, which shall neither be encreased nor

6 Superseded by the Twelfth Amendment.

diminished during the Period for which he shall have been elected, and he shall not receive within that Period any other Emolument from the United States, or any of them.

Before he enter on the Execution of his Office, he shall take the following Oath or Affirmation:—"I do solemnly swear (or affirm) that I will faithfully execute the Office of President of the United States, and will to the best of my Ability, preserve, protect and defend the Constitution of the United States."

Section 2. The President shall be Commander in Chief of the Army and Navy of the United States, and of the Militia of the several States, when called into the actual Service of the United States; he may require the Opinion, in writing, of the principal Officer in each of the executive Departments, upon any Subject relating to the Duties of their respective Offices, and he shall have Power to grant Reprieves and Pardons for Offenses against the United States, except in Cases of Impeachment.

He shall have Power, by and with the Advice and Consent of the Senate, to make Treaties, provided two thirds of the Senators present concur; and he shall nominate, and by and with the Advice and Consent of the Senate, shall appoint Ambassadors, other public Ministers and Consuls, Judges of the supreme Court, and all other Officers of the United States, whose Appointments are not herein otherwise provided for, and which shall be established by Law: but the Congress may by Law vest the Appointment of such inferior Officers, as they think proper, in the President alone, in the Courts of Law, or in the Heads of Departments.

The President shall have Power to fill up all Vacancies that may happen during the Recess of the Senate, by granting Commissions which shall expire at the End of their next Session.

Section 3. He shall from time to time give to the Congress Information of the State of the Union, and recommend to their Consideration such Measures as he shall judge necessary and expedient; he may, on extraordinary Occasions, convene both Houses, or either of them, and in Case of Disagreement between them, with Respect to the Time of Adjournment, he may adjourn them to such Time as he shall think proper; he shall receive Ambassadors and other public Ministers; he shall take Care that the Laws be faithfully executed, and shall Commission all Officers of the United States.

Section 4. The President, Vice President and all civil Officers of the United States, shall be removed from Office on Impeachment for, and Conviction of, Treason, Bribery, or other high Crimes and Misdemeanors.

Article III

Section 1. The judicial Power of the United States, shall be vested in one supreme Court, and in such inferior Courts as the Congress may from time to time ordain and establish. The Judges, both of the supreme and inferior Courts, shall hold their Offices during good Behaviour, and shall, at stated Times, receive for their Services, a Compensation, which shall not be diminished during their Continuance in Office.

Section 2. The judicial Power shall extend to all Cases, in Law and Equity, arising under this Constitution, the Laws of the United States, and Treaties made, or which shall be made, under their Authority;—to all Cases affecting Ambassadors, other public Ministers and Consuls;—to all Cases of admiralty and maritime Jurisdiction;—to Controversies to which the United States shall be a Party;—to Controversies between two or more States;—between a State and Citizens of another State;⁷—between Citizens of different States,—between Citizens of the same State claiming Lands under Grants of different States, and between a State, or the Citizens thereof, and foreign States, Citizens or Subjects.

In all cases affecting Ambassadors, other public Ministers and Consuls, and those in which a State shall be Party, the supreme Court shall have original Jurisdiction. In all the other Cases before mentioned, the supreme Court shall have appellate Jurisdiction, both as to Law and Fact, with such Exceptions, and under such Regulations as the Congress shall make.

⁷ Modified by the Eleventh Amendment.

The Trial of all Crimes, except in Cases of Impeachment, shall be by Jury; and such Trial shall be held in the State where the said Crimes shall have been committed; but when not committed within any State, the Trial shall be at such Place or Places as the Congress may by Law have directed.

Section 3. Treason against the United States, shall consist only in levying War against them, or in adhering to their Enemies, giving them Aid and Comfort. No Person shall be convicted of Treason unless on the Testimony of two Witnesses to the same overt Act, or on Confession in open Court.

The Congress shall have Power to declare the Punishment of Treason, but no Attainder of Treason shall work Corruption of Blood, or Forfeiture except during the Life of the Person attainted.

Article IV

Section 1. Full Faith and Credit shall be given in each State to the public Acts, Records, and judicial Proceedings of every other State. And the Congress may by general Laws prescribe the Manner in which such Acts, Records and Proceedings shall be proved, and the Effect thereof.

Section 2. The Citizens of each State shall be entitled to all Privileges and Immunities of Citizens in the several States.

A Person charged in any State with Treason, Felony, or other Crime, who shall flee from Justice, and be found in another State, shall on Demand of the executive Authority of the State from which he fled, be delivered up, to be removed to the State having Jurisdiction of the Crime.

No Person held to Service or Labour in one State, under the Laws thereof, escaping into another, shall, in Consequence of any Law or Regulation therein, be discharged from such Service or Labour, but shall be delivered up on Claim of the Party to whom such Service or Labour may be due.

Section 3. New States may be admitted by the Congress into this Union; but no new State shall be formed or erected within the Jurisdiction of any other State; nor any State be formed by the Junction of two or more States, or Parts of States, without the Consent of the Legislatures of the States concerned as well as of the Congress.

The Congress shall have Power to dispose of and make all needful Rules and Regulations respecting the Territory or other Property belonging to the United States; and nothing in this Constitution shall be so construed as to Prejudice any Claims of the United States, or of any particular State.

Section 4. The United States shall guarantee to every State in this Union a Republican Form of Government, and shall protect each of them against Invasion; and on Application of the Legislature, or of the Executive (when the Legislature cannot be convened) against domestic Violence.

Article V

The Congress, whenever two thirds of both Houses shall deem it necessary, shall propose Amendments to this Constitution, or, on the Application of the Legislatures of two thirds of the several States, shall call a Convention for proposing Amendments, which, in either Case, shall be valid to all Intents and Purposes, as Part of this Constitution, when ratified by the Legislatures of three fourths of the several States, or by Conventions in three fourths thereof, as the one or the other Mode of Ratification may be proposed by the Congress; Provided that no Amendment which may be made prior to the Year One thousand eight hundred and eight shall in any Manner affect the first and fourth Clauses in the Ninth Section of the first Article; and that no State, without its Consent, shall be deprived of its equal Suffrage in the Senate.

Article VI

All Debts contracted and Engagements entered into, before the Adoption of this Constitution, shall be as valid against the United States under this Constitution, as under the Confederation.

This Constitution, and the Laws of the United States which shall be made in Pursuance thereof; and all Treaties made, or which shall be made, under the Authority of the United States, shall be the supreme Law of the Land; and the Judges in every State shall be bound thereby, any Thing in the Constitution or Laws of any State to the Contrary notwithstanding.

The Senators and Representatives before mentioned, and the Members of the several State Legislatures, and all executive and judicial Officers, both of the United States and of the several States, shall be bound by Oath or Affirmation, to support this Constitution; but no religious Test shall ever be required as a Qualification to any Office or public Trust under the United States.

Article VII

The Ratification of the Conventions of nine States, shall be sufficient for the Establishment of this Constitution between the States so ratifying the Same.

[Signatures omitted.]

[AMENDMENTS]

ARTICLES in addition to, and Amendment of the Constitution of the United States of America, proposed by Congress, and ratified by the Legislatures of the several States, pursuant to the fifth Article of the original Constitution.

[The first ten articles proposed 25 Sept 1789; declared in force 15 Dec. 1791]

Article I

Congress shall make no law respecting an establishment of religion, or prohibiting the free exercise thereof; or abridging the freedom of speech, or of the press; or the right of the people peaceably to assemble, and to petition the Government for a redress of grievances.

Article II

A well regulated Militia, being necessary to the security of a free State, the right of the people to keep and bear Arms, shall not be infringed.

Article III

No Soldier shall, in time of peace, be quartered in any house, without the con sent of the Owner, nor in time of war, but in a manner to be prescribed by law.

Article IV

The right of the people to be secure in their persons, houses, papers, and effects, against unreasonable searches and seizures, shall not be violated, and no Warrants shall issue, but upon probable cause, supported by Oath or affirmation, and particularly describing the place to be searched, and the persons or things to be seized.

Article V

No person shall be held to answer for a capital, or otherwise infamous crime, unless on a presentment or indictment of a Grand Jury, except in cases arising in the land or naval forces, or in the Militia, when in actual service in time of War or public danger; nor shall any person be subject for the same offense to be twice put in jeopardy of life or limb; nor shall be compelled in any criminal case to be a witness against himself, nor be deprived of life, liberty, or property, without due process of law; nor shall private property be taken for public use, without just compensation.

Article VI

In all criminal prosecutions, the accused shall enjoy the right to a speedy and public trial, by an impartial jury of the State and district wherein the crime shall have been committed, which district shall have been previously ascertained by law, and to be informed of the nature and cause of the accusation; to be confronted with the witnesses against him; to have compulsory process for obtaining witnesses in his favor, and to have the Assistance of Counsel for his defense.

Article VII

In Suits at common law, where the value in controversy shall exceed twenty dollars, the right of trial by jury shall be preserved, and no fact tried by a jury, shall be otherwise re-examined in any Court of the United States, than according to the rules of the common law.

Article VIII

Excessive bail shall not be required, nor excessive fines imposed, nor cruel and unusual punishments inflicted.

Article IX

The enumeration in the Constitution, of certain rights, shall not be construed to deny or disparage others retained by the people.

Article X

The powers not delegated to the United States by the Constitution, nor prohibited by it to the States, are reserved to the States respectively, or to the people.

Article XI [proposed 5 Mar. 1794; declared ratified 8 Jan. 1798]

The Judicial power of the United States shall not be construed to extend to any suit in law or equity, commenced or prosecuted against one of the United States by Citizens of another State, or by Citizens or Subjects of any Foreign State.

Article XII [proposed 12 Dec. 1803; declared ratified 25 Sept. 1804]

The Electors shall meet in their respective states, and vote by ballot for President and Vice-President, one of whom, at least, shall not be an inhabitant of the same state with themselves; they shall name in their ballots the person voted for as President, and in distinct ballots the person voted for as Vice-President, and they shall make distinct lists of all persons voted for as President, and of all persons voted for as Vice-President, and of the number of votes for each, which lists they shall sign and certify, and transmit sealed to the seat of the government of the United States, directed to the President of the Senate;—The President of the Senate shall, in the presence of the Senate and House of Representatives, open all certificates and the votes shall then be counted;—The person having the greatest number of votes for President, shall be the President, if such number be a majority of the whole number of Electors appointed; and if no person have such majority, then from the persons having the highest numbers not exceeding three on the list of those voted for as President, the House of Representatives shall choose immediately, by ballot, the President. But in choosing the President, the votes shall be taken by states, the representation from each state having one vote; a quorum for this purpose shall consist of a member or members from two-thirds of the states, and a majority of all the states shall be necessary to a choice. And if the House of Representatives shall not choose a President whenever the right of choice shall devolve upon them, before the fourth day of March next following, then the Vice-President shall act as President, as in the case of the death or other constitutional disability of the President.— The person having the greatest number of votes as Vice-President, shall be the Vice-President, if such number be a majority of the whole number of Electors appointed, and if no person have a majority, then from the two highest numbers on the list, the Senate shall choose the Vice-President; a quorum for the purpose shall consist of two-thirds of the whole number of Senators, and a majority of the whole number shall be necessary to a choice. But no person constitutionally ineligible to the office of President shall be eligible to that of Vice-President of the United States.

Article XIII [proposed 1 Feb. 1865; declared ratified 18 Dec. 1865]

Section 1. Neither slavery nor involuntary servitude, except as a punishment for crime whereof the party shall have been duly convicted, shall exist within the United States, or any place subject to their jurisdiction.

Section 2. Congress shall have power to enforce this article by appropriate legislation.

Article XIV [proposed 16 June 1866; declared ratified 28 July 1868]

Section 1. All persons born or naturalized in the United States, and subject to the jurisdiction thereof, are citizens of the United States and of the State wherein they reside. No State shall make or enforce any law which shall abridge

the privileges or immunities of citizens of the United States; nor shall any State deprive any person of life, liberty, or property, without due process of law; nor deny to any person within its jurisdiction the equal protection of the laws.

Section 2. Representatives shall be apportioned among the several States according to their respective numbers, counting the whole number of persons in each State, excluding Indians not taxed. But when the right to vote at any election for the choice of electors for President and Vice President of the United States, Representatives in Congress, the Executive and Judicial officers of a State, or the members of the Legislature thereof, is denied to any of the male inhabitants of such State, being twenty-one years of age, and citizens of the United States, or in any way abridged, except for participation in rebellion, or other crime, the basis of representation therein shall be reduced in the proportion which the number of such male citizens shall bear to the whole number of male citizens twenty-one years of age in such State.

Section 3. No person shall be a Senator or Representative in Congress, or elector of President and Vice President, or hold any office, civil or military, under the United States, or under any State, who, having previously taken an oath, as a member of Congress, or as an officer of the United States, or as a member of any State legislature, or as an executive or judicial officer of any State, to support the Constitution of the United States, shall have engaged in insurrection or rebellion against the same, or given aid and comfort to the enemies thereof. But Congress may by a vote of two-thirds of each House, remove such disability.

Section 4. The validity of the public debt of the United State., authorized by law, including debts incurred for payment of pensions and bounties for services in suppressing insurrection or rebellion, shall not be questioned. But neither the United States nor any state shall assume or pay any debt or obligation incurred in aid of insurrection or rebellion against the United States, or any claim for the loss or emancipation of any slave; but all such debts, obligations, and claims shall be held illegal and void.

Section 5. The Congress shall have power to enforce, by appropriate legislation, the provisions of this article.

Article XV [proposed 27 Feb. 1869; declared ratified 30 Mar. 1870]

Section 1. The right of citizens of the United States to vote shall not be denied or abridged by the United States or by any State on account of race, color, or previous condition of servitude.

Section 2. The Congress shall have power to enforce this article by appropriate legislation.

Article XVI [proposed 12 July 1909; declared ratified 25 Feb. 1913]

The Congress shall have power to lay and collect taxes on incomes, from whatever source derived, without apportionment among the several States, and without regard to any census or enumeration.

Article XVII [proposed 16 May 1912; declared ratified 31 May 1913]

The Senate of the United States shall be composed of two Senators from each State, elected by the people thereof, for six years; and each Senator shall have one vote. The electors in each State shall have the qualifications requisite for electors of the most numerous branch of the State legislatures.

When vacancies happen in the representation of any State in the Senate, the executive authority of such State shall issue writs of election to fill such vacancies: *Provided,* That the legislature of any State may empower the executive thereof to make temporary appointments until the people fill the vacancies by election as the legislature may direct.

This amendment shall not be so construed as to affect the election or term of any Senator chosen before it becomes valid as part of the Constitution.

Article XVIII [proposed 18 Dec. 1917; declared ratified 29 Jan. 1919; repealed by the 21st Amendment]

Section 1. After one year from the ratification of this article the manufacture, sale, or transportation of intoxicating liquors within, the importation thereof into, or the exportation thereof from the United States and all territory subject to the jurisdiction thereof for beverage purposes is hereby prohibited.

Section 2. The Congress and the several States shall have concurrent power to enforce this article by appropriate legislation.

Section 3. This article shall be inoperative unless it shall have been ratified as an amendment to the Constitution by the legislatures of the several States, as provided in the Constitution, within seven years from the date of the submission hereof to the States by the Congress.[8]

Article XIX [proposed 4 June 1919; declared ratified 26 Aug. 1920]

The right of citizens of the United States to vote shall not be denied or abridged by the United States or by any State on account of sex.

Congress shall have power to enforce this article by appropriate legislation.

Article XX [proposed 2 Mar. 1932; declared ratified 6 Feb. 1933]

Section 1. The terms of the President and Vice President shall end at noon on the 20th day of January, and the terms of Senators and Representatives at noon on the 3d day of January, of the years in which such terms would have ended if this article had not been ratified; and the terms of their successors shall then begin.

Section 2. The Congress shall assemble at least once in every year, and such meeting shall begin at noon on the 3d day of January, unless they shall by law appoint a different day.

Section 3. If, at the time fixed for the beginning of the term of the President, the President elect shall have died, the Vice President elect shall become President. If a President shall not have been chosen before the time fixed for the beginning of his term, or if the President elect shall have failed to qualify, then the Vice President elect shall act as

8 Superseded by the Twenty-first Amendment.

President until a President shall have qualified; and the Congress may by law provide for the case wherein neither a President elect nor a Vice President elect shall have qualified, declaring who shall then act as President, or the manner in which one who is to act shall be selected, and such person shall act accordingly until a President or Vice President shall have qualified.

Section 4. The Congress may by law provide for the case of the death of any of the persons from whom the House of Representatives may choose a President whenever the right of choice shall have devolved upon them, and for the case of the death of any of the persons from whom the Senate may choose a Vice President whenever the right of choice shall have devolved upon them.

Section 5. Sections 1 and 2 shall take effect on the 15th day of October following the ratification of this article.

Section 6. This article shall be inoperative unless it shall have been ratified as an amendment to the Constitution by the legislatures of three-fourths of the several States within seven years from the date of its submission.

Article XXI [proposed 20 Feb. 1933; declared ratified 5 Dec. 1933]

Section 1. The Eighteenth article of amendment to the Constitution of the United States is hereby repealed.

Section 2. The transportation or importation into any State, Territory, or possession of the United States for de-livery or use therein of intoxicating liquors, in violation of the laws thereof, is hereby prohibited.

Section 3. This article shall be inoperative unless it shall have been ratified as an amendment to the Constitution by conventions in the several States, as provided in the Constitution, within seven years from the date of the submission hereof to the States by the Congress.

Article XXII [proposed 24 Mar. 1947; declared ratified 26 Feb. 1951]

Section 1. No person shall be elected to the office of the President more than twice, and no person who has held the office of President, or acted as President, for more than two years of a term to which some other person was elected President shall be elected to the office of the President more than once. But this Article shall not apply to any person holding the office of President when this Article was proposed by the Congress, and shall not prevent any person who may be holding the office of President, or acting as President, during the term within which this Article becomes operative from holding the office of President or acting as President during the remainder of such term.

Section 2. This article shall be inoperative unless it shall have been ratified as an amendment to the Constitution by the legislatures of three-fourths of the several States within seven years from the date of its submission to the States by the Congress.

Article XXIII (see p. 502)

JUSTICES OF THE UNITED STATES SUPREME COURT

Name *Chief Justices in Italics*	Service Term	Yrs.	Name *Chief Justices in Italics*	Service Term	Yrs.
John Jay, N.Y.	1789–1795	6	Samuel Chase, Md.	1796–1811	15
John Rutledge, S.C.	1789–1791	2	*Oliver Ellsworth,* Conn.	1796–1799	4
William Cushing, Mass.	1789–1810	21	Bushrod Washington, Va.	1798–1829	31
James Wilson, Pa.	1789–1798	9	Alfred Moore, N.C.	1799–1804	5
John Blair, Va.	1789–1796	7	*John Marshall,* Va.	1801–1835	34
Robert H. Harrison, Md.	1789–1790	1	William Johnson, S.C.	1804–1834	30
James Iredell, N.C.	1790–1799	9	Henry B. Livingston, N.Y.	1806–1823	17
Thomas Johnson, Md.	1791–1793	2	Thomas Todd, Ky.	1807–1826	19
William Paterson, N.J.	1793–1806	13	Joseph Story, Mass.	1811–1845	34
John Rutledge, S.C.*	1795–1795	..	Gabriel Duval, Md.	1811–1836	25

Acting chief justice; the Senate refused to confirm nomination.

Name Chief Justices in Italics	Service Term	Yrs.	Name Chief Justices in Italics	Service Term	Yrs.
Smith Thompson, N.Y.	1823–1843	20	Oliver W. Holmes, Mass.	1902–1932	29
Robert Trimble, Ky.	1826–1828	2	William R. Day, Ohio	1903–1922	19
John McLean, Ohio	1829–1861	32	William H. Moody, Mass.	1906–1910	4
Henry Baldwin, Pa.	1830–1844	14	Horace H. Lurton, Tenn.	1910–1914	5
James M. Wayne, Ga.	1835–1867	32	Charles E. Hughes, N.Y.	1910–1916	6
Roger B. Taney, Md.	1836–1864	28	Willis Van Devanter, Wyo.	1911–1937	26
Philip P. Barbour, Va.	1836–1841	5	Joseph R. Lamar, Ga.	1911–1916	6
John Catron, Tenn.	1837–1865	28	*Edward D. White, La.*	1910–1921	11
John McKinley, Ala.	1837–1852	15	Mahlon Pitney, N.J.	1912–1922	12
Peter V. Daniel, Va.	1841–1860	19	Jas. C. McReynolds, Tenn.	1914–1941	27
Samuel Nelson, N.Y.	1845–1872	27	Louis D. Brandeis, Mass.	1916–1939	23
Levi Woodbury, N.H.	1845–1851	6	John H. Clarke, Ohio	1916–1922	6
Robert C. Grier, Pa.	1846–1870	24	*William H. Taft, Conn.*	1921–1930	9
Benj. R. Curtis, Mass.	1851–1857	6	George Sutherland, Utah	1922–1938	16
John A. Campbell, Ala.	1853–1861	8	Pierce Butler, Minn.	1922–1939	17
Nathan Clifford, Me.	1858–1881	23	Edward T. Sanford, Tenn.	1923–1930	7
Noah H. Swayne, Ohio	1862–1881	20	Harlan F. Stone, N.Y.	1925–1941	16
Samuel F. Miller, Iowa	1862–1890	28	*Charles E. Hughes, N.Y.*	1930–1941	11
David Davis, Ill.	1862–1877	15	Owen J. Roberts, Penn.	1930–1945	15
Stephen J. Field, Cal.	1863–1897	34	Benjamin N. Cardozo, N.Y.	1932–1938	6
Salmon P. Chase, Ohio	1864–1873	9	Hugo Black, Ala.	1937–....	..
William Strong, Pa.	1870–1880	10	Stanley Reed, Ky.	1938–1957	19
Joseph P. Bradley, N.J.	1870–1892	22	Felix Frankfurter, Mass.	1939–....	..
Ward Hunt, N.Y.	1872–1882	10	William O. Douglas, Conn.	1939–....	..
Morrison R. Waite, Ohio	1874–1888	14	Frank Murphy, Mich.	1940–1949	9
John M. Harlan, Ky.	1877–1911	34	*Harlan F. Stone, N.Y.*	1941–1946	5
William B. Woods, Ga.	1880–1887	7	James F. Byrnes, S.C.	1941–1942	2
Stanley Matthews, Ohio	1881–1889	8	Robert H. Jackson, N.Y.	1941–1954	13
Horace Gray, Mass.	1881–1902	21	Wiley B. Rutledge, Iowa	1943–1949	6
Samuel Blatchford, N.Y.	1882–1893	11	Harold H. Burton, Ohio	1945–1958	13
Lucius Q. C. Lamar, Miss.	1888–1893	5	*Fred M. Vinson, Ky.*	1946–1953	7
Melville W. Fuller, Ill.	1888–1910	22	Thomas C. Clark, Tex.	1949–....	..
David J. Brewer, Kan.	1889–1910	21	Sherman Minton, Ind.	1949–1956	7
Henry B. Brown, Mich.	1890–1906	16	*Earl Warren, Calif.*	1953–....	..
George Shiras, Jr., Pa.	1892–1903	11	John Marshall Harlan, N.Y.	1955–....	..
Howell E. Jackson, Tenn.	1893–1895	2	William J. Brennan, Jr., N.J.	1956–....	..
Edward D. White, La.	1894–1910	16	Charles E. Whittaker, Mo.	1957–....	..
Rufus W. Peckham, N.Y.	1895–1910	14	Potter Stewart, Ohio	1958–....	..
Joseph McKenna, Cal.	1898–1925	27			

LEADING SUPREME COURT DECISIONS

1793. CHISHOLM v. GEORGIA (2 Dallas 419). The Constitution (Art. III, Sec. 2) gave the Federal courts explicit jurisdiction over "controversies between a state and citizens of another state." As executors for a British creditor, 2 S.C. citizens brought suit in the Supreme Court against the state of Ga. for the recovery of confiscated property. Ga. denied the Court's jurisdiction, and refused to appear. The Court decided in favor of Chisholm. The opinions of 4 majority justices (notably James Wilson) elaborated on the sovereignty and the nature of the Union. In a dissenting opinion, Justice James Iredell held that no constitutional sanction superseded the right (under English common law) of a sovereignty not to be sued without its consent. As a result of the decision, the 11th Amendment was proposed and ratified (p. 126).

1796. WARE v. HYLTON (3 Dallas 199). By the peace treaty with Great Britain (1783), no legal impediment was to be placed on the recovery of debts owed by Americans to British creditors. In this test case, the Court invalidated a Va. statute (1777) providing for the sequestration of debts owed to British subjects before the outbreak of the Revolution, on the ground that under the Constitution treaties are the supreme law of the land; hence paramount over state laws.

1796. HYLTON v. U.S. (3 Dallas 171) involved the question of whether a tax on carriages enacted in 1794 was an excise or a direct tax within the meaning of the Constitution. Holding that only land and capitation levies were direct taxes, the Court ruled that the carriage tax was indirect and hence could be levied without apportionment among the states. This was the 1st time the Court passed on the constitutionality of an Act of Congress.

1798. CALDER v. BULL (3 Dallas 386). The Court interpreted that provision of the Constitution (Art. I, Sec. 10) prohibiting state legislatures from enacting *ex post facto* laws as extending only to criminal, not civil, laws.

1803. MARBURY v. MADISON (1 Cranch 137), pp. 131, 132.

1810. FLETCHER v. PECK (6 Cranch 87) involved the claims arising under the Yazoo land frauds (p. 138). The Ga. legislature, many of its members having been bribed by land speculators, granted large tracts along the Yazoo River to land companies (1795). The grant was rescinded by the succeeding legislature on the ground that its enactment had been attended by fraud and corruption. Chief Justice Marshall rendered the opinion for a unanimous court, upholding the original grant on the grounds that (1) it was not within the province of the Court to inquire into the motives actuating a legislature, and (2) the rescinding act impaired the obligation of contracts, Marshall ruling that the contract clause made no distinction between public and private contracts. This was the first time the Court invalidated a state law as contrary to the Constitution.

1816. MARTIN v. HUNTER'S LESSEE (1 Wheaton 304) arose from the litigation over Virginia's confiscation of the Fairfax land grants and its statute prohibiting an alien from inheriting land, and involved the crucial question of the Court's appellate jurisdiction over the decisions of state courts. The first Court decision (1813), rendered against Va., stirred the defiance of the state court of appeals, which refused to obey the mandate and held that Sec. 25 of the Judiciary Act was unconstitutional. When the

case was again brought to the Supreme Court, Justice Story vigorously affirmed the Court's right to review decisions of state courts. Asserting the Court's role as the harmonizer of decisions emanating from inferior courts, Story ruled that the Constitutional grant of concurrent jurisdiction in specified cases did not deprive the Supreme Court of its appellate jurisdiction. The decision renewed the opposition of the Va. Republicans led by Judge Spencer Roane and set off a lively pamphleteering war.

1819. TRUSTEES OF DARTMOUTH COLLEGE v. WOODWARD (4 Wheaton 518), p. 158.

1819. STURGES v. CROWNINSHIELD (4 Wheaton 122) involved the constitutionality of a N.Y. statute (1811) relieving insolvent debtors of obligations contracted before the passage of the act. While Chief Justice Marshall held that state bankruptcy laws were permissible in the absence of Congressional legislation, he declared that the N.Y. statute impaired the obligation of contracts and was therefore unconstitutional. The decision served to restrict state action on bankruptcy during a period of financial chaos.

1819. M'CULLOCH v. MARYLAND (4 Wheaton 316), p. 158.

1821. COHENS v. VIRGINIA (6 Wheaton 264) arose from the conviction of the Cohens for selling lottery tickets in violation of a state law. The larger issues involved were the constitutionality of Sec. 25 of the Judiciary Act, under which the Cohens had appealed to the Supreme Court, and the interpretation of the 11th Amendment, under which Va. claimed exemption from Federal jurisdiction in this instance. On the merits, the Court decided in favor of Va., but Chief Justice Marshall issued a firm reply to the Va. Republicans who denied that state court decisions were subject to Court review. His comprehensive interpretation of the Court's scope of jurisdiction was based squarely on the doctrine of national supremacy.

1823. GREEN v. BIDDLE (8 Wheaton 1). Ruling that the contract clause applied to contracts between two states as well as those between private persons, the

Court nullified a Ky. law pertaining to land titles on the ground that it impaired the obligation of contracts deriving from a political agreement that Ky. made with Va. when the former state was organized. The Court also denied Ky.'s claim that agreement was invalid because Congress had not consented.

1824. GIBBONS v. OGDEN (9 Wheaton 1) involved a monopoly granted by the N.Y. legislature (1808) for the operation of steamboats in state waters. Aaron Ogden, successor to the exclusive right granted to Robert Fulton and Robert Livingston, sued Thomas Gibbons (who operated under a Federal license) to restrain him from engaging in steam navigation between N.Y. and N.J. The Court invalidated the New York grant. The opinion of Chief Justice Marshall was the 1st broad construction of the nature and scope of Congressional power under the commerce clause. Rejecting a narrow definition of commerce as "traffic" or simple exchange, Marshall construed it as embracing "every species of commercial intercourse," including navigation and other agencies of commerce. While he conceded that the regulation of wholly intrastate commerce was reserved to the state, he asserted that Congressional power to regulate interstate and foreign commerce "does not stop at the jurisdictional lines of the several states." This curb on state authority, coming at a time when many states had granted similar monopoly privileges, freed transportation from state restraints.

1824. OSBORN v. BANK OF THE U.S. (9 Wheaton 738) involved the validity of a circuit court decree restraining an Ohio tax and outlaw act directed against branches of the U.S. Bank within the state, and was a direct result of the opposition to the Court's decision in **M'Culloch v. Maryland**. The state auditor, Ralph Osborn, and other Ohio officials who seized Bank funds were sued for damages. The Court decision was in favor of the Bank. Chief Justice Marshall held that the agent of a state, when executing an unconstitutional statute, was personally responsible for damages caused by his enforcement of the act, and that a state could not invoke the protection of the 11th Amendment.

1827. MARTIN v. MOTT (12 Wheaton 19). During the War of 1812 state authorities in New England employed various means for effectively denying the authority of the Congress or President to call out the state militia. Justice Story held that the President, acting under Congressional authority, was the sole judge of the existence of those contingencies prescribed in the Constitution upon which the militia might be called out; that the President's decision was binding on state officials; and that state militia in Federal service were subject to the authority of officers commissioned by the President.

1827. OGDEN v. SAUNDERS (12 Wheaton 213). The Court ruled 4 to 3 that a N.Y. bankruptcy law (1801) did not violate the obligation of contracts entered into *after* the enactment of the law. Justice William Johnson of the majority, anticipating the later doctrine of the state's police power, declared that "all the contracts of men receive a relative, and not a positive interpretation: for the rights of all must be held and enjoyed in subserviency to the good of the whole." But the majority also declared that a state insolvency law could not discharge a contract of a citizen of another state. This was the first time Chief Justice Marshall was in a minority on the interpretation of a constitutional provision. He and Justice Story dissented on the ground that the contract clause protected all contracts, future as well as past, from impairment.

1827. BROWN v. MARYLAND (12 Wheaton 419) invalidated a Md. law requiring a special license for wholesalers dealing in foreign goods. Marking out the line between state and Federal control of commerce, Chief Justice Marshall laid down the **"original package"** doctrine: imported goods which became "incorporated and mixed up with the mass of property in the country" were subject to the state taxing power, but those which remained "in the original form or package" (i.e., the property of the importer) were still imports and hence subject to Congressional regulation.

1830. CRAIG v. MISSOURI (4 Peters 410). The Court, 4 to 3, upset a Mo. law authorizing the issuance of loan certificates receivable in discharge of taxes and debts due the state. Marshall narrowly construed the constitutional clause prohibiting states from emitting bills of credit, while the dissenting justices held the law to be a justifiable use of the state's borrowing power.

1831. CHEROKEE NATION v. GEORGIA (5 Peters 1), p. 171.

1832. WORCESTER v. GEORGIA (6 Peters 515), p. 171.

1833. BARRON v. BALTIMORE (7 Peters 243). Chief Justice Marshall held that the amendments included in the Bill of Rights were protection against infringement by the Federal government, but not binding upon the state governments.

1837. BRISCOE v. BANK OF KENTUCKY (11 Peters 257) upheld a Ky. law creating a state-owned bank empowered to issue notes for public circulation on the ground that the state had not pledged the redemption of the notes but had established for this purpose a public corporation capable of suing and being sued; hence, the state bank notes could not be construed as bills of credit. Story dissented. The decision paved the way for increased state regulation of currency and banking.

1837. CHARLES RIVER BRIDGE v. WARREN BRIDGE (11 Peters 420). The Mass. legislature authorized (1785) the Charles River Bridge Co. to construct and operate a toll bridge over the Charles River, and in 1792 extended the charter to 70 years. The grant did not confer exclusive privileges. The charter of the Warren Bridge (1828) provided that the structure (built a short distance from the Charles Bridge) should be turned over to the state upon the recovery of construction costs. The Charles River Bridge Co. brought suit for an injunction on the ground that the erection of the Warren Bridge constituted an impairment of the obligation of contracts. Rejecting the doctrine of vested rights invoked by the Charles River counsel, Chief Justice Taney ruled that the competing bridge was no such impairment, that a legislative charter must be construed narrowly, that no implied rights could be claimed beyond the specific terms of a grant, and

that ambiguous clauses must operate against the corporation in favor of the public. Taney's first pronouncement on a constitutional issue, the decision substantially modified Marshall's earlier contract doctrines.

1837. NEW YORK v. MILN (11 Peters 102) upheld the constitutionality of a N.Y. statute requiring masters of coastwise or transoceanic vessels entering N.Y. to furnish prescribed information concerning all passengers brought in, as a legitimate use of the state police power for purposes of internal health and welfare, not in conflict with the Federal commerce power. In a dissenting opinion, Story maintained that the statute infringed upon the exclusive Congressional power to regulate foreign commerce.

1839. BANK OF AUGUSTA v. EARLE (13 Peters 519) was the chief of the 3 Comity Cases of 1839, which arose from the attempt of Ala. to exclude corporations chartered by other states. A citizen of Ala. refused to honor the bills of exchange of a Ga. bank, contending that a "foreign" corporation had no lawful right to enter into a contract within a "sovereign" state. Chief Justice Taney recognized the general right of a corporation to do business under interstate comity with other states, but also upheld the right of states to exclude corporations by positive action. Taney rejected the argument that a corporation possessed all the legal rights guaranteed to natural persons under the Constitution.

1842. PRIGG v. PENNSYLVANIA (16 Peters 539) involved the constitutionality of the Federal fugitive slave law of 1793 and of a Pa. "personal liberty" law of 1826 banning forcible seizure and removal of a fugitive. For the majority, Story held (1) the state law unconstitutional, and (2) the execution of the fugitive slave clause in the Constitution exclusively a Federal power, hence no state was obliged to undertake the enforcement of the law. As a result, Northern states enacted a series of "personal liberty" laws forbidding state authorities from assisting in the return of fugitive slaves.

1847. LICENSE CASES (5 Howard 504). These 3 cases involved the legality of state laws restricting and taxing the sale of alcoholic liquors. The Mass. and R.I. statutes were upheld as not contrary to the "original package" dictum. The N.H. case, however, involved a tax upon liquor in the original and unbroken package. From the 9 opinions written by 6 justices emerged agreement on the view that a tax imposed as an exercise of the state police power is valid, even though the levy impinges on interstate commerce. Four justices (including Taney) indicated that in the absence of Federal legislation the states had a concurrent right to regulate interstate commerce unless they came in conflict with a law of Congress.

1849. LUTHER v. BORDEN (7 Howard 1) arose from the Dorr Rebellion in R.I. and involved the validity of the declaration of martial law by the existing state legislature. The Court decided that Congress had power under Art. IV, Sec. 4 of the Constitution to guarantee republican government in the states and to recognize the lawful government; the President by Act of Congress must decide in case of an armed conflict within a state which is the lawful government. Neither decision could be questioned by the Court.

1849. PASSENGER CASES (7 Howard 283). These 2 cases involved the legality of N.Y. and Mass. acts authorizing a head tax on each alien brought into the ports of these states and directing the tax collections to be used for internal welfare. The Court (5–4) held the acts unconstitutional on the ground that the power to regulate foreign commerce belonged exclusively to the Federal government and could not be exercised even in the absence of Congressional legislation. The dissenting justices maintained that the laws were a legitimate exercise of state police power. Taney contended that, failing positive Congressional regulation, the states had a concurrent power in this domain.

1851. COOLEY v. BOARD OF WARDENS (12 Howard 299) upheld the validity of a Pa. law regulating the employment of pilots in the port of Philadelphia. Justice Benjamin R. Curtis ruled that where commerce was national in character, the Federal power was exclusive;

but where local, the states had a concurrent power to legislate in the absence of Federal action.

1857. DRED SCOTT v. SANDFORD (19 Howard 393), p. 221.

1859. ABLEMAN v. BOOTH (21 Howard 506). This case arose when the Wis. Supreme Court (1854) freed the abolitionist editor, Sherman M. Booth, who had been convicted in Federal district court of violating the fugitive slave law of 1850. U.S. District Marshal Ableman obtained a writ of error in the U.S. Supreme Court to review the state court's findings. In an opinion notable for its affirmation of national supremacy and its analysis of divided sovereignty, Taney denied the right of the state judiciary to interfere in Federal cases and, in a brief obiter dictum, upheld the constitutionality of the fugitive slave law. His pronouncement led the Wis. legislature to adopt resolutions defending state sovereignty in the spirit of the Ky. and Va. resolutions.

1861. EX PARTE MERRYMAN (Fed. Cases No. 9487) involved military suspension of the privilege of the writ of habeas corpus, authorized in exceptional instances by President Lincoln. John Merryman, a Baltimore secessionist, arrested by military authority, successfully petitioned Chief Justice Taney (sitting as a circuit judge) for a writ of habeas corpus. That writ was rejected by the military commander. Taney, who cited the commander for contempt, filed an opinion denying that the Executive had the power to suspend the writ, holding such power to be vested in Congress, and condemning the suspension of constitutional rights by military order. Lincoln justified his course in his message to Congress (July 1861).

1863. PRIZE CASES (2 Black 635). Before Congress recognized a state of war, neutral shipping was seized under Lincoln's proclamations (19, 27 Apr. 1861) which authorized a blockade of Confederate ports. The Court (5–4) sustained the legality of the seizures, declaring that the President could not initiate war, but was fulfilling his lawful duties in resisting insurrection, and that insurrection was in fact war.

1864. EX PARTE VALLANDIGHAM (1 Wallace 243) involved arrests and trials of civilians by military commissions. Upon rejection of Vallandigham's petition for a writ of habeas corpus by a U.S. circuit court, his counsel appealed to the Supreme Court. The Court refused to review the case on the ground that its authority did not embrace the proceedings of a military commission.

1866. EX PARTE MILLIGAN (4 Wallace 2) involving the trial and conviction of civilians by military commission at Indianapolis, unanimously held the military commission authorized by the President to be void and released Milligan. A majority held that neither Congress nor the President had legal power to institute a military commission to try civilians in areas remote from the actual theater of war. Chief Justice Chase for the minority upheld Congress' power.

1867. TEST-OATH CASES: Cummings v. Missouri (4 Wallace 277), **Ex parte Garland** (4 Wallace 333). The **Cummings** case involved a Mo. constitutional (1865) provision requiring an oath of past allegiance from teachers, preachers, voters, and many others. The **Garland** case arose from a Federal loyalty oath requirement (1865) demanded of attorneys practicing in the Federal courts. Heard simultaneously, the Court split 5–4 in both decisions. The majority held such tests of past fidelity ex post facto and bills of attainder. The dissenters maintained that such requirements were valid expressions of a government's right to protect itself by laying down certain qualifications of its officers and voters.

1867. MISSISSIPPI v. JOHNSON (4 Wallace 475) concerned an attempt by Miss. to enjoin President Johnson from enforcing the 1867 Reconstruction Acts. Unanimously, the Court refused the injunction on the ground that purely Executive and political functions were not subject to judicial restraint, although mere ministerial acts might be. Similarly, a suit to enjoin the Secretary of War from enforcing these Acts was dismissed as involving political questions over which the Court had no jurisdiction; **Georgia v. Stanton** (6 Wallace 50).

1869. TEXAS v. WHITE (7 Wallace 700) involved the legality of financial actions of the Confederate government of Tex. The Court held that, secession being inadmissible, the Confederate state authorities had never legally existed. Chief Justice Chase, for the majority, analyzed the nature of the Union and the theories of secession and Reconstruction. "The Constitution," he said, ". . . looks to an indestructible Union, composed of indestructible states." While refraining from passing on the validity of the Reconstruction acts of Congress, the Court declared that Congress had the duty to provide guarantees of republican governments in the states.

1869. VEAZIE BANK v. FENNO (8 Wallace 533) dealt with the prohibitive 10% tax levied by Congress on state bank notes to promote the national banking system initiated during the Civil War. Chief Justice Chase, for the majority, upheld the tax as a legitimate exercise both of Congress' taxing power and of its authority to provide for a sound national currency.

1870. 1ST LEGAL TENDER CASE: Hepburn v. Griswold (8 Wallace 603). By a 5–3 decision, the Court held unconstitutional the Legal Tender Acts (1862, 1863), insofar as fulfillment of contracts made before their passage was concerned, as violating the obligation of contracts and due process clauses of the 5th Amendment. The minority held these acts to be legitimate exercises of the war power.

1871. 2ND LEGAL TENDER CASE: Knox v. Lee, Parker v. Davis (12 Wallace 457). Two new justices, J. P. Bradley and W. Strong, appointed by Grant, joined the minority of the **Hepburn** case to reverse the latter ruling. Legal tender was validated as a justifiable exercise of the national government's powers in time of emergency, not limited to war. While there is no evidence that Grant "packed the Court," he made no secret of his disapproval of the **Hepburn** decision, and was aware how his appointees stood on the issue.

1871. COLLECTOR v. DAY (11 Wallace 113). By an 8–1 decision, the Court held invalid a Federal income tax on the salary of a state official. From this decision there grew a large area of intergovernmental tax immunities, which was not ended until the **Graves** case (1939).

1873. SLAUGHTERHOUSE CASES (16 Wallace 36) were the first judicial pronouncement on the 14th Amendment. A monopoly grant of the La. legislature was contested as a violation of the privileges and immunities clause of that Amendment. By a 5–4 decision, the Court upheld the grant. For the majority, Justice Miller distinguished between state and national citizenship. Only the rights deriving from Federal citizenship were protected by the 14th Amendment, and those rights were narrowly defined. This interpretation placed the great body of civil rights under the protection of the state governments. The Court refused to consider the due process clause as a general substantive limitation upon the regulatory powers of the states, and held that the equal protection clause applied solely to state laws which discriminated against Negroes. The dissenting jurists held that the 14th Amendment was a safeguard against state violations of the privileges and immunities of U.S. citizens, and that impairment of property rights by statute violated due process.

1877. GRANGER CASES: Munn v. Illinois (94 U.S. 113). This case (one of a group known collectively as the Granger Cases) involved an Ill. law (1873) fixing maximum rates for grain storage. Chief Justice Waite, for the Court, upheld the law as a legitimate expression of the state's police power in regulating **businesses affected with ". . . a public interest."** He declared that appeal was "to the polls, not to the courts," and denied that the due process clause was substantively violated or that state regulation of intrastate commerce impaired Congress' unilateral control over interstate commerce. In dissent, Justice Field asserted that procedural due process was insufficient protection for property rights.

1881. SPRINGER v. U.S. (102 U.S. 586) upheld the constitutionality of the Federal income tax adopted during the Civil War on the ground that it was not a direct tax within the meaning of the Constitution, and did not require appor-tionment among the states in proportion to population.

1883. CIVIL RIGHTS CASES (109 U.S. 3) were 5 cases where Negroes had been refused equal accommodations or privileges, allegedly in defiance of the 1875 Civil Rights Act. That Act was declared invalid for protecting social rather than political rights. The Court held that the 14th Amendment prohibited invasion **by the states** of civil rights, but did not protect the invasion of civil rights **by individuals** unaided by state authority. This ruling virtually ended Federal attempts to protect the Negro against discrimination by private persons.

1884. JUILLIARD v. GREENMAN (110 U.S. 421). In issue was the 1878 Act of Congress which provided that Civil War legal tender notes should not be retired, but kept in circulation. Justice Gray for the Court upheld the act on the ground that the power of Congress to make notes legal tender was derived from its constitutional authority to provide a uniform national currency and did not rest solely on the war power. Dissenting, Justice Field stressed the alleged dangers of a doctrine which gave to government ". . . the power to alter the conditions of contracts."

1884. KU KLUX KLAN CASES: Ex parte Yarbrough (110 U.S. 651) upheld Congress' power to punish as a crime against Federal law private interference with the right of an American citizen to vote in a Federal election. Such right, held Justice Miller, is dependent on the Constitution and laws of the U.S., and not exclusively on state law.

1886. SANTA CLARA CO. v. SOUTHERN PACIFIC R.R. CO. (118 U.S. 394). In 1882 in **San Mateo Co. v. Southern Pacific R.R. Co.** (116 U.S. 138), Roscoe Conkling, counsel for the railroad and ex-senator from N.Y., contended that in Congressional committee the word "persons" in the 14th Amendment had been chosen to extend the protection of the due process clause to legal persons, i.e., corporations. In the **Santa Clara Co.** case Chief Justice Waite, for the Court, by way of dictum, announced acceptance of this doctrine, and thereby encouraged the substantive interpretation of the due process clause as a defense of corporate property rights.

1886. WABASH, ST. LOUIS & PA-CIFIC R.R. CO. v. ILLINOIS (118 U.S. 557) involved the validity of an Ill. statute prohibiting long-in-short-haul clauses in transportation contracts. The Court invalidated the law as an infringement on Congress' exclusive control over interstate commerce. The decision gravely weakened the ruling in the **Granger Cases** (1877) and created a "twilight zone" where neither the states nor the Federal government could operate.

1890. CHICAGO, MILWAUKEE & ST. PAUL R.R. CO. v. MINNESOTA (134 U.S. 418) invalidated a Minn. law (1887) providing for a rate-setting railroad and warehouse commission, to have final rate-fixing powers without permissible appeal to the courts, on the ground that denial of recourse to the courts was, substantively, deprivation of property without due process of law. The decision posed the question of the possibility of judicial review of rates prescribed by legislative bodies rather than by quasi-judicial commissions.

1894. REAGAN v. FARMERS' LOAN AND TRUST CO. (154 U.S. 362) upheld the right of the courts to review the fixing of rates by a Tex. commission, acting under state law. Justice Brewer declared: "It has always been a part of the judicial function to determine whether the act of one party . . . operates to divest another party of any rights of person or property."

1895. U.S. v. E. C. KNIGHT CO. (156 U.S. 1) involved the 1st judicial interpretation of the Sherman Antitrust Act. The government charged defendant with a near monopoly of sugar refining. In an 8–1 decision against the government Chief Justice Fuller, for the majority, drew a sharp line between commerce and manufacturing. "Commerce succeeds to manufacture," he asserted, "and is not a part of it." The Sherman Act was held inapplicable to intrastate manufacturing combinations. The effect of this decision was to impair seriously enforcement of the antitrust laws, and to place most monopolies beyond the reach of Federal control.

1895. INCOME TAX CASES: Pollock v. Farmers' Loan and Trust Co. (157 U.S. 429, 158 U.S. 601). These cases involved the validity of the Federal income tax clauses of the Wilson-Gorman Tariff Act (1894). In the 1st case the Court, 6–2, declared invalid that part of the tax statute imposing a tax on income from realty and municipal bonds. Such a tax, according to the Court, was a direct tax, and must be levied by apportionment among the states, while its incidence on income from municipal bonds was held a tax on an instrumentality of a state. Since no decision resulted on the issue of whether the income tax as a whole was voided, a rehearing was held. By 5–4 the Court invalidated the entire tax law, holding that taxes on personal property were direct taxes. As a result, the 16th Amendment was adopted to enable the Federal government to enact the income tax.

1895. IN RE DEBS (158 U.S. 564). The 1894 Pullman strike resulted in an injunction under the Sherman Antitrust Act against the union leaders. Debs, president of the American Railway Union, was cited for contempt in violating that injunction, and sued out a writ of habeas corpus in the Supreme Court. The writ was denied. The Court rested its judgment not on the Sherman Act, but on the broader ground that the relations of the Federal government to interstate commerce and the transportation of the mails authorized the use of the injunction to prevent forcible obstruction.

1896. PLESSY v. FERGUSON (163 U.S. 537) upheld a La. law requiring segregated railroad facilities. As long as equality of accommodation existed, the court held, segregation did not constitute discrimination, and the Negro was not deprived of equal protection of the laws under the 14th Amendment.

1897. U.S. v. TRANS-MISSOURI FREIGHT ASSOCIATION (166 U.S. 290). The Court ruled (5–4) an association of 18 railroads which existed to fix transportation rates to violate the Sherman Antitrust Act. The counsel for the railroads pleaded the "rule of reason"—that only those combinations were illegal which were in unreasonable restraint of trade. Although rejected in this instance, this doctrine was later to rule the Court.

1898. HOLDEN v. HARDY (169 U.S. 366) upheld (7–2) the validity of a Utah law (1896) limiting maximum work hours in mining industries as a reasonable exercise of the state's police functions. The right of freedom of contract must be modified when inequalities of bargaining power exist, the majority held. In addition, the Court stressed the peculiarly hazardous nature of the mining industry. This case served as a precedent for state regulation of labor conditions.

1898. SMYTH v. AMES (169 U.S. 466) invalidated a Neb. act of 1893 which had fixed railroad rates, on the ground that it constituted a deprivation of property without due process as guaranteed by the 14th Amendment. In order to be reasonable the rates fixed must yield a "fair" return on a "fair value" of the property involved. The rule was so vague as to leave to the courts for determination in each case the fairness of the rates contested.

1899. ADDYSTON PIPE AND STEEL CO. v. U.S. (175 U.S. 211) invalidated a market-allocation scheme as an infringement of the Sherman Act and as directly affecting interstate commerce. The ruling restored a degree of effectiveness to the Sherman Act, which had been impaired by the ruling in the Knight case (1895).

1901. INSULAR CASES: De Lima v. Bidwell (182 U.S. 1). The Court ruled (5–4) that Puerto Rico ceased to be a foreign nation at the formal close of the Spanish-American War. Thus, duties could not be levied upon goods imported from Puerto Rico without Congressional authority. **Dooley v. U.S.** (182 U.S. 222) held that U.S. goods shipped into Puerto Rico were free of duty. But **Downes v. Bidwell** (182 U.S. 244) asserted the principle that the Constitution did not automatically and immediately apply to the people of an annexed territory, nor did it confer upon them all the privileges of U.S. citizenship, but that it was for Congress specifically to extend such Constitutional provisions as it saw fit.

1903. LOTTERY CASE: Champion v. Ames (188 U.S. 321) upheld (5–4) a Federal law prohibiting the dissemination of lottery tickets through the mails under the commerce power, which, according to the majority, implied the power to prohibit as well as to regulate. For the minority, Chief Justice Fuller attacked the intent of the law as an infringement upon the police powers of the states under the guise of regulating interstate commerce. What was to become known as a "Federal police power" was given judicial sanction by this case.

1904. NORTHERN SECURITIES CO. v. U.S. (193 U.S. 197) rejuvenated the dormant Sherman Antitrust Act and upheld (5–4) the government in its suit against the railroad holding company. The majority held that stock transactions constituting an illegal combination (whether reasonable or unreasonable) in restraint of interstate commerce came within the scope of the Sherman Act. Justice Holmes, in dissent, pleaded for the "rule of reason."

1905. SWIFT & CO. v. U.S. (196 U.S. 375) upheld unanimously the government's antitrust prosecution of the "Beef Trust." For the Court, Justice Holmes expounded the "stream of commerce" concept, according to which certain local business agreements are regarded as integral parts of interstate commerce.

1905. LOCHNER v. NEW YORK (198 U.S. 45) involved the validity of a New York maximum-hours law for bakers. A bare majority of the Court held the law invalid as an unreasonable interference with the right of free contract, and an excessive use of the state's police powers. In a notable dissent, Justice Holmes criticized the majority's decision as based ". . . upon an economic theory which a large part of the country does not entertain. . . . The 14th Amendment does not enact Mr. Herbert Spencer's Social Statics." He insisted that the Constitution "is not intended to embody a particular economic theory, whether of paternalism . . . or of *laissez-faire.*"

1908. ADAIR v. U.S. (208 U.S. 161). The Erdman Act (1898) prohibited railroads engaged in interstate commerce from requiring as a condition of employment an agreement ("yellow-dog" contract) by workers not to join a labor union. The Court (6–2) invalidated this provision as an unreasonable violation of freedom of contract and property rights guaranteed by the 5th Amendment. Union membership, according to the majority, was not a subject of interstate commerce.

1908. LOEWE v. LAWLER (208 U.S. 274). This **"Danbury Hatters Case"** resulted in a unanimous decision by the Court that a **secondary boycott** (initiated 1902) by a labor union was a conspiracy in restraint of trade within the meaning of the Sherman Act. This was the 1st time the Act was applied to labor organizations.

1908. MULLER v. OREGON (208 U.S. 412) upheld an Ore. law limiting maximum working hours of women and denied that it impaired the liberty of contract guaranteed by the 14th Amendment. Notable was the use by Louis D. Brandeis, counsel for the state, of a brief ("**Brandeis Brief**") which amassed statistical, historical, sociological, and economic data to support his contentions, rather than traditional legal arguments.

1911. U.S. v. GRIMAUD (220 U.S. 506) upheld the validity of Federal laws (1891, 1905) relating to the disposition and administration of public lands which vested the Executive with a substantial measure of administrative discretion. The Court distinguished between "administrative discretion" and outright delegation of legislative power (the latter declared unconstitutional).

1911. STANDARD OIL CO. OF NEW JERSEY ET AL. v. U.S. (221 U.S. 1) upheld the dissolution of the company, applying the "rule of reason" to the Sherman Act. Harlan, in dissent, denounced the ruling as judicial usurpation.

1911. U.S. v. AMERICAN TOBACCO CO. (221 U.S. 106) ordered the reorganization of the "tobacco trust" rather than its complete dissolution on the basis of the "rule of reason" (White).

1913. MINNESOTA RATE CASES (230 U.S. 252) sustained the validity of an order by a state commission setting intrastate railroad rates. The Court held

that, while Congress' authority over interstate commerce was exclusive, a state might properly act in a field where it did not conflict with Federal laws.

1917. WILSON v. NEW (243 U.S. 332). Chief Justice White, for a bare majority of the Court, upheld the constitutionality of the Adamson Eight-Hour Act (1916), which specified 8 hrs. as a day's work on railroads operating in interstate commerce. Despite the fact that this was in effect a wage-fixing measure, the Court held that in an emergency Congress might establish a temporary standard.

1918. ARVER v. U.S. (245 U.S. 366), among the **Selective Draft Law Cases,** sustained the World War I conscription act. The power of a nation to secure military service from its residents was an incidence of sovereignty, the Court found, as well as a direct result of the Constitutional authorization to Congress "to declare war . . . to raise and support armies" (Art. 1, Sec. 8). Similarly, in 1919, in the **War Prohibition Cases** (251 U.S. 146), the Court upheld the wartime Prohibition measure as a legitimate exercise of the war power of the government. Again in 1919, the power granted the President to seize and operate the railroads in wartime was upheld under the war power in **Northern Pacific Railway Co. v. North Dakota** (250 U.S. 585).

1918. HAMMER v. DAGENHART (247 U.S. 251). The Keating-Owen Child Labor Act (1916) forbade interstate shipment of products of child labor. The Court split 5–4 on the issue of mutually restrictive areas of federal-state operations. Justice Day, for the majority, declared the act invalid as a regulation of local labor conditions rather than commerce. Holmes' dissent upheld Congress' right to regulate interstate commerce in unqualified terms, including the power to prohibit. **Bailey v. Drexel Furniture Company** (259 U.S. 20), in 1922, involved the 2nd Child Labor Act (1919), which levied prohibitive taxes upon the products of child labor in interstate commerce. Chief Justice Taft spoke for the majority of the Court in holding the law invalid on much the same grounds as in the **Hammer** decision.

1919. SCHENCK v. U.S. (249 U.S. 47). For a unanimous Court, Justice Holmes upheld the wartime Espionage Act as not violating the 1st Amendment. Applying the "clear and present danger" test, Holmes found that Schenck's pamphlets encouraged real resistance to the draft; that free speech is always under restraint, especially in time of war.

1919. ABRAMS v. U.S. (250 U.S. 616) upheld the 1918 Sedition Law. Applying the "bad tendency" test, Justice Clarke, for the majority, found pamphlets which criticized the U.S. expeditionary force to Siberia as falling within the scope of that Act and held that the invoking of disafection during wartime was not protected by the 1st Amendment. Holmes dissented.

1920. MISSOURI v. HOLLAND (252 U.S. 416), involving the constitutionality of the Migratory Bird Treaty of 3 July 1918, which sought to enforce a convention between the U.S. and Canada, held (7–2) that a treaty conferred powers upon Congress which it might not possess otherwise. Holmes for the majority asserted that treaties are made under the authority of the U.S., while acts of Congress are enacted under the authority of the Constitution. By implication, the powers of the central government are almost limitless if written into a treaty.

1921. DUPLEX PRINTING PRESS CO. v. DEERING (254 U.S. 443), the 1st Court pronouncement on the labor provisions of the Clayton Act, held that secondary boycotts were still enjoinable despite the anti-injunction provision of that Act. As a result, the Clayton Act furnished meager protection in the 1920's for labor union practices held by the courts to constitute illegal obstructions to interstate commerce and violations of the antitrust laws. In **Truax v. Corrigan** (257 U.S. 312), 1921, the Court invalidated a state statute forbidding the granting of injunctions against picketing as violating the due process and equal protection clauses of the 14th Amendment.

1923. MASSACHUSETTS v. MELLON (262 U.S. 447) involved the validity of the grants-in-aid provisions of the Sheppard-Towner Maternity Act, which the state attacked as coercion upon the states by the central government. While denying jurisdiction, the Court (Justice Sutherland) impliedly upheld the legitimacy of such grants. Since that date grants-in-aid have formed a vast complex of federal-state-municipal relationships.

1923. ADKINS v. CHILDREN'S HOSPITAL (261 U.S. 525) invalidated, as infringing upon the 5th Amendment, an Act of Congress (1918) authorizing the Wage Board for the District of Columbia to fix minimum wages for women. In dissent Holmes stated: "The criterion of constitutionality is not whether we believe the law to be for the public good."

1923. WOLFF PACKING CO. v. COURT OF INDUSTRIAL RELATIONS (262 U.S. 522) restricted the concept of public interest to the narrow monopoly definition. A mere declaration by a legislature that a business is affected with a public interest is not conclusive of the question whether its regulation is justified, declared Chief Justice Taft. Holmes' dissent in 1927 in **Tyson and Bros. v. Banton** (273 U.S. 418), where the Court invalidated a N.Y. law regulating resale theater ticket prices, attacked the doctrine of public interest and insisted that the state legislature could do whatever it saw fit unless specifically restrained by the Constitution. By 1934, in **Nebbia v. New York** (291 U.S. 502), involving a state law fixing retail milk prices, the majority (Roberts) upheld the right of the state to correct maladjustments in industries subject to regulation in the public interest, following Holmes' view that there is no closed category of business affected with a public interest.

1925–1932. GITLOW v. NEW YORK (268 U.S. 652), 1925; **WHITNEY v. CALIFORNIA** (274 U.S. 357), 1927; **STROMBERG v. CALIFORNIA** (283 U.S. 359), 1931; **NEAR v. MINNESOTA** (283 U.S. 697), 1931; **POWELL v. ALABAMA** (1ST SCOTTSBORO CASE [287 U.S. 45]), 1932—all extended the 14th Amendment to cover the 1st as well as an uncertain number of the remaining sections of the Bill of Rights. In later years some members of the court (notably Justice Black) advocated the inclusion of the entire Bill of Rights in the 14th Amendment, marking the shift of substantive due process from the economic to the civil rights area.

1935. GOLD CASES—Perry v. U.S. (294 U.S. 330), **U.S. v. Bankers Trust Co.** (294 U.S. 240), **Norman v. Baltimore & Ohio R.R. Co.** (294 U.S. 240), **Nortz v. U.S.** (294 U.S. 317)—involved the constitutionality of the Congressional Joint Resolution of 5 June 1933 which nullified the gold clause in private and public contracts. The government's power to so act in private contracts was affirmed in the **Bankers Trust, Norman,** and **Nortz** cases. In the **Perry** case Chief Justice Hughes held that government bonds were contractual obligations of the U.S. government. Hence, the Joint Resolution was unconstitutional. But since the plaintiff had suffered no more than nominal damages he could not sue in the Court of Claims. In effect, the government was upheld.

1935. SCHECHTER v. U.S. ("Sick Chicken Case" [295 U.S. 495]) unanimously invalidated the NIRA on 3 grounds (Chief Justice Hughes): (1) the excessive delegation of legislative power to the Executive, (2) the lack of constitutional authority for such legislation, and (3) the regulation of businesses wholly intrastate in character.

1935. RETIREMENT BOARD v. ALTON R.R. CO. (295 U.S. 330) invalidated (5–4) the Railroad Retirement Act as violating due process and the 5th Amendment and involving matters (pensions) outside the Federal commerce power (Justice Roberts).

1936. U.S. v. BUTLER (297 U.S. 1) invalidated (6–3) the AAA on the ground (Justice Roberts) that the processing tax in issue was not really a tax but a part of a system for regulating agricultural production and not within the purview of the welfare clause. Justice Stone in dissent attacked the trend toward judicial legislation. By the Soil Conservation and Domestic Allotment Act (1936) and the Second AAA (1938) the Court's objections were met.

1936. ASHWANDER v. TVA (297 U.S. 288) upheld the dams built under the TVA as legitimate exercise of the Fed-

eral government's power to control navigable streams and provide for adequate national defense.

1937. NEW DEAL CASES. During the struggle over President Roosevelt's court reorganization plan (p. 356) the Court upheld a series of important New Deal measures. **West Coast Hotel Co. v. Parris** (300 U.S. 379) upheld (5–4) a Wash. minimum wage law, overruling the **Adkins** precedent. The National Labor Relations Act was upheld (5–4) in **NLRB v. Jones and Laughlin Steel Corp.** (301 U.S. 1), where the majority stressed the broadest definition of the "stream of commerce" concept, and (5–4) in **NLRB v. Friedman-Harry Marks Clothing Co.** (301 U.S. 58), despite the local nature of the respondent's operations. The Social Security laws were upheld in **Steward Machine Co. v. Davis** (301 U.S. 548) and **Helvering v. Davis** (301 U.S. 619), by 5–4 in each instance. The **Steward** case upheld both the employer tax and the conditional Federal grant-in-aid. Justice Cardozo found no coercion of the states involved in such grants. The **Helvering** case upheld the old-age and benefit provisions.

1937–43. CIVIL LIBERTIES CASES. DE JONGE v. OREGON (299 U.S. 253), 1937, voided a conviction under an Ore. criminal syndicalist law by insisting that there was not a "clear and present danger" in a speech at an orderly meeting. **Herndon v. Lowry** (301 U.S. 242), 1937, reversed a Ga. conviction of a Communist organizer, with the Court squarely applying the "clear and present danger" doctrine. The **Flag Salute Cases:** The **Gobitis Case** (310 U.S. 586), 1940, sustained a state flag salute law; but this decision was reversed in **West Virginia State Board of Education v. Barnette** (319 U.S. 624), 1943, where a state law was invalidated as infringing the 1st Amendment.

PALKO v. CONNECTICUT (302 U.S. 319), 1937, held that the 14th Amendment did not include the double jeopardy provision of the 5th Amendment (a state could retry a person on criminal charges after he had been found innocent), but opened the way for the Court to investigate the scope of basic liberties which the states by the 14th Amendment were forbidden to infringe: (1) Peaceful picketing—**Thornhill v. Alabama** (310 U.S. 88), 1940. (2) Peaceable assemblage—**Hague v. C.I.O.** (207 U.S. 496), 1939. (3) The **Jehovah's Witnesses Cases** generally reaffirmed the right to disseminate religious literature without a license (**Lovell v. Griffin** [303 U.S. 444], 1938), and to solicit funds for religious ends (**Cantwell v. Connecticut** [310 U.S. 396], 1940) and without being subject to a tax (**Murdock v. Pennsylvania** [319 U.S. 105], 1943).

1938. MISSOURI EX REL. GAINES v. CANADA (305 U.S. 337) upheld the "equality" of educational opportunity for Negroes in segregated Missouri, specifically the petitioner's right to be admitted to the law school of the state university in the absence of other provision for his legal training; reaffirmed in **Sipuel v. University of Oklahoma** (332 U.S. 631), 1948.

1939. GRAVES v. NEW YORK EX REL. O'KEEFE (306 U.S. 466) put an end to intergovernmental tax immunities, which had deprived Federal and state governments of large potential sources of revenue, by holding that a state tax on Federal employees was no unconstitutional burden upon the Federal government.

1941. U.S. v. CLASSIC (313 U.S. 299) upheld the power of the Federal government to regulate a state primary where such an election was an integral part of the machinery for choosing a candidate for Federal office, reversing a previous decision that party primaries were private affairs.

1941. EDWARDS v. CALIFORNIA (314 U.S. 160) invalidated California's anti-"Okie" law designed to exclude indigent immigrants as a barrier to interstate commerce. In **Morgan v. Virginia** (328 U.S. 373), 1946, a Jim Crow law was voided as a barrier upon interstate commerce.

1941. U.S. v. DARBY (312 U.S. 100) unanimously overruled the **Hammer** case (1918) by upholding the Fair Labor Standards Act of 1938. Commerce was held a complete function, controllable by Congress to the point of prohibition.

This decision repudiated the doctrine of mutually exclusive spheres of Federal and state activities.

1943. HIRABAYASHI v. U.S. (320 U.S. 81) upheld military curfew regulations on the West Coast under the war powers, but refused to consider the issue of Japanese exclusion from that area.

1944. KOREMATSU v. U.S. (323 U.S. 214) upheld the exclusion of Japanese from the West Coast. The dissenters (Roberts, Murphy, and Jackson) termed the relocation program unconstitutional. In **Ex parte Endo** (323 U.S. 283), 1944, however, it was held that the War Relocation Authority could not detain a person whose loyalty had been established.

1944. SMITH v. ALLWRIGHT (321 U.S. 649) involved the exclusion of Negroes from voting in a primary in Texas, where Democratic party membership was restricted to whites. The Court held that in Tex. political party membership was equivalent to suffrage; hence, exclusion from the party on grounds of race violated the 15th Amendment.

1947. FRIEDMAN v. SCHWELLENBACH (330 U.S. 838). The Court here refused to review a lower court decision involving the dismissal of a Federal civil servant on disloyalty charges, and in effect upheld the President's 1947 Loyalty Order authorizing such removal.

1948. ILLINOIS EX REL. MCCOLLUM v. BOARD OF EDUCATION (333 U.S. 203) involved the "released time" plan (in this instance permitting public school students to receive religious instruction during school hours on school property but with private teachers). The Court held this particular program violated the 1st Amendment prescribing separation of Church and State, but left open the larger question of public aid to religious instruction. A N.Y. released time law was upheld (**Zorach v. Clauson**, 1952).

1948. SHELLEY v. KRAEMER (334 U.S. 1) held that a racially restrictive covenant violated the equal protection clause of the 14th Amendment.

1950. AMERICAN COMMUNICATIONS ASSN., C.I.O., ET AL. v.

DOUDS (339 U.S. 382) upheld Sec. 9h of the Taft-Hartley Act (1947), requiring a non-Communist affidavit from labor union officers under penalty of denying to the union involved certain statutory privileges. The majority denied that the oath was ex post facto, a bill of attainder, or an abridgement of the 1st Amendment. Justice Black in dissent stigmatized test oaths as "instrument[s] for inflicting penalties and disabilities on obnoxious minorities."

1951. DENNIS ET AL. v. U.S. (341 U.S. 494) upheld the Smith Act (1946) which made it a criminal offense to advocate the forceful overthrow of the government. Implicit in the majority opinion of Chief Justice Vinson was a revival of the "bad tendency" test criticized by Holmes. Dissenting, Justice Black called for a return to the "clear and present danger" doctrine and declared the Smith Act violated the 1st Amendment, and Justice Douglas differentiated between a "conspiracy to overthrow" the government and the teaching of "Marxist-Leninist doctrine."

1952. SAWYER, PETITIONER v. YOUNGSTOWN SHEET & TUBE CO., ET AL. (STEEL SEIZURE CASE) invalidated (6–3) the seizure of the steel companies by President Truman. Justice Black, for the majority, held that the President's power "must stem either from an act of Congress or from the Constitution itself." Chief Justice Vinson, for the minority, argued that there was no statute prohibiting seizure "as a method of enforcing legislative programs."

1952. UPDEGRAFF v. BOARD OF REGENTS held unconstitutional (8–0) an Okla. law requiring state employees to take an oath that they had not been, within the previous 5 yrs., members of an organization listed as subversive by the U.S. Attorney General. The court (Clark) distinguished the case from **Garner v. Bd. of Public Works** (341 U.S. 716, 1951), **Gerende v. Bd. of Supervisors** (341 U.S. 56, 1951), and **Adler v. Bd. of Education**, 342 U.S. 485 (1951) —all of which upheld loyalty oaths—on the ground that *knowledge* of the subversive nature of the organization was not involved in the Okla. statute.

1954. BROWN v. BOARD OF EDUCATION OF TOPEKA (347 U.S. 483) reversed **Plessy v. Ferguson** (1896), with its "separate but equal" doctrine. In 1950 **McLaurin v. Okla. State Regents** (339 U.S. 637) and **Sweatt v. Painter** (339 U.S. 629) had struck down state laws for the higher or professional education of Negroes as failing to meet the requirements of equality. In the Brown case, involving elementary education, the Court (Warren, Chief Justice) held unanimously that segregation in public education was a denial of the equal protection of the laws. The Court (349 U.S. 294, 1955) directed the lower courts to admit Negroes to public schools on a racially nondiscriminatory basis "with all deliberate speed." Reactions ranged from compliance in some border states to hostile gestures toward the Court. On 19 Jan. 1956, Ala. Senate passed "nullification" resolution; Va. legislature adopted (1 Feb.) an "interposition" resolution asserting the right of the state to "interpose its sovereignty" against the decision of the Court. On 11 Mar., 19 senators and 81 representatives issued a "Southern Manifesto" declaring their purpose to use "all lawful means" to reverse the desegregation decision. **Aaron v. Cooper** (358 U.S. 1, 1958) held that no scheme of racial discrimination against Negro children in school attendance can stand the test of the 14th Amendment if "there is state participation through any arrangement, management, funds or property."

1956. PENNSYLVANIA v. NELSON (350 U.S. 497) found Pa.'s antisubversive legislation, to the extent that it punished subversion against the U.S., to be unconstitutional, on the ground that Congress had pre-empted antisubversion enforcement. Since this is a field in which national interest is dominant, the Federal system must be assumed to preclude enforcement of state laws on the same subject.

1956. SLOCHOWER v. BOARD OF EDUCATION (350 U.S. 551) held that a public employee who pleaded self-incrimination was entitled to a fair hearing to determine whether, in the circumstances of his case, such a plea was a proper ground for dismissal. The exclusion of public servants from constitutional protection was held arbitrary and discriminatory.

1957. WATKINS v. U.S. (354 U.S. 178) reversed a contempt conviction of a labor union official who had testified before the House Committee on Un-American Activities about his earlier activities with respect to the Communist party, but refused to name others on the ground that such questions were not relevant to the work of the committee. The Court sustained Watkins on the ground of the lack of pertinency of the subject under inquiry and held that the resolution setting up the committee in 1938 was too vague and uncertain to give Watkins sufficient indication of the matter under inquiry.

1957. SWEEZY v. NEW HAMPSHIRE (354 U.S. 234) further limited the powers of the states to encroach upon the rights of public employees in their search for subversives. The Court divided 6–3; 4 of the majority invalidated a contempt conviction on the ground that the legislature, in its sweeping grant of discretionary authority to the Attorney General, had divested itself of all responsibility for the direction of the investigation. Two contended that the questions asked Sweezy deprived him of his constitutionally protected rights of academic freedom and political association. In 3 companion cases, **Quinn v. U.S.** (349 U.S. 155); **Emspak v. U.S.** (349 U.S. 190); **Bart v. U.S.** (349 U.S. 219), the Court dealt with the problem of recalcitrant witnesses before Congressional investigating committees, each of whom had been convicted of contempt of Congress. The Court ruled that there must be a clear disposition of the witness's objection before there can be a prosecution for contempt.

1957. YATES v. U.S. (354 U.S. 298) held that the govt. had too broadly construed its powers under the Smith Act to prosecute Communist leaders. Since the **Dennis Case** (1951), nearly 100 convictions and many more indictments had been obtained for Smith Act violations. The Court ruled that the Smith Act did not forbid advocacy and teaching of forcible overthrow as an abstract principle, divorced from any effort to incite action to that end.

1957. PEREZ v. BROWNELL (356 U.S. 44). In a review of deportation proceedings the Court held that a person born in the U.S. who voted in a Mexican election and remained outside the U.S. to avoid the draft forfeited his citizenship under the Nationality Act of 1940 under Congress' power to regulate relations with foreign countries. Chief Justice Warren, for the minority, argued that under the Constitution citizenship is an irrevocable "birthright."

1958. N.A.A.C.P. v. ALA. (357 U.S. 449). In reversing a contempt conviction by an Ala. court the Supreme Court held that the N.A.A.C.P. had a constitutional right to claim protection for its membership and to refuse to divulge its membership list.

1958. FIRST UNITARIAN CHURCH v. LOS ANGELES (357 U.S. 545) held that the denial of tax exemption for real property and buildings for religious worship, solely on the ground that the petitioners refused to subscribe to oaths stating that they did not advocate the violent overthrow of the govt. or support of foreign govts., violated the due-process clause of the 14th Amendment through procedures placing the burden of proof and persuasion on the taxpayer.

1958. UPHAUS v. WYMAN (360 U.S. 72) upheld a contempt conviction by the New Hampshire Supreme Court for refusal to produce the names of people attending appellant's summer camp on the ground that the state's interest in self-preservation as expressed in its Subversive Activities Act of 1951 outweighed individual rights in associational privacy. 3 justices joined Justice Brennan in dissenting on the ground that the New Hampshire act violated the Constitutional prohibition against states passing bills of attainder.

1959. ABBATE v. U.S. (359 U.S. 187) and **BARTKIS v. ILLINOIS** (359 U.S. 121) held that neither the constitutional prohibition against double jeopardy nor the guarantee of due process prevented the Federal and state govts. from successively prosecuting the same man for the same criminal act.

1959. BARENBLATT v. U.S. (360 U.S. 109) upheld the conviction (under 2 U.S. Code 192) of a university teaching fellow who refused to answer questions on Communist affiliation asked by the House Committee on Un-American Activities on the ground that the balance of defendant's and the govt.'s interest is struck in favor of the govt., and that the conviction does not transgress the 1st Amendment. Contrariwise, 3 justices (Justice Black) held that the committee was improperly seeking to try, convict, and punish, powers denied a legislative body.

1960. U.S. v. STATES OF LA., TEX., MISS., ALA., AND FLA. (80 Sup. Ct. Rep. 961) upheld the right of Texas to all her submerged lands within 3 leagues of the coast under the Tidelands Act, but ruled that, as regards Fla., Ala., Miss., and La., the act did not grant these states such rights beyond 3 geographic mi. from the coast. Previously, in **U.S. v. Calif.** (332 U.S. 19), 1945, the court had held, per Justice Black, that the U.S. had paramount rights to the 3-mi. belt of submerged lands off shore.

1960. HANNAH v. LARCHE (80 Sup. Ct. Rep. 1502) upheld the right of the Civil Rights Commission under the Civil Rights Act of 1957 to hold hearings in Louisiana and to adopt such procedures as do not violate rights protected by the due-process clause of the 5th Amendment.

1960. BOYNTON v. VIRGINIA (81 Sup. Ct. Rep. 182) extended **Morgan v. Va.** (1946) in holding that a bus terminal operated as an "integral" part of interstate bus service may not segregate passengers who are on a trip across state lines.

*   *

Article XXIII [proposed 16 June 1960; ratified 29 Mar. 1961]

Section 1. The district constituting the seat of government of the United States shall appoint in such manner as the Congress may direct:

A number of electors of President and Vice President equal to the whole number of Senators and Representatives in Congress to which the District would be entitled if it were a State, but in no event more than the least populous state; they shall be in addition to those appointed by the States, but they shall be considered, for the purpose of the election of President and Vice President, to be electors appointed by a State; and they shall meet in the District and perform such duties as provided by the twelfth article of amendment.

Section 2. The Congress shall have power to enforce this article by appropriate legislation.

THE AMERICAN ECONOMY

AGRICULTURE

IMPACT OF LAND TENURE. The organization of farm production was determined not alone by soil, climate, technology, and labor, but also by land tenure and land grant policies. **Free and common socage** (the tenure of the English peasant proprietors) was generally established by colonial charters. Land was held in **freehold,** which by 1607 had come to mean for an indefinite period of time. In New Netherland (later New York) and Md., where manorial systems were established, this tenure appeared in somewhat more feudalized form than in New England, but feudal services were generally limited to the reservation of a specific **quitrent** (in Pa., by 1775, 4s. for 100 acres). Owing to the opposition to quitrents on the ground that they constituted a source of private income instead of being devoted to public purposes, they were abolished (Va. and Pa., 1779; N.Y., 1786).

In New England and eastern Long Island grants of land were made to towns, generally 36 sq. mi. (a figure later adopted for the rectangular surveys of the U.S. public lands of the Northwest), and group settlement was fostered (by the 18th century the descendants of the original grantees [proprietors] were generally able to acquire ownership of the undistributed lands [against the non-commoners]). Except in R.I., N.E. land was inherited by the children equally, saving a double portion for the eldest son (held illegal by the Privy Council in *Winthrop* v. *Lechmere,* 1728; but reversed in *Phillips* v. *Savage,* 1737). N.Y., both under Dutch (patroonship of Rensselaerswyck [1630–37, 1685], 1 million acres) and English rule, fostered large grants

to proprietors and promoters, discouraging settlement. In the period, 1760–75, at least 6,000 tenant farmers dwelt in the colony, many of whom engaged in antirent demonstrations (1751–62), especially in Westchester, Dutchess, and Albany Counties (culminating in the uprising under Pendergrast, Apr.–Aug. 1766). Although N.J. followed a more democratic system of land distribution, uprisings broke out between squatters and proprietors (1745–48), finally quelled by 1755. The squatter problem was especially serious in western Pa.

In the Southern colonies large land accumulation was fostered by **headrights,** generally 50-acres per head to each person who transported an emigrant at his own expense. This system fostered land accumulation and speculation in land warrants which often raised the price of land beyond the means of servants who had worked out their time. As a result of modification of the system in 1705, after which date headrights were sold for cash, the system was in effect abolished and direct land purchases substituted.

Land accumulation in N.Y. and the South was fostered by the **entail,** a legal device to make land inalienable (Ga., 1750, enlarged all entails previously granted to absolute inheritances; Va., as a result of Jefferson's efforts, abolished entails, 1776; followed by the vast majority of states), and **primogeniture,** descent of land to the eldest son (abolished, Ga., 1777; N.C., 1784; Va., 1785; Md. and N.Y., 1786; S.C., 1791; R.I., 1798, with the New England states and Pa. abolishing the eldest son's double portion). Two instances where huge land grants were conferred without rights of government (unlike Md. and Pa.) were the holdings of Lord Fairfax of 5 million acres between the Potomac and Rappahannock Rivers, Va., and of Lord Granville, N.C. (1744); confiscated, 1777. The **confiscation of Loyalist estates** (p. 110) contributed eventually to the establishment of more moderate-sized farm holdings.

ABORIGINAL FARMING. Aside from hunting, fishing, and gathering, the Indians along the Atlantic seaboard generally engaged in hoe-type agriculture, utilizing natural clearings or clearing forest land by girdling, felling, or burning trees. Main products were maize (Indian corn), peas, and beans (cultivated in mounds—**hill culture**), squash, pumpkins, and tobacco. Fish was used as fertilizer along the Northern coast. The Indians lacked draft animals.

1607–1700. CEREAL CULTIVATION. European grains were initially unsuccessful. Because of its rapid ripening, its higher yield per acre ($c.40\%$ more), and its ease of cultivation (Indian-fashion) in stump-filled fields, **corn** quickly became the principal grain. **Wheat** was raised successfully in New Netherland by 1626, and by 1640 proved to be a close competitor to corn in the Connecticut Valley. The appearance of the wheat blast (black stem rust, 1660) served to check the introduction of the crop into older areas. **Rye**, better adapted to sandy soils, was successfully raised in eastern New England (1636), and by 1700 ranked second to corn. The Swedes and Finns on the Delaware preferred rye to wheat (from 1644), but later migrations into the area imposed a wheat culture (by 1680). **Barley** (for beer) was raised in scattered areas, and oats occasionally for feed (among the N.J. Scots for human consumption). By 1696 a **rice** crop had been successfully raised in S.C. from seed imported from Madagascar.

Livestock. Imported from Europe into Va., New Netherland, and Mass., livestock was largely uncared for (especially in the South), with wild herds of cattle, horses, and swine roaming in droves, subsisting on roots and herbs. By 1682 cattle grazing had become a major economic activity in S.C., and early expansion southward along the coast was primarily

to secure greater ranges. Since native grasses in the North (wild rye, broom straw) were not nutritious when dry, English grasses were introduced into New England by 1663 and spread to the Middle Colonies (direct importations from England to Pa., 1689).

1612–1700. EXPANSION OF TOBACCO CULTIVATION. After a short period of experimentation (1612–15), tobacco quickly became the cash crop of Va. Exports rose from 20,000 lbs. (1618) to 500,000 lbs. (1627). The crop was raised in Md. shortly after settlement. By the 1680's tobacco exports from the 2 colonies averaged 28 million lbs.

Other Crops. Va. experimented with viniculture (1612–22), silk culture (1613–22; bounties offered, 1658), hemp and flax (1611–21), indigo ($c.1622$), various exotic fruits, nuts, and spices (1609–21), as well as West Indies cotton (1607, 1611–12, 1622–23), without commercial success; although flax, hemp, and, to a lesser degree, cotton were cultivated for domestic consumption. Flax production, encouraged by Conn. (1640), was inconsequential in this period. The cultivation of fruits from England and northern Europe, better adapted to the country north of Cape Hatteras, proved successful, especially apples, while peaches did well in the warmer coastal regions (particularly Va.), where they were used to fatten hogs. European vegetables were introduced at settlement, with the largest varieties in New Netherland by 1650. However, pumpkins, squash, and native beans were still favored for human consumption. Potatoes were first introduced into Pa. in 1685.

1701–75. SOUTHERN TRENDS. The farm economy of S.C. and Ga. came to be based upon two staples, **rice** and **indigo** (especially after the successful experiments of **Eliza Lucas [Pinckney]** of St. Andrews' Parish, S.C., 1739–44, in producing indigo profitably with slave labor). Charleston rice exports mounted: 1699–1700, 1,800 bbls; 1734–35, 45,000 bbls; 1755–56, 90,000 bbls; 1772–73, 110,000 bbls. Savannah shipments: 1755–56, 2,000 bbls; 1772–73, 24,000 bbls. With the introduction of irrigation in rice cultivation ($c.1724$), the crop, originally confined to the inland river swamps, was by 1750 introduced into the tidal swamps. Indigo, especially adapted to the sandy uplands of the coastal region (by 1744), made sensational gains as a Charleston export: 1747–48, 138,334 lbs.; 1756–57, 393,531 lbs.; 1772–73, 720,591 lbs.; 1774–75, 1,122,218 lbs. (highest figure). Shipments from Savannah rose from about 5,000 lbs. (1755–56) to an annual average of 16,000 lbs. (1768–73). **Silk** production was constantly encouraged by bounties (S.C. acts of 1736 and 1755; Georgia Trustees established a nursery of mulberry trees at Savannah and 4 public filatures). Results were meager: Va., 300 lbs. of raw silk exported (1730); S.C., 651 lbs., 1742–55. High point of Georgia exports, 1766–67, 1,087 lbs.; declined, 1772–73, to 485 lbs. **Tobacco** exports rose sharply: 1709, 29 million lbs.; 1744–46, 47 million lbs. (annual average); 1771–75, 100 million lbs. Production techniques showed no substantial change from the colonial period to the Civil War. Exhaustion of the soil (after 3 yrs. fields generally turned over to other crops) required large holdings and the acquisition of newer acreage, with geographical shifts westward characteristic of tobacco farming. In some Tidewater areas grain displaced tobacco, but the substantial rise in grain exports (especially in wheat after 1742) in Md. and Va. was at least in part the result of the settlement of the Piedmont. **Livestock:** N.C. became the chief Southern meat-producing colony. Swine and cattle were driven to Va. and even as far north as Philadelphia to be fattened for slaughter (a practice introduced, c.1705, but not generally adopted in the South).

1701–75. NORTHERN TRENDS. Corn remained the chief cereal product of the North. **Wheat** cultivation shifted in New England from the eastern region and the Conn. Valley to western Mass. In the Middle Colonies the heavily fertilized (fish) lands on Long Island, the Hudson and Mohawk Valleys, and the Delaware and Susquehanna regions became the chief wheat-producing centers. **Flax** became a commercial crop, first in New England, and later in N.Y. (1740–60). The **plow** was used in grain growing, already having been introduced into corn cultivation in Conn. (before 1700), with

oxen extensively employed. **Livestock:** Yellow oxen (Danish) and a hardy breed of red milch cattle had been introduced by 1700. The Conestoga horse was raised in Pa. (by 1750) as a general work animal, and the Narragansett pacer was raised in R.I., largely for the West Indies trade. By 1749 the practice of sowing grasses on tilled land had become widespread, with timothy widely adopted in the Middle Colonies. Sheep raising was general in New England, where there was an average of 7 to 10 sheep per farm, but the Narragansett country specialized in livestock raising. Along the Delaware, in northern N.J., and around Hadley, Mass. (by 1750), stall feeding for the Philadelphia, New York, and Boston export markets had developed.

1789–1854. SCIENTIFIC AGRICULTURE. Although European scientific developments in agriculture had been called to the public's attention by **Jared Eliot** (1685–1763) with his *Essay upon Field Husbandry in New England* (1760) and by such agronomists as Jefferson and Washington, and modern techniques (rotation of crops, already practiced in eastern Pa., cultivation of legumes, use of fertilizer, and control of soil erosion) were already known, widespread adoption by American farmers proceeded slowly (rotation of crops in New England by 1800; in eastern N.Y., N.J., Va., and the older South by the 1840's). Public attention was called to the utility as fertilizers of lime, marl, gypsum, and other calcareous materials by **Edmund Ruffin** (1794–1865), Va. planter, through his *Essay on Calcareous Manures*, published in 1831, and the columns of the *Farmer's Register* (1836–42). Publication (1841) of Liebig's *Chemistry in Its Application to Agriculture and Physiology* promoted soil chemistry studies in the U.S. A further stimulus was given by **agricultural societies** (Philadelphia Society founded 1785); by **fairs**, a movement sponsored by **Elkanah Watson** (1758–1842), beginning in Pittsfield, Mass., 1807, with an exhibit of Merino sheep; and by **farm journals** (*American Farmer*, established by John P. Skinner, 1819; *Cultivator*, founded at Albany by Jesse Buel, 1834, was the first to attain national circulation). In 1839 the U.S.

Patent Office received an appropriation of $1,000 for work with agricultural statistics; budget increased to $35,000 by 1854.

1789–1860. SOUTHERN AGRICULTURE. Cotton: Sea Island or smooth-seed cotton was cultivated in S.C. as early as 1767, but the importation of Bahama strains (1786–87) caused production to expand along the Carolina coast. Exports rose from 9,840 lbs. (1789–90) to 8 million lbs. (1800–01). Short-staple or green-seed cotton was also grown in scattered areas before the Revolution. Rising British cotton imports (1784, 12 million lbs.; 1800, 56 million) combined with the loss of the British indigo market turned S.C. planters to this crop. The **invention of the cotton gin** (1793, p. 565) facilitated processing and encouraged extraordinary expansion. Out of the total national output of 100,000 bales (1801), S.C. produced half; Ga., a quarter; with the remainder largely raised in N.C. and Va. **Geographical Expansion:** Cultivation spread into the Yazoo delta region (by 1795), to La. (by 1802), and to central Tenn. (by 1796). National production rose from 171,000 bales (1810), to 731,000 bales (1830), to 2,133,000 (1850), and reached 5,387,000 bales (1859). States in order of production (1859): Miss., 1,203,000 bales; Ala., 990,000; La., 778,000; Ga., 701,000; while Tex. by 1860 already grew more cotton than S.C., as land values declined in the Southeast. The large **plantation system** developed in the rich lands along the Mississippi and in Ala., with 2% of the planters holding estates of more than 50 slaves. However, the intermediate planter and the yeoman farmer were more truly characteristic of the Southern landholding class. In 1850 only 18% of the farms and plantations of the South could be described as "plantations." Even in the Black Belt of Ala. almost 80% of the nonslaveholding landowners, who in 1850 constituted 44% of the region's farm population, owned farms ranging up to 200 acres. The small planters and yeoman farmers of the Black Belt owned 75% of the landed wealth. **Rice** production remained stable during the period and was confined largely to the coastal districts of S.C. and Ga. **Cane**

sugar production, after some experimentation (1791–95), rose from 20,000 tons (1823) to 270,000 tons (1861), of which La. produced 95%. **Tobacco** production, after reaching a new high (average of 110,000 hogsheads, 1790–92), stabilized until 1840, with exports rising on the eve of the Civil War to 160,000 hhds. Cultivation spread to Ky. (by 1783) and Tenn. (by 1789), and receipts at New Orleans rose from 24,000 hhds. (1818) to 25,500 hhds. (1831–34), and an average of 74,000 hhds. (1842–46). Va. remained the chief tobacco state (1839, 75 million lbs.; 1859, 124 million), with Ky. 2nd (1839, 53 million; 1859, 108 million). **Corn** was the only grain grown extensively in the Lower South (274,762,000 bu. out of U.S. total of 838,793,000, 1859). The border states (including Mo.) produced *c.*25% of the nation's wheat, *c.*17% of its rye, 19% of its oats. In addition to a more varied grain economy, the border states raised livestock (especially mules and horses in Ky. and Mo.) for the Southern market, and participated actively in the improvement of American breeds.

1789–1860. NORTHERN AGRICULTURE AND WESTERN COMPETITION. During the first quarter of the 19th century N.Y. and Pa. led in **wheat** production, but a westward shift was taking place even within their borders. The Genesee country supplanted the Hudson-Mohawk Valley (1810–25), but by the 30's lost ground to Ohio, which became an important wheat producer. By 1860 the top-ranking wheat states were Ill., Ind., and Wis. During 1850–60 production in the Northeast remained stabilized (around 30 million bu.), while increasing from 43,842,000 bu. to 95 million in the North Central states. **Corn** production in the North Central states, occupying a belt directly south of the wheat region, doubled from 222,209,000 bu. (1850) to 406,167,000 (1860), or about 50% of the total crop. In 1840, Ky., Tenn., and Va. were the leading corn states; in 1860, Ill., Ohio, Mo., and Ind. The North Atlantic states expanded **dairy** production, and by the end of this period produced about 70% of the nation's cheese, 50% of its butter, and continued to lead the country in the production of the lesser grains (rye, over 60%; barley, *c*.35%, buckwheat, *c*.75%) as well as Irish potatoes (*c*.58%).

Cattle Raising and Meat Packing. Hog raising in the Middle West was closely related to corn production. By 1818 a meat-packing industry had been established at **Cincinnati** (founded 1788), which was the leading center until 1860, when it was surpassed by **Chicago** (established at Fort Dearborn, 1830). In 1833 Cincinnati firms packed 85,000 hogs; in 1848, 500,000.

1820–60. INTRODUCTION OF AGRICULTURAL MACHINERY (also pp. 565, 566). The cradle was introduced in the North (*c*.1820) as a substitute for the sickle in reaping; in general use by 1840. The cast-iron plow replaced the wooden moldboard plow between 1825–40, and the steel plow (manufactured by **John Lane**, 1833, and **John Deere** [1804–86], 1837) replaced the iron plow on the prairies by 1845. The Hussey and McCormick reapers came into use in the East (*c*.1846) and the West (*c*.1848),

and replaced the cradle by 1860. Mowing (patented 1844), threshing, and haying machines, as well as seed drills and cultivators, were widely adopted in the 2 decades before the Civil War. The 1st grain elevator was constructed in Buffalo, 1842.

1841–63. RISE OF PACIFIC AND MOUNTAIN STATES AGRICULTURE. The arrival of settlers in Willamette Valley (Ore.), 1841–43, opened the Pacific coast to the American farmer, and the settlement of the Salt Lake Valley, 1846, opened the Mountain States. The California gold rush (1849–50) created a demand for food products. Cattle increased from *c*.250,000 head (1849) to over 2 million head (1860). After being obliged to import 740,000 bags of grain (1853), California became self-sufficient by 1855, even producing a surplus the next year, while garden crops and viniculture expanded rapidly. The Pike's Peak rush (1859) had a similar effect on farm conditions in the Denver region.

PER ACRE MAN-HOUR REQUIREMENTS IN WHEAT PRODUCTION
(U.S. Dept. of Agriculture, *Yearbook*, 1941)

Date	Man-Hours 20 bu. per acre	Implements
1822	50–60	Walking plow, bundle of brush for harrow, hand broadcast of seed, sickle harvesting, flail threshing
1890	8–10	Gang plow, seeder, harrow, binder, reaper, harvester, thresher, wagons, and horses
1930	3–4	3-bottom gang plow, tractor, 10-ft. tandem disk, harrow, 12-ft. combine, and trucks.

1861–70. SOUTHERN AGRICULTURAL PROBLEMS. During the Civil War, with the dislocation of foreign markets, cotton production dropped from an annual average of 4,500,000 bales (1859–61) to 1,597,000 (1862), reaching a low in 1864 of 299,000. Southern planters were further impoverished by the depreciation of Southern currency and securities, the wartime confiscatory policies of the Federal government, the instability of the labor market, and the effects of 2 drought years (1865, 1867). In 1870 cotton production was only 51% of prewar figures, cattle and swine 60%, rice

40%, sugar under 50%. While average holdings in the Cotton Belt declined from 402 to 230 acres (1870–80), the holdings of sharecroppers and tenants were included in the census, distorting the nature of the breakup. By 1869 the gang labor system, the first approach to tillage under free labor, was largely superseded by **sharecropping** (a seasonal arrangement where the landlord determines the crop and arranges the market, with division of the proceeds: one third for labor, one third for land, one third for implements, seeds, fertilizer, etc.); **tenancy**, a leasehold arrangement; and the **crop-lien** system, under which the small farmer pledges his crop to be marketed by the merchant-creditor.

1862–1916. EXPANSION OF FEDERAL ACTIVITIES. The U.S. Department of Agriculture was established 15 May 1862 to expand and continue the activities of the agricultural division of the Patent Office. Chemical, entomological, statistical, and forestry divisions were set up (by 1881), and a Bureau of Animal Husbandry, 1884. Appropriations rose from $64,000 (1862) to over $1 million (1889). The commissioner was raised to Cabinet rank (1889) and entrusted with the protection of national forests (1905), enforcement of the Pure Food and Drug Act (1906), Meat Inspection Act (1907), the inspection of dairy products for export (1908), and the Warehouse, Cotton Futures, and Grain Standards Acts (1916).

1866–1900. AGRICULTURAL EXPANSION. With the expansion of both domestic and foreign markets, the number of farms increased from around 2,660,000 to 5,377,000; total farm acreage from 493 million to 839 million (1870–1900).

Agricultural Expansion (in million acres)

	corn	wheat	oats	cotton	hay
1866–75	40	22	11	9	20
1896–1901	91	47	30	24	42

Livestock Expansion (in million head)

	cattle	milk cows	hogs	horses	mules
1870	24	8.9	25	7	1
1900	52	17	63	17	3

1870–90. GROWTH OF REGIONAL SPECIALIZATION. Rise of production (in million bu.) in west North Central States from 67 (1869) to 307 (1899) accounted for almost half of U.S. total wheat crop. Production in Pacific states rose from 19 to 72 and in Okla. and Tex. to 33 by 1899. **Wool** production (in million lbs.) rose in the Mountain States from 1 (1869) to 123 (1899). **Corn** remained the most widely distributed of the grains, but the west North Central States produced over 40% of the national crop (1899), as well as 50% of the **barley** and over 95% of the **flaxseed.** Ill. and Iowa produced over 35% of the **oats,** Pa. and N.Y. 70% of the **buckwheat,** Va. and N.C. 70% of the **peanuts,** and 4 states (Ky., N.C., Va., and Tenn.)

over 70% of the **tobacco,** with Ky. accounting for 35%. **Rice** production moved from S.C. and Ga. to La., which by 1899 produced almost 70% of the national crop. Four states (N.Y., Wis., Iowa, and Ill.) produced over 50% of the whole **milk,** with over 20% from N.Y.

1870–1900. TECHNOLOGICAL ADVANCES. Total value of farm implements and machinery increased from $271 million (1870) to $750 million (1900), or from $102 per farm to $130. Efficiency was promoted by the twine binder (1878), spring tooth harrow (after 1877), disc harrow (after 1892 in the Prairie States), gang plow (after 1880 in the Pacific states), cotton seed planters and special plows (by 1900), corn shucking and fodder shredding machine (1890), corn binder (1892), and giant combine harvester thresher (1880's in Pacific states). The centrifugal cream separator (1879) became common in all dairy regions (40,000 in use, 1900). Consumption of commercial fertilizer increased from 321,000 short tons (1870) to 2,730,000 (1900).

1870–1900. FARM DIFFICULTIES. In the face of vast expansion the wholesale price index of farm products generally declined:

FARM PRODUCTS WHOLESALE PRICE INDEX
(Warren and Pearson)

1910–14 = 100	
1866	140
1870	112
1876	89
1880	80
1882	99
1886	68
1890	71
1896	56
1900	71

Mortgages and Tenancy. Estimated average equity of farm operators in land they farmed was 62% (1880). This figure declined at an average rate of 4% each decade until 1935. In some prairie counties 90% of the farms changed hands during the 1890's; 11,000 foreclosures in Kansas (1889–93). Tenancy increased from 26% of total farms (1880) to 35% (1900), with marked rises in the cotton and wheat states.

GRANGER MOVEMENT (pp. 248, 257).

1900–14. AGRICULTURAL TRENDS.
Agriculture stabilized in this period. Farms increased from 5,737,000 to 6,480,000; wheat acreage expanded from an average of 7 million bu. to *c.*8 million; and corn expanded gradually but steadily. Notable production gains were scored in (1) cotton (from 10 million bales, 1900, to 16 million, 1914), (2) tobacco, and (3) citrus fruits; while a sharp decline occurred in the exports of beef (352 million lbs., 1898, to 194 million, 1913) and bacon (from 650 million lbs., 1898, to 194 million, 1913), largely the result of increase in world production of these products.

1914. SMITH-LEVER EXTENSION ACT, providing for a nationwide extension of the county-agent system (p. 275).

1914–18. EFFECT OF WORLD WAR I.
Wheat production rose to an average of *c.*870 million bu., although corn production was relatively stable. Beginning with 1918 grain production reached into the most arid sections of the Great Plains. Wholesale price index of farm products (Warren and Pearson; 1910–14 = 100) rose from 100 (1914) to 208 (1918) and continued to rise until 1920 (211).

1921–33. FARM DEPRESSION.
Wholesale price index of farm products dropped to 121 (1921), rising slightly to 138 (1923), but even in the prosperous years 1926–29 it never exceeded 149 (1928), and with the depression dropped to 68 (1932), lowest since 1899. Wheat hit an all-time low of 32 cts. per bu. Total farm receipts declined by 1932 to one third of the amount of 1918, while farm mortgage debt rose from $7,857 million (1920) to a high of $10,785 million (1923). Forced sales (bankruptcies, foreclosures, tax delinquencies) rose from an average of 12 per 1,000 (1921–24) to 21 per 1,000 farms (1926–30) and 54 per 1,000 (1933), and were exceptionally heavy in the Dakotas and Iowa. The estimated equity of farm operators in their farm land dropped from 62% (1880) to 39% (1935).

1924–32. FARM RELIEF.
For the Farm Loan Act (1916), see p. 276. Under the Agricultural Credits Act (24 Aug. 1924)

loans were granted dealers and cooperative groups to permit them to hold farm goods for domestic and foreign trade in an effort to prevent bankruptcies and dumping; $304 million loaned, 1924–32. For the Agricultural Marketing Act (1929), see p. 337.

1933–40. NEW DEAL FARM PROGRAM.
By the Agricultural Adjustment Act (p. 343), the Cotton Control Act (p. 348), and the Tobacco Control Act (p. 350), the Federal government sought to curtail farm production. Contributing to crop curtailment was a severe drought, even more severe than in the late 80's, in the Prairie and Plains states (1934), as a result of which one third of the nation's grain crop was lost and "Okies" abandoned their Okla. farms to seek work in California. Total acreage in 52 major crops harvested fell from an average of 358 million (1929–32) to 321 million (1933–35). After these Acts were declared unconstitutional (p. 498), the Federal government continued its curtailment program through the Soil Conservation and Domestic Allotment Act (1936, p. 354), modified by the 2nd AAA (1938, p. 358). Cash receipts for farm products rose from $4,743 million (1932) to $7,659 million (1935) and remained over $8 billion (1936–40). Wholesale price index of farm products (Bureau of Labor Statistics; 1926 = 100) rose from 48.2 (1932) to 86.4 (1936), then declined until World War II to 65.3 (1939). Farm mortgage debt declined from $8,466 million (1933) to $6,586 million (1940), and forced sales dropped from 54 per 1,000 farms (1933) to 16 per 1,000 (1940).

1940–52. WORLD WAR II AND POST-WAR EXPANSION.
The index of gross farm production (1935–39 = 100) rose from 108 (1940) to 126 (1946), with a further high to 131 (1948), as cash receipts for farm products rose from $9,132 million (1940) to $22,286 million (1945). Value of farm implements and machinery rose from $2,153 million (1935) to an all-time high of $14,208 million (1950 est.). Expenditures for fertilizer and lime in 1945 approximated $508 million, more than treble the 1934 figure. Farm prices soared in this period: No. 1 wheat, $.90 per bu. (1940) to a

high of $2.88 (1948); cotton from an average of $.096 per lb. (1936–40) to $.319 (1947) as production decreased. Beef cattle prices per 100 lbs. continued to soar in the postwar period: $7.46 (1940) to $23.20 (1950 est.), as did hog prices: $5.39 (1940) to $23.10 (1948). The farm mortgage debt was reduced from $6,586 million (1940) to $4,681 million (1946), rose to $5,413 million (1950), but the ratio of mortgage debt to total farm value declined from 41.5% (1940) to 25% (1956).

1920–54. RISE AND DECLINE OF TENANCY. Tenancy rose during the farm depression: 38.1% of farm holdings (1920) to 42.2% (1935). World War II and postwar farm prosperity brought general declines: 24% (1954). World War II and postwar farm prosperity brought general decline to 24% (1954). Regional breakdown (1954) of tenants

as percentage of total farm operators: N.E., 3; Middle Atlantic, 7; East North Central, 18.9; West North Central, 27.1; Pacific, 9.9; Mountain States, 15; South, 29.4. Number of farms, 1,000 acres and over rose from 29,000 (1880) to 131,000 (1954).

1951–60. FARM PRICES AND INCOME. Index of prices of all farm products received by farmers (1910–14= 100) declined slightly from 258 (1950) to 240 (1959), but prices paid by farmers for all commodities' used for maintenance and in production rose from 256 (1950) to 297 (1959), sharpest increases being recorded in interest payable per acre (89 to 194), taxes (320 to 496), and wages for hired farm labor (425 to 615). Net income to persons on farms derived from farming declined from $15.7 million (1950) to $13.6 million (1959).

FARM MECHANIZATION, 1931–57
(*Hist. Statistics of U.S. to 1957*)

Year	Tractors	Motor Trucks	Combines	Corn Pickers	Farms with Milking Machines
1931	997,000	920,000	—	—	—
1941	1,665,000	1,095,000	225,000	120,000	210,000
1957 (prel.)	4,600,000	2,900,000	1,020,000	725,000	720,000

COMMERCE AND THE TARIFF

MERCANTILISM. The economic controls for the regulation of commerce, industry, and labor which were introduced into the English colonies were rooted in English experience and stemmed from a body of doctrine called "mercantilism," which had as its objective the creation of a prosperous and powerful national state or self-sufficing empire. Such prosperity and power were to be secured by (1) maintaining an adequate stock of precious metals; (2) protecting home industries against foreign competition; (3) making it possible for home industries to compete successfully in foreign markets through the assurance of necessary raw materials (from the colonies) and low production costs (subsistence labor). The **Acts of Trade and Navigation** (1650–

1767) provided for the external regulation and control of foreign trade and the subordination of colonial interests to those of the mother country. The principal regulatory trade measures relating to the colonies:

1620. EARLY ATTEMPTS. Under the early Stuarts Parliament left colonial economic development to the crown. By agreement between the crown and the Virginia Co., in return for a duty of 1s. per lb. on tobacco, English tobacco growing was to be prohibited (carried out by proclamation 29 June 1620).

1650–60. LEGISLATION DURING THE INTERREGNUM. To liberate English trade from Dutch control Parliament (1) forbade foreign ships from trading in the colonies without special license (3 Oct. 1650); (2) enacted (9 Oct. 1651) that no goods from Asia, Africa, or America could be imported into England, Ireland, or the colonies except in ships of which the owner, the master, and the **major** part of the crew were English (including colonials); (3) that no European goods could be imported into England, Ireland, or the colonies except in **English** ships or ships of the **country of origin;** (4) prohibited foreign goods from being imported into England except from the place of production; (5) prohibited the importation of fish by aliens; and (6) excluded all foreign ships from the English coasting trade. These comprehensive acts depended for enforcement upon (1) informers and (2) colonial governors. Complaints arose of the hardships of enforcement owing to England's lack of shipping to replace the Dutch. The Governors of Barbados and Antigua complained of supply shortages (1652, 1656) and the former colony petitioned for repeal of the Act of 1650. The Virginia Assembly declared that freedom of trade would be maintained and all merchants protected (1655), demanding bond of all sea captains not to molest foreign shipping (Mar. 1660). Mass. (1655), R.I. (1657), and Conn. (1660) publicly announced their intention of continuing trade with the Dutch.

1660. NAVIGATION ACT OF 1660, passed by the Convention Parliament, approved by the crown, 1 Oct. 1660, and confirmed by the 1st regular Restoration Parliament (27 July 1661), (1) provided that no goods or commodities, regardless of origin, could be imported into or exported out of any English colony except in English-built or owned ships (of which the master and **three fourths** of the crew were English); (2) required that **enumerated articles** (including **sugar, tobacco,** and **indigo**) of colonial growth and manufacture be shipped only to England or her colonies, with ships sailing from the colonies required to give bond that they would unload enumerated commodities in the realm.

1662. ACT OF FRAUDS provided that only **English-built** ships were to enjoy the privileges under the Act of 1660 (except ships bought before 1662).

1663. NAVIGATION ACT OF 1663 (passed to benefit English merchants) provided that, with the exception of certain specified commodities (salt for the New England and Newfoundland fisheries, wine from Madeira and the Azores, and provisions, servants, and horses from Scotland and Ireland), European goods destined for the colonies must be shipped from England and on English-built ships. Enforcement duties were placed upon colonial Governors, who customarily delegated responsibility to a **naval officer** (in practice appointed in England).

1673. NAVIGATION ACT OF 1673 assessed duties at the **ports of clearance** upon enumerated products when shipped from one plantation to another (in order to prevent colonial shippers from evading English duties by stopping at a colonial port en route to Europe) and provided for the appointment of **customs commissioners** to collect the duties.

1696. NAVIGATION ACT OF 1696 (1) confined all colonial trade to English-built ships; (2) gave the provincial customs officers the same powers as in England, including the right of forcible entry; (3) required that bonds be posted on enumerated commodities, even where plantation duties were paid; (4) enlarged the direct responsibility of the colonial naval officer; and (5) voided colonial laws contrary to the Navigation Acts.

1699. WOOL ACT (passed to meet competition from Ireland and potential competition from the American colonies) restricted woolen manufacture in Ireland and forbade the export of wool products from any American colony either overseas or in the intercolonial trade.

1705. ENUMERATED ARTICLES (to be shipped only to English ports) expanded with the broadening of colonial economic activity: **rice** (now an established crop in Carolina) and **molasses,** mainstay of the West Indies economy; **naval stores,** not only enumerated but also given **bounties** per ton as follows: pitch and tar, £4; rosin and turpentine, £3; hemp, £6; masts, yards, and bowsprits, £1.

1709–74. FURTHER NAVAL STORES ACTS. Bounties continued for 11 yrs.

after expiration (1713) of Act of 1705; on hemp continued for another 16 yrs. (1725); but on the other naval stores were allowed to lapse (1725–29). When renewed in 1729 the rates were changed per ton: pitch, £1; turpentine, £1 10s.; masts, £1; tar, £2 4s. Under this Act the cutting of white pines was restricted to those standing on private property; of white pines 24 in. in diameter or greater was permitted only on lands granted before 7 Oct. 1692 (such a restriction had been included in the Mass. charter of 1692). Bounties on naval stores were continued to 1774, except for hemp, which was allowed to lapse in 1741 (renewed 1764). Bounty payments totaled, 1706–74, £1,438,702.

1721. BEAVER SKINS, FURS, AND COPPER ENUMERATED and the duties on beaver skins lowered. Prior to this enactment 30–40% of New York's fur exports went to Continental Europe. In 1721 copper ore shipments had been made both to England and Holland from a newly opened N.J. mine.

1730–35. Rice shipments were permitted from S.C. to Europe south of Cape Finisterre (1730), and the privilege extended to Ga. (1735).

1732. HAT ACT. As a result of pressure upon Parliament from London felt makers, already suffering from French competition and fearing the effects of an expanding hat industry in the Northern colonies, Parliament (1) prohibited the exportation of hats from one colony to another; (2) limited the pursuit of this trade in the colonies to those who had served a 7-yr. apprenticeship and (3) the number of apprentices to 2 per shop; and (4) barred the employment of Negro apprentices. Enforcement sporadic.

1733. MOLASSES ACT, passed to protect the British West Indies planters from competition of the foreign West Indies, levied an almost prohibitive duty of 9d. per gallon on rum and spirits, 6d. on molasses, and 5s. per hundredweight on sugar imported to the continental colonies from the foreign West Indies. The Act proved unenforceable.

1748–63. INDIGO BOUNTIES of 6d. per lb. granted to encourage production of a dye used in the woolen industry; lowered (1763) to 4d. Bounties paid to 1776 exceeded £185,000 (chiefly to Carolina and Ga. planters).

1750, 1757. IRON ACTS. To maintain the colonial supply of bar and pig iron for the iron and steel industry of the English Midlands but check the expansion in the colonies of the iron-finishing industry, Parliament (1) forbade the erection henceforth in the colonies of rolling and slitting mills, tilt-hammer forges, and steel furnaces; (2) allowed pig and bar iron to enter England free of duties under certain special conditions, which were removed (1757), after which date plantation iron was admitted free into England.

1764. SUGAR ACT (also p. 72) (1) forbade the importation of rum and spirits from the foreign West Indies into the continental colonies; (2) lowered the duties on molasses; (3) placed on the enumerated list hides and skins, pot and pearl ashes (a newly produced commodity), iron and lumber for Europe, and two minor products, whale fins and raw silk.

1767. ALL NONENUMERATED GOODS destined for any part of Europe north of Cape Finisterre were required to be first shipped to England. Only about 4.3% of colonial exports were affected by this Act, for by 1770 it is estimated that, from the time of first enumeration, 96% of the tobacco exported from the colonies had been reexported from England, 79% of the rice, 40% of the indigo, 58% of the beaver skins, 95% of other furs, 26% of hides and skins, 13% of pot and pearl ashes. On the other hand, colonial naval stores (except for tar, 5% of which was reexported) and pig and bar iron were almost entirely utilized in English industry (L. A. Harper).

PATTERNS OF COLONIAL TRADE. Handicaps to Overseas Trade. In addition to (1) the **Acts of Trade,** which, while encouraging shipping, shipbuilding, and naval stores, were especially detrimental to the tobacco trade and to a lesser degree to certain branches of manufacturing, other obstacles existed, including (2) **piracy** (robbery committed upon ships of friendly nations). Under Act of 28 Hen. VIII, c. 8 (1536), providing that pirates be tried in England before a commission specially named, the accused were sent from the colonies to England for trial. Most notable instance was the trial of Capt. **William Kidd** (*c*.1645–1701) for murder and piracy in Old Bailey (hanged 23 May 1701). By 11 Wm. III, c. 7 (1699), pirates could be tried by commission in any colony. Under this Act **Stede Bonnet** (S.C., 1718) was tried, convicted, and hanged. By proclamation, 1717, pirates who surrendered were pardoned (including a large contingent on Providence Island, Bahamas). **Robert Teach** ("Blackbeard") was killed in an attack by a Virginia expedition (1718). Thereafter a major hazard was (3) **privateering** (authorized attacks and seizures of enemy ships in wartime). (4) **Lack of Money and Credit Facilities**: Since the exportation of coin from Great Britain was forbidden, the colonists in the early period were dependent upon **wampum** (Indian shell bead money); **barter; commodity money** or "country pay" (notably tobacco crop notes [warehouse receipts] in Md. and Va. and rice crop notes in S.C.); **local coinage**, confined to the Mass. "pine-tree shillings" coined between 1652–84; **foreign coins**, which were consistently overvalued to attract importation (despite Royal Proclamation, 1704, limiting such overvaluation to 33⅓%, and the Parliamentary Act of 1704 providing a prison term and fine for violations); **bills of exchange** (especially those secured in trade with the British West Indies); and **paper money** (begun by Mass., 1690). In the early stages paper money was lawful only in **public** payments; after 1720 it was used as legal tender in **all** payments. Inflation arose, primarily in New England, 1730–50, as a result of the failure to support such issues by adequate taxes. In Mass., 1740, a **land bank** was organized to issue £150,000 in bills secured by mortgages at 3% interest. In opposition the Boston merchants organized the Silver Bank, which issued notes based on silver. The operations of the land bank were declared illegal and void by Act of Parliament, 1741, which extended the Bubble Act, 1720, outlawing joint-stock companies operating without special authority of Parliament. By Act of 1751 Parliament prohibited the New England colonies from erecting new land banks and from making bills of credit legal tender except in times of war or other emergency, and by Act of 1764 (p. 73) forbade the further issuance of paper money throughout the colonies.

1621–1700. NORTHERN OVERSEAS TRADE. The "Triangular Trade" was in fact a series of geometrical patterns which were largely the result of the necessity of the Northern colonies (in the absence of English demand for their products) to raise enough money to pay England for imported manufactured goods (textiles and hardware). Among the "triangles": (1) New England (fish and lumber) or Middle Colonies (flour) to the English (or foreign) West Indies, in exchange for sugar, molasses, or rum, with a final haul to London or Bristol, returning with English goods; (2) New England to the West Indies for rum, shipped to West Africa for slaves, with numerous variations in these 2 patterns.

1607–1700. SOUTHERN OVERSEAS TRADE. Tobacco shipments from Va. after 1616 increased rapidly: 1619, 20,000 lbs.; 1627, 500,000 lbs. With the spread of cultivation to Md. and N.C., exports rose: 1663, 7,367,140 lbs.; 1669, 9,026,046 lbs.; and in the 1680's averaged 28 million lbs. Trade of the Carolinas (forest products and hides) was still at a low level and in the hands of outsiders (chiefly New Englanders).

1607–1775. INTERNAL AND INTERCOLONIAL COMMERCE. Aside from furs, the only frontier product that could bear the cost of overland haulage was **potash**, exchanged with the Middle Colonies for grain, primarily wheat (after 1720). Other New England ports depended on Boston for their European products, as did many Southern regions, notably N.C. Tonnage clearing Boston for the coastal trade (1714–17, 11,589) roughly equaled that clearing for Great Britain. As late as 1769 Boston still led in the coastal trade, with New York and Philadelphia close rivals for 2nd place. In that year tonnage of vessels engaged in the coastal trade entering and clearing at colonial ports amounted to 213,000 tons as against 189,000 to and from Great Britain and Ireland, and 191,000 to and from the British and foreign West Indies.

1701–74. EXPANSION OF THE COLONIAL OVERSEAS TRADE.

TRADE WITH GREAT BRITAIN

(Annual averages in thousands of £ sterling; D. Macpherson, *Annals of Commerce*)

Colony	Exports to England		
	1701–10	1731–40	1761–70
New England	37	64	113
New York	10	16	62
Pennsylvania	12	12	35
Md.-Va.	205	394	468
Carolinas	14	177	330
Georgia	—	—	36

Colony	Imports from England		
	1701–10	1731–40	1761–70
New England	86	197	358
New York	28	92	349
Pennsylvania	9	52	295
Md.-Va.	128	207	491
Carolinas	22	94	262
Georgia	—	3	40

Chief export to Britain was **tobacco** (*c.*£900,000 out of a total of £1,750,000 in 1770). Other principal exports in 1770 were **rice** (£170,000), indigo (£130,-000), whale products, naval stores, pot and pearl ashes, furs and skins, and iron. In the years 1700–20 Va. and Md. accounted for about 75% of exports; 1760–70, 50%, with the proportion of the Carolinas and Ga. (rice, indigo, and naval stores) growing from less than 10% to over 35% in the same periods. The proportion of the export trade of the Northern colonies increased, 1770–75, as a result of heavier grain shipments. Philadelphia's wheat shipments increased from 52,000 bu. (1771) to 182,000 (1773), while all grain shipments from New York rose from 110,000 bu. (1766) to 350,000 bu. (1774).

Trade with the West Indies. In 1769 the Northern colonies provided the bulk of the exports (New England, *c.*40%; Middle Colonies over 30%). The importance of the foreign West Indies is indicated by the following figures for imports of gallons of **molasses** (Harper):

	From Foreign West Indies	From British West Indies
1768–70	9,625,426	853,229

The relative importance to Great Britain of the West Indies trade as compared with that of the continental colonies is evidenced by the fact that the annual average combined British imports and exports to the former, 1761–70, amounted to £3,406,000; to the continental colonies, £2,843,000. By 1772 Philadelphia was first in the overseas trade (in tonnage cleared), with Boston, New York, and Charleston rivals for second place.

1700–73. UNFAVORABLE BALANCE OF TRADE of the continental colonies

with Great Britain is revealed by statistics of imports and exports showing excess of imports from England over exports rising from £50,680 (1700) to £754,000 (ann. av., 1761–70). While the sterling gap was greatest in the Northern colonies, all thirteen except the Carolinas had an unfavorable balance, 1761–70. For the period, 1700–73, the unfavorable trade balance amounted to £20,195,568.

1775–89. COMMERCE DURING THE REVOLUTION AND IN THE CONFEDERATION. During the war trade

between Great Britain and the U.S., restricted generally to the area held by British troops, shrank to less than 5% of its former level. As a result of large-scale "dumping" of manufactured goods, imports from Britain, 1783–89, averaged only 10% less than the prewar level, while exports, on the other hand, amounted to only 50% of the prewar figure. The export industries lost their preferential treatment in the British market, and restrictions on trade with the West Indies (1783–1828) deprived the Northern states of a major outlet for their goods, only in part compensated for by direct shipments to the Continent of Europe; by the opening of the China trade (*Empress of China* entered New York from Canton, 1785); and by the beginning of trade between New England and the Pacific Northwest for fur products (then traded in China for Oriental goods), opened as a result of the voyage of Captain **Robert Gray** (1755–1806) to Oregon and China (1787–90).

1789–1815. FOREIGN TRADE. After averaging $20 million annually (1790–92), U.S. exports rose sharply, reaching $94 million (1801), and, after a temporary setback (1802–04), made a new high of $108 million (1807). Imports rose from $23 million (1790) to $110 million (1801) and, after suffering contraction along with exports, reached a new high of $138.5 million (1807). The rise, in large measure the result of the position of the U.S. as a major neutral shipping nation, represented in appreciable degree reexports ($6.5 million, 1794; $47 million, 1801; $60 million, 1806). The British Continental blockade, Napoleon's retaliatory acts, and the Embargo (1807) negated this advantage. Exports shrank to $22 million (1808), rising gradually until the War of 1812 (averaging $60 million annually, 1809–11). During the war exports sank to an all-time low of $7 million (1814) and imports to $13 million. Cotton exports, increasing throughout the period ($5 million, 1802; $15 million, 1810), surpassed tobacco as early as 1803. Lumber and potash replaced fur and naval stores as major forest products exported.

1789–1830. INTERNAL COMMERCE. The rapidly increasing population of the Ohio and Mississippi Valleys (150,000, 1790; 1 million, 1810) utilized the interior river systems for shipment of commodities to **New Orleans,** especially after 1803. Receipts at the Gulf port rose from $5 million (1807) to $10 million (1816) and $22 million (1830). **Cincinnati** (population 10,000, 1818) became a principal shipping point for provisions (grain and hogs) and **Louisville** for tobacco. The introduction of the steamboat on Western waters (*Enterprise,* 1815, also p. 443) proved a great boon to this trade, and by 1825 half the river traffic was carried on steamboats. The Great Lakes region, slower in development, tended to ship to Montreal. Land haulage from the West continued ($18 million from Pittsburgh to Philadelphia, 1820).

1815–60. FOREIGN COMMERCE. Imports rose after the War of 1812 to an annual average of nearly $100 million (1815–20), declined to $72 million (1821–30), rising again in the following decades to $284 million (1851–60), with the greatest advances after 1850. Despite the growth of the domestic textile industry, **woolen and cotton manufactures** were the leading imports, amounting to 20% of the total, 1860, as against 29%, 1821, but rising in value from $12.7 million (1821) to $69.2 (1860). **Sugar** was the principal commodity imported, rising from 5% of the total imports (1821) to 9% (1860), with **coffee** in second place (6%, both years). **Exports** averaged $70 million (1815–20), remained steady during the next decade, but rose gradually to an average of $249 million (1851–60). **Cotton** remained the No. 1 export, rising in value from $321 million (1836–40) and 43% of exports to $744.6 million and 54% of total, 1856–60. Domestic manufactures amounted to 12% of total exports, 1856–60, wheat and flour 11%, while tobacco declined from 15% (1816–20) to 6% (1856–60). Beef and pork products rose from 2% of the total, 1812–20, to 6% (1856–60). **New York** and **New Orleans** shared 1st position among export ports, but 70% of imports entered New York. The bulk of exports went to the European market, with the West Indies declining in importance.

1831–60. DOMESTIC COMMERCE. The completion of the Erie Canal (p. 444) promoted the eastward flow of commerce. Ohio (by 1830), Ind. (by 1835), Mich. (by 1836), Ill. (by 1838), and Wis. (by 1841) shipped grain to the Erie Canal, and, later, to the Lakes termini of the railroads. Pork, lumber, copper (after 1845), and iron (after 1855) moved eastward. Chicago, drawing from more westerly farmlands (from 1849), became the chief grain-shipping center (20 million bu. by 1858), and its meat trade surpassed Cincinnati (by 1863). Cincinnati's trade, still oriented toward the South as late as 1850, switched to the East (by 1860). Mississippi traffic continued to grow, with receipts at New Orleans rising from $50 million (1840) to $185 million (1860). Cotton was the chief commodity handled, with livestock and provisions for the cotton and sugar plantations major items of river traffic.

1789–1860. MERCHANT MARINE. U.S.-owned tonnage entering U.S. ports increased from 127,000 (1789) to 1,116,-

000 (1807), but declined sharply during the War of 1812 to 60,000 (1814). Thereafter U.S. tonnage entering showed a steady growth (784,000, 1819; 1,577,-000, 1840; 5,921,000, 1860), but its proportion of the total tonnage of all vessels cleared in foreign trade declined from 90% (1821) to 71% (1860), reflecting rising U.S. shipbuilding costs and U.S. cost disadvantage in building **iron** ships. **Transatlantic packet lines** were inaugurated by New York merchants, 1818. By 1845, 52 transatlantic packets were sailing regularly from New York (three sailings weekly). Average time (Liverpool-New York), 1818–22, 39 days; 1848–52, 33.3 days (reflecting improved efficiency of ship design). **Clipper ships**, especially 1843–60, set numerous speed records: Boston to San Francisco, 89 days, 8 hrs. (*Flying Cloud*, 1854). **Steamboats** in transatlantic trade were used from 1838, but were not competitive with the packets until 1848. In 1840 a Canadian, Samuel Cunard, with the aid of a British government mail subsidy, established a steamboat line, Liverpool to Boston; challenged by Collins Line (U.S.) in 1850–57. Speed increased to 13 knots by 1860, but by that date steam navigation was largely in European hands. Factors leading to the decline of U.S. shipping: (1) reluctance of Americans to shift from sails to steam; (2) Federal subsidies for mail carrying, inaugurated 1845, were less liberal than the British and were discontinued by Congress in 1858; revived 1862; (3) U.S. shops were unable to produce large iron frames and large steam engines.

1861–65. FOREIGN AND DOMESTIC COMMERCE DURING THE CIVIL WAR. Value of exports declined from $400 million (1860) to an average of $248 million (1861–65), reflecting decline of cotton exports. Imports showed a much smaller decline, from $362 million (1860) to an average of $275 million (1861–65). Net tonnage of American vessels entering U.S. ports declined from 5,024,000 (1861) to 2,944,000 (1865), while foreign tonnage increased from 2,218,000 (1861) to 3,217,000 (1865). The tonnage moved through the Erie Canal increased one-fourth over 1856–60 as East-West trade expanded.

1866–1900. EXPANSION OF FOREIGN TRADE. Value of exports more than trebled from $434 million (1866) to $1,499 million (1900), while imports more than doubled (from $445 million, 1866, to $929 million, 1900). **Chief Exports:** Crude materials and foodstuffs declined from 70% (1860) to 40% (1900); **baled cotton** remained No. 1 export item ($192 million, 1860; $243 million, 1900), but its proportion declined from c.60% to c.17%. Meat exports rose to $176 million (1900) and exports of grain and grain products rose to $159 (1900). Both petroleum products and machinery ($84 million and $78 million respectively in 1900) became major exports during the period. Europe bought 80% of U.S. exports (1860) as against 76.7% (1901–05), while imports from Europe declined from 61.3% to 52.6% in the same period, during which exports to South America rose from 9.9% to 13.2% and to Asia from 8.3% to 14.6%.

1866–1900. INTERNAL TRADE. Industrial and agricultural growth and specialization of era were accompanied by a great expansion of internal trade. The railway network expanded from 36,801 mi. (1866) to 193,346 mi. (1900). Railroad freight rose from c.39 billion ton-miles (1861) to c.142 billion (1900). Tonnage of vessels engaged in coastwise and internal trade increased from c.2,720,000 (1866) to c.4,286,000 (1900), Great Lakes tonnage alone from 408,000 (1870) to 1,446,000 (1900), including, in addition to grain shipments, the now expanded output of Lake Superior copper and iron mines.

1866–1950. U.S. MERCHANT MARINE. In 1860 American ships carried two thirds of U.S. ocean-bound commerce, but this figure declined to 10% in 1914. Decline was due to unfavorable cost differentials in ship construction, repair, and operation, and the American policy of limiting registration of the national merchant marine to American-built ships. Expansion of the merchant marine during World War I was the result of (1) the activity of the U.S. Shipping Board (est. by Act of Congress, Sept. 1916); (2) seizure by the U.S. of German vessels (600,000 tons) upon

U.S. entry into the war; (3) chartering by Congress of the Emergency Fleet Corporation to build, own, and operate a merchant fleet for the U.S. government. Some 700 vessels (300 of them wooden) were completed by the armistice. Subsequently the Shipping Board disposed of c.1,100 vessels to U.S. citizens (for Merchant Marine Act [1920], see p. 330). In view of the decline of U.S. shipping from 18 million tons (1923) to 16 million (1928), Congress passed the **Jones-White Act** (1928, p. 336), providing for loans to private shipowners for new shipbuilding and for subsidies for mail carrying. The Act failed to stimulate substantial ship construction, but $176 million in mail subsidies were paid out by 1937. The **Merchant Marine Act** (1936, also p. 354) continued low-interest construction loans and inaugurated a policy of encouraging a merchant marine for national defense. The program expanded with the outbreak of World War II. U.S. tonnage entered rose to a record high (61,465,000) in 1945, but subsequently declined to 35,376,000 (1950). **Speed record** for the **transatlantic** crossing by a commercial vessel was set 7 July 1952 by S. S. *United States,* which in her maiden voyage crossed from Ambrose Light, N.Y., to Bishop's Rock, Eng., 3 days, 10 hrs., 40 mins., beating the previous record of the *Queen Mary* by 10 hrs., 2 mins. (Aug. 1938); westward crossing record beaten by *United States,* (14 July) by 9 hrs., 36 mins.

1901–60. INTERNAL TRADE. Railroad mileage (first-line track) continued to expand until 1929 (260,570 mi.); declined gradually (231,494, 1958). Ton-miles of freight carried fluctuated as follows (in billions): 1920, 414; 1929, 450; 1931–35, 270 (annual average); 1936–40, 341; 1941–45, 655; 1957, 626. Percentage of total freight traffic hauled by railroads declined from 62.34 (1939) to 46.31 (1957), during which period motor vehicular freight percentage rose from 9.72 to 19.29, oil pipelines from 10.23 to 17.21, and airplanes from .002 to 0.044. Rail passenger revenue dropped from wartime peak of $915 million (1944) to $412 million (1957). In same period domestic airline revenues rose from $160 million to $1,515 million. Ton-miles of freight flown by aircraft in domestic commerce (thousands): 1934, 597; 1940, 3,476; 1945, 22,197; 1957, 266,483; in foreign commerce (thousands): 1945, 8,717; 1950, 60,551; 1957, 123,335.

1901–60. FOREIGN TRADE

FOREIGN TRADE, 1901–18		
	Value of Exports (millions)	Value of Imports (millions)
1901	$1,600	$ 926
1914	2,532	1,991
1918	6,433	3,165

Europe was principal U.S. export market, 1911–20—63%; Canada and Latin America supplied 41% and Asia 22% of U.S. imports.

U.S. DIRECT FOREIGN INVESTMENTS, 1897–1958 ($ million)					
1897	1914	1919	1929	1935	1958
634.5	2,652.3	3,879.5	7,553.3	7,219.2	27,075 (prel.)

INTERNATIONAL INVESTMENT POSITION OF THE U.S., 1939–58 (Net debtor (—) or creditor (+) position, in $ million)			
1939	1946	1949	1958
—340	+4,166	+15,019	+24,339

Excess of U.S. exports over imports (especially since 1939) created a **dollar gap,** remediable only by large-scale loans or gifts. For Lend-Lease, see pp. 367, 390; Marshall Plan, p. 390; Foreign Aid Programs, p. 390.

1958–60. BALANCE OF PAYMENTS AND GOLD DRAIN. As a result of a sharp decline in exports, 1958–59, higher spending abroad by U.S. tourists, increased U.S. private investment abroad, foreign economic aid, and U.S. military expenditures overseas, the U.S. lost over $4 billion in gold in 1958–60, with gold stock dropping below $18 billion by Dec. 1960. To stem the deficit in balance of payments President Eisenhower ordered (16 Nov. 1960) substantial reduction in total number of dependents of military personnel abroad, to go into effect 1 Jan. 1961, as well as cuts in staffs of civilian agencies abroad and purchases of foreign goods.

1959. Ranking Exports: Finished manufactures, 60.33%; grains and preparations the major foodstuff, $1,414.2 million; followed by fats, oil, and oil seeds, $717.1 million; cotton, unmanufactured, $452.1 million (as against $1,024 million, 1950); tobacco and manufactures, $440.6 million. **Ranking imports** (millions): petroleum and products, $1,528.6; nonferrous metals and ferroalloys, $1,311.5; coffee, $1,093 (ranked 1st in 1950); paper and paper products, $1,089.4.

1862–1960. CHANGING RETAIL PATTERNS. (1) **A one-price policy,** following a practice instituted by New York merchants in the 1840's, was adhered to by R. H. Macy from its founding in New York, 1858. (2) The **department store** was developed by **Alexander Turney Stewart** (1807–76) in New York (1862), and in succeeding years by **John Wanamaker** (1838–1922) in Philadelphia (1876) and in New York (1896), and by **Marshall Field** (1834–1906) in Chicago (1865–81). (3) **Mail order houses:** Montgomery Ward & Co., opened in Chicago, 1872, to sell to the Grangers, and Sears Roebuck (1895) revolutionized rural retailing. (4) **Chain stores:** Great Atlantic & Pacific Tea Co. (1859); **Frank Winfield Woolworth** (1852–1919), who opened his first "5-and-10-cent" store in Utica, N.Y., 1879; United Cigar Stores (1892). Chain store percentage of total retail sales: 21.5 (1929), 27 (1933), 20.7 (1950). (5) **Advertising:** Participation of nationally advertised brands began with patent medicines on eve of the Civil War, but business consolidations in the postwar period promoted large-scale advertising which was greatly expanded after World War I. Brand names came to dominate many branches of retailing. Index of national advertising expenditures (1947–49=100): 41 (1940), 230 (1959 prel.); by media: magazines, 40 (1940), 180 (1959 prel.); network radio, 96 (1950), 25 (1959 prel.); network TV, 49 (1950),

487 (1959 prel.); newspapers, 41 (1940), 206 (1959 prel.); outdoor, 39 (1940), 121 (1959 prel.). (6) **Discount houses,** (7) **Supermarkets,** (8) **Suburban shopping centers,** and (9) the expanded use of **trading stamps** were the chief retailing trends of the 1950's. Total retail sales continued to soar in this period: 1951, $156,548 million; 1959, $215,413 million.

THE TARIFF

1789–1816. EARLY TARIFFS. Tariff of 1789 (4 July), designed chiefly for revenue, with moderately protectionist features, provided for (1) specific duties on 30 commodities including molasses, hemp, steel, and nails; (2) ad valorem rates (from 7½% to 15%, averaging 8½%) on listed articles; (3) 5% duty on all other goods (increased, 1792, to 7½%). A 10% reduction in duties was permitted on articles imported in U.S.-built or owned shipping. Ad valorem duties rose to c.12½% (by 1812) and later (during War of 1812) to c.25%. **Tonnage Act** (20 July 1789) taxed U.S.-built and owned vessels 6 cents per ton; U.S.-built but foreign-owned shipping, 30 cts.; foreign-built and owned shipping, 50 cts.

1816–28. RISE OF PROTECTION. Tariff of 1816 (27 Apr.) placed a duty of 25% on most woolen, cotton, and iron manufactures (reduced, 1819, to 20%). Cheap cottons were virtually excluded by setting a minimum valuation on cotton cloth of 25 cts. a sq. yd. Ad valorem rate of 30% on certain goods including paper, leather, and hats; 15% on all other commodities. Chief opposition came from New England shipping interests. **Tariff of 1818** (20 Apr.) increased rates on iron manufactures; 25% duty on cotton and woolens was extended to 1826 instead of being reduced to 20% in 1819, as provided in Act of 1816. **Tariff of 1824** (22 May) increased protection for iron, lead, glass, hemp, and cotton bagging. The 25% minimum duty on cotton and woolens was increased to 33⅓%, but rates for raw wool advanced 15%. New England commercial and shipping interests joined with the South in opposition. In the **"Tariff**

ot Abominations" (19 May 1828) protection reached its highest point before the Civil War. An ad valorem duty of 50% as well as a specific duty of 4 cts. per lb. were imposed on raw wool; 45% ad valorem on most woolens; duties on pig and bar iron and hemp sharply increased.

1832–60. LOWERING OF DUTIES. The **Tariff of 1832** (14 July) eliminated the features of the Tariff of 1828 objectionable to the manufacturers and commercial East; increased the duty on woolens, but admitted cheap raw wool and flax free. Hence, it was viewed in the South as a sectional measure. The **Compromise Tariff** (2 Mar. 1833) expanded the free list (including worsted goods and linens), and provided for a gradual reduction of all duties above 20% by removing, at 2-yr. intervals (from 1834 to 1842), one tenth from each impost in excess of that level. Chief opposition came from New England and the Middle States. The **Tariff of 1842** (30 Mar.), a Whig measure, returned the tariff to the level of 1832 with duties averaging (1842–45) between 23% and 35%. The **Walker Tariff** (30 July 1846), a Democratic measure, essentially for revenue, reversed the trend (since 1816) of substituting specific for ad valorem duties and dropped the minimum valuation principle. A few commodities were duty free. The **Tariff of 1857** (3 Mar.), another Democratic measure, reduced the tariff to a general level of 20%, the lowest rate since 1850, and enlarged the free list.

1861–97. TRIUMPH OF PROTECTION. The **Morrill Tariff** (2 Mar. 1861) once more substituted specific for ad valorem duties and raised duties generally (from 5% to 10%). Subsequent revisions (16 July 1862, 30 June 1864, 2 Mar. 1867, 24 Feb. 1869) increased duties to an average rate of 47%. The **Tariff of 1870** (14 July) reversed the trend, placing 130 articles, mostly raw materials, on the free list and provided for some small reductions in rates on other commodities. The **Tariff of 1872** (6 June) continued this trend, reducing by 10% the rates on all manufactured goods. Most of these reductions, however, were restored by the Act of 1875 (3 Mar.). The **Tariff of 1883** (3 Mar.), lowered schedules 5% but retained the protectionist principle. The **McKinley Tariff** (1 Oct. 1890) raised the average level to 49.5% and provided for reciprocal raising of duties to meet discrimination by foreign nations. Its successor, the **Wilson-Gorman Tariff** (28 Aug. 1894), which became law without President Cleveland's signature, put wool, copper, and lumber on the free list and lowered duties to the average level of 39.9%. The **Dingley Tariff** (7 July 1897) raised rates to a new high (average level 57%), imposed high duties on raw and manufactured wool, and restored hides to the dutiable list.

1909–21. PERIOD OF MODERATION. The **Payne-Aldrich Tariff** (9 Apr. 1909) lowered duties to *c*.38%. Its successor, the **Underwood Tariff** (3 Oct. 1913) lowered duties yet further to *c*.30% and put iron, steel, raw wool, and sugar (the latter in 1916) on the free list.

1921–34. RETURN TO PROTECTION. The **Emergency Tariff** (27 May 1921) reversed the downward trend of the Wilson administration by raising rates on most agricultural products. Its successor, the **Fordney-McCumber Tariff** (21 Sept. 1922) exceeded the rates of 1909 up to 25% on manufactured goods, with high duties imposed on farm products. The **Smoot-Hawley Tariff** (17 June 1931) raised rates upon agricultural raw materials from 38% to 49% and on other commodities from 31% to 34%, with special protection given to sugar and textile interests. Under the Fordney-McCumber Act the President was authorized to change individual tariff rates on recommendation of the **Tariff Commission** (est. 1916), but such changes were limited to 50% of the Congressional rates.

1934–60. RECENT TARIFF DEVELOPMENTS. The **Trade Agreements Act** (12 June 1934) authorized the President to enter into agreements with other governments for the reduction of specific duties by as much as 50%. Such agreements (1) did not require Congressional ratification; (2) were to be based on the unconditional most-favored-nation principle. By 1951 agreements had been concluded with 53 nations with which the U.S. did more than 80% of its normal foreign trade. The Act was extended for 3-yr. periods down to 1951 and by Act of 16 June 1951 for a 2-yr. period, with certain restrictions imposed on the President's power to make concessions and the requirement that "escape clauses" be included in all agreements. On 1 Aug. President Truman proclaimed cancellation of tariff concessions to countries under Soviet control. Three major international tariff conferences were held after World War II: (1) **Geneva**, where, 30 Oct. 1947, a general agreement on tariff and trade was concluded by 28 nations, with some two thirds of the trade items between the participating countries covered by concessions; (2) **Annecy**, France, 1949, where additional nations entered the Geneva Agreement and the U.S. granted concessions on about 400 items; (3) **Torquay**, England (Sept. 1950–Apr. 1951), where the U.S. received concessions on an estimated half billion dollars of 1949 exports. The ef-

fect of the Trade Agreements program had been to reduce U.S. tariffs from an average of 53%, 1930–33, to less than 15% by 1951.

Modifications of the New and Fair Deal tariff policy were introduced during the Eisenhower administration. On 21 June 1955 the Trade Agreements Act was extended for 3 yrs., with authority granted to the President to reduce tariffs 5% a yr. in return for foreign concessions, and on duties in excess of 50% ad valorem. On 20 Aug. 1958 the Act extended the President's authority for 4 yrs., but also authorized increasing rates 50% above rates in effect on 1 July 1934 (instead of previously specified date of 1 Jan. 1945). Quotas on the importation of oil from abroad, set in 1957, were lowered (27 Mar.) 14.8%, and quota restrictions were proclaimed (22 Sept.) on imports of lead and zinc to 80% of average for preceding 5 yrs. Japan was encouraged to continue to extend its practice of establishing quotas on its shipment of certain items to the U.S.

INDUSTRY

CAPITAL INVESTMENT to 1789. Both European and colonial sources furnished capital for industry. English capital financed the colonial fisheries, control of which soon passed into the hands of settlers; as well as a large part of the New England shipbuilding industry, the Lynn Iron Works (1643–44), the Principio Co. in Md. (1715), and the projects in N.J. and N.Y. of Peter Hasenclever, Prussian-trained ironmaster (*c.*1764). Government subsidies in various forms also aided industry. Colonial capitalists (with considerable fortunes acquired between 1750–83) generally preferred more conservative investments —real estate or British government securities—to industrial risks. Notable exceptions at the end of this period were **Robert Morris** (p. 756) and **William Duer** (1747–99).

FOREST INDUSTRIES to 1775. (1) **Lumbering** (white pine abundant in New

England) prospered despite royal conservation measures (p. 512). British navy sought a source of forest products to lessen dependence upon Baltic countries. (2) **Shipbuilding** (fostered by Navigation Act of 1660, p. 511): By 1760 one third of the total British tonnage (398,-000) was colonial-built; 1765–75, 25,000 tons built yearly in the colonies. Except during period of New England inflation (1730–50), ships were constructed in the colonies 20%–50% below European costs. (3) **Naval stores:** Tar, pitch, turpentine, and potash favored by British bounties (p. 511). Exports rose (1770) to 82,000 bbls. of tar, 9,000 pitch, 17,000 turpentine (value £175,000).

MARITIME INDUSTRIES to 1775. Fishing. From the presettlement period down to the present day, codfishing from New England to Labrador has been steadily pursued. There were three grades: (1) best—traded down the coast for flour and tobacco; (2) medium—sent to Southern Europe (Catholic) in exchange for salt and wine; (3) "refuse"—shipped to sugar isles to feed the slaves (H. A. Inniss). **Whaling** flourished to supply demand for spermaceti (for important candlemaking industry begun in R.I., *c*.1750, with attempted intercolonial monopoly and price-fixing agreements, 1761–75), sperm oil, whalebone, and ambergris (for drugs, confectionery, and perfumery). By 1774 a fleet of 360 ships collected 45,000 bbls. of sperm oil, 75,000 lbs. of whalebone.

TECHNOLOGY AND ORGANIZATION to 1789. (1) **Workshop crafts** made custom-made goods, with the leather and hat industries (beaver felt hats despite restrictions under the Hat Act [p. 512]) outstanding examples, and with high standards obtaining among silversmiths (e.g., Jeremiah Dummer of Boston, Simeon Soumaine and Myer Myers of New York), cabinetmakers (Joshua Delaplaine of New York, William Savery, Philadelphia), and clockmakers (the Claggetts and Willards of New England). (2) **Domestic or putting-out system**, notably in weaving (chiefly homespuns), encouraged by the Nonimportation Agreements (pp. 73–84) and shoemaking (organized in Lynn, Mass., for wholesale operations by 1760). (3) **Mills and factories:** Flourmilling, especially in the vicinity of New York and Philadelphia, produced for export. Oliver Evans' mill elevator (p. 565), with its conveyor belt and labor-saving, cost-cutting features, was introduced shortly after 1783 by Ellicott brothers on the Patapsco River. Notable strides took place in **iron manufacture** despite restrictions of Iron Act of 1750 (p. 512), with **Henry William Stiegel** (1729–85) outstanding (after 1760) as an ironmaster and glassware maker (after 1764). In 1700 the colonies produced one seventieth of the world's iron supply; in 1775, **one seventh,** with pig and bar iron production exceeding England and Wales combined. Bar iron exports, 1771, 2,234 tons. Other outstanding ironmasters include, for the 17th century, John Winthrop, Jr. (1606–76), in Mass. (at Lynn, 1643) and Conn.; for the 18th, Alexander Spotswood (1676-1740), who established iron furnaces on

the Rapidan River. (1714), Robert Carter (1663–1732), Peter Hasenclever (1716–93), John Jacob Faesch (1729–99), William Alexander ("Lord Stirling," 1726–83), Charles Carroll (1737–1832), and Philip Livingston (1716–78).

1789–1807. EXPANSION OF FACTORY PRODUCTION. Textiles. Samuel Slater, using Arkwright machinery, first spun cotton by power, 20 Dec. 1790, at Pawtucket, R.I., a venture financed by **Moses Brown** (1738–1836), a Quaker merchant. By 1800, 7 Arkwright mills, containing 2,000 spindles, were in operation. Attempts to apply power carding and spinning to wool had proved abortive as late as 1801.

Arms Manufacturing. Eli Whitney (p. 799), turning in 1798 to arms production for the U.S. government, succeeded in developing a system of interchangeable parts. **Simeon North** (1765–1852) of Conn. devised tools and machinery for the production of interchangeable parts in the manufacture of pistols, 1799. Many of the ideas came from techniques already worked out in woodworking and reproductive metal industries. Cards and nails were manufactured in uniform shapes by automatic mechanisms in the 1790's. **Eli Terry** (1772–1852) and **Seth Thomas** (1785–1859) began the manufacture of clocks at Plymouth Hollow, Conn., on the basis of interchangeable parts and quantity production (1807–12). Seth Thomas Clock Co. organized, 1853.

1808–18. Non-intercourse and the War of 1812 boomed domestic manufacturing. Gallatin's report (1810) listed 14 woolen mills and 87 cotton mills. By 1816 it was estimated that $12 million was invested in the woolen industry, which produced an annual product worth $19 million. The **Boston Manufacturing Co.** (also called the Waltham Co.), established at Waltham, Mass., 1813, was the 1st textile factory to conduct **all** operations for converting cotton into cloth by power under a single management (the "**Waltham System**"). Other features: large capital investment, recruitment of New England farm girls housed in dormitories, and the production of standardized coarse cloth requiring minimum skills of operatives.

1816–30. IRON INDUSTRY REOR-GANIZES. (1) The production of bar iron by **puddling and rolling** as a continuous process in western Pa. (at Plumstock), 1817; soon adopted by the iron industry at **Pittsburgh.** (2) Introduction in urban rolling mills of coal for refining pigs while rural blast furnaces continued to use charcoal.

Machinery Production. Although the manufacture of machinery as a separate branch of industry dates back as early as 1803, when **Oliver Evans** (1755–1819) established a shop to fabricate steam engines (**Mars Iron Works**), a **specialization** trend is more decided in this period. Among the largest units were the Allaire Works, 1816; the Merrimac Co. (textile machinery), 1820; and the Novelty Works, 1830. By 1830, 9 textile machinery works existed in Worcester, Mass., alone, with the Lowell and Lawrence shops among the largest. The founding of mills at **Lowell,** Mass., the "Manchester of America," 1822, by Jackson and Lowell, marked the rapid extension of the Waltham System in cotton manufacturing. By 1830 belt transmission of power, dating back to the 1790's, began to be widely employed in textile manufacturing.

Paper manufacture. Thomas Gilpin is credited with manufacturing the 1st machine-made paper in the U.S. (1817) near Wilmington, Del. **Fourdrinier proc-ess** of paper manufacture was introduced into the U.S. *c.*1825; placed in large-scale operation at Holyoke, Mass. (1853), by Parson Paper Co.

1830–50. STEAM ENGINES AND STEAM POWER. As steam engines came into common use, locomotive building was transferred from general machine shops to specialized works—Baldwin Works (1832), Norris Works (1834). Steam power, however, was not widely introduced in manufacturing until 1850. The expansion of steam utilization as well as puddling and rolling created a demand for **anthracite coal.** Anthracite production rose from 215,272 tons to over 1 million tons by 1837. Although Frederick W. Geisenheimer conducted successful experiments in smelting iron ore with anthracite, 1830, and the hot blast was introduced, 1834, charcoal remained practically the sole fuel used for smelting.

Textiles. Power weaving and the Waltham System were extended in wool manufacture, beginning at Lowell, Mass. (1830), and at Lawrence, Mass. (1845). A loom for the manufacture of figured woolens was successfully demonstrated, 1840, by William Crompton (1806–91), and the process improved by his son, George (1829–86). As a result, hand weaving in New England practically disappeared, but in frontier areas household manufactures actually expanded down to 1830. During this period the cotton industry about doubled its capacity, the number of spindles exceeding 2,280,000.

1840–50. RAPID PROGRESS IN THE IRON INDUSTRY resulted from (1) substitution of mineral coal for charcoal, (2) replacement of open forge by reverberatory-type closed furnace, (3) advances in refining and rolling (heavy rails successfully rolled, 1845), (4) large-scale adoption of steam power, and (5) expansion of the railroad system. On 4 July 1840 David Thomas (1794–1884) made the first successful attempt to produce pig iron by the use of anthracite coal in hot-blast furnace of the Lehigh Crane Ironworks at Catasauqua, Pa. Output of anthracite quadrupled, exceeding 4 million tons.

Machine shop products multiplied in variety on the basis of standardized parts and quantity production: plows, threshing machines, harvesters, reapers (McCormick factory, Chicago, 1847), revolving pistols, stoves, metal clocks, sewing machines (first practical sewing machine produced by the Singer factory, 1850).

Textiles. Installation of steam power operation in textile mills at Salem and New Bedford, 1847, freed the industry from the limitations of water power.

Household manufactures throughout the U.S. declined: Per capita value 1840, $1.70; 1850, $1.18; 1860, $.78.

1850–60. In 1859 the value of the products of U.S. industry ($1,885,862,000) exceeded for the 1st time the value of agricultural products. In gross value of products flour milling ranked 1st (1st commercial flour mill began operations at Minneapolis, 1854), followed by the iron industry. Anthracite iron held 1st place, followed in order by charcoal iron, and bituminous coal and coke iron. Lake

Superior ores were beginning to be used by 1860. In the 20 years ending in 1860 the consumption of raw cotton by the textile industry had almost quadrupled, and the number of spindles more than doubled (exceeding 5,235,000). In capital invested, labor employed, and **net value** of product, the cotton industry was 1st in the U.S. by 1860.

This period is also marked by the emergence of **machine toolmaking** as a separate industry. The manufacture of the **vernier caliper** (1851) by J. R. Brown of Providence (later known as Brown and Sharpe Mfg. Co.), making possible measurements in thousandths of an inch, inaugurated true precision manufacturing. The **turret lathe** manufactured by Robbins and Laurence at Windsor, Vt., 1854, proved essential to mass production techniques.

Expansion of Steam-Powered Factories. By 1860 almost one fourth of the Fall River spindles were steam-driven.

MANUFACTURING BY SECTIONS, 1860

Section	Number of Establishments	Capital Invested	Average Number of Laborers	Annual Value of Products
New England	20,671	$257,477,783	391,836	$468,599,287
Middle States	53,387	435,061,964	546,243	802,338,392
Western States	36,785	194,212,543	209,909	384,606,530
Southern States	20,631	95,975,185	110,721	155,531,281
Pacific States	8,777	23,380,334	50,204	71,229,989
Territories	282	3,747,906	2,333	3,556,197
Total	140,533	$1,009,855,715	1,311,246	$1,885,861,676

Phenomenal increase in manufacturing output Since 1860: The result of technological developments which have revolutionized (1) **mineral production** through deeper mining (improved ventilation and air-conditioning) and deeper drilling of oil wells (made possible by rotary drill and steel alloys); improved blasting techniques; the pneumatic rock drill, increasing drilling speed; power shovels; the cyanide process in gold and silver mining; the electrolytic process in aluminum, copper, zinc, and lead refining; the open-hearth method in steel production (man-hour production in mineral industry, 1902–39, multiplied 3.67 times, in oil and gas 5-fold); (2) **chemical industry** (rayon, rubber, oil, leather, plastics); (3) **alloyed metals** production; (4) **electric power** and the **internal combustion engine** (cheapening transportation and promoting farm production and marketing); (5) **large-scale organization** promoting industrial efficiency.

1861–65. IMPACT OF THE CIVIL WAR was variously felt, wool production expanding, cotton manufacturing being severely curtailed. The introduction of power-driven sewing machines in the manufacture of military uniforms and boots and shoes brought these industries into the factory system. Agricultural machinery output spurted, but locomotive production fell off sharply. Extensive use of condensed milk processed by **Gail Borden** (1801–74) on the basis of a patent (1856) encouraged development of food processing industry. Demands for iron for military use expanded, while curtailment was marked in structural iron and railroad equipment, in building construction, and in most types of raw-material production. The war encouraged technological developments by creating a demand for rolled-iron plates of considerable thickness. The Rodman process was successfully utilized in casting large cannon hollow, and progress was made in crucible steel.

1866–73. ESTABLISHMENT OF THE BESSEMER STEEL INDUSTRY, 1864. at Wyandotte, Mich. (also p. 567), to meet demand for rails was principal achievement. By 1873, 115,000 tons of Bessemer rails were rolled, but as yet nearly 7 tons of iron rails were rolled for every ton of Bessemer rails. With **Bethlehem Steel Co.** beginning operations in 1873 and the Edgar Thompson Steel Works under construction, the Bessemer industry was on a firm basis by the end of this period. The **Lake Superior** region (U.S. govt. surveyors discovered ore deposits near Marquette, 1844) became the most important single source of iron ore, with annual shipments exceeding 1 million tons by 1873 (ultimately a number of ranges were opened up in Mich. and Minn., including the Menominee, Gogebic, Vermilion, Mesabi, and Cuyuna). While the Pittsburgh district continued to maintain its leadership, new establishments on a large scale were constructed on the Great Lakes with convenient access to the ore (notably at Gary, Ind., and Chicago district). Other trends: (1) **Steam power** now surpassed water power as a source of industrial energy; (2) **coal production** almost doubled, with bituminous surpassing anthracite in physical output by 1870; (3) the **worsted industry** rapidly expanded.

1867-1911. PETROLEUM INDUSTRY AND STANDARD OIL. As a result of a scientific report by **Benjamin Silliman, Jr.** (1816-85), refining and drilling operations were begun in Pa. Oil was successfully drilled by **Edwin L. Drake** (1819-80) near Titusville, 1859, leading to an **oil boom**, as petroleum quickly ousted whale oil and burning fluids as an illuminant. After 1884 drilling became nationwide, with production in Ohio and W.Va., in the 90's in Wyo., and by the early 1900's in Tex., Indian Territory (Okla.), Kan., La., and Ill. First oil pipeline completed from Pithole, Pa. (1866). **John D. Rockefeller**, concentrating on control of (1) **refining**, merged the interests of the Rockefellers, Harkness, and Flagler, organizing, 1870, the **Standard Oil Co. of Ohio** (capital $1 million). (2) By special **rate agreements** with Eastern railroads Rockefeller secured a competitive transportation advantage over rivals. (3) Control of **pipelines**. By 1879 Standard Oil controlled 90-95% of the oil refined. Trust agreement, 1879; formally organized, 1882; broken by Ohio courts, 1892. **Standard Oil Co. of N.J.** formed, 1899, as a holding and operating company; dissolved, 1911 (p. 496), but since that date the business has been controlled by a number of corporations chartered in several states with a "community of interest," with strong competition appearing in the industry (Gulf Oil and Shell Union, 1922; Texas Corp., 1926).

1873-1904. CONCENTRATION OF ECONOMIC POWER. Devices employed: (1) **Pools** (1873-87), a combine of business units to control prices by apportioning markets; forbidden to railroads by Interstate Commerce Act, 1887 (p. 258), and by Supreme Court, 1897 (p. 494). For *Addyston Pipe and Steel Co.* v. *U.S.* (1899), which forbade pools among manufacturers shipping across state lines, see p. 495. (2) **Trusts**, a device whereby stockholders under a trust agreement deposit their stock with trustees—Standard Oil Co. (1879-82); "Cotton-Oil" Trust (1884); "Whisky Trust," "Sugar Trust," and "Lead Trust" (1887); illegal under the Sherman Act, 1890, p. 261; for Supreme Court interpretation, p. 494. (3) **Holding Companies** (esp. 1897-1904) controlling a portion of the stock in other corporations. Lax laws of states like N.J. encouraged this device. The most notable example was the **U.S. Steel Corporation**, organized, 1901, by a group of financiers headed by **Elbert H. Gary** (1846-1927), Chicago, and **J. P. Morgan**, New York, who bought out **Andrew Carnegie's** interest in the Carnegie Steel Co. (resulting from a series of consolidations of iron and steel works, ore properties, and shipping facilities, 1874-99). Capitalized at $1.4 billion, U.S. Steel was for many years the largest holding company in the U.S. Holding companies were partially curbed by (1) the dissolution of the Northern Securities Co., 1904 (p. 495); (2) the dissolution of the Standard Oil Co. (p. 496) and the American Tobacco Co. (p. 496); and (3) New Deal legislation (p. 353). Other monopolistic devices: straight mergers, outright purchases, and control of patent rights, as in glass and aluminum.

1874-80. Bessemer plant capacity increased. By 1880 Pittsburgh blast furnaces produced 1,200 tons a week as against a maximum output of 600 tons in the previous decade. As a result Bessemer steel output exceeded 1 million tons for the 1st time, with pig iron production, 1880, attaining a new high of 4,295,000 tons, a one-third increase over the boom year, 1873. Other developments include (1) application of **refrigeration** to transportation, with the meat-packing industry now producing for a national market on a year-round basis; (2) expansion of machine manufacture of shoes, especially marked after the merger of firm established by Charles Goodyear (1833–96) with his competitor, Gordon McKay (1880).

1881–90. EXPANSION IN THE STEEL INDUSTRY. The **Open-Hearth Process** introduced into the U.S. by **Abram S. Hewitt** at Trenton, N.J., 1868), removing sulphur and especially phosphorus, and consequently opening up a larger portion of the ore reserve of the U.S. (including scrap metal) than the Bessemer process, expanded its operatives 5-fold, especially after 1886. At the same time Bessemer steel ingots and castings rose from 1,074,262 to 3,658,871 long tons. By 1885 iron rails accounted for only 15,000 out of over 1 million tons, with the proportion devoted to other products constantly increasing. Structural iron, wire, pipe, tubes, and armored plate faced heavy competition from steel. Reflecting the marked growth in size per unit, the number of blast furnaces in Pa., chief U.S. producer, fell from 269 to 211. The northern Ala. and adjacent Tenn. district (center: **Birmingham**), with resources of coal as well as iron ore, spurted to 2nd place in pig iron production. By 1890 iron ore production amounted to 4 million tons, or 25% of the national total, but this area did not keep up the pace, 1893–1914. Lake Superior ore shipments rose from 2 million to 9 million tons, accounting for 56% of the total U.S. output.

Other developments: (1) **Rise of Southern textile production** (number of cotton spindles increased from 542,000 to 1,554,000, but in 1890 New England still accounted for 76% of total U.S. spindles); (2) **ready-made clothing industry** expanded as a result of the introduction of cutting machines and mechanical pressers, with the organization largely characterized by **sub-contract system** and **sweat shops**; (3) **shoe industry** expanded, with annual output of Good-

year welt shoes amounting to 12 million pairs by 1890.

1891–1900. ELECTRIC POWER AND INTERNAL COMBUSTION ENGINES. The introduction of steam turbines (1890) to drive dynamos for the generation of electric power and the development of the internal combustion engine were the chief industrial developments. The Niagara Falls plant (1894) inaugurated the era of hydroelectric power. Utilization of such power was still in its infancy. By 1899 horsepower of electric motors run by purchased current amounted to merely 1.8% of the total installed primary power in manufacturing industries, while installed horsepower of internal combustion engines amounted to 1.3%. The introduction (1891) of the electrolytic process of copper refining speeded up the complete displacement of steel wire by copper wire in the conduction of electricity. Other trends: (1) Southern cotton industry aided by the perfection of the Northrop loom (1889–95). By 1900, Southern mills consumed 1.5 million bales of cotton as against slightly under 2 million spun in Northern mills. (2) Meat-packing industry became centralized in the Middle West as receipts of live cattle in the East began to decline absolutely, beginning in 1890, and shipments of slaughtered cattle expanded. (3) Kerosene production declined relatively, amounting to one half of all petroleum refining in 1900 as against three quarters, 1890. During the same period petroleum output increased 40%. (4) Decline of relative importance of rails in the steel industry. By 1891 steel used for structural and other rolled products exceeded rails, with the ratio widening to 2–1 by 1896. In forging, hydraulic presses supplanted steam hammers. Open-hearth steel production outstripped Bessemer in rate of expansion.

1901–09. (1) Output of steel products rose from 10 million to almost 24 million tons, with open-hearth steel exceeding Bessemer output by 1908. In 1909 open-hearth accounted for 14,493,000 tons, Bessemer 9,330,000 tons. **Coke** (of major importance as a blast-furnace fuel after 1890) became the principal fuel in the steel industry. (2) Heavy chemical industry rapidly expanded as a result of the Solvay process and the electrolytic process. (3) Machine tool industry introduced electrically driven and high-speed cutting tools, power presses, heavy portable machine tools, and compressed air tools. (3) The **Automobile Industry,** not listed separately in the Census of 1900, rose rapidly by 1909, its output increasing 3,500% during the decade, with a corresponding increase in demand for alloys, glass, steel, rubber, and petroleum products. (4) Fuel oil production rose from 300 million gallons to 1.7 billion gallons. (5) Lagging industries included wheat flour milling, forest products (dropped 36%), and cotton and wool manufacturing, which kept pace with the population rise but not at the rate of knit goods and silk production.

1909–14. Steel Industry trends. Bessemer production declined from 9.5 million tons to 6.2 million tons annually, while open-hearth steel totaled 21.5 million in 1914, setting a trend which continued through the first half of the 20th century. 1945: Bessemer, 3,844,034 long tons; open-hearth, 64,231,788 long tons. Ore from the Mesabi Range (about 100 mi. long in N.E. Minn.) virtually supplanted ore from Wis. and Mich. fields, constituting over 70% of all Lake Superior region shipments in 1914.

Automotive Expansion from 21st to 6th place in relation to value of output. In 1913–14 the Ford Motor Co. started reorganizing the assembly process, including the manufacture of its own motors and other important parts, and the utilization of "continuous flow production." A corresponding expansion was recorded in the rubber industry, largely due to a 4-fold increase in the value of tire and inner-tube production.

Textiles. Cotton manufacturing in the Southern Piedmont was accelerated by the utilization of hydroelectric power. By 1914 the South had almost 13 million spindles as against less than 11 million for Mass. The former produced coarse cotton goods; New England specialized in finer cloth. Rapid advances were recorded in silk and knit goods. The value of silk products reached $254 million in 1914. The introduction of rayon in 1909 inaugurated a new **era of synthetics,** but

production remained small in 1914.

Electric power installed in manufacturing rose from 1.7 to 3.8 million horsepower. By 1914 energy run by purchased current reached 17.3% of all installed primary power in manufacturing.

1914–19. WORLD WAR I increased the demands for **alloys** and accelerated the rise of the **aluminum industry.** To meet the needs for special alloys, electric furnace production increased conspicuously, rising from 27,000 long tons, 1914, to 511,693 long tons, 1918. In the tool industry electrically produced steel displaced crucible steel. During the war period total steel ingots and castings rose from 23,513,030 long tons (1914) to 45,060,607 (1917). Ship construction rose from $211,319,000 (1914) to $775,-093,000 (1918). The enlarged demands for munitions placed a premium upon the construction of **by-product coking ovens** to supply coal tar for explosives, the number of such ovens doubling by 1919, by which date by-product coke amounted to 56.9% of 44.2 million tons total. Installed primary power represented by purchased current more than doubled, reaching 9,347,556 horsepower, or 31.6% of total horsepower of manufacturing industries. The **War Industries Board** (p. 278) supported increases in productive capacity, standardization and simplification of products and processes, and scientific management.

1920–29. RATE OF GROWTH IN MANUFACTURING. In terms of distribution of the national income and employment, manufacturing remained relatively constant, while advances were scored in aggregate physical output far greater than in nonmanufacturing industries. Rate of growth **uneven,** with a **recession** in older basic industries—coal, textiles, lumber, wheat flour milling. Expansion in steel and iron leveled off. **Marked expansion in automotive industry,** which now took 1st rank in terms of value of product as well as value added by manufacture, with 2,798,737 passenger cars manufactured in 1929. Output of tires and inner tubes doubled. Gasoline production increased 4-fold, accounting for 48% of all refined products, while fuel oil output doubled but declined from 52% to 42% of petroleum refining

Chemical industry expansion, given a fillip by World War I, made spectacular gains, especially in the fields of dyes (formerly imported from Germany) and synthetic fibers (rayon production rose from 3 million lbs., 1919, to 33 million lbs., 1929) and plastics. Electrical equipment manufacturing enjoyed boom conditions, with the value of heavy household appliances rising from $109 million to $268 million; portable household electric appliances, from $71 million to $106 million; radios and related apparatus, from $15 million to $338 million; and industrial electrical appliances, from $46 million to $976 million. By 1929 the rated capacity of horsepower equipment of motors run by purchased energy exceeded the rated horsepower capacity of all other prime movers in manufacturing.

1929–39. DEPRESSION AND TRANSITION. The index of physical output of all manufacturing rose from 364 in 1929 to 374 in 1939 (1899 = 100; 1865 = 8.5), but in only 2 years of the entire decade was the 1929 output exceeded. Physical production rose 2.8%, while population increased about 6%, with one half of all industries declining absolutely and over one half declining in relation to population. Growth industries included chemicals (plastics output rose from 50,000 tons, 1935, to 170,000 tons, 1939), electrical equipment (household refrigerator output rose from 890,000 units, 1929, to 2,824,000, 1937), and petroleum (gasoline production rose almost 50%, and the catalytic "cracking process" was developed). Uneven trends were marked in textiles (rayon used in the silk and rayon goods industry increased 4-fold, 1929–35, while silk consumption declined 50%, and by 1939 was relegated to full-fashioned hosiery only; cotton goods dropped from 22% of total physical output in textiles, 1929, to 16%, 1937) and in clothing (men's ready-made clothing showed a net rise in output of about 2%, while women's clothing advanced by almost 50%, 1929–37). Other trends: The introduction of cemented tungsten carbide (1928), followed by tantalum carbide, for cutting tools permitted "super-speed" cutting and practical cutting speeds on materials formerly unmachinable. Developments in

synthetic abrasives, electric drive and control, hydraulic feed, and pneumatic accessories led to widespread redesigning of machine tools. Such processes as electrical welding and such substitutes for metal cutting as pressing, stamping, and punching were increasingly applied in the auto and other mass production industries and, during World War II, in the aircraft and shipbuilding industries. Purchased power used in manufacturing rose from 48% to almost 60% of total primary power utilized.

1938–52. ECONOMIC CONCENTRATION. By 1929, 69.2% of the products of manufacturing were produced by firms doing a business in excess of $1 million as against 1.1% ($5,000–$20,-000) by small firms (*Statistical Abstract*, 1933). The depression accelerated this trend, according to the TNEC *Hearings and Final Report* (p. 359). In 1935 less than 6% of the tobacco corporations owned 92% of the assets; 3% of the chemicals, 86%; 4% of the rubber concerns, 80%; 2% of the metal and metal products concerns, 74%. In 1937 one company produced 100% of the virgin aluminum (Aluminum Co. of America); 3 companies, 86% of the autos; and 4 companies, 58% of the whisky (1938). By 1938, 30 corporations had assets in excess of $1 billion. The leaders:

Corporation	Assets in Billion Dollars
Metropolitan Life Insurance	4.23
Amer. Tel. & Tel. Co.	3.99
Prudential Insurance Co.	3.12
Pennsylvania R.R. Co.	2.86
N.Y. Central R.R. Co.	2.35
Chase National Bank	2.33
New York Life Insurance Co.	2.22
Standard Oil Co. (N.J.)	1.89
National City Bank of N.Y.	1.88
Guaranty Trust Co.	1.84
Equitable Life Assurance Co.	1.82
U.S. Steel Corp.	1.82
Allegheny Corp.	1.73
Southern Pacific R.R. Co.	1.67
General Motors Corp.	1.49
Consolidated Edison Co.	1.38
Bank of America	1.27

By 1952 the number of corporations with a billion or more in assets rose to 59 (24 industrial, utility, and railroad companies; 21 banks; 13 insurance companies; 1 finance company). Assets of Standard Oil Co. of N.J. rose to $4.7

billion; General Motors, to $3.67 billion; U.S. Steel, to $3.14 billion.

1940–52. WORLD WAR II, RECONVERSION, AND COLD WAR. As a result of a shift from civilian to military production (military production rose from 2% of total national output, 1939, to 40%, 1944), plant expansion, and labor mobilization, industrial production rose from 100 (1935–39) to **239** by 1943, and durable manufactured goods to **360.** Mineral production rose to 148 (1942), fuels to 145 (1944). Steel ingots and castings reached a peak output in 1944 of 80,037,130 long tons, almost 50% above 1929 output ("turbo-hearth," new steelmaking technique, introduced, 1949). Most striking industrial gains occurred in (1) **alloys and light metals** (aluminum production increased 6-fold; magnesium output rose from 2,500 tons, 1939, to a peak of 170,000 tons, 1943). (2) **synthetics** (synthetic rubber production rose from 2,000 tons, 1939, to 930,-000 tons, 1945, meeting most of U.S. needs, and compared with prewar annual imports of natural rubber ranging from 550,000–650,000 tons); and (3) **plastics** (output expanded 5-fold as light-metal shortages developed, equaling by 1945 nearly one half the tonnage of aluminum produced. **U.S. government financed five sixths of the new plant** construction ($160 million through the Defense Plants Corp.). By the end of World War II the government owned 90% of the plants for synthetic rubber, aircraft, magnesium, and shipbuilding; 70% of the aluminum capacity; and 50% of the machine tool facilities. In addition, 3,800 miles of oil pipes ("Big Inch" and "Little Inch") were constructed by the government to carry petroleum to the East Coast.

The reconversion shift at the end of the war was virtually completed by mid-1947. Civilian production sought to meet shortages in **autos** (5 million units produced annually by end of 1948), **consumers' durable goods** (6,200,000 refrigerators, 14.6 million radios, and 7.4 million television sets manufactured, 1950), and **residential dwellings** (curtailed by high construction costs and material and labor shortages, with peak construction, 1950, $11,525 million). Production was

further augmented by the European Recovery Program (p. 390). The "Cold War," beginning 1949, curtailed industrial reconversion and led to restrictions upon civilian production (autos, one third from 1950 levels by 1952; radios and television sets, 40%) in favor of rearmament requirements. Nevertheless, peak output figures were achieved in this period. Iron and steel production rose to approximately 260 by 1951 (1935–39 = 100) as against 208, highest war year (1943); petroleum and coal products to 267 as against a record war output of 236 (1945); chemical products to 242 as compared with 228 (1943); and aircraft manufacturing was accelerated to reach, by July 1952, a production rate of 250 military planes monthly, considerably below earlier estimates.

Income originating from manufacturing (1949) amounted to $62.8 billion out of total national income of $216.8 billion as against $7.5 billion (manufacturing) out of $39.5 billion total national income in 1933.

1950–60. RATE OF GROWTH. Index of industrial production (1957=100) continued to rise during the 1950's, from 75 (1950) to 110 (prel. 1st qr. 1960), with largest percentage increases in utilities output, 52 to 122; transportation equipment, 53 to 106; instruments, 59 to 118; rubber and plastic products, 72 to 116; and machinery, 70 to 109. Over all, America's economic rate of growth (average annual increase in gross natl. product per capita in constant 1954 dollars), 1950–59, was 1.4%, considerably behind the rates of growth of Western Europe and the U.S.S.R. for the same period.

1953–60. INDUSTRIAL TRENDS marked by (1) spread of **automation** and, closely related thereto, of automatic, high-speed **computers**; (2) increase in production of **synthetic** (nylon use in tires expanded beg. 1954), **acrylic,** and **polyester fibers** (last 2 gaining ground in clothing products); (3) rapid expansion of new **defense and space age industries,** geared to military technology, notably in field of spacecraft, electronics (guidance, control, and communications), along with expanded use of lightweight metals (beryllium, titanium, molybdenum) and the refractory metals; and production of high-energy fuels; (4) era of the "compacts," initiated by U.S. small-car models in fall of 1957 (Amer. Motors, Studebaker-Packard, followed by Big Three, 1958–60) to meet twofold rise in foreign-

car registrations and 31% drop in U.S. car production (1958). In 1960 "compacts" constituted est. 30% of total U.S. passenger car production of 6,500,000 units.

NATIONAL PUBLIC FINANCE

1789--1800. Hamilton's "Report on Public Credit" (9 Jan. 1790) placed the total public debt outstanding at **$77,-124,564** (foreign debt, $11,710,379; domestic debt, $40,414,086; state debts, $25 million, of which $18,271,786 was actually assumed). Customs duties constituted the principal source of revenue, as a number of excise taxes and, in 1798, a direct tax on houses, land, and slaves apportioned among the states on the basis of population proved unproductive.

1791. Bank of U.S. chartered (p. 123).

1792, 2 Apr. Mint Act (1) provided for decimal system of coinage; (2) valued U.S. dollar at 24.75 grains of gold; (3) established bimetallism, with silver and gold legal tender at a ratio of 15 to 1; (4) established a mint at Philadelphia. New discoveries of Mexican silver resulted in silver being overvalued at this ratio.

1801–11. The Jeffersonian Republicans were committed to **retrenchment**. Increasing customs receipts made it possible to repeal all excises (1802), except tax on salt (eliminated 1807), and to reduce the debt of $83 million inherited from the Federalist administration by almost 50%.

1812–15. The War of 1812 undid the economy moves of the preceding years. Heavy government borrowing (loans, c.$80 million; Treasury notes, c.$37 million) brought the debt to $127,335,000 ($15 per capita). Prewar annual expenditures of c.$11 million rose to $35 million, 1814, in which year Congress increased tariff rates; doubled the tax of 1813 on land, dwelling houses, and slaves; and increased items subject to internal revenue.

1816. Second Bank of U.S. chartered (p. 154).

1816–18. Large revenues permitted the

retirement or funding into stock of Treasury notes outstanding and the removal by 1817 of most war taxes.

1819–21. Annual deficits handicapped Treasury fiscal operations.

1822–29. The accrual of surpluses was used to liquidate the public debt by the purchase in the open market of government securities. In 1826 a Senate committee complained of "the serious inconvenience of an **overflowing Treasury**."

1830–35. Land speculation made receipts from the sales of public lands an important source of government revenue. Reduced to only $7 million by 1832, the entire debt was paid off by Jan. 1835.

1834, 28 June. Second Coinage Act authorized ratio of 16–1 between silver and gold and reduced weight of gold to 23.22 grains. Discovery of gold in California (p. 207) led to overvaluation of gold at this ratio.

1836. Income from land sales totaled $25 million, exceeding customs receipts for the 1st and only time. The government surplus exceeded $40 million.

11 July. Specie Circular (p. 177).

1837. $28 million of the surplus was distributed among the states in the form of a loan.

1837–43. Declining revenues brought deficits totaling $46.4 million. To finance government expenditures, over $47 million of Treasury notes were issued.

1840. Independent Treasury system established (p. 182), discontinued 1841 (p. 184), reestablished 1846 (p. 196), continuing until merged with Federal Reserve System (1913, p. 274), and finally abolished (1921) by Act of 1920.

1844–46. Reappearance of annual surpluses.

1846–49. The War with Mexico was

financed almost entirely by borrowing. The total deficits for the 3-yr. period amounted to $53.2 million. 1847 marked the record federal expenditure to date of $57 million.

1850–57. A period of large surpluses.

1853, 21 Feb. Coinage Act reduced silver in all small coins except the dollar and authorized coinage of $3 gold pieces.

1858–60. The Panic of 1857 was followed by annual deficits, annual expenditures increasing to $74 million in 1858, with government credit at low ebb.

1861–65. CIVIL WAR led to the introduction of a variety of taxes. An **income tax**, for the first time, was enacted, 5 Aug. 1861; its rates (3% on incomes in excess of $800) increased in succeeding years. Internal revenue surpassed customs duties as a source of government revenue. By 1865 the income tax produced almost 20% of the total Federal receipts, and the manufacturers' and sales taxes amounted to some 23%. However, the major portion of the war expenditures was financed by paper money issues and loans. In August, 1865, the public debt reached a peak of $2,845,900,000 (in excess of $75 per capita), while some $450 million of U.S. legal tender notes or "greenbacks" had been issued (authorized Feb. 1862).

1866–70. With certain exceptions, excise taxes were gradually removed and the inheritance tax expired in 1870. Yet revenue exceeded expenditures by $133 million, 1867. Most of the debt was converted into long-term bonds, and the greenbacks outstanding were moderately contracted to c.$356 million.

1871–74. The U.S. Treasury issued $26 million legal tender notes by purchasing bonds. The income tax expired in 1872.

1873. Fourth Coinage Act ("Crime of '73"), p. 251.

1875–93. Every single year showed an excess of revenue over expenditures (1881, $145 million). The major source of government income was customs duties unrelated to fiscal needs. In order not to drain off currency by retaining in the Treasury the mounting surpluses, the government applied the surplus to debt

reduction at an unprecedented rate, the net debt falling to $839 million and the bonded debt from about $1,800 million to less than $600 million.

1878–94. The struggle to monetize silver—bimetallism (pp. 251, 254)—**Bland-Allison Act,** 28 Feb. 1878 (p. 254), **Sherman Silver Purchase Act,** 14 July 1890 (p. 261), repealed 1 Nov. 1894 (p. 263).

1894. Federal revenue failed to exceed expenditures (deficit $61 million) for the 1st time since the Civil War.

1895–99. Each year showed a deficit, which rose to $89 million in 1899. The war with Spain created no serious fiscal problem, although borrowing constituted the major source of government receipts, with the deficit rising to only $127 million for the war period.

1900. Gold Standards Act (p. 265).

1900–13. Government expenditures increased, but frequently lagged behind revenue, with surpluses in 6 years and deficits in 7 years. The gross national debt was slightly reduced and the per capita debt fell from $16.60 to **$12.27.**

1914–16. Slightly heavier spending for military purposes increased the annual deficit to over $62 million in 1915.

1917–20. U.S. entry into World War I brought drastic tax increases. The largest revenue producer was the excess profits tax, yielding over $2 billion in 1918, in which year income taxes amounted to $663.1 million. Of the c$35.5 billion expended, including $9 billion loans to the Allies, approximately 25% was raised by taxes, the rest by borrowing. Public debt rose from $1,300 million in Apr., 1917, to a peak exceeding $26 billion in Aug., 1919 ($242 per capita).

1921–29. With "economy" the watchword of fiscal policy, tax reductions were effected, especially in the higher income brackets, and budgetary surpluses were applied to debt reduction. The national debt was reduced to $16 billion by 1930 ($131 per capita). However, expenditures after World War I remained permanently higher than before the war, averaging in this period around $3 billion.

1931–32. Owing to falling revenues and declining incomes annual deficits occurred

(1932, $2,529 million).

1933–36. In March, 1933, the gross national debt amounted to $20.9 billion. In 1936 it was in excess of $33 billion ($263 per capita). Revenue rose ($3,100 million, 1934, to $4,115 million, 1936), but expenditures mounted even more rapidly (from $6 billion, 1934, to $8,600 million, 1936). Relief expenditures constituted the largest single item in the "emergency" budgets. For **abandonment of gold standard** (19 Apr. 1933), p. 342; **gold devaluation** (25 Oct. 1933), p. 346; and **silver purchase proclamation** (9 Aug. 1935), p. 349.

1937. With recovery under way, President Roosevelt's budget message recommended sharp reductions in expenditures in the expectation of a balanced budget; but the acute business slump in the latter part of the year brought about a resumption of government spending to combat the downtrend: 1937, $8,177 million; 1938, $7,238 million.

1938–40. The public debt rose from $37 billion to $43 billion ($325 per capita), while the launching of an armament program in 1940 presaged larger deficits in the future.

1940–45. U.S. expenditures, 1 July 1940–30 June 1946, **$370 billion.** Despite the heaviest taxation in U.S. history revenue amounted to only $169 billion. The Treasury borrowed the remainder. The national debt exceeded $258 billion ($1,852.74 per capita), and annual interest payments to maintain the debt structure exceeded $5 billion.

1946–52. Slight surpluses were recorded in 1947–48, but military and diplomatic exigencies brought a return of deficits: $1.8 billion (1949), $3.1 billion (1950), $4 billion (1952), $10.3 billion (est. 1953). As a result of continuing high tax rates (1951 record receipts, $48.1 billion) the national public debt remained virtually stabilized at peak levels, with per capita debt, 1951, **$1,693.80;** total public debt, 30 June 1952, $259.1 billion.

1953–60. Total **budget expenditures** in billions: 74.2 (1953), 67.7 (1954), 64.5 (1955), 66.5 (1956), 69.4 (1957), 71.9 (1958), 80.6 (1959), 78.3 (est. 1960). **Deficits** were incurred in 5 out of 7 yrs., 1953–59, rising to record for peacetime of $12,427 million (1959). **Public debt** of U.S. subject to statutory debt limit rose to $284.7 billion (1959).

SOURCES OF FEDERAL REVENUE[1]
(U.S. Treasury, *Annual Report*, 1945)

1800	%	1836	%	1845	%
Customs	82.7	Customs	45.9	Customs	91.85
Int. Rev.	7.5	Public lands	48.9	Public ands	6.9
All others	10.8	All others	5.2	All others	1.25

1890	%	1925	%	1945	%
Customs	61.7	Customs	14.4	Individ. income	39.9
Liquor & tobacco	38.0	Tobacco	9.1	Corp. income	10.2
All others	3.0	Indiv. income	22.4	Excess profits	23.3
		Corp. income	24.2	Liquor	4.8
		Foreign debt	4.9	Tobacco	1.9
		Estate and gifts	2.9	All others	19.7
		All others	18.4		

[1] **1960.** Individual income and employment taxes rose to 62.1% of total internal revenue collections.

PER CAPITA NATIONAL DEBT

1790 (Beginning of National Govt.)	$19	1919 (After World War I)	240
1816 (After War of 1812)	15	1948 (After World War II)	1,720
1866 (After Civil War)	78	1958	1,630

Interest on the debt as a percentage of national income approximated 2.6% at the end of the Civil War, 2.0% after World War I, 2.8% after World War II.

BANKING AND CAPITAL MARKETS

1607–1810. CORPORATE form of organization developed very slowly. Early joint-stock companies (each member liable for the obligations of the joint enterprise) were principally **nonprofit** corporations for religious worship, philanthropy, education, or **land companies.** Commercial corporations make their appearance with a Conn. trading corporation (1723), a Mass. wharf company (1772), a number of early fire insurance (notably Philadelphia Contributionship, 1768) and water supply companies, and the United Co. of Philadelphia (1775), organized to promote manufactures. For the Mass. Land Bank (1740), see p. 513. During the period 1783–89 numerous corporations were organized for building roads, canals, and bridges, and for banking (the **Bank of North America,** chartered by Congress, 31 Dec. 1781, the first private commercial bank in the U.S., and the **Bank of New York** and the **Bank of Massachusetts,** 1784). Such banks were localized and limited in scope (an exception was Aaron Burr's **Manhattan Co.** [1799], chartered as a water company but with broad enough powers to permit banking), paying out their notes on loans, with customers mainly merchants and bank stock subscribers.

1791. 1ST BANK OF THE U.S. (p. 123) opened its main office at Philadelphia, 12 Dec. 1791. Its 8 branches, located in the principal commercial towns, acted as clearing agencies. The Bank acted as fiscal agent for the government, its notes had general acceptance, and its specie holdings made it a bank of last resort.

STOCK EXCHANGES. The first securities exchange was informally organized at **Philadelphia,** 1791, followed, 1792, in **New York.** Both dealt mainly in Federal "stock." Most **domestic** enterprise was financed by **local capital.** Local merchants and storekeepers maintaining open accounts were still important sources of commercial credit. **Foreign commerce,** in large proportion, was financed by British merchants extending liberal credit.

1801–11. EXPANSION OF STATE-CHARTERED BANKING. The number of state banks rose from 30 to 88, while their total capital increased about 3-fold. In Feb. 1811, Congress failed to recharter the Bank of the U.S. State-owned banks ("mixed" enterprises in which private banks owned stock) started in Vt. (c.1800) and reached their highest development in Ind., Ohio, and Va.

1811–60. EXPANSION OF CORPORATE DEVICE. Limitation of liability, almost invariably conferred in the early charters, was made general by judicial decisions and statutes limiting the risks of investors (Mass. between 1809–30, general acceptance by 1856). Beginning with the N.Y. law of 1811 general incorporation laws were substituted for the previous practice of negotiating with the state legislature for a charter. After the restraints of the Jacksonian period had been lifted (in N.Y. by the Constitution of 1846), general incorporation laws became increasingly loose (especially in Del., Md., and later Nev.). Down to 1860 only a minority of corporations were in manufacturing; in Pa. over 60% chartered, 1790–1860, were in transportation. By 1900, however, two thirds of all manufacturing was done by corporations, a percentage which rose to 69.2%, 1929.

1812–15. WAR OF 1812 induced a banking boom (120 new banks chartered).

1812–60. LIFE INSURANCE AND SAVINGS BANKS. Pennsylvania Co. for Insurance on Lives and Granting Annuities, 1st company specializing in life insurance, incorp. Philadelphia, 1812. Rapid development of life insurance companies after 1843. By 1860, $160 million life insurance in force. First incorporated savings bank chartered, Boston, 1816; New York, Baltimore, and Philadelphia inaugurated policy of paying interest on deposits (1819). Total savings deposits: 1835, $7 million; 1850, $43 million; 1860, $150 million (278 savings banks).

1816–18. 2ND BANK OF THE U.S. (p. 154), chartered, Apr. 1816, as a result of the efforts of **Alexander J. Dallas** (1759–1817), **Stephen Girard** (1750–1831), and **John Jacob Astor** (p. 670) to aid government fiscal operations and support government securities, functioned, as did its predecessor, as a central bank. Under the direction of **William Jones** (1760–1831), a Republican politician, the Bank was mismanaged and came close to bankruptcy.

1819–22. Administration of **Langdon Cheves** (1776–1857), of S.C., 2nd president of the Bank of the U.S., pursued a conservative and restrictive policy, restoring the Bank to a sound condition.

1820–40. RAPID EXPANSION OF STATE BANKS to meet demand for loans of persons without capital or credit resulted in basic weaknesses: (1) lack of adequate specie reserve to redeem bank notes; (2) legal office for redemption purposely located in inaccessible spots ("wildcat banks").

1823–36. BIDDLE AND THE BANK. On the resignation (fall 1823) of Cheves, **Nicholas Biddle** succeeded to the presidency. During his regime the Bank's operations and influence were aggressively expanded. Bank notes issued, 1823, averaged $4.5 million; 1831, $19 million. The Bank advanced necessary loans to the U.S. govt. and made credit and currency more abundant in the West and

South. The Bank's expansion of operations in domestic exchange led to the rise of documentary bills rivaling the promissory note as a type of short-term commercial paper. Such short-term paper in effect provided the nation with an "elastic" currency. However, after 1832 the Bank sought to check inflation and contributed markedly to the business contraction which occurred (pp. 173, 537). The Bank's Federal charter expired, 1836.

1825–40. "SUFFOLK SYSTEM," in full operation by 1825, by the Suffolk Bank, Boston (founded 1818), required country banks to keep deposits in the Suffolk Bank to insure honoring their notes. Result: discount on country bank notes disappeared. A similar system was set up by the Metropolitan Bank of New York (1851). However, this system of *de facto* clearing houses did not operate on a nationwide basis until the establishment of the National Banking System, 1863 (p. 239). In this period country banks began depositing surplus funds with correspondent banks in leading financial centers. In 1840 bankers' balances held by New York City banks reached nearly $8 million. These funds were increasingly concentrated (1857–72) in 6 or 7 out of a total of 50 banks (M. G. Myers).

1829. Safety Fund Act of New York, passed for the protection of bank creditors, established the principles of (1) insurance, (2) control by bank commissioners.

1830–40. NEW YORK'S FINANCIAL PREEMINENCE. New York Stock Exchange passed Philadelphia in volume of trading, beginning with the 1820's with the successful flotation of Erie Canal bonds. With the expiration of the 2nd Bank's charter, New York also supplanted Philadelphia in the commercial credit field. Other trends: Boston Stock Exchange, 1834, facilitated security tranactions of N.E. manufacturing companies. The **Anglo-American merchant bankers,** a group of British houses led by Baring Bros. & Co., floated large issues of state bonds for internal improvements. Until the 1830's lotteries were also extensively used for this purpose; prohibited by state laws, 1821–33. By this period commercial credit dealing had become a major phase of banking, with rates on commercial paper quoted regularly in leading financial journals.

1837–48. PANIC OF 1837 (p. 178) and the wholesale failures of state banks with deposits of Federal funds led to the establishment of the **Independent Treasury** on 4 July 1840; repealed 13 Aug. 1841, but reenacted in Aug. 1846. As a number of states repudiated their maturing obligations, American credit suffered abroad and foreign capital was curtailed.

1838. N.Y. FREE BANKING ACT introduced competition in the banking field by no longer requiring special legislation to obtain a charter. However, the state law required banks to keep a specie reserve of 12.5% against note issues. La., 1842, and Mass., 1858, introduced similar reserve requirements.

1841. Establishment by Lewis Tappan of the Mercantile Agency, the first credit-rating agency, which became Dun & Co., 1859; Bradstreet's est. 1855.

1847–48. U.S. govt. loans for the War with Mexico were handled by Corcoran & Riggs, Washington, D.C., outbidding New York firms.

1849–60. INVESTMENT OPERATIONS. Renewed foreign investments, particularly in railroads, raised U.S. foreign indebtedness to $1,375,000 by 1857. Nevertheless, the U.S. money market had now become the chief source of capital funds. Out of a total exceeding $2 billion of corporate securities outstanding, 1860, **over three fourths** were owned by Americans. The expansion of security dealings led to the rise of "investment houses," particularly in New York, as well as brokerage firms, and firmly established the preeminent position in security trading of the New York Stock Exchange.

1853, Oct. Establishment of New York Clearing House formalized clearing operations. (Clearing houses also established at Boston, 1855; Phila., Baltimore, and Cleveland, 1856.)

1857. PANIC OF 1857. Bankers' balances held in New York City surged from $17 million, 1850, to over $30 million. The withdrawal of balances during the fall, coupled with the failure of the Ohio Life Insurance and Trust Co., precipitated a panic (p. 537), during which specie payments were temporarily suspended.

1862. Employing new retail marketing techniques and stressing patriotic appeal, **Jay Cooke** successfully floated U.S. Civil War loan.

1863–65. National Bank Act (1863, p. 239) bore a striking resemblance to the N.Y. Free Banking Act, but provided a safer currency. With the 1st national bank organized at Philadelphia by Jay Cooke, 20 June 1863, some 450 banks were established by 1863, of which one third constituted former state banks. The enactment, 1865, of a prohibitory tax on state bank note issues (p. 239) forced an additional 700 state banks to become national banks and brought about a **uniform currency** (national bank notes).

1869, 24 Sept. Black Friday (p. 250).

1873. The failure of Jay Cooke & Co. contributed to the increased prominence in the investment banking field of the house of **J. P. Morgan** (associated with the Drexels since 1871). The practice now emerged of bankers demanding a share in management control before granting credit (financing of N.Y. Central R.R., 1879, although the general practice was not conspicuous until the 1890's). Concentration of bankers' balances in a few New York banks continued (Sprague), making possible the development of the **call loan market.** For Panic of 1873, see p. 251. Bank suspensions, 1873–75: 104 (17 national, 87 state).

1879–90. Investment bankers undertook a larger share of railroad financing, as they began to exert influence on management and to promote combinations.

1891–1900. Investment bankers promoted consolidations in the railroad, utility, and industrial field. Bank suspensions, 1893: 491 (69 national). State-chartered **trust companies** rose from 251 to 290, with their investments increasing from $192 million to $326 million.

1901–12. TRUST COMPANY EXPANSION, number 6-fold; capital, 4-fold; investments, $1.5 billion.

1907–8. Bank suspensions, which had averaged 100 a yr., rose to well over 200 in the years of the depression.

1913. Establishment of the **FEDERAL RESERVE SYSTEM** (p. 274) to remedy defects of the National Banking System: inelasticity of the currency; need for a "lender of last resort" to come to the aid of commercial banks when there was a drain on reserves (demonstrated by Panic of 1907).

1914–18. Financing World War I. Investment market handled unprecedented volume of securities, including loans to Allies (nearly $2 billion by 1916), as well as **Liberty Loans,** which encouraged widespread public acquaintance with security issues.

1917–20. Modifications of Federal Reserve System: (1) Federal Reserve banks authorized to issue Federal Reserve Notes on the basis of gold as well as discounted paper; (2) gold reserves of Reserve banks raised from approximately $600 million to nearly $1,300 million. The effort of the Federal Reserve Board to hold down interest rates had an inflationary impact.

1921–29. Corporations increasingly applied their earnings to satisfying capital needs, adopting a conservative dividend policy. The expansion of the securities market and the rapid growth of **investment trusts** led to by-passing established investment bankers. The business practices of reducing accounts outstanding, and stressing smaller inventories and rapid turnover, left commercial banks with idle funds. The volume of **call loans** on security collateral dangerously expanded, and commercial banks branched into other fields—real estate, time-deposit banking, and investment banking through investment affiliates. This period is also noted for large banking consolidations and the spread of branch banking.

1929–33. Following the initial phase of stock market decline and leveling off of industrial production, European financial stringency (p. 324) led to large withdrawals from the U.S. of foreign bank deposits. Decline of agricultural prices led to farm mortgage deterioration, with rapid increase in the mortality of country banks in 1930 and the undermining of the whole rural credit structure, 1931–32. Liquidation of collateral by banks caused a demoralization of security values. **Bank suspensions, 1929–33: 9,765** (member, 2,391), or over a third of all banks.

1933–39. For New Deal reforms relating to banking and capital markets including deposit insurance, see pp. 342–353. New Deal banking legislation forced investment bankers to choose between deposit banking and underwriting. Between 1934–39, 20 New York City investment firms managed 78.6% of securities registered with the SEC, with **Morgan, Stanley & Co.** in 1st position. The U.S. govt., especially through the medium of the RFC (p. 338) and various farm and mortgage credit agencies (pp. 339–357), became increasingly a supplier of capital funds for long and short terms, and Treasury officials largely supplanted the Federal Reserve Board as formulators of credit policy.

1940–45. The war years were marked by an enormous expansion of the government's role as supplier of capital needs. On 25 June 1940 the RFC was authorized to make loans for acquiring, producing, or stockpiling strategic raw materials and for constructing, expanding, and operating plants. Under an Executive order of 26 Mar. 1942 the government began to guarantee or participate in loans made by banks to finance war production. By 31 Dec. 1945, Federal Reserve banks had executed 7,999 agreements for credits, totaling $9.9 billion, 80% of which were loans of $1 million and above. The Smaller War Plants Corp. was set up by the government to provide funds for small businesses with war contracts; its functions were taken over by the RFC in 1945. As a result of the government's desire to issue its securities at low interest, the Federal Reserve Board acted as an agency to support the bond market, and temporarily abdicated control over the money market.

1946–60. New Investment Trends. As a result of a marked increase in the assets of life insurance companies (500% by 1938 over 1910; by 1948, assets of legal reserve companies, $56 billion), such companies began to purchase whole issues of securities direct from the borrowing corporation in competition with investment bankers. Other corporations, owing to high taxes, proceeded to finance themselves out of profits in lieu of increasing dividends. In decade of 1950's investment companies, notably **mutual funds**, greatly expanded, with the number of shareholders exceeding 2.5 million (1960). Savings-bank deposits rose from $63.2 billion (31 Dec. 1952) to $100.8 billion (31 Dec. 1959); life insurance in force, $276 billion (1 Jan. 1953),

$542 billion (1 Jan. 1960). Income tax on life insurance companies increased 25 June 1959.

Rising interest rates. To meet the record-breaking expansion of credit and bank loans (beg. fall 1950), the Federal Reserve Board increased bank reserve requirements (1951). U.S. govt. bonds sold below par for the 1st time in more than a decade, with long-term interest rates showing a tendency to rise. As an antiinflationary step, bank rates on loans rose gradually in the 1950's—short-term business loans (average) from 2.7% (1950) to 5% (1959), the highest level in 28 yrs.

BUSINESS CYCLES AND PRICE TRENDS

Duration of Major Depressions
(Sachs-Thorp)

Years	Months' duration
1762–65	36
1768–69	12
1772–75	30
1784–88	**44**
1796–98	36
1802–03	24
1807–09	27
1815–21	**71**
1825–26	13
1833–34	9
1837–43	**72**
1857–58	18
1866–67	18
1873–78	**66**
1882–85	36
1890–91	9
1893–97	**48**
1907–08	12
1913–14	20
1920–21	18
1929–33	**42**
1937–38	10

1760. Peak of the French and Indian War boom. CP [1]: **79.**

1762–65. Low point of business slump early 1765. CP: 1762, **87;** 1765, **72;** 1766, **73.**

1768. Currency contraction precipitated a business slump, especially acute in New York and Philadelphia. CP: **74.**

1770–71. The termination of nonimportation agreements, combined with rising prices and favorable exchange rates, fostered speculation and large importations of British goods. CP: 1770, **77;** 1772, **89.**

[1] CP represents commodity prices down to 1860, based on Warren-Pearson wholesale price index for all commodities, New York—1910–14=100.

1772. The British banking crisis of the summer, with the ensuing credit contraction, brought widespread inventory liquidation and distress to colonial importers.

1773–75. Business sagged. CP: 1773, **84;** 1775, **75.**

1776–83. The American Revolution produced a business boom, with a sharp price rise caused in large measure by sizable emissions of paper money and deficit financing. CP: 1776, **86;** 1779, **226;** 1781, **216** (in depreciated currency the percentage rise was far greater).

1784–88. Excessive importations of British goods after the war, combined with an unstable currency and fiscal situation, set off a downturn, with the British banking crisis of 1784 precipitating a sharp deflation in the U.S. Although the business decline was arrested in the course of 1787, the drop in commodity prices was not halted until late 1788. CP: 1785, **92;** 1789, **86** (Bezanson, Philadelphia prices, puts decline at c.30% for same period).

1789–1800. While previous business fluctuations were mainly associated with external factors, cyclical factors inherent in business now became faintly discernible. Except for a minor recession, 1796–98, the period was one of substantial prosperity. The European wars created a large demand for U.S. farm commodities and shipping. Prices climbed steadily until 1797. CP: 1790, **90;** 1797, **131;** 1800, **129.**

1801–02. The peace of Amiens halted

the war boom. CP: 1801, **142**; 1802, **117**.

1803–07. Another wave of prosperity followed renewal of the European war, only to be terminated by the Embargo Act, 22 Dec. 1807. CP: 1804, **126**; 1806, **134**; 1807, **130**.

1808–09. Depression spread inland, followed by revival, 1810–11. CP: 1810, **131**.

1812–14. The War of 1812 curbed foreign trade, but most other branches of economic activity enjoyed an uneven war boom, with manufacturing especially benefiting by the curtailment of British imports and the South depressed, 1813–14. Heavy government borrowing stimulated banking expansion. CP: 1813, **162**; 1814, **182**.

1815–21. Resumption of importations hurt U.S. manufacturing, but the downtrend was checked by European demand for American farm staples. As farm commodities soared and bank credit was liberalized, a wave of land speculation occurred. CP: 1815, **170**. However, with the collapse of foreign markets prices broke in the fall (1819) (CP: **125**), land values sank rapidly, and numerous banks and mercantile houses failed in the **1st major banking crisis** in U.S. history, with general business depressed until 1822. CP: 1821, **102**; 1822, **106**.

1823–34. Slow business recovery with minor fluctuations (downturns, 1825–26, 1833–early 34). CP ranged from **103** down to **95**. The recession of 1833 resulted from the removal of government deposits from the 2nd Bank of the U.S., with subsequent credit curtailment by the Bank (p. 533).

1834–36. Brisk business activity returned by the spring of 1834. Land speculation was fostered by (1) a boom in canal and railroad building, (2) the transfer of U.S. deposits to state banks, (3) an inflow of foreign capital. The Specie Circular (July 1836, p. 177) resulted in a sharp downturn in land sales by the latter part of that year. CP: 1834, **90**; 1836, **114**.

1837. The collapse in real estate was followed in the 2nd quarter of 1837 by a precipitate fall in stock and commodity prices and an acute banking crisis attributed to (1) Specie Circular; (2) distribution legislation of 1836, leading to government drafts on state banks; (3) high interest rates and calling in of loans by British bankers; (4) crop failures in 1835 and 1837; (5) mounting state debts; (6) unfavorable balance of trade which increased flow of specie to Europe. CP: 1838, **110**.

1838–43. The decline was briefly halted in 1838 as business activity appeared to be building toward a secondary boom, but a major break came in 1839 when the Bank of the U.S., now a Pa.-chartered bank, closed its doors after an unsuccessful attempt to sustain cotton prices. The crisis was followed by a protracted depression, with its low point near Feb. 1843. CP: 1839, **112**; 1843, **75**.

1844–48. Gradual recovery with mild fluctuations. CP: 1848, **82**.

1849–56. A marked expansion of business fed in part by the inflow of foreign (particularly British) capital, which revived railroad building, and by the discovery of gold in California, which facilitated payments of international balances, stimulated foreign trade, and encouraged loans by domestic banks. Prosperity was briefly interrupted by a panic on the New York Stock Exchange in the fall of 1854. CP: 1850, **84**; 1854, **108**; 1855, **110**; 1856, **105**.

1857–58. The failure of the Ohio Life Insurance and Trust Co. (Aug.) touched off a sharp, though shortlived, financial panic, basically caused by overspeculation in railroad securities and real estate. CP: 1857, **111**; 1858, **93**.

1859–65. Recovery set in quickly, with prosperity continuing until the outbreak of the Civil War. Business wavered with the coming of war (1861), but heavy government spending and an inflationary price rise produced a war boom. The collapse of currency and finance in the Confederacy (Mar. 1865) brought temporary chaos to the South. CP [2]: 1861, **61.3**; 1862, **71.7**; 1863, **90.5**; 1864, **116**; 1865, **132**.

1866–72. Postwar readjustment (1866–

[2] After 1860, CP is based on wholesale price index, all commodities, Bureau of Labor Statistics (1926 = 100).

EFFECT OF U.S. WARS ON WHOLESALE PRICES, 1770 - 1960 *

67) brought little distress to the North as a railroad boom steadily gained momentum; violent stock market fluctuations, mainly the result of speculative activity, had only a limited nationwide impact. Most spectacular incident was "Black Friday," 24 Sept. 1869 (p. 250). CP: 1868, **97.7**; 1870, **86.7**.

1873–78. The failure of the banking house of Jay Cooke and Co., 18 Sept. 1873, revealed the weakened speculative structure resultant upon overextension in railroad securities. With bankruptcies among banks and brokers multiplying, prices fell precipitately, as did national income. CP: 1874, **81.0**; 1879, **58.8**. SP [3]: 1872, **39.8**; 1877, **24.8**.

1873–96. Economists not infrequently characterize this period as a "long-wave" depression. The price level declined steadily (CP: 1885, **56.6**; 1896, **46.5**), with only 8 partly or wholly prosperous years. Nevertheless, vigorous business upswings occurred, with enormous extension of investment in industrial plants and equipment. Recovery began in 1878 and continued until 1882, when a depression, 1883–85, primarily financial in origin, occurred, followed by quick recovery again, 1885–90, a short recession (1890–91), then a further upturn particularly in heavy industry (1892). The failure of the Philadelphia and Reading R.R. and the National Cordage Co. early in 1893 gave warning that the boom was over. Uncertainty over the status of the gold standard was a further depressing factor as foreign investors proceeded to sell U.S. securities, capital left the country, the reserve fell, and wholesale liquidation was set in motion. Before 1893 had ended, 491 banks and over 15,000 commercial institutions were reported to have failed. Before the turning point was reached by 1897, almost one third of the total railroad mileage was in the hands of receivers. SP: 1892, **43.9**; 1896, **33.5**.

3 Index of Common Stock Prices, all stocks (1926=100) U. S. Bureau of the Census, *Hist. Stat. of U.S., 1789–1945.*

1897–1914. Recovery followed rapidly, with relative continuing prosperity save for brief financial crises in 1903 and 1907, a recession, 1910–11, and a downturn on the eve of World War I (1913–14). CP: 1897, **46.6**; 1900, **56.1**; 1910, **70.4**; 1913, **69.8**. SP: 1897, **35.2**; 1912, **75.5**, with a decline, 1913–14, to **63.8**.

1914–19. A financial reaction following the outbreak of war was succeeded by a war boom fed by Allied orders. The peak of business activity was reached in 1916, and sustained by America's participation in the war. Temporary hesitation after the Armistice gave way to soaring prices, sales, and production, resulting from credit expansion and speculation in inventories. CP: 1916, **85.5**; 1917, **117.5**; 1918, **131.3**; 1919, **138.8**. SP: 1914, **63.8**; 1920, **64.2**.

1920–21. Sharp deflation after May 1920. CP: 1920, **154.5**; 1921, **97.6**; 1922, **96.7**.

1922–29. A rising tide of prosperity was sustained by conspicuous expansion of the consumers' durable goods industry. A boom in construction and real estate also developed (**Florida real estate boom** collapsed in 1926). By 1927 residential construction, auto output, purchases of consumers' durable goods, and new investment in producers' durable goods had begun to decline; but the boom continued, fed almost entirely by **unprecedented securities speculation not reflected in commodity prices.** CP: 1923, **100.6**; 1929, **95.3**, as contrasted with SP: 1922, **67.7**; 1929, **190.3**. The spectacular crash of stock prices occurred in Oct.-Nov. 1929.

1930–33. The depression deepened **despite** efforts to ease money market and extend credits (pp. 338, 339). Low point of depression: **Mar. 1933**, with industrial production rising 15%, July-Oct. 1932, but declining sharply by Mar. 1933 as the **banking crisis** deepened and bank holidays blanketed the nation. Industrial output almost halved, unemployment mounted to about 15 million, one third

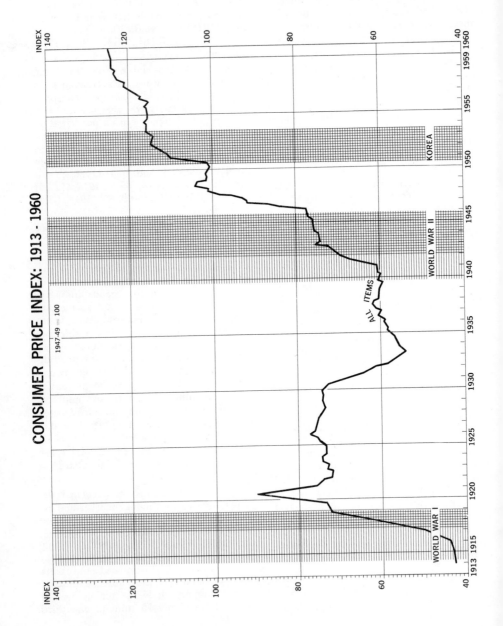

CONSUMER PRICE INDEX: 1913 - 1960

1947-49 = 100

ALL ITEMS

WORLD WAR I

WORLD WAR II

KOREA

INDEX

of the nation's railroad mileage was thrown into bankruptcy, and farm mortgage foreclosures were widespread. CP: 1930, 86.4; 1931, 73.0; 1932, 64.8; 1933, 65.9. SP: 1930, 149.8; 1932, 48.6. 1932: 48.6.

1933–37. New Deal intervention to halt the downward spiral took a variety of forms (pp. 341–358), including **deficit financing.** Business activity and prices rose. SP: 1934, 72.4; 1937, 111.8.

1935–37. The business recovery was interrupted by a brief, but acute, recession, Aug. 1937. CP: 1935, 80; 1937, 86.3.

1938–39. Deficit financing on an increasing scale contributed to recovery. Yet in Aug. 1939, about 10 million persons were still unemployed. Based on 1929 national income of $81 billion, the estimated loss of national income, 1930–38, totaled $132,600,000,000 (TNEC *Hearings*). CP: 1938, 78.6; 1939, 77.1.

1939–45. The outbreak of World War II in Europe was followed by a sudden spurt in economic activity. The index of industrial production standing at **105** (1935–39 = 100) in Aug. 1939 leaped to **125** in Dec., with unemployment falling 10%. By 1940 the effects of the U.S. military program were being felt in government expenditures, industrial output, and national income. The entry of the U.S. into the war brought large-scale mobilization of manpower and resources, with economic activity making giant strides. Peak levels were attained by 1944–45. The index of industrial production by 1944 reached **235**, and national income increased 2½ times.

MONEY IN CIRCULATION
(Hist. Statistics of U.S.)

1932	$5,695,171,000
1940	7,847,501,000
1945	26,746,438,000
1957	31,081,913,000

Despite wartime price and wage controls (p. 381) wholesale CP rose from **78.6** (1940) to **105.8** (1945).

1946–60. The inflationary upturn was accelerated by the removal of government economic controls, deferred postwar demand, and financing (in part deficit) for defense and foreign expenditures.

BLS Consumers' Price Index (1935–39=100)

June 1950	177.8	(pre-Korean intervention)
Jan. 1951	184.7	(U.S. govt. price "freeze")
Sept. 1952	191.1	(all-time high to 1952)

BOOM AND RECESSION. Period of general business expansion interrupted by 4 recessions: (1) 1948–49, decline in gross natl. product from $259.4 billion (1948) to $258.1 billion (1949), chiefly as a result of shift in inventory accumulation; unemployment reached 3.4 million in 1949; (2) 1953–54, resulting from inventory liquidation and decline in Federal expenditures for defense purposes, with 3.7 million persons unemployed by spring of 1954, and decline of gross natl. product from $364.9 billion (1953) to $356 billion (1954); (3) 1957–1958, resulting from overexpansion of plant capacity and drop in exports, with durable goods production chiefly hit; followed by rapid recovery until steel strike (15 July 1959); (4) beginning midsummer 1960, accompanied by falling off of demand for steel (below 40% capacity, Jan. 1961), autos, and appliances. Unemployment rose contraseasonally to 4 million (Nov. 1960) and est. 5.25 million (Jan. 1961). CP (1947–49=100) continued to rise, from 83.4 (1946) to 114.4 (1953) to 127.4 (Nov. 1960), with especially sharp increases in cost of housing, apparel, transportation, and medical care. (Care went from 90.6, 1947, to 155.0, Mar. 1960.) **Business cycle peak and trough** dates (as determined by the National Bureau of Economic Research):

Troughs	Oct. 1945	Oct. 1949	Aug. 1954	Apr. 1958
Peaks	Nov. 1948	July 1953	July 1957	May 1960

LABOR, SLAVERY, AND SOCIAL REFORM

SLAVERY TO 1789

1619, Aug. First Negroes (20) imported into Virginia as **bound servants.**

1619–90. Importations of African Ne-

groes continued on a moderate scale (only 3,000 Negroes estimated in Va., 1681), as white servants continued to perform bulk of farm labor.

1650–70. Judicial decisions and legislation in the tobacco provinces established slavery. Va. act of 1661 assumed that some Negroes served for life; act of 1670 declared that "all servants not being Christian" brought in by sea were slaves for life, the issue following the status of the mother. Laws passed between 1667–71 authorizing conversion of Negroes to Christianity did not bring release from servitude. Black Code, 1705, severely restrained the mobility of slaves and forbade miscegenation under heavy penalties, evidencing a racial as well as a legal differentiation between Negroes and whites. Md., 1663, provided life servitude for Negroes.

1672–1760. SLAVE TRADE. Royal African Co., a reorganized trading company, was granted a monopoly of the English slave trade, 1672; but owing to the protests of independent traders, the monopoly was lost, 1698. In the 18th century New England traders were active in the slave trade, with **Newport, R.I.,** a principal port of entry. For the relation of the slave trade to the Triangular Trade (in which the trip from Africa to the West Indies was called the "**Middle Passage**"), see p. 513. Colonial legislatures imposed duties on slave importations, but royal instructions, 1731, forbade governors consenting to such acts. The action of S.C., 1760, in prohibiting the slave trade entirely was disallowed by the King in Council. After 1690, slave importations mounted sharply. Va. had 12,000 Negroes by 1708, with about 1,000 Negroes being imported annually for the 3 preceding years. By 1715, the total had risen to 23,000 Negroes, to 42,000 by 1743, 120,156 by 1756, and 259,230 by 1782. Slave importations to the continental colonies increased from an annual average of 2,500 (1715–50) to 7,450 (1760–70), with S.C. averaging 2,800 (1753–73).

1712–40. NEGRO PLOTS AND INSURRECTIONS. Apr. 1712, the militia were called out to suppress a Negro insurrection in New York City; 21 Negroes executed. In 1739, 3 Negro uprisings broke out in S.C., most serious being the **Cato Conspiracy** (9 Sept.), which occurred at Stono, about 20 mi. southwest of Charleston, with 30 white and 44 Negro fatalities. As the result of uncovering a Negro plot in Charleston, Jan. 1740, 50 Negroes were hanged. Beginning with a burglary committed in **New York City, 28 Feb. 1741,** followed by a series of fires, panic seized the city as rumors spread that Negroes and poor whites had conspired to seize control. Despite insufficient evidence, 101 Negroes were convicted (18 Negroes and 4 whites were hanged, 13 Negroes burned alive, and 70 banished).

1749. Trustees' prohibition against slavery in Ga. was repealed and a fixed ratio of 4 male Negroes to 1 white servant adopted. As early as 1741, settlers had hired slaves for 100-yr. terms.

1776. Slavery and the Declaration of Independence. Jefferson's attack on the role of the crown in the slave trade ("He has prostituted his negative for suppressing every legislative attempt to prohibit or to restrain this execrable commerce") was unacceptable to the Southern delegates at the Continental Congress and was stricken from the document.

1776–89. ANTISLAVERY AND MANUMISSION MOVEMENTS. (1) The first antislavery society in the U.S. was organized by the Quakers in 1775, but their fight goes back to April 1688 when **Francis Pastorius** and the German Friends at Germantown declared that slavery was contrary to Christian principles. In 1696 the Yearly Meeting cautioned members against importing Negroes, and in 1755 ruled that all Friends who should thereafter import slaves would be excluded from the denomination. Antislavery societies spread in the Revolutionary Era. (2) The New York Society for Promoting Manumission, with John Jay as president, was established in 1785, with other states from Mass. to Va. following between 1788–92. The movement to manumit (free) slaves by will or deed continued in strength in the South during this period and down to c.1800. (3) The movement against the slave trade (prohibited in Md., 1783; curbed in N.C. by imposing a heavy duty on every Negro imported; repealed, 1790) culminated in the antislave-trade provision of the Federal Constitution (p. 479) as well as the provision relating to interstate fugitive slaves (p. 481). (4) Legislation was enacted, gradually abolishing slavery: Pa., 1780; Conn. and R.I., 1784; N.Y., 1785; N.J., 1786. By judicial decision, 1783, the Mass. Constitution of 1780, which held that "all men are born free and equal," was construed as having abolished slavery. In 1787 slavery was prohibited in the Northwest Territory (p. 117).

1790. POPULATION OF U.S. CLASSIFIED BY COLOR. White, 3,172,444; Free Negro, 59,557; Slaves, 697,624; Total, 3,929,625.

SLAVE DISTRIBUTION

Virginia	292,627
South Carolina	107,094
Maryland	103,036
North Carolina	100,783
Georgia	29,264
New York	21,193
Kentucky	12,430
New Jersey	11,423
Delaware	8,887
Pennsylvania	3,707
Southwest Terr.	3,417
Connecticut	2,648
Rhode Island	958
New Hampshire	157

In no state did the slave population exceed the white, but the ratio was higher in S.C., which had 140,178 white persons, and the highest average number of slaves per slaveholding family (12.1), as against 8.5 (est.) for Va. and 7.5 for Md. (W. S. Rossiter).

SLAVERY AND THE NEGRO, 1789–1860

1789–1831. MANUMISSION AND COLONIZATION PROJECTS. Chief impulse in this period for slavery reform came from the South. Out of 143 emancipation societies in the U.S. in 1826, 103 were in the South, including 4 abolition papers (1819–28). As far back as 1776, Jefferson proposed a plan for African colonization of the Negroes. Procolonization resolutions were passed by the Va. Assembly (1800, 1802, 1805, 1816). As a result, the **American Colonization Society** was established in 1817, headed at various times by Monroe, Madison, and John Marshall, and supported by **Henry Clay.** Free Negroes were first sent to Sierra Leone, and finally in 1821 a permanent location was purchased at Monrovia (settled, 1822); established as independent Republic of **Liberia** (named by **Robert Goodloe Harper [1765–1825]).** The **Mississippi Colonization Society** (founded, 1831) set up a separate African colony for Negro emigrants from that state. The colonization movement declined in the South after 1831. Total Negroes colonized by 1860 estimated at 15,000, of whom 12,000 were transported through the efforts of the American Colonization Society.

1790, 11 Feb. First petition to Congress for emancipation (presented by the Society of Friends). Many such petitions were presented prior to 1820.

1793. Invention of the **cotton gin** by Eli Whitney (p. 799), displacing the existing method of manual extraction of seed and increasing 50-fold the average daily output of clean short-staple cotton, promoted the rapid expansion of the **cotton kingdom,** firmly established the **plantation system** (also used for the cultivation of such staples as sugar cane, rice, and tobacco), and led to concentration of slaveholding. Of the more than 8 million whites in the South in 1860 only 383,637 were slaveholders. Of these, only 2,292 were large planters (holding 100 or more slaves).

1801, 30 Aug. GABRIEL PLOT in Richmond and elsewhere in Henrico County, Va., was suppressed by Governor Monroe; estimates of executions range from 16 to 35. Jefferson's comment: "We are truly to be pitied."

1804–60. UNDERGROUND RAILROAD, an apparatus for assisting slaves to escape from the South, was probably so named about 1831. At least 3,200 active workers have been identified (Siebert), outstanding among whom was the Quaker, **Levi Coffin** (1789–1877), and the escaped slave, **Harriet Tubman** (c.1821–1913), known as "Moses." Losses to the Underground Railroad were proportionally small (500–1,000 per annum after the passage of the Fugitive Slave Law, 1850 [p. 213], the period of its greatest expansion) and chiefly from the border states.

1808–60. SLAVE TRADE, FOREIGN AND DOMESTIC. Although Congress in 1808 prohibited the further importation of slaves, the illicit trade persisted, even after Congress declared it piracy (1820). Between 1854–60 every Southern commercial convention advocated reopening the trade. One estimate of the slaves brought into the U.S. illegally, 1808–60, places the total at 250,000. But the chief source of supply was the domestic slave trade, which by 1800 had already become regularized in response to the increasing demand for slaves. The Upper South found that the sale of surplus slaves in soil-exhausted areas was more profitable than crop cultivation. Chief marketing and distribution points: Richmond, Louisville, Charleston, Mobile, and New Orleans. A substantial part of the domestic trade was in prime field hands, ranging from 18 to 30 in age. Next in order of demand were the full hands used for household and industrial tasks. As a rule slave prices rose continuously after the closure of foreign trade, but were subject to considerable fluctuation in periods of agricultural prosperity and depression. The approximate price of a field hand in 1795 was $300; in 1860 it ranged between $1,200 and $1,800. **Slave hiring** supplemented slave purchases, and made possible the seasonal use of slaves in iron, lead, and coal mines and in factories (notably in tobacco and textile mills). Slave-hiring wages (paid to owners, but bonuses and incentive payments to slaves in addition) rose from $100 (1800) to $500–$600 per annum for a skilled artisan (1860).

1820. Missouri Compromise (p. 159).

1821, Jan. Publication of the *Genius of Universal Emancipation,* antislavery journal edited by **Benjamin Lundy** (1789–1839), advocate of colonization, who published first in Ohio, then in Tenn., and finally in Baltimore, where (1829) **William Lloyd Garrison** (p. 713) served as associate editor.

1822, 30 May. VESEY SLAVE PLOT in Charleston, S.C., led by a free Negro, Denmark Vesey, and urban slave artisans, was revealed by an informer and crushed; 37 executed (18 June–9 Aug.).

1826. Nashoba, a Utopian community near Memphis, Tenn., established by **Frances Wright** for the training of Negroes and their eventual resettlement outside the U.S. It was active until 1828.

1831, 1 Jan. First number of *The Liberator,* edited and published by **William Lloyd Garrison:** the organ of the militant abolitionist movement. "I will not retreat a single inch—AND I WILL BE HEARD."

13–23 Aug. NAT TURNER INSURRECTION in Southampton County, Va., led by Turner, a Negro preacher, in the course of which 57 whites—men, women, and children—were killed. Tracked down in a sensational manhunt (possibly 100 Negroes killed), 20 Negroes (including Turner) were executed after trials.

1831–32, winter. VIRGINIA CONVENTION, after debates covering every phase of the slavery problem, defeated by a small majority various proposals for emancipation. These debates mark a turning point in the handling of the slave problem by the South. Immediately thereafter, beginning with N.C., and spreading to all the slave states, the **slave codes were tightened** to curb the mobility of slaves (through a strict system of patrols and passes), prohibit their attendance at meetings, curtail their education, drastically restrict manumissions, and impose special disabilities on free Negroes. By 1860, 10 states had constitutional provisions curbing either statutory or voluntary emancipation or both.

1832–40. Organization by Garrison of the New England Anti-Slavery Society, which, with a New York group led by **Arthur** (1786–1865) and **Lewis Tappan** (1788–1873), merchants and philanthropists, formed the **American Antislavery Society** (1833). The Lane Theological Seminary debate at Cincinnati (1832) on colonization and abolition was followed by withdrawal (May 1833) of most of the students, led by **Theodore Weld** (1803–95), when the trustees ordered a halt to such discussions. After its organization (1833) Oberlin College (Ohio) was visited by Weld, who converted it into the center of Western abolitionism. The trustees of Oberlin, 1st college to admit women, voted (1835) to admit Negro students. Shortly afterward it became an important station on the Underground Railroad. In 1837 **James G. Birney** (Ky., 1792–1857) became secretary of the American Anti-Slavery Society. By 1838 a Garrisonian group in New England came out for passive resistance rather than physical force. With the Tappans and the **Grimké sisters** (Sarah Moore, 1792–1873; Angelina Emily, 1805–79), Weld launched the non-Garrisonian wing of the organized abolition movement—the **American and Foreign Antislavery Society,** which broke with the Garrison group in 1840.

1836. Adoption of the "**gag rule**" (p. 179).

1837, 7 Nov. A mob in Alton, Ill., attacked the office of **Elijah P. Lovejoy** (1802–37), an antislavery editor. In the ensuing battle Lovejoy was killed. Several persons were indicted, but found not guilty.

1839. *American Slavery As It Is,* by Theodore Weld and his wife, the former Angelina Grimké, was published. Consisting of extracts from Southern newspapers and the testimony of abolitionists who had seen slavery at first hand, this volume presented evidence of oppression. Additional eyewitness testimony was provided by a number of Negroes who participated in the abolition movement as speakers and agents, notably **Frederick Douglass** (p. 661), who escaped from slavery in 1838, and was active in Negro conventions and the Underground Railroad.

Formation of the **Liberty party** (p. 182).

1840. UNDERGROUND RAILROAD, a secret and shifting network of hiding places and routes for helping fugitive slaves escape to the North or Canada, was well established by this date. Without formal organization, it is known to have existed as early as 1786 and to have flourished in the Western Reserve after the War of 1812, but its spread through 14 Northern states did not come until 1830. The name (originally "Underground Road") supposedly dates from the time (1831) the Kentucky master of a fugitive slave named Tice Davids unsuccessfully pursued him across the Ohio River at Ripley, Ohio, and remarked that Davids "must have gone off an underground road." It is estimated that some 50,000 slaves escaped to freedom via the Underground Railroad, *c.*1830–60. A number of Northern states, including Penn., Conn., N.Y., Vt., and Ohio, passed a series of "**personal liberty laws**" (1820–40) which impeded the enforcement of the Federal fugitive slave law of 1793.

1848. "Free Soil" Convention (p. 209).

1850. COMPROMISE (p. 210) and **FUGITIVE SLAVE ISSUE,** 1850–58 (p. 214).

1852. *Uncle Tom's Cabin* (p. 215). *The Pro-Slavery Argument,* a collection of essays by **William Harper** (1790–1847), **Thomas R. Dew** (1802–46), **James H. Hammond** (1807–64), and others, defended slavery as a positive good on the basis of (1) the Scriptures, (2) its role in the prosperity of the South, (3) the alleged biological inferiority of the Negro, (4) slavery as the foundation for a culture based on white supremacy, and (5) as an agency for the education and adjustment of a barbarian people.

1854. *Sociology for the South; or, the Failure of Free Society,* by **George Fitzhugh** (1806–81), who also wrote *Cannibals All! or, Slaves Without Masters* (1857), praised the slave economy and social order of the South as superior to the laissez-faire capitalism of the North.

Kansas-Nebraska Act (p. 217).

1857. Dred Scott Decision (p. 221).

1859. John Brown's Raid (p. 225).

GROWTH OF SLAVE SYSTEM, 1790–1860 *

1790	697,624
1800	893,602
1810	1,191,362
1820	1,538,022
1830	2,009,043
1840	2,487,355
1850	3,204,313
1860	3,953,760

* Chief expansion was in the New South, where increase over 1810 was over 1,000% as against less than 100% in the Old South. Greatest increases: Ala., Miss., La., Tex., and Ark.

DISTRIBUTION OF SLAVES IN THE SLAVE STATES (1860)

Del.	1,798
Md. and D.C.	90,374
Va.	472,494
W.Va.*	18,371
N.C.	331,059
S.C.	402,406
Ga.	462,198
Ky.	225,483
Tenn.	275,719
Ala.	435,080
Miss.	436,631
La.	331,726
Ark.	111,115
Mo.	114,931
Fla.	61,745
Tex.	182,566

* Comprises counties set off from Va. to form W.Va., 1863–66, demonstrating marked difference in the regions with respect to slavery.

FREE AND BOUND LABOR TO 1789

Demand was met by (1) **free labor,** (2) **bound labor,** (3) **slaves.**

1621–1773. MAXIMUM WAGE AND PRICE CONTROLS adopted in certain periods because of labor shortages.

1621–40. Tobacco Provinces. Va. (1621–23) set specific wage and price scales. Md. (Oct. 1640) authorized county courts to regulate wages; expired in 2 yrs.

1630–75. New England. Mass. set maximum wages in the building trades (1630); repealed, 1631; revived and extended to farm labor, 1633; turned over to towns, Oct. 1636. Proposal to reestablish sweeping wage scales, 1670, 1672, defeated; but act of 1675, passed at time of King Philip's War, authorized selectmen to impose double penalty upon takers of excessive wages. Similar legislation enacted in Conn. (prior to 15 June 1640, and in 1641; repealed 1650; scales set in specific crafts, 1677) and New Haven (1640–41).

1671–1741. Rice and Sugar Colonies. In British West Indies minimum wage scales adopted to ensure adequate supply of white labor (e.g., Barbados, 1696); but maximum scales were drafted by S.C. authorities, 1671, and in Ga., 1739, 1741, for servants and laborers employed by the Trustees.

1690–1773. General wage scales and fees fell into disuse, but specific wages, fees, or prices were fixed by local authority in monopoly trades—carmen, porters, butchers, bakers, innkeepers, teachers, ministers, etc.

1774–83. REVOLUTIONARY WAGE AND PRICE CONTROLS. Congress and local committees set prices for scarce commodities as early as 1774. Major activity: **Providence, R.I., Convention,** 31 Dec. 1776, adopted sweeping wage and price regulations for New England states. **York, Pa., Convention,** Mar. 1777, failed to agree on schedules. **New Haven Convention,** Jan. 1778 (New England and Middle States), set up revised schedules. Subsequently town conventions in New England and Middle States continued to revise schedules to curb inflationary spiral (to 1780). Last regional convention, **Philadelphia, 1780.** Action of Congress, 18 Mar., fixing the value of Continental bills at not more than one fortieth of their face value (also p. 104), contributed ultimately to price and wage stabilization.

1636–1789. LABOR COMBINATIONS prior to permanent trade unionism fall into distinct categories: (1) **Combinations of master workers to maintain monopoly:** Mass., shipbuilding guild, 1644; shoemakers, 1648; N.Y., coopers, 1675; Westchester weavers, 1702; **Philadelphia,** cordwainers and tailors, 1718; **Carpenters' Co.,** 1724; **N.Y.,** building-trades workers, 1747, 1769; ship carpenters, 1784. (2) **Combinations of white servants to redress grievances by strikes or insurrections:** Va., York County, 1659, 1661; Gloucester, Sept. 1663 (4 executed for high treason); **Bacon's Rebellion,** 1676 (p. 28); **East Florida,** revolt of Minorcan immigrants at New Smyrna, 19 Aug. 1768 (2 leaders executed). (3) **Combinations of free white labor to bar their trades to Negroes:** Charleston, shipwrights, 1744; **N.C.,** river pilots, 1773. (4) **Joint political action by workmen and employers,** 1765–75: Sons of Liberty (p. 74), Sons of Neptune (mariners); Boston Massacre, 5 Mar. 1770, p. 79; strikes of mariners on British transports, N.Y., 1768; of workers on British fortifications, Boston, 1774. (5) **Strikes by journeymen to secure better working conditions:** Rare prior to 1775, but occur at least as early as 1636 when fishermen struck on Richmond Island off the Me. coast. Boston calkers, 1741, agreed not to accept notes in payment of wages; Savannah carpenters struck, 1746; N.Y. tailors struck for higher wages, 1768; printers, 1778, for raise of $3 a week, successful; Philadelphia seamen, 1779. **1783–89:** Increasing frequency of strikes and trade union organization: N.Y. shoe-makers, 1785; Philadelphia printers, 1786 (permanent organization by 1802); cord-wainers, 1789 ("Federal Society," 1794).

WAGE SCALES. Statistics, fragmentary and without data on supplementary in-come derived by labor from farming, in-dicate that wages exceeded English scale —skilled workers by up to 100%, un-skilled about 50%. Except during periods of inflation colonial real wages exceeded English by 30% to 100%. The differen-tial was noted by Alexander Hamilton, "Report on Manufactures," 1791. High wage scale favored land purchases by la-bor, contributing to maintaining labor shortages in this period. **Per diem wages:** Carpenters (Mass.), 1701, 58.4–61 cts.; 1712, 83.3 cts.; 1735–40, 45.6 cts. (spe-cie); 1743, 40 cts. (specie); 1751–75, 67 cts. **Common (unskilled) labor** (Mass.), 1752–57, 33 cts.; 1758–61, 25 cts.; 1762, 17.8 cts.; 1777, 22 cts.; 1779, 79 cts.

1619–1789. BOUND LABOR OR IN-DENTURED SERVITUDE, used prin-cipally in the Middle Colonies and the tobacco provinces, fell into 2 categories: (1) **voluntary,** (2) **involuntary.** The for-mer were either (a) **redemptioners** or "free willers," white immigrants who, in return for passage to America, bound themselves as servants for from 2 to 7 yrs. (4 yrs. average), estimated at from 60% to 77% of total immigration down to 1776; (b) **apprentices,** minors who were provided training in return for serv-ices in specified trades (in addition, poor children were bound out by public au-thority—1619, London Common Council

sent to Virginia 100 poor children as "bound apprentices"). The involuntary workers comprised (a) **British convict servants** transported to the colonies (prin-cipally Md., Va., or the West Indies) in commutation of death sentence—1655–99, 4,500 transported; 1750–70, 10,000 to Md. alone. Total to continental col-onies to 1775: approximately **50,000** (Butler). Terms of service fixed by Act of Parliament, 1718: **7 yrs.** for lesser crimes within benefit of clergy; **14 yrs.** for nonclergyable felonies (actually a number were transported for **life**). After the Revolution Britain continued convict dumping in the U.S. illegally as late as Aug. 1787, but eventually Australia re-placed America for this purpose. (b) **Victims of kidnaping,** mostly cases of forcible detaining of prospective emi-grants prior to taking passage for Eng-land committed by overzealous recruiting agents (called "spirits" or "crimps" in England; "newlanders" on the Conti-nent). (c) **Servitude in satisfaction of criminal sentences imposed by colonial courts,** particularly for **larceny** (usually punished in the colonies by multiple restitution, as contrasted with England, where larceny from the person above 12d. was capital) and **unlawful absence** from employer's service (punishable **10-fold** in Md. by act of 1661); continued in Delaware to 1839 for whites; to 1867 for Negroes. (d) **Servitude for debt,** gradually eliminated by legislation abol-ishing imprisonment for debt, chiefly in the period, 1820–60 (below), with sur-vivals in the form of post-Civil War **peonage,** or debt bondage, in the South.

LABOR AND SOCIAL REFORM, 1789–1860

1794–1815. ORIGINS OF TRADE UNIONS. Federal Society of Journey-men Cordwainers, Philadelphia (1794–1806), was the longest-lived of the early U.S. trade unions; struck, 1799. New York, printers struck (1794), cabinet-makers (1796); Pittsburgh, shoemakers (1809); Boston, printers (1809), and in other cities (1810–15). Objectives: higher wages, shorter hours, union con-trol of apprenticeship, closed shop.

1806–15. CONSPIRACY CASES. Trade unions were prosecuted for strikes as illegal conspiracies at common law. Issue drawn between Federalists (anti-labor) and Jeffersonian Republicans (pro-trade unions). Major cases: Philadelphia Cordwainers (1806), New York Cord-wainers (1809–10).

1817–48. DEBTOR RELIEF AND PRISON REFORM. N.Y. legislature

(1817) made $25 minimum debt for which a man could be imprisoned. Ky. (1821) abolished imprisonment for debt; Ohio followed, 1828; Vt. and N.J., 1830; N.Y., 1832; Conn., 1837; La., 1840; Mo., 1845; Ala., 1848. Prison reform stems from prison societies (Philadelphia, 1787; Boston, 1825; New York, 1845). Auburn (N.Y.) Penitentiary instituted (1824) **Auburn System**—cell blocks, silence, group labor. Opposing **Pennsylvania System** (exemplified by Eastern State Penitentiary, erected 1829) provided completely solitary confinement and solitary labor. By 1840, 12 Auburn-type prisons erected in the U.S. For treatment of the insane and role of Dorothea Lynde Dix, see p. 696.

1824. First recorded strike of women workers—Pawtucket, R.I., weavers.

1825. Establishment at **New Harmony, Ind.,** by **Robert Owen** (1771–1858), British social reformer, of a short-lived collectivist colony.

1827. CITY CENTRALS, or central trade councils in cities, first established in Philadelphia with Mechanics' Union of Trade Assns. By 1836, 13 cities had centrals.

1828–34. LABOR PARTIES. Participation of workers in politics was accelerated by **removal of property qualifications for voting** (new Western constitutions and Conn., 1818; Mass., 1820; N.Y., 1821; in R.I. not until 1843, after rebellion led by **Thomas W. Dorr** [1805–54]). First U.S. "labor" party organized in Philadelphia (May 1828); gained balance in the city council in the fall election. New York and Boston quickly followed. Leadership primarily not laborers but reformers and small businessmen. In Jacksonian period Eastern workers were divided in their allegiance. New York labor voted for Jackson; Philadelphia labor voted National Republican-Whig; Baltimore closely divided, as were the N.J. towns. Jackson drew greater support from the small Eastern farmers than from industrial areas. Labor platforms demanded (1) 10-hr. day; (2) abolition of imprisonment for debt (75,000 debtors in jail, 1829); (3) abolition of prison contract labor; (4) enactment of mechanics' lien laws (piecemeal extension

beg. Pa., 1803; N.Y., 1830; Va., 1843; Me., 1848); (5) abolition of discriminatory militia system; (6) curbs on licensed monopolies, particularly banks; (7) universal education. **Leadership.** New York: **Thomas Skidmore,** agrarian radical, and **William Leggett** (1801–39), editor and social reformer, as well as such extremists as **Robert Dale Owen** (1801–77), son of Robert Owen, and Scottish-born **Frances Wright** (1759–1852), pioneer agitator in U.S. for women's rights, who coedited (with Owen) the *Free Enquirer.* Philadelphia: **John Ferral** and **William English.** New England: **Seth Luther,** labor agitator, **Charles Douglas,** and **George Bancroft,** historian, who feared the effects of industrialization on labor. By 1834 the "labor" parties were defunct, being absorbed by the 2 major parties or reorganized as factions like **Loco-Focos** or Equal Rights faction, radical wings of the Democratic party in N.Y. and Pa.

1834, 29 Jan. 1ST USE OF FEDERAL TROOPS to intervene in a labor dispute (closed shop). President Jackson ordered the War Dept. to put down "riotous assembly" among Irish laborers constructing Chesapeake and Ohio Canal near Williamsport, Md.

1834–37. NATIONAL FEDERATIONS. City central movement spread from Philadelphia to New York (14 Aug. 1833), Baltimore, Boston, Louisville, Pittsburgh, and Cincinnati, with emphasis on nonpolitical, trade-union objectives. In 1834, New York General Trades Union called a convention of delegates from other city centrals, which organized the **National Trades Union,** headed by **Ely Moore,** elected to Congress on Tammany ticket. A number of trades held national conventions during this period, but the movement was aborted by the Panic of 1837 (p. 178). Mounting number of strikes in this period. In the decade, 1831–40, 126 strikes have been uncovered in Pennsylvania alone (W. A. Sullivan).

1835–42. In *People* v. *Fisher,* N.Y. court declared strikes illegal; but in Mass., in *Comm.* v. *Hunt* (1842), Chief Justice Lemuel Shaw (p. 778) ruled that trade unions were lawful and strikes for a closed shop legal.

1836–60. 10-HOUR MOVEMENT. Building trades workers in Eastern cities had obtained 10-hr. day by 1834, and the Whig municipal government of Philadelphia had prior to 1836 put the 10-hr. day into effect. As a result of a memorial to Congress by Ely Moore on behalf of the National Trades Union, and a local strike, President Jackson's Secretary of the Navy, Mahlon Dickerson, issued an order for a 10-hr. day in Philadelphia Navy Yard (31 Aug. 1836). Executive order of President Van Buren, 31 Mar. 1840, extended "10-hr. system" to all laborers and mechanics employed on Federal public works. Average daily hours of factory workers in 1840 estimated at 11.4. New England Convention (Oct. 1844) urged 10-hr. legislation; enacted: N.H., 1847; Me., 1848; Pa., 1848; Ohio, 1852; R.I., 1853; Calif., 1853; Conn., 1855; no action in Mass. Such laws were subject to evasion by contract. By 1860, 10-hr. day was standard among most skilled workers and common laborers, but had not yet been adopted in Lowell and Salem mills.

1840–52. SOCIAL REFORMS affected the labor movement, particularly the **Association** movement, an effort to draw men into cooperative programs: (1) Most notable example was the **Fourierist system** inspired by a French reformer, Charles Fourier (1772–1837) and endorsed in the U.S. by **Albert Brisbane** (1809–90), who expounded his ideas in Horace Greeley's N.Y. *Tribune*. This system provided for the setting up of **phalanxes**, communities of about 1,500 persons devoted to an agrarian-handicraft economy based upon voluntarism. Goods produced were the property of the phalanx, but private property and inheritance were not abolished. More than 40 phalanxes were established, from Mass. to Wis., all disappearing by 1860. Best known: **Brook Farm** (1841–46), established by **George Ripley** (1802–80), a Unitarian minister and Transcendentalist (p. 601), and numbering Nathaniel Hawthorne, Charles A. Dana, and John S. Dwight; in 1845 it was converted into a Fourierist phalanx, but was dissolved after a major fire in 1846. The short-lived **Sylvania Phalanx** in Pa. was organized, 1842, by Greeley

and others. The **North American Phalanx** near Red Bank, N.J., was established by Brisbane; disbanded, 1854. (2) **Owenite societies**, highly paternalistic collectivist communities, combining agriculture and factory production. In 1848 an Icarian community was settled in Tex. by European workingmen under the leadership of **Étienne Cabet** (1788–1856), whose *Le Voyage en Icarie* (1840) projected a social order on communist principles. The Tex. colony, like the one at Nauvoo, Ill. (1849), was unsuccessful. (3) **Cooperative societies** or protective unions (both producers' and consumers'). New England Protective Union, 1845, set up central agency to buy for retail stores; iron molders, Cincinnati, 1848; especially strong in New York City by 1851; more than 800 organized, 1845–60. (4) **Agrarian reform** agitated by the National Reform Association led by **George Henry Evans** (1805–56), editor of N.Y. *Working Man's Advocate* (1829–37, 1844–47), advocated free homesteads, exemption of homesteads from seizure for debt (p. 438), and foreshadowed Henry George's "single-tax" program (p. 463). (5) **Temperance crusade**, with roots in the colonial period, was stimulated by the writings of Dr. Benjamin Rush, the preaching of Lyman Beecher, and popularized by Timothy Shay Arthur (p. 603), as well as by the activities of the General Conference of the Methodist Church (1780, 1816), the American Temperance Union (1st national convention, 1836), and the Washingtonian Temperance Society (reformed drunkards, 1840). Under the leadership of **Neal Dow** (1804–97), Me. passed 1st statewide prohibition law in 1846; revision of 1851 served as model. Vt., R.I., and Minnesota Territory followed, 1852; Mich., 1853; Conn., 1854; and 8 other states by 1855.

1852–60. RISE OF NATIONAL TRADE UNIONS stressing business objectives: Natl. Typographical Union, 1852; Hat Finishers, 1854; Journeymen Stone Cutters Assn., 1855; United Cigarmakers, 1856; Iron Molders (led by **William Sylvis** (1828–69) and Machinists and Blacksmiths, 1859. The weaker nationals were shattered by the Panic of

1857. In decade, 1851–60, cost of living rose 12%; money wages rose 4%.

1860, 22 Feb. Strike of shoemakers in Lynn and Natick, Mass., for higher wages spread throughout New England and involved 20,000 workers, including women. Major demands won.

Years	(Index 1913=100)
1820–29	46
1830–39	48
1840–49	56
1850–59	52

INDEX OF REAL WAGES (Hansen)

LABOR AND OCCUPATIONAL TRENDS SINCE 1860

1861–65. IMPACT OF THE CIVIL WAR. Few strikes during war years, although by 1865 real wages had declined one third from 1860 level. Expansion of city centrals and national organizations was countered by the organization of employers' associations (as in Mich., 1864; N.Y. Master Builders Assn., 1869). Louisville Convention, Sept. 1865, representing 8 city centrals, attempted unsuccessfully to form a national labor federation. Consumers' cooperatives multiplied, inspired by the Rochdale pioneers in England (1844).

1864, 4 July. Passage of the Federal emigrant contract labor act, pledging wages of emigrants for terms not exceeding 12 mos., resulted in the setting up of the American Emigrant Co. to import laborers.

1864–73. NATIONAL TRADE UNION MOVEMENT. Organization of 26 national unions, with 6 previously established. Total trade union membership, 1870–72: 300,000. Most influential national was the Molders. Defeated in its fight against organized employers (1867–68), that union organized cooperative stove foundries, but the cooperators quickly became "capitalists." Railway brotherhoods originated in this period: Locomotive Engineers (1863), Railway Conductors (1868), Firemen (1873). Widespread utilization of shoe machinery, 1861–70, led to displacement of skilled mechanics by unskilled labor and prompted the organization of the Order of the Knights of St. Crispin (7 Mar. 1867). By 1870 its membership was estimated at 50,000. Major objective: protection of members against competition of "green hands" and apprentices. By the end of this period the shoeworkers' union had already begun to decline in membership.

1866, 20 Aug.–1872. NATIONAL LABOR UNION organized at Baltimore. Original objective: the 8-hour day, a movement led by Ira Stewart (1831–83), a Boston machinist, and George E. McNeill (1837–1906). As early as July 1862, Congress had provided that the hours and wages of employees in Federal navy yards should conform to those of private firms. Ill., N.Y., and Mo., 1867, enacted 8-hr.-day laws; not enforced; Wis. for women and children, but with loopholes. Failure of the 8-hr. demands led the National Labor Union, under the presidencies of Sylvis (1868) and Richard F. Trevellick (1869), head of Ship Carpenters and Caulkers Intl., to concentrate on political reform. In 1872 the federation was transformed into the National Labor Reform Party, with Judge David Davis (Ill.) its nominee for president (22 Feb.). The withdrawal of Davis caused the collapse of both party and federation. The period, 1868–72, was also marked by the establishment of numerous producers' cooperatives under union auspices.

1868. First Federal 8-hr. day enacted by Congress; confined to laborers and mechanics employed by or on behalf of the U.S. govt.

1873–78. DEPRESSION AND LABOR TURBULENCE. National unions dropped from 30 to 9 (1877), and unionized labor from 300,000 to *c.*50,000. Knights of St. Crispin disappeared by 1878. Outstanding manifestations of labor unrest: (1) Tompkins Square Riot, New York City, 13 Jan. 1874, where police charged radical labor meeting. (2) "Molly Maguires," a secret organization of miners, an outgrowth of the Ancient Order of Hibernians, organized in Ireland to oppose encroachments of landlords, promoted labor violence in Eastern Pa., beg. 1862. As a result of prosecution instituted by Philadelphia & Reading R.R. and evidence gathered by a Pinkerton detective, 24 Molly Maguires were convicted (fall 1875), 10 hanged for murder, the others sentenced to jail terms of 2–7 yrs. (1876), and the order was crushed. (3) General Strike. Railroad strikes, beg. 17 July 1877 on the B.&O. in protest against wage cuts, spread quickly to other lines east of the Mississippi and eventually to Western lines, with rioting in Baltimore, Pittsburgh, Chicago, and St. Louis. President Hayes sent Federal troops to restore order at Martinsburg, W.Va., after strikers had repulsed militia (9 persons killed), and at Pittsburgh, where, after resisting Philadelphia militia in a pitched battle (21 July, 26 killed), a mob tore up railroad tracks and burned down machine shops, the Union Depot, and other property, with damage estimated at from $5–$10 million. As a result of strike violence legislatures revived conspiracy laws.

EUROPEAN REVOLUTIONARY LABOR PROGRAMS made their appearance in this period. Three major groups: (1) Marxian Socialists, who split in 1872 with (2) the Anarcho-Communists, followers of Mikhail Bakunin, and moved the headquarters of the First International to New York City, under the leadership of a lieutenant of Karl Marx, Friedrich A. Sorge (1827–1906); formed Workingmen's party, 1876; name changed to Socialist-Labor party, 1877; worked in the trade-union movement especially through the Cigarmakers Union, headed by Adolph Strasser. (3) Lassallean Socialists, mostly German emigrants, followers of Ferdinand Lassalle, who favored political action.

1878, Jan.–1893. KNIGHTS OF LABOR organized on a national basis. The Knights originated, 1871, as a secret order at a tailors' meeting in Philadelphia called by Uriah Stephens (1821–82), who headed the Knights until 1879,

when he was succeeded by Terence V. Powderly (1849–1924), who held the post until 1893 (elected, 1878, mayor of Scranton on a labor ticket). The Knights was an industrial union headed by a General Assembly to which workers belonged as individuals, regardless of sex, race, or color. All gainfully employed persons, including unskilled workers (except certain professional groups) were eligible, but three fourths of each assembly were required to be wage earners. In the West farmers dominated; in the East trade unionists. Local assemblies rose from 484 (1882) to 5,892 (1886), with membership in excess of 700,000. Knights supported (1) 8-hr. day; (2) boycotts and arbitration (rather than strikes); (3) various political reforms, including adoption of graduated income tax; (4) consumers' and producers' cooperatives (135 set up, including the ownership and operation of a coal mine). Hard times, 1884–85, led to widespread boycotts and strikes, notably by railway shopmen of Union Pacific and the Southwest System (1884), both successful, and against the Wabash (1885), forcing Jay Gould to negotiate with the Knights and agree to end discriminatory practices. Decline after 1886 peak due to (1) failure of strike against Southwest R.R. System (1 Mar.–3 May 1886) led by Martin Irons, which Powderly sought to terminate by negotiation, and to unsuccessful results of strike waves in the latter half of 1886, including collapse of 8-hr.-day general strike at Chicago (begun 1 May 1886), and the packinghouse lockout of 1887; (2) Haymarket Incident (below). Agrarian control led to Powderly being replaced, 1893, by James R. Sovereign of Iowa.

1882, Sept. First Labor Day celebration held in New York City. By Act of Congress, 1894, 1st Monday in Sept. made an annual legal holiday.

1886, 4 May. HAYMARKET MASSACRE resulted when, after police broke up an Anarcho-Communist meeting at Haymarket Square, Chicago, a bomb exploded among the front rank of police, who then opened fire (7 police fatally injured; 70 wounded). The trial (19 June–20 Aug.) of August Spies, Albert

Parsons, Samuel J. Fielden, and other radical agitators before Judge Joseph E. Gary resulted in convictions (7 sentenced to death; 1 to 15 yrs. in prison). Conviction affirmed by Ill. Supreme Court, 14 Sept. 1887. As a result of petitions circulated by William Dean Howells (p. 730), Henry Demarest Lloyd (1847–1903), and labor groups for commutation of the death sentence, 2 prisoners were commuted by Gov. Oglesby to life terms. Remaining 4 executed on 11 Nov. 1887. Gov. John Peter Altgeld (1847–1902) freed 3 others, charging that the trial had been unfair (June 1893). The actual bomb thrower was never established. The incident damaged the labor movement.

1886, 8 Dec.–1914. AMERICAN FEDERATION OF LABOR organized at Columbus, Ohio, by some 25 labor groups representing about 150,000 members. First president, Samuel Gompers, who, with Strasser, had reorganized the Cigarmakers Union (by 1879) and had participated at the founding of the Federation of Organized Trades and Labor Unions (Pittsburgh, Nov. 1881), formed to protect the legislative interests of trade unions. The A.F. of L. immediately declared war on the Knights and accepted members and locals also in the latter body. Recognizing the autonomy of each trade, it confined its objectives chiefly to business unionism. After the depression, 1893–97, large gains in trade union membership took place. Despite antiunion campaign of National Association of Manufacturers (org., 1895), the A.F. of L. claimed, 1904, 1,676,200 out of 2,072,700 union members. After a brief decline, 1905–09, union membership rose again, 1910–14, by which date the A.F. of L. claimed 2,020,671 out of 2,687,100 union members (Wolman)— the greatest gains among coal miners, railroad workers, and in the building trades. The bulk of the unskilled and semiskilled workers were still unorganized. A.F. of L. unions, 1900–14, (1) stressed "job ownership," (2) favored immigration curbs, (3) demanded relief from technological unemployment, (4) enactment of labor legislation, and (5) collaboration with employers, as evidenced by labor participation (with employers and the public) in the National Civic Federation (1900) to promote mediation of labor disputes (particularly effective between 1900–05).

1892, 6 July. HOMESTEAD MASSACRE occurred when strikers at the Carnegie Steel Co. plant at Homestead, Pa., fired upon 2 barges being towed up the Monongahela with 300 Pinkerton detectives engaged by the company's general manager, Henry Clay Frick (1849–1919); 7 killed. Strike, broken by strikebreakers as state militia took over on 12 July, ended 20 Nov. On 23 July Alexander Berkman (1870–1936), a Russian-born Anarchist, shot and stabbed Frick, in an assault planned with Emma Goldman (1869–1940). Berkman was sentenced to 21 yrs. No effective steel union was organized until the 1930's.

14 July. Martial law declared in Coeur d'Alene silver mines in Ida. as result of violence between striking miners and strikebreakers. Federal troops dispatched to the area.

1894, 21 June–20 July. PULLMAN STRIKE called by American Railway Union (independent under Eugene V. Debs), with a boycott on Pullman cars. By the end of June the strike had tied up every Middle Western railroad. Attorney General Olney had 3,400 men sworn in as special deputies to keep trains running. When violence broke out, railroad association appealed to President Cleveland, who (over the protest of Governor Altgeld) sent Federal troops to restore order, safeguard the mail, and protect interstate commerce. On 2 July, a Federal court issued an injunction forbidding interference with the operation of the mails or interstate commerce. Debs was jailed for contempt and the strike was smashed. The incident dramatized the increasing use of the labor injunction (since 1883). Between 1901–28, 118 applications were officially reported for the Federal courts; 116 unreported (Frankfurter and Greene)— most of which ended strikes before a final decree was needed. State injunctions were widespread, and the courts frequently circumvented curbs imposed by legislatures.

1898–1934. ADJUSTMENT OF RAIL-ROAD LABOR DISPUTES. Although an Act of Congress of 1888 provided for arbitration by special boards set up by the parties in interest and for a Presidential commission to investigate and report where one of the parties refused the offer of the other to arbitrate, such machinery was ineffective in the Pullman strike. The **Erdman Act** (1 June 1898) provided for mediation by the chairman of the ICC and the commissioner of the Bureau of Labor, although neither official had legal power to initiate proceedings. Between 1906 and 1913, 61 railroad labor controversies were settled (26 by mediation). The **Newlands Act** (15 July 1913) created a Board of Mediation and Conciliation consisting of 4 members. Between 1913 and end of 1917 the Board settled 58 out of the 71 controversies which came before it. The **Adamson Act** (3 Sept. 1916) provided for an 8-hr. day and time and a half for overtime on interstate railroads. While the railroads were under Federal operation during and after World War I, 3 national adjustment boards were established, representing management and unions, to settle grievances. Under the **Esch-Cummins Act** (28 Feb. 1920; also p. 330) a Railroad Labor Board was established, comprising 9 members (3 each from the companies, the employees, and the public), whose authority stopped short of compulsory arbitration. Under the **Act of 1926** (20 May) the Labor Board was replaced by a Board of Mediation, an independent agency consisting of 5 members appointed by the President. By the **Railway Labor Act** of 1934 (27 June) a National Railroad Adjustment Board, with offices in Chicago, was established. The Act upheld the right of employees to organize and bargain collectively through representatives of their own choosing.

1902. ANTHRACITE COAL STRIKE, called (12 May) by United Mine Workers of America (UMW) President John Mitchell, when mine owners declined offer of arbitration, led to intervention (3 Oct.) by President Theodore Roosevelt, who (16 Oct.) appointed a commission to mediate the dispute. The strike was called off on 21 Oct., and on 22 Mar. 1903 the commission awarded the miners a wage increase of 10% but refused union recognition.

1902–08. DANBURY HATTERS' CASE (p. 496).

1905, June–1920. INDUSTRIAL WORKERS OF THE WORLD (I.W.W.), launched at Chicago convention, comprising Western Federation of Miners (1893) and the American Labor Union (org. 1898 as a rival of the A.F. of L.), emphasized revolutionary program: (1) **abolition of wage system,** and (2) **industrial unionism.** After eliminating the Socialist Labor faction headed by Daniel De Leon, the "Wobblies" stressed the organization in the West of **unskilled and migratory workers** in lumber, shipping, fruit growing, and textiles (largely the result of a successful strike at Lawrence, Mass., 1912). Most active organizer: **William D. ("Big Bill") Haywood** (1869–1928). As a result of vigilante action and Federal prosecutions, 1918–20, notably at **Centralia, Wash.,** the I.W.W. was eliminated as an effective power in the Northwest.

1909–11. INTERNATIONAL LADIES GARMENT WORKERS UNION made notable strides in eliminating evils in sweatshops in the shirtwaist trade, particularly after the **Triangle fire** (25 Mar. 1911), with 146 fatalities (proprietors indicted, 11 Apr.; acquitted, 7 Dec.), which led to enactment in New York of a drastically revised and stringent building code and a revision of the labor laws.

1910–12. ARBITRATION set up in protocol (1910) in N.Y. cloak and suit industry (initiated by Louis D. Brandeis) and in agreement negotiated (1911) by Sidney Hillman of the United Garment Workers with **Hart, Schaffner & Marx,** Chicago; latter developed into **impartial chairman** machinery (1912).

1912. First minimum wage act for women and minors passed in Mass.

1913. U.S. Dept. of Labor established.

1914. Clayton Act (p. 275).

1915. 4 Mar. La Follette Seamen's Act regulated conditions of employment for maritime workers.

1914–20. WORLD WAR I AND LA-

BOR. Union membership increased by 2,350,000, with A.F. of L. gaining 2,068,000 (Wolman). Strikes were successful during the "seller's market." A.F. of L. strongly supported the war; the Socialist party and the I.W.W. opposed U.S. entry. For prosecution of radicals, see p. 331. To maintain production schedules President Wilson set up a Mediation Commission, 1917, and the National War Labor Board, 8 Apr. 1918 (p. 279). Government agencies' general insistence that suppliers bargain collectively led to the rapid rise of company unions. After Federal labor agencies ceased operations strikes increased, with the number of wage earners involved rising from 1,239,989 (1918) to 4,160,348 (1919). Most notable was the steel strike, 1919. The refusal of Judge Elbert H. Gary (1846–1927), chairman of the board, U.S. Steel, to confer with the strike leaders brought on a strike call by the A.F. of L. at the urging of radical labor organizer, William Z. Foster (1881–). Strikers sought (1) union recognition, (2) collective bargaining rights, (3) abolition of the 12-hr. day and (4) of company unions, (5) wage increases. The strike began 22 Sept. 1919 and was abandoned 9 Jan. 1920.

1916, 1 Sept. FEDERAL CHILD LABOR LAW (Keating-Owen Act) barred from interstate commerce the products of child labor; declared unconstitutional 3 June 1918; Act of 24 Feb. 1919 declared unconstitutional 15 May 1922; 2 June 1924, Child Labor Amendment to the Constitution was submitted to the states for ratification. By 1950 only 26 of the necessary 36 states had ratified.

1921–32. LABOR SETBACKS. The sharp recession of 1921–22, strong opposition by employer associations, and unfavorable decisions by Federal courts weakened organized labor. Real wages and per capita income rose after 1923 (except in textiles and coal mining). Total union membership, 1929, 3,442,600 as against 5 million in 1921; A.F. of L., 2,961,096 against almost 4 million in 1921. Further drop by 1933 to 2,973,000, of whom 2,126,796 belonged to the A.F. of L. United Mine Workers under John L. Lewis shrank from 500,000 to 150,000.

Communist Agitation (Trade Union Education League headed by W. Z. Foster) within trade unions (particularly the I.L.G.W.U., Furriers, Amalgamated Clothing, and United Mine Workers) resulted in dual unions and forced progressives into alignments with conservative leaders against Communists.

Judicial Setbacks: See pp. 497, 553. Major Labor Gains: Railway Labor Act, 1926 (p. 553); Norris-La Guardia Anti-Injunction Act, 23 Mar. 1932, forbade injunctions to sustain antiunion employment contracts or to prevent strikes, boycotts, and picketing.

For A.F. of L. support of La Follette for President in 1924, see p. 335. William Green (1873–1952), of United Mine Workers, succeeded to the presidency of the A.F. of L. on the death of Gompers (1924), and kept the organization along craft union lines. Company unions expanded to over 400 by 1926, with a membership of 1,369,000, continuing to expand until 1935 to about 2,500,000. Chief violence occurred in textile strikes: Gastonia and Marion, N.C.; Elizabethtown, Tenn.; and Paterson, N.J.

1932. First Unemployment Insurance Law in the U.S. enacted in Wis.

1933–51. LABOR GAINS UNDER THE NEW DEAL AND FAIR DEAL. As a result of New Deal labor policies (pp. 346–359) total noncompany union membership approximated 4,400,000 in 1935, of which the A.F. of L. claimed 3,045,347. Further expansion was due in large measure to the Wagner Act (p. 351) and to the activities of industrial unions largely as the result of the formation, 9 Nov. 1935, within the A.F. of L. of the Committee for Industrial Organization (C.I.O.). In May 1938, leaders expelled from the A.F. of L. (John L. Lewis [1880–] had resigned as vice-president of the A.F. of L., 23 Nov. 1935) set up a rival organization under the leadership of Lewis—spectacularly successful in increasing the membership of the United Mine Workers—and Sidney Hillman (1887–1946) of the Amalgamated Clothing Workers. The C.I.O. was reorganized, 1938, as the Congress of Industrial Organizations. Philip Murray (1886–1952) succeeded to the presidency of the C.I.O. in Nov. 1940. By

1936 C.I.O. began to organize the motor and steel industries. On 31 Dec. 1936 a few hundred workers seized a number of General Motors plants at Flint, Mich., staging a spectacular **sit-down strike** which lasted 44 days; involved 40,000 workers directly and 110,000 indirectly. Sit-down strikes spread to rubber, steel, textiles, oil refining, shipbuilding, and involved a half million workers. Following a Supreme Court decision, 1939, declaring sit-down strikes illegal, this technique was discredited by organized labor.

1937, 30 May. MEMORIAL DAY MASSACRE. In the spring of 1937 the Steel Workers' Organizing Committee secured recognition by U.S. Steel as the bargaining agency, a wage boost of 10%, and a 40-hr. week with time and a half for overtime. Other employers challenged the constitutionality of the Wagner Act (upheld by Supreme Court, 1937, p. 498). "Little Steel" under the leadership of **Republic Steel**, headed by **Tom M. Girdler** (1877–   ), was adamant. The issue came to a head when a group of union demonstrators before the gates of the Republic plant in South Chicago were fired upon by police, with 4 killed, 84 injured. Finally, in 1941, virtually all of the independent steel companies signed agreements with the C.I.O.

Dec. Publication of a report of a Senate subcommittee, headed by **Robert M. La Follette, Jr.** (1895–1953), disclosed antilabor techniques employed to fight unions (1933–37), including blacklists, espionage, vigilante groups to curb labor organizers (**Mohawk Valley formula**), recruiting of strikebreaking services, private armed forces, and private arsenals (in the possession of the Youngstown Sheet and Tube Co. and the Republic Steel Corp.). The report singled out terrorism in Harlan Co., Ky.

1938. FAIR LABOR STANDARDS ACT (p. 360).

LABOR IN WORLD WAR II (p. 381). **SMITH-CONNALLY ACT** (1943, p. 382). For formation of C.I.O.-P.A.C. (1944), see p. 384.

UNION EXPANSION. A.F. of L. membership by 1943 had increased to almost 9 million; C.I.O. claimed 5,285,000, with a total of 13 million union members in the U.S. by early 1944 out of a total employment of 54 million. By 1947 union membership rose to 14 million (22.4% of labor force as against 6.6% in 1930).

1946, 1 Apr. United Mine Workers' strike of 400,000 bituminous coal miners began. President Truman seized the mines; the government retained control when the operators refused to accept a contract with the union negotiated by Federal authorities. A 2nd strike call on 21 Nov. by John L. Lewis in defiance of a government injunction led to his being held in contempt of court by a Federal district court (4 Dec.) and fined $10,000; United Mine Workers fined $3,500,000 (sustained by Supreme Court, 6 Mar. 1947, but fine subsequently reduced to $700,000). On 7 Dec. 1946 Lewis ordered the miners back to work.

1947, 23 June. TAFT-HARTLEY ACT, passed by Congress over President Truman's veto of 20 June, (1) banned the closed shop, which forbade the hiring of nonunion men; (2) permitted employers to sue unions for broken contracts or damages inflicted during strikes; (3) required unions to abide by a 60-day "cooling-off period" before striking; (4) required unions to make public their financial statements; (5) forbade union contributions to political campaigns; (6) ended the "check-off system," in which the employer collected union dues; (7) required union leaders to take an oath that they were not members of the Communist party. The Act was amended 22 Oct. 1951 to permit union-shop contracts without first polling employees.

1947–52. STRIKES AND WORK STOPPAGES increased in response to the inflationary cycle. By 1949 labor stressed pension plans and other "fringe" demands rather than higher wages. **Work stoppages**, relative to size of labor force, were lower in the postwar period (4,750 in 1945; 4,843 in 1950) than in 1903 (3,600) or 1917 (4,450), but were substantially higher than for the exceptional period, 1921–26 (c.1,500). When steel companies refused to abide by a Wage Mediation Board award (20 Mar. 1952) of higher wages to workers without rise in steel prices, President Truman under emergency powers seized the steel mills (8 Apr.). A preliminary injunction was granted 29 Apr. to nullify the seizure; on 2 June the Supreme Court ruled the seizure unconstitutional. The United Steel Workers Union called another strike, which was settled as a result of the intervention of President Truman (24 July), with the union obtaining a 16-ct. increase in wages, a rise of $5.20 per ton of steel, and a modified union shop.

1948. Mississippi became the 48th state to enact **workmen's compensation** legislation; 1st act, Md., 1902.

AVERAGE HOURLY EARNINGS IN MANUFACTURING

Year	Earnings	Productivity (1947 = 100)
1909	$0.193	36.6
1919	0.477	42.1
1929	0.566	72.5
1933	0.442	76.0
1937	0.624	83.6
1945	1.023	...
1957	2.070	...

OCCUPATIONAL TRENDS.

Shift of population from rural to urban life (p. 467) and technological progress were accompanied by far-reaching shifts in occupations:

NUMBER OF PERSONS, 10 YRS. OLD AND OVER, ENGAGED IN AGRICULTURAL AND NON-AGRICULTURAL PURSUITS

(U.S. Bureau of Census, *Hist. Stat. of U.S., 1789–1945;* 1960, 14 yrs. and over, *Stat. Abstract, 1960.*

	Nonagricultural	%	Agricultural	%
1820	812,042	28.2	2,068,958	71.8
1860	4,325,116	41.1	6,207,634	41.1
1900	18,161,235	62.5	10,911,998	37.5
1940	42,985,704	82.4	9,162,547	17.6
1950	52,500	83.1	7,500,000	16.9
1960	59,702,000	92.9	4,565,000	7.1

1952. Both A.F. of L. and C.I.O. endorsed Adlai E. Stevenson, the Democratic party's unsuccessful candidate for President, who favored repeal of the Taft-Hartley Act.

Upon the deaths of William Green and Philip Murray, **George Meany** and **Walter P. Reuther** succeeded to the presidency of the A.F. of L. and C.I.O. respectively.

DISTRIBUTION OF GAINFUL WORKERS
(in thousands of persons)

	1870	1900	1940
All gainful workers	12,920	29,070	53,300
Agriculture	6,730	10,950	9,000
Forestry and fisheries	60	210	140
Mining	190	750	1,110
Manufacturing and hand trades	2,130	6,250	11,940
Construction	700	1,640	3,510
Transportation and other public utilities	580	2,020	4,150
Trade	} 850 {	} 2,870	7,180
Finance and real estate			1,550
Education	190	650	1,680
Other professional services	140	510	2,320
Domestic service	940	1,740	2,610
Personal service	270	1,020	3,100
Govt., not elsewhere classified	100	300	1,690
Not allocated	40	160	3,330

WOMEN IN LABOR FORCE OR GAINFULLY OCCUPIED, 15 YRS. AND OVER

	Total No.	Married No.	%
1890	3,712,144	515,260	13.9
1920	8,346,796	1,920,281	23.0
1940	13,840,000	5,040,000	36.4
1957	21,523,000	11,529,000	53.4

1954. **"Right-to-work"** laws (outlawing union shop), on books of 13 states at beginning of yr., adopted in Utah and Kansas, but new bills defeated in 31 states.

1955. GUARANTEED ANNUAL WAGE. Provisions for payments during layoff periods were obtained by U.A.W. in a compromise settlement with Ford and General Motors; similar contracts were obtained by the C.I.O.-Steelworkers.

5 Dec. MERGER OF A.F. OF L. And C.I.O. made official, with **George Meany** (1894–   ) elected president. Under charter of the consolidated union, craft and industrial organizations were to have equal rank.

1957. RACKETEERING. A special senate committee under the chairmanship of Senator John L. McClellan to investigate racketeering in labor-management relations held hearings, largely concerned with the Teamsters Union and the activities of its president, **Dave Beck.** In

May Beck was expelled as vice-president of the A.F. of L.-C.I.O. He was convicted of embezzlement in a state court in Seattle, Dec. 1957. In addition, the union's vice-president, **James R. Hoffa,** was also charged with misappropriation of funds and close connections with gangsters. These disclosures led to the adoption by the A.F. of L.-C.I.O. of a Code of Ethics, the resignation of a number of union officials, and the suspension of several national affiliates in Oct. In Dec. the A.F. of L.-C.I.O. convention voted to expel the Teamsters Union, the Bakery Workers Union, and the Laundry Workers Union. Previously, 22 Sept. 1954, the Intl. Longshoremen's Assn. had been expelled from the A.F. of L. for refusing to rid itself of racketeering elements.

14 Sept. LABOR MANAGEMENT REPORTING AND DISCLOSURE ACT (p. 420).

1959, 15 July. Steel strike lasted until 7 Nov., when a federal court issued an 80-day injunction under the Taft-Hartley Act ordering the men back to work. The strike was settled by year end at an estimated increase of 41 cts. per hr. over 30 mos. Previous steel strike of 1956 ended with a wage rise of *c.*50 cts. per hr. by 1958 and rise in steel prices.

SCIENCE AND INVENTION

GENERAL SCIENCE

1665–1735. EARLY ASTRONOMY AND SEISMOLOGY. John Winthrop, Jr. (1606–76), probably the 1st colonial member of the Royal Society of London (Brasch), made the first systematic astronomical observations in the colonies (before 1665). Advanced astronomical knowledge was revealed by **Thomas Brattle** (1658–1713) in his *Almanack* (1678). His observations of Halley's comet (1680) were utilized and credited to him by Newton in his landmark *Principia mathematica* (1687). His account of a solar eclipse of 1694 was published in the *Philosophical Transactions* of the Royal Society (1704). He made significant observations of a later (1703) solar eclipse, 3 lunar eclipses (1700, 1703, 1707), and of variations of the magnetic needle (1708). **Thomas Robie** (1689–1729), Harvard astronomer and mathematician, described a meteor (1719) as a natural phenomenon. **Paul Dudley's** (1651–1751) report of an earthquake in New England (1727) and further data on such phenomena appeared in *Transactions* (1735).

1680–1725. NATURAL HISTORY. John Banister (*c.*1648–92) transmitted (1680) 52 species of American insects to Petiver, the English naturalist, and contributed a paper on American molluscs to the Royal Society (1693). His *Catalogus Plantarum in Virginia Observatarum* (published in Ray's *Historia Plantarum*) is probably the 1st systematic paper upon natural history written in the colonies. **Cotton Mather** contributed 13 letters on natural history and biology to *Transactions* (1712) and was credited by Petiver (1717) with specimens of bones and dried plants. **Paul Dudley** (1675–1751) contributed data on the swamp sumac,

bees, and the rattlesnake to the *Transactions* (1720–23). Work on New England fruit trees (1724) established him as the 1st colonial horticulturist. His *Natural History of Whales* (1725) became a standard work.

1708–51. PHYSICS AND MATHEMATICS. James Logan (1674–1751) is generally credited with formally introducing Newton's *Principia* into the colonies (1708), although information was already available through the *Transactions*. Cotton Mather's *Christian Philosopher* (1721) contained the 1st lengthy explanation of Newtonian physics (in the colonies). The 1st colonial chair in philosophy and mathematics was filled (1717) at William and Mary by Rev. Hugh Jones (*c.*1670–1760). More significant was the endowment of a chair in mathematics and natural philosophy at Harvard (1727); the 1st incumbent, **Isaac Greenwood** (1702–45), offered a course in fluxions (calculus).

1735–68. BOTANY AND ZOOLOGY. The correspondence between **John Bartram** (1699–1777) and Peter Collinson, English botanist, developed a channel for transmission of colonial plants and data abroad. Bartram, who established (1728) the 1st botanical garden in the colonies at Philadelphia, traveled widely through the colonies collecting specimens of rare plants and cultivating in North America plants received from abroad. He published (1751) his *Observations* of his trip to Lake Ontario. Together with his son, **William** (1739–1823), he explored the St. John's River, Fla., and there discovered the royal palm. William's list of 215 American birds (*Travels,* 1791) was the most complete pub. up to that time. Other pioneers in botany include John Clayton (1693–1773), best known for his *Flora Virginia* (1739); **John Mitchell** (1680–1768), who pioneered in applying the Linnaean system of plant classification; **James Logan,** who performed the 1st colonial experiments in physiological botany—on the fructification of maize (before 1739); **Cadwallader Colden** (1688–1776), whose work on the flora of N.Y. was published in *Acts* of the Royal Society of Upsala (1744); **Alexander Garden** (1728–92), who, from 1752, collected the flora of S.C. and discovered the Congo snake (an eel, before 1775); Rev. **Jared Eliot** (1685–1765), who published the 1st colonial work in the field of scientific agriculture (1760); and **Adam Kuhn** (1741–1817), who offered (1768) the 1st course in botany as professor of materia medica at the College of Philadelphia.

1739–69. ASTRONOMY. John Winthrop IV (1714–79), who succeeded Greenwood as professor of mathematics and natural philosophy at Harvard, wrote papers on sunspots (1739), on a transit of Venus and a lunar eclipse (1740), and on Halley's comet (1759). He journeyed to Newfoundland to record the transit of Venus (1761; also transit of 1768), and observed the transits of Mercury (1740, 1743, 1769). **Ezra Stiles** (1727–95), applying Newton, calculated the true position of the sun and moon (1745). **David Rittenhouse** (1732–96), Philadelphia clock and instrument maker, built the first orrery in the colonies (1767); made notable observations of the transits of Venus and Mercury (1769), and of Lexell's comet (1770).

1743–71. AMERICAN PHILOSOPHICAL SOCIETY. Although Cotton Mather formed a group interested in natural history (1681) and Franklin organized the **Junto** (1727), the first truly scientific society was the American Philosophical Society, organized in Philadelphia, with Thomas Hopkinson (1737–91) as 1st president and Franklin as secretary. Its meetings were held irregularly until it was reorganized (1769) with Franklin as president (until his death, 1790). *Transactions* 1st published, 1771.

1746–52. ELECTRICITY. John Winthrop IV gave the 1st lectures on electricity in the colonies (at Harvard, 1746). **Benjamin Franklin** began his 1st experiments in electricity (1747), discovered the phenomenon of plus and minus charges (1747–48), suggested (1749) that thunder and lightning could be explained electrically, and performed an experiment proving the electrical nature of lightning (1752). His *New Experiments and Observations on Electricity* went through 5 editions (1751–74). **James Bowdoin** (1726–90), author of numerous scientific papers, corrected Franklin's theory of electricity originating in the sea (1750).

1746–56. MATHEMATICS. Cadwallader Colden's *Principles of Action in Matter* (1745–51), a highly original supplement to Newton, propounded the theory that gravitation was a force exerted by an elastic, contractive form of matter. Winthrop at Harvard is reputed to have been the 1st to teach a course in Newtonian fluxions (calculus).

1780–94. SCIENTIFIC SOCIETIES. American Academy of Arts and Sciences founded 1780 at Boston largely through the efforts of John Adams; published *Memoirs* (1785). N.J. Society for the Promotion of Agriculture, Commerce, and Art (1781), with agricultural societies founded in S.C. and Pa. (1785), and the Chemical Society of Philadelphia (1792). Charles Willson Peale's Philadelphia Museum (1794) was the 1st independently established museum in the U.S.

1785. DESCRIPTIVE BOTANY. Publication of **Humphry Marshall's** (1722–1801) *Arbustrum Americanum,* a notable botanical essay based on the Linnaean system, and in the *Memoirs* of a paper by **Manasseh Cutler** (1742–1823), marked the beginning of systematic botany in New England.

1794–1860. DESCRIPTIVE ZOOLOGY. A paper on fish taken near Piscataqua, N.H., by **William Peck** (1763–1822) is considered the 1st paper on systematic zoology published in America (Coe). **Samuel Latham Mitchill** (1764–1831), professor of natural history at Columbia (1792–1801), established himself as a foremost zoologist with his work on the fish of New York (1814). **Thomas**

Say (1787–1834) published a paper (1817) and 2 books (1824–28) on entomology, followed by *American Conchology* (1830), both illustrated by Charles Alexander Leseur (1778–1846). **Constantine Samuel Rafinesque** (*c.*1783–1840) contributed papers on sponges, Western fishes, foxes, and on salivation of horses to Silliman's *Journal of Science* (1819–20). His *Ichthyologia Ohiensis* (1820) was notable in its field. **John D. Godman** (1794–1830) published his 3-vol. *American Natural History* (1826–28). With the encouragement of William Bartram, **Alexander Wilson** (1766–1813) began his *American Ornithology* (9 vols., 1808–13). **John James Audubon's** (p. 670) *Birds of America* began to appear in 1827; completed with publication of 5th vol., *Ornithological Guide* (1838). With John Bachman (1790–1874) he began work on the *Viviparous Quadrupeds of North America* (5 vols., 1842–54). **Louis Agassiz** (1807–73) became professor of zoology at Harvard (1848), founded the Museum of Comparative Zoology at Harvard (1859), and also established a pioneer marine station at Buzzard's Bay (1873).

1794–1860. CHEMISTRY. Arrival in U.S. of **Joseph Priestley** (1733–1804) stimulated interest in the field. First separate chair established at Princeton (1795) with **John MacLean** (1771–1814) as 1st incumbent. **Thomas Cooper** (1759–1839), as professor of chemistry and mineralogy at Dickinson College (1811–16), at the University of Pennsylvania (1817–19), and the University of South Carolina (1819–34), acted as a missionary for the new chemistry of Priestley, Lavoisier, and Davy. **Benjamin Silliman** (1779–1864), 1st professor of chemistry and natural history at Yale (1802–53), discovered that carbon was vaporized in an electric arc (1822), prepared hydrofluoric acid for the 1st time in the U.S. (1823), and detected bromine in a natural American brine (1830), was also founder of *American Journal of Science and Arts* (1818), which he edited to 1846. Other advances in chemical analysis: detection of boric acid in tourmaline (1822) and of beryllium in chrysoberyl (1824) by **Henry Seybert**, and development by **J. Lawrence Smith**

of a method for determining alkalies in minerals and destroying ammonium salts with aqua regia (1853). *Memoir on the Ammonia Cobalt Bases* (1857) by **Oliver Wolcott Gibbs** (1822–1908) and **Frederick A. Genth** (1820–93) constituted a solid achievement.

1797–1859. PALEONTOLOGY. **Thomas Jefferson** described a fossil found in Va. (1797) and in the remains of Proboscidea and other finds at Big Bone Lick, Ky. (1808). **Rembrandt Peale** wrote an account of the mastodon ("mammoth," 1802). **Edward Hitchcock** (1793–1864) pioneered on fossil footprints in the Connecticut Valley (1836), continuing his work in his *Final Report on the Geology of Mass.* (1841) and *Ichnology* and *Supplement* (1858, 1865). The arrival in the U.S. (1846) of **Louis Agassiz**, followed (1847) by work on fossils by Hiram A. Prout and S. D. Culbertson, focused attention on the prairie regions. Other notable contributions include the series of papers on the paleozoic vertebrates (1849) by **Isaac Lea** (1792–1886) and *The Ancient Fauna of Nebraska* (1853) by **Joseph Leidy** (1823–91), based on the findings of an expedition sent out by Spencer F. Baird (1823–87) of the Smithsonian Institution.

1798. BENJAMIN THOMPSON (Count Rumford, 1753–1814), a Loyalist exile who did all his scientific work abroad, reported the results of his experiments on the nature of heat as a form of motion. He endowed medals of the Royal Society (1st awarded, 1802) and the American Academy of Arts and Sciences (1st award, 1839) as well as the Rumford professorship of physics at Harvard (Jacob Bigelow, 1816, 1st incumbent).

1799. Publication of *Practical Navigator* by **Nathaniel Bowditch** (1773–1838), still a standard work of reference for mariners. Bowditch translated Laplace's *Mécanique céleste* (1814–17) and made observations on a meteor (1815).

1799–1804. WILLIAM DUNBAR (1749–1810) took the 1st important meteorological recordings in the Southwest and gave the 1st scientific account and analysis of the waters of Hot Springs.

1806–55. BENJAMIN SILLIMAN founded (at Yale) a notable school of geologists, including **Benjamin Silliman, Jr.** (1816–85), who made valuable investigations into the uses and preparation of petroleum products and wrote a report on petroleum in Pa.; **Edward Hitchcock** (1793–1864), who published notable reports on the geology of New England (1818, 1823); **Amos Eaton** (1776–1842), who published his *Index* to the geology of the North (1815); **Denison Olmstead** (1791–1859), whose report on the geology of N.C. (1824–25) was the 1st official state geological survey in the U.S.; and, most notable, **James Dwight Dana** (1813–95), who, on his return from the Wilkes expedition (p. 800) described for the 1st time 230 species of zoophytes and 536 of Crustacea, and published basic manuals on geology (1837, 1848, 1863). Other important geologists: **William Maclure** (1763–1840), whose *Observations on the Geology of the U.S.* (1809) contained the 1st geological map of America; revised, 1817; **Thomas Say** (1787–1834), the 1st American to point out the chronogenetic value of fossils (1819). The final integration of European and American chronologies was achieved through the efforts of **Isaac Lea** (1792–1886), **T. A. Conrad** (1803–77), and **James Hall** (1811–98).

1818–60. DESCRIPTIVE BOTANY. Notable work in this period contributed by **Gotthilf Muhlenberg** (1753–1815), with his catalogue of 2,800 species of North American plants (1813); **Thomas Nuttall** (1786–1859), *Genera of North American Plants* (1818); **John Torrey** (1796–1873), on flora of North and Middle States (1824): **Lewis David von Schweinitz** (1780–1834), on fungi (1831). For the work of **Asa Gray** both before and after 1860, see p. 717.

1829–46. ELECTRICITY. Following Franklin, electrical research was actively pursued in Europe (Galvani, current electricity, 1790; Volta, electric battery, 1800; Oersted, Ampère, Arago, electromagnetism, *c.*1820; Schweigger, galvanometer, 1820; Sturgeon, electromagnet, 1825). **Joseph Henry** (p. 725) began experiments in electricity (1827); improved the electromagnet (1829) and, independent of Faraday, discovered the method for producing induced currents of electricity

(1830–32); aided Morse in his experiments in telegraphy; discovered the oscillatory nature of electrical discharge of Leyden jar (1842); and anticipated later discoveries in radio and light waves (to 1846).

1831–61. METEOROLOGY. William C. Redfield's (1789–1857) pioneer observations (1831–37) and papers on wind motion during storms (1842, 1846) were challenged by **James P. Espy** (1785–1860), whose *Law of Cooling of Atmospheric Air* (1843) was one of the great U.S. contributions to the field. Further contributions in this field were made by **James H. Coffin** (1806–73) and **William Ferrel** (1817–91), who propounded (1856) Ferrel's Law, which expressed the fact that on account of the earth's rotation bodies on its surface are deflected to the right in the Northern Hemisphere and to the left in the Southern Hemisphere.

1840–59. ASTRONOMY. Astronomical observatory erected at Harvard (1840) by **William Cranch Bond** (1789–1859), its 1st director. With his son, **George Phillips Bond** (1825–65), he discovered 8th satellite of Saturn and single moon of Neptune, and invented electrochronograph for determining longitude. The Great Comet, which appeared in 1843, stimulated astronomical investigation. Notable work on the planet Neptune (discovered 1846) and the rings of Saturn done in this period by **Benjamin Peirce** (1809–80). **Maria Mitchell** (1818–89), of Nantucket, Mass., discovered a comet (1847) and became the 1st woman professor of astronomy in the U.S. (Vassar, 1865).

1846. SMITHSONIAN INSTITUTION founded by Act of Congress (1846), utilizing bequest (*c.*£100,000) of James Smithson, an English chemist and mineralogist; Joseph Henry named 1st director. **American Association for the Advancement of Science** organized, with William C. Redfield, president.

1847–56. HYDROGRAPHY AND OCEANOGRAPHY. Of great aid to worldwide exploration were the various *Wind and Current Charts* comp. by **Matthew Fontaine Maury** (1806–73), appointed (1842) superintendent of Dept.

of Charts and Instruments (later U.S. Naval Observatory and Hydrographic Office); cut sailing time from N.Y. to San Francisco (by 1855) from 180 to 130 days, with similar reductions in many other parts of the world. His *Physical Geography of the Sea* (1856) was widely translated.

1864–1903. CHEMISTRY. M. Carey Lea (1823–97) — platinum metals (1864); photochemistry (1865–93); discovery of photosalts (by 1880); notable work on colloidal suspensions, especially with silver (from 1889). Technics in volumetric analysis improved by **Josiah Parsons Cooke** (1827–94). Electrolytic analysis introduced by **Oliver Wolcott Gibbs** (1865) was improved by **Frank Austin Gooch** (before 1903) by the introduction of the rotating cathode. The completion by **Josiah Willard Gibbs** (p. 714) of his *On the Equilibrium of Heterogeneous Substances* (1875), followed by a further paper (1877–78), established him as the founder of "chemical energetics." He extended the method of thermodynamics, applying it to chemical problems, and introduced the "phase rule." **Ira Remsen** (1846–1927), who founded U.S. graduate research in chemistry at Johns Hopkins (1876), obtained benzoic sulfinide (saccharin) and enunciated "Remsen's Law" determining the protection of methyl and other groups from oxidation.

1864–1903. GEOLOGY. Calif. survey proved the presence of Upper Triassic (1864); found in Ida. (1877) and subsequently over most of the West. **F. V. Hayden** found marine Jurassic fossils in "Red Beds" of Rocky Mountain area, but it was not until the Jurassic strata were found in Calif. (1885) that the outlines of this formation could be drawn. Work of **Robert T. Hill** (on Tex. Cretaceous, 1887) and of **W. M. Gabb** and **J. D. Whitney** (on Calif. Cretaceous, 1869) contributed to rounding out the geological map of the U.S. Glacial formations described by Hilgard (Miss., 1866), Stevens (Va., 1873), Hall (Pa., 1876), and Rogers (Va. and N.C., 1876), with outstanding work (1873–82) by **Thomas C. Chamberlain** (1843–1928). **Grove K. Gilbert** (1843–1918) reported on extinct Lake Bonneville (1879). **William H. Dall** (1845–1927) made major contribu-

tions to stratigraphy (1885–1903). See also p. 454.

1864–1952. ASTRONOMY. Lewis M. Rutherfurd (1816–92) built astronomical camera and photographed the moon (1864), and invented micrometer to measure stars. **Henry Draper** (1837–82) obtained 1st successful photograph of the spectrum of a star (1872) and introduced photography of nebulae (1880). Using telescopes built by **Alvan Clark** (1808–87), **Asaph Hall** (1829–1907) discovered the moon of Mars (1877) and **James E. Keeler** (1857–1900) the composition of Saturn's rings (1886). **Samuel P. Langley** (1834–1906) devised the bolometer to detect temperatures and demonstrated a new way to test variations in surface temperatures of the sun (1881). **William H. Pickering** (1858–1938) discovered Phoebe, 9th satellite of Saturn (1898). As a result of prediction and research originated in 1905 by **Percival Lowell** (1855–1916), the planet Pluto was discovered (1930) by **Clyde W. Tombaugh** (1906–   ). **George Ellery Hale** (1868–1932) invented the spectroheliograph, with which he took the 1st successful photograph of solar prominence (1891). Through Hale's efforts the Mt. Wilson Observatory was opened (1906). Hale Telescope at Mt. Palomar opened in 1948. **Seth B. Nicholson** (1891–   ) discovered 9th, 10th, 11th moons of Jupiter 1914, 1938; 12th, 1952.

1866–1941. PALEONTOLOGY. Othniel Charles Marsh (1831–99), 1st professor of paleontology in the U.S. (Yale, 1866), led organized bone-hunting expeditions for Yale, and later (1881) for U.S. Geological Survey (discovered 500 new species, 225 new genera, 64 new families, 19 new orders). **Edward D. Cope** (1840–97) published 3 notable studies (1875, 1877, 1883) as a result of field expeditions he organized; his work on herpetology and ichthyology prepared the way for modern classification of North American reptiles, amphibians, and fishes. **Henry Fairfield Osborn** (1857–1935), professor of zoology at Columbia (1896–1910) and curator of vertebrate paleontology at American Museum of Natural History (1891–1910), popularized knowledge of the field. Dinosaur National Monument (Utah and

Col.) established (1915) to preserve area of great finds. The largest footprints yet found (4½ x 3 ft.) were discovered in the Texas Big Bend country (1941).

1870–84. MATHEMATICS. At Johns Hopkins, **James J. Sylvester** (1814–97), the British mathematician, advanced the studies in this field and founded the *American Journal of Mathematics*. At Yale **Josiah Willard Gibbs** (p. 714) published his *Elements of Vector Analysis* (*c.*1881–84).

1881–1920. VELOCITY OF LIGHT. **Albert A. Michelson** (p. 752) determined the velocity of light (1878–80) and invented the interferometer, by which length of standard meter was ascertained in terms of wave length of cadmium light (1887), and began investigations on existence of hypothetical ether (1881). Famous experiment with **Edward W. Morley** (1838–1923) in 1887 served as starting point for Einstein's Special Theory of Relativity (1905).

1909–26. STUDIES IN INHERITANCE. **Thomas Hunt Morgan** (p. 756) at Columbia used the fruit fly (drosophila) to test Mendel's laws of inheritance; first to use "gene" (1909) to describe individual parts of chromosomes controlling particular characteristics; discovered the phenomenon of sex-linked characteristics (1910) and later (1911, 1913) characteristics of different linkages. His students elaborated work on mutants and the gene theory. Work by **R. A. Emerson** (1873–1947) on mutations in corn (from 1914) tended to confirm Morgan. **Hermann J. Muller** (1890–) found that with X rays he could artificially increase the rate of mutation in the fruit fly (by 1926). Confirmation of findings provided by experiments with barley by **Lewis J. Stadler** (1896–) and with tobacco by **T. H. Goodspeed** (1887–).

1910. Trivalent carbon discovered by **Moses Gomberg** (1866–1947).

1910–25. ROBERT A. MILLIKAN (p. 753) announced (1910) he had measured the charge of an electron as a definite constant; elaborated results in his *The Electron* (1912; 2nd ed., 1925). He succeeded in proving Einstein's hitherto unproven photoelectric equation and in evaluating Planck's Constant (h).

1912–48. MEASURING THE UNIVERSE. **Henrietta Leavitt** (1868–1921) at Harvard announced her "period-luminosity" law; i.e., the period of fluctuation of brightness of a Cepheid star is directly proportional to its candlepower. **Harlow Shapley** (1885–), applying this law to globular clusters, was able (1917) to measure distances in the Milky Way. Data accumulated (by 1928) by Vestro M. Slipher (1875–), Lowell Observatory, on 43 spiral nebulae, using spectroscope and working with the "Doppler shift," showed that these nebulae were moving away from the earth at speeds increasing with distance. **Edwin Powell Hubble** (1899–1953), in conjunction with **Milton L. Humason** (1891–) at the Wilson Observatory, by adding the period-luminosity law to Slipher's technic (1929–43), worked out quantitative measurements of distance and speeds confirming Slipher.

1914–51. ATOMIC RESEARCH. **Gilbert N. Lewis** (p. 740) set forth new theory of the structure of the atom (1916); expanded by **Irving Langmuir** (p. 739) into the concentric shell theory (1919), which explained chemical activity of an element in terms of the completeness of its outer shell of electrons. **Theodore W. Richards** (1868–1928) at Harvard discovered an isotope of lead (1914, 2 isotopes of neon had been found in England, 1913). **William D. Harkins** (1873–1951), working on the problem of nuclei of atoms (1914–21), found that nitrogen bombarded by helium nuclei produced an oxygen isotope (atomic wt. 17) and predicted the neutron (1920), which was discovered in England (1932). **Arthur H. Compton** (p. 688) discovered the Compton effect, which showed that X rays have a corpuscular structure (1923). **Clinton J. Davisson** (p. 693) and **Lester H. Germer** (1896–) found that electrons shot against a nickel crystal were reflected in the same way as light waves, thus showing for the 1st time that matter has wavelike characteristics (1927). **Ernest O. Lawrence** (p. 739) constructed the 1st cyclotron, which made possible the acceleration of nuclear particles to energies of millions of volts for smashing atoms (1930). **Harold C. Urey** (p. 793) discovered hydrogen isotope of mass 2 (deuterium, or heavy hydrogen, 1931). **Arthur J. Dempster** (1886–1950) built improved mass spectrograph and isolated isotope uranium 235, later found to be the only natural fissionable element existing in relatively large quantities (1935). **Enrico Fermi** (1901–1954), **John R. Dunning** (1907–   ), and **George B. Pegram** (1876–1958) repeated uranium fission experiment of Otto Hahn and Fritz Strassman in Germany and Otto Frisch and Lise Meitner in Denmark, in which vast amounts of nuclear energy are released by the splitting of uranium 235 atoms with fast or slow neutrons, the discovery which led to the production of the atomic bomb and to the utilization of atomic energy. **Edwin M. McMillan** (p. 747) and Philip H. Abelson (1913–   ) isolated neptunium (element 93), first transuranic element (1940). **Glenn T. Seaborg** (p. 777) and **Emilio Segre** (1905–   ) produced plutonium, element 94, first man-made fissionable element (1941). First self-perpetuating nuclear chain reaction, demonstrating practicability of atomic bomb and industrial atomic power, on 2 Dec. 1942. Electromagnetic and gaseous diffusion plants for separation of isotope uranium 235 built at Oak Ridge, Tenn., 1943–44. Nuclear reactors for producing plutonium built at Hanford, Wash., 1943–44. **First atomic bomb** designed and constructed at Los Alamos, N.M., 1945; tested at Alamogordo, N.M., 16 July 1945. McMillan announced discovery of principle of synchrotron (1945). Seaborg *et al.* produced americium, curium, berkelium, and californium, elements 95, 96, 97, and 98 (1944–50). First production of electric power from nuclear reactor, Arco, Ida. (1951). Cosmotron at Brookhaven National Laboratory generated 2,250 million volts (10 June 1952).

1916–53. ALBERT EINSTEIN (1879–1955), continuing (1933) his life work at the Institute for Advanced Study, Princeton, N.J., disclosed (30 Mar. 1953) formulas as last step in his quest for a Unified Field Theory, a single mathematical system embracing electromagnetism and gravitation in 1 universal law, and eventually uniting the Relativity and Quantum theories.

1921–51. COSMIC RAYS. Millikan, with **Ira S. Bowen** (1898–   ) began investigations in Calif. on nature and origin of cosmic rays from outer space. **Arthur H. Compton** (p. 688) organized worldwide study (1931). **Carl D. Anderson** (p. 668) discovered the positron, particle with mass of negative electron but with a positive charge of equal magnitude, in cosmic rays (1932). Anderson with **Seth H. Neddermeyer** (1907–   ) discovered in the cosmic rays a new charged particle, intermediate in mass between the proton and the electron, which was named the meson (1936). **Jabez C. Street** (1906–   ) and **E. C. Stevenson** discovered same particle independently (1937). **Robert Marshak** (1916–   ) predicted on theoretical grounds the existence of heavier type of meson to account for nuclear forces, in accordance with earlier prediction by **Hideki Yukawa** of Japan (later at Columbia). Heavier meson, named pi-meson, later found in cosmic ray in British studies. Pi-meson produced artificially (1948) in giant synchrocyclotron at University of California, marking 1st time that matter was created out of energy in accordance with famous Einstein formula ($E = mc^2$).

1941, 28 June. Office of Scientific Research and Development (p. 382).

1954–57. NEW ELEMENTS. 99 (einsteinium, atomic weight 247) and 100 (fermium, atomic weight 254)—AEC's Argonne Natl. Laboratory and U. of Calif. (1954); 101 (mendelevium)—U. of Calif. (1955); 102 (nobelium)—Nobel Inst. and Argonne Lab. (1957).

1955. Nobel prize awards in physics to **Polykarp Kusch** (1911–   ), Columbia Univ., for precision determination of the magnetic moment of the electron, proving that energy level calculations of P. A. M. Dirac, British physicist, did not agree with experimental evidence, and to **Willis E. Lamb** (1913–   ), Stanford Univ., for discoveries regarding the hyperfine structure of the hydrogen spectrum.

18 Oct. ANTI-PROTON, a new atomic particle, discovered by **Emilio Segrè** and associates at U. of Calif.

1956. ANTI-NEUTRON identified at Bevatron Lab. of U. of Calif.

1957. SPONTANEOUS GENERA-TION. Amino acids, the basic substance of proteins, produced by exposing mixtures of methane, ammonium, water, and hydrogen to electrical charges comparable to lightning in experiment performed by **Stanley L. Miller** of Columbia Univ. Coll. of Physicians and Surgeons.

1957, July 1–1958, Dec. 31. INTER-NATIONAL GEOPHYSICAL YEAR, an 18-month period of intensive study of the earth, the oceans, the atmosphere, and the sun. U.S. scientists participated, with an appropriation of $39 million from Congress to Natl. Science Foundation.

INVENTIONS

1730–35. MARINER'S QUADRANT improved by **Thomas Godfrey** (1704–49), the mathematician. The theodolite, an instrument for measuring horizontal angles, improved by Roland Houghton (1735).

1730–40. LONG RIFLE (also Pa. and, later, Ky. Rifle) developed by Pa. gunsmiths by elongating barrel, narrowing and improving the rifling of bore, and adding grease patch. Prototype was introduced by German emigrants (1710–20).

1742–52. BENJAMIN FRANKLIN invented Franklin stove (Pa. fireplace), an adaptation of the German stove which permitted ventilation (1742), and the lightning rod (1752).

1750. FLATBOAT for inland navigation invented by Jacob Yoder (Pa.).

1750–60. CONESTOGA WAGON, adapted to frontier travel, made its 1st appearance in Pa.

1762. REV. JARED ELIOT (1685–1763) of Killingworth, Conn., developed a process for smelting iron from black magnetic sand (*Transactions,* 1762).

1775. DAVID BUSHNELL (*c.*1742–1824) built 1st American submarine, *American Turtle;* nearly succeeded in blowing up a British frigate in New York Harbor (1776).

c.1777–85. OLIVER EVANS (1755–1819) invented a card-making machine (*c.*1777–78) which could complete 150 pairs of cotton or wool cards from wire per day. During the same period he invented an **automatic flour mill** (cutting labor requirements by one half), which was first put into operation *c.*1785.

1781–87. STEAM ENGINES. First multitubular boiler (**John Stevens,** 1749–1838; patented, 1783). Noncondensing, high-pressure steam engine (**Oliver Evans,** 1787).

1783. Bifocal spectacles invented by Benjamin Franklin.

1785–87. 1ST STEAMBOATS. Steamboat invented by **John Fitch** (1743–89) franchised for N.J. waters 1786; launched on Delaware, 1787; patented, 1791. Second steamboat built by **James Rumsey** (1743–92), launched on Potomac, 1787; patented, 1791.

1790. First Federal patent granted to **Samuel Hopkins** (Vt., 1721–1803) for a process for the manufacture of pot and pearl ash. Machine to cut and head nails in 1 operation invented by **Jacob Perkins** (Mass., 1766–1849).

1790–91. SAMUEL SLATER (p. 780) reproduced Arkwright machinery, employing water power at Pawtucket, R.I.

1793–99. FARM INVENTIONS. Eli Whitney (p. 799) invented the **cotton gin,** cheapening the most costly process in refining cotton (1793). **Thomas Jefferson** invented the moldboard plow (1793). **Charles Newbold** patented the 1st cast-iron plow (1797). **Eliakim Spooner** invented a seeding machine (1799).

1798. Jig for guiding tools in operation invented by **Eli Whitney.**

1804–49. STEAM ENGINE AD-VANCES. Steam dredge by **Oliver Evans.** Jacob Perkins embodied experiments with steam of high pressure (1823) in numerous inventions down to 1849, including bathometer (to measure depth of water), plenometer (to record speed of vessel through water), piezometer (to measure compressibility of water)

1805. ROBERT FULTON (p. 711) built the 1st marine torpedo.

1807–08. PRACTICAL STEAM-BOATS. Although **John Stevens** designed a screw propeller (1802) and with it operated *Phoenix* to Philadelphia by sea (1808, 1st steam vessel in the U.S. to navigate the ocean), **Robert Fulton** built the 1st successful steamboat (*Clermont* sailed, 17 Aug. 1807, New York to Albany, 32 hrs.). The first ironclad vessel was built by Stevens (1813).

1807–54. MACHINERY. Manufacture of tacks (Jesse Reed, Conn., 1807), screw-cutting machine (Abel Stowel, Mass., 1809), circular saw (David Melville, 1814), profile lathe (1818, **Thomas Blanchard**, Mass. [1788–1864]); commercial vernier caliper by Brown and Sharp (1851); turret lathe, Robbins and Lawrence (Vt., 1854).

1816–27. PRINTING PRESS IM-PROVEMENTS. Hand printing press: George Clymer, Pa., 1816; with a toggle joint, Samuel Rust, 1827; improved, 1829.

1819–22. PLOW IMPROVEMENTS. Cast Iron 3-piece plow, (standardized interchangeable parts, **Jethrow Wood,** N.Y., 1819; lock colter devised by John Conant (Vt., 1822).

1819. Breech-loading flintlock (John Hall).

1822. ARTIFICIAL TEETH. First patent to C. M. Graham.

1826–37. LOCOMOTIVE with multitubular boiler (John Stevens, 1826; 1st patent to William Howard (1828). **Robert L. Stevens** (1788–1856), son of John Stevens, invented the balance valve for steam engines and the T-rail (1830). Other railroad improvements included pilot truck and bogie and double-slide cutoff for locomotives. **Peter Cooper** (p. 690) built 1st U.S. locomotive (1830). Swivel truck for locomotives devised by John B. Jervis (1831), equalizing lever by Joseph Harrison (1837).

1827–31. JOSEPH HENRY (p. 725) insulated wire; invented multiple coil magnet; built 1st magnetic and acoustic telegraph.

1831–34. REAPER invented by **Cyrus H. McCormick** (p. 746), 1831; patented, 1834; similar machine invented independently (1832–33) by **Obed Hussey** (1792–1860).

1833. STEEL-BLADE PLOWSHARE (John Lane, Ill.).

1834–39. ELECTRICAL MACHINERY. First actual electric motor invented by **Thomas Davenport** (1802–51), who also invented electric commutator (1835) and electric printing press (1839).

1835. REVOLVER patented by **Samuel Colt** (1814–62).

1836–43. JOHN ERICSSON (1803–89) improved screw propeller for steamships (1836). Going to U.S. (1840), designed *Princeton,* 1st warship to have propelling machinery below water line (1843). Other inventions in U.S.: telescopic smokestack, recoil mechanism for gun carriages, instrument for measuring distances at sea, gauges for fluids under pressure, alarm barometer, pyrometer, and self-registering deep-sea lead. For the *Monitor* (1861), see p. 236.

1837–40. FARM AND MILLING. Steel plow introduced (1837) in U.S. by **John Deere** (1804–86); thresher fanning mill (prototype of later improved threshers) built by Hiram A. and John Pitts (Me.).

1839. VULCANIZATION OF RUBBER discovered by **Charles Goodyear** (p. 716); patented (France, 1844).

1840–44. ADVANCES IN IRON AND COAL TECHNOLOGY. Hot blast iron furnace for anthracite coal (David Thomas, Conn.), anthracite coal breaker (Gideon Bast, 1840), roller and crusher for coal (J. and S. Battin, 1844).

1841. Drop cut-off gear for steam engines (perfected by Frederick E. Sickles).

1843–68. TYPEWRITER. Machine invented by **Charles Thurber** (Conn., 1843). First practical typewriter constructed, 1867, by **Christopher L. Sholes** (1819–90) in collaboration with Carlos Glidden and Samuel W. Soulé. Working alone, Sholes made numerous improved models and secured patents (1868); sold rights (1873) to E. Remington & Sons, who marketed it as Remington typewriter.

1844. TELEGRAPH. Samuel F. B. Morse (p. 757) developed the 1st practical telegraph (1832), following a large number of experiments; put into operation (24 May 1844) with message from **Alfred Vail** (1807–59) in Baltimore to

Morse in Washington, D.C. Morse invented Morse code (1838). Telegraphic printing technique invented by Vail (1844); patented by Royal E. House (1846).

1846–54. SEWING MACHINE invented by **Elias Howe** (p. 729); improved (1849–54) by **Allen B. Wilson** (1824–88) and (1851) by **Isaac Merritt Singer** (1811–75), who, with the aid of Edward Clark, opened plant in New York City (1853).

1846. ROTARY PRINTING PRESS invented by **Richard M. Hoe** (p. 727).

1847–64. FARM IMPLEMENTS. Revolving disc harrow (G. Page, 1847), agricultural binder (John E. Heath, 1850), chilled plow (**James Oliver**, 1855; improved by Marsh brothers, 1857), twine knotter (John F. Appleby, 1858), checkrower corn planter (John Thompson and John Ramsey, 1864).

1849. MODERN SAFETY PIN invented by Walter Hunt.

Pendulum press for can tops invented by Henry Evans.

1851–56. IRON AND STEEL ADVANCES. William Kelly (1811–88), Ky. ironmaster, developed a process for converting pig iron into steel by directing a current of air upon molten metal (1851), independently of Henry Bessemer in England, who perfected the technic (1856). First Bessemer converter built at Troy, N.Y. (1864); Kelly process at Wyandotte, Mich., same year. Rival claims compromised 1866. Wrought-iron I-beams rolled (1860) by **Peter Cooper** at Trenton, N. J.

1852. ELISHA G. OTIS (1811–61) invented 1st passenger elevator (making skyscraper possible).

1853. Sluicing process in mining perfected by E. E. Matteson.

1858–99. SHOE MACHINERY. Lyman R. Blake (1835–83) patented (1858) a machine capable of sewing soles of shoes to the uppers; promoted by **Gordon McKay** (1821–1903), who patented improved version (1862). The Blake-McKay machines were widely adopted by 1876. Charles Goodyear (1833–96), who acquired (1864–67) the welt-sewing machine, joined forces with McKay by 1880. Centralization of machine ownership brought about by formation (1899) of United Shoe Machinery Co.

1859. Successful **oil drilling** at Titusville, Pa., by **Edwin L. Drake** (1819–80).

1860. REPEATING RIFLE introduced by **Oliver F. Winchester** (1810–80).

1862. REVOLVING MACHINE GUN perfected by **Richard J. Gatling** (1818–1903).

1864. GEORGE M. PULLMAN (1831–97) built "Pioneer," 1st especially constructed sleeping car, and organized Pullman Palace Car Co. (1867).

1865. COMPRESSION ICE MACHINE invented by **Thaddeus Lowe** (1832–1913), who made 1st artificial ice in U.S., and in 1873 invented carbureted water-gas process.

1865–75. WEB PRINTING PRESS (using a web or roll of paper) invented by **William A. Bullock** (1813–63). **Rotary press** (printing on both sides of a sheet at the same time) attributed to Andrew Campbell and Stephen D. Tucker (1875).

1868–72. AIR BRAKE patented by **George Westinghouse** (p. 797); improved, 1872.

1869–99. CARPET SWEEPERS AND VACUUM CLEANERS. Suction-type vacuum cleaner patented by I. W. McGaffey (1869). Melville R. Bissell invented practical carpet sweeper (1876). First motor-driven vacuum cleaner patented by John Thurman (1899).

1869. ELECTRIC VOTING MACHINE invented by **Thomas A. Edison** (p. 701). First voting machine authorized for use, 1892.

1870–78. MOTION PICTURES: PIONEER STAGE. Experiments in depicting motion followed invention of zoetrope (designed in France, 1860), a series of pictures whirled on a drum to give effect of motion. Applying similar principle to magic lantern, Henry R. Heyl showed projected animated pictures (1870). Edward Muybridge set up a series of coordinated cameras to take successive photographs of a horse in motion (1878).

1871–74. TRANSPORTATION. Andrew S. Hallidie (1836–1900) invented cable streetcar (1871; in use in San Francisco, 1873). First electrically powered streetcar invented by **Stephen Dudley Field** successfully run in New York City, 1874.

Railroad coupler patented by **Eli H. Janney** (1831–1912).

1872. CELLULOID. Commercial production developed by **John W. Hyatt** (1837–1920).

1872–85. CALCULATING MACHINES. Edmund D. Barbour invented adding machine which printed totals and subtotals (1872). **Dorr Eugene Felt** (1862–1930) made 1st accurate comptometer (1884). First successful recording adding machine (1888) by **William S. Burroughs** (1857–1898).

1874. BARBED WIRE (p. 454).

1875–81. DYNAMOS. William A. Anthony (1835–1908) constructed 1st dynamo for outdoor lighting (1875, at Cornell Univ.); C. F. Brush (1876). Edison Machine Works constructed 1st successfully operating dynamo (27 tons, 1881).

1876–84. TELEPHONE invented by **Alexander Graham Bell** (p. 674) prior to 14 Feb. 1876; patent granted, 7 Mar.; 1st distinguishable conversation, 10 Mar.; outdoor transmission, 9 Oct.; 1st private home installation, 1877; New York to Boston, 1884.

1877–95. DISCOVERIES BY NIKOLA TESLA (p. 790). Tesla discovered the principle of the rotary magnetic field, applying it in a practical form to the induction motor and making possible the alternating current motor and the transmission of power by such current, employing what became known as 2-phase, 3-phase, multiphase, and polyphase systems, particularly on long distance lines (later used extensively). Also p. 790. Edison system of central power production introduced (1882) at New York City.

1878–83. ELECTRIC LIGHTING. Practical application of electric arc lamps (Philadelphia, 1878; Cleveland, 1879). Although Moses Gerrish of Salem had built an incandescent lamp as early as 1859, **Thomas A. Edison** (p. 701) invented the 1st practical incandescent bulb (1879); established factory (1880).

1878–1948. PHONOGRAPH patented by Edison (1878); practical machine made by firm of Bell and Tainter (1886). Electronic phonograph introduced 1924 by Western Electric Co., manufactured 1927 by RCA; 33⅓ rpm. microgroove record invented by Dr.

Peter Goldmark, marketed 1948.

1879–1923. AUTOMOBILE. Experimentation followed upon the building of an early steam-operated auto in the U.S. (by Henry A. House, 1866). George B. Selden applied for 1st auto patent (1879); took it out (1895). Storage-battery auto designed by William Morrison (1891). First gasoline-engine-driven motor built and operated by J. Frank Duryea (1895). Autocar Co. introduced shaft drive (1901) and circulating lubrication (1904). Pneumatic tire (1892) followed by clincher-type tire (1899), the demountable tire-carrying rim (1906), the nonskid tire (1908), the cord tire (1910), and the balloon tire (1923). Electric self-starter invented by Clyde J. Coleman (1899); perfected (1911) by **Charles F. Kettering** (1876–1958), who also invented lighting and ignition systems. Four-wheel auto brake patented, 1908. Bendix drive, 1914, by Vincent Bendix.

1880–88. CAMERA ADVANCES. George Eastman (1854–1932) patented 1st successful roll film (1880); perfected 1st "Kodak" hand camera (1888), resulting in popularization of photography.

1880–1931. RAZORS. Safety razor developed by Kampfe Bros., N.Y. First modern type with throwaway blades invented (1895) by **King C. Gillette** (1855–1932). Jacob Shick patented electric dry shaver 1928; marketed, 1931.

1882–1910. ELECTRIC APPLIANCES. Electric fan invented by **Schuyler Skaats Wheeler** (1860–1923). Patents granted for electric flatiron (1882, Henry W. Seely), electric stove (1896, William S. Hadaway), separable electric attachment plug (1904, Harvey Hubbell). Electric sewing machine developed (Singer Mfg. Co., 1889). Completely self-contained electric washing machine developed (1907, Hurling Machine Co.).

1884. FOUNTAIN PEN perfected by Lewis E. **Waterman** (1837–1901).

1884–89. LINOTYPE MACHINE invented by **Ottmar Mergenthaler** (p. 752); used commercially, 1886. **Mono**type machine patented 1887 by **Tolbert Lanston** (1844–1913).

1886. ELECTRIC WELDING MACHINE patented by **Elihu Thomson** (1853–1937), widely applied in auto industry and as a substitute for riveting in construction work; also patented cream separator, 1881.

Electrolytic process of refining aluminum discovered by **Charles Martin Hall** (1863–1914).

1890. PNEUMATIC HAMMER patented by Charles B. King.

1891–1917. RADIO. Predicted by James Maxwell (1865, England) and developed on the basis of studies of Heinrich Hertz (1887–88, Germany), the 1st radio patent in the U.S. was granted to Edison (1891). Nathan B. Stubblefield transmitted voice over the air without wires (1892), but major research was undertaken abroad (Marconi, Fleming) until **Reginald A. Fessenden** (1866–1932) patented (1901) an improved wireless transmitter, sending signals from Old Point Comfort to Cape Charles (1903) and demonstrating wireless telephone at Brant Rock, Mass., 11 Dec. 1906; and **Lee De Forest** (p. 694) invented the 3-element vacuum tube (1906, triode amplifier) and applied the microphone (ordinary telephone-type mouthpiece, 1907) to broadcasting. For Alexanderson's high frequency alternator, 1917, see p. 668.

1891. CARBORUNDUM (abrasive) discovered by **Edward G. Acheson** (1856–1931).

1893–96. MOTION PICTURES. Invention of photographic gun (E. J. Marey, France) and development of celluloid film (introduced by John Carbutt, 1883) led to invention of Edison's Kinetoscope (peepshow, 1893), which, employing a continuous roll of film, could be viewed by but 1 person at a time. Woodville Latham demonstrated the Pantoptiken (1895), a combination of the Kinetoscope with magic-lantern projection (simultaneously with the Cinematographe by the Lumières in France, the best projector at that time). C. Francis Jenkins (1867–1934) perfected the phantascope, modification of Edison's kinetoscope, and with Thomas Armat demonstrated the Vitascope (1896), prototype of the modern motion picture projector.

1896–1913. AIRPLANE. Orville and **Wilbur Wright** (p. 804) made 1st heavier-than-air flight at Kittyhawk, N.C., 17 Dec. 1903; previously, 8 Dec., Samuel P. Langley had made an unsuccessful attempt in a power-driven airplane. First American monoplane invented by Henry W. Walden (1909). **Gyroscope** stabilizer by **Elmer A. Sperry** (1860–1930) demonstrated on an airplane (1913), foreshadowing later instrument developments.

1897–1912. DIESEL ENGINES. Adolphus Busch (1839–1913) bought Diesel rights for the U.S. (1897); built 1st engine (1898); applied to submarine (1912, Vickers 4-cylinder).

1901. MERCURY VAPOR LAMP patented by **Peter C. Hewitt** (1861–1921).

1902–10. SYNTHETICS AND PLASTICS. Rayon (cellulose ester) patented (1902) by **Arthur D. Little** (1863–1935), with William H. Walker and Harry S. York; same group patented artificial silk (1902). First commercial production by American Viscose Co. (1910). **Leo H. Baekeland** (1863–1944) patented thermosetting plastic, 1909 (Bakelite).

1911. GYROCOMPASS pat. by Elmer A. Sperry (another pat. abroad by Anschütz-Kämpfe, 1908), who also perfected the gyroscope (invented by Foucault, 1852) and invented the automatic steersman.

1913. X RAY. Development by William D. Coolidge of new X-ray tube capable of sustained operation at 140,000 volts (later designed for 200,000 volts) revolutionized making of radiographs.

CRACKING PROCESS for gasoline patented by **William M. Burton.**

1914–26. EARLY ROCKETS. Robert H. Goddard (1882–1945) patented liquid fuel rocket (1914), using liquid ether and oxygen; demonstrated lifting force of rockets (1920); directed 1st rocket flight (1926).

1916. THOMPSON SUBMACHINE GUN invented by **John T. Thompson** (1860–1940). **National Research Council** organized 20 Sept. 1916 to promote wartime research; perpetuated by order of President Wilson 11 May 1918 to stimulate scientific research, programs, and information.

1918–52. HELICOPTER. First to rise successfully from ground built by Peter C. Hewitt and F. B. Crocker (1918). Developments in U.S. largely due to **Igor Sikorsky** (1889–   ), who arrived in U.S. in 1918. Improved product (VS-300) produced by Vought-Sikorsky Aircratt (1939).

1922. TECHNICOLOR process successfully developed by **Herbert T. Kalmus** (1881–   ).

1922–26. TELEPHOTO. C. Francis Jenkins sent photos over telephone wires; transcontinental photo (1925); transatlantic service (1926).

1922–46. RADAR. Based on studies of Hertz (1888), radio detection was 1st developed by **Albert H. Taylor** (1879–   ) and **Leo C. Young** (1922) for the U.S. Navy. True radar detection, using pulse-ranging technic, employed by **Gregory Breit** (1899–   ) and **Merle A. Tuve** (1901–   ) for ionospheric research (*c.*1926), and for naval detection by Taylor and Young (1930). Radar system developed by Naval Research Laboratory (1934–39) and U.S. Army Signal Corps (1936–38). By 1935 Great Britain had 5 radar detector stations in operation. Research accelerated under National Defense Research Committee (from July 1940). During World War II radar was employed both to direct artillery fire and to detect enemy submarines and aircraft. Radar signals sent to the moon and reflected back (from Belmar, N.J., 10 Jan. 1946).

1923–28. SOUND FILMS. Cameraphone, 1st sound moving picture, developed by Edison, 1904. Lee De Forest demonstrated sound on moving picture film, 1923; 1st public presentation of talking pictures, Aug. 1926; first full-length sound film, 1928. See also p. 628.

1925–51. TELEVISION. Background work on television largely European (Senlecq, France; Nipkow and Braun, Germany; Rosing, Russia; Swinton, England) until **Vladimir Zworykin** (p. 805) invented the iconoscope, basis of the electronic television camera, and **C. Francis Jenkins** demonstrated television with the Nipkow system (both in 1925). Radio Corp. of America demonstrated electronic transmission (using iconoscope and cathode ray tube, 1933). First transmission of television signals, New York to Washington, by Amer. Tel. & Tel. (1927). Full commercial television inaugurated 1941; British system, 1935). **Peter C. Goldmark** (1906–   ) of Columbia Broadcasting System (CBS) demonstrated "sequential method" of **color television** (1940). CBS and RCA evolved

independent systems by 1949. Hearings by FCC (1949–50) found CBS system sufficiently advanced to permit general transmission; production curtailed in interest of national defense (1951).

1927. MECHANICAL COTTON PICKER invented by **John Daniel Rust** (1892–   ) and **Mack Donald Rust** (1900–   ).

1928–34. AUTOGIRO 1st brought to U.S. from England (1928) by Harold F. Pitcairn; manufactured with closed cabin (1931) and applied to military uses (1934).

1930–31. TRACTORS. Diesel engine tractor manufactured (steam tractor, 1886; gasoline, 1892). Caterpillar tractor developed (1931).

1932. POLAROID GLASS invented by **Edwin H. Land** (1909–   ); polaroid camera 1947.

1934. RAILROAD DEVELOPMENTS. First streamlined high-speed train (2 Mar.), followed by all-steel Diesel-motored train (11 Nov.) and streamlined steam locomotive (14 Dec.).

23 May. NYLON. Wallace H. Carothers synthesized a superpolymer; marketed (1938) by Du Pont as nylon.

1935. SPECTROPHOTOMETER patented by **Arthur C. Hardy** (1895–   ).

1935–39. SYNTHETICS. Casein fiber developed by **Earl O. Whittier** (1891–   ) and **Stephen P. Gould** (1897–1939); patented, 1938. **Nylon:** commercial production begun (toothbrush bristles, Du Pont, 1938; followed by nylon yarn, 1939). **Fiberglas** technics patented (1938) by **Games Slayter** (1896–   ) and John H. Thomas.

1939. FREQUENCY MODULATION (FM) invented by **Edwin H. Armstrong** (1890–1954), who invented regenerative circuit (1912); superheterodyne circuit (1918).

1942–45. ROCKETS IN WORLD WAR II. "Bazooka," 1st U.S. rocket gun, developed by Capt. L. A. Skinner and C. N. Hickman; standardized, 1942. Germans 1st used V-1, 250–400-mph **pilotless aircraft, 12 June 1944, 6 days** after D-Day; shot down by Allied gunners aided by radar, M-9 director, and proximity fuse. V-2 (long-range rocket, 3,400 mph) began to land in London on 12 Sept. 1944. Rocket and guided-missile experiments pushed in postwar period. U.S. Navy guided missiles reported used in combat in Korea (1 Sept. 1952).

1942–60. JET PLANES. Jet engine 1st produced by British inventor, Frank Whittle, 1937. Jets 1st tested in U.S., 1942. In June 1944 a Lockheed P-80 with jet motor flew over 500 mph. Jet-propelled fighters were ordered by U.S. Air Force (1947); bombers developed (1947). By 1952, U.S. had developed B-52 bomber, with 8 turbojet engines, ceiling 50,000 ft., speed *c.* 600 mph.; B-47, *c.* 700 mph. B-70 supersonic heavy bomber (designed for speeds exceeding 2,000 mph) program drastically restricted by govt. 1 Dec. 1959. Bell X-2 rocket-powered research airplane set speed record in excess of 2,100 mph (1956); North American X-15 rocket plane made 1st successful flight under own power 17 Sept. 1959. Commercial jet transport initiated 15 Aug. 1958 with Boeing 707 (transatlantic service by Pan American Airways, 26 Oct. 1958), followed by Douglas DC-8 (1959), and Convair 880 (TWA, 1961).

1945–60. ATOMIC AND NUCLEAR DEVELOPMENTS. Atomic bomb completed and exploded (16 July 1945, p. 564). For **cyclotron,** see p. 739; **cosmotron,** p. 564. 1st **atomic-powered submarine,** U.S.S. Nautilus, commissioned 30 Sept. 1954, made 1st undersea crossing of the North Pole (5 Aug. 1958), submerging near Point Barrow, Alas., 1 Aug. and sailing under 50-ft.-thick ice-cap for 96 hrs. before surfacing. 6 days later submarine **Skate** covered same route from east to west. On 6 Oct. **Seawolf** surfaced after remaining submerged 60 days. Atomic-powered submarines were equipped (1960) with **Polaris** missiles, with nuclear warheads and range of 1,200 nautical mi. **Atomic-power projects,** p. 564. Controlled thermonuclear reaction created in U. of Calif. laboratories, 3 Nov. 1960.

1948. TRANSISTOR invented at Bell Tel. Laboratories by Walter Brattain, John Bardeen, and William Shockley—awarded Nobel Prize in physics, 1956.

1954. SOLAR BATTERY developed by 2 different laboratories—Bell Tel. and the Air Research and Development Command, Baltimore, Md.

1955, 18 May. NUCLEAR REACTOR patent issued to **Enrico Fermi** (d. 1954) and **Leo Szilard.**

4 Oct. 1957. DAWN OF THE SPACE AGE. The world's 1st artificial satellite ("Sputnik I") was launched as part of the Soviet participation in the Intl. Geophysical Year 1957–58. On 3 Nov. a 2nd artificial satellite ("Sputnik II"), carrying a dog, was launched. Sputnik III, a 2,925-lb. satellite, was launched 15 May 1958. In 1959 the U.S.S.R. launched 3 cosmic rockets: Lunik I, 2 Jan., reported 3 Jan. to have gone into permanent orbit around the sun as "1st artificial planet"; Lunik II, 12 Sept., making contact with the moon 14 Sept.; and Lunik III, 4 Oct., which circled the moon. A photograph of the hidden side of the moon was released 27 Oct. Sputnik IV was launched 15 May 1960, and space ships 14 May, 1 Dec.

1958–60. U.S. SATELLITE, ROCKET, and MISSILE EFFORT. The 1st U.S. artificial earth satellite (Explorer I) was placed in orbit by a modified Jupiter-C rocket, 31 Jan. 1958, followed 17 Mar. by the orbiting of a 3¼-lb. Navy satellite (Vanguard I), and 26 Mar. by a 31-lb. satellite (Explorer III). On 11 Oct. an Air Force Pioneer rocket failed to go into orbit around the moon but achieved a penetration of 79,173 statute miles into space. On 28 Nov. an Atlas inter-continental ballistic missile was successfully test-fired for a distance of 6,325 mi. On 18 Dec. an Atlas missile weighing *c.* 8,700 lbs. was placed in orbit around the earth. In 1959 space exploration was achieved by Vanguard II (17 Feb.), Vanguard III (18 Sept.), Discoverer I (28 Feb.), and other Discoverer satellites (13 Apr., 13 Aug., 19 Aug., 7 Nov.). On 3 Mar. Pioneer IV was propelled past the moon and entered a solar orbit. On 7 Aug. the "paddlewheel" satellite Explorer VI was launched and transmitted TV pictures of the earth. Explorer VII, VIII launched 13 Oct. 1959, 3 Nov. 1960. As of 12 Nov. 1960, when Discoverer XVII orbited, the U.S. had successfully orbited 29 earth satellites as against 8 launched by the U.S.S.R. Aerial recovery of Discoverer XIV capsule achieved 19 Aug., Discoverer XVII capsule 14 Nov. Camera-bearing weather satellites, Tiros I, Tiros II, orbited 1 Apr., 23 Nov. 1960. 21 Oct. A.T.&T. applied to FCC for permission to launch a communications space satellite.

3 **Nov.** Nobel prizes awarded to Donald A. Glaser for invention of **bubble bath**

chamber for photographing atomic particles and to Dr. Willard F. Libby for devising **Atomic time clock.**

MEDICINE AND PUBLIC HEALTH

1618–1776. EARLY EPIDEMICS. Smallpox: 1618–19, Mass. Indians, probably; 1631, 1635, 1638, 1648–49, 1666, N.E.; 1667, 1679–80, Va.; 1677–78, N.E.; 1689–90, Canada, N. E., N. Y.; 1696, Jamestown, Va.; 1702–03, 1721, Boston (over 50% infected, 1 in 7 deaths); 1730–31, Boston, N.Y., Phila.; 1737–38, N.E., Va., S.C.; 1746–47, Middle Colonies; 1751–52, Boston; 1756–57, Phila., Annapolis; 1758, N.Y.; 1759–60, Indians in S.C. and Ga.; 1760–61, 1764, N.E.; 1765, Md.; 1768, Reading, Pa. and Va.; 1774–76, throughout colonies. **Diphtheria:** 1659, N.E.; 1686, Va.; 1724, S.C.; 1735, N.H.; 1736–40, 1744–45, N.E., N.Y.; 1750–51, S.C.; 1754–55, N.E., N.Y.; 1763, Phila.; 1765, Boston; 1769, N.Y. **Scarlet fever:** 1702, 1735–36, Boston, Newport; 1764, Phila., N.C., S.C. **Measles:** 1657, Boston; 1687–88, N.E.; 1713–15, N.E. to Pa.; 1717, Va.; 1747–48, Conn., N.Y., Pa.; 1759, S.C., 1772–73, colonies generally. **Influenza:** 1647, N.E.; 1688, Va.; 1697–98, N.E.; 1722–23, colonies generally; 1756–57, 1761, 1767, 1770–72. **Pneumonia:** 1753–54, Mass. **Malaria:** 1658, 1668, 1683, N.E.; 1687, Va. Rising incidence in 18th cent., esp. in N.C. and S.C. **Dysentery:** 1669, N.E.; 1715, S.C.; 1731, Middle Colonies; 1751, S.C.; 1756, N.E.; 1757, Phila.; 1769, N.E. **Typhoid fever:** 1607, possibly, Jamestown; 1658, New Amsterdam; 1727, 1734, 1737, Conn. and Mass.; 1734, S.C.; 1741, N.E.; 1746, Albany, N.Y. By 1760 widely prevalent. **Typhus:** 1759, N.C.; 1764, 1766, Md. **Yellow fever:** 1st reported in Barbados, 1647; 1st clearly described in Phila., 1699, when it killed one-sixth of population; also Charleston; 1702, N.Y.; 1703, 1728, 1732, 1739, 1740, Charleston; 1741, Phila.; 1745, Charleston; 1747–48, Phila., Charleston; 1762, Phila.

1607–1750. EARLY PHYSICIANS, in addition to company physicians and ships' surgeons, included ministers like Revs. Gershom Bulkeley and Jared Eliot (Conn.) and emigrant physicans—**Cadwallader Colden, William Douglass**

(c.1691–1752), the elder **John Moultrie** (d.1771), **Alexander Garden** (1730–91). Native physicians in this period received their training through apprenticeship.

1716–66. SMALLPOX INOCULATION (serum from mildly infected human patients) was advocated by **Cotton Mather** through readings of the *Transactions,* 1714, 1716) and successfully put into practice (1721) by Dr. **Zabdiel Boylston** (1679–1766) prior to general acceptance in Europe (British royal children inoculated, 1722). Opposition led by **William Douglass** (died in smallpox epidemic, 1752), but practice spread to Philadelphia (1730) and S.C. (1738). Results reported by Benjamin Gale (Conn.) in *Transactions* (1766).

1735. First medical society in colonies founded at Boston.

First work describing lead poisoning from rum distilled with lead pipes published by **Thomas Cadwallader** (1708–79).

1736. First description of scarlet fever in the colonies by William Douglass.

1749–75. EUROPEAN MEDICAL TRAINING. Starting with **John Moultrie,** the Younger (1729–98), Americans began to study abroad, particularly at the University of Edinburgh (41 colonials in period), at private London lectures, and at the Universities of Leyden and Paris.

1752. EARLY HOSPITALS. Pesthouses were established at Boston (1717), Philadelphia (1742), Charleston (before 1752), New York (before 1757). A hospital for chronically ill patients was established at Charleston (1738). The 1st general hospital was established by **Thomas Bond** (1712–84) in Philadelphia (1752). New York Hospital, sponsored by Dr. **Samuel Bard** (1742–1821), was chartered 1771, but not opened until 1791. The first publicly supported mental hospital opened at Williamsburg, Va., 1773.

1754. *Opisthotonus and Tetanus* by Lionel Chalmers (d.1777), the most important work on tetanus produced in the course of the century.

1765–68. MEDICAL SCHOOLS. Medical faculty of College of Philadelphia (1765, largely through efforts of **John Morgan** [1725–89] and **William Shippen** [1736–1808] and King's College [1768]).

1775. First surgical textbook written in the colonies by **John Jones** (1729–91), *Remarks on the Treatment of Wounds and Fractures.*

1778. First American pharmacopoeia published by **William Brown** (1748–92).

1783–1810. MEDICAL SCHOOLS. Mass. Medical School, 1783. Faculties at Dartmouth (1798), Transylvania (1799), and Yale (1810). College of Medicine (Md.) organized, 1807; associated with University of Maryland, 1812. College of Physicians and Surgeons (1807) joined by the medical faculty of Columbia University (1813); reorganized as Medical Dept. of Columbia (1860).

1786–91. DISPENSARIES. Philadelphia Dispensary, opened, 1785, by Dr. **Benjamin Rush** (1745–1813); New York Dispensary, 1791.

c.1788–90. SURGERY. Dissection provoked serious rioting in New York City (1788). Dr. **John Jeffries** (1745–1819) —Loyalist physician who made a cross-channel balloon ascension with François Blanchard, 1785—had his 1st public lecture on anatomy (on return to Boston, 1789) broken up by a mob.

1793, Aug.–Oct. YELLOW FEVER EPIDEMIC in Philadelphia, worst in history of any U.S. city, led to improvement of urban sanitary conditions and water-supply systems. Croton Aqueduct for New York City's water supply built 1837–42. Other major epidemics: cholera (New York City, June–Oct. 1832; South, 1849; Middle West, 1850); smallpox, typhoid fever, typhus (Northern cities, 1865–71); yellow fever, cholera, and smallpox (Southern cities, 1873).

1797–1820. MEDICAL PERIODICALS. *Medical Repository* (quarterly, edited by **Samuel Latham Mitchill** [1764–1831]), followed in this period by 11 journals, including *New England Medical Rev. and Jl.* (1812, now *N.E. Jl. of Medicine*) and *Phila. Jl. of Medical and Physical Sciences* (1820, now *Amer. Jl. of Med. Sciences*).

1800–02. COWPOX VACCINATION introduced by Dr. **Benjamin Waterhouse** (Philadelphia, 1754–1846). Experiment by Boston Board of Health (Oct.–Nov. 1802) proved its efficacy and safety.

1808–20. PHARMACOPOEIAE. Mass. Medical Society published 1st official pharmacopoeia (1808; followed by New York Hospital, 1816). *U.S. Pharmacopoeia* prepared by representatives of state medical societies (1820), 1st to be nationally accepted.

1808. First work on **Naval Medicine** in U.S.: **Edward Cutbush's** (1772–1843) *Observations on the Means of Preserving the Health of Soldiers and Sailors.*

1809. First **ovariotomy** anywhere in the world performed by **Ephraim McDowell** (1771–1830) at Danville, Ky.

1810–40. MEDICAL EDUCATION. In this period 27 new medical schools were founded in U.S., foreshadowing later overexpansion. Middle Western pioneer was **Daniel Drake** (1785–1852).

1811. **John Syng Dorsey** (1783–1818) was the 1st in U.S. to ligate the external iliac artery for inguinal aneurism.

1812. *Diseases of the Mind* by **Benjamin Rush,** a pioneer work on mental disorders, earning for its author the sobriquet, "Father of American Psychiatry."

1817–50. CARE OF THE INSANE. Asylums opened at Frankford, Pa., 1817, and Boston (McLean) and New York (Bloomingdale), 1818, with general adoption by 1850. For work of **Dorothea L. Dix,** see p. 696.

1829. Publication of 1st U.S. textbook on pathology, by **William E. Horner** (1793–1853).

1831. **CHLOROFORM** discovered by **Samuel Guthrie** (1782–1848) simultaneously with, but independently of, von Liebig in Germany and Soubeiran in France. First used as anesthetic in England (1847); popularized in U.S. (1863) by **Gardner Q. Colton** (1814–98).

1833. GASTRIC PHYSIOLOGY. Publication of experiments by **William Beaumont** (p. 673).

1837. Typhus and typhoid fever clinically differentiated by **William W. Gerard** (1809–72).

1839. PATHOLOGY. *Elements of Pathological Anatomy* by **Samuel D. Gross**

(1805–84), 1st comprehensive work on the subject in English; also wrote significantly on intestinal lesions (1843), urinary bladder conditions (1851), respiratory organs (1854), and surgery (1859).

1839–41. DENTISTRY. *Amer. Jl. of Dental Science* (1839), College of Dental Surgery (Baltimore, 1840), American Soc. of Dental Surgeons (1840). Ala. introduced licensing of dentists (1841).

1842–46. ANESTHESIA. Although nitrous oxide (laughing gas) had been discovered by Joseph Priestley (1772) and its effects recognized by Humphrey Davy and William Allen (1800), neither it nor ether (whose effects were observed by Faraday, 1818) was used in surgery until William E. Clarke, a medical student, administered ether for a tooth extraction by Dr. Elijah Pope (Rochester, N.Y., Jan. 1842). For the claims of Long, Wells, and Morton, see p. 758.

1843. *Contagiousness of Puerperal Fever,* a paper by **Oliver Wendell Holmes** (p. 727), anticipated Semmelweiss in Vienna (1847; the latter's definitive report, 1861).

1844–47. NATIONAL MEDICAL ASSOCIATIONS. Assn. of Medical Superintendents of Amer. Institutions for the Insane (1844; now known as Amer. Psychiatric Assn.). Amer. Medical Assn. founded, 1847. Membership 1951, c.125,-000).

1844–85. MEDICAL JOURNALS. *Amer. Jl. of Psychiatry,* 1st specialized medical journal (1844); *Amer. Jl. of Obstetrics* (1868); followed by others, notably *Annals of Surgery* (1885).

1846. LARYNGOLOGY introduced into the U.S. by **Horace Green** (1802–66) with his *Treatise on Diseases of the Air Passages.* Introduction into U.S. of laryngoscope (1858) by **Ernest Krackowizer** (1821–75) expanded field.

1849. James M. Sims (1813–83) devised original operative treatment of vesicovaginal fistula.

1849–55. WOMEN IN MEDICINE. **Elizabeth Blackwell** (1821–1910), 1st woman medical graduate in the world, received M.D. degree from Medical School at Geneva, N.Y. Women's Medical College of Pa., 1st school of medicine entirely reserved for women (1850); Women's Hospital, New York (1855).

1850–54. ADVANCES IN PUBLIC HEALTH. Monumental *Report of Massachusetts Sanitary Commission* by **Lemuel Shattuck** (1793–1859). No action in Massachusetts until 1869 when a Board of Public Health was established; New Orleans, 1855. Daniel Drake's *Systematic Treatise* (1850–54) also aroused interest in subject.

1852. American Pharmaceutical Assn. founded.

1853. PEDIATRICS. Arrival in U.S. of **Abraham Jacobi** (1830–1919) promoted work in the field, as did **Job Lewis Smith** (1827–97) and **Thomas Morgan Rotch** (1849–1914).

1861. Kidney successfully removed by **Erastus B. Wolcott** (1804–80).

1867–68. ADVANCES IN ANESTHESIA. Gas inhaler covering nose and mouth introduced by S. S. White Dental Mfg. Co. (1867). **Edmund Andrews** (1824–1904) introduced use of oxygen with nitrous acid.

1868–85. MEDICAL JOURNALS. *Amer. Jl. of Obstetrics,* 1st specialized U.S. medical journal (1868); followed by others, notably *Annals of Surgery* (1885).

1869–72. PUBLIC HEALTH. First state board of health est. Mass. (1869). Amer. Public Health Assn. (1872) promoted work in field.

1872. Silas Weir Mitchell (1829–1914), pioneer U.S. neurologist, published his *Injuries of Nerves and their Consequences;* introduced "Weir Mitchell" treatment for certain types of nervous diseases. **Willard Parker** (1800–84) had distinguished (1856) between concussion of nerves and concussion of nerve centers.

1873. NURSING. Bellevue Hospital (N.Y.) est. school of nursing following principles of Florence Nightingale; rapidly spread: 15 schools by 1880; 432 schools by 1900.

1873–95. MEDICAL EDUCATION. From 1873–90, 112 medical schools were founded. Faulty distribution: Missouri first with 42; Cincinnati, 20; Chicago, 14; Louisville, 11. In an effort to raise professional level states tightened licensure; boards of examination by 1895 of the modern type in almost every state. Model was The Medical School at Johns

Hopkins University (founded 1893), with **William Henry Welch** (1850–1934) in pathology; **William S. Halsted** (1852–1922), surgery; Sir **William Osler** (1849–1919), the clinician.

1874–1930. OSTEOPATHY (emphasizing placement of bones in the body as key to health) founded by **Andrew Taylor Still** (1828–1917). Amer. Assn. of Advanced Osteopathy est., 1897. Three schools and 7,644 osteopaths in U.S. (1930).

1879–80. "INDEX MEDICUS" AND "INDEX-CATALOGUE." John Shaw **Billings** (1838–1913), curator of Army Medical Museum and Library, founded *Index Medicus* (1879), monthly list of newly published medical literature, and compiled great *Index-Catalogue to the Library of the Surgeon-General's Office* (1880), monumental bibliography of medical literature.

1884–99. ADVANCES IN ANESTHESIA. William Halsted injected cocaine into nerves to anesthetize peripheral regions (1884); **J. Leonard Corning** (1855–1923), using cocaine as spinal anesthetic, induced epidural anesthesia (1885) and used cocaine as local anesthetic (1887); spinal anesthesia used by Dudley Tait and Guido Caglieri in San Francisco and Rudolph Matas in New Orleans (1899).

1885–1913. ADVANCES IN SURGERY. Joseph O'Dwyer (1841–98) improved technic for intubation of the larynx in diphtheria (1885). Peroral endoscopy improved and modified by **Chevalier Jackson** (Philadelphia, 1865–1958). **Reginald Heber Fitz** (1843–1913) established "appendicitis" as a definite lesion (1886). First appendectomy following correct diagnosis of appendicitis performed by **Thomas George Morton** (1835–1903); technic improved by **John B. Murphy** (1857–1916), inventor of "Murphy Button" (1892), and **Charles McBurney** (1845–1913), who originated short incision. First successful removal in U.S. of brain tumor performed by **William W. Keen** (1837–1932; done in London, 1884). **William Steward Halsted** introduced the use of rubber gloves (*c.*1890), was the 1st to ligate the subclavian artery (1891), and perfected operations for hernia and breast removal. Founding of the **Mayo**

Clinic (1889) at Rochester, Minn. by the brothers **William James Mayo** (1861–1939) and **Charles Horace Mayo** (1865–1939) opened a new era in U.S. surgery, with stress on diagnosis as well as advanced technics. Advances in prevention of surgical shock and in operations for toxic goiter were made by **George W. Crile** (1864–1943). **Hugh H. Young** (1870–1945), urologist, devised a technic of prostatectomy. First thoracoplasty (1893) performed by **George Ryerson Fowler** (1848–1906). Amer. Coll. of Surgeons org. 1913 by **Franklin H. Martin** (1857–1935).

1885–1941. FIGHT AGAINST TUBERCULOSIS. Sanitarium at Saranac Lake, N.Y., founded (1884) by **Edward L. Trudeau** (1848–1915); established Saranac Laboratory for study of tuberculosis (1894). Early diagnosis aided by Roentgen's discovery of X ray (1895). For contribution of **Theobald Smith**, see p. 781. Natl. Assn. for Study and Prevention of Tuberculosis founded, 1904.

1889–1910. PREVENTIVE MEDICINE. Basic research in hog cholera, swine plague, and Texas fever in cattle by **Theobald Smith** (p. 781). **William Henry Welch** (1850–1934) discovered the bacillus of gas gangrene (1892). For the work in yellow fever of **Walter Reed** and associates, see p. 770. Col. **William Gorgas** (1854–1920), applying technics worked out by Reed, eliminated yellow fever from the Panama Canal Zone (1904–06). **Howard Taylor Ricketts** (1871–1910) demonstrated (*c.*1910) that typhus fever was caused by a new class of organisms now known as Rickettsiae (including Rocky Mountain fever, by a tick; trench fever, by a louse).

1895. CHIROPRACTICS founded by **Daniel D. Palmer** (1845–1904), emphasizing position of joints (especially of the spine) as key to health. Illegal in some states, there were 21 schools and 16,000 practitioners by 1930.

1896–1905. RADIUM AND X RAY IN THERAPY. X-ray treatment of breast cancer by **Emil H. Grube** (29 Jan. 1896) followed immediately upon publication of Roentgen's findings (5 Jan. 1896). Radium treatment for cancer used by **Robert Abbe** (1903); also 1st to treat cancer of womb with radium (1905).

1898–1927. HORMONES. Basic work

on isolating adrenalin done by **John J. Abel** (1857–1938); completed by **Jokichi Takamine** (1854–1922) on basis of Abel's findings (1901). For isolation of thyroxine by **Edward C. Kendall,** see p. 736. Work on insulin of Sir **Frederick G. Banting** and **J. J. R. MacLeod** (1922) utilized findings on the pancreas of **Moses Baron.** Isolation of substance in bull testes (later, androsterone and testosterone) accomplished (1927) by **Lemuel McGee.**

1901. ROCKEFELLER INSTITUTE OF MEDICAL RESEARCH founded (**William W. Welch** 1st head; succeeded, 1904, by **Simon Flexner** (1863–1946), who discovered (1905–07) serum for treating cerebrospinal meningitis and was 1st to transmit poliomyelitis to monkeys and to show it is caused by a virus (1909).

1906. "TYPHOID MARY," discovered by G. A. Soper, documented role of healthy carriers as sources of disease.

1908–50. MEDICAL EDUCATION. Report (1910) by **Abraham Flexner** (p. 707) for the Carnegie Foundation exposed abuses in medical education and proposed reforms. Large grants for medical schools and centers to Duke, Vanderbilt, George Washington, and Universities of Chicago, Rochester, and Iowa. Number of medical schools declined: 148 (1910), 76 (1932), 77 (1950). Number of graduates declined: Over 5,000 per annum (1900–06) to a low of 2,529 (1922, with a gradual rise to above 5,000 (1934–43). Number of physicians fluctuated slightly from 1 per 750 to 1 per 800. Studies abroad by many students (1,481 in 1931–32) cut off by World War II. Dental schools declined: 54 (1910), 39 (1945).

1909–52. PSYCHIATRY AND PSYCHOTHERAPY. Adolf Meyer (1866–1950), a founder (after 1892) of the mental hygiene movement in the U.S., enunciated the dynamic conception of dementia praecox, and with his associates discovered that serious mental disorders might yield to treatment involving introduction of malarial organisms into the blood stream. **Clifford W. Beers** (1876–1943) founded mental hospital movement (1909); **Elmer Ernest Southard** (1876–1920) made notable contributions in the field of neuropsychiatry and its social implications. Later U.S. psychiatrists

(since 1930) confirmed European discovery that dementia praecox could be cured by insulin or other shock treatment. First concerned with treatment of persons in asylums and mental hospitals, psychiatrists broadened their scope to include the origin of criminal behavior (with pioneer work on juvenile delinquency by Dr. **William Healy,** 1869–) and child guidance. Since 1940 considerable advances in psychotherapy and psychosomatic medicine have been achieved by **Franz Alexander** (1891–) and Dr. **William C. Menninger** (1899–) at the Menninger Clinic, Topeka, and as director of neuropsychiatry, Surgeon General's Office, U.S. Army, 1943–46. Lectures by **Sigmund Freud** and **Carl G. Jung** at Clark Univ. (1909) advanced psychoanalysis in U.S. **Psychoanalytic Rev.** est. (1913) by **William Alanson White** and S. E. Jelliffe. Recent psychoanalysis (since 1930) has emphasized social and cultural factors in neurosis and interpersonal aspect of analyst-patient relationship (**Karen Horney** [1885–1952], **Erich Fromm** [1900–], **Harry Stack Sullivan** [1892–1947]).

1912–32. NEUROLOGICAL SURGERY. Contributions of greatest U.S. figure in field, **Harvey Cushing,** at p. 692.

1913. Bela Schick (1877–) devised "Schick test," a skin test to determine susceptibility to diphtheria. Mass surveys, 1st in N.Y.C., followed by immunization of Schick-positive children by inactive toxin, drastically cut incidence of disease.

1914–48. VITAMIN RESEARCH. Beginning 1888, early work was conducted abroad (Eijkmann, Dutch East Indies; Funk and Hopkins, England; Frohlich and Holst, Norway; Pekelharing, Holland; Lunin, Switzerland). Vitamin A discovered (1912–14) by **Elmer V. McCollum** (1879–); Vitamin B. (1915–16); Vitamin D (1922). **Joseph Goldberger** (1874–1929), of U.S. Public Health Service, discovered (1915) that pellagra was a deficiency disease. **Harry Steenbock** (1886–) at the University of Wisconsin and Alfred Hess at Columbia University announced almost simultaneously (1924) methods for irradiating Vitamin D. Vitamin E isolated from wheat germ (1922) by **Herbert M. Evans** (1882–). Vitamin C isolated by Dr. Charles G. King (1932). R. J. Williams reported pantothenic acid (1933). Vitamin K discovered (1934) by **Edward A. Doisy** (1893–), simultaneously with Dam and Schønheyder in Denmark; synthesized (1939). Medical use of niacin discovered by **Conrad Elverhjem** (1901–). Thiamin synthesized (1936); pyridoxine isolated (1938); biotin's complex structure determined (1942). Para-amino benzoic acid synthesized (1943), in which year folic acid was discovered. By 1941 vitamin B was shown to be a complex of at least 5 distinct vitamins. Vitamin B$_{12}$ shown to be effective in treatment of pernicious anaemia (1948).

1918–19. INFLUENZA PANDEMIC spread from Western Front, with estimated 500,000 deaths in U.S. alone.

1920–43. TREATMENT OF EPILEPSY. Phenobarbital (discovered by Hauptmann, Germany, 1911) introduced in treatment by **Julius Grinker** (1920). Work of **William G. Lennox** (1884–) and **Tracy J. Putnam** (1894–) led to dilantin being synthesized and applied (1936). Tridione synthesized at Abbott Laboratories (1940); applied (1943).

1923–34. ANESTHESIA. Ethylene demonstrated by Arno B. Luckhardt; Sodium Amytal used on animals by F. J. Fulton and on humans intravenously by Leon G. Zerfas (1923). Cyclopropane (by Neff, Rovenstine, and Waters) and Nembutal (by R. H. Fitch, Waters, and Tatum) used as anesthetics (1930). Divinyl oxide, fastest yet devised, produced by Chauncey D. Leake (1930). Pentothal Sodium administered (1934) intravenously by John S. Lundy; also to permit free questioning by psychiatrists.

1927–28. IRON LUNG invented by Philip Drinker and Louis A. Shaw; used for poliomyelitis (1928).

1936–39. SULFA DRUGS. Perrin H. Long and Eleanor A. Bliss at Johns Hopkins proved the effectiveness of both prontosil (discovered by Domagk, Germany, 1932) and sufanilamide (discovered by Fourneau and Trèfouëls, France) on peritonitis, scarlet fever, tonsillitis, blood poisoning, and impetigo. These drugs were displaced, first by sulfapyridine (proved effective in the Sudan, 1939), and later by sulfathiazole, sulfa-diazine, and other sulfa compounds.

1939–52. ANTIBIOTICS. René J. Dubos (1901–) at Rockefeller Institute discovered tyrothricin in soil bacteria (effective in eye infections, ulcer, impetigo). **Selman Waksman** (1888–) discovered astinomycin (1940), streptothricin (1941)—both too destructive—and streptomycin (with Schatz, 1944; Nobel Prize for discovery, 1952), the last effective in meningitis, tuberculosis, dysentery, and bladder and kidney infections. Other antibiotics followed: chloromycetin (Ehrlich *et al.*, 1947); aureomycin (Duggar, 1948); terramycin (Finlay *et al.*, 1950); magnamycin (Pfizer Lab., 1952).

1941–43. PENICILLIN. Discovered by Dr. Alexander Fleming in London (1929); experiments by Dr. Howard W. Florey (1938) led to use on a human patient (1941). At beginning of World War II production of penicillin transferred to the U.S. under the wartime direction of Dr. Chester Keefer. Due to findings of Robert D. Coghill, production rose to 300 billion units (*c*.15 lbs.) per month (1945). Tests made by Florey abroad, and by Keefer, Leo Lowe, and John Mahoney, revealed effectiveness in most sulfa-resistant streptococcus and staphylococcus infections, including syphilis and subacute bacterial endocarditis (1943).

(1943). **Synthetic penicillin** developed in Beecham Laboratories, Eng. (1959), and Bristol-Myers, U.S.; introduced in U.S., 1960.

1943–50. ANTIHISTAMINES. Paralleling work at Pasteur Institute, U.S. researchers began work in field (1943). Benadril discovered by George Rieveschl, Jr. (1943); Pyrobenzamine (1946); Neohetramine (1948). Dramamine shown to be effective for control of seasickness (1948). Antihistamines used in treatment of allergies; promoted for common cold (1949–50), with debatable results.

1946–52. CORTISONE, a hormone of the cortex of the adrenal gland, synthesized by several groups (Sarett; Kendall, Mason, and Mattox; Julian; Gallagher, 1946; from carbon, oxygen, and hydrogen by Sarett, 1952). First used (1949) for rheumatic arthritis by Edward C. Kendall (p. 736) and Philip S. Hench (p. 725). ACTH, a hormone from the pituitary gland, was concentrated at Armour Laboratories and used by Hench *et al.* for rheumatoid arthritis.

1951–60. DRUG TRENDS. Tranquilizers: Miltown 1st synthesized 1950, in widespread use by 1955. Isolation (1952) of reserpine from old Indian shrub, along with introduction (1954) of thorazine, or chloropromazine (synthesized in France), with dramatic effects in treatment of patients with mental disorders. **Steroids:** In addition to corticosteroids (for arthritis), research and development progressed rapidly in field of sex steroids for treating endocrine deficiencies, of applying steroids as an anabolic agent for reconstruction of body and muscle tissues, and as cardiovascular agents. Synthesis of polypeptide hormone, oxytocin, by **Vincent du Vigneaud** (1901–), also synthesized hormone vasopressin, 1956) won him Nobel Prize in chemistry (1955). ACTH equivalent synthesized (1960) by Dr. Klaus Hofmann and associates. **Diabetes control:** Introduction (1957) of a nonbactericidal sulfonamide (Orinase) for treatment of mild diabetes of old age. **Fat-reducing diets:** Rockefeller Institute announced (1956) liquid formula based on glucose and corn oil, which served as basis of proprietary products, widely marketed beginning 1959.

1953. CANCER AND CIGARETTE SMOKING. Increase of incidence of cancer of the lung due to cancer-producing factor in cigarette smoking reported 8 Dec. 1953 by Dr. Alton Ochsner; statistical confirmation by Drs. Evarts A. Graham and Ernest L. Winder, 2 Feb. 1954; by British govt. study, 12 Feb.; and by statistical report of American Cancer Soc., 21 June.

1955, 12 Apr. SALK VACCINE. Widespread field tests of use of gamma globulin during polio epidemics in Utah, Tex., and Iowa, 1952, showed only short-term protection (*c.* 5 wks.). Earlier (1949) Drs. **John F. Enders** (1897–), **Thomas H. Weller** (1915–), and **Frederick C. Robbins** (1916–) of Harvard Medical School found that polio virus could be grown in cultures of non-nervous human and monkey tissues in test tubes, for which they were awarded the Nobel Prize in medicine and physiology (1954). This discovery paved the way for growth of the virus in quantities massive enough for use as vaccine. Using 3 strains of in-

activated polio, Dr. **Jonas E. Salk** (1914–) of Pittsburgh Univ. Medical School reported (26 Mar. 1953) hopeful results from a vaccine he prepared. In the largest medical field test in history, 1,830,000 school children participated in program to evaluate Salk vaccine. Evaluation report (12 Apr. 1955) disclosed that active immunity was provided for at least 6 mos., with more permanent protection by use of booster injections. As a result of a number of fatalities in the early stages, due to accidental inclusion of live virus in certain batches of vaccine, both the method of preparation and the strains of virus were modified for greater safety. The Poliomyelitis Vaccination Act (12 Aug. 1955) provided that the Public Health Service should allocate $30 million to the states to help them buy the vaccine, of which *c.* 20% was given free. Rise and decline in U.S. polio cases: (annual average) 1938–42, 6,400; 1942–47, 16,800; 1947–51, 34,000; 1952, *c.* 60,000; 1955, 37,771; 1957–58, *c.* 5,700; 1960, 3,277 (lowest since 1938).

1957. Pandemic of "Asian flu," a new strain of Type A influenza, spread from northern China and reached the U.S. in June, where it quickly became epidemic, although death rate remained low.

1958. GENETICS. Nobel Prize in medicine and physiology awarded to **Joshua Lederberg** (1925–) for discoveries concerning genetic recombination and organization of genetic material of bacteria, and to **George Wells Beadle** (1903–) and **Edward Lawrie Tatum** (1909–) for discovery that genes act by controlling specific chemical reactions.

1960. HEALTH INSURANCE. President Truman's Commission on the Health Needs of the Nation recommended (18 Dec. 1952) a program falling between the compulsory health insurance proposals of the Truman administration and the limited voluntary prepayment plan advocated by the American Medical Assn. By 1959 more than 70% of the population had hospitalization insurance and more than 60% some type of surgical and medical insurance. For Medical Care Bill (13 Sept. 1960) for needy aged, see p. 420. In Presidential campaign of 1960 Senator Kennedy proposed linking medical care program to social security.

THOUGHT AND CULTURE

RELIGION

1609. CHURCH OF ENGLAND was established by law in Va. A statute (1610), reenacted when Va. became a royal colony, but never rigidly enforced, provided for compulsory church attendance. The Anglican Church was also established in the lower counties of N.Y. (1693), and in Md. (1702), S.C. (1706), N.C. (nominally, 1711), and Ga. (1758). The first Anglican church in New York City, Trinity Church, was founded in 1697, with Rev. William Vesey as rector. In Mass. Anglican worship was introduced by Governor Andros (1686). In Pa. Christ Church, Philadelphia, was organized in 1694 and gained ground following the Quaker schism. Anglicanism was introduced in N.J. (1702) and in Conn. (1706). The influence of the Church was restricted by the predominantly mediocre quality of the colonial clergy, by oversized parishes, low salaries, neglect of discipline, and lay control. In the absence of a resident bishop confirmation and ordination could not be administered in the colonies. The latter served to discourage the growth of a native ministry. The **Bishop of London** was placed in charge of colonial churches in 1635, and was represented in the colonies by **commissaries**, notably by **James Blair** (1655–1743) in Va., 1689–1743, and **Thomas Bray** (1656–1730) in Md. The latter founded (1701) the **Venerable Society for the Propagation of the Gospel in Foreign Parts** (S.P.G.), which engaged in missionary activities and founded churches (notably in the Carolinas). After the first quarter of the 18th century the Anglican Church gained ground as a result of a split among Calvinists. Repeated agitation for an **American episcopate** (1700–70) failed because

of the opposition of governmental officials, dissenters, and Southern laymen who insisted on the right to choose their own curates. The first bishop in America was **Samuel Seabury** (1729–96), consecrated in Aberdeen by nonjuring bishops (1784).

1620. CONGREGATIONAL CHURCHES were introduced by the Pilgrims in Plymouth (1620) and by the Puritans in Massachusetts Bay (1630). The principal difference was that the former (Independents) repudiated the Church of England; the latter (Nonconformists) did not openly break with the Established Church. The Puritan theological system stressed 3 covenants—between God and man, between the Church and its members, and between the State and its citizens. Since the Church never controlled the State officially, Mass. never achieved a true theocracy, but rather a "Bible Commonwealth" in which the civil rulers, seeking to rule in accordance with the will of God, sought counsel of the divines (Calvinist "consociation"). Factors contributing to the decline of the Church in New England were (1) the disappearance of the distinction in civil matters between the "elect" and all others, (2) gradual dispersal of the population on farms, and (3) the growth of rationalism. The **Halfway Covenant** (1657–62), which admitted to baptism the children of baptized persons who themselves had not experienced conversion, served to erase the distinction between the "elect" and all others. Rationalist influences: (1) the revulsion against the Salem Witchcraft Trials (1692–93), (2) the ouster of the orthodox Increase Mather as president of Harvard College (1701); (3) the founding of the Brattle Street Church in Boston (1699), the 1st Puritan church not to require a public confession of faith for admission to communion. The religious monopoly of the Congregationalists was challenged by the Baptists under **Roger Williams** (p. 801) and **Henry Dunster** (1609–59), who was forced to resign (1654) the presidency of Harvard College because of his opposition to infant baptism; by the Presbyterians, as evidenced in the remonstrance of Dr. Robert Child (1646), the later attempt of Increase Mather to Presbyterianize the church, resisted by Rev. **John Wise** (1710–17), and the **Saybrook Platform** (1708), by which Conn. Congregationalists placed themselves under a Presbyterian-type government; and by the Quakers (p. 37); and was terminated as a result of the revocation of the old charter (1684).

1628. DUTCH REFORMED CHURCH (a Calvinist, Presbyterian group) was organized in New Amsterdam by Rev. Jonas Michaëlius (1628), placed under the jurisdiction of the Classis of Amsterdam, and established by the Freedoms and Exemptions (1640). A Coetus or synod of ministers and elders was formed in 1747. Between 1755 and 1771 a cleavage developed between the **Coetus** (demanding virtual self-government) and the **Conferentie** (conservative), which was settled by Rev. **John Henry Livingston** (1770–1825), with substantial independence for the Coetus. The organization of a General Synod, 1792, made the American church independent.

1633. ROMAN CATHOLIC CHURCH had previously been established in North America as a result of Spanish and French missionary activity (pp. 50, 51, 60, 61), but the 1st group of Catholics to arrive in the English colonies came to Md., which had been founded (1632) to provide refuge for that denomination. For the Toleration Act (1649) and its repeal (1654), see p. 29. The Revolution of 1689 in Md., leading to Protestant ascendancy, resulted in the passage of anti-Catholic legislation (1) imposing poll tax on Irish Catholic immigrant servants; (2) requiring that children of mixed marriages be reared as Protestants; (3) imposing a fine for sending children to Catholic schools abroad. In N.Y. Roman Catholics enjoyed toleration under the administration of the Catholic Governor, Thomas Dongan (1682–88), but in the beginning of the 18th century R.I. and Pa. were the only colonies in which Roman Catholics enjoyed religious and civil rights. For Protestant opposition to the Quebec Act, 1774, see p. 83. By 1775 public worship by Roman Catholics was confined to Pa. (with Jesuit churches and chapels in Philadelphia, Conewago, Goschenhoppen, Lancaster, and Reading).

1639. BAPTISTS (opposed to infant baptism and stressing the separation of Church and State) were organized as a church by **Roger Williams** (p. 801) at Providence, R.I., followed by Newport (1644). Large gains were made in the Middle Colonies among the Welsh and as a result of the Quaker schism. In addition, their membership expanded as a result of (1) the Great Awakening and (2) the American Revolution. Under such leaders as **Isaac Backus** (1724–1806) and **John Leland** (1754–1841), they were active on behalf of religious liberty and the separation of Church and State.

1640. LUTHERAN CHURCH. Rev. **Reorus Torkillus**, 1st Lutheran minister to serve in the New World, arrived in New Sweden (spring 1640). The 1st synod was not organized until 1748 under Rev. **Heinrich Mühlenberg** (1711–87). The organization of the Ministerium of Pa. led ultimately to the independence of the Lutheran Church in the U.S., with some 130 congregations, chiefly in Pa., at the outbreak of the Revolution.

1654. JEWS. Despite the efforts of Stuyvesant to deprive them of civil rights, the 1st group of Jews, arriving in New Amsterdam (1654) from Curaçao, induced the Dutch West India Co. (7 Jews were among the 167 stockholders) to permit them to reside and engage in wholesale trade (1655–56). In 1657 they were admitted to the retail trades. In 1685 they demanded the right of public worship, denied under Dutch rule, and a synagogue (Shearith Israel, "Remnant of Israel") was known to exist in New York City in 1695. In 1737 their right to vote for the N.Y. Assembly was denied. Admitted in R.I. to the freemanship (1665), they were later denied political rights (1728), which were reestablished by the state constitution (1777). Similarly, in S.C. voting was confined to Christians (1721), but at least 1 Jew was elected to public office—Francis Salvador, Jr., to the 1st provincial congress. In Savannah, Ga., Jews held minor public office (1765–88), with David Emanuel elected governor (1801). The disqualification of the Md. constitution of 1776, barring Jews from public office, was finally removed in 1826; in N.C., not until 1868. The Jews prior to 1789 were mainly **Sephardim** (of Spanish, Portuguese, and Dutch origin).

1656. QUAKERS (SOCIETY OF FRIENDS), founded by George Fox (1624–91), stressed "inner light," separation of Church and State, opposition to war and oaths. Except in R.I., they were persecuted in the period, 1656–70 (p. 37). Expansion of this sect is attributed to the visit of Fox to America (1671) and to Penn's "Holy Experiment" (1681, pp. 48, 49). As a result of a schism in 1692 between Penn and **George Keith** (c.1638–1716), principal of the Penn Charter School, the latter founded a sect known as Christian, or Baptist, Quakers, or "Keithians," and then was ordained in the Church of England (1700).

1683. MENNONITES, led by **Francis Daniel Pastorius** (1651–c.1720), settled in Germantown, Pa. They advocated separation of Church and State, religious liberty, adult baptism, a church of the elect, pacifism, refusal to take oaths, and drew up the 1st protest against slavery (1688). Most conservative of this group were the **Amish**. The Old Amish Order still uses the German language exclusively and is opposed to innovation.

1706. PRESBYTERIANS. The 1st presbytery was organized in Philadelphia by **Francis Makemie** (1658–1708); the 1st synod in 1718. The Adoption Act, the 1st constitution of American Presbyterianism, was adopted (1729). Expansion was due to the founding of "log colleges," especially the one by Rev. **William Tennent** at Neshaminy (1736), and by the establishment of the College of New

Jersey (1746). Synod of 1786 provided for a General Assembly, the 1st meeting of which was held in Philadelphia (1789).

1721. Hollis Chair in Divinity, the 1st professorship in theology, was established at Harvard.

1723. DUNKARDS, OR GERMAN BAPTISTS, were organized under the leadership of **Alexander Mack**. Their distinctive features were triple immersion, pacifism, and agape feasts.

1726–56. GREAT AWAKENING, a series of revivals, usually dates from the preaching of Domine **Theodorus Frelinghuysen**, a Dutch Reformed minister in N.J., the establishment of Tennent's log college (1736), and the 1st visit of George **Whitefield** (p. 799) to Ga. (1738) and his later itinerant preaching from Me. to Ga. In New England, undisputed leadership in the movement was assumed by **Jonathan Edwards** (p. 701), beginning with his sermons of 1734. In Va. it attained its peak, 1748–49, under Rev. **Samuel Davies** (1723–61). Stubal Stearns and Daniel Marshall spread the movement among the Va. Baptists. The Methodist phase, under Rev. Devereux Jarrett, reached its climax, 1775–85. Among Presbyterians, the Great Awakening led to a schism between "New Side" (revivalists, who organized an independent synod, 1745) and "Old Side" (conservatives), which was healed in 1758. Among Congregationalists a similar division developed, with the more conservative joining the Anglican Church.

1732. EPHRATA SOCIETY, an offshoot of the German Baptists, was founded by **Johann Conrad Beissel**. The group stressed the monastic life, chastity, and the 7th-day sabbath. For contributions to music, see p. 646.

1734. SCHWENKENFELDERS made their 1st appearance in Pa., but lacked formal organization until 1782.

1735. MORAVIANS, OR UNITED BRETHREN, comprising Hussites and German Pietists, came to Ga. in 1735, and, under Count **Nikolaus Zinzendorf** (1700–60), founded a settlement at Bethlehem, Pa. (1741). **Augustus Gottlieb Spangenberg** (1704–92) was consecrated bishop of the Church in America (1744).

In that year a semicommunistic General Economy was established at Bethlehem (at Winston-Salem, N.C., 1753), but was dissolved, 1762, when the crafts and trades returned to private management. Control was exercised from Herrnhut, Saxony. Not until 1857 was the American Church given a constitution with relative independence from German control. Renowned for church music, notably part-singing of congregations.

1747. GERMAN REFORMED CHURCH, organized by Michael Schlatter as a subordinate body of the Dutch Reformed Church, made large gains among the Pa. Germans. The Church remained under Dutch control until 1793.

c.1750. RISE OF RATIONALISM. Rev. Jonathan Mayhew (1720–66) and Charles Chauncey (1705–87), by stressing the function of reason apart from revelation (p. 595), laid the foundation for Unitarianism.

1766. METHODISM began in America, as in England, as a movement within the Church of England. It appeared 1st in New York City (1766) with the organization by **Philip Embury** (1728–73) of the John Street Church, and was expanded by the activities of itinerant preachers sent out by Wesley (1771), notably **Francis Asbury** (1745–1815). In Va., Rev. **Devereux Jarratt** (1733–1801), an Anglican minister, acted as unofficial chaplain to the Methodists. It is estimated that by 1777 some two thirds of all American Methodists lived in the vicinity of Jarratt's parish. In 1784 Asbury was consecrated bishop.

1774. SHAKERS, OR "MILLENNIAL CHURCH," a Protestant monastic group, led by Mother **Ann Lee** (1736–84), 1st arrived in the colonies, settling at Watervliet, N.Y.

1775–83. CHURCHES AND THE REVOLUTION. The Anglican clergy throughout the colonies were Loyalist, the Southern laity overwhelmingly Patriot. The Congregational and Presbyterian clergy took a Patriot stand. The Methodist missionaries were Loyalist. Lutherans and Roman Catholics were divided in loyalty. The Quakers, officially neutral, leaned toward the Loyalists, as did the Shakers.

RELIGIOUS CENSUS, 1775 (Based on Rough Estimates—3,105 Religious Organizations and Congregations)

Congregationalists	575,000
Anglicans	500,000
Presbyterians	410,000
Dutch Reformed	75,000
German Churches (incl. German Reformed, 50,000, and Lutheran in Pa., 75,000)	200,000
Quakers	40,000
Baptists	25,000
Roman Catholics	25,000
Methodists	5,000
Jews	2,000

1776–89. DISESTABLISHMENT. Under the leadership of Baptists and Presbyterians the movement for religious freedom and separation of Church and State gained headway in Va. in the Revolutionary period. Mainly the work of **George Mason** (1725–92) and **James Madison,** the Va. **Declaration of Rights** (12 June 1776) advocated "free exercise of religion." An Act of 1776 suspending payment of tithes (becoming effective 1 Jan. 1777) really disestablished the Church of England, although final steps were taken in Jefferson's Bill for Establishing Religious Freedom, passed through Madison's efforts (1785), and preceded by the latter's "Memorial and Remonstrance against Religious Assessments" (1784). Elsewhere the Church was disestablished: 1776—Pa., Del., and N.J.; 1777—N.Y., N.C., and Ga. (partially, completely in 1789); 1790—S.C.

1780. UNIVERSALISTS. The 1st American Universalist church, built by Rev. John Murray (1741–1815) in Gloucester, Mass., favored separation of Church and State. "Winchester Program" adopted, 1803. General Convention, governing body, est. 1833; incorporated, 1866.

1782. 1ST PAROCHIAL SCHOOL erected by St. Mary's Church, Philadelphia ("Mother School"). The system was officially sanctioned in Baltimore (1829). By 1840, there were 200 parochial schools in the U.S. In 1951, there were 236 colleges with 236,636 students, 1,628 high schools (diocesan and parochial) with 337,414 students, and 8,202 elementary schools (parochial) with 2,575,329 students.

1784. THEOLOGICAL SCHOOLS. The first theological college in the U.S. was established at New Brunswick, N.J. Other important seminaries were Andover (founded to oppose Unitarian trends at Harvard, 1808), Princeton (1812), General (1817), Auburn (1818), Virginia (1823), Hartford (1834), and Union Theological (1836).

1789. PROTESTANT EPISCOPAL CHURCH, depleted by Loyalist emigration, now independent of the Church of England, was organized at its first triennial convention in Philadelphia, and adopted canons along with revised prayers. By 1792 five bishops had been named.

1790. ROMAN CATHOLIC EPISCOPATE was established with the consecration of Rev. **John Carroll** (1735–1815); nominated, 1788; previously, 1784, appointed superior with power to administer confirmation. Political discrimination against Catholics continued until 1835 (N.C.).

1792. RUSSIAN ORTHODOX CHURCH began missionary activities in Alaska, with a resident bishop at Sitka, 1798. The episcopal see was moved to San Francisco (1872), and in 1905 to New York City.

1794. DEISM gained ground after the publication of Tom Paine's *Age of Reason*. Previously such views had been expounded in Ethan Allen's *Reason the Only Oracle of Man* (1784), but deism's most influential exponent in America was **Elihu Palmer,** ex-Baptist preacher, whose *Principles of Nature* (1797) attacked the orthodox tenets of Christianity. Deists established ties with pro-Jacobin democratic societies after 1794.

1797. GREAT REVIVALS began on the frontier with the preaching of **James McGready** (*c.*1758–1817). His camp-meeting movement was climaxed by the **Cane Ridge Meeting** (Aug. 1801). A schism among revivalists resulted in the organization of the Cumberland Presbyterian Church (1810). In Ky., the revival of **Barton W. Stone** (1774–1844) led to the New Light ("Stoneite") schism (1803; ultimately merging with Methodist and Baptist groups as the "Christian Church"). In New England the revival was led by the Edwardeans,

who were opposed by (1) the **old covenant theologians** (Timothy Dwight [1752–1817] and **Lyman Beecher** [1775–1863]), and (2) by the **rationalists** and **Unitarians.**

1800. UNITED BRETHREN IN CHRIST, an Arminian group, was founded by **Martin Boehm** (1725–1812) and **Philip W. Otterbein** (1726–1813), 1st bishops; merged (1946) with the Evangelical Church, founded, 1800, by **Jacob Albright** (1769–1808).

1801. Adoption of the Presbyterian-Congregational Plan of Union to eliminate competition in regions where one or the other was already established.

1805. RAPPISTS, a group of German pietists led by **George Rapp** (1755–1847), was organized in Pa., founded New Harmony, Ind. (1815), sold to Robert Owen (1824), and then moved to Economy, near Pittsburgh. A celibate, authoritarian sect, it declined following Rapp's death, and its affairs were terminated (1905).

1808. METHODIST CHURCH adopted a constitution. Previously, a schism led by James O'Kelley, who opposed Asbury's appointive powers, had resulted in the organization of the Republican Methodist Church (1792). The Methodist Protestants seceded (1830).

1810. Organization of the **AMERICAN BOARD OF COMMISSIONERS FOR FOREIGN MISSIONS** (Congregational), which became interdenominational (1812), marked the beginning of American missionary interest. The American Bible Society (1816), the Home Missionary Society (1826), and the American Tract Society (1825) followed. In 1814 the General Missionary Convention of the Baptists for Foreign Missions initiated home missions movement. In 1832 the Baptist Home Missionary Society was organized to operate in the South and West.

DISCIPLES OF CHRIST, a group of progressive Presbyterians opposed to closed communion, founded the Independent Church of Christ at **Brush Run, Pa.** Two groups, 1 founded by Rev. **Barton Warren Stone** (1774–1844) and the other by Rev. **Thomas Campbell** (1763–

1854) and his son, Alexander (1788–1866) united at Lexington, Ky. (1832).

1813–17. Large Negro groups formed independent churches, including African Methodist Episcopal Church (Philadelphia, 1816). The 1st Negro Baptist church was founded in Ga. (1773). In 1861 there were 200,000 Negro members of the Methodist Episcopal Church, South; 150,000 Negro Baptists.

1818. Conn. constitution disestablished the Congregational Church.

1819. UNITARIAN CHURCH (stressing unity of God and denying Trinitarianism) founded by **William Ellery Channing** (p. 685). The Dedham Case (Mass., 1820) allowed Unitarians, even though a minority, to retain church property they were occupying after a majority of orthodox had withdrawn, thereby strengthening the denomination.

1820–60. General Synod of the Lutheran Church held at Hagerstown, Md. (Oct. 1820). German (Missouri) Synod est. 1847; Norwegian Synod, 1853, ultimately Norwegian Lutheran Church of America. Augustana, Swedish Synod, est. 1860.

1824–50. REVIVALISM in Pa., N.Y., and Mass. led by **Charles G. Finney** (1792–1875), licensed to preach as a Presbyterian. The Broadway Tabernacle was established for him in New York City (1834). His followers withdrew from Presbyterianism (1836) and adopted Congregationalism. In the Middle West revivalism was led by such itinerant preachers as **Peter Cartwright** (1785–1872) and **James B. Finley** (1781–1856).

1827–28. Schism between **Orthodox** and **Hicksite** Quakers.

1828. Presbyterian schism between Old School (orthodox Calvinists) and New School (Western liberals).

1829–54. ANTI-CATHOLIC AGITATION, following the founding of the Society for the Propagation of the Faith (Lyons, France, 1822) and the Leopold Association (Vienna, 1829) to promote Roman Catholic missions in America, resulted in such publications as *The Protestant* and *Priestcraft Unmasked,* of anti-Catholic sermons by Rev. **Lyman Beecher** and writings by **Samuel F. B. Morse** (p.

757), and of acts of violence, such as the burning of the Ursuline Convent at Charlestown, Mass. (11 Aug. 1834). For nativism and the Know-Nothing movement of the 40's and 50's, see pp. 187, 218.

1830. LATTER-DAY SAINTS, OR MORMONS, owe their origin to the publication of the *Book of Mormon,* based on a revelation claimed by **Joseph Smith** (1805–44), followed by the founding of the Church at Fayette, N.Y., the same year. As a result of opposition, the Mormons left N.Y. (1831) for Kirkland, Ohio, and Independence, Mo. Expelled from Mo., they settled at Nauvoo, Ill. Violence followed them, culminating in the lynching of Smith in the jail at Carthage. Driven from Nauvoo (1846), the Saints settled in the valley of the Great Salt Lake in Utah (1848) under the leadership of **Brigham Young** (p. 805).

1832–69. SLAVERY AND THE CHURCHES. The issue of abolitionism came to a head when Theodore Dwight Weld, a student at Lane Theological Seminary, Cincinnati, withdrew from that institution when the trustees suppressed an antislavery society. In the North abolitionism quickly became part of revivalism. The issue divided the Protestant churches. The Southern Baptists withdrew (1843) to organize the Southern Baptist Convention. The Methodist Church, South, set up a separate organization (1844). An abolitionist group of New School Presbyterians organized the Synod of Free Presbyterian Churches, Ohio (1847), followed by a major schism in the New School (1857), when the United Synod of the South was established. Old School Presbyterians split (1861), and the Presbyterian Church in the Confederate States was founded. The Ohio Synod and the New School Presbyterians united in 1862. In 1864 the Southern groups united as the Presbyterian Church in the U.S. The Northern groups united as the Presbyterian Church in the U.S.A. (1869). Division on this issue was avoided in the Protestant Episcopal Church.

1833. Mass. disestablished the Church by constitutional amendment, ratified by popular vote of 32,234 to 3,273.

**1840–60. REFORM and CONSERVA-
TIVE JUDAISM.** Rabbi Isaac Mayer
Wise (1819–1900), through *The Israelite,* established in Cincinnati, advocated
the idea of reform. In 1873 he organized the Union of American Hebrew
Congregations, followed (1875) by Hebrew Union College in Cincinnati
(merged with the Jewish Institute of
Religion, New York City, 1948) and
(1889) the Central Conference of American Rabbis. A conservative movement in
opposition was headed by Rabbis **Isaac
Leeser** (1806–68) and **Sabato Morais**
(1823–97) of Philadelphia. The Jewish
Theological Seminary (conservative)
was founded (1886).

**c.1840–60. GOSPEL OF INDIVIDU-
ALISM,** combining rationalism and
evangelical Protestantism, was expounded by **Francis Wayland** (1796–
1865), president of Brown University,
and author of *Elements of Moral Science*
(1835).

1843. MILLERISM, an Adventist movement, resulted from the preaching of
William Miller (1782–1849), who proph-
esied the 2nd coming of Christ between
1843–44. His followers founded the Adventist Church (1845). The **Seventh-
Day Adventists** separated from the parent body (1846).

1847. THEOLOGICAL LIBERALISM
was exemplified by the publication of
Rev. **Horace Bushnell's** (1802–76) *Christian Nurture,* stressing mysticism, free
will, and Christian nurture, rather than
election, as the road to salvation.

1874. The publication of *Outlines of
Cosmic Philosophy* by **John Fiske** (1842–
1901), with its attempt to reconcile the-
ism with Darwinian evolution, brought
theological liberalism (advocated by Rev.
Henry Ward Beecher [1813–87], Rev.
Lyman Abbott [1835–1922], **Washington
Gladden** [1836–1918], Rev. **Phillips
Brooks** [p. 680], **John William Draper**
[1811–82], and **Andrew D. White** [1832–
1918]) into open conflict with orthodoxy.

1875–86. Archbishop **John McClosky**
became the 1st American cardinal. Archbishop **James Gibbons** (p. 714) was
elected to the same rank (1886). The
Catholic University of America was

founded at Washington, D.C., by the 3rd
plenary council (1884).

1875–92. CHRISTIAN SCIENCE textbook, *Science and Health,* by **Mary
Baker Eddy** (p. 700), was published and
the Christian Science Association organized. The 1st church was established at
Boston, 1879; reorganized, 1892.

**1876. SOCIETY FOR ETHICAL CUL-
TURE** established in New York by **Felix
Adler** (1851–1933).

1880. SALVATION ARMY, evangelistic
organization, after being 1st established
by Gen. William Booth in England, was
organized in the U.S.

1892. HIGHER CRITICISM resulted
in several heresy trials, notably that of
Charles A. Briggs (1841–1913), professor at Union Theological Seminary.
Tried (1892) and acquitted, he was suspended from the Presbyterian ministry
and subsequently entered the ministry
of the Protestant Episcopal Church.

1895. National Baptist Convention of
the U.S.A., representing merger of Negro
Baptist groups, formed at Atlanta; incorporated (1915). The National Baptist
Convention of America separated (1916).

1902. Five Years Meeting (a loose confederation) formed by 13 Yearly Meetings of the Society of Friends. Kan. and
Ore. have since withdrawn. Three Yearly
Meetings from outside the U.S. have
joined.

1905. The Federal Council of Churches
of Christ in America, 1st major interdenominational organization, was founded;
succeeded (1950) by the National Council of Churches of Christ in the U.S.A.

1907. SOCIAL GOSPEL. Publication
of *Christianity and the Social Crisis* by
Walter Rauschenbusch (1861–1918),
with its criticism of capitalism and the
industrial revolution and its stress on cooperation rather than competition.

1908. Home Missions Council established
to direct noncompetitive missionary activity.

**1909–25. FUNDAMENTALIST REAC-
TION,** inspired by such traveling evan-
gelists as William Jennings Bryan (p.
680), William A. ("Billy") Sunday, and
John Alexander Dowie, reached its cli-

max at Dayton, Tenn. (10–21 July 1925), in the trial and conviction of **John Scopes**, a Tenn. schoolteacher, for teaching evolution. Scopes was opposed by Bryan; defended by Clarence Darrow and Dudley Field Malone.

1918. United Lutheran Church in U.S. formed, placing 45 synods on the same doctrinal basis.

1931. JEHOVAH'S WITNESSES, under the leadership of Judge J. F. Rutherford (originating with the Russellites, incorporated by Pastor Charles T. Russell, 1884), were incorporated (1939) as The Watch Tower Bible and Tract Society. For Jehovah's Witnesses cases, see p. 499.

c.1935. NEO-ORTHODOXY, a synthesis of the socioeconomic liberalism of the Social Gospel and a rediscovery of Biblical theology, with stress on the fall of man and the judgment of God, secured a wide following among American Protestants under the leadership of **Reinhold Niebuhr** (p. 759).

1939. Methodist Episcopal Church, Methodist Episcopal Church, South, and the Methodist Protestant Church were reunited.

1952. Bible, Revised Standard Version (Natl. Council, Churches of Christ, U.S.A.), best seller; also Roman Catholic Confraternity translation, vol. I.

1950–60. PROTESTANT CHURCH

UNITY TREND. Natl. Council of the Churches of Christ in the U.S.A. formed 29 Nov. 1950 by 25 Protestant denominations and 5 Eastern Orthodox bodies embracing 37 million church members. Congregational Christian Churches and the Evangelical Reformed Church united (June, 1957) to form the United Church of Christ. Presbyterian Church in the U.S.A. and United Presbyterian Church joined 28 May, 1958 to form the United Presbyterian Church in the U.S.A. On 4 Dec. 1960 the chief executive officer of the United Presbyterian Church proposed a merger into a new church of the Methodist, Protestant Episcopal, and United Presbyterian Churches and the United Church of Christ, with total membership of 12,-250,000 for the 4 churches.

1954–57. Evangelist **Rev. Dr. Billy Graham** (1918–   ), who began a series of popular evangelistic campaigns in 1946, toured Great Britain and western Europe in 1954–55, and conducted a 16 wks. campaign in N.Y.C., culminating 27 Oct. 1957.

1958. CHIEF GAINS IN CHURCH ROLLS since 1950 reported by Churches of Christ, with membership rise to 2 million (100%); Latter-day Saints, 1,541,000 (38%); Roman Catholic Church, 39,510,000 (34%); Southern Baptist Convention, 9,200,000 (29%).

1926–50 Gains in Church Rolls

	1926	1950	% Increase
American Baptist Convention	1,289,966	1,561,073	21
Southern Baptist Convention	3,524,378	7,079,889	100.9
National Baptist Convention U.S.A., Inc.... }	3,196,623	7,091,394	121.8
National Baptist Convention of America..... }			
Churches of Christ	433,714	1,000,000	130.6
Congregational Christian	994,491	1,204,789	21.1
Disciples of Christ	1,377,595	1,767,964	28.3
Greek Orthodox Church (Hellenic)	119,495	1,000,000	736.9
Evangelical and Reformed	675,804	726,361	7.5
Evangelical United Brethren	583,516	717,531	23
Jewish Congregations	4,081,242	5,000,000	22.5
Church of Jesus Christ of Latter-day Saints.	542,194	1,111,314	105
American Lutheran Church	474,923	692,484	45.8
Evangelical Lutheran Church of America....	496,707	813,837	63.8
Lutheran Church—Missouri Synod	1,040,275	1,674,901	61
United Lutheran Church	1,214,340	1,954,342	60.9
African Methodist Episcopal	545,814	1,166,301	113.7
African Methodist Episcopal Zion	456,813	530,116	16
The Methodist Church	6,760,642	8,935,647	32.2
Presbyterian Church in the U.S.A.	1,894,030	2,318,615	22.4
Presbyterian Church in the United States...	451,043	678,206	50.4
Protestant Episcopal Church	1,859,086	2,540,548	36.7
Roman Catholic Church	18,605,003	28,634,878	53.9

EDUCATION

1636–1775. E L E M E N T A R Y SCHOOLS. Diversity in the 3 major regional systems was the result of (1) religious differences at the time of settlement and (2) divergences in the economic and social structure of the areas. **New England** (influenced by Calvinist emphasis upon individual responsibility for salvation and the concomitant necessity of each individual's reading the Bible) was committed to the **compulsory maintenance** program as developed in 2 Mass. laws:

1642. Act imposed fines for neglect of education.

1647. Act required all towns of 50 families to provide a teacher for instruction in reading and writing; all towns of 100 families to establish a Latin grammar school (already set up in Boston, 1636). The act made it optional whether the school was to be tax-supported or fee-supported, and imposed a penalty of £5 (raised in 1671 to £10) for noncompliance. Similar acts passed by Conn., 1650; Plymouth, 1671; N.H., 1689; with R.I. only exception. Although historians disagree as to the extent of enforcement of this law, statistical evidence points to a higher degree of **literacy** in New England than elsewhere (1640–1700, 95% literacy [Shipton] as against 54%–60% for males in Va. [Bruce]).

1692. Disallowance of Mass. statute reviving compulsory education laws resulted in adoption of policy whereby selectmen or overseers of poor were empowered to bind out as apprentices "any poor children."

1765. At least 48 out of the 140 Mass. towns with a population of 100 families or more were maintaining Latin schools.

The **Middle Colonies** adopted a **parochial school** program, both as a result of private and church efforts. New Amsterdam: 1638, 1st school under Adam Roelantsen, Dutch Reformed auspices but town-supported; 1659, classical school established. N.Y.: despite act of 1702 to encourage a free grammar school in New York City, activity was left to the Venerable Society (S.P.G.), which in 1710 founded the Trinity School. Chief emphasis thereafter was upon charity and private schools. Pa.: 1689, Friends' School, Philadelphia (chartered, 1697, later known as William Penn Charter School). In the Northern and Middle colonies **apprenticeship** generally imposed educational requirements, such as one quarter's schooling each year, necessitating the establishment in the 18th century of **evening schools** in the larger towns.

In the **South** apprenticeship was the leading method for educating the poor (in Va. book education provided by act of 1705), supplemented by the establishment of **pauper schools** (county pauper schools est. Md., 1723). Children of planters were educated by tutors or through private fee-supported schools.

1750–1860. ACADEMY (with a broader and more practical curriculum) came to supplant the Latin grammar school. **Franklin's Academy** (1751) had 3 curricula: English, mathematical, and classical; **Phillips Exeter** (1778) 2 curricula: classical and English. Although especially popular in the South, the Academy was by no means confined to that area (Mass., 1840, had 112 chartered academies).

1636–1775. HIGHER EDUCATION. Nine colleges founded before the Revolution.

1636. Harvard (Congregational) est. by bequest of John Harvard and a grant from the Mass. General Court.

1693. William and Mary (Anglican) through efforts of Rev. **James Blair** (1655–1743).

1701. Yale (Congregational), located at New Haven, 1716; named in honor of benefactor, Elihu Yale, 1718.

1746. College of New Jersey (Presbyterian); name changed to Princeton 1896.

1751. Franklin's Academy (originally nonsectarian), chartered 1754; became the University of Pennsylvania, 1791.

1754. King's College (nonsectarian under Anglican control), largely suspended activities, 1776–84; reopened 1784 as Columbia College.

1764. Rhode Island College (Baptist); renamed Brown University, 1804, in honor of Nicholas Brown, benefactor.

1766. Queen's College (Dutch Reformed); renamed Rutgers, 1825, in honor of benefactor, Col. Henry Rutgers.

1769. Dartmouth College (Congregational), named for Lord Dartmouth, patron; originally Rev. Eleazar Wheelock's (1711–79) Indian school, est. at Lebanon, Conn.; moved to Hanover, N.H., 1770.

1765–1817. PROFESSIONAL TRAINING was 1st provided in **medicine** by the College of Philadelphia, 1765 (affiliated with the University of Pennsylvania, 1791), and by the medical department of King's College, 1767. The first **law** lectures were offered by Chancellor **George Wythe** (1726–1806) at William and Mary, 1779–89. In the post-Revolutionary period law schools were established by Judge Tapping Reeve at **Litchfield**, Conn. (1784–1833), and Peter Van Schaack at **Kinderhook**, N.Y. (1786–1830's), and law lectures at Pennsylvania (1790), Columbia (1797), and Transylvania (1799). A law faculty was organized at the University of Maryland (1812) and a law school was opened at Harvard (1817).

1776, 5 Dec. Phi Beta Kappa (national scholarship fraternity) founded at William and Mary, Williamsburg, Va.

1779–86. Introduction by **Thomas Jefferson** of a school bill into the Va. legislature containing the 1st definite proposal for a modern state school system (free tuition to all free children for 3 yrs., with attendance voluntary; outstanding students to be given grammar school education, with superior scholars furnished an additional 3-yrs. at William and Mary). No action by the legislature.

1805–67. ORIGINS OF THE FREE PUBLIC SCHOOL:

1805. Establishment of Free School Society (later known as Public School Society) of New York, a private philanthropic body, opposed to the pauper school system. **De Witt Clinton** 1st president of board of trustees.

1806. First Bell-Lancastrian school in the U.S. (employing monitorial system of mass instruction) established at New York City; reduced teaching costs.

1834–67. Free School vs. Pauper School. Pa. Free School Act, 1834, created school districts with option (supplanting act of 1802 for educating paupers at public expense); attempted repeal, 1835, blocked through efforts of **Thaddeus Stevens**; fully adopted, 1873. N.Y. held two referenda, 1849–50—cities (majority) favored having state assume rate bills by general tax; rural districts opposed. Result: a compromise (poor children entitled to free education with local option) adopted; in force until 1867, by which date public schools were free to all. Conn., R.I., Mich., and N.J. followed by 1871.

1837–39. Major school reforms effected by **Horace Mann** (p. 748), secretary of the newly established Mass. State Board of Education (1st state normal school in U.S. established at Lexington, Mass., 1839) and by **Henry Barnard** (p. 672), appointed secretary of the Conn. Board of School Commissioners, 1838.

1816–1902. EDUCATIONAL EXTENSION:

1816–73. Infant school introduced in Boston, 1816, and included in the public school system, 1818; admitted children at 4 yrs.; N.Y., 1827. First German **kindergarten** (Froebel) introduced in the U.S. at Watertown, Wis., 1855, by Mrs. Carl Schurz; 1st English kindergarten at Boston, 1860, by **Elizabeth Peabody** (1804–94); 1st public school kindergarten by Susan Blow at St. Louis (1873) under sponsorship of **William Torrey Harris** (1835–1908), superintendent of schools (national Commissioner of Education, 1889–1906).

1821–27. First **high school** in U.S. established in Boston, 1821, with broad, liberal curriculum. Mass. act of 1827 required every town of 500 families to establish a high school.

1826–83. Josiah Holbrook (1788–1854) instituted adult education and self-improvement courses at Millbury, Conn., where he established the Millbury Lyceum No. 1, branch of the American Lyceum, thus inaugurating the **lyceum** movement. The National American Lyceum was organized at New York in 1831. By 1834 there were 3,000 town lyceums in 15 states. In 1874 Bishop **John H. Vincent** (1832–1920) and Lewis Miller organized the 1st **Chautauqua Assembly.** Home reading program est. by 1878. **William Rainey Harper** (later president of the University of Chicago) appointed educational director, 1883; attracted outstanding lecturers. Young Men's Christian Assn. set up evening classes in the 1880's. In 1888 the New York City Board of Education established public lectures for working people. Other public lectures provided by Lowell Institute of Boston (inaugurated by Benjamin Silliman, 1839); Peabody Institute, Baltimore (1857); Cooper Union, New York (1857–59), endowed by **Peter Cooper** (p. 690).

1821–36. WOMEN'S EDUCATION:

1821. The Troy (N.Y.) Female Seminary, the 1st women's high school in the U.S., established by **Emma Willard** (p. 800).

1833. Oberlin College (Oberlin, Ohio) opened its doors to women, thus becoming the 1st coeducational college in the U.S.

1836. Mount Holyoke Female Seminary (later Mount Holyoke College), South Hadley, Mass., 1st permanent women's college, founded by **Mary Lyon.**

By 1902 women made up 25% of the undergraduates, 26% of graduate students, 3% of professional enrollment, with 128 women's colleges founded by 1901.

1789–1860. RISE OF STATE UNIVERSITIES. University of North Carolina (1789) 1st state university to begin instruction (1795). University of Georgia 1st state university to be chartered (1785), but not established until 1801. Other early state universities: Vermont, 1800; University of South Carolina, 1801; University of Virginia, 1819, a project conceived by Jefferson. Although the national government, beginning with Ohio, 1802, granted 2 townships to each new Western state for a university, there were only 17 state universities out of a total of 246 in 1860.

1862–1952. FEDERAL LEGISLATION. Morrill Act (p. 464) provided for grants of land to states to aid the establishment of agricultural colleges. Resulted in vast expansion of agricultural and engineering schools and served as the keystone of higher education in the Middle West and

Far West. Extension of Federal aid provided by Hatch Act (1887, p. 259), Smith-Lever Act (1914, p. 275), Smith-Hughes Act (1917, p. 277).

1944–52. "G.I. Bill" provided subsistence allowance, tuition fees, and supplies for the education of veterans of World War II. End of program 25 July 1956. Similar educational and readjustment payments provided for Korean war veterans (1952).

1861–1952. MAIN TRENDS IN HIGHER EDUCATION. Elective System fully in effect at Harvard under the administration of President **Charles W. Eliot** (p. 703); swing to free electives accelerated, 1885–1918. Eliot's ideas supported by Presidents **Andrew Dickson White** (1832–1918) of Cornell, **James Burrill Angell** (1829–1916) of Michigan, **David Starr Jordan** (1851–1931) of Stanford, and **Arthur T. Hadley** (1856–1930) of Yale; opposed by Hadley's predecessor, **Noah Porter** (1811–92) and by **James McCosh** (1811–84) of Princeton. After 1918 free elective trend was checked, with emphasis placed upon a prescribed core of basic study for early college years. **Graduate Study:** First Ph.D. degree in U.S. awarded at Yale, 1861. Graduate work organized at Yale and Harvard, 1870. In 1876 Johns Hopkins (under presidency of **Daniel Coit Gilman,** 1831–1908) opened as an institution of purely graduate study, followed by Clark University (1887), Worcester, Mass., especially under the presidency of the eminent psychologist, **Granville Stanley Hall** (1844–1924). Other leaders in the expansion of graduate instruction and research were **Charles Kendall Adams** (1835–1902) at Michigan, **John W. Burgess** (1844–1931) at Columbia, and Presidents **Frederick Augustus Porter Barnard** (1809–89) and **Nicholas Murray Butler** (1862–1947) of Columbia. **General Education,** with emphasis upon orientation courses, was established at Columbia 1918–19 with the course in Contemporary Civilization, and there were notable innovations in the University of Chicago Plan, 1931.

1885–1918. EXPANSION OF PRIVATELY ENDOWED COLLEGES AND UNIVERSITIES. Among the more notable endowments were those of Leland Stanford University (1885), by Leland

Stanford, of the University of Chicago (1891) by John D. Rockefeller, and of Duke University (1924, formerly Trinity College) by James B. Duke. Endowed institutions (notably in the South) have been the recipients of large grants from such foundations as the Peabody Education Fund, est. by George Peabody (1795–1869); the Julius Rosenwald Fund (1917; dissolved, 1948); the Rockefeller Foundation (1913), including the Rocke-feller Institute for Medical Research, the General Education Board, and the Laura Spelman Rockefeller Memorial; the Carnegie Endowment, including the Carnegie Institution of Washington (1902), the Carnegie Foundation for the Advancement of Teaching (1905), the Carnegie Endowment for International Peace (1910), and the Carnegie Corporation of N.Y. (1911); and the Commonwealth Fund, est. by Mrs. Stephen V. Harkness (1918).

RANKING ENDOWED UNIVERSITIES, 1960
(*Amer. Univ. and Colleges*, 8th ed., 1960; market value unless otherwise indicated)

Harvard University	$539,266,000
University of Texas	357,337,554 (bk. val.)
Yale University	238,316,505 (bk. val.)
Columbia University	220,000,000
University of Chicago	210,780,797
Princeton University	175,000,000
University of Rochester	165,222,220
Mass. Inst. of Technology	155,777,000
Stanford University	124,630,817
University of California	123,800,000
Johns Hopkins University	100,751,275

RECENT EDUCATIONAL TRENDS. Educational Testing, the application of statistical measurement to mental and other human traits, developed in the U.S. notably by **Edward Lee Thorndike,** chiefly after 1902. **Progressive Education,** largely inspired by the instrumentalist philosophy of **John Dewey** (p. 695), with emphasis on **problems** instead of rote learning (Progressive Education Association organized, 1918); more recently opposed by National Council of American Education, Allan A. Zoll, director). **Modern School Plans** include the **Gary,** or platoon, school, 1st brought to public notice at Gary, Ind., by W. A. Wirt, 1908; the **Dalton** plan (individual instruction on laboratory plan), 1st used extensively by Helen Parkhurst at Dalton, Mass., 1920; the **Winnetka** plan (individual instruction supplemented by group activity), introduced by F. L. Burke of the San Francisco Normal School (1913) and C. W. Washburne at Winnetka, Ill. **Junior High School,** organized in Richmond, Ind., 1896, spread to Columbus, Ohio, 1908, and elsewhere. Numbers increased from 387 (1922) to 2,372 (1938). **Junior Col-**lege, organized by President Harper in Joliet, Ill., 1902. Numbers increased from 74 (1915) to 584 (1945). **Community colleges** multiplied in 1950s to meet postwar population bulge.

SCHOOL ATTENDANCE (% of population): 1910, 59.2; 1920, 64.3; 1930 69.9; 1940, 70.8.

ENROLLMENT IN ELEMENTARY AND SECONDARY SCHOOLS, 1870–1946

	1870	1900	1946
% of total population— 5–17-yr.-olds	31.3	28.3	20.5
Pupils enrolled—% of population 5–17 yrs.	57.0	72.43	80.5

1947, Oct. ILLITERACY (persons unable to read or write any language). Total, 14 yrs. of age and over: 2.7% of population (urban, 2%; rural nonfarm, 2.4%; rural farm, 5.3%), as compared with 20.0% (1870), 10.7% (1900), 4.3% (1930).

1951–60. FOUNDATIONS AND EDUCATION. Foundations expanded rapidly after 1940, with only 600 reporting up to 1939 as against 3,564 reporting, 1940–55. They were the subject of an investigation by a special committee of the House of Representatives in 1954. A record educational grant of $550 million was made in 1955 by the Ford Foundation to 4,157 privately supported colleges, universities, and hospitals, to help raise salaries and improve services, with an additional $455.5 million granted in 1956, including $8 million for educational TV.

1955, 28 Nov.–1 Dec. WHITE HOUSE CONFERENCE ON EDUCATION focused attention on educational goals as well as needs, teacher training and recruitment, and school financing, with the participants approving, 2–1, the proposition that the federal govt. should increase its financial participation in public education.

1957, 11 Nov. U.S. Office of Education released 2-yr. study of Soviet educational system, revealing vast strides being made in secondary and technical education in U.S.S.R., with stress on science subjects; findings confirmed by govt.-sponsored study of Soviet education by U.S. educators, May-June, 1958, pointing out widespread teaching of foreign languages.

1958. NATIONAL DEFENSE EDUCATION ACT (p. 419).

LITERATURE

PIONEER PERIOD, 1607–60

Best Seller: *Bay Psalm Book* (1640); reached 27 editions before 1750.

REPORTERS, ANNALISTS, AND HISTORIANS. 1608–29. Capt. John Smith (p. 780), adventurer, explorer, and Va. pioneer, 1607–09, published an account of the founding of Jamestown: *A True Relation of Occurrences in Virginia* (1608); subsequently recounted his exploring expedition along the New England coast in *A Description of New England* (1619) and *New England's Trials* (1620). His account of his rescue by Pocahontas 1st appeared in *The Generall Historie of Virginia* (1624), and its authenticity has been questioned. Despite embroidery, Smith's narration is unsurpassed for vivid and dramatic description of pioneer struggles. **1622–47. William Bradford** (p. 679) is generally believed to have collaborated with **Edward Winslow** (1595–1655) in compiling materials subsequently published in England (1622) by **George Morton** (1585–1624) and known because of its preface (signed "G. Mourt") as "Mourt's" *Relation*, a journal of events in Plymouth, 1620–21. Bradford's major historical work was his *History of Plimouth Plantation,* written 1630–47, but not published until 1856 (although drawn upon by **Nathaniel Morton** [1613–86] in his *New England's Memorial,* 1669). **Edward Winslow** (1595–1655) added further light on early New England history in his *Good News from New England,* 1624, and *Brief Narration,* 1646. **1630–49:** Comparable in importance for the early history of Mass. with the Pilgrim Bradford's *History* was the Puritan **John Winthrop's** (p. 803) *Journal* (or *History of New England*), a diary record from Mar. 1630 to 1649, which remained unpublished until 1790 (subsequently revised, 1825, and again, 1929–31). In addition to accounts of the relations of the Mass. authorities with such major critics as Roger Williams and Anne Hutchinson, the *Journal* includes Winthrop's General Court speech, 1645, on the nature of liberty (which he maintained must be under authority and restraint). While en route to the Bay Colony, Winthrop wrote his *Model of Christian Charity* (1630), emphasizing self-denial and cooperation ("We must be knit together in this work as one man"). A leading critic of affairs in Plymouth and Mass., **Thomas Morton** (1575–1647) satirized colonial policy in his *New English Canaan* (1637). **1654:** To counteract hostile reports of the Puritan colonization, which he considered a sacred crusade, **Edward Johnson** (1598–1672) wrote his *Wonder-Working Providences of Sion's Saviour in New England* (1654), an apologia for theocratic rule.

THEOLOGICAL AND RELIGIOUS WRITERS. "Chief stewards of the theocracy." **1638–40: Thomas Hooker** (?1586–1647), in his *Survey of the Summe of Church Discipline* (1648), postulated the principle of divine absolutism. This book and his orthodox Calvinist sermons reveal literary power and the author's conviction that it was his duty to "fasten the nail of terror deep" into the hearts of sinners. **1641–60: Thomas Shepard** (1605–49), "soul-melting preacher," whose *Sincere Convert* (1641) preached a gospel of love; *Theses Sabbaticae* (1649), Sabbath origin and observance; *Parable of the Ten Virgins* (1660). **1642–48: John Cotton** (1584–1652), major spokesman of theocracy, preeminent as scholar and theologian ("They could hardly believe God would suffer Mr. Cotton to err"—Roger Williams). His numerous writings include *The Keyes of the Kingdom of Heaven* (1644), stressing consociation of church and state; *Milk for Babes, Drawn out of the Breasts of Both Testaments* (1646), for the religious instruction of children; and *The Bloudy Tenent, Washed and Made White*

in the Bloud of the Lamb (1647), in refutation of Roger Williams and opposing freedom to "sinful error." **Minor figures** of the period include **Nathaniel Ward** (?1578–1652), author of the first Mass. Code of Laws, the Body of Liberties (1641), and a humorist and satirist (*Simple Cobbler of Aggawamm,* 1647); and **John Eliot** (1604–90), translator of the Bible into the Indian tongue, 1663, and author of *The Christian Commonwealth* (1659) and an Indian grammar (1666) and primer (1669).

Critic of the Established Order: Roger Williams (*c.*1603–83), radical in religious and political outlook; advocated separation of Church and State as early as 1635; as ardent in polemics as his opponents. Writings include *A Key into the Language of America* (1643); *The Bloudy Tenent of Persecution for the Cause of Conscience* (1644), attack on the conservative ideas of Cotton. The latter's vindictive reply elicited from Williams *The Bloudy Tenent Made Yet More Bloudy* (1652). His *George Fox Digged out of his Burrowes* (1676) was a criticism of Quaker views.

POETS. 1641: *The Bay Psalm Book* (*The Whole Book of Psalms Faithfully Translated into English Metre*), the 1st book printed in the colonies,[1] was a translation of the Psalms purposefully sacrificing beauty to accuracy by **Thomas Welde, Richard Mather** (1596–1669), and **John Eliot,** an uninspired rendition. **1650:** Publication in London of *The Tenth Muse,* a collection of didactic poems by **Anne Bradstreet** (?1612–72), influenced by Spenser, Quarles, and Du Bartas. Emancipated from her literary models, she produced her most distinguished poem, *Contemplations,* written late in life (pub. 1678).

---

[1] The 1st piece of printing was "The Freeman's Oath," followed by an almanac, both in 1639.

FIRST CENTURY OF NATIVE LITERATURE, 1661–1760

BEST SELLERS BY COLONIAL WRITERS 2

1640. *Bay Psalm Book*
1662. Michael Wigglesworth, *Day of Doom*
1682. Mary Rowlandson, *Captivity and Restoration*
1683? *New England Primer*, comp. and pub. by Benj. Harris (total sales estimated at 6 to 8 million)
1699. Jonathan Dickinson, *God's Protecting Providence*
1707. John Williams, *The Redeemed Captive*
1719. *Mother Goose's Melodies for Children*
1725–64. Nathaniel Ames, comp., *Astronomical Diary and Almanack*
1732–57. Benjamin Franklin, *Poor Richard's Almanack*
1741. William Penn, *No Cross, No Crown*

NARRATIVES OF INDIAN WARS AND CAPTIVITIES. c.1670: Capt. John Mason (1600–72) wrote *A Brief History of the Pequot War* (partly published by Increase Mather, 1677; completely, 1736). 1674: Daniel Gookin (1612–87), *Historical Collections of the Indians in New England* (1792), a description of Indian mores, and *An Historical Account of the Doings and Sufferings of the Christian Indians* (completed 1677, published 1836), a vindication of their role in King Philip's War. 1676: Increase Mather (1639–1723), *A Brief History of the War with the Indians* (1676). 1677: William Hubbard (1621–1704), *A Narrative of the Troubles with the Indians* (hostile toward the Indians); also wrote *A General History of New England* (to 1680), not published until 1815. 1682: Mary White Rowlandson (c.1635–c.1678), captured by the Indians in a raid on Lancaster, 1676, wrote the most popular captivity account, *The Sovereignty and Goodness of God*, republished many times by its subtitle, *The Narrative of the Captivity and Restoration of Mrs. Mary Rowlandson*. 1699: A straightforward, graphic account of captivity in Fla. was told by an English Quaker merchant who later became chief justice of Pa., Jonathan

Dickinson (1663–1722), *Journal, or God's Protecting Providence.* 1698: Gabriel Thomas. *An Historical and Geographical Account of the Province of Pennsylvania and West New Jersey,* a Quaker's humorous and favorable account.

TRAVELERS AND EXPLORERS. 1704: Sarah Kemble Knight (1666–1727), Boston schoolmistress, wrote a lively account of a horseback journey to N.Y. (*Journal*, published for the first time, 1825), with refreshing sidelights on rural conditions. 1728–33: Col. William Byrd, 2nd (1674–1744) of Westover, a great Va. estate owner, educated abroad, left a collection of manuscripts of absorbing interest, consisting of both travels and explorations (not published until 1841), and a shorthand diary, a frank and racy document, deciphered and published in part, 1709–12 (1941), 1739–41 (1942). His major work of exploration was *History of the Dividing Line Run in the Year 1728,* an account of experiences with a party surveying the Va.–N.C. boundary line. A satirical version, *The Secret History of the Dividing Line* (not published until 1929) is the most interesting and uninhibited travel book of the colonial period. His other works include *A Journey to the Land of Eden* (1732) and *A Progress to the Mines* (1736), published 1841. 1744: Dr. Alexander Hamilton (1712–56), of Annapolis, whose *Itinerarium* describing his journey from Annapolis, Md., to Portsmouth, N.H., is one of the most entertaining and informative travel books of the colonial period. 1751: John Bartram (1699–1777), the Pa. botanist, published an account of a scientific expedition to western N.Y. and Lake Ontario in 1751 (*Observations*).

REPORTERS, ANNALISTS, DIARISTS, AND HISTORIANS. 1666: George Alsop (1638–?), who served a term as an indentured servant in Md., wrote a colorful and humorous defense of that colony, *A Character of the Province of Maryland.* 1670: Daniel Denton (d.1696), in his *Brief Description of New York,* provided a graphic account of a "terrestrial Canaan." 1673–1729: Samuel Sewall (1652–1730) left the fullest diary of the period (1674–1729, with gaps 1677–85), invaluable for the social historian (not published until 1879–82). His tract, *The Selling of Joseph* (1700), was an early antislavery appeal. **1676:** The *Burwell Papers,* attributed to **John Colton** (published 1814; revised, 1866), a spirited, if affected, account of the course of Bacon's Rebellion, closing with an eloquent eulogy of Bacon. **1676–93: Increase Mather** (1639–1723), president of Harvard, 1685–1701, upholder of the theocratic tradition of John Cotton, wrote *A Brief History of the War with the Indians in New England* (1676) and an uncritical compilation of other people's narratives of providential events, published, 1684, as *An Essay for the Recording of Illustrious Providences* (commonly known as *Remarkable Providences*). **1693–1702:** His son, **Cotton Mather** (1663–1728), the most prolific colonial author (over 400 published works), served as annalist of the Salem witchcraft episode (1692) in his book, *The Wonders of the Invisible World* (1693). His apologia for the trial and execution of the accused was effectively answered by **Robert Calef** (1648–1719), a Boston merchant, whose *More Wonders of the Invisible World* (1700) was publicly burned in the Harvard yard upon order of Increase Mather. Cotton Mather's major work is his *Magnalia Christi Americana, or, The Ecclesiastical History of New England, 1620–98* (1702), which set forth the splendor of government by God's elect, combining accurate information with fable and gross misrepresentation. For his scientific contributions, see pp. 558, 572.

1697: Rev. James Blair (1655–1743), an Anglican clergyman, collaborated with **Henry Hartwell** and **Edward Chilton**, on a report, *The Present State of Virginia and the College* (published 1727).

1705: Robert Beverley (1675–1716), *The History and Present State of Virginia* (revised 1722), a lucid account of a land where "nobody is poor enough to beg or want food." **1724: Hugh Jones** (*c.*1670–1760), clergyman, *The Present State of Virginia,* a frank and factual account, with a dismal picture of educational standards at William and Mary College, where he was a teacher of mathematics.

1727–47: Cadwallader Colden (1688–1776), scientist and later lieutenant gov-

ernor of New York, wrote a valuable account of the Iroquois tribes, *The History of the Five Indian Nations,* the most substantial colonial treatise on the Indians. **1736–56: Thomas Prince** (1687–1758), *Chronological History of New England,* arid but scholarly annals. **1740:** Patrick Tailfer's *A True and Historical Narrative of the Colony of Georgia,* a documented history attacking Oglethorpe. **1747: William Stith** (1689–1755), President of William and Mary, 1752–55, *History of the First Discovery and Settlement of Virginia* (from Jamestown to 1624), drew heavily upon Captain John Smith. **1748–53: William Douglass** (1691–1752), Scottish physician who settled in Boston, 1718, and wrote innumerable pamphlets against religious revivalism, paper money, etc., produced a caustic, partisan, and disorganized *Summary, Historical and Political, of the First Planting, Progressive Improvements and Present State of the British Settlements in North America.* **1756: William Livingston** (1723–90), educator, statesman, governor of N.J. (1776–90), *A Review of the Military Operations in North America,* 1753–56, frank and significant history. **1757: William Smith** (1728–93), jurist and later Loyalist, *The History of the Province of New York* (to 1732), reprinted (1829) with his continuations to 1762, an able, if partisan, historical account, with valuable insights on contemporary N.Y. society (supplemented by his massive unpublished diary in the New York Public Library).

THEOLOGICAL AND RELIGIOUS WRITERS. 1669–1717: Representative of the conservative theological tradition were **Increase Mather** and his son, **Cotton.** The former, a great pulpit orator, published 92 titles (1669–1723), mostly sermons. The latter, a child prodigy, published innumerable sermons and religious and moral tracts, one of the most notable being *Bonifacius* (1710), endorsing the performance of good deeds on business principles—a work which influenced Benjamin Franklin. Representative of liberalism and opposition to the Mather hierarchy, was **John Wise** (1652–1725), minister at Ipswich, who, in addition to his notable fight against Governor Andros over the payment of unauthorized taxes, was the author of 2 pamphlets opposing the plan of the Mathers for reorganizing the churches along Presbyterian lines, and favoring democratic Congregationalism: *The Churches' Quarrel Espoused* (1710), and *A Vindication of the Government of the New England Churches* (1717).

1720–54: Jonathan Edwards (p. 701), pastor at Northampton, was a major writer on theological and moral questions, a logical thinker who devoted his energies to a regeneration of religious values, defended the "revival" as a legitimate device for quickening spiritual values, and opposed Locke's idealism with emphasis on mystical experience. His "Notes on the Mind" was a venture in Berkeleyan idealism. Typical of his later revivalist sermons emphasizing hell-fire and brimstone was *Sinners in the Hands of an Angry God* (Enfield, 9 July 1741). His greatest intellectual effort was *A Careful and Strict Enquiry into the Modern Prevailing Notions of Freedom of the Will* (1754), an exposition of his understanding of Calvinist predestination, followed 4 years later by the posthumous publication of *The Great Christian Doctrine of Original Sin Defended.* In his 2nd dissertation "Concerning the End for Which ⁴God Created the World" (written 1755) he returned to the mystic pantheism of his youth and foreshadowed Transcendentalism. Foremost opponents of revivalism were **Charles Chauncy** (1705–87), Boston Congregationalist pastor, whose notable sermon, *Seasonable Thoughts on the State of Religion in New England* (1743), stressing divine benevolence assuring man a rational place in a world of free choice, dates the start of the controversy between the **New** and **Old Lights;** and **Samuel Johnson** (1696–1772), convert to Anglicanism and 1st president (1754–63) of King's College (Columbia), who became the chief exponent in the colonies of the doctrines of the English philosopher, George Berkeley, as exemplified by *Elementa Ethica* (1746), republished by Benjamin Franklin in enlarged form as *Elementa Philosophica* (1752), stressing rationalism in religion and the concepts of the Enlightenment. Very different in form and spirit were the works of the N.J. Quaker, **John Woolman** (1720–72), whose *Journal,* written 1756–72, published 1774, reveals his simplicity and purity. Sensitive to social injustice, he criticized the institution of slavery in *Some Considerations on the Keeping of Negroes* (1754–62), a plea for racial equality; and his *Considerations on the True Harmony of Mankind* (1770) revealed his concern about growing antagonisms between labor and capital.

POETS include **Michael Wigglesworth** (1631–1705), whose *Day of Doom* (1662), in jog-trot ballad measure, was a Calvinist version of the last judgment (unbaptized infants assigned to the "easiest room in hell"); **Edward Taylor** (*c*.1644–1729), English-born pastor of Westfield, Mass., whose sensuous poetry, rich in imagery, imaginative and dramatic, and the most inspired American verse of the 17th century, was discovered (1937) with the publication of some of his poems from MS.; the anonymous author ("Eben. Cook, Gent.") of *The Sot-Weed Factor* (1708) and *Sot-Weed Redivivus* (1730), satirical burlesques on the inhabitants of Md.; and 2 Mass. Loyalists who produced poetry in the pre-Revolutionary era—**Mather Byles** (1707–88), an imitator of Pope (*Elegy addressed to Governor Belcher on the Death of his Lady,* 1732, and *The Conflagration,* 1744) and **Benjamin Church** (1734; lost at sea, 1776), whose *The Choice* (1757) was modeled upon a poem of Pomfret (1700), who also influenced the poetry of **William Livingston** (*The Philosophic Solitude,* 1747).

REVOLUTIONARY GENERATION, 1763–89

Best Sellers

1768. John Dickinson, *Letters from a Farmer in Pennsylvania*
1775–76. John Trumbull, *McFingal* (1st complete ed. 1782)
1776. Thomas Paine, *Common Sense*
1776–83. Thomas Paine, *The American Crisis*
1783. Noah Webster, *American Spelling Book* (*Blue-Backed Speller* — estimated total sale 70 million copies by 1883)
1787–88. Alexander Hamilton, James Madison, and John Jay, *The Federalist*

LITERATURE OF POLITICS: 1762: A year after his renowned arguments against the issuance of writs of assistance (24 Feb. 1761), **James Otis**, Boston lawyer, published his 1st political pamphlet, *A Vindication of the Conduct of the House of Representatives* (Mass.), in which he affirmed the privileges of the colonies under the British constitution. 1764: His ablest effort, called forth by the Sugar Act, was *The Rights of the British Colonies Asserted* (July), in which he raised the argument of no taxation without representation. Other critics of the new imperial policy included **Oxenbridge Thacher**, *Sentiments of a British American;* and R.I.'s governor, **Stephen Hopkins** (1707–85), *The Rights of the Colonies Examined* (1765; answered by Martin Howard, a Newport lawyer, *A Letter from a Gentleman at Halifax*). 1765: The Stamp Act prompted a series of articles by **John Adams** in the Boston *Gazette*, republished, 1768, in revised form, as *A Dissertation on the Canon and Feudal Law;* and 2 notable pamphlets, one by **John Dickinson** (1732–1808), *Considerations upon the Rights of the Colonists to the Privileges of British Subjects,* the other by **Daniel Dulany** (1722–97), a Md. lawyer and later Loyalist, *Considerations on the Propriety of Imposing Taxes* (p. 74). 1766: Most vigorous of the New England clergy in opposing Parliamentary measures was **Jonathan Mayhew** (1720–66), a rationalist who anticipated later Unitarian doctrines. As early as 1750 in his *Discourse Concerning Unlimited Submission* he had asserted: "Britons will not be slaves." On the repeal of the Stamp Act he wrote his last published sermon, *The Snare Broken*. 1768: The passage of the Townshend Acts prompted the issuance by Dickinson of a widely distributed pamphlet (at least 12 editions in the colonies and abroad), *Letters from a Farmer in Pennsylvania to the Inhabitants of the British Colonies* (p. 76). 1773: The qualities of **Benjamin Franklin** as a political satirist are exemplified by his imaginary "An Edict of the King of Prussia" (*Gentleman's Mag.,* Oct.) and his renowned *Rules for Reducing a Great Empire to a Small One*. 1774: The Loyalist argument was forcefully presented by Rev. **Samuel Seabury** (1729–96), later 1st bishop of the Protestant Episcopal Church in the U.S., in a series of four *Westchester Farmer* pamphlets attacking the aims and policy of the 1st Continental Congress (answered effectively by young **Alexander Hamilton**, in *A Full Vindication of the Measures of Congress* [1774] and *A Farmer Refuted*) and by **Daniel Leonard** (1740–1829), in a series of 17 letters to the newspapers under the pen name of "Massachusettensis," in which the unconstitutional character of the Revolutionary position was stressed. For **John Adams'** refutation, see p. 84. The plan of union proposed by **Joseph Galloway** (1731–1803; p. 83) was published the following year in *A Candid Examination of the Mutual Claims of Great Britain and the Colonies*. The development of patriot thinking by this date was best exemplified in **James Wilson's** (1742–98) *Considerations of the Nature and Extent of the Legislative Authority of Great Britain* (p. 84), and **Thomas Jefferson's** *A Summary View of the Rights of British America* (p. 84). 1776: Most influential of all Revolutionary pamphlets was **Thomas Paine's** *Common Sense* (p. 90), which was followed by a series of 16 irregularly issued (1776–83) essays called *The Crisis*, designed to lift patriot morale, the 1st words of the 1st number being: "These are the times that try men's souls." 1782–87: Thomas Jefferson's *Notes on Virginia*, a reply to a series of questions by the Marquis de Barbé-Marbois, is representative of his political thought. Written, 1782, it was 1st printed privately in Paris, 1785, then in London, 1787.

1787–88: The ratification of the Constitution was opposed in a considerable number of pamphlets, most notably by **Richard Henry Lee** (Va., 1732–94), (*Observations Leading to a Fair Examination* [1787] and *An Additional Number of Letters* [1788]) and **George Mason** (Va., 1725–92), (*Objections to the Proposed Federal Constitution*). Supporters of ratification included the lexicographer, **Noah Webster** (1758–1843), *An Examination into the Leading Principles of the Federal Constitution;* the political economist, **Pelatiah Webster** (1725–95), *The Weakness of Brutus Exposed;* **Tench Coxe** (1755–1824), political economist and industrialist, *An Examination of the Con-*

stitution, and **John Dickinson** (*Letters of Fabius*); but most influential were the papers produced by **Hamilton, Madison, and Jay,** published as *The Federalist* in book form 1788 (p. 119).

FRANKLIN'S AUTOBIOGRAPHY.

Ranking as an American classic is Franklin's *Autobiography* (covering the events of his life to the end of 1759), written between 1771 and 1789, published in part in France, 1791, and not in complete form until 1867, and exemplifying the Yankee-Puritan spirit which could accept the Enlightenment and follow the literary models of Defoe and Addison. For Franklin's journalistic enterprises, see p. 613; for his scientific contributions, p. 559. Franklin wrote for the amusement of his friends urbane bagatelles: *The Ephemera* (1778), *The Morals of Chess* (1779), *The Whistle* (1779), *The Dialogue between Franklin and the Gout* (1780).

HISTORIANS. 1764–67: Thomas Hutchinson

(1711–80), lieutenant governor of Mass., produced the major historical writing of the period. The 1st volume of *The History of the Colony of Massachusetts Bay* (1628–91) appeared in 1764; the 2nd (down to 1750) appeared in 1767; and the 3rd (1750–74) was published posthumously in 1828. The earlier volumes are marked by more detachment than the last, which is in part a defense of his own administration. Although an outstanding Loyalist he managed in the main to make judicious and objective valuations. **1780:** Another Loyalist, **George Chalmers** (1742–1825), published an account of colonial history down to 1763 (*Political Annals*) which largely reflects the official British attitude. **1782:** Chalmers' *Introduction to the History of the Revolt of the American Colonies* was a legalistic and unsympathetic approach to colonial problems based largely on official records. **1784: Jeremy Belknap** (1744–98) wrote a scholarly *History of New Hampshire* (2nd vol. to 1790, pub. 1791) based upon prodigious research. **1788:** A more biased, but nevertheless notable, firsthand account of Shays' Rebellion was **George Minot's** (1758–1802) *History of the Insurrections in Massachusetts in the Year 1786,* a conservative's view of the issues and events.

TRAVELERS. 1778: Jonathan Carver

(1710–80), a New Englander, wrote a travel book based upon an exploring expedition to the Great Lakes and the Upper Mississippi, containing much information on natural history and Indian mores, *Travels through the Interior Parts of North America.* **1782:** A fresh recorder of rural life was **J. Hector St. John de Crèvecoeur** (1735–1813), born in France, served under Montcalm, traveled through the Great Lakes and Ohio Valley, and settled down on a farm in Orange Co., N.Y. (1769). His book of impressions of America, which attained wide popularity abroad, was published as *Letters from an American Farmer.* Crèvecoeur saw the American environment transforming the European from a peasant to a freeholder. To him the American was an amalgam of all nations, and his ultimate role in world affairs was dimly foreseen. **1784:** A Kentucky pioneer, **John Filson** (*c.*1747–88), prepared an account of *The Discovery, Settlement, and Present State of Kentucke,* to which was appended a purported autobiography of **Daniel Boone.**

POETS. 1776–88: The major poet of

the period was **Philip Freneau** (1752–1832), whose poetry reflects 18th-century deism, love of nature, idealization of the "noble savage," the idea of progress, and hostility to tyranny. His more notable efforts include "The Beauties of Santa Cruz" (1776), lyric; "The House of Night" (1779), a powerful poem in the graveyard tradition; an elegy to the war heroes, "To the Memory of Brave Americans" or "Eutaw Springs" (1781); perhaps his most beautiful lyric, "To a Wild Honeysuckle" (1786); "The Indian Burying Ground" (1788); and a number of sea poems, including "The Memorable Victory of Paul Jones" and "The Battle of Lake Erie." For his pro-Jefferson paper, *National Gazette,* see p. 615.

1778: "The Battle of the Kegs," a satirical poem by **Francis Hopkinson** (1737–91), also the author of several satirical essays as well as musical compositions (p. 647), was one of the most popular poems of the war period.

CONNECTICUT (HARTFORD) WITS

patterned themselves after the Augustan wits. Essentially conservative, opposing deism and egalitarianism and clinging to Calvinism and Federalism, they celebrated America's independence by extolling its history and society. Members included **John Trumbull** (1750–1831), *The Progress of Dullness* (1772–73), a Hudibrastic satire on education, and the enormously popular *McFingal*, an epic satire on the Tories (1775–82). **Joel Barlow** (1754–1812), land speculator, diplomat, and later an ardent democrat, whose most ambitious patriotic poem was *The Vision of Columbus* (1787), subsequently (1807) enlarged as *The Columbiad*, but who is best remembered for his charming poem, *Hasty Pudding* (1796). His volume of political essays, *Advice to the Privileged Orders* (1792), a radical defense of the French Revolution, was proscribed by the British government. **Timothy Dwight** (1752–1817), a Congregational minister and president of Yale, 1795–1817, whose *Triumph of Infidelity* (1788) was a defense of orthodoxy, also wrote an important multivolume work on theology (1818–19) and a book of *Travels in New England and New York* (1821–22). Two of the minor Connecticut wits, **David Humphreys** (1752–1818) and **Lemuel Hopkins** (1750–1801), in collaboration with Barlow and Trumbull, pilloried New England radicals in the *Anarchiad* (1786–87), a satire on mob rule, currency inflation, and other nostrums.

1696–1760. EARLY LIBRARIES. Dr. **Thomas Bray** (1656–1730), cofounder of the Society for the Propagation of the Gospel in Foreign Parts (1701), on becoming Commissary in Md. (1696), established free circulating libraries in most of the 30 parishes in that province, beginning with Annapolis. Other libraries were established under his auspices in N.Y. (Trinity Parish, 1698) and Charleston (1699). Although the largest libraries prior to 1789 were either those of private individuals (Cotton Mather, 3,000 vols.; William Byrd II, 4,000, 1788) or of colleges, the semipublic **subscription library** was the most common. Between 1731–60, 21 were founded, notably:

1731. Library Co. of Philadelphia, an outgrowth of the Junto, a debating society organized by Benjamin Franklin, 1727.

1747. Redwood Library, Newport, R.I. (Ezra Stiles librarian, 1755–75).

1748. Charleston Library Society.

1754. New York Society Library.

1789–1860

1791. Susanna Rowson, *Charlotte Temple*
1792. Hugh H. Brackenridge, *Modern Chivalry*
1794. Benjamin Franklin, *Autobiography*
1794–95. Thomas Paine, *Age of Reason*
1800. Mason L. Weems, *Life of Washington*
1809. Washington Irving, *History of New York*

NOVELISTS. 1789: *The Power of Sympathy* by **William Hill Brown** (1765–93) is generally considered the 1st American novel. **1790: Susanna Haswell Rowson** (*c.*1762–1824), English-born actress, dramatist, novelist, and Boston schoolteacher, wrote an exceptionally popular sentimental novel, *Charlotte Temple*. **1789–1801: Charles Brockden Brown** (1771–1810) wrote a series of Gothic romances revealing some of the moral purpose of Godwin, the sentimentalism of Richardson, and above all the horrors of the school of Mrs. Radcliffe: *Wieland* (1798), an attack on superstition; *Arthur Mervyn* (1799), a realistic picture of the yellow fever epidemic in Philadelphia; *Ormond* (1799); *Edgar Huntley* (1799), crimes committed by a sleepwalker; *Clara Howard* (1801); and *Jane Talbot* (1801). His *Alcuin* (1798) was a treatise on women's rights. **1792–1815: Hugh Henry Brackenridge** (1748–1816), editor and jurist, wrote *Modern Chivalry* (1792), a satire, realistically depicting frontier conditions and reflecting the influence of Cervantes.

1819. Washington Irving, *Sketch Book* *
1821. James Fenimore Cooper, *Spy* *
1823. James Fenimore Cooper. *Pilot* *
1823. James Fenimore Cooper, *The Pioneers* *
1824. James Everett Seaver, *Life of Mrs. Jemison* (Indian captivity)
1826. James Fenimore Cooper, *The Last of the Mohicans* *
1827. James Fenimore Cooper, *The Prairie* *
1832. Rev. Jacob Abbott, *The Young Christian*
1836. Maria Monk, *Awful Disclosures* (as novice in a Montreal nunnery, an imposture)
1837. Hannah Farnham Lee, *Three Experiments of Living*

1839. Henry Wadsworth Longfellow, *Voices of the Night* *; Jared Sparks, *Life of Washington*

1840. Richard Henry Dana, Jr., *Two Years before the Mast* *

1842. Rufus Wilmot Griswold, ed., *Poets and Poetry of America* (outstandingly popular anthology)

1843. Robert Sears, *The Wonders of the World*

1844. George Lippard, *The Monks of Monk Hall*, printed 1845 as *The Quaker City* *

1846. Joel Tyler Headley, *Napoleon and His Marshals* *

1850. Nathaniel Hawthorne, *The Scarlet Letter* *; Ik Marvel (Donald Grant Mitchell), *Reveries of a Bachelor* *; Susan Bogert Warner, *The Wide, Wide World* *

1852. Mrs. E. D. E. N. Southworth, *The Curse of Clifton* *; Harriet Beecher Stowe, *Uncle Tom's Cabin* *

1854. Phineas T. Barnum, *Struggles and Triumphs;* Maria Susanna Cummins, *The Lamplighter* *; Mary Jane Holmes, *Tempest and Sunshine* *; Timothy Shay Arthur, *Ten Nights in a Bar-Room*

1855. Joseph Holt Ingraham, *The Prince of the House of David*

1856. Mary Jane Holmes, *Lena Rivers* *

1859. Augusta Jane Evans [Wilson], *Beulah;* Mrs. E. D. E. N. Southworth, *The Hidden Hand* *

1860. Edward Sylvester Ellis, *Seth Jones* (a dime novel); Miriam Coles Harris, *Rutledge;* Ann Sophia Stephens, *Malaeska* (1st of the Beadle Dime Novels)

BEST SELLERS IN LATER PERIODS

1837. Robert Montgomery Bird, *Nick of the Woods* (forerunner of dime-novel thrillers); Nathaniel Hawthorne, *Twice-Told Tales*

1839. Daniel Pierce Thompson, *The Green Mountain Boys*

1840. James Fenimore Cooper, *The Pathfinder*

1841. James Fenimore Cooper, *Deerslayer;* Ralph Waldo Emerson, *Essays*

1843. William Hickling Prescott, *Conquest of Mexico*

1845. Edgar Allan Poe, *The Raven and Other Poems*

1849. John G. Whittier, *Poems*

1851. Nathaniel Hawthorne, *The House of the Seven Gables;* Herman Melville, *Moby-Dick*

1854. Henry D. Thoreau, *Walden*

1855. Walt Whitman, *Leaves of Grass*

1809–60. KNICKERBOCKER SCHOOL.

For some 2 decades after 1815 the foremost native literary figures were **Washington Irving** (p. 732), **James Fenimore Cooper** (p. 690), and **William Cullen Bryant** (p. 681). Irving and Bryant were identified with the Knickerbocker School of writers at New York, a group which took its name from Ir-

* Also best sellers after their period, including cheap reprints.

ving's satirical *A History of New York . . . by Diedrich Knickerbocker* (1809). Cooper's conventional association with the school is based almost wholly upon geographical circumstances.

Leaving the U.S. in 1815, Irving produced in 1819–20 *The Sketch Book,* which included such tales as "Rip Van Winkle" and "The Legend of Sleepy Hollow." His literary activity on the Continent resulted in *Bracebridge Hall* (1822), *The Life and Voyages of Columbus* (1828), *The Conquest of Granada* (1829), *Tales of a Traveller* (1829), and *The Alhambra* (1832). He returned to the U.S. in 1832 and maintained his popularity with *A Tour on the Prairies* (1835), *Astoria* (1836), and *The Adventures of Captain Bonneville* (1837), the U.S. army officer who led an expedition into the Rocky Mountain region. The most important of Irving's later works was the *Life of Washington* (1855–59), facilitated by the publication of *The Writings of Washington* (1833–39), ed. by **Jared Sparks** (1789–1866).

Cooper's first novel, *Precaution* (1820), portrayed English society life. In *The Spy* (1821), the 1st of his works using an American theme and setting, Cooper displayed his capacity for picturing forest life and creating authentic American character. With *The Pioneers* (1823), Cooper inaugurated the *Leatherstocking Tales* for which he is best remembered, completing the series with *The Last of the Mohicans* (1826), *The Prairie* (1827, last in narrative order), *The Pathfinder* (1840), and *The Deerslayer* (1841). Almost singlehanded Cooper established the historical romance of the American scene and made American fiction's greatest statement about the clash between primitive and civilized values on the frontier. He is also noted for his sea tales, e.g., *The Pilot* (1823) and *The Red Rover* (1827–28), and his novels of social criticism, e.g., the Antirent series begun with *Satanstoe* (1845). Unlike Irving's continued popularity, Cooper's waned after 1833 when his aristocratic social ideals expressed in *A Letter to His Countrymen* (1834), *The American Democrat* (1839), and many novels antagonized his fellow citizens.

Bryant's fame began with the publication of "Thanatopsis" in the *North American Review* (1817, enlarged version in 1821), a poem notable for its handling of the theme of death and for its lyrical treatment of nature; and "To a Waterfowl" (1818), generally considered his masterpiece. In 1825 Bryant left Mass. and settled at New York, joining (1828) the staff of the N.Y. *Evening Post,* of which he was editor (1829–78). He published *The Fountain* (1842), *The White-Footed Deer* (1844), and *A Forest Hymn* (1860), but his absorption in newspaper work weakened his powers as a poet.

Among the other members of the Knickerbocker School were **James Kirke Paulding** (1778–1860), author of *The Diverting History of John Bull and Brother Jonathan* (1812), the historical novels *Koningsmarke* (1823) and *The Dutchman's Fireside* (1831), and *The Book of St. Nicholas* (1836); **Fitz-Greene Halleck** (1790–1867), author of *Alnwick Castle, with Other Poems* (1827), who collaborated with another Knickerbocker writer, **Joseph Rodman Drake** (1795–1820), on the "Croaker Papers" (1819), a set of satirical verses; **Gulian C. Verplanck** (1786–1870), who divided his time between politics and literature; **Nathaniel P. Willis** (1806–67), writer of popular verse and travel sketches; and **Charles Fenno Hoffman** (1806–84), journalist and novelist.

1815–60. NEW ENGLAND RENAISSANCE. The community of thought which drew its vitality from New England Transcendentalism made the most fruitful and enduring contributions to American letters before the Civil War. After the War of 1812 the focal point of national literature gradually shifted to Boston, Cambridge, and the New England hinterland, where the successive ferments of Unitarianism and Transcendentalism gave to the nation that period later characterized as the "flowering of New England." Boston remained the intellectual capital of the country until after the Civil War. The "**Unitarian Controversy,**" which came to a climax in 1815 under the leadership of **William Ellery Channing** (p. 685), was a spiritual revolt against the confinements of orthodox Congregationalism which exerted a potent liberating influence over the New England mind.

1836–50. When Unitarianism in turn fell into the ways of orthodoxy, it was challenged by **Transcendentalism,** whose doctrines received their most comprehensive exposition in *Nature* (1836), by **Ralph Waldo Emerson** (p. 703). *Nature* appeared in the year when the Transcendental Club became active at Boston and Concord. Transcendentalism was a mood or cast of mind rather than a systematically articulated philosophy. Despite their diversity of outlook, the Transcendentalists agreed on the sacredness, uniqueness, and authority of the individual apprehension of experience. Man was of the divine essence. His insights, drawn from a conception of the mystic unity of nature, might enable the discovery of truth without reference to dogma and established authority. The self-reliance and self-determination exalted by Transcendentalism gave to American writers a freedom that vitalized the 1st great period in national letters.

Emerson was the seer of Transcendentalism. Between 1826 and 1832, when he held a Unitarian pulpit, he formulated the basic elements of his moral vision. His retirement from the Church formalized his revolt against orthodoxy. After his journey to Europe in 1833 he became the spokesman of his generation. *The American Scholar,* delivered as the Phi Beta Kappa address at Harvard (1837), was an eloquent expression of the Emersonian creed of individualism, independence, and self-sufficiency. His address (1838) before the Harvard Divinity School challenged conservative Unitarianism. The luminous passages of the *Essays* (1841, 1844) contained the mature fruits of his thought. In the years before the Civil War, Emerson also expounded Transcendentalism from lecture platforms throughout the North and West. This period witnessed the publication of his *Poems* (1847), *Representative Men* (1850), *English Traits* (1856), and *The Conduct of Life* (1860).

In **Henry David Thoreau** (p. 791) the individualism of the Transcendentalist movement reached its most intense and uncompromising form. Thoreau's views, molded by a long and extraordinary process of self-discipline, had already become confirmed principles by the time he went to live at Walden Pond in 1845. His 2-year sojourn was a criticism by example of the materialism of a social order that he regarded as a block to man's capacity for free development. Thoreau's 1st book, *A Week on the Concord and Merrimack Rivers* (1849), was received coldly by the public and by the few critics who noticed its appearance. *Walden* (1854) fared somewhat better, but general recognition of Thoreau came only after his death. Thoreau's literary artistry attained its high point in *Walden*. His philosophy of nature, supported by concrete instance, showed how man's rediscovery of himself could bring his freedom. The essay on "Civil Disobedience" (1849), which posed the sovereign rights of conscience against the claims of the state, was one of Thoreau's most moving utterances of an individualism grounded on high moral conviction.

Among the other members of the Transcendentalist movement were **Margaret Fuller** (p. 711), editor of *The Dial;* **Bronson Alcott** (1799–1888); **Jones Very** (1813–80); **George Ripley** (1802–80); **Theodore Parker** (1810–60); **Orestes A. Brownson** (1803–76); **James Freeman Clarke** (1810–88); and **Christopher P. Cranch** (1813–92).

One of New England's most popular writers, and a leader of literary society in the Boston he christened the "hub of the Universe," was the Harvard medical professor, **Oliver Wendell Holmes** (p. 727). Mingled with his charming wit and light touch was a rationalism that appeared in his humorous parable of orthodox Calvinism, "The Deacon's Masterpiece; or, The Wonderful 'One-Hoss Shay,' " included (1858) in *The Autocrat of the Breakfast-Table* (1831–32 in the *N.E. Mag.* and 1857 as an installment in the initial number of the *Atlantic Monthly*). Holmes also published *The Professor at the Breakfast-Table* (1860), another collection of intimate and congenial essays; 3 psychiatric novels (including *Elsie Venner*, 1861); and poems ("Old Ironsides") and humorous ballads.

1837–52. HAWTHORNE, MELVILLE, WHITMAN, AND POE. The currents of Transcendentalism touched **Nathaniel Hawthorne** (1804–64) and **Herman Melville** (1819–91), although at a divergent angle. They did not share Emerson's optimism; for them the problem of evil was the most meaningful and enduring element in life.

Hawthorne's focus was relatively narrow, but it was intense. With a craftsmanship of the 1st order, he gave a somber portrayal of the Puritan mind of New England, searching out the play of evil and the ramifications of sin, guilt, and remorse. His finest achievement is embraced by *Twice-Told Tales* (1837), *The Scarlet Letter* (1850), *The House of the Seven Gables* (1851), *The Blithedale Romance* (1852), and *The Snow-Image and Other Twice-Told Tales* (1852).

Melville, who had been a sailor, set his great romances against the background of the sea. *Typee* (1846), *Omoo* (1847), and *Mardi* (1849) were based on experiences in the South Seas. *Redburn* (1849) drew upon his experiences on the Atlantic and in England. In *White-Jacket* (1850) Melville's portrayal of the brutality that prevailed aboard the warships of the U.S. Navy ranked with the revelation of stern treatment in *Two Years Before the Mast* (1840) by **Richard Henry Dana, Jr.** (1815–82). Melville's masterpiece was *Moby-Dick* (1851), a novel of a whaling voyage allegorically conceived as a great tragedy imbued with philosophic significance.

Together with *Leaves of Grass* (1855; enlarged in successive editions to 1892) by **Walt Whitman** (p. 799), *Moby-Dick* was proof that American writers had shaped their own idiom. Whitman utilized a simple poetic style devoid of the ordinary usages of rhyme, meter, or ornament, and distinguished by a natural organic growth. Whitman had a profound belief in the perfectibility of man and in democracy. Among his later poems inspired by the events of the Civil War were "The Wound-Dresser" and 2 poems called forth by grief over Lincoln's death —"When Lilacs Last in the Dooryard Bloom'd" and "O Captain! My Captain!" (1865). His poetry is also marked by the frank though frequently symbolic treatment of sex—"Children of Adam" and "Calamus" (1860). His most important prose works were *Democratic Vistas* (1871) and *Specimen Days and Collect* (1882).

The greatest literary figure produced by the South during this period was **Edgar Allan Poe** (p. 766), but his productive years were passed in Philadelphia and New York after 1837 and his art was independent of historical and geographical association. One of the most complex personalities in American letters, Poe is remembered as an innovator in fields as different as poetry and the detective story. He did pioneer work as a literary critic. His "The Philosophy of Composition," "The Rationale of Verse," and "The Poetic Principle" revealed his conception of poetic unity to be one of mood or emotion, with emphasis upon the beauty of melancholy. He preferred the short story to the novel on the same basis that he preferred the short poem to the long. These stories were either of horror or of careful reasoning. The latter set the standard for the modern detective story. Poe's aesthetic principles had a marked influence upon the French *Symbolistes* as well as upon such Americans as Bierce and Hart Crane and such Englishmen as Rosetti, Swinburne, Dowson, and Stevenson. Among his works are *Tales of the Grotesque and Arabesque* (1840), "The Murders in the Rue Morgue" (1843), and *The Raven and Other Poems* (1845).

SOUTH. The representative Southern writers of the time concentrated on local themes. In *Swallow Barn* (1832), **John Pendleton Kennedy** (1795–1870) wrote a series of sketches portraying plantation life in Va. Working in a more realistic vein, **Augustus Baldwin Longstreet** (1790–1870) produced *Georgia Scenes, Characters, and Incidents* (1835), dealing with life in the backwoods. It was notable for its handling of dialect. The most prolific Southern writer was **William Gilmore Simms** (1806–70), who published poetry, historical romances, history, and biography. His best works include *Guy Rivers* (1834), one of his Border Romances; *The Partisan* (1835), one of his Revolutionary Romances; and *The Yemassee* (1835), a panel in the series of romances dealing with the colonial period. In the 1st rank of the Southern poets of

this period were **Henry Timrod** (1828–67) and **Paul Hamilton Hayne** (1830–86), both born in S.C.

1838–58. POETS. Henry Wadsworth Longfellow (p. 744) was the most popular American poet of his day. Many of his lines, for all of their lack of originality and firsthand observation, quickly became American household favorites. His popularity was based on such works as *Voices of the Night* (1839), *Evangeline* (1847), *The Song of Hiawatha* (1855), and *The Courtship of Miles Standish* (1858). When **John Greenleaf Whittier** (1807–92) did not turn his hand to antislavery agitation, as in *Poems Written During the Progress of the Abolition Question* (1838) and in individual pieces like "Massachusetts to Virginia" (1843) and "Ichabod" (1850), he produced ballads and narrative poems based on New England life and legend, as in "The Barefoot Boy" and "Maud Muller" (both 1856). **James Russell Lowell** (1819–91) used Yankee dialect to good advantage in offering a Northern Whig's satirical view of the Mexican War in the *Biglow Papers* (1st series, 1848) and attacking slavery (2nd series, 1867). Other antislavery poems include "Prometheus" (1843), "The Present Crisis" (1845), and "On the Capture of Certain Fugitives near Washington" (1845). Lowell characterized contemporary authors in *A Fable for Critics* (1848) and reached a wide audience with *The Vision of Sir Launfal* (1848).

1834–60. HISTORIANS. William Hickling Prescott (p. 768), author of the *History of the Reign of Ferdinand and Isabella* (1838), *History of the Conquest of Mexico* (1843), *History of the Conquest of Peru* (1847), and *History of the Reign of Philip the Second* (1855–58), worked in the dramatic vein of William Robertson and Sir Walter Scott. **George Ticknor** (1791–1871), **George Bancroft** (p. 671), and **John Lothrop Motley** (p. 758) were schooled in high standards of historical scholarship at German universities. Ticknor's *History of Spanish Literature* was published in 1849. In 1834 Bancroft brought out the 1st volume of his *History of the United States,* a work which ultimately ran to 11 volumes and concluded with the establishment of the

LITERATURE

603

national government. It was noteworthy both for its patriotic tone and its research in original materials. In 1856 Motley published *The Rise of the Dutch Republic.* Motley's concept of the vitalizing influence of Protestantism was shared by **Francis Parkman** (1823–93), who began the grand design of his epic of France and England in North America to 1763 with the *History of the Conspiracy of Pontiac* (1851). Parkman did not write the bulk of his work until after the Civil War, but he had already won fame with his travel account, *The California and Oregon Trail* (1849). In conscious contrast to Bancroft's oratorical prose, **Richard Hildreth** (1807–65) employed a sparse, dry style in his *History of the United States,* whose 6 volumes covering the period 1492–1821 appeared between 1849 and 1852. Virtually ignored by contemporary readers, Hildreth's work has a high degree of factual accuracy and penetrating insights into economic interests. Two collections of source materials published at government expense were important in encouraging the writing of American history: the *Debates, Resolutions, and Other Proceedings in Convention on the Adoption of the Federal Constitution,* brought out between 1827 and 1845 under the editorship of **Jonathan Elliot** (1784–1846); and the *American Archives* (covering the years 1774–76), ed. by **Peter Force** (1790–1868) and brought out between 1837 and 1853.

1848–60. REFORM NOVEL. The novel of propaganda, instruction and uplift flourished during this period of reform. *Uncle Tom's Cabin* (1852), by **Harriet Beecher Stowe** (p. 785), was the most successful of the many tracts for the times largely because its publication coincided with the national impact of the antislavery crusade. Her 2nd novel in this genre was *Dred, A Tale of the Great Dismal Swamp* (1856). Where *Uncle Tom's Cabin* (p. 215) fixed its attention on the evils of slavery as an institution, and was remarkably free from attacks upon Southerners, *Dred* sought to show the mark the institution left upon those who lived by it. Supposedly the 1st novels based on the antislavery theme were *Northwood, or Life North and South* (1827), by Sarah Josepha Hale (1788–1879), and *The Slave; or, Memoirs of Archy Moore* (1836), by Richard Hildreth.

Another reform impulse that was embodied in literature was the temperance movement, which reached its height in the 1850's. **Timothy Shay Arthur** (1809–85), best known for *Ten Nights in a Bar-Room and What I Saw There* (1854), published some 100 tracts and stories of which 1,000,000 copies had been printed by 1860. Also popular as a temperance writer was Lucius Manlius Sargent (1786–1867), whose *Temperance Tales* (1848) included such best-selling stories as "My Mother's Gold Ring" and "Groggy Harbor," originally issued between 1833 and 1843.

1840–60. POPULAR LITERATURE. The growth of the middle class, along with the extension of free public education, the establishment of subscription libraries, and the lyceum movement, had a direct influence on book publishing and literary standards. The mass audience widened the market for books of practical social instruction and sentimental novels of moral uplift. In addition to the best sellers listed above, etiquette books, juveniles (notably the moralistic *Peter Parley* juveniles, which sold approximately 7 million copies from 1827–60 and were written on a mass production basis by authors employed by **Samuel G. Goodrich** [1793–1860]), and anthologies were widely sold in this period. Two anthologist-editors, **Rufus W. Griswold** (1815–57) and **Evert A. Duyckinck** (1816–78), editor of the *Literary World,* had a substantial impact on reading taste. With **Park Benjamin** (1809–64), Griswold began in 1839 to serialize pirated fiction in *Brother Jonathan.* The first dime novel, *Malaeska* by **Ann Sophia Stephens** (1813–86), appeared in 1860. The last decade of this period is often called the "Feminine Fifties," a tribute to the number of women authors who wrote best sellers, easily outselling the works by Emerson, Hawthorne, Melville, and Whitman.

1802–60. BOOK PUBLISHING. Matthew Carey (1760–1839), Philadelphia publisher and economist, and founder of Carey and Lea (1785), promoted the American Co. of Booksellers, which managed 5 book fairs, 1802–06. More effective distribution was achieved by Harper & Bros. (est. N.Y., 1817, as J. & J. Harper), with the adoption in 1830 of the stereotyping of plates for "omnibus editions" of English reprints, and in the 1840's with the issuance of 25-ct. English novels. Carey & Hart (Philadelphia, 1829) followed suit. Scott, Dickens, and other foreign authors were printed in enormous pirated editions before the International Copyright Law (1891). Other major publishing houses included D. Appleton & Co. (1825); J. B. Lippincott & Co. (Philadelphia, 1836); Dodd, Mead & Co. (1839, 1870); the Boston firms of Little, Brown (1847), Houghton, Mifflin (1852) and E. P. Dutton (1852; moved to N.Y., 1869); and Charles Scribner's Sons (Baker & Scribner, 1846).

1800–60. PUBLIC LIBRARY MOVEMENT. Library of Congress, Washington, D.C., established 1800 with the library of Thomas Jefferson as a nucleus. Its greatest expansion occurred under the librarianship of **Herbert Putnam** (1861–1955), 1899–1939. In 1951 its holdings totaled 9,400,000 books and pamphlets. **Beginning of Tax-Supported Local Libraries. 1803:** Founding of a children's library in Salisbury, Conn., by a gift from Caleb Bingham, Boston publisher, supplemented by occasional grants of town money. **1833:** Under the leadership of Rev. Abiel Abbot a social library was established at Peterborough, N.H., supported by a small membership fee and a portion of the state bank tax set aside by the town to purchase books. **1850:** Public library at Wayland, Mass., established by gift of President Francis Wayland (1796–1865) of Brown University, matched by town donation and supported by regular tax funds. **1851:** Enactment in Mass. of a law permitting towns to tax inhabitants for the support of free libraries. Founding of the **Boston Public Library,** largely as a result of the activities of **Edward Everett** (1794–1865), orator, statesman, and scholar, and **George Ticknor,** with private book donations, money gifts, and a city appropriation.

TRENDS SINCE 1860

BEST SELLERS

1862. William G. Brownlow, *Parson Brownlow's Book*

1863. Mrs. E. D. E. N. Southworth, *The Fatal Marriage* *; Mrs. A. D. T. Whitney, *Faith Gartney's Girlhood*

1864. Mrs. E. D. E. N. Southworth, *Ishmael* *

1865. Mary Mapes Dodge, *Hans Brinker and His Silver Skates* *

1867. Horatio Alger, Jr., *Ragged Dick* *; Augusta J. Evans Wilson, *St. Elmo*

1868. Elizabeth S. P. Ward, *The Gates Ajar* *; Louisa May Alcott, *Little Women* *

1869. Mark Twain, *Innocents Abroad* *

1870. Bret Harte, *The Luck of Roaring Camp* *

1871. Louisa May Alcott, *Little Men* *; Edward Eggleston, *The Hoosier Schoolmaster* *

1872. Edward Payson Roe, *Barriers Burned Away;* Mark Twain, *Roughing It* *

1874. Edward Payson Roe, *Opening a Chestnut Burr*

1876. John Habberton, *Helen's Babies* *; Mark Twain, *Tom Sawyer* *

1878. Anna Katharine Green, *The Leavenworth Case* *

1879. Henry George, *Progress and Poverty* *

1880. Joel Chandler Harris, *Uncle Remus* *; Harriet Lothrop (Margaret Sidney), *Five Little Peppers and How They Grew* *; Lew Wallace, *Ben-Hur* *

1883. James Whitcomb Riley, *The Old Swimmin'-Hole* *; Mark Twain, *Life on the Mississippi* * (chief sales in 1940's in pocket size)

1885. Mark Twain, *Huckleberry Finn* *; Ulysses S. Grant, *Personal Memoirs*

1886. Frances Hodgson Burnett, *Little Lord Fauntleroy* *

1887. Archibald C. Gunter, *Mr. Barnes of New York* *

1888. Edward Bellamy, *Looking Backward* *

1894. William Hope Harvey, *Coin's Financial School* (free-silver argument)

1895. Opie Read, *The Jucklins;* Stephen Crane, *The Red Badge of Courage* *

1896. Harold Frederic, *The Damnation of Theron Ware*

1897. Charles Monroe Sheldon, *In His Steps* * (sales *c.*8 million to 1945)

1898. Edward Noyes Westcott, *David Harum* *

1899. Charles Major, *When Knighthood Was in Flower;* Winston Churchill, *Richard Carvel;* Paul Leicester Ford, *Janice Meredith;* Elbert Hubbard, *A Message to Garcia* *

1900. Mary Johnston, *To Have and to Hold;* Irving Bacheller, *Eben Holden*

1901. George Barr McCutcheon, *Graustark;* Alice Hegan Rice, *Mrs. Wiggs of the Cabbage Patch;* Winston Churchill, *The Crisis*

1902. Owen Wister, *The Virginian* *

1903. John Fox, Jr., *The Little Shepherd of Kingdom Come;* Kate Douglas Wiggin, *Rebecca of Sunnybrook Farm;* Jack London, *The Call of the Wild* *

1904. Jack London, *The Sea Wolf* *; Gene Stratton Porter, *Freckles*

1906. Zane Grey, *The Spirit of the Border* *

1907. Harold Bell Wright, *The Shepherd of the Hills* *

1908. John Fox, Jr., *The Trail of the Lonesome Pine;* Mary Roberts Rinehart, *The Circular Staircase*

1909. Gene Stratton Porter, *A Girl of the Limberlost;* Harold Bell Wright, *The Calling of Dan Matthews* *

1911. Kathleen Norris, *Mother;* Gene Stratton Porter, *The Harvester;* Harold Bell Wright, *The Winning of Barbara Worth* *

1912. Zane Grey, *The Riders of the Purple Sage* *

1913. Eleanor Hodgman Porter, *Pollyanna;* Gene Stratton Porter, *Laddie*

1914. Edgar Rice Burroughs, *Tarzan of the Apes* *; Booth Tarkington, *Penrod* *; Harold Bell Wright, *The Eyes of the World* *

1915. Gene Stratton Porter, *Michael O'Halloran*

1916. Edgar A. Guest, *A Heap o' Livin'* *; Harold Bell Wright, *When a Man's a Man* *

1918. Edward Streeter, *Dere Mable;* Henry Adams, *The Education of Henry Adams;* Zane Grey, *The U.P. Trail* *

1920. Edward W. Bok, *The Americanization of Edward Bok;* Sinclair Lewis, *Main Street* *

1921. Dorothy Canfield, *The Brimming Cup*

1923. Emily Post, *Etiquette* *

1924. Edna Ferber, *So Big*

1925. John Erskine, *The Private Life of Helen of Troy;* Anita Loos, *Gentlemen Prefer Blondes;* Bruce Barton, *The Man Nobody Knows*

1926. Sinclair Lewis, *Elmer Gantry;* Will Durant, *The Story of Philosophy* *; Thorne Smith, *Topper* *

1927. Thornton Wilder, *The Bridge of San Luis Rey*

1929. Lloyd C. Douglas, *The Magnificent Obsession;* Robert L. Ripley, *Believe It or Not* *

1930. Edna Ferber. *Cimarron*

1931. Pearl Buck, *The Good Earth* *; Ellery Queen, *The Dutch Shoe Mystery* *

1932. Ellery Queen, *The Egyptian Cross Mystery* *

1933. Hervey Allen, *Anthony Adverse;* Erle Stanley Gardner, *The Case of the Sulky Girl* *

1934. Erle Stanley Gardner, *The Case of the Curious Bride* *; Ellery Queen, *The Chinese Orange Mystery* *

1935. Lloyd C. Douglas, *Green Light;* Erle Stanley Gardner, *The Case of the Counterfeit Eye* *

1936. Dale Carnegie, *How to Win Friends and Influence People* *; Erle Stanley Gardner, *The Case of the Stuttering Bishop* *; Margaret Mitchell, *Gone with the Wind* *

1937. Erle Stanley Gardner, *The Case of the Dangerous Dowager* *; *The Case of the Lame Canary* *

1938. Marco Page, *Fast Company;* Marjorie K. Rawlings, *The Yearling;* Max Brand

(Frederick Faust), *Singing Guns* *; Erle Stanley Gardner, *The Case of the Substitute Face* *; Damon Runyon, *The Best of Damon Runyon* *

1939. John Steinbeck, *The Grapes of Wrath* *

1940. Ellery Queen, *New Adventures of Ellery Queen* *; Ernest Hemingway, *For Whom the Bell Tolls* *

1942. Lloyd C. Douglas, *The Robe;* Marion Hargrove, *See Here, Private Hargrove*

1943. Ernie Pyle, *Here Is Your War;* Betty Smith, *A Tree Grows in Brooklyn;* Wendell Willkie, *One World*

1944. Ernie Pyle, *Brave Men;* Kathleen Winsor, *Forever Amber;* Lillian Smith, *Strange Fruit*

1945. Thomas Bertram Costain, *The Black Rose;* Betty MacDonald, *The Egg and I;* Samuel Shellabarger, *Captain from Castile*

1946. Joshua Loth Liebman, *Peace of Mind;* Frank Yerby, *Foxes of Harrow;* Taylor Caldwell, *This Side of Innocence*

1947. John Gunther, *Inside U.S.A.;* Laura Z. Hobson, *Gentleman's Agreement;* Sinclair Lewis, *Kingsblood Royal;* Samuel Shellabarger, *The Prince of Foxes*

1948. Frank Yerby, *The Golden Hawk;* Alfred C. Kinsey, *Sexual Behavior in the Human Male;* Frances Parkinson Keyes, *Dinner at Antoine's;* Thomas Costain, *High Towers;* Norman Mailer, *The Naked and the Dead*

1949. Lloyd C. Douglas, *The Big Fisherman;* Frank Yerby, *Pride's Castle*

1950. Henry Morton Robinson, *The Cardinal*

1951. Rachel Carson, *The Sea Around Us;* Herman Wouk, *The Caine Mutiny;* James Jones, *From Here to Eternity;* Gaylord Hauser, *Look Younger, Live Longer*

1952. Thomas B. Costain, *The Silver Chalice* *; *The Holy Bible: Revised Standard Version* *

1953. Lloyd C. Douglas, *The Robe* (reissue); Catherine Marshall, *A Man Called Peter*

1954. Norman Vincent Peale, *The Power of Positive Thinking*

1955. Herman Wouk, *Marjorie Morningstar;* Anne Morrow Lindbergh, *Gift from the Sea*

1956. Edwin O'Connor, *The Last Hurrah;* Grace Metalious, *Peyton Place* *; Morey Bernstein, *The Search for Bridey Murphy*

1957. James G. Cozzens, *By Love Possessed;* Meyer Levin, *Compulsion;* Vance Packard, *The Hidden Persuaders*

1958. Robert Traver, *Anatomy of a Murder;* James Jones, *Some Came Running*

1959. Leon Uris, *Exodus;* Moss Hart, *Act One;* Harry Golden, *Only in America;* D. C. Jarvis, *Folk Medicine*

1960. Allen Drury, *Advise and Consent;* James A. Michener, *Hawaii*

1865–1900. LITERATURE OF AMERICA'S REDISCOVERY. The West: Samuel Langhorne Clemens (Mark

---

* Also best sellers after their period, including cheap reprints (but not dictionaries, almanacs manuals, textbooks, cookbooks, comic books, or government publications).

Twain, also p. 686), the great voice of the West of his generation, won a worldwide reputation by his defiantly American outlook, his uncompromising democracy (hostility to slavery, snobbery, and the tyrannies of chivalry), and his pungent colloquial style. Of all contemporary humorists (including **John Phoenix** [George Horatio Derby, 1823–61], **Josh Billings** [Henry Wheeler Shaw, 1818–85] **Maj. Jack Downing** [Seba Smith, 1792–1868], **Bill Arp** [Charles Henry Smith. 1826–1903], **Petroleum V. Nasby** [David Ross Locke, 1833–88], and **Artemas Ward** [Charles Farrar Browne, 1834–67]), Clemens alone created great literature. His experience on the frontiers in the Old Southwest and the Far West (the latter depicted in *Roughing It,* 1872) prepared him to use regional tall tales and realism with his own idiom, as in *The Celebrated Jumping Frog of Calaveras County* (1865), a brilliant reworking of a California folk tale. His frontier irreverence for ancient culture, displayed in *The Innocents Abroad* (1869), the 1st of several travel books, is in contrast to his enthusiasm in the 1st part of *Life on the Mississippi* (1883). *The Gilded Age* (1873), written with Charles Dudley Warner (1829–1900), was his 1st novel, marked like others by its episodic improvisation, but it lacks the distinction of *The Adventures of Tom Sawyer* (1878) and particularly *The Adventures of Huckleberry Finn* (1884), picaresque portrayals of regional character and frontier experience centered on the adventures of 2 boys. His later pessimism is seen in *The Man That Corrupted Hadleyburg* (1900) and *The Mysterious Stranger* (1916). The Western **Local-Colorists** (concerned with commonplace local scenes, utilizing regional dialects, and presenting character types) include **Bret Harte** (1836–1902), who, using stock characters and plots, created a romantic legendary view of Calif. in stories and sketches (notably *The Luck of Roaring Camp,* 1870, called "the father of all Western local color stories," and *Mrs. Skaggs's Husbands,* 1873), as well as poems, the most popular being the satiric comic ballad, "Plain Language from Truthful James" (1870), familiarly known under the pirated name, "The Heathen Chinee." The vogue for vernacular Western poetry was further solidified

by *The Pike County Ballads* (1871) of **John Hay** (p. 724), whose prose works include *Castilian Days* (1871), an attack upon the Catholic Church; *The Bread-Winners* (1883), an antilabor novel; and, in collaboration with J. G. Nicolay, the classic 10-vol. *Abraham Lincoln: A History* (1890); and by **Joaquin Miller** (Cincinnatus Hiner Miller, *c.*1839–1913). Miller romanticized some of his early experiences in *Life Amongst the Modocs* (1873), but in Ore. and Calif. he was by turn horse thief, lawyer, newspaperman, and Indian fighter. His extravagantly romantic poems, e.g., *Songs of the Sierras,* were first hailed as products of a primitive, but he dwindled into a hack writer although the late *Songs of the Soul* (1896) includes his well-known "Columbus." Other balladists of the West: **Will Carleton** (1845–1912), *Farm Ballads* (1873), including the poem "Over the Hills to the Poor House"; **James Whitcomb Riley** (1849–1916), Indiana poet; and **Eugene Field** (1850–95), Chicago *Daily News* columnist, whose best-known poem was "Little Boy Blue." **Edward Eggleston** (1837–1902), in addition to writing pioneer historical works on American cultural history, notably *The Transit of Civilization* (1901), founded the **Hoosier School** with his novels of the middle border, notably *The Hoosier Schoolmaster* (1871), *The Circuit Rider* (1874), *Roxy* (1878), and *The Graysons* (1888).

The South: **Joel Chandler Harris,** 1848–1908, creator of many "Uncle Remus" stories, humorous animal legendary reflecting Negro folk life, furnished an authentic picture of the Georgia Negro under slavery and Reconstruction, notably in *Free Joe and Other Georgian Sketches* (1887), and of the "cracker" or "poor white" (*Mingo and Other Sketches in Black and White,* 1884). Other Southern Local-Colorists included **George Washington Cable** (1844–1925), with short stories (*Old Creole Days,* 1879) and novels of Creole life (*The Grandissimes,* 1880; *Dr. Sevier,* 1885; *Bonaventure,* 1888); **Thomas Nelson Page** (1853–1922), who idealized Tidewater Virginia of antebellum days (*Red Rock,* 1898, a study of the Negro problem); and **James Lane Allen** (1849–1925), who used the central Kentucky plateau around his native Lexington for the locale of his novels (*A Kentucky Cardinal*, 1894; *Summer in Arcady*, 1896; *The Choir Invisible*, 1897; *The Reign of Law*, 1900).

New England: Regional fiction found its most accomplished exponent in **Sarah Orne Jewett** (1849–1909), who revealed social and psychological problems in the declining Maine seaport settlements, beginning with *Deephaven* (1877) and culminating in her masterpiece, *The Country of the Pointed Firs* (1896). Another exponent of the Local-Colorist School was **Mary Eleanor Wilkins** [Freeman] (1852–1930), whose early short stories (*A Humble Romance*, 1887, and *A New England Nun*, 1891) represent her most important work.

1865–1892. RISE OF REALISM. An early realist was **John William De Forest** (1826–1906), whose Civil War novel, *Miss Ravenel's Conversion from Secession to Loyalty* (1867), and story of a S.C. feud, *Kate Beaumont* (1872), are frank accounts of the seamy, brutal, and corrupting aspects of life. Most popular exponent of the realists was **William Dean Howells** (also p. 730), with his masterpiece, *The Rise of Silas Lapham* (1885), a sympathetic study of the *nouveaux riches*. Howells' novels provide a penetrating analysis of the post-Civil War American economy. His sympathy with socialism (by 1887) is evident in such novels of social protest as *A Hazard of New Fortunes* (1890). His critical theories are summarized in *Criticism and Fiction* (1891), in which he championed realism, whose sources he ascribed not only to science but to democracy. He insisted that art must serve morality. His economic novels showed the influence of the Utopian socialist novel of **Edward Bellamy** (1850–98), *Looking Backward, or 2000–1887* (1888). Howells' realistic approach was adopted by Garland, Stephen Crane, Frank Norris, and Robert Herrick. **Hamlin Garland** (1860–1940), an advocate of "veritism," or honest realism (*Crumbling Idols,* 1894), wrote a number of propaganda novels of prairie life and agrarian conditions (1887–94). His major work was *Main-Travelled Roads* (1891), stories of the burdens of farm life. His autobiography, *A Son of the Middle Border* (1917), presents the everyday life of a group of migrating families to the prairies and the plains

(1840–95).

1875–1941. HENRY JAMES (also p. 733) **AND THE NOVELISTS OF MANNERS.** A detached observer contrasting American and European cultures and moral standards in relation to social conventions, James was a leader in psychological realism, a sensitive interpreter of subtle characters, and a master of a complex style and the formal architecture of fiction. His many novels of contrasting characters developed in subtlety from *The American* (1877) through *The Portrait of a Lady* (1881) to the later major period of *The Wings of the Dove* (1902), *The Ambassadors* (1903), and *The Golden Bowl* (1904). His short stories (e.g., "The Turn of the Screw," 1898) and his criticism (e.g., the prefaces to his revised collected novels and tales, 1907–09) are as distinguished as his longer fiction. James' most articulate disciple in portraying upper-class American society was **Edith Wharton** (1862–1937), whose major novels of New York's social elite include *The House of Mirth* (1905), *The Age of Innocence* (1920), and *The Old Maid* (1924). In *Ethan Frome* (1911), a tale of sordid misery in the New England hills, she produced a work of dignified simplicity. **Ellen Glasgow** (1874–1945) dealt with the ironies of a decaying Va. society (*Barren Ground*, 1925; *The Romantic Comedians*, 1926; *In This Our Life*, 1941), and **Willa Cather** (p. 685) produced chronicles in which environment and character are deftly interwoven: *O Pioneer!* (1913), *My Ántonia* (1918), *A Lost Lady* (1923), *Death Comes for the Archbishop* (1927), and *Shadows on the Rock* (1931).

1893–1949. NATURALISM AND THE PROPAGANDA NOVEL. Nineteenth-century theories of biological and economic determinism shaped the literary theory of naturalism, with its frankness, objectivity, determinism, and fatalism. Notable among the fiction writers of this school were **Stephen Crane** (p. 691), **Frank Norris** (1870–1902), **Robert Herrick** (1868–1938), and **Jack London** (1876–1916). The influence of Zola was found in Crane's *Maggie: A Girl of the Streets* (1893), an impressionistic novelette; but his masterpiece was *The Red Badge of Courage* (1895), a lyrical and intense novel of the Civil War, influenced by both Zola and Tolstoi. Among his most successful short stories were "The Open Boat" and "Blue Hotel." *McTeague* (1899) by Norris was a major naturalistic American novel, a study in character disintegration under economic pressure. *The Octopus* (1901), the 1st of his "Epic of the Wheat" trilogy, a struggle between the wheat growers and the Southern Pacific Railroad, was followed (1903) by *The Pit* (Chicago grain market). *The Wolf*, 3rd of the trilogy, was never written. Social protest against the forces of acquisitiveness found expression in Herrick's novels, notably in the *Memoirs of an American Citizen* (1905), *Clark's Field* (1914), and in *Waste* (1924), where the engineer, Thornton, finds "a sense of corruption working at the very roots of life." Most widely read in the U.S. and abroad of any of these writers was London, among whose 49 vols. of fiction, drama, and essays was *The Call of the Wild* (1903), the story of a dog in the far North who escapes from civilization to lead a wolf pack; *The Sea Wolf* (1904), a ruthless captain of a sealing ship; *Martin Eden* (1909), a writer's struggle; and *The Valley of the Moon* (1913), in which economic problems are solved by a return to the land.

Other problem novelists of the period who diverged from the path of naturalism and produced straight propaganda novels include **Winston Churchill** (1871–1947), a middle-class progressive, who, in addition to historical romances like *Richard Carvel* (1899) and *The Crisis* (1910), wrote political and economic novels—*Coniston* (1900), *Mr. Crewe's Career* (1908), *A Far Country* (1915), *The Dwelling Place of Light* (1917); **Ernest Poole** (1880–1950), *The Harbor* (1915); **David Graham Phillips** (1867–1911), *The Great God Success* (1901) and *Susan Lenox: Her Fall and Rise* (written 1908, pub. 1917), an epic of slum life and political corruption; and **Upton Sinclair** (1878–   ), whose major novels include *The Jungle* (1906, corruption in meat packing and labor exploitation) and a series of expository and propagandist works: *The Profits of Religion* (1918), on the church; *The Brass Check* (1919), the press; *The Goose Step* (1923) and *The Goslings*

(1924), on the schools; *Mammonart* (1925) and *Money Writes* (1927), on the arts. Other exposé novels include *Oil!* (1927), a story of corruption in the Harding era; *Boston* (1928), based on the Sacco-Vanzetti case; and the "Lanny Budd" series (1940–49), a personal interpretation of the two World Wars (1940–49).

1899–1901. FIN-DE-SIÈCLE ROMANCE was exemplified in the works of **Paul Leicester Ford** (1865–1902), *Janice Meredith* (1899); **Mary Johnston** (1875–1936), *To Have and to Hold* (1900); and **Booth Tarkington** (1869–1946), *Monsieur Beaucaire* (1900). Tarkington's best work dates from the end of World War I and includes *The Magnificent Ambersons* (1918) and *Alice Adams* (1921).

1900–25. NATURALISM OF THEODORE DREISER (p. 698). *Sister Carrie* by Dreiser, the story of the realization of her own personality by a poor young girl (1900), remained largely unread until its 3rd edition, 1912, a year after the appearance of *Jennie Gerhardt*, on a similar theme. Dreiser's preoccupation with Social Darwinism is given expression in the notable trilogy, *The Financier* (1912), *The Titan* (1914), and *The Stoic* (1947), with the masterly character delineation of Cowperwood, prototype of worldly success. Another victim of social and biological forces is Clyde Griffiths in *An American Tragedy* (1925). Objective, amoral, Dreiser, despite lack of style and undistinguished language, achieved a powerful projection of reality.

1918–39. BETWEEN WORLD WARS. "Lost generation" was the name applied by **Gertrude Stein** (1874–1946) to the disillusioned intellectuals and aesthetes of post-World War I years. This group was typified by **F. Scott Fitzgerald** (1896–1940), whose *This Side of Paradise* (1920) is an expression of jazz-age cynicism, and *The Great Gatsby* (1925) of disillusion about quickly acquired riches. That cynicism and disillusionment were also reflected in the writings of **Sinclair Lewis** (1885–1951) in a revolt against small-town meanness (*Main Street*, 1920) and the dullness of the businessman (*Babbitt*, 1922). His writing is closer to caricature than to photographic realism. Other novels include *Arrow-*

smith (1924), an exposé of the medical profession; *Dodsworth* (1929), a sympathetic portrayal of a retired American manufacturer; *It Can't Happen Here* (1935), concerned with a future fascist revolt in the U.S.; and *Kingsblood Royal* (1947), a novel about race prejudice. Lewis became (1930) the 1st American author to be awarded the Nobel prize for literature. This period was also marked by the literature of the **escapists**, including **James Branch Cabell** (1879–1958), with *Jurgen* (1919) and *Figures of Earth* (1921); **Joseph Hergesheimer** (1880–   ), with *The Three Black Pennys* (1917) and *Java Head* (1919); **Elinor Wylie** (1885–1928), poet and novelist; and **Thornton Wilder** (1897–   ), *The Bridge of San Luis Rey* (1927), *Ides of March* (1948) (also p. 627); and by experiments with words rather than ideas carried on by **Gertrude Stein** in many books written between *Three Lives* (1909) and *The Autobiography of Alice B. Toklas* (1933). The most powerful literary impact upon the new generation of American writers was that of **Ernest Hemingway** (p. 725), with his plain, factual, but evocative style (*The Sun Also Rises,* 1926, a depiction of an expatriate group; and *A Farewell to Arms* [1929], the best American novel of World War I). Other writers of the period include **Sherwood Anderson** (1876–1941), with *Winesburg, Ohio* (1919), stories of small-town life, a naturalistic interpreter of America; and **Ring Lardner** (1885–1933), a sardonic humorist exposing foibles through conversational speech—*How to Write Short Stories* (1924), a collection; *What of It* (1925); *Round Up* (1929); *First and Last* (1934).

The pervasive economic depression of the 30's resulted in a revitalized social problem novel, as exemplified by such writers as **James T. Farrell** (1904–   ), whose *Studs Lonigan* trilogy (1932–35) constitutes a naturalistic portrayal of squalor among the Chicago Irish; **Erskine Caldwell** (1903–   ), whose most popular novel, *Tobacco Road* (1932), recreates the contemporary Jukes and Kallikaks of the South; and **John Dos Passos** (1896–   ), whose outlook and style reached maturity in *Manhattan Transfer* (1925). His *U.S.A.* trilogy (1930, 1932, 1936), a Domesday Book of economic malpractices, employs several distinctive fictional devices, including a panoramic background, or "newsreel," and the "Camera Eye," the author's point of view toward his subject matter expressed in stream-of-consciousness passages. **John Steinbeck's** (1902–   ) *The Grapes of Wrath* (1939) is a memorable recreation of the economic dislocation of the Okies and the tragedy of the Dust Bowl (other outstanding novels: *Tortilla Flat* 1935), *Of Mice and Men* (1937), *East of Eden* (1952). **William Faulkner** (p. 705) wrote a series of novels constituting a bitter comedy of plantation family decadence (*The Sound and The Fury,* 1929, decadence as seen through the eyes of an idiot son; *As I Lay Dying,* 1930, psychology of a subnormal poor-white family with its use of naturalism to highlight the dominance of the irrational in human nature; *Sanctuary,* 1931, a sadistic horror story; *Light in August,* 1932, the ordeal of a pregnant girl; *Intruder in the Dust,* 1948). **Richard Wright** (1909–60) was a contemporary Negro novelist.

1861–1950. CHANGING FASHIONS IN POETRY. Despite her individualism, the influence of **Emily Dickinson** (p. 695), whose pieces were distinguished by sharp and unexpected imagery and poignant feeling, has been profound. Her metaphors made her seem to Amy Lowell a precursor of the Imagist School. Among the **conservative** poets of the earlier period were **Bayard Taylor** (1825–78); **Edmund Clarence Stedman** (1833–1908); **Thomas Bailey Aldrich** (1836–1907), editor of the *Atlantic* (1881–90); **Richard Watson Gilder** (1844–1909), reflecting the influence of Rossetti and other Pre-Raphaelites; **Edward Rowland Sill** (1841–87), whose *Poems* (1902) are marked by a classic finish and stoic idealism; **John Banister Tabb** (1845–1909), poet-priest whose poetry has been compared to Emily Dickinson and to the 17th-century English metaphysical poets; **Sidney Lanier** (1842–81), the outstanding Southern poet of the period, who attempted to produce in verse the sound patterns of music, revealing in his poetry exceptional melodic gifts and a fine rhythmical feeling ("The Song of the Chattahoochee," "The Symphony," and "The Marshes of Glynn"). Others in the period include **Richard Hovey** (1864–1900), a chauvinist, whose poetry reveled in the joys of the open road (*Songs from*

Vagabondia, 1894), **William Vaughan Moody** (1869–1910), best known for his verse dramas (p. 625), whose poetry combined lyrical treatment with attention to political questions treated along anti-imperialist lines; **Edwin Markham** (1852–1940), whose most popular poem, "The Man with the Hoe" (1899), was inspired by Millet's painting; and **Joyce Kilmer** (1886–1918), *Trees and Other Poems* (1914).

The **revolt against traditionalism** was led by **Ezra Pound** (1885–), who served as an editor of *Poetry* (founded Chicago, 1912), a leader of the Imagists and a sponsor of diverse authors. His disciplined metrical experiments, concern with a continuum of culture, and use of medieval and Chinese literature brought powerful new forces to play on modern poetry. His works include *Personae* (1926) and *Cantos* (1919–). An expatriate (1908–45), he espoused Fascism in Italy, was brought to the U.S. to be tried for treason, but was confined without trial because he was adjudged "paranoid." Pound's impact was especially notable in the work of **T.[homas] S.[tearns] Eliot** (1888–), American-born poet who became a British subject in 1927, with *The Waste Land* (1922), his major poetic effort, an epic compressed into 400 lines. In *Ash-Wednesday* (1930) he made clear his allegiance to the Church of England, and its value as a medium of social action is affirmed in *Murder in the Cathedral* (1935), a latter-day morality play. Eliot considers poetry as an escape from emotion and personality. His influence in turn was felt in the work of **Hart Crane** (1899–1932).

Other principal poets of the post-World War I period (many of whom published major works prior to 1914) include **Edwin Arlington Robinson** (p. 770), heir to the New England tradition of Puritanism and Transcendentalism, who dealt primarily with ethical conflicts within the individual; **Amy Lowell** (1874–1925), a free-verse Imagist; **Robert Frost** (p. 710), whose lyrics are marked by an intense but restrained emotion and a brilliant insight into New England character; **Vachel Lindsay** (1879–1931), known for his vivid imagery, vigorous rhythm, and dramatic conception (*Congo and Other Poems*, 1914); **Carl Sandburg** (1878–), also author of a monumental biography of Lincoln (1926–43), whose realism captures the American idiom; **Edgar Lee Masters** (1869–1947), *Spoon River Anthology* (1915), a bitter commentary on American urban standards; **Robinson Jeffers** (1887–), *Tamar* (1924), *Roan Stallion* (1925), poems of violence set in the headlands and valleys of Calif.; **Conrad Aiken** (1889–), whose subjective poetry is marked by subtle musical rhythms; **Stephen Vincent Benét** (1898–1943), *John Brown's Body* (1928), a narrative poem of the Civil War; **Edna St. Vincent Millay** (1892–1950), whose *Renascence and Other Poems* (1917) exhibited technical virtuosity, freshness, and a hunger for beauty—her mastery of the sonnet form was demonstrated by *The Buck in the Snow* (1928) and *Fatal Interview* (1931); **Marianne Moore** (1887–), *Collected Poems* (1951); and **Wallace Stevens** (1879–1955), whose poems exhibit intensity, precision, and command of imagery; *Collected Poems* (1954).

1890–1930. LITERATURE AND SOCIAL CRITICISM. Chief critics of the period who considered literature from the point of view of social values were **Randolph Bourne** (1886–1918), *Youth and Life* (1913) and *Untimely Papers* (1919); and **Van Wyck Brooks** (1886–), who, in *The Wine of the Puritans* (1909), developed the thesis that the Puritan tradition crushed American culture, views which have been altered in later works, notably his 5 studies in cultural history, *Movers and Makers,* begun in 1936. His *America's Coming of Age* (1915) affirmed the prewar idealism of the younger generation. The most notable achievement in socioliterary criticism was *Main Currents in American Thought* (1927–30) by **Vernon Louis Parrington** (1871–1929). **Henry L. Mencken** (1880–1956), founder with **George Jean Nathan** (1882–1958) of *The American Mercury* (1924), which he edited to 1933, is best known for his aggressive iconoclasm toward American democracy and the cultural gaucheries of the American scene. His most important scholarly work is *The American Language* (1919–48). Leaders of **conservative criticism** were **Paul Elmer More** (1864–1937), **Irving Babbitt** (1865–1933), **Stuart Pratt Sherman** (1881–1926), and

William Crary Brownell (1851–1928), with a neohumanist movement launched (1930) by **Norman Foerster** (1887–) and supported by More and Babbitt. Opposing were critics of such diverse schools as Edmund Wilson (1895–), Lewis Mumford (1895–), Kenneth Burke (1899–), and Allen Tate (1899–).

1861–1939. HISTORIANS. The major impact on historical writing in the post-Civil War period derived from the "scientific school," as evidenced in the writings of **Henry Harisse** (1829–1910) and **Justin Winsor** (1831–97) and in the introduction of the seminar method in the universities by Charles K. Adams at Michigan (1869), by Henry Adams at Harvard (1871), and notably after 1880 at Johns Hopkins under Herbert Baxter Adams (1850–1901) and at Columbia under John W. Burgess (1844–1931). The founding of the American Historical Association, 1884 (with its *Review* appearing 1895), and the establishment of the *Political Science Quarterly*, 1886, were early evidences of the new trend. Major historians of the period include **Henry Adams** (p. 666); **James Ford Rhodes** (1848–1927), with his multivolume history of the U.S. since 1850; **John Fiske** (1842–1901), notable as well for his fight for Spencerian evolution (*The Outlines of Cosmic Philosophy,* 1874) as for his vitalizing early American history and stressing the European genesis of American institutions; **John Bach McMaster** (1852–1932), 1st of the important social historians; and a new group of objective analysts of (1) the colonial period: **Herbert Levi Osgood** (1855–1918), **George Louis Beer** (1872–1920), and **Charles McLean Andrews** (1863–1943), and (2) Reconstruction: **William Archibald Dunning** (1857–1922) and his disciples. But the chief impulse to the newer group of 20th-century historians came from the writing of **Frederick Jackson Turner** (1861–1932) and **Charles Austin Beard** (1874–1948). In a paper entitled "The Significance of the Frontier in American History" (1893) Turner pointed out that the frontier has been the 1 great determinant of American civilization, a point of departure from previous writers who stressed continuity of American institutions with Europe.

Despite significant correctives of this thesis, it has had an exceptional impact upon the study of the roles of environment and geographical sections in U.S. history. The widest reading public in the post-World War period was achieved by Beard, whose major research was embodied in 2 early monographs, *An Economic Interpretation of the Constitution* (1913) and *The Economic Origins of Jeffersonian Democracy* (1915). *The Rise of American Civilization* (2 vols., pub. in 1927 with Mary Beard; vol. 3, *America in Midpassage,* 1939) revealed that Beard was no longer an economic determinist and stressed pluralism in historical causation. **James Harvey Robinson** (1863–1936) in *The New History* (1912) insisted that the historian had a duty to explain how things came to be as they are, to study all kinds of social facts, and to make "syntheses." Although Beard in later life distinguished between **history as actuality** and the **historical record** (involving selection and interpretation of the facts), and Robert L. Schuyler cautioned against the "present-mindedness" of recent historians, the prevailing trend down to the mid-century was to stress social, economic, and intellectual history and to relate historical data to contemporary problems.

In the 1930's and 40's historical biography reacted from the earlier muckraking school, as well as from the critical and psychoanalytical studies of the 20's (W. E. Woodward's Grant; Van Wyck Brooks, *Ordeal of Mark Twain*) to providing fuller and more sympathetic factual biographies (Carl Van Doren's Franklin, Douglas S. Freeman's Lee, Allan Nevins' Grover Cleveland, Carl Sandburg's and James G. Randall's multivol. Lincoln, and Dumas Malone's Jefferson).

1861–1952. LIBRARIES: MAJOR TRENDS. System and Technique: In 1876 the American Library Association held its 1st convention; established *Library Journal,* 1876. The introduction of methods of business efficiency and cataloguing was largely the result of the efforts of **Melvil Dewey** (1851–1931), who founded the New York State Library School (1887) and originated the Dewey "decimal classification." **Free Library**

Movement: In 1881 **Andrew Carnegie** (p. 683) made his original offer to donate buildings for public libraries provided that each municipality would establish and adequately finance such a library by annual tax appropriations. By 1900 there were 1,700 free libraries in the U.S. with over 5,000 vols.; by 1947 there were more than 7,100 public libraries and 4,200 libraries of other kinds. The free library movement was further accelerated by the enactment in 1893 of the 1st state law (in N.H.) requiring townships to create libraries. **Founding of the New York Public Library,** 23 May 1895, out of the consolidation of the Astor (1848) and Lenox (1870) Libraries, and the Tilden Trust created by the will of Samuel J. Tilden (d. 1886). By 1952 it had in excess of 5 million volumes and was the largest public library in the U.S. **Growth of University and Reference Libraries:** Among the largest university libraries at the end of the period were Harvard, 5,400,000 vols.; Yale, 3,980,000; California (including branches), 2,717,000; Illinois, 2,384,000; Columbia, 2,000,000. Notable among the specialized reference libraries: American Antiquarian Society, Worcester, Mass. (older newspapers); Henry E. Huntington Library and Art Gallery, San Marino, Calif. (English and U.S. literature and history); Smithsonian Institution (1846), Washington, D.C., scientific and learned societies publications; Library of the Surgeon General's Office, U.S. Army, Washington, D.C. (beg. 1818), medical science; Folger Shakespeare Library, Washington, D.C., English books, 1475–1640.

1861–1960. PUBLISHING TRENDS. Dime novels had a sensational vogue, 1860–1900, inspired by the success of the "penny dreadfuls" in England and published by such firms as Beadle & Adams and Street & Smith. The pen name "Nick Carter" was used by such writers as John Russell Coryell, Frederick William Davis, Frederick Van Rensselaer Day, and others. **Juveniles:** Conspicuously successful down to World War I were the works of **Louisa May Alcott** (p. 668); **Frances Hodgson Burnett** (1849–1924), *Little Lord Fauntleroy* (1886); and **Booth Tarkington,** *Penrod* (1914). Despite serious competition from comic books, juveniles came to command an increasing share of publishers' attention after 1940, constituting in 1950, after fiction, the largest single category. **Consolidation** among major firms took place throughout the period, notably in the formation, 1890, of the American Book Co. to publish school texts. Greater centralization of publishing in the New York area developed. Other firms founded prior to 1901 included Henry Holt & Co. (1866 as Leypoldt & Holt); Macmillan Co., 1870; Doubleday, 1900 (merged with Doran, 1927). Of considerable advantage to U.S. writers was the enactment, 3 Mar. 1891, of an international **copyright law** to prevent pirating the works of foreign authors; revised 4 Mar. 1909 (amended through 3 June 1949). New literary and distribution trends were encouraged by the rise of new publishing houses in the 20th century, notably B. W. Huebsch, 1905 (absorbed by Viking, 1925); Alfred A. Knopf, 1915, with emphasis upon books by outstanding European authors; Boni & Liveright, 1917, with the moderate-priced "Modern Library" series (acquired by Bennett A. Cerf, 1925; since 1927 by Random House); Harcourt Brace, 1919; Simon & Schuster, 1924; Random House, 1927; and, in the field of scholarly and scientific works, by the establishment of **university presses,** notably Columbia, Harvard, Chicago, Yale, Princeton, and North Carolina. Two major distributing trends after World War I were the establishment of **book clubs** (Book-of-the-Month Club and Literary Guild both began distribution in 1926), with over 50 different clubs by 1947; and the successful distribution of reprints of popular books in the 25ct.–35ct. range, with Pocket Books (1939), Bantam Books (1946), and Signet-Mentor (New American Library) the 3 major organizations in the field by 1952.

1960 witnessed a rash of mergers in the book publishing business, including Henry Holt & Co. with Rinehart and Winston, the acquisition of Meridian by World, of the New American Library by the Los Angeles *Times-Mirror,* of Macmillan by Crowell-Collier, of Appleton-Century-Crofts by Meredith, and of Alfred A. Knopf, Inc., by Random House. Financing was chiefly done by public sale of stock, in most cases mergers being prompted by desire to expand in the textbook field.

1951–60. POETRY TRENDS. The 1950's were marked by the revival of lyrical verse and increasing examples of intellectual poetry—Conrad Aiken's *Selected Poems* (1953), Stephen Vincent Benét's *Western Star* (1943), Karl Shapiro's *Poems, 1942–53* (1953), W. H. Auden's *The Age of Anxiety* (1947), Peter Viereck's *Terror and Decorum* (1948) and *New Poems* (1952), Archibald MacLeish's *Collected Poems* (1953) and *J.B.* (poetic drama, 1957), Robert Penn Warren's *Promises* (1957), Stanley Kunitz's *Selected Poems* (1958), and E. E. Cummings' *Poems, 1923–54* (1954). The **"beat"** generation of postwar America was captured in free verse by Allen Ginsberg's **Howl** (1956) and reported by Jack Kerouac in his novel **On the Road** (1957).

NEWSPAPER AND PERIODICAL PRESS

1690–1736. HARRIS TO ZENGER. *Public Occurrences* (Boston; Benjamin Harris [fl.1673–1728]), suppressed by the government after 1 issue for critical comments on conduct of the war. First continuous colonial newspaper: Boston *News-Letter* (1704, John Campbell; discontinued, 1776), contained 1st illustration in colonial paper (19 Jan. 1708). Other papers: Boston *Gazette* (1719, William Brooker); Phila. *American Mercury* (1719, Andrew Bradford [1686–1742], employed Benj. Franklin; disc. 1749); *N.E. Courant* (1721, Boston, James Franklin; issued by brother Benjamin when editor jailed for criticizing government; disc. 1726); N.Y. *Gazette* (1725, William Bradford [1663–1752]; sold to James Parker, 1743, and merged with N.Y. *Post-Boy or Gazette*); *N.E. Weekly Journal* (1727, Samuel Kneeland; merged with Gazette, 1741); *Md. Gazette* (1727, William Parker (c.1698–1750); disc. 1734; revived, 1745, by Jonas Green; cont. to 1839); *Universal Instructor . . . and Pa. Gazette* (1728, Phila., Samuel Keimer; bought by **Benjamin Franklin**, 1729, continued as *Pa. Gazette;* David Hall proprietor after 1766; disc. 1815). *Weekly Rehearsal* (1731, Boston, Jeremy Gridley, forerunner of Boston *Eve. Post;* disc. 1775 after pursuing neutral course); *S.C. Gazette* (1732, Charleston, Thomas Whitmarsh with Franklin's support; later edited by Peter Timothy; became *Gazette of State of S.C.,* 1777; then *State Gazette of S.C.;* disc. 1802); *R.I. State Gazette* (1732, Newport, James Franklin, disc. 1773); N.Y. *Weekly Journal,* 5 Nov. 1733, **John Peter Zenger** (p. 805). For Zenger Trial (1734–35), in which Andrew Hamilton successfully argued that truth was a defense to seditious libel, see p. 805. Boston *Post-Boy* (1734), leading Tory organ. *Va. Gazette* (1736), Williamsburg, William Parks; disc. 1750; succeeded by 4 other weeklies of this name, in order: Hunter, 1751–78; Rind, 1766–76; Purdie, 1775–80; and Dixon & Nicholson, 1779–80.

1739–78. FOREIGN LANGUAGE PRESS. The 1st foreign language newspaper in the colonies was the Phila. *Zeitung* (1732, Benj. Franklin); it quickly expired. The most lasting were the Germantown *Zeitung* (1739, **Christopher Sower**, 1693–1758, later a Loyalist) and *Wöchentliche Philadelphische Staatsbote* (1762–79, Heinrich Miller).

1741–1775. EVE OF THE REVOLUTION. *American Magazine,* 1st magazine in the colonies (Jan. 1741, Phila., Andrew Bradford; disc. Mar. 1741); *General Magazine and Historical Chronicle* (Jan. 1741, Phila., Benjamin Franklin; disc. June 1741); *Pa. Journal* (1742, Phila., William Bradford, III; later *Patriot;* disc. 1793); N.Y. *Post-Boy* (1743, James Parker; disc. 1773); Boston *Weekly Museum* (1743, Gamaliel Rogers and John Fowle, disc. 1743); *Christian History* (1743, a weekly to report Great Awakening, disc. 1745); N.Y. *Eve. Post* (1744, Henry DeForest; disc. 1752); *American Magazine and Historical Chronicle* (1746, Boston, Rogers and Fowle; disc. Dec. 1746); *Independent Advertiser* (1748, Boston, Rogers and Fowle); N.Y. *Weekly Mercury* (1752, **Hugh Gaine** [1727–1807]; 2 editions published during Revolution—Loyalist in N.Y.; Patriot in Newark, N.J.); *Independent Reflector* (1752, James Parker; disc. 1753). *Pa. Gazette* carried 1st colonial cartoon (attributed to Franklin), depicting a cut-up snake and the caption: "Join or Die" (9 May 1754). Boston *Gazette* (1755, **Benjamin Edes** [1732–1803] and John Gill), leading Patriot organ, with such contributors as Sam and John Adams, Josiah Quincy, Jr., and Joseph Warren. *Conn. Gazette* (1755, New Haven, James Parker; disc. 1768); *N.H. Gazette* (1756, Portsmouth, **Daniel Fowle** [1715–87]), still published; *American Magazine and Monthly Chronicle* (1757. Phila., William Bradford, III, with Rev. William Smith, provost of College of Philadelphia, as editor), 1st well-edited colonial magazine; disc. 1757. *New American Magazine* (1758, Woodbridge, N.J., Judge Samuel Nevill; disc. 1760); Newport *Mercury* (1758, James Franklin, nephew of Benj. Franklin), still published; N.Y. *Gazette* (1759, William Weyman; merged with *Mercury,* 1768); *American Chronicle* (1762, New York, Samuel Farley; disc. July); Providence *Gazette* (1762, William Goddard; disc. 1825); *Ga. Gazette* (1763, James Johnston), Loyalist; published under British occupation during Revolution as *Royal Georgia Gazette,* 1779–82. N.Y. *Pacquet* (1763, Benjamin Mecom; disc. Aug.); *Connecticut Courant* (1764, Hartford, Thomas Green), still published); N.Y. *Journal or General Advertiser* (1766, **John Holt** [1721–84], Patriot organ published during Revolution in Kingston and Poughkeepsie; merged, 1793, with *Greenleaf's N.Y. Journal); Essex Gazette* (1768, Salem; removed to Cambridge 1775 as *N.E. Chronicle;* to Boston, 1776, as *Independent Chronicle;* cont. as *Semi-Weekly Advertiser,* 1840–76); N.Y. *Chronicle* (1769, James Robertson; disc. 1770); *Mass. Spy* (1770, Boston, **Isaiah Thomas** [p. 790]), Patriot; removed to Worcester, 3 May 1775, carrying story of Lexington and Concord; became Worcester *Gazette,* 1781). McDougall libel case (p. 79). *Pa. Packet* (1771, Phila., John Dunlap; disc. 1790); *Rivington's New York Gazetteer* (1773, **James Rivington** [1724–1802], Loyalist; disc. 1775, resumed, 1777, as *Loyal New York Gazette;* disc. 1783). *Royal Amer-*

ican Magazine (1774, Boston, Isaiah Thomas, Patriot; disc. Mar. 1775); *Pa. Magazine* (1775, Phila., Robert Aitken; **Thomas Paine** (p. 761) editor, Feb. 1775–May 1776; disc. July 1776).

1775. POLITICS AND CIRCULATION. There were 37 newspapers in the colonies (23 Patriot, 7 Loyalist, 7 neutral or doubtful in loyalty). Average weekly circulation rose from *c.*600 (1765) to as much as 3,500 (1775, *Mass. Spy*). Price ranged from 2s. 6d.–6s. per quarter. Phila. *Eve. Post* (1775, Benjamin Towne, later Loyalist; disc. 1784), 1st American daily, sold for 2d. an issue.

1776–89. N.Y. *Packet* (1776, **Samuel Loudon** [1727–1813]; pub. at Fishkill, Jan. 1777; returned to N.Y., 1783; became daily; disc. 1792). N.Y. *Evening Post* (1782, Christopher Sower *et al.;* became *Morning Post,* 1783; disc. 1792); *Boston Magazine* (1783, John Eliot, James Freeman, George R. Minot; disc. 1786); N.Y. *Independent Journal* (1783, semiweekly; later a daily as *Daily Gazette;* published *Federalist Papers;* disc. 1795); *Mass Centinel and Republican Journal* (1784, Boston, Benjamin Russell and William Warden, supported Constitution; as *Columbian Centinel,* beg. 1790, was a leading Federalist paper; disc. 1840). N.Y. *Daily Advertiser* (1785; disc. 1806); *New Haven Gazette and Connecticut Magazine* (1786, Josiah Meigs and Eleutheros Dana; disc. 1789); *Worcester Magazine* (1786, Isaiah Thomas; disc. 1788); *Columbian Magazine* (1786, Philadelphia, ed. by Mathew Carey *et al.;* merged 1790 with *Universal Asylum;* disc. 1792); *Pittsburgh Gazette* (1786, John Sculland and Joseph Hall; 1st newspaper west of the Alleghenies; Federalist; cont. after merger (1927) as *Post-Gazette*); *American Museum* (1787, Philadelphia, **Mathew Carey** [1760–1839]; disc. 1792; *American Magazine* (1787, New York, **Noah Webster** [1758–1843]; disc. 1788); *Gazette of the U.S.* (1789, New York; Phila. beg. 1790; **John Fenno** [1751–98]; leading Federalist organ; known, 1804–18, as *U.S. Gazette*).

1790–1860. NEWSPAPER GROWTH. There were 92 newspapers in U.S., 1790 —8 dailies, 70 weeklies, 14 semiweekly or at other intervals; 3,725 newspapers,

1860—387 dailies, 3,173 weeklies, 79 semiweeklies, 86 triweeklies.

1790–1804. FEDERALIST AND REPUBLICAN PRESS. *General Advertiser,* 1790, Phila., **Benjamin F. Bache** (1769–98); later (1794) known as *Aurora,* succeeding *National Gazette* as leading Republican organ; later ed. by **William Duane** (1760–1835); disc. 1835. *National Gazette,* 1791, Phila., ed. **Philip Freneau** (1752–1832), anti-Federalist; disc. 1793. *Mass. Mercury* (1793, Boston); known as *N.E. Palladium,* 1803–14. *N.H. Journal* (1793, Walpole, N.H.), best known beg. 1797 as *The Farmer's Weekly Museum,* a famous village weekly; **Joseph Dennie** (1768–1812) ed., 1796–99; shared literary column with **Royall Tyler** (1757–1826), beg. 1794; disc. 1810. *Centinel of the North-Western Territory* (1793, Cincinnati); 1st paper in present Ohio; later known as *Freeman's Journal;* merged with *Scioto Gazette* (Chillicothe), started by Nathaniel Willis; still published. *American Minerva* (1793, N.Y., **Noah Webster**), Federalist; became (1797) *Commercial Advertiser;* renamed *Globe and Commercial Advertiser,* 1904; absorbed by N.Y. *Sun,* 1923. Dunlap and Claypoole's *American Daily Advertiser,* 1793, Phila.; became (1800) *Poulson's American Daily Advertiser;* absorbed (1839) by the Phila. *North American.* N.Y. *Argus* (1795, Thomas Greenleaf, a Burr Republican; name changed, 1800, to *American Citizen).* *Federal Gazette* (1796, Baltimore; disc. 1825); *Porcupine's Gazette and U.S. Advertiser* (1797, Phila., **William Cobbett** [1763–1835], Federalist; disc. 1799). *Palladium* (1798, Frankfort, Ky., disc. *c.*1817). **Sedition Act** prosecutions, 1798 (p. 129). Baltimore *American* (1799). *Western Spy* (1799, Cincinnati; disc. 1822). Raleigh (N.C.) *Register* (1799, **Joseph Gales** [1761–1841]). *Washington Federalist* (1800, Georgetown; disc. 1809). Charleston (S.C.) *Times* (1800). *National Intelligencer* (1800, Washington, D.C.); purchased (1807) by **Joseph Gales, Jr.** (1786–1860); from 1812–60 by Gales and **William W. Seaton** (1785–1866); leading political organ (Whig); disc. 1869. N.Y. *Evening Post* (1801), **Alexander Hamilton** *et al.,* Federalist; **William Cullen Bryant** (p. 681), editor in

chief, 1829–78, supported Democratic party. Charleston (S.C.) *Courier* (1803); later as *News and Courier,* Unionist during Nullification. Richmond (Va.) *Enquirer* (1804), **Thomas Ritchie** (1778–1854) sole publisher in 1805; a leading Southern paper; disc. 1877. *Indiana Gazette* (1804, Vincennes) became (1807) *Western Sun;* later (1879) *Sun-Commercial.*

1804. CROSWELL LIBEL CASE. Harry Croswell, publisher of the Hudson (N.Y.) *Wasp,* convicted for a criminal libel upon President Jefferson. On appeal Alexander Hamilton, his counsel, reaffirmed and modified defense contention in Zenger case (p. 805), arguing that truth published "with good motives and justifiable ends" was a defense. Although **James Kent** (p. 737), then dominating the N.Y. Supreme Court, supported Hamilton, the motion for a new trial was denied by a divided court, but the prosecution was dropped. A N.Y. act of 6 Apr. 1805 adopting Hamilton's formula (incorporated into constitutions of 1821 and 1846) served as a model for the press guarantees of many state constitutions.

1806–20. WESTERN EXPANSION. *Western World* (1806, Frankfort, Ky., Joseph M. Street) exposed Burr Conspiracy (p. 135); disc. 1810. *Democratic Press* (1807, Phila.; disc. 1829). *Argus of Western America* (1808, Frankfort, Ky., **Amos Kendall** [1789–1869] coeditor, 1816–29; disc. *c.*1838). *Federal Republican* (1808, Baltimore); plant destroyed by mob for opposition to War of 1812; resumed, 1816; disc. 1834). *Mo. Gazette* (1808, St. Louis; disc. 1822). *N.H. Patriot* (1809, Concord, **Isaac Hill** [1789–1851], Democrat; disc. *c.*1921). *Mobile Centinel* (1811, Fort Stoddert, 1st paper in present Ala.). *Ohio State Journal* (1811, Columbus; daily since 1837). *Niles' Weekly Register* (1811, Baltimore, **Hezekiah Niles** [1777–1839], Whig, with a nationwide influence; distinguished for factual reporting; disc. 1849). Albany *Argus* (1813), later organ of the "Albany Regency," disc. *c.*1894. Boston *Daily Advertiser* (1813, Whig; disc. 1929). *Illinois Herald* (1814, Kaskaskia); 1st paper in Ill. Territory. *West-*

ern Journal (1815, St. Louis); later known as *Enquirer,* with **Thomas Hart Benton** (1782–1858) among early editors. *Ohio Monitor* (1816, Columbus); became (1838) *Ohio Statesman,* Democratic. Detroit *Gazette* (1817), 1st successful paper in present Michigan; disc. 1830. *Texas Republican* (1819, Nacogdoches); 1st English-language paper in Texas. *Arkansas Gazette,* 1819, Arkansas Post; removed (1822) to Little Rock. *National Gazette* (1820, Phila.; disc. 1842).

1820. Out of some 1,634 newspapers established between 1704 and 1820 only 4 had lasted 50 years or more.

1821–33. CONTINUED EXPANSION. Mobile *Register* (1821). Charleston *Mercury* (1822, Henry Laurens Pinckney ed., 1823–32; chief secessionist organ). Richmond *Whig,* 1824, **John H. Pleasants** (1797–1846); disc. 1888. Boston *Courier* (1824, **Joseph T. Buckingham** [1779–1861]; disc. 1864). *National Journal* (1824, Washington, D.C.; disc. 1832). *U.S. Telegraph* (1826, Washington; **Duff Green** [1791–1875]; chief Jackson organ until *c.*1831; disc. 1837). N.Y. *Morning Courier* (1827) became (1829) *Courier and Enquirer* (Whig) after merging with N.Y. *Enquirer;* **James Watson Webb** (1802–84); merged with *World* (1861). Baltimore *Republican* (1827; actually Democratic; disc. 1863); Cincinnati *Daily Gazette* (1827; disc. 1883). *Journal of Commerce* (1827, N.Y., **Arthur Tappan** [1786–1865]). *Cherokee Phoenix* (1828, New Echota, Ga.), Indian newspaper printed in characters devised by Sequoyah (?1770–1843); disc. 1835. *Pa. Inquirer* (1829; later Phila. *Inquirer*). Albany *Eve. Journal,* 1830, **Thurlow Weed** (1797–1882), Whig; disc. 1925. *Eve. Transcript* (1830, Boston, L. M. Walter, cultural organ; disc. 1941). Louisville (Ky.) *Journal,* 1830, **George D. Prentice** (1802–70); later (1868) merged with *Democrat* (1843) and *Courier* (1844) as *Courier-Journal,* ed. by **Henry Watterson** ("Marse Henry," 1840–1921). Washington *Globe,* 1830, **Francis P. Blair** (1791–1876); Jackson organ; disc. 1845. Boston *Morning Post* (1831; Democratic). Boston *Atlas* (1832; disc. 1861). *Pennsylvanian,* 1832, Phila., ed. for a time by John W. Forney (1817–81); leading Democratic

paper in state; disc. 1861. *Mercantile Journal* (1833, Boston); became *Eve. Journal,* 1845; absorbed (1917) by Boston *Herald.* *Weekly Democrat* (1833, Chicago; disc. 1861). Green Bay *Intelligencer* (1833; 1st paper in Wisconsin Territory; disc. *c.*1836).

1828–34. EARLY LABOR PRESS. *Mechanics' Free Press* (1828, Phila.; 1st labor paper in U.S.; disc. *c.*1835). *Working Man's Advocate,* 1829, N.Y., **George Henry Evans** (1805–56); disc. *c.*1851. *Man* (1834, N.Y., **George Henry Evans**; disc. 1835).

1834–56. GERMAN PRESS. New York *Staats-Zeitung* (1834, **Jacob Uhl**); tri-weekly, 1842; daily 1848; claimed largest German language circulation of any newspaper in the world. *Volksblatt* (1836, Cincinnati). There were 56 German newspapers in U.S., 1856.

1833–37. RISE OF THE PENNY PRESS. N.Y. *Sun,* 1833, **Benjamin H. Day** (1810–89); 1st successful penny daily in the U.S.; celebrated "Moon Hoax" appeared in its papers in 1835; in 1868 purchased by **Charles A. Dana** (1819–97) and others; absorbed (1950) by N.Y. *World-Telegram.* N.Y. *Transcript* (1834; disc. *c.*1839). N.Y. *Morning Herald,* 1835, **James Gordon Bennett** (p. 674); chief rival of *Sun;* pioneered in reporting crime and society news; following merger (1924), became *Herald Tribune.* Phila. *Public Ledger,* 1836; merged (1934) in the *Inquirer.* Boston *Daily Times,* 1836; merged (1857) with Boston *Herald.* Baltimore *Sun* (1837, Swain, Abell, and Simmons).

1835–60. ANTE-BELLUM EXPANSION. *Telegraph and Texas Register,* 1835, San Felipe; later Houston *Telegraph;* disc. 1877. *Union* (1835, Nashville, Tenn.; supported Polk's candidacy; disc. 1875). Detroit *Free Press* (1835). New Orleans *Picayune,* 1836, **George W. Kendall** (1809–67); noteworthy coverage of War with Mexico; later the *Times-Picayune.* N.Y. *Morning Express* (1836); Whig; disc. *c.*1864). Milwaukee *Advertiser* (1836; disc. 1841); Milwaukee *Sentinel,* 1837; became (1844) 1st daily in Wis. Phila. *North American* (1839; Whig; disc. 1925). N.Y. *Tribune,* 1841, **Horace Greeley** (p. 717); Whig-Republican; *Weekly Tribune,* 1841, with wider circulation especially in Northern rural areas; merger (1924) created *Herald Tribune.* Cincinnati *Commercial* (1843; disc. 1930). Springfield (Mass.) *Republican,* 1844, Whig, pioneer in independent journalism; est. as daily by **Samuel Bowles** (1826–77); previously a weekly since 1824; still published. *Plain Dealer* (1845, Cleveland, Ohio). New Orleans *Delta* (1845; disc. 1863). Rotary press invented by **Richard M. Hoe** (p. 727) revolutionized newspaper printing; 1st used (1847) by Phila. *Public Ledger. Oregon Spectator* (1846, Oregon City; 1st newspaper on Pacific Coast; disc. 1855). *Californian* (1846, Monterey); 1st newspaper in California; became (1849) the *Alta Californian,* 1st daily in California; disc. 1891. *Republican* (1847, Santa Fe); 1st successful paper in present New Mexico. Chicago *Daily Tribune,* 1847; under **Horace White** (1834–1916) supported Lincoln in 1856 and 1860; came under control of **Joseph Medill** (1823–99) in 1874. Toledo (Ohio) *Blade* (1848). New Orleans *Crescent* (1848; disc. 1869). Organization of a group of N.Y. newspapers later known as the **Associated Press** (1848). *Minnesota Pioneer* (1849, St. Paul; disc. 1875). *Deseret News* (1850, Salt Lake City). *Weekly Oregonian* (1850, Portland; became daily, 1861). N.Y. *Daily Times,* 1851, **Henry J. Raymond** (1820–69); Whig-Republican; became (1857) *The New York Times. Missouri Democrat* (1852, St. Louis, later *Globe-Democrat*). *Columbia* (1852, Olympia, Wash.); later *Washington Pioneer;* disc. 1861. St. Paul (Minn.) *Daily Pioneer,* 1854; later (1875) *Pioneer-Press. Nebraska Palladium* (1854, Bellevue, Neb.); 1st paper printed in Neb.; issued 1st number in Iowa. Chicago *Times* (1854; disc. 1895). *Kansas Weekly Herald* (1854, Leavenworth; disc. 1861). Two Free-Soil papers est. (1855) at Lawrence, Kan.: *Kansas Free State* and *Herald of Freedom;* latter disc. 1860. Proslavery *Squatter Sovereign* (1855, Atchison, Kan.); became (1858) *Freedom's Champion* and (1868) *Atchison Champion;* disc. 1917. San Francisco *Bulletin* (1855), **James King;** killed in 1856 for opposing lawlessness; later ed. by **Fremont Older** (1856–1935),

who fought political machine; merged (1929) by W. R. Hearst with San Francisco *Call* (founded 1856). *Territorial Enterprise* (1858, Genoa); later removed to Carson City and Virginia City; 1st newspaper in present-day Nev.; Mark Twain was reporter, 1862–63. Richmond *Examiner* (1859; disc. 1867); *Weekly Arizonian* (1859, Tubac; later removed to Tucson; disc. 1871). *Democrat* (1859, Sioux Falls, S.D.). Des Moines *Register* (1860). N.Y. *World* (1860, Alexander Cummings); sold 1 July 1861 to August Belmont and Fernando Wood, with **Manton Marble** (1835–1917) as editor (to 1867).

1801–60. PERIODICALS. 1801: *Port Folio* (Phila., **Joseph Dennie** [1768–1812]; a leading literary journal; disc. 1827). **1803:** *Mass. Baptist Missionary Mag.* (later *Amer. Baptist Mag.,* Boston, disc. 1909). *Literary Mag. and Amer. Reg.* (Phila., **Charles Brockden Brown** [1771–1810]; disc. 1807). **1808:** *Amer. Law Jl.* (Phila.; disc. 1817). **1813:** *Analectic Mag.* (later *Literary Gazette,* Phila.; disc. 1821). *Religious Remembrancer* (later *Christian Observer,* Phila.). **1815:** *North American Rev.* (Boston, **William Tudor** [1779–1830], a leading intellectual organ; other early editors included **Edward Everett** and **Jared Sparks;** disc. 1939). **1816:** *Portico* (Baltimore; disc. 1818); *Cobbett's Amer. Pol. Reg.* (N.Y.; disc. 1818). **1818:** *Methodist Mag.* (later *Methodist Rev.,* N.Y.). **1819.** *Amer. Farmer* (Baltimore; disc. 1897); *Universalist Mag.* (later *Universalist Leader*), Boston. **1821:** *Genius of Universal Emancipation* (Mt. Pleasant, Ohio, antislavery monthly, **Benjamin Lundy** [1789–1839]; disc. 1839); *Saturday Eve. Post* (Phila., Charles Alexander and Samuel C. Atkinson); claims descent from *Pa. Gazette,* founded, 1728; originally a newspaper, changed gradually to a weekly mag. by 1871. Bought 1897 by **Cyrus H. K. Curtis** (1850–1933). **1822:** *U.S. Catholic Miscellany* (Charleston; disc. 1832). *N.E. Farmer* (Boston; disc. 1846). **1823:** *Zion's Herald* (Boston); N.Y. *Mirror* (a leading weekly; disc. c.1857); *Christian Examiner* (Boston; disc. 1869). **1825:** *Biblical Repertory* (later *Princeton Rev.,* Princeton, N.J.; disc. 1884). *New Harmony Gazette* (later *Free Enquirer,* New Harmony, Ind.; disc. 1835). **1826:** *Amer. Jl. of Education* (later *Amer. Annals of Education,* Boston; disc. 1839). *Casket* (Phila.; disc. 1840); *Franklin Jl.* (later *Jl. of the Franklin Instit.,* Phila.); *Christian Advocate* (N.Y.). **1827:** *Amer. Qly. Rev.* (Phila.; disc. 1837). *Youth's Companion* (Boston; famous children's mag.; disc. 1929). **1828:** *Southern Agriculturalist* (Charleston; disc. 1846). *Southern Rev.* (Charleston; disc. 1832). **1829:** *Amer. Jurist and Law Mag.* (Boston; disc. 1843). **1830:** *Lady's Book* (later *Godey's Lady's Book,* Phila.; most important of early women's mags.; disc. 1898). **1831:** *The Liberator,* 1 Jan., Boston, abolitionist organ, **William Lloyd Garrison** (p. 713); disc. 29 Dec. 1865. *Biblical Repository* (Andover, Mass.; disc. 1850). *Spirit of the Times* (N.Y.; disc. 1861). **1833:** *Knickerbocker Mag.* (N.Y.; 1st popular monthly; **Lewis Gaylord Clark** [1808–73]; disc. 1865); *Parley's Mag.* (N.Y.; disc. 1844). **1834:** *Southern Literary Messenger* (Richmond; leading Southern mag.; Poe, Simms, Matthew F. Maury among contributors; disc. 1864). **1837:** *U.S. Mag. and Democratic Rev.* (Washington, D.C.; **John L. O'Sullivan** and Samuel D. Langstreet; later known as *Democratic Rev.;* jingoist; introduced term "Manifest Destiny" [p. 193]; disc. 1859). **1838:** *Pa. Freeman* (Phila., antislavery; disc. 1854). *Conn. Common School Jl.* (Hartford; disc. 1866). *Common School Jl.* (Boston; disc. 1852). **1839:** *Brother Jonathan* (N.Y.; disc. c.1845). *Merchants' Mag. and Commercial Rev.* (later *Hunts' Merchants' Mag.,* N.Y.; disc. 1870). *Dial* (Boston; Transcendentalist organ; edited 1st by **Margaret Fuller** [p. 703], then by **Ralph Waldo Emerson** [p. 711]; disc. 1844). *Lowell Offering* (Lowell, Mass.; printed contributions by young women mill operatives; disc. 1845). *Graham's Mag.* (Phila., **Edgar Allan Poe** lit. ed., 1841–42; disc. 1858). **1842:** *Pa. Law Jl.* (later *Amer. Law Jl.*), Phila.; disc. 1852. *Amer. Agriculturist* (N.Y., now Ithaca; oldest farm jl. still published). *Peterson's Ladies National Mag.* (Phila.; close competitor to *Godey's;* disc. 1898). **1843:** *New Englander* (later *Yale Rev.*), New Haven, Conn. **1844:** *Brownson's Qly. Rev.* (Boston; disc. 1875). *Littell's Living Age*

(Boston; disc. 1941). **1845:** *Amer. Rev.* (later *Whig Rev.,* N.Y.; disc. 1852). *Harbinger* (Brook Farm, West Roxbury, Mass., **George Ripley** (1802–80), Fourierist; disc. 1849); *Scientific American* (N.Y.). **1846:** *Commercial Rev. of the South and West* (later *De Bow's Rev.,* New Orleans; outstanding for economic coverage of ante-bellum South; disc. 1880). **1847:** *Natl. Era* (Washington, D.C., **Gamaliel Bailey** [1807–59], antislavery jl.; disc. 1860). **1848:** *The Independent* (N.Y.; disc. 1928). **1850:** *Harper's New Monthly Mag.* (later *Harper's Mag.*), N.Y.; circulation 200,000 by 1860. *Waverley Mag.* (Boston; disc. 1908). **1851:** *N.Y. Ledger* (**Robert Bonner** [1824–99], weekly; circulation 400,000 by 1860; disc. 1903). *Gleason's Pictorial Drawing-Room Companion* (Boston; 1st illustrated mag. in the U.S.; disc. 1859). **1852:** *Amer. Law Reg. and Rev.* (later *Univ. of Pa. Law Rev.,* Phila.). **1853:** *Putnam's Monthly Mag.* (N.Y.; disc. 1857). *Country Gentleman* (Albany; now Phila.). **1855:** *Amer. Jl. of Education* (N.Y.; disc. 1882). *Frank Leslie's Illustrated Newspaper* (later *Leslie's Weekly,* N.Y.; disc. 1922). **1856:** *Jl. of Agriculture* (St. Louis; disc. 1921). **1857:** *Atlantic Monthly* (Boston, **James Russell Lowell** [p. 744]). *Harper's Weekly* (N.Y., a news weekly; disc. 1916).

1861–65. NEWSPAPERS: CIVIL WAR.

The Northern press was divided in its support of the war. Only 5 out of 17 New York dailies were unquestionably loyal. To protect military secrets courtsmartial were authorized where news was released considered as aiding the enemy; telegraph wires from Washington were placed under State Dept. censorship. For open hostility to the war effort, the New York *Daily News* lost its postal privilege (Aug. 1861; suspended 18 mos.). The Columbus *Copperhead* (1861), the New York *Copperhead* (1863), and the Phila. *Eve. Journal* were suppressed for support of Vallandigham, and the Chicago *Times* and Phila. *Christian Observer* were seized by the Federal authorities.

1861–82. SYNDICATES AND PRESS ASSOCIATIONS.

First newspaper syndicate organized (1861) by Ansell N. Kellogg of the Baraboc (Wis.) *Republic,* providing "readyprint" for local papers. United Press organized (1882); expired 1893. A 2nd United Press founded (1907, below). McClure Newspaper Syndicate organized 1884 by Samuel S. McClure.

1864–96. NEWSPAPER CHANGES. St. Louis *Dispatch,* 1864; acquired by **Joseph Pulitzer** (p. 768) in 1848 and combined with St. Louis *Post,* est. by John A. Dillon, 1875. San Francisco *Chronicle* (1865, Charles and Michael De Young). Atlanta *Constitution* (1868, W. A. Hemphill). N.Y. *Sun* acquired (1868) by **Charles A. Dana** (1819–97). Its issue of 8 Nov. 1876 (Hayes-Tilden election story) had record sale of 220,000 copies. Sold to *World-Telegram,* 1950. *Public Record* (Phila., 1870, W. J. Swain). Boston *Globe* (1872, Maturin Ballou; eve. ed. begun 1877). **Whitelaw Reid** (1837–1912) succeeded Horace Greeley (1872) as editor of N.Y. *Tribune.* N.Y. *Daily Graphic* (1873; featuring news pictures; disc. 1889). Chicago *Daily News,* 1876, **Melville E. Stone** (1848–1929). Washington *Post* (1877; sold to John R. McLean 1905). Kansas City *Star* (1880, W. R. Nelson). N.Y. *Eve. Post* sold (1881) to **Henry Villard** (1835–1900), with Carl Schurz (p. 776) as editor. **Edwin L. Godkin** (p. 715) became editor in chief, 1883. N.Y. *Morning Journal* (1882, Albert Pulitzer); sold, 1884, to John R. McLean; **William Randolph Hearst** (1863–1951) became owner in 1895; merged with N.Y. *Eve. Jl.* (1937) to become *Journal-American.* N.Y. *World* acquired by Joseph Pulitzer. News coverage innovations, editorials, and 2-ct. price boosted circulation from 20,000 (1883) to 250,000 (1886). N.Y. *Eve. World* (1887, S.S. Carvallo; disc. 1931). Ownership of San Francisco *Examiner* (1865) transferred (1887) from George Hearst to his son, **William Randolph Hearst.** Emporia *Gazette* (1890); acquired, 1895, by **William Allen White** (1868–1944), whose editorials, e.g., "What's the Matter with Kansas?" (1896) were nationally read. **Adolph S. Ochs** (p. 760) acquired (1896) the N.Y. *Times.*

1880–1914. Daily circulation of German papers in St. Louis (1880) amounted to 21% of aggregate; in New York, 10%; in Cincinnati, 28%, with 80 German dailies, 466 weeklies, and 95 other German periodicals. In addition: 13 Bohemian periodicals, 49 Scandinavian, 41 French, 26 Spanish, 4 Italian, 5 Welsh. *Jewish Daily Forward* (N.Y., 1897), ed. **Abraham Cahan** (1860–1951). There were 1,300 foreign language newspapers and periodicals in the U.S., 1914; 140 dailies (one third German). New York had 32 (including 10 German, 5 Yiddish, 3 Italian).

1897–1933. CHAIN NEWSPAPER ERA (paralleling trends in industry and merchandising) was inaugurated with the organization (1897) by Edward Wyllis Scripps and Milton Alexander McRae of the Scripps-McRae League of Newspapers; Scripps-McRae Press Assn., 1897. Together with the Publisher's Press (1904), it was the forerunner of the 2nd **United Press** (1907). Between 1892–1914 the Scripps chain had a controlling interest in 13 newspapers, acquired principally by establishing new papers in smaller cities. With the addition of Roy W. Howard to the board in 1922 the organization became the Scripps-Howard chain. The **Munsey Chain** began (1901) with the purchase by Frank A. Munsey of the Washington *Times* and N.Y. *Daily News,* followed by the acquisition of the Boston *Journal* (1902), the Baltimore *Evening News* (1908), and the Philadelphia *Eve. Times* (1908). The **Hearst Chain** acquired 30 papers (1913–34) in addition to control of 2 wire services, the King Features Syndicate, 6 magazines, a newsreel, and the *American Weekly* (a Sunday supplement). The 5 other leading chains (1933, Patterson-McCormick, Scripps-Howard, Paul Block, Ridder, and Gannett) controlled 81 dailies, with combined total circulation of 9,250,000.

1897–1907. COMIC STRIPS appeared in the comic weeklies of the 70's and 80's; color sequence in the N.Y. *Sunday World* (1894). Real origin dates from Rudolph Dirks' "Katzenjammer Kids" (N.Y. *Journal,* 1897). First 6-days-a-week strip was H. C. "Bud" Fisher's "A. Mutt" (San Francisco *Chronicle,* 1907); later "Mutt and Jeff."

1898. SPANISH-AMERICAN WAR. N.Y. *Journal* and *World* outdistanced all other "yellows" in agitating for U.S. intervention in Cuba as well as in coverage of the war.

1908–12. JOURNALISM SCHOOLS. School of Journalism est. at University of Missouri (1908; courses offered as early as 1878). Columbia University School of Journalism est. (1912) by a bequest from Joseph Pulitzer.

1917. PULITZER PRIZE AWARDS inaugurated by the trustees of Columbia University, granted on recommendation of the Advisory Board of the Columbia School of Journalism. Awards have been made to newspapers for meritorious public service and to working newspapermen in various branches of journalism. In addition, awards are made for (1) novel, (2) drama, (3) U.S. history, (4) biography, (5) poetry, (6) music.

1918. The *Stars and Stripes* published by the American Expeditionary Force in France; disc. 1919; revived in Washington, D.C., 1919–26.

1919–24. TABLOIDS. The N.Y. *Daily News* est. by the McCormick-Patterson chain. A tabloid featuring sensational news, crime, and sex stories, it attained the largest daily circulation in the U.S. in 1924 (1,750,000). By 1944, 2 million daily, 4 million Sundays. Its success led to the establishment in 1924 of the N.Y. *Daily Mirror* by W. R. Hearst and the *Daily Graphic* by Bernarr Macfadden.

1940. *PM* (N.Y., Marshall Field; disc. 1946).

1941. Chicago *Sun* (Marshall Field).

1942–45. ARMY PAPERS. *Stars and Stripes* est. as a weekly (17 Apr.; a daily by 2 Nov.; coined phrase "GI Joe"). *Yank*, 24-page weekly tabloid est., with ultimately 21 editions in various war theaters.

1944, Nov. Thomas E. Dewey was supported for President by 796 newspapers (68.5% of total circulation); 291 (17.7% of circulation) supported F. D. Roosevelt (lowest press support since Bryan's campaign against McKinley, 1896). Similarly proportionate press support for Dewey v. Truman, 1948, and Eisenhower v. Stevenson, 1952.

1949, 1 Oct. There were 1,780 dailies with a circulation of 52,845,551; 546 Sunday papers with a circulation of 46,-498,968 (*Editor and Publisher*).

1862–1900. PERIODICALS. 1862: *The Old Guard* (N.Y., C. Chauncey Burr; Copperhead; disc. 1870). **1863:** *Army and Navy Jl.* (N.Y., William Conant Church, ed., 1863–1917). **1865:** *The Catholic World* (N.Y., Paulist Fathers). *The Nation* (N.Y., weekly jl. of politics, literature, science and the arts); first ed., E. L. Godkin (p. 715), to 1881; later eds. include **Oswald Garrison Villard** (1918–32), **Joseph Wood Krutch** (1933–37), and **Freda Kirchwey** (since 1933). **1866:** *The Galaxy* (N.Y., monthly literary mag., William Conant Church and Francis Pharcellus; disc. 1878). **1867:** *The Southern Rev.* (Baltimore, Albert Taylor Bledsoe; disc. 1879). *Jl. of Speculative Philosophy* (St. Louis, **William Torrey Harris**; disc. 1893). *Harper's Bazaar* (N.Y., weekly women's mag.; Fletcher Harper; became monthly, 1901; purchased by Hearst, 1913). **1868:** *Overland Monthly* (San Francisco; California regional mag., **Bret Harte**, ed.; suspended 1876–82; cont. again until 1935). *Lippincott's Mag.* (Phila., literary monthly; John Foster Kirk ed. until 1884; 1915 moved to N.Y. as *McBride's Mag.;* merged with *Scribner's Mag.,* 1916). *Vanity Fair* (N.Y., ed. for a time by **Frank Harris**; absorbed by *Vogue,* 1936, a woman's fashion mag.). **1869:** *Appleton's Jl.* (N.Y., literary weekly; became monthly 1876; disc. 1881). **1870:** *Christian Union* (N.Y., "family mag.," Henry Ward Beecher and Lyman Abbott; name changed, 1893, to *The Outlook,* with more emphasis on political commentary; disc. 1935). *Scribner's Monthly* (N.Y., literary jl., ed., Josiah G. Holland); after absorbing *Putnam's* (1870), it was continued as the *Century* (1881); merged 1930 with *The Forum* (est. 1886), with **Walter Hines Page**, ed., a mag. of controversy; merged with *Current History* (1940). **1872:** *Publisher's Weekly* (N.Y., Frederick Leypoldt); *Popular Science Monthly* (N.Y., Edward L. Youmans). **1873:** *The Delineator* (N.Y., E. Butterick & Co., fashion mag.; later of general circulation; disc. 1937). *Woman's Home Companion* (Cleveland, Ohio, originally a semimonthly under name of *Home Companion;* since 1897 a monthly). *St. Nicholas* (N.Y., children's mag.; ed. 1873–1905 by Mrs.

Mary Mapes Dodge; disc. 1940). **1876:** *Frank Leslie's Popular Monthly* (N.Y., name changed, 1906, to *The American Mag.*, published by a group of muckraking authors including Ida Tarbell, Lincoln Steffens, *et al.*). **1877:** *Puck* (N.Y., a comic mag., Joseph Keppler and A. Schwarzmann; disc. 1912). **1880:** *The Dial* (Chicago, conservative rev.; became fortnightly 1892, when it was moved to N.Y. as a radical jl. of opinion and chief of the "little magazines"; eds. included **Conrad Aiken, Randolph Bourne, Van Wyck Brooks**; disc. 1929). **1881:** *The Critic* (N.Y., weekly literary rev.; Jeannette and Joseph Gilder; disc. 1906). *Judge* (N.Y., comic weekly by authors and artists who seceded from *Puck;* disc. 1939). **1883:** *Ladies Home Jl.* (Phila., monthly; **Cyrus H. K. Curtis;** popularized by its 2nd ed., **Edward W. Bok** [1863–1930], ed. 1899–1920). **1884:** *The Christian Century* (Chicago). *The Journalist* (N.Y.; 1st professional mag. for journalists; consolidated 1907 with *Editor and Publisher*). **1887:** *Scribner's Mag.* (N.Y., literary jl.; purchased 1939 by *The Commentator* and renamed *Scribner's Commentator*). *The Cosmopolitan* (Rochester, a conservative family monthly; but removed to N.Y., 1887, and became popular mag.; after 1900 entered muckraking movement; purchased by Hearst, 1925). **1888:** *Collier's* (N.Y., weekly; under ed. of **Norman Hapgood** [1903–12] and **Mark Sullivan** [1914–17] was a leading liberal-muckraking publication). **1889:** *The Arena* (Boston, Benjamin O. Flower; 1st muckraking periodical; disc. 1909). *Life* (N.Y. humor mag., featuring **Charles Dana Gibson**, and his "Gibson Girl"; disc., 1936, when its title was acquired by a news weekly. *Munsey's Mag.* (N.Y., Frank A. Munsey; merged 1929 with *Argosy All-Story Weekly*). **1890:** *The Literary Digest* (N.Y., newspaper and mag. of comment; its straw poll erroneously predicting the election of Landon in 1936 contributed to its demise, 1938). *Smart Set* (N.Y., jl. of society; Mencken and Nathan, eds., 1914–24, when purchased by Hearst; disc. 1930). **1891:** *Review of Reviews* (N.Y., monthly of comments on events; **Albert Shaw** ed. from 1894; merged with *Literary Digest* 1937).

1893: *McClure's Mag.* (N.Y., S. S. McClure; merged, 1929, with *New Smart Set*). **1899:** *Everybody's Mag.* (N.Y., absorbed by *Romance,* 1929). **1900:** *World's Work* (N.Y., monthly record of current events; **Walter Hines Page;** absorbed, 1932, by *Rev. of Revs.*).

1905–16. 1905: *Variety* (N.Y., theatrical trade jl., Sime Silverman, 1873–1933). **1911.** *Masses* (N.Y., proletarian monthly; superseded, 1918, by *The Liberator; New Masses,* 1926). **1912:** *Poetry* (Chicago, **Harriet Monroe,** organ for new trends in poetry). **1914:** *New Republic* (N.Y., Herbert Croly and **Walter Lippmann**). *The Little Rev.* (Chicago, moving to N.Y. and then Paris; best known for its serialization of Joyce's *Ulysses;* disc. 1929). **1916:** *Theater Arts Mag.* (N.Y., qly. jl., cont. since 1924 as *Theatre Arts Monthly*).

1922–36. 1922: *The Reader's Digest* (Pleasantville, N.Y., condensation of reprints of other periodicals, **De Witt Wallace;** circulation, 1944, exceeded 9 million, with another 4 million among its foreign editions). **1923:** *Time* (N.Y., news weekly, **Henry R. Luce** and Briton Hadden). **1924:** *American Mercury* (N.Y., critical and literary, H. L. Mencken and **George Jean Nathan**). *The Saturday Rev. of Literature* (N.Y., **Henry Seidel Canby** ed. to 1936). **1925:** *The New Yorker* (N.Y., weekly humorous mag. for the "caviar sophisticates"; **Harold Wallace Ross** [1892–1951]). **1930:** *Fortune* (N.Y., monthly mag. of business, finance, and industry; **Henry R. Luce**). **1933:** *Newsweek* (N.Y., news mag.). *Esquire* (N.Y., monthly, short stories and humorous illustrations). **1936:** *Life* (N.Y., **Henry R. Luce,** news and features through photos).

1951, 30 June (period ending). INROADS OF COMICS revealed by the net paid circulation of leading U.S. magazines (A.B.C. Publishers' statements):

Marvel Comic Group	11,057,832
Reader's Digest (in excess of)	8,500,000
National Comics Group	7,906,688
Harvey Comics Group	5,458,861
Life	5,301,331
True Story Women's Group	5,068,968
Ladies' Home Journal	4,458,219
McCall's	4,011,643
Woman's Home Companion	3,992,005
Woman's Day	3,866,062

Fawcett Comic Group 3,569,927
Archie Comic Group 3,569,927
Better Homes and Gardens 3,563,856
Look 3,260,927

1954, 27 Oct. Adoption of comic book code to be voluntarily enforced by 26 publishing firms to bar vulgar, obscene, and terror comics. By 1955, 13 states had passed laws to police comics.

1952–60. PERIODICAL TRENDS. While a few new periodicals quickly achieved success (*TV Guide, Confidential,* 1952; *Sports Illustrated, American Herit-*

age, 1954), the long-term trend was toward mergers and discontinuance. In 1956 *Collier's, American,* and *Woman's Home Companion* ended publication, followed (1957) by *Town Journal* (successor, 1953, to *Pathfinder*), *Omnibook,* and *Étude.*

1953, 28 Nov.–8 Dec. 11-day strike of photoengravers left New York City without a major daily newspaper for 1st time since 1778.

1958. United Press Assn. and Intl. News Service merged to form United Press Intl.

THE THEATER, MOTION PICTURES, AND TV

1665. *Ye Bare and Ye Cubb,* the 1st English play known to have been performed in the colonies, was written and produced by 3 amateurs of Accomac Co., Va.; prosecuted but acquitted.

1714. *Androborus,* a satirical farce by Gov. Robert Hunter (N.Y., d.1734), printed but not produced.

1716. First theater in the colonies was erected at Williamsburg. Foreclosed 1723, it became the Town Hall in 1745.

1749–50. First American acting company was organized in Philadelphia by Thomas Kean and Walter Murray. Staged Addison's *Cato.* The company opened in New York (1750) in *Richard III* with Kean in the title role. Fourteen other Shakespearean plays were produced in the colonies. In addition to *Richard III,* the most popular were *King Lear* and *Katharine and Petruchio* (*The Taming of the Shrew*). The Kean-Murray company's New York repertoire included 24 plays (by Addison, Cibber, Congreve, Dryden, Farquhar, Fielding, Garrick, Lillo, and Otway). The company also performed in Williamsburg, Fredericksburg, and Annapolis.

1752. HALLAM COMPANY, sent to America by William Hallam and headed by his brother, **Lewis,** opened at Williamsburg with *The Merchant of Venice.* This company had a repertoire of over 40 plays, chiefly from Elizabethan and Restoration dramatists. Played also in New York and Philadelphia; disbanded in Jamaica, 1754.

1758. David Douglass, organizer of the

American Company, opened in New York with Rowe's *Jane Shore.*

1766. Southwark Theater in Philadelphia, the 1st permanent theater built in the colonies, opened with Shakespeare's *Katharine and Petruchio.*

Ponteach; or The Savages of America, by Maj. **Robert Rogers;** 1st tragedy written on a native subject; unproduced.

1767. *The Prince of Parthia,* a tragedy (written before 1763) by **Thomas Godfrey** (1736–63), pioneer American dramatist, performed at Southwark Theater, Philadelphia; 1st native play to be professionally staged.

1775–83. REVOLUTIONARY THEATER. During the war most theatrical companies moved to Jamaica. Resolutions of the Continental Congress (24 Oct. 1774 and 12 Oct. 1778) recommended legislation prohibiting public entertainments. However, regular performances were given by the British troops in occupied towns. Howe's Thespians, an amateur group directed by Surgeon General Beaumont, opened its season in New York in 1777 and in Philadelphia in 1778. Clinton's Thespians gave their 1st performance at the John Street Theater (built 1767), New York, and continued intermittently until 1782. A number of propaganda plays were written in this period. Tory plays included *A Dialogue between a Southern Delegate and His Spouse on His Return from the Grand Continental Congress* (anon., 1774), Jonathan Mitchell Sewell's *Cure for the Spleen,* and General Burgoyne's *The Blockade of Boston* (both in 1775). The Patriot playwrights included Mrs. **Mercy Warren** (1728–1814), whose 1st play, *The Adulateur,* a satire on Gov. Hutchinson (1773), was followed by *The Group* (1775), based on the revocation of the Mass. charter (neither play produced). Other Patriot plays included *The Fall of British Tyranny* (1776), attributed to John or Joseph Leacock (1776); an anonymous farce, *The Blockheads* (1776); and 3 plays by **Hugh Henry Brackenridge** (1748–1816), *The Battle of Bunker's Hill* (1776), *The Rising Glory of America* (1771), and *The Death of General Montgomery* (1777).

1787. *The Contrast,* by **Royall Tyler** (1757–1826; later chief justice of Vt.), the 1st American comedy to be produced by a professional company, performed in New York.

1789–97. EARLY AMERICAN PLAYWRIGHTS of this period included **William Dunlap** (1766–1839)—*The Father, or American Shandyism* (1789), *The Fatal Deception* (1794; published, 1806, as *Leicester*) and *Fontainville Abbey,* a Gothic drama (1795); **Samuel Low**—*The Politician Outwitted,* Federalist satire, published 1789; **Susanna Haswell Rowson** (*c.*1762–1824)—*Slaves in Algiers* (1794) and *The Volunteers,* a play dealing with the Whisky Insurrection (1795); **John Daly Burk** (*c.*1775–1808)—*Bunker Hill,* patriotic drama (1797); **Royall Tyler**—*A Georgia Spec, or Land in the Moon,* based on the Yazoo land frauds (1797).

1797. The tragedy *Douglas,* performed at Washington, Ky., the 1st recorded performance of an English-language drama west of the Alleghenies.

1799. NEGRO MINSTRELSY. At the close of the 2nd act of *Oroonoko,* a play produced in Boston, Gottlieb Graupner, said to have been made up in Negro character, sang "The Gay Negro Boy," accompanying himself on the banjo; one of the earliest known origins of Negro minstrelsy, subsequently developed and popularized by Andrew Jackson Allen, Thomas Dartmouth Rice, Bob Farrell, and George Washington Dixon.

1806–18. Leading American playwrights included **John Howard Payne** (1791–1852)—*Julia, or the Wanderer* (1806, at New York's leading theater, Park Theater, built, 1798; destroyed by fire, 1820);

Payne wrote 64 plays; including *Brutus, or the Fall of Tarquin,* a tragedy produced at the Drury Lane, London (1818; N.Y., 1819). **James Nelson Barker** (1784–1858)—*Tears and Smiles* (1807); *The Indian Princess,* 1st Indian play by a native American to be performed (Philadelphia, 1808); its production at the Drury Lane, London (1820), under the title of *Pocahontas,* made it the 1st American play performed overseas after initial production at home; *Marmion,* based on Scott's poem (1812).

1817–32. ACTING DEBUTS. Noah Miller Ludlow (1795–1886), a leading figure in the theatrical history of the West, embarked on his career as actor-manager (1817); **Edwin Forrest** (p. 708), 1st native-born actor to attain top rank, made his debut at the Walnut Street Theater, Philadelphia, as Young Norval in the tragedy *Douglas* (1820); **Edmund Kean** (1787–1833), the English tragedian, made his American debut in New York as Richard III (1820); **Junius Brutus Booth** (1796–1852), English actor, made his American debut at the Richmond (Va.) Theater as Richard III (1821). **James H. Hackett** (1800–71) made his New York debut in *Love in a Village* (1826); **William Charles Macready** (1793–1873), English actor, made his American debut at the Park Theater, N.Y., in the role of Virginius (1826); **Fanny Kemble** (1809–93), British actress, made her American debut at the Park Theater, N.Y., as Bianca in *Fazio.*

1823–35. Notable American plays of this period included *Clari, or The Maid of Milan,* by John Howard Payne (1823, Covent Garden, London; N.Y., 1823; included the song "Home, Sweet Home"); *Superstition,* James Nelson Barker's best play (1824); *Charles the Second, or the Merry Monarch,* a comedy by John Howard Payne in collaboration with Washington Irving (London and N.Y., 1824); *Metamora, or the Last of the Wampanoags,* a tragedy by **John Augustus Stone** (1800–34), N.Y., 1829; 1st surviving dramatization of Rip Van Winkle by John Kerr (1829); *The Triumph of Plattsburgh,* by **Richard Penn Smith** (1799–1854), a play celebrating McDonough's victory in 1814 (1830); *Pocahontas,* by **George Washington Parke**

Custis (1781–1857), 1830; *The Gladiator,* by **Robert Montgomery Bird** (1806–54), a drama of democracy, including antislavery sentiments (1831); *The Broker of Bogota,* a domestic tragedy by Bird (1834); *Jack Cade,* a play by Robert T. Conrad, dealing with a Kentish peasant uprising in 1450.

1828. The minstrel character and song, *Jim Crow,* introduced in Louisville, Ky., by **Thomas Dartmouth ("Daddy") Rice** (1808–60).

1832. Publication of *A History of the American Theatre* by **William Dunlap,** a pioneer work.

1836. CHARLOTTE CUSHMAN (p. 692), American tragedienne and 1st native-born actress to attain top rank, made her New York debut (1836) at the Bowery Theater (opened 1826) as Lady Macbeth.

1837–48. Notable American plays included *Bianca Visconti* (1837), tragedy by **Nathaniel P. Willis** (1806–67), and Willis' romantic comedy, *Tortesa the Usurer* (1839); *The People's Lawyer* (1839), by **Joseph Stevens Jones** (1809–77), with the central character the Yankee type, Solon Shingle; *Fashion* (1845), an outstandingly popular social comedy by Mrs. **Anna Cora Mowatt** (1819–70); *Witchcraft, or The Martyrs of Salem* (1846), historical drama by **Cornelius Mathews** (1817–89); *The Bucktails; or, Americans in England* (pub., 1847), a satirical play by **James Kirke Paulding** (1778–1860); *A Glance at New York* (1848), one of the 1st "city" plays, by **Benjamin A. Baker** (1818–90).

1842. PHINEAS T. BARNUM (p. 672) opened Barnum's American Museum at New York.

1843. Virginia Minstrels, a quartette that included **Daniel Decatur Emmett** (1815–1904), appeared at the Masonic Temple, Boston, in what is regarded as the 1st accurately dated public performance of a genuine full-length minstrel show. Among the popular minstrel companies of the following 2 decades were the Dixie Minstrels, the Columbia Minstrels, the Christy Minstrels, Bryant's Minstrels, White's Serenaders, the Congo Minstrels, the Kentucky Rattlers, and the Nightingale Serenaders.

1849, 10 May. ASTOR PLACE RIOT, which took lives of 22 persons and caused injuries to 36 others, occurred outside the Astor Place Opera House, New York City. A manifestation of revived anti-British sentiment, it involved the partisans of Edwin Forrest and William Charles Macready.

1849–60. Notable plays included *Calaynos,* a tragedy by **George Henry Boker** (1823–90), produced at the Sadler's Wells Theater, London (1849); in the U.S., 1851. Other plays of Boker: *The Betrothal,* a comedy (1850); *Leonor de Guzman,* a tragedy (1853); *Francesca da Rimini,* a tragedy and his most highly esteemed work (1855). In addition, *Uncle Tom's Cabin* (1852), dramatized by **George L. Aiken** (1830–76); *Ten Nights in a Bar Room* (1858), a play by William W. Pratt based on the novel of Timothy Shay Arthur.

1849–60. NOTABLE DEBUTS. Edwin Booth (p. 678) at the Boston Museum as Tressel in Cibber's version of *Richard III* (1849); **Joseph Jefferson** (1829–1905) at the National Theater, N.Y., as Jack Rackbottle in *Jonathan Bradford* (1849); **Lola Montez** (1818–61), American debut in *Betty the Tyrolean* at the Broadway Theater, N.Y.; **Edward Askew Sothern** (1826–81), American debut at National Theater, Boston, as Dr. Pangloss in *The Heir at Law;* achieved fame as Lord Dundreary in *Our American Cousin* (1858); **Laura Keene** (*c.*1826–73), British actress, made her American debut at Wallack's Theater, N.Y.; subsequently became the 1st woman manager in the U.S. **Dion Boucicault** (1820–90), Irish actor-playwright, made his American debut at the Old Broadway Theater as Sir Charles Coldstream in his own farce, *Used Up;* several of his plays produced in this period, including *The Poor of New York* (1857), *The Octoroon* (1859), *The Colleen Bawn* (1860); organized the **road show** (1860). **Lotta Crabtree** (1847–1924) made her 1st stage appearance at the mining camp of Rabbit Creek, Calif.

1856. First copyright law passed protecting dramatists against literary piracy.

1861–1900. VOGUE OF DION BOUCICAULT. After 1860 his most important plays included *Arrah-no-Pogue* (London, 22 Mar. 1865), *The Shaugh-*

raun (New York, 14 Nov. 1874), and the revision of Charles Burke's version of Washington Irving's *Rip Van Winkle* (London, 4 Sept. 1865).

1867–75. IMPACT OF (JOHN) AUGUSTIN DALY (1838–99), both as playwright and theatrical manager. His 1st play was *Leah the Forsaken* (1862). *Under the Gaslight* (a realistic drama of New York life) produced in New York 12 Aug. 1867. Original plays include *Divorce* (5 Sept. 1870), *Horizon* (25 Mar. 1871), and *Pique* (14 Dec. 1875). Daly organized a stock company (1867) and opened his own theater in New York, 1869, starring **John Drew** (1853–1927), Adelaide Neilson (1848–1880), and **Maurice Barrymore** (1847–1905).

1870–89. COMEDY OF MANNERS. The influence of the French drama was reflected in the popular plays of **Bronson Howard** (1842–1908), including *Saratoga* (21 Dec. 1870), *The Banker's Daughter* (30 Sept. 1870), *The Young Mrs. Winthrop* (9 Oct. 1882), *The Henrietta* (26 Sept. 1887), and *Shenandoah*, the 1st successful drama of the Civil War (9 Sept. 1887). Other exponents of the social comedy form were **Augustus Thomas** (1875–1934), whose most notable plays include *Alabama,* a romance of Reconstruction (1891); *In Mizzoula* (1893); *The Earl of Pawtucket* (1903); *Mrs. Leffingwell's Boots* (1905); *The Witching Hour* (1907), the 1st of his realistic dramas; *The Harvest Moon* (1909); *As a Man Thinks* (1911); and *The Copperhead* (1919), starring Lionel Barrymore; and **William Clyde Fitch** (1865–1909), with his 1st success, *Beau Brummel* (1890), written for Richard Mansfield. His 30 plays include *The Climbers* (1901); *The Girl with the Green Eyes* (1902), generally considered his best play; *Truth Again* (1907); *The City* (1909). Best known of his 17 adaptations was *Sappho*.

1872–79. THE WEST IN THE DRAMA. *Davy Crockett* (1872), a frontier drama by **Frank Hitchcock Murdock**; Daly's *Big Bonanza* (1875), satire on speculation; Bret Harte's *The Two Men of Sandy Bat* (1876); Joaquin Miller's *The Danites in the Sierras* (1877); Bartley Campbell's *My Partner* (1879).

1880–1930. ERA OF THE THEATRICAL MANAGER. Dramatist, actor, and producer, **David Belasco** (1854–1931) wrote or adapted 75 plays and made pioneer contributions to realistic staging. His successful plays include *The Darling of the Gods* (1902), *Madam Butterfly* (1900, in collaboration with John Luther Long), *The Return of Peter Grimm* (1911), and *The Girl of the Golden West* (1905). Coming to New York in 1880, he became stage manager of the Madison Sq. Theater, was later an associate of Daniel Frohman, and opened the Belasco Theater in 1902. Other notable theatrical managers of the period include **Charles Frohman** (1860–1915), who organized a stock company in 1890, opened the Empire Theater in 1893, and formed in 1896 the 1st theatrical syndicate, including Sam Nixon, Fred Zimmerman, Al Hayman, Marc Klaw, and Abraham Erlanger, who gradually extended its control throughout the U.S. From 1897 until his death (on the *Lusitania*) Frohman was the leading American manager, placing emphasis upon the "star system" (Maude Adams, Ethel Barrymore, and Otis Skinner) and the productions of established British dramatists. His brother, **Daniel Frohman** (1851–1940), opened the Lyceum Theater, N.Y. (1885), and was an exponent of the stock company. More commercialized was the impact of J. J., Lee, and Sam S. Shubert, who, beginning with the Herald Sq. Theater, N.Y., controlled some 70 theaters in N.Y. and other principal cities by 1924. During the period 1905–13 a **vaudeville empire** was erected by Benjamin F. Keith and Edward F. Albee, although the most conspicuously successful managers in that field were Oscar and William Hammerstein. Marcus Loew and William Fox rapidly accumulated theater chains.

1880–92. EARLY REALISM was exemplified in the plays of **James A. Herne** (1839–1901), notably his *Hearts of Oak* (1880), with David Belasco; *Margaret Fleming* (1890); and *Shore Acres* (1892).

1895–1913. Notable plays at the turn of the century included **William Gillette's** (1855–1937) *Secret Service* (1895), a Civil War theme, and *Sherlock Holmes* (1899); **William Vaughan Moody's** (1869–1910) *The Great Divide* (1906);

Langdon Mitchell's (1862–1935) *The New York Idea* (1906), critical of the marriage institution; **Eugene Walter's** (1874–1941) *The Easiest Way* (1909); and **Edward Sheldon's** (1886–1946) *The Nigger* (1909), *The Boss* (1911), and *Romance* (1913), with Doris Keane as Madame Cavallini.

1900–19. LITTLE-THEATER MOVEMENT. The 1st "little theater" in the U.S. was constructed (1900) for the Hull House Players, Chicago; the 1st in the academic world was **G. P. Baker's** (1866–1935) *47 Workshop* at Harvard (1912), later at Yale. Civic theaters developed rapidly, beginning (1919) with the Théâtre du Vieux Carré in New Orleans.

1908–48. MUSICALS. *The Black Crook* (1866) was the 1st long-run musical extravaganza produced in the U.S. **Florenz Ziegfeld** (1869–1932) originated a series of revues called the *Ziegfeld Follies,* featuring beautiful girls ("glorifying the American girl"), scenic invention, and comic sketches, and including such actors as W. C. Fields, Eddie Cantor, Fannie Brice, and Bert Williams. The **musical comedy,** a highly developed form in the U.S., combining opera, comedy, and ballet, flourished in the early 1900's with *The Merry Widow* and *The Chocolate Soldier,* but major innovations appeared in the 1920's largely as a result of the efforts of **Jerome Kern** (1885–1945), with his notable *Show Boat* (1928); **George** and **Ira Gershwin; Cole Porter;** and the team of **Richard Rodgers** and **Lorenz Hart** (beg. with *Garrick Gaieties,* 1925). An outstanding success was *Of Thee I Sing* (1931), book by George S. Kaufman and Morrie Ryskind. An innovation in the field was *Pal Joey* (1941), a modern *Beggar's Opera,* music by Rodgers, lyrics by Hart, and book by John O'Hara. The most striking success was the presentation in 1943 of *Oklahoma!* by **Richard Rodgers** (1902–   ) and **Oscar Hammerstein II** (1895–1960), followed in 1947 by *South Pacific* (with Mary Martin and Ezio Pinza). The introduction of **ballet** by **Agnes De Mille,** dancer and choreographer, in such productions as *Oklahoma!, Bloomer Girl* (1944), *Carousel* (1945), and *Brigadoon* (1947) gave to the musical comedy of the 40's its major innovating feature.

1915–52. SCENIC DESIGN. Chief impact upon modern scenic design in the U.S. stems from 1915, with the designs of **Robert Edmond Jones** (1887–1954) for *The Man Who Married a Dumb Wife;* later *Hamlet* (1922), *Richard III, Othello* (1936), and *The Philadelphia Story* (1939). Other notable contributors in this field: **Norman Bel-Geddes** (1893–1958), *The Miracle* (1923), *Dead End* (1935); **Lee Simonson** (1888–   ), *Lilliom,* O'Neill's *Dynamo;* **Jo Mielziner** (1901–   ), *Winterset* (1935), *High Tor* (1937).

1916–46. EUGENE O'NEILL (p. 760), the most notable American playwright, whose works were 1st performed at the Provincetown Playhouse, New York (*S.S. Glencairn*), a group interested in experimental drama. His plays varied from the naturalism of *Anna Christie* (1921) to the expressionism of *The Hairy Ape* (1922), and from the symbolism of *The Great God Brown* (1926) to experiments in combining Greek tragedy and Freudian psychology, as in *Mourning Becomes Electra* (1931).

Pulitzer Prize Plays, 1918–51

1918.	*Why Marry?* By Jesse Lynch Williams
1920.	*Beyond the Horizon.* By Eugene O'Neill
1921.	*Miss Lulu Bett.* By Zona Gale
1922.	*Anna Christie.* By Eugene O'Neill
1923.	*Icebound.* By Owen Davis
1924.	*Hell-Bent Fer Heaven.* By Hatcher Hughes
1925.	*They Knew What They Wanted.* By Sidney Howard
1926.	*Craig's Wife.* By George Kelly
1927.	*In Abraham's Bosom.* By Paul Green
1928.	*Strange Interlude.* By Eugene O'Neill
1929.	*Street Scene.* By Elmer L. Rice
1930.	*The Green Pastures.* By Marc Connelly
1931.	*Alison's House.* By Susan Glaspell
1932.	*Of Thee I Sing.* By George S. Kaufman, Morrie Ryskind, and George and Ira Gershwin
1933.	*Both Your Houses.* By Maxwell Anderson
1934.	*Men in White.* By Sidney Kingsley
1935.	*The Old Maid.* By Zoe Akins
1936.	*Idiot's Delight.* By Robert E. Sherwood
1937.	*You Can't Take It With You.* By Moss Hart and George S. Kaufman
1938.	*Our Town.* By Thornton Wilder
1939.	*Abe Lincoln in Illinois.* By Robert E. Sherwood
1940.	*The Time of Your Life.* By William Saroyan
1941.	*There Shall Be No Night.* By Robert E. Sherwood
1943.	*The Skin of Our Teeth.* By Thornton Wilder
1945.	*Harvey.* By Mary Chase
1946.	*State of the Union.* By Russel Crouse and Howard Lindsay
1948.	*A Streetcar Named Desire.* By Tennessee Williams

1949. *Death of a Salesman.* By Arthur Miller
1950. *South Pacific.* By Richard Rodgers, Oscar Hammerstein II, and Joshua Logan
1951. *The Shrike.* By Joseph Kramm

1919, 19 Apr. First production of the **Theater Guild,** Jacinto Benavente's *The Bonds of Interest,* at the Garrick Theater, followed by St. John Ervine's *John Ferguson.* Under the direction of **Theresa Helburn** the Guild, a subscription group dedicated to raising the level of the American stage, scored brilliant successes in the 20's with *Porgy,* Shaw's *St. Joan,* O'Neill's *Strange Interlude,* Molnar's *The Guardsman* (Alfred Lunt and Lynn Fontanne), and Sidney Howard's *They Knew What They Wanted.*

1924–48. POETIC AND IMAGINATIVE DRAMA. Maxwell Anderson (1888–), coauthor, with Laurence Stallings, of the most popular U.S. war play of the 20's, *What Price Glory* (1924), wrote such notable tragedies as *Elizabeth the Queen* (1930), *Mary of Scotland* (1933), *Winterset* (1935), *Key Largo* (1939), *The Eve of St. Mark* (1942, war play), and *Joan of Lorraine* (1947). In addition, he wrote a romantic verse comedy, *High Tor* (1937), and a musical comedy, *Knickerbocker Holiday* (1938). Other exemplars of the imaginative drama were **Paul Green** (1894–), whose plays include *In Abraham's Bosom* (1926), *The Field God* (1927), *The House of Connelly* (1931), *Tread the Green Grass* (1932), *Roll, Sweet Chariot* (1934), and *The Common Glory* (1948); **Marc Connelly** (1890–), who, in addition to collaborating with **George S. Kaufman** (1889–1961) on satires and comedies (*Dulcy,* 1921; *Beggar on Horseback,* 1924), wrote *The Green Pastures* (1930); and **Thornton Wilder** (1897–), *Our Town* (1938), *The Skin of Our Teeth* (1942).

1924–39. TRENDS. Drawing-room comedy done with wit and craftsmanship was notably exemplified by **S. N. Behrman** (*The Second Man,* 1927; *Rain From Heaven,* 1934; and *No Time for Comedy,* 1939) and by **Philip Barry** (*Holiday,* 1928; *Animal Kingdom,* 1932; and *The Philadelphia Story,* 1939). **Sidney Howard** (1891–1939) contributed to realism with *They Knew What They Wanted* (1924), *Ned McCobb's Daughter* (1926),

and *The Silver Cord* (1926). **Elmer Rice** (1892–), who had contributed an expressionistic play, *Adding Machine* (1923), wrote a naturalistic drama, *Street Scene* (1929). An individualistic approach is found in **William Saroyan's** (1908–) *The Time of Your Life* (1940).

1935–39. WPA FEDERAL THEATER PROJECT, under the national direction of Mrs. **Hallie Flanagan** of Vassar College, brought back the theater to the road with low-priced productions of T. S. Eliot's *Murder in the Cathedral,* the Negro *Macbeth,* Orson Welles' and John Housman's *Doctor Faustus,* and *Pinocchio.* Most notable was its contribution of a new form to the American theater, the Living Newspaper, in which headlines were dramatized, including *Triple A Ploughed Under* (1936), *Power* (1937), *One Third of a Nation* (1938).

1935–47. PLAYS OF PROPAGANDA AND SOCIAL CRITICISM were especially popular during the depression and in the early years of World War II. Representative were **Clifford Odets** (*Awake and Sing,* 1935; *Waiting for Lefty,* 1935; *Golden Boy,* 1937; *Rocket to the Moon,* 1938), **Lillian Hellman** (*The Children's Hour,* 1934; *The Little Foxes,* 1939; *Watch on the Rhine,* 1941; *Another Part of the Forest,* 1947), and **Robert E. Sherwood** (1896–1955, *The Petrified Forest,* 1934; *Idiot's Delight,* 1936; *There Shall Be No Night,* 1940).

1951–60. OFF-BROADWAY THEATER continued its remarkable growth, stressing daring and experimental plays (*The Threepenny Opera* and the revival of O'Neill's *The Iceman Cometh*) and attracting performers of rank.

Pulitzer Prize Plays, 1952–59

1952. *The Shrike.* By Joseph Kramm
1953. *Picnic.* By William Inge
1954. *The Teahouse of the August Moon.* By John Patrick
1955. *Cat on a Hot Tin Roof.* By Tennessee Williams
1956. *The Diary of Anne Frank.* By Frances Goodrich and Albert Hackett
1957. *Long Day's Journey into Night.* By Eugene O'Neill
1958. *Look Homeward, Angel.* By K. Frings
1959. *Fiorello!* By J. Bock, S. Harnick, Jerome Weidman, and G. Abbott

LONGEST RUNS ON BROADWAY, 31 DEC. 1960

Plays	No. of Performances
Life with Father	3,224
Tobacco Road	3,182
My Fair Lady	2,406
Abie's Irish Rose	2,327
Oklahoma!	2,248
South Pacific (to 9 Jan. 1961)	2,000
Harvey	1,775
Born Yesterday	1,642
The Voice of the Turtle	1,557
Arsenic and Old Lace	1,444
Hellzapoppin	1,404
Angel Street	1,295
Lightnin'	1,291
The King and I	1,246
Guys and Dolls	1,200
Mister Roberts	1,157
Annie Get Your Gun	1,147

1944–60. Notable playwrights in the mid-century included **Tennessee Williams** (1914–), *The Glass Menagerie* (1944), *A Streetcar Named Desire* (1947), *Cat on a Hot Tin Roof* (1954), *Garden District* (1958), *Period of Adjustment* (1960); and **Arthur Miller** (1915–), *Death of a Salesman* (1949), *The Crucible* (1953), *View from the Bridge* (1955).

MOTION PICTURES AND TV

1896, 23 Apr. The 1st motion picture commercially exhibited was shown at Koster and Bial's Music Hall, New York.

1900. *Cinderella,* the 1st film to use "artificially arranged scenes" in progressive continuity was produced by **Georges Melies**, French producer.

1903. *The Great Train Robbery* earned for **Edwin S. Porter**, its producer, recognition as the "father of the story film."

1905. **NICKELODEON,** early movie house, established in Pittsburgh by John P. Harris and Harry Davis. By 1908 between 8,000 and 10,000 were in operation, augmenting the need for expansion of film production facilities.

1909–35. ERA OF TRUSTS AND CONSOLIDATIONS. Edison, Biograph, Vitagraph, 3 pioneer companies, and several others formed Motion Picture Patents Co., 1909, but, as a result of a lawsuit brought by **William Fox** (1879–1952), independent distributor, the trust was inactive by 1914. The independents had by 1913 made **Hollywood** the cen-

ter of the industry, supplanting New York. Famous Players Films Co. (reorganized as Paramount) was organized in 1912 and innovated **"block booking."** Loew's (Metro-Goldwyn-Mayer, 1924) followed in 1920, Warner Bros. in 1923, Columbia in 1924, and Radio-Keith-Orpheum in 1928. Last of the major combines was Twentieth-Century Fox (1935).

1913. SERIALS. *What Happened to Mary,* a serial film, evidenced growing interest in this type of picture. Queens of the serial were Pearl White (*Perils of Pauline*) and Ruth Roland (*Ruth of the Rockies*).

1913–16. Mack Sennett's 2-reel comedies (Keystone), with burlesque satire and trick photography, launched a new school of "slapstick" comedians, notably **Charles Chaplin** (1889–), whose burlesque was gradually sharpened into satire: *The Tramp* (1915), *The Pawnshop* (1916), *Easy Street* (1917), *A Dog's Life* (1918), *Shoulder Arms* (1918), *The Kid* (1921). Later successes include *The Gold Rush* (1925), *City Lights* (1931), *Modern Times* (1936), *The Dictator* (1940), *Monsieur Verdoux* (1947), and *Limelight* (1952).

1913–29. STAR SYSTEM. Stars of the silent film included Mary Pickford, Douglas Fairbanks, Harold Lloyd and Buster Keaton (comics), Lillian and Dorothy Gish, Rudolph Valentino, Gloria Swanson, and Greta Garbo.

1914–39. WESTERNS attained worldwide popularity, starring William S. Hart and Tom Mix. A notable early production was *The Covered Wagon* (1923), directed by **James Cruze.** The outstanding Western of the later period was *Stagecoach* (1939), directed by **John Ford.**

1915, 3 Mar. *The Birth of a Nation,* a 12-reeler, produced by **D. W. Griffith** (p. 718), was first publicly exhibited. Improved photographic techniques, constant shifting of scenes, the use of symbolism, increased use of orchestral music, and brilliant film editing made the film a phenomenal box-office success; but its controversial theme (Reconstruction) aroused a storm of protest. Griffith's *Intolerance,* a financial failure, followed in 1916.

1919. PRODUCERS AND DIRECTORS. Cecil B. de Mille (1881–1959) began a series of lavish film productions emphasizing sex and sensation with *Male and Female,* and culminating in his most spectacular picture, *The King of Kings,* a religious spectacle (1927). Other producers of spectacles included Thomas Ince (*The Wrath of the Gods,* 1914) and Rex Ingram (*Four Horsemen of the Apocalypse,* 1921).

1921. *The Cabinet of Doctor Caligari,* a German film emphasizing new art forms, produced in 1919, was exhibited in the U.S. Other notable foreign influences in the period include the exhibition in the U.S. of Eisenstein's *Potemkin* (1926) and *Ten Days That Shook the World* (1927), with montage as an innovation.

1922. *Nanook of the North,* pioneer documentary film, was produced by **Robert Flaherty** (1884–   ). Other documentaries include Pare Lorentz' *The Plow That Broke the Plains* (1936) and *The River* (1937), and *The City* (1939, Oscar Serles, Ralph Steiner, and Willard Van Dyke).

"HAYS OFFICE" (Motion Picture Producers and Distributors Assn.) established with Will H. Hays as president; stressed self-regulation. Eric Johnston succeeded to post, 1945.

1923. Eric von Stroheim, pioneer realist, produced *Greed* (1923). Other notable realistic films of the period include King Vidor's *The Crowd* (1928), Victor Seastrom's *The Wind* (1928), W. S. Van Dyke's *The Thin Man* (1934), and Fritz Lang's *Fury* (1936). In addition, important directing was done by Ernst Lubitsch (*Student Prince,* 1927; *The Patriot,* 1928) and Josef von Sternberg (*Underworld,* 1927; and Marlene Dietrich's pictures, beg. with *Morocco,* 1930).

1925–51. Technical advances in TV (p. 570).

1926, 26 Aug. The 1st motion picture with **sound** accompaniment was Warner Brothers' *Don Juan.* The success of **talking pictures** was established by Warners' *The Jazz Singer* (6 Oct. 1927) with Al Jolson.

1928. *Plane Crazy,* the 1st **Walt Disney** (1901–   ) cartoon, was released. Other popular favorites followed (*The Three Little Pigs,* and *Mickey Mouse* and

Silly Symphony series). His *Flowers and Trees* (1935) was the 1st picture which successfully utilized the 3-color method of **Technicolor.** Disney's 1st full-length picture (also in Technicolor), was *Snow White and the Seven Dwarfs* (1938).

1934. Production of Frank Capra's sensational success, *It Happened One Night* (starring Claudette Colbert and Clark Gable).

1939. *Gone With the Wind* (Hollywood's top-grossing film), based on Margaret Mitchell's novel.

1946. *Variety* half-century poll: All-time best films: (1) *Gone With the Wind,* (2) *Birth of a Nation,* (3) *Best Years of Our Lives.* Top stars: Charles Chaplin and Greta Garbo. Best producers: (1) Irving Thalberg, (2) Darryl F. Zanuck (producer of *Gentlemen's Agreement,* 1946; *Pinky, Snake Pit*), (3) Sam Goldwyn. Best director: (1) D. W. Griffith, (2) Cecil B. de Mille, (3) William Wyler.

1948. Major film companies required under Supreme Court ruling to dispose of theater units.

1952. **3-dimensional movies** (Cinerama and Natural Vision) launched.

1953. **CinemaScope,** introduced with 20th Cent.-Fox production of *The Robe,* widely adopted in 1954. **25 May.** 1st educational TV station in U.S., KUHT, operated by Univ. of Houston, began broadcasting. 47 educational TV stations operating on a nonprofit basis by 1960; 6 being built. **21 Dec.** 1st colorcast of a commercial program: *Amahl and the Night Visitors* (NBC-TV).

1955. **MOVIES ON TV.** Sale by RKO of pre-1948 films to TV, followed shortly by other major companies; contributed to decline of "live" and original TV, represented in the mid-1950s by such quality programs as *Omnibus, Philco Playhouse, Wide Wide World, See It Now, You Are There, Firestone Hour,* as Westerns, quiz programs, and situation comedies gained ground on network TV. Columbia, 1960, 1st major film company to sell post-1948 films to TV (1960).

1955–60. **QUIZ PROGRAM SCANDALS.** *$64,000 Question* (CBS-TV) quickly won top video rating, which it shared (1957) with *Twenty-One* (NBC). Revelations (Aug.-Dec. 1958) that contestants in *Twenty-One* and *The $64,000 Challenge* (CBS-TV) had been given answers to questions led to House subcommittee hearing (6–10 Oct., 1959). Further probes brought out allegations of "payola" to disk jockeys (21 Nov., 4 Dec.). The result was the passage (30 Aug. 1960) of a federal law designed to curb payola and quiz-show rigging, which required radio and TV stations to announce whether they had received money or anything of value for broadcasting material and outlawed clandestine aid to contestants in purportedly bona fide contests, with maximum penalties of $10,000 fine and 1 yr. imprisonment fixed. Public reaction spurred increase of public service and educational programming (1958–60).

1956. Michael Todd (1909–58) pro-

duced *Around the World in 80 Days* in Todd-AO.

1956-60. INDEPENDENT PRODUCERS set new trend in picturemaking, with wide shake-up in production chiefs in major studios (1956). By 1958, 50% of the new movies were made by "independents," although usually released through major studios.

1960, Oct. TV CAMPAIGN DEBATES. Campaign history was made when the Presidential candidates, Richard M. Nixon (Rep.) and John F. Kennedy (Dem.), debated the campaign issues over TV (7, 13, 21, and 26 Oct.).

14, 21 Nov. Eugene O'Neill's *The Iceman Cometh* given 4-hr. presentation on WNTA's *Play of the Week*, considered a milestone in TV drama.

ALL-TIME FILM LEADERS
(Estimated gross film rentals from U.S. and Canada, *Variety*, 4 Jan. 1961)

Title and Release	Estimated Gross Film Rentals (overseas excluded)
The Ten Commandments (Paramount, 1957)	$34,200,000
Gone with the Wind (Selznick—MGM, 1939)	33,500,000
Ben Hur (MGM, 1960—projected est.)	33,000,000
Around the World in Eighty Days (Todd—UA, 1957)	22,000,000
The Robe (20th Century-Fox, 1953)	17,500,000
South Pacific (20th Century-Fox, 1958)	16,300,000
Bridge on the River Kwai (Columbia, 1958)	15,000,000
Greatest Show on Earth (Paramount, 1952)	12,800,000
From Here to Eternity (Columbia, 1953)	12,500,000
This Is Cinerama (Cinerama, 1952)	12,500,000
White Christmas (Paramount, 1954)	12,000,000
Giant (Warner Bros., 1956)	12,000,000

FINE ARTS AND ARCHITECTURE

1650–1721. EARLY AMERICAN PAINTING. The limners, the earliest American painters, were probably self-taught. Their portraits are characterized by an excess of realistic detail and a refreshing naïveté (*The Mason Children, c.*1670; *Mrs. Freake and Baby Mary, c.*1674). Among the earliest known limners were John Foster (1648–81) and **Thomas Smith**, a sea captain, whose paintings shared the Puritan obsession with death. Later New England limners after 1700 reflect English influence more directly. The earlier rugged energy is replaced by shallow elegance and a looser technique (Pierpont limner, 1711; Nathaniel Emmons [d. 1740]; J. Cooper [active *c.*1714–18]; the Pollard limner, 1721). In New Netherland and New

York the **patroon painters**, 1660–*c.*1710 (Stuyvesant limner, Provoost limner [*c.*1700]; *Grootje Vas*, 1723, possibly by Pieter Vanderlyn), portrayed the upper class in an attempted style of elegance after European models.

1708–17. German-born Justus Englehardt Kühn introduced at Annapolis a provincial translation of the European tradition of aristocratic portraiture (*Eleanor Darnall, c.*1712).

1729–50. NEW ENGLAND REVIVAL was inaugurated by **John Smibert** (1688–1751), who staged the 1st art exhibition in the American colonies in Boston, 1730. His severe middle-class realism, variant of the English portrait tradition (*Bishop Berkeley and his Entourage*), created a school that was to include the colonial masters **Robert Feke** (*c*.1705–*c*.1750) and **John Singleton Copley** (p. 691). Feke, the 1st supposedly American-born painter of recognized talent, painted chiefly in Newport (R.I.), Boston, and Philadelphia, between *c*.1741 and *c*.1750. He was a skillful draftsman with a fine sense of color (*Isaac Royall and Family*, 1741; *Rev. Thos. Hiscox*, 1745; *Mrs. Charles Willing*, 1746; *Charles Apthorp*, 1748), but no naturalist.

1740–74. In Charleston, S.C., the Swiss, Jeremiah Theüs, dominated local portraiture with his version of the "international" style derived from Lely and Kneller.

1760–63. BENJAMIN WEST (1738–1820) left Philadelphia for Rome to study, setting up his studio 3 years later in London.

1760–74. In Boston **Copley** (p. 691) painted his early realistic masterpieces (*Boy with Squirrel* [Henry Pelham], *c*.1765).

1761. John Hesselius (1728–78), son of the Swedish-born painter Gustavus Hesselius, painted his *Charles Calvert and His Colored Slave*.

1765–81. In his famous London studio **West** played host to American artists, determining in large measure the character of American painting. His group included Matthew Pratt (1734–1805; returned to America, 1768), Earl, Charles Willson Peale, Copley, Stuart, and Trumbull. His romanticized characterization of *The Death of Wolfe* (1771), containing recognizable portraits, achieved wide popularity. In 1772 West became historical painter to George III.

1778–92. RALPH EARL (1751–1801), after whose paintings Amos Doolittle made popular engravings of 4 scenes of the early Revolution, went to London to study (probably with West); returned to the U.S., 1785. His mature portraits (*Chief Justice Oliver Ellsworth and His Wife*, 1792) are notable for the importance of setting and landscape having personal relationships to his sitters.

1781–93. The highly successful London period of **Gilbert Stuart** (p. 785). In this period also **Charles Willson Peale** (1741–1827) established himself at Philadelphia (*Benjamin Franklin*, 1787).

1792. Benjamin West succeeded **Sir** Joshua Reynolds as president of the Royal Academy.

c.1681–1789. EARLY SCULPTURE. Seventeenth-century efforts were chiefly in the field of gravestone carving in New England (Thomas Child, 1655–1706). Native sculptors were slow in appearing. Eighteenth-century activity was chiefly the carving of ship figureheads (Senior Simeon Skillin, *c*.1741) and weathervanes (Shem Drowne). **Patience Lovell Wright** (1725–86), a wax sculptress, was a U.S. secret agent in Great Britain during the Revolution (modeling George III, Queen Charlotte, and other notables), and her son, **Joseph** (1756–93), who studied under Trumbull and West, was commissioned to make a statue of Washington, but all that survived are 2 medallions based on a life mask (1783–84). Appointed (1792) diesinker of the U.S. Mint, he designed numerous coins and medals. When Franklin was commissioned by Congress, 1776, to find a sculptor to carve the memorial tablet to Gen. Richard Montgomery, he selected Jean-Jacques Caffieri; and Jefferson subsequently selected **Jean-Antoine Houdon** to make a marble effigy of Washington, which he executed from a life mask (1785).

EARLY ARCHITECTURE. In their early architecture the colonists attempted to duplicate in their new homes the forms and atmosphere of those they had left, in areas with different materials and different climates. Three European countries provided the chief models—Spain, in Fla., later in the Southwest and Calif.; France, in the Mississippi Valley; and England, along the Atlantic coast—with 3 diverging types developing: **Spanish** (*Fort of San Marco*, 1672; the Cathedral [1793–97]; and a few early houses), **French** (New Orleans, planned 1721; Ste. Genevieve, early houses; Cahokia, Ill., *Courthouse*, *c*.1737), and **English** (which eventually became the major influence).

1607–c.1640. EARLIEST ENGLISH HOUSES were shacks based either on Indian "wigwams" (round-roofed structures of oblong plan) or palisadoed dwellings (reconstruction of old Salem); but in Va. timber-framed and even brick houses were built in urban fashion by 1612, and in the more northern areas permanent timber-framed houses were the rule by the 1630's or 40's. **Log cabins** (logs laid around **horizontally**) were unknown in England, and were introduced by the Swedes on the Delaware (*Lower Log House,* Darby, Pa., 1640); ultimately the Scotch-Irish made them the prevailing frontier dwelling.

1641–1700. Evolution of the "Colonial" Style. Seventeenth-century architecture remained largely medieval, a product of unsophisticated craftsmanship, but with variants from European standards, chiefly caused by the more severe climate. Characteristic clapboard or shingle-covered walls (found occasionally in southeastern England) were used, rather than typical English "half-timber" filled with brick or plaster, because they were more weatherproof. Windows were small leaded casements. Early examples of this type (upper story overhang, small windows, inconspicuous doorways, central chimney, and often characteristic "salt box" roof sloping to the rear) have survived in Conn., R.I., and Mass. The smaller houses of the less well-to-do settlers were frame structures of from 1 to 1½ stories, with relatively tall and simple gable or gambrel roofs. Roof slopes tended to become less steep in accordance with weather conditions.

The current English **Jacobean** style was introduced in details, especially in the South, notably in Bacon's Castle (*c.*1655), Surrey Co., Va., a good example of full Jacobean design, with its geometrical gables, clustered chimneys, and stair tower, and in **Fairfield,** or Carter's Creek, Va. (1692). The style was also found in Middleton Place, Ashley River, S.C.; in the old *Landgrave Smith Back River* plantation house; and in the *Peter Sergeant House (Province House),* Boston. *Malvern Hill,* Va., represents the transition from Jacobean to more classic Renaissance. Timber construction continued to prevail in New England; brick, stone, and wood were used in the Middle Colonies (with stone predominating in portions of Pa., N.J., and Del.); and brick houses were generally constructed in the South (in Va. as early as 1636), becoming the prevailing material for the

better dwellings. The brick was sometimes stuccoed in Charleston; wood was more general in N.C.).

1700–50. Increasing prosperity, greater numbers of skilled craftsmen, and the increased importation of architectural books and building details rapidly modified the earlier trends, and permitted a more sophisticated following of the fashions of the mother country. The English **baroque** style (of Wren and Gibbs) was now adopted for more pretentious homes, with symmetrical façades, the double-hung window (replacing the casement type), and the elimination of overhangs. Pediments and pilasters were added in the later period to embellish the central doorway. The better houses were in brick or stone, but wooden houses often imitated stone details.

c.1751–89. Growing national feeling and closer commercial and political contacts produced increasing similarities in colonial architecture and a greater freedom in using English precedent. An American architecture was being created. The term **Georgian** came to be applied to houses of 2 or 3 stories built upon a strictly rectangular plan, with windows regularly spaced, the use of dormers, with horizontal lines emphasized, the small entry, or porch, replaced by a spacious center hall, with 2 chimneys, one on each side of the hall, in place of the central chimney (*Hooper House,* Marblehead, 1745; *Longfellow House,* Cambridge, Mass., 1759).

In N.Y. the earlier **Dutch** style of New Amsterdam and the Hudson Valley (stepped gables, *Widow Sturtevant House,* Albany) and the **Flemish** style (projecting roof curved or flared at the ends) of parts of Long Island and N.J. were ultimately supplanted by the Georgian. Classicism was evident in *Johnson Hall,* Johnstown, 1762, and the *Morris (Jumel) Mansion,* 1765. In the Hudson River Valley simple houses of stone masonry, long low rectilinear structures with chimneys at either end, were built after the English conquest (*Senate House,* Kingston, 1676–95; *Freer House,* New Paltz, 1720). Until 1750 the simple Quaker style dominated the Philadelphia area, but Georgian rapidly came into vogue (*Mt. Pleasant,* 1761, brick, stone, and stucco; *Woodford, c.*1750, brick, both with Doric doorways; *Cliveden,* Germantown, 1770, American Palladian style). **Pennsylvania-Dutch** architecture of the Upper Rhine Valley immigrants radiated from Bethlehem, Pa., down the Great Valley into S.C., with its generally stone construction and its square plan for a number of rooms clustered about a central flue (*Miller's House,* Milbach).

In the South the baroque style of colonial Georgian was adopted in such plantation houses as the *Hammond House,* Annapolis, 1770, designed by **William Buckland,** who came from England in 1755; in Va. at *Stratford Hall,* Westmoreland Co. (*c.*1725), and at *Westover,* Charles City Co. (*c.*1730), with the Palladian influence notably present in *Mount Airy,* Warsaw (1755–58), and in *Mount Vernon* (1758–86). Charleston's brick and stucco mansions adapted the West Indian style of long porches or piazzas, with houses often standing endwise to the street. The galleries (most existing galleries are post-Revolutionary additions) faced the gardens, rooms were high-ceilinged and spacious, and the ground-floor story was raised several feet above the ground, with curving wrought-iron stair rails. Outstanding examples: *Izard House* (before 1757); the Miles Brewton House (1765–69), with its double portico, Doric columns on the 1st floor and Ionic on the 2nd, evidencing the growing classical influence. The **Huguenot** type, based on French architectural styles, was also found in S.C., *c.*1690–1800 (*The Mulberry,* Berkeley Co., with its mansard roof; *Brick House,* Edisto Island, *c.*1725).

Churches. Early churches were simple, in the South following English Gothic small parish churches (*St. Luke's,* Smithfield, Va., 1682); in the North, because of the Puritan religious-government system, taking the form of meeting houses—large rectangular structures with entrance on 1 long side, galleries on 3 sides, and the high pulpit on the long side opposite the entrance (*"Old Ship" Meeting House,* Hingham, Mass., 1681). By 1750, however, English influence, introducing the type of towered church developed by Sir Christopher Wren and James Gibbs, almost completely effaced the earlier types, even for dissenting churches

(*St. Michael's Church,* Charleston, S.C., 1752–61, possibly the work of **Peter Harrison** [1716–75], patterned after Gibbs' St. Martin's-in-the-Fields; Harrison's *King's Chapel,* Boston, 1749–54, also after Gibbs; and his *Touro Synagogue,* Newport, 1759–63, influenced by Inigo Jones and Gibbs).

Public Buildings were notably represented by the *Old State House,* Boston (1712–28); *Carpenter's Hall,* Philadelphia (1724); *Independence Hall,* designed by Andrew Hamilton, Philadelphia (1732–41); the *Pennsylvania Hospital* (1755); and the *Maryland State House,* Annapolis (1772), which helped to set the domed type which has become almost universal in state capitol buildings. The *Capitol* (1701–05) and the *College of William and Mary* (1695–1702) at Williamsburg (restoration begun 1927) show, in reconstructed and restored fashion, the most highly developed types; the latter was built from drawings supplied by Wren.

1793–1828. PAINTING. Portraiture. After his return from England in 1792 **Gilbert Stuart** (p. 785) was active in New York, Philadelphia, Washington, and Boston, producing a gallery of life-size bust portraits limning worthies of the Federal and Republican eras. His canvases, bearing the strong impress of the British tradition of Reynolds, Gainsborough, and Raeburn, possessed a high technical finish and a mastery of color tones. Among his portraits are many of *George Washington,* and those of *Mrs. Richard Yates, Mrs. Timothy Pickering, Mrs. Perez Morton* (*c.*1802), and *Nathaniel Bowditch.*

At Philadelphia, **Charles Willson Peale** (1741–1827), who had made his mark before 1789, finished *The Family Group* (1809) and also painted *The Staircase Group* (*c.*1795), *Exhuming the Mastodon* (1806), and *Self-Portrait in His Museum* (1824). These works were all innovations in American painting, possibly because Peale's interest in the Natural History Museum gave him an objective approach to nature. Because he believed anyone could learn to paint he taught many of his family to follow his trade, including his brother James (1749–1831) and his sons, Rembrandt (1778–

1860) and Raphaelle (1774–1825).

Stuart's work helped make the life-size portrait bust in oil the favorite medium of the age. Active at New York were Samuel Lovett Waldo (1783–1861) and William Jewett (1795–1874), and at Philadelphia, Thomas Sully (1783–1872).

c.1800–25. Miniature painters included Edward Green Malbone (1777–1807) and Benjamin Trott (*c*.1790–*c*.1841).

1830–50. Among portrait painters active near the mid-century, many of whom show the mark of their competition with **photography** from its rise, *c*.1840, were Henry Inman (1801–46), John Neagle (1796–1865), Charles Loring Elliott (1812–68), Thomas Hicks (1823–90), George P. A. Healy (1812–94), and Chester Harding (1792–1866). Mention should also be made of the Negro painter, Robert S. Duncanson (1821–71).

1790–1860. HISTORICAL PAINTING. The genres of historical, religious, and panoramic painting were developed about 1789. **John Trumbull** (1756–1843) painted *The Battle of Bunker's Hill* in West's studio in London in 1785 and *The Declaration of Independence*, one of the 4 murals in the National Capitol, between 1786–94. **John Vanderlyn** (1776–1852) painted the *Panorama of Versailles, The Death of Jane McCrea, The Landing of Columbus, Marius Musing amid the Ruins of Carthage*, and his *Ariadne* (1810), one of the early nudes in American painting, and thought to be in such poor taste that it blighted his career. Edward Savage (1761–1817), who did a canvas of Washington's family, also painted a panorama of London. Henry Sargent (1770–1845) painted *The Landing of the Pilgrims* and *Christ Entering Jerusalem*. The versatile **William Dunlap** (1766–1839) painted *Calvary, The Bearing of the Cross*, and *The Attack on the Louvre*. Dunlap's *History of the Rise and Progress of the Arts of Design in the United States* (1834) was the 1st treatment of that subject.

Washington Allston (1779–1843) struck the 1st vibrant note of romanticism in American painting. His poetic-philosophic bent for religious themes was exhibited in the famous unfinished *Belshazzar's Feast, The Deluge, Uriel in the Sun*, and *The Dead Man Restored to Life*

by the Bones of Elijah. A pupil of Allston was **Samuel F. B. Morse** (p. 757), who made his mark as a portraitist before his association with the development of the telegraph. Among his portraits are those of De Witt Clinton, Lafayette, and President James Monroe. His *Exhibition Gallery of the Louvre* is a *tour de force*.

The school of historical painting that emerged by the mid-century included Robert Walker Weir (1803–89), *Embarkation of the Pilgrims;* John Gadsby Chapman (1808–89), *Baptism of Pocahontas;* James Walker (1819–89), *Battle of Chapultepec;* William Henry Powell (1823–79), *Perry's Victory on Lake Erie;* Emmanuel Leutze (1816–68), *Washington Crossing the Delaware* and *Westward the Course of Empire Takes Its Way;* Daniel Huntington (1816–1906), *Mercy's Dream* and *Pilgrim's Progress;* and Thomas P. Rossiter (1818–71), *Washington and Lafayette at Mount Vernon, 1776*. Perhaps the most deliberate of the historical-genre painters was George Caleb Bingham (1811–77), who recorded contemporary river and frontier life in *Daniel Boone Coming Through Cumberland Gap, Fur Traders Descending the Missouri, The Jolly Flatboatmen*, and *The Verdict of the People*.

1830–60. LANDSCAPE PAINTING. The early landscape painters included Alvan Fisher (1792–1863), Thomas Birch (1779–1851), James Hamilton (1818–78), and Robert Salmon (fl. 1800–40). A distinctive school of American landscape emerged only with the achievement of **Thomas Doughty** (1793–1856), the 1st American painter who made a successful career in this genre; **Asher Brown Durand** (1796–1886), and **Thomas Cole** (1801–52). These 3 pioneers were the leaders of the **Hudson River School**, which also included John W. Casilear (1811–93), John Frederick Kensett (1818–72), the early work of **George Inness** (p. 731), Jasper F. Cropsey (1828–1900), Sanford R. Gifford (1823–80), Worthington Whittredge (1820–1910), Frederick Edwin Church (1826–1900), Jervis McEntee (1828–91), William M. Hart (1823–94), and James M. Hart (1828–1901).

ANECDOTAL GENRE PAINTING. The work of such early storytelling painters as Charles Cattron (1756–1819) and John Lewis Kimmel (1789–1821) became more fully developed in the anecdotal paintings of William Sidney Mount (1807–68), the 1st American to establish himself in this genre; also James Henry Beard (1812–93), William Holbrook Beard (1824–1900), William Ranney (1813–57), Tompkins M. Matteson (1813–84), and David Gilmor Blythe (1815–65). The life of the North American Indian and the Far West was recorded in the paintings of George Catlin (1796–1872), Alfred Jacob Miller (1810–74), Seth Eastman (1808–75), John Mix Stanley (1814–72), Frank B. Mayer (1827–99), and Carl Wimar (1828–62).

In the field of art reproductions, John James Audubon (p. 670) issued his superb aquatint plates of the *Birds of America* (1827–38). On a popular level, the prints of Currier & Ives were based on the work of such artists as George Henry Durrie (1820–63) and Arthur Fitzwilliam Tait (1819–1905). The development of commercial lithography created a wide market for art reproductions in the medium of the "chromolith."

1789–1830. SCULPTURE. The work of the early artisan carvers displays technical ingenuity and artistic integrity, notably William Rush (1756–1833), who enjoyed a busy career as a woodcarver of ships' figureheads, among them *The Genius of the United States* and *Nature,* both of which were mounted on U.S. frigates. His Indian figures, e.g., the *Indian Trader* (on the ship *William Penn*), were among his best works. Another woodcarver, who later worked in marble, was Hezekiah Augur (1791–1858), whose best-known work is *Jephthah and His Daughter.* John Frazee (1790–1852) began as a N.J. stonecutter, was wholly self-taught as a sculptor, and did not carve his 1st marble bust until c.1825. Among his marble portraits are those of John Jay, John Marshall, and Daniel Webster. Although the work of John Henri Isaac Browere (1792–1834) may be classified as life masks rather than sculpture, his portraits of prominent Americans are valuable as authentic historical records.

1830–60. ITALIAN NEO-CLASSICISM. In the 1830's U.S. sculptors began to pursue professional training abroad (particularly in Italy). The 1st American who deliberately chose sculpture as a profession was **Horatio Greenough** (1805–52), best known for the heroic, half-draped statue of Washington that stands on the Capitol grounds. Other sculptors who performed all or most of their work in Italy were William Wetmore Story (1819–95) and Harriet G. Hosmer (1830–1908). Among Story's works were a statue of his father, Justice Joseph Story, and *Saul, Moses, Cleopatra,* and *Medea.* Those by Hosmer include *Beatrice, Zenobia,* and the statue of *Thomas Hart Benton* at St. Louis.

Hiram Powers (1805–73) shares with Greenough the distinction of being the 1st professionally trained native sculptor. He did many portrait busts of American statesmen in an age when the marble bust predominated, but his best-known work is the *Greek Slave,* which created a sensation in its time. Powers was the 1st American sculptor to win a European reputation.

Other sculptors noted for their busts and figures in white marble include Erastus D. Palmer (1817–1904) and Thomas Ball (1819–1911). Palmer is best known for *Indian Girl, White Captive,* and the bust of Washington Irving. **Ball** did the equestrian statue of Washington at the Boston Public Gardens and the *Emancipation* group at the National Capitol. William Rimmer (1816–79), whose works include *Falling Gladiator* and *Head of Saint Stephen,* was noted for his mastery of anatomical knowledge.

Thomas Crawford (1813–57) was one of the outstanding pioneers of American sculpture. Among his works are the statue of *Armed Freedom* on the dome of the Capitol, the group called *Past and Present of America* on the pediment of the Senate wing, and the *Washington Monument* at Richmond.

Henry Kirke Brown (1814–86) is best known for his equestrian statue of *Washington* in Union Square, N.Y., where his statue of *Lincoln* also stands. **Clark Mills** (1815–83) made the 1st equestrian statue cast in the U.S., that of *Gen. Andrew*

Jackson (erected 1853) which stands near the White House.

Randolph Rogers (1825–92) did the bronze doors of the Capitol rotunda and the *Genius of Connecticut* on the dome of the State House at Hartford, as well as *Nydia* and *Lost Pleiad*. **John Rogers** (1829–1904) gained wide popularity with his "Rogers groups," the mass-produced plaster statuettes that found their way into thousands of American homes. His folk artistry and sharp delineation are displayed in such representative works as *Checkers up at the Farm, Town Pump, The Fugitive's Story, Union Refugees, Council of War,* and *The Wounded Scout.*

1789–1860. ARCHITECTURE: CLASSIC REVIVAL. The American Revolution brought with it a demand (recognized by Jefferson in his *Notes on Virginia*) for a new American architecture, expressive of the new nation. Yet for some time the older building ways and the older dependence on England continued. Thus the **Adam** style continued as a major influence for 2 or 3 decades. Jefferson saw the source of inspiration for the new work in the ancient classic architecture of Rome and Greece, and eventually a **Roman Revival** (1789–*c.*1820) and a **Greek Revival** (*c.*1820–60) became dominant. One of the foremost practitioners in the persisting Adamesque manner was **Samuel McIntire** (1757–1811), who built houses and mansions for the Salem merchants, among them the Derbys and Crowninshields. Other adapters of this mode were **Asher Benjamin** (1773–1845), who worked at the beginning of his career in the Connecticut Valley and was the author of the popular handbook, *The Country Builder's Assistant* (1797) and many other similar books; and **Charles Bulfinch** (p. 681), who embodied it in many distinguished houses in Boston. It was characteristic of the time that McIntire and Benjamin practiced as carpenter-builders rather than professional architects.

1789–*c.*1820. ROMAN REVIVAL saw the emergence of the professional architect in the U.S. Its vogue was due to (1) direct importation from Europe; (2) the analogy with the Roman Republic drawn by Americans of the early national period. Chiefly influential in this initial phase

were **Thomas Jefferson** (p. 734) and **William Thornton** (1759–1828). Jefferson's design for the *Virginia Capitol* at Richmond (1785–89), the 1st American structure after the Roman style, was based on the ancient Roman temple at Nîmes, France, known as the Maison Carrée. His plan for the *University of Virginia* at Charlottesville, with its systematic use of the various orders, represents the high mark of the Roman Revival. Charles Bulfinch, among the 1st native professional architects, later shifted to the style of the Roman and, rarely, the Greek Revivals. In houses, the new classicism shows chiefly in the creation of a restrained, clear simplicity, with a diminution in decorative adjuncts. These are often called **Federal** in style. French influence appears occasionally. Perhaps the finest example of this type is the New York *City Hall* (1803–12), whose design was shared by **John McComb, Jr.** (1763–1853), and **Joseph F. Mangin** (fl.1794–1818).

1793–1830. NATIONAL CAPITOL expressed the idealism of the new nation. After Maj. **Pierre Charles L'Enfant** (1754–1825) had designed the Washington city plan, President Washington, as the result of a competition, selected **William Thornton** as architect of the Capitol. **Stephen Hallet** (fl.1789–65), who succeeded Thornton, shares the credit for the basic conception—the large central dome and the flanking Senate and House wings. Beginning in 1803, **Benjamin Henry Latrobe** (p. 739) modified the somewhat impractical original design and used Greek inspiration in the details, working on the Capitol (which was burned by the British in 1814) until 1817. **Charles Bulfinch** brought Latrobe's plans to completion (1817–30). The architect of the **Executive Mansion** was **James Hoban** (*c.*1762–1831), who also designed the State House at Charleston, S.C. In the White House the east and west porticoes were built from Latrobe's designs. After the British burned the White House, Hoban rebuilt it with Latrobe's modifications.

***c.*1820–60. GREEK REVIVAL** is attributable to the renewed Continental interest in classic forms, to the influx of foreign architects, and to American enthusiasm for the Greeks in their struggle for independence. This period saw the dominance of the carpenter-builder, when handbooks came into use, e.g., Asher Benjamin's widely reprinted *The Practical House Carpenter* (1830) and the 3 books by **Minard Lefever** (1797–1854)—*Young Builder's General Instructor* (1829), *Modern Builder's Guide* (1833), and *Beauties of Modern Architecture* (1835), even more important in spreading the Greek Revival throughout the country. Many Federal and state government buildings, merchants' exchanges, banks, and churches were designed in this style, generally a free inventive rendering of Greek forms based on such Greek structures as the Parthenon, the Erectheum, and the monument of Lysicrates. Among the prominent characteristics of the style were the use of the Greek orders, doors and mantels with creative versions of Greek inspiration, great variety in house plans, and, in public buildings, magnificent fireproof masonry-vaulted construction. Chiefly responsible for introducing the Greek Revival was **Benjamin Henry Latrobe** (p. 739). The 1st Greek building in America was his Bank of Pennsylvania at Philadelphia, characteristic in its free adaptation of ancient precedent and in its fireproof vaulted construction. Two of his pupils were **Robert Mills** (1781–1855) and **William Strickland** (*c.*1787–1854). Mills, the designer of many houses, customhouses, and other Federal buildings, is best known for the *Treasury Building, Patent Office,* and *Washington Monument* (begun 1836). Strickland built the *Merchants Exchange,* Philadelphia, and the *Capitol,* Nashville, Tenn. A pupil of Strickland was **Thomas U. Walker** (1804–87), who designed *Girard College,* Philadelphia, and brought the U.S. Capitol to final completion (1850–65). Others identified with this style include **Minard Lefever; Gideon Shryock; Isaiah Rogers** (1800–69), who created the modern hotel concept in the *Tremont House* (Boston, 1828), and built the *Merchants Exchange* at New York; and **Alexander Jackson Davis** (1803–92), in partnership with **Ithiel Town** (1784–1844) until 1844, who designed the New York *Custom House* (1832) and several state capitols.

1840–60. BEGINNING OF THE GOTHIC REVIVAL. Groundwork was laid by **A. J. Davis; Richard Upjohn** (1802–78), 1st president of the American Institute of Architects, founded, 1857, who designed the new Trinity Church and Trinity Chapel; and **James Renwick** (1818–95), Grace Church, 1843–46, and St. Patrick's Cathedral, 1850–79. The many-times-republished books of **Andrew J. Downing** (1815–52), dealing with landscape and rural architecture, had great influence in spreading the Gothic Revival, as well as in stimulating romantic gardens; he is also one of the fathers of the city park in the U.S. The eclecticism of the period did not go unchallenged. In 3 important works on architecture Horatio Greenough attacked current trends (*American Architecture* [1843], *Aesthetics at Washington* [1851], and *Structure and Organization* [1852]), anticipating by a half century Louis Sullivan's functional approach.

1861–1910. PAINTING. Portrait and Figure. Still active after 1860 were many of the portraitists, among them Daniel Huntington and Charles Loring Elliott, who before the Civil War shaped a technique of sober and almost photographic realism. The Lincoln theme made its early appearance in a series of studies by Francis Bicknell Carpenter (1830–1900), including *The Lincoln Family in 1861* and *The Reading of the Emancipation Proclamation.* Portraits of public figures were a specialty of Alonzo Chappell (1828–87), whose pictures reached a wide audience through the medium of the steel engraving.

The absorption of Continental influences appeared in the work of a later generation: Gustave H. Mosler (1841–1920), Francis D. Millet (1846–1912), Frank Duveneck (1848–1919), William Merritt Chase (1849–1916), Wyatt Eaton (1849–96), and Kenyon Cox (1856–1919). The most successful portrait painter of the time was **John Singer Sargent** (1856–1925), who did most of his work abroad. His technical finish is evident in such characteristic portraits as those of *Ada Rehan, Ellen Terry, Mrs. John L. Gardner, Coventry Patmore, Madame X, The Four Doctors,* and *The Misses Hunter.* Another American portraitist who did virtually all of his work in Europe was **James A. McNeill Whistler**

(p. 798), whose work includes *Portrait of the Artist's Mother, Thomas Carlyle,* and *Miss Alexander.* Whistler's *Nocturnes* and *Symphonies* used color and mass with fresh inventiveness, and his etchings of Venetian and London waterside subjects exhibit a brilliant Impressionist technique.

Figure painting in the U.S. reached a new level with the work of Eastman Johnson (1824–1906), *Old Kentucky Home* and *In the Fields;* William Morris Hunt (1824–79), *The Bathers;* George Fuller (1822–84); Robert L. Newman (1827–1912); Abbott H. Thayer (1849–1921); Thomas Dewing (1851–1938); Frederic Remington (1861–1909); and John W. Alexander (1865–1915).

Historical, Mural, Anecdotal, and Still Life. The pre-Civil War tradition of historical painting was continued by Constantino Brumidi (1805–80), whose work at the National Capitol includes *Apotheosis of Washington;* and by William De La Montagne Cary (1840–1922), Henry F. Farny (1847–1916), and John Mulvaney (1844–1906). Among the outstanding mural painters were John La Farge (1835–1910), who was also a prolific worker in stained glass; Kenyon Cox; Edwin Austin Abbey (1852–1911); Elihu Vedder (1836–1923); Edwin H. Blashfield (1848–1936); John W. Alexander; and Robert F. Blum (1857–1903). Anecdotal painters of the time included John George Brown (1831–1913), *The Music Lesson;* Thomas Waterman Wood (1823–1913), *The Village Post Office;* and Edward Lamson Henry (1841–1919), *The 9:45 Accommodation.* Among the still-life painters were George Henry Hall (1825–1913), Andrew J. H. Way (1826–88), William Michael Harnett (?1848–92), William Merritt Chase, John Frederick Peto (1854–1907), and John Haberle (1856–1933).

Landscape. Those who continued to produce repetitions or variations of the Hudson River School included William Rickaby Miller (1818–93), Frederick Edwin Church (1826–1900), Albert Bierstadt (1830–1902), Samuel Colman (1832–1920), James David Smillie (1833–1909), Thomas Moran (1837–1926), George Henry Smillie (1840–1921), and Robert Swain Gifford (1840–

1905). **George Inness,** who before the Civil War had been a follower of the Hudson River School, shaped a fresher idiom in such canvases as *Peace and Plenty, Autumn Oaks, Delaware Water Gap,* and *Home of the Heron.* Other landscape painters included Alexander H. Wyant (1836–92), *Falls of the Ohio and Louisville, Mohawk Valley,* and *An Old Clearing;* Homer D. Martin (1836–97), *View of the Seine* (best-known as *Harp of the Winds*); Ralph Albert Blakelock (1847–1919), *Brook by Moonlight;* and Abbott H. Thayer, *Monadnock.*

1860–80. TRANSITION TO OBJECTIVE REALISM. Homer and **Eakins.** American painting took on a greater power, resourcefulness, and maturity with the work of **Winslow Homer** (p. 728) and **Thomas Eakins** (p. 700).

Homer, who began as a magazine illustrator, 1st came to prominence in 1866 with *Prisoners from the Front,* a canvas based on his Civil War experience as a pictorial reporter; this reminiscent phase was continued in *Rainy Day in Camp* and *Sunday Morning in Virginia.* After 1880, when he began living in Me., Homer abandoned illustrative and anecdotal subjects. Along the Me. seacoast, and during his stay in the Caribbean, Homer developed an original vein which appears in *All's Well, Winter Coast, Rowing Home, The Gulf Stream,* and *After the Tornado, Bahamas.* As a water-colorist, Homer is of the 1st rank.

Eakins brought to portrait and figure painting a strength and character based on a profound study of the human form and an intimate acquaintance with the work of the French and Spanish masters. His choice and treatment of subject signaled the rise of a new realism reflected in such paintings as *The Swimming Hole, The Agnew Clinic, The Gross Clinic, The Thinker, Max Schmitt in a Single Scull, The Concert Singer,* and *Katherine.*

1877. Opening of the first American Salon des Réfusés by the Society of American Artists (early exhibitors included La Farge, Inness, Ryder, and Eakins); amalgamated with the Academy in New York, 1906, to form the present National Academy of Design.

1880–1910. MYSTICISM. The poetic intensity of **Albert Pinkham Ryder** (p. 775) produced canvases weighted with heavy yet luminous color and with strange masses and forms drawn from an imaginary world. A solitary worker during his lifetime, it was only after his death that Ryder won general recognition. Among his paintings are *Macbeth and the Witches, The Flying Dutchman, Jonah and the Whale, Toilers of the Sea,* and *Pegasus.*

1880–1910. IMPRESSIONIST MOVEMENT. French Impressionism, a school preoccupied with the subtle and iridescent play of light over forms, developed *c.*1871, *et seq.,* with the work of such painters as Claude Monet, Berthe Morisot, Camille Pissarro, and Alfred Sisley. American painting's 1st direct acquaintance with Impressionism began with **Mary Cassatt** (1845–1926), known for such characteristic pieces as *Caresse Maternelle* and *Mother and Child.* The only American invited to exhibit with the French Impressionists, she did all of her work abroad. It remained for Theodore Robinson (1852–96) to introduce Impressionism into America. The influence of Monet is apparent in Robinson's *Spring in Giverny.* Impressionism combined with American themes in the work of J. Alden Weir (1852–1919), *A Factory Village, Visiting Neighbors, Ploughing for Buckwheat,* and *Nocturne, Queensboro Bridge;* John H. Twachtman (1853–1902), *The White Bridge, Snow-bound, Waterfall, Summer,* and *October;* and Childe Hassam (1859–1935), *Union Square in Spring, Church at Old Lyme, The 17th of October,* and *Central Park from the Plaza.* In 1898 Hassam, Twachtman, Weir, and others banded together as "Ten American Painters" and held the 1st exhibition of U.S. Impressionists.

1900–1910. REALISTS. In the early 20th century there emerged a group of painters who concentrated on homely incident, subject, and character, basing their content on direct observation and their technique on European masters such as Hals, Goya, Hogarth, and Daumier. Known as "The Ash Can School" (and sometimes, with Maurice Prendergast [1859–1924] and others, as "The Eight"), this group included Robert Henri (1865–1929), *Martche in a White Dress* and *Boy with a Piccolo;* George Luks (1867–1933), *The Old Duchess, The Little Milliner,* and *The Spielers;* William Glackens (1870–1938), *Chez Mouquin* and *Roller Skating Rink;* John Sloan (1871–1951), *The Wake of the Ferry, Dust Storm, Election Night,* and *McSorley's Bar* (organizer of the Society of Independent Artists, 1917, in protest against the conservatism of the National Academy of Design); George Bellows (1882–1925), *Stag at Sharkey's, Edith Cavell,* and *Day in June;* and Everett Shinn (1876–   ), best known for his treatments of stage subjects, as in *Revue* and *White Ballet.*

1913. ARMORY SHOW, which opened at the 69th Regiment Armory in New York on 17 Feb. 1913, was organized by the Association of Painters and Sculptors, whose president was Arthur B. Davies (1862–1928). It had a 2-fold purpose: to introduce to an American audience in coherent and integrated form the origins and evolution of the modern European art tradition, and to create a more favorable atmosphere for the reception of artists working outside the established academic tradition. In addition to exhibiting works by Ingres, Delacroix, Courbet, and the French Impressionists, the Armory Show included the post-Impressionists (Cézanne, Van Gogh, Seurat, and others), and Cubist and abstractionist painters like Picasso, Matisse, Duchamp, and Kandinsky. In the work of Brancusi, Maillol, and Lehmbruck, Americans saw new experiments in sculpture.

A landmark in the history of American art, the Army Show signified a definite break in the hold exerted by the academic school and had a lasting influence over a wide range of media, including interior design and advertising art. Its notes were heard in the art criticism of Willard Huntington Wright, Leo Stein, and Walter Pach. The Armory Show paved the way for the acceptance of a new generation of American painters, among them Louis M. Eilshemius (1864–1941), Jerome Myers (1867–1940), George ("Pop") Hart (1868–1933), Alfred Maurer (1868–1932), John Marin (p. 749), Eugene Higgins (1874–   ), Kenneth Hayes Miller (1876–   ),

Maurice Sterne (1877–   ), Marsden Hartley (1877–1943), Arthur G. Dove (1880–1946), Walt Kuhn (1880–   ), Max Weber (1881–   ), Rockwell Kent (1882–   ), Edward Hopper (1882–   ), Charles Demuth (1883–1935), Charles Sheeler (1883–   ), Guy Pène du Bois (1884–   ), and Georgia O'Keeffe (1887–   ).

1861–85. SCULPTURE. The sculptors of the post-Civil War era alternated between realism and classicism until *c.*1885, when the influence of the Italian Renaissance began to make itself strongly felt in monumental and ornamental sculpture. The leading sculptors up to *c.*1880 included Launt Thompson (1833–94), who executed *Rocky Mountain Trapper,* the statue of *Abraham Pierson* at Yale University, and the equestrian statues of *Gen. John Sedgwick* at West Point and of *Gen. Winfield Scott* at Washington, D.C.; Larkin G. Mead (1835–1910), *Lincoln Monument* at Springfield, Ill., the statue of *Ethan Allen* at the National Capitol, and *The Father of Waters;* George Bissell (1839–1920), statues of *Chancellor James Kent* at the Congressional Library, *President Arthur* in Madison Square Park, N.Y., and *Chancellor James Watts* at Trinity Church, N.Y.; Franklin Simmons (1839–1913), the *Naval Monument* at Washington, D.C., and statues of *Roger Williams* and *Gov. William King* at the National Capitol; Martin Milmore (1844–83), *Soldiers' and Sailors' Monument* on Boston Common; and Olin L. Warner (1844–96), known for his portrait busts of *J. Alden Weir* and *William Crary Brownell,* the statue of *William Lloyd Garrison* at Boston, and a series of relief portraits of North American Indians.

1885–1938. American sculpture attained a new mark of craftsmanship and conception with the work of the Irish-born **Augustus Saint-Gaudens** (1848–1907) and that of **Daniel Chester French** (1850–1931) and **George Grey Barnard** (1863–1938). Saint-Gaudens executed the statue of *Lincoln* at Lincoln Park, Chicago; the *Adams Memorial* (the noted hooded figure sometimes called *Grief*) in Rock Creek Cemetery, Washington, D.C.; the *Shaw Memorial* at Bos-

ton; the *Sherman* and *Farragut Memorials,* both at New York; *Amor Caritas;* and *Diana* (the figure on the tower of the old Madison Square Garden at New York). Among French's many works are *The Minute-Man* and *Ralph Waldo Emerson* at Concord, Mass.; the statue of *Lincoln* at the Lincoln Memorial, Washington, D.C.; the statue of *John Harvard* and the *Longfellow Memorial* at Cambridge, Mass.; the statue of *Lewis Cass* at the National Capitol; the massive figure of *The Republic* at the World's Columbian Exposition; *Gallaudet and His First Deaf-Mute Pupil* at Washington, D.C.; the *Parkman Memorial* at Boston; and *Death and the Young Sculptor* at Roxbury, Mass. Barnard's works include *The Two Natures, The Prodigal Son, The Hewer,* the group at the State Capitol at Harrisburg, Pa., and the uncompleted colossal World War I memorial.

Other leading sculptors of the period were Frederick W. MacMonnies (1863–1937), who executed *Civic Virtue,* formerly at City Hall Park, N.Y., the site of his statue of *Nathan Hale; Bacchante,* at Boston; *Victory,* at West Point, N.Y.; the *Soldiers' and Sailors' Memorial* at Grand Army Plaza, Brooklyn, N.Y., on which Thomas Eakins collaborated; the statue of *Shakespeare* at the Congressional Library; and the *Columbian Fountain* at the World's Columbian Exposition; Herbert Adams (1858–1945), best known for his polychrome portrait busts, including *Primavera, The Rabbi's Daughter,* and *Julia Marlowe;* Paul Wayland Bartlett (1865–1925), *The Ghost Dancer, The Bear Tamer, The Genius of Man,* and statues of *Michelangelo* and *Columbus* at the Congressional Library; Karl Bitter (1867–1915), *Carl Schurz Memorial* at New York, monumental reliefs at the Broad Street Station, Philadelphia, and *The Standard Bearers* at the Pan-American Exposition held at Buffalo; and James Earle Fraser (1876–   ), *End of the Trail, Alexander Hamilton* at the Treasury Department Building, Washington, D.C., group for the Theodore Roosevelt Memorial at New York, figures of *Thomas Jefferson* and *Lewis and Clark* at the Missouri State Capitol, and the statue of *Franklin* at the Franklin Institute, Philadelphia.

c.1861–c.1885. ARCHITECTURE.
Rapid industrialization profoundly changed older ideas; cast iron came into wide use in commercial buildings, and glass in large sheets became available for the 1st time. New fortunes placed a premium on lavish, showy design. This period witnessed the 1st practical passenger elevators (p. 567), and the beginnings of the typical city office building as well as the large department store.

VICTORIAN GOTHIC (English), marked by an Italianate strain, appeared in numerous guises, ranging from the filigree jigsaw detail of "carpenter's Gothic" to polished careful designs that reflected the influence of John Ruskin. Used for public buildings and in many town and country houses, the style featured polychrome masonry, squat pointed arches, high ceilings, arcaded windows, and elaborate bays and oriels. Among the best examples: old *Boston Museum of Fine Arts* (1872–75), designed by **Russell Sturgis** (1836–1909; better known for his critical writings and *A History of Architecture*, 4 vols., 1906–15); library and *Memorial Hall* at Harvard University (completed 1874), designed by **William Robert Ware** (1832–1915) and **Henry Van Brunt** (1832–1903); and the *State House,* Hartford, Conn. (completed 1885), designed by **Upjohn.**

FRENCH RENAISSANCE REVIVAL was the architectural hallmark of the "Gilded Age." Among its prominent characteristics were mansard roofs, lavish and heavy ornamentation, coupled columns and pilasters, large cornices, and an undiscriminating use of the architectural orders. This style was employed in many types of buildings—churches, hotels, hospitals, schools, railroad stations, and public buildings. One of the most active exemplars was A. B. Mullett (?–1890), who as government architect designed the *State, War and Navy Building,* Washington, D.C., and the old *Post Offices* at Boston and New York. An important offshoot of this mode was the **brownstone-front house,** adopted on a wide scale in New York City during the 1870's and 1880's. The style achieved a fresh delicacy in the work of **Richard Morris Hunt** (1828–95), trained in Paris, designer of numerous houses for merchant princes at New York, Newport, R.I., and elsewhere, including those for the Vanderbilts.

COLLEGIATE ARCHITECTURAL EDUCATION began in the U.S. in this period. The 1st architectural school was opened at the Massachusetts Institute of Technology (1866) under the direction of William Robert Ware. Architectural courses were subsequently introduced at the University of Illinois (1870), Cornell (1871), Columbia (1883), and Harvard (1890). The influence of the École des Beaux Arts in Paris, where many Americans were trained in the 1870's, was dominant in the majority.

1876. PHILADELPHIA CENTENNIAL EXPOSITION (U.S. International Exposition), with its 249 buildings occupying 465 acres of Fairmount Park, constituted a grandiose summation of the architectural styles of the period; its dominant modes were the Queen Anne variation of Victorian Gothic, French mansard, and Swiss châlet derivations. In it, however, the influence of new constructional ideas gave rise to a few prophetic and independent exteriors important as reflecting the new forms industrialized engineering might produce. Foreign art exhibits, particularly in the crafts, left a deep mark on public taste.

c.1876–c.1894. ROMANESQUE REVIVAL. Although derived from the Romanesque of southern France, it was not based on any current European revival; its leading force was **Henry Hobson Richardson** (p. 770), who received his training at the École des Beaux Arts. At the outset of his career he employed Victorian Gothic (design for the *Church of the Unity*, Springfield, Mass.), but turned to his own adaptation of French Romanesque in his plans for the *Brattle Square Church,* Boston. His integrated use of mass, space, and line, and his imaginative treatment of ornament, rank him among the foremost U.S. architects. His most famous work is *Trinity Church* at Boston (opened 1877). His other outstanding designs include *Crane Library,* Quincy, Mass.; the libraries at Malden, Mass., and Burlington, Vt.; the *Allegheny Courthouse and Jail*, Pittsburgh; the *Marshall Field Wholesale Store,* Chicago; the now demolished *Hay-Adams* houses at Washington, D.C.; and railroad stations for the Boston and Albany line. Especially influential in New England and the West, the Romanesque Revival was frequently employed in the latter area by the partners, **Daniel H. Burnham** (1846–1912) and **John Wellborn Root** (1850–91), who designed the old *Chicago Art Institute* and the *Montauk, Phoenix, Rookery,* and *Rialto* buildings, all at Chicago.

1884–1914. COMING OF THE SKYSCRAPER. An indigenous American contribution, the skyscraper was made possible by cheap and abundant structural steel, the passenger elevator, inexpensive fireproofing, and resourceful solutions of the structural problems of foundations. Because its problems were new, the skyscraper induced architects to work out solutions based on function rather than style. Customarily accredited as the 1st tall structure embodying in part the basic principles of metal frame construction is the *Home Insurance Building* at Chicago (built 1884–85), designed by **William LeBaron Jenney** (1832–1907), who used cast-iron columns and wrought-iron beams. The 1st building erected completely of wrought-iron skeleton construction was the 13-story *Tacoma Building* at Chicago (built 1887–88), designed by Holabird and Roche. Precursors of the functional form were the *Wainwright Building* at St. Louis (1890), the characteristic nontraditional skyscraper design of the early 20th century, and the horizontal emphasis in the *Carson, Pirie, and Scott Building* at Chicago (1899), both by **Louis H. Sullivan** (p. 787). Prevailing eclecticism governed architectural style at the turn of the 20th century. Characteristic of this style, all in New York City: *Singer Building,* by **Ernest Flagg** (1857–1947); *Metropolitan Life Insurance Co. Tower* (1906), by N. LeBrun & Sons; the *"Flatiron" Building,* by Daniel H. Burnham; and the *Woolworth Building* (1911–13), with its overlay of Gothic motifs, by **Cass Gilbert** (1859–1934).

1893–1917. NEW CLASSICAL REVIVAL AND ECLECTICISM. The **Chicago World's Fair** (World's Columbian Exposition, 1893) provided the major impetus for the general adoption of Greek, Roman, and Renaissance forms and the gradual abandonment of the Romanesque. The Roman Classical mode for the grounds and buildings on 686 acres of Jackson Park, along Lake Michigan, was chosen by a group of architects working under the direction of Daniel H. Burnham, including Richard M. Hunt, McKim, Mead & White, and George B. Post. The most important building at the "White City" which did not bear the classic stamp was the *Transportation Building* by Sullivan. The classic-eclectic tradition of exposition architecture was continued at the **Pan-American Exposition** (1901) and the **Louisiana Purchase Exposition** (1904) at St. Louis. Among leading exponents of classic eclecticism was the firm of **McKim, Mead & White,** of which the most important members were **Charles F. McKim** (1849–1909) and **Stanford White** (1853–1906). Their work includes the *Henry Villard House* (1885), the *Century Club* (1890), the earlier (Low) *Columbia University Library* (1893), the *Herald Building* (1894), the *J. Pierpont Morgan Library* (1906), all at New York City, and the *Boston Public Library* (1888). Other exemplars were Carrère and Hastings, who designed the *New York Public Library* and the *Senate* and *House Office Buildings,* Washington, D.C.; and **Cass Gilbert,** who designed the *Minnesota State Capitol,* the *U.S. Custom House* at New York City, the *U.S. Treasury Annex,* and the *Supreme Court Building,* Washington, D.C. Eclecticism marked the work of **Henry J. Hardenbergh** (1847–1918), who designed the old *Waldorf-Astoria Hotel* (1891–96) and the *Plaza Hotel* (1907), both at New York City, and the *Copley Plaza* (1910) at Boston; and the work of **George B. Post** (1837–1913), who designed the *Pulitzer Building* (1889–92), the *New York Produce Exchange* (1881–85), the *New York Cotton Exchange* (1883–86), the *St. Paul Building* (1897–99), the *College of the City of New York* (1902–11), the *New York Stock Exchange* (1904), and the *Wisconsin State Capitol.* Gothic eclecticism found its most brilliant expression in **Ralph Adams Cram** (1863–1942), member of the firm of Cram, Goodhue &

Ferguson. Among the structures which bear his distinctive mark are *St. Stephen's Church,* Cohasset, Mass.; *West Point Academy* (1904); *St. Thomas's Church,* New York City (1911–13); *Calvary Church,* Pittsburgh (1907); and the *Fourth Presbyterian Church,* Chicago (1912). In his latter days **Bertram Grosvenor Goodhue** (1869–1924) broke with the Gothic style. His plan for the *Capitol* at Lincoln, Neb., marked a new expression of the classic tradition, with a free and daring use of decorative sculpture.

SULLIVAN AND WRIGHT. During the Classical Revival the quest for a functional, indigenous style was carried forward by **Louis H. Sullivan** and his disciple, **Frank Lloyd Wright** (p. 804). Sullivan was in partnership with Dankmar Adler at Chicago (1881–1900), and here Wright served his apprenticeship. Among Sullivan's most notable structures: *Chicago Auditorium* (1889), *Chicago Stock Exchange Building* (1894), *Bayard Building,* New York City (1898), and the *National Farmers Bank,* Owatonna, Minn. (1908). Toward the turn of the 20th century Wright began to develop his distinctive **"prairie house"** style in the Midwest. His first important commercial structure was the *Larkin Administration Building,* Buffalo, N.Y. (1904). One of his most successful suburban dwellings was the *Robie House,* Chicago (1908).

1914. World War I found U.S. architecture in a confused state. The brilliance of the planning in many of the great classic-eclectic monuments blinded many to the basic superficiality of its approach. Office buildings, department stores, mass housing, and factories of undreamed of complexity and size constituted pressing challenges to which rational and beautiful answers were still rare. Industrial production of building materials was breaking down hand craftsmanship and curtailed building appropriations discouraged lavishness on the earlier scale. Only a completely new creative architecture, then only in its infancy, could provide the answer.

1914–29. REIGN OF PARIS ABSTRACTION. With the outbreak of World War I French artists (Gleizer, Picabia, and Duchamp) came to the U.S.

and spread ideas of **cubism,** which in the period 1919–29 was changed into a purist style by Demuth, Sheiler, and Preston Dickinson (1891–1930). The mid-20's saw the apogee of Paris Abstraction in the work of such artists as Weber, Maurer, and **John Marin** (p. 749).

1919–29. FROM REALISM TO SOCIAL REALISM. The influence of Robert Henri in emulating the work of Manet and Velasquez is found in the works of such students as **George Bellows** (p. 674), notable for his career as an illustrator and lithographer and for his prize fight scenes (*Dempsey and Firpo,* 1923); Edward Hopper, who classicized the facts of daily life in the U.S. (*Automat; The City; Compartment C, Car 293*); Edward Speicher (1883– ; *Katharine Cornell, Graziana*); Alexander Brook (1898– ; *Morning*); and Rockwell Kent (1882–), with his Alaskan and marine scenes. During the same period Georgia O'Keeffe and Charles Burchfield (1898–) painted objective records of the local scene.

1930–40. The social realism of the "Ash Can School" was intensified by the depression and by the organization in 1935 of the **WPA Federal Art Projects.** The newer artists divested slum scenes of poetry or sentimentality and used them as a medium of social protest. Robert Gwathmey (1903– ; *End of Day*) projected his message through complex semi-abstract types; Jack Levine (1915–) caricatured the privileged (*The Reluctant Ploughshare*); Mitchell Siporin (1910–) portrayed the heroes of the class struggle in allegorical groupings. Among the most effective exponents of social realism were William Gropper (1897– ; *The Opposition*), Philip Evergood (1901– ; *Suburban Landscape*), and Ben Shahn (1898– ; *Vacant Lot, Sunday Football*). A sympathetic treatment of working people was notably expressed in the work of the three Soyer brothers, Moses, Raphael, and Isaac.

1930–40. REGIONALISTS OR ISOLATIONISTS. In reaction to the influence of Picasso, Matisse, and the Parisian school, a trio of U.S. artists stressed native Midwestern scenes, particularly after

1932: Grant Wood (1892–1942; *Dinner for Threshers, Return from Bohemia, American Gothic*), John Steuart Curry (1897–1946; *My Mother and Father, Baptism in Kansas, Roadworkers' Camp*), and Thomas Hart Benton (1889– ; *First Crop*). Ultimately the trend ran its course and revealed its sterility.

1930–40. Abstract traditions were maintained by Stuart Davis (1894–), Karl Knaths (1891–), and Dove. When the **Bauhaus** closed in 1934, some of its leaders came to the U.S. (Gropius, Moholy-Nagy, and Josef Albers), as well as the expressionist, George Grosz (1893–).

1939–48. With the rise of Fascism many European artists found refuge in the U.S. (Marc Chagall, Lipschutz, Tchelitchew, and Dali). Socially conscious painting declined after the Nazi-Soviet pact (the American Artists Congress, a left-wing group founded in 1936, broke up in 1940), and abstractions and surrealist works enjoyed an increase in popularity (Peter Blume, *The Eternal City*). New experimentation appeared in the "magic realism" of Byron Thomas (1902– ; *Night Ball Game*) and the abstractionism of German-born Werner-Drewes (1899–). In addition, the WPA Index of American Design revived interest in U.S. primitives and encouraged the self-taught artists, including in this period Grandma Moses (1860–), with her anecdotal detail, and the Negro artist, Horace Pippin (1888–1946; *The Trial of John Brown*). A personal art form was still being developed by Yasuo Kuniyoshi (1893–).

1914–52. TRENDS IN SCULPTURE. A revived interest in the architectonic aspects of sculpture developed after 1914. Important work in direct carving was done by Jacob Epstein (1880–), U.S.-born expatriate who lives in London, William Zorach (1887– ; *Mother and Child, Affection*), Gaston Lachaise (1882–1935; *Figure of a Woman*), Maurice Sterne (1878– ; *Rogers-Kennedy Memorial*), Elie Nadelman (1882–1946; *Seated Woman, Head in Marble*), Robert Laurent (1890– ; *Charity, Kneeling Figure*). In contrast to the rugged quality of Jo Davidson's (1883–) work (*Gertrude Stein, Dr. Albert Einstein*) were the creations of Paul Manship

(1886–), reflecting Renaissance, archaic, and Oriental influence (*Dancer and Gazelles, Centaur and Dryad, The Indian Hunter*). Outstanding for his animal sculpture was John B. Flannagan (1898–1942; *Chimpanzee*). The newer group of sculptors include Charles Alston, abstractionist, Ahron Ben-Shmuel (*The Boxers, Young Poet*), and Hugo Robus, with archaic qualities incorporated into his streamlined figure studies (*Girl Reading, Girl Washing Her Hair*). Some of the most significant work continued to be contributed by Swedish-American Carl Milles (1875–1955); *Astronomer, Dancing Girls*).

1918–60. ARCHITECTURAL TRENDS. The confused state of taste in 1914 yielded to more creative tendencies, despite the widespread wave of "colonialism" in domestic architecture—final manifestation of eclecticism. Shortly after World War I strong influences from the new architecture of Europe (especially of France and Germany) were dominant. The form this new architecture took in the 1920's was primarily ascetic, geometrical, and antihistorical, even deliberately avoiding the use of traditional building materials and techniques. This is sometimes called the **international style**. It influenced domestic, school, and factory architecture profoundly, but its disregard of regional and national differences in materials, climate, and ways of living proved it too limited for wide U.S. application, although some of its basic ideals of truth to structure and material and its geometrical quality were absorbed into the U.S. tradition. The **Chicago World's Fair** (1933) and the **New York** and **San Francisco World's Fairs** (1939) were important chiefly as indicating public acceptance of the objectives of modern architecture. By 1940 its dominance was at an end. Instead, the best U.S. architecture sought much freer, though equally new and logical, solutions, using the traditional brick, stone, and wood in new ways, with marked regional differences (e.g., houses in Fla. compared to Calif.). In this development the influence of **Wright**, who had always stood for a humane and nonmechanized ideal, was of primary importance.

In the 1950's, in protest against the neo-classicism of **Ludwig Mies van der Rohe** (1886–), with its stress on form rather than site (860 Lake Shore Dr., Chicago; Seagram Bldg., N.Y.C.), new forms emerged—**Hugh Stebbins'** Congress Hall in Berlin, **Eero Saarinen's** auditorium for M.I.T. and hockey rink for Yale; or texture stressed—**Edward D. Stone's** U.S. Embassy at New Delhi and **Harry Weese's** U.S. Embassy at Accra. Other trends in the 1950's; striking airport design—Lambert Field, St. Louis, by Hellmuth, Yamasee, and Leinweber; regional shopping centers—Northland, for suburban Detroit; and school design stressing site-planning and building arrangement—Perkins and Wills' Heathcote School, Scarsdale, N.Y.

MID-CENTURY PAINTINGS AND SCULPTURE. (1) **Realism** was exemplified in paintings by Walt Kuhn, Andrew Wyeth, and Edward Hopper, and the sculpture of William Zorach, Robert Laurent, José de Creeft, Alexander Archipenko, Chaim Gross, and Oronzio Malderelli; (2) the **primitives** by Horace Pippin and Grandma Moses. (3) **Abstrac-**tion in its purer form was exemplified by a small group of painters, including Stuart Davis, George L. K. Morris, and Irene Rice Pereira. (4) The **"romantic-abstractionists,"** a larger group, had surrealist overtones and were concerned with personal symbolism and metaphysics (William Baziotes, Mark Rothko, Jackson Pollock, Theodore Stamos, and the sculpture of Theodore J. Roszak, Herbert Ferber, David Smith, and Isamu Noguchi). (5) **Abstract expressionism** gained ground in the 1950s, in individual works of many of the aforementioned artists, and in the pictures of Hans Hofmann, Vaclav Vytacil, Willem de Kooning, Franz Kline, Robert Motherwell, Adolph Gottlieb, and the sculpture of Seymour Lipton, David Smith, Ibram Lassau, and Theodore Roszak. The wire constructions of Richard Lippold elaborated on the early work of such artists as Alexander Calder. Other artists, notably Jack Levine, Abraham Rattner, Yasuo Kuniyoshi, Peter Blume, and Ben Shahn, utilized expressionism, surrealism, and abstraction to make social comments.

MUSIC

1640–1764. *Bay Psalm Book* (also p. 592) published at Cambridge, Mass.; the 1st hymn book printed in the English colonies; adopted throughout New England and as far south as Philadelphia. This psalm collection was printed without tunes, leaving choice of psalmody to the individual congregation. As a result psalm singing became a confused cacophony. The 9th ed. (1698) included 13 tunes (1st book with music printed in the colonies). In 1712 Rev. John Tufts of Boston published *A Very Plain and Easy Introduction to the Whole Art of Singing Psalm Tunes,* containing 28 tunes in 3-part harmony, the 1st instruc-tion book on singing to be compiled in the colonies. In 1764 Josiah Flagg of Boston published *A Collection of Best Psalm Tunes,* engraved by Paul Revere.

1703–87. ORGAN. First recorded use in a colonial church, Gloria Dei Church (Swedish) in present Philadelphia. First organ to be built in the colonies was constructed by Dr. Thomas Witt of Philadelphia (1704). The 1st imported into New England was in 1711 by Thomas Brattle of Boston (still in existence in Portsmouth, N.H.). The 1st to be constructed (1745–46) by a native American was built by Edward Bromfield, Jr., of Boston. In 1756 the new organ constructed by Gilbert Ash was dedicated at City Hall, N.Y. A pipe organ was used for the 1st time in a colonial Congregational Church in Philadelphia, 1770. The 1st pipe organ west of the Alleghenies was built (1787) in Cookstown (now Fayette City), Pa., by Joseph Downer of Brookline, Mass.; instrument now at Carnegie Institute, Pittsburgh.

1707–37. HYMNS, as a replacement of psalm renderings, were popularized by Isaac Watts' famous English hymnal (1707). John Wesley, influenced by Moravian hymn singing, was arraigned by the Savannah, Ga., grand jury (1737), charged, among other counts, with introducing unauthorized psalms and hymns into the Anglican Church service. The folk hymnody of the Methodists and Baptists on the frontier continued this tradition.

c.1715. MOTHER GOOSE rhymes composed by "Mother Goose," mother-in-law of Thomas Fleet, Boston printer, who came to live with Thomas and her daughter Elizabeth after the birth of their baby, and sang to him. Fleet published the nursery rhymes under the title, *Songs for Nursery or Mother Goose Melodies for Children.*

1720–30. EPHRATA CLOISTER, founded by German Dunkers, 50 miles west of Philadelphia. Women copied and illuminated hymn books. Hymns were sung in 4-, 5-, 6-, and 7-part harmony (while in the rest of the colonies congregations sang only in unison). Ephrata Hymnbook (*Gottliche Lieben und Lobes Gethöne*) published by Benjamin Franklin (1730). More than 1,000 of the hymns are attributed to **Johann Conrad Beissel** (1690–1768), supposed to be the 1st composer in the colonies whose works were published.

1731–32. EARLY CONCERTS. First authentic record in the English colonies of a public concert at Mr. Pelham's (*Boston News-Letter,* Dec. 16, 23). First recorded concert in Charleston, S.C., a few months later.

1732–33. Karl Theodore Pachelbel, son of the famous organist, the 1st European musician of note to visit Boston; gave the 1st recorded concert in New York (1736), playing the harpsichord.

1735–50. BALLAD OPERAS. The ballad opera, *Flora, or Hob in the Well,* at the Courtroom, Charleston, S.C. (1735), the 1st recorded operatic performance in the colonies. *The Mock Doctor* (1750), the 1st performed ballad opera in New York, was followed that year by *The Beggar's Opera.*

1742. MORAVIAN MUSIC. First singstunde in Bethlehem, Pa. (settled, 1741, by Moravians). **Collegium musicum,** founded 1744, credited with early performance of parts of several oratorios; continued until 1820, when it was succeeded by the Philharmonic Society. Most notable among the Revolutionary generation of Moravian musicians was **John Frederick Peter** (1746–1813), a composer of chamber music as well as organist of the Moravian congregation. The 1st copies of Haydn's quartets and symphonies were imported from Europe to Bethlehem, which also gave the 1st performances in America of *The Creation* and *The Seasons* by Handel. Bethlehem Bach Choir org. 1900.

1752. First use of an orchestra in an operatic performance in the colonies: *The Beggar's Opera,* given in Upper Marlboro, Md., by the Kean and Murray Co.

1753. William Tuckey (1708–81), on arrival in New York, became organist and choirmaster of Trinity Church; directed 1st performance in the colonies of excerpts from Handel's *Messiah* (1770).

1754–63. CONCERT HALLS AND OUTDOOR CONCERTS. First concert hall in Boston opened by Gilbert Deblois (1754). Ranelagh Gardens' series of open-air summer concerts announced in N.Y. *Mercury;* continued for 4 yrs.

1756–89. FRENCH HORNS AND OBOE. Franklin records the 1st instance of the use of French horns in the colonies in commenting on the excellent music in the Moravian Church at Bethlehem, where flutes, oboes, French horns, and trumpets were used with the organ. In New England the 1st mention of French horns was 1761, at a concert given by Mr. Dipper, organist of King's Chapel, Boston. First mention of oboe in New England was at a concert at Salem, Mass., by Gottlieb Graupner (1789).

1757. Dr. Arne's *Masque of Alfred* performed by students of College of Philadelphia.

1759–88. SECULAR SONGS. First secular song by a native American, "My Days Have Been So Wondrous Free," music by **Francis Hopkinson** (1737–91), poem by Thomas Parnell. Hopkinson, a Philadelphian and the 1st native composer, was later a signer of the Declaration of Independence, a member of the Constitutional Convention, the 1st judge of the Admiralty Court of Pa., and author of many pamphlets and poems; his *Seven Songs,* 1788.

1761–87. MUSICAL SOCIETIES. St. Cecilia Society, oldest musical society, founded at Charleston, S.C.; continued until 1912; gave several concerts each year, including St. Cecilia's Day, 22 Nov. The orchestra was composed of "gentlemen performers," supplemented by professional musicians engaged by the season. Harmonic Soc., N.Y., gave concert series (1773–74) presenting 1st French and Italian virtuosi. Handel Society (Dartmouth College, 1780), Harmonic Society (Fredericksburg, Va., 1784), Musical Society of Boston (1785–89) performed excerpts from Handel's works. Stoughton (Mass.) Musical Society organized by William Billings, probably the oldest singing society still in existence in the U.S.; held 1st singing contest in U.S. at Dorchester (1790), competing against First Parish of Dorchester. Uranian Society est. (Phila., 1787–1800) to improve church music.

1763. EARLY MUSIC SCHOOL. James Bremner opened a music school in Philadelphia; subsequently active in city's musical life; pupils reputed to have included Francis Hopkinson.

1765. Concert of "musical glasses" in Philadelphia; a harmonica seen in England in 1762 by Franklin, who introduced an improved model into the colonies.

1767. "YANKEE DOODLE," mentioned in 1st American opera libretto, Andrew Barton's *The Disappointment, or the Force of Credulity.* First American printing, as part of an instrumental medley, in *Federal Overture* (1794), arranged by **Benjamin Carr** (1769–1831) and published by him in Philadelphia and New York (1795). Nonsensical text ("Father

and I went down to camp, along with Capt. Goodwin") dates back to 1775. First American edition to use words and music published by G. Willig (1798).

1769, 16 Nov. Symphony by **John Gualdo** (d. 1771), Italian emigrant, performed in Phila.

1769–74. SPINET AND PIANOFORTE. First American spinet made by John Harris in Boston; first American pianoforte by John Behrent, Philadelphia.

1770. Milton's *Masque of Comus* performed by Hallam Co., Phila. 1st performance in colonies of Handel's *Messiah* (overture and 16 nos.) at Trinity Church, N.Y., cond. and org. by William Tuckey. *New England Psalmsinger* by **William Billings** (1746–1800), 1st N.E. composer, organizer of singing societies; composer of *Fuguing Tunes, Chester,* and numerous popular patriotic songs during the Revolution.

1783. Fortnightly City Concert est. at Philadelphia by John Bentley, subsequently leader of the orchestra of the old American Co., which he founded.

1791–1835. EARLY SONG AND HARMONY BOOKS. *Harmonia Americana,* by Samuel Holyoke (1791); *The American Harmony,* by Oliver Holden (1792), and Holden's *The Union Harmony* (1793), with 1st printing of "Coronation" (later the hymn, "All Hail the Power of Jesus' Name"); *Rural Harmony,* by Jacob Kimball (1793); *The Continental Harmony,* by **William Billings** (1794); *Boston Handel and Haydn Society's Collection of Sacred Music* (1822), comp. by **Lowell Mason** (1792–1872), pioneer in U.S. musical education, called "the father of American church music"; *The Southern Harmony and Musical Companion,* by William Walker (1835).

1793–98. POPULAR SONGS. "The President's March" (*c.*1793), variously attributed to Philip Roth and Philip Phile; "Adams and Liberty" (1798), words by Robert Treat Paine; words of "Hail, Columbia," by Joseph Hopkinson, set to tune of "The President's March" (1798).

1794–96. EARLY AMERICAN OPERAS. *Tammany,* by **James Hewitt** (1770–1827), sometimes claimed to be the 1st American opera, produced at New York under the auspices of the Tammany Society (1794). *The Archers, or the Mountaineers of Switzerland,* libretto by **William Dunlap,** music by **Benjamin Carr** (1768–1831); and *Edwin and Angelina,* libretto by Elihu H. Smith, music by Victor Pelissier (both N.Y., 1796).

1796–1847.[1] FOREIGN COMPOSERS IN AMERICA. Gluck: Overture to *Iphegenie en Aulide* performed in Charleston, S.C., by an orchestra of some 30 instruments (1796). **Haydn:** *Stabat Mater,* Charleston, S.C., 1796; Haydn societies org. Phila., 1809; Cincinnati, 1819; 1st complete perf., *Creation,* Boston, 1819. **Handel:** *Messiah,* Univ. of Pa. (1801); 1st complete performance, probably HH (1818); oratorio, *Israel in Egypt,* Seguin Opera Co., N.Y. (1842). **Beethoven:** *1st Symph.,* MFSP (1821); *6th* (Pastoral) and *2nd,* Boston (1842); *5th,* PS (1843); *Egmont Overture,* Boston (1844); *9th,* PS (1846). **Mozart:** *Jupiter Symph.* (No. 41), PS (1844); *3rd,* PS (1847); Mozart Society org., Chicago (1847). **Weber:** *Jubilee Overture,* Boston (1842). **Rossini:** *Stabat Mater,* HH (1843). **Mendelssohn:** Oratorio, *St. Paul,* N.Y. (1838); oratorio, *Elijah,* HH (1840); *Hebrides Overture,* PS (1844); *Scotch Symph.,* PS (1845); Mendelssohn Festival, Castle Garden, N.Y. (1847). **Schumann:** *1st Symph.,* MFSB (1841).

1800–52. MUSICAL PERIODICALS. *American Musical Mag.* (Northampton, Mass., 1800; disc. 1801); *Boston Musical Gaz.* (1838; disc. 1846); *Musical World* (N.Y., 1849; disc. 1860); *Amer. Monthly Musical Rev.* (N.Y., 1850; disc. 1852); *Dwight's Jl. of Music* (Boston, 1852; pioneered in musical criticism; disc. 1881).

1803–53. PIANOS. First authenticated American piano made by Benjamin Crehorne of Milton, Mass. (1803); firm of Stewart and Chickering, piano manufac-

turers, est. at Boston (1823). **Jonas Chickering** (1798–1853) patented (1837) the 1st successful casting of a full iron piano frame capable of withstanding powerful tension without deflecting pitch. **Wilhelm Knabe** (1803–64) est. at Baltimore the firm of Knabe & Co. (*c.*1837). Henry Steinway & Sons established at New York City (1853).

1805. DA PONTE. Lorenzo Da Ponte (1749–1838), Italian poet who wrote the libretti for Mozart's *Don Giovanni* and *Marriage of Figaro,* arrived in the U.S. (1805); held professorship of Italian literature at Columbia College; was active (1825–26) in establishing Garcia's Opera Co.; and backed the French tenor, Montrésor, in opening a season in New York with Rossini's *La Cenerentola* (1832). He also promoted the building of the Italian Opera House in N.Y. (1833).

c.1810–50. ORCHESTRAS. Boston Philharmonic Society founded by **Gottlieb Graupner** (1767–1836); credited as the 1st genuine and regular orchestra in the U.S.; gave its last concert, 1824. Philharmonic Society of New York founded (1842) chiefly through the efforts of Ureli C. Hill, its 1st president; first concert 7 Dec. Chicago Philharmonic Soc., 1850; disbanded *c.*1854.

1814. "STAR-SPANGLED BANNER." "The Defence of Fort McHenry," by **Francis Scott Key** (1779–1843), published (1814) in the Baltimore *Patriot.* This poem, based on the author's observation of the British bombardment of Ft. McHenry (13–14 Sept. 1814), was issued in handbill form almost immediately after its composition. On or about 19 Oct. 1814 the title was changed to "The Star-Spangled Banner," which by Act of Congress (1931) was designated as the national anthem. The tune, a familiar one in post-Revolutionary days, is that of "To Anacreon in Heaven," variously credited to the British composers Samuel Arnold and John Stafford Smith.

1815–56. CHORAL SOCIETIES. Handel and Haydn Society, organized at Boston (1815) under the leadership of Gottlieb Graupner, Thomas Smith Webb, and others. Lowell Mason president and conductor beg. 1827. German Männerchor organized by Philip Wolsifer at Phil-

1 *Abbreviations*

HH Handel and Haydn Society, Boston (1815)
MFSP Musical Fund Society, Philadelphia (1820)
MFSN Musical Fund Society, New York (c.1828)
MFSB Musical Fund Society, Boston (1847)
PS Philharmonic Society of New York (1842)

adelphia (1835); oldest German singing society in the U.S. Chicago Sacred Music Society est. 1842. Deutsche Liederkranz, N.Y., 1847. Milwaukee Musikverein, 1849. *Saengerfest* held at Cincinnati (1849) brought together for the 1st time the German singing societies of the Midwest. Chicago Männergesang-Verein (1852; disbanded, 1859). Arion Society, a German choral group (N.Y., 1854; merged, 1918, with the Liederkranz Society). Cecilia Soc. and Harmonic Soc. (Cincinnati, 1856).

1819–60. FOREIGN OPERA. Rossini: *Barber of Seville* (English, N.Y., 1819; Italian, by Manual Garcia troupe, N.Y., 1825; 6 operas given at Italian Opera House, N.Y., 1833, including *La Gazza Ladra*). **Mozart:** *Marriage of Figaro* (Bishop's English version, N.Y., 1823; in Italian, N.Y., 1858); *Don Giovanni* (N.Y., 1825); *Die Zauberflöte* (Phila., 1832). **Weber:** *Der Freischütz* (English, N.Y., 1825); *Oberon* (Phila., 1827). **Meyerbeer:** *Roberto il Diavolo* (English, N.Y., 1834); New Orleans productions of *Les Huguenots* (1839), *L'Etoile du Nord* (1850), *Il Profeta* (1850). **Bellini:** *La Straniera* (N.Y., 1834); *La Sonnambula* (English, N.Y., 1834); *Norma* (Phila., 1841). **Donizetti:** *L'Elisir d'Amore* (N.Y., 1838); *Lucia di Lammermoor* (New Orleans, 1841); *La Favorita* and *The Daughter of the Regiment* (New Orleans, 1843); *Gemma di Vergi* (N.Y., 1843); and 8 others by 1850. **Verdi:** Havana Opera Co. productions of *I Lombardi* and *Ernani* (N.Y., 1847); *Nabucco* (N.Y., 1848); *Attila* (N.Y., 1848); *Macbeth* (N.Y., 1850); *Luisa Miller* (Phila., 1852); *Il Trovatore* (N.Y., 1855); *La Traviata* (N.Y., 1856); *Rigoletto* (New Orleans, 1860). **Wagner:** *Tannhaüser* and *Lohengrin* (N.Y., 1859). **Halévy:** New Orleans operatic season, 1858–59, probable 1st performances of *Jaquarita l'Indienne, La Juive,* and *Reine de Chypre.*

1825–60. MUSIC SCHOOLS AND EDUCATION. Musical Fund Soc. established a music school at Philadelphia (1825); 1st important institution of its kind in the U.S. Music school of Boston Academy of Music (established by Lowell Mason, 1832) introduced 1st significant advances in musical education in the U.S. First music school in Chicago, 1834. Lowell Mason introduced (1838) the teaching of music into the Boston public schools. Boston Music School est. (1850) by Benjamin F. Baker; dissolved, 1868. Class system of pianoforte instruction begun (1851) by Eben Tourjée at Providence, R.I.

1827–60. POPULAR SONGS. "The Minstrel's Return from the War," by John Hill Hewitt (1827). "The Old Oaken Bucket" (1834), words by Samuel Woodworth, who wrote the poem in 1818. "Zip Coon" (*c.*1834, later known as "Turkey in the Straw"). "Woodman, Spare That Tree" (1837), words by George P. Morris, music by Henry Russell. "Tippecanoe and Tyler, Too" (1840), political campaign song used by the Whig party; words by Alexander C. Ross to the tune of "Little Pigs." "We Won't Go Home Till Morning" (1842), words by William Clifton; based on the old French melody "Malbrouck." "Old Dan Tucker" (1843), generally credited to **Daniel D. Emmett** (1815–1904), also thought to be the composer of "The Blue Tail Fly" (also called "Jim Crack Corn," 1846). "Oh! Susanna" (1848), by **Stephen C. Foster** (p. 708). "Ben Bolt" (1848), words by Thomas Dunn English. "De Camptown Races" (1850) by Foster. "Old Folks at Home" (1851, often called "Swanee River"), also by Foster. "Massa's in de Cold, Cold Ground" (1852) by Foster. Original version of "Frankie and Johnny" (1850); later reputedly sung at siege of Vicksburg (1863); more than 100 different versions uncovered, chiefly after 1899. "My Old Kentucky Home" (1853) by Foster. "Listen to the Mocking Bird" (1855), music by Septimus Winner (1826–1902). "Darling Nelly Gray" (1856) by Benjamin Russel Hanby. "Jingle Bells" (1857) by J. S. Pierpont. "Dixie's Land" (written 1859, commonly called "Dixie"), by Daniel D. Emmett; 1st performed by Bryant's Minstrels (N.Y., 1859); played at the inauguration of Jefferson Davis, Montgomery, Ala., 18 Feb. 1861, it quickly became the symbol of the Confederacy. "Old Black Joe" (1860) by Foster.

1827–35. MUSIC PUBLISHERS. Carl Fischer (N.Y., 1827); Oliver Ditson (Boston, 1835).

1831–43. PATRIOTIC SONGS. Words of the national hymn "America" written by Rev. Samuel Francis Smith (1808–95); 1st performed at the Park St. Church, Boston (1831). The tune is that of the English national anthem, "God Save the King." "Columbia, the Gem of the Ocean" (1843) is usually credited to Thomas A. Beckett, but sometimes claimed for David T. Shaw.

1835–59. MUSICAL DEBUTS. Charlotte Cushman, actress, made her debut as a singer in *The Marriage of Figaro* (Boston, 1835). Ole Bull, Norwegian violinist (N.Y., 1843); **Jenny Lind,** Swedish soprano (Castle Garden, N.Y., 11 Sept. 1850); **Henriette Sontag,** German dramatic soprano (N.Y., 1853); **Louis M. Gottschalk** (1829–69), native-born composer and pianist (N.Y., 1853); **Marietta Alboni,** Italian operatic soprano (U.S. tour, 1853); **Adelina Patti** (in *Lucia,* N.Y., 1859).

1837. Harvard Musical Assn. founded by John S. Dwight.

c.1840–60. "SINGING FAMILY" TROUPES (the Hutchinsons, Cheneys, Bakers, Harmoneons, and Father Kemp's Old Folks), group performers of popular choral and instrumental music.

1845. *Leonora,* an opera by **William H. Fry** (?1815–64), Phila., the 1st grand opera to be composed by a native American.

1847. Havana Opera Co., acclaimed as the best opera company to visit the U.S. up to that time; second tour, 1848.

1847–52. OPERA HOUSES AND CONCERT HALLS. Astor Place Opera House opened in N.Y. (1847). N.Y. Academy of Music and Boston Music Hall (1852). Academy of Music, Phila. (1856).

1848. REVOLUTIONS OF '48 led to the migration of many musical artists to the U.S. The Germania Orchestra (N.Y., 1848) introduced Wagner's music into the U.S. Counterparts were organized at Boston, Philadelphia, and other cities. Among the composers and instrumentalists of the Germania group who later became well known were **Carl Bergmann** (1821–76), **Carl Zerrahn** (1826–1909), **Theodor Eisfeld** (1816–82), and **Otto Dresel** (1826–90).

1848–60. FOREIGN COMPOSERS IN AMERICA. Beethoven: *7th Symph.,* MFSB (1850); *Leonore Overture, No. 3* (Boston, 1850); *Egmont,* music complete (Boston, 1859). **Mozart:** *G min. Symph.* (No. 40), MFSB (1850); *Requiem,* HH (1857); *E flat maj. Piano Concerto* (Boston, 1859). **Mendelssohn:** *Midsummer Night's Dream,* Germania Orch. (N.Y., 1848); *Italian Symph.* (Boston, 1851). **Schumann:** cantata, *Paradise and the Peri,* Musical Institute, N.Y. (1848); *Symph. in D.,* PS (1857); *Manfred Overture,* PS (1857); *A minor Piano Concerto* (op. 54), PS (1859). **Berlioz:** *King Lear Overture,* PS (1846); *Roman Carnival Overture* (1857). **Donizetti:** *Il Poliuto,* performed as oratorio, HH (1849). **Schubert:** *C maj. Symph.,* PS (1851). **Wagner:** Overture to *Rienzi* played from manuscript by Germania Orch. (Boston, 1853); *Faust Overture* (Boston, 1857); Prelude to *Lohengrin,* PS (1857).

1849. ENSEMBLES. Mendelssohn Quintet Club, the 1st important string chamber music group in the U.S., est. at Boston.

1853–58. CONDUCTORS. American debut of the French conductor, **Louis Antoine Jullien,** who toured the U.S. with his orchestra (1853–54), conducting 200 concerts, and directing a "Grand Musical Congress" made up of 1,500 instrumentalists and 16 choral societies performing oratorios and symphonies (1854). **Carl Zerrahn** (1826–1909) named conductor of the Handel and Haydn Society at Boston; later (1865–82) conducted the concerts of the Harvard Musical Assn. **Theodore Thomas** (p. 791), who arrived in the U.S. from Germany in 1845, joined **William Mason** (1829–1908) in organizing a string quartet, which introduced music of Schumann and Brahms into the U.S.; Thomas named conductor of N.Y. Academy of Music (1858).

1861–65. CIVIL WAR SONGS. "John Brown's Body," most widely sung Federal song, has been credited to Thomas B. Bishop, the musical adaptation of a Negro Carolina low-country melody to James E. Greenleaf. A ribald parody, beginning "Hang Jeff Davis on a sour apple tree," appeared in 1865. "Battle Hymn of the

Republic," written by **Julia Ward Howe** (1819–1910) to the tune of "John Brown's Body" (pub. Feb. 1862). Next to Emmett's "Dixie" (1859), the most popular Southern marching song was "The Bonnie Blue Flag" (1862), words by Mrs. Annie Chambers-Ketchum, music by Henry McCarthy. "Maryland, My Maryland" (1861), by James Ryder Randall, sung to German folk song "O Tannenbaum." "We Are Coming, Father Abraham" (1862), by James Sloan Gibbons, abolitionist writer in answer to a plea to the states by Lincoln to raise "300,000 more" soldiers; musical settings by Orlando Emerson (1820–1915) and Stephen Foster. Walter Kittredge's "Tenting Tonight" (1862). "When Johnny Comes Marching Home" (1863), by **Patrick Sarsfield Gilmore** (1829–92). "Tramp, Tramp, Tramp" (1864), by George Root. "Marching Through Georgia" (1865), by **Henry Clay Work** (1832–84), who also wrote "Father, Dear Father, Come Home with Me Now."

1861–1946.[2] VERDI TO SHOSTAKOVICH: FOREIGN COMPOSERS IN AMERICA. Verdi: *Un Ballo in Maschera* (N.Y., 1861); *La Forza Del Destino* (1865); *Aïda* (1873); *Requiem Mass,* Italian Opera Co. (N.Y., 1875); *Don Carlo,* Havana Opera Co. (1877); *Otello,* Campanini, conduct. (N.Y., 1888); *Falstaff,* MO (1895). **C. P. E. Bach:** *Symph in D maj.* (N.Y., 1862); *Symph. in C* (N.Y., 1866); **J. S. Bach:** *Toccata in F* and *Passacaglia,* Theo. Thomas (N.Y., 1865); *Suite in D,* PS (1869); *St. Matthew's Passion,* in part, HH (1874), complete (1879); *Christmas Oratorio,* pts. 1 & 2, HH, with Emma Thursby (1877); *Mass in B min.,* Bach Festival, Bethlehem, Pa. (1900); *Brandenburg Concerto, F maj.* (1901); *1st Violin Concerto,* BS (1902); *2d,* BS (1904). **Beethoven:** *2nd Piano Concerto,* Bklyn. Philh. Soc. (1865); *Choral Fantasia* (1866); *Prometheus music,* Theo. Thomas (1867); *Grand Quartet* (op.

2 Abbreviations

BS   Boston Symphony Orchestra (1881)
CO   Chicago Opera Assn. (1910)
HH   Handel and Haydn Society, Boston (1815)
MO   Metropolitan Opera, New York (1883)
PH   Philadelphia Orchestra (1900)
PS   Philharmonic Society of New York (1842, later Philarmonic-Symphony Society)
SS   Symphony Society of New York (1878)

131), scored for full orchestra by Carl M. Berghaus, BS (1884). **Tschaikovsky:** Frequent performances beginning with *1st Piano Concerto,* Hans von Bülow, soloist (Boston, 1875); *Romeo and Juliet Overture,* PS (1876). First complete performance of *Violin Concerto,* Maude Powell (N.Y., 1889); *4th Symph.,* SS (1890); *Nutcracker Suite,* Chicago Symph. Orch. (1892); *1812 Overture,* Theo. Thomas (Chicago, 1893); opera, *Eugene Onegin,* in concert form, SS (1908); operatic version, MO (1910). **Wagner:** *Flying Dutchman* music, Theo. Thomas (N.Y., 1862); prelude to *Tristan,* PS (1866); "Ride of the Valkyries," Theo. Thomas (N.Y., 1872); "Wotan's Farewell" and "Magic Fire Scene" from *Die Walküre,* Thomas (Phila., 1865); "Centennial March," Centennial Exposition, Thomas (Phila., 11 May 1876); "Good Friday Spell" from *Parsifal,* SS (1883). *Die Meistersinger,* MO (1886); *Tristan,* MO (1886); *Der Ring des Nibelungen,* MO (1888); *Parsifal,* 1st performance in German outside of Bayreuth, Alfred Hertz conduct., MO (1903). **Brahms:** *German Requiem,* N.Y. Oratorio Soc. (1877); *1st Symph.,* Damrosch and Thomas (1877); *2d,* Thomas (1878); *3d* (BS, 1884); *4th* (BS, 1886); *Academic Festival Overture,* Thomas (Boston, 1881); *2nd Piano Concerto,* PS, Rafael Joseffy soloist (1882); *Violin* (BS, 1889). **Gounod:** *Faust* (Phila. and N.Y., 1863). **Bizet:** *Carmen* (N.Y., 1878). **Johann Strauss:** *Die Fledermaus* (N.Y., 1885). **Leoncavallo:** *I Pagliacci* (N.Y., 1894). **Humperdinck,** *Hansel and Gretel* (English, N.Y., 1895). **Richard Strauss:** *F min. Symph.,* Thomas (N.Y., 1884); tone poem, *Don Juan,* BS, A. Nikisch (1891); *Tod und Verklärung,* PS, Thomas (1892); *Ein Heldenleben,* Chicago Symph. (1900); operas: *Salome,* MO (1907), aroused storm of protest; barred from MO repertory (1907); banned in Boston (1909); *Elektra,* MO (1910), *Der Rosenkavalier,* MO (1913). **Dvořák:** *Carnival* and *Otello* overtures at concert honoring composer's 1st U.S. appearance, Nat. Conserv. of Mus. (N.Y., 1892); *New World Symph.,* PS (1893); *Concerto for Violin,* SS (1894). **Schubert:** Overture to *Fierabras,* Harvard Mus.

Assn. (Boston, 1866); extracts from *Rosamunde,* Theo. Thomas (N.Y., 1867); *Unfinished Symph.,* Theo. Thomas (1867); *Octet for Strings; C. maj. Symph.,* Theo. Thomas (N.Y., 1875). **Berlioz:** *Symphonie Fantastique,* N.Y. (1866); *Damnation of Faust,* N.Y. Symph. (1880). **Franck:** *D min. Symph.,* BS (1899). **Mahler:** *4th Symph.,* SS (1903); *5th Symph. (Giant),* Cincinnati Symph. (1905); *1st Symph.,* PS (1909); *8th Symph.,* PH with more than 1,000 performers (1916). **Rachmaninoff:** *2nd Symph.,* composer conduct., Russian Symph. Orch. (N.Y., 1909); *2nd Piano Concerto,* composer soloist, SS (1909); *Isle of the Dead* (tone poem), Chicago Symph. (1909). **Sibelius:** *2nd Symph.,* BS, 1904; *1st,* BS, 1907; *Finlandia,* BS, 1908; *Swan of Tuonela,* BS, 1911. On visit to the U.S. he conducted *Pohjala's Daughter, King Christian II, Swan of Tuonela,* Litchfield, Conn., Choral Union (1914). **Puccini:** *Manon Lescaut* (Phila., 1894); *La Bohème,* Royal Italian Op. (San Francisco, (1898); *Tosca,* MO (1901); *Mme. Butterfly* (English, Washington, D.C., 1908); world *première* of *Il Tabarro, Gianni Schicchi,* and *Suor Angelica,* MO (Farrar, Easton, De Luca, 1918); *Turandot,* MO (1926). **Debussy:** *Pelléas et Mélisande,* Manhattan Op. (Mary Garden, 1908); *L'Enfant Prodigue* (Boston, 1910). **Moussorgsky:** *Boris Godunov,* MO (Anna Case, Louise Homer, 1913). **Stravinsky:** *Feuerwerk,* Russian Symph. Orch., N.Y. (1910); BS (1914); Orch. suite from *Petrouchka,* BS (1920); *Sacre du Printemps,* PH (1922); *Symph. of Psalms* for orch. and chorus, BS (1930). **Schoenberg:** *5 Pieces for Orch.,* BS (1914); *Verklärte Nacht,* sextet, BS (1921). **Prokofieff:** *Concerto for Violin and Orch.,* BS (1924); *Concerto No. 3,* piano and orch., BS (1926); *Classical Symph.,* BS (1927); *Concerto No. 2,* piano and orch., BS (1930). **Ravel:** *Rhapsodie Espagnole,* BS (1914); *Daphnis et Chloë,* 1st suite, BS (1918); 2d suite, BS (1917); *Bolero,* Toscanini, PS (1929). **Hindemith:** *Nusch-Nuschi Dances,* PH (1924–25); *Concerto for Orch.,* BS (1926); *Konzertmusik for String and Brass Instruments,* BS (1931). **Milhaud:** *2d Orch. Suite,* BS (1921);

Le Carnaval d'Aix, BS (1926). **Vaughan Williams:** *London Symph.,* N.Y. Symph. (1920); *Fantasia on a Theme by Thos. Tallis,* N.Y. Symph. (1922); *Norfolk Rhapsody No. 1,* BS (1926). **Shostakovich:** *1st Symph.,* BS (1928); *7th,* Toscanini, NBC Orch. (1942); *8th,* PS (1944); *9th* (Tanglewood, 1946).

1862–1928. DEBUTS OF MUSICAL ARTISTS. Teresa Carreño, Venezuelan pianist (N.Y., 1862); *Carlotta Patti* in opera *La Sonnambula* (N.Y., 1862); **Christine Nilsson** (N.Y., 1870); **Anton Rubinstein,** pianist, and **Henri Wieniawski,** violinist (N.Y., 1872; **Hans von Bülow,** pianist (Boston, 1875); **Marcella Sembrich** in *Lucia di Lammermoor,* MO (1883); gave violin, piano, and vocal concert 21 Apr. 1884; **Lillian Norton (Nordica)** as Margaret in *Faust* (N.Y., 1883); **Lilli Lehmann,** soprano, as Carmen, MO (1885); **Maude Powell,** American violinist (Orange, N.J., 1885); **Josef Hofmann,** pianist (N.Y., 1887); **Tamagno,** Italian tenor, as *Otello,* MO (1890); **Ignace Paderewski** (N.Y., 1891); **Jean** (tenor) and **Edouard** (bass) de Reszke in *Romeo and Juliet,* MO (1891); **Emma Calvé,** French mezzosoprano, as Santuzza in *Cavalleria Rusticanà,* MO (1893); **Nellie Melba,** Australian soprano, in *Lucia di Lammermoor,* MO (1893); **Ernestine Schumann-Heink** as Ortrud in *Lohengrin* (Chicago, 1898); **Antonio Scotti** in *Don Giovanni,* MO (1899); **Louise Homer,** contralto, as Amneris in *Aïda,* MO (1900); **Ossip Gabrilowitsch,** pianist (N.Y., 1900); **Enrico Caruso** as the Duke in *Rigoletto,* MO (1903); **Geraldine Farrar** as Juliette in *Romeo et Juliette,* MO (1906); **Emmy Destinn** as Aïda, Toscanini conduct., MO (1908); **Alma Gluck** as Sophie in *Werther,* MO (1909); **Amelita Galli-Curci** as Gilda in *Rigoletto,* Chicago Op. (1916); **Jascha Heifetz,** violinist (N.Y., 1917). Last appearance of Caruso, *La Juive* (24 Dec. 1920); d. Naples, 2 Aug. 1921; farewell appearance of Farrar in *Zaza* (22 Apr. 1923). Debuts of **Yehudi Menuhin,** violinist, San Francisco Orch. (1923); PS (1926); and **Vladimir Horowitz,** pianist (PS, 1928).

1865–1945. FESTIVALS AND CONCERT SERIES. Peabody Institute Concerts (Baltimore, Md., 1865); World Peace Jubilee, org. Boston (1869) by Patrick S. Gilmore, employed chorus of 10,000 and orchestra of 1,000 pieces; imported Johann Strauss to conduct *Blue Danube Waltz*. First annual Cincinnati Festival, dir. Theo. Thomas (1873); Bach *B min. Mass,* Bach choir, Bethlehem, Pa., as part of Bach Festival begun 1900. MacDowell Festival est. Peterboro, N.H. (1910). Music festival at Pittsfield, Mass., est. by Elizabeth Sprague Coolidge (1918), marking the beginning of her active participation in chamber music; Elizabeth Sprague Coolidge Foundation for sponsoring festivals of music at the Library of Congress est. 1925; 1st Festival of Chamber Music, 28 Oct. First Festival of Contemporary American Music, Yaddo, Saratoga Springs, N.Y. (1932); 1st annual summer Berkshire Music Festival, Lenox (Tanglewood), Mass. (1934); Koussevitzy Music Foundation est. by Serge Koussevitzky (1942); 1st annual Festival of Contemporary American Music, sponsored by Alice M. Ditson Fund, Columbia University (1945).

1862–1948. EXPANSION OF THE SYMPHONY ORCHESTRA. First concert by **Theodore Thomas'** own orchestra (N.Y., 1862); summer night concerts at Terrace Gardens, N.Y., begun by Thomas (1866); 1st of 22 annual tours by Thomas orchestra (1869). Germania Orch. (Pittsburgh, 1873). Symphony Soc. of N.Y., **Leopold Damrosch** (1832–85), conductor (1878); **Walter Damrosch** (1862-1950) succeeding his father (1885); merged with the N.Y. Philh., 1928. Boston Symphony Orch., est. (1881) by Henry L. Higginson, with Georg Henschel conducting 1st concert; Chicago Symph. Orch. under Hans Balatka (1886), Frederick Stock, conduct., beg. 1905; Pittsburgh Symph. under Frederick Archer (1893), Victor Herbert conduct., 1898; Cincinnati Orch. Assn., Frank von der Stucken, conduct. (1895), succeeded (1909–12) by **Leopold Stokowski** (1887–), Fritz Reiner replaced (1922) Eugène Ysaye as conduct.; Philadelphia Orch., Fritz Scheel, conduct. (1900), succeeded by Stokowski (1914–36); St. Paul Symph., Walter Rothwell conduct. (1905); St. Louis (1907), Max

Zach conduct.; Rudolph Ganz, 1921–27; Seattle, Michael Kegrizi conduct. (1908), Henry K. Hadley (1909); Kansas City, Mo., Carl Busch (1911); San Francisco, Henry K. Hadley (1911), reorg. under Alfred Hertz (1915); Baltimore, Gustav Strube (1915); New Orleans (1917); Detroit, Gabrilowitsch (1917); Cleveland, Nikolai Sokoloff (1918). Decade, 1921–30, marked by **phenomenal increase** in professional orchestras, with notable conductors engaged: **Pierre Monteux** (1875–) to conduct Boston (1920), succeeded (1924) by **Serge Koussevitsky** (1874–1951); **Willem Mengelberg** from Amsterdam as guest conductor of Bodanzky's National Symph. Orch. (1921), succeeding Josef Stransky when the N.Y. Philharmonic merged with Bodanzky's Symphony (1922); **Wilhelm Furtwängler** of Leipzig Gewandhaus and Berlin Philharmonic to conduct N.Y. Philh. (1925), with **Arturo Toscanini** (1867–1957) made regular conductor (1928–36), inaugurating the orchestra's most successful decade. Toscanini was organizer and conductor of National Broadcasting Co. (NBC) Symphony Orch., beg. 1937. **Leonard Bernstein** (1918–), who replaced (14 Nov. 1943) Bruno Walter as guest conductor of the N.Y. Philh. upon the latter's illness, succeeded Stokowski as conductor of the N.Y. City Symphony (1945–48).

1872–1942. MUSICAL SOCIETIES. Mendelssohn Soc. (N.Y., 1863–72), Cecilia Soc. (Boston, 1874), Music Teachers Natl. Assn. (1876). Society of American Musicians and Composers (1899). Organization (1913) of American Society of Composers, Authors, and Publishers (ASCAP) by Victor Herbert, Sousa, Witmark, and others to protect musical copyright interests. Friends of Music Soc. (N.Y.), 1st concert 7 Dec. 1913; produced Schoenberg, Bloch, and Bach; disc. after 1931. Organization (1923) of League of Composers to promote contemporary compositions. New Friends of Music founded (N.Y., 1936), "to give the best in the literature of chamber music and lieder." Founding of the American Composers' Alliance (1938). ASCAP, after a struggle with radio networks and rival organization, Broadcast Music, Inc., over royalties, reached settlement (1941).

1917–24. JAZZ. Dixie Jass (*sic*) Band of New Orleans opened at Reisenweber's Cabaret, Chicago (26 Jan. 1917); jazz band reported in N.Y. by *Variety* (2 Feb. 1917). Paul Whiteman's concert at Aeolian Hall, N.Y. (1924), to bring artistic respectability to jazz, introduced **George Gershwin's** (p. 713) *Rhapsody in Blue.*

1935. FEDERAL MUSIC PROJECT of the WPA established to relieve unemployment among musicians, under direction of Nikolai Sokoloff; 1935–39, $50 million expended, 225,000 performances financed, 700 projects launched, 15,000 musicians employed. Among its most significant achievements was the establishment (1935) of the Composers' Forum-Laboratory devoted to the works of living American composers.

1865–1940. CONSERVATORIES. Oberlin College (1834), conservatory (1865). Boston Conservatory, New England Conservatory, Cincinnati Conservatory, Chicago Academy of Music (later Chicago Musical College)—all 1867; Ill. Conservatory of Music, Jacksonville (1871); Northwestern Univ. (1873); Cincinnati College of Music, Theo. Thomas dir. (1878); Chicago Conservatory (1884); Amer. Inst. of Applied Music, Kate Chittenden (N.Y., 1885); Amer. Conservatory of Music, J. J. Haffstaedt (1886); Institute of Musical Art (1905), Frank Damrosch, financed by a $500,000 bequest; George Eastman School of Music (1918), est. by George Eastman as an affiliate of Rochester Univ. (Howard Hansen dir. since 1925). Juilliard Graduate School est. (1924) with an endowment of $15 million, Ernest Hutcheson dean. In 1926 the Institute of Musical Art became the preparatory school of the Juilliard. Curtis Institute of Music (Phila., 1924) by an endowment of $12,-500,000 from Mrs. Mary Louise Bok (Josef Hofmann, dir., 1927). Berkshire Music Center org. at Tanglewood (1940) by Koussevitzky.

1861–85. MUSIC PUBLISHERS. Beer and Schirmer took over C. Breusing; after 1866 G. Schirmer; Thomas B. Harms (N.Y., 1881), after 1922, Harms, Inc.; Theo. Presser (Phila., 1884); M. Witmark & Sons (N.Y., 1885).

1865–1950. OPERA COMPANIES. Performance of 24 operas in San Francisco (1865); Crosby Opera House (Chicago, 1865); French *opéra bouffe* (N.Y., 1867), Offenbach's *La Grande Duchesse de Gérolstein* ran 180 nights); 6 nights of Russian opera given at Théâtre Française (N.Y., 1869); Col. Mapleson's 1st operatic tour of U.S. (1878–79); opening of **Metropolitan Opera House** (23 Oct. 1883; destroyed by fire, 27 Aug. 1892; new opera house opened 1893); American Opera Co. (N.Y., 1886–87), Theo. Thomas conduct.; Tivoli Opera House (San Francisco, 1877); grand opera given in U.S. by Henry E. Abbey Co. (1883–84), with cast including Nilsson and Sembrich; Abbey and Schoeffel (1890), with cast including Patti, Nordica, Tamagno (1890). **Oscar Hammerstein** (1847–1919) opened 1st Manhattan Opera House (1892); the 2nd and better known (1906), with such artists as Melba, Nordica, Tetrazzini, and Garden, to become a serious rival of the Metropolitan; sold out to Metropolitan (1910). **Giulio Gatti-Casazza** (1869–1940) appointed manager of Metropolitan (1908). Boston Opera House (1909). Chicago Opera Co. (1910), Andreas Dippel, dir. **Mary Garden** (1877–) succeeded (1919) Campanini as impresario of the Chicago Opera, to become the 1st woman impresario; in turn succeeded (1923) by Giorgio Polacco. Edward Johnson, tenor, became manager MO (1935), and Rudolf Bing (1950). Metropolitan debut (1935) of Kirsten Flagstad as Sieglinde in *Die Walküre* marked the inauguration of a highly successful Wagnerian series. New York City Center Opera Co. founded, 1944.

1921–52. OPERAS BY FOREIGN COMPOSERS. Prokofiev: *Love for Three Oranges,* Chicago Op. Assn. (1921); **Berg:** *Wozzeck,* Phila. Grand Op. Co. (19 Mar. 1931); **Gian-Carlo Menotti:** *Amelia Goes to the Ball* (Phila., 1937), MO (1938); *The Old Maid and the Thief,* broadcast over NBC (1939), 1st stage performance, Phila. Op. (1941); *The Medium* and *The Telephone* (N.Y., 1947); *The Consul* (N.Y., 1950); *Amahl,* TV, 1950; **Benjamin Britten:** *Peter Grimes* (Tanglewood, 1946); *Billy Budd,* TV, 1952.

1896–1952. OPERAS BY AMERICAN COMPOSERS. Walter Damrosch: *Scarlet Letter* (Boston, 1896), *Cyrano de Bergerac,* MO (1913); Frederick Converse: *Pipe of Desire,* 1st American opera to be performed MO, with entirely American cast (1910); Victor Herbert: *Natoma* (Phila., 1911), *Madeleine,* MO (1914); Horatio T. Parker: *Mona,* MO (1912, awarded $10,000 prize); Reginald de Koven: *Rip Van Winkle,* Chicago Op. Assn. (1920); Deems Taylor: *King's Henchmen,* libretto by Edna St. Vincent Millay, MO (1927), *Peter Ibbetson,* MO (1931); Howard Hanson: *Merrymount,* MO (1934); George Gershwin: *Porgy and Bess,* setting of DuBose Heyward play, *Porgy,* with an entire Negro cast (Boston, 1935); Douglas Moore: *Devil and Daniel Webster* (1939), *Giants in the Earth* (N.Y., 1951); Virgil Thomson: *Four Saints in Three Acts,* based on text by Gertrude Stein, with Negro cast (Hartford, Conn., 1934), *The Mother of Us All* (1947); Bernard Rogers: *The Warrior* (book by Norman Corwin), awarded $1,500 Ditson prize (1946); MO (1947); Leonard Bernstein: *Trouble in Tahiti* (Tanglewood and TV, 1952).

1860–1951. PERFORMANCES OF AMERICAN COMPOSITIONS. John Knowles Paine (1839–1906): *Oratorio* (Portland, Me., 1873); *1st Symph.,* Theo. Thomas (Boston, 1876); *Spring Symph.* (Cambridge, Mass., 1880); symphonic poem, *An Island Fantasy,* BS (1889). George W. Chadwick (1854–1931): Overture to *Rip Van Winkle* (Boston, 1879); royalty of $13 by BS for performance of *2nd Symph.* (1886) established a precedent; *3rd Symph.,* BS (1894); *Judith,* choral work (Worcester, 1901); *Cleopatra,* symphonic poem, Chicago Orch. (1905). George F. Bristow (1825–98): *Arcadian Symph.,* PS (1874). Arthur Foote (1853–1937): Overture *In the Mountains,* BS (1887); *Suite for Strings* (1889). Edward A. MacDowell (p. 746); *1st Piano Concerto* Theo. Thomas (N.Y., 1889); symphonic poem, *Lancelot and Elaine,* BS (1890); *Suite in A min.,* Worcester Festival (1891); *Indian Suite,* BS (N.Y., 1896). Dudley Buck (1839–1909): Prize symphonic cantata, *Golden Legend,* Cincin-

nati Festival (1880); *Romance for 4 Horns and Orch.* (N.Y., 1891); *Star Spangled Banner Overture* (N.Y., 1891). Victor Herbert (1859–1924): Dramatic cantata, *The Captive,* Worcester Festival (1891); also composer of operas and numerous comic operas. Charles M. T. Loeffler (1861–1935): *Concerto Fantastique,* BS (1894); *La Mort de Tintagiles* (1898). Amy M. Beach (Mrs. H. H. A.; 1867–1944): *Gallic Symph.,* BS (1896). Charles T. Griffes (1884–1920), *Pleasure Dome of Kubla Khan,* BS (1919); *Three Songs,* soprano and orch., PH (1919); *Clouds* and *White Peacock,* BS (1922). Henry K. Hadley (1871–1937): Symph., *The Four Seasons* (Chicago, 1902); *The Culprit Fay* (Grand Rapids, Mich., 1909), *5th Symph.* (1949). John Alden Carpenter (1876–1951): Orchestral suite, *Adventures in a Perambulator,* Chicago Symph. (1915); *Concertino* (1916). Ernest Bloch (1880–   ; came to U.S. 1917; naturalized, 1924): *Israel Symph.* and *Schelomo,* Soc. of Friends of Music (N.Y., 1916); *Three Hebrew Poems,* BS (1917); *Symph. in C sharp min.,* PS (1918); *Piano Quartet,* inaugural concert, League of Composers (N.Y., 1923); *America,* epic rhapsody, PS (1928). George Gershwin (p. 713): *An American in Paris,* symphonic poem (N.Y., 1928). Aaron Copland (1900–   ): *1st Symph.,* SS (1925); *Concerto for Piano and Orch.,* BS (1927); *Symphonic Ode,* BS (1932); ballet, *Billy the Kid* (1938); *Appalachian Spring* (1945), *3rd Symph.,* BS (1946). Douglas Moore (1893–   ): *2nd Symph.,* Paris Radio Orch. (1946). Charles Ives (1874–1954): *3rd Symph.* (1946), *2nd Symph.,* PS (1951). Frederick Jacobi (1891–1952): *Symph. in C,* San Francisco Symph. (1948). Walter Piston (1894–   ): *2nd Symph.* (1943), *3rd Symph.,* BS (1948). Roger Sessions (1896–   ): *1st Symph.,* BS (1927), *2nd Symph.,* PS (1951). William Schuman (1910–   ): *1st Symph.* (1936), *2nd Symph.* (1937), *3rd Symph.* (1938), *Symph. for Strings,* BS (1947). Howard Hanson (1876–   ): *Nordic Symph.* (1924), *4th Symph.* (*Requiem*) (1943), *Piano Concerto,* BS (1948). Samuel Barber (1910–   ): *Adagio for Strings* and *Essay for Orch.,* NBC Orch., Toscanini (1938), *Symph. in One Movement*

(Rome, 1936), *Violin Concerto* (1940), *2nd Essay for Orch.*, PS (1942), *2nd Symph.*, BS (1944), *Capricorn Concerto* (1944), *Concerto for Violoncello and Orch.*, BS (1946). **Virgil Thomson** (1896–): *Suite for Orch.*, PH (1948); **Lukas Foss** (1922–): *Song of Songs*, BS (1947), *Recordare*, orch. threnody, BS (1948). **David Diamond** (1915–): *2nd Symph.*, BS (1944), *Rounds for Orch.* (1944). **Roy Harris** (1898–): *3rd Symph.*, BS (1939), *6th Symph.*, BS (1944). **Leonard Bernstein** (1918–): *Jeremiah Symph.*, PS (1944); symph., *The Age of Anxiety*, awarded $1,000 BS prize (1949). **William Grant Still** (1895–): *Afro-American Symph.* (1931), *Symph. in G min.* (1937). **Marc Blitzstein** (1905–): *Airborne Symph.* (1946).

1907–52. RADIO AND TV PERFORMANCES. Lee De Forest (p. 694) transmitted (5 Mar. 1907) Rossini's *William Tell* overture by wireless from the Telharmonic Hall, N.Y., to the Brooklyn Navy Yard, the 1st broadcast of a musical composition. First broadcast from the stage of the Metropolitan (20 Jan. 1910), when portions of *Cavalleria Rusticana* and *Pagliacci*, both with Caruso, were picked up by radio amateurs. First major orchestral broadcast, BS over NBC (1926). First regular series of opera broadcasts from stage of Chicago Civic Opera (1927). In the same year concerts broadcast from BS and PS. Regular Sunday broadcasts inaugurated by PS (1929). First broadcast of a full opera from MO, *Hänsel und Gretel* (1931). First opera written expressly for radio, *The Willow Tree*, by Charles W. Cadman, broadcast, NBC (1931); for television, Gian-Carlo Menotti's *Amahl and the Night Visitors*, NBC (1951; again 1952). First telecast of a major symphony concert, Ormandy, PH (20 Mar. 1948); Toscanini, NBC Orch., 1 hr. later.

1953–60. •PERFORMANCES OF FOREIGN COMPOSERS. Shostakovich: *10th Symph.*, PS(1954); **Menotti:** *2nd Piano Concerto*, PS (1958); *Saint of Bleecker St.* (N.Y., 1954); *Maria Golovin*, NBC Opera Co. at Brussels World's Fair (1958); **Prokofiev;** *War and Peace*, NBC Opera Co., TV (1957);

Verdi: *Nabucco*, MO (1960); **Hindemith:** *Angelico Veloces*, Aspen, Colo. (1958); *Octette* and *Ten Madrigals*, Natl. Artists Chamber Orch., N.Y. (1959); **Vaughan Williams:** *9th Symph.*, Cont. Music Soc., N.Y. (1958); **Handel:** *Hercules*, Amer. Op. Soc., N.Y. (1960).

1953–60. OPERAS BY AMERICAN COMPOSERS. Igor Stravinsky: *Rake's Progress*, MO (1953); Aaron Copland: *Tender Land*, N.Y.C. Opera Co. (1953); Norman Dello Joio: *Trial at Rouen*, NBC–TV (1956), *The Ruby* (N.Y., 1957); William Bergsma: *Wife of Martin Guerre* (N.Y., 1956); Barber: *Vanessa*, MO (1958); Douglas Moore and J. Latouche, *Ballad of Baby Doe*, N.Y.C. Opera Co. (1958); Carlisle Floyd: *Susannah*, U. of Fla., Tallahassee (1955), N.Y.C. Opera Co. (1959).

1953–60. PERFORMANCES OF AMERICAN COMPOSITIONS. Harris: Symph. Fantasy (Pittsburgh, 1954); **Darius Milhaud:** *6th Symph.*, BS (1955); **Walter Piston:** *5th Symph.*, BS (1955); *Concerto for Violin and Orch.* (1958); **Ives:** *He Is There*, Norwalk, Conn. (1959); **Stravinsky:** *Canticum Sacrum* (Los Angeles, 1957), ballet score *Agon*, N.Y.C. Ballet (1957)—both on occasion of 75th birthday, *Threni*, Schola Cantorum, N.Y. (1959), *Movements for Piano and Orch.* Columbia Symph. Orch., N.Y. (1960); **Peter Mennen:** *Piano Concerto*, Cleveland Symph., N.Y. (1958); **Barber:** *Toccata Festifa*, PH (1960); **Foss:** *Time Cycle, for Soprano and Orch.* PS (1960); *Vittorio Giannini*, *4th Symph.*, Juilliard Schl. of Music, N.Y. (1960).

1954, 4 Apr. TOSCANINI RETIRES as conductor of NBC Symp. Orch.; reorg. as Symph. of the Air, with 1st concert, N. Y. (27 Oct.).

1954–59. FOUNDATION GRANTS. Through a grant from the Rockefeller Foundation (Apr. 1953) the Louisville Orch. initiated (2 Jan. 1954) series of commissioned works by 65 American and foreign composers. Grants broadened to include other orchestras (1957). In spring of 1958 N.Y.C. Opera Co. presented 5-wk. season of 10 American operas under Ford grant. 4 opera cos. shared 1959 Ford grant to foster American opera.

1954–60. FESTIVALS. American Jazz Festival began (1954) annual summer concerts at Newport, R.I. Pablo Casals moved to Puerto Rico (1956) and directed annual festivals at San Juan. During the 1950's other festivals, some long established, flourished, including Berkshire (Tanglewood, Mass.); Aspen, Colo.; Caramoor (Katonah, N.Y.); Empire State (Ellenville, N.Y.); Eastman School (Rochester, N.Y.); Lewisohn Stadium Concerts (N.Y.C.); Robin Hood Dell Concerts (Phila.); Ravinia Park (Chicago); Cincinnati Zoo; Central City, Colo.

1955, 7 Jan. MARIAN ANDERSON, contralto, made her debut at MO; 1st Negro to sing in its 71-yr. history.

19 Nov. LEONARD BERNSTEIN (1918–   ) named musical director of PS to succeed Dimitri Mitropolous; in Sept. his musical, *West Side Story,* opened on Broadway; *Candide* (1956); presented TV shows on music (*Omnibus,* 1954–58).

1955–60. MUSICAL THAW IN COLD WAR. Exchange of visits of Soviet and American musicians included visits to U.S. of Emil Gilels and David Oistrakh (1955); Moiseyev Dance Co. (1958); Bolshoi Ballet, Soviet composers, including D. Shostakovich (1959); Moscow State Symph.; Leonid Kogan; Sviatoslav Richter (1960). U.S. artists who toured the U.S.S.R. included Isaac Stern and Jan Peerce (1956), BS (1956), PS (1959, 1960). In addition Louis ("Satchmo") Armstrong (1900–   ), Dixieland trumpeter and jazz-band leader, made a triumphal tour of the Middle East, Mediterranean countries, and Western Europe (1956) and of Africa (1960).

1958, 11 Apr. HARVEY K. ("VAN") CLIBURN, Jr., 23-yr. old Texan, won 1st prize at Intl. Tchaikovsky Piano Competition in Moscow; on return to the U.S. he drew huge audiences at Chicago's Grant Park, Hollywood Bowl, and Lewisohn Stadium.

THE TWENTY-FIVE ALL-TIME SONG HITS, 1892–1959

Daisybelle (On a bicycle built for 2), w., m., Harry Dacre	1892
The Sidewalks of New York, w., m., Charles B. Lawler and James W. Blake	1894
The Stars and Stripes Forever, m., John Philip Sousa	1897
Sweet Adeline, w. Richard H. Gerard [Husch]; m., Harry Armstrong	1903
Kiss Me Again, w., Henry Blossom; m., Victor Herbert	1905
Shine on Harvest Moon, w., m., Nora Bayes and Jack Norworth	1908
Ah! Sweet Mystery of Life, w., Rida Johnson Young; m., Victor Herbert	1910
A Perfect Day, w., m., Carrie Jacobs Bond	1910
Alexander's Ragtime Band, w., m., Irving Berlin	1911
When Irish Eyes Are Smiling, w., Chauncey Olcott and George Graff, Jr., m., Ernest R. Ball	1912
St. Louis Blues, w., m., W. C. Handy	1914
Swanee, w., Irving Caesar; m., George Gershwin	1919
Tea for Two, w., Irving Caesar; m., Vincent Youmans	1924
Dinah, w., Sam M. Lewis and Joe Young; m., Harry Akst	1925
Ol' Man River, w., Oscar Hammerstein 2nd; m., Jerome Kern	1927
Star Dust, w., Mitchell Parish; m., Hoagy Carmichael	1929
Dancing In The Dark, w., Howard Dietz; m., Arthur Schwartz	1931
Easter Parade, w., m., Irving Berlin	1933
Begin the Beguine, w., m., Cole Porter	1935
September Song, w., Maxwell Anderson; m., Kurt Weill	1938
God Bless America, w., m., Irving Berlin	1939
White Christmas, w., m., Irving Berlin	1942
Some Enchanted Evening, w., Oscar Hammerstein, 2nd; m., Richard Rodgers[1]	1949
I Could Have Danced All Night, w., Alan Jay Lerner; m., Frederick Loewe[1]	1956
Mack the Knife, German w., Berthold Brecht; English w., Marc Blitzstein; m., Kurt Weill[1]	1959

[1] A projection, as time insufficient to determine all-time-hit status.

III

Four Hundred Notable Americans

(Biographical Section)

THIS Biographical Section, confined by reason of space limitations to 400 eminent figures, is meant to be used as a handy reference source. It underscores the contribution that individuals made to the building of the nation, from the settlement of Jamestown to the Nuclear Space Age. The 400 are representative of top-level achievement for their own time in a range of fields crowded with significant names.

Making selections involved some arbitrary choices. Thus, John Augustus Roebling has been chosen to symbolize the 19th-century achievements in bridgebuilding, although a more extended list would have included James Buchanan Eads. In the steel industry Andrew Carnegie was selected in preference to either Henry Clay Frick or Charles M. Schwab, likewise substantial figures. In the areas of general science, of medicine and public health, and of invention and technology an effort has been made to give representation to earlier and less creative periods of American history, but the worldwide impact of American scientific achievement in the 20th century justifies adequate recognition. Much technical knowledge and experiments by others contributed to the range of inventions covered herein, but the persons singled out for biographical treatment were those who developed, perfected, and usually patented their "inventions."

To qualify as an American on the list of the 400 one must have spent a major portion of his career in the original Thirteen Colonies (hence the exclusion of such towering figures as William Penn and James Edward Oglethorpe) or, after 1776, made substantial contributions as citizens of the U.S. On this ground Charles Chaplin has been excluded as well as such expatriates as Benjamin Thompson (Count Rumford), the physicist, and T. S. Eliot. An exception has been made in the case of Henry James, who became a British subject at the very end of his career. Naturalized citizens are included as well as natural-born. All 34 Presidents receive biographical treatments, but their relative historical importance is suggested by respective space allocations.

The table preceding the biographical articles lists the subjects by major fields of activity. A word of caution, however. The allocation by categories has been done rather arbitrarily. Men as versatile as Benjamin Franklin, Thomas Jefferson, Albert Gallatin, Increase Mather, Samuel F. B. Morse, Theodore Roosevelt, and Benjamin Rush were conspicuous in more than one field. Scientists who were more effective in the diffusion of knowledge than in original and creative work appear in the table as Educators.

Finally, it should be pointed out that a great many notable Americans not herein included are referred to elsewhere in the *Encyclopedia* and appear in the **Index**.

THE PRESIDENTS (34)[1]

JURISTS and LAWYERS (27)

Hugo L. Black
Louis D. Brandeis
Benjamin N. Cardozo
Salmon P. Chase

1 Listed pp. 422–425. Cleveland, who served 2 nonconsecutive terms, is considered the 22nd and 24th President. Hence, Kennedy is technically the 35th President, but in fact the 34th.

Thomas M. Cooley
Clarence Darrow
William Maxwell Evarts
David Dudley Field
Stephen J. Field
Felix Frankfurter
Learned Hand
John M. Harlan
Oliver Wendell Holmes, Jr.
Charles E. Hughes
John Jay

James Kent
Edward Livingston
John Marshall
Samuel Freeman Miller
Lemuel Shaw
Harlan Fiske Stone
Joseph Story
Roger B. Taney
Morrison R. Waite
Earl Warren
Edward D. White
James Wilson

STATESMEN (57)

Charles Francis Adams
Samuel Adams
John Peter Altgeld
Stephen F. Austin
Thomas Hart Benton
Sir William Berkeley
James G. Blaine
William E. Borah
William Bradford
William Jennings Bryan
Aaron Burr
John C. Calhoun
Lewis Cass
Henry Clay
De Witt Clinton
George Clinton
Jefferson Davis
John Dickinson
Sanford B. Dole
Stephen A. Douglas
John Foster Dulles
Hamilton Fish
Benjamin Franklin
Albert Gallatin
Joseph Galloway
Alexander Hamilton
John Hancock
Townsend Harris
John Hay
Patrick Henry
Sam Houston
Thomas Hutchinson
Sir William Johnson
Robert La Follette
Fiorello La Guardia
Richard Henry Lee
Robert Livingston
Huey Long
George Mason
Increase Mather
George Norris

James Otis
John Randolph of Roanoke
Elihu Root
Carl Schurz
William H. Seward
Alfred E. Smith
Alexander H. Stephens
Thaddeus Stevens
Adlai E. Stevenson
Henry L. Stimson
Peter Stuyvesant
Charles Sumner
Robert Taft
Samuel J. Tilden
Daniel Webster
John Winthrop

MILITARY and NAVAL FIGURES (26)[2]

Benedict Arnold
George Rogers Clark
Stephen Decatur
George Dewey
David G. Farragut
Nathanael Greene
Thomas J. Jackson
Joseph E. Johnston
John Paul Jones
Robert E. Lee
Douglas MacArthur
George B. McClellan
Alfred T. Mahan
Francis Marion
George C. Marshall
William Mitchell
Daniel Morgan
Chester W. Nimitz
Matthew C. Perry
Oliver H. Perry
John J. Pershing
Winfield Scott
Philip Henry Sheridan
William T. Sherman
J. E. B. Stuart
George H. Thomas

BELLES LETTRES (33)

Louisa May Alcott
Willa Cather
Samuel L. Clemens
James Fenimore Cooper
Stephen Crane

[2] Other notable military figures are included with the Presidents: Washington, Andrew Jackson, Taylor, Grant, and Eisenhower.

Emily Dickinson
Theodore Dreiser
William Faulkner
F. Scott Fitzgerald
Robert Frost
Joel Chandler Harris
Nathaniel Hawthorne
Ernest Hemingway
Oliver Wendell Holmes, Sr.
William Dean Howells
Washington Irving
Henry James
Henry Wadsworth Longfellow
James Russell Lowell
Archibald MacLeish
Herman Melville
H. L. Mencken
Edna St. Vincent Millay
Thomas Paine
Edgar Allan Poe
Ezra Pound
Edwin Arlington Robinson
Carl Sandburg
William Gilmore Simms
Harriet Beecher Stowe
Henry David Thoreau
Walt Whitman
John Greenleaf Whittier

HISTORY, PHILOSOPHY, and SOCIAL SCIENCES (17)

Henry Adams
George Bancroft
Charles A. Beard
Franz Boas
John Dewey
Ralph Waldo Emerson
William James
Lewis Henry Morgan
John Lothrop Motley
Francis Parkman
Charles S. Peirce
William H. Prescott
Josiah Royce
William Graham Sumner
Frederick Jackson Turner
Thorstein Veblen
Lester Frank Ward

ARTISTS (17)[3]

John J. Audubon
George W. Bellows
John S. Copley
Thomas Eakins

3 Includes photography.

Winslow Homer
George Inness
John La Farge
John Marin
Thomas Nast
Charles Willson Peale
Jackson Pollock
Albert P. Ryder
Augustus Saint-Gaudens
John Singer Sargent
Alfred Stieglitz
Gilbert Stuart
James A. M. Whistler

ARCHITECTS (6)

Charles Bulfinch
Benjamin H. Latrobe
Frederick Law Olmsted
Henry H. Richardson
Louis H. Sullivan
Frank Lloyd Wright

THEATER and ALLIED ARTS (10)

Phineas T. Barnum
Edwin Booth
Charlotte Cushman
Isadora Duncan
Edwin Forrest
David W. Griffith
Oscar Hammerstein, 2nd
Arthur Miller
Eugene O'Neill
Tennessee Williams

MUSICIANS and COMPOSERS (8)

Irving Berlin
Leonard Bernstein
Aaron Copland
Stephen C. Foster
George Gershwin
Edward MacDowell
Richard Rodgers
Theodore Thomas

RELIGIOUS LEADERS (16)

Henry Ward Beecher
Phillips Brooks
William Ellery Channing
John Cotton
Mary Baker Eddy
Jonathan Edwards
James Gibbons
Anne Hutchinson

Dwight L. Moody
Reinhold Niebuhr
Theodore Parker
Walter Rauschenbusch
George Whitefield
Roger Williams
Isaac Mayer Wise
Brigham Young

EDUCATORS (18)

Louis Agassiz
Henry Barnard
Nicholas Murray Butler
James Bryant Conant
Charles W. Eliot
Abraham Flexner
Daniel Coit Gilman
William Rainey Harper
Christopher C. Langdell
Mary Lyon
Horace Mann
William H. McGuffey
Benjamin Silliman
Edward L. Thorndike
Noah Webster
Andrew Dickson White
Emma Willard
John Witherspoon

SOCIAL REFORMERS and LABOR LEADERS (24)

Jane Addams
Susan B. Anthony
Clara Barton
John Brown
Peter Cooper
Eugene V. Debs
Dorothea L. Dix
Frederick Douglass
Neal Dow
W. E. B. Du Bois
Margaret Fuller
William Lloyd Garrison
Henry George
Samuel Gompers
Sidney Hillman
Samuel Gridley Howe
John L. Lewis
Wendell Phillips
Terence V. Powderly
Eleanor Roosevelt
Elizabeth Cady Stanton
Lincoln Steffens
Booker T. Washington
Frances Willard

JOURNALISTS, EDITORS, and PUBLISHERS (9)

James Gordon Bennett
William Cullen Bryant
Herbert Croly
Edwin L. Godkin
Horace Greeley
Adolph Ochs
Joseph Pulitzer
Isaiah Thomas
John Peter Zenger

PIONEERS and EXPLORERS (10)

Daniel Boone
Richard E. Byrd
John C. Frémont
Meriwether Lewis and William Clark
Robert E. Peary
Zebulon M. Pike
John Wesley Powell
John Smith
Charles Wilkes

BUSINESS LEADERS (19)

John Jacob Astor
Nicholas Biddle
Andrew Carnegie
Jay Cooke
James B. Duke
Eleuthère Irénée du Pont
Cyrus W. Field
Marshall Field
Henry Ford
Daniel Guggenheim
Marcus A. Hanna
James J. Hill
Cyrus H. McCormick
J. Pierpont Morgan
Robert Morris
John D. Rockefeller
Samuel Slater
Leland Stanford
Cornelius Vanderbilt

MEDICINE (incl. Psychiatry) and PUBLIC HEALTH (12)

William Beaumont
Edwin J. Cohn
William Crawford Gorgas
Philip S. Hench
William J. and Charles H. Mayo
William T. G. Morton
Walter Reed
Benjamin Rush

Jonas E. Salk
Theobald Smith
Harry Stack Sullivan
Selman A. Waksman

GENERAL SCIENCE (29)

Nathaniel Bowditch
George Washington Carver
Arthur H. Compton
Clinton J. Davisson
Albert Einstein
John Franklin Enders
Enrico Fermi
Josiah Willard Gibbs
Asa Gray
Joseph Henry
Edward C. Kendall
Joshua Lederberg
Gilbert N. Lewis
Fritz Albert Lipmann
Edwin M. McMillan
Matthew Fontaine Maury
Albert A. Michelson
Robert A. Millikan
Thomas Hunt Morgan
Hermann J. Muller
Linus Pauling
I. I. Rabi
Henry A. Rowland
Glenn T. Seaborg
Wendell M. Stanley
Edward Teller

Harold C. Urey
John von Neumann
Robert Burns Woodward

INVENTION and TECHNOLOGY (28)

Ernst F. W. Alexanderson
Edwin H. Armstrong
Leo H. Baekeland
Alexander Graham Bell
Wallace H. Carothers
Lee De Forest
George Eastman
Thomas Alva Edison
John Ericsson
Robert Fulton
Robert H. Goddard
George W. Goethals
Charles Goodyear
Richard M. Hoe
Elias Howe
Charles F. Kettering
Irving Langmuir
Ernest O. Lawrence
Ottmar Mergenthaler
Samuel F. B. Morse
Michael Pupin
John Augustus Roebling
William B. Shockley
Nikola Tesla
George Westinghouse
Eli Whitney
Wilbur and Orville Wright
Vladimir K. Zworykin

Adams, Charles Francis (b. Boston, Mass., 18 Aug. 1807; d. there, 21 Nov. 1886), diplomat and statesman, son of John Quincy Adams and father of Henry Adams, was graduated from Harvard (1825), and admitted to the bar in 1829, establishing his practice at Boston. A member (1841–44) of the Mass. house of representatives, he also served (1844–45) in the state senate. His growing antislavery convictions led him to establish the Boston *Whig* as an organ of opposition to conservative Whiggery, and in 1848 he was the unsuccessful Free-Soil candidate for Vice-President on the ticket with Martin Van Buren. Elected to Congress as a Republican, he served from 4 Mar. 1859 to 1 May 1861, and in the months before the outbreak of the

Civil War headed the Northern forces of concession and conciliation in the House of Representatives. He resigned from Congress to accept appointment by President Lincoln as Minister to England, a post he held until 1868. During the first half of the Civil War, when British official sympathy for the Confederacy was at its height, Adams handled with exemplary tact and firmness vital diplomatic matters such as the *Trent* affair (p. 233) and the armored rams built by the Lairds for the Confederacy. (Adams to Lord Russell: "This is war.") In 1872 the Liberal Republicans considered him for a time as a likely candidate for the Presidency. He brought out the *Works of John Adams* (10 vols., 1850–56) and the *Memoirs of John Quincy Adams* (12 vols., 1874–77).

Adams, Henry Brooks (b. Boston, Mass., 16 Feb. 1838; d. Washington, D.C., 27 Mar. 1918), historian and man of letters, grandson of John Quincy Adams (1767–1848). He was graduated from Harvard (1858), pursued postgraduate study in Germany, and during the Civil War served as secretary to his father, Charles Francis Adams (1807–86), U.S. Minister to England. He returned to Washington (1868), was active as a journalist (1869–70), and from 1870 to 1877 was assistant professor of history at Harvard, meanwhile serving during most of his period at Cambridge as editor of the *North American Review*. He married (1872) Marian Hooper, whose suicide (1885) had a tragic impact on his life. While at Harvard and Washington, D.C., he brought out the following works: *Essays on Anglo-Saxon Law* (1876) and *Documents Relating to New England Federalism, 1800–1815* (1877), both of which he edited; *The Life of Albert Gallatin* (1879), *The Writings of Albert Gallatin* (1879); 2 novels, *Democracy* (1880) and *Esther* (1884), both of which were published anonymously; *John Randolph* (1882); and the *History of the United States During the Administrations of Jefferson and Madison* (9 vols., 1889–91), a diplomatic, political, and military account that ranks as one of the landmarks in American historical writing. The latter part of his life was spent in travel in Europe and the South Seas. He is best remembered for *The Education of Henry Adams* (1907), which, with the writings collected in *The Degradation of the Democratic Dogma* (1919), sets forth his formulation of the dynamic theory of history and expresses his doubts that technological advance reflect progress. He also wrote *Mont-Saint-Michel and Chartres* (1904).

Adams, John (b. Braintree (now Quincy), Mass., 19 Oct. 1735; d. there, 4 July 1826), 2nd President of the U.S., was graduated from Harvard (1755) and admitted to the Massachusetts bar in 1758. He attacked the Stamp Act in a series of articles in the Boston *Gazette* (1765), and after removal to Boston (1768) de-fended the British soldiers tried for murder in the "Boston Massacre" (1770). He served in the General Court (1770–71) and the Revolutionary Provincial Congress (1774–75), and his constitutional views were expounded in *Novanglus* (1774), written in reply to the Loyalist, Daniel Leonard. As a delegate to the 1st and 2nd Continental Congresses (1774–78) he helped draft the petition to the king and the petition of rights, recommended Washington for command of the army, and defended the Declaration of Independence in its passage through Congress. He served as chairman of the Board of War and Ordnance and superseded Silas Deane as Commissioner to France (1778). He was a delegate to the convention which framed the Massachusetts Constitution (1780), of which he was the principal author. With Franklin and Jay he negotiated the Paris peace treaty with Great Britain (1783), and was U.S. Minister to Great Britain (1785–88). He was 1st Vice-President of the U.S. (1789–97), casting votes in Senate ties no less than 20 times, and succeeded Washington as President (1797–1801). His feud with Hamilton, along with the Alien and Sedition Acts, for which he had no direct responsibility, contributed to his loss of popularity and the downfall of the Federalist party. In retirement he lived in Quincy and renewed his relations with Jefferson.

Adams, John Quincy (b. Braintree (now Quincy), Mass., 11 July 1767; d. Washington, D.C., 23 Feb. 1848), 6th President of the U.S., eldest son of John and Abigail (Smith) Adams, studied in France (1778–79) and Holland (1780), and served as secretary to Francis Dana in Russia (1781) and to his father in Great Britain (1782–83). Returning to the U.S., he was graduated from Harvard (1787), admitted to the bar (1790), and practiced in Boston. Under Washington he served as Minister to the Netherlands (1794–96) and, under his father, to Prussia (1797–1801). He was defeated for Congress in 1802, but elected to the U.S. Senate the following year. As a result of his support of the administration in the Embargo of 1807, which he favored as an alternative to war, he was forced to resign (1808). He served briefly as a professor of rhetoric at Harvard; was Minister to Russia, 1809–14, chairman of the peace commission that negotiated the Treaty of Ghent (1814), and Minister to Great Britain, 1815–17. Appointed Monroe's Secretary of State (1817–25), he obtained the cession of Fla. (1819) and shared with Monroe credit for formulating the Monroe Doctrine (1823). In the Presidential election of 1824, he was 2nd to Jackson in electoral votes. In the House of Representatives Clay threw his support to Adams (resulting in an unsubstantiated charge of a "corrupt bargain") and Adams was elected President. During his administration he favored a broad national program of internal improvements, but refused to build up a personal political machine. Defeated by Jackson (1828), he was elected to Congress (1831–48). He opposed the annexation of Tex. (1836) and the extension of slavery. Every year (1836–44) he opposed without success the adoption of the "gag rule," forbidding discussion or action in the House on antislavery petitions, until its defeat (1844). He was further identified with the antislavery cause by his argument before the Supreme Court vindicating the right to freedom of the *Amistad* captives (1841).

Adams, Samuel (b. Boston, Mass., 27 Sept. 1722; d. there, 2 Oct. 1803), Revolutionary patriot leader, 2nd cousin of John Adams (1735–1826), was graduated from Harvard (1740); joined his father in the brewery business, which he later inherited and lost; and served (1756–64) as a tax collector. A member of the Boston "Caucus Club," he was by 1764 a power in local politics. He took a leading role in whipping up opposition to the Sugar Act (1764), the Stamp Act (1765), and the Townshend Acts (1767), was one of the organizers of the Non-Importation Association (1768), and played an important part in the agitation that culminated in the Boston Massacre (1770). He helped organize the Sons of Liberty (1765) and was a member (1765–74) of the Mass. House of Representatives, of which he served as recording clerk (1766–74). In writings for the press he enunciated many of the basic arguments that later became familiar Revolutionary doctrine, and kept the spirit of controversy alive during the period of comparative calm and conservative ascendancy (1770–72). He initiated the Mass. committee of correspondence (1772), drafted the Boston declaration of rights (1772), was the leading force behind the Boston Tea Party (1773), and with John Hancock was singled out by the British government for punishment. As a delegate (1774–81) to the Continental Congress, he favored immediate independence, proposed an intercolonial confederation of independent states, voted for and signed the Declaration of Independence, and opposed compromise with Great Britain. He was a delegate to the Mass. constitutional convention (1779–80) and to the state convention (1788) for ratifying the Federal Constitution. He served as lieutenant governor (1789–93) and governor (1794–97) of Massachusetts.

Addams, Jane (b. Cedarville, Ill., 6 Sept. 1860; d. Chicago, Ill., 21 May 1935), humanitarian and social reformer. She was graduated from Rockford College (A.B., 1882), attended the Woman's Medical College in Philadelphia, and during a trip to England (1887–88) became interested in social reform. With Ellen Gates Starr, she founded (1889) Hull House at Chicago, a settlement house devoted to the improvement of community and civic life in the Chicago slums, the 1st of its kind in the U.S. Active (1915–34) as a crusader against war, she was named chairman in 1915 of the Woman's Peace party and president of the International Congress of Women at The Hague. She served as president of the Women's International League for Peace and Freedom. In 1931 she was co-recipient (with Nicholas Murray Butler) of the Nobel Peace Prize. Her writings on social reconstruction include *Democracy and Social Ethics* (1902), *Newer Ideals of Peace* (1907), *The Spirit of Youth and the City Streets* (1909), *Twenty Years at Hull-House* (1910), *A New Conscience and an Ancient Evil* (1912), *The Second Twenty Years at Hull-House* (1930), and *The Excellent*

Becomes the Permanent (1932).

Agassiz, Jean Louis Rodolphe (b. 28 May 1807, Canton Fribourg, Switzerland; d. Cambridge, Mass., 14 Dec. 1873), educator, zoologist, and geologist, studied at the Universities of Zurich, Erlangen (Ph.D. 1829), Heidelberg, and Munich (M.D., 1830). After an early contribution to zoology (*The Fishes of Brazil,* 1829), he studied fossil fish under Cuvier in Paris (1831), publishing in that field *Recherches sur les poissons fossiles* (1833–44) and *Études critiques sur les mollusques fossiles* (1840–45). Professor of natural history at Neuchâtel Univ. (1832–46), he made extensive investigations of glacial phenomena in Europe (*Études sur les glaciers,* 2 vols., 1840). Coming to the U.S. (1846), he accepted (1848) the chair of natural history at the newly established Lawrence Scientific School at Harvard, where he founded the Harvard Museum of Comparative Zoology (1859). Interested in the natural history and geology of the Western Hemisphere (*Contributions to the Natural History of the U.S.,* 1857), he made extensive field trips to Brazil (1865) and to the U.S. West (1868, 1871), but his career in the U.S. was chiefly notable as teacher and lecturer and promoter of scientific study. His teleological view of natural history prompted him to take the leadership in the U.S. in opposing Darwinian evolution with its theory of natural selection, and his scientific reputation suffered as a result. He founded (1873) the Anderson School of Natural History on Penikese Island in Buzzard's Bay to train teachers of natural history.

Alcott, Louisa May (b. Germantown, Pa., 29 Nov. 1832; d. Boston, Mass., 6 Mar. 1888), author, daughter of Amos Bronson Alcott (1799–1888), was reared in Boston and Concord and received most of her education from her father. Her 1st book, written at the age of 16, was *Flower Fables* (1854). During the Civil War she served as a nurse in a Union hospital at Georgetown until her health was impaired. A volume of her letters, *Hospital Sketches* (1863), was followed by her 1st novel, *Moods* (1864). She became (1867) editor of *Merry's Museum,*

a children's magazine. Her most popular work is *Little Women* (2 vols., 1868, 1869), whose familiar characters of Jo, Amy, Beth, and Meg were drawn from her family life. These books enjoyed a phenomenal sale. Among her later works are *An Old Fashioned Girl* (1870), *Little Men* (1871), *Aunt Jo's Scrap-Bag* (6 vols., 1872–82), *Work* (1873), *Eight Cousins* (1875), *Rose in Bloom* (1876), *Silver Pitchers* (1876), *Under the Lilacs* (1878), *Proverb Stories* (1882), *Jo's Boys* (1886), and *A Garland for Girls* (1888).

Alexanderson, Ernst Frederik Werner (b. Upsala, Sweden, 25 Jan. 1878–), electrical engineer and inventor, was graduated (1900) from the Royal Institute of Technology, Stockholm, and pursued postgraduate studies at Berlin. Arriving in the U.S. in 1901, he joined the staff (1902) of the General Electric Company at Schenectady, N.Y., of which he is now consulting engineer. His association with General Electric has been unbroken except for his service as chief engineer (1920–24) of the Radio Corporation of America. He was naturalized in 1908. The holder of patents for more than 300 inventions, many of which have revolutionized the field of radio communications, he is the inventor (1917) of the Alexanderson high frequency alternator making world-wide wireless possible, and has also done pioneering work in electric ship propulsion, radio electronics, railroad electrification, and television. Among his inventions are the tuned radio frequency receiver, the vacuum tube radio telephone transmitter, and the multiple tuned antenna.

Anderson, Carl David (b. New York City, 3 Sept. 1905–), physicist, was graduated from the California Institute of Technology (B.S., 1927; Ph.D., 1930), where he has been a member of the faculty since 1928. From 1927 to 1930 he carried out research on X-ray photoelectrons, and since 1930 has been engaged in research on gamma and cosmic rays. In 1932 he discovered the positron (positively charged electron) in the cosmic radiation (predicted by the electron theory of Dirac), for which discovery he was awarded a Nobel prize in physics (1936), and in 1936 discovered the heavy electron, or mesotron, with a mass some 200 times that of an electron.

Anthony, Susan Brownell (b. Adams, Mass., 15 Feb. 1820; d. Rochester, N.Y., 13 Mar. 1906), social reformer and woman suffrage leader. Reared in a Quaker household, she was educated at her father's school and became a schoolteacher, serving (1846–49) as head of the Female Department of the Canajoharie (N.Y.) Academy. Abandoning education for reform activities, she devoted her 1st efforts to temperance, and was among the organizers of the Woman's State Temperance Society of New York, the 1st body of its kind. She also took part in the abolitionist cause, being among the 1st to advocate Negro suffrage after the Civil War, but gradually shifted her main energies to the woman suffrage movement. She attempted to have inserted in the 14th Amendment a provision guaranteeing the franchise to women as well as to male Negroes. She was involved in a celebrated case that was touched off when she registered and voted at the Rochester city elections (1872) in a plan to test the legality of woman suffrage. She became president (1869) of the National Woman Suffrage Association and was president (1892–1900) of the National American Woman Suffrage Association.

Armstrong, Edwin Howard (b. New York City, 18 Dec. 1890; d. there, 1 Feb. 1954), engineer and inventor, studied at Columbia Univ. (E.E., 1913) under Michael Pupin (*q.v.*), succeeding him (1934) as professor of electrical engineering at Columbia University. His regenerative circuit (1912) won him engineering acclaim along with a patent controversy with Lee De Forest (*q.v.*). As a Signal Corps officer in World War I he developed the principles of his superheterodyne circuit (1918), basic to radio receivers. In 1920 he devised the super-regenerative circuit, used in 2-way police and aircraft radio systems. "Father of FM," Armstrong perfected (1939) his system of static-free radio through frequency modulation, widely adopted in the

U.S., England, and Germany. At the time of his death by suicide he was involved in litigating claims against leading broadcasting and electronic manufacturing firms for patent infringement. In 1947 he was awarded the Medal of Merit for his contributions to military communications during World War II.

Arnold, Benedict (b. Norwich, Conn., 14 Jan. 1741; d. London, 14 June 1801), Revolutionary patriot and traitor, served in the French and Indian War, became a druggist and bookseller as well as active in the West India trade. Capt. in the Conn. militia, he undertook as col., with Ethan Allen of Vt., the successful attack on Ft. Ticonderoga (1775). Heading an expedition across the Maine wilderness to Quebec, he was wounded in the assault on that city, but made brig. gen. (10 Jan. 1776) for his conspicuous role. At Valcour Island he held up Carleton's invasion force on Lake Champlain (11 Oct. 1776), forcing the British to abandon the invasion of N.Y. Promoted maj. gen. as a result of actions at Ridgefield and Norwalk (1777), he played a leading role in frustrating Burgoyne's invasion of N.Y., raising the siege of Ft. Stanwix (1777), anticipated Burgoyne's movement to turn the American left at Freeman's Farm, and was wounded in a frontal assault on Breymann's redoubt at Bemis Heights. Military commander of Phila. (1778), he was court-martialed (1779) and found guilty of using military forces for his own private purposes. Gently reprimanded by Washington, his steadfast supporter, he was given command of West Point. Entering into treasonable correspondence with Sir Henry Clinton (in which his wife Margaret Shippen Arnold was involved) to surrender the key fort to the British, he was forced to flee to the British army when Major André was captured and the plot exposed. He received £6,315 for his treason and made brig. gen. of provincial troops by the British. He carried out a marauding expedition into Virginia (1780) and raided New London, Conn. (1781). He sailed for England Dec. 1781, and was held there in scorn.

Arthur, Chester Alan (b. Fairfield, Vt.,

5 Oct. 1830; d. New York City, 18 Nov. 1886), 21st President of the U.S., was graduated from Union College (1848) and admitted to the N.Y. bar (1853). An abolitionist, he was counsel for the state in the case of Jonathan Lemmon, securing a decision that slaves brought into N.Y. while in transit between 2 slave states were thereby made free. During the Civil War he served as quartermaster general of New York, was appointed collector of the Port of New York by President Grant (1871), but was removed (1878) by President Hayes for violating an Executive order (1876) forbidding Federal officials from participating in party management and campaigns. Elected Vice-President of the U.S. (1880), he became President following the death of Garfield (19 Sept. 1881). His administration continued the prosecution of the "Star Route" mail frauds (1882–83) and secured enactment of the Pendleton Civil Service Act (1883). In addition, he began the rebuilding of the U.S. Navy and vetoed a Chinese exclusion bill. He was denied renomination in 1884.

Astor, John Jacob (b. John Jakob Ashdour, Waldorf, Germany, 17 July 1763; d. New York City, 29 Mar. 1848), fur trader and merchant. Migrated to London, 1780; to the U.S., 1783; obtained a job in a fur store in New York City, mastered the business, and in 1786 opened his own establishment. The provisions of Jay's Treaty and the subsequent evacuation of frontier posts by the British (1796) enabled Astor to trade with the British North West Co. His business expanded rapidly; by 1800, when he had a fortune of $250,000, he was the chief factor in the fur trade. He became active in the shipping trade to the Far East and made prudent investments in New York City real estate. Following the acquisition of La. and the Lewis and Clark expedition, he made plans for penetrating the West. He established the American Fur Co. (1808) and the Pacific Fur Co. (1810). With Montreal merchants as partners, he formed the South West Fur Co. (1811) for the purpose of supplying goods to both the British and his own fur companies free of customs duties. He established Astoria at the mouth of the Columbia River (1811) for transshipment of furs to Canton. He lost the post during the War of 1812, but managed to retain the South West and American Fur Cos. and to carry on trade with the British in the Great Lakes region throughout the conflict. After 1815, he established posts in the Mississippi Valley (old North West Co. posts) and expanded his fur-trading operations by establishing the Western Dept. of the American Fur Co. (1822). After absorbing the Columbia Fur Co. (1827), he held a monopoly in the upper Missouri territory, but after failing to eliminate the Rocky Mountain Fur Co., retired from business. At his death he was the richest man in America. He left a fortune of more than $20 million.

Altgeld, John Peter (b. Nieder Selters, Germany, 30 Dec. 1847; d. Chicago, 12 Mar. 1902), governor of Ill., reformer, came to Richmond County, Ohio, with his parents as an infant and was largely self-taught. Elected state's attorney for Andrew County, Mo. (1874), he moved (1875) to Chicago, where he served as judge and chief justice of the Superior Court of Cook County (1886–91). Elected 1st Democratic governor of Ill. (1893–97), he outraged public opinion by pardoning (1893) the anarchists Fielden, Schwab, and Neebe, convicted of complicity in the Haymarket murders (1886). Conservatives were equally critical of his opposition on constitutional grounds to President Cleveland's use of regular army troops in the Pullman strike (1894). Supporter of free silver in the Democratic National Convention (1896), he was defeated that year for a 2nd gubernatorial term by John R. Tanner. His treatise on crime, *Our Penal Machinery and Its Victims* (1884), expressed the view that the poor lacked equal opportunity before the law.

Audubon, John James (b. Les Cayes, Santo Domingo [now Haiti], 26 Apr. 1785; d. New York City, 27 Jan. 1851), artist and naturalist, pioneer American ornithologist. Taken to France in 1789, he was educated at Nantes and arrived (1803) in the U.S., where he began his ornithological studies in the Pa. countryside. He made (Apr. 1804) the 1st experimental banding on the young of an American wild bird. Beginning in 1807, he made his home in Ky., where he was a merchant at Louisville and Henderson, and there continued his paintings and sketches of birds. Following a series of business reverses, he became (1820) a taxidermist at the Western Museum in Cincinnati. In 1826 he went to England and Scotland, where he secured the 1st subscriptions for the projected publication of his drawings and obtained the services of Robert Havell, Jr., a London engraver who brought out Audubon's monumental work, *The Birds of America* (1827–38), containing more than 1,000 life-size figures of about 500 species. After 1827 Audubon spent much of his time at Edinburgh, where he brought out his *Ornithological Biography* (with the assistance of William MacGillivray; 5 vols., 1831–39) and *Synopsis of the Birds of North America* (1839), and in 1842 made his home at the present site of Audubon Park, New York City. He collaborated with Rev. John Bachman on the *Viviparous Quadrupeds of North America* (2 vols. of plates, 1842–45; text, 3 vols., 1846–54). The Audubon Societies were founded in his memory.

Austin, Stephen Fuller (b. Wythe Co., Va., 3 Nov. 1793; d. Austin, Tex., 27 Dec. 1836), founder of Tex., moved with his parents to Mo. (1798), to which he returned (1810) after studying near New Haven, Conn., and at Transylvania University. He planted the 1st legal settlement of Anglo-Americans in Tex. (1822), obtaining confirmation of his grant when Mexico achieved independence. Until 1828 he was executive, lawmaker, supreme judge, and military commandant, and kept a steady stream of emigrants coming into Tex. In 1828 he obtained the enactment of a contract labor law permitting the continued introduction of slaves as indentured servants. In pressing the claim of the convention of 1833 for a state government (against his own judgment), he was arrested and held by the Mexican government on the baseless charge of fomenting revolution in Tex. and annexation to the U.S. He was re-

leased in July 1835. When the War of the Texas Revolution broke out, Austin was called to command the army, then sent to Washington to negotiate a loan and enlist support. He returned to Texas (June 1836) and was defeated for the presidency of the Republic of Texas by Sam Houston, whose secretary of state he became for the brief period remaining until his death.

Baekeland, Leo Hendrik (b. Ghent, Belgium, 14 Nov. 1863; d. Beacon, N.Y., 23 Feb. 1944), chemist, inventor, received his B.S. from the Univ. of Ghent (1882), where he taught until emigrating to the U.S. (1889) to serve as consultant to A. & H. T. Anthony (later Ansco) of New York City, a photographic firm. In 1888 he patented a dry plate which could be developed in water. Founding with Leonard Jacobi the Nepara Chemical Co. to produce a photographic paper (Velox) he invented, he sold his rights (1899) to Eastman Kodak for $1 million. Attacking the problem of chemical synthesis, he produced a plastic which he exhibited (Feb. 1909) as Bakelite, the 1st of a long series of resins to revolutionize modern economic and technological life. Organizer (1910) of the General Bakelite Co., Perth Amboy, N.J., he was president until 1939, when it was acquired by Union Carbon and Carbide Corp. He received the Franklin Medal in 1940. He wrote *Some Aspects of Industrial Chemistry* (1914).

Bancroft, George (b. Worcester, Mass., 3 Oct. 1800; d. Washington, D.C., 17 Jan. 1891), historian, diplomat, and Cabinet officer, was graduated from Harvard (1817) and in 1820 received the degrees of Ph.D. and M.A. from the University of Göttingen. With Joseph Green Cogswell, he founded (1823) the Round Hill School at Northampton, Mass., but abandoned teaching in 1831 to begin research for his *History of the United States* (10 vols., 1834–76), covering the span between the discovery of America and the close of the Revolutionary War. Bancroft was active in the Jacksonian movement in Mass. in the 1830's; in 1844, when he was an unsuccessful candidate for the governorship of Mass., he was instrumental in securing the Democratic Presidential nomination for James K. Polk. As Secretary of the Navy (1845–46), he established the U.S. Naval Academy at Annapolis and gave the orders to Commodore Sloat which upon the outbreak of the Mexican War facilitated early American success in the California area. As acting Secretary of War (May 1845) he signed the order which sent Gen. Zachary Taylor across the Tex. frontier and brought on the clash with Mexico. Bancroft served as U.S. Minister to Great Britain (1846–49) and Germany (1867–74), meanwhile tirelessly searching out materials in private and public collections for use in his *History*. In 1865 he wrote President Andrew Johnson's 1st annual message. In 1876 he brought out a revised edition (the "Centenary Edition") of his history in 6 vols. His final revision (6 vols., 1883–85) included the *History of the Formation of the Constitution* (1882). He also wrote *Poems* (1823), *Literary and Historical Miscellanies* (1855), and *Martin Van Buren to the End of His Public Career* (1889).

Barnard, Henry (b. Hartford, Conn., 24 Jan. 1811; d. there, 5 July 1900), educator. He was educated at the Monson (Mass.) Academy and at the Hopkins Grammar School in Hartford, was graduated from Yale (1830), read law privately and attended the Yale Law School (1833–34), and was admitted to the bar (*c.*1835). He was a member (1837–40) of the Conn. General Assembly, where he sponsored legislation for the improvement of the common schools; secretary (1838–42) of the board of school commissioners in Conn.; school commissioner (1843–49) of R.I.; superintendent (1850–54) of the Conn. state schools; chancellor (1858–60) of the University of Wisconsin; and president (1866–67) of St. John's College, Annapolis, Md. In 1867 he became the 1st U.S. Commissioner of Education, serving in that post until 1870. A leader in the public school movement, he published the *American Journal of Education* (1855–82) and founded the Conn. *Common School Journal*.

Barnum, Phineas Taylor (b. Bethel, Conn., 5 July 1810; d. Bridgeport, Conn.,

7 Apr. 1891), showman and promoter. Until 1834, when he came to New York City, he pursued a variety of occupations, including the editing of an abolitionist newspaper at Danbury, Conn. His career in show business began with his purchase and exhibition (1835) of Joice Heth, a Negress purported to be the nurse of George Washington and 161 years old (she was actually about 80 years old). He bought (1841) Scudder's American Museum and Peale's Museum, using their collections for his American Museum (opened at New York in 1842), where he exhibited the dwarf, Gen. Tom Thumb, and other freaks, and delighted the public with hoaxes. With Tom Thumb, Barnum made a successful tour of the Continent in 1844. In 1850 he brought the Swedish singer, Jenny Lind, to the U.S. for a concert tour, and in 1855 retired to Iranistan, his lavish home at Bridgeport, Conn. In 1871 he made his return as a showman, opening his circus ("The Greatest Show on Earth") at Brooklyn. In 1881 he combined forces with a rival to form the Barnum & Bailey Circus, and imported from the Royal Zoological Society at London the elephant known as Jumbo. One of the colorful aspects of his showmanship was the elaborate advertising he used to whet the public appetite for his bizarre exhibitions.

Barton, Clara (b. Oxford, Mass., 25 Dec. 1821; d. Glen Echo, Md., 12 Apr. 1912), humanitarian. After teaching school in N.J., she went to Washington, D.C. (1854), where at the outbreak of the Civil War she organized supply and nursing services for sick and wounded Union troops. Without receiving compensation or accreditation, she performed her work behind the lines and on battlefields, including that of the Wilderness. In 1864, when she accompanied the Army of the James, she acted as superintendent of nurses under authority of Gen. Benjamin Butler. After the war she was in charge (1865–69) of a government-sponsored search for missing soldiers. During the Franco-Prussian War she was active in relief activities in association with the International Red Cross of Geneva. Upon her return to the U.S. she undertook a campaign to establish an American Red

Cross, and it was through her efforts that a National Society of the Red Cross was organized (1881). Miss Barton served as its president until 1904. She was active in relieving suffering caused by wars and disasters, such as the Spanish-American War, the Boer War, and the Galveston flood (8 Sept. 1900), and was responsible for the introduction of the "American Amendment" at the Geneva International Conference (1884), specifying that in extreme peacetime emergencies the Red Cross should carry out humanitarian work similar to that assumed by it during wars.

Beard, Charles Austin (b. Knightstown, Ind., 27 Nov. 1874; d. New Haven, Conn., 1 Sept. 1948), historian, political scientist, was graduated from De Pauw Univ. (1908), studied English local govt. at Oxford, and received his M.A. (1903) and Ph.D. (1904) from Columbia. Teaching history and politics at Columbia (1904–17), he resigned (1917) on an academic freedom issue, and cofounded (1919) the New School for Social Research. He was adviser (1922) to the Institute of Municipal Research in Tokyo. With James Harvey Robinson, he coauthored *The Development of Modern Europe* (1907) and an accompanying book of readings—pioneer text and source book offering a brilliant synthesis of political, social, and cultural history. *An Economic Interpretation of the Constitution* (1913), attributing the work of the Federal Convention to the self-interest of the Founding Fathers (in line with J. Allen Smith [1907] and Arthur F. Bentley [1908]) and introducing a strong element of economic determinism, had an enormous vogue. It was followed by *Economic Origins of Jeffersonian Democracy* (1915) and *The Economic Basis of Politics* (1910). He later repudiated such economic determinism in *The Republic* (1943), and more recent critics have challenged both his methodology and his evidence. With his wife Mary Ritter Beard he wrote *The Rise of American Civilization* (1927) and its sequels *America in Midpassage* (1939) and *The American Spirit* (1943), a notable and popular historical synthesis, stressing the Civil War as a 2nd American Revolution.

He also wrote *The Supreme Court and the Constitution* (1912) and *President Roosevelt and the Coming of the War, 1941* (1948), an isolationist critique.

Beaumont, William (b. Lebanon, Conn., 21 Nov. 1785; d. St. Louis, Mo., 25 Apr. 1853), army surgeon, pioneer in gastric physiology. He served his medical apprenticeship under Dr. Benjamin Chandler of St. Albans, Vt., was licensed (June 1812) by the Third Medical Society of Vermont, and was commissioned (13 Sept. 1812) a surgeon's mate to the 6th Infantry at Plattsburg, N.Y. After the close of the War of 1812, he resigned from the service and established a private practice at Plattsburg. He enlisted again (1820) and was assigned to Fort Mackinac (in present-day Mich.) as a surgeon. It was there, on 6 June 1822, that Alexis St. Martin, a Canadian youth, was accidentally shot and suffered a powder-and-shot wound that left a portion of his stomach punctured and protruding from the abdominal cavity. St. Martin was brought to the military hospital for treatment. After a time a flap of the inner stomach closed the puncture, but the lid could be pushed back to expose the interior. Early in 1825 Beaumont undertook scientific studies in digestion, observing St. Martin's stomach temperature during digestion, the movements of his stomach walls, the relative digestibility of certain foods, and the workings of gastric juice under artificial conditions. These studies eventuated in the publication of *Experiments and Observations on the Gastric Juice and the Physiology of Digestion* (1833), revolutionary in its impact upon the existing knowledge and theories of the physiology of the stomach and the chemistry of gastric digestion, much of it still valid.

Beecher, Henry Ward (b. Litchfield, Conn., 24 June 1813; d. Brooklyn, N.Y., 8 Nov. 1887), clergyman and orator, son of Lyman Beecher (1775–1863) and brother of Harriet Beecher Stowe, was graduated from Amherst (1834) and attended the Lane Theological Seminary, Cincinnati, in which city he began preaching as an independent Presbyterian. Called (10 Oct. 1847) to the Plymouth Congregational Church, Brooklyn, N.Y., he drew weekly audiences averaging 2,500, with notable sermons printed in pamphlet form and widely circulated. His influence was extended in editorials in the *Independent* (1861–64) and the *Christian Union,* which he edited 1870–81. An antislavery leader, he opposed interference in the slave states but counseled disobedience of the Fugitive Slave Law. In 1863 he visited England and defended the Union cause before hostile audiences. A modernist, he supported woman suffrage and civil service reform, accepted evolution, but clung to his belief in miracles. His Christianity stressed the love of God and the joy and glory of the religious life. His personal life became a public issue in the Beecher-Tilton adultery case (1874), in which his defense was upheld by a divided jury.

Bell, Alexander Graham (b. Edinburgh, Scotland, 3 Mar. 1847; d. Cape Breton Island, Nova Scotia, 2 Aug. 1922), inventor of the telephone and educator of the deaf. He was educated at McLauren's Academy in Edinburgh and at the Royal High School; became (*c.*1867) assistant in London to his father, Alexander Melville Bell (1819–1905), inventor of the Visible Speech System; accompanied his family to Canada (1870); and in 1871 began giving special instruction in his father's speech system to teachers of the deaf in cities throughout New England. He opened a normal training school at Boston (1872) and served (1873–77) as professor of vocal physiology and the mechanics of speech in the School of Oratory of Boston University. His work for the deaf and his interest in the science of acoustics were related to the experiments which he meanwhile pursued (1873–76) to invent a multiple telegraph and an electric speaking telegraph or telephone. These experiments led to his invention of the harmonic multiple telegraph (1874) and the telephonic telegraphic receiver (1874), in the course of which he gained a thorough knowledge of electrical wave transmission. His preoccupation with the idea of a machine for the electrical transmission of speech finally resulted in the 1st practical demonstration (at Boston, 10 Mar. 1876) of the first magneto-electric telephone. The Bell Telephone Co., the 1st organization of its kind, was founded in 1877, and thereafter the commercial development and application of the telephone proceeded rapidly. Bell became an American citizen in 1882. His career as an inventor did not interrupt his activities as an educator of the deaf. Among his other inventions were the photophone for the transmission of sound by light (1880), the telephone probe for locating metallic masses in the human body (1881), the spectrophone (1881), and the tetrahedral kite (1903). He was associated (1884–86) with the invention of the wax cylinder record for phonographs.

Bellows, George Wesley (b. Columbus, Ohio, 12 Aug. 1882; d. New York City, 8 Jan. 1925), painter, lithographer, and illustrator, was graduated from Ohio State University (1903), studied painting in New York under Robert Henri, and, in his early painting, was inspired by city crowds (*42 Kids,* 1907) and prize fights (*Stag at Sharkey's,* 1907), following directly in the tradition of Eakins' realism. He taught at the Art Students League, beginning in 1910, and also at the Chicago Art Institute in 1919. His paintings show the influence of Goya and Daumier, and later of Greco and Renoir, but are stamped with his own personality. Among his larger canvases are *Edith Cavell* (1918), with dramatic use of light and dark; *The Return of the Useless* (1918); and *The Pic-nic* (1924). Turning to lithography (1916), he soon became a master of that medium.

Bennett, James Gordon (b. Newmills, near Keith, Scotland, 1795; d. New York City, 1 June 1872), editor, emigrated to Halifax, Nova Scotia (1819), thence to Boston and New York, where he wrote for the press and acquired the *Sunday Courier* (1825). He was appointed associate editor of the New York *Enquirer* (1826) and coedited the combined *Courier & Enquirer* (1829). On 6 May 1835 he founded the New York *Herald,* a penny paper. Its sensational and comprehensive news coverage (in the Civil War it employed 63 war correspondents) and personalized editorial style raised its circulation to 100,000 (by 1864). Editorially, Bennett generally supported the Democrats, Douglas against Lincoln, and secession; but after Ft. Sumter, when a mob threatened him, he executed an about face and backed the war, although he did not give Lincoln his full support until 1864.

Benton, Thomas Hart (b. Harts Mill near Hillsboro, N.C., 14 Mar. 1782; d. Washington, D.C., 10 Apr. 1858), statesman, studied at Chapel Hill Coll. (now U. of N.C.) and the law dept. of Wm. and Mary. Tenn. state senator (1809), he was admitted to the bar at Nashville (1806), served in the War of 1812 as aide-de-camp to Jackson, then removed to St. Louis (1815), where he practiced law and edited the *Missouri Inquirer*. In 1817 he killed Charles Lucas, U.S. district attorney in a 2nd duel after wounding him in the 1st. Elected (1820) to the U.S. Senate, he was the 1st senator to serve 30 consecutive yrs. (1821–51). Supporting Jackson (1828) as Senate floor leader in the war against the Bank and in his advocacy of hard money, "Old Bullion" secured a change in the ratio of gold and silver from 15 to 1 to 16 to 1. He sponsored the resolution to expunge from the Senate journal the resolution of censure of President Jackson. Advocate of free homesteads of 160 acres, anticipating the later Homestead Act, he opposed the annexation of Texas but supported the War with Mexico. Preferring compromise to war over the Oregon issue, he favored the 49th parallel, the boundary finally secured. Opposing Calhoun's proslavery resolution of 1850 as well as Clay's compromise, he lost his seat in the Senate, but in the House (1853–55) fought the Missouri Compromise repeal, which lost him his seat and his campaign for governor (1856). He supported Buchanan for President (1856) against his own son-in-law John C. Frémont (*q.v.*). He wrote a notable autobiography, *Thirty Years' View* (1854–56) and compiled *Abridgment of the Debates of Congress, 1789–1856* (1857–61).

Berkeley, Sir William (b. at or near London, 1606; d. England, 13 July 1677), colonial governor, received his B.A. (1624) and M.A. (1629) from Oxford. Knighted by Charles I (1639), he became royal governor of Virginia (1642), where he inaugurated vigorous and constructive policies, heading an expedition (1644) against the Indians which established a generation of peace and encouraging crop diversification and manufactures. Anglican and Royalist, he denied toleration to nonconformists, defied Parliament after the execution of Charles I, and, confronted by a naval force dispatched to Virginia by Parliament to establish its authority, worked out a compromise but yielded his own office. Back in office with the Restoration, his 2nd administration, though continuing some of his constructive policies, was increasingly arbitrary, with no new elections of the burgesses called between 1660 and 1674. The unrest stemming from tax policies, bad crops, and Indian attacks, which Nathaniel Bacon exploited, found the governor obdurate. In the ensuing insurrection (1676) he was driven out of Jamestown, but on Bacon's death returned to power, rescinded recent reform measures, and despite royal promise of pardon hanged 23 rebels. Refusing to yield office to a royal investigating commission, he resigned on ground of ill health, returned to England, and, failing to obtain an audience with Charles II, died soon after.

Berlin, Irving [Isidore Baline] (b. Temun, Russia, 11 May 1888–   ), songwriter and composer, came to the U.S. in 1893, studied in the New York City public schools for 2 yrs., then worked as a song-plugger on the Bowery and as a singing waiter (1904). His 1st song hit, "Dorando," was published in 1909. Graduating to Broadway, he appeared in *Up and Down Broadway* (1910) and his "Alexander's Ragtime Band" (1911) quickly became a top hit. In 1912 he wrote the score for Ziegfeld's *Follies*. During World War I he became a U.S. citizen, and as an army sergeant he wrote an all-soldier show, *Yip-Yip-Yaphank*, while stationed at Camp Upton, Yaphank, L.I. Among his top hits was his musical comedy all-soldier revue *This Is the Army*, which opened on Broadway (1942), with Berlin singing "Oh, How I Hate to Get Up in the Morning," and wearing his World War I sergeant's uniform. For this show, the profits of which went to Army Emergency Relief, he was awarded the Medal of Merit, and for his song "God Bless America" (1917, but introduced in 1938) he received a Congressional gold medal (1954). Other stage successes include *Annie Get Your Gun* (1947), *Call Me Madam* (1950, with Howard Lindsay and Russel Crouse), and the film musical *Easter Parade* (1933). Lacking formal musical instruction, he played tunes in one key, F sharp, and used a piano adapted to change keys mechanically. Among his innumerable song hits are "Remember," "Always," "What'll I Do?," "All Alone," "A Pretty Girl Is Like a Melody," "Blue Skies," "White Christmas." He was married twice. His 1st wife, Dorothy Goetz, died 8 mos. after their marriage in 1913. In 1926 he married Ellin, daughter of Clarence H. Mackay.

Bernstein, Leonard (b. Lawrence, Mass., 25 Aug. 1918–), received his B.A. (1939) from Harvard, studying composition with Walter Piston, and at the Curtis Inst. of Music, from which he was graduated (1941; piano with Isabella Vengerova and conducting with Fritz Reiner). Assistant to Serge Koussevitsky at the Berkshire Music Center (1943–44), he achieved fame overnight when in 1943 as Asst. Conductor he conducted the N.Y. Philharmonic Symph. upon the illness of Bruno Walter. Conductor of the N.Y.C. Symph. (1945–48), co-conductor of the N.Y. Philharmonic (1957–58), and its musical director since 1958, he has been outstanding as music educator and popularizer. He headed the conducting dept. of the Berkshire Music Center beg. 1948, was professor of music at Brandeis Univ., 1951–56, a frequent music interpreter on TV (*Omnibus,* 1957; children's concerts), and inaugurator of the Thurs. night previews of the N.Y. Philharmonic. His compositions include *Clarinet Sonata* (1942), *Symph. No. 1* (*Jeremiah,* 1942), *Symph. No. 2 The Age of Anxiety* (1949). A musical virtuoso, he also wrote *Trouble in Tahiti,* a 1-act opera (1952); the scores for the musical shows *On the Town* (1944), *Wonderful Town* (1953), *Candide*

(1956), and *West Side Story* (1957); and the film score for *On the Waterfront* (1954). He wrote *The Joy of Music* (1959).

Biddle, Nicholas (b. Philadelphia, 8 Jan. 1766; d. "Andalusia," near Philadelphia, 27 Feb. 1844), financier and editor, was graduated from the College of New Jersey (1801) and served abroad (1804) as secretary to John Armstrong, U.S. Minister to France, and to Monroe, Minister to Great Britain (1806). On his return to the U.S. (1807) he settled in Philadelphia and became associate editor (1806–12) of the *Port Folio* with Joseph Dennie and sole editor (1812). In collaboration with Paul Allen he prepared the *History of the Expedition of Captains Lewis and Clark* (1814). He served in Congress (1810–11) and in the Pa. state senate (1814–18). President Monroe appointed him a government director of the 2nd Bank of the U.S., of which he became president (1822) and served in that capacity until it closed its doors (1836) on failure to secure renewal of the charter. Following a conservative policy, Biddle made the Bank of the U.S. a paramount influence in the national economy, only to arouse the enmity of advocates of an "easy money" policy. His fatal error was to make the Bank an issue in the Presidential election of 1832. Jackson's overwhelming victory left no doubt about the issue. Under a charter from Pa. Biddle continued to act as president of the bank, which finally failed (1841), although the creditors were fully paid.

Black, Hugo La Fayette (b. Harlan, Ala., 27 Feb. 1886–), jurist, received his LL.B. (1906) from the Univ. of Ala., practiced law in Birmingham (1907), where he served as police judge (1910–11) and later as solicitor of Jefferson County (1915–17). Democratic senator from Ala. (1927–37), he resigned to accept appointment as associate justice of the Supreme Court (1937). When appointed, considerable criticism was aroused by the revelation that he had once been a member of the Ku Klux Klan (1923–25), although his record in the Senate had been consistently progressive, notably in his investigation of the public utility lobby. His role as a liberal activist on the bench soon silenced some of his critics. Taking an absolutist position regarding much of the Bill of Rights, especially the 1st Amendment (*Bridges* v. *Calif.,* 1941; dissent in *Yates* v. *U.S.,* 1957), he opposed setting limits to the right to picket (*Milk Wagon Drivers Union* v. *Meadowmoor Dairies,* 1941). His dissenting opinion in *Conn. Gen. Life Ins. Co.* v. *Johnson* (1938) denied the right of corporations to claim protection under the 14th Amendment. In dissent in *Adamson* v. *Calif.* (1947) he asserted that the 14th Amendment extended to all the people the complete protection of the Bill of Rights. He upheld the right to distribute religious literature in a company town (*Marsh* v. *Ala.,* 1946), and in *Everson* v. *Bd. of Education* (1947) ruled that a N.J. law expending tax money for transportation to parochial schools did not constitute support of religion. Although he held that the exclusion order relating to Japanese-Americans during World War II was within the federal war powers (*Korematsu* v. *U.S.,* 1944), he invalidated the military courts set up in Hawaii during the war (*Duncan* v. *Kahanamoku,* 1946). He attacked non-Communist affidavits required of labor union officers as abridging the 1st Amendment (*Amer. Comm. Assn.* v. *Douds,* 1950), and, in dissent in *Dennis* v. *U.S.* (1951), held the Smith Act unconstitutional as violating the 1st Amendment.

Blaine, James Gillespie (b. West Brownsville, Pa., 30 Jan. 1830; d. Washington, D.C., 27 Jan. 1893), statesman, was graduated from Washington College (1847); taught school (1848–54); studied law, moving to Augusta, Me., where he edited the Kennebec *Journal* (1854–57). While Republican state legislator (1859–62), he became speaker (1861–62). He served in Congress (1862–76) and was Speaker of the House (1869–76). The "Mulligan letters" (1876), which accused Blaine of using his position as Speaker for personal gain by giving a land grant to the Little Rock & Ft. Smith R.R., blasted his hopes for the Presidential nomination that year. He

again failed to secure the nomination in 1880. As Garfield's Secretary of State (1881) he planned the 1st Pan-American Conference and proposed to Great Britain a modification of the Clayton-Bulwer Treaty. Republican nominee for President (1884), his defeat has been attributed in no small part to the indiscreet reference by one of his supporters to the Democratic party as the party of "Rum, Romanism, and Rebellion," which might well have lost the crucial state of N.Y. He supported Harrison (1888), and became Secretary of State (1889–92). His constructive achievements include the convening of the first Pan-American Conference (1889) and the settlement of the Bering seal dispute with Great Britain. He favored Hawaiian annexation.

Blalock, Alfred (b. Colloden, Ga., 5 Apr. 1899–), surgeon, was graduated from the University of Georgia (B.A., 1918) and from Johns Hopkins (M.D., 1922), was on the medical faculty in surgery (1927–41) at the Vanderbilt University Medical School, and in 1941 became director of the department of surgery at the Johns Hopkins University and surgeon in chief of the Johns Hopkins Hospital. His most notable work has been done in surgical shock and in regulation of the circulation. Testing a theory advanced by Dr. Helen Brooke Taussig (1898–), he operated (9 Nov. 1944) on a "blue baby," by-passing the pulmonary artery. As a result thousands of "blue babies" regained their health by the Blalock operation.

Boas, Franz (b. Minden, Westphalia, Germany, 9 July 1858; d. New York City, 21 Dec. 1942), anthropologist. He studied at Heidelberg and Bonn, received the degree of Ph.D. (1881) at Kiel, and as a member of a German Arctic expedition (1883–84) studied Eskimo life in Baffin Land. He served (1885–86) as an assistant at the Royal Ethnological Museum in Berlin and as *Privatdocent* in geography at the University of Berlin. Arriving in the U.S. in 1886, he was an editorial staff member (1886–88) of *Science* and instructor in anthropology (1888–92) at Clark University. In 1896 he was named lecturer in anthropology at Columbia University, where he became professor in 1899. He was curator of anthropology (1901–05) in the American Museum of Natural History; organized the Jesup North Pacific Expedition (1902), and edited its *Reports;* was president (1907–08) of the American Anthropological Society; and president (1910) of the New York Academy of Sciences. His numerous papers and studies, based upon the scientific fact-finding technique of the field survey, modified earlier concepts of cultural evolution. His publications on the Kwakiutl Indians are classics in their field. Among his writings are *Baffin Land* (1885), *The Central Eskimos* (1888), *The Mind of Primitive Man* (1911, 1938), *Anthropology and Modern Life* (1928), *General Anthropology* (1938), and *Race, Language and Culture* (1940).

Boone, Daniel (b. near Reading, Pa., 2 Nov. 1734; d. near St. Charles, Mo., 26 Sept. 1820), pioneer. Becoming a hunter at the age of 12, he settled (1751) at Buffalo Lick in the Yadkin Valley of N.C.; served as a teamster and blacksmith in Braddock's campaign (1755); made his 1st trip into Ky. (1767); and in 1767 led a party through Cumberland Gap over a trail later known as the Wilderness Road, living and exploring in central Ky. with his brother-in-law John Stuart Finley and others until his return to N.C. in 1771. Serving as the agent of Col. Richard Henderson of the Transylvania Co., he returned to Ky. with a party of settlers (1775) and established a fort at what became the site of Boonesborough. Captured and adopted by the Shawnees (1778), he escaped. After Va. repudiated Henderson's land titles and made Ky. a county of Va., Boone served as lt. col. of the Fayette County militia, was chosen a delegate to the legislature, and was made sheriff and county lieutenant (1782). He moved to Maysville in 1786 and in 1788 left Ky., going to Point Pleasant in what is now W.Va. Because of failure to make proper entry of his land holdings, he lost all of his claims. After being ejected from his last holding, he moved (*c.*1798) to present-day Mo., where he received a land grant and continued his hunting and trapping. One of the folk heroes of American history, Boone is popularly credited with deeds, such as the discovery of Kentucky, which have no foundation in fact.

Booth, Edwin Thomas (b. near Bel Air, Md., 13 Nov. 1833; d. New York City, 7 June 1893), actor, son of Junius Brutus Booth (1796–1852), brother of John Wilkes Booth (1838–65). He made his debut (10 Sept. 1849) at Boston as Tressel in Cibber's version of *Richard III* and up to 1856 did most of his acting in Calif., where he emerged as an accomplished tragedian. Returning to the East in 1856, he scored a great success at Boston (20 Apr. 1857) in the role of Sir Giles Overreach. His appearances at New York and in the South and West established him as the leading American actor of his day. Among his favorite roles were those of Shylock, Hamlet, Romeo, and Othello. Between 1869 and 1874 he reached the peak of his career in performances given at Booth's Theater, built by him at New York City. Because of financial difficulties brought on by the Panic of 1873, Booth went into bankruptcy (1874) and for the remainder of his life was a roving player in the U.S. and Europe. He was the founder (1888) and 1st president of the Players' Club, to which he gave its present building on Gramercy Park, New York City.

Borah, William Edgar (b. Jasper Township, Ill., 29 June 1865; d. Washington, D.C., 19 Jan. 1940), statesman, studied at the Univ. of Kansas (1885–86), read law, was admitted to the bar (1889), and quickly gained prominence in Boise, Ida., as a criminal lawyer as well as counsel for timber and mining interests. Special prosecutor in the trial (1907) of William D. Haywood and others for the murder of Gov. Frank D. Steunenberg, he himself was unsuccessfully prosecuted (1907) for timber frauds. Elected to the U.S. Senate (1907), he served in that body until his death. Orator, reformer, and political maverick, he supported labor reform legislation and fought for the income tax and direct election of senators. Though a supporter of Theodore Roosevelt, he refused to follow him into the Progressive party in 1912. Opposing most of Wilson's progressive legislation, including women's suffrage, he favored national prohibition. Leader of the irreconcilables opposed to the League of Nations, he refused, with Henry Cabot Lodge, to compromise on that issue. Responsible for calling the Washington Disarmament Conference (1921) he exercised, as chairman of the Senate Committee on Foreign Relations (beg. 1924), enormous influence on U.S. foreign policy, favoring recognition of Russia but opposing U.S. intervention in Latin America as well as membership in the World Court. He induced Secy. of State Kellogg to substitute a multinational for a bilateral pact outlawing war (1928). He opposed Hoover's farm and tariff policies, supported much of the New Deal domestic program, but was an outstanding critic of the NRA and Franklin D. Roosevelt's Supreme Court bill. Supporting the Neutrality Act of 1935, he remained an isolationist to the end, advocating nonintervention in World War II.

Bowditch, Nathaniel (b. Salem, Mass., 26 Mar. 1773; d. there, 17 Mar. 1838), astronomer, mathematician, was completely self-educated, learning algebra at 14 and studying Latin at 17 in order to read Newton's *Principia*. On his 5 sea voyages (1795–1803) as clerk, supercargo, or master, he perfected his knowledge of mathematics and navigation. He corrected J. H. Moore's *The Practical Navigator,* and from the 13th English edition published (with his brother William's collaboration) the 1st American edition (1799). The 3rd American edition, extensively altered, appeared under his name as *The New Practical American Navigator* (1802). Nine other editions of this classic appeared in his lifetime and at least 56 more since. *Bowditch's Useful Tables* were reprinted (1844) from the work. In addition, he published (1804–20) 23 important nautical and astronomical papers in the *Memoirs* of the Amer. Academy of Arts and Sciences and translated the 1st 4 vols. of La Place's *Mécanique céleste* (1828–39). In addition to his numerous scientific honors he was president of the Essex Fire and Marine Insurance Co. (beg. 1804) and actuary of the Mass. Hospital Life Insurance Co. (1823–38).

Bradford, William (b. Austerfield, Yorkshire, England, 1590; d. Plymouth Colony, now Mass., 19 May 1657), Pilgrim leader. While still a boy he attended the Separatist group meetings held at William Brewster's house in Scrooby, and in 1609 accompanied the Scrooby congregation to Amsterdam and later to Leyden. He came to America (1620) in the *Mayflower* and was elected Governor (1621) of Plymouth Colony following the death of John Carver. Between 1622 and 1656 he was reelected to the Governorship in every year except 1633, 1634, 1636, 1638, and 1644, when he served as an assistant. The leading statesman of the Plymouth Colony, he exercised (1622–36) broad authority in governmental and religious matters. Plymouth Colony was placed on a firm economic footing when Bradford and other Pilgrim Fathers assumed (1627) the original investment of the merchant adventurers who had financed the settlement. Bradford took part in drafting (1636) a body of laws that endowed the office of Governor with a quasi-constitutional status. Although he believed in maintaining the Plymouth Colony as a separate and compact settlement, Bradford cooperated in larger undertakings such as the Pequot War and the New England Confederation. He began (c.1630) writing his *History of Plimmoth Plantation,* completing it in 1651. It was not published in full until 1856.

Brandeis, Louis Dembitz (b. Louisville, Ky., 13 Nov. 1856; d. Washington, D.C., 5 Oct. 1941), jurist, studied in Germany (1873–75), was graduated from Harvard Law School (1878), and practiced in Boston until 1916. Because of his advocacy of public causes he came to be known as the "people's attorney." Attorney for the policyholders in the investigation of the Equitable Life (1906), he devised and secured enactment in Massachusetts of the issue of low-cost life insurance through savings banks (1907). His mastery of the facts and his firm grasp of economics were demonstrated in his pathmaking brief in *Muller* v. *Oregon* (1908), largely devoted to an analysis of the injurious effect of hard labor upon the physique of women. An opponent of bigness in business or government, his advice was sought by President Wilson on trust legislation, currency, and labor problems. His appointment as associate justice of the U.S. Supreme Court (1916) was confirmed over strong opposition by the organized bar. Serving until retirement (1939), he was aligned in dissent with Holmes and (after 1932) with Cardozo and Stone. He cautioned the Court against curbing social and economic experimentation by the states (*New State Ice Co.*, 1932) and sought, in public-utility rate making, a measurement of value according to "prudent investment" (*Southwestern Bell Telephone Co.*, 1923).

Brooks, Phillips (b. Boston, Mass., 13 Dec. 1835; d. there, 23 Jan. 1893), Episcopal bishop. He attended Harvard; studied in the seminary at Alexandria, Va., where he was ordained a deacon (1859); and occupied his 1st ministry in the Church of the Advent in Philadelphia from 1859 to 1862. Here his eloquent and lofty preaching soon won wide attention. He served as rector (1862–69) of Holy Trinity in Philadelphia, and in 1865 made the prayer at the Harvard commemoration day. Brooks was rector (1869–91) of Trinity Church in Boston, where he brought into Episcopal preaching fresh currents of piety and conviction. His definition of preaching as "the bringing of truth through personality" was the central idea of the Lyman Beecher Lectures on Preaching given by Brooks at the Yale Divinity School (Jan.–Feb. 1877). In 1880, when he preached in Westminster Abbey, he won the distinction of being the 1st American to preach before a crowned head in the Royal Chapel at Windsor. In 1891 he was elected and consecrated Bishop of Mass., a post he held until his death.

Brown, John (b. Torrington, Conn., 9 May 1800; d. Charlestown, W. Va., 2 Dec. 1859), reformer son of an abolitionist and "underground railway" agent, Owen Brown, and Ruth Mills Brown (who died insane), had an unsuccessful business career as a tanner, land speculator, and shepherd in 10 different locations. Convinced of the need for a slave insurrection, he left Ohio in 1855 to join 5 of his sons in the Ossawatomie colony in Kansas, where he became capt. of the local militia company. As Free-Soil crusaders, Brown and a party of 6 (4 of whom were his sons) planned and executed the massacre of 5 proslavery men (24 May 1856). "Old Ossawatomie Brown" and his company were eventually dispersed and the colony burned in retaliation. Supplied with arms and money by leading abolitionists, Brown and a band of 21 men, aiming to liberate the slaves, seized (16 Oct. 1859) the Harper's Ferry armory, and bridges leading to the Ferry, a blow which inflamed the South. Forced to surrender to Col. Robert E. Lee, he was tried for treason to Virginia and speedily convicted. During and subsequent to the trial he conducted himself with dignity, protesting that his only desire was to free the slaves. Hanged at Charlestown, he was hailed as a martyr by antislavery elements.

Bryan, William Jennings (b. Salem, Ill., 19 Mar. 1860; d. Dayton, Tenn., 26 July 1925), political leader and orator, was graduated from Illinois College, Jacksonville, Ill. (1881), and from the Union College of Law in Chicago (1883); practiced law in Jacksonville (1883–87); and in 1887 moved to Lincoln, Neb., where he became active in Democratic politics. Elected to Congress in 1890, and reelected in 1892, he became a member of the silver bloc. An unsuccessful candidate for the Senate in 1894, he became editor in chief of the Omaha *World-Herald*, and at about this time began his long association with the Chautauqua lecture platform. Having already demonstrated in Congress his powers as an orator, he was much sought after as a public speaker advocating the free coinage of silver, and during 1894–95 went on speaking tours that augmented his reputation by the time the Democratic National Convention met at Chicago in 1896. His "Cross of Gold" speech (8 July 1896), his most famous oration, won him the Presidential nomination. Conducting a brilliant and energetic campaign on the platform of the free coinage of silver in a sectional battle that saw the agrarian South and West aligned against the industrial and commercial Northeast, Bryan lost to William McKinley by 600,000 votes out of a total of 13,600,000. From 1896 until 1912 he was the virtually undisputed leader of the Democratic party. He advised Democrats in the Senate to approve the treaty of peace with Spain, but fought the Presidential campaign of 1900 on the issue of anti-imperialism, receiving less votes than he had in 1896. In 1901 he established the weekly newspaper, the *Commoner,* which he edited and published until 1913, and in 1908 was again an unsuccessful Presidential candidate. At the Democratic Convention of 1912, held in Baltimore, Bryan wielded considerable influence in securing the nomination of Woodrow Wilson on a liberal platform. As Secretary of State in Wilson's Cabinet (1913–15) he adhered, after the outbreak of World War I, to strict neutrality. Differences with Wilson over the second *Lusitania* note led to his resignation from the Cabinet (9 June 1915). A fundamentalist in religion, he drafted state legislation forbidding the teaching of evolution in public schools. When John T. Scopes, a teacher in Dayton, Tenn., was indicted for violating a state law of this nature, Bryan, on the prosecution staff, was subjected to withering examination by Clarence Darrow, a defense attorney (1925).

Bryant, William Cullen (b. Cummington, Mass., 3 Nov. 1794; d. New York City, 12 June 1878), poet and editor, attended Williams College (1810–11); wrote the Federalist satire, *The Embargo: or Sketches of the Times, a Satire; by a Youth of Thirteen* (1808); and in 1811 the 1st draft of the poem, "Thanatopsis," 1st published in the *North American Review* in 1817. He studied law privately, was admitted to the bar in 1815, and finally established his practice at Great Barrington, Mass. He published *Poems* (1821), which included "The Ages," "To a Waterfowl," and "The Yellow Violet." His contributions (1824–25) to the *United States Literary Gazette* included "Monument Mountain" and the "Forest Hymn." By 1825 he had gained wide recognition as a poet. Abandoning his law practice, he moved to New York City in 1825 and for a year was coeditor of the *New York Review and Athenaeum Mag-*

azine. In 1826 he was made assistant editor of the New York *Evening Post;* becoming its editor in 1829, he served in that capacity until his death. During his 1st decade as a newspaper editor he wrote relatively little poetry. A Jacksonian Democrat and a free trader, Bryant broke with the Democratic party in 1848, when he supported the Free-Soil ticket, and in 1856 became a Republican spokesman. During the Civil War, he took a radical stand on emancipation and the prosecution of the war, but afterward favored a liberal policy toward the South. He also published *Poems* (1832), *The Fountain, and Other Poems* (1842), and *The White-Footed Doe, and Other Poems* (1844). He ranks as one of the finest American lyric poets of nature.

Buchanan, James (b. near Mercersburg, Pa., 23 Apr. 1791; d. Wheatland, near Lancaster, Pa., 1 June 1868), 15th President of the U.S., was graduated from Dickinson College (1809), admitted to the Pennsylvania bar (1812), and practiced at Lancaster. Federalist state legislator (1815–16) and congressman (1820–31), he served as U.S. Minister to Russia (1832–33), negotiating a commercial treaty, and was Democratic U.S. senator (1835–45). He entered Polk's Cabinet as Secretary of State (1845–49), settled the Oregon dispute, and offered to purchase Cuba from Spain. Minister to Great Britain (1853–56), he joined with Mason and Soulé in drafting the "Ostend Manifesto" (1854). Democratic President of the U.S. (1857–61), he held slavery to be a moral wrong but urged acceptance of the Lecompton Constitution in Kansas (1858). Denying the right of states to secede, he failed to find the legal authority to meet secession and favored an amendment to the Constitution expressly recognizing slavery and the right to recover fugitive slaves. Although he endorsed Breckinridge in 1860, he supported the Federal government during the Civil War.

Bulfinch, Charles (b. Boston, Mass., 8 Aug. 1763; d. there, 4 Apr. 1844), architect, was graduated from Harvard in 1781 and made a tour (1785–86) of England and the Continent, where, at

Jefferson's suggestion, he studied the classical architecture of France and Italy that was to leave a lasting imprint on his style. He designed the old Hollis Street Church in Boston (1788), churches at Taunton and Pittsfield, the Beacon Monument (1789), the Boston Theater, the Massachusetts State House at Boston, and the State House at Hartford. His introduction of the Adamesque style (1792 *et seq.*), as in the Coolidge, Barrell, and Derby houses, led to a general adoption of that mode for New England residences during the early Federal period and influenced architect-builders such as Samuel McIntire and Asher Benjamin. Bulfinch also drew up plans for the Franklin Crescent (1793), the Harrison Gray Otis houses, India Wharf, the Boylston Market, additions to Faneuil Hall, the New South Church (1814), and the old courthouse, all at Boston; Christ Church at Lancaster (1816–17); the State Prison at Charlestown; the Massachusetts General Hospital (1817–20); and the State Capitol at Augusta, Me. (1828–31). As chairman (1799–1817) of the Boston board of selectmen, he was largely responsible for the renovation and development of old Boston. He succeeded (1817) Benjamin H. Latrobe as architect of the Capitol Building at Washington, D.C., remaining in that post until the structure's completion in 1830.

Burr, Aaron (b. Newark, N.J., 6 Feb. 1756; d. Port Richmond, N.Y., 14 Sept. 1836), statesman, was graduated from the College of New Jersey (1772); studied theology briefly and then law. In 1775 he served in Arnold's expedition to Canada and, subsequently, on Washington's staff and then on Putnam's, becoming lt. col. (1777). Admitted to the bar (1782), he moved from Albany to New York City (1783); became attorney general of N.Y. (1789–91) and U.S. senator (1791–97). Defeated for reelection (1796), he served in the N.Y. Assembly (1797–99). In the Presidential election of 1800 he tied Jefferson. When the House of Representatives chose the latter, Burr became 3rd Vice-President of the U.S. He was defeated for governor of New York (1804). Provoked by published accusations made by his political foe,

Alexander Hamilton, Burr mortally wounded Hamilton in a duel at Weehawken, N.J. (11 July 1804). He fled southward, but returned to preside over the impeachment trial of Supreme Court Justice Samuel Chase. In 1806 he became involved in a conspiracy which, whether to seize Mexico for the U.S. or to have the Western states secede from the Union, has never been clarified. Arrested by co-conspirator Gen. James Wilkinson, he was brought before Chief Justice Marshall (30 Mar. 1807), sitting at Richmond in the U.S. Circuit Court. Acquitted both of treason and of high misdemeanor, he resided in Europe (1808–12) and then practiced law in New York City.

Butler, Nicholas Murray (b. Elizabeth, N.J., 2 Apr. 1862; d. New York City, 7 Dec. 1947), educator and author, was graduated from Columbia (A.B., 1882; A.M., 1883; Ph.D., 1884), studied at Berlin and Paris (1884–85), and served at Columbia as an assistant (1885–86), tutor (1886–89), and adjunct professor of philosophy (1889–90). In 1889 he established the *Educational Review,* of which he was the 1st editor (1889–1920). He was the organizer and 1st president (1886–91) of Teachers College and, as president of Columbia University from 1901 until his retirement in 1945, he was outstandingly successful in expanding the university's effectiveness and prestige. Active in public affairs, Butler was Republican Vice-Presidential nominee in 1912. He was appointed (1905) a trustee of the Carnegie Foundation for the Advancement of Teaching, served as president (1925–45) of the Carnegie Endowment for International Peace, and was chairman (1937–45) of the Carnegie Corporation. In 1931 he shared the Nobel Peace Prize with Jane Addams.

Byrd, Richard Evelyn (b. Winchester, Va., 25 Oct. 1888; d. Boston, Mass., 11 Mar. 1957), naval officer, explorer, was graduated from the U.S. Naval Academy (1912), entered the Aviation Service (1917); and was commander July–Nov. 1918) of the U.S. air forces in Canada. He made a dirigible flight across the Atlantic (1921) and was commander

(1925) of the aviation unit of the Navy-MacMillan Polar Expedition. With Floyd Bennett, he made an airplane flight (9 May 1926) over the North Pole, for which he was awarded the Congressional Medal of Honor. With 3 companions, he made a 4,200-mile flight from New York to France (29 June–1 July 1927). He made his 1st expedition to the Antarctic in 1928–30, flying over the South Pole (29 Nov. 1929) from his base at "Little America." In his 2nd expedition to the Antarctic (1933–35) he recorded important scientific data near the South Pole and discovered and named Maria Byrd Land and the Edsel Ford Mountains, and on his 3rd (1939) he made flights that resulted in the discovery of 5 islands, 5 mountain ranges, and 100,000 sq. mi. of land area. He commanded the U.S. Navy Expedition (1946–47) which explored 1,700,000 sq. mi., tested equipment, made weather observations, and carried out a geological survey of the South Pole region.

Calhoun, John Caldwell (b. Abbeville District, S.C., 18 Mar. 1782; d. Washington, D.C., 30 Mar. 1850), statesman, was graduated from Yale (1804) and admitted to the S.C. bar (1807). After a term in the S.C. legislature (1808–09), he was in Congress (1811–17), where he became a leader of the "war hawks" and supported nationalistic legislation after the War of 1812, including the protective Tariff of 1816. He served as Secretary of War under Monroe (1817–25), was a candidate for President (1824), but was elected Vice-President of the U.S., serving 1st under John Quincy Adams (1825–29) and then under Jackson (1829–32). In his "South Carolina Exposition" (1828), written in opposition to the Tariff of 1828, he postulated the principles of states' rights and nullification. Breaking with Jackson over Peggy Eaton and nullification, he resigned as Vice-President (1832). As U.S. senator (1832–44) he became the leading proponent of states' rights. While Tyler's Secretary of State (1844–45), he secured the annexation of Tex. Again senator (1845–50), he opposed the Mexican War, the admission of Calif. to statehood (because its constitution forbade slavery), and the

Wilmot Proviso. In his last speech, on the Compromise of 1850, read to the Senate by Sen. Mason of Va. (4 Mar. 1850), he approved the purpose of the Act but criticized it for its failure to provide the South with adequate guarantees. In his "Discourse on the Constitution," posthumously published, he proposed a dual Executive (from North and South), each armed with a veto.

Cardozo, Benjamin Nathan (b. New York City, 24 May 1870; d. Port Chester, N.Y., 9 July 1938), jurist, was graduated from Columbia (1889), admitted to the New York bar (1891), practicing law in New York until his election to the state supreme court (1913). Appointed to the state court of appeals (1917) and elected its chief judge (1927), he established that court's preeminent prestige and was the obvious choice to succeed O. W. Holmes on his retirement from the U.S. Supreme Court. Appointed by Hoover associate justice (1932), he aligned himself with the liberal wing (Brandeis and Stone) on social and economic issues. Although he vigorously concurred in the *Schechter Case* (1935) in opposition to "delegation running riot," he just as vigorously dissented from the tendency of the majority to curb distasteful governmental policies (*Carter Case,* 1936), and upheld the Social Security Act under the general welfare clause (*Stevens Machine Co.* and *Helvering* v. *Davis,* 1937). His ideas of sociological jurisprudence and his position that adherence to precedent should be relaxed in the face of changing conditions were expressed in his writings (*The Nature of the Judicial Process,* 1921, *The Growth of the Law,* 1924; and *The Paradoxes of Legal Science,* 1928).

Carnegie, Andrew (b. Dunfermline, Scotland, 25 Nov. 1835; d. Lenox, Mass., 11 Aug. 1919), industrialist and philanthropist. Coming to the U.S with his poverty-stricken parents (1848), he began his career in Allegheny, Pa., as a bobbin boy employed at $1.20 a week, then (1849) a messenger in the Pittsburgh telegraph office. At the age of 16 he became one of the 1st operators in the U.S. able to take messages by sound. In 1853 he became private secretary and personal telegrapher to Thomas A. Scott, general superintendent of the Pennsylvania R.R. Upon Scott's appointment (1860) as vice-president of the road, Carnegie was named superintendent of the Pittsburgh division; and when Scott was named assistant secretary of war (1861), Carnegie became superintendent of the eastern military and telegraph lines, performing notable services for the Union forces during the Civil War. Having reorganized the Keystone Bridge Works (1862), Carnegie resigned from the Pennsylvania R.R. (1865) to devote himself to the iron, oil, and other businesses. He established (1868) the Union Iron Mills, and beginning in 1873 concentrated solely on the steel industry. In the following 3 decades, during which the U.S. took the lead over British steel production, the rapid expansion of U.S. steel manufactures was largely his creation. Carnegie progressively added to his holdings by lease or purchase, and in 1888 took over the Homestead Steel Works. By 1900, the Carnegie Steel Co., which had been organized in 1899, controlled the bulk of U.S. steel production. After selling his company to the interests that formed the U.S. Steel Corp. (1901), Carnegie retired and devoted himself to philanthropy. He set up the Carnegie trusts and foundations, among them the Carnegie Institution of Washington (1902), the Carnegie Foundation for the Advancement of Teaching (1906), the Carnegie Endowment for International Peace (1910), the Carnegie Corp. of New York (1911), and the Carnegie United Kingdom Trust (1913). He endowed numerous libraries throughout the world. He wrote *The Gospel of Wealth* (1900).

Carothers, Wallace Hume (27 Apr. 1896, Burlington, Iowa; d. Philadelphia, 29 Apr. 1937), chemist, inventor, received his B.S. (1920) from Tarkio College, Mo., and his M.S. (1921) and Ph.D. (1924) from the Univ. of Ill. His 1st independent papers, "Isosterism of Phenal Isocyanate and Diazobenzene-Imide" (1923) and "The Double Bond" (1924), revealed his creativity in the field of theoretical organic chemistry. Instructor at Harvard (1926–28), he left to direct a fundamental research program in organic chemistry at E. I. du Pont de Nemours and Co. in Wilmington, Del. His interest in unsaturated compounds led to the production of a rubberlike polymer (1930) and to the commercial development of a synthetic rubber known as neoprene. The research of Carothers and his associates (1929–37) provided a general theory of polymerization processes, culminating (23 May 1934) in the synthesizing of a superpolymer, which led (1939) to the commercial production of nylon, the 1st completely synthetic fiber. Despondent over the death of his sister (1937), he committed suicide.

Carver, George Washington (b. near Diamond Grove, Mo., *c*.1864; d. Tuskegee, Ala., 5 Jan. 1943), Negro agricultural chemist. Born of slave parents, he was illiterate until he was almost 20 years old. He worked his way through the Minneapolis (Kan.) high school and through the Iowa State College of Agriculture and Mechanic Arts (B.S., 1894; M.S., 1896), where he was head of the college greenhouse and of bacterial laboratory work in systematic botany (1894–96). In 1896 he became director of the department of agricultural research at Tuskegee Institute, Ala., where he remained for the rest of his life. Essentially a practical chemist, he used empirical methods in his work on the diversified utilization of common agricultural products, including the peanut, sweet potato, and soy bean. His achievements exercised an important influence on the shift of the Southern agricultural economy from a single-crop basis to a diversified and more prosperous foundation. From the peanut and the sweet potato he developed more than a hundred different products, including plastics, lubricants, dyes, medicines, ink, wood stains, face creams, tapioca, and molasses. He also evolved the cross between the short-stalk and tall-stalk cotton known as "Carver's Hybrid." In 1940 he gave his life savings to establish the Carver Foundation for research in creative chemistry.

Cass, Lewis (b. Exeter, N.H., 9 Oct. 1782; d. Detroit, Mich., 17 June 1866), soldier, diplomat, statesman, attended

Exeter Academy. Setting out on foot from Wilmington, Del., for the Northwest Territory in 1801, he studied law under Gov. Meigs in Marietta, Ohio, and was admitted to the Ohio bar (1802). In the Ohio legislature (1806), he was U.S. Marshal for Ohio (1807–12), when he resigned to enlist in the army. Col. and brig. gen., he played an important role in Harrison's victories over the British and Indians in the War of 1812. Governor of Mich. Terr. (1813–31), he concluded treaties with the Indians. Jackson's Secy. of War (1831–36), he directed the Black Hawk War. Minister to France (1836–42), he resigned because of differences with Secy. of State Webster over a 5-party treaty legalizing the right of search, which he opposed. In a bid for the Democratic Presidential nomination, he urged (Hannegan Letter, 10 May 1844) annexation of Texas. A nationalist and expansionist, he backed Polk's Oregon policy and opposed the Wilmot Proviso as senator from Mich. (1845–48). He resigned to run as the Democratic nominee for President in 1848, suffering defeat by Taylor as a result of party defection in N.Y. and Pa. Senator again (1849–57), he favored the Compromise of 1850. As Buchanan's Secy. of State (1857–60), he resigned 12 Dec. 1860 in protest against the President's decision not to reinforce the Charleston forts.

Cather, Willa (b. Winchester, Va., 7 Dec. 1876; d. New York City, 24 Apr. 1947), novelist, moved with her parents to Neb. (1884) and graduated from the University of Nebraska (1895). She taught school, did newspaper work in Pittsburgh, and published her 1st book of stories (1905). Editor, *McClure's Magazine* (1907–12), she resigned to devote herself to creative writing. Her novels, poignant recollections of a pioneer past stressing the supremacy of moral and spiritual over material values, are economically constructed and marked by a graceful, lucid style. They include: *O Pioneers!* (1913), *The Song of the Lark* (1915), *My Antonia* (1918), *One of Ours* (1922, a Pulitzer prize-winner), *A Lost Lady* (1923, often regarded as her best work), *Death Comes for the Archbishop* (1927), and *Shadows on the Rock* (1931).

Channing, William Ellery (b. Newport, R.I., 7 Apr. 1780; d. Bennington, Vt., 2 Oct. 1842), Unitarian clergyman. Graduating from Harvard in 1798, he was ordained and installed (1803) as minister of the Federal Street Church at Boston, a pastorate he held until his death. His humane and liberal theology touched off the "Unitarian Controversy" that saw Channing and his followers ranged against orthodox Calvinists. The controversy reached its height c.1815. Expressing the viewpoint of members of Congregationalist and other sects who were dissatisfied with Calvinist doctrine, particularly its emphasis on the depravity of man, he preached the gospel of goodness and love, the dignity and perfectibility of man, the validity of reason, and freedom of will and moral responsibility, but accepted the supernatural in Christianity. Channing became the acknowledged head of the Unitarians, whose formal emergence was precipitated by the sermon he delivered at Baltimore (1819) at the ordination of Jared Sparks, an address in which he formulated the Unitarian creed. Channing organized the Berry Street conference of liberal ministers (1820), the predecessor of the American Unitarian Association (1825). After 1825 his influence spread beyond religious circles. His addresses on education, literature, slavery, and war attracted wide attention; some of them were published in pamphlet form, including *Remarks on American Literature* (1830), *Slavery* (1835), *The Abolitionist* (1836), and *Duty of the Free States* (1842). The moral and religious forces which he liberated were the bases of New England Transcendentalism.

Chase, Salmon Portland (b. Cornish, N.H., 13 Jan. 1808; d. New York City, 7 May 1873), statesman, was graduated from Dartmouth (1826), admitted to the bar (1829), and commenced law practice in Cincinnati (1830). Through his defense of fugitive slaves he became a leader of the antislavery movement, an organizer (1841) of the Liberty party, and a founder (1848) of the Free-Soil party. As U.S. senator (1849–55) he opposed the Compromise of 1850 and the Kansas-Nebraska Bill. Republican governor of Ohio (1855–60), he was again elected to the U.S. Senate (1860). Unsuccessful candidate for President in that year, he became Lincoln's Secretary of the Treasury, maintaining credit and funds to prosecute the Civil War and recommending the National Banking Act (1863). Opposing Seward in the Cabinet, his resignation was finally accepted (June 1864), but in Dec. of that year Lincoln appointed him Chief Justice of the U.S. Supreme Court. He reorganized the Federal courts in the South, presided over the trial of Jefferson Davis and favored quashing the indictment (1867), and over the Senate impeachment proceedings against President Johnson (1868). In the *Hepburn Case* (1870) he declared the opinion of the court invalidating the Legal Tender Act of 1862 making "greenbacks" (issued by him as Secretary of the Treasury) legal tender, and dissented from the reversal (1871). He stood with the majority of the Court in decisions upholding the Republican policy of Reconstruction.

Clark, George Rogers (19 Nov. 1752, Charlottesville, Va.; d. 13 Feb. 1818, Louisville, Ky.), conqueror of the Northwest, explored the Ohio (1772) and Kentucky rivers (1774), the latter as surveyor for the Ohio Co. Commissioned maj. in charge of the defense of the Kentucky area when the Revolution broke out, his plan for the conquest of the Illinois country was endorsed by Virginia's gov. Patrick Henry (*q.v.*). As lt. col. he set out with a company of 175 men, capturing Kaskaskia and Vincennes (1778), soon lost to British counterattack. In a heroic winter march of 180 mi. he recaptured Vincennes (1779), forcing Lt. Gov. Henry Hamilton to surrender. In 1780 he met a British threat to the Spanish outpost in St. Louis, was on the defensive in 1781, but held fast to the key bastion of Ft. Nelson on the Falls of the Ohio (1782). The close of the war found Kentucky in U.S. hands and much of Ohio and Ill., and by the Treaty of Paris (1783) the Northwest was given to the U.S. In 1786 James Wilkinson made political capital out of Clark's seizure of Spanish goods at Vincennes (1786) in order to provision his garrison. Involved in 2 French projects (1793, 1798) to lead an expedition against the Spanish for the reconquest of Louisiana, he refused a U.S. demand to surrender his generaliship in the French army, taking refuge in St. Louis. In later life he was interested in Indian history and archaeology.

Clark, William, see **Lewis, Meriwether,** and **Clark, William.**

Clay, Henry (b. Hanover Co., Va., 12 Apr. 1777; d. Washington, D.C., 29 June 1852), statesman, studied law in Richmond, was admitted to the bar (1797), and practiced in Lexington, Ky. Ky. legislator (1803–06), he filled an unexpired term in the U.S. Senate (1806–07), became speaker of the state legislature (1807–09), and filled another unexpired term in the Senate (1809–10). While Congressman (1811–25), he became Speaker (1811–20 and 1823–25) and was a leader of the "war hawks." A commissioner to negotiate peace with Great Britain (1814), he urged recognition of South American republics by the U.S. (1817) and was influential in framing the Missouri Compromise (1820). As a candidate for President (1824), he was 4th in the number of electoral votes, throwing his support to John Quincy Adams, whose Secretary of State (1825–29) he became. Senator (1831–42 and 1849–52), Clay was the Whig candidate for President (1832), but was defeated by Jackson largely because of his support of the 2nd Bank of the U.S. His "American System" was based upon tariff protection and Federal aid for internal improvements. He sponsored the compromise Tariff of 1833, failed to secure the Whig nomination in 1840, and ran in 1844, losing because of his noncommittal stand on Texas. His sponsorship of the Compromise of 1850 earned him the title of "The Great Pacificator."

Clemens, Samuel Langhorne [pseudonym **Mark Twain**] (b. Florida, Mo., 30 Nov. 1835; d. Redding, Conn., 21 Apr. 1910), novelist and humorist, was reared in Hannibal, Mo. (1839–53), where, at the age of 12, he was apprenticed to a printer. As a journeyman printer he worked (1853–57) in cities in the Old West and along the Eastern seaboard, and from 1857 to 1861 served successively as apprentice pilot and licensed pilot on Mississippi steamboats. In 1861 he became secretary to his brother Orion, who had just been named secretary to the territorial governor of Nev. After an unsuccessful attempt at prospecting and mining, he became (1862) a reporter on the *Territorial Enterprise* in Virginia City, using for the 1st time the pseudonym Mark Twain (a river term indicating 2 fathoms deep), by which he is best known. This had been the nom de plume of Capt. Isaiah Sellers (d. 1863). Going to California in 1864, he wrote in the following year the humorous story, "The Celebrated Jumping Frog of Calaveras County," which was reprinted in newspapers throughout the U.S. and served as the title of his 1st book (1867). After taking an assignment as a roving correspondent in the Sandwich Islands, he began (1866) his long career as a lecturer. A commission as a travel correspondent for a San Francisco newspaper took him to the Mediterranean and the Holy Land, a trip that provided the material for *The Innocents Abroad* (1869), a book that brought him a national reputation. He lived in Buffalo (1869–71), writing for the Buffalo *Express,* and married (1870) Olivia Langdon of Elmira, N.Y. His outstanding books include *Roughing It* (1872), *The Adventures of Tom Sawyer* (1876), *Life on the Mississippi* (1883), *The Adventures of Huckleberry Finn* (1884), *A Connecticut Yankee at King Arthur's Court* (1889), and *The Tragedy of Pudd'nhead Wilson* (1894). See also p. 605. *Mark Twain's Autobiography* was published in 1924. A growing despair and bitterness toward the end of his life was reflected in *What is Man?* (1906) and *The Mysterious Stranger* (1916). At his best, Twain raised to the level of universal human appeal the lusty humor of the frontier.

Cleveland, Stephen Grover (b. Caldwell, N.J., 18 Mar. 1837; d. Princeton, N.J., 24 June 1908), 22nd and 24th President of the U.S., studied law in Buffalo and was admitted to the N.Y. bar (1859). Assistant district attorney of Erie County (1863), elected Democratic sheriff (1869), mayor of Buffalo (1881–82), and governor of N.Y. (1882–84), he was elected Democratic President of the U.S. (1885–89). He married Frances Folsom (1886) at the White House. His conciliatory attitude toward the South, his vetoes of over two thirds of bills presented to him (mostly private pension bills), and his tariff reduction proposal (1887) contributed to his defeat by Harrison in 1888. Again elected President (1892), serving, 1893–97, he took a "hard money" stand and had Congress repeal the Sherman Silver Purchase Act (1893) following the panic of that year. By sending troops into Ill. to break the Pullman strike and permitting Attorney General Olney to employ a railroad attorney as special counsel to the government (4 July 1894), he alienated labor. Cleveland intervened in the boundary dispute between Great Britain and Venezuela (1895). An anti-imperialist, he withdrew the U.S. treaty of annexation of Hawaii (1893), although he recognized the republic the following year.

Clinton, De Witt (b. Little Britain, Orange Co., N.Y., 2 Mar. 1769; d. Albany, 11 Feb. 1828), statesman, was graduated from Columbia (1786), studied law, was admitted to the N.Y. bar (1788), and became private secretary (1790–95) to his uncle George Clinton, governor of N.Y. State assemblyman (1797–98) and state senator (1798–1802), he is credited with introducing the "spoils system" when serving on the Council of Appointment. In the legislature he sponsored relief for prisoners for debt, the abolition of slavery, and the promotion of steam navigation. Elected to the U.S. Senate (1802), he resigned to become mayor of New York City (1803–15, except for 1807–08 and 1810–11), in which office his record was outstanding. As chief organizer of the Public School Society (1805) and sponsor of the Lancastrian school system, he laid the foundation of the public school system in N.Y. Candidate of the New York Republicans (1812) in the Presidential race of that year, he was defeated by Madison, 128–89. Appointed (1817) commissioner to examine and survey the route for the Erie Canal, he was chiefly responsible for its successful completion in 1825. Elected governor (1817) and re-elected (1820), he retired from office in 1823 when the "Albany Regency" became supreme. Public reaction to his removal from office as canal commissioner (1824) led to his reelection as governor (1825–28).

Clinton, George (b. Little Britain, N.Y., 26 July, 1739; d. Washington, D.C., 20 Apr. 1812), statesman, studied law under William Smith in New York City and returned to practice in Ulster County. In the N.Y. Assembly (1768) and the 2nd Continental Congress (1775–76), as brig. gen. of militia he unsuccessfully defended Fort Montgomery against Sir Henry Clinton (1777). Seven-term gov. of N.Y., serving from 1777–95 and from 1801–04, he may be considered the "father" of the state. Leader of the N.Y. Antifederalists, he was outspoken in opposition to the Constitution, unwilling to surrender either his own power or any significant vestige of state sovereignty. As "Cato" his arguments in the N.Y. *Journal* against the Constitution were answered by "Caesar" (allegedly Hamilton) in the *Daily Advertiser*. His plan (1783) for a series of canals connecting the Hudson with Lakes Ontario and Champlain (1783) were later carried out by his nephew De Witt Clinton (*q.v.*). Elected Vice-President (1804 and again 1808), he registered his old animosity against Hamilton and his contempt for Madison by casting (1811) the deciding vote against the bill to recharter the Bank of the U.S.

Cohn, Edwin Joseph (b. New York City, 17 Dec. 1892; d. Boston, Mass., 2 Oct. 1953), biochemist, was graduated from the University of Chicago (B.S., 1914; Ph.D., 1917), held a National Research Council fellowship (1919–22) during his studies at the Carlsberg Laboratory in Copenhagen and at Cambridge University, and became (1922) assistant professor of physical chemistry at the Harvard Medical School, where he served (1935–49) as professor of biochemistry and head of the department of physical chemistry, and after 1949 as director of the physical chemistry laboratory at Harvard. His most notable researches have been made in the protein fractionization of blood, particularly the isolation of albumin. Serum albumin, as precipitated by Cohn and his associates, is a nontoxic, stable, and compact blood substitute better suited to emergency conditions than stored whole blood or dried plasma and widely used in the U.S. armed services after Pearl Harbor. Gamma globulin contains antibodies which help prevent or treat diseases like measles and jaundice. Other pure plasma proteins isolated by fractionization (such as thrombin and fibrinogen, in combination as a blood-clotting agency) serve a variety of uses in medicine and surgery. He wrote *Proteins, Amino Acids and Peptides* (with J. T. Edsall in 1943).

Compton, Arthur Holly (b. Wooster, Ohio, 10 Sept. 1892–), physicist and educator, was graduated from the College of Wooster (B.S., 1913) and Princeton (M.A., 1914; Ph.D., 1916); was an instructor in physics (1916–17) at the University of Minnesota; research engineer (1917–19) for the Westinghouse Lamp Co.; research fellow (1919–20) at the Cavendish Laboratory, Cambridge University; professor of physics (1920–23) at Washington University, St. Louis, and (1923–45) at the University of Chicago. Chancellor of Washington University (1945–53), he then became distinguished service professor of natural philosophy. His investigations (1923 *et seq.*) of the scattering of X rays by matter led to his discovery of the change of wave length known as the Compton effect. He also discovered the total reflection and (with C. H. Hagenow) polarization of X rays. With C. T. R. Wilson, he was the joint recipient (1927) of the Nobel prize in physics. He also did important work on cosmic rays, in which field he directed a worldwide study (1931–33) and showed the electrical composition of cosmic rays and their variation with altitude and latitude. As wartime director (1942–45) of plutonium research for the U.S. atomic bomb project, he guided the development of the 1st quantity production of plutonium.

Conant, James Bryant (b. Dorchester, Mass., 26 Mar. 1893–), chemist, diplomat, educator, received his A.B. (1913)

and Ph.D. (1916) from Harvard, where he taught chemistry (1916–33), with an interruption during World War I for service as lt., Sanitary Corps, U.S. army, and maj. in the Chemical Warfare Service. He did notable research in the field of organic chemistry, specifically on the structure of chlorophyll and hemoglobin. President of Harvard (1933–53), he introduced significant reforms as regards admissions and curriculum. Chairman (1941–46) of the National Defense Research Comm., he had a key role in the production of the atomic bomb, was instrumental in the creation of the National Science Foundation (1950), and was a member of the general advisory committee, AEC (1947–52). High commissioner to West Germany (1953–55) and U.S. ambassador there (1955–57), he made an extensive investigation of U.S. high schools under a Carnegie grant (1957–58), publishing *The American High School Today* (1959) and *The Child, the Parent, and the State* (1959). For his work in education he received (1959) the Woodrow Wilson Distinguished Service Award (1959). He wrote numerous works in organic chemistry, including *Organic Chemistry* (1928) and *The Chemistry of Organic Compounds* (1933).

Cooke, Jay (b. in present-day Sandusky, Ohio, 10 Aug. 1821; d. Ogontz, Pa., 16 Feb. 1905), banker and financier, was a clerk at St. Louis and at Philadelphia, where he entered (1839) the banking house of E. W. Clark & Co., from which he retired (1857) to participate in the general banking business. In 1861 he formed with his brother-in-law the banking house of Jay Cooke & Co. at Philadelphia, which during the Civil War acted as agent for the U.S. government in floating bond issues for meeting military requirements. In 1865 he was appointed fiscal agent of the Treasury Department. During the course of the war he floated $2,500 million worth of bonds at virtually no profit to himself. His firm became financial agent for the Northern Pacific R.R. Its connection with that enterprise led to its failure (18 Sept. 1873), precipitating the panic of that year. Compelled to go into bankruptcy, Cooke later

repaid his creditors and recouped his fortune.

Cooley, Thomas McIntyre (b. near Attica, N.Y., 6 Jan. 1824; d. Ann Arbor, Mich., 12 Sept. 1898), jurist, was admitted to the Mich. bar (1846) and practiced in Tecumseh and Adrian. He compiled the state statutes (1857), became reporter for the state supreme court (1858), and published his *Digest of Michigan Reports* (1866). Professor of law (1859–84) and of American history (1884–98) at the University of Michigan, he was justice of the state supreme court (1864–85) and chairman of the Interstate Commerce Commission (1887–91), where he was largely responsible for turning it into a quasi-judicial body and for formulating ruling principles of rate regulation. His most important writings were on constitutional law. *The Constitutional Limitations Which Rest upon the Legislative Power of the States of the American Union* (1868), with its doctrine of implied constitutional limitations upon the state's legislative power, was the basis for widening the scope of the doctrine of judicial review, while his concept of due process provided the courts with authority to curb government intervention in the economic and social sphere. With Story, he ranks as the most influential commentator on the Constitution. Other works include *The Law of Taxation* (1876), *Treatise on the Law of Torts* (1879), and *General Principles of Constitutional Law in the U.S.* (1880).

Coolidge, Calvin (b. Plymouth, Vt., 4 July 1872; d. Northampton, Mass., 5 Jan. 1933), 30th President of the U.S., was graduated from Amherst (1895) and practiced law at Northampton (1897). Member of the Mass. General Court (1907–08), mayor of Northampton (1910–11), state senator (1912–15, serving as president of that body, 1914–15), and lieutenant governor (1916–18), he came into national prominence as governor (1919–20) through his suppression of the Boston police strike (1919). Elected Republican Vice-President of the U.S., he became President on Harding's death (2 Aug. 1923), and was elected President (1924), serving 1925–29. He twice vetoed the McNary-Haugen Farm Relief Bill, refused to intervene in the general coal strike (1927), and did not "choose" to run for President in 1928. On 4 Dec. 1928 he told Congress: "The country . . . can anticipate the future with optimism." He left office before the 1929 crisis.

Cooper, James Fenimore (b. Burlington, N.J., 15 Sept. 1789; d. Cooperstown, N.Y., 14 Sept. 1851), novelist, historian, and social critic, was expelled from Yale, where he was a member of the class of 1806. He shipped before the mast (1806–07), was commissioned midshipman in the U.S. Navy (1808), and resigned from the service in 1810. From 1811 to 1822 he followed the life of a country squire. His first novel, *Precaution* (1820), was a conventional story with an English background that he wrote for his own satisfaction, but in *The Spy* (1821), where Cooper used a native setting for a theme drawn from the Revolutionary period, he showed signs of his powerful narrative gift. The novel enjoyed an international success. In 1822 Cooper moved to New York to follow a literary career. His most famous work, the Leatherstocking series, includes the following novels: *The Pioneers* (1823), *The Last of the Mohicans* (1826), *The Prairie* (1827), *The Pathfinder* (1840), and *The Deerslayer* (1841). He also wrote *The Pilot* (1824) and *Lionel Lincoln* (1825) before going to Europe (1826), where he found the themes and settings for the novels, *The Bravo* (1831), *The Heidenmauer* (1832), and *The Headsman* (1833). During his European stay he also published novels with an American background, such as *The Red Rover* (1828), *The Wept of Wish-ton-Wish* (1829), and *The Water-Witch* (1831), and gathered the material for the following travel accounts: *Sketches of Switzerland* (1836), *Gleanings in Europe* (1837), *Gleanings in Europe: England* (1837), and *Gleanings in Europe: Italy* (1838). Upon his return to the U.S. in 1833 he published *A Letter to His Countrymen* (1834) and *The American Democrat* (1838), forthright criticisms of the provincialism of his native land that precipitated a quarrel between Cooper

and his public that lasted for several years. The same critical viewpoint was incorporated in novels such as *Homeward Bound* (1838) and *Home as Found* (1838), and, to some extent, in *The Monikins* (1835). After 1834, when Cooper lived at Cooperstown, he enjoyed his most productive period, including the writing of a scholarly *History of the Navy of the United States of America* (1839).

Cooper, Peter (b. New York City, 12 Feb. 1791; d. there, 4 Apr. 1883), manufacturer, inventor, and philanthropist. After brief formal schooling, he was apprenticed (1808) to a New York coachmaker, and later manufactured clothshearing machines of his own invention, glue, and isinglass. In partnership with 2 others, he established (1828) the Canton Iron Works at Baltimore. In 1830 he designed and constructed for the Baltimore & Ohio R.R. the 1st steam locomotive (popularly known as "Tom Thumb") built in America. In 1845 established at Trenton, N.J., a rolling mill where the 1st structural iron for fireproof buildings was rolled (1854); and in 1856 became the 1st U.S. iron manufacturer to use the Bessemer converter. Cooper was the chief financial supporter of Cyrus Field's Atlantic cable project and was president of the New York, Newfoundland & London Telegraph Co. He founded (1857–59) Cooper Union, an educational institute at New York City "for the advancement of science and art." He was the Presidential candidate (1876) of the Greenback party and outlined his position on currency and other matters in *Political and Financial Ideas of Peter Cooper with an Autobiography* (1877) and *Ideas for a Science of Good Government* (1883).

Copland, Aaron (b. Brooklyn, N.Y., 14 Nov. 1900–), composer, studied harmony and composition with Rubin Goldmark (1917) and in Paris (1921) with Nadia Boulanger, who introduced him to Koussevitsky, from then on an ardent Copland admirer. His *Symphony for Organ and Orchestra* was introduced to the U.S. in Boston and N.Y. (1925) and was rescored without organ as *1st Symph.* (1928). The jazz element appeared in his work with *Music for Theater* (1925), a suite for chamber orchestra. A new phase, with greater dissonance predominating, is found in *Piano Variations* (1930) and *Short Symph.* (1933). He wrote scores for the ballet, including *Billy the Kid* (1938), *Rodeo* (1942), and *Appalachian Spring* (1944); the last, commissioned for Martha Graham, won the Pulitzer Prize in Music. He also wrote the *3rd Symph.* (1946), an opera *Tender Land* (1954), and film scores for such movies as *The City* (1939), *Of Mice and Men* (1939), *Our Town* (1940), and *The Heiress* (1948, Academy Award 1950). With Roger Sessions he founded the Copland-Sessions Concerts (1928–31) and org. (1932) the Amer. Festival of Contemporary Music at Yaddo, Saratoga Springs, N. Y. He wrote *What to Listen for in Music* (1939, rev. 1957) and *Our New Music* (1941).

Copley, John Singleton (b. Boston, Mass., 1738; d. London, 9 Sept. 1815), painter, probably received his early training under his stepfather, the painter and engraver Peter Pelham, and at about the age of 18 became a professional portraitist. In the 1760's and early 1770's he painted many of the prominent personages of New England. In 1766, following the exhibition in London of Copley's *The Boy with the Squirrel,* he was elected a Fellow of the Society of Artists of Great Britain. In 1771–72 he held sittings at New York and in 1774, partly at the urging of Benjamin West, left Boston. He made the Continental tour and settled (1775) in London, where he painted portraits and also historical subjects, notably *The Death of Lord Chatham.* In 1783 he was elected a member of the Royal Academy. Among his many portraits are those of John Adams, Samuel Adams, Mr. and Mrs. Thomas Mifflin, and Mr. and Mrs. Isaac Winslow.

Cotton, John (b. Derby, Derbyshire, England, 4 Dec. 1584; d. Boston, Mass., 23 Dec. 1652), Puritan divine and author. He was graduated from Cambridge (A.B., 1603; A.M., 1606), was ordained deacon and priest (1610), and served as head lecturer and dean of Emmanuel College, Cambridge. In 1613 he received his divinity degree. While serving as vicar of St. Botolph's at Boston, Lincolnshire, he was attracted (*c.*1615) to Puritan tenets. A friend of John Winthrop, he preached the farewell sermon at Southampton when the *Arbella* departed for America (1630). In 1633 Cotton arrived at Boston aboard the *Griffin* and became teacher of the church at Boston. His change from liberalism to orthodox conformity is evidenced in the Antinomian controversy, during which his initial defense of Anne Hutchinson gave way to support of her excommunication and banishment from Massachusetts Bay. A prolific author, he prepared a code of laws for the colony, "Moses his Judicialls" (1636), which was not adopted, and wrote treatises on Congregationalism, such as *The Keyes of the Kingdom of Heaven* (1644), *The Way of the Churches of Christ in New England* (1645), and *The Way of the Congregational Churches Cleared* (1648). He also wrote *Milk for Babes* (1646), a children's catechism which long remained standard in New England. Cotton's controversy with Roger Williams, which led the latter to write *The Bloudy Tenent of Persecution* (1644), brought in reply Cotton's *The Bloudy Tenent Washed and Made White* (1647).

Crane, Stephen (b. Newark, N.J., 1 Nov. 1871; d. Badenweiler, Germany, 5 June 1900), novelist and short-story writer, worked as a newspaper correspondent in Asbury Park, N.J., and attended Lafayette College and Syracuse University (1890–91). He settled in New York City, where he was a reporter for the *Tribune* and *Herald,* and in 1892 published at his own expense his first novel, *Maggie: A Girl of the Streets,* a study of New York slum life that revealed Crane's strong bent for realism. His Civil War novel, *The Red Badge of Courage* (1895), brought him instant fame. In 1896 his adventures with a filibustering expedition bound for Cuba provided him with the substance of the short story, "The Open Boat." As a war correspondent he covered the Spanish-American and Greco-Turkish wars. His last 2 years were spent in England, where he formed friendships with such authors as Joseph Conrad, Henry James, and H. G. Wells.

He died of tuberculosis. Among his works are *The Black Riders and Other Lines* (1895, verse), *The Little Regiment and Other Episodes of the Civil War* (1896), *George's Mother* (1896), *The Third Violet* (1897), *Active Service* (1899), *Wounds in the Rain* (1900), *The Monster* (1899), *War is Kind* (1899, verse), *Whilomville Stories* (1900), *The O'Ruddy* (1903), and *Men, Women, and Boats* (1921).

Croly, Herbert David (b. New York City, 23 Jan. 1869; d. Santa Barbara, Calif., 17 May 1930), editor, reformer, studied intermittently (1893–99) at Harvard with William James, Josiah Royce, and George Santayana, but did not receive his B.A. until 1910. Editor of the *Architectural Record* (1900–06), he gave up the editorship to write *The Promise of American Life* (1909), a Progressive classic. Combining a Hamiltonian belief in strong central govt. with advocacy of a positive program for social goals, it was a source of T.R.'s New Nationalism and of Wilson's New Freedom. Editor of the *New Republic*, founded 1914, he played a significant role in bringing about U.S. entry into World War I, but broke with Wilson after publication of the Treaty of Versailles. His opposition to treaty ratification injured the magazine's circulation and influence. Other books include *Progressive Democracy* (1914) and *Marcus Alonzo Hanna, His Life and Work* (1912).

Cushing, Harvey William (b. Cleveland, Ohio, 8 Apr. 1869; d. New Haven, Conn., 7 Oct. 1939), neurological surgeon, specialist in brain surgery. He was graduated from Yale (A.B., 1891) and Harvard (A.M., M.D., 1895), was a practicing surgeon at Cleveland (1895–1902), and served as associate professor of surgery (1902–12) at the Johns Hopkins University, spending the years 1901–03 abroad studying under leading Continental surgeons. In 1912 he became professor of surgery at Harvard and surgeon in chief to the Peter Bent Brigham Hospital at Boston, holding these posts until 1932. During World War I he was senior consultant in neurological surgery to the A.E.F. He was Sterling professor of neurosurgery (1933–37) at Yale, where he was director in the history of medicine from 1937 until his death. During his service at the Peter B. Brigham Hospital he evolved a notable school of brain surgery based on experimental research in neurophysiology. He did important work on the operative treatment of facial paralysis, cerebral tumors, nerve block, and the intracranial hemorrhage of new-born babies; invented surgical instruments; pioneered in using the X ray and blood-pressure determination in the U.S.; and made contributions to endocrinology. He wrote the biography, *The Life of Sir William Osler* (2 vols., 1925), which was awarded the Pulitzer prize. Among his medical writings are *The Pituitary Body and Its Disorders* (1912), *Tumors of the Nervus Acusticus* (1917), *A Classification of the Glioma Group* (1926), *Intracranial Tumors* (1932), *Pituitary Body and Hypothalmus* (1932), and *Meningomas* (1939).

Cushman, Charlotte Saunders (b. Boston, Mass., 23 July 1816; d. there, 17 Feb. 1876), actress. In 1835 she made her debut as an operatic singer, but while performing at New Orleans in that year abandoned opera for the dramatic stage, appearing as Lady Macbeth. She came to New York (*c.*1836) and appeared (8 May 1837) for the 1st time as Meg Merrilies in *Guy Mannering,* one of her best-known roles. She won acclaim as Nancy Sykes in *Oliver Twist* (1837), was stage manager (1842–44) of the Walnut Street Theater at Philadelphia, and made her London debut (14 Feb. 1845) as Bianca in *Fazio.* Emerging in England as a Shakespearean actress of the 1st rank, she toured the U.S. (1849–52), playing male as well as female roles, and was received as the leading actress of the American stage. She lived in England until 1857, but gave frequent "farewell performances" in the U.S., to which she returned in 1870.

Darrow, Clarence (b. Kinsman, Ohio, 18 Apr. 1857; d. Chicago, 13 Mar. 1938), lawyer and reformer, attended Allegheny College and spent a year at Univ. of Mich. Law School. Admitted to the Ohio bar (1878), he removed to Chicago

(1887), where he was junior law partner of John Peter Altgeld (*q.v.*). Supporter of many reform movements and opponent of capital punishment, he won a reputation as a pre-eminent trial lawyer by his defense of more than 50 persons charged with 1st-degree murder, of whom only one, Robert Prendergast (1894), was lost to the executioner. His defense of Eugene Debs (*q.v.*) in the injunction proceedings and conspiracy charges resulting from the rail strike of 1894 gave him national prominence. He successfully defended Haywood, Moyer, and Pettibone (1907), charged with being accessories to the murder of Gov. Steunenberg of Idaho. Undertaking the defense (1924) of Nathan Leopold and Richard Loeb, tried for the kidnapping and murder of Robert Franks, his introduction of psychiatric evidence and his masterly summation resulted in the prisoners receiving a life sentence. In the Scopes evolution trial (1925) he had a celebrated courtroom encounter with William Jennings Bryan (*q.v.*), whom he subjected to a merciless cross-examination. Normally on the side of the underdog, he surprised his admirers by acting as defense counsel in the Massie case (1932), a sensational Honolulu trial for the murder and kidnapping of a Hawaiian, in which he secured for his clients a nominal sentence.

Davis, Jefferson (b. Todd Co., Ky., 3 June 1808; d. New Orleans, La., 6 Dec. 1889), president of the Confederacy, was graduated from West Point (1828) and served in the Black Hawk War (1830–31). Resigning his commission (1835), he married Zachary Taylor's daughter (who died within 3 months) and became a Miss. planter (married Varina Howell, 1845). Democratic congressman (1845–46), he resigned to command the Mississippi Rifles in the War with Mexico and was wounded at Buena Vista. U.S. senator (1847–51), he resigned to run for governor (1851), being narrowly defeated by Henry S. Foote. As Pierce's Secretary of War he strengthened the army and coast defenses, directed surveys for the transcontinental Southern route, and urged the President to sign the Kansas-Nebraska Bill (1854). Again senator (1857–61), he resigned 21 Jan. 1861, when Miss. seceded. On 18 Feb. 1861 he was inaugurated at Montgomery as provisional president of the provisional Confederate government, and was then elected for a 6-yr. term and inaugurated at Richmond (22 Feb. 1862). His autocratic methods and interference in military affairs aroused hostility among Confederate leaders. When Richmond fell he moved the executive offices to Danville, Va., and thence to Greensboro, N.C. At final cabinet meeting held at Charlotte (24 Apr. 1865), he conceded the end of the Confederacy. He was captured at Irwinville, Ga., and imprisoned at Ft. Monroe (1865–67). In 1866 he was indicted for treason; released on bail the following year, and the trial dropped. After travel abroad he made his home at Beauvoir, Miss., and wrote *Rise and Fall of the Confederate Government* (1881).

Davisson, Clinton Joseph (b. Bloomington, Ill., 22 Oct. 1881 d. Charlottesville, Va., 1 Feb. 1958), physicist, was graduated from the University of Chicago (B.S., 1908) and Princeton University (Ph.D., 1911); was an instructor in physics (1911–17) at the Carnegie Institute of Technology, Pittsburgh; and (1917–46) was a member of the research staff of the Bell Telephone laboratories (originally the engineering department of the Western Electric Co.) at New York. Beginning his researches on the electron in 1923, he discovered (1927, with Dr. L. H. Germer) the principle of electron diffraction (the exhibiting by electrons of wavelike as well as corpuscular properties). In 1928 he was awarded the Comstock Prize for the "most important research in electricity, magnetism, and radiant energy made in North America" during the preceding 5 yrs. In 1937 Davisson and Germer discovered that the wave length of electrons depends on their velocity, confirming De Broglie's law (1932). He was awarded the Nobel prize in physics in 1937.

Debs, Eugene Victor (b. Terre Haute, Ind., 5 Nov. 1855; d. Elmhurst, Ill., 20 Oct. 1926), Socialist and labor leader. In 1870 he became a worker in the shops of the Terre Haute & Indianapolis R.R., subsequently becoming a locomotive fireman, and in 1875 took part in the organization of a Terre Haute lodge of the Brotherhood of Locomotive Firemen, becoming secretary of the lodge. Debs was named (1880) national secretary and treasurer of the Brotherhood and editor of the *Firemen's Magazine.* An advocate of industrial unionism, he participated in the organization (1893) of the American Railway Union, of which he was made president. During the Pullman strike of 1894 he and other union leaders were held in contempt of court and sentenced to 6 months in jail. He emerged from his imprisonment a convert to socialism, and in 1897 founded the Social Democratic party of America, which in 1900 was formally united with a faction of the Socialist Labor party to form the Socialist party of America. He was 5 times a candidate for President on the Socialist ticket (1900, 1904, 1908, 1912, 1920). Sentenced to jail (1918) for 10 yrs. on charge of violating the sedition provisions of the Espionage Act, he received during his confinement in the Atlanta penitentiary more than 900,000 votes as Socialist candidate for the Presidency. Debs was released (1921) by order of President Harding, but his citizenship was not restored. He was an editor of the *Appeal to Reason,* a Socialist weekly, and editor (1925–26) of the *American Appeal,* organ of Socialist and Progressive elements.

Decatur, Stephen (b. Sinepuxent, Md., 5 Jan. 1779; d. near Bladensburg, Md., 22 Mar. 1820), naval officer. During the naval war with France he was commissioned midshipman (30 Apr. 1798) and served in West Indian waters. He won fame during his service under Commodore Preble in the Tripolitan War. On the evening of 16 Feb. 1804 Decatur and a boarding party recaptured the U.S. frigate *Philadelphia,* which had been stranded off Tripoli, and destroyed it, thus denying its use to the enemy. He was commissioned a captain and took part in the bombardments (3, 7 Aug. 1804) and subsequent assaults on Tripoli. He served (1808) as a member of the court-martial that suspended Capt. James Barron following the *Chesapeake-Leopard* encounter. During the War of 1812 he commanded the *United States* and the *President,* taking several valuable prizes, and was wounded in an engagement with the British blockading force off Long Island. In 1815 he commanded the squadron which compelled the Tripolitans to end their exactions of tribute and the other Barbary pirates to make compensation for damages inflicted by them during the War of 1812. Acclaimed as a hero on his return to the U.S., Decatur responded to a toast made at a dinner given in his honor: "Our country! In her intercourse with foreign nations may she always be in the right; but our country, right or wrong." He served (1815–20) on the Board of Navy Commissioners and was killed in a duel with Capt. James Barron.

De Forest, Lee (b. Council Bluffs, Iowa, 26 Aug. 1837; d. Hollywood, Cal., 30 June 1961), radio engineer and inventor, pioneer in the development of wireless communications, received his Ph.B. (1896) and Ph.D. (1899) from Yale, joined the experimental telephone laboratory of the Western Electric Co. at Chicago, and while engaged in working on wireless telegraphy for the Armour Institute of Technology at Chicago (1900–02) designed the alternating current transmitter. He was the 1st to use the electrolytic receiver (a type of telephone receiver). He established (1902) the American De Forest (later United) Wireless Telegraph Co. at Jersey City, N.J., which installed at 5 U.S. Navy bases the 1st high-power naval radio stations. De Forest also developed several types of antennae, including the loop and direction antennae. His invention of the Audion amplifier (1905 *et seq.*), and in its improved form the 3-electrode vacuum tube, made possible transcontinental telephony after his telephone repeater rights were sold to the American Telephone and Telegraph Co. (1912). His invention of the oscillating Audion, 1st demonstrated in 1913, paved the way for the developments which earned him the sobriquet, "the father of radio broadcasting." In 1934 he established Lee De Forest, Inc., at Los Angeles, Calif. The holder of more than 300 patents, he perfected the phonofilm method of sound recording, the glow-light recording of sound films, contributed to the development of television and high-speed facsimile transmission, and invented radiotherapy and the radio knife.

Dewey, George (b. Montpelier, Vt., 26 Dec. 1837; d. Washington, D.C., 16 Jan. 1917), naval officer, was graduated (1858) from the U.S. Naval Academy and became executive officer of the *Mississippi,* which was part of Farragut's fleet at the Battle of New Orleans (1862). Dewey became (1889) chief of the Bureau of Equipment in the Navy Department, and was appointed (1895) president of the Board of Inspection. He attained the rank of commodore and was ordered (Nov. 1897) to assume command of the Asiatic Squadron, which he led during the Spanish-American War. Learning (26 Apr. 1898) that war had been declared, Dewey led his squadron, which he had been holding in readiness for such a contingency, from Mirs Bay to Manila, 600 miles away. He entered Manila Bay at dawn on 1 May 1898 and in 7 hrs. of fighting destroyed 8 Spanish warships, thus eliminating the enemy's naval power in the Far East. The victory assured the U.S. possession of the Philippines and made Dewey a national hero. Congress created for him the rank of admiral of the navy. He served (1900–17) as president of the General Board of the Navy Department.

Dewey, John (b. Burlington, Vt., 20 Oct. 1859; d. New York City, 1 June 1952), philosopher and educator, was graduated from the University of Vermont (B.A., 1879) and Johns Hopkins (Ph.D., 1884); taught philosophy at the University of Michigan (1884–88, 1890–94) and the University of Minnesota (1889); headed the philosophy department at the University of Chicago (1894–1904), where he was also director of the school of education (1902–04); and in 1904 joined the faculty of Columbia University. As a philosopher, Dewey was the foremost exponent of the pragmatism of William James and evolved a view of environmental and functional reality called "instrumentalism" that has been widely influential in American social

thought. In the field of education, he has been the major force in the development of progressive education. Among his many works are *The School and Society* (1899), *The Child and the Curriculum* (1902), *How We Think* (1909), *The Influence of Darwin on Philosophy and Other Essays in Contemporary Thought* (1910), *Essays in Experimental Logic* (1916), *Democracy and Education* (1916), *Human Nature and Conduct* (1922), *Experience and Nature* (1925), *The Quest for Certainty* (1929), *Philosophy and Civilization* (1931), *Art as Experience* (1934), *Experience and Education* (1938), *Freedom and Culture* (1939), and *Problems of Men* (1946).

Dickinson, Emily Elizabeth (b. Amherst, Mass., 10 Dec. 1830; d. there, 15 May 1886), poet, attended Amherst Academy and Mt. Holyoke Female Seminary (1847–48). Except for a trip to Washington and Philadelphia (1854) and 2 journeys to Boston (1864, 1865), she never left Amherst, where she gradually withdrew from society. She never married. During her lifetime only 2 of her poems were published. Her intense spiritual life was expressed in poetry whose directness of vision and vivid imagery are found in posthumously published works that include *Poems* (1890), *Poems: Second Series* (1891), *Poems: Third Series* (1896), *The Single Hound* (1914), *Further Poems* (1929), and *Unpublished Poems* (1936).

Dickinson, John (b. Talbot Co., Md., 8 Nov. 1732; d. Wilmington, Del., 14 Feb. 1808), statesman, moved with his parents in 1740 to Dover, where he studied privately under a tutor. In 1750 he began the study of law in the office of John Moland of the Philadelphia bar. After three years at the Middle Temple in London he returned in 1757 to Philadelphia, where he began to practice law and quickly rose to eminence in his profession. Elected to the Delaware Assembly (1760–62) and the Pennsylvania Assembly (1762–65 and 1770–76), he opposed Benjamin Franklin and defended the proprietary system. His pamphlet *The Late Regulations Respecting the British Colonies* (1765), showing the economic injury to the British business interests resulting from the Sugar and Stamp Acts, led to his designation by the Pennsylvania legislature as a delegate to the Stamp Act Congress in New York, where he drafted the resolutions petitioning the King and Parliament for the repeal of the Stamp Act. His pamphlet *Letters from a Farmer in Pennsylvania to the Inhabitants of the British Colonies* (1768), written in opposition to the Townshend Acts, denied the authority of Parliament to tax the colonies in whatever form. It proved enormously influential in shaping colonial opinion. Thereafter he pursued an increasingly conservative course, opposing the use of force by the colonists. In the 1st Continental Congress from Pennslyvania he drew up the Petition to the King and the Address to the People of Canada. In the 2d Continental Congress as a Delaware member (1776, 1777, 1779, 1780), in his 2d Petition to the King, or "Olive Branch Petition." Co-author with Thomas Jefferson of the "Declaration of the Causes of Taking up Arms" (1775), he opposed the Declaration of Independence but stayed away from the final vote. In Congress he headed a committee which drafted (1776) the Articles of Confederation. Subsequently he served (1781) as president of the Delaware Supreme Executive Council and as president of Pennsylvania, 1782–85, and was a delegate and signer from Delaware to the Federal Convention. In the "Fabius" letters he advocated the adoption of the Constitution. His political writings in 2 vols. were 1st published in 1801. He was a founder (1783) of Dickinson College, Carlisle, Pa., which was named for him.

Dix, Dorothea Lynde (b. Hampden, Me., 4 Apr. 1802; d. Trenton, N.J., 17 July 1887), humanitarian. She operated the Dix Mansion at Boston (1821–34), a school for girls, went abroad for her health, and upon her return to Boston (1838) devoted herself to the reform of conditions in prisons, houses of correction, almshouses, and insane asylums. Her *Memorial to the Legislature of Massachusetts* (Jan. 1843), an indictment of prevailing conditions and treatment of the insane, was followed by similar investigations and exposés in other states. According to her own estimate, she visited in 3 yrs. (*c*.1841–44) 18 state penitentiaries, 300 county jails and houses of correction, and more than 500 almshouses and other institutions, in addition to hospitals and houses of refuge. She was directly responsible for the enlargement or founding of state-supported hospitals for the insane in 15 states and in Canada and England. At the outbreak of the Civil War she offered her services to the surgeon general and was appointed (10 June 1861) superintendent of women nurses, in which capacity ·she was in charge of hospital nursing for ·the Union forces.

Dole, Sanford Ballard (b. Honolulu, 23 Apr. 1844; d. there, 9 June 1926), statesman, jurist, son of the missionary Daniel Dole, was educated in missionary schools, attended Williams College (1866–67), and studied law. Admitted to the Mass. bar, he returned to Hawaii to practice. In the legislature in 1884 and 1886, he supported the monarchy but advocated reforms. He was a leader in the revolution (1887) which ended the Gibson regime and forced King Kalakaua to grant a new constitution. Associate justice of the Hawaii Supreme Court (1887–93), he joined the 2nd Hawaiian revolution aimed at overthrow of the monarchy, which failed to support the reforms, and annexation to the U.S. Heading the provisional govt. (1893), he refused, as minister of foreign affairs, to comply with Cleveland's demand (Dec. 1893) for the restoration of Queen Liliuokalani, denying the President's right to interfere in Hawaii's internal affairs but favoring ultimate union with the U.S. Declared President (1894) of the newly formed republic, he visited Washington (1898) in the interests of the newly negotiated annexation treaty. First gov. of the Territory of Hawaii (1901), he resigned to become judge of the U.S. district court for Hawaii (1903–15).

Douglas, Stephen Arnold (b. Brandon, Vt., 23 Apr. 1813; d. Chicago, Ill., 3 June 1861), statesman. He attended the Canandaigua (N.Y.) Academy, and in 1833 set out for the Old Northwest, finally settling in Jacksonville, Ill., where he taught school and read law. Licensed to practice (1834), he became state's attorney (1835), state legislator (1835–37), secretary of state for Illinois (1840), and judge of the state supreme court (1841–43). During his 2 terms in the U.S. House of Representatives (1843–47), he was an expansionist on the Oregon issue, vigorously supported the Mexican War, and was chairman of the Committee on Territories. Elected (1847) to the Senate, where he served until his death, he was made chairman of the Committee on Territories. In the Compromise of 1850, he drafted bills providing territorial governments for Utah and N.M. which left those governments free to enact laws concerning slavery. Known as the "Little Giant," he led the "Young America" wing of the Democratic party in the early 1850's and zealously championed sectional compromise. His principle of "popular sovereignty," an adaptation of "squatter sovereignty," was incorporated in his Kansas-Nebraska Bill (1854) and precipitated further sectional strife. Douglas was an unsuccessful contender for the Democratic Presidential nomination in 1852 and 1856. In 1857–58, during the Senate debate over the Lecompton constitution, his denunciation of that constitution as a violation of the "popular sovereignty" principle led to a break between him and the Buchanan administration and alienated the proslavery wing of the Democratic party. In the Ill. campaign of 1858, he conducted with his opponent, Abraham Lincoln, a series of 7 joint debates commonly known as the Lincoln-Douglas debates, during the course of which he formulated the "Freeport doctrine," further angering Southern Democrats, with whom he finally broke in 1859. In 1860, when Douglas won the Democratic nomination for the Presidency, the Southern faction withdrew and chose John C. Breckinridge as their candidate. The rift contributed to the election of Lincoln. In the closing days of the Buchanan administration, Douglas made further attempts at compromise, but upon the outbreak of the Civil War gave his complete support to Lincoln's measures to preserve the Union.

Douglass, Frederick (b. Tuckahoe, near Easton, Md., c.Feb. 1817; d. Washington, D.C., 20 Feb. 1895), Negro abolitionist, writer, and orator. The son of a Negro slave and a white father, he was originally named Frederick Augustus Washington Bailey, taking the name of Douglass after he escaped to freedom from Baltimore (3 Sept. 1838), where he had learned to read and write while a house servant. Going to New York, and thence to New Bedford, Mass., where he supported himself by working as a common laborer, Douglass in 1841 attended a convention of the Massachusetts Antislavery Society at Nantucket. A speech he delivered there was so moving that he was immediately named as a lecturing agent of the society. Mobbed and assaulted in the performance of his duties, he became the leading figure in the "One Hundred Conventions" of the New England Antislavery Society and published a frank account, *Narrative of the Life of Frederick Douglass* (1845). To avoid possible reenslavement, Douglass stayed in Great Britain and Ireland (1845–47), where he collected enough money to buy his freedom upon returning to the U.S. He established an abolitionist newspaper, the *North Star,* at Rochester, N.Y., was active as a lecturer, and supported industrial education for Negroes and woman suffrage. One of the advisers of John Brown, he fled to Canada and then to the British Isles after Brown was arrested for the raid on Harpers Ferry. During the Civil War he assisted in raising Negro regiments and agitated for Negro suffrage and civil rights. He was secretary of the Santo Domingo Commission (1871), marshal (1877–81) and recorder of deeds (1881–86) of the District of Columbia, and U.S. consul general to Haiti (1889–91).

Dow, Neal (b. Portland, Me., 20 Mars 1804, d. there 2 Oct. 1897), temperance reformer, was a son of Quaker parents and reared according to the principles of the Friends, although he was eventually excluded from the Society because of his views on arms. At 24 he made his first temperance speech as a clerk of the Deluge Engine Co., opposing liquor at a company dinner. In 1838 he was instrumental in founding the Maine Temperance Union, committed to total abstinence and prohibitory legislation (1845). The 1st law (1846) proved inadequate, and Dow, elected mayor of Portland (1851), headed a committee urging more stringent legislation. With the passage of the "Maine Law" (2 June 1851) Dow achieved world renown for temperance reform, speaking on tours, serving (1853) as president of the World's Temperance Convention in N.Y.C. In his 2nd term as mayor (1855) the "June riot," led by antiprohibitionists, caused the repeal of the "Maine Law," but it was enacted again in 1857. As opposed to slavery as he was to liquor, Dow became col. (1861), 13th Reg. of Maine Volunteers, during the Civil War and was commissioned brig. gen. (1862). He was twice wounded at Port Hudson and imprisoned for 8 months in Libby Prison and at Mobile. He ran for President (1880) as a Prohibitionist.

Dreiser, Theodore (b. Terre Haute, Ind., 27 Aug. 1871; d. Hollywood, Calif., 28 Dec. 1945), novelist. Born into a poverty-stricken family, he was reared chiefly in Warsaw, Ind., attended Indiana University (1889–90), and was a newspaper reporter (1892–94) in Chicago, St. Louis, and Pittsburgh. In 1894, when he settled in New York, he began a career as a magazine editor and free-lance writer that closed with his post as editor in chief (1907–10) of the Butterick Publications. His novels bear the deep impress of a deterministic philosophy drawn from his reading of Spencer, Huxley, Tyndall, and Haeckel. His view of life as a welter of blind, amoral forces was the underpinning of his first novel, *Sister Carrie* (1900), whose bold social realism (particularly its treatment of sexual mores) brought threats of censorship. The novel was withdrawn by the publisher; its reissuance was a victory for literary realism. Dreiser's naturalism and realism permeated his other novels: *Jennie Gerhardt* (1911); the trilogy based on the career of the traction magnate, Charles T. Yerkes, *The Financier* (1912), *The Titan* (1914), and *The Stoic* (1947); *The Genius* (1915); and the novel which found Dreiser's widest audience, *An American Tragedy* (1925). *The Bulwark* (1946) showed evidences of a return to religious conviction. In the years after World War I, Dreiser embraced socialism, writing *Dreiser Looks at Russia* (1928), *Tragic America* (1932), and *America is Worth Saving* (1941).

Du Bois, William Edward Burghardt (b. Great Barrington, Mass., 23 Feb. 1868–), writer, reformer. Of slave descent, he received his A.B. at Fisk Univ. (1888), then 3 degrees at Harvard (A.B., 1890); A.M., 1891; Ph.D., 1895). Professor of history and economics at Atlanta Univ. (1896–1910), he devoted himself to Negro sociological and historical problems. Taking a militant position on race relations, as opposed to Booker T. Washington (*q.v.*), he helped launch (1905) the Niagara Movement for racial equality and became (1910) director of publicity and research of the Natl. Assn. for the Advancement of Colored People, a post which he held for 24 yrs. He organized the Pan-African Congress (1919) and called the 1st Intl. Congress of Colored Peoples during the Versailles Peace Conference (1918). Heading the dept. of sociology at Atlanta Univ. (1933–44), he returned to the N.A.A.C.P. as head of a dept. of special research (1944–48). Candidate for senator in N.Y. on the American Labor party ticket (1948), he subsequently served as vice-chairman of the Council on African Affairs (1949–54) and was prominent in organizations favoring friendlier postwar relations with the U.S.S.R. His numerous writings include *The Suppression of the African Slave Trade* (1896), *The Philadelphia Negro* (1899), *The Souls of Black Folk* (1903), *The Negro* (1915), and *Black Reconstruction* (1935). In addition he edited the *Encyclopedia of the Negro* (1933–45) and the *Crisis* magazine, 1910–32.

Duke, James Buchanan (b. near Durham, N.C., 23 Dec. 1856; d. New York City, 10 Oct. 1925), industrialist and philanthropist. Shortly after the Civil War, he and his brother, Benjamin Newton Buchanan (1855–1929), helped their father put up packaged leaf tobacco which they sold on the road in N.C. The firm of W. Duke & Sons, of which he became a member in 1884, began in 1881 the manufacturing of cigarettes by hand and shortly thereafter turned them out by machine. In 1884 the Duke firm opened a branch factory at New York City and by adroit price and advertising policies commanded by 1889 half of the total U.S. production of cigarettes. The "tobacco war," a contest among 5 chief cigarette manufacturers, led to the organization (1890) of the American Tobacco Co., which merged the rival concerns. Named president, J. B. Duke was also president of the combination of plug manufacturers known as the Continental Tobacco Co. (formed 1898). In succession, he organized the American Snuff Co. (1900), the American Cigar Co. (1901), the Consolidated Tobacco Co. (1901), and the United Cigar Stores Co. In 1911, by which year Duke's various combinations controlled 150 factories capitalized at $502 million, the U.S. Supreme Court ordered the dissolution of the American Tobacco Co. as a combination in restraint of trade. Duke was also active in forming (1905) and developing the Southern Power Co. In 1924 he created a trust fund for Trinity College, subsequently renamed Duke University.

Dulles, John Foster (b. Washington, D.C., 25 Feb. 1888; d. there 24 May 1959), lawyer, statesman, received his B.A. from Princeton (1908), studied at the Sorbonne (1908–09), and obtained his Ll.B. from George Washington Univ. (1911). Beginning in 1911, he spent his entire legal career with Sullivan & Cromwell, which firm he headed from 1927. An outstanding international lawyer, he was chief counsel for U.S. bondholders of Kreuger & Toll, the intl. match trust. During World War I, in addition to service in the armed forces, he was special agent of the State Dept. in Central America (1917), assistant to the chairman, War Trade Board (1918), and counsel to the American Peace Commission (1918–19). Delegate to the San Francisco Conference (1945) and to the UN (1946–50), he also served as adviser to the Secy. of State at the Council of Foreign Ministers at London (1945, 1947). Appointed interim U.S. senator from N.Y. (1949), he acted as adviser to

the State Dept. (1950–53) and was the chief architect of the Japanese Peace Treaty (1951). Secy. of State (1953–59) in the Eisenhower administration, he was the major force in U.S. foreign policy in that period, personally engaging in innumerable missions abroad, traveling over 500,000 mi. during his term. Holding Truman's policy of "containment" of Communism to be inadequate, he espoused "liberation" of Communist-controlled areas, held firm against Red Chinese threats to seize Quemoy and Matsu, forced Britain and France to abandon the Suez Canal attack (1956), was responsible for the Eisenhower Doctrine (1957) designed to preserve peace in the Middle East, and committed the U.S. to hold West Berlin, if necessary by force (1958). Resuming his duties after an operation for abdominal cancer (1957), he died of that disease.

du Pont, Eleuthère Irénée (Paris, 24 June 1771; d. Philadelphia, 31 Oct. 1834), manufacturer, son of the economist Pierre Samuel du Pont de Nemours, was given his baptismal name by Minister of Finance Turgot, his godfather. In 1788 Lavoisier, a friend of his father's, took him into the royal powder works at Essonne. He married at 20, fighting 2 duels over his fiancée. In 1797 the du Pont publishing business was suppressed, and the family left for the U.S. Here, Irénée investigated gunpowder manufacture and returned to Paris to procure machinery and designs for its manufacture in the U.S. He set up his works (1801) on the Brandywine River, near Wilmington, Del. In 1804 powder was ready for sale, and military orders, greatly increasing with the War of 1812, established the firm's position as the principal manufacturer of powder for the govt. The plant also supplied South American govts. In 1833 he turned down a $24,000 cash order from the S.C. Nullifiers. In spite of opposition from his partner Peter Bauduy, the company was called E. I. du Pont de Nemours & Co., the name by which it is still known.

Duncan, Isadora (b. San Francisco, 27 May 1878; d. Nice, France, 14 Sept.

1927), dancer, quit school at the age of 10 to devote herself entirely to dancing, and with her sister, Elizabeth, taught a system of movements interpretative of nature, music, and poetry which had some vogue in her native city. She made her 1st appearance in New York (1895) in the Augustin Daly company. Disillusioned by the formalism of dance in America, she left with her family for London on a cattle boat. Joining Loie Fuller's company on tour to Germany, she went on alone to Budapest, Munich, Vienna, and Berlin, taking them by storm. Failing in her attempt to build a temple of dance on a hill outside Athens, she opened (1904) a school of the dance on the outskirts of Berlin and returned to the stage, with tours of France, Germany, Russia, and the U.S. (1906–08). Performing barefoot and in flowing costumes, she was a notable interpreter of classical music and popularized the dance as an art in the U.S., awakening an enthusiasm upon which such later figures as Martha Graham and Agnes de Mille were able to build a more solid structure. Pagan in her advocacy of free love, she had one child of Edward Gordon Craig and another of "Lohengrin," a wealthy patron. The children were both drowned in an accident. In Moscow, where she established a dance school at the invitation (1921) of the Soviet govt., she finally married Sergei Yessenin, later a suicide. A moment after saying, *"Je vais à la gloire,"* she came to a dramatic end when her long scarf caught in the wheel of a moving auto, breaking her neck.

Eakins, Thomas (b. Philadelphia, 25 July 1844; d. there, 25 June 1916), artist and teacher, attended the Pennsylvania Academy of Fine Arts; was a student (1866–69) at the École des Beaux Arts in Paris, where he worked under Bonnat and Gérôme; in 1869 traveled in Spain, where his study of the realist painters, such as Velasquez and Goya, was influential in forming his style; and in 1870 returned to Philadelphia, where his study of anatomy at the Jefferson Medical College helped to make him a master of the human figure and resulted in two of his best compositions, *The Gross Clinic* and *The Agnew Clinic*. In 1873 he became a

teacher (and subsequently dean) at the Pennsylvania Academy of Fine Arts, and also taught at the Art Students' League. Among his paintings, both portrait and figure, are *The Writing Master, The Thinker, The Chess Players, Max Schmitt in a Single Scull, Whistling for Plover, Salutat, Between Rounds, The Concert Singer, The Swimming Hole,* and *Edith Mahon.* He also modeled sculpture, including 2 reliefs on the battle monument at Trenton, N.J.

Eastman, George (b. Waterville, N.Y., 12 July 1854; d. Rochester, N.Y., 14 Mar. 1932), inventor, manufacturer, philanthropist, became interested in photography at an early age. Patenting his invention of a dry-plate process in 1880, he began manufacturing dry plates in Rochester. Forming a partnership with Henry A. Strong, he invented a paper-backed flexible film (1884), soon put into production as roll film, and then a small box camera, the Kodak. Developing motion-picture film on the basis of patents he held jointly with Henry M. Reichenbach, the inventor, he formed the Eastman Kodak Co. (1892), recapitalizing and expanding its operations until by 1901 it was the world's largest industrial plant devoted to the manufacture of photographic supplies. Stressing research, Eastman's technicians constantly improved the firm's products and his welfare and profit-sharing programs built up a loyal labor force. His philanthropies by grant and bequest exceeded $100 million and included such institutions as the Univ. of Rochester, M.I.T., Tuskegee and Hampton institutes, the establishment of a chair of American studies at Balliol College, Oxford, and founding the Eastman School of Music in Rochester. Ironically, he preferred anonymity and was rarely photographed. He had no family, and leaving a note, "My work is done, why wait?" he took his own life.

Eddy, Mary Baker (b. Bow, N.H., 16 July 1821; d. Chestnut Hill, Newton, Mass., 3 Dec. 1910), founder of the practice of Christian Science and of the Church of Christ, Scientist. She married (1843) George Washington Glover, by whom, a few months after his death, she had a son, George (born in Sept. 1844). In 1853 she married Dr. Daniel Patterson, a N.H. dentist and homeopathist, from whom she was separated in 1866 and divorced in 1873. She practiced intermittently (1866–70) a system of mental healing after undergoing treatment from Dr. Phineas P. Quimby (1802–66) of Portland, Me., in 1862. The principles later associated with Christian Science were formulated by her (c.1866), supposedly after making through "divine revelation, reason and demonstration" a remarkable recovery from a serious injury. Setting up a spiritual-healing prac- at Lynn, Mass. (1870), she published *Science and Health with Key to the Scriptures* (1875, and numerous revised editions), in which she set forth the basic doctrines of Christian Science. She married (1877) Asa Gilbert Eddy, one of her disciples; he died in 1882. The Christian Scientists' Association, established in 1876, was chartered (1879) as The Church of Christ, Scientist. In 1881 Mrs. Eddy obtained a charter for the Massachusetts Medical College, a training institution for Christian Science practitioners. In 1883 she began publishing the *Journal of Christian Science*. She and 12 followers established at Boston (1892) The First Church of Christ, Scientist, the mother church of the national religious organization. In her last years she founded *The Christian Science Monitor*.

Edison, Thomas Alva (b. Milan, Ohio, 11 Feb. 1847; d. West Orange, N.J., 18 Oct. 1931), inventor. Taken out of school after a few months because he was a slow learner, he received his education at home from his mother. As a boy, he sold newspapers, candy, and other articles on trains; becoming acquainted with telegraph operators during his trips, he became one himself (1863), continuing in the meantime his keen interest in chemistry. In 1868, he joined the Western Union Telegraph Co. at Boston, patenting (1869) his 1st invention, an electrographic vote recorder. Moving to New York that year, he entered into partnership in the electrical engineering firm of Pope, Edison & Co. When the firm was bought out in 1870, Edison received $40,000 as his share, and with this money established his own business, early initiating his policy of hiring assistants capable of collaborating on inventions under his guidance. During the period 1870–75 he was active in the improvement of the telegraph. In 1876 he built an establishment at Menlo Park, N.J., and in 1887 transferred the Edison research laboratories to larger quarters at Orange, N.J. His ventures were ultimately combined into the Edison General Electric Co., later absorbed by the General Electric Co. In 1877 he produced one of his most important inventions, the phonograph. Beginning in 1879 he introduced improvements that made possible the commercial production of the incandescent electric lamp. During his work on this device he made his 1st and only significant discovery in pure science when he observed the "Edison effect," demonstrating that the incandescent lamp could be utilized as a valve admitting negative but not positive electricity. (In 1904 the principle of the "Edison effect" was employed by J. Ambrose Fleming, inventor of the electron tube.) In the field of motion pictures, Edison acquired and improved the projector invented by Thomas Armat (1895) and placed it on the market as the Edison Vitascope. Although Edison was granted a total of more than 1,000 patents, most of them were the fruit of collective effort in his research laboratories. Among the inventions or improvements produced at the Edison laboratories were the storage battery, dictaphone, mimeograph, district telegraph signal box, Sprague motor, ore separator, composition brick, compressing dies, electric safety lantern, electric dynamo, and electric locomotive.

Edwards, Jonathan (b. East Windsor, Conn., 5 Oct. 1703; d. Princeton, N.J., 22 Mar. 1758), Congregational theologian and philosopher. After his graduation from Yale (1720), he studied theology there, and in 1722 became minister of a Presbyterian church in New York, where he remained until 1723. He was a tutor at Yale (1725–26), and in 1727 became assistant pastor to his grandfather, Solomon Stoddard, in the church at Northampton, Mass. Edwards became its sole pastor in 1729. His preaching initiated the New England phase of the religious revival known as the "Great Awakening" (*c.*1730–50). At Northampton, Edwards expounded doctrines fusing rationalism and mysticism and aimed at stemming the rising tide of liberal thought. He stressed the rationality of Scriptural knowledge, the intuitive apprehension of spiritual experience, and the metaphysical concepts of understanding and will as moral agencies under the supreme and arbitrary power of God. In 1750, following a controversy over church doctrine and practices, he was dismissed from the Northampton pastorate. Edwards settled at Stockbridge, Mass., as pastor of the church and missionary to the Indians, and there wrote his most important treatises. In 1757 he was chosen as president of the College of New Jersey at Princeton, but died a few months after taking the post. For his principal works, see p. 595.

Einstein, Albert (b. Ulm Donnau, Germany, 14 Mar. 1879; d. Princeton, N.J., 18 Apr. 1955), physicist, was graduated (1900) from the Federal Institute of Tech. at Zurich and received his doctorate (1905) at the Univ. of Zurich. His special theory of relativity (1905), his equation $E = mc^2$ (1905, keystone in the modern concept of the atom), and his contributions to quantum theory (1905) were followed by his general theory of relativity (1915) and work on the photoelectric effect of light, for which he received the Nobel Prize (1921). He taught at the Federal Institute of Tech. at Zurich (1912–14) and in 1914 assumed the post of director of the Kaiser Wilhelm Institute in Berlin. With the advent of Hitler he came to the U.S. (1932), accepted a post at the Institute for Advanced Study at Princeton (1933–45), and on 2 Aug. 1939 sent a historic letter to President Roosevelt stressing the urgency of research on the atomic bomb. His major work in the U.S. was his formulation (30 Mar. 1953) of a unified field theory, the mathematical expression of which appeared in 1950 as an appendix to *The Meaning of Relativity* (1922; Eng. tr., 4th ed., 1950). He also wrote *Relativity:*

the Special and the General Theory (1918), and was active in the peace movement and in Zionism.

Eisenhower, Dwight David (b. Denison, Tex., 14 Oct. 1890–), 34th President of the U.S., soldier, spent his boyhood in Abilene, Kan.; was graduated (1915) from the U.S. Military Academy; served (1915–17) with the 19th Infantry at Fort Sam Houston; Tex.; and during World War I, when he organized Camp Colt for the training of tank troops, attained the rank of capt. He was graduated (1926) from the Command and General Staff School at Ft. Leavenworth, Kan.; (1929) from the Army War College, Washington, D.C.; and (1932) from the Army Industrial College. He was named (1933) special assistant to Gen. Douglas MacArthur, then chief of staff, under whom he served (1935–39) as assistant military adviser to the Philippine Commonwealth. Promoted to lt. col. in 1936, he returned to the U.S. in 1939 and was named (Feb. 1942) chief of the War Plans Division in the Office of Chief of Staff, subsequently became chief of the Operations Division, and in June 1942, was appointed commander of U.S. forces in the European Theater. He commanded the Allied invasion of North Africa that began on 8 Nov. 1942; was named (Jan. 1944) Supreme Commander of the Allied Expeditionary Force in Western Europe and set up his headquarters (SHAEF) near London. After the invasion of Europe (6 June 1944 *et seq.*) and the surrender of Germany (7 May 1945) he served as commander of the U.S. occupation zone of Germany. Gen. of the army (Dec. 1944), he succeeded (Nov. 1945) Gen. George C. Marshall as chief of staff, became (7 June 1948) president of Columbia University, and took a leave of absence from Columbia to become (1951) Supreme Commander of the Allied Powers in Europe (SHAPE). He resigned that command in 1952 to campaign for the Presidency, was the Republican nominee that year, and was elected with the largest popular vote in U.S. history. Reelected (1956), he advocated personal top-level diplomacy, sought to contain Soviet expansion in the Middle East and to achieve a balanced budget in the face of mounting defense needs. He is author of *Crusade in Europe* (1948).

Eliot, Charles William (b. Boston, Mass., 20 Mar. 1834; d. Northeast Harbor, Me., 22 Aug. 1926), educator, was graduated from Harvard (1853), where he taught mathematics and chemistry (1854–63). After 2 years of study on the Continent, he was appointed (1865) professor of chemistry at the Massachusetts Institute of Technology. Early in 1869 he published in the *Atlantic Monthly* 2 articles on "The New Education: Its Organization," which drew wide notice, and in the same year was appointed and inaugurated president of Harvard, a post he held until his retirement in 1909. During his administration the elective system and sabbatical year were introduced at Harvard College; Harvard University was expanded in enrollment and size to include units such as the graduate schools of arts and sciences, applied science, and business administration; and the standards of the professional schools were raised. In 1892, as chairman of the National Education Association's Committee on Secondary School Studies, he prepared a report on the functions and curricula of public schools which led to the organization (1901) of the Board of College Entrance Examinations. He edited the *Harvard Classics* (popularly called the "five-foot shelf").

Emerson, Ralph Waldo (b. Boston, Mass., 25 May 1803; d. Concord, Mass., 27 Apr. 1882), philosopher, poet, essayist, and lecturer, was graduated from Harvard (1821), where he was class poet, taught school at Boston and at Roxbury, Mass., and for a brief period in 1825 attended the Harvard Divinity School. Admitted (1826) as a candidate for the Unitarian ministry, he resigned his pastorate at the 2nd Church of Boston (1829–31) when he decided that he could not conform in the administration of the Lord's Supper. He made a tour of England and the Continent (1832–33), meeting Coleridge, Wordsworth, and Carlyle, through whom he became acquainted with the doctrines of German idealism which, together with infusions from neo-

Platonism and the sacred books of the East, influenced the molding of Transcendentalist thought. After his return to Boston, he resumed preaching, but gradually abandoned it for the lyceum and lecture platform. Settling at Concord in 1835, he formed friendships with Thoreau, Bronson Alcott, Margaret Fuller, and Nathaniel Hawthorne. His 1st publication, *Nature* (1836), was a fundamental exposition of Transcendentalism, a philosophical and literary reaction against Unitarian intellectualism. His address, "The American Scholar," delivered as the Phi Beta Kappa oration at Harvard (1837), called for an indigenous national culture and defined the functions of the intellectual in the light of Transcendentalism. His "Divinity School Address," also delivered at Harvard (1838), indicted orthodox Christianity and brought pointed attacks on Emerson from the ministry. With Margaret Fuller and other Transcendentalists, he edited *The Dial* (1840–44). The quarter century after 1840 constituted the period of his greatest activity as a lecturer in the North and the West. He published the *Essays* (1st series, 1841; 2nd series, 1844), which established his reputation in the U.S. and Europe; *Poems* (1847), including "May-Day," "Threnody," and "Concord Hymn"; *Addresses and Lectures* (1849); *Representative Men* (1850); and *English Traits* (1856). Active in the antislavery movement, he wrote *The Conduct of Life* (1860) and *Society and Solitude* (1870), gave a course of lectures at Harvard that was published as *Natural History of Intellect* (1893), and published *Letters and Social Aims* (1876). The *Journals* (10 vols., 1909–14) were edited by his son, Edward Waldo Emerson; the *Letters* (6 vols., 1939), by Ralph L. Rusk.

Enders, John Franklin (b. West Hartford, Conn., 10 Feb. 1897–), bacteriologist, received his B.A. (1920) from Yale and his M.A. (1922) and Ph.D. (1930) from Harvard, where he taught in the dept. of bacteriology and immunology (1929–56); since then has served as chief of the research dept. of infectious diseases, Children's Hospital, Harvard Medical School. Civilian consultant to the Secy. of War on epidemic diseases (1942–46), and member of the Comm. on Viral Infections, Armed Forces Epidemiological Bd. (1945–49), he received the Nobel Prize in Medicine and Physiology (1954) for culturing poliomyelitis viruses in living tissues, laying the foundations for the production of the Salk vaccine. He edited *Journal of Immunology* (1942–58).

Ericsson, John (b. Langbanshyttan, Sweden, 31 July 1803; d. New York City, 8 Mar. 1889), inventor and engineer, grew up in the midst of mining works, and at 11 designed and constructed a miniature sawmill. Admiral Count Platen, celebrated engineer, recognizing his ability, appointed him a cadet in the mechanical engineer corps. At 17 he enlisted in the Swedish army, where he was detailed to do topographical surveying. In London for 12 years, beginning in 1826, he made various marine inventions, and developed the screw propeller, which revolutionized navigation. Coming to New York in 1839, he furnished (1840) designs for the screw warship *Princeton* (which suffered an explosion on trials in 1844), the 1st ship to have its propelling machinery under water and out of firing range. In 1861 he designed and built for the Union the ironclad *Monitor* with a circular armored revolving turret. Following the victory of the *Monitor* over the *Merrimac* at Hampton Roads, Va. (9 Mar. 1862), he was kept busy designing and building other ironclads. He also made notable contributions to the improvement of the steam engine. After his death Ericsson's body was carried back to Sweden with great ceremony, appropriately in a new steel naval vessel.

Evarts, William Maxwell (b. Boston, Mass., 6 Feb. 1818; d. New York City, 28 Feb. 1901), lawyer and statesman, was graduated from Yale (1837), studied at Harvard Law School, and was admitted to the N.Y. bar (1841). An assistant U.S. attorney for the southern district of N.Y., 1849–53, and unsuccessful candidate for the U.S. Senate (1860), he argued in behalf of N.Y. State the Lemmon slave case in dispute with Va. (1860) and represented the Federal government before the Supreme Court during the Civil War in asserting the right to treat captured vessels as maritime prizes. Among the preeminent leaders of the bar, he was President Johnson's chief defense counsel in the impeachment trial before the Senate (1868), winning an acquittal, and from 15 July until the close of Johnson's administration was U.S. Attorney General. He was U.S. counsel in the Geneva Arbitration (1871–72) over the *Alabama* claims, chief counsel for Hayes in the Presidential election dispute of 1876, and senior counsel for defendant in *Tilton* v. *Henry Ward Beecher* (1874–75). As Hayes' Secretary of State (1877–81) he asserted the "paramount interest" of the U.S. in an isthmian canal (1880). He was U.S. senator from N.Y. (1885–91).

Farragut, David Glasgow (b. Campbell's Station, near Knoxville, Tenn., 5 July 1801; d. Portsmouth, N.H., 14 Aug. 1870), naval officer. Adopted (*c*.1808) by Commander David Porter of the New Orleans naval station, he was appointed (1810) midshipman, and during the War of 1812 served aboard the frigate *Essex* in the Pacific. He saw duty in the Mediterranean (1815–20), and during the middle 1850's established the navy yard at Mare Island. Farragut was appointed (9 Jan. 1862) commander of the West Gulf Blockading Squadron with orders to open the Mississippi River and to attack and invest New Orleans. Departing from Hampton Roads aboard his flagship, the steam sloop *Hartford,* Farragut, with 17 ships and a mortar flotilla at his disposal, opened the Battle of New Orleans on 18 Apr. 1862. At his orders the Union warships ran by the Confederate defenses before they were reduced and destroyed most of the Confederate fleet, thus hastening the fall of New Orleans (28 Apr.). In recognition of his achievement, Farragut was commissioned a rear adm. (30 July 1862), becoming the 1st to hold that grade. His victory (5 Aug. 1864) in the Battle of Mobile Bay, when to the warning of "Torpedoes ahead!" he replied, "Damn the torpedoes!" brought him the commission of vice-adm. (23 Dec. 1864), an office created for him, as was the commission of adm. (26 July 1866). He led the European Squadron on a good-will tour (1867–68) of Continental ports.

Faulkner, William (b. New Albany, Miss., 25 Sept. 1897–), novelist and short-story writer, served as a pilot with the Canadian Royal Air Force in 1918 and attended the University of Mississippi from 1919 to 1921. Most of his novels and stories comprise a saga of the Compson, Sartoris, Snopes, McCaslin, and other families living in imaginary Yoknapatawpha County, with its county seat of Jefferson, in northern Miss., a powerful narrative of decay and corruption portraying Southern life from early frontier days to the coming of modern industrialism. His works include *Soldier's Pay* (1926), *Mosquitoes* (1927), *Sartoris* (1929), *The Sound and the Fury* (1929), *As I Lay Dying* (1930), *Sanctuary* (1931), *These Thirteen* (1931), *Light in August* (1932), *Doctor Martino, and Other Stories* (1934), *Pylon* (1935), *Absalom, Absalom!* (1936), *The Unvanquished* (1938), *The Wild Palms* (1939), *The Hamlet* (1940), *Go Down, Moses, and Other Stories* (1942), *Intruder in the Dust* (1948), *Knight's Gambit* (1949) *Collected Stories* (1950), *Requiem for a Nun* (1951), *A Fable* (1954)—Pulitzer Prize (1955). In 1950 he was awarded the Nobel prize in literature.

Fermi, Enrico (b. Rome, Italy, 29 Sept. 1901; d. Chicago, 28 Nov. 1954), physicist, was graduated from the Univ. of Pisa (1922), taught physics at Florence (1924) and Rome (1926–38) before coming to the U.S. (1939). His early experiments in artificial radioactivity, using slow neutrons, led directly to the discovery of uranium fission and brought him the Nobel Prize in physics (1938). In the U.S. he set the 1st atomic furnace into successful operation (2 Dec. 1942). The U.S. atomic bomb project was not only materially aided by his research abroad, but it benefited from his active participation in the project at Los Alamos. Professor of physics at Columbia (1939–45) and thereafter at Chicago, his numerous contributions to the new physics include his postulating the existence of an atomic particle (neutrino), his discovery of element 93 (neptunium), and his formulation of the theory of beta-ray emission in radioactivity. For work on the A-bomb he received the 1st Special Award ($25,000) of the AEC (1954). He wrote *Thermodynamics* (1937), *Elementary Particles* (1951).

Field, Cyrus West (b. Stockbridge, Mass., 30 Nov. 1819; d. New York City, 12 July 1892), financier, promoter of the first transatlantic cable, brother of David Dudley and Stephen Johnson Field. At the age of 15 he settled in New York City, where he became an errand boy in A. T. Stewart's dry-goods store. In 1837 he went to Lee, Mass., where he was assistant to his brother, Matthew, a paper manufacturer, and about 2 years later organized his own paper mill at Westfield, Mass. Soon afterward he became a junior partner in the wholesale-paper-dealing firm of E. Root & Co. at New York. When this establishment failed (1841), he founded Cyrus W. Field & Co., and within 10 years paid all his debts and retired with a fortune of $250,-000. His interest in the project of a transatlantic cable from Newfoundland was aroused when he met (1854) Frederick N. Gisborne, a Canadian engineer. Field vigorously promoted the idea and won the support of a group of New Yorkers who subscribed $1,500,000 for the project. After surmounting many disheartening technical and financial obstacles, the company completed the laying of the telegraph cable joining Valentia, Ireland, and Trinity Bay, Newfoundland (5 Aug. 1858). On 16 Aug. 1858 Queen Victoria sent over the line a message to President Buchanan. Soon thereafter, the cable stopped working. Field suffered heavy financial loss, but continued to press for support of the project. After the Civil War he secured the *Great Eastern*, at that time the largest steamboat afloat, and with it relaid an improved cable. Subsequent investments in railroad and elevated railway stocks cost him his fortune.

Field, David Dudley (b. Haddam, Conn., 13 Feb. 1805; d. New York City, 13 Apr.

1894), lawyer and jurist, was graduated from Williams College (1825), admitted to the N.Y. bar (1828), and practiced in New York City. A Democrat, he opposed the extension of slavery and supported Frémont (1856) and Lincoln (1860), returning to the Democratic party in 1876, with 3 mos. service in Congress. Although notable as a lawyer (counsel for Milligan in *Ex parte Milligan,* 1867; for McCardle in a case involving the constitutionality of the Reconstruction Act of 1867; for Jay Gould and James Fiske in the Erie R.R. litigation, 1869; chief counsel for "Boss" Tweed, 1873–78; and counsel for Tilden before the Electoral Commission, 1876), his major contribution was as a law reformer and codifier. Appointed (1847) to a commission for codification of N.Y. State laws and to another for reform of procedure, he drafted a code of civil procedure which was enacted by the legislature (1848). Codes based on his reforms were soon passed in many states, notably in the West, and ultimately influenced English judicial reforms. Chairman of a new commission (1857) to prepare penal and civil codes, a task completed by 1865, his proposals were opposed by James C. Carter (1827–1905) and only the penal code became law (1881). His *Draft Outline of an International Code* (2 vols., 1872) gained recognition by the courts of many nations. He was a founder and 1st president of the Association for Reform and Codification of the Law of Nations (now International Law Association).

Field, Marshall (b. near Conway, Mass., 18 Aug. 1835; d. New York City, 16 Jan. 1906), merchant and philanthropist. His formal schooling ended when, at the age of 17, he became a clerk in a dry-goods store at Pittsfield, Mass. Moving to Chicago in 1856, he became a clerk and traveling salesman in the wholesale dry-goods establishment of Cooley, Wadsworth & Co., of which he became general manager (1861) and a partner (1862). In 1865 the store became known as Field, Palmer & Leiter, and in 1881 became Marshall Field & Co., with Field as major proprietor. He eventually bought out the other interests in the concern. Field made

several pioneering innovations in retail merchandising: the making of wholesale purchases of goods in anticipation of consumer demand in order to improve his position on the open market, the segregation of wholesale and retail departments in his store, the operation of buying agencies throughout the world, the purchase of the entire output of manufacturing plants, and the establishment of his own factories as sources of supply. Among his philanthropies were the founding of the Chicago Manual Training School, the donation of the site of the University of Chicago, and the Columbian Museum at the Chicago World's Fair of 1893, a structure that was later converted, through a provision in his will, into the Field Museum of Natural History.

Field, Stephen Johnson (b. Haddam, Conn., 4 Nov. 1816; d. Washington, D.C., 9 Apr. 1899), jurist, was graduated from Williams College (1837), admitted to the N.Y. bar (1841), and practiced in New York City with his brother, David Dudley. He went to Calif. (1849) and was elected to the state legislature (1850), serving on the judicial committee which reorganized the judicial code of Calif. along lines laid down by his brother, and securing passage of basic mining laws. Judge of the state supreme court (1857–59) and chief justice (1857–63), he was appointed by Lincoln associate justice of the U.S. Supreme Court (1863–97), serving 34 years and 7 months, the longest term of any member of that bench. His most notable opinions were dissents, acting as a curb upon the centralizing tendencies of the majority. His dissents in the *Slaughterhouse Cases* (1873) and *Munn* v. *Ill.* (1876) forecast later recognized constitutional principles. He upheld Congress' paramount power over interstate commerce, even denying to the states the right to prohibit imports or exports of articles not recognized by them as legitimate subjects of commerce. With the majority in *Pollock* v. *Farmers' Loan* (1894), he opposed the income tax as an "assault upon capital." As presiding judge in his home circuit he courageously defied local sentiment on the Chinese question (*Chinese*

Immigration Case; Queue Case).

Fillmore, Millard (b. Locke, N.Y., 7 Jan. 1800; d. Buffalo, 8 Mar. 1874), 13th President of the U.S., read law, was admitted to the bar (1823), practiced in East Aurora until 1830, and then moved to Buffalo. As a protégé of Thurlow Weed he was sent to the state Assembly (1829–31) on the Anti-Masonic ticket. Congressman (1833–35 and 1837–43), he joined the Whig party (1834) and became its leader in the House. As chairman of the Ways and Means Committee he drafted the tariff bill of 1842. Defeated as Whig nominee for governor of New York (1844), he was elected Vice-President of the U.S. (1848), having been nominated on the ticket with Zachary Taylor to placate the Clay wing of the Whig party. On Taylor's death he succeeded to the Presidency (9 July 1850–4 Mar. 1853), signed the Clay Compromise of 1850, and sought to enforce the Fugitive Slave Act at the cost of much popularity in the North. He approved the Perry Treaty opening relations with Japan. Denied renomination in 1852, he was the nominee of the American (Know-Nothing) party for the Presidency in 1856, running a poor 3rd.

Fish, Hamilton (b. New York City, 3 Aug. 1808; d. there, 6 Sept. 1893), statesman. Graduated from Columbia (1827), he was admitted to the N.Y. bar (1830), and in 1842 was elected to Congress on the Whig ticket, serving 1 term. He was lieutenant governor (1847–48) and governor (1849–50) of N.Y., and served (1851–57) in the U.S. Senate, during which time he moved into the Republican party. During the Civil War he was a member of the Union defense committee of N.Y. State and was a Federal commissioner for the relief of prisoners. As Secretary of State (1869–77) under President Grant, he negotiated the Treaty of Washington (1871), which settled the *Alabama* controversy and other matters of dispute between the U.S. and Great Britain; handled the *Virginius* crisis that arose (Nov. 1873) with Spain; negotiated a treaty of commercial reciprocity with Hawaii (1875); and reached a general settlement with Spain (1876) concerning American claims in Cuba.

Fitzgerald, Francis Scott Key (b. St. Paul, Minn., 24 Sept. 1896; d. Hollywood, 21 Dec. 1940), novelist, lived between the poles of success and despair, much like the lost-rich characters of his novels. Entering Princeton in 1913, he left in 1917 to enlist in the army. His first novel, rewritten for the third time in St. Paul, *This Side of Paradise* (1920), depicted the younger generation of the "Jazz Age." On the strength of its financial success he married the beautiful Zelda Sayre, and they began the life of desperate gaiety which took a heavy toll of both. In 1922 he published *The Beautiful and the Damned*. In 1924, he and his wife moved to Europe, where they hoped to live more cheaply, and remained there until 1930. Zelda Sayre suffered two mental breakdowns from which she never recovered, and Fitzgerald began drinking heavily. His most brilliant book, *The Great Gatsby* (1925), was a critical success but a financial failure, and *Tender is the Night* was a critical failure as well (1933). He retreated to a small southern town, where he wrote *The Crack-Up* (1936), and then left for Hollywood, where he wrote for the movies.

Flexner, Abraham (b. Louisville, Ky., 13 Nov. 1866 d. Washington, D.C., 21 Sept. 1959), educational administrator, was graduated from Johns Hopkins (A.B., 1886). After 19 yrs. as secondary school teacher and principal he took graduate work at Harvard (M.A., 1906) and the Univ. of Berlin (1906–07). In 1908 he joined the research staff of the Carnegie Foundation for the Advancement of Teaching. His reports, *Medical Education in the U.S. and Canada* (1910) and *Medical Education in Europe* (1912) hastened much-needed reforms in teaching, curricula, and standards of American medical schools. His pamphlet, *A Modern School* (1916), led to the founding of the Lincoln Experimental School of Teachers College, Columbia University. A member of the General Education Board, 1912–25, he was influential in guiding philanthropies of the

Rockefellers, the Carnegie trusts, and George Eastman. His *Universities—American, English, German* (1930) criticized abuses of the elective system in the U.S. and the trend toward noncultural subjects. As 1st director of the Institute for Advanced Study, Princeton, N.J., he profoundly influenced its plan, scope, and original membership. His other works include *I Remember: An Autobiography* (1940) and biographies of H. S. Pritchett (1943) and Daniel Coit Gilman (1946).

Ford, Henry (b. near Dearborn, Mich., 30 July 1863; d. Dearborn, Mich., 7 Apr. 1947), industrialist. His formal schooling at Greenfield, Mich., ended in 1878, and in the following year he moved to Detroit, where he worked (1879–84) as a machine-shop apprentice and as a traveling repair man for a farm machinery firm. After operating a sawmill for several years, he became (1887) chief engineer of the Edison Illuminating Co. in Detroit. His 1st automobile was developed and built by 1896. For a time he was associated with the Detroit Automobile Co., manufacturers of custombuilt vehicles. After manufacturing his 1st racing car, the "999," Ford organized (1903) the Ford Motor Co., which in 1909 produced the first "Model T" (popularly known as the "flivver"), a standardized vehicle turned out on a mass-production assembly line. The factory assembly methods evolved by Ford engineers made him a worldwide symbol of American industrial technique. Ford's victory in the suit (1903–11) brought against him by the Association of Licensed Automobile Manufacturers (the Selden Patent Suit) freed the industry from the hold of an agreement that threatened to retard the development of automobile manufacture. In 1914 Ford attracted national attention by introducing into his plants the 8-hr. day with a minimum daily wage of $5. At the same time he inaugurated a profit-sharing plan for his employees. Late in 1915, Ford chartered the *Oscar II* (commonly known as the Ford Peace Ship), which took to the Scandinavian nations a group of pacifists, feminists, and other idealists in an attempt to halt World War I by neutral

mediation. During that war he manufactured a wide range of equipment for the U.S. government, including gun carriages and Liberty motors. In 1918 he was an unsuccessful candidate for U.S. senator from Mich. He served as president of the Ford Motor Co. until 1919, when he was succeeded by his son, Edsel B. Ford; upon the death of the latter, he again became president (1943) and served until his death. The Ford Foundation was established by Henry and Edsel Ford in 1936. Its operations were conducted on a relatively modest scale until 1951, when with vastly increased assets the Ford Foundation undertook a diversified program in educational philanthropy and other fields.

Forrest, Edwin (b. Philadelphia, Pa., 9 Mar. 1806; d. there, 12 Dec. 1872), actor. He made his debut (27 Nov. 1820) at the Walnut Street Theater, Philadelphia, in the role of Young Norval, and subsequently was a member of a roving company on the frontier circuit. He played at New Orleans as a member of James H. Caldwell's company and supported Edmund Kean in an engagement at Albany (1825). He made his New York debut (23 June 1826) at the Park Theater as Othello and in the ensuing decade became a leading American actor, appearing in Shakespearean tragic roles and in plays such as John H. Stone's *Metamora* (1829) and Robert M. Bird's tragedy, *The Gladiator,* both of which won prizes offered by Forrest to encourage plays by native dramatists. In 1834 Forrest went to Europe, where he was acclaimed as the 1st great American-born actor. His rivalry with the British actor Macready resulted in the Astor Place Riot (10 May 1849) at New York, in which 22 persons lost their lives. The last 2 decades of Forrest's life were darkened by domestic difficulties that took on the dimensions of public scandals, and by a growing personal bitterness and isolation. The house he bought at Philadelphia is now maintained as the Forrest Home for aged actors.

Foster, Stephen Collins (b. Allegheny City, Pa., 4 July 1826; d. New York City, 13 Jan. 1864), composer, for a brief period in 1841 attended Jefferson College. He worked (1846) as a book-keeper for his brother at Cincinnati, where several Negro ballads composed by Foster, such as "O Susanna," "Away Down South," and "Uncle Ned," were used by a local publisher who brought out *Songs of the Sable Harmonists* (1848). Thereafter Foster devoted himself to songwriting, producing ballads and songs, most of them for Negro minstrels. He made an agreement (1851) with E. P. Christy giving 1st performance rights to Christy's Minstrels and publication rights to himself. Among Foster's songs are "Nelly Was a Lady" (1849), "De Camptown Races" (1850), "The Old Folks at Home" (1851; also known as "Swanee River"), "Massa's in de Cold, Cold Ground" (1852), "My Old Kentucky Home" (1853), "Old Dog Tray" (1853), "Jeannie With the Light Brown Hair" (1854), and "Old Black Joe" (1860). Spending his last years in poverty, Foster died in a Bowery roominghouse.

Frankfurter, Felix (b. Vienna, Austria, 15 Nov. 1882–), jurist, came to the U.S. in 1894, received his A.B. (1902) from the Coll. of the City of N.Y. and his LL.B. (highest honors, 1906) from the Harvard Law School. Asst. U.S. atty., Southern Dist. of N.Y., 1906–10, he served as law officer in the Bureau of Insular Affairs (1911–14), and joined the faculty of the Harvard Law School in 1914, where he taught administrative law until 1939. During World War I he served as asst. to the Secy. of War, counsel to the President's Mediation Bd. (1917–18), and chairman, War Labor Policies Bd. (1918). He argued or filed briefs before the Supreme Court in *Bunting* v. *Oregon* (1917) and *Adkins* v. *Children's Hospital* (1923), and gained national prominence by his critique of the Sacco-Vanzetti trial (*The Case of Sacco and Vanzetti*, 1927). Close adviser to President Franklin D. Roosevelt, he was influential in recruiting personnel for the New Deal. Appointed associate justice of the Supreme Court (1939), he quickly assumed leadership in opposing the Black-Douglas position that the 1st Amendment rights were absolute, whereas he considered that amendment a generic pro-

vision requiring definition by present experience. The view that freedom is not absolute but must be weighed against legislative judgment he expressed in the *Gobitis Case* (1940), sustaining a state flag salute law. "One who belongs to the most vilified and persecuted minority in history is not likely to be insensible to the freedoms guaranteed by our Constitution," he declared in dissenting to the reversal in *W. Va. Bd. of Educ.* v. *Barnette* (1943). In setting boundaries to the right to picket (*Milk Drivers Union* v. *Meadowmoor Dairies* (1941), he said: "Utterance in a context of violence can lose its significance as an appeal to reason and become part of an instrument of force." In the *Dennis Case* (1951) he repudiated the "clear and present danger" formula, holding that advocacy of overthrow of the govt. deserves little protection. He wrote numerous works in the field of constitutional and administrative law, including *The Commerce Clause under Marshall, Taney and Waite* (1937) and *Felix Frankfurter Reminisces* (1960, recorded by H. B. Phillips).

Franklin, Benjamin (b. Boston, Mass., 17 Jan. 1706; d. Philadelphia, 17 Apr. 1790), statesman, diplomat, editor, and scientist, attended school briefly; worked in his father's tallow shop and then in his brother's printing shop. In 1723 he went to Philadelphia and worked as a printer, acquiring an interest in (1729) and sole ownership of the *Pennsylvania Gazette,* which he edited until 1748, and publishing annually (1732–57) *Poor Richard's Almanack.* Leader in cultural movements, he founded the Junto, a debating club (1727) which developed into the American Philosophical Society (1743); a circulating library (1731); Philadelphia's 1st fire company (1736); and an academy (1751), nucleus of the University of Pennsylvania. His international fame as scientist and inventor began with the invention of the Franklin stove (1742). The identity of lightning and electricity was demonstrated in France (1752) by methods he suggested, and he later confirmed it by his kite experiment. Clerk of the Pa. Assembly (1736–51), he was a member of that body (1751–64), deputy postmaster at Philadelphia (1737–53), and, jointly with William Hunter, postmaster general for the colonies (1753–74). In this office he improved the postal service and placed it on a profitable basis. Delegate to the Albany Congress (1754), he drafted a Plan of Union which the Congress adopted but which both Great Britain and the colonies rejected for opposing reasons. He went to England (1757) to press the claims of the Pa. Assembly to tax the proprietary estates, and acted as agent in England for Pa. (1764–75), for Ga. (after 1768), and for Mass. (after 1770). He was instrumental in securing the repeal of the Stamp Act (1766), but was publicly censured for allowing publication of the "Hutchinson letters" (1774). Returning to Philadelphia (1775), he was a member of the 2nd Continental Congress and became the 1st Postmaster General (1775–76). He was one of 3 commissioners sent (1776) to secure the aid of Canada, helped draft the Declaration of Independence, and was a signer. One of the 3 agents dispatched to France (1776–85), where his fame preceded him, he secured loans and concluded a treaty of alliance (1778). He was one of the negotiators of the Treaty of Peace with Great Britain (1783). President of the Executive Council of Pa. (1785–88), he was a member of the Constitutional Convention (1787), where he was influential in framing the compromise between the large and small states on the question of representation in the House of Representatives. His most famous book was his unfinished *Autobiography*, 1706–59 (written between 1771 and 1789).

Frémont, John Charles (b. Savannah, Ga., 31 Jan. 1813; d. New York City, 13 July 1890), explorer, politician, and soldier. He attended Charleston (S.C.) College, 1829–31, and in 1835 became an assistant engineer in the U.S. Topographical Corps, in which he was commissioned a 2nd lt. (1838). In 1838 he assisted Joseph N. Nicollet in exploring the plateau between the upper Mississippi and Missouri rivers. He married (1841) Jessie Benton, daughter of Sen. Thomas Hart Benton (Mo.), who used his influence to further Frémont's expeditions. Frémont made 3 important explorations that earned for him the sobriquet, "the Pathfinder": a scientific investigation of the Oregon Trail that took him to the Wind River chain of the Rockies and through South Pass (1842); to the Great Basin between the Rockies and the Sierras (1843–44); and to the Sierra Nevada by way of the headwaters of the Arkansas, Rio Grande, and Colorado rivers. The 3rd exploration was made on the eve of the Mexican War; when he reached the Pacific Coast, Frémont played a leading and controversial role in the conquest of Calif. His quarrel with Gen. Stephen W. Kearny resulted in a courtmartial at Washington, D.C. (Nov. 1847–Jan. 1848), that found Frémont guilty of mutiny and disobedience. Despite President Polk's remission of the sentence, Frémont resigned from the army. Returning to California, Frémont served a brief term as U.S. senator from that state and in 1853–54 made winter expeditions for a southern railway route to the Pacific. In 1856 he was the 1st Presidential candidate of the newly organized Republican party on an antislavery platform, losing to Buchanan by about 500,000 votes. At the outbreak of the Civil War he was appointed maj. gen. in charge of the Department of the West, with headquarters at St. Louis. When his radical policy toward slaveholders brought him into conflict with the Lincoln administration, he was removed from his post and given a command in western Va., but resigned when he was placed under General Pope, with whom he was on unfriendly terms. After making unsuccessful attempts at railroad promotion, he served as territorial governor of Ariz. (1878–83) and in 1890 was restored to the rank of maj. gen. with retirement pay.

Frost, Robert (b. San Francisco, Calif., 26 Mar. 1875–), poet. He attended Dartmouth and Harvard; worked in New England as a shoemaker, teacher, country editor, and farmer; and in 1912 went to England, where he brought out his 1st volume of poetry, *A Boy's Will* (1913). Following the publication of *North of Boston* (1914), he returned to the U.S. (1915), where he soon won recognition as a poet of the 1st rank, who has been awarded the Pulitzer prize 4 times (1924, 1931, 1937, 1943). Most of his poetry is based on themes drawn from New England rural life. His works include *Mountain Interval* (1916), *New Hampshire* (1923), *West-Running Brook* (1928), *Collected Poems* (1930, 1939), *Selected Poems* (1937), *A Further Range* (1937), and *A Witness Tree* (1943). Among his individual poems are "Mowing," "The Death of the Hired Man," "Home Burial," "Mending Wall," "Birches," and "Fire and Ice." He was the 1st poet to participate in a Presidential inaugural ceremony (1961).

Fuller, Margaret [full name **Sarah Margaret Fuller**; title **Marchioness Ossoli**] (b. Cambridgeport, Mass., 23 May 1810; d. off Fire Island, N.Y., 19 July 1850), feminist, critic, and journalist. A precocious child, she received most of her education from her father and at an early age formed friendships with New England intellectual leaders such as James Freeman Clarke and Frederic Henry Hedge. She conducted (1839–44) her "conversations" at the Boston residence of Elizabeth Peabody, drawing her pupils from leading circles of the city. The material of her "conversations" appeared in her feminist work, *Woman in the Nineteenth Century* (1845). With Ralph Waldo Emerson and George Ripley, she edited (1840–42) *The Dial,* Transcendentalist journal. Her book, *Summer on the Lakes, in 1843* (1844), drew the attention of Horace Greeley, who offered her a staff job with the New York *Tribune.* Her significant writings as literary critic of the *Tribune* from 1844 to 1846 were published as *Literature and Art* (1846). She went abroad in 1846 and while in Italy had a son (1848) by the Marquis Angelo Ossoli, whom she married in 1849. With her husband, an ardent follower of Mazzini, she took part in the Roman Revolution. She and her family died in a shipwreck while returning to America.

Fulton, Robert (b. Little Britain, now Fulton, Pa., 14 Nov. 1765; d. New York City, 24 Feb. 1815), artist, civil engineer, and inventor, pioneer in steam navigation. During his boyhood he showed a talent for drawing and mechanical crafts, becoming an expert gunsmith in nearby Lancaster. Going to Philadelphia in 1783, he worked as an artist and draftsman; in 1786 he went abroad, where he remained for 20 years. Although his 1st years in London were devoted to painting, he soon shifted his interest to science and engineering. He invented an apparatus (the double inclined plane) for raising and lowering canal boats, a power shovel for digging canal channels, a device for sawing marble, and a flax-spinning machine. His chief interest was in internal improvements, particularly inland waterways. In 1794 he settled in Paris, where he painted what is held to be the 1st panorama. He published *A Treatise on the Improvement of Canal Navigation* (1796), a comprehensive work of its kind, and submitted to the Board of Agriculture of Great Britain detailed plans and proposals (1796) for the construction of cast-iron aqueducts requiring simplified casting and building operations. One of these structures was later reared across the Dee near Chester. Fulton also proposed cast-iron bridges of his own design which were built at several points in England. For 9 years, beginning in 1797, he devoted himself to the development of the submarine mine and torpedo; failing to gain the financial support of the French government, he secured the aid of Joel Barlow and made short-lived experiments with a self-propelled submarine torpedo. In 1801, after Napoleon showed interest in Fulton's project, Fulton made successful experiments with his submarine boat, the *Nautilus;* but upon his failure to make a satisfactory demonstration under actual combat conditions, the French authorities quickly lost interest. In 1804 he placed his invention at the disposal of the British government, which finally refused to adopt it despite a successful test carried out in 1805. Returning to the U.S. (1805), Fulton continued the experiments with steamboats that had begun along the Seine in 1803 with the assistance of the U.S. Minister to France, Robert R. Livingston. Fulton designed the *Clermont,* a boat with 2 side paddlewheels. During the course of its construction, he demonstrated in New York Harbor (20 July 1807) the effectiveness of his torpedo device. The *Clermont* was completed in the spring of 1807 and the Watt steam engine was installed later. Starting out from New York on 17 Aug. 1807, the *Clermont* made its voyage to Albany and back in 5 days (62 hours of actual operating time). Until his death Fulton was active in organizing and managing steamboat lines. In 1814 he constructed for the U.S. government the *Fulton the First,* a huge paddlewheel steam warship, never tested in warfare.

Gallatin, Albert [full name **Abraham Alfonse Albert Gallatin**] (b. Geneva, Switzerland, 29 Jan. 1761; d. Astoria, Long Island, N.Y., 12 Aug. 1849), statesman, diplomat, and ethnologist. He was graduated (1779) from Geneva Academy; emigrated to Mass. (1780); settled in the Pa. back country (1784), where he made unsuccessful ventures in land speculation; and as a member (1790–92) of the Pa. legislature emerged as a leader of the nascent Republican forces in the western part of the state. He was elected (28 Feb. 1793) to the U.S. Senate, but a Federalist majority deprived him of his seat (28 Feb. 1794) on the ground that he had not been a U.S. citizen for 9 yrs. An opponent of the Federal excise tax of 1791, he took a moderate stand during the Whisky Rebellion of 1794 and was instrumental in averting serious bloodshed. As a member of Congress (1795–1801), he became the recognized leader of the Republican minority in the House. His able grasp of finance and his criticism of the Federalist policy in the Treasury Department led to the creation of a standing committee on finance. As Secretary of the Treasury (1801–14) under Jefferson and Madison, he carried out a program of financial reform and economy which after 1807 was virtually destroyed by embroilments in the Napoleonic Wars and by the War of 1812. He was a member of the commission (1814) which negotiated the Treaty of Ghent, served as Minister to France (1816–23) and to England (1826–27), and from 1831 to 1839 was president of the National Bank at New York City. Called "the father of American ethnology," he wrote *Synopsis of the Indian Tribes . . . of North America* (1836) and founded (1842) the American Ethnological Society.

Galloway, Joseph (b. West River, Anne Arundel Co., Md., *c*.1731; d. Watford, England, 29 Aug. 1803), colonial statesman, studied law in Philadelphia, where he rose to eminence at the bar. Assemblyman (1756–76, except for 1764–65), he joined Franklin in attempts to tax the Penns' land, and eventually, with Franklin, petitioned the Crown to substitute royal for proprietary govt. An imperial statesman, he saw the need for a revenue for America, but opposed parliamentary taxation. Instead, he advocated a written constitution for the empire. In the 1st Continenal Congress (1774) he proposed the Galloway Plan for an imperial legislature, defeated by a close vote. Refusing to be a delegate to the 2nd Congress, he criticized its predecessor in *A Candid Examination of the Mutual Claims of Great Britain and the Colonies* (1775). Civil administrator of Philadelphia during Gen. Howe's occupation of the city, he left for London with the recapture of the city (1778), and became the spokesman for the Loyalists. His estates confiscated by Pa. and his petition (1793) to return denied, he spent his last 20 yrs. in exile.

Garfield, James Abram (b. Cuyahoga Co., Ohio, 19 Nov. 1831; d. Elberon, N.J., 19 Sept. 1881), 20th President of the U.S., was graduated from Williams College (1856), served as president of Western Reserve Eclectic Institute (later Hiram College), 1857–61, was admitted to the bar, and elected to the Ohio Senate as a Republican (1859). During the Civil War he distinguished himself in engagements at Middle Creek, Ky., Shiloh, and Chickamauga; was a member of the court of inquiry in the Fitz John Porter case (1862); and was on the staff of General Rosecrans. Congressman (1863–81), his prestige as orator and parliamentarian made him Blaine's rival for influence with that body. Although charged, without proof, of corruption in connection with Crédit Mobilier, he was elected to the U.S. Senate (1880), and in that same year nominated and elected President. In the midst of involvements over appointments to office, prompting the resignation of Roscoe Conkling and T. C. Platt from the U.S. Senate, he was fatally shot in the Washington railroad station by Charles J. Guiteau, a disappointed office seeker.

Garrison, William Lloyd (b. Newburyport, Mass., 10 Dec. 1805; d. New York City, 24 May 1879), abolitionist. After brief schooling, he was apprenticed (1818) to the editor of the Newburyport *Herald;* became (1826) editor of the Newburyport *Free Press;* when that newspaper failed, he moved to Boston and became (1828) coeditor of the *National Philanthropist,* an organ devoted to reform causes. At about this time he met Benjamin Lundy, a Quaker antislavery writer and journalist, whom he joined at Baltimore (1829) as coeditor of *The Genius of Universal Emancipation.* Garrison's tirades in the columns of this paper resulted in his imprisonment for libel (1830), but he was released after the New York merchant and abolitionist sympathizer, Arthur Tappan, paid his fine. Returning to Boston (1830), he founded and published the *Liberator,* in which he was joined by his partner, Isaac Knapp. The 1st issue of this abolitionist paper, dated 1 Jan. 1831, announced the uncompromising attitude that henceforth characterized Garrison's crusade against slavery and slaveholders. He remained its editor until the last issue of the *Liberator* appeared 35 years later. Garrison demanded immediate and complete emancipation of slaves. He was one of the founders of the New England Antislavery Society (1831) and organized the American Antislavery Society (1833). Resentment in the North against the abolitionists was so strong that Garrison was dragged through the streets by a Boston mob and almost killed (21 Oct. 1835). His opposition to political action resulted in a split in the organized antislavery ranks in the late 1830's. During that period Garrison embraced disunionism, demanding that the North withdraw from a compact that sheltered slavery. Under his influence the Massachusetts Antislavery Society resolved (1843) that the Constitution of the U.S. was "a covenant with death and an agreement with hell." On 4 July 1854, before a gathering at Framingham, Mass., he publicly burned the Constitution, saying: "So perish all compromises with tyranny!" During the Civil War he gave his full support to Lincoln after the issuance of the Emancipation Proclamation. In the years after the war he was allied with reform causes, including prohibition and women's suffrage.

George, Henry (b. Philadelphia, Pa., 2 Sept. 1839; d. New York City, 29 Oct. 1897), economist and reformer. After a brief period of formal schooling, he went to sea as a foremast boy (1855), became a typesetter (1856), was a prospector in the Pacific Northwest (1858), and until 1880, when he moved to New York, was a printer and newspaperman, chiefly at San Francisco. He published (1871) a pamphlet, *Our Land and Land Policy,* which set forth the basic elements of the single-tax theory elaborated by him in *Progress and Poverty* (1879). Holding that taxes should be confined to the economic rent derived from land, George asserted that the accumulation of such unearned increment tended to impoverish society, and that the single tax, by eliminating all other government levies, would enable the unimpeded and benevolent operation of the economic mechanism. After publishing *The Irish Land Question* (1881), he served as a correspondent in the British Isles for the *Irish World.* He was also active as a lecturer. In 1886, as the liberal and labor candidate for mayor of New York, he was defeated in a contest with Abram S. Hewitt and Theodore Roosevelt. In 1897 he was the independent Democratic candidate for mayor of New York, and died while campaigning for that office.

Gershwin, George (b. Brooklyn, N.Y., 26 Sept. 1898; d. Hollywood, Calif., 11 July 1937), composer, was educated in the New York public schools, studied the piano with Charles Hambitzer and harmony with Rubin Goldmark, and worked as a song plugger in Tin Pan Alley. His 1st song, "When You Want 'Em You Can't Get 'Em," was published in 1916; his first musical comedy score was written for *La, La, Lucille* (1919). Gershwin's use of the native jazz idiom in serious music 1st appeared in *Rhapsody in Blue* (1st performance given by Paul Whiteman and his orchestra at Aeolian Hall, New York City, 12 Feb. 1924). In this vein Gershwin also wrote *Concerto in F* (1925), *An American in Paris* (1928), *Second Rhadsody* (1931), *Cuban Overture* (1932), and the opera *Porgy and Bess* (1935). Among Gershwin's popular musical comedies were *George White's Scandals* (1920–24), *Lady Be Good* (1924), *Rosalie* (1927), *Strike Up the Band* (1927), *Show Girl* (1929), *Girl Crazy* (1930), *Of Thee I Sing* (1931; 1st musical comedy awarded the Pulitzer prize), and *Let 'Em Eat Cake* (1933). His best-known songs include "I'll Build a Stairway to Paradise" (1922), "Somebody Loves Me" (1924), "It Ain't Necessarily So" (1935), and "Summertime" (1935).

Gibbons, James (b. Baltimore, Md., 23 July 1834; d. there, 24 Mar. 1921), Roman Catholic prelate, was graduated (1858) from St. Charles College, near Baltimore, took advanced training for the priesthood at St. Mary's Seminary, Baltimore, and was ordained (1861). He took charge of St. Bridget's Church in the suburb of Canton and during the Civil War was chaplain at Ft. McHenry. Invited to take the post of secretary to Archbishop Spalding, he became (1866) assistant chancellor of the Second Plenary Council of Baltimore and head of the newly established Vicarate Apostolic of N.C. Consecrated bishop of Adramyttum (16 Aug. 1868), he was at that time the youngest of all Catholic bishops. He served (1870) as the youngest member of the Ecumenical Council of the Vatican; succeeded (1872) to the bishopric of Richmond; was appointed (May 1877) coadjutor archbishop of Baltimore; and, upon the death of Archbishop James R. Bayley (Oct. 1877), became head of the See of Baltimore. He organized and conducted the Third Plenary Council of Baltimore (1884), over which he presided as apostolic delegate. In 1885 he was named the 2nd American cardinal and was formally installed at Baltimore (1886) and at Rome (1887), where he made a memorable pronouncement expressing his attachment to American in-

stitutions. Sympathetic to the cause of labor, he secured at Rome ecclesiastical assurances that the Knights of Labor would not be condemned in the U.S., and was instrumental in obtaining the removal of the hierarchical ban against that body in Canada. He laid the cornerstone of the Catholic University of America at Washington, D.C. (1888), and served as chancellor until his death. In 1903 he was the 1st American to participate in the election of a pope.

Gibbs, Josiah Willard (b. New Haven, Conn., 11 Feb. 1839; d. there, 28 Apr. 1903), mathematical physicist. He was graduated from Yale (1858), where he received the degree of Ph.D. (1863), served as a tutor at Yale, and in 1866 went to the Continent, where he continued his studies at Paris (1866–67), Berlin (1867–68), and Heidelberg (1868–69). He was appointed (1871) professor of mathematical physics in Yale College, holding that post until his death. His chief contributions were his theory of thermodynamics, the basis for the major part of modern physical chemistry and chemical engineering. Among the papers he published are "Graphical Methods in the Thermodynamics of Fluids" (1873), "A Method of Geometrical Representation of the Thermodynamic Properties of Substances by Means of Surfaces" (1873), and "Electrochemical Thermodynamics" (1886). His most important single paper, "On the Equilibrium of Heterogeneous Substances" (1876), contained his formulation of the phase rule, one of the revolutionary laws of theoretical physics. Between 1880 and 1884 he evolved a system of vector analysis adapted to the needs of mathematical physicists, publishing papers such as "On the Role of Quaternions in the Algebra of Vectors" (1891) and "Quaternions and Vector Analysis" (1893). From 1882 to 1889 he devoted himself principally to theories of optics, developing an electromagnetic theory of light. In 1902 he published *Elementary Principles in Statistical Mechanics*. His *Collected Works* were published in 1928.

Gilman, Daniel Coit (b. Norwich, Conn., 6 July 1831; d. there, 13 Oct. 1908), educational administrator. He was graduated from Yale (1852), served as an attaché (1853–55) of the U.S. legation at St. Petersburg, and drew up the plan for the Sheffield Scientific School at Yale, where he served (1855–72) as librarian and professor of physical and political geography. With Eliot of Harvard and White of Cornell he was the chief maker of the modern American university, serving as president (1872–75) of the University of California, and as the 1st president (1876–1901) of the Johns Hopkins University, which he made into a leading center of creative study and research. He was instrumental in founding the Johns Hopkins Hospital (1889) and Medical School (1893), and raised the general level of medical training in the U.S.

Goddard, Robert Hutchins (b. Worcester, Mass., 5 Oct. 1882; d. Baltimore, Md., 10 Aug., 1945), physicist, "father of the modern rocket," attended the Worcester Polytechnical Inst. (B.S., 1908) and Clark University (M.A., 1910; Ph.D., 1911), where he became professor of physics (1919). In 1912 he began his work on rocketry, developing a general theory of rocket action, including the "optimum velocity" principle. Engaged in research during World War I for the U.S. Signal Corps at Mt. Wilson, he pressed developments in rocketry. His paper, "A Method of Reaching Extreme Altitudes" (1920), predicted the use of rockets to explore high altitudes. In 1926 he completed and successfully launched the world's 1st liquid-fuel rocket (prototype of the German V-2) and 4 yrs. later fired a rocket to a height of 2,000 ft. at a speed of 500 mi. an hr. During World War II he directed research in jet propulsion for the navy, and produced rockets attaining speeds of 700 mi. an hr. In 1960 the U.S. govt. paid $1 million for use of Goddard's patents, which had been assigned to the Daniel and Florence Guggenheim Foundation in return for its support.

Godkin, Edwin Lawrence (b. Moyne, County Wicklow, Ireland, 2 Oct. 1831; d. Brixham, England, 21 May 1902), editor. He was graduated (1851) from Queen's College, Belfast; worked in the London publishing house of Cassell, which brought out his *History of Hungary and the Magyars* (1853); was correspondent (1853–55) for the London *Daily News* during the Crimean War; and came to the U.S. in 1856. As the 1st editor (1865–1900) of the weekly *Nation*, and as editor (1883–1900) of the New York *Evening Post*, Godkin established new standards of American political journalism. An ardent exponent of civil service reform, he was an implacable foe of the spoils system. He pursued an independent liberal course in politics and in 1884 took a leading role in the Mugwump revolt against James G. Blaine.

Goethals, George Washington (b. Brooklyn, N.Y., 29 June 1858; d. New York City, 21 Jan. 1928), army officer and engineer, builder of the Panama Canal. He attended the College of the City of New York and was graduated from the U.S. Military Academy (1880). He served (1882–1905) in the Engineer Corps of the U.S. Army and (1903–07) on the Army General Staff. In the spring of 1907, when he held the rank of lt. col., he was appointed by President Theodore Roosevelt as chairman and chief engineer of the Isthmian Canal Commission. In this capacity, Goethals bore virtually sole responsibility for the successful administration of the canal project. His organizing ability overcame numerous serious difficulties involving engineering problems, employee grievances, housing and sanitation, and the establishment of a law enforcement system. He was made (1914) the 1st civil governor of the Panama Canal Zone, serving in that post until 1916, and was promoted to maj. gen. and received the thanks of Congress (1915). From Apr. to July 1917, he was general manager of the Emergency Fleet Corporation. Although he was transferred to the retired list in 1916, he was recalled to duty (1917–19) as acting quartermaster general and director of purchase, storage, and supplies, responsible for the supply and transportation of all U.S. troops at home and abroad.

Gompers, Samuel (b. London, England,

27 Jan. 1850; d. San Antonio, Tex., 13 Dec. 1924), labor leader. Apprenticed as a cigarmaker in London, he arrived in the U.S. in 1863 and joined (1864) the Cigarmakers' Union, of which he became president in 1877. He was one of the main figures in the organization (1881) of the Federation of Organized Trades and Labor Unions of the U.S. and Canada, reorganized (1886) as the American Federation of Labor. Gompers was chosen president of the A.F. of L. and, with the exception of the year 1895, served in that capacity until his death. During that period he was the acknowledged head of the American labor movement. An exponent of craft unionism, Gompers stressed practical demands such as wages and hours, and was an avowed opponent of theorists and radicals in the labor movement. He was opposed to an independent labor party and eschewed political commitments by labor organizations to any of the existing parties. During World War I he organized a War Committee on Labor that was instrumental in maintaining national unity. Among his works are *Labor in Europe and America* (1910), *American Labor and the War* (1919), and *Seventy Years of Life and Labor* (2 vols., 1925).

Goodyear, Charles (b. New Haven, Conn., 29 Dec. 1800; d. New York City, 1 July 1860), inventor, pioneer of the rubber industry in the U.S. Until 1830, when he was declared bankrupt, he was in the hardware business at New Haven and Philadelphia. In 1834 he became interested in improving the process for curing India rubber. In the following years, despite poverty and time spent in debtors' prison, he experimented with raw rubber in an attempt to make a product that would not melt or decompose at high and low temperatures. He patented a process (17 June 1837) which he used in making articles such as shoes, tablecloths, and piano covers. From Nathaniel M. Hayward, who had devised a process that included the use of sulphur, Goodyear acquired a patent in 1839, and in the same year accidentally dropped a rubber and sulphur mixture on a hot stove, thus discovering the vulcanizing process. Borrowing a total of more than $50,000, Goodyear perfected the process and received a patent for it (15 June 1844). Financial obligations forced him to sell licenses and to establish royalties that were far less than the true value of the rights; consequently, the profits derived from his discoveries accrued to others. His subsequent years in Europe (1851–59) and America were marked by unsuccessful lawsuits and increasing debt.

Gorgas, William Crawford (b. Toulminville, Ala., 3 Oct. 1854; d. London, 3 July 1920), sanitarian, received his B.A. (1875) from the Univ. of the South. Unable to enter West Point, he was graduated from Bellevue Hospital Medical College (1879). After a year's internship at Bellevue, he was appointed (1880) to the U.S. Army Medical Corps. Surviving an epidemic of yellow fever at Fort Brown, Tex., he was, due to his immunity, often assigned to posts where yellow fever was rampant. In 1898, following the occupation of Havana, he became chief sanitation officer of the city. Once the cause of yellow fever was established by Walter Reed, Gorgas succeeded in ridding the city of the disease by destroying the breeding places of the *Stegomyia* mosquito. Despite criticism, he introduced (1904) the same measures in the Panama Canal Zone, making Panama and Colón models of sanitation, and winning a worldwide reputation as a top sanitary expert. Appointed surgeon general of the army with the rank of brig. gen. (1914), he was sent (1916) by the Intl. Health Board to Central and South America on yellow fever missions. During World War I he served as head of the army Medical Service, and, when the war ended, on a yellow fever mission to the west coast of Africa. He wrote *Sanitation in Panama* (1915).

Grant, Ulysses Simpson (b. Point Pleasant, Ohio, 27 Apr. 1822; d. Mt. McGregor near Saratoga, N.Y., 23 July 1885), 18th President of the U.S., was graduated from the U.S. Military Academy (1843). During the War with Mexico he served under Zachary Taylor and Winfield Scott (1845–48), being breveted capt. for gallantry at Chapultepec. He served in Calif. and Ore. until resigning from the army (1854), when he engaged in farming and real estate in St. Louis, Mo. (1854–60), and then clerked in his father's leather store in Galena, Ill. At the outbreak of the Civil War he was commissioned col., 21st Illinois Volunteer Infantry; then brig. gen. of volunteers; and after capturing Forts Henry and Donelson (winning in the latter operation the sobriquet of "Unconditional Surrender Grant"), he was promoted maj. gen. of volunteers (1862). Victor at Shiloh (Apr. 1862), he captured Vicksburg (4 July 1863) and won the Battle of Chattanooga (23–25 Nov. 1863). After driving the Confederates from Missionary Ridge and raising the siege of Chattanooga, he was given supreme command of the Union forces, with revived rank of lt. gen. (Mar. 1864). In a campaign of attrition (Wilderness, Spotsylvania, Cold Harbor, 5 May–3 June 1864), he wore down Lee's resistance and, finally, by capturing Petersburg forced his surrender at Appomattox, Va. (9 Apr. 1865). Commissioned gen. (1866), he was appointed Secretary of War ad interim (Apr. 1867–Jan. 1868). Republican nominee, he was elected and reelected President of the U.S. (1869–77). Among the constructive achievements of his administration were the funding of the national debt, the resumption of specie payments (1875), the inauguration of civil service reform, and the negotiation of the Treaty of Washington with Great Britain (8 May 1871). On the debit side were involvements in scandals, notably the Fisk-Gould attempt to corner the gold market (1869); Crédit Mobilier (1873); the resignation of Secretary of the Treasury W. A. Richardson (1874) to escape a vote of censure by Congress; the implication in the Whisky Ring of O. E. Babcock, Grant's private secretary; and the resignation of Secretary of War W. W. Belknap (1876) to escape impeachment for bribe taking. His administration also had to weather the severe depression which followed the Panic of 1873. After a world tour (1877–80), Grant lost his fortune through the bankruptcy of Grant & Ward (1884), but it was recouped by his writing his *Personal Memoirs* (1885), which earned nearly $500,000.

Gray, Asa (b. Sauquoit, Oneida County, N.Y., 18 Nov. 1810; d. Cambridge, Mass., 30 Jan. 1888), botanist, received his M.D. (1831) from the Fairfield (N.Y.) Medical School, but soon he abandoned medicine for his study of plants and brought out his 1st independent publication, *North American Gramineae and Cyperaceae* (2 pts., 1834–35). He published his 1st botanical textbook, *Elements of Botany* (1836), and with John Torrey collaborated on *The Flora of North America* (2 vols., 1838–43). In 1842, when he published the 1st edition of his *Botanical Text-Book,* he was appointed Fisher professor of natural history in Harvard University, a post he held until his retirement in 1873. The leading American botanist of his time, he was one of the founders of the National Academy of Science, president (1863–73) of the American Academy of Arts and Sciences, and president (1872) of the American Association for the Advancement of Science. He made valuable contributions to the descriptive botany of North America, in which his most important work was *Manual of the Botany of the Northern United States* (1848 and subsequent editions). He also elaborated the botanical findings of the Wilkes Expedition in *United States Exploring Expedition during the Years 1838–42* (1854–57, 1874). It was to Gray that Charles Darwin wrote the letter (5 Sept. 1857) 1st outlining his theory of evolution. Gray became the chief American exponent of the Darwinian concepts, defending them against the attacks of Louis Agassiz (1807–73).

Greeley, Horace (b. Amherst, N.H., 3 Feb. 1811; d. New York City, 29 Nov. 1872), newspaper editor and reformer. He served his newspaper apprenticeship (*c.*1825–30) with the *Northern Spectator* at East Poultney, Vt.; arrived (1831) at New York City, where he engaged in job printing and founded (1834) a weekly literary and news journal, the *New Yorker;* and edited and published 2 Whig journals, the *Jeffersonian* (1838) and the *Log Cabin* (1840). He founded (1841) the New York *Tribune,* which in its daily and weekly editions was influential in shaping political opinion in the Northern and Western parts of the U.S., and served as the vehicle for Greeley's social and economic views, including Fourierism, antislavery sentiment, temperance, women's rights, homestead legislation, and the protective tariff. He originated the phrase "Go West, young man." Until 1854 he maintained a political alliance with William H. Seward and Thurlow Weed. One of the founders of the Republican party, he supported the nomination of Lincoln at the Chicago convention (1860), but during the war aligned himself with the radical antislavery faction and at times pursued an erratic course on the prosecution of the war. His attempt to bring about direct peace negotiations in the summer of 1864 ended in a fiasco. After the war he favored a liberal policy toward the South. In 1872, as the Liberal Republican candidate for the Presidency, he made a poor showing against Grant.

Greene, Nathanael (b. Potowomut, now Warwick, R.I., 7 Aug. 1742; d. Mulberry Grove, near Savannah, Ga., 19 June 1786), Revolutionary general, served as deputy (1770–72, 1775) to the R.I. General Assembly, was appointed brig. (May 1775) in charge of 3 regiments authorized by R.I., and was named (22 June 1775) a brig. gen. in the Continental Army. He served through the siege of Boston, and after its evacuation by the British (Mar. 1776) was placed in command of the army of occupation. He was promoted (9 Aug. 1776) to maj. gen. in the Continental army, took part in the defensive operations in and around New York City, and played an important role in Washington's surprise assault on the British at Trenton (Dec. 1776). He participated in the Battle of Germantown (1777), went into winter quarters at Valley Forge, and was appointed (25 Feb. 1778) quartermaster general, in which capacity he reorganized and improved the supply system. He took part in the battles of Monmouth (1778) and Newport (1778). Difficulties with Congress and members of the "Conway Cabal" led to his resignation as quartermaster general. He was acting commander of the Continental army when Benedict Arnold's plot was brought to light, and served

(1780) as president of the board of general officers which condemned John André to the gallows. Following the defeat of Gen. Horatio Gates at Camden, S.C. (1780), Washington chose Greene (14 Oct. 1780) to command the Revolutionary forces in the Southern theater. Carrying out an extensive program of reorganization and refitting, Greene assembled an army that included subordinate commanders such as Henry Lee and Francis Marion. He divided the British forces under Lord Cornwallis, won the Battle of Cowpens (17 Jan. 1781), drained British strength in engagements at Guilford Court House, N.C. (15 Mar. 1781) and Hobkirk's Hill (26 Apr. 1781), and forced the British withdrawal from Camden. He defeated the British at the Battle of Eutaw Springs (8 Sept. 1781) and compelled the enemy to fall back on Charleston. The triumph of the Patriot forces in the South was largely due to his generalship.

Griffith, David Lewelyn Wark (b. La Grange, Ky., 22 Jan. 1875; d. Hollywood, Calif., 23 July 1948), motion picture director and producer. After being connected with the stage for almost a decade, he played his 1st movie role in *The Eagle's Nest,* made at the Edison Studio, and in 1908 joined the Biograph Company as an assistant director, remaining with that unit until 1912. His 1st film was *The Adventures of Dollie.* Griffith won fame with *The Birth of a Nation,* which was made in 1914 and had its premiere at New York City on 3 Mar. 1915. Based on *The Clansman,* a novel by Thomas Dixon, Jr., *The Birth of a Nation* was produced on a $100,000 budget and earned approximately $48 million by the time Griffith died. Among the better known of the 500 pictures directed and produced by Griffith are *Intolerance* (1916), *Broken Blossoms* (1919), *Way Down East* (1920), *Orphans of the Storm* (1922), and *America* (1924). He was one of the founders of the United Artists Corporation in 1919, and retired in 1932. Among the foremost pioneers in the art of the motion picture, Griffith introduced technical devices such as the fade-out and fade-in, the close-up, long shots for crowd scenes, high and low angle shots, soft focus, mist photography, the vignette, and backlighting. His *Judith of Bethulia* was the 1st four-reeler.

Guggenheim, Daniel (b. Philadelphia, Pa., 9 July 1856; d. near Port Washington, Long Island, N.Y., 28 Sept. 1930), industrialist and philanthropist, served his mercantile apprenticeship in Switzerland and upon his return to the U.S. (1884) became active in the copper mining and smelting business in which his father, Meyer Guggenheim (1828–1905), had made heavy investments. He soon became the leading figure among the 7 Guggenheim sons. It was largely due to his planning that the combination and integration of copper mining, smelting, and refining took place on a large scale. With his brothers, he took control (1901) of the reorganized American Smelting & Refining Co., of which he served as president or chairman of the board at different times between 1901 and 1919. Under his guidance the enterprise took shape as a vast industrial empire. It extended its activities to South America and Africa; developed nitrate fields in Chile, tin mines in Bolivia, and rubber plantations and diamond fields in the Belgian Congo; set up subsidiaries such as the Utah Copper Co., the Guggenheim Exploration Company, the Chile Copper Co., the Chile Nitrate Co., and the Utah Copper Co.; and introduced mass production methods and technological improvements in mining and metallurgy. He established the Daniel and Florence Guggenheim Foundation and the Daniel Guggenheim Fund for the Promotion of Aeronautics; his brother, Simon (1867–1941), with his wife, the John Simon Guggenheim Memorial Foundation.

Hamilton, Alexander (b. Nevis, B.W.I., 11 Jan. 1755; d. New York City, 11 July 1804), statesman, after clerking at St. Croix, left for New York in 1773, in which year he entered King's College, where he wrote pamphlets in the Patriot cause (1774–75). At the outbreak of the Revolution he organized an artillery company and gained Washington's attention by his skillful conduct in campaigns around New York City. With rank of lt. col. he served as Washington's private secretary and aide-de-camp (1777–81). At his request he was given command of troops and fought at Yorktown (1781). Married Elizabeth, daughter of Philip Schuyler (1780). After a year in Congress (1782–83), he began law practice in New York. As a delegate from New York to the Annapolis Convention (1786) he drafted report which led to the assembling of the Constitutional Convention (1787), where he advocated an extremely strong central government. He worked wholeheartedly for the ratification of the Constitution, writing more than half of the *Federalist* papers (1787–88), and carrying the New York convention (1788) despite strong opposition. As 1st Secretary of the Treasury (1789–95), he devised the U.S. fiscal program (1790), recommending the funding of both the foreign and domestic debt at par, assumption by the Federal government of Revolutionary state debts, and supplementing revenue from duties with an excise tax to bring national authority home to every citizen. He also recommended the creation of a national bank (1791), which he justified under the "implied powers" of the Constitution, and tariffs for industry, bounties for agriculture, and Federally sponsored internal improvements (1791). His policies ("Hamiltonian system") were supported by the Federalists and opposed by the Jeffersonian Republicans (1792). Resigning from the Cabinet, he resumed law practice in New York, interrupted by assuming command of the army, 2nd only to Washington, when war with France appeared likely (1798–1800). Federalist leader of New York, he was in opposition to President John Adams. By throwing support to Jefferson (1800) he thwarted Aaron Burr's ambitions for the Presidency and killed his chances for the governorship of New York (1804). Challenged by Burr to a duel on account of his acrimonious comments, he was fatally shot at Weehawken, N.J., and died the following day.

Hammerstein, Oscar, 2nd (b. 12 July 1895, New York City; d. Doylestown, Pa., 23 Aug. 1960), librettist, was graduated from Columbia (B.A., 1916), and quickly won acclaim for the books and lyrics he wrote, often in collaboration, for many

Broadway musicals. Notable among his early productions were *Rose Marie* (music by Rudolf Friml, 1924); the *Desert Song* (1926) and *New Moon* (1928), for both of which Sigmund Romberg wrote the music; and his adaptation of Edna Ferber's novel *Show Boat* (1927) to Jerome Kern's score. His collaboration with Richard Rodgers (*q.v.*) established the musical comedy, employing serious plots and sometimes serious overtones, as a distinctively American contribution to the drama. Their first smash hit, *Oklahoma* (1943, Special Pulitzer Award, 1944), was followed by *Carousel* (1945), based on Molnar's *Liliom;* the international success, *South Pacific* (Pulitzer Prize Award for the Drama, 1949); and *The King and I* (1951). At the time of Hammerstein's death their last joint production, *The Sound of Music,* was playing on Broadway. The songs of Rodgers and Hammerstein quickly became American classics, among them "The Surrey with the Fringe on Top," "Some Enchanted Evening," "Bali H'ai," "I'm in Love with a Wonderful Guy."

Hancock, John (b. North Braintree, now Quincy, Mass., 12 Jan. 1737; d. there, 8 Oct. 1793), merchant and Revolutionary leader, 1st signer of the Declaration of Independence. He was graduated from Harvard (1754) and entered the shipping trade; became (1763) a partner in the leading Boston mercantile house of Thomas Hancock & Co., and its head in 1764. He took part in the protest (1765) against the Stamp Act and in 1768 was defended by John Adams in a *cause célèbre* involving the seizure by customs officers of Hancock's sloop *Liberty* on charges of illegal trading. He was elected (1769) to the Massachusetts General Court, became (1770) head of the Boston town committee, and thereafter took a leading part in the Patriot cause. Elected (1774) president of the Mass. Provincial Congress, he and Samuel Adams were singled out for punishment in Governor Gage's proclamation (12 June 1775) and expressly denied amnesty. In 1775 he was chosen delegate to the 2nd Continental Congress, of which he served as president (24 May 1775–29 Oct. 1777). Alone with Charles Thomson, sec-

retary of the Congress, he signed the Declaration of Independence 4 July 1776. The other delegates attached their signatures later. In 1780 he was elected the 1st governor of Mass., serving (1780–85, 1787–93) in that capacity for 9 terms. Again elected president of the Continental Congress on 23 Nov. 1785, illness prevented him from serving, and he resigned on 29 May 1786. He presided (1788) over the Mass. convention for ratifying the Federal Constitution.

Hand, Learned (b. Albany, N.Y., 27 Jan. 1872–   ), jurist, was graduated summa cum laude from Harvard (1893); returned to secure his M.A. the following year, and his LL.B. from Harvard Law School (1896). Admitted to the N.Y. bar (1897), he clerked or practiced in Albany (1897–1902), then moved to New York City (1902), becoming a member (1904) of the firm of Gould & Wilkie. U.S. District Judge, Southern District of N.Y. (1909–24), he ran unsuccessfully (1913) as a Progressive for the post of Chief Judge of the N.Y. Court of Appeals. He served as Judge of the U.S. Circuit Court, 2nd Circuit, from 1924 until his retirement (1951), rendering notable opinions in the fields of maritime law, taxation, banking, trade-marks, and labor law. In the antitrust suit against the Aluminum Co. of America he declared: "Congress did not condone 'good trusts' and condemn 'bad' ones; it forbade all." He upheld (1950) the conviction of the 11 Communist leaders under the Smith Act, interpreting Justice Holmes's "clear and present danger" test to mean that the courts must ascertain "whether the gravity of the 'evil,' discounted by its improbability, justifies such invasion of free speech as is necessary to avoid the danger." A literary craftsman and master of epigram, he made numerous addresses, including his eloquent "The Spirit of Liberty" delivered (1944) at an "I Am an American Day" ceremony in Central Park, N.Y. (pub. with other papers, 1952). Recognizing the values of detachment, skepticism, and nonconformity, he regarded the key to his philosophy to be epitomized in Oliver Cromwell's plea before the Battle of Dunbar: "I beseech ye in the bowells of Christ, think that ye may be mistaken."

Hanna, Marcus Alonzo (b. New Lisbon, Ohio, 24 Sept. 1837; d. Washington, D.C., 15 Feb. 1904), businessman and politician, attended Western Reserve College for a brief time, entered the grocery and commission business at Cleveland, and in 1867 transferred his interests to the coal and iron trade in that city, becoming (1885) head of the firm of M. A. Hanna & Co. He also helped establish the Union National Bank, became owner of the Cleveland Opera House and the Cleveland *Herald,* and dominated the city's street railway system. Active in local politics, he was chosen a member of the Republican state committee and soon became a power in Ohio politics. A break between him and Joseph B. Foraker in 1888 led Hanna to support Congressman William McKinley, whom he backed for the Ohio governorship (1891, 1893) and groomed as a Presidential candidate. In 1894–95 Hanna withdrew from business activity to devote himself to launching a McKinley boom. A skilled and astute political manager, Hanna conducted a preconvention McKinley campaign for which he paid most of the financial cost. McKinley was nominated on the 1st ballot at the Republican convention in 1896. In recognition of his political ability, Hanna was chosen chairman of the Republican national committee. Chiefly by levies on businessmen and corporations, Hanna raised the unprecedented sum of $3,500,000 for the Republican national campaign. He was elected (1897) to the Senate, where he defended large corporate enterprises and supported ship subsidies and the Panama route for an isthmian canal. He was an intimate adviser to Presidents McKinley and Theodore Roosevelt. Although Hanna became in the public mind almost synonymous with big business, he supported labor's right to organize and was chairman of the executive committee of the National Civic Federation. Shortly before his death there were signs that powerful Republican elements in the East were hoping to secure for him the Presidential nomination in 1904.

Harding, Warren Gamaliel (b. Corsica, Ohio, 2 Nov. 1865; d. San Francisco, Cal., 2 Aug. 1923), 29th President of the U.S., attended Ohio Central College, Iberia (1879–82), studied law briefly, and (1884) became owner and editor of Marion *Star,* weekly, later a daily. He entered Republican politics as a protégé of Sen. Joseph B. Foraker, was elected to the state senate (1900–04), became lieutenant governor (1904–06), but was defeated in the gubernatorial election (1910). U.S. senator from Ohio (1915–21), he supported the 18th Amendment and the Volstead Act, and was known for his party regularity. At the Republican National Convention (1920) he was designated by the party leaders and nominated after a deadlock in the balloting between Gen. Leonard Wood and Frank O. Lowden. Straddling the League issue and pledging a "return to normalcy," he was elected by a landslide vote. Despite appointments to his Cabinet of men of such standing as Hughes and Hoover, many of his choices were mediocrities (Attorney General Harry M. Daugherty of the "Ohio Gang" and Secretary of the Interior Albert B. Fall). The major achievement of his administration was the Washington Conference for naval limitation (1921–22). On a return trip from Alaska he died suddenly at San Francisco. Subsequent exposure of corruption in the Departments of Interior, Justice, and Navy, the Veterans Bureau, and Alien Property Custodian stamped his administration as both corrupt and incompetent.

Harlan, John Marshall (b. Boyle Co., Ky., 1 June 1833; d. Washington, D.C., 14 Oct. 1911), jurist, was graduated from Centre College (1850), studied law at Transylvania University, and was admitted to the Ky. bar (1859). Adjutant general of Ky. (1851) and Judge of Franklin County (1858), he served in the Civil War as col., 10th Kentucky Infantry (1861–63). State attorney general (1863–67), unsuccessful candidate for governor in 1871 and again in 1875, he was appointed by President Hayes associate justice of the U.S. Supreme Court (1877–1911). His dissents (in 316 cases) were notable. He dissented in the sugar-trust cases (1895), opposing the majority's narrow interpretation of the commerce power; vigorously challenged the majority of the court which held the income tax unconstitutional (1895); and dissented in *Lochner* v. *N.Y.* (1905) on the ground that limiting hours of employment in an unhealthful occupation was a justifiable infringement on liberty of contract. He wrote the majority opinion dissolving the Northern Securities Co. (1904) and sustaining the Sherman Antitrust Act, maintained in the *Insular Cases* (1901) that "the Constitution followed the flag," and declared Federal legislation barring "yellow-dog" contracts in railroad employment to infringe upon the 5th Amendment (1907).

Harper, William Rainey (b. New Concord, Ohio, 24 July 1856; d. Chicago, Ill., 10 Jan. 1906), educator and scholar, was graduated (1870) from Muskingum College (Ohio), where he taught Hebrew (1872–73), and in 1874, at the age of 18, received the degree of Ph.D. at Yale. He taught at Denison University, Granville, Ohio, from 1876 to 1879, when he became teacher of Semitic languages at the Baptist Union Theological Seminary in Chicago, and at Yale (1881–86), and was active in the Chautauqua movement, giving summer courses in Semitic languages and Biblical studies. In 1891 he assumed the presidency of the newly founded University of Chicago, a post he held until his death. He introduced such features as the university press, university extension, the summer quarter, and the division of the academic year into 4 quarters. He guided the University of Chicago through its complex period of initial growth and was instrumental in assembling there a faculty that was among the most brilliant of its time. His work as a Hebraist produced *The Priestly Element in the Old Testament* (1902), *The Prophetic Element in the Old Testament* (1905), and *Critical and Exegetical Commentary on Amos and Hosea* (1905).

Harris, Joel Chandler (b. near Eatonton, Ga., 9 Dec. 1848; d. Atlanta, 3 July 1908), journalist, author, became (1862) printer's devil for Joseph Addison Turner's *Countryman*. He worked for 6 mos. (1866) for the publisher of the New Orleans *Crescent Monthly*, but thereafter never left his home state except for brief trips. A growing reputation as a humorist earned him a position on the Savannah *Morning News*, and then with the Atlanta *Constitution*. His "Uncle Remus Stories," 1st published in the Atlanta *Constitution*, made that paper nationally famous. His 1st collection, *Uncle Remus, His Songs and His Sayings* (1880), was enormously popular, especially the "Tar-Baby" story, and was followed by a series down to 1918. A master of dialect, he used folk tales, but the dialogue and character of Uncle Remus and the world of animals were uniquely his own. In *Mingo and Other Sketches in Black and White* (1884) and *Free Joe and Other Sketches* (1887), he captured the white Georgia cracker on printed page.

Harris, Townsend (b. Sandy Hill, N.Y., 3 Oct. 1804; d. New York City, 25 Feb. 1873), diplomat, was largely self-educated, beginning work in a drygoods store in New York City at 13. Later he established a family partnership for importing china. Elected to the Bd. of Education as a Democrat (1846), he launched a vigorous campaign, against strong opposition, for a free city college, and carried through the necessary legislation to establish (1847) the College of the City of New York. Following his mother's death (1847), the bachelor Harris bought a trading ship and made trips in the Pacific and Indian oceans. In 1853 he applied for a consular post. First assigned (1855) to Ningpo, he managed, through the influence of Secy. of State William L. Marcy and Seward, to be named consul general to Japan, a post resulting from ratification of the Perry Treaty. Responsible for the 1st U.S.-Japanese commercial agreement (17 June 1857) and the treaty of 29 July 1858, he exercised at Yeddo (Tokyo) great influence over the Japanese govt. Resigning his post with Lincoln's election, he returned to N.Y. and became a War Democrat.

Harrison, Benjamin (b. North Bend, Ohio, 20 Aug. 1833; d. Indianapolis, Ind., 13 Mar. 1901), 23rd President of the U.S., grandson of William Henry Harrison, 9th President, was graduated from Miami University (1852), admitted to the Cincinnati bar (1853), commenced practice in Indianapolis (1854), and was reporter of the Ind. supreme court, 1860–62, and again, 1864–68, after service in the Civil War (commissioned 2nd lt.; raised 70th Indiana Regiment and became its col.). Defeated as Republican candidate for governor of Ind. (1876), he declined a post in Garfield's Cabinet, having been elected to the U.S. Senate (1881–87), where he opposed Cleveland's pension vetoes and advocated civil service reform. Defeated for reelection, he was the Republican nominee for President (1888) and defeated Cleveland. During his administration (1889–93) the McKinley Tariff and Sherman Silver Act were passed, Civil War pensions were augmented, and imperialist policies pressed in the Pacific. Renominated (1892), he was defeated by Cleveland, and resumed his law practice, serving as chief counsel for Venezuela in arbitration of her boundary dispute with Great Britain.

Harrison, Ross Granville (b. Germantown, Pa., 13 Jan. 1870–), biologist. He was graduated from Johns Hopkins (A.B., 1889; Ph.D., 1894) and the University of Bonn (M.D., 1899), was a lecturer in morphology (1894–95) at Bryn Mawr College, and taught anatomy at Johns Hopkins (1896–1907) and anatomy and biology at Yale (1907–38). He was chairman (1938–46) of the National Research Council, managing editor (1904–46) of the *Journal of Experimental Zoology,* and coeditor (1907–10) of the *Journal of Morphology.* He was the 1st to adapt (1907) the hanging-drop culture method to the study of embryonic tissues and demonstrated the histogenesis of the peripheral nervous system. He has done important researches in the development of fins of fishes, transplantation in amphibian larvae, and cultivation of tissues outside the organism. Among the honors held by him is the John Scott Medal and Premium of the City of Philadelphia (1925) for inventing devices for tissue grafting and tissue culture.

Harrison, William Henry (b. Berkeley, Charles City Co., Va., 9 Feb. 1773; d. Washington, D.C., 4 Apr. 1841), 9th President of the U.S., attended Hampden-Sidney College (1787–90), studied medicine briefly at the University of Pennsylvania, then entered the army, attaining a captaincy, resigning (1798) to accept appointment as Secretary of the Northwest Territory. He was elected its 1st delegate to Congress (1799) and was the drafter of the Land Act of 1800. Appointed by President John Adams 1st governor of Indiana Territory (1801–12) and a special commissioner to deal with the Indians, he negotiated several boundary treaties. Confronted with Indian resistance under Tecumseh to further white encroachments, he won a nominal victory at Tippecanoe (7 Nov. 1811), and during the War of 1812, when he held the rank of maj. gen., he decisively defeated both the British and the Indians at the Battle of the Thames (5 Oct. 1813). Congressman from Ohio (1816–19), state senator (1819–21), U.S. senator from Ohio (1825–28), he was appointed U.S. Minister to Colombia (1828), but recalled by Jackson the following year. Retiring to North Bend, Ohio, he became clerk of the common pleas court of Hamilton County. Candidate for the Presidency on one of the Whig tickets (1836), with Anti-Masonic support, he was defeated by Van Buren, but was the successful Whig nominee (1840), staging his "log cabin and hard cider" campaign. He died of pneumonia a month after his inauguration.

Hawthorne, Nathaniel (b. Salem, Mass., 4 July 1804; d. Plymouth, N.H., 18/19 May 1864), novelist and writer of tales. Born of Puritan ancestry, he was graduated from Bowdoin College (1825) and returned to Salem, where he led a secluded life devoted to the mastery of his craft. He issued at his own expense the anonymously published novel, *Fanshawe* (1828), and began publishing in the *Token,* an annual brought out by Samuel G. Goodrich, the stories later collected in *Twice-Told Tales* (1837; enlarged ed., 1842). He was editor (1836) of the *American Magazine of Useful and Entertaining Knowledge,* also published by Goodrich, for whom he compiled *Peter Parley's Universal History* (1837) and wrote children's books such as *Grand-*

father's Chair (1841), *Famous Old People* (1841), *Liberty Tree* (1841), and *Biographical Stories for Children* (1842). With the aid of Franklin Pierce, whom he had known at Bowdoin, he secured a post as weigher and gauger (1839–41) in the Boston Custom House. He spent several months (1841–42) at Brook Farm, which furnished him with the setting for *The Blithedale Romance* (1852); was married (9 July 1842) to Sophia Amelia Peabody of Salem; settled in the Old Manse at Concord (1842–45); and was surveyor of the port of Salem from 1846 to 1849, during which time he published *Mosses from an Old Manse* (1846). His best-known novel, *The Scarlet Letter* (1850), dealt with the moral decadence of 17th-century New England Puritanism, and was followed by *The House of the Seven Gables* (1851), *The Snow Image and Other Twice-Told Tales* (1852), *A Wonder-Book for Girls and Boys* (1852), and *Tanglewood Tales for Girls and Boys* (1853). In 1850 Hawthorne moved to Lenox, Mass., where he became acquainted with Herman Melville, but in a few years returned to Concord. As a reward for writing a campaign biography, *The Life of Franklin Pierce* (1852), he was appointed (1853) U.S. consul at Liverpool, a post he held until 1860. The last books by him published during his lifetime were *The Marble Faun* (1860) and *Our Old Home* (1863). Among his other works are *Passages from the American Notebooks* (1868), *Passages from the English Notebooks* (1870), *Septimius Felton* (1871), *Passages from the French and Italian Notebooks* (1871), *The Dolliver Romance* (1876), *Dr. Grimshawe's Secret* (1883), and *The Ancestral Footstep* (1883). Among his better-known tales are "Ethan Brand," "The Great Stone Face," "The Maypole of Merrymount," "Dr. Heidegger's Experiment," and "The Ambitious Guest."

Hay, John Milton (b. Salem, Ind., 12 Oct. 1838; d. Lake Sunapee, N.H., 1 July 1905), was graduated from Brown University (1858), admitted to the Ill. bar (1861), and practiced in Springfield, where he was drawn into the Lincoln circle. Accompanying Lincoln to Washington as assistant private secretary, he served until the President's death. Subsequently he was 1st secretary of legation at Paris (1865–67) and Madrid (1868–70) and chargé d'affaires at Vienna (1867–68). On his return to the U.S. (1870), he became an editorial writer on the New York *Tribune* (1870–75), then moved to Cleveland, returning to Washington as assistant secretary of state under William M. Evarts (1879–81). McKinley's Ambassador to Great Britain (1897–98) and thereafter, until his death, McKinley's and Theodore Roosevelt's Secretary of State (1898–1905), he supported the Open Door policy in China, and concluded the Hay-Pauncefote Treaty with Great Britain (1900–01) and the Hay-Herrán and Hay-Bunau-Varilla treaties with Colombia and Panama respectively. Poet and novelist, as well as historian, he published *Pike County Ballads* and *Castilian Days* (1871), the antilabor union novel *The Bread Winners* (anon., 1883), and, in collaboration with John G. Nicolay, *Abraham Lincoln: A History* (10 vols., 1890), and *Abraham Lincoln: Complete Works* (2 vols. 1894).

Hayes, Rutherford Birchard (b. Delaware, Ohio, 4 Oct. 1822; d. Fremont, Ohio, 17 Jan. 1893), 19th President of the U.S., was graduated from Kenyon College (1842) and Harvard Law School (1845); was admitted to the Ohio bar and commenced practice at Fremont (1845), removing to Cincinnati (1849). A Whig and then a Republican (from 1854), he was city solicitor (1858–61), resigning to become governor of Ohio (1868–72). Running on a "sound money" platform, he was elected for a 3rd term (1875) and established himself as the logical candidate of the anti-Blaine forces at the Republican National Convention the following year, where he won the nomination. Although Tilden, the Democratic candidate, secured a larger popular vote, Hayes was adjudged by the partisan Electoral Commission to have obtained 1 more electoral vote (185–184). Despite party factional disputes and Democratic control of the Lower House (1876) and of both Houses (1878), his administration ended military reconstruction by withdrawal of Federal troops from S.C. (1877) and made indecisive efforts toward civil service reform. On issues of labor and finance he was conservative, calling out Federal troops to suppress the railroad strike (1877) and vetoing the Bland-Allison Silver Coinage Act (1878), which was passed over his veto.

Hemingway, Ernest (b. Oak Park, Ill., 21 July 1898; d. Ketchum, Idaho, 2 July 1961), novelist and short-story writer. After working as a reporter on the Kansas City *Star*, he went to France as a volunteer ambulance driver in World War I and then enlisted in the Italian army, winning 2 medals for battle actions in which he was wounded. After the war he served as a newspaper correspondent in the Near East for the Toronto *Star* and then settled in Paris, where he became associated with the expatriates of the "lost generation," whose leading spokesman he became. Hemingway has spent most of his life abroad, chiefly in Europe and Cuba, and was a war correspondent during the Spanish Civil War and in France during World War II. His stories and novels, most of which are concerned with the disintegration of private values in a world between wars, are marked by a high level of craftsmanship and a terse prose style that has had a wide influence on writing in the U.S. and elsewhere. Hemingway's novels include *The Sun Also Rises* (1926), *A Farewell to Arms* (1929), *To Have and Have Not* (1937), *For Whom the Bell Tolls* (1940), *Across the River and into the Trees* (1950), and *The Old Man and the Sea* (1952). His volumes of short stories are *In Our Time* (1924), *Men Without Women* (1927), and *Winner Take Nothing* (1933), collected in *The Fifth Column and the First Forty-Nine Stories* (1938). *Death in the Afternoon* (1932) deals with bullfighting and *Green Hills of Africa* (1935) is about big-game hunting. He was awarded the Nobel Prize in Literature in 1954 for *The Old Man and the Sea* (1952).

Hench, Philip Showalter (b. Pittsburgh, Pa., 28 Feb. 1896–), physician. He was graduated from Lafayette College (B.A., 1916) and the University of Pittsburgh (M.D., 1920), and was a fellow (1921–23) and 1st assistant in medicine (1923–25) at the Mayo Clinic, Rochester, Minn., where he became (1926) staff consultant and head of the section on rheumatic diseases. Since 1928 he has taught at the Mayo Foundation and Graduate School of Medicine at the University of Minnesota. He has done pioneering work on cortisone and ACTH therapy in crippling rheumatic diseases, particularly rheumatoid arthritis, and received the Nobel prize (1950) for discoveries concerning hormones of the adrenal cortex.

Henry, Joseph (b. Albany, N.Y., 17 Dec. 1797; d. Washington, D.C., 13 May 1878), physicist. He attended the Albany Academy, where he became (1826) professor of mathematics and natural philosophy and carried out experiments in the magnetic fields created by electrical currents. In the course of these researches he improved William Sturgeon's electromagnet, increasing the magnetic condition of its core by an arrangement that is still the basis of the modern electromagnet. In a paper published in the *American Journal of Science* (Jan. 1831), Henry described his discovery of the quantity and intensity magnets, correctly predicting that the latter type would be used in the electromagnetic telegraph. His findings were indispensable to the commercial development of the telegraph. Another paper published by him on electromagnetic induction (July 1832) paralleled contemporaneous and independent researches by Faraday and led to Henry's important discoveries in self-induction (the modern practical unit of inductance, the henry, is named after him). In 1832 he was named professor of natural philosophy in the College of New Jersey, where his continued researches foreshadowed many of the developments in the modern science of electricity. He discovered (1842) the oscillatory nature of electrical discharge. In 1846 he was appointed the 1st secretary and director of the Smithsonian Institution at Washington, D.C.; his 1st report to its Board of Regents laid down the broad policies, particularly those relating to original research and the free diffusion of knowledge, that have since guided the Smithsonian. Henry introduced ($c.$1850) the system of transmitting weather reports by telegraph and using them for forecasting weather conditions, thus laying the foundation for the U.S. Weather Bureau. He also made valuable researches in fog signaling. One of the organizers of the American Association for the Advancement of Science, he was chosen its president (1849) and served as president of the National Academy of Science (1868–78).

Henry, Patrick (b. Hanover County, Va., 29 May 1736; d. at his plantation, "Red Hill," Charlotte County, Va., 6 June 1799), Revolutionary patriot, orator, and statesman. After an early career as a storekeeper and farmer, he read law, was licensed to practice (1760), and soon became one of the leading lawyers in western Va. His fame as an orator began in 1763, when he appeared for the defense in the "parson's cause" and invoked the theory of mutual compact in making a plea against the royal disallowance of the "twopenny act" passed by the Va. Assembly. In 1765 he became a member of the House of Burgesses and emerged as a leader of the frontier and backcountry elements in their contest with the conservative Tidewater interests. With the adoption of the Stamp Act, he proposed 7 resolutions (29 May 1765), one of which contended that Va. enjoyed complete legislative autonomy, and in their behalf made the speech later reputed to have closed with the famous injunction: "Caesar had his Brutus— Charles the first, his Cromwell—and George the third—may profit by their example. . . . If *this* be treason, make the most of it." Under his leadership the legislators gathered at Raleigh Tavern (27 May 1774), after Lord Dunmore dissolved the colonial assembly, and issued the calls for a Va. convention and a continental congress. On 23 Mar. 1775, in a speech urging resistance to British policy and in advocating the establishment of an armed force, he declared: "Give me liberty, or give me death!" He was outlawed in a proclamation issued by Lord Dunmore (6 May 1775). Henry took his seat in the Continental Congress on 18 May 1775, helped draft the Va. constitution of 1776, and as governor of Va. (1776–79) dispatched in 1778

George Rogers Clark on a military mission to the Illinois country. After the war, Henry's political views changed sharply. He served again as governor (1784–86), but at the Va. convention (1788) for ratifying the Constitution opposed its adoption as inimical to state sovereignty. A leader in the movement for the Bill of Rights, he wrote the Va. appeal to the 1st Congress and the other states for amendments to the Constitution. In his closing years he was a Federalist.

Hill, James Jerome (b. near Rockwood, Ontario, Canada, 16 Sept. 1838; d. St. Paul, Minn., 29 May 1916), railroad builder, went to work at the age of 14 as a clerk in a village store, lost the sight of 1 eye by the accidental discharge of an arrow, and in 1856 became clerk in St. Paul, Minn., in a steamboat transportation firm. By 1865 he had gone into the forwarding and transportation business for himself, organized (1870) the Red River Transportation Co., and joined (1878) a syndicate that built the Canadian Pacific R.R. and purchased (1878) the St. Paul and Pacific R.R., which was expanded (1890) into the Great Northern R.R., from Lake Superior to Puget Sound. Without the aid of government land grants, Hill's line weathered financial storms. Together with J. P. Morgan, Hill was involved in a struggle with Edward H. Harriman and Jacob H. Schiff for control of the Northern Pacific R.R., which precipitated the stock market panic of 1901. The Northern Security Co., organized (1901) as a holding company of all Hill's interests, was dissolved by the U. S. Supreme Court (1904) as violating the Sherman Act. Because of his notable role in the development of the Northwest, Hill has been called the "empire builder."

Hillman, Sidney (b. Zagare, Lithuania, 23 Mar. 1887; d. Point Lookout, N.Y., 10 July, 1946), labor leader, was educated at the Slobodka Rabbinical Seminary in Lithuania, and came to the U.S. in 1907, becoming a clothing worker with the Chicago firm of Hart, Schaffner, and Marx. The agreement which he negotiated with that firm (1911) formed the basis for the impartial chairman plan

(1912), adopted by other industries. First president of the Amalgamated Clothing Workers (1914), he organized the N.Y., Rochester, Philadelphia, and Chicago industries and initiated such union activities as cooperative housing and banking. An advocate of industrial unionism, he quit the A.F. of L. (1935) to cofound the C.I.O., of which he became vice-president (1935–40) and headed the textile workers' organizing drive. Codirector of the Office of Production Management, later WPB (1940–42), he cofounded Labor's Non-Partisan League (1936) to support the re-election of Franklin D. Roosevelt and headed (1943) the C.I.O.–P.A.C. to support Roosevelt and congressmen sympathetic to labor. A central figure at the Democratic National Convention of 1944 ("Clear it with Sidney," F.D.R. told the party managers), he threw his support to Harry S. Truman for the Vice-Presidential nomination. Founder and chairman (1944–45) of the American Labor party, he was instrumental in setting up the World Federation of Trade Unions (1945).

Hoe, Richard March (b. New York City, 12 Sept. 1812; d. Florence, Italy, 7 June 1886), inventor and manufacturer. Educated in the public schools of New York, he entered (1827) the printing-press factory owned by his father, whom he succeeded in 1830. At about that time the Hoe Company was manufacturing a single small cylinder press; in 1837 the double small cylinder press improved by Hoe was perfected and put into production; and during the same period Hoe designed and introduced the single large cylinder press, the 1st flat bed and cylinder press ever used in America. To meet the demands of newspaper publishers, Hoe invented and designed (1845–46) the rotary printing press, the 1st of which, capable of printing 8,000 papers an hour, was installed (1847) in the plant of the Philadelphia *Public Ledger*. This machine was the predecessor of the web press (1871) designed by Hoe and Stephen D. Tucker. First installed in the plant of the New York *Tribune,* the web press printed simultaneously from a continuous roll of paper both sides of a sheet at the rate of 18,000 papers an hour. Hoe also intro-

duced the stop cylinder press (1853) and devised the triangular form folder (1881). The latter, in combination with the web press and the curved stereotype plate, is the foundation of the modern newspaper printing press.

Holmes, Oliver Wendell (b. Cambridge, Mass., 29 Aug. 1809; d. Boston, 7 Oct. 1894), author and physician, was graduated from Harvard College (1829), studied law for a year, and then turned to medicine, graduating from Harvard Medical School (1836) and studying in Paris (1833–35). He commenced practice in Boston (1836); was professor of anatomy at Dartmouth (1838–40) and Parkman professor of anatomy and physiology at Harvard Medical School (1847–82) as well as dean (1847–53). His medical papers include "Homeopathy and Its Kindred Delusions" (1842) and, most notable, "The Contagiousness of Puerperal Fever" (1843), in which he demonstrated, statistically, that the disease was spread by contagion, a position which, despite criticism, was entirely vindicated by Semmelweis' study (1861). Accomplished as a poet ("Old Ironsides," 1830; "The Chambered Nautilus," "Wonderful One-Hoss Shay"), he was especially renowned as lecturer, conversationalist, and essayist, contributing extensively to the *Atlantic Monthly* after its founding (1857) and publishing *The Autocrat at the Breakfast Table* (1858), followed by *The Professor at the Breakfast Table* (1860) and *The Poet at the Breakfast Table* (1872). In addition, he published 3 novels of heredity and psychology (*Elsie Venner,* 1861; *The Guardian Angel,* 1867; and *A Mortal Antipathy,* 1885) and biographies of Motley (1879) and Emerson (1885).

Holmes, Oliver Wendell, Jr. (b. Boston, 8 Mar. 1841; d. Washington, D.C., 6 Mar. 1935), jurist, son of Oliver Wendell Holmes, was graduated from Harvard (1861) and served in the Civil War for 3 years, being wounded at Ball's Bluff, Antietam, and Fredericksburg, and attaining the rank of lt. col. On graduation from the Harvard Law School (1866) he practiced in Boston and became instructor in constitutional law at Harvard (1870–

71), professor of law (1882), and editor of the *American Law Review* (1870–73). Associate justice (1882) of the Mass. supreme judicial court, and chief justice (1899–1902), he was appointed by President Theodore Roosevelt an associate justice of the U.S. Supreme Court (1902), serving until his retirement at the age of 90 (12 Jan. 1932). The court's most notable dissenter and leader of its liberal wing, he sharply criticized the Sherman Antitrust Act (*Northern Securities' Case*), but his conception of a "current of commerce" (*Swift Case*, 1905) paved the way for increasingly broad interpretations of the commerce clause. In his dissent in *Lochner* v. *N.Y.* (1905) he declared that "the 14th Amendment does not enact Mr. Herbert Spencer's *Social Statics*." His opposition to the rule in the *Adair* (1908) and *Coppage* (1915) cases foreshadowed later reversals by the court. He also dissented in *Hammer* v. *Dagenhart* (1918), where the majority invalidated the Federal child labor law. In *Schenck* v. *U.S.* (1919) he enunciated the "clear and present danger" doctrine to govern the interpretation of the 1st Amendment, although in the *Abrams Case* (1919) he made an eloquent plea for "free trade in ideas." In later opinions he attacked wiretapping as "dirty business" (1928) and denounced the use of the 14th Amendment to "prevent the making of social experiments" (*Truax* v. *Corrigan*, 1921). He refused to accept the common law as a fundamental all-pervasive set of principles and denied that it was "a brooding omnipresence in the sky." He edited the 12th edition of Kent's *Commentaries* (1873); his published works include *The Common Law* (1881) and *Collected Legal Papers* (1920).

Homer, Winslow (b. Boston, Mass., 24 Feb. 1836; d. Scarboro, Me., 29 Sept. 1910), painter and illustrator. After serving his apprenticeship under Bufford, a lithographer in Boston, he established his studio there (1857), drew illustrations for *Ballou's Pictorial* and *Harper's Weekly,* and in 1859 moved to New York, where he continued his training at the National Academy of Design. During the Civil War he drew battlefield scenes for *Harper's Weekly* and recorded these impressions in such paintings as *Rainy Day in Camp, Sharpshooter on Picket Duty,* and *Prisoners from the Front.* He gradually abandoned magazine illustration and anecdotal painting, and after 1882, when he established his home at Scarboro, Me., began work on the long line of marine pieces that occupied the rest of his life. In Me., and during his annual journeys to the Caribbean, he produced oil paintings and water colors marked by original design, virile draftsmanship, and vivid color. His works include *The Life Line, Eight Bells, Sun and Cloud, Summer Night, The Fallen Deer, Northeaster, Cannon Rock,* and *The Wreck* (also p. 638).

Hoover, Herbert Clark (b. West Branch, Iowa, 10 Aug. 1874–   ), 31st President of the U.S., moved to Ore. and was graduated from Stanford University (1895) as a mining engineer. After several years in the U.S. he engaged in mining operations abroad, 1st in Australia, then in China, Africa, Central and South America, and Russia. During World War I he was notably effective as chairman of the American Relief Committee in London, as chairman of the Commission for Relief in Belgium, and as U.S. Food Administrator. Appointed Secretary of Commerce (1921–28), he served in both the Harding and Coolidge Cabinets, expanding the activities of that department and fostering trade associations. Republican nominee, he was elected President (1928). To deal with the economic collapse which occurred in the 1st year of his administration, he counted upon economic forces to bring about a revival and was hesitant to extend Federal activities, although at the end of his term he signed an act creating the Reconstruction Finance Corporation (1932) to extend loans to banks and large business enterprises. On 20 June 1931 he announced a 1-yr. moratorium on all intergovernmental debts. Renominated, he was defeated (1932) by Franklin D. Roosevelt. He served (1947–49, 1953–55) as chairman of the Commissions on Organization of the Executive Branch of the Government (Hoover Commissions). An isolationist prior to 1941, he advocated

(1952) U.S. military withdrawal from Western Europe. His works include *Memoirs* (3 vols., 1951–52) and *The Ordeal of Woodrow Wilson* (1958).

Houston, Samuel (b. near Lexington, Va., 2 Mar. 1793; d. San Antonio, Tex., 26 July 1863), soldier and statesman, removed to Blount Co., Tenn. (1807), clerked in a trader's store, left home, and lived nearly 3 years with the Cherokee. On return, he taught in a country school. In the War of 1812 he served under Andrew Jackson against the Creeks and was wounded at Horseshoe Bend (28 Mar. 1814). After assisting in the removal of the Cherokee from Tennessee to present Ark. (1817–18), he resigned from the army, studied law in Nashville, and was admitted to the bar. Congressman, 1823–27, and governor of Tenn., 1827–29, he resigned after his wife left him and was adopted into the Cherokee nation. Jackson sent him to Tex. to negotiate a treaty with the Indians (1832) and he settled at Nacogdoches (1833). He was elected a delegate to the San Felipe constitutional convention, which petitioned for separation of Tex. from Cohuila (1833). With the outbreak of the War for Texan Independence he became commander in chief of the Texan army (1835). He surprised and routed Santa Anna at San Jacinto (21 Apr. 1836), thereby achieving Texan independence. The newly founded (1836) city of Houston was named for him. Elected president of Tex. (1836–38) and reelected (1841–44), he secured recognition of the republic by the U.S. After Tex. was admitted to the Union (1845), he became one of the 1st 2 senators (1846–59). A Union Democrat, he opposed the Kansas-Nebraska Bill (1854). Elected governor of Tex. (1859), he opposed secession, refused to espouse the Confederate cause, and was deposed (18 Mar. 1861).

Howe, Elias (b. Spencer, Mass., 9 July 1819; d. Brooklyn, N.Y., 3 Oct. 1867), inventor of the sewing machine. He was an apprentice (1835–37) in a cotton machinery factory in Lowell, Mass., and subsequently, while working in an instrument maker's shop in Cambridge, Mass., designed and constructed a sewing machine which he improved during the winter of 1844–45. The patent for the machine was issued on 10 Sept. 1846. Encountering indifference in the U.S., Howe marketed his machine in England to William Thomas, a London corset manufacturer, who also bought the English rights from Howe. After a quarrel that led to a break with Thomas, Howe returned to the U.S. to find that the English reputation of his machine had spread to his homeland. The lawsuits which Howe instituted against those (like Isaac M. Singer) whom he accused of infringing his patent lasted from 1849 to 1854 and ended in Howe's favor with the award of a royalty on every sewing machine that infringed his rights. His royalties for the period 1861–67 often amounted to $4,000 a week. He established (1865) the Howe Machine Co. of Bridgeport, Conn., whose perfected machine won the gold medal at the Paris Exhibition of 1867.

Howe, Samuel Gridley (b. Boston, Mass., 10 Nov. 1801; d. there, 9 Jan. 1876), humanitarian, reformer, was graduated from Brown Univ. (1821) and received his M.D. from Harvard (1824). Drawn to the Greek cause like other romantics of his time, he spent 6 yrs. fighting against the Turks, distributing food and clothing supplies, and aiding reconstruction. Appointed (1831) to run a Mass. school for the blind, he established it in his father's home and later in the Perkins mansion (Perkins Institution). His work with the blind demonstrated that the sightless could be economically and socially competent. During his 45 yrs. with the school he trained a staff in educating the blind, visiting 17 states to advance this cause. He taught the deaf and blind child Laura Bridgeman, demonstrating to an incredulous world the values of such training, and promoted the oral, as against the sign, method for instructing the deaf. From 1865–74 he headed the Mass. State Bd. of Charities, the 1st of its kind in the U.S. With his gifted wife, Julia Ward Howe (1819–1910), whom he married in 1843, he coedited the antislavery paper *The Commonwealth* and aided and abetted John Brown. He backed Horace Mann's fight for better schools, helped

Dorothea Dix in her campaign for care of the insane, and agitated for prison reform.

Howells, William Dean (b. Martin's Ferry, Belmont County, Ohio, 1 Mar. 1837; d. New York City, 11 May 1920), novelist and critic, spent his boyhood in several Ohio towns, including Dayton and Ashtabula, had little formal schooling, and at the age of 9 began setting type in his father's printing office. He served (1856–61) on the editorial staff of the *Ohio State Journal,* in association with John J. Piatt published *Poems of Two Friends* (1860), and after writing a campaign life of Lincoln (1860) served as U.S. consul at Venice (1861–65) and published *Venetian Life* (1866) and *Italian Journeys* (1867). Returning to the U.S. in 1865, he worked for the *Nation* and in 1866 became subeditor of the *Atlantic Monthly,* of which he was editor in chief from 1871 to 1881. During this period he formed his friendship with Henry James and gained an intimate knowledge of Boston and New England society. The novels published during this period were *Their Wedding Journey* (1872), *A Chance Acquaintance* (1873), *A Foregone Conclusion* (1875), *The Lady of the Aroostook* (1879), *The Undiscovered Country* (1880), *A Fearful Responsibility* (1881), and *Dr. Breen's Practice* (1881). After leaving the *Atlantic* he wrote serials for the *Century Magazine,* contributed (1886–91) influential critical writings to the "Editor's Study" in *Harper's Monthly,* and in 1891 moved to New York. After the Haymarket affair, Howells developed a deep interest in social and economic problems. During his middle and later period he wrote *A Modern Instance* (1881), *A Woman's Reason* (1883), *The Rise of Silas Lapham* (1885), *Indian Summer* (1886), *The Minister's Charge* (1887), *April Hopes* (1888), *Annie Kilburn* (1889), *A Hazard of New Fortunes* (1890), *The Quality of Mercy* (1892), *An Imperative Duty* (1893), *The World of Chance* (1893), *The Coast of Bohemia* (1893), *A Traveler from Altruria* (1894), *The Landlord at Lion's Head* (1897), and *Through the Eye of the Needle* (1907). His last novel was *The Leather-*

wood God (1916). He also wrote works of reminiscence, such as *Boys' Town* (1890), *My Year in a Log Cabin* (1893), *My Literary Passions* (1895), *Impressions and Experiences* (1896), *Literary Friends and Acquaintances* (1900), *My Mark Twain* (1910), and *Years of My Youth* (1916). His critical works, among them *Criticism and Fiction* (1891) and *Literature and Life* (1902), helped pave the way for the acceptance of realism in the American novel. Howells gave encouragement to such realist writers as Frank Norris, Stephen Crane, and Hamlin Garland.

Hughes, Charles Evans (b. Glen Falls, N.Y., 11 Apr. 1862; d. Osterville, Mass., 27 Aug. 1948), 10th chief justice of the U.S., was graduated from Brown University (1881) and received his law degree from Columbia (1884). His practice in New York City was temporarily interrupted by his professorship of law at Cornell University (1891–93). He was counsel for the Stevens Gas Commission investigating utility practices in N.Y. (1906) and attained nationwide reputation as counsel for the Armstrong Commission which exposed abuses in the life insurance field (1906–07). Republican governor of N.Y. (1906–10), his administration was notable for its reforms, including the establishment of a Public Service Commission. Appointed associate justice of the U.S. Supreme Court (1910), he resigned (1916) to accept the Republican nomination for President. His close defeat by President Wilson was attributed in no small measure to tactical errors he made during an electioneering tour of Calif., the loss of which state gave Wilson a majority in the Electoral College. After a period of law practice, he served as Secretary of State in the administrations of Harding and Coolidge (1921–26), organized the Washington Conference on Naval Limitation of Armaments, and negotiated a series of multipartite treaties. Member of the Permanent Court of Arbitration (1926–30) and judge on the Permanent Court of International Justice (1930), he was chosen chief justice of the U.S. Supreme Court that same year, serving until his retirement (1941). In the alignment between liberals and conservatives, he, together with Associate Justice Roberts, occupied a middle ground and contributed to a cautious reshaping of the law to meet social change. He upheld civil liberties and the freedom of the press, curbed the judicial power of administrative agencies, spoke for a unanimous court in invalidating the NIRA (*Schechter Case, 1935*), but sustained the Wagner Act (1937). He effectively opposed President Franklin D. Roosevelt's court reorganization plan (1937).

Hutchinson, Anne (b. Alford, Lincolnshire, England, 1591; d. Eastchester, N.Y., Aug. or Sept. 1643), religious leader. Born Anne Marbury, she married (1612) William Hutchinson, and in 1634 came with her husband and family to Massachusetts Bay, where her openly avowed religious views provoked keen antagonism among the orthodox. She attacked the religious polity of the Mass. colony as a "covenant of works" and advocated a "covenant of grace" based on a direct personal apprehension of divine grace and love. Characterized as an Antinomian by her enemies, she was backed by Rev. John Cotton, Rev. John Wheelwright, and Gov. Henry Vane; but lost her support when Cotton recanted, Wheelwright was banished, and Vane departed for England. Brought to trial for sedition and contempt of the magistrates, she was sentenced to banishment and was later formally excommunicated from the Church for heresy, after refusing to make a public recantation. With her family, she emigrated (1638) to the colony on the island of Aquidneck (now part of R.I.). For her subsequent career and death, see p. 34.

Hutchinson, Thomas (b. Boston, 9 Sept. 1711; d. Brompton, England, 3 June 1780), Loyalist statesman, received his B.A. (1727) and his M.A. (1730) from Harvard, and after serving in his father's business was elected to the Mass. House of Representatives (1737). Serving there (1737–49), he was speaker (1746–48). An advocate of hard money, he opposed the Mass. Land Bank, and sponsored legislation to redeem the colony's bills of credit. Serving in the Council (1749 66), he represented Mass. at the Albany Congress (1754), where he collaborated with and supported Franklin in a plan of union. Lieut. gov., beg. 1758, he also served as chief justice from 1760. In the latter capacity he granted the writs of assistance (1761). His support of enforcement of both the Sugar and Stamp Acts marked him as the leader of the Court party. On 26 Aug. 1765 his home was sacked and his books and papers scattered in reprisal. Royal governor (1770–74), he argued for the supremacy of Parliament over the colonies. Publication in Boston (1773) of letters he sent to England urging the govt. to assert more vigorously its authority over the colonies created a sensation. His insistence that clearance papers would not be given to the tea ships until the tea was landed brought on the Boston Tea Party (1773). Reporting personally to George III (1774), he now advocated a conciliatory policy, but remained in exile, hopeful to the last of laying his "bones in New England." His most important writings were his notably objective *History of the Colony of Mass. Bay* (3 vols., 1764–1828) and *A Collection of Original Papers Relative to the History of Mass. Bay* (1769).

Inness, George (b. near Newburgh, N.Y., 1 May 1825; d. Bridge of Allan, Scotland, 3 Aug. 1894), painter, received brief instruction in the studio of Régis Gignoux, New York City, but was virtually self-taught. He studied in Italy (1847, 1851, and 1871) and in France (1854), but did most of his painting in Medfield, Mass., and later in Montclair, N.J., and New York City. His early work was in the tradition of the Hudson River School, but his style broadened (*Delaware Meadows*, 1867) in the direction of lyricism and subjectivity, with a feeling for light and air achieved by his color patterns. Foremost American landscapist, his paintings are in the Art Institute, Chicago; the Metropolitan Museum, New York; and the National Gallery, Washington, D.C. They include *Peace and Plenty* (1865), *Coming Storm* (1878), *Sunset in the Woods* (1883), *Niagara Falls* (1884), and *March Breezes* (1885).

Irving, Washington (b. New York City, 3 Apr. 1783; d. Tarrytown, N.Y., 28 Nov. 1859), man of letters. He began reading law in 1798 and for a short time practiced law at New York, but soon abandoned this calling for writing and travel. Beginning in 1802 he published in New York City journals "The Letters of Jonathan Oldstyle, Gent.," and in 1807–08 brought out a collection of essays, *Salamagundi: or, the Whim-Whams and Opinions of Launcelot Langstaff, Esq. and Others*. The spirit of these lively satirical pieces was carried over into his comic account, *History of New York . . . by Diedrich Knickerbocker* (1809), which gave its name to the Knickerbocker School of writers. In 1815 he sailed for Europe, remaining there until 1832. During his stay in England he wrote *The Sketch Book of Geoffrey Crayon, Gent.* (1819–20), which included essays such as "Westminster Abbey" and "The Mutability of Literature," and tales such as "Rip Van Winkle" and "The Legend of Sleepy Hollow." He also published *Bracebridge Hall* (1822). Leaving England in 1822, he went to Germany and France, and in 1826 went to Spain, where he served (1826–29) on the staff of the U.S. embassy. At Madrid, and in the Alhambra at Granada, he wrote *The History of the Life and Voyages of Christopher Columbus* (1828), *A Chronicle of the Conquest of Granada* (1829), and *The Alhambra: A Series of Tales and Sketches of the Moors and Spaniards* (1832). Irving served as attaché (1829–32) at the U.S. legation in London, and upon his return to the U.S. was hailed as the nation's leading man of letters. His travels to the West produced *A Tour on the Prairies* (1835), *Astoria* (1836), and *The Adventures of Captain Bonneville, U.S.A.* (1837). He settled at "Sunnyside," near Tarrytown, N.Y., and, except for the years 1842–46, when he was U.S. Minister to Spain, lived there until his death. Among his other works are *Tales of a Traveller* (1824), *The Crayon Miscellany* (1835), *Oliver Goldsmith* (1849), *Mahomet and His Successors* (2 vols., 1849–50), *Wolfert's Roost* (1855), and *Life of George Washington* (5 vols., 1855–59). Irving was the 1st American to gain an international reputation as a man of letters and to make writing his full-time profession.

Jackson, Andrew (b. Waxhaw, S.C., 15 Mar. 1767; d. near Nashville, Tenn., 8 June 1845), 7th President of the U.S., served briefly in the American Revolution (1781), when he was taken prisoner by the British, studied law in Salisbury, N.C., was admitted to the bar (1787), and began practice in Martinsville. Appointed (1788) prosecuting attorney for western district of N.C. (now Tenn.), he moved to Nashville. Married (1791) Mrs. Rachel Robards (née Donelson), mistakenly believing that she had already obtained a divorce (actually granted 2 yrs. later). Member of state constitutional convention (1796), 1st congressman from Tenn. (Dec. 1796–Mar. 1797), U.S. senator (1797), he resigned and became judge of the Tenn. supreme court (1798–1804). In one of several duels he killed Charles Dickinson (1806). Personal feuds with President Jefferson (partly growing out of his attachment to Aaron Burr) and Gov. John Sevier (Tenn.) led to his temporary retirement from public life. As maj. gen. of militia he defeated the Creeks (1813–14). Commissioned maj. gen. in U.S. Army, he decisively defeated the British at New Orleans (8 Jan. 1815) after the treaty of peace had been signed at Ghent. Commanding in the Seminole War, he invaded Fla. (1818), captured Pensacola, and created an international incident by the hanging of 2 British subjects (Arbuthnot and Ambrister). Military governor of Fla. (1821) and U.S. senator (1823–25), he received the largest number of electoral votes for the Presidency (1824), but, failing of a majority, was defeated in the House of Representatives, which elected John Quincy Adams (1825). He won easily 4 years later. His administration (1829–37) initiated the spoils system, set up a "Kitchen Cabinet" of intimate advisers (Amos Kendall, Duff Green, William Berkeley Lewis), and checked the program of Federal internal improvements (Maysville veto, 1830). He reorganized his Cabinet (1831) when Mrs. Calhoun and other wives of Cabinet members refused to meet Mrs. J. H. (Peggy) Eaton. He finally broke with Calhoun on learning that the latter had favored censuring him for his conduct in Fla. in 1818 and over the issue of nullification, which Jackson vigorously opposed, taking military measures to enforce S.C.'s respect for Federal authority (1832). Favoring hard money, he warred on the Bank of the U.S., vetoed its recharter (1832), and ordered withdrawal of U.S. funds. His Indian policy consisted of relocation on lands west of the Mississippi. His administration is notable for expansion of the Presidential power. After the inauguration of Van Buren, his choice for the Presidency, he retired to his home, "The Hermitage," near Nashville.

Jackson, Thomas Jonathan [commonly called "Stonewall" Jackson] (b. Clarksburg, Va., now W.Va., 21 Jan. 1824; d. Guiney's Station, Va., 10 May 1863), Confederate gen., was graduated (1846) from the U.S. Military Academy; was breveted maj. during the Mexican War; became (1851) professor of artillery tactics and natural philosophy at the Virginia Military Institute, Lexington, Va.; and resigned from the army in 1852. He commanded the cadet corps at the hanging of John Brown (2 Dec. 1859). Commissioned (17 June 1861) a brig. gen. in the Confederate forces, he earned his sobriquet "Stonewall" at 1st Bull Run when his troops held off a strong Union assault (21 July 1861). Jackson was made a maj. gen. (7 Oct. 1861) and took command (5 Nov. 1861) of Confederate forces in the Shenandoah Valley. The Valley campaign (Mar.–June 1862) demonstrated Jackson's brilliance as a field tactician. Despite numerical inferiority, he defeated the Union force under Gen. Nathaniel P. Banks at Front Royal (23 May 1862) and Winchester (24–25 May 1862), and prevented the main enemy forces from uniting. During the 7 Days before Richmond, Jackson took part in the actions at Gaines' Mill (27 June 1862) and White Oak Swamp (30 June 1862). After destroying the Union advanced base at Manassas Junction (27 Aug. 1862), he helped defeat Pope at 2nd Bull Run (30–31 Aug. 1862). He also took part in the battles of Antietam (17 Sept. 1862) and Fredericksburg (13 Dec. 1862). After forcing a Union retreat at Chancellorsville (2 May 1863), Jackson was accidentally wounded by the fire of Confederate pickets and died of pneumonia shortly afterward. His death deprived Lee of the greatest of his lieutenants.

James, Henry (b. New York City, 15 Apr. 1843; d. London 28 Feb. 1916), novelist and essayist, son of Henry James (1811–82) the theologian, and brother of William James, was educated in France, entered Harvard Law School (1862), but turned to letters, contributing to the *Nation,* the *Atlantic,* and *Galaxy.* Returning to Europe for several visits in the 1870's, he finally settled in London (1876), becoming a British subject (July 1915). A master of the fiction technique, he established himself in the forefront of the analytical school of novelists with his subtle treatment of British and American society and his romanticizing of aristocratic European culture. In his early works (*The Americans,* 1877; *Daisy Miller,* 1878; *The Bostonians,* 1886), his leading characters are Americans, although the scene is often abroad; but in his 2nd period (*The Princess Casamassima,* 1886; *The Sacred Fount,* 1901), his novels are confined to English society. In his 3rd period (*The Wings of a Dove,* 1902; *The Ambassadors,* 1903; *The Golden Bowl,* 1904; and his unfinished novels), he returned to his theme of the American abroad.

James, William (b. New York City, 11 Jan. 1842; d. Chocorua, N.H., 26 Aug. 1910), psychologist and philosopher, was educated abroad. After accompanying Agassiz on the Thayer expedition to the Amazon (1865–66), he entered Harvard Medical School, then pursued medical studies in Germany, and obtained a Harvard M.D. (1869). Harvard lecturer on anatomy and physiology (1872), assistant professor of physiology (1876), he transferred to the Department of Philosophy as assistant professor (1880), becoming a full professor (1885–1907). His works include *The Principles of Psychology* (1890), *The Varieties of Religious Experience* (1907), *A Pluralistic Universe* (1909), *The Meaning of Truth* (1909), and *Essays in Radical Empiricism* (1912).

A radical empiricist, he evolved the method of pragmatism (the testing of truth by practical consequences), with its emphasis upon individuality, free initiative, spontaneity, and novelty. His conception of the world as one of changes, chance, and plurality largely anticipated trends in the physical sciences.

Jay, John (b. New York City, 12 Dec. 1745; d. Bedford, N.Y., 17 May 1829), 1st Chief Justice of the U.S., was graduated from King's College (1764), studied law, was admitted to the bar (1768), and practiced in N.Y. Secretary of the N.Y.-N.J. boundary commission (1773), he was a member of the 1st and 2nd Continental Congresses (1775–76) and of the N.Y. Provincial Congress (1776–77). Chairman of the committee which drew up the N.Y. state constitution (1777), he became chief justice of N.Y. in that year and also a member of Congress, becoming its president (10 Dec. 1778). Sent to Spain as Minister Plenipotentiary, his mission (1780–82) failed owing to Spanish hostility to U.S. independence. Member of the U.S. delegation to negotiate peace with Great Britain, he was instrumental in the decision to deal with Great Britain independent of France (1782). Secretary of Foreign Affairs (1784–90), his agreement with Gardoqui to settle differences with Spain (1785), which involved restricting U.S. use of the Mississippi, was defeated in Congress. Advocate of the new Constitution, he wrote 5 of *The Federalist* papers. Chief Justice of the U.S. (4 Mar. 1789), he was sent to Great Britain (1794) to settle outstanding differences with that country. Jay's Treaty was denounced by Jeffersonian Republicans for its concessions to England, but it averted war at that time. His most important Supreme Court decision, *Chisholm* v. *Georgia* (1793), holding that a state could be sued by a citizen of another state, led to the 11th Amendment to the Constitution. He resigned from the Court (1795) to accept the governorship of New York (1795–1801).

Jefferson, Thomas (b. Shadwell, Albemarle Co., Va., 13 Apr. 1743; d. Monticello, 4 July 1826), 3rd President of the U.S., was graduated from William and Mary (1762), studied law, and was admitted to the bar (1767), practicing until 1770 and managing his estate. Sent to the House of Burgesses (1769–75), he published (1774) *A Summary View of the Rights of British America.* A delegate to the Continental Congress (1775–76), he drafted the Declaration of Independence. Returning to the Va. legislature, he supported measures providing "a foundation for a government truly republican"— abolition of primogeniture and entails, separation of Church and State, establishment of a public school system. He also favored discontinuing the slave trade and gradual emancipation. Succeeding Patrick Henry as governor of Va. (1779–81), he directed without conspicuous success resistance to British invasion. Returning to Congress (1783–84), he devised a plan for a decimal monetary system and drafted the Land Ordinance of 1784, the basis for the later organization of the territories. Succeeding Franklin as Minister to France (1785–89), he published his *Notes on Virginia* (Paris, 1785) and witnessed the beginnings of the French Revolution. Washington's first Secretary of State, he supported Hamilton's funding and assumption plan on condition that the national capital be located on the Potomac. He served until 1793, when he resigned in protest against Hamilton's fiscal and centralizing policies. Leader in retirement of the Democratic-Republican party, he was Vice-President under John Adams (1797–1801). Opposing the Alien and Sedition Acts, he prepared, with Madison, the Virginia and Kentucky Resolutions (1798), implying that a state could nullify Congressional legislation. In the election of 1800 he tied with Aaron Burr in electoral votes and was chosen President by the House of Representatives with Hamilton's support. His administration (1801–09) was marked by simplicity and economy, the successful war against the Barbary pirates (1801–05), the Louisiana Purchase (1803), the Lewis and Clark and Pike expeditions, the Burr treason trial (1807), and the Embargo Act (1807), adopted to preserve U.S. neutral rights, but repealed (1809). In retirement at Monticello, Jefferson founded the University of Virginia (1819) and contributed notably to the revival of classical architecture in the U.S. A philosopher-statesman of the Enlightenment, he favored a society of self-sufficing free farmers and decentralized governmental powers.

Johnson, Andrew (b. Raleigh, N.C., 29 Dec. 1808; d. Carter Station, Tenn., 31 July 1875), 17th President of the U.S., was self-educated, becoming a tailor in Greenville, Tenn. Soon engaging in politics, where he came to stand for a more equitable land policy, he was alderman (1828–30), mayor (1830–33), Democratic member of the state's lower house (1835–37 and 1839–41) and of the state senate (1841–43), he was elected Democratic congressman (1843–53), served as governor of Tenn. (1853–57), and U.S. senator, 1857–62, where he distinguished himself as the only Southern senator to support the Union during the Civil War. Appointed by Lincoln military governor of Tenn. with the rank of brig. gen. (4 Mar. 1862), he was Lincoln's running mate (1864) on the Union-Republican ticket and was elected Vice-President, becoming President upon Lincoln's death (1865). His attempt to carry out Lincoln's conciliatory Reconstruction policy led him into conflict with the Radical Republicans, who passed over his veto their own Reconstruction Act (1867) which enfranchised Negroes and disfranchised ex-Confederates. In violation of the Tenure of Office Act (passed 2 Mar. 1867 over his veto and declared unconstitutional by the Supreme Court, 1926), Johnson dismissed Edwin M. Stanton, Secretary of War. Impeachment by the House of Representatives failed by 1 vote (May 1868) in the trial before the Senate. Reelected senator (1875), he died the same year.

Johnson, Sir William (b. Smithtown, County Meath, Ireland, 1715; d. Johnstown, N.Y., 11 July 1774), colonial official and diplomat, came to America in 1737, settling on the Mohawk, trading with the Indians, amassing a fortune as well as huge landholdings, and founding (1762) Johnstown. On intimate terms with the Six Nations, particularly the Mohawks, he was largely responsible for keeping them on the British side during King George's War. In 1746 he was made col. and commissary of N.Y. for Indian affairs, resigning the latter office in 1750. At the start of the French and Indian War, he attended, as a member of the N. Y. Council, the Albany Congress (1754), helping to formulate Indian policy. In 1755 Braddock gave him command of the force against Crown Point and "sole management" of the Six Nations. Though he failed to capture Crown Point, he warded off the French threat to the northern colonies and was made (1755) a baronet for his achievements and superintendent of Indian affairs (1756). He advocated centralized control of the fur trade and a boundary line between white settlement and Indian hunting lands. Such a boundary he negotiated (1768) at Ft. Stanwix, opening up to settlement large tracts in N.Y., Pa., and Va. An imperialist, he secured by his policies the attachment of most of the Iroquois to the British side after his death when the Revolution broke out.

Johnston, Joseph Eggleston (b. "Cherry Grove," Prince Edward County, Va., 3 Feb. 1807; d. Washington, D.C., 21 Mar. 1891), Confederate gen. Graduated (1829) from the U.S. Military Academy, he served in the Mexican War, in which he was wounded 5 times, and was promoted to lt. col. in 1855 and brig. gen. in 1860. With the secession of Va., Johnston resigned from the U.S. Army and was appointed (May 1861) brig. gen. in the Confederate Army. After turning back the Union forces at 1st Bull Run (21 July 1861), where he shared the field with Beauregard against McDowell, Johnston was commissioned a gen. and was wounded while commanding (31 May–1 June) at the Battle of Seven Pines (Fair Oaks). He was placed in command (Nov. 1862) of the Confederate forces in Tenn. and Miss., and after the fall of Vicksburg, which contributed to a worsening of Johnston's relations with Jefferson Davis, was assigned (Dec. 1863) to the Army of the Tennessee before Chattanooga. Late in the spring of 1864 Johnston fell back before Sherman's assault and was relieved from his command (17 July 1864) before Atlanta. The Confederate Congress passed a resolution asking for the reinstatement of Johnston, who had been replaced by Gen. John B. Hood. Restored (23 Feb. 1865) to the Army of the Tennessee, Johnston signed an armistice (18 Apr. 1865) with Sherman which the Union government rejected. When Johnston was ordered by Jefferson Davis to continue the war in the interior, he refused and surrendered his force to Sherman near Durham Station, N.C. (26 Apr. 1865). He served in Congress (1879–81) and was appointed (1885) a Federal commissioner of railroads.

Jones, John Paul (b. Kirkbean, Kirkcudbrightshire, Scotland, 6 July 1747; d. Paris, France, 18 July 1792), naval officer. Until *c*.1773, when he arrived in America, he was known as **John Paul.** He was commissioned (7 Dec. 1775) a lt. in the newly organized Continental navy, captured 16 prizes as commander of the *Providence,* and in 1776 was promoted to capt. Appointed (14 June 1777) commander of the sloop *Ranger,* he carried out raids on British shipping, using Brest as a base of operations. Early in 1779 he was given command of an old East Indiaman which he christened the *Bonhomme Richard* (*Poor Richard*) in honor of Benjamin Franklin. On 14 Aug. 1779 he set out from Lorient at the head of a small fleet to prey upon the British coast. On 23 Sept. 1779 there took place off Flamborough Head the naval engagement between the *Bonhomme Richard* and the larger and more heavily armed British warship *Serapis.* Although the *Richard* was sunk, the *Serapis* was captured by Jones, who on this occasion is reported to have said in reply to the British demand for surrender: "I have not yet begun to fight." He was made commander (26 June 1781) of the warship *America,* whose construction he supervised. When the navy was discontinued (1783), Jones went abroad. By unanimous resolve, Congress authorized (16 Oct. 1787) the presentation of a gold medal to Jones, the only Continental naval officer so honored. Late in 1787 Jones decided to enter the Russian naval service and, as a rear adm., took command (26 May 1788) of a fleet on the Black Sea. He resigned from the Russian navy in 1789 and returned to Paris. In 1905 what are thought to be his remains were brought to the U.S. and now rest in the crypt of the chapel of the U.S. Naval Academy.

Kendall, Edward Calvin (b. South Norwalk, Conn., 8 Mar. 1886–), biochemist, was graduated from Columbia (B.S., 1908; M.S., 1909; Ph.D., 1910), where he was a Goldschmidt fellow. He served as a research chemist with Parke, Davis & Co. at Detroit (1910–11) and with St. Luke's Hospital at New York (1911–14). Since 1914 he has been head of the biochemistry section at the Mayo Foundation, Rochester, Minn., and professor of physiological chemistry under the Mayo Foundation at the University of Minnesota. His 1st notable achievement was to isolate thyroxine from the thyroid gland (1914); then he isolated glutathione from yeast (1929). For isolating and synthesizing the principal hormone of the adrenal cortex (cortisone), he won a Nobel prize in 1950 (with Hench and Reichstein).

Kennedy, John Fitzgerald (b. Brookline, Mass., 29 May 1917–), 35th President of the U.S., son of Joseph P. Kennedy, banker and realtor, received his B.S. cum laude (1940) from Harvard, spending six mos. during his junior year working in the London embassy while his father was ambassador to Great Britain. His observations inspired *Why England Slept* (1940). In the navy (1941–45), he was awarded the Navy and Marine Corps Medals and the Purple Heart for action as commander of a PT boat in the Solomons. After a brief period as a news correspondent, covering the UN organization meetings and the Potsdam Conference, he was elected Democratic congressman from Mass. for 3 terms (1947–53). His defeat of Henry Cabot Lodge in the senatorial race of 1952 was a major upset. He lost a close race to Estes Kefauver for the Democratic Vice-Presidential nomination in 1956, but was re-elected to the Senate (1958) by an 875,000-vote margin. Defeating Senator Hubert H. Humphrey, Jr. (Minn.), in primary races in Wis. and W. Va., he won the Democratic nomination for the Presidency (1960) on the 1st ballot. Elected in the closest Presidential election since 1884, he became the 1st Catholic and youngest man to be elected to that office. His *Profiles in Courage* (1956) was awarded the Pulitzer Prize in Biography (1957).

Kent, James (b. Fredericksburg, N.Y., 31 July 1763; d. New York City, 12 Dec. 1847), jurist, was graduated from Yale (1781), admitted to the N.Y. bar (1785), and practiced in Poughkeepsie until 1793 and thereafter in New York City until his elevation to the bench. Professor of law at Columbia (1794–98 and 1824–26), he became master in chancery (1796), justice (1798), and chief justice (1804) of the state supreme court, where he introduced much French civil law into the N.Y. legal system as well as the practice of written opinions. Appointed chancellor (1814–23), his decisions, along with the work of Story, laid the foundations of equity jurisprudence in the U.S. His Columbia lectures, which followed the model of Blackstone, were expanded into *Commentaries on the American Law* (1826–30), called by Justice Story "our first judicial classic," and soon accepted as an authoritative exposition of the English common law in the U.S. and a standard interpretation of the Constitution. The most notable edition was the 12th by O. W. Holmes, Jr. (1873). A lifelong Federalist, Kent vigorously opposed universal suffrage at the N.Y. Constitutional Convention (1821).

Kettering, Charles Franklin (b. London-ville, Ohio, 29 Aug. 1876; d. Dayton, Ohio, 25 Nov. 1958), inventor, received his E.E. degree (1904) from Ohio State Univ. He began work with the Star Telephone Co., Ashland, and then, with the National Cash Register Co., Dayton, he invented an electric motor for cash registers. In 1909 he organized the Dayton Engineering Laboratories Co. (Delco), and within 2 yrs. made notable improvements in automobile ignition and lighting systems. His perfection (1911) of the self-starter, 1st installed in the Cadillac, enormously expanded the market for the motor car. As general manager of General Motors' research laboratories (1925–47)

he directed research on improving Diesel engines and the development of a non-toxic and noninflammable refrigerant. He also originated and guided researches resulting in higher octane gasoline, adding tetraethyl lead. In 1951 he developed a new high-compression engine. Founder and chairman of the Charles F. Kettering Foundation (1927), he directed research in the natural sciences, working on chlorophyll and photosynthesis, artificial-fever therapy, and cancer. He was cofounder of the Sloan-Kettering Institute for Cancer Research.

La Farge, John (b. New York City, 31 Mar. 1835; d. Providence, R.I., 14 Nov. 1910), artist and writer. He was graduated (1853) from Mount St. Mary's College at Emmitsburg, Md.; in 1856 went to Paris, where he worked briefly under the painter Couture and then made studies of the old masters during a tour of Northwestern Europe; returned to the U.S. in 1858, studied under William Morris Hunt, and subsequently experimented with luminism in painting, anticipating the colorist treatments of the French Impressionists. From easel work he moved into mural painting, in which his outstanding achievements are decorations for Trinity Church at Boston, *The Ascension* in the Church of the Ascension at New York, panels for the Church of the Incarnation at New York, and lunettes at the State Capitol at St. Paul, Minn. La Farge also attained eminence as a worker in stained glass, reviving that field as a craft and an industry. He invented opaline glass and designed and manufactured hundreds of windows. With Henry Adams, he visited Japan and the South Seas in 1886, recording his journey in *An Artist's Letters from Japan* (1897) and *Reminiscences of the South Seas* (1912), illustrated by his paintings and sketches.

La Follette, Robert Marion (b. Primrose, Wis., 14 June 1855; d. Washington, D.C., 18 June 1925), statesman, was graduated from the University of Wisconsin (1879), studied law privately and at the university law school, was admitted to the bar in 1880, and practiced at Madison, Wis. As a Republican, he opposed the regular political leaders of Dane County, of which he was elected (1880) district attorney, and in 1884 was elected to Congress, where he served from 1885 to 1891. His fight against the political leadership of U.S. Sen. Philetus Sawyer led to an open break between La Follette and the party bosses. Although failing to win the Republican nomination for governor in 1896 and 1898, his fight against the entrenched political groups brought him (1900) nomination by acclamation. He took office as governor (1901) with a program that soon became known as the "Wisconsin Idea" and served as a model of progressive government: opposition to political bosses, direct appeal to the people, and the employment of technical experts; and specific proposals for direct primary legislation, railroad control, and tax reform. The primary law was enacted in 1903; a railroad commission was set up in 1905. La Follette was reelected governor in 1902 and 1904, and in 1906 took his seat in the U.S. Senate, to which he was reelected 3 times. As a Progressive leader in the Senate, he opposed the Payne-Aldrich Tariff, advocated the physical valuation of railroads as a basis for rate making, and sponsored the La Follette Seamen's Act (1915). He established (1909) *La Follette's Weekly Magazine.* In 1911 he drafted the program for the National Progressive Republican League, campaigned for the Progressive nomination in 1911–12, but lost it to Theodore Roosevelt, partly as a result of a temporary breakdown (Feb. 1912) suffered in public. He opposed Wilson's foreign policy and early in 1917, as one of the "little group of willful men" (in Wilson's phrase), prevented passage of the armed merchant ship bill. He voted against the declaration of war on Germany, but supported most of the war measures. He opposed U.S. participation in the League of Nations and the World Court. A liberal leader in the postwar years, he was the author of a resolution for a Senate inquiry into the Teapot Dome and other naval oil leases made during the Harding administration. The Progressive candidate for President in 1924, he received nearly 5,000,000 votes. He published his *Autobiography* (1913).

La Guardia, Fiorello Henry (b. New York City, 11 Dec. 1882; d. there 20 Dec. 1947), congressman, mayor of New York, reformer, received his early education in Arizona, where he wrote for the Phoenix *Morning Courier.* During the Spanish-American War he was a Florida correspondent for the St. Louis *Post-Dispatch.* He worked (1901–04) for the U.S. consular service in Budapest, Trieste, and Fiume, then for the U.S. Immigration Service at Ellis Island, N.Y. (1907–10) while studying law at New York Univ. (LL.B., 1910), and was admitted to the New York bar that year. Victor over Tammany, he was elected to Congress as a Republican (1917) and joined in the successful fight for the liberalization of the House rules, but resigned to command the U.S. air forces on the Italo-Austrian front in World War I. President of the bd. of aldermen (1920–21), he returned to Congress (1923–33), where he fought for labor reforms and cosponsored the Norris-La Guardia anti-injunction bill (1932). Elected Fusion mayor of New York (1933) and re-elected (1937, 1941), the "Little Flower" (from his 1st name) proved indefatigable, incorruptible, and colorful in executing a vast program of reform and public works and bringing about the adoption (1938) of a new city charter. He served (1946) as director of the UN Relief and Rehabilitation Administration.

Langdell, Christopher Columbus (b. New Boston, N.H., 22 May 1826; d. Cambridge, Mass., 6 July 1906), jurist and law teacher. He was graduated from Harvard (1851) and the Harvard Law School, practiced law at New York City (1854–70), and in 1870 was named Dane professor of law in the Harvard Law School, a post he held until 1900, as well as that of dean (1870–95). His fame rests on his introduction of the case method of teaching law, with its emphasis upon the formulation of legal principles from a study of specific court decisions, as expounded in his *A Selection of Cases on the Law of Contracts* (1871). He also wrote *A Summary of Equity Pleading* (1877) and works in the field of contracts.

Langmuir, Irving (b. Brooklyn, N.Y., 31 Jan. 1881; d. Schenectady, N.Y., 16 Aug. 1957), physical chemist, was graduated from the Columbia University School of Mines (1903) and the University of Göttingen (Ph.D., 1906), was an instructor in chemistry (1906–09) at Stevens Institute, and in 1909 joined the General Electric Co. as a research chemist and physicist. He was assistant (1909–32) and associate director (1932–51) of the General Electric Research Laboratory. In 1912 he developed a high-intensity tungsten electric lamp filled with nitrogen (later argon), a great improvement over the vacuum-type lamp. He has done pioneer work in surface tension and with Gilbert N. Lewis formulated the Lewis-Langmuir theory of atomic structure and valence. He has also carried out important investigations in colloid chemistry, the kinetics of gas reactions at low pressures, the production of artificial snow, the dissociation of hydrogen, acoustic devices for detecting submarines, and the vapor pressures of metals. In 1932 he received the Nobel prize in chemistry.

Latrobe, Benjamin Henry (b. Fulneck, Yorkshire, England, 1 May 1764; d. New Orleans, La., 3 Sept. 1820), architect and civil engineer. Educated in Germany, he took his professional training in England under the architect Samuel Pepys Cockerell and the civil engineer John Smeaton. He came to the U.S. in 1796; improved the navigation of the Appomattox and James rivers; designed (1797) the penitentiary at Richmond, Va.; and completed the façade of the Virginia State Capitol designed by Jefferson. The leading exponent of the Greek Revival in the U.S., Latrobe designed in that style the Bank of Pennsylvania at Philadelphia, where he also built (1799–1801) the city water works on the Schuylkill. He improved the navigation of the Susquehanna River, served as engineer of the Chesapeake & Delaware Canal, and constructed the Washington City Canal. In 1803 President Jefferson named him surveyor of the public buildings, in which capacity Latrobe revised the plans for the National Capitol drawn up by William Thornton. He intermittently continued work on the Capitol, including its rebuilding after its destruction by fire in 1814, until his retirement from Federal service in 1817. He also drew up plans for the Marine Hospital and St. John's Church, both at Washington, D.C.; the Baltimore Cathedral; the Bank of Philadelphia; the old Pennsylvania Academy of Fine Arts, the Markoe and Waln houses, and the 2nd Bank of the U.S., all at Philadelphia; the Henry Clay house at Ashland, Ky.; and the Exchange (including the Bank of the U.S. and the Custom House) at Baltimore. In his last years he was engaged on the water supply system for New Orleans. Almost singlehanded, Latrobe raised architectural practice in the U.S. to the status of a profession.

Lawrence, Ernest Orlando (b. Canton, S.D., 8 Aug. 1901; d. Palo Alto, Calif., 27 Aug. 1958), nuclear physicist, inventor of the cyclotron, was graduated from the Univ. of South Dakota (A.B., 1922), the Univ. of Minnesota (A.M., 1923), and Yale (Ph.D., 1925), taught physics at Yale (1925–28), and since 1928 at the University of California, where he directed the radiation laboratory beginning 1936. His major contribution is the development of the cyclotron (atom-smashing machine), a mechanism which produces atomic transmutation through bombardment of matter with high-energy particles. Lawrence outlined the fundamental concept of the cyclotron as early as 1930 and, with his associates, constructed the 1st cyclotron in 1932, thereafter making improvements. In 1936 he transmuted other elements into gold. For his invention of the cyclotron, he was awarded (1939) the Nobel prize in physics. In World War II the cyclotron was used for separating U-235 from natural uranium during research on the atomic bomb, a project in which Lawrence took part. In 1957 he received the Fermi Award given by the U.S. Atomic Energy Commission.

Lederberg, Joshua (b. Montclair, N.J., 23 May 1925–), geneticist, was graduated from Columbia (B.A., 1944), studied at the Coll. of Physicians and Surgeons (1944–46), receiving his Ph.D. at Yale (1947), where he worked with Dr.

Edward L. Tatum (1909–) on sexual reproduction in bacteria. He taught genetics at the Univ. of Wis. (1947–57) and became (1959) professor of genetics at the Stanford Sch. of Medicine. In 1958 he received the Nobel Prize in Physiology and Medicine for his discoveries concerning genetic recombination and organization of the genetic material of bacteria. His work in virus breeding and cross-breeding is basic to research on the control of virus diseases.

Lee, Richard Henry (b. "Stratford," Westmoreland Co., Va., 20 Jan. 1732; d. neighboring "Chantilly," 19 June 1732), Revolutionary statesman, studied under private tutors, completing his education at the academy at Wakefield, in Yorkshire, England. Entering the House of Burgesses (1758), he opposed (1764) the Sugar Act and organized (1766) the Westmoreland Association, initiating the nonimportation association movement. With Henry and Jefferson, he originated (1773) the plan for intercolonial committees of correspondence. At the 1st Continental Congress (1774) he formed close personal and political ties with Sam Adams and backed the Continental Association. In the 2nd Continental Congress he introduced (7 June 1776) the resolution calling for a declaration of independence, foreign alliances, and a confederation of the American states. To make the Confederation possible, he advocated the surrender by Virginia of her claims to western lands and supported his brother Arthur in his dispute with Silas Deane, which divided Congress into 2 camps. President of Congress (1784–85), he declined to serve as a delegate to the Constitutional Convention. Leader of the opposition to ratifying the Constitution in Va., he urged in *Letters of the Federal Farmer* (1787) the need for a bill of rights and a more democratic lower house. Senator from Virginia (1789–92), his chief proposals were embodied in the 1st 10 Amendments.

Lee, Robert Edward (b. Stratford, Va., 19 Jan. 1807; d. Lexington, Va., 12 Oct. 1870), soldier, was graduated from the U.S. Military Academy (1829) and commissioned in the engineers. He married Mary Custis (1831), great-granddaughter of Martha Washington. Serving in the War with Mexico under Scott, he was superintendent of West Point (1852–53), and lt. col. of cavalry on frontier duty in Tex. (1855–61), with the exception of 2 yrs. (1857–59) spent on leave at Arlington. He commanded the troops which put down John Brown's raid (1859). At the outbreak of the Civil War he declined field command of the U.S. Army offered by Lincoln (18 Apr. 1861) but accepted command of Va.'s military forces, soon receiving the rank of gen. When J. E. Johnston was wounded he was assigned to command the Army of Northern Virginia (1 June 1862), removing McClellan's threat to Richmond in the 7 Days' Battles (25 June–1 July 1862). He routed Pope at 2nd Bull Run (29–30 Aug.), was checked at Antietam (17 Sept.), and defeated Burnside at Fredericksburg (13 Dec.) and Hooker at Chancellorsville (2–4 May 1863). His defeat and withdrawal at Gettysburg (1–3 July) constituted the turning point of the war. He opposed Grant (May–June 1864) in the battles of Wilderness, Spotsylvania, and Cold Harbor, and was appointed general in chief of all Confederate armies (Feb. 1865). He surrendered to Grant at Appomattox Courthouse (9 Apr. 1865) and advised the South to create a new and better section within the Union. After the war he accepted the presidency of Washington College (later renamed Washington and Lee University in his honor).

Lewis, Gilbert Newton (b. Weymouth, Mass., 23 Oct. 1875; d. Berkeley, Calif., 23 Mar. 1946), physical chemist. He was graduated from Harvard (A.B., 1896; A.M., 1898; Ph.D., 1899), attended the universities of Leipzig and Göttingen (1900–01), and taught chemistry at Harvard (1899–1906), the Massachusetts Institute of Technology (1907–12), and the University of California (1912–46). During World War I he headed the defense division of the gas service of the A.E.F. One of the most versatile of American physical chemists, he evolved the "octet" theory of molecular structure, did important work on the absorption bands and phosphorescence spectra of dyes, improved thermodynamic methods by the concepts of "fugacity" and "activity," collaborated with Dr. Ernest O. Lawrence in inventing the cyclotron (atom-smashing machine), and with Dr. Irving Langmuir formulated the Lewis-Langmuir theory of atomic structure and valence. He wrote *Thermodynamics and the Free Energy of Chemical Substances* (with M. Randall, 1923), *Valence and the Structure of Atoms and Molecules* (1923), and *The Anatomy of Science* (1926).

Lewis, John Llewellyn (b. Lucas, Iowa, 12 Feb. 1880–), labor leader, son of a Welsh miner, joined his father as a laborer in a Lucas coal mine at the age of 16. As state legislative agent for District 12 of the United Mine Workers of America (1909–11), he secured the passage of workmen's compensation and mine safety laws in Ill. Field and legislative representative of the A.F. of L., he rose to the presidency of the U.M.W. (1920), which post he held until his retirement (1960). A militant unionist and formidable bargainer, he called the crippling bituminous coal strikes of 1919 and 1922, scoring notable victories in each case. In a period of economic distress for the coal industry, he fought off (1930) an ouster move by insurgents. Vice-president of the A.F. of L. (1934), he resigned (1935) to form, with Sidney Hillman (*q.v.*) and David Dubinsky (1892–), the Congress of Industrial Organization (later C.I.O.), A.F. of L.'s giant rival. With Hillman he organized (1936) Labor's Non-Partisan League, supporting the re-election of Franklin D. Roosevelt, with whom he later broke. His April, 1946, coal strike precipitated U.S. govt. seizure of the mines (21 May) and was ended by an injunction and a contempt conviction, although when the mines were returned to their owners (June, 1947) Lewis secured all his demands.

Lewis, Meriwether (b. in Albemarle County, Va., 18 Aug. 1774; d. in central Tenn., 11 Oct. 1809), and **Clark, William** (b. in Caroline County, Va., 1 Aug. 1770; d. St. Louis, Mo., 1 Sept. 1838), explorers and territorial governors, leaders of the Lewis and Clark overland expedition to the U.S. Northwest (1803–06). Both were officers in the U.S. Army, Clark being the brother of the Revolutionary soldier, George Rogers Clark (1752–1818). In 1801 Lewis became private secretary to President Jefferson, who selected him as commander of an overland expedition to the Pacific. Lewis chose Capt. Clark as his companion officer, and they shared authority. The expedition was fitted out in Ill. during the winter of 1803–04 and was later transferred to St. Louis. Clark joined Lewis at St. Charles, Mo. Their party, consisting of 23 soldiers, 3 interpreters and 1 slave, set out in the spring of 1804 and followed the Missouri River in a 1,600-mile journey to the Mandan villages in N.D., where it went into winter quarters near the site of present-day Bismarck, N.D. Resuming the journey on 7 Apr. 1805, the expedition reached the mouth of the Yellowstone (26 Apr.), the triple fork of the Missouri (25 July), and descended the Columbia, reaching the Pacific Ocean on 15 Nov. On the return journey (23 Mar.–23 Sept. 1806) to St. Louis, the party divided and, after exploring much of what is now the state of Mont., reunited below the mouth of the Yellowstone. The records of the Lewis and Clark expedition, including the diaries kept by both leaders and the maps and drawings made by Clark, constituted valuable scientific findings. Lewis, appointed governor of Louisiana Territory (1806), died either by suicide or killing. Clark, appointed superintendent of Indian affairs at St. Louis (1807) and governor of Missouri Territory (1813), concluded treaties with the Indians after the War of 1812.

Lincoln, Abraham (b. Hardin, Ky., 12 Feb. 1809; d. Washington, D.C., 15 Apr. 1865), 16th President of the U.S., moved with his parents (Thomas and Nancy Hanks Lincoln) to Spencer Co., Ind. (1816), then settled in southern Ill. (1830), where he clerked in a store at New Salem. He became captain of volunteers in the Black Hawk War (1832), but did not see action. He operated a store, practiced surveying, and served as postmaster at New Salem (1833–36) while he studied law and was admitted to the bar (1836). He moved to Springfield (1837), where he opened a law office and quickly obtained a reputation on the circuit as an outstanding jury lawyer. Whig state legislator (1834–42), he was elected to Congress (1846), but did not stand for reelection. In his Peoria speech (1854) he denounced the Kansas-Nebraska Act. Joining the Republican party (1856), he ran for the Senate against Stephen A. Douglas (1858), accepting the nomination (17 June) with a speech in which he declared: "A house divided against itself cannot stand." In the course of 7 campaign debates with Douglas he forced the latter to announce the so-called Freeport Doctrine. Losing the election, Lincoln had established himself as a national figure. Although he won the Republican nomination for the Presidency in 1860 because of his conservative views on slavery, his election was regarded in the South as forecasting an attack on the "peculiar institution." By 4 Mar. 1861, 7 states had already seceded. In his 1st inaugural Lincoln reiterated his constitutional doctrine that the contract between the states was binding and irrevocable. Against the advice of his Cabinet, he ordered the provisioning of Ft. Sumter and when war began called out the state militia, suspended the writ of habeas corpus, proclaimed a blockade of Southern ports, and in other ways did not hesitate to use the dictatorial powers with which he was invested. He largely countermanded Frémont's proclamation (30 Aug. 1861) emancipating the slaves of rebels in Mo. and proposed his own plan for compensated emancipation (Dec. 1861, 12 July and 1 Dec. 1862). "My paramount object is to save the Union, and not either to save or destroy slavery," he stated (22 Aug. 1862). After Antietam he prepared a draft of emancipation, proclaimed formally 1 Jan. 1863. A diplomat in the handling of both his Cabinet and his generals, his reelection in 1864, when he easily defeated McClellan, was assured by the military victories of Grant, Sherman, and Sheridan. His plan of Reconstruction (8 Dec. 1863) was based on the prompt restoration of the Southern states to "their proper practical relation with the Union." He pocket-vetoed the harsher Wade-Davis Bill (8 July 1864). He personally attended the Hampton Roads Conference (3 Feb. 1865) to discuss peace terms with Confederate leaders. His most notable speeches were his Gettysburg Address (19 Nov. 1863) and his 2nd Inaugural (4 Mar. 1865), in which he appealed to the nation to "finish the work we are in . . . with malice toward none, with charity for all." Shortly after Lee's surrender he was shot by John Wilkes Booth in Ford's Theater, Washington (14 Apr. 1865), and died the next day.

Lipmann, Fritz Albert (b. Konigsberg, Prussia, 12 June 1899–), biochemist, received his M.D. (1922) and Ph.D. (1927) from the Univ. of Berlin, became research assistant at the Kaiser Wilhelm Institute in the laboratory of Otto Meyerhof, where he began investigating the mechanism of fluoride effects and, from 1930–31, the field of tissue culture. Winner of a Rockefeller fellowship, he began work at the Rockefeller Inst. (1931) on phosphorus mechanisms, then returned to Europe (1932), spending 7 yrs. as research associate in the Biol. Inst. of the Carlsberg Foundation at Copenhagen. Returning to the U.S. (1939) as a research fellow at the Cornell Univ. Medical Coll., he became (1941) senior biochemist at the Mass. Gen. Hospital and since 1946 has taught biochemistry at the Harvard Medical Sch. During World War II he served as a civilian scientist with the Office of Scientific Research and Development. He became a U.S. citizen (1944). Experiments in 1937 started him on a series of investigations during which he developed the idea of phosphate bond energy. He isolated acetyl phosphate (1942) and with his coworkers synthesized it (1944). He received the Nobel Prize in Medicine and Physiology (1953) for isolating and identifying coenzyme A (1945) as a crucial element in providing usable energy for the body-building process and demonstrating how coenzyme A brought forth the construction of fatty acids and steroids necessary to the body's renewal and growth. He later did research in the structure of cancer cells and investigated pantothenic acid and the action of the energy-regulating thyroid hormone.

Livingston, Edward (b. "Clermont," Columbia Co., N.Y., 28 May 1764; d. "Montgomery Place," N.Y., 23 May 1836), jurist, statesman, and diplomat, was graduated from the College of New Jersey (1781), studied law in Albany, and was admitted to the N.Y. bar (1785). In Congress as a Jeffersonian Republican (1795–1801), he was U.S. district attorney of N.Y. (1801). Elected mayor of New York City (1801–03), he reformed the rules of procedure of the mayor's court. When a custom-house clerk misappropriated public funds, he sold his own property to meet the deficit and moved to New Orleans (1803), where he resumed law practice. Purchaser (1808) of the Gravier estate, he improved the *batture* (an alluvial deposit or river beach), was dispossessed on Jefferson's orders, but was the ultimate victor in a celebrated litigation. In the lower house of the La. legislature (1820), congressman (1822–29), U.S. senator (1829–31), he was President Jackson's Secretary of State (1831–33) and wrote the Nullification Proclamation. U.S. Minister to France (1833–35), he futilely endeavored to secure payment of U.S. spoliation claims. His fame rests upon his work as a codifier of the laws. After reading Bentham he drafted a code of procedure which was adopted by the La. legislature (1805), the 1st real code in the U.S. At the request of the legislature he began his comprehensive criminal code (1820), completed (1824), and published (1833). Although not adopted in his own state, it was acclaimed abroad and became the model of state penal codes in the U.S., foreshadowing many later reforms in penology. Sir Henry Maine called Livingston "the first legal genius of modern times."

Livingston, Robert R. (b. New York City, 27 Nov. 1746; d. "Clermont," N.Y., 26 Feb. 1813), Revolutionary patriot, jurist, diplomat, was graduated from King's College (1765). Admitted to the bar (1770), he practiced law briefly with John Jay (*q.v.*). In the Continental Congress (1775–76, 1779–81, 1784–85),

he was on the committee which drafted the Declaration of Independence, but, owing to lack of instructions from the N.Y. Convention, neither voted for nor signed the document. Member of the committee which drafted the N.Y. Constitution (1777), he was Chancellor of N.Y. (1777–1801), administering the oath to Washington in 1789. First Secy. of Foreign Affairs (1781–83), he criticized the U.S. peace commissioners for their distrust of France, but supported the treaty they negotiated. With Hamilton and Jay, he was a leading supporter of the Constitution at the N.Y. ratifying convention, but broke with the Federalists over the patronage and used his family and public influence to oppose Jay's Treaty. Defeated by Jay for governor (1795), he was appointed by Jefferson (1801) minister to France, where his most conspicuous achievement was the successful negotiation of the Louisiana Purchase (1803). Patron of the arts, he was interested both in scientific agriculture and technology, and financed Robert Fulton's (*q.v.*) experiments in steam navigation. The steamboat *Clermont* was named for his estate. With Fulton, he secured and maintained during his lifetime a monopoly of steam navigation on the Hudson, which involved him in litigation and was terminated by *Gibbons* v. *Ogden* (1824).

Long, Huey Pierce (b. near Winnfield, La., 30 Aug. 1893; d. Baton Rouge, 10 Sept. 1935), politician, worked as a traveling salesman before studying law (1914) at Tulane Univ. Admitted to the La. bar (1915), he won a reputation as a poor man's lawyer by specializing in workmen's compensation cases. Elected and re-elected railroad (later public service) commissioner (1921–26), as chairman he brought about telephone rate reductions and prevented streetcar fare rises. Defeated for the governorship (1924), he won election (1928), trouncing the New Orleans Democratic machine. An oil property owner himself and long known for his vindictive opposition to the Standard Oil Co., he pushed through the legislature a constitutional amendment to tax the oil interests and use the revenue for highways and education. Impeached by the lower house

(1929) for bribery and gross misconduct, he rounded up enough state senators (the "Famous 15") to avoid conviction. Elected to the U.S. Senate (1930), he ruled La. (1930–34) by alliance with the New Orleans machine, retaining the governorship and sponsoring a vast highway program and the expansion of Louisiana State Univ. As U.S. senator, the "Kingfish" failed to secure President Roosevelt's backing for his social program and organized (Jan. 1934) a Share-Our-Wealth Society, promising a homestead allowance of $6,000 and a minimum annual income of $2,500 for every American family. Meantime, to keep control in La., he reorganized the state govt. (1934–35), abolishing local govt. and creating a virtual dictatorship. Announcing his own candidacy for the Presidency (Mar. 1935), he was fatally wounded on the steps of the Baton Rouge Capitol by Dr. Carl Weiss, who was shot and killed by Long's bodyguard. His death ended a threat to the New Deal of a 3rd party, but his program, along with parallel proposals of Dr. Francis E. Townsend and Rev. Charles E. Coughlin, provided the impetus for the later New Deal social security legislation. Of all Southern demagogues Long posed the most serious threat to democracy.

Longfellow, Henry Wadsworth (b. Portland, Me., 27 Feb. 1807; d. Cambridge, Mass., 24 Mar. 1882), poet. He was graduated (1825) from Bowdoin College; studied modern languages in France, Spain, Italy, and Germany from 1826 to 1829; was professor and librarian at Bowdoin (1829–35); and served (1836–54) as Smith professor of modern languages and belles-lettres at Harvard. His 1st book of poetry was *Voices of the Night* (1839). His *Ballads and Other Poems* (1841) included "The Village Blacksmith," "Excelsior," and "The Wreck of the Hesperus." When he died he was the most popular American poet. Among other works of poetry by him are *Poems on Slavery* (1842), *Evangeline* (1847), *The Belfry of Bruges and Other Poems* (1845), *The Seaside and the Fireside* (1849), *Hiawatha* (1855), *The Courtship of Miles Standish* (1858), *Tales of a Wayside Inn* (1863–74, which includes "Paul Revere's Ride"), *The Masque of Pandora* (1875), *Ultima Thule* (1880), and *In the Harbor* (1882). He translated *The Divine Comedy of Dante Alighieri* (3 vols., 1865–67).

Lowell, James Russell (b. Cambridge, Mass., 22 Feb. 1819; d. there, 12 Aug. 1891), author, editor, teacher, and diplomat. He was graduated from Harvard (1838) and from the Harvard Law School (1840), published *A Year's Life* (1841) and *Poems* (1844), and coedited (Jan.-Mar. 1843) *The Pioneer: A Literary and Critical Magazine.* Through the influence of Maria White, whom he married in 1844, he became interested in the antislavery movement, and was an editorial writer (1845) for the *Pennsylvania Freeman* and a contributor and corresponding editor of the *National Anti-Slavery Standard.* He established himself as a writer with the following, all published in 1848: *Poems by James Russell Lowell, 2nd Series, A Fable for Critics, The Vision of Sir Launfal,* and *The Biglow Papers* (1st series), a satire on the Mexican War written in the Yankee vernacular. He succeeded Longfellow (1855), as Smith professor of modern languages and belles-lettres at Harvard, was the 1st editor (1857–61) of the *Atlantic Monthly,* and joint editor (with Charles Eliot Norton) of the *North American Review* from 1864 to 1872. He was Minister to Spain (1877–80) and to England (1880–85). His critical and other writings include *Fireside Travels* (1864), *Biglow Papers* (2nd series, 1867), *Under the Willows* (1868), *The Cathedral* (1870), *Among My Books* (1st and 2nd series, 1870, 1876), *My Study Windows* (1871), *Heartease and Rue* (1888), *Political Essays* (1888), *Latest Literary Essays and Addresses* (1891); and *The Old English Dramatists* (1892). One of his best-known poems is "Ode Recited at the Harvard Commemoration" (1865).

Lyon, Mary (b. Buckland, Mass., 28 Feb. 1797; d. South Hadley, Mass., 5 Mar. 1849), educator. She attended seminaries at Ashfield and Amherst, Mass., and in 1821 studied at the Byfield (Mass.) Seminary. She was a teacher (1821–34) at Ashfield and Ipswich, Mass., and at

Londonderry, N.H. Between 1834 and 1837 she worked on a plan to establish a seminary for the education of girls of moderate means, raising the funds for the project and shaping the curriculum (which was based on that at Amherst College). Mount Holyoke Female Seminary (later Mount Holyoke College), of which she served as principal until her death, was opened at South Hadley, Mass., on 8 Nov. 1837. It was the 1st permanent institution devoted to the higher education of women. Miss Lyon made valuable contributions to educational theory and wrote *Tendencies of the Principles Embraced and the System Adopted in the Mount Holyoke Seminary* (1840).

MacArthur, Douglas (b. Little Rock, Ark., 26 Jan. 1880–   ), soldier. Graduated (1903) from the U.S. Military Academy, he saw service in the Philippines (1903–04) and Japan (1905–06), was aide-de-camp (1906–07) to President Theodore Roosevelt and served on the army general staff (1913–15, 1916–17). In Aug. 1917 he was named chief of staff of the 42nd (Rainbow) Div., on 6 Aug. 1918 commanding gen. of the 84th Infantry Brigade, and on Nov. 1918 commanding gen. of the 42nd Div. He took part in the major U.S. offensives of World War I and was twice wounded in action. He served (Nov. 1918–Apr. 1919) with the army of occupation in Germany, was appointed (12 June 1919) superintendent of the U.S. Military Academy, and was promoted to brig. gen. in 1920. He served in the Philippines (1922–25) as commander of the Manila District, was promoted to maj. gen. (1925) and gen. (1930), and in 1928 became commander of the Philippine Department. After serving as chief of staff (1930–35) of the U.S. Army, he became (1935) director of the organization of national defense for the Philippine Commonwealth. Appointed (1936) a field marshal in the Philippine Army, he retired (1937) from the U.S. Army, but was recalled to active service (26 July 1941) as commander of the U.S. forces in the Far East, and subsequently assumed his former rank of gen. Following the Japanese attack on the Philippines,

MacArthur led a skillful defense, made a planned retreat to Bataan Peninsula, and set up his headquarters on Corregidor. Appointed (22 Feb. 1942) Supreme Allied Commander of forces in the Southwest Pacific, he escaped to Australia and commanded the Allied campaigns against Japanese forces in that area. He was made (Dec. 1944) a gen. of the army, and in Aug. 1945 was appointed supreme commander to accept the formal surrender of Japan, where he subsequently served as commander of the occupational forces. Following the Communist invasion of South Korea (25 June 1950), he was made commander of the United Nations forces fighting there. On 10 Apr. 1951 President Truman relieved him of his Far Eastern commands.

McClellan, George Brinton (b. Philadelphia, 3 Dec. 1826; d. Woodstock, Conn., 29 Oct. 1885), soldier, studied at the Univ. of Penn. (1840–42) and was graduated from West Point (1846) No. 2 in his class. He saw service during the Mexican War at Contreras, Chirubusco, and Chapultepec. Asst. engineer for the construction of Ft. Delaware (1851), he accompanied Capt. R. B. Marcy on an exploration to trace the source of the Red River (Ark.), then did river and harbor work in Texas, and commanded an expedition to survey a railroad route across the Cascade Mts. After a year in Europe observing the siege of Sevastopol (1855), he resigned from the army (1857) to become chief engineer of the Ill. Central R.R. and then (1860) president of the Ohio and Miss. R.R. At the outbreak of the Civil War he was commissioned maj. gen. of the Ohio volunteers, and on 3 May 1861 appointed maj. gen. of the regular army in command of the Dept. of Ohio. He cleared western Virginia of Confederate troops and was given command of the Division of the Potomac, succeeding (Nov. 1861) Winfield Scott (*q.v.*) as general in chief. His Peninsular campaign ended in the bloody Seven Days' Battles (26 June–2 July 1862). His troops were detached from him and assigned to Gen. Pope's Army of Virginia, but after Pope's defeat at 2nd Manassas, he was called upon to defend Washington. Defeating Lee at

South Mountain (12 Sept.) and Antietam (17 Sept.), he allowed the Confederates to withdraw across the Potomac. Criticized 13 Oct. 1862 by Lincoln for being "overcautious," he was removed from command 7 Nov. Democratic candidate for the Presidency (1864), he was defeated by Lincoln, 212–12 electoral votes. After residing in Europe (1864–68) he served as chief engineer of the Dept. of Docks, N.Y.C. (1870–72), and governor of N.J. (1878–81).

McCormick, Cyrus Hall (b. in Rockbridge County, Va., 15 Feb. 1809; d. Chicago, 13 May 1884), inventor and manufacturer. He invented and patented a hillside plow (1831) and in 1832 designed and constructed a reaper which avoided the errors of the mechanism upon which his father, the inventor Robert McCormick (1780–1846), had been engaged for 2 decades. Successfully demonstrated in 1832, the reaper had the basic components of the modern reaper: the divider, reel, straight reciprocating knife, fingers or guards, platform, main wheel and gearing, and the front-side draft traction. McCormick added improvements to his machine during the 1830's and began its commercial manufacture (*c.*1840) at his birthplace. In 1847 he set up his own plant at Chicago, Ill. Despite widespread competition following the expiration of his patent in 1848, he developed a nationwide business by 1850. In 1851, on the occasion of the world's fair at London, he introduced the reaper into Europe; the machine won major prizes at London, Paris, Hamburg, Lille, Vienna, and elsewhere. Not less important than McCormick's achievement as an inventor was his contribution to modern industrial and business methods. He pioneered in the use of labor-saving, mass-production factory machinery, and in the use of field trials, cash and deferred payments, and guarantees and testimonials in advertising. His reaper increased the food output of the North during the Civil War, and made possible the export grain trade to Europe that helped to bolster the finances of the Union government; it tied agriculture even closer to the market economy, accelerated the settlement of vacant Western lands, and released manpower from the farms for industrial enterprises and urban settlement.

MacDowell, Edward Alexander (b. New York City, 18 Dec. 1861; d. there, 23 Jan. 1908), composer and teacher. In 1876 he went to Paris, where he studied with Marmontel and Savard; subsequently at Wiesbaden and at the Frankfort Conservatory; and in 1881 became chief piano teacher at the Darmstadt Conservatory. By the time he returned to America (1888), he had composed his 1st and 2nd *Modern Suites,* 2 concertos, and a symphonic poem, *Hamlet and Ophelia.* From 1888 to 1896 he lived in Boston, where in addition to teaching and composing he gave recitals. During these years he wrote *Woodland Sketches, Sonata Eroica, Sonata Tragica, Twelve Virtuoso Studies,* and the 1st and 2nd *Indian Suites* for orchestra. He became (1896) professor of music at Columbia University, but resigned in 1904 after a conflict over policy. His health declined rapidly beginning in 1905. Among the works of his last active period are *Sea Pieces, New England Idylls, Norse Sonata,* and *Keltic Sonata.* After his death, MacDowell's farm at Peterboro, N.H., was established by his widow as the MacDowell Colony for artists, writers, and composers.

McGuffey, William Holmes (b. near Claysville, Pa., 23 Sept. 1800; d. Charlottesville, Va., 4 May 1873), educator and compiler of school readers, was graduated from Washington College (1826) and served (1826–36) as professor of languages, philosophy, and philology at Miami University, Oxford, Ohio. He was appointed (1836) president of Cincinnati College and was instrumental in securing the enactment of the law under which the common schools of Ohio were 1st established. He served as president (1839–43) of Ohio University, as professor (1843–45) at Woodward College, Cincinnati, and as professor of moral philosophy (1845–73) at the University of Virginia. He is best remembered for his *Eclectic Readers* (commonly called McGuffey's Readers), 6 schoolbooks for elementary grades that were published between 1836 and 1857 and went through numerous editions that sold an estimated total of 122 million copies. The *Readers,* in part extracts from standard English writers, were an amalgam of entertaining literature, self-improvement themes, and patriotic and moral instruction.

McKinley, William (b. Niles, Ohio, 29 Jan. 1843; d. Buffalo, N.Y., 14 Sept. 1901), 25th President of the U.S., studied at Allegheny College; served in the Union Army during the Civil War, with fighting at South Mountain, Antietam, Winchester, and Cedar Creek (breveted maj., 1865); studied law in Albany, N.Y., and was admitted to the Ohio bar, 1867, commencing practice in Canton. Elected prosecuting attorney of Stark Co. (1869), he was Republican congressman (1876–90, excepting 1882). High-tariff advocate, he sponsored the McKinley Tariff (1890). Defeated on this issue (1890), he was elected governor of Ohio in 1891 and again in 1893. With the support of Marcus A. Hanna, he was Republican nominee for President (1896) on a protective tariff, sound money (gold standard) platform, defeating Bryan. His administration was marked by revision of the tariff upward to the highest rate in U.S. history (Dingley Tariff, 1897), the passage of the Gold Standard Act (1900), and the annexation of Hawaii (7 July 1898). After the blowing up of the battleship *Maine* (15 Feb. 1898), he yielded to press clamor for war and recommended intervention in Cuba (11 Apr.), despite a note received from Spain (10 Apr.) promising to order immediate cessation of hostilities on that island. The acquisition of Puerto Rico, the Philippines, and Guam (1899) as a result of the War with Spain established the U.S. as a world power. He again defeated Bryan for President (1900) in a "full dinner pail" campaign, but was assassinated (6 Sept. 1901) by an anarchist, Leon Czolgosz, on a visit to the Pan-American Exposition in Buffalo.

MacLeish, Archibald (b. Glencoe, Ill., 7 May 1892–   ), poet and public official, was educated at Yale (A.B., 1915) and Harvard (LL.B., 1919). He served from private to capt. in World War I, then practiced law in Boston (1920–23), but left the law for poetry, studying in France (1923–28). Turning from personal and subjective poetry (*Poems, 1924–33* [1933]), he won a Pulitzer Prize with his narrative poem of the conquest of Mexico, *Conquistador* (1932). In a radio verse drama, *The Fall of the City* (1937), as well as in prose writings (*The Irresponsibles* [1940], *A Time to Speak* [1941]), he spoke out on behalf of democratic values and against fascism. Librarian of Congress (1939–44), his appointment aroused criticism because of his lack of special training. He resigned this post to serve as asst. secy. of state (1944–45). During World War II he had also served as dir. of the Office of Facts and Figures (1941–42) and asst. dir. of the Office of War Information (1942–43). In the postwar period he was active in UNESCO and in 1949 became Boylston Professor at Harvard. His *Collected Poems, 1917–52* (1952) earned him another Pulitzer award, as well as the Bollingen and National Book Awards, and a third Pulitzer Prize came to him (1958) for *J B,* his dramatic verse adaptation of the story of Job.

McMillan, Edwin Mattison (b. Redondo Beach, Calif., 18 Sept. 1907–   ), nuclear physicist. He was graduated from the California Institute of Technology (B.S., 1928; M.S., 1929) and received his Ph.D. in physics at Princeton University in 1932. In 1934 he joined the staff of the Radiation Laboratory (director since 1958) at Univ. of Calif., where he has taught physics. During World War II he worked on microwave radar and on sonar (underwater sound detection) at the Navy Radio and Sound Laboratory at San Diego, Calif., and was on the staff of the Los Alamos (N.M.) Atomic Bomb Laboratory. He has made important researches in nuclear physics, particularly in the field of artificial radioactivity. The discoverer of neptunium (element 93), he laid the foundation for the production of plutonium (element 94) by Glenn T. Seaborg and others. In 1951 he and Seaborg were joint recipients of the Nobel prize in chemistry for their discoveries in the chemistry of the transuranic elements. The construction of cyclotrons, such as the synchrotron, synchrocyclotron, cosmotron, and bevatron, with an atom-smashing potential exceeding that of earlier models, was made possible by his theory of phase stability.

Madison, James (b. Port Conway, Va., 16 Mar. 1751; d. Montpelier, Va., 28 June 1836), 4th President of the U.S., was graduated from the College of New Jersey (1771), was chairman of the committee of public safety for Orange Co., Va. (1775), and helped draft the state constitution in the Va. Convention (1776). Member of the Va. Council of State (1778–79), he served in the Continental Congress (1780–83), drafted instructions to Jay to demand of Spain free navigation of the Mississippi, and drew up the compromise plan whereby Va. ceded her Western lands to the U.S. A member of the Va. House of Delegates (1784–86), he was the author of the "Memorial and Remonstrance" (1784) in which he opposed taxation to support religious teachers, and secured the enactment of Jefferson's bill for religious freedom. Active in the call for the Alexandria and Mount Vernon conferences (1785), the Annapolis Convention (1786), and the Federal Convention (1787), he played a most influential role in the adoption of the Constitution, drafting the Va. large-state plan presented by Randolph, and acting as reporter of the proceedings. Author of 28 of the *Federalist* papers, he was largely responsible for securing ratification in Va. Congressman (1789–97), he proposed the 1st 10 amendments to the Constitution known as the Bill of Rights. Parting with Hamilton over debt assumption and later opposing his pro-British leanings, he became a leader of the Jeffersonian Republicans. He married Dolly Payne Todd (1794). He drew up the Va. Resolves (adopted by the state legislature, Dec. 1798), condemning the Alien and Sedition Acts. While Jefferson's Secretary of State (1801–09), he was involved in controversies with France and Great Britain over neutral rights. President (1809–17), being elected over C. C. Pinckney (1808) and over De Witt Clinton (1812), he lost popularity largely as a result of his inept leadership of the War of 1812 ("Mr. Madison's War"), which the U.S.

entered unprepared and disunited. His signing in his 2nd administration of a bill chartering the 2nd Bank of the U.S. and raising tariff rates marked a trend toward Hamiltonian nationalism.

Mahan, Alfred Thayer (b. West Point, N.Y., 27 Sept. 1840; d. Quogue, N.Y., 1 Dec. 1914), naval officer and historian, was graduated from the U.S. Naval Academy (1859) and an officer in the U.S. Navy down to 1896, lecturer on naval history and tactics at Newport War College (1866), and its president (1866–89 and 1892–93). His monumental work, *The Influence of Sea Power upon History, 1660–1783* (1890), examined naval strategy and sea power, to which he gave pivotal importance. His *The Influence of Sea Power upon the French Revolution, 1793–1812* showed how British sea power nullified Napoleon's victories on the Continent. He also wrote *Major Operations of the Navy in the War of American Independence* (1913). His arguments in favor of a big U.S. Navy, a strong merchant marine, naval bases, and colonial possessions had an enormous impact on U.S. political thought and were influential abroad, notably in Germany before World War I.

Mann, Horace (b. Franklin, Mass., 4 May 1796; d. Yellow Springs, Ohio, 2 Aug. 1859), educator, pioneer in the improvement of the common school system. With little formal schooling up to his 17th year, he was graduated with high honors from Brown University (1819), where he was a tutor in Latin and Greek (1819–21). He attended the Litchfield (Conn.) Law School, was admitted to the Mass. bar (1823), and practiced at Dedham (Mass.) and Boston until 1837, meanwhile serving in the Mass. house (1827–33) and senate (1833–37). He was active in humanitarian and reform movements and, as president (1836–37) of the state senate, signed the education bill (1837) providing for a state board of education. As secretary of the board (1837–48) he eliminated many of the evils of the decentralized state school-district system that had been in force for about a half century and instituted the following reforms: a minimum school year of 6 mos., appropriations for public education more than doubled, about 50 new high schools established, public school-teachers' salaries increased, curriculum and methods of instruction revamped, the operations of local schools linked to a central authority, and professional training of teachers improved and regularized. During the period of his secretaryship Mann advanced the principle of non-sectarian education, established and edited the *Common School Journal,* and made illuminating surveys of existing conditions and needs in 12 annual reports that exercised a wide influence on the course of public education in the U.S. In 1839 he established at Lexington, Mass., the 1st state normal school in the U.S. His 7th annual report was devoted to a survey of European educational conditions made by him during a 5-month tour in 1843. He resigned his secretaryship (1848) to occupy the Congressional seat made vacant by the death of John Quincy Adams. He was defeated (1852) as the Free-Soil candidate for the Mass. governorship, and from 1853 until his death served as president of Antioch College, Yellow Springs, Ohio.

Marin, John (b. Rutherford, N.J., 23 Dec. 1872; d. Addison, Maine, 1 Oct. 1953), painter, studied at the Stevens Institute, then in an architect's office, at the Pennsylvania Academy of Fine Arts, the Art Students League, and in Paris. In 1906 he did an oil which was accepted by the Luxembourg. In New York his work was sponsored by Alfred Stieglitz (1864–1946). His annual 1-man shows of sea (notably his Maine seascapes) and landscape, beginning 1909, brought to the attention of the art world an individual mode of painting, reflecting the influence of the Chinese school and both the method of abstract cubism and of expressionism. By 1932 he was producing important work in water color, and by 1936, when a 1-man show was assembled at the Museum of Modern Art, his reputation in the top rank of American artists was secure.

Marion, Francis (b. probably in St. John's Parish, Berkeley County, S.C., c.1732; d. there, 26 Feb. 1795), Revolutionary soldier, popularly known as "the Swamp Fox." He took part (1759, 1761) in campaigns against the Cherokee; was elected to the S.C. Provincial Congress of 1775; became a captain in the S.C. militia; and, as a lt. col. of the Continental Line, commanded a regiment in the attack on Savannah (1779). When the Revolutionary forces under Gen. Horatio Gates were routed at Camden, S.C., Marion resorted to guerrilla warfare against British lines of communication, using Williamsburg as his base of operations and taking refuge in the swamps when numerically superior enemy forces faced him. By also weakening Loyalist potential in S.C., Marion helped to wrest the initiative from the British in the South. In 1781, as a brig. gen. of militia, Marion was instrumental in retaking S.C. from the enemy. He served under Gen. Nathanael Greene at the Battle of Eutaw Springs (8 Sept. 1781), which forced the British to fall back on Charleston.

Marshall, George Catlett (b. Uniontown, Pa., 31 Dec. 1880; d. Washington, D.C., 17 Oct. 1959), soldier and statesman, was graduated from Virginia Military Institute (1901) and commissioned in the U.S. Army (1902). With the A.E.F. (1917–19), he was detailed to the general staff, 1st Div.; was chief of operations, 1st Army; chief of staff, 8th Army Corps; and aided in planning the St. Mihiel and Meuse-Argonne offensives (1918). Aide to Gen. Pershing (1919–24), assistant commandant of the Infantry School, Ft. Benning, Ga. (1927–32), he was detailed to the general staff as chief of the war plans division (1938), and was appointed chief of staff with rank of gen. (1939–45) and gen. of the army (1944). As chairman of combined chiefs of staff he was the principal Allied strategist in World War II. Special Ambassador to China (1945), he served as Secretary of State under President Truman (1947–49), responsible for the "Marshall Plan" (ERP) and in formulating the "Truman Doctrine" (Mar. 1947). In 1950–51 he served as Secretary of Defense, responsible for rebuilding U.S. armed forces and for over-all military planning in defense of Korea. He was awarded the Nobel Peace Prize in 1953.

Marshall, John (b. Germantown [now Midland], Va., 24 Sept. 1755; d. Philadelphia, Pa., 6 July 1835), 3rd Chief Justice of the U.S., served in the American Revolution (1776–79), 1st as lt., then capt.; attended law lectures at William and Mary (May–June 1780), was admitted to the bar, and began practice in Fauquier Co. and (1783) in Richmond. Member of the Va. Assembly (1782–91 and 1795–97), delegate to the state convention which ratified the Federal Constitution (1788), he declined the Attorney Generalship offered by Washington (1795) and the post of Minister to France (1796), but served as a member of the "X.Y.Z." mission to that country (1797–98). Federalist congressman (1799–1800) and then Secretary of State under John Adams (June 1800–Mar. 1801), he was in the meantime appointed Chief Justice of the U.S. Supreme Court (from 31 Jan. 1801). His 34 yrs. on the bench established the prestige of the court. Taking upon himself the task of writing most of the important opinions, he used the Court and the Constitution to curb interference by the states with vested rights. His major opinions include *Marbury* v. *Madison* (1803), with its assertion of the right of judicial review; *Fletcher* v. *Peck* (1810), the *Dartmouth College Case* (1819), and *Ogden* v. *Saunders* (dissenting opinion, 1827), sustaining the contract clause of the Constitution; *McCulloch* v. *Maryland* (1819), with its doctrine of implied powers; and *Gibbons* v. *Ogden* (1824), with its broad interpretation of the commerce clause.

Mason, George (b. near Pasbytanzy, Northern Neck, Va., 1725; d. "Gunston Hall," Va., 7 Oct., 1792), Revolutionary statesman, was educated by private tutors and studied law under John Mercer. He began his political association with Washington in the House of Burgesses (1759), joined with him in anti-Stamp Act activity (1766), and prepared the non-importation resolutions, successfully proposed by Washington to the dissolved burgesses. Author of the Fairfax Resolves (18 July, 1774), restating the colonial position toward the Crown, he framed for the Virginia Convention the Bill of Rights (12 June 1776), model for the 1st part of Jefferson's Declaration of Independence and basis of the 1st 10 Amendments to the federal Constitution, and the major part of the Va. Constitution (29 June 1776). In collaboration with Jefferson, Patrick Henry, and George Wythe, he revised Virginia's legal system. Backer of George Rogers Clark's (*q.v.*) campaign, he also initiated the plan for the cession of Virginia's western lands and influenced Jefferson's 1st Territorial Ordinance (1784). A leading figure at the Federal Convention, he refused to sign the Constitution and campaigned against its ratification, insisting on the inclusion of a Bill of Rights and opposing especially the compromise on the slave trade, which he denounced as "disgraceful to mankind."

Mather, Increase (b. Dorchester, Mass., 21 June 1639; d. Boston, 23 Aug. 1723), Puritan clergyman and political leader, was graduated from Harvard (1656), and received his A.M. from Trinity College, Dublin (1658). Before returning to Mass. (1661), he preached at Great Torrington, Devonshire, Gloucester, and on Guernsey. Teacher of the 2nd Church in Boston (1664), he ultimately (1675) supported the Half-Way Covenant. Acting president of Harvard (1685) and rector (1686–1701), he supported the study of science and sought to maintain Congregational influence. He urged Bostonians (1683) to resist the royal authorities in the *quo warranto* proceedings against the Mass. charter. Representing the Congregational churches, he personally appealed (1688) to James II for renewal of the charter, which he finally obtained from William III. The charter, more liberal than the Puritans expected, gave the lower house the right to elect the Council, a unique feature. In 1692 he returned to Boston with William Phips, the governor whom he had nominated. Unlike his son and supporter Cotton Mather (1663–1728), most prolific of American Puritan writers, he took a cautious attitude toward the Salem witch trials. His *Cases of Conscience Concerning Evil Spirits* (1693), disapproving of spectral evidence, induced Phips to stop the execution of the convicted "witches." Other writings include *Wo to Drunkards* (1673), an early temperance tract, *A Brief History of the Warr with the Indians* (1676), and *Remarkable Providences* (1684).

Maury, Matthew Fontaine (b. near Fredericksburg, Va., 14 Jan. 1806; d. Lexington, Va., 1 Feb. 1873), oceanographer, naval officer, went to school in Tenn. Becoming a midshipman (1825), he made 3 extended cruises in the following 9 yrs. In his leisure time he worked on navigation, publishing (1836) *A New Theoretical and Practical Treatise on Navigation*. In a series of anonymous articles in the Richmond *Whig* (1838) and the *Southern Literary Messenger* (1840–41) he criticized the Dept. of the Navy and proposed reforms. Permanently lamed by a stagecoach accident (1839), he was appointed supt. of the Dept. of Charts and Instruments of the Navy Dept. (1842), devoting himself to hydrographic and meteorological research, and publishing (1847) *Wind and Current Chart of the North Atlantic* and related works (1850–51). The uniform system of recording oceanographic data which he advocated was adopted at the Brussels Intl. Congress (1853) for worldwide use by naval vessels and merchant ships. His charts reduced the time of passage from N.Y. to San Francisco by 47 days (1855). His *The Physical Geography of the Sea* (1855) was the 1st text of modern oceanography. Dropped from active service (1855), but restored (1858), he resigned (1861) to accept a commission as commander in the Confederate States Navy, where he began experiments with electric mines. In England as special Confederate agent, he secured ships of war for the Confederacy. After the Civil War he was involved in an abortive colonization scheme to send ex-Confederates to Mexico. After a stay in England again, he returned to the U.S. (1868) to accept a professorship of meteorology at the Va. Military Inst.

Mayo, William James (b. Le Sueur, Minn., 29 June, 1861; d. Rochester, Minn., 28 July 1939) and his brother, **Charles Horace** (b. Rochester, Minn., 19 July 1865; d. Chicago, 26 May 1939), surgeons, sons of Dr. William Worrall Mayo (1820–1911), pioneer surgeon of the Northwest, both took medical degrees, William at the Univ. of Mich. (1883), Charles at the Chicago Medical College (1888). They gradually took over their father's large practice in Rochester, and father and sons constituted the medical and surgical staff of St. Mary's Hospital, opened in 1889. Observing clinical and surgical practice in Europe and America, they incorporated the latest surgical techniques and originated much, William in abdominal surgery, Charles in surgery of the thyroid gland. Developing a cooperative group clinic, they added general practitioners, surgeons, and laboratory scientists. Out of this grew the Mayo Clinic, a group of some 200 doctors, each a specialist, engaged in cooperative practice. The 1st Mayo Clinic building was constructed in 1912, and in 1915 the brothers donated $1,500,000 (increased to $2,500,000 by 1934) to establish the Mayo Foundation for Medical Education and Research, which became an affiliate of the graduate school of the Univ. of Minn. During World War I they served as chief army consultants for surgical service, receiving the rank of brig. gen. (1921). They published *Collected Papers of the Mayo Clinic and the Mayo Foundation* (1932).

Melville, Herman (b. New York City, 1 Aug. 1819; d. there, 28 Sept. 1891), author. His only formal schooling, which he received at the Albany Academy, ended at the age of 15. He worked as a bank and store clerk, farmer, and teacher, and in 1837 shipped to Liverpool as a cabin boy. In 1841–42 he made a voyage to the South Seas aboard the whaler *Acushnet*. Deserting at the Marquesas Islands, he lived among the natives, went to Tahiti, and in 1843 enlisted as an ordinary seaman on the frigate *United States*. He was discharged at Boston in 1844 and immediately set to work on the novels that were based on his adventures: *Typee* (1846), *Omoo* (1847), *Mardi* (1849), *Redburn* (1849), and *White-Jacket* (1850). Moving (1850) to a farm near Pittsfield, Mass., he formed here his friendship with Nathaniel Hawthorne and wrote his masterpiece, *Moby-Dick* (1851).

This was followed by a period of uneven achievement: *Pierre: or the Ambiguities* (1852), *Israel Potter* (1855), *The Piazza Tales* (1856), and *The Confidence Man* (1857). In 1863 he moved to New York, where he worked as a customs inspector (1866–85) and lived in obscurity. His works of poetry date from this period: *Battle-Pieces and Aspects of the War* (1866), *Clarel* (1876), *John Marr and Other Sailors* (1888), and *Timoleon* (1891). The novelette, *Billy Budd*, completed in his last year, was not published until 1924, following a revival of interest in Melville.

Mencken, Henry Louis (b. Baltimore, Md., 12 Sept. 1880, d. there, 29 Jan. 1956), journalist, literary critic, was graduated from Polytechnic Institute at the head of his class. Police reporter (1899), then city editor (1903) of the Baltimore *Morning Herald,* he joined the staff of the Baltimore *Sun* (1906). In the era following World War I, Mencken's vogue was enormous. Nietzschean iconoclast and debunker, he was critical of his age and cynical about democracy and the "Boobus Americanus." His literary criticism helped bring to the fore such writers as Dreiser, D. H. Lawrence, Ford Maddox Ford, and Sherwood Anderson. With George Jean Nathan, he collaborated on *The Smart Set,* later (1924) on *The American Mercury,* of which Mencken was sole editor, 1925–33. His monumental *The American Language,* published in several editions (1919–48), is a more durable contribution to letters. His popularity waned during the depression, when his former admirers sought more constructive values.

Mergenthaler, Ottmar (b. Hachtel, Germany, 11 May 1854; d. Baltimore, Md., 28 Oct. 1899), inventor of the linotype. After serving his apprenticeship (1868–72) to a watchmaker at Bietigheim, he came to the U.S. in 1872 and was engaged in the making of scientific instruments in the establishments of August Hahl at Washington, D.C. (1872–76) and Baltimore (1876–82). During the early part of this period Mergenthaler worked on the improvement of a writing machine (originated by James O. Cle-

phane and devised by Charles Moore) aimed at the lithographic reproduction of print. A full-scale model failing to operate successfully, Mergenthaler began experimenting with a machine that would eliminate typesetting by hand and supplant stereotyping with the lithographic process. Difficulties compelled Mergenthaler to abandon the project (1879); but shortly after he opened his own establishment (1883), he secured from Clephane an order to construct a typesetting machine capable of obtaining clean type from a matrix. When this device proved to be unsatisfactory, Mergenthaler devised a plan for the stamping and casting of type metal in the same machine; by July 1884, he had successfully incorporated this principle in the first direct-casting linotype. The machine was patented on 26 Aug. 1884, and for its manufacture he and Clephane organized the National Typographic Co. of W.Va.; a subsidiary, the Mergenthaler Printing Company, was established in 1885. By the time of his death Mergenthaler had made an aggregate of more than 50 patented improvements. The linotype revolutionized mass-circulation newspaper production.

Michelson, Albert Abraham (b. Strelno, Prussia, 19 Dec. 1852; d. Pasadena, Calif., 9 May 1931), physicist. Brought to the U.S. as an infant (1854), he was educated at Virginia City, Nev., and San Francisco, Calif., and was graduated (1873) from the U.S. Naval Academy, where he served (1875–77) as an instructor in physics and chemistry. He pursued postgraduate studies (1880–81) at Heidelberg, Berlin, and Paris; taught physics at the Case School of Applied Science, Cleveland, Ohio (1883–89), and at Clark University (1889–92); and in 1892 was made chief professor in the Ryerson Physical Laboratory and head of the physics department at the newly established University of Chicago, where he served until his retirement in 1931. Virtually all of his experiments and researches lay in the field of optics and were marked by skillfully designed apparatuses for attaining precise measurement. His improvements of the Foucault apparatus for measuring the speed of light enabled him to determine the velocity of light with a margin of error of less than 1 in 100,000. He designed (1887) an interferometer with which he determined linear distances in terms of the wave length of light. Using the interferometer, he made (with Edward Williams Morley) the famous experiment (1887) designed to detect the relative motion of the earth through the ether. The findings of the Michelson-Morley experiment contributed much to the development of the theory of relativity. Michelson also determined the length of the meter in terms of the wave length of lines in the cadmium spectrum, was the first to measure the angular diameter of a star, devised the echelon spectrometer, and measured the tides in the solid earth. He was awarded the Nobel prize in physics (1907). He wrote *Light Waves and Their Uses* (1903).

Millay, Edna St. Vincent (b. Rockland, Me., 22 Feb. 1892; d. Austerlitz, N.Y., 19 Oct. 1950), poet, wrote her 1st long poem, "Renascence," at 19. Published in *The Lyric Year,* a prize anthology (1912), it won her critical acclaim. Her education at Barnard and Vassar (A.B., 1917) was financed by a woman admirer of that poem. Entering enthusiastically into Bohemian life in Greenwich Village, N.Y.C., she published in that period *A Few Figs from Thistles* (1920) and *Aria da Capo* (1921), an antiwar piece. In protest against the Sacco-Vanzetti trial, she wrote the poem "Justice Denied in Mass." (1927) and was arrested for participating in the "death watch" demonstration outside the Boston State House. Recognizing the Nazi threat to Western civilization, she wrote *There Are No Islands Any More* (1940), a plea for U.S. aid to Britain and France, and *The Murder of Lidice* (1942). An advocate of sexual equality for women, her love poetry is characterized by an ironic poignance and a clarity of style. Her works include *Buck in the Snow* (1928); *Fatal Interview* (1931), a collection of sonnets; *Huntsman, What Quarry?* (1939); *Collected Sonnets* (1941). She was awarded the Pulitzer Prize in Poetry (1923).

Miller, Arthur (b. New York City, 7 Oct. 1917–), playwright, was graduated from the Univ. of Mich. (1938). Writing plays while at college, he later joined the Federal Theater Project in N.Y. In 1944 *Situation Normal* examined army conditions, and *Focus* (1945), a novel, dealt with anti-Semitism. His 1st Broadway play, *The Man Who Had All the Luck* (1944), was followed by *All My Sons* (1947; N.Y. Drama Critics Circle award). His Pulitzer Prize-winning *Death of a Salesman* (1949), depicting the drama of a small man destroyed by an empty society, has been called the modern American tragedy and brought Miller worldwide attention. Other plays include *The Crucible* (1953) and *View from the Bridge* (1955). He was sentenced (1957) for contempt of Congress for refusing to name persons who had attended Communist meetings with him, but his conviction was reversed on appeal. Married to movie star Marilyn Monroe (1956, divorced 1961), he wrote for the screen (*The Misfits*).

Miller, Samuel Freeman (b. Richmond, Ky., 5 Apr. 1816; d. Washington, D.C., 13 Oct. 1890), jurist, was graduated from the medical school of Transylvania University (1838), practiced for 12 years, then turned to the law, and was admitted to the bar (1847). Becoming an abolitionist, he moved to Keokuk, Iowa (1850) and became a state leader of the Republican party. Lincoln appointee as associate justice of the U.S. Supreme Court (1862), he was a stanch supporter of the national authority. In his dissent in the *Test-Oath Cases* (1867) he upheld the loyalty oath. In the *Slaughterhouse Case* (1873) he denied that the 14th Amendment was applicable to business corporations, but restricted it to Negroes. In dissent in *Hepburn* v. *Griswold* (1870) he upheld the legality of the Legal Tender Act, and in *Ex parte Yarbrough* (1884) he upheld the authority of the Federal government to supervise Congressional elections in the states (1884). He voted with the Republican majority in the Electoral Commission (1876).

Millikan, Robert Andrews (b. Morrison, Ill., 22 Mar. 1868; d. Pasadena, Calif.,

19 Dec. 1953), physicist. He was graduated from Oberlin College (A.B., 1891; A.M., 1893), received the degree of Ph.D. at Columbia (1895), and studied at Berlin and Göttingen (1895–96). He was a member of the physics staff (1896–1921) at the University of Chicago, and in 1921 became director of the Norman Bridge Laboratory of Physics at the California Institute of Technology at Pasadena. He received the Nobel prize in physics (1923) for his determination of the exact values of the mass and charge of the electron. He also made important investigations in the laws of reflection of gas molecules, cosmic rays, the absorption of X rays, the polarization of light from incandescent surfaces, the effect of temperature on photoelectric discharge, and the velocities of electrons discharged from metals under the influence of ultraviolet light. He was the author of *Mechanics, Molecular Physics and Heat* (1901), *Electricity, Sound and Light* (1908), *The Electron* (1917), *Cosmic Rays* (1939), and others.

Mitchell, William Lendrum (b. Nice, France, 29 Dec. 1879; d. New York City, 19 Feb. 1936), military aviation officer and pioneer exponent of air power, popularly known as "Billy" Mitchell. He attended Racine College, Wis., was graduated from George Washington University, enlisted as a private at the outbreak of the Spanish-American War (1898), and in the same year was commissioned an officer in the U.S. Army Signal Corps. He was graduated (1909) from the Army Staff College, served on the Mexican border (1912), and in 1913 became the youngest officer ever appointed to the army general staff. During World War I he was chief of air service for several units, including the U.S. 1st Corps and the U.S. 1st and 2nd Armies, and after the war was promoted to the rank of brig. gen. and named director of military aviation. As assistant chief of the Army Air Service from 1920 to 1924, Mitchell openly criticized national aviation policy and demonstrated his confidence in air power as a major arm of warfare by sinking target battleships with aerial bombs. He called for a unified command of the armed forces. In 1925, while serving as air officer for the 8th Corps Area, he accused the high military and naval command of "incompetency, criminal negligence, and almost treasonal administration of national defense." He was court-martialed, found guilty, and suspended for 5 yrs. without pay or allowances. While President Coolidge upheld the suspension, he granted Mitchell half pay and restored his allowances; Mitchell, however, resigned from the service (1 Feb. 1926) and continued his criticism of official military aviation policy. He was posthumously restored to the service (1942) with the rank of maj. gen.

Monroe, James (b. Westmoreland Co., Va., 28 Apr. 1758; d. New York City, 4 July 1831), 5th President of the U.S., left William and Mary (1774–76) to serve in the Continental Army, fighting at Harlem Heights, White Plains, Trenton, Brandywine, Germantown, and Monmouth. He studied law under Jefferson (1780–83), and entered the Va. House of Delegates (1782) and the Continental Congress (1783–86). In the Va. Convention (1788) he opposed the Federal Constitution. As U.S. senator (1790–94), he joined the Jeffersonian Republicans. Minister to France (1794–96), he was recalled for failure to allay resentment caused by the Jay Treaty. Governor of Va. (1799–1802), he returned to France as envoy extraordinary (1802–03), joining R. R. Livingston with instructions to buy New Orleans from France and West Fla. from Spain. Exceeding instructions, he acquired all La. Subsequently he served as Minister to Great Britain (1803–06) and, with Charles Pinckney, went to Madrid (1804–05) in a futile effort to settle a boundary dispute. Again governor of Va. (1811), he resigned to become Madison's Secretary of State (1811–17) and to serve for a time as Secretary of War (1814–15). Elected President (1816) and reelected (1820) with all but 1 electoral vote, his administration was characterized as an "Era of Good Feelings" following a quarter century of rivalry between Federalists and Republicans. He settled boundaries with Canada and eliminated border forts, acquired Fla. (1819), and formulated, with modifications suggested by J. Q. Adams, the

Monroe Doctrine (2 Dec. 1823), which he decided to issue unilaterally.

Moody, Dwight Lyman (b. Northfield, Mass., 5 Feb. 1837; d. there, 22 Dec. 1899), evangelist, was admitted to membership in the Congregational Church at Boston (1856), but moved to Chicago, where he combined a career as a shoe salesman with church work. In 1860 he abandoned business to become an independent city missionary; in 1866, after having served with the U.S. Christian Commission during the Civil War, he was made president of the Chicago Young Men's Christian Association. He made his mark as a lay preacher dedicated to the saving of souls. In 1873–75, during his 3rd trip to Great Britain, he and the organist and singer, Ira D. Sankey, conducted a series of revivalist meetings which were attended by an estimated total of 2,530,000 people and led to an almost unprecedented religious awakening in the British Isles. Upon his return to the U.S., he and Sankey conducted evangelistic campaigns (1875–76) in Philadelphia, New York, and Brooklyn, and between 1877 and 1881 preached in cities including Chicago, Hartford, Baltimore, St. Louis, and San Francisco. Subsequent evangelistic campaigns in Great Britain (1881–84, 1891–92) equaled the success of his British tour of 1873–75. Between 1884 and 1891 Moody was active as an evangelist in many small cities in the U.S. and Canada. He founded the Chicago Bible Institute (1889) and the Bible Institute Colportage Association (1894). The spiritual awakening he stimulated in American colleges led to the organization of the Student Volunteer Movement, a group devoted to foreign missionary service.

Morgan, Daniel (b. 6 July 1736, Hunterdon County, N.J.; d. Winchester, Va., 6 July 1802), Revolutionary soldier, ran away from home, worked as a farm laborer and teamster in the Shenandoah Valley in Virginia, was a lieut. in Pontiac's War, and accompanied (1774) Lord Dunmore's expedition to western Pa. Commissioned (22 June 1775) capt. of a company of Va. riflemen, he traveled from Winchester to Boston in 21 days.

On the march to Quebec with Benedict Arnold (q.v.), he took command after Arnold was wounded there, captured the 1st barrier, and penetrated to the lower city, but was forced to surrender to overwhelming odds. Released (12 Nov. 1776), he was commissioned col. of a Va. regt. and, rejoining Washington, organized a corps of 500 sharpshooters. His part at Saratoga was notable. At Freeman's Farm his riflemen checked the movement to turn the American left and at Bemis Heights he took his men on a wide circuit around the enemy's right and from the flank and rear of the British poured deadly fire on Lord Balcarre's troops. Sent (1780) by Nathanael Greene (q.v.) to harass British outposts, he inflicted a disastrous defeat upon Tarleton in the battle of Cowpens (17 Jan. 1781), a military classic and model for Greene at Guilford Courthouse and Eutaw Springs. In command of the Va. militia (1794) he assisted in putting down the Whisky Rebellion. He served 1 term in Congress (1797–99).

Morgan, John Pierpont (b. Hartford, Conn., 17 Apr. 1837; d. Rome, Italy, 31 Mar. 1913), financier. After being educated at Boston, he received further schooling at Vevey, Switzerland, and at the University of Göttingen; entered (1856) his father's banking house at London; and came to New York (1857), where he established J.P. Morgan & Co. (1860), which acted as agent for his father's firm. During the Civil War he was engaged in foreign exchange and gold speculation. In 1864 he became a member of the firm of Dabney, Morgan & Co., and in 1869 won control of the Albany & Susquehanna R.R. from Jay Gould and Jim Fisk. In 1871 he established the New York firm of Drexel, Morgan & Co., which in 1895 became known as J. P. Morgan & Co. Together with its allied houses in London and Paris, this firm became one of the leading and most influential banking houses in the world. An exponent of combination, integration, and centralized financial control in the business and industrial world, Morgan played an important role in the reorganization of American railroads (1885 *et seq.*). After the Panic of 1893, the Cleveland administration called upon him to relieve the pressure on the Treasury. Morgan took part in the financing and organization of the United States Steel Corp. (1901) and the International Harvester Co. (1902). In alliance with James J. Hill, he became embroiled in a struggle with Edward H. Harriman for control of the Northern Pacific R.R. that ultimately came before the Supreme Court in the *Northern Securities Case* (1904). During the panic of 1907 he helped stabilize financial conditions. In 1912 he became the chief target of the Pujo investigation of the so-called "Money Trust." Perhaps the leading private art collector of his time, he left at his death valuable collections of books, manuscripts, and art objects now housed in the Pierpont Morgan Wing of the Metropolitan Museum and in the Pierpont Morgan Library, both in New York City.

Morgan, Lewis Henry (b. Aurora, N.Y., 21 Nov. 1818; d. Rochester, N.Y., 17 Dec. 1881), ethnologist and anthropologist, was graduated from Union College (1840), studied law, and moved to Rochester, where he practiced in partnership with George F. Danforth. Member of the N.Y. Assembly (1861–68) and State Senate (1868–69), he is best known for his work in ethnology and as the "father of American anthropology." His 1st research was an investigation of the customs and institutions of the Iroquois, inspired by his adoption (1 Oct. 1847) into the Hawk clan of the Seneca in appreciation of his services in defeating ratification of a treaty unfavorable to the Seneca. His *League of the Ho-dé-no-sau-nee, or Iroquois* (1851), written in collaboration with Ely S. Parker, was the 1st scientific account of an Indian tribe. In addition to his Iroquois research, he made ethnological investigations (1859–62) of the Prairie Indians and observed similarities between the kinship systems of the Iroquois and other Indian tribes in North America. These observations led to his *Systems of Consanguinity and Affinity of the Human Family* (1870), a comprehensive collection of the kinship systems of the world. In *Ancient Society* (1877) he formulated his social evolu-

tionary scheme of culture as having developed in stages from savagery to barbarism and then to civilization. His postulate of unilateral evolution has been modified basically by later anthropology. He also wrote *Houses and Houselife of the American Aborigines* (1881).

Morgan, Thomas Hunt (b. Lexington, Ky., 25 Sept. 1866; d. Pasadena, Calif., 4 Dec. 1945), biologist. He was graduated from the State College of Kentucky (B.S., 1886; M.S., 1888) and from Johns Hopkins (Ph.D., 1890), served as professor of biology (1891–1904) at Bryn Mawr College, was professor of experimental zoology (1904–28) at Columbia, and in 1928 was named director of biological science at Calif. Inst. of Technology. After carrying out his initial researches in experimental embryology and regeneration, he made his more noted experiments and studies on heredity and mutation in the fruit fly (Drosophila). His findings made valuable contributions to the knowledge of the genes and the nature of mutations, and provided the basis for the development of the science of genetics. For his work in the phenomena of heredity, Morgan received the Nobel prize in physiology and medicine (1933). Among his publications are *Regeneration* (1901), *Evolution and Adaptation* (1903), *Heredity and Sex* (1913), *Mechanism of Mendelian Heredity* (1915), *Critique of the Theory of Evolution* (1916), *The Physical Basis of Heredity* (1919), and *The Theory of the Genes* (1926).

Morris, Robert (b. at or near Liverpool, England, 31 Jan. 1734; d. Philadelphia, Pa., 8 May 1806), financier of the American Revolution. He received a brief schooling at Philadelphia, where he joined the shipping and mercantile house of Charles Willing, becoming partner of the latter's son Thomas (1754), under the firm name of Willing & Morris. Morris was not definitely committed to the Patriot cause until 1775. The Pa. Assembly named him (30 June 1775) a member of the council of safety. He also served on the committee of correspondence and was chosen (Nov. 1775) as a delegate to the Continental Congress, in which he served until 1778. He was a member of several committees, including the secret committee for procuring munitions. He was occasionally assigned banking business by Congress; meanwhile, he continued his private activities as a member of his Philadelphia firm in importing military supplies. Although he voted against the Declaration of Independence in July 1776 on the ground that it was premature, he signed it in Aug. When Congress fled from Philadelphia (Dec. 1776), Morris remained there to continue the work of the committee of secret correspondence to which he had been appointed in Jan. 1776. He borrowed money and purchased supplies that were of crucial importance to the weakened Revolutionary forces. During the critical financial period, 1780–81, Morris was appointed by Congress (20 Feb. 1781) as superintendent of finance. In this capacity, he wielded the powers of a financial dictator. He strengthened the public credit, instituted an economy program, and at times used notes based on his personal credit. He also served as marine agent for the government. His efforts contributed directly to the victory over Cornwallis at Yorktown. A loan he secured from the French enabled the organization (1781–82) of the Bank of North America. He resigned his government post on 24 Jan. 1783. Morris was a delegate to the Annapolis Convention (1786) and, as a delegate to the Federal Convention of 1787, supported a strong central government. He declined Washington's offer of the post of Secretary of the Treasury in the 1st administration, and served (1789–95) as U.S. senator from Pennsylvania. His involvement in various land speculations, including a large interest he held in the present site of Washington, D.C., brought his financial ruin. Confined to the Philadelphia debtors' prison (1798–1801), he never regained his fortune.

Morse, Samuel Finley Breese (b. Charlestown, Mass., 27 Apr. 1791; d. New York City, 2 Apr. 1872), artist and inventor. The son of the Congregational clergyman, Jedidiah Morse (1761–1826; known as the "father of American geography"), he

was graduated from Yale (1810), and in 1811 accompanied the painter Washington Allston to England. Morse spent the next 4 yrs. studying under Allston and at the Royal Academy in London. Returning to Boston (1815), he opened a studio, but the lack of sufficient portrait commissions compelled him to seek patrons elsewhere. He scored his 1st success at Charleston, S.C., where he passed the winters from 1818 to 1821, and in 1823 settled at New York. In 1825 he executed at Washington his 2 portraits of Lafayette. He was the chief founder of the National Academy of Design and served as its 1st president (1826–42). He went to Europe in 1829, and upon his return in 1832 was appointed professor of painting and sculpture in the University of the City of New York (later New York University). During the period 1832–35 he was active in the Native American movement and was its candidate (1836) for mayor of New York. Morse abandoned painting (c.1837) to devote himself to experimenting with the transmission of signals by electricity, an idea 1st broached to him during his return voyage from Europe in 1832; at that time Morse had set down his original conception of an electromagnetic recording telegraph. While working on the apparatus, which after many experiments was improved by the addition of Joseph Henry's intensity magnet, Morse devised a code of dots and dashes that was named after him (Morse code). Morse's most important contribution was his system of electromagnetic renewers or relays for the transmission of messages over great distances and through any number of stations and branch lines. In the development of the telegraph, he received financial support from Alfred Vail, who became his partner in 1837. Although Morse filed for a patent in 1837, he did not receive it until 1844. Congress appropriated (1843) $30,000 for an experimental line from Washington to Baltimore that was constructed by Ezra Cornell. On 24 May 1844 Morse transmitted over this line the message, "What hath God wrought!" When the government refused to buy the rights to the apparatus, Morse and his associates formed a company for the manufacture of the telegraph.

Morton, William Thomas Green (b. Charlton, Mass., 9 Aug. 1819; d. New York City, 15 July 1868), dentist and pioneer in surgical anesthesia. He was educated at academies in Northfield and Leicester, entered (1840) the College of Dental Surgery at Baltimore, Md., and in 1842 began his practice at Farmington, Conn. In 1842–43 he set up a joint practice at Boston with Dr. Horace Wells of Hartford, Conn., who in 1844 was to use nitrous oxide (laughing gas) in the extraction of teeth. When the partnership was terminated in late 1843, Morton remained in Boston. He matriculated (1844) at Harvard Medical School, but attended only for a brief period. At about this time, at the suggestion of Prof. Charles T. Jackson, a chemist, Morton employed ether in drops as a local anesthetic in filling a tooth. Jackson had also demonstrated that the inhalation of sulphuric ether induced loss of consciousness; it was this method that Morton used in experiments on animals and himself. He performed the painless extraction of an ulcerated tooth (30 Sept. 1846) after using ether inhalation on the patient. Following other successful painless extractions, Dr. John Collins Warren, a Boston surgeon, arranged for the use of Morton's discovery in an operation at the Massachusetts General Hospital. On 16 Oct. 1846, with Morton administering the anesthetic in the presence of physician spectators, Warren removed a vascular tumor from the neck of a patient. Formal announcement of the discovery was made on 18 Nov. 1846 in the *Boston Medical and Surgical Journal*. Morton patented his discovery under the name of "letheon" (12 Nov. 1846). When the French Academy of Medicine awarded a joint prize of 5,000 francs (1847) to Jackson and Morton, the latter did not accept his share, asserting that the discovery was his alone. Morton's claims led Dr. Crawford W. Long (1815–1878) of Athens, Ga., to publish accounts (1848, 1853) of independent discoveries he had made with sulphuric ether in 8 operations on human beings performed between 1842 and 1846. To Morton, however, goes the major credit for the discovery, for he was the 1st to make a public demonstration with assumption of full responsibility for the consequences.

Motley, John Lothrop (b. Dorchester, Mass., 15 Apr. 1814; d. in Dorsetshire, England, 29 May 1877), historian and diplomat. He was graduated from Harvard (1831), studied at Göttingen and Berlin, and after returning to Boston wrote two novels, *Morton's Hope* (1839) and *Merrymount* (1849). He served (1841–42) as secretary of legation at St. Petersburg and in 1847 began work on the historical subject that was to occupy the rest of his life. To further his researches in archives in Germany and Holland, he went to Europe in 1851. *The Rise of the Dutch Republic* (3 vols., 1856) indicated the main lines of Motley's history and his point of view: his dramatic narrative treatment, his preoccupation with political and religious developments, and his studied contrast of liberty and absolutism. He also published *The History of the United Netherlands* (4 vols., 1860, 1867) and *The Life and Death of John of Barneveld* (2 vols., 1874). From 1861 to 1867 Motley was Minister to Austria and from 1869 to 1870 Minister to Great Britain.

Muller, Hermann Joseph (b. New York City, 21 Dec. 1890–), geneticist, received his degrees at Columbia (B.A., 1910; M.A., 1911; Ph.D., 1915), and taught at Cornell, Rice Inst., Columbia, and the Univ. of Texas. Senior geneticist (1933–37) of the Inst. of Genetics in Moscow, he has since 1945 been professor of zoology, Indiana Univ. His genetics research was begun in 1911 and conducted mainly by breeding experiments in the fruit fly, *Drosophila*. Working with Thomas Hunt Morgan (*q.v.*), he established the principle of linear linkage, accounting for the inheritance of characteristics on the basis of a linear arrangement of genes. He made a special study of mutations leading to permanently altered, hereditary characteristics, and described the gene as probably a single molecule. For his discovery of hereditary changes or mutations produced by X rays, he was awarded the Nobel Prize (1946). His writings include *The Mechanism of Mendelian Heredity* (with others, 1915), *Out of the Night* (1935), and *Genetics,*

Medicine, and Man (with others, 1947).

Nast, Thomas (b. Landau, Bavaria, 27 Sept. 1840; d. Guayaquil, Ecuador, 7 Dec. 1902), artist and cartoonist, came to New York in 1846, studied art under Theodore Kaufman and at the National Academy of Design, and at 15 became draftsman for *Frank Leslie's Illustrated Weekly*. He was sent to London by the New York *Illustrated News* (1860), and accompanied Garibaldi as artist of the *Illustrated London News* and *Le Monde Illustré* (Paris). Returning to New York (1861), he became a staff artist of *Harper's Weekly*, with war drawings (*Emancipation*, 24 Jan. 1863; *Compromise with the South*, 3 Sept. 1864), which influenced public opinion. His fame rests largely on his dramatic cartoons exposing the Tweed Ring in New York City (1869–72), notably *Let Us Prey* and *Tiger Loose*. His adaptation of the tiger to represent Tammany proved a potent weapon of municipal reform. He also invented the elephant for the Republican party and popularized the donkey for the Democrats. The line and texture of his bold, graphic style lost none of their bite in being engraved in wood.

Niebuhr, Reinhold (b. Wright City, Mo., 21 June 1892–), clergyman and theologian. He was graduated from the Yale Divinity School (B.D., 1914; A.M., 1915), was ordained (1915) as a minister in the Evangelical Synod of North America, and served as a pastor at Detroit (1915–28). In 1928 he became assistant professor of the philosophy of religion at the Union Theological Seminary in New York, where he has been professor of applied Christianity since 1930. Primarily concerned with social ethics and politically oriented, Niebuhr's theology combines the political liberalism of the Social Gospel with Biblical theology, stressing original sin and God's judgment. It differs from Continental Neo-orthodoxy (Karl Barth and Emil Brunner) in its refusal to consider man as having lost contact with God. Among his works are *Does Civilization Need Religion?* (1927), *Moral Man and Immoral Society* (1932), *Reflections on the End of an Era* (1934), *An Interpretation of Christian Ethics* (1935), *Beyond Tragedy* (1937), *Christianity and Power Politics* (1940), *The Nature and Destiny of Man* (1941–43), *Faith and History* (1949), and *The Irony of American History* (1952).

Nimitz, Chester William (b. Fredericksburg, Tex., 23 Feb. 1885–), naval officer, was graduated from the U.S. Naval Academy (1905), and served as chief of staff to the commander of the U.S. Atlantic submarine fleet during World War I. In 1939 he was made chief of the Bureau of Navigation with the rank of rear adm. After the Pearl Harbor attack he took over command of the Pacific Fleet from Admiral Husband E. Kimmel. Commander of the Pacific Fleet and the Pacific Ocean Areas with the rank of adm., his initial strategy was to defend the Hawaiian approaches and the lines of mainland communication. Given much of the credit for the strategy of "island hopping," he began his offensive with the amphibious landing on Guadalcanal (7 Aug. 1942) and the decisive victory in the naval Battle of Guadalcanal (12–15 Nov.). In 1943 he pursued his offensive aimed at seizing the Solomons, the Gilberts and Marshalls, and the Bonin Islands to come within effective bombing distance of Japan. At the time of Japan's surrender he commanded 6,256 ships and 4,847 combat aircraft, the largest fighting fleet in history. At the Japanes surrender ceremonies in Tokyo Bay he signed for the U. S. Chief of Naval Operations, 1945–47, and special assist. to the Secy. of the Navy since 1947, he headed (1949) the UN mediation commission in the dispute over Kashmir.

Norris, George William (b. Sandusky, Ohio, 11 July 1861; d. McCook, Neb., 2 Sept. 1944), statesman, was graduated in law (1882) from Northern Indiana Normal School (now Valparaiso University), moved to Beaver City, Neb. (1885), and served 3 terms as prosecuting attorney of Furnas Co. and then as a district judge (1895–1902). Congressman (1903–18), U.S. senator from Neb. (1913–42), as a progressive Republican he supported the Bull Moose movement (1912), opposed U.S. entry into World War I as well as participation in the League of Nations, but endorsed U.S. participation in World War II. Sponsor of the Norris-La Guardia Anti-injunction Act (1932) and of the 20th (Lame Duck) Amendment to the Federal Constitution (1933), his most notable service was his fight for federal water power regulation and for public ownership and operation of hydroelectric plants. In 1928 he secured passage of a bill providing for government operation of the dam at Muscle Shoals, but it was vetoed by Coolidge. Another bill (1931) was vetoed by Hoover. The Tennessee Valley Authority (TVA) constituted the culmination of his efforts. Norris Dam (near Knoxville) was named in his honor.

Ochs, Adolph Simon (b. Cincinnati, Ohio, 12 Mar. 1858; d. Chattanooga, Tenn., 8 Apr. 1935), newspaper publisher. He received most of his schooling from his parents and during his boyhood served his apprenticeship in the newspaper business on the Knoxville (Tenn.) *Chronicle*. In 1878 he purchased the controlling interest in the Chattanooga *Times*, then on the brink of failure, and instituted a policy of full, accurate, and reliable reporting that characterized his subsequent career (1896–1935) as publisher of *The New York Times*. Taking over the *Times* when it was on the verge of bankruptcy, Ochs reorganized the newspaper according to the canons of responsible journalism in a day when the influence of the sensational press in New York City was at its height. By 1900 he had made the *Times* a profitable venture, and under his guidance it became known as the "newspaper of record" because of its extensive coverage of public events and its intelligent specialized reporting. His view of the responsibility of a free press is expressed in the motto he selected for the *Times:* "All the news that's fit to print."

Olmsted, Frederick Law (b. Hartford, Conn., 26 Apr. 1822; d. Waverly, Mass., 28 Aug. 1903), landscape architect and author. He attended Yale (1842–43) and from 1847 to 1857 engaged in experimental farming in Conn. and Staten Island. In 1850 he made an overseas tour,

recording his observations in *The Walks and Talks of an American Farmer in England* (1852). His 3 journeys in the South (1852 *et seq.*) were described in as many volumes, comprising one of the most valuable factual records of Southern social and economic life on the eve of the Civil War: *A Journey in the Seaboard Slave States* (1856), *A Journey Through Texas* (1857), and *A Journey in the Back Country* (1860), all 3 of which were condensed in *The Cotton Kingdom* (2 vols., 1861). In 1857 he was appointed superintendent of Central Park, New York City, and in 1858, in collaboration with Calvert Vaux (1824–95), he won the prize competition for its new design. In 1858 he was named chief architect of Central Park, a pioneer enterprise of American municipal planning. In numerous commissions, most of them executed between 1865 and 1895, Olmsted laid the foundations of American landscape architecture and made the public park a significant factor in urban life. Among his works are Prospect Park, Brooklyn; Riverside Park, New York; the grounds of the National Capitol, Washington, D.C.; the park systems of Boston, Hartford, and Louisville; Mount Royal Park, Montreal; the grounds of the World's Fair (1893) at Chicago; Roland Park, Baltimore; Belle Isle Park, Detroit; and the grounds of Stanford University and the University of California.

O'Neill, Eugene Gladstone (b. New York City, 16 Oct. 1888; d. Boston, Mass., 27 Nov. 1953), dramatist. The son of the actor James O'Neill, he attended Princeton (1906) and, after a period of travel and adventure, was a student (1914–15) in the 47 Workshop of George Pierce Baker at Harvard. He became associated (1916) with the Provincetown Players, who produced (1916–20) 10 of his 1-act plays, including *Bound East for Cardiff* and *The Moon of the Caribbees*. With the Broadway production of *Beyond the Horizon* (1920), which was awarded the Pulitzer prize, O'Neill took his place as the foremost American dramatist of his day. He also won the Pulitzer prize for *Anna Christie* (1921) and *Strange Interlude* (1928), both of which were later produced as motion pictures, and in 1936 was awarded the Nobel prize in literature. A resourceful and inventive dramatist, whose work has passed through several stages of development including naturalism, expressionism, symbolism, romanticism, and a combination of Greek tragedy and Freudian psychology, O'Neill has written *The Emperor Jones* (1920), *Diff'rent* (1921), *The Hairy Ape* (1922), *All God's Chillun Got Wings* (1924), *Desire Under the Elms* (1924), *The Great God Brown* (1926), *Lazarus Laughed* (1927), *Marco Millions* (1928), *Dynamo* (1929), *Mourning Becomes Electra* (1931), *Ah, Wilderness!* (1933), *Days Without End* (1934), and *The Iceman Cometh* (1946). Unproduced before his death were *A Touch of the Poet* (1957) and *Long Day's Journey into Night* (1956), Pulitzer Prize play, 1957.

Otis, James (b. West Barnstable, Mass., 5 Feb. 1725; d. Andover, Mass., 23 May, 1783), pre-Revolutionary leader, was admitted to the Plymouth County bar (1748), and 2 yrs. later moved to Boston. He resigned his office as King's advocate general of the vice-admiralty court to appear on behalf of a group of Boston merchants to oppose (1761) as unconstitutional the issuance by the superior court of writs of assistance—general search warrants to aid the enforcement of the Sugar Act of 1733. Writing years later, John Adams asserted: "Then and there the child Independence was born." Although the court issued the writs, Otis took the battle to the general court, to which he was elected that year. Chief target of Otis was Thomas Hutchinson (*q.v.*), whose appointment as chief justice in place of Otis's father, James, senior, an active candidate, aroused the enmity of father and son. A vigorous pamphleteer, he expounded his constitutional views in *A Vindication of the Conduct of the House of Representatives* (1762) and most notably in *The Rights of the British Colonies Asserted and Proved* (1764). Participating in the Stamp Act Congress (1765), which had been summoned at his suggestion, he advocated colonial representation in Parliament and conceded the supremacy of Parliament (*A Vindication of the British Colonies* [1765]). By the time of the Townshend Acts he had become even more moderate in his political views, although he was increasingly abusive and unbalanced in personal behavior and was caned in a coffeehouse brawl by John Robinson, a customs officer. In 1771 his younger brother Samuel A. Otis was appointed his guardian, and he took no part in the Revolution. His death was dramatic; he was struck down by lightning in the Isaac Osgood farmhouse.

Paine, Thomas (b. Thetford, Norfolk, England, 29 Jan. 1737; d. New York City, 8 June 1809), Revolutionary propagandist. The son of a Quaker corsetmaker, he was engaged in a wide variety of occupations before coming to America in 1774. He settled at Philadelphia, where he contributed to the *Pennsylvania Magazine* and wrote *Common Sense*, an anonymous pamphlet published on 10 Jan. 1776. In *Common Sense*, reputed to have sold 120,000 copies in 3 mos. and to have attained a total sale of 500,000, Paine advocated the immediate declaration of independence on both practical and ideological grounds. Joining the Revolutionary army, he took part in the retreat across N.J., writing at Newark the 1st of his *Crisis* papers (1776–83), of which the opening passage was: "These are the times that try men's souls. The summer soldier and the sunshine patriot will, in this crisis, shrink from the service of their country." The pamphlet, ordered read to the troops in the Revolutionary encampments, resolved by its eloquent patriotism the hesitation of many in and out of the army. In subsequent *Crisis* papers Paine favored a strong Federal union and called for effective fiscal measures. He served (1777–79) as secretary to the committee on foreign affairs of the Continental Congress, and in 1779 was named clerk of the Pa. assembly. After peace was concluded with Great Britain, he lived at New York and at Bordentown, N.J., until 1787, when he went to France and England. In the *Rights of Man* (1791–92), Paine defended republican government and the practical measures of the early phases of the French Revolution in reply to Edmund Burke's *Reflections on the French Revolution* (1790). *The Rights of Man*, which contained some seditious passages, was suppressed by the British government, and Paine, at that time in France, was tried for treason and was outlawed (1792). Made a citizen by the French Assembly (1792), Paine was elected to the Convention. He associated himself with the Girondist party; with the fall of the Girondins, he was stripped of his French citizenship and imprisoned (Dec. 1793). He remained in jail until Nov. 1794, when he was released through the intervention of the U.S. Minister, James Monroe. While in jail he began work on *The Age of Reason* (1794–96), a deistic work, beginning: "I believe in one God, and no more; and I hope for happiness beyond this life." In his closing years, spent in N.J. and N.Y., Paine lived in poverty and obscurity. He was buried on his farm in New Rochelle, N.Y.; in 1819 William Cobbett exhumed the remains and took them to England.

Parker, Theodore (b. Lexington, Mass., 24 Aug. 1810; d. Florence, Italy, 10 May 1860), clergyman, theologian, and author, graduated (1836) from the Harvard Divinity School, was ordained (1837) at the West Roxbury (Mass.) Church, and during the course of the Unitarian controversy supported the radical wing, enunciating his position in his sermon on "The Transient and Permanent in Christianity" (1841), which endorsed the views set forth by Emerson in the "Divinity School Address" (1838). His interpretation of Christianity as the high point of evolutionary progress, and his call for a new theology based on the immanence of God in human experience and in nature, appeared in *A Discourse of Matters Pertaining to Religion* (1842). His Transcendentalist views brought him into open conflict with the orthodox Unitarians and with the liberal clergy of the Boston Association of Ministers, and led to his resignation from the West Roxbury pulpit (1852) and to his installation as minister of the newly created 28th Congregational Society of Boston. An erudite scholar, Parker was also active in humanitarian and reform movements. He wrote *A Letter to the People of the United States Touching the Matter of Slavery* (1848), aided in the escape of fugitive slaves, and

played a notable role in the defense of Anthony Burns (1854). He supported the New England Emigrant Aid Society and was a member of a secret committee that abetted John Brown's raid on Harpers Ferry (1859). His writings were collected in *Theodore Parker's Works* (14 vols., 1863–70).

Parkman, Francis (b. Boston, Mass., 16 Sept. 1823; d. Jamaica Plain, Mass., 8 Nov. 1893), historian. He was graduated from Harvard (1844), received the degree of LL.B. (1846) from the Harvard Law School, and in 1846 made the journey to the Far West which he recorded in *The California and Oregon Trail* (1849; commonly called *The Oregon Trail*). The strenuous expedition taxed his already impaired health and, soon after returning from the West, he suffered a physical and nervous breakdown. Although he was for the rest of his life a semi-invalid suffering from weak eyesight bordering on blindness and from a nervous disorder that prevented unbroken concentration, Parkman eventually won a place as the leading American historian of his time. His historical series dealing with the struggle of England and France for the domination of North America is based on a scholarly use of original sources, and is marked by a sweeping narrative power and vivid descriptive passages dealing with life in the primitive wilderness. In order of their publication, the volumes of his series are *History of the Conspiracy of Pontiac* (1851), *Pioneers of France in the New World* (1865), *The Jesuits in North America* (1867), *The Discovery of the Great West* (1869), *The Old Régime in Canada* (1874), *Count Frontenac and New France under Louis XIV* (1877), *Montcalm and Wolfe* (2 vols., 1884), and *A Half-Century of Conflict* (2 vols., 1892).

Pauling, Linus Carl (b. Portland, Ore., 28 Feb. 1901–), chemist, received his B.S. from Oregon State College (1922) and his Ph.D. from the California Institute of Technology (1925), where since 1931 he has been professor of chemistry, chairman of the division of chemistry and chemical engineering, and since 1937 director of the Gates and Crellin laboratories of chemistry. He is renowned for his theory of resonance in the molecular structure of organic chemicals, leading to a better understanding of certain properties of the carbon compounds, especially the aromatics, and for his contributions to immunology, notably on the nature of serological reactions and the molecular structure of antitoxins. With Campbell and Pressman he produced synthetic antibodies. He has also done important work in applying the quantum theory to chemistry, in crystal structure, and in the theory of electrolytes. He has written many scientific papers, including *The Nature of the Chemical Bond* (1939). He was awarded the Nobel Prize in Chemistry in 1954 for discoveries of forces holding proteins and molecules together.

Peale, Charles Willson (b. Queen Anne County, Md., 15 Apr. 1741; d. Phila., 22 Feb. 1827), portrait painter, naturalist, was apprenticed as a saddler at 13. He began portrait painting at 20, studying with John Hesselius, then in Boston under Copley (*q.v.*) and in London (1767) in Benjamin West's studio. Lieut. in the Phila. militia, he fought at Trenton, Princeton, and Germantown, and served 1 term (beg. 1779) in the Pa. Assembly. A naturalist as well as a painter, he opened (1802) Peale's Museum of Natural History Objects and Portraits (later the Phila. Museum) and founded (1805) the Pa. Academy of Fine Arts. Renowned as the painter of Washington, he painted the first portrait of the Virginian in 1772, 7 additional ones from sittings, and a total of 60 in all. Of all Washington's portraits, Peale's are the most faithful and uncompromising. He painted other leading patriots, faithfully reproducing their dress and manner, but adding little character interpretation. He also painted *Christ Healing the Sick at the Pool of Bethesda* (1822). His sons, Raphael, Rembrandt, Titian, and Rubens, were painters and naturalists like their father.

Peary, Robert Edwin (b. Cresson, Pa., 6 May 1856; d. Washington, D.C., 20 Feb. 1920), naval officer and Arctic explorer. Graduating from Bowdoin College (1877), he became a county surveyor, entered the U.S. Coast and Geodetic Survey in 1879, and was commissioned a lt. (1881) in the U.S. Navy corps of civil engineers. While on leave in the summer of 1886, he explored the west coast of Greenland, at that time still unknown territory, reaching the ice cap 100 miles inland at an elevation of 7,500 feet above sea level. After further tours of duty in Nicaragua and along the Atlantic coast, he secured support from scientific and geographical societies in the U.S. for another Greenland expedition, which he made (1891–92) in the company of 5 others, including his wife. Peary made a 1,300-mile return journey to the northeast coast of Greenland from his base on the northwest coast, determining the insularity of Greenland and the northernmost limit of the ice cap. The party returned to the U.S. with valuable scientific data. He made further trips (1893–95, 1896) in order to bring to the U.S. large meteorites discovered by him. In 1898 he made a voyage on the *Windward*, a vessel presented by Lord Northcliffe; reaching the shores of the Polar Sea, he marked the region of Smith Sound and made his nearest approach yet to the North Pole, returning to the U.S. in 1902. His next trip (1905–06), made in the *Roosevelt*, saw him come within 174 miles of the North Pole, the closest approach made up to that time. Starting out again in the *Roosevelt* (1908), Peary, with his Negro servant Matthew Henson, 4 Eskimos, and 40 dogs, reached the North Pole by sledge on 6 Apr. 1909. Shortly before Peary's ship put in at Labrador, where he announced his discovery, a similar claim was made by Dr. Frederick A. Cook, who asserted he had reached the North Pole on 21 Apr. 1908. The bitter controversy which followed was finally resolved by the scientific world in Peary's favor.

Peirce, Charles Sanders (b. Cambridge, Mass., 10 Sept. 1839; d. Milford, Pa., 19 Apr. 1914), philosopher, logician, and scientist. The son of the Harvard mathematician and astronomer, Benjamin Peirce (1809–80), he was graduated from Harvard (1859), where he also received the degrees of M.A. (1862) and Sc.B. (1863). As a staff member (1861–91) of the U.S. Coast Survey, he was the 1st American delegate to the International Geodetic Congress (1877) and made researches in pendulum work and geodesy. During the same period he was an assistant (1869–72) at the Harvard Observatory; the astronomical observations made there by him between 1872 and 1875 provided the material for the only book by Peirce that appeared during his lifetime, *Photometric Researches* (1878). He lectured on science and logic at Harvard (1864, 1869, 1870), the Lowell Institute (1866, 1892, 1903), and Johns Hopkins (1879–84). His most significant contributions were made in formal logic and philosophy. He laid the basis for the logic of relations in mathematical logic, and made vital contributions to the theory of probability, induction, and the logic of scientific methodology. Among the concepts developed by him were tychism (theory of the reality of absolute chance) and synechism (doctrine of continuity). Peirce is best known as the creator (1877–78) of the principle of pragmatism, as well as the term itself. The latter 1st appeared in print in 1898, when William James used it. Peirce's views, however, differed from those of James, and Peirce later called his doctrine "pragmaticism" to stress the distinction. Most of his voluminous papers remained unpublished until after his death. His studies covered a wide range of subjects including religion, philology, psychology, meteorology, and chemistry.

Perry, Matthew Calbraith (b. Newport, R.I., 10 Apr. 1794; d. New York City, 4 Mar. 1858), naval officer, brother of Oliver Hazard Perry. Entering the navy as a midshipman (1809), he served under his brother on the *Revenge* and took part in the War of 1812. After a varied tour of duty, he was named (1833) 2nd officer of the New York navy yard, where he organized the U.S. Naval Lyceum, an educational body for naval officers, and served as its president. His plan for a naval apprentice system was adopted by Congress in 1837. Promoted to capt. (1837), he took command of the *Fulton*, one of the 1st naval steam-powered vessels, aboard which he conducted (1839–40) the 1st American naval school of gun

practice. He organized the 1st naval engineer corps and was appointed (1841) commandant of the New York navy yard. After another tour of duty that included the command (1843 *et seq.*) of the African Squadron for aiding in the suppression of the slave trade, service in the Mexican War (including command of the naval force that helped take Vera Cruz in 1847), and special duty at New York (1848–52) as superintendent of ocean mail steamship construction, he was chosen by President Fillmore to negotiate a treaty with Japan, which at that time barred all intercourse with the West. In command of the augmented Eastern Squadron, Perry anchored in Yedo Bay (8 July 1853), where he stayed 9 days; the Japanese officials, impressed with his show of naval strength, agreed to transmit Fillmore's proposals to high dignitaries. Perry sailed for China and returned to Yedo Bay (Feb. 1854), and concluded at Yokohama (31 Mar. 1854) a treaty that opened Japan to the Occidental nations. His official report is in *Narrative of the Expedition of an American Squadron to the China Seas and Japan* (3 vols., 1856).

Perry, Oliver Hazard (b. South Kingston, R.I., 20 Aug. 1785; d. along the Orinoco River, Venezuela, 23 Aug. 1819), naval officer, became a midshipman in the U.S. Navy (1799), saw service in West Indian waters during the naval war with France, and was on tours of duty (1802–03, 1804–06) in the Mediterranean during the Tripolitan War. After the outbreak of the War of 1812, he was ordered (1813) to join Commodore Isaac Chauncey's force at Sackett's Harbor, N.Y., and was given command of the U.S. naval forces on Lake Erie. Perry went to Erie, Pa., where he spent the spring and summer constructing and equipping a fleet of 10 vessels, of which the largest were the *Lawrence* and the *Niagara*. The Battle of Lake Erie (10 Sept. 1813), in which Perry defeated the British fleet under Commander Robert H. Barclay, was one of the decisive battles of the war. It gave the Americans control of Lake Erie and enabled Gen. William Henry Harrison (to whom Perry sent the message: "We have met the enemy and they are ours") to seize much of upper Canada. Perry was promoted to capt. (1813), received the thanks of Congress (1814), and was acclaimed a national hero. He later took part in the operations against Detroit and in the Battle of the Thames. He commanded the *Java* on a Mediterranean tour (1815–16) and died of yellow fever after completing a diplomatic mission to the Venezuelan government.

Pershing, John Joseph (b. near Laclede, Linn County, Mo., 13 Sept. 1860; d. Washington, D.C., 15 July 1948), soldier, commander of the A.E.F. in World War I, was graduated (1886) from the U.S. Military Academy, and served as a cavalry officer in operations (1886–90) against Indians in the Southwest and in S.D. He was a military instructor (1891–95) at the University of Nebraska, from which he received the degree of LL.B. (1893), was an instructor in military tactics (1897–98) at the U.S. Military Academy, and served in the Spanish-American War. He was on a tour of duty in the Philippines (1899–1903), served on the army general staff (1903–05), was a military observer with the Japanese forces during the Russo-Japanese War, and was promoted (1906) from capt. to brig. gen. He again served in the Philippines (1906–13), was named (1913) commander of the Eighth Cavalry Brigade, with headquarters at the Presidio, San Francisco, commanded the Mexican border operations (1916), and was promoted (1916) to maj. gen. He was appointed (May 1917) commander of the American Expeditionary Forces (A.E.F.), which he led in France during World War I. It was mainly through his insistence that the American forces operated as a separate command. He was promoted (Oct. 1917) to the rank of full gen. and received (Sept. 1919) the title of "General of the Armies of the United States." He served as army chief of staff from 1921 until his retirement from the service in 1924.

Phillips, Wendell (b. Boston, 29 Nov. 1811; d. there, 2 Feb. 1884), reformer, orator, obtained his B.A. (1831) and LL.B. (1834) from Harvard and practiced law briefly in Boston. In a speech at Faneuil Hall (1837) he publicly identified himself with abolitionism, speaking out against the murder of Elijah P. Lovejoy, abolitionist editor. Frequent contributor to Garrison's *Liberator,* he was delegate from Mass. to the World Anti-Slavery Convention at London (1840) and was outspoken and uncompromising in his stand against slavery, opposing the annexation of Texas, the Mexican War, and Webster's stand on the Compromise of 1850. In the Civil War, he attacked Lincoln for his moderation on the slavery question and opposed his renomination. Succeeding Garrison (1865) as president of the American Antislavery Society, he kept it active until the adoption of the 15th Amendment. Phillips was sympathetic with the broad spectrum of reform, advocating the abolition of capital punishment, currency and Indian reform, votes for women, and the rights of labor. Gubernatorial nominee of the Labor Reform party and the Prohibitionists (1870), he drew up the Labor Reform platform (1871), advocating the overthrow of the profit system. An orator of the stature of Edward Everett and Daniel Webster (*q.v.*), although his style was easy and colloquial, his most popular lectures and orations include "The Lost Arts" (delivered over 2,000 times), "The Scholar in a Republic," and "Toussaint L'Ouverture." Two series of his *Speeches, Lectures, and Letters* were published (1863, 1891).

Pierce, Franklin (b. Hillsboro, N.H., 23 Nov. 1804; d. Concord, N.H., 8 Oct. 1869), 14th President of the U.S., was graduated from Bowdoin (1824), studied law, and was admitted to the N.H. bar (1827). In the state legislature (1829–32; as speaker, 1831–32), he became a Democratic congressman (1833–37) and U.S. senator (1837–42), when he resigned to resume law practice in Concord, N.H. In the War with Mexico he became brig. gen. of volunteers, serving under Winfield Scott. Democratic nominee (1852) on the 49th ballot over Buchanan, Cass, and Douglas, he defeated Scott. His administration was under proslavery influence. He extended the U.S. southern border through the Gadsden Purchase (1853), sent Perry to Japan

(1853), signed the Kansas-Nebraska Act (1854), and recognized the Walker regime in Nicaragua. His "bleeding Kansas" policy lost him the support of Northern Democrats and the renomination (1856).

Pike, Zebulon Montgomery (b. Lamberton, now part of Trenton, N.J., 5 Jan. 1779; d. York, now Toronto, Canada, 27 Apr. 1813), soldier and explorer. Entering the army as a cadet (1794), he was commissioned (1805) by Gen. James Wilkinson to take an exploring party to the source of the Mississippi. His expedition, based on St. Louis, explored (9 Aug. 1805–30 Apr. 1806) the upper Mississippi region of the Louisiana Purchase, but did not find the true source of the river. Promoted to capt. in 1806, Pike led a 2nd expedition (1806–07) which explored what is now Col. and N.M. He sighted but did not succeed in climbing the summit that was later named Pikes Peak. He explored the headwaters of the Arkansas and Red rivers; was arrested by the Spaniards in Santa Fe, but was soon set free; and published *An Account of Expeditions to the Sources of the Mississippi and through the Western Parts of Louisiana* (1810). After the outbreak of the War of 1812, he was commissioned a brig. gen. (1813) and was killed in the explosion of a powder magazine while leading the assault on York.

Poe, Edgar Allan (b. Boston, Mass., 19 Jan. 1809; d. Baltimore, Md., 7 Oct. 1849), poet, short-story writer, and critic. Orphaned when he was about 3 yrs. old, he was reared by a Richmond (Va.) tobacco merchant, John Allan, whose name he used as his middle name after 1824. He was admitted (1826) to the University of Virginia, but left after 1 term because of gambling debts. His 1st volume, *Tamerlane and Other Poems* (1827), was published anonymously at Boston. Poe served (1827–29) in the U.S. Army, was admitted (1830) to West Point, and was dismissed (1831) for gross neglect of duty. His 2nd volume, *Al Aaraaf, Tamerlane, and Minor Poems* (1829), was published at Baltimore; *Poems by Edgar A. Poe* (1831) was published at New York. He 1st won public notice with "A

MS. Found in a Bottle," which was awarded (1833) a prize by a Baltimore publication. He contributed to the *Southern Literary Messenger,* of which he became (1835) assistant editor. He married (1836) his 14-year-old cousin, Virginia Clemm, and moved to New York City (1837), where he published *The Narrative of Arthur Gordon Pym* (1838). He moved to Philadelphia (1838), where he coedited (1839–40) *Burton's Gentleman's Magazine* and was literary editor (1841–42) of *Graham's Lady's and Gentleman's Magazine.* He published *Tales of the Grotesque and Arabesque* (2 vols., 1840) and won a prize (1843) for his story, "The Gold Bug." He returned (1844) to New York, where he did free-lance writing (the "Balloon Hoax" was published in the New York *Sun* on 13 Apr. 1844) and published his poem, "The Raven," which brought him his 1st fame. He became (1845) editor and proprietor of the *Broadway Journal* and published (1845) *Tales* and *The Raven and Other Poems.* His chronic poverty, alcoholism, and poor health worsened after the death of his wife (1847). He returned to Richmond (1849) and died in Baltimore after being found semiconscious in a saloon. A lyric poet of the 1st rank, he exerted an important influence upon poetry in the U.S. and abroad, particularly on the French Symbolists; was one of the originators of the detective story genre; and made important contributions as a literary critic, notably in his essays, "The Poetic Principle" and "The Philosophy of Composition."

Polk, James Knox (b. Mecklenberg Co., N.C., 2 Nov. 1795; d. Nashville, Tenn., 15 June 1849), 11th President of the U.S., moved with his parents (1806) to central Tenn., was graduated from the University of North Carolina (1818), read law, was admitted to the bar (1820), and began practice in Columbia, Tenn. State legislator (1823–25), congressman (1825–39; served as speaker, 1835–39), he was governor of Tenn. (1839–41), but was defeated for reelection in 1841 and again in 1843. He was Democratic nominee (1844) on the 9th ballot when Van Buren failed of the necessary two-thirds vote. He defeated Clay in the ensuing election. As President he accomplished all his major objectives; settled the Oregon question by a compromise on the 49th parallel (1846); achieved tariff reduction (1846) and the reestablishment of the independent treasury system originated under Van Buren. Dispute over the Tex. boundary led to War with Mexico (1846–48). An expansionist rather than an imperialist, he approved the acquisition of Tex., Calif., and N.M., but opposed retaining Mexico by force. He did not seek reelection.

Pollock, Jackson (b. near Cody, Wyo., 28 Jan. 1912; d. Southampton, L.I., 11 Aug. 1956), painter, left Los Angeles high school at 17, receiving his formal training at the Art Student's League, N.Y., under Thomas Hart Benton. On the Federal Arts Project (1939–42), he gave his 1st 1-man show in N.Y. (1943). His work in his 1st period was characterized by violence and passion still under control (*Male and Female in Search of a Symbol, Wounded Animal*). In the mid-1940's he broke away from American realism to develop his own distinctive abstract style, abandoning the easel for drippings of color on canvas and creating "rhythmic labyrinths" or "dripped mazes" (*Sleeping Effort, Portrait with a Dream, Eastern, Totem, Scent*, and others simply given numbers). Before his death in an auto accident, he had become a leading figure among abstract expressionists, giving 1-man shows abroad, at Venice and Milan (1950) and Paris (1952). His paintings quickly acquired a phenomenal posthumous success.

Pound, Ezra Loomis (b. Hailey, Ida., 30 Oct. 1885–), poet, studied at Hamilton Coll. (Ph.B., 1905) and the Univ. of Penn. (M.A., 1906) and taught 4 mos. at Wabash Coll. before leaving the U.S. (1907) to travel through Spain, France, and Italy, eventually settling in England. His *Personae* and *Exultations* (1909), followed by *Canzoni* (1911) *and Ripostes* (1912), demonstrated his poetic gifts. Leader of the Imagists, he edited (1917–19) the *Literary Review* (London) and was Paris correspondent (1920) for *The Dial*. His *Cantos* (1925–48), still un-finished, drawing upon legend, Oriental poetry, troubadour ballads, and modern jargon, constitute his most substantial work. Resident of Italy since 1924, he began (1941) broadcasting Fascist propaganda from Rome to the U.S. during World War II. Brought back to the U.S. on a charge of treason (1945), he was adjudged insane and hospitalized, but continued to write poetry. The award (1949) of the Bollingen Prize for his *Pisan Cantos* (1948, part of the *Cantos*) evoked a storm of protest. Released from St. Elizabeth's Hospital (1956), he returned to Italy with his wife, Dorothy Shakespeare Pound, after treason charges were dropped.

Powderly, Terence Vincent (b. Carbondale, Pa., 22 Jan. 1849; d. Washington, D.C., 24 June 1924), labor leader, reformer, attended school until 13, then worked on the railroad. Apprenticed to the machinist trade at 17, he worked at that trade until 1877. President of the Machinist and Blacksmith's Natl. Union (1872), he was initiated into the secret order of the Knights of Labor (1874), became its Grand Master Workman (1879) and held that office until 1893. Heading the largest and most powerful labor organization of its day, he was basically a reformer, placing little stress on immediate demands for wages and hours, opposing strikes; but advocating producers' cooperatives, trust regulation, currency reform, and the abolition of child labor. He was instrumental in the passage of the alien contract labor law (1885). Elected mayor of Scranton on a Greenback-Labor ticket (1878), he was twice re-elected (1880, 1882), but supported the Republican ticket beginning in 1894. Commissioner general of Immigration (1897–1902), he was chief of the division of information in the Bureau of Immigration (1907–21). He wrote *Thirty Years of Labor, 1859–1889* (1889) and an autobiography, *The Path I Trod* (1940).

Powell, John Wesley (b. Mt. Morris, N.Y., 24 Mar. 1834; d. Haven, Me., 23 Sept. 1902), geologist and explorer, attended Illinois, Oberlin, and Wheaton colleges, and while still a youth made solitary botanizing trips on the Ohio and Mississippi rivers. He enlisted in the Union army at the outbreak of the Civil War, lost his right arm at the elbow as the result of a wound received at the battle of Shiloh (1862), and rose to the rank of maj. of artillery. He served as professor of geology in the Illinois Wesleyan College at Bloomington and as lecturer and curator of the museum of the Illinois Normal University. In 1869, on a grant from the Federal government and the Smithsonian Institution, he led an exploring party along some 900 miles of the Green and Colorado rivers, being the 1st white man to make this expedition, and continued his Western explorations in 1871, 1874, and 1875. He became (1875) director of the 2nd division of the U.S. Geological and Geographical Survey of the Territories, which in 1877 became known as the Survey of the Rocky Mountain Region, and in 1879 issued the *Report on the Lands of the Arid Region of the United States* whose recommendations subsequently became a part of national land policy. When the Western explorations were consolidated (1879) as the U.S. Geological Survey under Clarence King, Powell was placed in charge of anthropological investigations under the Smithsonian Institution. From 1880 to 1894 Powell served as director of the U.S. Geological Survey. His most important contributions in the field of physiographic geology were made in *Explorations of the Colorado River of the West and Its Tributaries* (1875; issued in 1895 in revised and enlarged form as *Canyons of the Colorado*).

Prescott, William Hickling (b. Salem, Mass., 14 May 1796; d. Boston, Mass., 28 Jan. 1859), historian. He was graduated from Harvard (1814), where an accidental blow blinded his left eye (1813); in 1815 an inflammation of his right eye virtually deprived him of his sight. In the research and composition of his histories, he was aided by a noctograph (a visual-aid device), by secretaries who read aloud to him, and by a tenacious memory. On the history of Spain and Spanish conquest, which he chose as his special subject, he wrote *History of the Reign of Ferdinand and Isabella* (3 vols., 1838), *History of the Conquest of Mexico* (3 vols., 1843), *History of the Conquest of Peru* (2 vols., 1847), and *History of the Reign of Philip the Second* (3 vols., 1855, 1858). His histories, narrative rather than analytical, and romantic in conception, are based on rigid standards of scholarship which justify the claim that he was the 1st American scientific historian. His stress on literary form popularized the reading of history by Americans.

Pulitzer, Joseph (b. Mako, Hungary, 10 Apr. 1847; d. Charleston, S.C., 29 Oct. 1911), journalist and newspaper publisher. Arriving in the U.S. in 1864, he served briefly in the Union army, became (1868) a reporter on the St. Louis *Westliche Post*, and in 1869 was elected to the Mo. legislature. He soon became a figure of some importance in St. Louis politics, served as a city police commissioner, and was active as a supporter of the Liberal Republican movement (1870–72). He was part owner (1871–73) of the *Westliche Post* and was admitted to the bar (1876) in the District of Columbia. He purchased (1878) the St. Louis *Post* and the *Dispatch*, combining them as the *Post-Dispatch*, a journal which under his leadership became one of the foremost organs in the Midwest. In 1883 he purchased the New York *World* from Jay Gould and, following a policy of sensational journalism that included recourse to large headlines, comic strips, and crime stories, converted the *World* into a profitable enterprise. The *Evening World* was established in 1887. During the period 1896–98 the *World* rivaled Hearst's *Evening Journal* in its "yellow journalism." Both newspapers shared responsibility for arousing public opinion for war against Spain. In subsequent years, however, the *World* became a responsible and politically independent journal that observed high standards. Pulitzer's announced intention (1903) to establish a school of journalism at Columbia University resulted in the provision in his will of $2 million for the School of Journalism (1912) and for the Pulitzer prizes awarded annually in many fields of achievement.

Pupin, Michael Idvorsky (b. Idvor, Banat, Austria, 4 Oct. 1858; d. New York City, 12 Mar. 1935), physicist, inventor, grew up in an atmosphere supercharged with Serbian hostility to Hapsburg rule. He went to Prague (1873) to study, but left for the U.S. in 1874. He held odd jobs in Delaware and New York, picking up English, Latin, and Greek. Entering Columbia (1879), he obtained his A.B. degree and his U.S. citizenship papers in 1883. He then studied mathematics with John Edward Routh at Cambridge Univ. and physics with Helmholtz at Berlin (Ph.D., 1889). Returning to N.Y., he taught mathematical physics and electromechanics at Columbia (1889–1931). Inventor of numerous electrical devices relating to long-distance telephony and multiplex telegraphy, his "pupinized" cable, transmitting sound over long distances, solved the problem of sound attenuation and distortion. He conducted research in X ray, was the 1st in the U.S. to obtain an X-ray photograph (1896), and discovered X-radiation. He was adviser to the Yugoslav delegation at the Peace Conference (1919). In addition to his Pulitzer Prize-winning autobiography, *From Immigrant to Inventor* (1923), he wrote *Thermodynamics of Reversible Cycles in Gases and Saturated Vapors* (1894), *New Reformation* (1927), and *The Romance of the Machine* (1930).

Rabi, Isidor Isaac (b. Rymanow, Austrian Galicia, 29 July 1898–), physicist. He was brought to the U.S. in his infancy, was graduated from Cornell (B. Chem., 1919) and from Columbia (Ph. D., 1927), and as a fellow of the International Education Board took postgraduate study (1928–29) in Munich, Copenhagen, Hamburg, Leipzig, and Zurich. In 1929 he joined the physics faculty at Columbia, and in 1940 became associate director of the radiation laboratory at the Massachusetts Institute of Technology, where he was engaged in radar research (1940–45) during World War II. He was also wartime consultant to the Los Alamos atomic bomb laboratory. He has made notable advances in the study of magnetic properties of molecules, atoms, and atomic nuclei and in quantum mechanics, nuclear physics, and molecular beams, and was awarded the Nobel prize in physics (1944) for his precision work in neutrons. He was vice-president of the Intl. Conferences on Peaceful Uses of Atomic Energy at Geneva, 1955, 1958.

Randolph, John, of Roanoke (b. "Cawsons," Prince George Co., Va., 2 June 1773; d. Philadelphia, 24 May 1833), statesman, orator, studied at the Coll. of N.J. (1787) and at Wm. and Mary (1792–93). A restless person, his education was casual and varied, but he was widely read. Elected to Congress in 1799 as a Jeffersonian, he became at 28 chairman of the Ways and Means Committee and administration leader under Jefferson. He mismanaged the prosecution in the impeachment trial of Judge Samuel Chase and was held responsible for the failure to convict. Heading a faction called the "Quids," he blocked the bill (1804–05) awarding land to holders of Yazoo land warrants, losing his party leadership thereby. Opposing the Embargo and Madison's candidacy in 1808, he was defeated for re-election (1813) as a result of his opposition to the War of 1812. Returning to Congress (1815), he opposed chartering the 2nd Bank of the U.S. and the tariff. Maligning the Adams-Clay alliance as the combination of the "puritan and the blackleg," he fought a duel with Clay (1826). In the Senate (1825–27) and again in the House (1827–29), he headed the opposition to President J. Q. Adams. Delegate to the Va. Convention (1829), he sided with the conservative forces. U.S. Minister to Russia under Jackson, he remained there only a month because of his health. Incomparable orator and master of invective, champion of lost causes and strict constructionist, he was, with his high soprano voice and increasingly unbalanced behavior, a figure both brilliant and pathetic.

Rauschenbusch, Walter (b. Rochester, N.Y., 4 Oct. 1861; d. New York City, 25 July 1918), clergyman, was graduated from the Gymnasium of Gütersloh, Westphalia (1883), received his A.B. (1884) from the Univ. of Rochester, and 2 yrs. later was graduated from the Rochester

Theological Seminary. Ordained a Baptist minister, he took charge of the 2nd German Baptist Church, New York City, working with German immigrants. Studying economics and theology at the Univ. of Berlin (1891–92) and industrial conditions in England, he was influenced by the Fabian movement and by the work of the Salvation Army and the Consumers' Cooperatives. Succeeding his father, Rev. Augustus Rauschenbusch, to the chair of New Testament interpretation at the Rochester Theological Seminary (1897), he gained prominence as an advocate of the "social gospel," the application of Christian principles to social problems, by his *Christianity and the Social Crisis* (1907). This positive reaction to social Darwinism was also expounded in *Prayers of the Social Awakening* (1910), *Christianizing the Social Order* (1912), *The Social Principles of Jesus* (1916), and *A Theology for the Social Gospel* (1917).

Reed, Walter (b. Belroi, Va., 13 Sept. 1851; d. Washington, D.C., 22 Nov. 1902), army surgeon and bacteriologist. He was graduated from the University of Virginia (1869) and the Bellevue Hospital Medical School, New York City (M.D., 1870). In 1875, after having served on the boards of health in New York and Brooklyn, he entered the Medical Corps of the U.S. Army with the rank of 1st lt. and was assigned to duty as an assistant surgeon. Ordered to Baltimore (1890) as attending surgeon and examiner of recruits, he studied at the Johns Hopkins Hospital and was attached to the pathological laboratory, where, under Dr. William H. Welch and others, he specialized in the then emerging science of bacteriology. In 1893, he was made curator of the Army Medical Museum at Washington, D.C., and named professor of bacteriology and clinical microscopy at the newly established Army Medical School. In the years immediately preceding the outbreak of the Spanish-American War he carried out researches in the bacteriology of erysipelas and diphtheria. In 1898 he was made chairman of a committee for investigating typhoid fever, at that time rife in the volunteer camps. The commission's report

(1904) pointed to the importance of transmission by flies, dust, and other hitherto ignored agencies. In 1897–99 Reed and Dr. James Carroll disproved the theory propounded by Dr. Giuseppe Sanarelli of Italy concerning the causative agency of yellow fever. Named as head of the U.S. Army Yellow Fever Commission (1900), Reed and his associates (Carroll, Lazear, and Agramonte) carried out in Cuba experiments with soldier and other volunteers which conclusively proved the theory of mosquito transmission of yellow fever (through the agency of *Stegomyia fasciata,* later classified as *Aëdes ægypti*). The commission's findings made it possible to control yellow fever and virtually eliminate the disease in the U.S. and Cuba. The general hospital of the army medical center at Washington, D.C., is named for Reed.

Richardson, Henry Hobson (b. St. James Parish, La., 29 Sept. 1838; d. Brookline, Mass., 27 Apr. 1886), architect. Graduated from Harvard (1859) and admitted (1860) to the École des Beaux Arts in Paris, he made his early reputation with prize-winning designs for churches at Springfield and West Medford, Mass. With the Brattle Square Church at Boston he abandoned Victorian Gothic for the style that became his hallmark and reached its flower in Trinity Church, Boston, for which he was awarded the prize commission in 1872. Richardson was the leader in introducing the Romanesque Revival into the U.S. Adapted chiefly from the forms of Southern French Romanesque, this mode was widely used in the American Northeast and West until it gave way to the Classical Revival. Toward the close of his life Richardson was evolving a functionalist architecture, as in the John H. Pray Co. Bldg. at Boston (*c.*1886), that foreshadowed the modernism of Louis H. Sullivan and others. For other outstanding designs, see p. 641.

Robinson, Edwin Arlington (b. Head Tide, Me., 22 Dec. 1869; d. New York City, 6 Apr. 1935), poet, attended Harvard from 1891 to 1893. His 1st volume of poetry, *The Torrent and the Night Before* (1896; reprinted with additions in 1897 as *The Children of the Night*), was published at his own expense. In 1899 he settled at New York, where poverty forced him to work as a timekeeper (1904) on the subway construction project. When his plight came to the attention of President Theodore Roosevelt, an admirer of Robinson's poetry, Robinson received (1905) a clerkship in the customs service at New York, a post he held until 1909. The following years brought him general recognition and fame in the U.S. and abroad. His poetry, which bears the stamp of his Calvinistic New England background, deals with traditional themes and reveals a masterly command of blank verse technique. His works include *Captain Craig and Other Poems* (1902), *The Town Down the River* (1910), *The Man against the Sky* (1916), *Merlin* (1917), *Collected Poems* (1921), *Avon's Harvest* (1921), *Roman Bartholow* (1923), *The Man Who Died Twice* (1924), *Tristram* (1927), *Cavender's House* (1929), *Matthias at the Door* (1931), *Amaranth* (1934), and *King Jasper* (1935). He was awarded three Pulitzer prizes.

Rockefeller, John Davison (b. Richford, N.Y., 8 July 1839; d. Ormond Beach, Fla., 23 May 1937), industrialist and philanthropist, was educated in Cleveland, Ohio, where he worked as a clerk and bookkeeper and became a member of the firm of Clark & Rockefeller. Following the discovery of oil at Titusville, Pa. (1859), he became associated with Samuel Andrews, inventor of a cheaper process of refining oil, and in 1865 joined his brother, William Rockefeller (1841–1922), in establishing the firm of William Rockefeller & Co. and the Standard Oil Works at Cleveland. The Standard Oil Co., organized in 1867 and incorporated in 1870 with John D. Rockefeller as president, became the largest unit in the American oil industry and the 1st great effective industrial combination of its time. By the mid-1870's it had absorbed or eliminated most of its rival concerns; by the end of that decade it exercised a virtual monopoly over oil refining and transportation. The company became known (1881) as the Standard Oil Trust, a unit that was outlawed by the Supreme

Court of Ohio (1892) and dissolved in 1899. It was replaced by the Standard Oil Co. of N.J., which functioned as a holding company for the Rockefeller interests until its dissolution was ordered by the U.S. Supreme Court (1911). At about that time the active management of the business was handed over to his son, John D. Rockefeller, Jr. (1874–1960). The senior Rockefeller retired with a fortune estimated a $1 billion. The immense financial resources built up by him were devoted to a variety of philanthropies, including the endowment of University of Chicago (1892), the Rockefeller Institute of Medical Research (1901), the General Education Board (1902), and the Rockefeller Foundation (1913).

Rodgers, Richard (b. New York City, 28 June 1902–), composer, studied at Columbia Univ. (1919–21) and the Inst. of Musical Art, N.Y. (1921–23). He was the 1st Columbia freshman to win the competition for the annual varsity show, *Fly With Me*. As an outstanding composer for musical comedy, his greatest achievements were in collaboration with Lorenz Hart (1895–1943), whom he met in 1919, and, beginning in 1943, with Oscar Hammerstein, 2nd (*q.v.*). He and Hart had their 1st musical hit with *Garrick Gaieties* (1925). They worked together on *The Girl Friend* (1926), *A Connecticut Yankee* (1927), *I'd Rather Be Right* (1937), *Pal Joey* (1940), and *By Jupiter* (1942), in which Rodgers collaborated on the script. Among their song hits of the 20's were "Thou Swell," "With a Song in My Heart," and in the 30's, "Bewitched, Bothered and Bewildered." His association with Oscar Hammerstein started with a signal success, *Oklahoma!* (1943-special Pulitzer award), and was continued with *Carousel* (1945), *Allegro* (1947), the Pulitzer Prize-winning *South Pacific* (1949), and *The King and I* (1951). Their song hits quickly became American classics, among them "Oh, What a Beautiful Mornin'," "People Will Say We're in Love," "Some Enchanted Evening," and "I'm Gonna Wash That Man Right Outa My Hair." Rodgers also wrote film scores for numerous motion pictures, including *State*

Fair (1945). He received the U.S. Navy Distinguished Public Service Award (1953) for his score of the Peabody Award-winning TV Series *Victory at Sea.*

Roebling, John Augustus (b. Mühlhausen, Thuringia, Germany, 12 June 1806; d. Brooklyn, N.Y., 22 July 1869), engineer, bridge builder, and manufacturer. He was educated at Mühlhausen and at the Royal Polytechnic Institute at Berlin, where he received the degree of civil engineer (1826), and for the next 3 yrs. worked on road construction in Westphalia, meanwhile making special studies of bridge construction. He came to the U.S. in 1831. After a period of unsuccessful farming in western Pa., he became a state engineer in the same year (1837) that he was naturalized. His work on the Allegheny Portage Railroad provided the stimulus for his manufacture at Saxonburg, Pa. (1841), of the 1st wire rope made in America. The factory, subsequently transferred to Trenton, N.J., is today known as the John A. Roebling's Sons Co. He built his 1st suspension bridge (1846) over the Monongahela River at Pittsburgh. After constructing other bridges, including the railroad suspension span at Niagara Falls (1851–55), Roebling suggested in 1857 the possibility of an East River bridge joining lower Manhattan and Brooklyn (Brooklyn Bridge). When the charter was granted, Roebling was named chief engineer, and his plans were approved by the bridge commission in 1869. Construction was about to begin when, as the result of an accident suffered by him at the bridge site (28 June 1869), he developed tetanus and died. The bridge was completed under the general supervision of his son, Washington Augustus Roebling (1837–1926). With James Buchanan Eads (1820–1887), who constructed the bridge across the Mississippi at St. Louis (1867–74), J. A. Roebling ranks as the greatest American bridge builder of the 19th century.

Roosevelt, Anna Eleanor (b. New York City, 11 Oct. 1884–   ), humanitarian, was educated in private schools, and married her distant cousin, Franklin D. Roosevelt (17 Mar. 1905). Active since World War I in educational and social reform, she participated in her husband's gubernatorial campaigns (1928 and 1930) and aided him in his campaign for the Presidential nomination (1932). Her notable public career after entering the White House (1933–45) was unrivaled by any other President's wife. Lecturer and newspaper columnist, champion of the underprivileged and minority groups, she served the President as an invaluable source of public opinion. During World War II she served as assistant director, Office of Civilian Defense, and toured military bases abroad. After her husband's death she accepted appointment as U.S. delegate to the UN General Assembly (1945, 1949–52), and served as chairman, commission on human rights, Economic and Social Council (1946). Author of several books, her most successful was *This I Remember* (1949).

Roosevelt, Franklin Delano (b. Hyde Park, N.Y., 30 Jan. 1882; d. Warm Springs, Ga., 12 Apr. 1945), 32nd President of the U.S., was graduated from Harvard (1904), studied law at Columbia Law School, was admitted to the bar (1907), and practiced in N.Y. Democratic state senator (1911–13), he served as assistant secretary of the navy (1913–20). James M. Cox's running mate on the Democratic ticket (1920), he was defeated in the Republican landslide of that year. Stricken with infantile paralysis (Aug. 1921), he recovered partial use of his legs and established the Warm Springs (Ga.) Foundation for those so afflicted. At the Democratic conventions of 1924 and 1928 he placed in nomination Gov. Alfred E. Smith, the "Happy Warrior." Elected governor of N.Y. (1928) and reelected (1930), he was the Democratic nominee for President in 1932, defeating Herbert Hoover. His 1st inaugural, in which he exhorted that "the only thing we have to fear is fear itself" and promised "direct, vigorous action," keynoted his 1st administration, which was largely concerned with "New Deal" economic and social legislation to overcome the depression—relief and public works (resulting in deficit financing), labor legislation to implement collective bargaining (Wagner act), and farm legislation to support agricultural prices. Largely responsible for U.S. aid to Great Britain after the fall of France (1940), he contributed notably to achieving interallied unity during World War II and conducted his own foreign relations. His "unconditional surrender" announcement (24 Jan. 1944) and his conferences with allied leaders at Casablanca, Cairo, Quebec, Teheran, and Yalta determined the bases of the postwar world. First President to break the 3rd-term tradition (1940) by defeating Wendell L. Willkie, he was elected to a 4th term (1944), winning over Gov. Thomas E. Dewey. Three months after his 4th term had begun, and on the verge of victory against Germany and Japan, he was stricken with a cerebral hemorrhage and died.

Roosevelt, Theodore (b. New York City, 27 Oct. 1858; d. Oyster Bay, N.Y., 6 Jan. 1919), 26th President of the U.S., was graduated from Harvard (1880), read law briefly, and engaged in historical writing (*The Naval War of 1812*, 1882; *The Winning of the West*, 1889–96). After a term in the state Assembly (1882–84), he lived on a N.D. cattle ranch (1884–86). Returning to New York City, he was unsuccessful candidate for mayor (1886) and a notably effective U.S. civil service commissioner (1889–95) and president of the board of police commissioners of New York (1895–97). Assistant secretary of the navy (1897–98), he helped prepare the navy for the War with Spain. When war broke out he resigned and, with Leonard Wood, organized the 1st U.S. Volunteer Cavalry ("Rough Riders"), and as its col. led the charge up San Juan Hill. Elected governor of New York (1898), his reform administration alarmed the political bosses, notably T. C. Platt, who arranged to have him nominated as McKinley's running mate (1900). On McKinley's death he became President and was reelected (1904), decisively defeating Alton B. Parker. Known as a trust buster, he dissolved the Northern Securities Co., but distinguished between "good" and "bad" trusts. His most notable achievements on the domestic front were his sponsorship of conservation of natural resources and

of food inspection and railway rate legislation. Hastily recognizing the Republic of Panama, he secured the right to construct the Panama Canal (1903). For his successful intervention in the Russo-Japanese War (1905) he was awarded the Nobel peace prize. He supported his Secretary of War, William Howard Taft, as his successor; but after traveling abroad (1909–10), he reentered politics. Failing to secure the Republican nomination (1912), he was the nominee of the Progressive ("Bull Moose") party, losing in a 3-cornered contest to Woodrow Wilson. On an expedition to Brazil (1914) he explored the "River of Doubt," named Rio Teodoro in his honor. At the outbreak of World War I he favored the Allies and criticized Wilson's neutrality policy.

Root, Elihu (b. Clinton, N.Y., 15 Feb. 1845; d. New York City, 7 Feb. 1937), statesman, jurist, and diplomat, was graduated from Hamilton (1865) and in law from New York University (1867). He began practice in N.Y., was U.S. attorney for southern district of N.Y. (1883–85) and chairman of the judiciary committee of the state constitutional convention (1894). While Secretary of War under McKinley and Theodore Roosevelt (1899–1904) he created a general staff for the army, drew up a constitution for the Philippines, and formulated the Platt Amendment (1901) for the government of Cuba. As Secretary of State under Roosevelt (1905–09), he reorganized the consular service and negotiated the Root-Takahira Open-Door Agreement with Japan (1908). Republican senator from N.Y. (1909–15), he served as chief counsel for the U.S. in the North Atlantic Fisheries Arbitration (1910) and was also, from 1910, a member of the Permanent Court of Arbitration at The Hague. In recognition of his services as president of the Carnegie Endowment for International Peace (1910–25) he was awarded the Nobel prize (1912). Advocate of U.S. entry into the League of Nations, he was a member of the committee of jurists at The Hague which devised the Permanent Court of International Justice (1920–21). He was a U.S. delegate to the Washington Conference on Limitation of Armaments (1921), and as a member of the commission to revise the World Court statute (1929), he devised a formula to facilitate U.S. entry.

Rowland, Henry Augustus (b. Honesdale, Pa., 27 Nov. 1848; d. Baltimore, Md., 16 Apr. 1901), physicist, was graduated as a civil engineer (1870) from the Rensselaer Polytechnic Institute at Troy, N.Y., where he taught physics (1872–75). In 1876 he became the 1st professor of physics in the newly established Johns Hopkins University, where he served for the remainder of his life. His achievements as a pioneer in the fields of optics, magnetism, the spectra of the elements, and the electron were marked by a combination of practical mechanics and mastery of theory. His researches into optics resulted in diffraction gratings which are still used in spectrum analysis. His work on the magnetic lines of force produced his paper, "On Magnetic Permeability, and the Maximum of Magnetism of Iron, Steel, and Nickel," published in the *Philosophical Magazine* (1873), which served as the foundation for later researches into permanent and induced magnetization, and was essential to the design of transformers and dynamos. His experiments in electromagnetism (1875–76) in the Berlin laboratory of von Helmholtz made significant contributions to the modern theory of electrons. He made accurate measurements of the values which are still standard for the mechanical equivalent of heat, the wave lengths of various spectra and the ohm, carried out researches in the theory of alternating currents, and was consultant for the installation of equipment at the Niagara Falls power plant.

Royce, Josiah (b. Grass Valley, Nevada County, Calif., 20 Nov. 1855; d. Cambridge, Mass., 14 Sept. 1916), philosopher and teacher, was graduated from the University of California (1875) and in 1878 received the Ph.D. degree from Johns Hopkins. He taught English at the University of California (1878–82) and in 1882, with the aid of William James, received an appointment at Harvard, where he taught philosophy for 34 yrs. His greatest metaphysical work, *The*

World and the Individual (2 vols., 1900–01), expounded his view that the life of an absolute purpose required the moral independence of the individual. His *Studies in Good and Evil* (1898) and *Outline of Psychology* (1903) provided the psychological basis for this theory. In the *Philosophy of Loyalty* (1908) and *The Hope of the Great Community* (1916) he established the metaphysical basis of loyalty.

Rush, Benjamin (b. Byberry, Pa., 24 Dec. 1745; d. Philadelphia, 19 Apr. 1813), physician, Revolutionary patriot, obtained his A.B. (1760) from the Coll. of N.J., then studied medicine under Dr. John Redman (1761–66), completing his medical education at the Univ. of Edinburgh (M.D., 1768) and St. Thomas' Hospital, London (1768). Returning to Philadelphia (1769), he began the practice of medicine and served as a professor of chemistry at the Coll. of Philadelphia, publishing (1770) the 1st American text on the subject. Member of the 2nd Continental Congress and signer of the Declaration of Independence, he was surgeon general of the armies of the Middle Dept. (1777), but resigned in a dispute with Dr. William Shippen when he was not supported by Washington. In turn, he became a critic of Washington's military competence, favoring the general's replacement by Gates or Conway. With James Wilson, he led the successful fight in the Pa. ratifying convention for the adoption of the Constitution, and was treasurer of the U.S. Mint (1797–1813). On the staff of the Pa. Hospital from 1783, he established the 1st free dispensary in the U.S. (1786) and held chairs at the College of Phila. (1789) and the new Univ. of Pa. (beg. 1792), in medical theory and practice, exercising an enormous influence as a teacher in medicine and clinical practice. Stoutly advocating the view that disease was due to spasms in the blood vessels, he favored extensive bleedings, which he practiced during the yellow fever epidemic of 1793 in Phila., doubtless increasing the mortality rates. His principal works were *An Account of the Bilious Remitting Yellow Fever* (1794), where he stressed the need for sanitation, and *Medical In-*

quiries and Observations upon Diseases of the Mind (1812), with its pioneer insights into mental healing and psychiatry.

Ryder, Albert Pinkham (b. New Bedford, Mass., 19 Mar. 1847; d. Elmhurst, Long Island, N.Y., 28 Mar. 1917), painter. He took his early training at New York City under the painter William E. Marshall and, beginning in 1871, studied at the National Academy of Design. Although Ryder was a member of the Society of American Artists and was elected to the National Academy in 1906, he received scant recognition during his lifetime, most of which he spent as a recluse in New York. His paintings, the bulk of which were produced between 1873 and 1898, derived from an intense poetic vision and rank among the finest imaginative works of modern art. His works include *Toilers of the Sea, The Flying Dutchman, Moonlight at Sea, Death on a Pale Horse, Forest of Arden, Macbeth and the Witches, Jonah and the Whale, Ophelia, Temple of the Mind,* and *Pegasus.*

Saint-Gaudens, Augustus (b. Dublin, Ireland, 1 Mar. 1848; d. Cornish, N.H., 3 Aug. 1907), sculptor. Brought to the U.S. in his infancy, he was apprenticed to cameo cutters during his boyhood at New York City. He studied drawing in night classes at Cooper Union and attended the National Academy of Design; went to France (1867), was admitted to the École des Beaux Arts in Paris; and then went to Rome, where he came under the influence of the Renaissance tradition and won his 1st commissions. His *Hiawatha, Silence,* and bust of *William Maxwell Evarts* were followed by *Admiral Farragut* (1881; in Madison Square, New York City), which demonstrated the forceful characterization and original design that appeared in later works such as *The Puritan* (1885), *Lincoln* (1887; in Lincoln Park, Chicago), the *Shaw Memorial* (1897) at Boston, the equestrian statue of *Gen. John A. Logan* (1897) at Chicago, and the equestrian statue of *Gen. William T. Sherman* (1903) in New York City. Among other works by Saint-Gaudens are *Diana* (1892; figure modeled for the tower of

the old Madison Square Garden), *Amor Caritas,* reliefs of *Homer Saint-Gaudens* and *Bastien-Lepage,* the *Adams Memorial* (the figure sometimes called *Grief*) at Rock Creek Cemetery, Washington, D.C., and the *Parnell Monument* at Dublin.

Salk, Jonas (b. New York City, 28 Oct. 1914–), virologist, received his B.S. (1934) from City College, New York, and his M.D. (1939) from N.Y.U. Coll. of Medicine, where he carried on virus research under Thomas Francis, Jr. Joining Francis (1944) at the Univ. of Michigan's School of Public Health, he did research on influenza vaccine. He joined (1947) the staff of the Univ. of Pittsburgh School of Medicine and became director of its Virus Research Laboratory. With funds from the Natl. Foundation for Infantile Paralysis, Salk began work on a polio preventive in 1951. Using a technique reported (1949) by Dr. J. F. Enders (*q.v.*) for growing polio virus in cultures of non-nervous tissues, he announced (1953) a trial vaccine against polio, made by cultivating 3 strains of virus separately in monkey tissue and killing the viruses in the vaccine with formaldehyde. Tested during a mass trial conducted by Francis in 1954, the vaccine was pronounced safe (1955) and 80–90% effective. First recipient (1955) of the Medal for Distinguished Civilian Achievement awarded by Congress, Salk was given a special chair of preventive medicine at Pittsburgh (1950).

Sandburg, Carl (b. Galesburg, Ill., 6 Jan. 1878–), poet, son of a Swedish blacksmith, left school at 13, enlisted in the army, and saw active service in Puerto Rico in the Spanish-American War. He attended Lombard College in Galesburg (1898–1902), but never graduated. He served as a private secy. to the mayor of Milwaukee (1910–12) and as a newspaperman. First recognition as a poet came to him in 1914, when *Poetry* magazine awarded him the Helen Haire Levinson Prize. His *Chicago Poems* (1915) established his reputation. In his rugged poems Middle Western vernacular is mixed with lyric passages. His *Collected Poems* received the Pulitzer Prize for poetry (1951). A prodigious Lincoln scholar, he published the 1st vol. of his multivol. Lincoln biography, *The Prairie Years* (1926), followed by *The War Years* (1939, Pulitzer Prize in History). He wrote *Rootabaga Stories* for children (1922). Collector and singer of American folk music, he edited his own collection, *The American Songbag* (1927). Other works include *The People, Yes* (1936); a novel, *Remembrance Rock* (1948); and his autobiography, *Always the Young Strangers* (1953).

Sargent, John Singer (b. Florence, Italy, 12 Jan. 1856; d. London, 15 Apr. 1925), painter, of American parentage, studied at the Academy of Fine Arts, Florence, and, when his parents moved to Paris (1874), at the École des Beaux-Arts there under Carolus Duran. After a 1st trip to the U.S. (1876), he returned to Paris, painting *Gitana* and exhibiting at the salons (1877–81). Following Spanish and Moroccan trips (1880) and a visit to Venice, he whipped up a storm of criticism in Paris by his *Madame Gautreau,* and at 28 established a studio in London. His triumphant *Carnation, Lily, Lily, Rose* (1884–86), 1st of a long series of pictures of children, brought him commissions in the U.S., where (1857) he painted Mrs. H. G. Marquand, Mrs. Charles Inches, and Mrs. John L. Gardner. Exhibiting in Boston (Dec. 1887), he made many visits to that city and was commissioned to do murals for the Boston Public Library (completed 1916), the Art Museum, and Harvard's Widener Library. A brilliant technician and a stylist both exotic and elegant, he was considered by contemporaries 1st of all as a portraitist (*Carmencita,* the Wertheimer family, and portraits of Theodore Roosevelt, Henry James, and Woodrow Wilson), but he did original and charming work as a painter of genre (*The Weavers, Neapolitan Children Bathing*), and his swiftly executed and luminous water colors (*Melon Boats, White Ships*), painted during his later years, were to be considered his masterpieces. Declining a knighthood (1907) on the ground that he considered himself a U.S. citizen, he was sent to the front in northern France by the British govt. during World War I, where he painted *Gassed* (1919).

Schurz, Carl (b. Liblar, near Cologne, Germany, 2 Mar. 1829; d. New York City, 14 May 1906), soldier, statesman, diplomat, and author. Taking part in the unsuccessful German revolutionary movement (1848–49) while a student at the University of Bonn, he emigrated to the U.S. (1852) and in 1856 settled at Watertown, Wis. He became active in politics, helped organize the Republican party in Wis., and, as an antislavery man, actively supported Lincoln against Douglas in the Ill. senatorial campaign of 1858. He was admitted to the Wis. bar (1858) and practiced law at Milwaukee. As chairman of the Wis. delegation to the Chicago Republican Convention (1860) he backed Lincoln's nomination, was appointed (1860) Minister to Spain, returned to the U.S. (1862), and was appointed brig. gen. of volunteers. He commanded a division at 2nd Bull Run (1862), was promoted to maj. gen. (1863), and in 1863 took part in the battles of Chancellorsville and Gettysburg. At President Johnson's request he made a survey (July–Sept. 1865) of the postwar South, was Washington correspondent (1865–66) of the New York *Tribune,* editor (1866–67) of the Detroit *Post,* and joint editor and owner (1867–69) of the St. Louis *Westliche Post.* An anti-Grant Republican, he served (1869–75) in the Senate as a member from Mo. and was one of the chief organizers of the Liberal Republican movement (1870–72). An exponent of civil service reform and of a liberal policy toward the South, he supported Hayes in 1876 and served (1877–81) as Secretary of the Interior, carrying out signal reforms in the treatment of the Indians. He lived in New York after 1881 and was an editor (1881–83) of the New York *Evening Post,* chief editorial writer (1892–98) for *Harper's Weekly,* and president (1892–1900) of the National Civil Service Reform League. He wrote *Henry Clay* (2 vols., 1887), a penetrating essay on Lincoln (1891), and *The Reminiscences of Carl Schurz* (3 vols., 1907–08).

Scott, Winfield (b. "Laurel Branch," near Petersburg, Va., 13 June 1786; d. West Point, N.Y., 29 May 1866), soldier, popularly called "Old Fuss and Feathers." He attended the College of William and Mary; served in the War of 1812, attaining the rank of brig. gen. (1814) and performing gallantly at the battles of Chippewa and Lundy's Lane (1814), for which he was breveted a maj. gen. and acclaimed as a military hero. He served in the Black Hawk War and in the campaigns against the Seminole and Creek Indians, and in 1838, following the *Caroline* crisis in Anglo-American relations, restored peace on the Canadian border. He became (June 1841) general in chief of the U.S. Army, and in the Mexican War commanded the amphibious operation that took Vera Cruz (26 Mar. 1847) and led the overland advance over mountainous terrain, winning the battles of Cerro Gordo, Churubusco, Molino del Rey, and Chapultepec, and finally taking Mexico City (14 Sept. 1847). After the war his strained relations with Polk resulted in the preferring of charges against Scott; the charges, however, were withdrawn, and in 1852 Congress passed a resolution giving Scott the pay and rank of a lt. gen. The Whig candidate for the Presidency in the campaign of 1852, he was decisively defeated by Franklin Pierce. In 1859 he again acted as peacemaker between the U.S. and Great Britain, on this occasion averting serious trouble in the dispute over the possession of San Juan Island in Puget Sound. Despite his Virginian background, he remained loyal to the Union when the Civil War broke out, and as commander of the U.S. Army made preparations for defending the capital. He retired on 1 Nov. 1861.

Seaborg, Glenn Theodore (b. Ishpeming, Mich., 19 Apr. 1912–), physical chemist. He was graduated (1934) from the University of California, where he received the degree of Ph.D. in 1937 and became a full professor in 1945. With associates, including Dr. Edward M. McMillan, with whom he shared the Nobel prize in chemistry (1951) for their work in the transuranic elements, he discovered plutonium, which supplied the fuel for the atomic bomb. The researches of Seaborg and his associates on heavier-than-uranium substances led to the discovery of 4 other elements: americum (95) and curium (96); and berkelium (97) and californium (98), produced by the alpha bombardment of americum and curium. The instruments and methods which were devised for the determination of these transuranic elements included the use of the Berkeley 184-inch cyclotron, and virtually created the new technique of ultramicrochemistry. Chancellor of the Univ. of Calif. at Berkeley, 1958–61, he became (1961) chairman of the A.E.C.

Seward, William Henry (b. Florida, Orange Co., N.Y., 16 May 1801; d. Auburn, N.Y., 10 Oct. 1872), statesman, was graduated from Union College (1820), admitted to the bar (1822), and commenced practice in Auburn. Affiliated with the Anti-Masonic party, he was elected to the state senate (1830–34), but defeated for reelection (1832), and was unsuccessful Whig nominee for governor (1834). After election (1838) and reelection (1840) as governor, he resumed the practice of law with notable success in criminal cases and in the patent field. Elected to the U.S. Senate (1848) and reelected (1854), he took an advanced stand against slavery. In his speech of 11 Mar. 1850 attacking the Compromise of 1850 he enunciated "a higher law" than the Constitution. Opposed to the Kansas-Nebraska Bill, he declared at Rochester on 25 Oct. 1858 that the slavery struggle was "an irrepressible conflict" between North and South. Prominent in the new Republican party, he was unsuccessful candidate for President in 1856 and again in 1860, but entered Lincoln's Cabinet as Secretary of State. His advocacy of a strong foreign policy to unify the country faced with civil war was fortunately not heeded by Lincoln. His most notable achievements were his negotiations with Great Britain of the *Trent* affair and the *Alabama* claims. At the end of the war he forced France to agree to withdrawal from Mexico within a specified time limit. Coincident with Lincoln's assassination, he was wounded by Lewis Powell, coconspirator with John Wilkes Booth. On his recovery he continued in the Cabinet of Johnson and supported him against the Radical

Republicans. An expansionist, he acquired Alaska from Russia (1867) for $7,200,000 ("Seward's Folly"), negotiated a treaty for the purchase of the Danish West Indies which the Senate failed to ratify, and advocated the annexation of Hawaii.

Shaw, Lemuel (b. Braintree, Mass., 9 Jan. 1781; d. Boston, 30 Mar. 1861), jurist, was graduated from Harvard (1800), was admitted to the bar (1804), and began practice in Boston. Representative in the General Court (1811–14, 1820, and 1829), he was also state senator (1821–22), and a member of the constitutional convention of 1820. He became chief justice of Mass. in 1830 and served for 30 years. On the bench he reshaped the state common law in accordance with changing industrial and social conditions, with especially notable contributions in the field of railway and public utility law. He invariably construed public grants in favor of the community and against private interests. His ruling (*Lombard* v. *Stearns*, 1849) that a water company was under an obligation to serve the public was a judicial landmark, as was his decision in *Comm.* v. *Hunt* (1842, p. 519), supporting legitimate trade union activity. On the other hand, in expounding the "fellow-servant rule," holding a company not liable when an employee was injured owing to the negligence of another employee, he materially delayed the expansion of workmen's compensation. Shaw presided (1850) over the trial of Prof. John W. Webster for the murder of Dr. George Parkman, and refused (1851) to release Sims, the fugitive slave, on habeas corpus, bowing to the Constitution and the law although personally opposed to slavery.

Sheridan, Philip Henry (b. Albany, N.Y., 6 Mar. 1831; d. Nonquitt, Mass., 5 Aug. 1885), Union soldier, was reared in Ohio, had little schooling, clerked in a store at 14, and was appointed to West Point in 1848. Suspended a year for misconduct, he was graduated in 1853. He first saw service along the Rio Grande and against the Indians in the Northwest. When war broke out he was made capt. in the 13th

Infantry (1861), with service in the Corinth campaign, then (1862) col. of the 2nd Mich. Cavalry, and for his victory at Booneville, Mo., made brig. gen. a little over a month later. Maj. gen. of volunteers (31 Dec. 1862), he commanded the 20th Corps, Army of the Cumberland, at Chickamauga, and his charge over Missionary Ridge at Chattanooga contributed largely to Grant's victory. Taking command (Apr. 1864) of the cavalry of the Army of the Potomac, he protected the flanks of Grant's army and attacked Confederate communications around Richmond. In Aug. 1864 he was given command of the Army of the Shenandoah, with orders to push the enemy south and destroy all supplies in the Valley. He defeated Jubal Early at Opequon Creek, Fisher's Hall, and Cedar Creek, making his renowned ride to the battlefield from Winchester 20 mi. away to turn a near defeat into victory. Following this raid, he turned the flank of the Confederate army (1 Apr. 1865), forcing it to evacuate Petersburg and retreat to Appomattox. Military governor of the 5th Dist., La. and Tex., with headquarters at New Orleans, he pursued stern policies and earned President Johnson's disapproval and transfer to the Dept. of Mo., where he launched military operations against hostile Indians, whom he forced to settle on reservations allotted them. Lieut. gen. (1869), he went to Europe (1870) to observe the Franco-Prussian War, and was made a full gen. (1888). He wrote *Personal Memoirs* (1888).

Sherman, William Tecumseh (b. Lancaster, Ohio, 8 Feb. 1820; d. New York City, 14 Feb. 1891), soldier, was graduated from West Point (1840), served in the War with Mexico (1846–47), resigning from the army (1855) to engage in banking in San Francisco. After his bank failed, he practiced law briefly in Leavenworth, Kan., and then served as superintendent of the military academy at Alexandria, La. (1859–61). At the outbreak of the Civil War he rejoined the U.S. Army, commanded a brigade at 1st Bull Run, was given command in Ky. (Oct. 1861), promoted to maj. gen. for conduct at Shiloh (6–7 Apr. 1862), participated in Grant's final Vicksburg campaign, and, as commander of the Army of the Tennessee, in the Battle of Chattanooga. He succeeded Grant (Mar. 1864) in command of the military division of the Mississippi, set out from Chattanooga (May), and began his invasion of Ga. with a brilliant campaign against J. E. Johnston and later Hooker. Taking Atlanta (1 Sept.), he made his "March to the Sea" with 62,000 men without supplies, capturing Savannah (21 Dec.). Under orders to live off the country and to destroy war supplies, public buildings, railroads, and factories, his army exceeded instructions by acts of pillage. In bringing the war home to civilians by destruction of goods rather than life, Sherman has been considered the 1st modern general. Turning northward, he marched through the Carolinas to join Grant in Va., receiving the surrender of J. E. Johnston at Durham, N.C. (26 Apr. 1865). In 1869 he succeeded Grant in command of the army, until his retirement (1884). His *Memoirs* (2 vols.) appeared in 1875.

Shockley, William Bradford (b. London, Eng., 13 Feb. 1910–), physicist and inventor, received his B.S. (1932) from the Calif. Inst. of Technology, and his Ph.D. from M.I.T. (1936), in which year he joined the technical staff of the Bell Telephone Laboratories. During World War II he directed (1942–44) research at Columbia for the antisubmarine warfare operations program, and in the postwar period served as director of the research weapons system evaluations group, Dept. of Defense (1955–58). Known for his studies of semiconductivity and other aspects of solid-state physics, he shared with John Bardeen and W. H. Brattain the 1958 Nobel Prize in Physics for developing (1948) the transistor, a semiconductor and substitute for the vacuum tube. He is the inventor of the junction transistor (1951). He wrote *Electrons and Holes in Semiconductors* (1950) and edited *Imperfections in Nearly Perfect Crystals* (1952).

Silliman, Benjamin (b. Trumbull, Conn., 8 Aug. 1779; d. New Haven, Conn., 24 Nov. 1864), educator, scientist, was graduated from Yale (1796), studied law at New Haven, and was admitted to the Conn. bar (1802), but abandoned the career for chemistry and natural history. Professor of chemistry and natural history at Yale from 1802 to 1853, he was extraordinarily influential as a teacher and popularizer of science. His interest in geology was aroused on a trip to England and the Continent (1805). Utilizing the mineral collection of Col. George Gibbs, he introduced (1813) an illustrated lecture course in mineralogy and geology, and was one of the organizers of the Yale Medical School (1818). He began to give (1818) scientific lectures, utilizing experiments as demonstrations, open to the public of New Haven, and, responding to popular demand, lectured in N.Y., N.E., and other parts of the country. He initiated the lecture series of the Lowell Institute (1839–40). He founded (1818) the influential *American Journal of Science and Arts*, which he edited for 20 yrs. In addition to many scientific papers, he wrote *A Journal of Travels in England, Holland and Scotland* (1810), *A Visit to Europe in 1851* (1853), and edited *The Elements of Experimental Chemistry* (1814).

Simms, William Gilmore (b. Charleston, S.C., 17 Apr. 1806; d. there, 11 June 1870), author, studied law privately and in 1827 was admitted to the Charleston bar. Writing in a Byronic vein, he produced 5 vols. of verse by 1832. Also active as a journalist, he was editor (1828–33) of the Charleston *City Gazette*. His 1st novel was *Martin Faber* (1833), a study of a criminal. With *Guy Rivers* (1834) and *The Yemassee* (1835), Simms inaugurated the series of romances based on S.C. history and Southern frontier life by which he is chiefly remembered: The Border Romances, including *Richard Hurdis* (1838), *Border Beagles* (1840), *Beauchampe* (1842), *Helen Halsey* (1845), *Charlemont* (1856), *Voltmeier* (1869) and *The Cub of the Panther* (1869); and the Revolutionary Romances, including *Mellichampe* (1836), *The Kinsmen* (1841; published as *The Scout* in 1854), *Katharine Walton* (1851), *The Sword and the Distaff* (1853; published as *Woodcraft* in 1854), *The For-*

ayers (1855), and *Eutaw* (1856). A prolific writer who is the most representative of the men of letters of the Old South, he also wrote plays, a *History* (1840) and *Geography* (1843) of S.C., biographies of Francis Marion (1844) and Nathanael Greene (1849), and contributed to *The Pro-Slavery Argument* (1852).

Slater, Samuel (b. Belper, Derbyshire, England, 9 June 1768; d. Webster, Mass., 21 Apr. 1835), pioneer of cotton manufacture in the U.S. Apprenticed (1783) to Jedediah Strutt, a partner of Richard Arkwright in the development of cotton textile machinery, Slater became thoroughly skilled in all aspects of the business. At a time when the British government forbade the emigration of textile workers and the export of textile machinery or data, Slater memorized the details of the machinery made by Crompton, Arkwright, and Hargreaves, and, attracted by the bounties offered by American state legislatures, emigrated to the U.S. (1789). He met (1790) Moses Brown at Providence, R.I., and for the firm of Almy & Brown reproduced from memory Arkwright's cotton machinery, thus ushering in the American cotton industry. He became (1793) a member of the firm of Almy, Brown & Slater, which built a plant at Pawtucket, R.I. In 1798 he formed a partnership under the name of Samuel Slater & Co., which established plants at Pawtucket, Smithfield (later Slatersville), R.I.; East Webster, Mass.; Amoskeag Falls, N.H.; and Oxford (later Webster), Mass. In 1815 he began the manufacture of woolen cloth in his plants.

Smith, Alfred Emanuel (b. New York City, 30 Oct. 1873; d. there, 5 Oct. 1944), governor of New York, grew up on Manhattan's lower East Side, attended parochial school, and worked in the Fulton Fish Market. Tammany assemblyman (1903–15) and majority leader of the Assembly, he was identified with reform legislation, playing with Robert Wagner a leading role in the N.Y. State Factory Investigation Comm., which secured the passage of safety laws after the Triangle fire (1911). Sheriff of N.Y. County (1915–17) and president of the N.Y.C. Bd. of Aldermen (1917), he was governor

of N.Y. for 4 terms (1918–21, 1923–28). An outstanding state executive, he demonstrated exceptional talent for political administration and progressive legislation in the fields of labor, housing, and public works. Nominated for President by Franklin D. Roosevelt at the Democratic National Convention in 1924, he was opposed by William G. McAdoo, both withdrawing after 95 ballots, making possible the nomination of John W. Davis. First Roman Catholic nominee for President (1928) and advocate of the repeal of the 18th Amendment, he was defeated by Herbert Hoover. Failing to secure the Democratic nomination in 1932, he retired from politics and engaged in business. An organizer of the American Liberty League (1934), he aligned himself with the opponents of the New Deal.

Smith, John (b. Willoughby, Lincolnshire, England, *c.*1579; d. London, England, 21 June 1631), soldier of fortune, explorer and author, was apprenticed to a merchant, and then sought adventure as a soldier on the Continent, serving against the Turks. Returning to England (*c.* 1604), where according to his own claim he participated in the organization of the London Co. (1606), he left for Va. in Dec. 1606, as one of the party of 144 colonists aboard 3 ships and disembarked at Jamestown on 24 May 1607. He was made a member of the governing council, was active in exploration, and performed his most valuable services in securing food from the Indians for the hard-pressed colony. According to Smith's account in his *General Historie of Virginia* (1624), he was taken prisoner by the Indians, was condemned to death, and was saved by the intercession of Pocahontas, daughter of the chief Powhatan. When Smith returned to Jamestown (Jan. 1608), he found his enemies had seized control, was arrested and sentenced to hang, but was saved by the arrival of Capt. Christopher Newport with supplies and colonists from England. In the summer of 1608 Smith explored the Potomac and Rappahannock rivers and Chesapeake Bay. To Newport, who sailed for England in June 1608, he gave the manuscript of the account of Va.'s settlement brought out that year as *A True Relation.* Elected president by the council in late 1608, he governed the colony until 1609, returning to England in Oct. of that year. He published *A Map of Virginia* (1612). In Mar. 1614, he went on an expedition along the New England coast on behalf of London merchants. He returned with an excellent cargo of fish and furs, and in *A Description of New England* (1616), which fixed the name on that region, included a valuable map, and stressed the importance of fishing.

Smith, Theobald (b. Albany, N.Y., 31 July 1859; d. New York City, 10 Dec. 1934), pathologist and parasitologist. He was graduated from Cornell (Ph.B., 1881) and the Albany Medical College (M.D., 1883), and pursued postgraduate studies in biology at Johns Hopkins, Cornell, and the University of Toronto. In 1884 he was named director of the newly established pathological laboratory in the Bureau of Animal Industry, Department of Agriculture. In 1886 he organized at the Columbian (later George Washington) University the 1st department of bacteriology in any U.S. medical school, and was professor at that institution from 1886 to 1895. With Dr. Daniel E. Salmon he made studies in the diseases of hogs, set forth in *Special Report on the Cause and Prevention of Swine Plague* (1891), and showed that the alarming mortality among pigs was caused chiefly by hog cholera and swine plague. He also demonstrated (1886) the practicability of immunizing man to cholera by injection of the filtered virus of hogs. He published studies (1898, 1902) on the differentiation of the human and bovine types of the bacillus of tuberculosis. His researches in Texas fever of cattle resulted in the publication of *Investigations into the Nature, Causation, and Prevention of Texas or Southern Cattle Fever* (in collaboration with F. L. Kilborne, 1893), which set forth the discovery of the transmission of the protozoan parasite *Babesia bigemina* by the cattle tick *Boophilus annulatus*, a study which for the 1st time demonstrated the transmission of diseases by insect carriers. Smith served as director (1895–1915) of the pathological laboratory of the Massachusetts Board of Health, professor of comparative pathology (1896–1915) in the Harvard Medical School, and was director (1915–29) of the department of animal pathology of the Rockefeller Institute for Medicine. In 1933 he became president of the Rockefeller Institute. Among his many publications are *Studies in Vaccinal Immunity Towards Diseases of the Bovine Placenta due to Bacillus Abortus* (1923) and *Parasitism and Disease* (1934). The debt of the American livestock industry to Smith is almost incalculable.

Stanford, Leland (b. Watervliet, N.Y., 9 Mar. 1824; d. Palo Alto, Calif., 21 June 1893), railroad builder, attended school at Clinton and Cazenovia, N.Y., entered an Albany law firm at the age of 21, and was admitted to the bar 3 yrs. later. After the burning of his law office at Port Washington (1852), he followed his younger brothers to the Pacific coast, setting up in the merchandise business in El Dorado Co., and then Sacramento. Republican nominee for governor (1859), he was decisively defeated, but was elected in 1861 due to a split in the Democratic party. As governor he held California in the union. Interested by Theodore Dehone Judah (1826–63), engineer, in a transcontinental railroad, he joined with Mark Hopkins (1813–78), Charles Crocker (1822–88), and Collis P. Huntington (1821–1900) in organizing the Central Pacific R.R. (1861), which benefited by grants and other state assistance while he was governor. At the expiration (1863) of his term of office, he devoted himself entirely to railroad affairs, handling the financial and political interests of the Central Pacific, while Crocker took charge of construction and Huntington acted as chief railroad lobbyist back East. He was president and director of the Central Pacific R.R. from the beginning until his death and director of the Southern Pacific Co. (1885–93) and president (1885–90), as well as a shareholder in the railroad construction companies. His election as U.S. Senator (1885–93) caused a break with Huntington, who succeeded in supplanting him as president of the Southern Pacific. He founded (1885) and endowed Stanford University in memory of his son

Leland Stanford, Jr. (d. 1884) and selected David Starr Jordan (1851–1931) as president.

Stanley, Wendell Meredith (b. Ridgeville, Ind., 16 Aug. 1904–), biochemist. He was graduated from Earlham College (B.S., 1926) at Richmond, Ind., and from the University of Illinois (M.S., 1927; Ph.D., 1929), where he was a research associate and instructor in chemistry (1929–30). As a National Research fellow he studied at Munich (1930–31) and was associated with the Rockefeller Institute for Medical Research (1931–48). Since 1948 he has been professor of biochemistry and director of the virus laboratory at the University of California. He was the first to isolate and crystallize a virus (the tobacco mosaic virus) and has done notable work on the chemical nature of influenza and other viruses, and in the fields of diphenyl sterochemistry and lepracidal compounds. In 1946 he shared the Nobel prize in chemistry with J. H. Northrop.

Stanton, Elizabeth Cady (b. Johnstown, N.Y., 12 Nov. 1815; d. New York City, 26 Oct. 1902), social reformer and militant feminist, was graduated (1832) from the Troy (N.Y.) Female Seminary, and in 1840 married the lawyer and reformer, Henry Brewster Stanton. In 1840, while attending a London antislavery convention where Lucretia C. Mott and other American women were refused official accreditation because of their sex, Mrs. Stanton joined with Mrs. Mott in planning a women's rights convention in the U.S. This gathering, held at the Wesleyan Methodist Church in Seneca Falls, N.Y. (19–20 July 1848), ushered in the modern feminist movement. Mrs. Stanton was also active in the abolition and temperance movements, but devoted her chief efforts to the crusade for women's rights. After 1851 she worked in close cooperation with Susan B. Anthony. She was president of the National Woman Suffrage Association and its successor body, and was coeditor (1868 *et seq.*) of the *Revolution,* an organ of the feminist movement.

Steffens, Lincoln (b. San Francisco, 6 Apr. 1866; d. Carmel, Calif., 9 Aug. 1936), journalist, reformer, obtained a Ph.B. from the Univ. of Calif. (1889), then studied abroad at Heidelberg, Munich, Leipzig, and the Sorbonne. Returning to New York (1892), he worked as a reporter for the *Evening Post,* covering the Lexow Committee's exposé of vice, and as city editor of the *Commercial Advertiser* (1897). Joining (1901) the staff of *McClure's Magazine,* which included Ida Tarbell and Ray Stannard Baker, he wrote a series of articles, "Tweed Days in St. Louis" (1902), a pioneer "muckraking" article, focusing attention on municipal corruption in St. Louis, and following with an exposé of Minneapolis. His *Shame of the Cities* (1904) stressed the link between business and politics, maintaining that privilege was the enemy rather than the corruptionists. With Tarbell and Baker, he took over (1906) the *American Magazine,* which quickly became a major reform publication, but quit the following year to write as a free lance. He sponsored Walter Lippmann, whom he made his secy., and John Reed, and after a trip to Russia (1917) he lectured in favor of a just peace. On the William C. Bullitt mission to Russia (1919), he met Lenin. ("I have seen the future; and it works.") His *Autobiography* (1931) evidenced disillusionment with the early reform efforts and a more revolutionary approach.

Stephens, Alexander Hamilton (b. in present-day Taliaferro County, Ga., 11 Feb. 1812; d. Atlanta, Ga., 4 Mar. 1883), statesman, author, and Confederate vice-president, was graduated (1832) from the University of Georgia, admitted to the Ga. bar (1834), and practiced law at Crawfordville, Ga. He served in the state legislature (1836–42) and was a Whig (later Democratic) representative in Congress (1843–59). While he opposed the Mexican War, he resisted efforts to restrict slavery in the territory won from Mexico. In 1852 he entered the Democratic ranks. During the critical pre-Civil War years he advocated sectional moderation and conciliation, but became increasingly firm on the slavery issue. At the Georgia secessionist convention (Jan. 1861) he opposed immediate separation, but when the ordinance of secession was adopted he took part in organizing the new government and was elected (9 Feb. 1861) Vice-President of the Confederate States of America. In his "cornerstone speech" delivered at Savannah (21 Mar. 1861), he termed slavery the basic foundation of the Confederate government. During the war his zeal for states' rights and civil liberties brought him into conflict with Jefferson Davis. He was head of the Confederate peace mission at the Hampton Roads Conference (1865). After the war he was held prisoner for 5 mos. at Ft. Warren in Boston Harbor. Although elected (1866) to the U.S. Senate, he was not permitted to take his seat. He was an editor and part proprietor (1871–73) of the Atlanta *Southern Sun,* served in Congress (1873–82), and in 1882 was elected governor of Ga. He wrote *A Constitutional View of the Late War Between the States* (2 vols., 1868, 1870) and *The Reviewers Reviewed* (1872).

Stevens, Thaddeus (b. Danville, Vt., 4 Apr. 1792; d. Washington, D.C., 11 Aug. 1868), statesman, was graduated (1814) from Dartmouth College; moved (1814) to York, Pa., where he studied law; and after being admitted to the bar settled (1816) in Gettysburg, Pa., and practiced law, soon becoming one of the leading attorneys in his part of the state. His strong antislavery convictions led him to defend many fugitive slaves without fee. In 1826 he became a partner in the iron works of James D. Paxton & Co., which in 1828 became Stevens & Paxton. Elected on the Anti-Masonic ticket, he was a member of the Pa. house of representatives (1833–35, 1837, 1841) and served as a delegate to the state constitutional convention (1838). In 1842 he moved to Lancaster, Pa. Elected (1848) to Congress on the Whig ticket, he served until 1853, becoming one of the leading antislavery spokesmen. He took an important part in the formation of the Republican party in Pa., and was elected (1858) as a Republican to the 36th and the 4 succeeding Congresses, serving from 1859 until his death. In 1860 he opposed concessions to the South. He was made chairman of the Ways and Means Committee, thus increasing his power in

Congress; and during the Civil War became the foremost exponent of a stern policy toward the South, opposing Lincoln's plan of reconstruction in favor of harsh measures. As chairman of the House group of the Joint Committee on Reconstruction, he was the leader of the Congressional Radical Republicans. He broke with President Andrew Johnson over the Freedmen's Bureau Bill (1866), imposed military Reconstruction on the South (1867), and was chairman of the managers appointed by the House of Representatives in 1868 to conduct the impeachment proceedings against President Johnson, but was prevented by failing health from taking an important part in the trial.

Stevenson, Adlai Ewing (b. Los Angeles, Calif., 5 Feb. 1900–), statesman, served in the U.S. Naval Reserve (1918) as apprentice seaman, was graduated from Princeton University (A.B., 1922), attended Harvard Law School and received his law degree from Northwestern University (1926), when he was admitted to the Ill. bar. He practiced law in Chicago (1927–41), except for the years (1933–35) when he served as special counsel to the new AAA (1933–34) and Asst. Gen. Counsel, Fed. Alcohol Administration (1934). During World War II he was Special Assistant to the Secy. of the Navy (1941–44). Assigned to the Foreign Economic Administration, he headed a mission to Italy (1943). Subsequently (1944) he returned to Europe for the War Dept. as a member of an Air Force mission. Special Assistant to Secretaries of State Stettinius and Byrnes (1945), he was a member of the U.S. delegation to the UN Conference at San Francisco (Apr. 1945), Senior Adviser to the U.S. delegation to the UN (1946), and alternate delegate (1946–47). Elected Democratic governor of Ill. (Nov. 1948) by an unprecedented 572,067 plurality, he overhauled and reorganized the state administration, attacked gambling and corruption, introduced state economies, vetoed a loyalty oath bill, and fought unsuccessfully for a state FEPC. Democratic nominee for President (1952, 1956), he was defeated both times by Dwight D Eisenhower. In 1961 he was made U.S. Ambassador to the UN.

Stieglitz, Alfred (b. Hoboken, N.J., 1 Jan. 1864; d. New York City, 13 Apr. 1946), photographer, studied at the College of the City of New York (1879–81) and the Berlin Polytechnic Laboratory (1881–90), where he experimented in new photographic techniques. Returning to New York (1890) after winning numerous photographic awards abroad, he edited a series of photo magazines, *American Amateur Photographer* (1892–96), *Camera Notes* (1897–1902), and *Camera Work* (1902–17), organ of the photo-secessionists. A master of the commonplace who used photographs to symbolize an extraordinary range of thoughts and feelings, he achieved for photography recognition as a fine art. Championing the newest art trends, Stieglitz, in his notable photographic and art galleries—291 Fifth Avenue (1905–07), the Intimate (1925–30), and the American Place (1930–46)—introduced the works of Cézanne, Picasso, Matisse, Lautrec, and Brancusi, and was responsible for making known the works of such American artists as Max Weber, John Marin (*q.v.*), Charles Demuth, and Georgia O'Keeffe (1887–   ), whom he married in 1924.

Stimson, Henry Lewis (b. New York City, 21 Sept. 1867; d. Huntington, Long Island, N.Y., 20 Oct. 1950), statesman, was graduated from Yale (B.A., 1888), Harvard (M.A., 1889), and the Harvard Law School (1889–90), and was admitted to the bar in 1891. He was in private practice in New York City until 1906, when President Theodore Roosevelt appointed him U.S. attorney for the southern district of N.Y., a post he held until 1909. The unsuccessful Republican candidate for the governorship of New York (1910), he was named (1911) Secretary of War by President Taft and served until 1913. As a delegate to the N.Y. constitutional convention (1915), he was responsible for many of the principal reforms effected by it. During World War I he served with the A.E.F. in France as a col. of field artillery. In 1927 he was named by President Coolidge as special representative to Nicaragua, where by

arbitration he settled a political dispute that had brought on civil war. He served as governor general of the Philippines (1927–29), and as secretary of state (1929–33) in President Herbert Hoover's Cabinet was chairman of the U.S. delegations to the London Naval Conference (1930) and to the Geneva Disarmament Conference (1932). He formulated and announced the "Stimson Doctrine" (1931) of nonrecognition of territories and agreements obtained by acts of aggression. Resuming his private law practice in 1933, he supported many of President Franklin D. Roosevelt's foreign policy measures, and called for aid to Great Britain and for compulsory military training. Named Secretary of War (July 1940), he served through World War II and retired in Sept. 1945, when he resigned from President Truman's Cabinet. Stimson was the 1st American to serve in the Cabinets of 4 presidents. He was the author of *American Policy in Nicaragua* (1927) and *On Active Service in Peace and War* (with McGeorge Bundy, 1948).

Stone, Harlan Fiske (b. Chesterfield, N.H., 11 Oct. 1872; d. Washington, D.C., 22 Apr. 1946), 11th Chief Justice of the U.S., was graduated from Amherst (1894) and Columbia Law School (1898), commenced practice in New York City, and joined the faculty of Columbia Law School (1899), serving as dean (1907 and from 1910–23, when he returned to private practice). Appointed U.S. Attorney General in Coolidge's Cabinet (1924), he reorganized the Federal Bureau of Investigation. As an associate justice of the U.S. Supreme Court (1925), becoming Chief Justice (1941), he was early identified with Holmes and Brandeis in dissents on social issues and after 1932 generally supported the New Deal program. In his dissent in *U.S.* v. *Butler* (1935), where the AAA processing tax was held unconstitutional, he declared: "Courts are not the only agencies of government that must be assumed to have capacity to govern." He sustained Federal and state social security legislation. In a lone dissent in the *Jehovah's Witnesses' Case* (1940), he opposed state legislation compelling belief or expression violating religious convictions, but upheld restrictions imposed at the time of World War II upon U.S. citizens of Japanese origin as being within the war powers (1943). During the war he opposed the use of members of the Court for non-judicial activities.

Story, Joseph (b. Marblehead, Mass., 18 Sept. 1779; d. Cambridge, Mass., 10 Sept. 1845), jurist, was graduated from Harvard (1798), studied law under Chief Justice Sewall and later under Samuel Putnam, was admitted to the bar (1801), and practiced in Salem. A Jeffersonian Republican, he served in the state legislature (1805–08) and in the U.S. House of Representatives (1808–09), where he favored repeal of the embargo. Again in the state legislature (1811) he was appointed in that year by President Madison as associate justice of the U.S. Supreme Court. His decisions in admiralty and prize cases during the War of 1812 became classic expositions of international law. A nationalist along with Marshall, he went so far as to maintain that the power of Congress to regulate interstate and foreign commerce was exclusive (dissent in *N.Y.* v. *Miln,* 1837). He upheld the property rights of private corporations (*Terrett* v. *Taylor,* 1815) as well as the obligation of contracts, although outvoted by the Jacksonian majority in the *Charles River Bridge Case.* After Marshall's death (1835) he upheld, in dissent, the broad construction of the Constitution. His antislavery views were evident in the *Amistad Case* (1839), where he freed slaves as "property rescued from pirates," and in *Prigg* v. *Pa.* (1842), where he held that the enforcement of the Federal fugitive slave laws vested exclusively in the national government. Appointed (1829) to the newly established Dane professorship of Law at Harvard, where he taught until his death, he made a notable contribution both as a teacher and a writer on the law, particularly to the development of American equity jurisprudence (1836) and through his treatise on the conflict of laws (1834). He also published his *Commentaries on the Constitution of the U.S.* (3 vols., 1833).

Stowe, Harriet Elizabeth Beecher (b. Litchfield, Conn., 14 June 1811; d. Hart-ford, Conn., 1 July 1896), author, daughter of Lyman Beecher (1775–1863), sister of Henry Ward Beecher (1813–87). She was educated at Litchfield and Hartford, moved to Cincinnati (1832), where she produced her 1st published writings and developed antislavery sympathies, and married (1836) Calvin E. Stowe, professor of Biblical literature in the Lane Theological Seminary, of which her father was president. She left Cincinnati in 1850, when her husband became professor at Bowdoin College. The agitation over the Fugitive Slave Law of 1850 led her to write *Uncle Tom's Cabin, or Life Among the Lowly* (2 vols., 1852), originally published in serial form (5 June 1851–1 Apr. 1852) in the *National Era,* an antislavery newspaper brought out at Washington, D.C. The book sold 300,000 copies within a year, aroused deep hostility in the South, and won her an international reputation. She answered her critics in *A Key to Uncle Tom's Cabin* (1853). She also wrote a 2nd antislavery novel, *Dred; a Tale of the Great Dismal Swamp* (1856). Among her later works were *The Minister's Wooing* (1859), *The Pearl of Orr's Island* (1862), *Oldtown Folks* (1869), *Sam Lawson's Oldtown Fireside Stories* (1872), and *Poganuc People* (1878).

Stuart, Gilbert (b. North Kingston, R.I., 3 Dec. 1755; d. Boston, Mass., 9 July 1828), painter. He received his 1st professional training (*c.*1769 *et seq.*) under Cosmo Hamilton, a Scotch painter at Newport whom he accompanied to Edinburgh. Returning to America after Hamilton's death (1772), he went to London (1775) and became the pupil (1776–*c.*1781) of Benjamin West. His *Portrait of a Gentleman Skating* (1782) brought him public notice, and thereafter Stuart enjoyed a wide patronage in London, where he won a place as a leading portrait painter and exhibited with the Royal Academy until 1785. In 1787 he went to Ireland to continue his success as a portraitist. He came to the U.S. (*c.*1793), set up a studio in New York City, and in 1794 opened a studio in Philadelphia, where he produced many notable portraits of women and his 1st 2 life portraits of George Washington.

He moved to Germantown in 1796 and in 1803 went to Washington, D.C., where he painted his gallery of statesmen of the early Republic, including Jefferson, Madison, and Monroe, by which he is best remembered. In 1805 he moved to Boston. Among his many portraits are those of Benjamin West, Colonel Isaac Barré, Rev. Joseph Stevens Buckminster, Gen. Henry Knox, James Sullivan, Joseph Story, Samuel Eliot, James Perkins, Oliver Wolcott, Albert Gallatin, Mrs. Perez Morton, John Trumbull, and John Randolph. These and many other lifelike and luminous paintings left him an unrivaled reputation in American portraiture.

Stuart, James Ewell Brown (b. Patrick County, Va., 6 Feb. 1833; d. Richmond, Va., 12 May 1864), soldier, attended Emory and Henry Coll., 1848–50, was graduated from West Point (1854), and joined the U.S. cavalry. He served with Lee in suppressing John Brown's raid at Harper's Ferry (1859). Resigning his commission at the outbreak of the Civil War, he was made a capt. of Confederate cavalry (24 May 1861). At the 1st Battle of Bull Run he protected the Confederate left and was made brig. gen. (21 Sept. 1861). He covered the Confederate withdrawal to the Chickahominy in the Peninsular campaign and rode completely around McClellan's army on reconnaissance. In a raid to the rear of Pope's forces he burned stores and captured headquarters documents disclosing the strength and position of the Union forces. Promoted maj. gen. (25 July 1862), he fought at the 2nd Battle of Bull Run and in the Antietam campaign. He fought at Fredericksburg and Chancellorsville, and, after Jackson had been wounded, assumed command of the 2nd Army Corps. His most controversial action took place in the Gettysburg campaign, where he allowed himself to be held up in interposing his cavalry between the Union army and Washington before attempting to make contact with Ewell, as a result of which Lee was deprived for 3 days of information about Union movements. At Yellow Tavern he turned off Sheridan's columns from the direct road to Richmond and was fatally wounded. A spectacular cavalry officer, "Jeb" Stuart was regarded by Lee as the "eyes of the army."

Stuyvesant, Petrus [Peter] b. Scherpenzeel, Friesland, Holland, c. 1610; d. New York City, Feb. 1672), colonial governor, enrolled at the Univ. of Franeker (c. 1628), then pursued a military career, followed (1635) by service with the Dutch West India Co., becoming governor of Curaçao (1644). His right leg was amputated as the result of an injury sustained in leading an expedition (Mar.-Apr. 1644) against the island of St. Martin. Commissioned (1646) director general of New Netherland, he arrived on Manhattan in 1647. His career was notable for its progressive measures and reforming zeal. He curbed the sale of liquor to the Indians, enforced Sabbath observance, and taxed imports to construct public works. He promoted intercolonial relations with the English, negotiating (1650) the Treaty of Hartford fixing a boundary line with Conn. He drove the Swedes from the Delaware (1655), which was incorporated into New Netherland. On the debit side, he was arbitrary and dictatorial, banished his critics, and, although instituting (1649) a Board of Nine Men to assist him, he only yielded (1653) under pressure to the demands of the burghers for municipal self-govt. in New Amsterdam. Devout Dutch Reformed adherent, he was intolerant toward other sects and, in a move aimed primarily against the Lutherans, forbade meetings by other religions. Reproved by the directors of the Company in Amsterdam, he was forced to back down, as he was in his efforts to bar the Jews from settlement and burgher rights (1655–56). On 6 Sept. 1664 he surrendered the colony to the English, but after returning to the Netherlands (1665) to defend his official conduct, he went back to New York (1667), living the remainder of his life on "Stuyvesant's Bouwery," the farm conveyed to him (1650) by the Company.

Sullivan, Harry Stack (b. Norwich, N.Y., 21 Feb. 1892; d. Paris, France, 15 Jan. 1949), physician and psychiatrist, worked his way through Chicago Coll. of Medicine and Surgery (M.D., 1917). During

World War I he served as a 1st lieut. attached to the Bd. of Examiners for the Medical Corps, and after the war was medical executive officer, Federal Bd. for Vocational Education (1919–20), drafting policy and procedures for handling soldiers disabled by neuropsychiatric conditions. As psychiatrist, Public Health Institute (1921–22), and veterans' liaison officer at St. Elizabeth's Hospital (1922–23), where he worked in association with William Alanson White, he launched his career in psychiatry. As director of clinical research at Sheppard and Enoch Pratt Hospital, near Baltimore (1923–25), he pursued intensive studies of schizophrenic disorders. Convinced that psychoanalysis needed to be supplemented by consideration of the impact of cultural forces upon personality, he developed his theory of interpersonal relations. He taught psychiatry at the Maryland Med. Schl. (1923–39) and became professor and head of the dept. at Georgetown Schl. of Med. (1939). Previously, he investigated schizophrenia and obsessional neurosis while practicing psychiatry in N.Y.C., beginning 1931, and as head of both the William Alanson White Foundation (1933–43) and the Washington School of Psychiatry (1936–47). Co-editor and editor of *Psychiatry* (1938–49), he gathered a number of his papers in *Conceptions of Modern Psychiatry* (1940). During World War II he was consultant in psychiatry for the Selective Service System and medical adviser, personnel section, War Dept. General Staff

Sullivan, Louis Henri (b. Boston, Mass., 3 Sept. 1856; d. Chicago, 14 Apr. 1924), architect. He attended (1872–73) the Massachusetts Institute of Technology, worked (1873) in the architectural office of William LeBaron Jenney at Chicago, and was admitted (1874) to the École des Beaux Arts at Paris. As a partner in the architectural firm of Adler and Sullivan (1881–95), he became the leading figure in the so-called Chicago School of architecture. His abandonment of the modes of Victorian Gothic and Romanesque Revival became evident in his plans for the interior of the Chicago Auditorium (built 1886–90), where he used the delicate ornamentation that became associated with his style. In his designs for the Wainwright Building at St. Louis (1890), the Schiller Building (1892) and the Gage Building (1898) at Chicago, and the Prudential Building at Buffalo, N.Y. (1895), he evolved resourceful solutions of the architectural and structural problems posed by the skyscraper, and was among the 1st to stress the vertical lines of steel skeleton construction. His root idea, "form follows function," established the basis of the modern organic architecture created by his disciple, Frank Lloyd Wright. For his other notable designs, see p. 643.

Sumner, Charles (b. Boston, Mass., 6 Jan. 1811; d. Washington, D.C., 11 Mar. 1874), statesman, was graduated from Harvard (1830) and the Harvard Law School (1833). Admitted to the bar in 1834, he was appointed reporter of the U.S. circuit court and lectured at the Harvard Law School (1835–37). After a sojourn on the Continent (1837–40), he became active in the movement for outlawing war and in an address (1849) before the American Peace Society urged the establishment of a "Congress of Nations." An opponent of the Mexican War, he helped found the Free-Soil party (1848) and was the Senatorial candidate of a coalition of Free-Soilers and Democrats. Following a prolonged contest in the Mass. legislature, he took his Senate seat in 1851, and was reelected as a Republican in 1857, 1863, and 1869, serving until his death. An outspoken antagonist of slavery, he made a stirring indictment (1852) of the Fugitive Slave Law of 1850, opposed the Kansas-Nebraska Bill (1854), and helped organize the Republican party. After making "The Crime Against Kansas" speech (20 May 1856), Sumner was violently assaulted (22 May 1856) on the Senate floor by Rep. Preston Brooks (S.C.); the injuries he received compelled his absence from the Senate until 5 Dec. 1859. He became (1861) chairman of the Foreign Relations Committee; beginning late in 1861 he was an ardent exponent of emancipation; and in 1862 formulated the "state suicide" theory of Reconstruction, holding that the Confederate states had relinquished all rights under the Constitution. After the war, however, he gradually adopted a more sympathetic attitude toward the South. He championed equal suffrage for whites and Negroes. Differences with President Grant and Secretary of State Hamilton Fish led to his removal (1872) from the chairmanship of the Foreign Relations Committee.

Sumner, William Graham (b. Paterson, N.J., 30 Oct. 1840; d. Englewood, N.J., 12 Apr. 1910), economist, political and social scientist, and teacher, was graduated from Yale (1863), studied for the ministry in Germany and England, was a tutor at Yale (1866–69), and in 1869 was ordained a priest of the Protestant Episcopal Church. He remained in the ministry until 1872, when he was invited to occupy the newly established chair of political and social science at Yale, a post he held for the remainder of his life. An exponent of laissez faire, he opposed trade unions, social legislation, and government regulation. As an economist, he favored free trade and opposed free silver and bimetallism. As a sociologist, he pioneered in establishing a general science of society based on the study and interrelationships of all social institutions, making his most illuminating contribution in *Folkways* (1907). Among his works are *A History of American Currency* (1874), *What Social Classes Owe to Each Other* (1883), *Protectionism* (1885), *The Financier and Finances of the American Revolution* (2 vols., 1891), *War and Other Essays* (1911), and *The Forgotten Man and Other Essays* (1919). The posthumously published *Science of Society* (4 vols., 1927) was completed by Albert G. Keller.

Taft, Robert Alphonso (b. Cincinnati, Ohio, 8 Sept. 1889; d. Washington, D.C., 31 July 1953), lawyer, statesman, son of President William Howard Taft, was graduated from Yale (1910) and studied law at Harvard (LL.B., 1913), practicing in Cincinnati with Maxwell & Ramsey, later (1923) becoming senior partner of Taft, Stettinius & Hollister. Member of the state House of Representatives (1921–26), he was elected U.S. senator from Ohio (1938) and served until his death. He consistently opposed the New

Deal program, spearheaded the isolationist bloc in Congress, and fought the Lend-Lease bill, but later backed U.S. participation in the UN. Cosponsor of the Taft-Hartley Labor Act (1957), he was 3-time candidate for the Republican Presidential nomination (1940, 1948, 1952), supporting Gen. Eisenhower in return for the latter's acceptance (12 Sept. 1952) of most of Taft's program. After Eisenhower's election he became Senate floor leader.

Taft, William Howard (b. Cincinnati, Ohio, 15 Sept. 1857; d. Washington, D.C., 8 Mar. 1930), 27th President of the U.S. and 9th Chief Justice, was graduated from Yale (1878) and Cincinnati Law College (1880); practiced law in Cincinnati; and was assistant county prosecutor (1881–82, 1885–86), collector of internal revenue, 1st dist. of Ohio (1882–83), superior court judge (1887–90), and U.S. Solicitor General under Harrison (1890–92). While Federal judge for 6th Circuit (1892–1900), he was also dean of the University of Cincinnati Law School. Appointed by McKinley president of the Philippine Commission (1900), he became the 1st civil governor (1901–04), credited with notable reforms, the restoration of peace, solving the problem of church lands, and establishing limited self-government. Theodore Roosevelt's Secretary of War (1904–08), he was the President's personal choice as Republican nominee (1908), defeating Bryan for the Presidency. Although he continued a number of Roosevelt's policies, notably a vigorous enforcement of the antitrust laws (Standard Oil and American Tobacco trusts dissolved), he split with the progressives over the Payne-Aldrich Tariff (1909). Renominated (1912), he was defeated in a 3-cornered race with Theodore Roosevelt and Woodrow Wilson. Kent professor of law at Yale (1913–21), he was appointed by Harding as Chief Justice of the U.S. Supreme Court (1921–30). An intelligent conservative, he upheld the president's removal power (*Myers' Case,* 1926), and his dissent in *Adkins* v. *Children's Hospital* was later upheld by the Court. However, his labor decisions curtailed the Clayton Act, permitted injunctions in secondary boycotts, made unions liable to be sued even though unincorporated, and invalidated the attempt of Congress to impose a tax on the interstate products of child labor.

Taney, Roger Brooke (b. Calvert Co., Md., 17 Mar. 1777; d. Washington, D.C., 12 Oct. 1864), 4th Chief Justice of the U.S., was graduated from Dickinson College (1795), read law, and was admitted to the bar (1799), practicing in Calvert Co. (1799–1801), Fredericksburg (1801–23), and Baltimore. Federalist state legislator (1799–1800), he broke with the Federalists (1812) and led a dissenting faction (the "Coodies"). State senator (1816–21), he supported Jackson (1824) and resigned his post as Md. attorney general (1827–31) to enter Jackson's Cabinet as U.S. Attorney General. He drafted that part of Jackson's bank-charter veto message (10 July 1832) in which contention was made that the President was not bound by the interpretation placed upon the Constitution by the Supreme Court. When the Senate refused confirmation of his appointment as Secretary of the Treasury to succeed William J. Duane (1833), he was given a recess appointment to remove Federal deposits from the 2nd Bank of the U.S. and to set up a system of government depositories. On Marshall's death (6 July 1835) he was appointed Chief Justice of the U.S. Supreme Court over bitter Whig opposition. Reversing the court's nationalist trend, his most notable decision was the *Charles River Bridge Case* (1837), which curtailed the scope of the *Dartmouth College Case* and curbed the growth of monopolies. "We must not forget that the community also have rights," he declared on that occasion. His most fateful decision was the *Dred Scott Case* (1857), where, under cover of a discussion of jurisdiction, he declared invalid the Missouri Compromise and the Compromise of 1850, and furnished a major cause of the Civil War. In *Ex parte Merryman* (1861) he defended the rights of civilians in wartime.

Taylor, Zachary (b. Montebello, Va., 24 Nov. 1784; d. Washington, D.C., 9 July 1850), 12th President of the U.S., moved with his family to Ky., was privately tutored, and served as a volunteer in the Ky. militia (1806). His commission as 1st lt., 7th U.S. Infantry (1808), inaugurated 40 yrs. service in the U.S. Army. He successfully defended Ft. Harrison, Indiana Territory (4–5 Sept. 1812); fought in the Black Hawk (1832–33) and Seminole (1837) Wars, with a victory at Lake Okeechobee (25 Dec.); and commanded the department of Fla., 1838–40. Commanding the Army of Occupation on the Mexican Border (1845–46), his forces engaged in hostilities which precipitated War with Mexico (Matamoras, 23 Apr. 1846). Victor at Palo Alto (8 May) and Resaca de la Palma (9 May), he was appointed maj. gen. and, ignoring Polk's order to fight on defense, advanced into Mexico, capturing Monterrey (23 Sept.). Compelled to detach many of his best troops to reinforce Winfield Scott, he continued his invasion, decisively defeating Santa Anna at Buena Vista (23 Feb. 1847). "Old Rough and Ready," now a national hero, was the Whig nominee for President (1848) and was elected over his Democratic opponent, Lewis Cass. Opposing appeasement of the South, he died suddenly in the midst of the struggle over the Compromise of 1850.

Teller, Edward (b. Budapest, Hungary, 15 Jan. 1908–), physicist, obtained his Ph.D. at the Univ. of Leipzig (1930), studied at Copenhagen with Niels Bohr, and left Germany when Hitler came to power. After lecturing at the Univ. of London, he came to George Washington Univ. as visiting professor (1935), collaborating on research with Dr. George Gamow. He worked on the A-bomb project (1941–45). Joining the physics dept. of the Univ. of Chicago (1945), he returned to work at Los Alamos Laboratory (1949). Following Russia's successful A-bomb test and the revelations (Jan. 1950) of Klaus Fuchs' atomic espionage, he became a leading proponent of a crash program for producing a thermonuclear weapon, and has been called "the principal architect of the H-bomb," although he himself had little to do with its actual building. Placed in charge of the new H-bomb laboratory of the AEC at Livermore, Calif. (1952), he brought the H-bomb issue to national attention by testifying before the AEC's Gray Committee in the Oppenheimer case (April 1954). In subsequent international controversy over the dangers of H-bomb testing, he opposed cessation of tests and advised that a "clean" bomb, with little fallout, was practicable.

Tesla, Nikola (b. Smiljan, Lika, Austria-Hungary, 9 July 1856; d. New York City, 7 Jan. 1943), inventor. He was educated at Karlstadt and Gratz, where he specialized in mechanics, mathematics, and physics, studied philosophy at the University of Prague, and in 1881 settled in Budapest, where he invented the telephone repeater and discovered the principle of the rotating magnetic field. He arrived in the U.S. in 1884, became a naturalized citizen, and for several years was associated with George Westinghouse and Thomas A. Edison. His best-known inventions are the alternating current motor (1888) and the Tesla coil or transformer (1891). Principally known for his researches in alternating currents of high frequency and high potential, Tesla's discoveries and inventions include an arc lighting system (1886); incandescent lamps; an alternating current power transmission system (1888); an electrical conversion and distribution system based on oscillatory discharges (1889); high frequency current generators (1890); mechanical oscillators and generators of electrical oscillations (1894–95); radiations, material streams and emanations (1896–98); and a high-potential magnifying transmitter (1897). He worked (1897–1905) on a system of transmission of power without wires and subsequently devoted himself to the fields of telephony and telegraphy.

Thomas, George Henry (b. Southampton County, Va., 31 July 1816; d. San Francisco, 28 Mar. 1870), soldier, often called "the Rock of Chickamauga." He was graduated (1840) from the U.S. Military Academy; during service in the Mexican War was promoted to brevet capt. and maj. for gallantry at Monterrey and Buena Vista; and was an instructor in artillery and cavalry (1851–54) at West Point. Despite his Southern

ties, Thomas adhered to the Union cause at the outbreak of the Civil War. He was commissioned (17 Aug. 1861) brig. gen. of volunteers; as commander, 1st Div., Army of the Ohio, won the Battle of Mill Springs (19 Jan. 1862); was promoted (25 Apr. 1862) to maj. gen. of volunteers; and was a corps commander at Stone River (31 Dec. 1862–3 Jan. 1863) and in the Tullahoma campaign (June–July 1863) in Tenn. As commander of the XIV Corps of the Army of the Cumberland, Thomas withstood a fierce assault by Bragg and Longstreet during a general Northern rout at the Battle of Chickamauga (19–20 Sept. 1863). Promoted (27 Oct. 1863) to brig. gen. in the regular army, Thomas relieved Rosecrans as commander of the Army of the Cumberland and held Chattanooga against a siege. In the Battle of Chattanooga (24–25 Nov. 1863), his troops captured Lookout Mountain and Missionary Ridge. In the Atlanta campaign, the Army of the Cumberland under Thomas made up over half of Sherman's force. At Nashville (15–16 Dec. 1864) Thomas decisively defeated the Confederate army under Hood.

Thomas, Isaiah (b. Boston, Mass., 30 Jan. 1750; d. Worcester, Mass., 4 Apr. 1831), printer and publisher. He learned the printing trade at Boston during his apprenticeship to Zechariah Fowle, whose partner he became in 1770, and founded the *Massachusetts Spy*, a patriot newspaper. He joined Paul Revere in warning the countryside (18 Apr. 1775) and as a minuteman participated in the fighting at Lexington and Concord. Removing his printing plant to Worcester, he resumed publishing the *Spy* on 3 May, and quickly ranked as the leading publisher of the time, producing books distinguished for their typography and format. Also active as a bookseller, he maintained branches in Boston, Albany, Portsmouth, Baltimore, and elsewhere. He published the *Royal American Magazine* (1774–75), the *Worcester Magazine* (1786–88), and the *Massachusetts Magazine* (1789–96). Between 1771 and 1822 he published the almanac which, beginning in 1775, was known as *Thomas's New England Almanack*. He published the 1st dictionary (William Perry's) printed in America and the 1st English illustrated folio Bible in U.S. Included in his prolific output were editions of more than 100 children's books, including *Mother Goose's Melody* (1768). He wrote *The History of Printing in America* (2 vols., 1810), long a standard authority, and founded and incorporated (1812) the American Antiquarian Society, of which he served as 1st president.

Thomas, Theodore [full name **Christian Friedrich Theodore Thomas**] (b. Esens, Germany, 11 Oct. 1835; d. Chicago, 4 Jan. 1905), musician and conductor. He received his musical training as a violinist under his father, arrived (1845) in New York with his parents, made a concert tour (1850) of the South, and played 1st violin (1853) with the American orchestra of Louis Antoine Jullien. He was made (1854) a member of the Philharmonic Society of New York; took part with William Mason in the Mason-Thomas chamber music concerts (1855) at New York, where he appeared (1857–58) as a violin soloist; and in 1860 became an operatic conductor at New York. He organized (1862) his own orchestra, which he took on frequent tours; became (1866) conductor of the Brooklyn Philharmonic Society; conducted the Philadelphia Centennial concerts (1876); and was director (1878) of the College of Music in Cincinnati. He served as conductor (1877, 1880 *et seq.*) of the N.Y. Philharmonic Society; became (1885) director of the American Opera Co.; was conductor (1891–1905) of the Chicago Symphony Orchestra and music director for the Chicago World's Fair (1893). Through his orchestral tours and astute program planning, Thomas advanced popular musical taste in America.

Thoreau, Henry David (b. Concord, Mass., 12 July 1817; d. there, 6 May 1862), poet and essayist, was graduated from Harvard (1837), taught school intermittently (1837–41), and from 1841 to 1843, when he lived in Emerson's home, became acquainted with the Transcendentalist circle. He lived at Walden Pond from 4 July 1845 to 6 Sept. 1847. His antislavery convictions led him to refuse the payment of the Mass. poll tax during the Mexican War, which he regarded as an expansionist scheme of the slave power. He was arrested and jailed, and later related his experiences in his essay on "Civil Disobedience," which subsequently became one of the leading works on passive resistance. Thoreau left Concord only to make his nature tours, or for lecture engagements, and toward the end of his life became an outspoken advocate of abolition. A poet-naturalist whose prose has a homely strength, Thoreau was also a social critic who believed in moral imperatives superior to the institutions fashioned by men. His works include *A Week on the Concord and Merrimack Rivers* (1849), *Walden* (1854), *Excursions* (1863), *The Maine Woods* (1864), *Cape Cod* (1865), and *A Yankee in Canada* (1866). Among his speeches and lectures are "Slavery in Massachusetts" (1854) and "A Plea for Captain John Brown," "The Last Days of John Brown," and "After the Death of John Brown" (1859).

Thorndike, Edward Lee (b. Williamsburg, Mass., 31 Aug. 1871; d. Montrose, N.Y., 9 Aug. 1949), educator, studied at Wesleyan, Harvard, and Columbia, then taught education at Western Reserve University for a year before going to Teachers College, Columbia, where he taught until his retirement (1941). Starting with his early books (*Educational Psychology*, 1903; *Mental and Social Measurements*, 1904; *The Principles of Teaching*, 1905), he emphasized the application of scientific method in education, especially statistical techniques, and placed stress on practical education. His psychological testing methods employed in the U.S. Army in World War I set the pattern for personnel, placement, and educational guidance. His doctrine of innate differences in the aptitudes of pupils constituted an important modification of the idea of equality of educational opportunity. His later views in educational psychology are embodied in *The Measurement of Intelligence* (1926).

Tilden, Samuel Jones (b. New Lebanon, N.Y., 9 Feb. 1814; d. Yonkers, N.Y., 4 Aug. 1886), governor of New York, reformer, spent one term at Yale (1834), studied at N.Y.U. Law School (1838–41), and was admitted to the bar (1841), practicing law in New York City. Corporation counsel of the city (1843), he rose rapidly in the Democratic party, co-founding with John L. O'Sullivan the N.Y. *Morning News* to help Polk carry N.Y. in 1844. In the subsequent party split Tilden joined the Barnburners opposing Marcy's Hunkers. Although Tilden was in the state legislature (1846), was prominent at the constitutional convention of that year, and ran unsuccessfully for attorney general (1855), his prominence in the pre-Civil War years was at the bar rather than in politics. The defense (1856) of Azariah C. Flagg in a vote fraud case was one of his more sensational trial appearances, but more important was his huge railroad practice which laid the foundations for his great fortune. During the Civil War he sought to build up the Democratic party as a "constitutional opposition" and supported Johnson's reconstruction policy. He gained national attention by his role as chairman of the Democratic state committee in ousting the "Tweed Ring" (1872), helping in prosecuting its members, securing legislation reforming the New York City government, and impeaching corrupt judges. Elected governor (1874), he introduced tax reforms and shattered the "Canal Ring." Democratic nominee for President (1876), he won a majority of 250,000 votes over Hayes, but lost the election when a partisan Electoral Commission awarded Hayes the electoral votes of all the contested states. He bequeathed the Tilden Trust, which after protracted litigation made possible the establishment of the N.Y. Public Library.

Truman, Harry S. (b. Lamar, Mo., 8 May 1884–), 33rd President of the U.S., was educated in the public schools; operated the family farm near Independence, Mo. (1906–17); and saw service in World War I as 1st lt. and capt., 129th Field Artillery, 35th Div., participating in the Vosges operation and the St. Mihiel and Meuse-Argonne offensives. He studied nights at Kansas City School of Law (1923–25); was, with the back-ing of "Boss" Tom Prendergast, made judge of Jackson Co. court (1922–24) and presiding judge (1926–34), and was elected U.S. senator from Mo. (1934) and reelected (1940), where he achieved prominence as chairman of the Senate Committee to Investigate the National Defense Program. Franklin D. Roosevelt's choice as compromise running mate (1944), he was elected Vice-President, succeeding to the Presidency on the death of Roosevelt (12 Apr. 1945). With little preparation he was forced to make decisions for carrying the war to a successful conclusion (authorizing the use of the A-bomb against Japan) and for planning the postwar world (at Potsdam, July 1945). Losing control of Congress (1946), his sponsorship of the "Fair Deal," civil rights legislation, and repeal of the Taft-Hartley Act (1947), as well as his vigorous election campaign, won him a surprise victory over Gov. Thomas E. Dewey (1948). His 2nd term was largely concerned with the Cold War against Russia, the Marshall and Truman plans, the resistance (after June 1950) to North Korean and later Chinese aggression in South Korea, the organization of the defense of Western Europe, and the negotiation of the Japanese (1951) and German (1952) peace treaties. He is the author of 2 vols. of memoirs (1955, 1956).

Turner, Frederick Jackson (b. Portage, Wis., 14 Nov. 1861; d. Pasadena, Calif., 14 Mar. 1932), historian, received his B.A. (1884) and M.A. (1888) from the Univ. of Wisc. and his Ph.D. (1890) from Johns Hopkins. Elaborating on his doctoral thesis, "The Character and Influence of the Indian Trade in Wisconsin" (1891), he delivered at a meeting of the American Historical Association (1893) a seminal paper, "The Significance of the Frontier in American History," in which he brilliantly outlined his interpretation of the effect of the frontier on the advance of American democracy and individualism. Influenced by Achille Loria, Friedrich Ratzel, and the evolutionary school, Turner had opened up a concept of the central and liberating role of the contracting frontier which enormously shaped the next generation of

American historical writing. He himself modified his determinism and Darwinism in his *The Significance of Sections in American History* (1932, Pulitzer Award) and *The United States, 1830–50* (posthumously pub. 1935), and a number of critics have taken exception to various parts of his thesis. He taught at the Univ of Wisc. (1892–1910) and Harvard (1910–24).

Twain, Mark, see **Clemens, Samuel Langhorne.**

Tyler, John (b. Greenway, Va., 29 Mar. 1790; d. Richmond, Va., 18 Jan. 1862), 10th President of the U.S., was graduated from William and Mary (1807), admitted to the bar (1809), and practiced in Charles Co., Va. State legislator (1811–16), he entered Congress as a Jeffersonian Democrat (1816–21), served as governor of Va. (1825–27), and was U.S. senator (1827–36). He broke with Jackson over the Bank of the U.S., resigning his seat when ordered by the Va. legislature to support Benton's resolution expunging Clay's censure of Jackson for removal of deposits from the Bank. Joining the states' rights group cooperating with the Whigs, he was state legislator (1838–40) and was nominated Vice-President on the Whig ticket with Harrison (1840) and elected in the "Tippecanoe and Tyler, too" campaign. He became President on Harrison's death (4 Apr. 1841). His veto of Clay's bank bill led to resignation of the entire Whig Cabinet (12 Sept. 1841) except Daniel Webster, who also withdrew (May 1843) after negotiating the Webster-Ashburton Treaty. He reorganized his Cabinet with both Whigs and Democrats, with Calhoun as Secretary of State (May 1844). The principal achievements of his administration were the Preemption Act (1841), a victory for the frontier, and the annexation of Tex. through joint Congressional resolution. Retiring to "Sherwood Forest," his Va. home, he emerged briefly in 1861 as chairman of a peace convention at Washington, served in the Confederate Provisional Congress, and was elected to the Confederate Congress, but died before that body assembled.

Urey, Harold Clayton (b. Walkerton, Ind., 29 Apr. 1893–), physical chemist. He was graduated from the University of Montana (B.S., 1917), where he was an instructor in chemistry (1919–21); received the degree of Ph.D. (1923) from the University of California; and studied at Copenhagen (1923–24). He taught chemistry at Johns Hopkins (1924–29), Columbia (1929–45), Chicago (1945–58), and the Univ. of Calif. (since 1958). He was awarded the Nobel prize in chemistry (1934) for having been the 1st to isolate (1932) heavy water (deuterium oxide), which led to the discovery of the heavy isotope of hydrogen named deuterium. Research director (1942–45) of the Manhattan District project that produced the materials for the atomic bomb, he worked on the separation of uranium 235 and heavy water. One of the foremost authorities on the separation of isotopes, he has also done work on atomic and molecular structure, absorption spectra, the thermodynamic properties of gases, and the measurement of paleotemperatures.

Van Buren, Martin (b. Kinderhook, N.Y., 5 Dec. 1782; d. there, 24 July 1862), 8th President of the U.S., was admitted to the bar (1803) and practiced in Kinderhook (1807–16) and Albany. Surrogate of Columbia Co. (1808–13), state senator (1812–20), and state attorney general (1815–19), he headed a political organization known as the "Albany Regency." U.S. senator (1821–28), he supported Crawford in 1824 and Jackson in 1828. Governor of N.Y. (1 Jan. 1829), he resigned (5 Mar.) to accept appointment in Jackson's Cabinet as Secretary of State. After securing Great Britain's consent to opening direct trade with the British West Indies (1830), he resigned (Aug. 1831) to become Minister to Great Britain, but returned from London when Calhoun blocked confirmation in the Senate. Vice-President under Jackson (1833–37), he was Jackson's choice for President, defeating Harrison (1836). His Independent Treasury policy reflected the views of the hard-money Democrats, but the Panic of 1837 undermined his popularity. Although nominated (1840), he was defeated by Harrison. His opposition to the immediate annexation of Tex. cost him the nomination in 1844. Active among New York "Barnburners" opposing extension of slavery, he was the Free-Soil nominee for President (1848). He later returned to the Democratic party but opposed secession.

Vanderbilt, Cornelius (b. 27 May 1794, Staten Island, N.Y.; d. New York City, 4 Jan. 1877), steamship and railroad promoter, financier, quit school after the age of 11, bought a small boat at 16, and began a freight and passenger service between Staten Island and New York. At 19 he married his cousin, Sophia Johnson, who bore him 13 children. During the War of 1812 he had a govt. contract to provision forts in N.Y. harbor and in 1814 built a schooner for service to Long Island Sound. Working as a capt. (1818–29) for Thomas Gibbons' shipping line, he moved to New Brunswick, where his wife ran "Bellona Hall," a stopping place for travelers. between New York and Philadelphia. Competing aggressively with Daniel Drew in steamboat operations on the Hudson, he amassed over a half-million dollars by the age of 40. During the Gold Rush, he organized the Accessory Transit Co. and secured a charter from the Nicaraguan govt. to operate a passenger route (water and highway) across that isthmus, 2 days shorter than the Panama route, enabling him to cut the N.Y.-San Francisco passenger fare. Selling out his Panama concern to rivals, he entered (1855) into competition for the Atlantic trade with the Cunard and Collins Lines. After the Civil War he turned his attention to railroads, winning control of the N.Y. & Harlem R.R., then combining the Hudson River R.R. with the N.Y. Central, and leasing the Harlem to the combination, creating a single line. At his death his fortune was estimated at $100 million. Late in life he gave $1 million to Vanderbilt (previously Central) University, Nashville, Tenn.

Veblen, Thorstein Bunde (b. in Cato township, Manitowoc County, Wis., 30 July 1857; d. Palo Alto, Calif., 3 Aug. 1929), economist and writer. He was graduated (1880) from Carleton College,

Northfield, Minn., and pursued postgraduate studies at Johns Hopkins, Yale (Ph.D., 1884), and Cornell. He taught at the University of Chicago (1893–1906), at Stanford (1906–09), the University of Missouri (1911–18), and the New School for Social Research, N.Y. (1918–20). His 1st published book, *The Theory of the Leisure Class* (1899), an analysis of the pecuniary values of the business and middle classes, won him public notice. It was followed by *The Theory of Business Enterprise* (1904). A seminal social thinker, he conceived of the existing economic system as a price system, whose recurrent crises testified to its inability to adjust. As an alternative he suggested in his later works a system in which production and distribution would be controlled by the engineers, foreshadowing "Technocracy." Other works by him include *The Instinct of Workmanship* (1914), *Imperial Germany and the Industrial Revolution* (1915), *An Inquiry into the Nature of Peace* (1917), *The Higher Learning in America* (1918), *The Vested Interests and the State of the Industrial Arts* (1919), *The Engineers and the Price System* (1921), and *Absentee Ownership and Business Enterprise in Recent Times* (1923).

von Neumann, John (b. 28 Dec. 1903, Budapest, Hungary; d. Washington, D.C., 8 Feb. 1957), mathematician, studied at the Universities of Berlin (1921–23) and Zurich (1923–25), obtained a Ph.D. from Budapest Univ. (1926), and came to the U.S. in 1930, becoming a citizen in 1937. He taught at Princeton and after 1933 was a member of the Institute of Advanced Study. Cofounder with Oskar Morganstern of the theory of games, a mathematical approach to the study of economic behavior, sociology, and military strategy, he also made important contributions to quantum theory. He worked on the A-bomb and the H-bomb projects and was a leader in the design and development of high-speed computers, notably MANIAC (mathematical analyzer, numerical integrator, and computer) developed at the Institute, and utilized in advanced govt. research projects, notably in building and testing the H-bomb. He was a member of the Atomic Energy Commission (1954–57).

Waite, Morrison Remick (b. Lyme, Conn., 29 Nov. 1816; d. Washington, D.C., 23 Mar. 1888), 6th Chief Justice of the U.S., was graduated from Yale (1837), studied law, and began practice (1839) in Maumee, Ohio, moving to Toledo (1850). Ohio state legislator (1849–50), he was, with William M. Evarts and Caleb Cushing, counsel for the U.S. before the *Alabama* tribunal in Geneva (1871–72) and president of the Ohio constitutional convention (1873–74). Appointed Chief Justice of the U.S. Supreme Court (1874), his most notable opinions were rendered in the *Granger Cases* (1877), where he stated that "business affected with a public interest" must be controlled by the public for the common good; upheld state legislation fixing rates; and declared that, until Congress acted, a state regulation of railroads was valid "even though it may indirectly affect those without." This position was reversed in the *Wabash Case* (1886), with Waite dissenting. He also laid the foundation for the modern interpretation of due process as a limitation of state power, insisting on reasonable regulation (*Stone v. Farmers' Loan* (1886).

Waksman, Selman Abraham (b. Priluka, Russia, 22 July 1888–   ), microbiologist, came to the U.S. (1910), receiving his B.S. from Rutgers Univ. (1915) and his Ph.D. from the Univ. of Calif. (1918) and becoming a citizen in 1916. Microbiologist at the N.J. Agricultural Experiment Station (1921–24), he taught soil microbiology at Rutgers (1918–58). The discoverer of streptomycin (Nobel Prize in Medicine and Physiology, 1952), an antibiotic derived from a soil fungus and effective against tuberculosis, he turned over (1948) to Rutgers the funds accruing from the patent rights, making possible the establishment of the Institute of Microbiology at Rutgers. Its 1st director, he retired in 1958. His writings include *Streptomycin, Its Nature and Application* (1949), *Soil Microbiology* (1952), *My Life with the Microbes* (1954), *Neomycin, Nature and Application* (1958).

Ward, Lester Frank (b. Joliet, Ill., 18 June 1841; d. Washington, D.C., 18 Apr. 1913), sociologist. He attended (1861–62) the Susquehanna Collegiate Institute at Towanda, Pa., enlisted (1862) in the Union army, was wounded at Chancellorsville (1863), and was discharged in 1864. He served (1865–81) with the U.S. Treasury Department at Washington, D.C., meanwhile attending Columbian College (later George Washington University), A.B., 1869; LL.B., 1871; A.M., 1872). He took posts as a geologist (1883 *et seq.*) and paleontologist (1892 *et seq.*) with the U.S. Geological Survey; served as president of the Institut International de Sociologie (1900–03) and 1st president of the American Sociological Society (1906–07). In 1906 he was named professor of sociology at Brown University, where he served until his death. A pioneer of American evolutionary sociology, Ward stressed the role of mind and education in human progress and the necessity of intelligent and systematic planning for the furthering of rational social development, in opposition both to the laissez-faire school and to the evolutionary determinism of Spencer. His works include *Dynamic Sociology* (1883), *The Psychic Factors of Civilization* (1893), *Outlines of Sociology* (1898), *Pure Sociology* (1903), and *Glimpses of the Cosmos* (6 vols., 1913–18).

Warren, Earl (b. Los Angeles, Calif., 19 Mar. 1891–   ), 13th Chief Justice of the U.S., received his B.L. (1912) and his J.D. (1914) from the Univ. of Calif., was admitted to the bar in 1914, and practiced in San Francisco and Oakland. District attorney of Alameda County, 1925–39, and attorney general of Calif. (1939–43), he was governor of Calif. for 3 terms (1942–53), winning both the Democratic and Republican nominations in 1946. Republican nominee for Vice-President of the U.S. in 1948, he resigned the governorship to become Chief Justice of the U.S. Supreme Court (Sept. 1953). Generally aligning himself with the liberals, he delivered a number of notable opinions, including *Brown v. Bd. of Education* (1954), abolishing the separate-but-equal doctrine and upholding desegregation in public education; *Penn* v. *Nelson* (1956), holding in effect that the states have no authority to punish subversive actions against the U.S.; and *Watkins* v. *U.S.* (1957), where he enunciated principles defining limitations on the power to investigate, including those springing from the 1st Amendment.

Washington, Booker Taliaferro (b. Hale's Ford, Franklin County, Va., 5 Apr. 1856; d. Tuskegee, Ala., 14 Nov. 1915), Negro educator. The son of a Negro slave and a white father, he worked (*c.*1865 *et seq.*) in a salt furnace and coal mine at Malden, W. Va., meanwhile attending school. He entered (1872) Hampton Institute, the Negro vocational school in Va., where he earned his board by working as a janitor, and graduated in 1875. He was a school teacher at Malden (1875–77) and a student (1878–79) at Wayland Seminary, Washington, D.C., and in 1879 returned to Hampton Institute, where he took charge of the Indian dormitory and night school. Chosen (1881) to organize at Tuskegee a Negro normal school that had been chartered by the Ala. legislature, Washington founded there the Normal and Industrial Institute for Negroes. He soon became the foremost advocate of Negro education and was active as a public speaker on race relations, stressing industrial education and gradual adjustment rather than political and civil rights. He wrote *The Future of the American Negro* (1899), *Sowing and Reaping* (1900), the autobiographical *Up From Slavery* (1901), and *Frederick Douglass* (1907).

Washington, George (b. Bridges Creek, Westmoreland Co., Va., 22 Feb. 1732; d. Mount Vernon, Va., 13· Dec. 1799), 1st President of the U.S. After his father's death (1743) he lived chiefly at Mount Vernon, and worked as a surveyor. He visited Barbados with his half-brother, Lawrence (1751–52). Sent by Gov. Dinwiddie to warn the French from encroaching on land in the Ohio Valley (1753), he served in the French and Indian Wars (1755–59) with the rank of lt. col., was obliged to surrender Ft. Necessity (3 July 1754), distinguished himself in the engagement known as Braddock's Defeat (9 July 1755), and participated in the capture of Ft. Duquesne (1759). Inheriting Mount Vernon from Lawrence (1752), he married Martha Dandridge Custis (6 Jan. 1759), entering the Va. House of Burgesses that same year. A leader in the movement for independence, he was a delegate to the 1st and 2nd Continental Congresses. On 15 June 1775 he was chosen to command the Continental Army and took up duties before Boston (3 July). When the British evacuated that city, he attempted to defend New York, but was forced to withdraw to Westchester Co. and thence into N.J. (1776). Brilliant successes at Trenton (24 Dec. 1776) and Princeton (3 Jan. 1777) raised Patriot morale. After defeats at Brandywine (11 Sept. 1777) and Germantown (4 Oct.), he evacuated Philadelphia and endured a winter of semistarvation at Valley Forge (1777–78). The exposé of the alleged Conway Cabal (1777–78) to displace Washington left him secure in his command. His most brilliant achievement was his secret and rapid march from the Hudson to Chesapeake Bay, resulting in the surrender of Cornwallis at Yorktown (19 Oct. 1781), ending the war. He denounced the Newburgh Address (1783), which had hinted at monarchy, and took leave of his officers at Fraunces' Tavern, New York (4 Dec. 1783), retiring to Mount Vernon. Returning to public life, he attended the Annapolis Convention (1786) and presided over the Federal Convention (1787) which adopted the Constitution. Unanimously elected 1st president, he was inaugurated in New York (30 Apr. 1789) and administered the office for 2 terms, during which Hamiltonian fiscal policies were followed, neutrality was observed (1793), the Whisky Rebellion suppressed (1794), and Jay's Treaty (1795) upheld. Declining a 3rd term as President, he advised his countrymen in his Farewell Address (19 Sept. 1796) "to steer clear of permanent alliances . . . [trusting] to temporary alliances for extraordinary measures." When war with France threatened (1798), he was called from retirement as commander in chief, but hostilities were averted.

Webster, Daniel (b. Salisbury, N.H., 18

Jan. 1782; d. Marshfield, Mass., 24 Oct. 1852), statesman and orator, was graduated from Dartmouth (1801), read law at Salisbury and Boston, and was admitted to the Boston bar in 1805. He moved (1807) to Portsmouth, N.H., where he engaged in politics as a Federalist advocate of regional interests opposing Jefferson's embargo. His "Rockingham Memorial" (Aug. 1812), a forceful condemnation of the War of 1812, led to his election (Nov. 1812) to Congress. Reelected in 1816, he opposed the protective features of the Tariff of 1816 as inimical to New England commerce and shipping, and in the same year moved to Boston. In the following years he devoted himself to his law practice, appearing before the U.S. Supreme Court in cases including the *Dartmouth College Case, McCulloch* v. *Maryland, Gibbons* v. *Ogden,* and *Ogden* v. *Saunders,* and gaining a reputation as one of the foremost constitutional lawyers in the country. His standing as an orator was established by his Plymouth speech (22 Dec. 1820), his speech on Greek independence (19 Jan. 1824), and his Bunker Hill oration (17 June 1825). Elected to Congress in 1823, he opposed the Tariff of 1824, and in 1827 was elected to the U.S. Senate. Reflecting the shift in the economic development of New England, Webster supported the Tariff of 1828 and thereafter was an ardent protectionist. A champion of nationalism, he made one of his great orations during the nullification controversy, when he engaged Sen. Robert Y. Hayne (S.C.) in the debate that stimulated Webster's utterance, "Liberty *and* Union, now and forever, one and inseparable!" Opposed to Jackson's financial policies, he supported a national bank and fought Van Buren's subtreasury proposal. In 1836 and 1840 he was an unsuccessful contender for the Whig nomination for the Presidency. He served as Secretary of State under Presidents William Henry Harrison and John Tyler, negotiated the Webster-Ashburton Treaty of 1842, and resigned from the Cabinet in 1843. Elected to the Senate in 1844, he served there until 1850. Although he consistently supported the Wilmot Proviso, he held the preservation of the Union as paramount and backed the Compromise of 1850, answering secessionists and abolitionists alike in his famous 7th of March speech: "I wish to speak today, not as a Massachusetts man, nor as a northern man, but as an American. . . . I speak today for the preservation of the Union. 'Hear me for my cause.' " As Fillmore's Secretary of State, he wrote the nationalistic "Hülsemann letter." With Calhoun and Clay, he comprised the great Senatorial triumvirate; and to the conservatives of New England was known as "the godlike Daniel."

Webster, Noah (b. West Hartford, Conn., 16 Oct. 1758; d. New Haven, Conn., 28 May 1843), lexicographer, philologist, and journalist. After graduating from Yale (B.A., 1778), he read law and was admitted to the bar at Hartford, but practiced for only a short period (1789–93). While teaching at Goshen, N.Y. (1782), he prepared the 1st part of what later became his *Spelling Book* (*Blue-Backed Speller*) for the use of school children. Published (1783) as *A Grammatical Institute of the English Language,* and completed with a grammar (1784) and a reader (1785), the work, designed to meet American needs, was influential in standardizing spelling and pronunciation in the U.S. as distinguished from prevailing British forms. The *Spelling Book* had an estimated printing of 15 million copies by 1837; by 1890 of more than 70 million. Webster wrote *Sketches of American Policy* (1785) and was later active as a Federalist pamphleteer and journalist, editing the *American Minerva* and *Herald,* both at New York (1793–1803). He abandoned journalism for lexicography and, moving to New Haven, brought out *A Compendious Dictionary of the English Language* (1806). This small work was succeeded by the scholarly *An American Dictionary of the English Language* (2 vols., 1828), which assured Webster's reputation in the U.S. and abroad as a pioneer in the science of lexicography.

Westinghouse, George (b. Central Bridge, N.Y., 6 Oct. 1846; d. New York City, 12 Mar. 1914), inventor and manufacturer. He served in the Union army until he was honorably discharged in 1864, and for the remainder of the Civil War was an engineer in the Union navy. Interested in mechanical inventions, he abandoned his education at Union College, Schenectady, N.Y., to enter his father's agricultural implement shop. In 1865 he obtained patents for a rotary steam engine and a car replacer, and in 1868–69 developed a railroad frog. In 1869, when he secured the 1st air-brake patent, he incorporated the Westinghouse Air Brake Co. This compressed air apparatus had a revolutionary impact on railroad transportation, making high-speed rail travel safe, and is still used as standard equipment. Westinghouse also invented an automatic air brake for long freight trains, and next turned his attention to railroad signaling by electrical controls. He organized (1882) the Union Switch and Signal Co. and later, after he became interested in natural gas and electrical power, formed the Philadelphia Co., the Westinghouse Machine Co., and the Westinghouse Electric Co. In the field of natural gas, he developed a long-distance transmission system. His interest in electrical inventions began in 1885, when he promoted the development and construction of transformers which enabled the introduction into the U.S. of high-tension systems using single-phase alternating currents. In 1886 he purchased the patents held by Nikola Tesla and developed a 2-phase system suitable for lamps and motors. Westinghouse held more than 400 patents, among them shock absorbers, marine steam turbines, a trolley car motor, and an electrical brake for subway cars.

Whistler, James Abbott McNeill (b. Lowell, Mass., 10 July 1834; d. London, 17 July 1903), painter and etcher. During his childhood he traveled with his parents in Russia and England; entered the U.S. Military Academy (1851), from which he was dismissed in 1854; served as a draftsman (1854–55) with the U.S. Coast Survey; and went to Paris (1855), where he took professional training and brought out his 1st etchings (1858). After c.1870 he did most of his work in England. The famous libel suit (1878) against John Ruskin, which resulted from the latter's excoriating com-

ments on Whistler's *Black and Gold— The Falling Rocket,* ended with a 1-farthing verdict in favor of Whistler. The 2 dominant influences in his painting were Velasquez and Japanese art patterns. For Whistler, the essence of painting was arrangement in color. Among his works are the *Portrait of My Mother,* portraits of Thomas Carlyle, Theodore Duret, Rosa Corder, and Lady Meux, and a series of *Nocturnes* and *Symphonies* (such as *Battersea Bridge*) in which he experimented with color harmonies. A brilliant etcher, his etchings and dry-points of London river scenes and Venetian subjects show a complete authority in the medium. He wrote *The Gentle Art of Making Enemies* (1890).

White, Andrew Dickson (b. Homer, N.Y., 7 Nov. 1832; d. Ithaca, N.Y., 4 Nov. 1918), educator, diplomat, and historian. He was graduated from Yale (1853), served as an attaché (1854–55) to the U.S. legation at St. Petersburg, and in 1857, after taking his master's degree at Yale, became professor of history at the University of Michigan, where he remained until 1863. He was elected (1863) to the N.Y. senate and during his incumbency (1864–67) served as chairman of the committee on education, created the state system of normal schools, and was the leading spirit in planning and securing the charter for Cornell University, of which he became (1867) 1st president, serving in that capacity until 1885. At Cornell he introduced such innovations as the nonsegregation of the humanities, the natural sciences, and technical arts, and the employment of leading scholars as "nonresident professors." He also taught history at Cornell, and was one of the founders and the 1st president of the American Historical Association (1884). He served as U.S. Minister to Germany (1879–81), Minister to Russia (1892–94), Ambassador to Germany (1897–1902), and was president of the International Peace Conference at The Hague (1899). His works include *History of the Warfare of Science with Theology in Christendom* (2 vols., 1896), which accepted Darwinism, and *Autobiography* (2 vols., 1905).

White, Edward Douglass (b. Parish Lafourche, La., 3 Nov. 1845; d. Washington, D.C., 19 May 1921), 8th Chief Justice of the U.S., studied at Jesuit College, New Orleans, and at Georgetown, enlisted in the Confederate army at the age of 16, was taken prisoner at Port Hudson, La., and paroled. Admitted to the state bar (1868), he practiced in New Orleans, was state senator (1874–78), and judge of the state supreme court (1879–80). Democratic U.S. senator (1891–94), he was appointed by Cleveland as associate justice of the U.S. Supreme Court (1894) and made Chief Justice by Taft (1910). On the high court he followed a middle-of-the-road policy, taking a liberal position in his dissent in *Lochner* v. *N.Y.* (1905) and in *Wilson* v. *New* (1917), upholding the Adamson Act providing an 8-hr. day for railroad workers, but he dissented in *Bunting* v. *Oregon* (1917), which upheld the Oregon 10-hr. law. Dissenting in the *Northern Securities Case* (1904), he laid down the "rule of reason" opinion dissolving the *Standard Oil Co.* and the *American Tobacco Co.* (1911).

Whitefield, George (b. Gloucester, England, 16 Dec. 1715; d. Newburyport, Mass., 30 Sept. 1770), evangelist. He was graduated from Oxford, where he became associated with John and Charles Wesley and the Methodist movement. During the absence of the Wesleys in Georgia (which Whitefield visited in May–Sept. 1738), he acted as the leader of the Methodist movement. When virtually all of the churches in England closed their doors against him, Whitefield took to preaching outdoor sermons, soon attracting large audiences and wide attention with his impassioned oratory and expert histrionics. In 1739 he returned to America, where he was the most important single influence in stirring the religious revival commonly called the Great Awakening. Upon his return to England (1741) Whitefield, who had become a Calvinist, broke with the Wesleys and assumed the leadership of the Calvinistic Methodist movement. He made subsequent visits to America in 1744–48, 1751, 1754–55, 1763–64, and 1769–70.

Whitman, Walt (b. West Hills, Huntington, Long Island, N.Y., 31 May 1819; d. Camden, N.J., 26 Mar. 1892), poet, worked as a printer's devil, taught school, and edited (1838–39) the *Long Islander.* From 1841 to 1848 he was associated with newspapers and magazines at New York, editing (1846–48) the *Brooklyn Eagle* and publishing a temperance novel, *Franklin Evans; or, The Inebriate, a Tale of the Times* (1842). He went to New Orleans (1848), where he worked for the *Crescent,* and after his return to Brooklyn wrote for the Free-Soil daily, the *Freeman,* during 1848–49, and edited 1857–59) the Brooklyn *Times.* He published *Leaves of Grass* (1855), which struck a new and indigenous note in American poetry, and to which many pieces were added in subsequent editions. During the Civil War, Whitman was a volunteer nurse at Washington, D.C., where he also worked as a clerk in the Department of the Interior. Following a paralytic stroke suffered by him in 1873, he moved to Camden, N.J., where he resided for the rest of his life. Sometimes called "the Good Gray Poet," Whitman is the bard of democracy who, in celebrating his own identity, extolled both the average man and the uniqueness of the individual. Among his works are *Drum Taps* (1865), *Passage to India* (1871), *Democratic Vistas* (1871, prose work), *Specimen Days and Collect* (1882–83, prose work), and *Good-bye, My Fancy* (1891). Among his individual poems are "Pioneers! O Pioneers!" "The Song of the Broad Axe," "Once I Pass'd through a Populous City," "When Lilacs Last in the Dooryard Bloom'd," and "O Captain! My Captain!"

Whitney, Eli (b. Westboro, Mass., 8 Dec. 1765; d. New Haven, Conn., 8 Jan. 1825), inventor. As a boy and young man he became familiar with mechanical crafts in his father's metalworking shop. He entered Yale in 1789 and was graduated in 1792. While in the South, where he began his law studies on the Georgia plantation of the widow of Gen. Nathanael Greene, his attention was called to the tedious method of cleaning green seed cotton, at that time an unprofitable crop because of the costly manual process of separating the staple. Whitney designed a cotton gin and, after successive experiments, built a large and improved model (1793) with which a single slave could maintain a daily output of 50 lbs. of cleaned cotton. Before Whitney obtained his patent (1794), many imitations were placed on the market; in the various infringement suits he undertook, Whitney did not secure a favorable verdict until 1807, and most of the little money he made from the invention went for law costs. His cotton gin revolutionized the course of Southern agriculture and territorial expansion. In New Haven, Whitney undertook the manufacture of firearms. He obtained from the Federal government a contract for 10,000 muskets (1798). For their manufacture he devised a system of interchangeable parts (1800), also devised independently (before 1808) by Simeon North (1765–1852), the Conn. gunsmith. Whitney established a factory near New Haven, at the site of present-day Whitneyville, and designed and built the machinery for producing muskets with precision parts turned out by relatively inexperienced workmen engaged in simple operations.

Whittier, John Greenleaf (b. Haverhill, Mass., 17 Dec. 1807; d. Hampton Falls, N.H., 7 Sept. 1892), poet and abolitionist, published his 1st poems (1826 *et seq.*) in the Newburyport (Mass.) *Free Press* edited by William Lloyd Garrison. He attended (1827–28) Haverhill Academy, became (1829) editor of *The American Manufacturer* at Boston, and edited (1831) the *New England Weekly Review* at Hartford, Conn. He published *Legends of New England in Prose and Verse* (1831) and *Moll Pitcher* (1832), and under the influence of Garrison became an active abolitionist (after *c.*1833). He served (1835) in the Mass. legislature, edited (1838–40) the *Pennsylvania Freeman* and published *Poems Written During the Progress of the Abolition Question* (1838). He helped establish the American and Foreign Antislavery Society and ran for Congress on the Liberty party ticket. He became (1847) corresponding editor of the antislavery journal, the *National Era*. His volumes of poetry include *Lays of My Home*

(1843), *Voices of Freedom* (1846), *Songs of Labor* (1850), *The Chapel of the Hermits* (1853), *The Panorama and Other Poems* (1856), *In War Time and Other Poems* (1864), *Snow-Bound* (1866), *The Tent on the Beach* (1867), *Ballads of New England* (1870), and *At Sundown* (1890). His best-known individual poems include "Maud Muller," "Barefoot Boy," "Massachusetts to Virginia," "Ichabod," and "Barbara Frietchie."

Wilkes, Charles (b. New York City, 3 Apr. 1798; d. Washington, D.C., 8 Feb. 1877), naval officer and explorer, was commissioned midshipman in the U.S. Navy (1818) and given charge of the Department of Charts and Instruments (1833), out of which developed the Naval Observatory and Hydrographic Office. In 1838 he was given command of the 1st national marine exploration and surveyed routes in the Pacific Ocean and South Seas frequented by American whalers. In Jan. 1840 he claimed discovery of the Continent of Antarctica, coasting along part of the Antarctic barrier from about 150°E to 108°E, subsequently named Wilkes Land in his honor. He supervised the preparation of the 19-vol. report of the expedition and personally prepared *Narrative* (1844), *Meteorology* (1851), and *Hydrography* (1861). Commanding the *San Jacinto* in the Civil War, he stopped the British mail steamer *Trent* in the old Bahama Channel (8 Nov. 1861) and seized the Confederate commissioners, James M. Mason and John Slidell, en route to Europe. Although thanked by Congress, his action was disavowed by Lincoln as a breach of international law, and Mason and Slidell were surrendered to Britain.

Willard, Emma Hart (b. Berlin, Conn., 23 Feb. 1787; d. Troy, N.Y., 15 Apr. 1870), educator. She attended the Berlin Academy, and from 1807 until 1809, when she married John Willard, was head of the Middlebury (Vt.) Female Academy. In 1814 she established the Middlebury Female Seminary, where she made innovations in women's education. She sent to Governor DeWitt Clinton of New York *An Address . . . Proposing a Plan* *for Improving Female Education* (1819), in which she advocated educational equality for women. Although her proposals led the N.Y. legislature to charter (1819) the Waterford Academy established by her, the state failed to provide financial aid. At the invitation of citizens of Troy, N.Y., she established there (1821) the Troy Female Seminary, the first U.S. college-level institution for women. It provided instruction in subjects such as mathematics and philosophy from which women had been traditionally excluded. Mrs. Willard wrote history and geography textbooks that were used in many schools and trained hundreds of teachers who spread her doctrines. She retired in 1838, thereafter devoting herself to the improvement of common schools. She was the author of a volume of poetry, *The Fulfilment of a Promise* (1831), which included "Rocked in the Cradle of the Deep."

Willard, Frances (b. Churchville, N.Y., 28 Sept. 1839; d. New York City, 18 Feb. 1898), reformer, was graduated from Northwestern Female College (1859) and settled in Evanston, Ill., where she began teaching (1860) and became president of the Evanston College for Ladies (1871–74). She resigned to join the temperance crusade and served as president (from 1879) of the National Woman's Christian Temperance Union (W.C.T.U.) and of the World Woman's Christian Temperance Union (from 1887). She helped organize the Prohibition party and participated in the women's suffrage movement.

Williams, Roger (b. London, England, *c.*1603; d. Providence, R.I., between 26 Jan. and 25 Mar. 1683), religious leader, founder of the Rhode Island Colony. Protégé of the lawyer, Sir Edward Coke, who helped Williams secure his education, he was graduated from Cambridge (B.A., 1627), took holy orders in the Church of England (*c.*1628), and as chaplain to Sir William Masham became acquainted with Puritan circles. Immigrating to Mass. (1631), he antagonized the magistracy by his contentions that the civil government was not empowered to enforce the religious precepts of the

Ten Commandments and that the royal charter illegally expropriated the land rights of the Indians. After serving in churches at Plymouth and Salem, he was tried by the General Court, which ordered his banishment (1635). With some of his followers he founded (1636) the earliest R.I. settlement at Providence, adopting a humane policy toward the Indians. Having already taken a position more radical than Separatism, he now viewed with skepticism all established churches. After a brief period as a Baptist, he became (1639) a Seeker, i.e., one who adhered to the basic tenets of Christianity but refused to recognize any creed. First champion of complete religious toleration in America, he also espoused a liberal political order in the R.I. colony, which was founded on the compact theory of the state and featured a democratic land association. To safeguard his colony against the encroachments of the New England Confederation, he went to England (1643) and secured a charter (1644). During his stay in England he wrote pamphlets on behalf of the liberal wing of Puritanism, including *Queries of Highest Consideration* (1644), which opposed the establishment of a national church, and *The Bloudy Tenent of Persecution* (1644), which advocated unqualified religious and political freedom. He returned to R.I. (1644) to find that William Coddington of Newport had organized opposition to Williams' plans for the union of the 4 R.I. settlements. With John Clarke, Williams again went to England (1651), where he succeeded in having Coddington's commission withdrawn. During this period he wrote *The Bloudy Tenent Yet More Bloudy* (1652) in reply to John Cotton's *The Bloudy Tenent Washed and Made White* (1647). Upon his return to R.I., Williams served for 3 terms (1654–57) as president of the colony, which in 1663 obtained a new charter from Charles II.

Williams, Tennessee [Thomas Lanier] (b. Columbus, Miss., 26 Mar. 1914–   ), playwright, moved to St. Louis at 12, attended the Univ. of Missouri (1931–33), but left during the depression to clerk with a shoe company. After a year at Washington Univ., St. Louis (1936–37), he finished his college course at the Univ. of Iowa (B.A., 1938). A Rockefeller fellow in 1940, he quickly established a reputation as a talented and prolific playwright. His early plays include *Battle of Angels* (1940) and *The Glass Menagerie* (1945). His Pulitzer Prize-winning *Streetcar Named Desire* (1947) established his reputation. His plays, often concerned with the destruction of innocence by inexorable forces and with individual depravity, reached a broad audience through adaptation for the screen. Among his later plays are *The Rose Tattoo* (1948), *Cat on a Hot Tin Roof* (1955, Pulitzer Prize), *Sweet Bird of Youth* (1959). Screenplays of importance are *Baby Doll* and *The Fugitive Kind*.

Wilson, James (b. Carskerdo, Scotland, 14 Sept. 1742; d. Edenton, N.C., 21 Aug. 1798), Revolutionary statesman, jurist, attended St. Andrews, Glasgow, and Edinburgh universities (1757–63). Leaving Scotland for America, he arrived in N.Y. during the Stamp Act crisis and obtained a post as Latin tutor at the College of Philadelphia (1766). Studying law with John Dickinson (*q.v.*), he was admitted to the bar (1767), practiced in Reading (1768), and moved to Carlisle, where by 1774 he had amassed a huge practice. Heading a Committee of Correspondence at Carlisle (1774), he published in that year his notable *Considerations on the Nature and Extent of the Legislative Authority of the British Parliament,* denying Parliament's authority over the colonies and anticipating a British Commonwealth. Signer of the Declaration, he sought in the 2nd Continental Congress to strengthen the national government. An opponent of the radical Pa. constitution of 1776, he became leader of the conservative forces in Philadelphia, to which he moved in 1778. Incurring animosity for his defense of the Penn family and of profiteering merchants, he and his friends barricaded themselves against a mob (4 Oct. 1779). In Congress (1785–87), he played a leading role at the Federal Convention and successfully fought for adoption of the Constitution in Pa. Law lecturer at the College of Philadelphia (1789), he was associate justice of the U.S. Supreme Court (1789–98), and wrote a notable opinion in *Chisholm* v. *Georgia* (1793), upholding the national against the states' authority. Throughout his life a heavy land speculator, he fled to N.C. to avoid arrest for debt and died under a cloud.

Wilson [Thomas] Woodrow (b. Staunton, Va., 28 Dec. 1856; d. Washington, D.C., 3 Feb. 1924), 28th President of the U.S., was graduated from Princeton University (1879), studied law at the University of Virginia (1880), was admitted to the bar (1881), and, after opening a law office in Atlanta, entered the graduate school at Johns Hopkins (1883), where he completed his notable doctoral thesis, *Congressional Government* (1885). After teaching history at Bryn Mawr (1885–88) and Wesleyan (1888–90), he became professor of jurisprudence and political economics at Princeton (1890–1902), quickly establishing himself as a preeminent authority in his field and in wide demand as a public lecturer. Appointed first nonclerical president of Princeton (1902–10), he became 2nd only to Eliot of Harvard as an educational leader. Defeated in his plans for the graduate school, his position became untenable, and he resigned to accept the Democratic nomination for governor of N.J. His term (1911–12) was marked by reforms and a courageous fight against the Democratic political machine. Put forward as a conservative Democrat to defeat W. J. Bryan, he obtained the Democratic nomination for President (1912) and was elected as a result of a split in Republican ranks. His 1st administration was notable for such reforms as the Underwood Tariff, the Federal Reserve Act (1913), the Federal Trade Commission, and the Clayton Act (1914). He sent a punitive expedition across the Mexican border (1916) and sought to maintain U.S. neutrality after the outbreak of World War I despite infringement of American rights. Reelected President (1916) on the campaign slogan "he kept us out of war," he called for war (2 Apr. 1917) after Germany renewed unrestricted submarine warfare. "The world must be made safe for democracy," he then declared. On 8 Jan.

1918 he laid down 14 Points as the basis of peace and stated (27 Sept.) that the League of Nations was the "most essential part" of the peace settlement. Heading the U.S. peace delegation, he was given an unprecedented reception in Paris (14 Dec. 1918) and in other European capitals, but became involved in disputes with Allied leaders and was forced to compromise numerous of the 14 Points in order to save the League. When the Senate refused to ratify the Treaty of Versailles without reservations unacceptable to him, he set out from Washington (3 Sept. 1919) to carry to the people his case against "the little group of willful men." He collapsed at Pueblo (26 Sept. 1919) and never fully recovered.

Winthrop, John (b. Edwardstone, Suffolk, England, 22 Jan. 1588; d. Boston, Mass., 26 Mar. 1649), colonial Puritan statesman, 1st governor of Massachusetts Bay. He attended Cambridge, was admitted at Gray's Inn (1613), and practiced law in London, being admitted to the Inner Temple in 1628. A country squire, his Puritan convictions led him to take an interest in the Massachusetts Bay Co., of which he was chosen governor (1629). He signed the Cambridge Agreement (1629) by which 12 members pledged that if the charter and company could be legally transferred to New England they would go there with their families. He sailed from Southampton (1630) aboard the *Arbella,* part of a fleet transporting to Salem some 700 passengers, the 1st large contingent of the Puritan migration, and settled at the present site of Boston. Winthrop and his Puritan associates laid the foundation of the "Bible Commonwealth." He served as governor (1629–34, 1637–40, 1642–44, 1646–49) and was deputy governor for a total of ten years. As early as 1637 he advocated a New England Confederation, particularly for reasons of defense, and was the 1st president of the confederation when it was formed in 1643. The 1st 2 volumes of his manuscript *Journal* (1630–44) appeared in 1790, and it was published in full as *The History of New England* (2 vols., 1825–26).

Wise, Isaac Mayer (b. Steingrub, Bo-

hemia, 29 Mar. 1819; d. Cincinnati, Ohio, 26 Mar. 1900), religious leader, entered (1835) a rabbinical school in Jenikau, then attended the Univ. of Prague for 2 yrs. and the Univ. of Vienna for a year. Admitted to the rabbinate, he was elected (1843) rabbi of the congregation of Radnitz, but opposing govt. control and censorship, he left Bohemia for the U.S. (1846). Rabbi in Albany, N.Y. (1846–54), he accepted a call to the Bene Yeshurun Congregation in Cincinnati, where he was rabbi (1854–1900). His weekly newspaper, the *Israelite* (later *American Israelite*), advocated adjusting Judaism to American life and institutions, including the use of English in religious services and a simplification of ritual observances. Founder of Reformed Judaism in the U.S., he appealed (1848) for a union of congregations, which saw fruition in the Union of American Hebrew Congregations (1873); founded the Hebrew Union College (1875), 1st native institution for training rabbis; and established a rabbinical organization, the Central Conference of Amer. Rabbis (1889), of which he was president until his death. His writings include *History of the Israelitish Nation from Abraham to the Present Time* (1854), *The Cosmic God* (1876), and *Pronaos to Holy Writ* (1891).

Witherspoon, John (b. Yester, near Edinburgh, Scotland, 5 Feb. 1723; d. New Jersey, 15 Nov. 1794), religious leader, educator, and Revolutionary patriot. He received his divinity degree (1743) from the University of Edinburgh, was ordained in the Presbyterian ministry in 1745, and held pulpits in Scotland until 1768, when he came to America to occupy the presidency of the College of New Jersey (now Princeton). As an educator, he revamped methods of instruction and the college curriculum, and was an exponent of the Scottish "common sense" philosophy. As a religious leader, he closed the factional breach between the "Old Side" and "New Side" Presbyterians in the colonies, was partly responsible for the rapid growth of the Presbyterian Church in America on the eve of the Revolution, and was a stanch advocate of religious liberty. Delegate to the

Continental Congress in 1776, he favored the Declaration of Independence, of which he was a signer. He served intermittently in Congress until 1782, and was a signer of the Articles of Confederation. He was a member (1783, 1789) of the N.J. legislature and of the state convention that ratified (1787) the Federal Constitution, and was active (1785–89) in furthering the national organization of the Presbyterian Church. He coined the term "Americanism" in an article on language in the *Pennsylvania Journal* (1781). His *Works* (4 vols.) were published in 1800–01.

Woodward, Robert Burns (b. Boston, 10 Apr. 1917–   ), chemist, obtained his B.S. (1936) from M.I.T. and his Ph.D. a year later. Joining the Harvard faculty that year, he achieved, with Dr. William E. Doering, the 1st total synthesis of quinine (1944). His synthesis, with C. H. Schramm, of protein analogues (1947), materials resembling natural proteins found in animal and plant life, came closer than ever before to duplicating a natural growth process, and proved valuable in plastics, antibiotics, and medical research. First to synthesize a steroid (1951), he announced later that year the total synthesis of cortisone. For this and other achievements he has received numerous national and intl. scientific honors.

Wright, Frank Lloyd (b. Richland Center, Wis., 8 June 1869; d. Phoenix, Ariz., 10 Apr., 1959), architect. He studied civil engineering (1884–88) at the University of Wisconsin and was a draftsman (1889–94) with architectural firms at Chicago, including Adler & Sullivan, for whom he worked on plans for the Transportation Building at the Chicago World's Fair (1893) and the James Charnley house at Chicago. In 1894 he established independent practice at Oak Park, Ill., and in 1911 moved to Spring Green, Wis., where he designed his own residences, "Taliesin I" and "Taliesin II." His "prairie house" style appeared as early as *c.*1894 in the W. H. Winslow house at River Forest, Ill. A disciple of Louis H. Sullivan, Wright became the foremost American innovator and expo-

nent of an organic architecture based on the integration of form, function, building site, and materials, and on the subordination of style to human needs. His preoccupation with the social relations of architecture is expressed in his model for the projected community of Broadacre City. His designs have exerted a pervasive influence on modern European architecture, particularly in France, Holland, Germany, and the Scandinavian countries. Among his works are Unity Temple, Oak Park, Ill.; the Larkin Administration Bldg. and the Darwin Martin house, both at Buffalo, N.Y.; the Coonley Playhouse and Kindergarten, Riverside, Ill.; the Ward H. Willits house, Highland Park, Ill.; the F. C. Robie house, Francisco Terrace, and Midway Gardens, all at Chicago; the Aline Barnsdall house, Los Angeles, Calif.; the Imperial Hotel at Tokyo, which withstood the earthquake of 1923; "Taliesin West" at Paradise Valley, Phoenix, Ariz.; the Johnson Wax Company Administration Bldg., Racine, Wis.; the Jacobs house, Madison, Wis.; the Jones house, Tulsa, Okla.; and the Kaufmann house at Bear Run, Pa. In 1956 he completed work on the Price Tower in Bartlesville, Okla., and began construction of Guggenheim Museum, N.Y.C.

Wright, Wilbur (b. Millville, near New Castle, Ind., 16 Apr. 1867; d. Dayton, Ohio, 30 May 1912), and his brother, **Orville** (b. Dayton, Ohio, 19 Aug. 1871; d. there, 30 Jan. 1948), aviation pioneers and inventors. The sons of Bishop Milton Wright of the United Brethren in Christ, they had only brief formal schooling, neither completing high school. In 1892 they established a bicycle shop at Dayton, where they began (1895) the manufacture of bicycles. Their interest in aviation having been aroused (*c.*1898), they read articles and books on aeronautics, built a biplane kite (1899), and conducted two man-carrying glider experiments (1900, 1901) at Kitty Hawk, N.C. Finding a relative paucity of scientific information in the field of aircraft design and construction, they built a wind tunnel (1901) in which they tested and verified the operation of some 200 wing and biplane surfaces. They worked out major innovations in aircraft control systems and, on the basis of their painstaking compilation of scientific data, began (Oct. 1902) the construction of a powered aircraft with a total weight of 750 lbs. and carrying a 170-lb., 12-horsepower gasoline engine. This machine was completed at Kitty Hawk, where, on 17 Dec. 1903, Orville Wright made the 1st piloted flight in a powered airplane, remaining aloft for 12 seconds over a distance of about 120 ft. Of the 4 flights made on that day, Wilbur flew the longest one: 59 seconds over a distance of 852 ft. Returning to Dayton, the Wright brothers improved their machine. Toward the close of 1905 they made in it a flight of about 38 minutes over a distance of more than 24 mi. around Huffman Field, Dayton. They obtained a patent for their aircraft on 22 May 1906. In 1908–09 Wilbur toured England, France, and Italy, setting records for altitude and distance. Their machine, after being subjected to tests at Ft. Myer, Va., was accepted by the U.S. Army (2 Aug. 1909). The commercial development and manufacture of the Wright airplane was begun in 1909 with the organization of the Wright Co.

Young, Brigham (b. Whitingham, Vt., 1 June 1801; d. Salt Lake City, 29 Aug. 1877), Mormon leader and colonizer. In his infancy he was taken by his family to the "burnt-over" district in western New York, a region of intense evangelical activity. After working as a house painter and glazier, he settled (1829) on a farm at Mendon, N.Y., about 40 miles from Palmyra, N.Y., where Joseph Smith (1805–44) published The Book of Mormon and founded the Church of Jesus Christ of Latter-Day Saints. Young became a convert to Mormonism (1832) and devoted the rest of his life to the upbuilding of the Mormon Church. In 1835 he became the 3rd ranking member of the Quorum of the 12 Apostles, the administrative body of the Church, and by 1838 was its senior member. During these years he was active as a Mormon missionary. Upon the death of Joseph Smith at Carthage, Ill., he became head of the Church. In this role Young demonstrated his brilliance, energy, and determination

as a practical organizer. He led the Mormon mass migrations to the Valley of the Great Salt Lake and directed the settlement of Deseret, which in 1850 was organized by Congress as Utah Territory. Young was named territorial governor, and although removed from his post (1857) during the Mormon controversy with the Federal government, remained the effective leader of the community. His lasting contribution was the shaping of an administrative machinery that enabled the survival and development of the Mormon Church. He adopted polygamy, had about a score of wives, and fathered 56 children.

Zenger, John Peter (b. in Germany, 1697; d. New York City, 28 July 1746), printer and journalist. He arrived at New York in 1710 and served his apprenticeship (1711–19) to the printer William Bradford, with whom he formed (1725) a short-lived partnership. In 1726 Zenger established an independent business. In 1733, after Gov. Cosby adopted arbitrary measures, Zenger became the editor and publisher of the New-York Weekly Journal, set up by him and prominent New Yorkers in opposition to the provincial administration and its organ, Bradford's New York Gazette. The polemical articles which appeared in the Weekly Journal were probably written by Zenger's associates; under existing law, however, the publisher was held responsible. In 1734 Zenger was arrested and imprisoned, and held incommunicado for about 10 months. Brought to trial (1735) for seditious libel, he was defended by Andrew Hamilton of Philadelphia. Despite the court's refusal to admit evidence establishing the truth of the libel, Hamilton succeeded in securing Zenger's acquittal. The case is a landmark in the history of the freedom of the press in America. Zenger became public printer for the colony of N.Y. (1737) and the colony of N.J. (1738).

Zworykin, Vladimir (b. Mourom, Russia, 30 July 1889–), electronics engineer, pioneer in the development of television. He was graduated from the Petrograd Institute of Technology (E.E., 1912), came to the U.S. in 1916, was naturalized in 1924, and served as research engineer (1920–29) with the Westinghouse Electrical and Manufacturing Co. He applied (1925) for the patent on the iconoscope (the essential basis of the electronic television camera), the 1st practical application and predecessor of modern television. He served as director of electronic research (1929–42) for the RCA Manufacturing Co., and was associate director (1942–45) of the RCA Laboratories, of which he was named director of electronic research (1946) and vice-president and technical consultant (1947). In 1933, employing the iconoscope and the cathode-ray tube, he made a successful demonstration of television over a radio-wave relay between New York and Philadelphia. He has also done work in the fields of electron optics and the electron microscope. He is the author of *Photocells and Their Applications* (1932) and *Television* (1940).

INDEX

We the People

of the United States, in Order to form a more perfect Union, establish Justice, insure domestic Tranquility, provide for the common defence, promote the general Welfare, and secure the Blessings of Liberty to ourselves and our Posterity, do ordain and establish this Constitution for the United States of America.

Article. I.

Section. 1. All legislative Powers herein granted shall be vested in a Congress of the United States, which shall consist of a Senate and House of Representatives.

Section. 2. The House of Representatives shall be composed of Members chosen every second Year by the People of the several States, and the Electors in each State shall have the Qualifications requisite for Electors of the most numerous Branch of the State Legislature.

No Person shall be a Representative who shall not have attained to the Age of twenty five Years, and been seven Years a Citizen of the United States, and who shall not, when elected, be an Inhabitant of that State in which he shall be chosen.

Representatives and direct Taxes shall be apportioned among the several States which may be included within this Union, according to their respective Numbers, which shall be determined by adding to the whole Number of free Persons, including those bound to Service for a Term of Years, and excluding Indians not taxed, three fifths of all other Persons. The actual Enumeration shall be made within three Years after the first Meeting of the Congress of the United States, and within every subsequent Term of ten Years, in such Manner as they shall by Law direct. The Number of Representatives shall not exceed one for every thirty Thousand, but each State shall have at Least one Representative; and until such enumeration shall be made, the State of New Hampshire shall be entitled to chuse three, Massachusetts eight, Rhode-Island and Providence Plantations one, Connecticut five, New-York six, New Jersey four, Pennsylvania eight, Delaware one, Maryland six, Virginia ten, North Carolina five, South Carolina five, and Georgia three.

When vacancies happen in the Representation from any State, the Executive Authority thereof shall issue Writs of Election to fill such Vacancies.

The House of Representatives shall chuse their Speaker and other Officers; and shall have the sole Power of Impeachment.

Section. 3. The Senate of the United States shall be composed of two Senators from each State, chosen by the Legislature thereof, for six Years; and each Senator shall have one Vote.

Immediately after they shall be assembled in Consequence of the first Election, they shall be divided as equally as may be into three Classes. The Seats of the Senators of the first Class shall be vacated at the Expiration of the second Year, of the second Class at the Expiration of the fourth Year, and of the third Class at the Expiration of the sixth Year, so that one third may be chosen every second Year; and if Vacancies happen by Resignation, or otherwise, during the Recess of the Legislature of any State, the Executive thereof may make temporary Appointments until the next Meeting of the Legislature, which shall then fill such Vacancies.

No Person shall be a Senator who shall not have attained to the Age of thirty Years, and been nine Years a Citizen of the United States, and who shall not, when elected, be an Inhabitant of that State for which he shall be chosen.

The Vice President of the United States shall be President of the Senate, but shall have no Vote, unless they be equally divided.

The Senate shall chuse their other Officers, and also a President pro tempore, in the Absence of the Vice President, or when he shall exercise the Office of President of the United States.

The Senate shall have the sole Power to try all Impeachments. When sitting for that Purpose, they shall be on Oath or Affirmation. When the President of the United States is tried, the Chief Justice shall preside: And no Person shall be convicted without the Concurrence of two thirds of the Members present.